SMITHSONIAN INSTITUTION
BUREAU OF AMERICAN ETHNOLOGY
BULLETIN 30

# HANDBOOK

OF

# AMERICAN INDIANS

## NORTH OF MEXICO

EDITED BY

FREDERICK WEBB HODGE

VOLUME I   A to G

WASHINGTON
GOVERNMENT PRINTING OFFICE
(Fourth impression, September, 1912)

SMITHSONIAN INSTITUTION
BUREAU OF AMERICAN ETHNOLOGY
BULLETIN 30

# HANDBOOK

OF

# AMERICAN INDIANS

NORTH OF MEXICO

EDITED BY

FREDERICK WEBB HODGE

TRADEPAPER:

VOLUME I     A-G     ISBN     1-58218-748-7
VOLUME II    H-M     ISBN     1-58218-749-5
VOLUME III   N-S     ISBN     1-58218-750-9
VOLUME IV    T-Z     ISBN     1-58218-751-7

Digital Scanning and Publishing is a leader in the electronic republication of historical books and documents. We publish many of our titles as eBooks, as well as traditional hardcover and trade paper editions. DSI is committed to bringing many traditional and little known books back to life, retaining the look and feel of the original work.

©2003 DSI Digital Reproduction
First DSI Printing: July 2003

Published by DIGITAL SCANNING, INC.
Scituate, MA 02066
www.digitalscanning.com

# LETTER OF TRANSMITTAL

SMITHSONIAN INSTITUTION,
BUREAU OF AMERICAN ETHNOLOGY,
*Washington, D. C., July 1, 1905.*

SIR: I have the honor to submit herewith the manuscript of Bulletin 30 of the Bureau of American Ethnology, entitled "Handbook of American Indians," which has been in preparation for a number of years and has been completed for publication under the editorship of Mr F. W. Hodge. The Handbook contains a descriptive list of the stocks, confederacies, tribes, tribal divisions, and settlements north of Mexico, accompanied with the various names by which these have been known, together with biographies of Indians of note, sketches of their history, archeology, manners, arts, customs, and institutions, and the aboriginal words incorporated into the English language.

Respectfully,

W. H. HOLMES, *Chief.*

The SECRETARY OF THE SMITHSONIAN INSTITUTION,
*Washington, D. C.*

III

# PREFACE

During the early exploration and settlement of North America, a multitude of Indian tribes were encountered, having diverse customs and languages. Lack of knowledge of the aborigines and of their languages led to many curious errors on the part of the early explorers and settlers: names were applied to the Indians that had no relation whatever to their aboriginal names; sometimes nicknames were bestowed, owing perhaps to personal characteristics, fancied or real; sometimes tribes came to be known by names given by other tribes, which were often opprobrious; frequently the designation by which a tribal group was known to itself was employed, and as such names are oftentimes unpronounceable by alien tongues and unrepresentable by civilized alphabets, the result was a sorry corruption, varying according as the sounds were impressed on Spanish, English, French, Dutch, German, Russian, or Swedish ears. Sometimes, again, bands of a single tribe were given distinctive tribal names, while clans and gentes were often regarded as independent autonomous groups to which separate tribal designations likewise were applied. Consequently, in the literature relating to the American Indians, which is practically coextensive with the literature of the first three centuries of the New World, thousands of such names are recorded, the significance and application of which are to be understood only after much study.

The need of a comprehensive work on the subject has been felt ever since scientific interest in the Indians was first aroused. Many lists of tribes have been published, but the scientific student, as well as the general reader, until the present time has been practically without the means of knowing any more about a given confederacy, tribe, clan, or settlement of Indians than was to be gleaned from casual references to it.

The work of which this Handbook is an outgrowth had its inception as early as 1873, when Prof. Otis T. Mason, now of the United States National Museum, began the preparation of a list of the tribal names mentioned in the vast literature pertaining to the Indians, and in due time several thousand names were recorded, with references to the works in which they appear. The work was continued by him until after the establishment of the Bureau, when other duties compelled its suspension. Later the task was assigned to Col. Garrick Mallery, who, however, soon abandoned it for investigations in a field which proved to be his life work, namely, the pictography and sign language of the American Indians. Meanwhile Mr James Mooney was engaged in compiling a similar list of tribes, with their synonymy, classified chiefly on a geographic basis and covering the entire Western Hemisphere—a work begun in 1873 and continued for twelve years before either he or the members of the Bureau of American Ethnology knew of the labors of each other in this field.

Soon after the organization of the Bureau in 1879, the work of recording a tribal synonymy was formally assigned to Mr Henry W. Henshaw. Up to this time a complete linguistic classification of the tribes north of Mexico, particularly in the West and Northwest, was not possible, since sufficient data had not been gathered for determining their linguistic affinities. Mr Henshaw soon perceived that a linguistic classification of the Indian tribes, a work long contemplated by Major Powell, must precede and form the basis for a tribal synonymy, and to him, therefore, as a necessary preliminary, was intrusted the supervision of such a linguistic classification. By 1885 the Bureau's researches in this direction had reached a stage that warranted the grouping of practically all the known tribes by linguistic stocks. This classification is published in the Seventh Annual Report of the Bureau, and on it is based, with few exceptions, the present Handbook.

Immediately on the completion of the linguistic classification, the entire force of the Bureau, under Mr Henshaw's immediate direction, was assigned to the work that had now grown into a Dictionary and Synonymy of the Indian Tribes North of Mexico. As his special field Mr Henshaw devoted attention to several of the Californian stocks, and to those of the North Pacific coast, north of Oregon, including the Eskimo. To Mr Mooney were given the great and historically important Algonquian and Iroquoian families, and through his wide general knowledge of Indian history and customs he rendered aid in many other directions. A list of Linguistic Families of the Indian Tribes North of Mexico, with Provisional List of the Principal Tribal Names and Synonyms (55 pp., octavo), was at once printed for use by the collaborators of the Bureau in connection with the complete compilation, and although the list does not include the Californian tribes, it proved of great service in the earlier stages of the work. The 2,500 tribal names and synonyms appearing in this list were taken chiefly from Mr Mooney's manuscript; the linguistic classification was the result of the work that the Bureau had been conducting under Mr Henshaw's supervision.

Rev. J. Owen Dorsey assumed charge of the work on the Siouan, Caddoan, and Athapascan stocks; Dr W. J. Hoffman, under the personal direction of Major Powell, devoted his energies to the Shoshonean family, and Mr Jeremiah Curtin, by reason of his familiarity with a number of the Californian tribes, rendered direct aid to Mr Henshaw in that field. Dr Albert S. Gatschet employed his time and long experience in the preparation of the material pertaining to the Muskhogean tribes of southeastern United States, the Yuman tribes of the lower Colorado drainage and of Lower California, and various smaller linguistic groups. To Col. Garrick Mallery were assigned the French authors bearing on the general subject. With such aid the work received a pronounced impetus, and before the close of 1885 a large body of additional material had been recorded. Four years later the elaboration of the material pertaining to the Yuman, Piman, Keresan, Tanoan, and Zuñian stocks of the extreme Southwest was placed in charge of Mr. F. W. Hodge, who brought it to completion.

The work was continued under Mr Henshaw's supervision until, in 1893, ill health compelled his abandonment of the task. This is the more to be regretted as Mr Henshaw had in course of preparation a classification and nomenclature of the minor divisions of the linguistic stocks, which is essential to a proper presentation and a clear understanding of the subject. After Mr Henshaw's relinquishment of the work, Mr Hodge was given entire charge of it. But other official duties of members of the staff prevented the Handbook as a whole from making marked progress until 1899, when Dr Cyrus Thomas was intrusted with the task of revising the recorded material bearing on the Algonquian, Siouan, and Muskhogean families.

In 1902 the work on the Handbook was again systematically taken up, at the instance of Secretary Langley, who detailed Mr Hodge, at that time connected immediately with the Smithsonian Institution, to undertake its general editorial supervision. The scope of the subject-matter was enlarged to include the relations between the aborigines and the Government; their archeology, manners, customs, arts, and industries; brief biographies of Indians of note; and words of aboriginal origin that have found their way into the English language. It was proposed also to include Indian names that are purely geographic, but by reason of the vast number of these it was subsequently deemed advisable to embody them eventually in an independent work. Moreover, it was provided that the work should be illustrated as adequately as time and the illustrative material available would admit, a feature not originally contemplated. To fully cover this vast field at the present time is impossible, by reason of the fact that research among the native tribes, notwithstanding the extensive and important work that has been accomplished in recent years, has not advanced far beyond the first stage, even when is taken into account the sum of knowledge derived from the researches of the Bureau and of other institutions, as well as of individuals.

The lack of completeness of our present knowledge of the tribes was, perhaps, never better shown than when an attempt was made to carry out the enlarged plan of the Handbook. With its limited force the

Bureau could scarcely hope to cover the entire range of the subject within a reasonable time; consequently various specialists not directly connected with the Bureau were invited to assist—an invitation that was accepted in a manner most gratifying. It is owing to the generous aid of these students that a work so complete as the Handbook is intended to be was made possible, and to them the Bureau owes its deep appreciation. That the Handbook has many imperfections there is no doubt, but it is hoped that in future editions the weak points may be strengthened and the gaps filled, until, as researches among the tribes are continued, the compilation will eventually represent a complete summary of existing knowledge respecting the aborigines of northern America.

The scope of the Handbook is as comprehensive as its function necessitates. It treats of all the tribes north of Mexico, including the Eskimo, and those tribes south of the boundary more or less affiliated with those in the United States. It has been the aim to give a brief description of every linguistic stock, confederacy, tribe, subtribe or tribal division, and settlement known to history or even to tradition, as well as the origin and derivation of every name treated, whenever such is known, and to record under each every form of the name and every other appellation that could be learned. These synonyms, in alphabetic order, are assembled as cross references in Part 2.

Under the tribal descriptions a brief account of the ethnic relations of the tribe, its history, its location at various periods, statistics of population, etc., are included. Accompanying each synonym (the earliest known date always being given) a reference to the authority is noted, and these references form practically a bibliography of the tribe for those who desire to pursue the subject further. It is not claimed that every spelling of every tribal name that occurs in print is given, but it is believed that a sufficient number of forms is recorded to enable the student to identify practically every name by which any group of Indians has been known, as well as to trace the origin of many of the terms that have been incorporated into our geographic nomenclature.

In many instances the treatises are satisfactorily illustrated; in others, much necessarily has been left to a future edition in order that the present publication may not be further delayed. The work of illustration was intrusted largely to Mr De Lancey Gill.

The contributors to Part 1, in addition to those who have rendered valued assistance by affording information, correcting proofs, and in other ways, are as follows, the names being arranged in the alphabetical order of the initials attached to the signed articles:

A. C. F.      Alice C. Fletcher of Washington.
A. F. C.      Alexander F. Chamberlain of Clark University.
A. H.         A. Hrdlicka of the United States National Museum.

| | |
|---|---|
| A. L. D. | Anna L. Dawes of Pittsfield, Mass. |
| A. L. K. | A. L. Kroeber of the University of California. |
| A. S. G. | Albert S. Gatschet, formerly of the Bureau of American Ethnology. |
| C. M. F. | Cora M. Folsom of the Hampton Normal and Agricultural Institute, Hampton, Va. |
| C. T. | Cyrus Thomas of the Bureau of American Ethnology. |
| E. G. E. | Elaine Goodale Eastman of Amherst, Mass. |
| E. L. H. | Edgar L. Hewett of Washington. |
| F. B. | Franz Boas of Columbia University. |
| F. H. | Frank Huntington, formerly of the Bureau of American Ethnology. |
| F. H. C. | The late Frank Hamilton Cushing of the Bureau of American Ethnology. |
| F. V. C. | F. V. Coville of the United States Department of Agriculture. |
| F. W. H. | F. W. Hodge of the Bureau of American Ethnology. |
| G. A. D. | George A. Dorsey of the Field Museum of Natural History. |
| G. B. G. | George Bird Grinnell of New York. |
| G. F. | Gerard Fowke of Saint Louis. |
| G. P. M. | George P. Merrill of the United States National Museum. |
| H. E. B. | Herbert E. Bolton of the University of Texas. |
| H. W. H. | Henry W. Henshaw, formerly of the Bureau of American Ethnology. |
| J. C. | The late Jeremiah Curtin of the Bureau of American Ethnology. |
| J. D. M. | Joseph D. McGuire of Washington. |
| J. H. D. | Josiah H. Dortch of the Office of Indian Affairs. |
| J. M. | James Mooney of the Bureau of American Ethnology. |
| J. McL. | James McLaughlin of the Office of Indian Affairs. |
| J. N. B. H. | J. N. B. Hewitt of the Bureau of American Ethnology. |
| J. O. D. | The late J. Owen Dorsey of the Bureau of American Ethnology. |
| J. R. S. | John R. Swanton of the Bureau of American Ethnology. |
| J. W. F. | J. Walter Fewkes of the Bureau of American Ethnology. |
| L. F. | Livingston Farrand of Columbia University. |
| M. E. G. | Merrill E. Gates of the Board of Indian Commissioners. |
| M. K. S. | M. K. Sniffen of the Indian Rights Association. |
| O. T. M. | Otis T. Mason of the United States National Museum. |
| P. E. B. | Paul Edmond Beckwith of the United States National Museum. |
| P. E. G. | P. E. Goddard of the University of California. |
| R. B. D. | Roland B. Dixon of Harvard University. |
| R. H. L. | Robert H. Lowie of New York. |
| S. A. B. | S. A. Barrett of the University of California. |
| S. C. | Stewart Culin of the Brooklyn Institute Museum. |
| S. M. B. | S. M. Brosius of the Indian Rights Association. |
| W. E. | Wilberforce Eames of the New York Public Library. |
| W. H. | Walter Hough of the United States National Museum. |
| W. H. H. | William H. Holmes of the Bureau of American Ethnology. |
| W. J. | William Jones of the Field Museum of Natural History. |
| W. M. | The late Washington Matthews, United States Army. |

F. W. HODGE.

BUREAU OF AMERICAN ETHNOLOGY,
*December, 1906.*

# HANDBOOK OF THE INDIANS

**AANETUN.** An extinct village of the Tututni, a Pacific Athapascan group formerly living on the Oregon coast.
'A'ă-ne'-tûn.—Dorsey in Journ. Am. Folk-lore, III, 236, 1890.

**Aatsosni** ('narrow gorge'). A Navaho clan.
Aatsósni.—Matthews, Navaho Legends, 30, 1897.

**Ababco.** An eastern Algonquian tribe or subtribe. Although mentioned in the original records of 1741 (Bacon, Laws of Maryland, 1765) in connection with the Hutsawaps and Tequassimoes as a distinct tribe, they were probably only a division of the Choptank. This name is not mentioned in John Smith's narrative of his exploration of Chesapeake bay. The band lived on Choptank r., Md., and in 1741 the Colonial government confirmed them in the possession of their lands on the s. side of that stream, in Dorchester co., near Secretary cr. By 1837 the entire tribe to which they belonged had dwindled to a few individuals of mixed Indian and African blood. (J. M.)
Ababeves.—Bozman, Hist. Maryland, I, 115, 1837.

**Abascal.** A Diegueño rancheria near San Diego, s. Cal.—Ortega (1795) quoted by Bancroft, Hist. Cal., I, 253, 1886.
Abuscal.—Ibid. Aguscal.—Ibid.

**Abayoa.** A Tequesta village at the s. extremity of Florida pen., mentioned in connection with the expedition of Ponce de Leon (1512).—Barcia, Ensayo, 2, 1723.

**Abbatotine** ('bighorn people'). A Nahane tribe living in upper Pelly, Macmillan, and Stewart r. valleys, Yukon T.
Abbāto-tenā'.—Dall in Cont. N. A. Ethnol., I, 32, 1877. Abba-to-tenah.—Dall in Proc. A. A. A. S., 271, 1870. Abbato-tinneh.—Bancroft, Nat. Races, III, 587, 1882. Affats-tena.—Ibid., I, 149 (misprint). Ah-bah-to din-ne.—Hardisty in Smithson. Rep. 1866, 311, 1872. Ambahtawoot.—Prichard, Phys. Hist., v, 377, 1847. Ambah-tawút-dinni.—Latham in Trans. Philol. Soc. Lond., 69, 1856 (trans. 'mountain sheep men'). Amba-ta-ut' tinè.—Richardson, Arct. Exped., II, 7, 1851. Am-ba-ta-ut' tinè.—Petitot, Dict. Dènè Dindjié, xx, 1876. Ambatawwoot.—Schoolcraft, Ind. Tribes, II, 28, 1852. Ambawtamoot.—Ibid., III, 525, 1853. Ambawtawhootdinneh.—Franklin, Narr., II, 84, 1824. Ambawtawhoot Tinneh.—Bancroft, Nat. Races, v, 640, 1882. Ambawtawoot.—Gallatin in Trans. Am. Antiq. Soc., II, 19, 1836. Ambawtowhoot.—Balbi, Atlas Ethnog., 821, 1826. **Mountain Sheep Men.**—Latham in Trans. Philol. Soc. Lond., 69, 1856. **Sheep Indians.**—Franklin, Narr., II, 84, 1824. **Sheep People.**—Richardson, op. cit.

**Abbigadasset.** An Abnaki sachem whose residence was on the coast of Maine near the mouth of Kennebec r. He conveyed tracts of land to Englishmen conjointly with Kennebis. In 1667 he deeded Swans id. to Humphrey Davy.—Drake, Bk. Inds., bk. 3, 101, 1837.

**Abechiu** (a Tewa onomatope representing the screech of an owl.—E. L. Hewett). A prehistoric Tewa pueblo at a place called La Puente, on a bluff close to the s. bank of Rio Chama, 3 m. s. E. of the present town of Abiquiu, Rio Arriba co., N. Mex.—Bandelier in Arch. Inst. Papers, IV, 56, 58, 1892.
Abe-chiu.—Bandelier, op. cit., 39 (aboriginal name). Oj-po-re-ge.—Ibid., 58 (Santa Clara name: 'place where metates are made rough.')

**Abercronk.** A former (Potawatomi?) village on L. Michigan, in N. E. Porter co., Ind.—Hough, map in Indiana Geol. Rep. for 1882–3, 1883.

**Aberginian.** A collective term used by the early settlers on Massachusetts bay for the tribes to the northward. Johnson, in 1654, says they consisted of the "Massachuset," "Wippanap," and "Tarratines." The name may be a corruption of Abnaki, or a misspelling for "aborigines." The Wippanap are evidently the Abnaki, while the Tarratines are the same Indians, or a part of them. (J. M.)
Abarginny.—Johnson (1628) in Mass. Hist. Soc. Coll., 2d s., II, 66, 1814. Abergeny.—Williams (1643), ibid., 1st s., III, 204, 1794. Aberginians.—Wood (1634) quoted by Schoolcraft, Pers. Mem., 644, 1851. Aberieney.—Levett (1628) in Mass. Hist. Soc. Coll., 3d s., VIII, 174, 1843. Aborginny.—Humphrey's Acc't, 281, 1730 (incorrectly quoting Johnson, 1628).

**Abihka.** One of the oldest of the Upper Creek towns; exact location unknown, but it was near upper Coosa r., Ala.
Abacoes.—ten Kate, Reizen in N. A., 462, 1885. Abchas.—McKenney and Hall, Ind. Tribes, III, 79, 1854 (probably a misprint of Abekas). Abecaes.—Coxe, Carolana, 25, 1741. Abecas.—Ibid., map. Abecka.—Romans, Florida, 309, 1775. Abeicas.—Alcedo, Dicc. Geográfica, I, 3, 1786. Abeikas.—Pénicaut (1708) in French, Hist. Coll. La., n. s., I, 101, 1869. Abekas.—Bossu (1759), Travels in Louisiana, I, 229, 1771. Abicas.—La Harpe (1703) in French, Hist. Coll. La., III, 29, 1851. Abi'hka.—Gatschet, Creek Migr. Leg., I, 124, 1884. Abikas.—La Harpe (1707) in French, Hist. Coll. La., III, 36, 1851. Abikaws.—Rivers, Early Hist. So. Car., 94, 1874. Albikas.—La Harpe (1714) in French, Hist. Coll. La., III, 43, 1851. Apiscas.—Williams, Florida, 75, 1837 (same?). Au-be-cuh.—Hawkins (1799), Sketch of Creek Country, 42, 1848. Aubocoes.—Macomb (1802) in Am. State Papers, Ind. Aff., I, 680, 1832. Becaes.—Coxe, Carolana, 25, 1741. Beicas.—Gatschet, Creek Migr. Leg., I, 125, 1884. Obekaws.—Von der Reck in Urlsperger, Ausführliche Nachricht von den Saltzburgischen Emigranten, 871, 1735. Obika.—Gatschet, Creek Migr. Leg., I, 125, 1884. Sak'hútka.—Gatschet, in-

formation (symbolic name, sig. 'door,' as the town was situated at the N. limits of the Creek country, and thus defended it against hostile inroads).

**Abihka.** A town of the Creek Nation on the s. side of North fork of Canadian r., Tp. 11 N., R. 8 E., Ind. T.

Abí'hka.—Gatschet, Creek Migr. Leg., II, 185, 1888. Arbeka.—U. S. P. O. Guide, 366, 1904.

**Abikudshi** ('Little Abihka'). A former Upper Creek town in N. Talladega co., Ala., on the right bank of Tallahatchee cr., 5 m. E. of Coosa r. It was settled by Oakfuskee Indians and some of the Natchez. Bartram (1775) states that the inhabitants spoke a dialect of Chickasaw, which could have been true of only a part.

Abacooches.—Bartram, Travels, 461, 1791. Abacouchees.—U. S. Ind. Treaties (1797), 68, 1837. Abbacoochees.—Swan (1791) in Schoolcraft, Ind. Tribes, V, 262, 1855. Abecoche.—Jefferys, Am. Atlas, 5, 1776. Abecochi.—Alcedo, Dicc. Geog., I, 3, 1786. Abecoochee.—U. S. Ind. Treaties (1814), 162, 1837. Abecothee.—Lattré, Carte des États-Unis, 1784. Abécouéchis.—Baudry de Lozières, Voy. Louisiane, 241, 1802. Abuobochu.—H. R. Ex. Doc. 276, 24th Cong., 1st sess., 315, 1836. Arbiccoochee.—Sen. Ex. Doc. 425, 24th Cong., 1st sess., 301, 1836. Au-ba-coo-che.—Hawkins (1814) in Am. State Papers, Ind. Aff., I, 837, 1832. Au-be-cooche.—Hawkins (1798–99), Sketch, 41, 1848.

**Abikudshi.** A town of the Creek Nation on Deep fork of Canadian r., above Ocmulgee, Ind. T.

Abi'hkúdshi.—Gatschet, Creek Migr. Leg., II, 185, 1888.

**Abiquiu** (from *Abechiu*, q. v.). A pueblo founded by the Spaniards prior to 1747 at the site of the prehistoric Tewa pueblo of Fejiu, on the Rio Chama, Rio Arriba co., N. Mex. In Aug., 1747, it was raided by the Ute, who killed a number of the inhabitants and compelled its abandonment. It was resettled soon afterward, and in 1748 contained 20 families, but, owing to further depredations by the Ute and Navaho, was again abandoned, and in 1754 reoccupied. In 1765 the settlement (the mission name of which was Santa Rosa, later changed to Santo Tomas) contained 166 persons, and in the vicinity were 612 others. In 1779 the pueblo had 851 inhabitants, and at least as early as 1794 it was peopled in part by Genizaros, or Indian captives and fugitives, chiefly Hopi, whom the Spaniards had rescued or purchased. In 1808 Abiquiu contained 122 Indians and 1,816 whites and mestizos. The town was thoroughly Mexicanized by 1854. See Bancroft, Ariz. and N. Mex., 280, 1889; Bandelier in Arch. Inst. Papers, IV, 54, 1892. (F. W. H.)

Abequin.—Kern in Schoolcraft, Ind. Tribes, IV, 39, 1854. Abicu.—Arrowsmith, Map of N. A., 1795, ed. 1814. Abicui.—Humboldt, Atlas Nouv. Espagne, carte 1, 1811. Abiguin.—Ward in Ind. Aff. Rep. 1867, 210, 1868. Abiquico.—Lane (1854) in Schoolcraft, Ind. Tribes, V, 689, 1855. Abiquieu.—Escudero, Noticias Nuevo-Méx., 14, 1849. Abiquin.—Hezio (1797–98) in Meline, Two Thousand Miles, 260, 1867. Abiquíri.—Mühlenpfordt, Mejico, II, 533, 1844. Abiquiu.—Ms. of 1750 cited by Bandelier in Arch. Inst. Papers, III, 174, 1890. Abricu.—Pike, Exped., map, 1810. Abuquin.—

Johnston in Emory, Recon., 569, 1848. Albiquin.—Simpson, Rep., 2, 1850. Aluquia.—Buschmann, N. Mex., 245, 1858. Jo-so-ge.—Bandelier in Arch. Inst. Papers, IV, 54, 1892 (Tewa name; from *Jo-so*, their name for the Hopi, because most of the inhabitants were of that tribe). Santa Rosa de Abiquiú.—Dominguez y Escalante (1776) in Doc. Hist. Mex., 2d s., I, 378, 1854. San Tomas de Abiquiu.—Ward in Ind. Aff. Rep. 1867, 213, 1868. Santo Tomás de Abicui.—Orozco y Berra in Anales Minis. Fom., VI, 255, 1882. Santo Tomas de Abiquiu.—Alencaster (1805) in Meline, Two Thousand Miles, 212, 1867. Sta Rosa Abiquiú.—Bancroft, Ariz. and N. Mex., 252, 1889.

**Abittibi** (*abi'ta*, 'half,' 'middle,' 'intermediate'; *bi*, a secondary stem referring to a state or condition, here alluding to water; -*g*, a locative suffix: hence 'halfway-across water,' referring to the situation of Abittibi lake.—W. Jones). A little known Algonkin band whose habitat has been the shores of Abittibi lake, Ont. The first recorded notice of them is in the Jesuit Relation for 1640. It is said in the Relation of 1660 that the Iroquois had warred upon them and two other tribes of the same locality. Du Lhut (1684) includes them in the list of nations of the region N. of L. Superior whose trade it was desirable should be turned from the English of Hudson bay to the French. Chauvignerie (1736) seems to connect this tribe, estimated at 140 warriors, with the Têtes de Boule. He mentions as totems the partridge and the eagle. They were reported by the Canadian Indian Office to number 450 in 1878, after which date they are not officially mentioned. (J. M. C. T.)

Abbetikis.—Chauvignerie (1736) quoted by Schoolcraft, Ind. Tribes, III, 556, 1853. Abbitibbes.—Keane in Stanford, Compendium, 498, 1878. Abitibis.—Harris, Voy. and Trav., I, map, 1705. Abittbbes.—Walch, map, 1805. Abittibis.—Chauvignerie (1736) in N. Y. Doc. Hist., IX, 1054, 1855. Outabitibek.—Jesuit Rel. 1660, III, 12, 1858. Outabytibis.—Bacqueville de la Potherie, II, 49, 1753. Outatibes.—Harris, Voy. and Trav., I, map, 1705. Tabitibis.—Du Lhut (1684) in Margry, Déc., VI, 51, 1886. Tabittibis.—Chauvignerie (1736) in N. Y. Doc. Hist., IX, 1053, 1855. Tabittikis.—Schoolcraft, Ind. Tribes, III, 555, 1853. Tibitibis.—Hennepin, New Disc., map, 1698.

**Abmoctac.** A former Costanoan village connected with Dolores mission, San Francisco, Cal.—Taylor in Cal. Farmer, Oct. 18, 1861.

**Abnaki.** (*Wábŭna'ki*, from *wábŭn*, a term associated with 'light,' 'white,' and refers to the morning and the east; *a'ki* 'earth,' 'land'; hence *Wábŭna'ki* is an inanimate singular term signifying 'eastland,' or 'morning-land,' the elements referring to animate dwellers of the east being wanting.—Jones). A name used by the English and French of the colonial period to designate an Algonquian confederacy centering in the present state of Maine, and by the Algonquian tribes to include all those of their own stock resident on the Atlantic seaboard, more particularly the "Abnaki" in the N and the Delawares in the s. More recently it has been applied also to the emigrant Oneida,

Stockbridges, and Munsee about Green bay, Wis. By the Puritans they were generally called Tarrateens, a term apparently obtained from the southern New England tribes; and though that is the general conclusion of modern authorities, there is some doubt as to the aboriginal origin of this term. In later times, after the main body of the Abnaki had removed to Canada, the name was applied more especially to the Penobscot tribe. The Iroquois called them Owenunga, which seems to be merely a modification of Abnaki, or Abnaqui, the name applied by the French and used by most modern writers. The form Openango has been used more especially to designate the eastern tribes. Maurault (Hist. des Aben., 2, 1866) says: "Some English authors have called these savages Wabanoaks, 'those of the east'; this is the reason they are called 'Abenakis' by some among us. This name was given them because they were toward the east with reference to the Narragansetts."

*Ethnic relations.*—In his tentative arrangement Brinton (Len. Leg., 11, 1885) brings into one group the Nascapee, Micmac, Malecite, Etchimin, and Abnaki, but this is more of a geographic than a linguistic grouping. Vetromile (Abnakis, 20, 1866), following other authors, says that we should "embrace under this term all the tribes of the Algic [Algonquian] family, who occupy or have occupied the E. or N. E. shore of North America; thus, all the Indians of the seashores, from Virginia to Nova Scotia, were Abnaki." Maurault gives the following as the principal tribes of the Abnaki confederacy: Kanibesinnoaks (Norridgewock in part; see *Kennebec* and *Norridgewock*); Patsuikets (Sokoki in part); Sokouakiaks (Sokoki); Nurhantsuaks (Norridgewock); Pentagoets (Penobscot); Etemankiaks (Etchimin); Ouarastegouiaks (Malecite), the name Abnaki being applied in the restricted sense to the Indians of Kennebec r. All these tribes spoke substantially the same language, the chief dialectal differences being between the Etchimin and the other tribes of the group. The Etchimin, who formed a subgroup of the Abnaki confederacy, included the Passamaquoddy and Malecite. Linguistically the Abnaki do not appear to be more closely related to the Micmac than to the Delaware group, and Dr William Jones finds the Abnaki closely related to the central Algonquian languages. In customs and beliefs they are more nearly related to the Micmac, and their ethnic relations appear to be with the tribes N. of the St Lawrence.

*History.*—The history of the Abnaki may be said to begin with Verrazano's visit in 1524. The mythical accounts of Norumbega (q. v.) of the early writers and navigators finally dwindled to a village of a few bark-covered huts under the name Agguncia, situated near the mouth of Penobscot r., in the country of the Abnaki. In 1604 Champlain ascended the Penobscot to the vicinity of the present Bangor, and met the "lord" of Norumbega, doubtless an Abnaki chief. From that time the Abnaki formed an important factor in the history of the region now embraced in the state of Maine. From the time of their discovery until their partial withdrawal to Canada they occupied the general region from the St Johns to the Saco; but the earliest English accounts indicate that about 1605–20 the s. w. part of the coast of Maine was occupied by other Indians, whose chief seat was near Pemaquid, and who were at war with the Abnaki, or Tarrateen, as the English termed them, who were more to the N; but these other tribes were finally conquered by the Abnaki and probably

GROUP OF ABNAKI (PASSAMAQUODDY)

absorbed by them. Who these Indians were is unknown. The Abnaki formed an early attachment for the French, chiefly through the influence of their missionaries, and carried on an almost constant war with the English until the fall of the French power in America. The accounts of these struggles during the settlement of Maine are familiar episodes in American history. As the whites encroached on them the Abnaki gradually withdrew to Canada and settled chiefly at Bécancour and Sillery, the latter being afterward abandoned by them for St Francis, near Pierreville, Quebec. The Penobscot, Passamaquoddy, and Malecite, however, remained in their ancient homes, and in 1749 the Penobscot, as the leading tribe, made peace with the English, accepting fixed bounds. Since that period the different tribes have gradually dwindled into insignificance. The descendants of those who emigrated from Maine, together with remnants of other New England tribes, are now at St Francis and Bécancour, in Quebec, where, under the name of Abnaki, they numbered 395 in 1903. At the same time the Malecite, or Amalicite, were numbered at 801 in several villages in New Brunswick and Quebec, with about 625 Penobscot and Passamaquoddy in Maine. The present Penobscot say they number between 300 and 400, while the Passamaquoddy claim as many as 800 souls.

*Customs and beliefs.*—According to the writers on early Maine, the Abnaki were more gentle in manners and more docile than their western congeners. Yet they were implacable enemies and, as Maurault states, watched for opportunities of revenge, as did other Indians. Notwithstanding Vetromile's statement to the contrary, if Maurault's assertion (Hist. Abenakis, 25, 1866) applies to this tribe, as seems evident, they, like most other tribes, were guilty of torturing their prisoners, except in the case of females, who were kindly treated. Although relying for subsistence to a large extent on hunting, and still more on fishing, maize was an important article of diet, especially in winter. Sagard states that in his day they cultivated the soil in the manner of the Huron. They used the rejected and superfluous fish to fertilize their fields, one or two fish being placed near the roots of the plant. Their houses or wigwams were conical in form and covered with birch-bark or with woven mats, and several families occupied a single dwelling. Their villages were, in some cases at least, inclosed with palisades. Each village had its council house of considerable size, oblong in form and roofed with bark; and similar structures were used by the males of the village who preferred to club together in social fellowship. Polygamy was practised but little, and the marriage ceremony was of the simplest character; presents were offered, and on their acceptance marriage was consummated. Each tribe had a war chief, and also a civil chief whose duty it was to preserve order, though this was accomplished through advice rather than by command. They had two councils, the grand and the general. The former, consisting of the chiefs and two men from each family, determined matters that were of great importance to the tribe, and pronounced sentence of death on those deserving that punishment. The general council, composed of all the tribe, including males and females, decided questions relating to war. The Abnaki believed in the immortality of the soul. Their chief deities were Kechi Niwaskw and Machi Niwaskw, representing, re-

spectively, the good and the evil; the former, they believed, resided on an island in the Atlantic; Machi Niwaskw was the more powerful. According to Maurault they believed that the first man and woman were created out of a stone, but that Kechi Niwaskw, not being satisfied with these, destroyed them and created two more out of wood, from whom the Indians are descended. They buried their dead in graves excavated in the soil.

*Tribal divisions.*—The tribes included in the confederacy as noted by Maurault have already been given. In a letter sent by the Abnaki in 1721 to the governor of New England their divisions are given as follows: Narantsouuk (Norridgewock), Pentugouet (Penobscot), Narakamigou (Rocameca), Anmissoukanti (Amaseconti), Muanbissek, Pegouakki (Pequawket, Me.), Medoktek (Medoctec), Kwapahag, Pesmokanti (Passamaquoddy), Arsikantegou (Arosaguntacook), Ouanwinak (Wewenoc, s. edge of N. H.). The following is a full list of Abnaki tribes: Accominta, Amaseconti, Arosaguntacook, Etchimin, Malecite, Missiassik, Norridgewock (the Abnaki in the most limited sense), Passamaquoddy, Penobscot, Pequawket, Rocameca, Sokoki, and Wewenoc. The bands residing on St Croix and St Johns rs. spoke a different dialect from those to the southward, and were known collectively as Etchimin. They are now known as Passamaquoddy and Malecite. Although really a part of the Abnaki, they were frequently classed as a distinct body, while on the other hand the Pennacook tribes, although distinct from the Abnaki, were often classed with them on account of their connection during the Indian wars and after their removal to Canada. According to Morgan they had fourteen gentes: 1, Mals′-sŭm, Wolf; 2, Pis-suh′, Black Wildcat; 3, Ah-weh′-soos, Bear; 4, Skooke, Snake; 5, Ah-lunk-soo, Spotted Animal; 6, Ta-mä′-kwa, Beaver; 7, Maguh-le-boo′, Caribou; 8, Kä-bäh′-seh, Sturgeon; 9, Moos-kwă-suh′, Muskrat; 10, K′-che-gä-gong′-go, Pigeon Hawk; 11, Meh-ko-ă′, Squirrel; 12, Che-gwä′-lis, Spotted Frog; 13, Koos-koo′, Crane; 14, Mä-dä′-weh-soos, Porcupine. According to Chauvignerie their principal totems were the pigeon and the bear, while they also had the partridge, beaver, and otter totems.

The Abnaki villages, so far as their names have been recorded, were Amaseconti, Ammoncongan, Aquadocta (?), Arosaguntacook, Asnela, Aucocisco, Bagaduce, Bécancour, Calais (Passamaquoddy) Gunasquamekook (Passamaquoddy), Imnarkuan (Passamaquoddy), Kennebec, Ketangheanycke, Lincoln Island, Masherosqueck, Mattawamkeag

(Penobscot), Mattinacook (Penobscot), Mecadacut, Medoctec (Malecite), Meecombe, Missiassik (Missiassik), Moratiggon (?), Moshoquen, Muanbissek (?), Muscongus, Negas, Negusset (?), Norridgewock, Norumbega, Okpaak (Malecite), Olamon (Penobscot), Old Town (Penobscot), Ossaghrage, Ouwerage, Pasharanack, Passadumkeag (Penobscot), Passamaquoddy (village?), Pauhuntanuc, Pemaquid, Penobscot, Pequawket, Pocopassum, Precaute, Rocameca, Sabino, Sagadahoc, Sainte Anne (Malecite), St Francis, Satquin, Sebaik (Passamaquoddy), Segocket, Segotago, Sillery, Sokoki (village?), Taconnet, Tobique (Malecite), Unyjaware, Viger (Malecite), Wabigganus, Waccogo, Wewenoc (village?). (J. M. C. T.)

**Abanakees.**—Ross, Fur Hunters, I, 98, 1855. **Abanakis.**—Doc. of 1755 in N. Y. Doc. Col. Hist., X, 342, 1858. **Abanaquis.**—Report of 1821, Mass. Hist. Soc. Coll., 2d s., X, 127, 1823. **Abanaquois.**—Vetromile in Maine Hist. Soc. Coll., VI, 214, 1859 (old form). **Abenaguis.**—La Potherie, Hist. Am., I, 199, 1753. **Abenaka.**—Ibid. **Abena'kes.**—Boyd, Ind. Local Names, 1, 1885. **Abenakias.**—Boudinot, Star in the West, 125, 1816. **Abénakis.**—Du Lhut (1679) in Margry, Découvertes, VI, 22, 1886 (mentioned as distinct from the Openagos). **Abena'kiss.**—Boyd, Ind. Local Names, 1, 1885. **Abenakkis.**—Jefferys, French Dominions, pt. I, map, 118, 1761. **Abenaques.**—Buchanan, N. Am. Inds., I, 139, 1824. **Abenaquioicts.**—Champlain (1632), Œuvres, v, pt. 2, 214, 1870. **Abenaquiois.**—Champlain (1632), Œuvres, v, pt. 2, 233, 1870. **Abenaquioue.**—Sagard (1636), Canada, IV, 889, 1866. **Abenaquis.**—French document (1651) in N. Y. Doc. Col. Hist., IX, 5, 1855 (the same form is used for the Delawares by Maximilian, Travels, 35, 1843). **Abenati.**—Hennepin, Cont. of New Disc., 95, 1698. **Abenequas.**—Hoyt, Antiquarian Researches, 90, 1824. **Abenquois.**—Hind, Labrador Pen., I, 5, 1863. **Abernaquis.**—Perkins and Peck, Annals of the West, 680, 1850. **Abinaqui.**—Schoolcraft, Ind. Tribes, VI, 174, 1857. **Abinohkie.**—Dalton (1783) in Mass. Hist. Soc. Coll., 1st s., X, 123, 1809. **Abnakis.**—Vetromile in Maine Hist. Soc. Coll., VI, 208, 1859. **Abnaquies.**—Willis in Maine Hist. Soc. Coll., IV, 95, 1856. **Abnaquiois.**—Jesuit Relation, 1639, 25, 1858. **Abnaquis.**—Historical Mag., 2d s., I, 61, 1867. **Abnaquois.**—Vetromile in Maine Hist. Soc. Coll., VI, 214, 1859. **Abnaquotii.**—Du Creux, map (1660) in Maine Hist. Soc. Coll., VI, 210, 1859. **Abnasque.**—Vetromile, Abnakis, 26, 1866 (possible French form). **Abnekais.**—Albany conference (1754) in N. Y. Doc. Col. Hist., VI, 886, 1855. **Abonakies.**—Croghan (1765) in Monthly Am. Jour. Geol., 272, 1831. **Abonnekee.**—Allen in Maine Hist. Soc. Coll., I, 515, 1831. **Aguanoχgi.**—Gatschet, Cherokee MS., B. A. E., 1881 (Cherokee name for one Delaware; plural, Anáguanoχgi). **Akotsakannha.**—Cuoq in Brinton, Lenape Leg., 255, 1885 (Iroquois name: 'foreigner'). **Ak8anake.**—Le Jeune (1641) in Jes. Rel., I, 72, 1858 (Huron pronunciation of Wabanaki or Abanaki, 'east land'). **Albenaquioue.**—Sagard (1636), Canada, IV, 889, 1866. **Albenaquis.**—Du Pratz in Drake, Book of Inds., bk. IV, 40, 1848. **Alnânbaï.**—Vassal in Can. Ind. Aff. 1884, 27, 1885 (own name: 'Indians' or 'men'). **Anagonges.**—Bayard (1689) in N. Y. Doc. Col. Hist., III, 621, 1853. **Anaguanoχgi.**—Gatschet, Cherokee MS., B. A. E., 1881 (Cherokee name for the Delawares; see Aguanoχgi above). **Annogonges.**—Bayard (1689) in N. Y. Doc. Col. Hist., III, 611, 1853. **Anogongaars.**—Livingston (1730) in N. Y. Doc. Col. Hist., v, 912, 1855. **A-pa-năχ'-ke.**—ten Kate, Synonymie, 11, 1884 (given as Choctaw name for the Pawnee, but really for the Delawares). **Aquannaque.**—Sagard (1626), Voyage du Hurons, pt. 2, Dict., "nations," 1865 (Huron pronunciation; qu=b of 'Abnaki' or 'Wabanaki,' and applied by them to

the 'Algoumequin' or Algonkin). **Aubinaukee.**—Jones, Ojebway Inds., 178, 1861. **Bashabas.**—Gorges (1658) in Maine Hist. Soc. Coll., II, 62, 1847 (plural form of the name or title of the ruling chief about Pemaquid; used by Gorges as the name of his tribe). **Bénaquis.**—Gatschet, Caughnawaga MS., B. A. E., 1882 (name used by French Canadians). **Cannon-gageh-ronnons.**—Lamberville (1684) in Doc. Hist. N. Y., I, 142, 1849 (Mohawk name). **Eastlanders.**—Schoolcraft, Ind. Tribes, III, 353, 1853 (given as meaning of 'Wabanakis'). **Moassones.**—Popham (1607) in Maine Hist. Soc. Coll., V, 357, 1857 (Latin form, from Moasson, Mawooshen, or Moasham, used by early English writers for the Abnaki country. Ballard, U. S. Coast Survey Rep. 252, 1871, thinks it is the Penobscot word Maweshenook, 'berry place'). **Moassons.**—Willis (?) in Maine Hist. Soc. Coll., V, 359, 1857 (from Popham's form, Moassones). **Narānkamigdok epitsik arenanbak.**—Vetromile, Abnakis, 23, 1866 ('men living on the high shores of the river': given as collective term used by Abnaki to designate all their villages; real meaning 'villages of the Narānkamigdog'). **Natio Euporum.**—Du Creux, map (1660) in Maine Hist. Soc. Coll., VI, 211, 1859 (misprint of the following). **Natio Luporum.**—Same in Vetromile, Abnakis, 21, 1866 ('wolf nation'). **Natságana.**—Gatschet, Caughnawaga MS., B. A. E., 1882 (Caughnawaga name; singular, Rutságana). **Ŏ-bén-aki.**—O. T. Mason, oral information, 1903 (name as pronounced by a native). **Obenaquiouoit.**—Champlain (1629), Œuvres, v, pt. 2, 196, 1870. **Obinacks.**—Clinton (1745) in N. Y. Doc. Col. Hist., VI, 276, 1855. **Obunegos.**—Schoolcraft, Ind. Tribes, V, 196, 1855 (=Delawares). **Olinacks.**—Clinton (1745) in N. Y. Doc. Col. Hist., VI, 281, 1855 (misprint). **Onagongues.**—Bellomont (1701) in N. Y. Doc. Col. Hist., IV, 834, 1854. **Onagonque.**—Schuyler (1693), ibid., 64. **Onagunga.**—Colden (1727) quoted by Schoolcraft, Ind. Tribes, VI, 174, 1857. **Onagungees.**—Johnson (1750) in N. Y. Doc. Col. Hist., VI, 592, 1855. **Onconntehocks.**—La Montagne (1664), ibid., XIII, 378, 1881 (same?). **Ondiakes.**—Albany treaty (1664), ibid., III, 68, 1853. **Onejages.**—Document of 1664, ibid., XIII, 389, 1881 (same?). **Onnagonges.**—Bayard (1689), ibid., III, 621, 1853. **Onnagongues.**—Document of 1688, ibid., 565, 1853. **Onnagongwe.**—Bellomont (1700), ibid., IV, 758, 1854 (used as the Iroquois name of one of the Abnaki villages). **Onnagonques.**—Schuyler (1687), ibid., III, 482, 1853. **Onnogonges.**—Ft Orange conference (1664), ibid., XIII, 379, 1881. **Onnagongwaes.**—Schuyler (1701), ibid., IV, 836, 1854. **Onnongonges.**—Bayard (1689), ibid., III, 611, 1853. **Onoconcquehagas.**—Schelluyne (1663), ibid., XIII, 309, 1881. **Onoganges.**—Dareth (1664), ibid., 381. **Onogongoes.**—Schuyler (1724) in Hist. Mag., 1st s., X, 116, 1866. **Onogonguas.**—Stoddert (1753) in N. Y. Doc. Col. Hist., VI, 780, 1855. **Onogungos.**—Governor of Canada (1695), ibid., IV, 120, 1854. **Onokonquehaga.**—Ft Orange conference (1663), ibid., XIII, 298, 1881. **Onongongues.**—Bayard (1689), ibid., III, 621, 1853. **Openadyo.**—Williamson in Mass. Hist. Soc. Coll., 3d s., IX, 92, 1846. **Openagi.**—Sanford, U. S., cxxiv, 1819. **Openagos.**—Du Lhut (1679) in Margry, Déc., VI, 22, 1886. **Openangos.**—La Hontan, New Voy., I, 230, 1703 (sometimes used specifically for the Passamaquoddy). **O-po-nagh-ke.**—H. R. Rep. 299, 44th Cong. 1st sess., 1, 1876 (Delawares). **Oppenago.**—Cadillac (1703) in Margry, Déc., v, 304, 1883 ('Oppenago ou Loups,' near Detroit, probably the Delawares). **O-puh-nar'-ke.**—Morgan, Consanguinity and Affinity, 289, 1871 ('people of the east': the Delawares). **Ouabenakiouek.**—Champlain (1629), Œuvres, v, pt. 2, note, 196, 1870. **8abenakis.**—Lusignan (1749) in N. Y. Doc. Col. Hist., VI, 519, 1855. **Ouabenaquis.**—La Salle (1683) in Margry, Déc., II, 363, 1877. **Ouabnaquia.**—Ibid., II, 157, 1877 (used in collective sense). **Oubenakis.**—Chauvignerie (1736) in Schoolcraft, Ind. Tribes, III, 553, 1853. **8benakis.**—Chauvignerie (1736) in N. Y. Doc. Col. Hist., IX, 1052, 1855. **Owenagungas.**—Colden (1727), Five Nat., 95, 1747 (so called by Iroquois). **Owenagunges.**—Boudinot, Star in the West, 99, 1816. **Owenagungies.**—Macauley, N. Y., II, 174,

1829. **Owenungas.**—Schoolcraft, Ind. Tribes, III, 513, 1853 (Iroquois name for the Abnaki, Micmac, etc.). **Pánaχki.**—Gatschet, Tonkawe and Caddo MS. vocab., B. A. E., 1884 (Caddo name for Delawares). **Pĕn′ikis.**—Hewitt, oral information, 1886 (Tuscarora name for Abnaki living with the Tuscarora). **Skacewanilom.**—Vassal in Can. Ind. Aff., 28, 1885 (so called by Iroquois). **Taranteens.**—Shea, Mississippi Val., 165, 1852. **Tarateens.**—Barstow, Hist. New Hamp., 13, 1853. **Tarenteens.**—Godfrey, in Maine Hist. Soc. Coll., VII, 99, 1876. **Tarentines.**—Mourt (1622) in Mass. Hist. Soc. Coll., 2d s., IX, 57, 1822. **Tarentins.**—Bradford (1650?) in Mass. Hist. Soc. Coll., 4th s., III, 104, 1856. **Tarranteeris.**—Hist. Mag., 1st s., x, 116, 1866 (misprint). **Tarrantens.**—Levett (1628) in Maine Hist. Soc. Coll., II, 93, 1847. **Tarrantines.**—Smith (1616) in Mass. Hist. Soc. Coll., 3d s., VI, 117, 1837. **Tarrateens.**—Smith (1631) in Maine Hist. Soc. Coll., VII, 101, 1876. **Tarratines.**—Wonder-working Providence (1654) in Mass. Hist. Soc. Coll., 2d s., II, 66, 1814. **Tarratins.**—Keane in Stanford, Compen., 537, 1878. **Tarrenteenes.**—Wood (1639) in Barton, New Views, xix, 1798. **Tarrenteens.**—Richardson, Arctic Exp., II, 38, 1851. **Tarrentens.**—Levett (1628) in Mass. Hist. Soc. Coll., 3d s., VIII, 175, 1843. **Tarrentines.**—Smith (1629) Virginia, II, 192, reprint 1819. **Terentines.**—Smith (1631) in Mass. Hist. Soc. Coll., 3d s., III, 22, 1833. **Terentynes.**—Smith (1616), ibid., VI, 131, 1837. **Unagoungas.**—Salisbury (1678) in N. Y. Doc. Col. Hist., XIII, 519, 1881. **Vnnagoungos.**—Brockhols (1678) in Maine Hist. Soc. Coll., v, 31, 1857 (old style). **Wabanackies.**—McKenney, Memoirs and Travels, I, 81, 1846. **Wabanakees.**—Schoolcraft, Ind. Tribes, I, 304, 1853 (used collectively). **Wabanakis.**—Ibid., III, 353, note, 1853. **Wábaníka.**—Dorsey, MS. Çegiha Dict., B. A. E., 1878 (Omaha and Ponka name for Delawares). **Wábaníke.**—Dorsey, MS. Kansas vocab., B. A. E., 1882 (Kansa name for Delawares). **Wabanoaks.**—Maurault, Hist. des Aben., 2, 1866 (English form). **Wabanocky.**—McKenney (1827) in McKenney and Hall, Ind. Tribes, III, 134, 1854 (used for emigrant Oneida, Munsee, and Stockbridges at Green bay, Wis.). **Wabenakies.**—Kendall, Travels, III, 61, 1809. **Wabĕnáki senobe.**—Gatschet, Penobscot MS., B. A. E., 1887 (Penobscot name). **Wabenauki.**—McKenney and Hall, Ind. Tribes, III, 97, 1854 (applied by other Indians to those of Hudson r.). **Wâb-na-ki.**—Hist. Mag., 1st s., IV, 180, 1860. **Wampum-makers.**—Gale, Upper Miss., 166, 1867 (said to be the French name for the Delawares in 1666; evidently a corruption of Wapanachki). **Wānbānaghi.**—Vetromile, Abnakis, 19, 1866 (proper form). **Wanbanaghi.**—Ibid., 27 (proper form, the first *an* being strongly nasal). **Wānbanaki.**—Vetromile, Abnakis, 27–42, 1866 (proper form; *an* in first syllable strongly nasal). **Wanbanakkie.**—Kidder in Maine Hist. Soc. Coll., VI, 231, 1859 (given as a correct form). **Wānb-naghi.**—Vetromile in Maine Hist. Soc. Coll., VI, 214, 1859. **Wapanachk.**—Heckeweder quoted by Vetromile, Abnakis, 23, 1866 (given by Heckewelder for Delawares). **Wapanachki.**—Barton, New Views, xxvii, 1798 (name given to Delawares by western tribes). **Wapanaki.**—Vetromile, Abnakis, 27–42, 1866 (Delaware form). **Wâpa′na′kiᵃ.**—Wm. Jones, inf'n, 1905 (sing. anim. form of the name in Sauk, Fox, and Kickapoo; *Wápana′kihagi*, pl. anim. form). **Wâpanákihak,**—Gatschet, Sac and Fox MS., B. A. E., 1882 (Fox name for Delawares; singular, Wâpanáki). **Wapanaχki há-akon.**—Gatschet, Tonkawe and Caddo MS. vocab., B. A. E., 1884 (Tonkawa name for Delaware man). **Wapanends.**—Rafinesque, Am. Nations, I, 147, 1836. **Wápaniu′kyu.**—Dorsey, MS. Osage vocab., B. A. E., 1883 (Osage name for Delawares). **Wapenacki.**—Ruttenber, Tribes Hudson R., 51, 1872 (applied to all the eastern tribes). **Wappenackie.**—Ibid., 355 (used either for Delawares or for Wappingers). **Wappenos.**—Ibid., 51 (applied to all eastern tribes). **Wa-pu-nah-ki′.**—Grayson, MS. Creek vocab., B. A. E., 1885 (Creek name applied to the Delawares). **Wau-ba-na-kees.**—Wis. Hist. Soc. Coll., v, 182, 1868 (Stockbridges and Oneidas at Green bay, Wis.). **Waub-un-uk-eeg.**—Warren (1852) in Minn. Hist. Soc. Coll., v, 32 1885 (Chippewa name for Delawares). **Waw-, bunukkeeg.**—Tanner, Narrative, 315, 1830 (Ottawa

name for Stockbridge Indians in Wisconsin). **W'Banankee.**—Kidder in Maine Hist. Soc. Coll., VI, 244, 1859 (name used by themselves, as nearly as can be represented in English, accenting last syllable). **Whippanaps.**—Humphrey, Acct., 281, 1730 (after Johnson). **Wippanaps.**—Johnson (1654) in Mass. Hist. Soc. Coll., 2d s., II, 66, 1814 (mentioned as part of the "Abarginny men" and distinct from the "Tarratines"). **Wo-a-pranach-ki.**—Macauley, N. Y., II, 164, 1829 (used as synonymous with Lenni Lenape for tribes of eastern Pennsylvania, New Jersey, New York, Delaware, and Connecticut). **Wobanaki.**—Kidder in Maine Hist. Soc. Coll., VI, 243, 1859 (title of spelling book of 1830).

**Abo** (*A-bo′*). A former pueblo of the Tompiros division of the Piros, on the Arroyo del Empedradillo, about 25 m. E. of the Rio Grande and 20 m. s. of Manzano, in Valencia co., N. Mex. Whether the pueblo was built on both sides of the arroyo, or whether there were two pueblos successively occupied, has not been determined. It was first mentioned in 1598 by Juan de Oñate; it became the seat of the mission of San Gregorio, founded in 1629 by Fray Francisco de Acevedo, who erected a large church and monastery, the walls of which are still standing, and died there Aug. 1, 1644. Tenabo and Tabira were the visitas of Abo mission. Considering the ruins now on both banks of the arroyo as those of a single pueblo, the population during the early mission period was probably 2,000. Owing to Apache depredations many of the inhabitants fled to El Paso as early as 1671, and prior to the Pueblo insurrection of 1680 the village was entirely abandoned for the same cause. The Piros of Senecu del Sur claim to be the last descendants of the Abo people. See Vetancurt (1697), Crónica, 325, repr. 1871; Bandelier in Arch. Inst. Papers, IV, 270, 1892; Abert in Emory, Recon., 488, 1848. (F. W. H.)

**Abbo.**—Oñate (1598) in Doc. Inéd., XVI, 114, 1871. **Abio.**—Abert in Emory, Reconnoissance, 490, 1848. **Abo.**—Oñate, op. cit., 123. **Ako.**—Simpson in Smithson, Rep. 1869, map, 1872 (misprint). **Avo.**—Wislizenus, Memoir, 24, 1848. **San Gregorio Abbo.**—Vetancurt, Crónica, 325, repr. 1871. **S. Gregoio de Abo.**—Senex, map, 1710 (misprint). **S. Gregoria.**—Güssefeld, Charte America, 1797 (wrongly located on Rio Grande). **S. Gregorio de Abo.**—De l'Isle, Carte Mexique et Floride, 1703. **Sᵗ Gregory.**—Kitchin, Map N. A., 1787.

**Abon.** See *Pone.*

**Aboreachic.** A small Tarahumare pueblo not far from Norogachic, in Chihuahua, Mexico. The name is apparently a corruption of *aoreachic* 'where there is mountain cedar,' but should not be confounded with that of the village of Aoreachic.—Lumholtz, inf'n, 1894.

**Abrading Implements.** In shaping their numerous implements, utensils, and ornaments of stone, wood, bone, shell, and metal, the native tribes were largely dependent on abrading implements, of which there are many varieties. Of first importance are grinding stones and whetstones of more or less gritty rock, while less effectual are potsherds and rasp-like surfaces, such as that of the skin of the dogfish. Of the same general class are all sawing, drilling, and scraping tools and devices, which are described under separate heads. The smoothing and polishing implements into which the grinding stones imperceptibly grade are also separately treated. The smaller grinding stones were held in the hand, and were usually unshaped fragments, the arrowshaft rubber and the slender nephrite whetstone of the Eskimo being exceptions.

ABRADING STONE, NEW JERSEY. (LENGTH, 3 1-2 INCHES.)

The larger ones were slabs, bowlders, or fragments, which rested on the ground or were held in the lap while in use. In many localities exposed surfaces of rock in place were utilized, and these as well as the movable varieties are often covered with the grooves produced by the grinding work. These markings range from narrow, shal-

ARROWSHAFT RUBBER, CALIFORNIA. (LENGTH, 4 INCHES.)

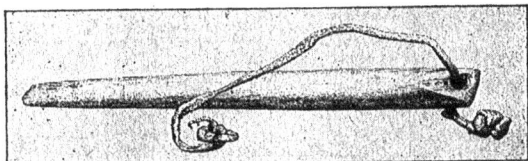

WHETSTONE OF NEPHRITE, ESKIMO. (LENGTH, 5 INCHES.)

low lines, produced by shaping pointed objects, to broad channels made in shaping large implements and utensils. Reference to the various forms of abrading implements is made in numerous works and articles treating of the technology of the native tribes. The more important of these are cited under *Archeology, Bonework, Stonework, Shellwork.* (W. H. H.)

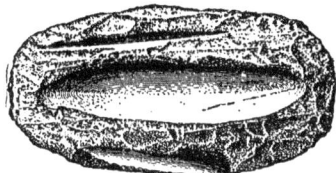

GRINDING STONE, TENNESSEE (LENGTH, 21 INCHES)

**Abraham,** also called Little Abraham. A Mohawk chief of considerable oratorical power who succeeded the so-called King Hendrick after the battle of L. George in 1755, in which the latter was killed. He espoused the English cause in the American Revolution, but was of a pacific character. He was present at the last meeting of the Mohawk with the American commissioners at Albany in Sept., 1775, after which he drops from notice. He was succeeded by Brant. (C. T.)

**Absayruc.** A Costanoan village mentioned as formerly connected with the mission of San Juan Bautista, Cal.—

Engelhardt, Franciscans in Cal., 398, 1897.

**Absentee.** A division of the Shawnee who about 1845 left the rest of the tribe, then in Kansas, and removed to Ind. T. In 1904 they numbered 459, under the Shawnee school superintendent in Oklahoma. (J. M.)
Ginetéwi Sawanógi.—Gatschet, Shawnee MS., B. A. E., 1879 (so called sometimes by the other Shawnee; Ginetéwi is derived from the name of Canadian r., on which they live). Pépua-hapítski Sawanógi.—Ibid. ('Away-from-here Shawnee,' commonly so called by the other Shawnee).

**Acacafui.** Mentioned by Juan de Oñate (Doc. Inéd., XVI, 115, 1871), in connection with Puaray, apparently as a pueblo of the Tigua of New Mexico in 1598.

**Acacagua.** An unidentified pueblo of New Mexico in 1598.—Oñate (1598) in Doc. Inéd., XVI, 103, 1871.

**Acachin.** A Papago rancheria in s. Arizona; pop. 47 in 1865.—Ind. Aff. Rep., 135, 1865.

**Acadialite.** A reddish chabazite (Dana, Text-book of Mineral.,458,1898), so called from Acadia, an early and still a literary name of Nova Scotia and New Brunswick; a latinization, helped out by analogy with the classical Arcadia, of a word formed by the early French explorers on the basis of a suffix of many place names, which in the Micmac dialect of Algonquian signifies 'where a thing is plentiful.' The *lite* represents the Greek λιθος, stone. (A. F. C.)

**Acapachiqui.** An unidentified town in s. Georgia, visited by De Soto in March, 1540.—Biedma in French, Hist. Coll. La., II, 99, 1850.
Capachiqui.—Gentleman of Elvas (1557) in French, op. cit., 137.

**Accohanoc.** A tribe of the Powhatan confederacy that formerly lived on the river of the same name, in Accomac and Northampton cos., Va. They had 40 warriors in 1608. Their principal village bore the name of the tribe. They became mixed with negroes in later times, and the remnant was driven off at the time of the Nat Turner insurrection, about 1833. (J. M.)
Accahanock.—Herrman, map (1670) in Maps to Accompany the Rep't of the Com'rs on the B'nd'ry Line bet. Va. and Md., 1873. Accohanock.—Strachey (ca. 1612), Virginia, 41, 1849. Accotronacks.—Boudinot, Star in the West, 125, 1816. Acohanock.—Smith (1629), Virginia, I, 120, repr. 1819. Aquohanock.—Ibid., II, 61. Occahanock.—Beverly, Virginia, 199, 1722. Ochahannanke.—Strachey (ca. 1612), Virginia, 62, 1849.

**Accomac.** (According to Trumbull the word means 'the other-side place,' or 'on-the-other-side-of-water place.' In the Massachuset language *ogkomé* or *akawiné* means 'beyond'; and *ac, aki,* or *ahki* in various Algonquian dialects means 'land.' According to Dr Wm. Jones (inf'n, 1905) the term is probably akin to the Chippewa *ăgaming,* 'the other shore,' and to the Sauk, Fox, and Kickapoo *ŭgámähèg i, ing* in the one case and *-gi* in the other being variations of the same suffix expressing 'place where'). A tribe of the Powhatan confederacy of Virginia that formerly lived in Accomac and Northampton cos., E. of Chesapeake bay, and according to Jefferson their principal village, which bore the tribal name, was about Cheriton, on Cherrystone inlet, Northampton co. In 1608 they had 80 warriors. As they declined in numbers and importance they lost their tribal identity, and the name became applied to all the Indians E. of Chesapeake bay. Up to 1812 they held their lands in common and were known under the names of Accomacs, living chiefly in upper Accomac co., and Gingaskins (see *Gangasco*), living near Eastville, Northampton co. They had become much mixed with negroes, and in the Nat Turner insurrection, about 1833, were treated as such and driven off. (J. M.)

Accawmacke.—Smith (1629), Va., I, 133, repr. 1819. Accomack.—Ibid., 120. Accowmack.—Ibid., map. Acomack.—Ibid., II, 61. Acomak.—Drake, Book of Indians, v, 1848.

**Accominta** (possibly related to the Chippewa *ä'ku'kŭmiga'k*, a locative expression referring to the place where land and water meet, hence, specifically, 'shore,' 'shore-line.'—Wm. Jones. The name was given by the Indians to York r.). A small tribe or band of the Pennacook confederacy, commonly called Agamenticus or Accominticus, that occupied a village of the same name at or near the site of the present York, York co., Me., to which the name "Boston" was given on some early maps. Capt. John Smith (Virginia, II, 183, repr. 1819) says that the people of this place were allied to those immediately N. of them, and were subject to the bashabees of Penobscot, which would seem to place them in the Abnaki confederacy, though they are now generally and apparently correctly included in the Pennacook confederacy. Schoolcraft (Ind. Tribes, v, 222, 1856) includes this area in the Pennacook dominion. Under what name the Accominta people were subsequently recognized is not known. (J. M. C. T.)

Accomentas.—Hoyt, Antiquarian Res., 90, 1824. Accomíntas.—Gookin (1674) in Mass. Hist. Soc. Coll., 1st s, I, 149, 1806. Accominticus.—Smith (1616), ibid., 3d s., VI, 97, 1837. Accomintycous.—Smith (1629), Virginia, II, 195, repr. 1819. Accomynticus.—Ibid., 183. Agamenticus—Ballard in Coast Surv. Rep., 246, 1871. An-ghem-ak-ti-koos.—Ibid. (given as proper name).

**Acconoc.** A village of the Powhatan confederacy in 1608, situated between Chickahominy and Pamunkey rs., New Kent co., Va.—Smith (1629), Virginia, I, map, repr. 1819.

**Accoqueck** (probably cognate with Chippewa *ä'ku'kwäg*, 'whirlpool,' or 'turn in the bend' of a river or road.—Wm. Jones). A Powhatan village, situate in 1608 on Rappahannock r., above Secobec, Caroline co., Va.—Smith (1629), Virginia, I, map, repr. 1819.

**Accossuwinck** (possibly cognate with the Chippewa *ä kosowing*, 'point where the tail and body meet'; or with *ä'kosink*, 'as far up as the place rises.'—Wm. Jones). A Powhatan village, existing in 1608 on Pamunkey r., King William co., Va.—Smith (1629), Virginia, I, map, repr. 1819.

**Acela.** A small village in w. central Florida, visited by De Soto in 1539. Ocilla r. derives its name from the place. See Gentleman of Elvas (1557) in French, Hist. Coll. La., II, 129, 1850.

**Achasta.** A former village of the Rumsen division of the Costanoan family, on the spot now occupied by the town of Monterey, Cal. The Rumsen were sometimes called Achastliens from the name of this settlement.—Taylor in Cal. Farmer, Apr. 20, 1860.

Achiesta.—Taylor, ibid.

**Acheha.** A Timucua phratry which included the Hiyaraba, Cayahasomi, Efaca, Hobatinequasi, and Chehelu clans.—Pareja (1612–14) quoted by Gatschet in Am. Philos. Soc. Proc., XVII, 492, 1878.

**Achepabecha** ('prairie dog'). A Crow band.

Ache-pä-be'-cha.—Morgan, Anc. Soc., 159, 1877. Rich Prairie Dog.—Culbertson in Smithson. Rep. 1850, 144, 1851.

**Achigan** (*ŭ'shigŭn*, sing. anim. noun.—Wm. Jones). A French-Canadian name of the small-mouthed black bass (*Micropterus dolomieu*), occasionally found in English writings. The word is old in French, Hennepin using it in 1688. *Ashigan* is the name of this fish in Chippewa and closely related Algonquian dialects. (A. F. C.)

**Achiligouan.** A tribe or band living between 1640 and 1670 on the N. shore of L. Huron, about the mouth of French r. and westward nearly to Sault Ste Marie. In 1670 they were attached to the mission at the Sault. In the Jesuit Relation of 1640 their position is given on the N. shore of L. Huron, at the mouth of French r. The Amikwa are mentioned in the same connection as residing on this stream. In the Relation of 1658 they appear to be placed farther N. on the river, and it is stated that they traded with the Cree. In the Relation of 1670 they are said to have been attached to the mission of Sault Ste Marie, but only as going there to fish. It is probable that they were a Chippewa or a Nipissing band. (J. M. C. T.)

Achiligouans.—Heriot, Travels, 194, 1807. Achiligoüiane.—Jesuit Rel., 1670, 79, 1858. Achiligouans.—Ibid., 1646, 81. Archirigouan.—Ibid., 1643, 61, 1858. Atchiligoüan.—Ibid., 1640, 34, 1858.

**Achilla.** A Costanoan village of Santa Cruz mission, Santa Cruz co., Cal., in 1819.—Taylor in Cal. Farmer, Apr. 5, 1860.

**Achillimo.** A Chumashan village formerly existing near Santa Inés mission, Santa Barbara co., Cal.—Taylor in Cal. Farmer, Oct. 18, 1861.

**Achois.** A native place in Encina valley, s. Cal., at which the mission of San Fernando was established, Sept. 8, 1797. **Achoic Comihavit.**—Coues, Garcés Diary, 266, 1900. **Achois.**—Ibid.

**Achomawi** (from *adzúma*, or *achóma*, 'river.'—Dixon). A division of the Shastan family formerly occupying the Pit r. country of N. E. Cal., except Burney, Dixie, and Hat cr. valleys, which were inhabited by the Atsugewi. A principal village was near Fallriver Mills, Shasta co. The languages of the Achomawi and the Atsugewi, while unquestionably related, are strikingly unlike. The term Achomawi was also employed by Powers to denote all the Indians of the Palaihnihan family of Powell, popularly known as Pit River Indians. See *Shastan Family.* **Achomáwes.**—Powers in Overland Mo., XII, 412, 1874. **A-cho-mâ'-wi.**—Powers in Cont. N. A. Ethnol., III, 267, 1877. **Adzumáwi.**—Curtin, Ilmawi vocab., B. A. E., 1889. **Kō'm-maidüm.**—Dixon, inf'n, 1904 ('snow people': Maidu name). **Shawash.**—Kroeber, inf'n, 1903 (Yuki name for the Achomawi taken to Round Valley res.).

**Achougoula** (probably 'pipe people,' from Choctaw *ashunga*, 'pipe'). One of the 9 villages constituting the Natchez confederacy in 1699.—Iberville in Margry, Déc., IV, 179, 1880.

**Achpoan.** See *Pone.*

**Achsinnink** (cognate with the Chippewa *â'kusîning*, 'at the place of rough rock,' meaning a place where many bowlders lie scattered about, or a rocky place hard to travel through.—Wm. Jones). A village of the Unalachtigo Delawares existing about 1770 on Hocking r., Ohio.—Heckewelder in Trans. Am. Philos. Soc., IV, 390, 1834.

**Achusi.** The port on the N. coast of the Gulf of Mexico, within the Muskhogean area, in which the fleet of De Soto wintered in 1539–40. It took its name from a neighboring town and is commonly identified with Pensacola bay. **Achusi.**—Garcilasso de la Vega, Fla., 299, 1723. **Achusse.**—Shipp, De Soto and Fla., 682, note, 1881. **Achussi.**—Ibid., 334. **Acusy.**—Margry, Déc., IV, 310, 1880. **Chuse.**—Biedma (1540) in French, Hist. Coll. La., II, 102, 1850. **Ochus.**—Gentleman of Elvas (1557), ibid., 136. **Ocus.**—Ibid., 145.

**Achyarachki** (*Ách-yä-rach'-ki;* 'where there is an old man,' in allusion to a stone pinnacle resembling a human form). A Tarahumare rancheria 16 m. s. of Rekorichic, Chihuahua, Mexico, about lat. 27° 5′, long. 106° 45′.—Lumholtz, inf'n, 1894.

**Ackia.** A Chickasaw village in N. Mississippi, attacked by the French and

Choctaw in 1736.—Gayarré, Louisiana, I, 480, 1851.

**Aclutoy.** A village supposed to be of the Patwin division of the Copehan family which formerly lived in Napa and Yolo cos., Cal. Its inhabitants concluded a treaty with Gov. Vallejo in 1836.—Bancroft, Hist. Cal., IV, 71, 1886.

**Acnagis.** A former village, presumably Costanoan, connected with Dolores mission, San Francisco, Cal.—Taylor in Cal. Farmer, Oct. 18, 1861.

**Acochis** (evidently from the Wichita *ha-kwi-chis*, 'metal,' interpreted 'gold' by the Spaniards). Given by an Indian nicknamed "Turk," q. v., as the name for gold in the language of the people of Quivira or Harahey, identified as the Wichita and Pawnee, respectively. By misinterpretation the name has been given to Quivira itself. See Castañeda and Jaramillo in 14th Rep. B. A. E., 493, 510, 1896; Davis, Span. Conq. N. Mex., 226, 1869; Hodge in Brower, Harahey, 70, 1899. (F. W. H.)

**Acolapissa.** An indefinite group, of Choctaw lineage, formerly living on L. Ponchartrain, about the coast lagoons, and on the Mississippi, in Louisiana. Early French writers derived the name from the Choctaw *háklo pisa*, 'those who listen and see.' Allen Wright, governor of the Choctaw nation, suggests *okla pisa*, 'those who look out for people'; that is, watchmen, guardians, spies, which probably refers to their position, where they could observe entrance into or departure from the lake and river. The name appears to have been made by early authors to include several tribes, the Bayogoula, Mugulasha, and others. According to Iberville the Acolapissa had 7 towns; but one of their villages was occupied by the Tangiboa, who appear to have been a different tribe. The Acolapissa are said to have suffered severely from an epidemic about 1700, and Iberville says they united with the Mugulasha; if so, they must have been included in those massacred by the Bayogoula, but this is rendered doubtful by the statement of Pénicaut (French, Hist. Coll. La., n. s., I, 144, 1869) that in 1718 the Colapissa, who inhabited the N. shore of L. Ponchartrain, removed to the Mississippi and settled 13 leagues above New Orleans. (C. T.) **Aqueloa pissas.**—Jefferys, French Dom. Am., I, 162, 1761. **Aquelon Pissas.**—Bossu (1751), Travels, I, 34, 1771. **Aquelou pissas.**—Du Pratz, Hist. La., II, 219, 1758. **Calopissas.**—Pénicaut (1713) in Margry, Déc., V, 507, 1883. **Cenepisa.**—La Salle, ibid., I, 564, 1875. **Colapessas.**—Gravier in Shea, Early Voy., 159, 1861. **Colapissas.**—Pénicaut (1699) in French, Hist. Coll. La., n. s., I, 38, 1869. **Colipasa.**—Drake, Bk. Inds., VI, 1848. **Collapissas.**—Bossu (1751), Travels, I, 34, 1771. **Coulapissas.**—Sauvole (1700) in Margry, Déc., IV, 462, 1880. **Equinipichas.**—Sauvole in French, Hist. Coll. La., III, 225, 1851. **Goulapissas.**—B. des Lozières, Voy.

à la Le., 242, 1802. **Kinipissa.**—Tonti in Margry, Déc., I, 604, 1875. **Kolapissas.**—Gravier (1700) in French, Hist. Coll. La., II, 88, 1875. **Nipissa.**—Iberville in Margry, Déc., IV, 101, 1880. **Piniscas.**—Sauvole (1700) in French, Hist. Coll. La., III, 235, 1851 (probably the same). **Quenipisa.**—La Salle in Margry, Déc., I, 564, 1875. **Quinipisas.**—French, Hist. Coll. La., II, 23, 1875. **Quinipissa.**—Tonti (1682), ibid., I, 63, 1846. **Quiniquissa.**—Hennepin (1680), ibid., 206. **Quinnipissas.**—La Melairie (1682), ibid., II, 50, 1875.

**Acoli.** Mentioned by Oñate (Doc. Ined., XVI, 114, 1871) as a pueblo of New Mexico in 1598. Probably situated in the Salinas, in the vicinity of Abo, and in all probability a Tigua or Piros village.

**Acoma** (from the native name *Akóme*, 'people of the white rock,' now commonly pronounced *A'-ko-ma*. Their name for their town is *A'ko*). A tribe and pueblo of the Keresan family, the latter situate on a rock mesa, or peñol, 357 ft. in height, about 60 m. w. of the Rio Grande, in Valencia co., N. Mex. Acoma is mentioned as early as 1539 by Fray Marcos de Niza, under the name Acus, a corruption of Hakukia, the Zuñi name of the pueblo; but it was first visited the following year by members of Coronado's army, who recorded the name as Acuco. The strength of the position of the village, which has the distinction of being the oldest inhabited settlement in the United States, is remarked by the early Spanish chroniclers, who estimated its houses at 200 and its warriors at the same number. Antonio de Espejo also visited Acoma in 1583, designating it by the name under which it is now known, attributing to it the exaggerated population of 6,000, and mentioning its dizzy trail cut in the rock and its cultivated fields "two leagues away," probably those still tilled at Acomita (Tichuna) and Pueblito (Titsiap), their two summer, or farming, villages, 15 m. distant. Juan de Oñate, the colonizer of New Mexico, visited Acoma in 1598, when, during his governorship, Fray Andrés Corchado was assigned a mission field which included that pueblo, but no mission was actually established there at so early a date. The Acoma had been hostile to the surrounding village tribes during this period, and as early as 1540 are mentioned as "feared by the whole country round about." Juan de Zaldivar, of Oñate's force, visited Acoma in Dec., 1598, with 30 men; they were surprised by the Indians, who killed 14 of the Spaniards outright, including Zaldivar and 2 other captains, and caused 4 others to leap over the cliff, 3 of whom were miraculously saved. In Jan., 1599, an avenging party of 70 Spaniards were dispatched under Zaldivar's brother Vicente, who, after a battle which lasted 3 days, succeeded in killing half the tribe of about 3,000 and in partly burning the town. The first missionary labor performed at Acoma was by Fray Gerónimo de Zarate-Salmeron, prior to 1629; but Fray Juan Ramirez, who went to Acoma in the spring of 1629, and remained there many years, was its first permanent missionary and the builder of the first church, which was replaced in or after 1699 by the present great structure of adobe. The Acoma participated in the general Pueblo revolt against the Spaniards in 1680 (see *Pueblos*), killing their missionary, Fray Lucas Maldonado; but, largely on account of their isolation and the inaccessibility of their village site, they were not so severely dealt with by the Spaniards as were most of the more easterly pueblos.

ACOMA MAN

An attempt was made to reconquer the village by Gov. Vargas in Aug., 1696, but he succeeded only in destroying their crops and in capturing 5 warriors. The villagers held out until July 6, 1699, when they submitted to Gov. Cubero, who changed the name of the pueblo from San Estevan de Acoma to San Pedro; but the former name was subsequently restored and is still retained. The population of Acoma dwindled from about 1,500 at the beginning of the revolt to 1,052 in 1760. In 1782 the mission was reduced to a visita of Laguna, and by the close of the century its population was only a few more than 800. The present (1902) number is 566. The Acoma are agriculturists, cultivating by irrigation corn, wheat, melons, calabashes, etc., and raising sheep, goats, horses, and donkeys. In prehistoric and early historic times they had flocks of domesticated turkeys. They are expert potters, but now do little or no weaving. The villages which they traditionally occupied after leaving Shipapu, their mythical place of origin in the N., were Kashkachuti, Washpashuka, Kuchtya, Tsiama, Tapitsiama, and Katzimo (q. v.), or the Enchanted mesa. Heashkowa and Kowina were also pueblos occupied by Acoma clans in prehistoric times. The following are the clans of the tribe, those marked by an asterisk being extinct: Tsits (Water), Kochinish (Yellow corn), Kukanish (Red corn), *Kuishkosh (Blue corn), *Kuishtiti (Brown corn), Kusesh (White corn), Tyami (Eagle), Shawiti (Parrot), Osach (Sun), Shask (Road-runner), Hapanyi (Oak), Shquwi (Rattlesnake), Kuwhaia (Bear), Tsina (Turkey), Tanyi (Calabash), Kurts (Antelope), Huwaka (Sky), *Moshaich (Buffalo), *Haka (Fire), Sii (Ant). The land grant of the tribe, made by Spain and confirmed by the United States, comprises 95,792 acres. See Winship, Coronado Exped., 14th Rep. B. A. E., 1896; Espejo (1583) in Doc. Inéd. de Indias, XV, 100, 151, 1871; Villagran, Hist. Nueva Mexico, 1610, repr. 1900; Vetancurt, Crónica, and Menologia, repr. 1871; Bandelier, (1) Hist. Introd., 1881, (2) Contributions, 1890, (3) Final Report, 1890–92; Bancroft, Hist. Ariz. and N. Mex., 1889; Lummis, Land of Poco Tiempo, 1893; Hodge, (1) Katzimo the Enchanted, 1898, (2) Ascent of the Enchanted Mesa, 1898. (F. W. H.)

Aacus.—Barcia, Ensayo, 21, 1723. Abucios.—Duro, Don Diego de Peñalosa, 23, 1882 (the Acus of Niza). Acmaat.—Evans (1888) in Compte Rendu Cong. Int. Am., VII, 229, 1890. A-co.—Bandelier in Arch. Inst. Papers, III, pt. 1, 132, 1890 (or Acoma). Acogiya.—Oñate (1598) in Doc. Inéd., XVI, 102, 1871 (from Zuñi name Hakukia). Acoma.—Espejo (1583), ibid., XV, 116, 1871. Acóma.—Oñate (1598), ibid., XVI, 127, 1871. Acoman.—Hakluyt, Voy., 469, 1600 (or Acoma; citing Espejo, 1583). Acomas.—Alcedo, Dic. Geog., II, 523, 549, 1787 ("pueblo de Acomas"). Acome.—MS. of 1764 in Schoolcraft, Ind. Tribes, III, 304, 1853. Acomenses.—Bancroft, Ariz. and N. Mex., 145, 1889. Acomeses.—Villagran, Hist. Nueva Mexico, 158, 1610. Acomo.—Mota-Padilla, Hist. de la Conquista, 169, 1742. Acona.—Emory, Recon., 133, 1848. Aconia.—Ward in Ind. Aff. Rep. 1864, 191, 1865. Acquia.—Benavides (1630) misquoted in Nouv. Ann. Voy., 5th ser., XXVII, 307, 1851. Acu.—Ogilby, America, 392, 1671. Acuca.—Ramusio, Nav. et Viaggi, III, 1, 1565. Acucans.—Whipple in Pac. R. R. Rep., III, pt. 3, 90, 1856. Acuco.—Castañeda (1540) in Winship, Coronado Exped., 519, 1896. Acucu.—Coronado (1540), ibid., 560. Acus.—Nica (1539) in Hakluyt, Voy., III, 440. 1600. Acux.—Mota-Padilla, Hist. de la Conq., 111, 1742. Ago.—Bandelier in Arch. Inst. Papers, I, 14, 1881 (proper Queres name). Ah-co.—Lummis, Land of Poco Tiempo, 63, 1893. Ah-ko.—Lummis, Man Who Married the Moon, 207, 1894. A'ikoka.—Stephen in 8th Rep. B. A. E., 30, 1891 (Hopi name of pueblo). Aioma.—Linschoten, Descrip. de l'Amérique, 336, map, 1638. Aiomo.—Ogilby, America, map, 1671. Ako.—Loew (1875)

in Wheeler Surv. Rep., VII, 339, 345, 1879. Akókovi.—Voth, Traditions of the Hopi, 145, 1905 (Hopi name of pueblo). Ako-ma.—Bandelier in Arch. Inst. Papers, V, 173, 1890 (tribal name). Akómë.—Hodge, field notes, B. A. E., 1895 (own name: 'people of the white rock'). Alcuco.—Barcia, Ensayo, 21, 1723. Alomas.—Mota-Padilla, Hist. de la Conq., 515, 1742 (probably the same). A-qo.—Bandelier in Mag. West. Hist., 668, Sept., 1886 (native name of pueblo). Aquia.—Jefferys, Am. Atlas, map 5, 1776 (doubtless the same, but he locates also San Estevan de Acoma). Atlachaco.—Mota-Padilla (1742), op. cit., 159. Coco.—Alvarado (1540) in Winship, Coronado Exped., 594, 1896. Hab-koo-kee-ah.—Domenech, Des. N. A., II, 53, 1860. Hacu.—Bandelier in Mag. West. Hist., 668, Sept., 1886 (Navaho name of pueblo). Hacuqua.—Bandelier, Gilded Man, 149, 1893 (given as Zuñi name of pueblo; should be Hakukia). Ha-cu-quin.—Bandelier in Mag. West. Hist., 668, Sept., 1886 (Zuñi name of pueblo). Hacús.—Niça (1539) cited by Coronado (1540) in Doc. Inéd., XIV, 322, 1870 (same as Niça's Acus). Hah-kóo-kee-ah.—Eaton quoted by Schoolcraft, Ind. Tribes, IV, 220, 1854 (Zuñi name of pueblo). Hak-koo-kee-ah.—Simpson in Smithson. Rep. 1869, 333, 1871. Haku.—Bandelier in Arch. Inst. Papers, V, 173, 1890 (given as Zuñi name of pueblo). Ha-ku Kue.—Ibid., III, pt. 1, 132, 1890 (improperly given as Zuñi name of pueblo). Ha-kus.—Ibid., V, 173, 1890 (Navaho name of pueblo; see Hacu, above). Peñol.—Alcedo, Dic. Geog., IV, 149, 1788 (so named from the mesa). Peñoles.—Perea, Verdadera Rel., 3, 1632. Quebec of the Southwest.—Lummis, Land of Poco Tiempo, 57, 1893. Quéres Gibraltar.—Ibid., 57. San Estéban de Acoma.—Vetancurt, Teatro Mex., III, 319, 1871 (mission name). San Estéban de Acoma.—Orozco y Berra in Anales Minis. Fom., VI, 255, 1882 (misprint s for c). San Pedro.—Bancroft, Ariz. and N. Mex., 221, 1889 (mission name after July, 1699). S. Estevan de Acoma.—Jefferys, Am. Atlas, map 5, 1776. S. Estevau de Acama.—Brion de la Tour, map l'Amér., 1779 (misprint). St Estevan.—Kitchin, map N. A. (1785) in Raynal, Indies, VI, 1788. St Estevan Acoma.—De l'Isle, Carte Mex. et Floride, 1703. St Estevan Queres.—Ibid., Atlas Nouveau, map 60, 1733. Suco.—Galvano (1563) in Hakluyt Soc. Pub., XXX, 227, 1862 (misquoting Acuco, of Coronado; also applied to Cicuic = Pecos). Ti'lawehuide.—Gatschet, Isleta MS. vocab., B. A. E., 1885 (Isleta name of the people; pl. Ti'lawehun). Ti'lawéi.—Ibid. (Isleta name; compare Tuthlahuay). Tu'hlawaí.—Hodge, field-notes, B. A. E., 1895 (Sandia name; probably refers to a tree or plant). Tŭ'hlawé.—Ibid. (Isleta name). Tülawéi.—Gatschet, Isleta MS. vocab., B. A. E., 1885 (another Isleta name). Tuthea-uáy.—Bandelier, Gilded Man, 211, 1893 (Tigua name of pueblo). Tuthla-huay.—Bandelier in Arch. Inst. Papers, IV, 235, 1892 (Tigua name). Tuth-lanay.—Bandelier, Gilded Man, 149, 1893 (misprint n for u). Vacus.—Niça, Relation, in Ramusio, Nav. et Viaggi, III, 357, 1565. Vsacus.—Ibid. Yacco.—Oñate (1598) in Doc. Inéd., XVI, 115, 1871 (Spanish y Acco = 'and Acco'). Yaco. — Columbus Memorial Vol., 155, 1893 (misprint of Oñate's "Yacco").

**Acomita.** An Acoma summer village about 15 m. N. of the pueblo of Acoma, near McCartys station on the Santa Fé Pacific railroad, Valencia co., N. Mex.

Aconista.—Pullen in Harper's Weekly, 594, Aug. 2, 1890. Tichuna.—Hodge, field notes, B. A. E., 1895 (native name).

**Aconchi.** An Opata pueblo on the E. bank of Rio Sonora, about lat. 29° 45′, N. W. Mexico. It was the seat of the Spanish mission of San Pedro, founded in 1639. Pop. 580 in 1678, 285 in 1730. (Orozco y Berra, Geog., 344, 1864.)

San Pedro Aconchi.—Zapata (1678) quoted by Bancroft, No. Mex. States, I, 246, 1884.

**Acoomemeck.** A town, perhaps Nipmuc, in E. Massachusetts in the 17th century.—Winthrop (1638) in Drake, Book of Inds., bk. II, 27, 1848.

**Acoti.** A locality, apparently Indian, on a w. branch of the Rio Grande, w. of Taos, in N. N. Mex., and indicated as the "birth place of Montezuma" on an Indian map reproduced in Whipple, Pac. R. R. Rep., III, pt. 3, 10, 1856. See *Shipapulima*.

Acota.—Meline, Two Thousand Miles, 202, 1867.
Acotí.—Whipple, op. cit.

**Acous.** The principal village of the Chaicclesaht, situate on Battle bay, Ououkinish inlet, w. coast of Vancouver id.—Can. Ind. Aff., 264, 1902.

**Acpactaniche.** A town, probably Muskhogean, located on De l'Isle's map of 1703 on the headwaters of Coosa r., Ala.

**Acquack** (possibly related to the Chippewa *ä'kwa kwäyag*, a locative term expressing the line between cover and open; its particular sense is 'at the edge of the woods,' the point of view being from the open; the idea of woods is expressed by the secondary stem *-a'k-*.—Wm. Jones). A village of the Powhatan confederacy of Virginia in 1608, on the N. bank of Rappahannock r., Richmond co.—Smith (1629), Virginia, I, map, repr. 1819.

Atquacke.—Ibid., II, 91.

**Acquaskac.** A village situated in 1608 on the w. bank of Patuxent r., St Marys co., Md. The word may be related to Aquascogoc and Weckquaesgoek.

Acquaseack.—Bozman, Hist. Md., I, 141, 1837.
Acquaskack.—Smith (1620), Virginia, I, map, repr. 1819.

**Acquera.** An Utina tribe or band in N. Florida.—Laudonnière (1564) in French, Hist. Coll. La., n. s., I, 243, 1869.

Acuera.—Garcilasso de la Vega, Florida, 47, 1723.
Aequeya.—Barcia, Ensayo, 48, 1723 (given as the cacique's name).

**Acquintanacsuak.** A tribe or subtribe which Capt. John Smith (Virginia, I, 118, 1629; Arber ed., 53, 1884) locates on the w. bank of Patuxent r., St Mary's co., Md. They were near to and in friendship with the Patuxent and Mattapanient, the 3 tribes numbering 200 warriors. The principal village bore the tribal name and is supposed by Bozman to have been situated at the mouth of a small creek about 2½ m. above Cole's inspection house. Smith describes them as "the most civill to give entertainement." Although this people had their werowance, or chief, it is doubtful whether they formed a distinct tribe; it is not impossible that they were a band or division of the Patuxent. A number of local names mentioned by early writers as those of Indian tribes of Maryland subsequently dropped from notice without indication of the extinction of the people, very likely because subsequent and more correct information showed that these referred merely to divisions of well-known tribes. (J. M. C. T.)

Ac-quin-a-nack-su-acks.—Macauley, N. Y., II, 168, 1829. Acquintanacksuah.—Bozman, Hist. Md., I, 140, 1837. Acquintanacksuak.—Smith (1629), Va., I, 118, repr. 1819. Acquintanacsuck.—Ibid., map. Acquintunachsuah.—Bozman, Hist. Md., II, 467, 1837. Acquitanases.—De Laet, Hist. du Nouv. Monde, 85, 1640.

**Actinolite.** A variety of amphibolite much used for implements by the ancient Pueblos of Arizona and New Mexico. It occurs in small bodies in connection with various crystalline formations, especially serpentine, and is much diversified in color, the mottlings of various hues of red, yellow, green, and gray giving very pleasing effects. Analysis shows silica, 60; magnesia, 21; lime, 14; specific gravity, 3 to 3.1. Illustrations are given by Nordenskiold, Cliff Dwellers, 1893; Putnam in Surv. W. 100th Merid., VII, 1879; Wilson in Rep. Nat. Mus. 1896, 1898. (W. H. H.)

**Acubadaos.** A tribe known to Cabeza de Vaca (Smith transl., 84, 1851) during his sojourn in Texas, 1527–34, as living "in the rear" of or more inland than the Atayos (Toho).

**Acuragna.** A former Gabrieleño village in Los Angeles co., Cal., at a place later called La Presa.—Ried (1852) quoted by Taylor in Cal. Farmer, June 8, 1860.

**Acushnet.** A village of Praying Indians in 1698, probably about Acushnet, Bristol co., Mass. "Acchusnutt" is said to have been the Indian name of New Bedford.—Rawson and Danforth (1698) in Mass. Hist. Soc. Coll., 1st s., x, 129–134, 1809.

**Acyum.** A former village, presumably Costanoan, connected with Dolores mission, San Francisco, Cal.—Taylor in Cal. Farmer, Oct. 18, 1861.

**Adac.** A Cochimi rancheria belonging to Santa Gertrudis mission, E. side of Lower California, about lat. 27° 58′.—Taylor in Cal. Farmer, Jan. 17, 1862.

**Adai.** A tribe of the Caddo confederacy, speaking a dialect closely related to that of the Kadohadacho, Hainai, and Anadarko. The mission of San Miguel de Linares was founded among them in 1716; it was destroyed by the French, with Natchitoch and Caddo allies, in 1719, but was restored in 1721 and the presidio of Nuestra Señora del Pilar de los Adaes established. When Iberville ascended Red r. of Louisiana in 1699 he heard of the Adai and called them Natao, stating that their village was on the river near that of the Yatasi. According to La Harpe (1719) the tribe was very useful to the French traders and explorers, particularly when making portages. At that time the villages of the Adai extended from Red r. southward beyond the Sabine, in Texas, known in the 18th century as Rio de los Adais. The trail which from ancient times had connected the Adai villages became the noted "contraband trail" over which traders and travelers journeyed between the French and Spanish provinces, and one of the villages was a station on the road between the French fort at Natchitoches and the Spanish fort at San Antonio. As the villages of the tribe were scattered over a territory one portion of which was under the control of the French and the other under that of the Spaniards, the Indians were subjected to all the adverse influences of the white race and suffered from their wars and from the new diseases and intoxicants which they introduced, so that by 1778 they were reported by Mezières (Bancroft, No. Mex. States, I, 661, 1886) as almost exterminated. About 1792, 14 families of the tribe, together with a number of Mexicans, emigrated to a region s. of San Antonio de Bejar, but they soon melted away and were lost among other Indians. Those who remained numbered about 100. In 1805 Sibley reported a small settlement of these Indians on Lac Macdon, near an affluent of Red r.; it contained only 20 men, but a larger number of women. This Adai remnant had never left their ancient locality, but they had not escaped the vicissitudes of their kindred. In 1715 Domingo Ramon, with a company of Franciscans, traversed the Adai territory and started settlements. In 1716 the mission of San Miguel de Linares was founded among them, and there were Adai also in the mission of San Francisco de los Tejas, established in 1690. About 1735 a military post called Nuestra Señora del Pilar was added, and 5 years later this garrison became the Presidio de los Adayes. Later, when the country was districted for the jurisdiction of Indians, the Adai tribe was placed under the division having its official headquarters at Nacogdoches. In all essentials of living and ceremony they resembled the other Caddo, by whom the remnant was finally absorbed.　　　　(A. C. F.)

Adaes.—Rivera, Diario, leg. 2,602, 1736. **Adæs.**—Bollaert in J. Ethnol. Soc. Lond., II, 265, 1850. **Adage.**—Tanner, Nar., 327, 1830. **Adahi.**—Latham, Elem. Comp. Philol., 467, 1862. **Ăda′-i.**—Mooney, Caddo MS., B. A. E., 1891. **Adaïces.**—Ann. de la Prop. de la Foi, III, 508, 1828. **Adaics.**—Boudinot, Star in the West, 125, 1816. **Adaies.**—Pénicaut (1701) in French, Hist. Coll. La., n. s. I, 73, 1869. **Adaihe.**—Latham, Elem. Comp. Philol., 469, 1862. **Adais.**—Mota-Padilla (1742), Hist. de la Conq., 177, 1870. **Adaisses.**—Bollaert in J. Ethnol. Soc. Lond., II, 280, 1850. **Adaize.**—Sibley, Hist. Sketches, 67, 1806. **Adayes.**—La Harpe (1719) in Margry, Déc., VI, 303, 1886. **Adays.**—La Harpe in French, Hist. Coll. La., III, 47, 1851. **Addaise.**—Schermerhorn (1812) in Mass. Hist. Coll., 2d s., II, 24, 1814. **Addaize.**—Brackenridge, Views of La., 81, 1814. **Addees.**—U. S. Ind. Treaties, 465, 1826. **Addies.**—Clark and Cass (1829) quoted by Schoolcraft, Ind. Tribes, III, 596, 1853. **Adees.**—Keane in Stanford, Compend., 499, 1878. **Adeyches.**—Martin, Hist. La., I, 202, 1827. **Adiais.**—Jefferys, Am. Atlas, map 5, 1776. **Adoses.**—Villa-Señor, Theatro Am., II, 329, 1748. **Adyes.**—Pike, Exped., 277, 1810. **Andayes.**—Baudry des Lozières, Voy. Louisiane, 241, 1802. **Atayos.**—Cabeça de Vaca (1529), Smith transl., 121, 1871. **Atoyos.**—Davis,

Span. Conq., N. Mex., 82, 1869. **Azadyze.**—Woodward, Reminis., 78, 1859. **Hadaí.**—Gatschet, Creek Migr. Leg., I, 43, 1884. **Hadaies.**—Doc. of 18th century quoted by Smith, Cabeça de Vaca, 127, note, 1871. **Natao.**—Iberville (1699) in Margry, Déc., IV, 178, 1880.

**Adario.** A Tionontate chief, known also as Kondiaronk, Sastaretsi, and The Rat. He had a high reputation for bravery and sagacity, and was courted by the French, who made a treaty with him in 1688 by which he agreed to lead an expedition against the Iroquois, his hereditary enemies. Starting out for the war with a picked band, he was surprised to hear, on reaching Cataracouy, that the French were negotiating peace with the Iroquois, who were about to send envoys to Montreal with hostages from each tribe. Concealing his surprise and chagrin, he secretly determined to intercept the embassy. Departing as though to return to his own country in compliance with the admonition of the French commandant, he placed his men in ambush and made prisoners of the members of the Iroquois mission, telling the chief of the embassy that the French had commissioned him to surprise and destroy the party. Keeping only one prisoner to answer for the death of a Huron who was killed in the fight, he set the others free, saying that he hoped they would repay the French for their treachery. Taking his captive to Michilimackinac, he delivered him over to the French commander, who put him to death, having no knowledge of the arrangement of peace. He then released a captive Iroquois whom he had long held at his village that he might return to inform his people of the act of the French commander. An expedition of 1,200 Iroquois fell upon Montreal Aug. 25, 1689, when the French felt secure in the anticipation of peace, slew hundreds of the settlers and burned and sacked the place. Other posts were abandoned by the French, and only the excellent fortifications of others saved them from being driven out of the country. Adario led a delegation of Huron chiefs who went to Montreal to conclude a peace, and while there he died, Aug. 1, 1701, and was buried by the French with military honors.　　　　(F. H.)

**Adirondack** (Mohawk: *Hatiroñ′tăks*, 'they eat trees', a name given in allusion to the eating of the bark of trees in time of famine.—Hewitt). The Algonquian tribes N. of the St Lawrence with which the Iroquois were acquainted, particularly those along Ottawa and St Maurice rs., who were afterward settled at Three Rivers and Oka, Quebec. Jefferys in 1761 seems to apply the term to the Chippewa.　　　　(J. M.)

Adirondacs.—Barton, New Views, xxxviii, 1798. **Adirondacks.**—Garangula (1684) quoted by Williams, Vermont, I, 504, 1809. **Adirondaks.**—Homann heirs map, 1756. **Adirondax.**—Livingston

(1701) in N. Y. Doc. Col. Hist., IV, 899, 1854. **Adirontak.**—Vetromile, Abnakis, 51, 1866. **Adisonkas.**—Martin, North Carolina, I, 76, 1829. **Adnondecks.**—McKenney and Hall, Ind. Tribes, III, 79, 1854. **Arundacs.**—Johnson (1763) in N. Y. Doc. Col. Hist., VII, 582, 1856. **Arundax.**—Ft Johnson conference (1756), ibid., 233. **Honanduk.**—Coxe, Carolana, map, 1741 (on E. shore of L. Huron; same?). **Iroondocks.**—Carver, Travels, 120, 1778. **Lătĭlēntasks.**—King, Jour. to Arctic Ocean, I, 11, 1836 (at Oka). **Orendakes.**—Martin, North Carolina, I, 65, 1829. **Orondacks.**—Johnson (1751) in N. Y. Doc. Col. Hist., VI, 729, 1855. **Orondocks.**—Stoddart (1750), ibid., 582 (at Oka). **Orondoes.**—Imlay, Western Ter., 292, 1797. **Oroondoks.**—Stoddart (1753) in N. Y. Doc. Col. Hist., VI, 780, 1855. **Oroonducks.**—Lindesay (1749), ibid., 538. **Orundacks.**—Dinwiddie (1754), ibid., 827. **Rarondaks.**—Vater, Mithridates, pt. 3, sec. 3, 309, 1816. **Ratirúntaks.**—Gatschet, Caughnawaga MS., B. A. E., 1882 (Mohawk name; sing. Rarúntaks). **Rondax.**—Glen (1699) in N. Y. Doc. Col. Hist., IV, 559, 1854. **Rondaxe.**—Von der Donck (1656) in N. Y. Hist. Soc. Coll., 2d s., I, 209, 1841.

**Adjuitsuppa.** An Eskimo settlement and Danish trading station in s. w. Greenland, lat. 60° 27′.—Meddelelser om Grönland, XVI, map, 1896.

**Südpröven.**—Koldewey, German Arct. Exped., 182, 1874. **Sydpröven.**—Meddelelser om Grönland, XVI, map, 1896.

**Adlet.** A fabulous people that the Eskimo believe to be descended from a dog. A woman married a red dog and bore five dogs, which she cast adrift in a boat, and also five children of monstrous shape. The dogs reached the other side of the ocean and begot the white people. The monsters engendered the Adlet, terrible beings, identified by the Labrador Eskimo with the Indians, of whom they formerly lived in dread, also by the Eskimo of the western shores of Hudson bay, who, however, called this misbegotten and bloodthirsty race Erqigdlit. The Eskimo of Greenland and Baffin land, having no Indian neighbors, pictured the tribe of monsters with human heads, arms, and trunks joined to the hind legs of dogs. See Boas (1) in Trans. Roy. Soc. Can., V, sec. 2, 35, 1888; (2) in 6th Rep. B. A. E., 640, 1888.

**Adla.**—Boas in Trans. Roy. Soc. Can., op. cit. (sing. form of *Adlat*). **Adlähsuin.**—Stein in Petermanns Mitt., no. 9, map, 1902. **Adlat.**—Boas, op. cit. **Adlet.**—Boas in 6th Rep. B. A. E., 640, 1888. **Erqiglit.**—Ibid.

**Adobe** (a word traceable to an Egyptian hieroglyph signifying 'brick,' thence to Arabic *at-ṭōb*, *al-ṭob*, whence the Spanish *adobar*, 'to daub,' 'to plaster'; adopted in the United States from Mexico). Large sun-dried bricks, much used by the Pueblo Indians of New Mexico in building houses and garden walls. The process of molding adobes in a wooden frame was not employed by the aborigines of the United States before the advent of the Spaniards in the 16th century. In 1540 the Pueblo method of preparing the material and of erecting masonry, when stone was not available, is thus described by Castañeda (14th Rep. B. A. E., 520, 1896): "They gather a great pile of twigs of thyme [sagebrush] and sedge

grass and set it afire, and when it is half coals and ashes they throw a quantity of dirt and water on it and mix it all together. They make round balls of this, which they use instead of stones after they are dry, fixing them with the same mixture, which comes to be like a stiff clay." After the introduction of wheat by the Spaniards the straw crushed by the hoofs of horses in stamping out the grain on a threshing floor was substituted by the Indians for the charred brush. The character of much of the soil of the arid region is such that no foreign admixture, excepting the straw, is required. A requisite of adobe-making is a good supply of water; consequently the industry is conducted generally on the banks of streams, near which pueblos are usually built. When molded, the adobes are set on edge to dry, slanted slightly to shed rain. Adobes vary in size, but are generally about 18 in. long, 8 to 10 in. wide, and 4 to 6 in. thick. In setting them in walls mortar of the same material is used, as is the case with stone masonry. In the S. W., where the average precipitation is not great, structures built of adobes last indefinitely with reasonable repair, the greatest amount of disintegration being at the base of the walls during seasons of rain, although prolonged sand storms also erode the surfaces. For the sake of appearance, as well as to aid in protecting it against weathering, adobe masonry is usually plastered (the Indian women using their hands as trowels), when it presents a pleasing appearance, varying in color from gray to a rich reddish brown, according to the color of the earth of which the plaster is made. The interior walls and likewise also the borders of the windows and doors are sometimes whitewashed with gypsum. Away from streams, as at Acoma, stone is usually employed for house masonry; but a noteworthy exception is the immense adobe church at this pueblo, built by the Indians about 1699, under the direction of the Spanish fathers, of material carried from the plain below, the summit of the Acoma mesa being bare rock. Another kind of earth-masonry in the arid region is that known as pisé. This was made by erecting a double framework of poles, wattled with reeds or grass, forming two parallel surfaces as far apart as the desired thickness of the wall, and into the enclosed space adobe grout was rammed. In the celebrated ruin of Casa Grande (q. v.) the framework was evidently built about 5 ft. long and 3 or 4 ft. wide, and when the grout became dry the frame was moved sideways or upward to receive the next course (see Mindeleff in 13th Rep. B.

A. E. 309, 1896; Cushing, ibid., 360). Houses constructed of adobes are very comfortable, being warm in winter and cool in summer. For this reason, and owing to the availability and cheapness of the material, adobe forms an important factor in the domestic economy of both white and Indian inhabitants of the S. W. (F. W. H.)

**Adoeette** (*ado* 'tree,' *e-et* 'great,' *te* personal suffix: ' Big Tree '). A Kiowa chief, born about 1845. In consequence of Custer's vigorous campaign on the Washita in the fall of 1868 the Kiowa and confederated tribes had been compelled to come in upon their reservation, in what is now s. w. Oklahoma, but still kept up frequent raids into Texas notwithstanding the establishment of Ft

ADOEETTE (KIOWA)

Sill in their midst. In May, 1871, a large party of warriors led by Satanta (properly Set-t'aiñ-te, White Bear), q. v., and accompanied by Satank (properly Set-ängyä, Sitting Bear), q. v., and Big Tree, attacked a wagon train, killing 7 men and taking 41 mules. For their part in this deed, which they openly avowed, the three chiefs named were arrested at Ft Sill to stand trial in Texas. Setängyä made resistance and was killed by the guard. The other two were confined in the Texas penitentiary until Oct., 1873, when they were released on promise of good behavior of their tribe. Satanta was subsequently rearrested and committed suicide in prison. During the latter part of the outbreak of 1874–75 Big Tree, with other chiefs believed to be secretly hostile, were confined as prisoners at Ft Sill. Since that

time the tribe has remained at peace. Big Tree is still living upon his allotment on the former reservation and is now a professed Christian. See Mooney, Calendar Hist. Kiowa Inds., 17th Rep. B. A. E., 1898.

**Adoption.** An almost universal political and social institution which originally dealt only with persons but later with families, clans or gentes, bands, and tribes. It had its beginnings far back in the history of primitive society and, after passing through many forms and losing much ceremonial garb, appears to-day in the civilized institution of naturalization. In the primitive mind the fundamental motive underlying adoption was to defeat the evil purpose of death to remove a member of the kinship group by actually replacing in person the lost or dead member. In primitive philosophy, birth and death are the results of magic power; birth increases and death decreases the *orenda* (q. v.) of the clan or family of the group affected. In order to preserve that magic power intact, society, by the exercise of constructive *orenda*, resuscitates the dead in the person of another in whom is embodied the blood and person of the dead. As the diminution of the number of the kindred was regarded as having been caused by magic power—by the *orenda* of some hostile agency—so the prevention or reparation of that loss must be accomplished by a like power, manifested in ritualistic liturgy and ceremonial. From the view point of the primitive mind adoption serves to change, by a fiction of law, the personality as well as the political status of the adopted person. For example, there were captured two white persons (sisters) by the Seneca, and instead of both being adopted into one clan, one was adopted by the Deer and the other by the Heron clan, and thus the blood of the two sisters was changed by the rite of adoption in such wise that their children could intermarry. Furthermore, to satisfy the underlying concept of the rite, the adopted person must be brought into one of the strains of kinship in order to define the standing of such person in the community, and the kinship name which the person receives declares his relation to all other persons in the family group; that is to say, should the adopted person be named son rather than uncle by the adopter, his status in the community would differ accordingly. From the political adoption of the Tuscarora by the Five Nations, about 1726, it is evident that tribes, families, clans, and groups of people could be adopted like persons. A fictitious age might be conferred upon the person adopted, since age largely governed the rights, duties, and position of persons in the community. In this wise, by the action of the constituted authorities, the age of an adopted group was fixed and its social and political importance thereby determined. Owing to the peculiar circumstances of the expulsion of the Tuscarora from North Carolina it was deemed best by the Five Nations, in view of their relation to the Colonies at that time, to give an asylum to the Tuscarora simply by means of the institution of adoption rather than by the political recognition of the Tuscarora as a member of the League. Therefore the Oneida made a motion in the federal council of the Five Nations that they adopt the Tuscarora as a nursling still swathed to the cradleboard. This having prevailed, the Five Nations, by the spokesman of the Oneida, said: "We have set up for ourselves a cradle-board in the extended house," that is, in the dominions of the League. After due probation the Tuscarora, by separate resolutions of the council, on separate motions of the Oneida, were made successively a boy, a young man, a man, an assistant to the official woman cooks, a warrior, and lastly a peer, having the right of chiefship in the council on an equal footing with the chiefs of the other tribes. From this it is seen that a tribe or other group of people may be adopted upon any one of several planes of political growth, corresponding to the various ages of human growth. This seems to explain the problem of the alleged subjugation and degradation of the Delawares by the Iroquois, which is said to have been enacted in open council. When it is understood that the Five Nations adopted the Delaware tribe as men assistants to the official cooks of the League it becomes clear that no taint of slavery and degradation was designed to be given by the act. It merely made the Delawares probationary heirs to citizenship in the League, and citizenship would be conferred upon them after suitable tutelage. In this they were treated with much greater consideration than were the Tuscarora, who are of the language and lineage of the Five Nations. The Delawares were not adopted as warriors or chiefs, but as assistant cooks; neither were they adopted, like the Tuscarora, as infants, but as men whose duty it was to assist the women whose official function was to cook for the people at public assemblies. Their office was hence well exemplified by the possession of a corn pestle, a hoe, and petticoats. This fact, misunderstood, perhaps intentionally misrepresented, seems to explain the mystery concerning the "making women" of the Delawares. This kind of adoption was virtually a state of probation, which could be made long or short.

The adoption of a chief's son by a fellow chief, customary in some of the tribes of the N. W. coast, differs in motive and effect from that defined above, which concerns persons alien to the tribe, upon whom it confers citizenship in the clan, gens, and tribe, as this deals only with intratribal persons for the purpose of conferring some degree of honor upon them rather than citizenship and political authority.

The Iroquois, in order to recruit the great losses incurred in their many wars, put into systematic practice the adoption not only of individuals but also of entire clans and tribes. The Tutelo, the Saponi, the Nanticoke, and other tribes and portions of tribes were forced to incorporate with the several tribes of the Iroquois confederation by formal adoption.

After the Pequot war the Narraganset adopted a large body of the Pequot. The Chickasaw adopted a section of the Natchez, and the Uchee were incorporated with the Creeks. In the various accounts of the American Indian tribes references to formal adoption and incorporation of one people by another are abundant. It is natural that formal adoption as a definite institution was most in vogue wherever the clan and gentile systems were more or less fully developed. (J. N. B. H.)

**Adornment.** The motive of personal adornment, aside from the desire to appear attractive, seems to have been to mark individual, tribal, or ceremonial distinction. The use of paint on the face, hair, and body, both in color and design, generally had reference to individual or clan beliefs, or it indicated relationship or personal bereavement, or was an act of courtesy. It was always employed in ceremonies, religious and secular, and was an accompaniment of gala dress donned to honor a guest or to celebrate an occasion. The face of the dead was frequently painted in accordance with tribal or religious symbolism. The practice of painting was widespread and was observed by both sexes. Paint was also put on the faces of adults and children as a protection against wind and sun. Plucking the hair from the face and body was generally practised. Deformation, as head flattening, and tattooing, according to some writers, were personal embellishments. Fats were used to beautify the hair and to ceremonially anoint the face and body. Sweet grass and seeds, as those of the columbine, served as perfume.

Ear ornaments were a mark of family thrift, wealth, or distinction, and indicated honor shown to the wearer by his kindred. Ceremonies, occasionally religious in character, some of which seem to relate to sacrificial rites, usually attended the boring of the ear.    Each perforation cost the parent of the child or the kindred of the adult gifts of a standard value, and sometimes these perforations extended round the entire rim of the ear. The pendants were of haliotis or other valued shell, or were made of metal or bone, or were long woven bands of dentalium which reached nearly to the waist.

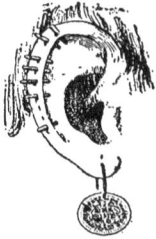

SEMINOLE EAR ORNAMENTS

Labrets were used by the Eskimo, the N. Pacific coast tribes, and some of the Gulf coast Indians. Among some the labret was worn only by men, in some by women, and where worn by both sexes it was of two different styles. At puberty an incision was made in the lip or at the corner of the mouth, and a slender pin was inserted, which was replaced by larger ones until the opening could admit a stud of the size desired. The Eskimo, when traveling, removed his labret to prevent freezing of the lip, but inserted it when en-

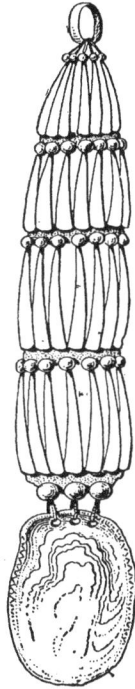

PENDANT OF DENTALIUM AND ABALONE SHELL

tering a village.    Among some of the northern and southern tribes the septum of the nose was pierced, and feathers, bark, or rings were inserted.

ESKIMO GIRL WITH NOSE-RING

Elaborate ornamentation of garments was reserved for the gala dress.    The Eskimo combined bits of fur of different colors and quality in a pleasing pattern for trimming their garments, and fishskin dyed in brilliant colors and the plumage of birds were also used for the same purpose.    Outer garments were made of the breasts of sea birds skilfully joined together.    Among the inland tribes the earlier designs for porcupine and feather quillwork were reproduced later in beads of European manufacture.    Feathers were widely used to decorate the robes and garments of warriors and other distinguished persons, and were woven into mantles by the cliff-dwellers and by tribes formerly living near the Gulf of Mexico.    Among the Plains Indians the milk teeth of the elk were the most costly of adornments.    They were fastened in rows on a woman's tunic, giving the garment a value of several hundred dollars.

Headbands, armlets, bracelets, belts, necklaces, and garters, of metal, seeds,

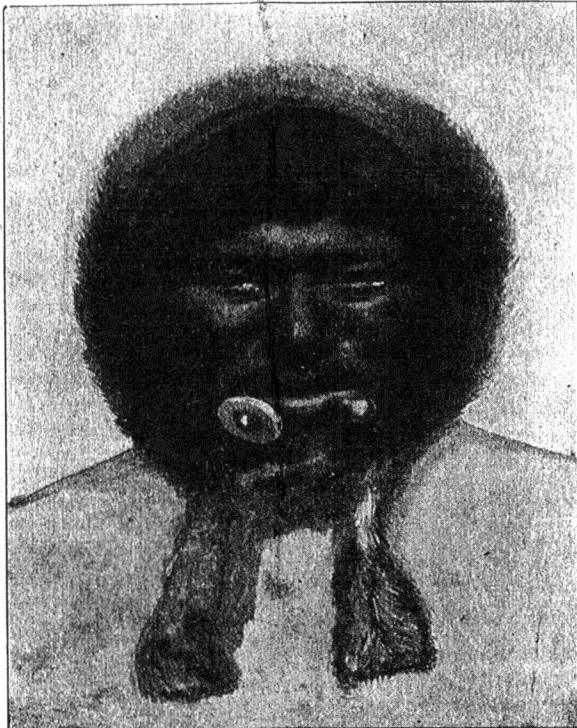

SILVER BRACELETS, HAIDA.    (NIBLACK)

embroidered buckskin, peculiar pelts, or woven fiber, had their practical use, but

LABRETS, WESTERN ESKIMO.    (NELSON)

57008°—Bull. 30—12——2

were made decorative, and often were symbolic. Archeological testimony shows that sea-shell beads, worn as necklaces or woven into belts, were widely used, and they probably found their way into the

CROW WOMAN WITH ELK-TOOTH DRESS

interior through barter or as ceremonial, or friendly gifts. Wampum belts figured largely in the official transactions between the early settlers and the eastern tribes. Disks cut from the conch shell were worn as ornaments and were also offered in certain religious rites; they ranked among the northern tribes as did the turquoise among the people of the S. W. With the Plains Indians a necklace of bear's claws marked the man of distinction. The headdress varied in different parts of the country and was generally significant of a man's kinship, ceremonial office, rank, or totemic de-

CHILKAT CEREMONIAL ROBE. (NIBLACK)

pendence, as was also the ornamentation upon his weapons and his shield.

In the S. W. blankets bordered with a design woven in colors were used on ceremonial occasions, and with the broad

belts, white robes, and fringed sashes worn at marriage are interesting specimens of weaving and color treatment. The brilliant Navaho blankets with their cosmic symbols are well known. The most remarkable example of the native weaver's skill is the ceremonial blanket and apron of the Chilkat tribe of Alaska; it is made of the wool of the mountain goat, dyed black, yellow, and green with native dyes over a warp of cedar-bark strings. A design of elaborate totemic forms covered the entire space within the border lines, and the ends and lower edge were heavily fringed. According to Boas these garments probably originated among the Tsimshian. In the buffalo country women seldom ornamented their own robes, but embroidered those worn by men. Sometimes a man painted his robe in accordance with a dream, or pictured upon it a yearly record of his own

SIHASAPA (BLACKFOOT SIOUX) COSTUME

deeds or of the prominent events of the tribe. Women wore the buffalo robe differently from the men, who gathered it about the person in a way that emphasized their action or the expression of emotion.

It was common for a tribe to have its peculiar cut and decoration of the moccasin, so that a man's tribe was proclaimed by his foot gear. The war shirt was frequently painted to represent the wearer's prayer, having the design on the back for protection and one on the breast for victory. The shirt was occasionally decorated with a fringe of human hair, locks being generally contributed by female relatives; it rarely displayed war trophies. The most imposing article of the warrior's regalia was the bonnet with its crown of golden-eagle feathers. Before the introduction of the horse the flap at the back rarely extended below the waist, but when the warriors got to be mounted "the spine," with its ruff of feathers, was so lengthened as to equal or exceed the height of the man. Song and ceremony accompanied the making of a war bonnet by warriors of the tribe, and a war honor was recounted upon each feather before it was placed in position. A bonnet could not be made without the consent of warriors, and it stood as a

HOPI MAIDEN. (JAMES)

record of tribal valor as well as a distinction granted to a man by his fellow tribesmen.

The gala and ceremonial dress of the Pueblo tribes of the S. W., of those for-

merly dwelling on the plains, and of those of the Pacific coast, was replete with ornamentation which, either in design or material, suggested rites or past experiences and thus kept alive beliefs and historic memories among the people. Such

HUPA GIRL IN GALA DRESS. (GODDARD)

were the woman's dress of the Yurok of California; the fringe of the skirt was wrapped with the same vegetal materials as she used in her basketry, and her apron was an elaborate network of the same on which depended strands of shells with pendants cut from the abalone. In the same connection may be mentioned the manner of dressing the hair of a Hopi maiden; the whorl on each side of her head symbolizes the flower of the squash, a sacred emblem of the tribe. The horses of warriors were often painted to indicate the dreams or the war experiences of their riders. Accouterments were sometimes elaborately ornamented.

Consult Abbott, Prim. Indus., 1881; Beauchamp (1) in Bull. N. Y. State Mus., no. 41, 1901, (2) ibid., no. 73, 1903; Boas

(1) in Rep. Nat. Mus. 1895, 1897, (2) in Mem. Am. Mus. Nat. Hist., Anthr. I, pt. I, 1898; Dall in 3d Rep. B. A. E., 1884; Fewkes in 19th Rep. B. A. E., 1900; Fletcher in Pubs. Peabody Mus.; Matthews (1) in Mem. Am. Mus. Nat. Hist., VI, 1903, (2) in 3d Rep. B. A. E., 1884; Mooney in 19th Rep. B. A. E., 1900; Moorehead, Prehist. Impls., 1900; Nelson in 18th Rep. B. A. E., 1899; Putnam in Peabody Mus. Rep., III, no. 2, 1882; Voth in Am. Anthrop., II, 1900; Wissler in Bull. Am. Mus. Nat. Hist., XVIII, pt. 3, 1904. See *Art, Artificial Head Deformation, Beadwork, Clothing, Dyes and Pigments, Featherwork, Hairdressing, Labrets, Painting, Ornament, Quillwork, Shellwork, Tattooing.* (A. C. F.)

**Adshusheer.** A tribe associated with the Eno and Shakori in North Carolina in 1701. Mooney (Bull. 22, B. A. E., 1894) says: " It is doubtful if they, at least the Eno and Shoccoree, were of Siouan stock, as they seem to have differed in physique and habit from their neighbors; but as nothing is left of their language, and as their alliances were all with Siouan tribes, they can not well be discriminated." There is but a single mention of the Adshusheer. Lawson (1701) tells of " the Shoccorie Indians, mixed with the Enoe and those of the nation of the Adshusheer, ruled by Enoe Will, a Shocorrie," the latter residing at Adshusheer, 14 m. from Achonechy, and ruling as far w. as Haw, or Reatkin, r. (Hist. Carolina, 96, 97, 1860). The village of the 3 tribes was called Adshusheer, which Mooney locates near the present town of Hillsboro, Durham co., N. C. Nothing is known of their subsequent history. The Adshusheer were probably absorbed by one of the tribes with which they were associated. (C. T.)

**Adzes.** Cutting, scraping, or gouging implements in prehistoric and early historic times, made usually of stone, but not infrequently of shell, bone, or copper. Iron and steel are much used by

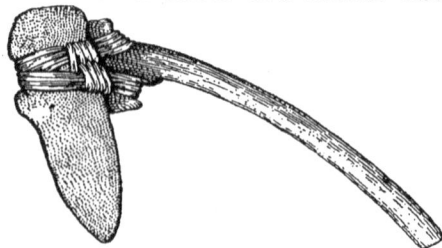

STONE ADZ WITH WOODEN HAFT, HAIDA.   (NELSON)

the tribes at the present day. The blade resembles that of a celt, although often somewhat curved by chipping or by grinding at the proper angle to make it most effectual. Some are grooved for hafting, after the manner of the grooved ax, but the groove does not extend over the flat face against which the handle is fastened.

The hafting takes various forms according to the shape and size of the blade. The adz is primarily a wood-working tool, but it serves also for scraping, as in the dressing of skins and in other arts, and, no doubt also on occasion, for digging. The edge of the primitive adz was probably not sharp enough to make it effectual in working wood save in connection with the process of charring. The distribution of this implement was very general over the area north of Mexico, but it probably reached its highest development and specialization among the wood-

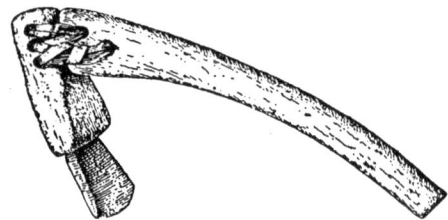

IRON ADZ WITH IVORY HAFT, ESKIMO.   (MURDOCH)

working tribes of the N. Pacific coast. The scraper and the gouge have many uses in common with the adz.

For various examples of the adz, ancient and modern, consult Beauchamp in Bull. N. Y. State Mus., no. 18, 1897; Fowke in 13th Rep. B. A. E., 1896; Moorehead, Prehist. Impls., 1900; Murdoch in 9th Rep. B. A. E., 1892; Nelson in 18th Rep. B. A. E., 1899; Niblack in Rep. Nat. Mus. 1888, 1890; Rau in Smithson. Cont., XXII, 1876. (W. H. H.   G. F.)

**Aegakotcheising** (*Aegakötchëising*).—An Ottawa village in Michigan in 1851.—Schoolcraft, Ind. Tribes, I, 478, 1851.

**Aepjin** (Dutch for 'little ape'). A Mahican village, known as Aepjin's castle, from the name of the resident chief, situated in the 17th century at or near Schodac, Rensselaer co., N. Y.—Ruttenber, Tribes Hudson R., 86, 1872.

**Aestaca.** A Costanoan rancheria connected with Santa Cruz mission, Cal., in 1819.—Olbez quoted by Taylor in Cal. Farmer, Apr. 5, 1860.

**Afegua** ('bird island'). An island off the w. coast of Lower California, about lat. 31°, on which was once a Cochimi rancheria.—Venegas, Hist. Cal., II, 436, 1757.

**Afognak.** A Kaniagmiut settlement consisting of 3 villages on Afognak id., s. of Cook inlet, Alaska (Bruce, Alaska, map, 1895). Pop. 339 in 1880, 409 in 1890, 307 in 1900.

**Agacay.** A former Timuquanan town on St Johns r., Florida, about 150 m. from the mouth.—Fontaneda (1565) in French, Hist. Coll. La., 2d s., 264, 1875.

**Agaihtikara** ('fish-eaters'). A division of the Paviotso living in 1866 in the vicinity of Walker r. and lake and Car-

son r. and lake, Nev. They were under Chief Oderie and numbered about 1,500.
**A-gai-du-ka.**—Powell, Paviotso MS., B. A. E., 1881. **Aga'ih-tïka'ra.**—Mooney in 14th Rep. B. A. E., 1051, 1896. **A'-gai-ti-kút-teh.**—Powers, Inds. W., Nev., MS., B. A. E., 1876. **Ahgy-tecitteh.**—Powers in Smithson. Rep. 1876, 452, 1877. **Ahgyweit.**—Ibid. **Ocki Pah-Utes.**—Campbell in Ind. Aff. Rep., 113, 1870. **Ocki-Pi-Utes.**—Ibid., 119, 1866. **Octi.**—Ibid. **Walker River Pi-Utes.**—Ibid.

**Agaivanuna** (*A-gai-va-nu'-na*). A Paviotso division formerly living at Summit lake, w. Nevada.—Powell, Paviotso MS., B. A. E., 1881.

**Agamagus.** See *Moxus.*

**Aganustata.** See *Oconostota.*

**Agate.** See *Chalcedony.*

**Agawam** ('fish-curing [place]'.—Hewitt). A name of frequent occurrence in s. New England and on Long Island, and by which was designated at least 3 Indian villages or tribes in Massachusetts.

The most important was at Ipswich, Essex co., Mass. The site was sold by the chief in 1638. Its jurisdiction included the land on Newbury r., and the tribe was a part of the Pennacook confederacy. It was almost extinct in 1658, but as late as 1726 there were still 3 families living near Wigwam hill.

The second tribe or band of that name had its chief town on Long hill, near Springfield, Hampden co., Mass. Springfield was sold in 1635 and the Indian town was in existence in 1675. This tribe was commonly classed with the Pocomtuc.

The third was about Wareham, Plymouth co., Mass., the site of which was sold in 1655. It was probably subject to the Wampanoag, but joined in the plot against the English in 1621. (J. M.)
**Agawaam.**—Records (1672) in Mass. Hist. Soc. Coll., 2d s., IV, 86, 1816. **Agawam.**—Pynchon (1663) in N. Y. Doc. Col. Hist., XIII, 308, 1881. **Agawom.**—Smith (1629), Virginia, II, 174, repr. 1819. **Agawomes.**—Gookin (1674) in Mass. Hist. Soc. Coll., 1st s., I, 149, 1806. **Aggawam.**—Smith (1616), ibid., 3d s., VI, 97, 1837. **Aggawom.**—Smith (1629), Virginia, II, 177, repr. 1819. **Agissawamg.**—Johnson (1654) in Mass. Hist. Soc. Coll., 2d s., II, 66, 1814. **Agowaun.**—Williams (1638), ibid., 4th s., VI, 248, 1863. **Agowaywam.**—Mount (1622), ibid., 1st s., VIII, 262, 1802. **Aguwom.**—Underhill (1638), ibid., 3d s., VI, 1, 1837. **Angawom.**—New Eng. Mem. quoted by Drake, Ind. Wars, 95, note, 1825. **Angoum.**—Mourt (1622) in Mass. Hist. Soc. Coll., 2d s., IX, 37, 1822. **Anguum.**—Ibid. **Augawam.**—Dee in Smith (1629), Virginia, II, 235, repr. 1819. **Augawoam.**—Smith (1631) in Mass. Hist. Soc. Coll., 3d s., III, 22, 1833. **Augoam.**—Smith (1616), ibid., VI, 97, 1837. **Augoan.**—Smith (1629), Virginia, II, 193, repr. 1819. **Auguan.**—Smith (1631) in Mass. Hist. Soc. Coll., 3d s., III, 87, 1833.

**Agawano** (*A-ga'-wa-no*). A prehistoric pueblo of the Nambe, situated in the mountains about 7 m. E. of the Rio Grande, on Rio Santa Cruz, lat. 36°, New Mexico.—Bandelier in Arch. Inst. Papers, IV, 84, 1892.
**A-ga Uo-no.**—Bandelier, op. cit.

**Agawesh.** A Modoc settlement and camping place on Lower Klamath lake, N. Cal., and on Hot cr. The name is primarily that of Lower Klamath lake, and the people of the settlement were called Agaweshkni. (L. F.)

**Agáwesh.**—Gatschet in Cont. N. A. Ethnol., II, pt. I, xxxii, 1890. **Agáweshkni.**—Ibid., 19 ('people of Agáwesh'). **Agáweshni.**—Ibid. **Aka-ush.**—Ibid., 16. **Aká-uskni.**—Ibid., 19. .**Hot creek Indians.**—Meacham, Wigwam and Warpath, 577, 1875. **Okkowish.**—Steele in Ind. Aff. Rep., 121, 1864 (said erroneously to be the Modoc name for themselves).

**Agdluitsok.** An Eskimo village and Danish post in s. w. Greenland, lat. 60° 31'.—Meddelelser om Grönland, XVI, map, 1896.
**Lichtenau.**—Koldewey, German Arct. Exped., 182, 1874.

**Agency System.** Indian affairs are conducted under the administrative bureau in Washington by local Indian agents. This agency system was gradually developed to meet the various exigencies arising from the rapid displacement of Indian tribes by white settlers.

*History.*—During the colonial period the spread of trade brought a large number of tribes in contact with the French and the English, and each nation strove to make allies among the natives. Their rivalry led to the French and Indian war, and its effects were felt as late as the first half of the 19th century. When the Revolution began the attitude of the Indians became a matter of importance, and plans were speedily devised to secure their friendship for the colonists and to thwart English influence. One of the means employed was the appointment of agents to reside among the tribes living near the settlements. These men were charged to watch the movements of the Indians and through the maintenance of trade to secure their good will toward the colonists. As the war went on the western trading posts of the British became military camps, which drew the colonial troops into a hitherto unknown country. Conditions arose which necessitated new methods for the control of Indians, and in 1786 Congress, to which the Articles of Confederation gave exclusive right and power to manage Indian affairs, established two districts— a northern district, to include all tribes N. of Ohio r. and w. of Hudson r., and a southern district, to include all tribes s. of Ohio r. A bonded superintendent was placed over each, and power was given to him to appoint two bonded deputies. Every tribe within these districts laid claim to a definite tract as its own territory, and these tribal districts came to be recognized as tribal lands. The old trading posts became in time industrial centers, and the Indians were called on to cede the adjoining lands. The right of way from one post to another was next acquired. As settlers advanced more land was secured, and so rapidly were the tribes constrained to move westward that it became necessary to recast the districts established in 1786. The plan of districting the country under bonded officers was continued, but on a new basis—that of tribal holdings, or, as they came to be called, reservations, which were grouped geographically into superintendencies, each presided over by a bonded superintendent, who was directly responsible to the Commissioner of Indian Affairs at Washington. The reservations were in charge of bonded agents, who reported to the district superintendents. This plan continued in force until about the middle of the 19th century, when the office of superintendent was abolished and agents became directly responsible to the Commissioner. For more than 80 years the office of agent had been almost exclusively filled by civilians. The powers of the agents had expanded until both life and property were subject to their dictum. While many men filled the difficult position with honor and labored unselfishly for the welfare of the Indians, others abused their trust and brought discredit upon the service. President Grant, in 1868–69, sought to remedy this evil by the appointment of army officers as Indian agents, but Congress, in 1870, prohibited "the employment of army officers in any civil capacity." The President then appealed to the religious denominations to suggest candidates for Indian agencies, and to facilitate this arrangement the reservations were apportioned among the various denominations. The plan led to the amelioration of the service through the concentration of the attention of religious bodies upon particular tribes, thus awakening an intelligent interest in their welfare. About this time commissioners were appointed to visit and report on the various tribes, and in this way many facts and conditions hitherto unknown were brought to the knowledge of the Government authorities and the public. As a result new forces were evoked in behalf of the natives. Industrial schools were multiplied both on and off the reservations; Indians became agency employees; lands were allotted in severalty; and through citizenship legal rights were secured. These radical changes, brought about within the two decades following 1873, led up to the act of Mar. 3, 1893, which permits the abolishment of agencies, where conditions are suitable, giving to the bonded superintendent of the reservation school the power to act as agent in the transaction of business between the United States Government and the tribe.

*Administrative department.*—The adoption of the Constitution in 1789 brought about changes in the administration of Indian affairs at Washington. On the organization of the War Department the management of the Indians passed from a standing committee of Congress to the Secretary of War. By the act of Mar. 1, 1793, the President was authorized to appoint "temporary agents to reside among the Indians." The act of Apr. 16, 1818, inaugurated the present policy: the President nominates and the Senate approves the appointment of all Indian agents. The office of Indian Commissioner was created by the act of Congress of July 9, 1832, and by an act of June 30, 1834, the office of Indian Affairs was created. On the institution of the Department of the Interior, in accordance with the act of Mar. 3, 1849, the office of Indian Affairs was transferred from the War Department to the Interior Department, where it still remains.

Congress established the office of inspector by the act of Feb. 14, 1873. There are 5 inspectors, nominated by the President and confirmed by the Senate. They hold their office for 4 years and report directly to the Secretary of the Interior. They are charged with the duty of visiting and reporting on agencies, and have power to suspend an agent or employee and to enforce laws with the aid of the United States district attorney. The salary is $2,500, with necessary traveling expenses. In 1879 Congress provided for special agents. These are appointed by the Secretary of the Interior. Their duties are similar to those of the inspectors, but they may be required to take charge of agencies, and are bonded sufficiently for that purpose. They report direct to the Commissioner of Indian Affairs. The salary is $2,000. Special agents are also detailed by the Indian Bureau to investigate special matters or to transact special business. Special allotting agents, whose duties are to allot, on specified reservations, the land in severalty to the Indians, are appointed by the President. The inspectors and special agents are the intermediaries between the Indian Bureau at Washington and its field organization.

*Field organization.*—The Indian agent holds his office for 4 years or until his successor is appointed and qualified. He must give a bond with not fewer than two sureties, and the several sums in which the sureties justify must aggregate at least double the penalty of the bond. If required, an agent shall perform the duties of two agencies for one salary, and he shall not depart from the limits of his agency without permission (see U. S. Stat. L., XXII, 87; XVIII, 147; IV, 736). Cessions of lands by the tribes to the United States were always made for a consideration, to be paid to the Indians in money or merchandise. Most of these payments extended over a series of years, and the disbursing of them devolved on the agent. He was also charged with the preservation of order on the reservation, the removal from the Indian country of all persons found therein contrary to law, the oversight of employees, the protection of the rights of the Indians in the matter of trade, the suppression of the traffic in intoxicating liquors, the investigation of depredation claims, the protection of the Indians on their land held in severalty, the care of all Government property, the care of agency stock, the proper receipt and distribution of all supplies received, the disbursement of money received, and the supervision of schools (see U. S. Stat. L., IV, 564, 732, 736, 738; X, 701; XI, 80, 169; XII, 427; XIII, 29; XVIII, 449; XIX, 244, 293; XXIII, 94). In addition to the correspondence and other clerical work incident to the current business of his office, each agent is required to keep a book of itemized expenditures of every kind, with a record of all contracts, together with receipts of money from all sources, of which a true transcript is to be forwarded quarterly to the Commissioner of Indian Affairs (see U. S. Stat. L., XVIII, 451). The salaries of Indian agents range from $1,000 to $3,000 per annum. The employees under the agent are clerks, interpreters, police, farmers, carpenters, blacksmiths, millers, butchers, teamsters, herders, laborers, watchmen, engineers, and physicians, besides the school employees. A large proportion of these employees are provided in accordance with treaty stipulations. The salaries range from $200 to $1,200 per annum.

*Interpreters.*—This class of employees stood between the Indian and the white race, between the tribe and the Government, and have exercised a far-reaching influence on Indian affairs. The translations of these men were the sole means by which the two races understood or misunderstood each other. Until recently most interpreters picked up colloquial English from trappers, traders, and other adventurers in the Indian country. They were generally mixed-bloods whose knowledge of the language and the culture of both the white and the Indian races was necessarily limited. It was impossible for them, with the best intentions, to render the dignified and thoughtful speech of the Indian into adequate English, and thus they gravely prejudiced the reputation of the native's mental capacity. The agency interpreter received his salary from the Government through the agent, and, as was natural, he generally strove to make himself acceptable to that officer. His position was a responsible and trying one, since questions frequently arose between the Indians and the agent which demanded courage, prudence, and unswerving honesty on the part of the interpreter,

who was the mouthpiece of both parties. Of late years the spread of English among the younger people through the medium of the schools, while it has not done away with the official interpreter, has lessened his difficulties and, at the same time, diminished the power he once held.

*Indian police.*—This force was authorized by act of Congress of May 27, 1878. Its duties are to preserve order on the reservation, to prevent illegal liquor traffic and arrest offenders in this matter, to act as guards when rations are issued and annuities paid, to take charge of and protect at all times Government property, to restore lost or stolen property to its rightful owners, to drive out timber thieves and other trespassers, to return truant pupils to school, and to make arrests for disorderly conduct and other offenses. Such a force is organized at all the agencies, and the faithfulness of the Indian police in the discharge of their duties is well attested. The pay is from $10 to $15 a month, usually also with a small house and extra rations.

*Annuities.*—Although the right of eminent domain over all territories of the United States is vested in the Government, still the Indians' "right of occupancy" has always been recognized. The indemnity paid by the United States to the Indians when these made cessions of land was intended to extinguish this right. These payments were made in money or merchandise, or both. The entire amount to be paid to a tribe was placed to its credit in the United States Treasury. In some instances only the interest on this sum was paid annually to the tribe; in other cases the principal was extinguished by a stated annual payment. These annuities (annual payments under treaty obligations) had to be voted each year by Congress and were distinct from the sums appropriated as special gratuities to be used for cases of peculiar need. During the early part of the 19th century cash annuities were handed over by the agents to the chief, who receipted for the money and distributed it among the tribe, but for the last fifty years or more an enrolment of the tribe has been made by the agent prior to each payment, and the money has been divided pro rata and receipted for individually.

A large proportion of the payments made to Indians was originally in merchandise. This mode of payment was abused, and inured to the advantage of white manufacturers and traders, but was injurious to the tribe, as it tended to kill all native industries and helped toward the general demoralization of the Indian. Payments in goods are now made only in cases where an isolated situation or other conditions make this method suited to the interests of the Indians.

*Rations.*—These were a part of the merchandise payments. They were at first urged upon the tribes in order to keep them confined within the reservations instead of wandering in the pursuit of game. After the destruction of the buffalo herds the beef ration became a necessity to the Plains Indians until they were able to raise their own stock. Except in a few instances, where treaties still require this method of payment, rations are not now issued unless great poverty or some disaster makes it necessary.

A movement is now on foot for the division of all tribal money held in the United States Treasury, an arrangement that would do away with many disadvantages that are connected with payments in annuities and rations.

See *Governmental Policy, Reservations, Treaties.* (A. C. F.)

**Aggavacaamanc** ('arroyo of the gulls' (?)). A rancheria, probably Cochimi, connected with Purísima (Cadegomo) mission, w. Lower California, in the 18th century.—Doc. Hist. Mex., 4th s., v, 189, 1857.

**Aggey.** Mentioned by Oñate (Doc. Inéd., xvi, 113, 1871) as a pueblo of New Mexico in 1598. Doubtless situated in the Salinas, in the vicinity of Abo, E. of the Rio Grande, and in all probability occupied at that time by the Tigua or the Piros.

**Agiukchuk.** A Kaialigamiut village opposite the s. shore of Nelson id., Alaska; pop. 35 in 1880, 81 in 1890.
Agiukchugumut.—Nelson in 18th Rep. B. A. E., map, 1899. Ighiakchaghamiut.—11th Census, Alaska, 110, 1893.

**Agivavik.** A Nushagagmiut village on Nushagak r., Alaska; pop. 52 in 1880, 30 in 1890.
Agivarik.—Post route map, 1903. Agivavik.—Petroff, 10th Census, Alaska, map, 1884.

**Aglemiut.** An Eskimo tribe inhabiting the N. w. coast of Alaska from the mouth of Nushagak r. s. w. to the valley of the Ugashik, extending E. to the highlands (Dall in Cont. N. A. Ethnol., I, 19, 1877). They numbered only 767 in 1890. They dwell on the coast, hunting the walrus and occasionally putting out to sea in pursuit of whales. Although Christians, they retain their native beliefs and customs, resembling their neighbors in dress, except that they use reindeer skins for winter garments. They carve ivory as skilfully as the northern tribes. Subdivisions are the Kiatagmiut, Ugagogmiut, and Ugashigmiut. The villages are Igagik, Ikak, Kingiak, Paugwik, Ugashik, and Unangashik.
Achkugmjuten.—Holmberg, Ethnol. Skizz., 4, 1855 (applied to Aglemiut and Kaniagmiut by the people of Norton sd.) Aglahmutes.—Elliott, Cond. Aff. in Alaska, 29, 1874. Aglaxtana.—Doroschin in Radloff, Wörterb. d. Kinai-Spr., 29, 1874

(Knaiakhotana name). Aglegmguten.—Holmberg, Ethnol. Skizz., 4, 1855. Aglĕgmiut.—Worman quoted by Dall in Cont. N. A. Ethnol., I, 19, 1877. Aglemüt.—Radloff, Wörterb. d. Kinai-Spr., 29, 1874. Agolĕgmiut.—Turner quoted by Dall, op. cit., 19. Agolegmutes.—Latham (1845) in J. Ethnol. Soc. Lond., I, 183, 1848. Agolemüten.—Wrangell, Ethnog. Nachr., 121, 1839. Agoolmutes.—Elliott, Cond. Aff. in Alaska, 29, 1874. Aguljmjuten.—Holmberg, Ethnol. Skizz., 5, 1855. Agulmüten.—Wrangell, Ethnog. Nachr., 122, 1839. Dog-drivers.—Petroff, 10th Census Alaska, 164, 1884. Oglemut.—Dall, op. cit., 19. Oglemutes.—Dall in Proc. A. A. A. S., 267, 1869. O'gŭlmüt.—Dall in Cont. N. A. Ethnol., I, 19, 1877. Sewernowskije.—Radloff, Wörterb. d. Kinai-Spr., 29, 1874('northerner': Russian name). Svernofftsi.—Dall in Cont. N. A. Ethnol., I, 19, 1877. Tchouktchi americani.—Balbi quoted by Dall, ibid. Tịndị šuxtana.—Dawydof quoted by Radloff, Wörterb. d. Kinai-Spr., 29, 1874 (Kinai name). Tuntu šuxtana.—Doroschin quoted, ibid. Tyndysiukhtana.—Petroff, Alaska, 164, 1884.

**Aglutok.** An Eskimo settlement in s. w. Greenland. Ruins found there are supposed to be those of former Norse settlers.—Crantz, Hist. Greenland, I, 18, 1767.

**Agomekelenanak.** An Eskimo village in the Kuskokwim district, Alaska. Pop. 15 in 1890.
Ahgomekhelanaghamiut.—11th Census, Alaska, 164, 1893.

**Agomiut** ('people of the weather side'). A tribe of Eskimo inhabiting a region of N. Baffin land bordering on Lancaster sd., consisting of two subtribes—the Tununirusirmiut in the w., about Admiralty inlet, and the Tununirmiut in the E., about Eclipse sd. They hunt the narwhal and the white whale in Eclipse sd., and in search of seals sometimes cross the ice on sledges to North Devon, there coming in contact with the natives of Ellesmere land.

**Agreements.** See *Governmental Policy, Reservations, Treaties.*

**Agriculture.** An opinion long prevailed in the minds of the people that the Indians N. of Mexico were, previous to and at the time Europeans began to settle that part of the continent, virtually nomads, having no fixed abodes, and hence practising agriculture to a very limited extent. Why this opinion has been entertained by the masses, who have learned it from tales and traditions of Indian life and warfare as they have been since the establishment of European colonies, can be readily understood, but why writers who have had access to the older records should thus speak of them is not easily explained, when these records, speaking of the temperate regions, almost without exception notice the fact that the Indians were generally found, from the border of the western plains to the Atlantic, dwelling in settled villages and cultivating the soil. De Soto found all the tribes that he visited, from the Florida peninsula to the western part of Arkansas, cultivating maize and various other food plants. The early voyagers found the same thing true along the Atlantic from Florida to Massachusetts. Capt. John Smith and his Jamestown colony, indeed all the early colonies, depended at first very largely for subsistence on the products of Indian cultivation. Jacques Cartier, the first European who ascended the St Lawrence, found the Indians of Hochelaga (Montreal id.) cultivating the soil. "They have," he remarks, "good and large fields of corn." Champlain and other early French explorers testify to the large reliance of the Iroquois on the cultivation of the soil for subsistence. La Salle and his companions observed the Indians of Illinois, and thence southward along the Mississippi, cultivating and to a large extent subsisting on maize.

Sagard, an eyewitness of what he reports, says, in speaking of the agriculture of the Hurons in 1623–26, that they dug a round place at every 2 feet or less, where they planted in the month of May in each hole nine or ten grains of corn which they had previously selected, culled, and soaked for several days in water. And every year they thus planted their corn in the same places and spots, which they renovated with their small wooden shovels. He indicates the height of the corn by the statement that he lost his way quicker in these fields than in the prairies or forests (Hist. du Canada, I, 265–266, 1636, repr. 1866).

Indian corn, the great American cereal, "was found in cultivation from the southern extremity of Chile to the 50th parallel of N. latitude" (Brinton, Myths of the New World, 22, 1868). "All the nations who inhabit from the sea as far as the Illinois, and even farther, carefully cultivate the maize corn, which they make their principal subsistence" (Du Pratz, Hist. La., II, 239, 1763). "The whole of the tribes situated in the Mississippi valley, in Ohio, and the lakes reaching on both sides of the Alleghenies, quite to Massachusetts and other parts of New England, cultivated Indian corn. It was the staple product" (Schoolcraft, Ind. Tribes, I, 80, 1851).

The great length of the period previous to the discovery during which maize had been in cultivation is proved by its differentiation into varieties, of which there were four in Virginia; by the fact that charred corn and impressions of corn on burnt clay have been found in the mounds and in the ruins of prehistoric pueblos in the S. W.; by the Delaware tradition (see *Walam Olum*); and by the fact that the builders of the oldest mounds must have been tillers of the soil.

Some idea of the extent of the cultivation of maize by some of the tribes may be gained from the following estimates: The amount of corn (probably in the ear) of the Iroquois destroyed by Denonville

in 1687 was estimated at 1,000,000 bushels (Charlevoix, Hist. Nouv. Fr., II, 355, 1744; also Doc. Hist. N. Y., I, 238, 1849). According to Tonti, who accompanied the expedition, they were engaged seven days in cutting up the corn of 4 villages. Gen. Sullivan, in his expedition into the Iroquois country, destroyed 160,000 bushels of corn and cut down the Indian orchards; in one orchard alone 1,500 apple trees were destroyed (Hist. N. Y. During the Revolutionary War, II, 334, 1879). Gen. Wayne, writing from Grand Glaize in 1794, says: "The margins of these beautiful rivers—the Miami of the Lake and the Au Glaize—appear like one continuous village for a number of miles, both above and below this place; nor have I ever before beheld such immense fields of

PUEBLO CORN PLANTING

corn in any part of America from Canada to Florida" (Manypenny, Ind. Wards, 84, 1880).

If we are indebted to the Indians for maize, without which the peopling of America would probably have been delayed for a century, it is also from them that the whites learned the methods of planting, storing, and using it. The ordinary corncribs, set on posts, are copies of those in use among the Indians, which Lawson described in 1701 (Hist. Car., 35, repr. 1860).

Beans, squashes, pumpkins, sweet potatoes, tobacco, gourds, and the sunflower were also cultivated to some extent, especially in what are now the southern states. According to Beverly (Hist. Va., 125–128, 1722), the Indians had two varieties of sweet potatoes. Marquette, speaking of the Illinois Indians, says that in addition to maize, "they also sow beans and melons, which are excellent, especially those with a red seed. Their squashes are not of the best; they dry them in the sun to eat in the winter and spring" (Voy. and Discov., in French, Hist. Coll. La., IV, 33, 1852).

The foregoing applies chiefly to the region E. of the Rocky mts., but the native population of the section now embraced in New Mexico and Arizona not only cultivated the soil, but relied on agriculture to a large extent for subsistence. No corn was raised or agriculture practised anywhere on the Pacific slope N. of the lower Rio Colorado, but frequent mention is made by the chroniclers of Coronado's expedition to New Mexico of the general cultivation of maize by the Indians of that section, and also of the cultivation of cotton. It is stated in the Relacion del Suceso (Winship in 14th Rep. B. A. E., 575, 1896) that those who lived near the Rio Grande raised cotton, but the others did not. The writer, speaking of the Rio Grande valley, adds: "There is much corn here."

"From the earliest information we have of these nations [the Pueblo Indians] they are known to have been tillers of the soil, and though the implements used and their methods of cultivation were both simple and primitive, cotton, corn, wheat [after its introduction], beans, with many varieties of fruits were raised in abundance" (Bancroft, Nat. Rac., I, 538, 1882). Chile and onions are extensively cultivated by the Pueblo tribes, as also are grapes and peaches, but these latter, like wheat, were introduced by the Spaniards.

The Indians of New Mexico and Arizona had learned the art of irrigating their fields before the appearance of the white man on the continent. This is shown not only by the statements of early explorers, but by the still existing remains of their ditches. "In the valleys of the Salado and Gila, in s. Arizona, however, casual observation is sufficient to demonstrate that the ancient inhabitants engaged in agriculture by artificial irrigation to a vast extent. . . . Judging from the remains of extensive ancient works of irrigation, many of which may still be seen passing through tracts cultivated to-day as well as across densely wooded stretches considerably beyond the present nonirrigated area, it is safe to say that the principal canals constructed and used by the ancient inhabitants of the Salado valley controlled the irrigation of at least 250,000 acres" (Hodge in Am. Anthrop., July, 1893). Remains of ancient irrigating ditches and canals are also found elsewhere in these territories.

The sunflower was cultivated to a limited extent both by the Indians of the Atlantic slope and those of the Pueblo region for its seeds, which were eaten after being parched and ground into meal between two stones. The limits of the cultivation of tobacco at the time of the discovery has not yet been well defined. That it was cultivated to some extent on the Atlantic side is known; it was used aboriginally all over California, and indeed a plant called tobacco by the natives was cultivated as far N. as Yakutat bay, Alaska.

Although it has been stated that the Indians did not use fertilizers, there is evidence that they did. The Plymouth colonists were told by the Indians to add fish to the old grounds (Bradford, Hist. Plym. Plant., Mass. Hist. Soc. Coll., 4th s., III, 100, 1856). It is also stated that the Iroquois manured their land. Lescarbot says the Armouchiquois, Virginia Indians, and others "enrich their fields with shells and fish." The implements they used

HOE, FROM AN ENGRAVING IN DE BRY, SIXTEENTH CENTURY

in cultivating the ground are described as "wooden howes" and "spades made of hardwood." "Florida Indians dig their ground with an instrument of wood fashioned like a broad mattock," "use hoes made of shoulder blades of animals fixed on staves," "use the shoulder blade of a deer or a tortoise shell, sharpened upon a stone and fastened to a stick, instead of a hoe;" "a

IMPLEMENT OF SHELL, FLORIDA

piece of wood, 3 inches broad, bent at one end and fastened to a long handle sufficed them to free the land from weeds and turn it up lightly." Mention is also

FLINT SPADE, MIDDLE MIS-
SISSIPPI VALLEY

FLINT HOE, MIDDLE MIS-
SISSIPPI VALLEY

made of shells used as digging implements, and Moore and Cushing have found in Florida many large conchs that had served this purpose.

Such are some of the earlier statements in regard to the agricultural implements used by the Indians; however, certain stone implements have been found in vast numbers which are generally conceded to have been used in breaking the soil. Of these the most characteristic are the hoes and spades of the middle Mississippi valley.

Formerly the field work was generally done by the women. Hariot (Hakluyt, Voy., III, 329, 1810) says, "The women, with short pickers or parers (because they use them sitting) of a foot long, and about 5 inches in breadth, do only break the upper part of the ground to raise up the weeds, grass, and old stubs or cornstalks with their roots." It was a general custom to burn over the ground before planting in order to free it from weeds and rubbish. In the forest region patches were cleared by girdling the trees, thus causing them to die, and afterward burning them down.

Though the Indians as a rule have been somewhat slow in adopting the plants and methods introduced by the whites, this has not been wholly because of their dislike of labor, but in some cases has been due largely to their removals by the Government and to the unproductiveness of the soil of many of the reservations assigned them. Where tribes or portions of tribes, as parts of the Cherokee and Iroquois, were allowed to remain in their original territory, they were not slow in bringing into use the introduced plants and farming methods of the whites, the fruit trees, livestock, plows, etc.

According to the Report of the Commissioner of Indian Affairs for 1904 the following is a summary of the agricultural industries of the Indians, exclusive of the Five Civilized Tribes, during that year:

| | | |
|---|---|---|
| Land cultivated | acres | 365,469 |
| Land broken | " | 30,644 |
| Land under fence (1903) | " | 1,836,245 |
| Fencing built | rods | 269,578 |
| Families living on and cultivating lands in severalty | | 10,846 |
| Crops raised: | | |
| Wheat | bushels | 750,788 |
| Oats and barley | " | 1,246,960 |
| Corn | " | 949,815 |
| Vegetables | " | 606,023 |
| Flax | " | 26,290 |
| Hay | tons | 405,627 |
| Miscellaneous products of Indian labor: | | |
| Butter made | pounds | 157,057 |
| Lumber sawed | feet | 5,563,000 |
| Timber marketed | " | 107,032,000 |
| Wood cut | cords | 118,493 |
| Stock owned by Indians: | | |
| Horses, mules, and burros | | 295,466 |
| Cattle | | 497,611 |
| Swine | | 40,898 |
| Sheep | | 792,620 |
| Goats | | 135,417 |
| Domestic fowls | | 267,574 |
| Freight transported by Indians with their own teams | pounds | 23,717,000 |
| Amount earned by such freighting | | $113,641 |

| | | |
|---|---|---|
| Value of products of Indian labor sold by Indians: | | |
| To Government | | $456,026 |
| Otherwise | | $1,878,462 |
| Roads made | miles | 570 |
| Roads repaired | " | 3,045 |
| Days' labor expended on roads | | 125,813 |

Much additional information regarding agriculture among the Indians may be found in the Annual Reports of the Bureau of American Ethnology. See also *Food, Gourds, Irrigation, Maize, Tobacco, Wild Rice*, etc., and for agricultural implements see *Hoes, Implements and Utensils, Spades*. (C. T.)

**Agtism.** Mentioned as a Costanoan village near Santa Cruz mission, Cal., in 1819.—Olbez quoted by Taylor in Cal. Farmer, Apr. 5, 1860.

**Agua Caliente** (Span.: 'warm water'). A small Cahuilla division on the headwaters of San Luis Rey r., s. Cal., forming one linguistic group with the Kawia, Luiseño, and Juaneño. Villages: Gupa and Wilakal. The people of Wilakal are included in Los Coyotes res. (see *Pachawal*). By decision of the U. S. Supreme Court the title of the Indians in the other village and in several small Diegueño rancherias, collectively better known as "Warner's Ranch Indians," was disproved, and under act of Congress of May 27, 1902, a tract was added to Pala res., and these and neighboring Indians were removed thereto in 1903 (Ind. Aff. Reps., 1902, 1903). At that time they aggregated about 300.

Agua Caliente.—Kroeber, inf'n, 1905. Hekwach.—Ibid. (so called by Dieguenos of San Felipe). Warner's Ranch Indians.—Popular name for inhabitants of Gupa and some Diegueño rancherias in the neighborhood. Xagua'tc.—Boas in Proc. Am. Asso. Adv. Sci., XLIV, 261, 1895 (so called by Dieguenos of Tekumak).

**Aguacay.** A large village, probably belonging to a division of a southern Caddoan tribe, formerly in the vicinity of Washita r., Ark., where salt was manufactured both for home consumption and for trade. It was visited by the DeSoto expedition in 1542. See Gentl. of Elvas (1557) in French, Hist. Coll. La., II, 194, 1850; Hakluyt Soc. Pub., 197, 1851; Harris, Voy. and Trav., I, 810, 1705. (A. C. F.)

**Aguachacha.** The Yavapai name of a tribe, evidently Yuman, living on the lower Colorado in Arizona or California in the 18th century.—Garcés (1776), Diary, 404, 1900.

Aquachacha.—José Cortez (1799) quoted in Pac. R. R. Rep., III, pt. 3, 126, 1856.

**Agua Escondida** (Span.: 'hidden water'). Apparently a Pima or Papago rancheria s. w. of Tubac, s. Arizona, in 1774.—Bancroft, Ariz. and N. Mex., 389, 1889.

**Agua Fresca** (Span.: 'fresh water'). A Timuquanan district in N. Florida about the year 1600.—Pareja (1614), Arte Tim., xxi, 1886.

**Agua Fria** (Span.: 'cold water'). A village, probably Piman, on Gila River res., s. Arizona; pop. 527 in 1863. Bailey makes the pop. 770 in 1858, and Browne gives it as 533 in 1869.
Agua Rias.—Taylor in Cal. Farmer, June 19, 1863 (misprint). Aqua Baiz.—Browne, Apache Country, 290, 1869. Arizo del Aqua.—Bailey in Ind. Aff. Rep., 208, 1858.

**Aguama.** A former Chumashan village near Santa Inés mission, Santa Barbara co., Cal.—Taylor in Cal. Farmer, Oct. 18, 1861.

**Agua Nueva** (Span.: 'new water'). A former pueblo, doubtless of the Piros, on the Rio Grande between Socorro and Sevilleta, N. Mex. It was apparently abandoned shortly before Gov. Otermin's second visit in 1681, during the Pueblo revolt.—Davis, Span. Conq. N. Mex., 313, 1869.

**Aguaquiri.** An Indian village, probably in central N. Car. or N. E. Ga., visited by Juan Pardo in 1565.—Vandera (1567) in Smith, Coll. Docs. Fla., I, 17, 1857.

**Agua Salada** (Span.: 'salt water'). A Navaho division in 1799, mentioned as a village by Cortez (Pac. R. R. Rep., III, pt. 3, 119, 1856). As the Navaho are not villagers, the Thodhokongzhi (Saline water, or Bitter water) clan was probably intended.

**Agua Salada.** A district in Florida where one of the various Timuquanan dialects was spoken.—Pareja (1614), Arte Tim., 88, 1886.

**Aguas Calientes** (Span.: 'warm waters'). A province with 3 towns visited by Coronado in 1541; identified by J. H. Simpson with the Jemez ruins at Jemez Hot Springs, near the head of Jemez r., Sandoval co., N. Mex.
Aguas Calientes.—Castañeda (1596) in 14th Rep. B. A. E., 525, 1896. Aquas-Calientes.—Castañeda (1596) misquoted by Ternaux-Compans, Voy., IX, 182, 1838. Oji Caliente.—Bell in J. Ethnol. Soc. Lond., N. s., I, 262, 1869 (misprint).

**Aguastayas.** A tribe, possibly Coahuiltecan, mentioned by Rivera (Diario, leg. 1,994, 2,602, 1736) in connection with the Mesquites and Payayas, as residing s. s. E. of San Antonio presidio, Tex. The three tribes mentioned numbered 250 people.

**Aguile.** A town in N. Florida, visited by DeSoto in 1539, possibly in the neighborhood of Ocilla r.—Biedma in Smith, Coll. Docs. Fla., I, 48, 1857.

**Aguin.** A Chumashan village w. of the Shuku village at Ventura, Ventura co., Cal., in 1542; placed by Taylor (Cal. Farmer, Apr. 17, 1863) on the beach of Las Llagas.

**Agulakpak.** An Eskimo village near Kuskokwim r., Alaska. Pop. 19 in 1890.
Ahgulakhpaghamiut.—11th Census, Alaska, 164, 1893.

**Aguliak.** A Kuskwogmiut village on the E. shore of Kuskokwim bay, Alaska. Pop. 120 in 1880, 94 in 1890.

Aguliagamiut.—11th Census, Alaska, 164, 1893. Aguliagamute.—Petroff, Rep. on Alaska, map, 1884. Aguligamute.—Petroff, ibid., 17.
**Agulok.** A former Aleut village on Unalaska id., Alaska.—Coxe, Russ. Discov., 159, 1787.

**Agulukpuk.** An Eskimo village in the Nushagak district, Alaska; pop. 22 in 1890.
Agulukpukmiut.—11th Census, Alaska, 164, 1893.
**Agumak.** A Kuskwogmiut village in Alaska; pop. 41 in 1890.—11th Census, Alaska, 164, 1893.

**Ahachik** ('moving lodges'). A Crow band.
Ah-hä-chick.—Morgan, Anc. Soc., 159, 1877. Lodges charged upon.—Culbertson in Smithson. Rep. 1850, 144, 1851.

**Ahadzooas.** The principal village of the Oiaht, on Diana id., w. coast of Vancouver id.—Can. Ind. Aff., 263, 1902.

**Ahaharopirnopa.** A division or band of the Crows.
Ahâh-âr-ro'-pir-no-pah.—Lewis and Clark, Disc., 41, 1806.

**Ahahpitape** (*aah'-pŭn* 'blood,' *tŭppe* 'people': 'bloody band'). A division of the Piegan tribe of the Siksika.
Ah-ah'-pi-tä-pe.—Morgan, Anc. Soc., 171, 1877. Ah'-pai-tup-iks.—Grinnell, Blackfoot Lodge Tales, 209, 1892. A'-pe-tup-i.—Hayden, Ethnog. and Philol. Mo.Val., 264, 1862. Bloody Piedgans.—Culbertson in Smithson. Rep. 1850, 144, 1851.

**Ahahswinnis.** The principal village of the Opitchesaht, on the E. bank of Somass r., Vancouver id.—Can. Ind. Aff., 263, 1902.

**Ahahweh** (*ä'häwe*, 'a swan.'—Wm. Jones). A phratry of the Chippewa. According to Morgan it is the Duck gens of the tribe.
A-auh-wauh.—Ramsey in Ind. Aff. Rep., 83, 1850. Ah-ah-wai.—Schoolcraft, Ind. Tribes, I, 304, 1853. Ah-ah-wauk.—Warren in Minn. Hist. Soc. Coll., V, 44, 1885. Ah-ah'-weh.—Morgan, Anc. Soc., 166, 1877. A-auh-wauh.—Ramsey in Ind Aff. Rep., 91, 1850. Ah-auh-wauh-ug.—Warren in Minn. Hist. Soc. Coll., V, 87, 1885 (plural). Ahawh-wauk.—Schoolcraft, Ind. Tribes, II, 142, 1852.

**Ahalakalgi** (from *aha* 'sweet potato', *algi* 'people'). One of the 20 Creek clans.
Ah'-ah.—Morgan. Anc. Soc., 161, 1877. Ahala-χálgi.—Gatschet, Creek Migr. Leg., I, 155, 1884.

**Ahantchuyuk.** A division of the Kalapooian family on and about Pudding r., an E. tributary of the Willamette, emptying into it about 10 m. s. of Oregon City, Oreg.
Ahándshiyuk.—Gatschet, Calapooya MS. vocab., B. A. E. (own name). Ahandshuyuk amim.—Gatschet, Lakmiut MS., B. A. E., 1877 (Lakmiut name). Ahántchuyuk amim.—Gatschet, Atfálati MS. vocab., B. A. E., 1877 (so called by the Calapooya proper). French Prairie Indians.—So called by early settlers. Pudding River Indians.—So called by various authors.

**Ahapchingas.** A former Gabrieleño rancheria in Los Angeles co., Cal., between Los Angeles and San Juan Capistrano.—Taylor in Cal. Farmer, May 11, 1860.

**Ahapopka** ('eating the *ahi*,' or bog potato). A former Seminole town, probably on or near the lake of the same name and near the head of Ocklawaha r., N. central Florida.

**Ahapapka.**—H. R. Ex. Doc. 74 (1823), 19th Cong., 1st, sess., 27, 1826. **Ahapopka.**—Bell in Morse, Rep. to Sec. War, 306, 1822. **Hapapka.**—Jesup (1837) in H. R. Doc. 78, 25th Cong., 2d sess., 65, 1838.

**Ahasimus** (possibly related to the Chippewa *animush*, 'dog'; the Sauk, Fox, and Kickapoo word for dog is *únemòᵃ*, and for a puppy, *unémohä ᵃ*, but when the word becomes the name of a boy of the Wolf gens, it assumes another form of the diminutive, *únimòs ᵃ*.—W. Jones). A village in N. New Jersey in 1655, probably of the Unami Delawares (N. Y. Doc. Col. Hist., XIII, 55, 1881). As the name of a later white settlement the word occurs in a number of forms.

**Ahchawat.** A summer village of the Makah at C. Flattery, Wash.—Swan in Smithson. Cont., XVI, 6, 1870.

**Hatch-áh-wat.**—Gibbs, MS. 248, B. A. E.

**Ahdik** (*údi'k*, 'caribou'—W. Jones). A gens of the Chippewa, often translated 'reindeer.'

**Addick.**—Warren in Minn. Hist. Soc. Coll., v, 44, 1885. **Ad-dik.**—Tanner, Narrative, 314, 1830. **Addik'.**—Morgan, Anc. Soc., 166, 1877. **Ătik'.**—Gatschet *fide* Tomazin, Indian informant.

**Ahealt.** A Koluschan division in the neighborhood of Pt Stewart, Alaska. The name can not be identified, but a clan called Hehlqoan, q. v., now living at Wrangell, formerly occupied this region. (J. R. S.)

**A-he-alt.**—Kane, Wand. in N. A., app., 1859. **Ahialt.**—Petroff in Tenth Census, Alaska, 36, 1884 (quoted from a Hudson Bay Co. census taken in 1839). **Port Stuart Indians.**—Kane, op. cit.

**Ahehouen.** A former village or tribe between Matagorda bay and Maligne (Colorado) r., Tex. The name was told to Joutel in 1687 by the Ebahamo Indians, who lived in that region, and probably applied to a tribe or division closely affiliated to the Karankawa. Tribes belonging to the Tonkawan family also roamed in this vicinity, and those of the Caddoan family sometimes visited the country. See Gatschet in Peabody Museum Papers, I, 35, 46, 1891. (A. C. F.)

**Ahehoen.**—Joutel (1687) in French, Hist. Coll. La., I, 137, 1846. **Ahehoenes.**—Barcia, Ensayo, 271, 1723. **Ahehouen.**—Joutel (1687) in Margry, Déc., III, 288, 1878. **Ahekouen.**—Joutel (1687) in French, Hist. Coll. La., I, 152, 1846.

**Ahkaiksumiks.** A subtribe or gens of the Kainah.

**Ah-kaik'-sum-iks.**—Grinnell, Blackfoot Lodge Tales, 209, 1892.

**Ahkaipokaks** (*ah-kai-ĭm'* 'many', *po-ka'* 'child': 'many children.'—Grinnell). A subtribe or gens of the Kainah.

**Ah-kai'-po-kaks.**—Grinnell, Blackfoot Lodge Tales, 209, 1892.

**Ahkaiyikokakiniks** ('white breasts'). A band or gens of the Piegan.

**Ah-kai-yi-ko-ka'-kin-iks.**—Grinnell, Blackfoot Lodge Tales, 209, 1892. **Kai'-it-ko-ki'-ki-naks.**—Hayden, Ethnog. and Philol. Mo. Val., 264, 1862.

**Ahkotashiks** ('many beasts [horses]'). A subtribe or gens of the Kainah.

**Ahk-o'-tash-iks.**—Grinnell, Blackfoot Lodge Tales, 209, 1892.

**Ahkwonistsists** ('many lodge poles'). A subtribe or gens of the Kainah.

**Ah-kwo'-nis-tsists.**—Grinnell, Blackfoot Lodge Tales, 209, 1892.

**Ahlunksoo** ('spotted animal'). A gens of the Abnaki.

**Ah-lunk'-soo.**—Morgan, Anc. Soc., 174, 1877.

**Ahmeekkwun-eninnewug** (Chippewa: *Ŭmĭ'kuwĭ'nĭnĭwŭg*, 'beaver people'). A tribe living, according to Tanner (Narr., 316, 1830), among the Fall Indians, by which name he seems to mean the Atsina or, possibly, the Amikwa.

**Ahmik** ('beaver'). A gens of the Chippewa.

**Ah-meek.**—Tanner, Narrative, 314, 1830. **Ahmik'.**—Morgan, Anc. Soc., 166, 1877. **Amik.**—Warren in Minn. Hist. Soc. Coll., v, 45, 1885. **Ŭmi'k.**—Jones, inf'n, 1905 (correct form).

**Ahnahanamete** (supposed to indicate some animal). A Hidatsa band, regarded by Matthews as possibly the same as the Amahami.

**Ah-naħ-ha-nä'-me-te.**—Morgan, Anc. Soc., 159, 1877.

**Ahome.** (Buelna says the aboriginal name is *Jaomeme*, 'where the man ran.' In Cahita, *ho-me* means 'to inhabit,' 'to live,' and in Nahuatl *ahome* might be derived from *atl* water, *ome* two, 'two waters,' referring to the ocean tide which ascends the river to this point; but after all the word may be of Vacoregue origin.) A subdivision of the Cahita, speaking the Vacoregue dialect, and the name of its pueblo, situated 4 leagues above the mouth of Rio del Fuerte, N. W. Sinaloa, Mexico. The tradition exists among them that they came from the N.; in that country they fixed paradise and the dwelling place of the souls of their dead. They were of agreeable disposition and of larger size than the other inhabitants of the river valley. They are said to have uttered cries and lamentations for their dead during one entire year, for an hour at sunrise and another at sunset. Although speaking the same language as the inhabitants of a number of neighboring pueblos, the Ahome formed a distinct organization. The pueblo of Ahome became the center of the Batucari settlement under the Jesuit missionaries. (F. W. H.)

**Ahome.**—Kino, map (1702) in Stöcklein, Neue Welt-Bott, 1726. **Hoomi.**—Doc. Hist. Mex., quoted by Buelna, Peregr. Aztecas, 123, 1892. **Jaomeme.**—Buelna, ibid. **Omi.**—Hardy, Trav. in Mex., 438, 1829.

**Ahosulga.** A former Seminole town 5 m. s. of New Mickasuky town, probably in Lafayette co., Fla.—H. R. Ex. Doc. 74 (1823), 19th Cong., 27, 1826.

**Ahouerhopihein** (probably a combination of Ahouergomahe and Kemahopihein of Joutel's list; see Margry, Déc., III, 288, 289, 1878). A village or possibly two villages in Texas. The people are mentioned by Joutel as living in 1687 between Matagorda bay and Maligne (Colorado) r., Tex. The region was inhabited by Karankawan tribes, and the name was given by the Ebahamo, who were probably closely affiliated to that group. See Gatschet, Karankawa Indians, 35, 46, 1891. (A. C. F.)

**Abonerhopiheim.**—Joutel (1687) in French, Hist. Coll, La., I, 152, 1846. **Ahonerhopiheim.**—Ibid., 137. **Ahouerhopiheim.**—Shea, note in Charlevoix, New France, IV, 78, 1870.

**Ahousaht.** A Nootka tribe about Clayoquot sd., w. coast of Vancouver id.; pop. 273 in 1902. Their principal village is Mahktosis. (J. R. S.)

**Ahhousaht.**—Can. Ind. Aff., 188, 1883. **Ahosett.**—Swan in Smithson. Cont., XVI, 56, 1870. **Ahousaht.**—Sproat, Sav. Life, 308, 1868. **Ahousĕt.**—Mayne, Brit. Col., 251, 1862. **Ahowartz.**—Armstrong, Oreg., 136, 1857. **Ahowsaht.**—Powell in 7th Rep. B. A. E., 130, 1891. **Ah-owz-arts.**—Jewitt, Narr., 36, 1849. **Arhosett.**—Swan, MS., B. A. E. **Asonsaht.**—Can. Ind. Aff., 7, 1872.

**Ahoyabe.** A small town, possibly Muskhogean, subject to the Hoya, and lying between them and the Coosa, on the coast of s. S. C., in 1567.—Vandera in Smith, Coll. Docs. Fla., I, 16, 1857.

**Ahpakosea** ('buzzard'). A gens of the Miami.

**Ah-pă'-kose-e-ă.**—Morgan, Anc. Soc., 168, 1877.

**Ahseponna** ('raccoon'). A gens of the Miami.

**Ah-se-pon'-nä.**—Morgan, Anc. Soc., 168, 1877. **Ä'sepŭnᵃ.**—Wm. Jones, inf'n., 1905 (Sauk, Fox, and Kickapoo form).

**Ahtena** ('ice people'). An Athapascan tribe occupying the basin of Copper r., Alaska. Their permanent villages are situated 100 m. or more from the sea, on Copper r., the mouth of which Nagaieff discovered in 1781. An expedition in 1796 under Samoylof failed on account of the hostility of the natives, as did a second under Lastóchkin in 1798, and one under Klimoffsky in 1819. Gregorief in 1844 renewed the attempt with like result. In 1848 Serebránnikof ventured up the river, but his disregard for the natives cost the lives of himself and 3 of his party (Dall, Alaska, 343, 1877). Dall met a trading party of Ahtena in 1874 at Port Etches, and in 1882 a trader named Holt ascended the river as far as Taral, but on a subsequent visit was murdered by the natives. Lieut. Abercrombie in 1884 explored a part of the river, and in the following year Lieut. Allen made an extended exploration, visiting the Ahtena villages on Copper r. and its chief tributaries. The natives strongly resemble the Koyukukhotana in appearance, the men being tall, straight, of good physique, with clear olive complexion, arched eyebrows, beardless faces, and long, straight, black hair, worn loose or in a single scalp-lock. Petroff (10th Census, Alaska, 164, 1884) states that prior to 1880 the women had never been seen by any white man who lived to describe them. On account of the hostile nature of these people but little is known of their customs and beliefs. Their clothing ordinarily consists of two garments, trousers and boots forming one, a parka the other. The clothing is decorated with beads or, more commonly, with fringe and porcupine quills, since beads are used in trade with the tribes on Tanana r. They have a cap of skin detached from the parka. The chief occupation of the men is hunting and fishing, supplemented by a yearly trading trip as middlemen between the coast tribes and those of the interior. In visiting the coast they travel in large skin-covered boats purchased from traders or from the coast tribes. The chief articles of trade are beads, cotton prints, and tobacco, which are exchanged for furs and copper. Their chief weapon is the bow and arrow, although a few old-fashioned guns are occasionally found. The men have both nose and ears pierced, the women the latter only. The houses are of two kinds, permanent, for use in winter, and temporary, used only as shelters during hunting trips. To the permanent dwellings are attached subterranean bath-rooms, in which steam is created by pouring water on red-hot stones. They live in small villages, of one or two houses; the headman is called a *tyone*, and his near relatives, the next in rank, are called *skillies*. There is usually a shaman in every village, and slaves of varying degrees of servitude are kept. Polygamy is practised to a limited extent; it is said that the women are treated with very little consideration and valued in proportion to their ability to work (Allen, Rep. on Alaska, 266, 1887). According to Allen (ibid., 259) the Ahtena are divided into two branches: those on Copper r., from its mouth to Tazlina r., and on Chitina r. and its branches he calls the Midnusky; those above the Tazlina, Tatlatan. Petroff in 1880 stated that the Ahtena did not number more than 300. Allen in 1885 gave the entire number of natives on the river and its branches as 366, of whom 128 were men, 98 women, and 140 children, distributed as follows: On Chitina r. and its branches, 30; on Tazlina r. and lake, 20; on Copper r., between Taral and the Tazlina, 209; Tatlatans, 117. According to Hoffman (MS. vocab., B. A. E., 1882) the tribe consists of six divisions: Ikherkhamut, Kangikhlukhmut, Kulushut, Shukhtutakhlit, Vikhit, and he includes also the Kulchana. The census of 1890 makes the total number of Ahtena 142, consisting of 89 males and 53 females. Their villages are: Alaganik, Batzulnetas, Liebestag, Miduuski, Skatalis, Skolai, Slana, Titlogat, Toral. (F. H.)

**Áh-tená.**—Dall, Alaska, 429, 1870 (own name). **Ahtna-khotana.**—Petroff, 10th Census, Alaska, 164, 1884. **Artez-kutchi.**—Richardson, Arct. Exped.,

I, 397, 1851. **Artez-kutshi.**—Latham, Nat. Races Russ. Emp., 293, 1854. **Artez-Kuttchin.**—Petitot, Dict. Dènè-Dindjié, xx, 1876. **Atakhtans.**—Erman quoted by Dall in Cont. N. A. Ethnol., I, 34, 1877. **Atenâs.**—Harmon, Journ., 190, 1820. **Athnaer.**—Holmberg, Ethnol. Skizz., 7, 1855. **Atnachtjaner.**—Erman, Archiv, VII, 128, 1849. **Atnäer.**—Richardson, Arct. Exped., I, 402, 1851. **Atnahs.**—Pinart in Rev. de Philol. et d'Ethnol., no. 2, 1, 1875. **Atnans.**—Petitot, Autour du lac des Esclaves, 362, 1891. **Atnas.**—Scouler in Journ. Geog. Soc. Lond., I, 218, 1841. **Atnatána.**—Allen, Rep., 62, 1887. **Atnatena.**—11th Census, Alaska, 67, 1893. **Atnaxthynné.**—Pinart, Sur les Atnahs, 1, 1875. **Copper Indians.**—Mahoney in Ind. Aff. Rep. for 1869, 575, 1870. **Copper River Indians.**—Colyer, ibid., 535. **Intsi Dindjich.**—Petitot, Autour du lac des Esclaves, 165, 1891 ('men of iron': Kutchin name). **Ketschetnäer.**—Wrangell, quoted by Baer and Helmersen, Beiträge, I, 98, 1839 ('ice people': Russian name). **Kolshína.**—Dall, Alaska, 429, 1870 (so called by Russians). **Madnussky.**—Mahoney in Ind. Aff. Rep. 1869, 575, 1870 (corruption of Russian *Miednovski*, from *miednaia*, 'copper,' the name given to the river). **Maidnorskie.**—Elliott, Cond. Aff. Alaska, 29, 1874. **Mednoftsi.**—Hoffman, MS. vocab., B. A. E., 1882 ('Copper r. people': Russian name). **Mednovtze.**—11th Census, Alaska, 156, 1893. **Midnóoskies.**—Allen, Rep., 22, 1887 (Russian name). **Midnóvtsi.**—Ibid., 128 (Russian name). **Miednoffskoi.**—Worman quoted by Dall in Cont. N. A. Ethnol., I, 34, 1877. **Miednofskie.**—Pinart in Rev. de Philol. et d'Ethnol., no. 2, 1, 1875. **Minóosky.**—Allen, Rep., 128, 1887. **Minúsky.**—Ibid. **Nehannes.**—Keane in Stanford, Compend., 525, 1878. **Nehaunee.**—Dall, Alaska, 429, 1870. **Nehaunee Indians.**—Ross, MS. map quoted by Dall in Cont. N. A. Ethnol., I, 34, 1877 (Yellowknife or). **Neine Katlene.**—Doroschin in Radloff, Wörterbuch d. Kinai-Spr., 29, 1874 (own name). **Onossky.**—Mahony in Sen. Ex. Doc. 68, 41st Cong., 2d sess., 19, 1870. **Otno-khotana.**—Petroff in 10th Census, Alaska, 164, 1884 (so-called by Knaiakhotana). **Otnox tana.**—Dawydow quoted by Radloff, Wörterbuch d. Kinai-Spr., 29, 1874. **Utunx tana.**—Doroschin, ibid. **Yellowknife Indians.**—Ross, MS. map cited by Dall in Cont. N. A. Ethnol., I, 34, 1877 (Nehaunee or; so called by English). **Yullit.**—Petroff in 10th Census, Alaska, 165, 1884 (Ugalakmiut name).

**Ahuamhoue.** A former Chumashan village near Santa Inés mission, Santa Barbara co., Cal.—Taylor in Cal. Farmer, Oct. 18, 1861.

**Ahuanga.** A Luiseño settlement, consisting of 2 villages, about 30 m. from the coast, lat. 33°, 25′, in San Diego co., Cal.—Hayes (*ca.* 1850) quoted by Bancroft, Nat. Races, I, 460, 1882.

**Ahulka** (*A-hul-qa*). A village of the Ntlakyapamuk, on Fraser r., British Columbia, just below Siska; pop. 5 in 1897, the last time the name appears. **Ahulqa.**—Hill-Tout in Rep. Ethnol. Surv. Can., 5, 1899. **Halaha.**—Can. Ind. Aff. for 1885, 196 (probably the same).

**Ahwaste.** A division of the Costanoan family formerly living near San Francisco bay, Cal., and connected with Dolores mission. **Aguasajuchium.**—Taylor in Cal. Farmer, Oct. 18, 1861 (Aguasa and Juchium [Uchium] combined). **Aguasto.**—Ibid. **Ah-wash-tes.**—Schoolcraft, Ind. Tribes, II, 506, 1852. **Ahwastes.**—Latham in Proc. Philol. Soc. Lond., VI, 79, 1854. **Apuasto.**—Taylor in Cal. Farmer, Oct. 18, 1861. **Habasto.**—Ibid.

**Ahwehsoos** ('bear'). A gens of the Abnaki. **Ah-weli′-soos.**—Morgan, Anc. Soc., 174, 1877. **Awasos.**—J. D. Prince, inf'n, 1905 (modern St Francis Abnaki form).

**Aiachagiuk.** A Chnagmiut village on the right bank of the Yukon, near the head of the delta. **Aiachagiuk.**—Baker, Geog. Dict. Alaska, 1901. **Ayachaghayuk.**—Coast Surv. map, 1898.

**Aiacheruk.** A Kaviagmiut Eskimo village near C. Nome, Alaska; pop. 60 in 1880. **Ahyoksekawik.**—11th Census, Alaska, 162, 1893. **Aiacheruk.**—Jackson, Reindeer in Alaska, map, 1894. **Ayacheruk.**—Petroff, Rep. on Alaska, 59, 1880.

**Aiaktalik.** A Kaniagmiut village on one of the Goose ids. near Kodiak, Alaska; pop. 101 in 1880, 106 in 1890. **Aiakhatalik.**—Petroff, 10th Census, Alaska, map, 1884. **Aiaktalik.**—Baker, Geog. Dict. Alaska, 1901. **Anayachtalik.**—Sauer, Exped., 1802. **Ayaktalik.**—11th Census, Alaska, 163, 1893. **Ayakhtalik.**—Petroff, op. cit., 29.

**Aiapai.** Mentioned by Powers (Cont. N. A. Ethnol., III, 370, 1877) as a division of the Yokuts at Soda Spring, on Tule r., Cal., but it is merely the name of a locality at which the Yaudanchi or perhaps other divisions once lived. (A. L. K.)

**Aicatum.** A Maricopa rancheria on the Rio Gila, Ariz., in 1744.—Sedelmair (1774) quoted by Bancroft, Ariz. and N. Mex., 366, 1889.

**Aigspaluma** (Shahaptian: 'people of the chipmunks'). The Klamath, Modoc, Shoshoni, and Paiute living on Klamath res. and its vicinity in Oregon.—Gatschet in Cont. N. A. Ethnol., II, pt. I, xxxiii, 1890. **Aigspalo.**—Gatschet, ibid. (abbreviated form). **Aikspalu.**—Ibid. **I-uke-spi-ule.**—Huntington in Ind. Aff. Rep., 466, 1865.

**Aika.** A former Shasta village near Hamburg Bar, on Klamath r., Siskiyou co., Cal. (R. B. D.) **Ika.**—Steele in Ind. Aff. Rep. 1864, 120, 1865.

**Aimgua.** A former Chnagmiut village near the mouth of Yukon r., Alaska.—Zagoskin in Nouv. Ann. Voy., 5th s., XXI, map, 1850.

**Aingshi** ('bear'). A Zuñi clan. **Aiñ′shi-kwe.**—Cushing in 13th Rep. B. A. E., 368, 1896 (*kwe* = 'people'). **Aiŋshi-kwe.**—Ibid., 386. **Än-shi-i-que.**—Stevenson in 5th Rep. B. A. E., 541, 1887.

**Ainslie Creek.** A band of Ntlakyapamuk on Fraser r., above Spuzzum, Brit. Col.—Can. Ind. Aff., 79, 1878.

**Aiodjus** (*ᵍaiᵍodjus*, 'all fat [meat]'). A Skittagetan town on the w. side of the mouth of Masset inlet, Queen Charlotte ids. It was occupied by the Aokeawai before they moved to Alaska.—Swanton, Cont. Haida, 281, 1905.

**Ais.** A rude tribe of unknown affinity formerly occupying the E. coast of Florida, from about Cape Cañaveral s. to about Santa Lucia inlet, or about the present Brevard co. They planted nothing, but subsisted entirely on fish and wild fruits, and were more or less subject to the Calusa. (J. M.) **Ais.**—De Canzo Rep. (1600) in Brooks Coll. MS., Lib. Cong. **Aïs.**—Gatschet, Creek Migr. Leg., I, 12, 1884. **Aïsa.**—Romans, Florida, I, 281, 1775 (the lagoon). **Ays.**—Mexia Report (1586) in Brooks Coll. MS., Lib. Cong. **Chaas.**—Penière (1821) as quoted by Morse, Rep. to Sec. War, 311, 1822. **Chiaas.**—Penière, ibid., 150. **Chias.**—Penière, ibid., 149. **Is.**—Barcia, Ensayo, 95, 1723. **Jece.**—Dickenson (1699), Narr., 47, 1803. **Ys.**—Fairbanks, Florida, 175, 1871.

**Aisikstukiks** ('biters'). A band of the Siksika.
**Ai-sik′-stŭk-iks.**—Grinnell, Blackfoot Lodge Tales, 209, 1892.

**Aitacomanes**. Mentioned with the Otocomanes as a people occupying a province that had been visited by the Dutch and "where the abundance of gold and silver is such that all the vessels for their use are of silver, and in some cases of gold." The locality is not given, and the province is probably as imaginary as the expedition in connection with which it is mentioned. See Freytas, Exped. of Peñalosa (1662), Shea transl., 67, 1882.

**Aivilik** ('having walrus'). An Eskimo village on Repulse bay, Franklin dist., Brit. Am., the principal winter settlement of the Aivilirmiut.—Boas in 6th Rep. B. A. E., 449, 1888.
**A′-wee-lik.**—McClintock, Voy. of Fox, 163, 1881. **Ay-wee-lik.**—Lyons, Priv. Journ., 161, 1825. **Eiwili.**—Klutschak, Unter d. Eskimo, map, 48, 1881. **Iwillichs.**—Gilder, Schwatka's Search, 294, 1881. **Iwillie.**—Ibid., 304. **Iwillik.**—Ibid., 181.

**Aivilirmiut** ('people of the walrus place'). A Central Eskimo tribe on the N. shores of Hudson bay from Chesterfield inlet to Fox channel, among whom Rae sojourned in 1846–47, C. F. Hall in 1864–69, and Schwatka in 1877–79. They kill deer, muskoxen, seal, walrus, trout, and salmon, caching a part of the meat and blubber, which before winter they bring to one of their central settlements. Their chief villages are Akugdlit, Aivilik, Iglulik, Maluksilak, Nuvung, Pikuliak, Ugluriak, Ukusiksalik; summer villages are Inugsulik, Kariak, Naujan, Pitiktaujang.—Boas in 6th Rep. B. A. E., 445, 1888.
**Ahaknañĕlet.**—Petitot in Bib. Ling. et Ethnol. Am., III, xi, 1876 (so called by the Chiglit of Liverpool bay: sig. 'women'). **A-hak-nan-helet.**—Richardson, Arct. Exped., I, 362, 1851. **Ahaknanhelik.**—Richardson, Polar Regions, 300, 1861. **Ahwhacknanhelett.**—Franklin, Journey to Polar Sea, II, 42, 1824. **Aivillirmiut.**—Boas in 6th Rep. B. A. E., 445, 1888. **Eivillinmiut.**—Boas in Trans. Anthrop. Soc. Wash., III, 102, 1885. **Eiwillik.**—Boas in Zeitschr. Ges. f. Erdk., 226, 1883.

**Aivino.** A division of the Nevome in a pueblo of the same name on the w. tributary of the Rio Yaqui, lat. 29°, s. central Sonora, Mexico. The inhabitants spoke a dialect differing somewhat from the Nevome proper, and their customs were similar to those of the Sisibotari.
**Aibina.**—Balbi quoted by Orozco y Berra, Geog., 352, 1864. **Aibinos.**—Kino et al. (1694) in Doc. Hist. Mex., 4th s., I, 399, 1856. **Aivino.**—Ribas, Hist. Trium. Sa. Fee, 370, 1645. **Aybino.**—Kino et al., op. cit.

**Aiwanat** (*Aiwánat*, pl. of *Aiwan*). The Chukchi name for the Yuit Eskimo residing at and near the vicinity of Indian point, N. E. Siberia, as distinguished from those who speak the dialect of the vil-

lage of Nabukak on East cape and that of Cherinak near C. Ulakhpen.—Bogoras, Chukchee, 20, 1904.

**Aiyaho** (a red-topped plant). A Zuñi clan, by tradition originally a part of the Asa people who afterward became Hopi.
**Aiwahokwe.**—Fewkes in 19th Rep. B. A. E., 606, 1900. **Aíyaho-kwe.**—Cushing in 13th Rep. B. A. E., 368, 1896 (*kwe* = 'people'). **Aiyáhokwi.**—Stephen and Mindeleff in 8th Rep. B. A. E., 30–31, 1891. **Olla-jocue.**—Cushing misquoted by Donaldson, Moqui Pueblo Inds., 88, 1893 (incorrectly given as "Blue seed grass" people). **Pétâa-kwe.**—Ibid., 386 (former name).

**Aiyansh** ('eternal bloom.'—Dorsey). A mission village on the lower course of Nass r., British Columbia, founded in 1871, its inhabitants being drawn from Niska villages. Pop. 133 in 1901.
**Aiyansh.**—Can. Ind. Aff., 271, 1889. **Aiyaush.**—Dorsey in Am. Antiq., XIX, 281, 1897 (misprint).

**Akachumas.** A former Chumashan village near Santa Inés mission, Santa Barbara co., Cal.—Gatschet in Chief Eng. Rep., pt. III, 553, 1876.

**Akachwa** ('pine grove'). A Tarahumare rancheria near Palanquo, Chihuahua, Mexico.—Lumholtz, inf'n, 1894.

**Akaitchis.** A tribe said to have resided on Columbia r. not far from the mouth of the Umatilla, in Oregon (Nouv. Ann. des Voy., X, 78, 1821). Their location would indicate a Shahaptian division, but they can not be identified.

**Akaitsuk.** A former Chumashan village about Santa Inés mission, Santa Barbara co., Cal.
**A-kai′t-sŭk.**—Henshaw, Santa Inez MS. vocab., B. A. E., 1884.

**Akak.** An Eskimo settlement in the Nushagak district, Alaska, of only 9 people in 1890.
**Akakhpuk.**—11th Census, Alaska, 164, 1893.

**Akamnik.** A tribe of the Upper Kutenai living around Ft Steele and the mission of St Eugène on upper Kootenai r., Brit. Col.
**Aqk′amnik.**—Boas in 5th Rep. N. W. Tribes Can., 10, 1889. **Aqk′ā′mnik.**—Chamberlain in 8th Rep. N. W. Tribes Can., 6, 1892.

**Akanaquint** ('green river'). A Ute division formerly living on Green r., Utah, belonging probably to the Yampa.
**Akanaquint.**—Beckwith in Pac. R. R. Rep., II, 61, 1855. **Chaguaguanos.**—Escudero, Not. Nuevo Méx., 83, 1849. **Changuaguanes.**—Orozco y Berra, Geog., 59, 1864 (given as Faraon Apache). **Green river band.**—Cummings in Ind. Aff. Rep., 153, 1866. **Green river Utahs.**—Beckwith in Pac. R. R. Rep., II, 61, 1855. **Sabaguanas.**—Dominguez and Escalante (1776) in Doc. Hist. Mex., 2a s., I, 537, 1854. **Sabuagana Gutas.**—Escalante (1776) misquoted by Harry in Simpson, Rep. of Explor. across Utah in 1859, 494, 1876. **Sabuaganas.**—Dominguez and Escalante, op. cit., 421. **Saguaguana.**—Escudero, Not. Estad. de Chihuahua, 231, 1834. **Yutas sabuaganas.**—Dominguez and Escalante (1776) in Doc. Hist. Mex., 2a s., I, 415, 1854. **Zaguaganas.**—Cortez (1799) in Pac. R. R. Rep., III, pt. 3, 120, 1856. **Zaguaguas.**—Villa Señor, Theatro Am., II, 413, 1748.

**Akanekunik** ('Indians on a river'). A tribe of the Upper Kutenai on Kootenai r. at the Tobacco plains, Brit. Col.
**Aqk′anequnik.**—Boas in 5th Rep. N. W. Tribes Can., 10, 1889. **Aqk′āneqũ′nik.**—Chamberlain in 8th Rep. N. W. Tribes Can., 6, 1892. **Tobacco**

**Plains Kootanie.**—Tolmie and Dawson, Comp. Vocabs., 124B, 1884. **Tobacco Plains Kootenay.**—Chamberlain, op. cit., table opp. 41. **Yaket-ahnoklatak-makanay.**—Tolmie and Dawson, op. cit. **Yā′k′ēt aqkinūqtlē′ēt āqkts′mā′kinik.**—Chamberlain, op. cit., 6 ('Indians of the Tobacco plains,' from *yā′k′ēt* tobacco, *āqkinūqtlē′ēt* plain, *āqkts′mā′kinik* Indians).

**Akasquy.** An extinct tribe, probably Caddoan, visited by La Salle in Jan., 1687, when its people resided between the Palaquesson and the Penoy in the vicinity of Brazos r., Tex. They made cloth of buffalo wool and mantles decorated with bird feathers and the "hair of animals of every color." See Cavelier in Shea, Early Voy., 39, 1861. (A. C. F.)

**Akatlik.** A Yuit village on Plover bay, Siberia.
**Akatlak.**—Krause in Deutsche Geogr. Blätter, v, 80, map, 1882. **Akatlik.**—Nelson in 18th Rep. B. A. E., map, 1899.

**Akawenchaka** (Onondaga: *A-ka-wĕnch-hă-kă*). A small band that formerly lived in North Carolina, now numbering about 20 individuals, incorporated with the Tuscarora in New York. They are not regarded as true Tuscarora.—Hewitt, Onondaga MS., B. A. E., 1888.
**Kauwetsaka.**—Cusick (1825) quoted by Macauley, N. Y., II, 178, 1829 (mentioned as a settlement in N. C.). **Kauwetseka.**—Cusick, Sketches Six Nations, 34, 1828.

**Akawiruchic** ('place of much fungus'). A Tarahumare rancheria near Palanquo, Mexico.—Lumholtz, inf'n, 1894.

**Akchadak-kochkond.** A coast village of the Malemiut in Alaska.—Zagoskin in Nouv. Ann. Voy., 5th s., XXI, map, 1850.

**Akerninak.** A settlement of East Greenland Eskimo on Sermilik fiord; pop. 12 in 1884.—Holm, Ethnol. Skizze af Angmagsalikerne, 14, 1887.

**Akgulurigiglak.** An Eskimo village in the Nushagak district, Alaska; pop. 61 in 1890.—Eleventh Census, Alaska, 164, 1893.

**Akhiok.** A Kaniagmiut village on Alitak bay, Kodiak id., Alaska; pop. 114 in 1880, slightly more than 100 in 1900.
**Achiok.**—Holmberg, Ethnol. Skizz., map, 142, 1855. **Akhiok.**—Petroff, 10th Census, Alaska, 29, 1884. **Alitak.**—11th Census, Alaska, 5, 1893. **Kaschjukwagmjut.**—Holmberg, op. cit. **Kashukvagmiut.**—Russ. Am. Co., map, 1849. **Oohaiack.**—Lisianski, Voy. (1805), quoted by Baker, Geog. Dict. Alaska, 1901. **Uhaiak.**—Baker, ibid.

**Akiachak.** A Kuskwogmiut village on Kuskokwim r., Alaska; pop. 43 in 1890, 165 in 1900.
**Akiakchagmiut.**—11th Census, Alaska, 164, 1893. **Akiatshágamut.**—Spurr and Post quoted by Baker, Geog. Dict. Alaska, 1901.

**Akiak.** A Kuskwogmiut village on Kuskokwim r., 30 m. above Bethel; pop. 175 in 1880, 97 in 1890.
**Ackiagmute.**—Petroff, Rep. on Alaska, map, 1884. **Akiagamiut.**—11th Census, Alaska, 104, 1893. **Akiagamute.**—Hallock in Nat. Geog. Mag., IX, 1898. **Akiágmut.**—Spurr and Post quoted by Baker, Geog. Dict. Alaska, 1901. **Akkiagamute.**—Petroff, op. cit., 53. **Akkiagmute.**—Ibid., 17.

**Akiskenukinik** ('people of the two lakes'). A tribe of the Upper Kutenai living on the Columbia lakes, having their chief settlement at Windermere, Brit. Col. They numbered 72 in 1902.
**Akiskinookaniks.**—Wilson in Trans. Ethnol. Soc. Lond., 304, 1866. **AqkiskanūkEnik.**—Boas in 5th Rep. N. W. Tribes Can., 10, 1889. **Aqki′sk′Enū′kinik.**—Chamberlain in 8th Rep. N. W. Tribes Can., 6, 1892. **Columbia Lakes.**—Ibid., 7.

**Akiyenik** (*Aqkīyē′nik*, 'people of the leggings'). A tribe of the Upper Kutenai living on L. Pend d'Oreille, Idaho.—Boas in 5th Rep. N. W. Tribes Can., 10, 1889.

**Aklut** ('provisions'). A Kuskwogmiut village on Kuskokwim r. at the mouth of the Eek, Alaska; pop. 162 in 1880, 106 in 1890.
**Ahguliagamut.**—11th Census, Alaska, 164, 1893. **Aklukwagamut.**—Spurr and Post quoted by Baker, Geog. Dict. Alaska, 1901. **Akooligamute.**—Petroff, Rep. on Alaska, 17, 1884; Nelson (1878) quoted by Baker, op. cit.

**Akmiut.** A Kuskwogmiut village on Kuskokwim r., 10 m. above Kolmakof, Alaska.
**Akmute.**—Petroff, 10th Census, Alaska, map, 1884.

**Akol** (*Ā′kol*). An organization among the Pima, apparently gentile, belonging to the Suwuki Ohimal, or Red Ants, phratral group.—Russell, Pima MS., B. A. E., 313, 1903.

**Akonapi** (possibly related to the Chippewa *a′kunabäwĭsĭ*, 'he is good at getting game'; *-nap-* is a secondary stem referring to a human person. Another form is *a′kuwĭnĭnĭ; ĭnĭnĭ* refers to 'man.'—Wm. Jones). A people mentioned in the ancient *Walam Olum* record of the Delawares (Brinton, Lenâpe Legends, 190, 231, 1885), with whom they fought during their migrations. Brinton, who identifies them with the Akowini of the same tradition, thinks it probable that they lived immediately N. of Ohio r. in Ohio or Indiana. He regards Akowini as "correspondent" with Sinako, and Towakon with Towako; the latter he identifies with the Ottawa, called by the Delawares *Taway*. If this identification be correct, it is likely that the Akonapi were the Sinago branch of the Ottawa. (C. T.)
**Ahkonapi.**—Walam Olum (1833) in Brinton, Lenâpe Leg., 190, 1885. **Akhonapi.**—Ibid. **Akowini.**—Ibid., 198.

**Akonye** ('people of the canyon'). An Apache band at San Carlos agency and Ft Apache, Ariz., in 1881; probably coordinate with the Khonagani clan of the Navaho.—Bourke in Journ. Am. Folk-Lore, III, 111, 1890.
**Nar-go′-des-giz′-zen.**—White, Apache Names of Ind. Tribes, MS., B. A. E.

**Akorninarmiut.** A village of the southern group of East Greenland Eskimo, between lat. 63° and 64°; pop., with three other villages, 135.—Rink in Geog. Blätter, VIII, 346, 1886.

**Akpaliut.** A Kaviagmiut village w. of Golofnin bay, on Norton sd., Alaska; possibly the same as Chiukak.
**Acpalliut.**—W. U. Tel. map, 1867, cited by Baker, Geog. Dict. Alaska, 1901.

**Akpan** ('auks'). An Ita Eskimo settlement on Saunders id., N. Greenland. The name is applied to many bird cliffs in E. Arctic America.
Akbat.—Hayes, Arct. Boat Journ., 241, 1854. Akpani.—Peary, My Arct. Jour., 80, 1893.

**Aktayatsalgi.** One of the 20 Creek clans.—Gatschet, Creek Migr. Leg., I, 155, 1884.

**Aktese.** A village of the Kyuquot on Village id., Kyuquot sd., w. coast of Vancouver id.—Can. Ind. Aff., 264, 1902.

**Akuch.** The extinct Ivy clan of the Sia.
A'küch-háno.—Hodge in Am. Anthrop., IX, 351, 1896 (háno='people').

**Akuchiny.** A former Pima village s. w. of Maricopa station, s. Arizona.—Russell, Pima MS., B. A. E., 16, 1902. Cf. *Aquitun.*

**Akudnirmiut** ('people of the intervening country'). An Eskimo tribe of E. Baffin land, on the shore of Home bay and northward. They migrate between their various stations, in winter as well as in summer, in search of deer, bear, seal, walrus, and salmon, having ceased to capture whales from the floe edge since the advent of whaling ships; pop. 83 in 1883 (Boas in 6th Rep. B. A. E., 440, 1888). Their winter settlements are not permanent. Their villages and camping places are: Arbaktung, Avaudjelling, Ekalualuin, Ijelirtung, Ipiutelling, Karmakdjuin, Kaudjukdjuak, Kivitung, Niakonaujang, Nudlung, Sirmiling.

**Akugdlit.** A village of the Aivilirmiut at the s. end of the Gulf of Boothia, on Committee bay.—Boas in 6th Rep. B. A. E., 445, 1888.

**Akuli.** An Iglulirmiut village on the isthmus of Melville peninsula; pop. 50.
Ao-cool-le.—Ross, Sec. Voy., 316, 1835. Accoulee.—Ibid., map facing p. 262. Ackoolee.—Ibid., 254. Akkoolee.—Parry, Sec. Voy., 449, 1824.

**Akuliak.** An Akuliarmiut winter village on the N. shore of Hudson str., where there was an American whaling station; pop. 200.
Akuliaq.—Boas in 6th Rep. B. A. E., map, 1888.

**Akuliarmiut** ('people of the point between two large bays'). An Eskimo tribe settled on the N. shore of Hudson strait (Boas in 6th Rep. B. A. E., 421, 1888). They go to Amakdjuak through White Bear sd. to hunt, where they meet the Nugumiut.
Akkolear.—Gilder, Schwatka's Search, 181, 1881. Akudliarmiut.—Boas in Trans. Anthrop. Soc. Wash., III, 96, 1885. Akuliak-Eskimos.—Boas in Petermanns Mitt., 68, 1885.

**Akuliukpak** ('many provisions'). A Nushagagmiut Eskimo settlement on Pamiek lake, Alaska; pop. 83 in 1880.
Akuliakhpuk.—Petroff, Rep. on Alaska, 17, 1884.

**Akulivikchuk.** A Nushagagmiut village on Nushagak r., Alaska; pop. 72 in 1880.
Akulvikchuk.—Petroff, Rep. on Alaska, 17, 1884.

**Akun** ('distant'). A former Aleut village on a small island of the same name between Unalaska and Unimak, Aleutian group, Alaska; pop. 55 in 1880. The inhabitants have deserted it for Akutan.
Akoon.—Schwatka, Mil. Recon. in Alaska, 360, 1885.

**Akuninak** (á'kuni 'bone,' -nawe 'town,' 'country,' -ki 'place where': 'at the bone place'). A group of Sauk and Foxes who lived together in a village near where some huge bones, probably of a mastodon, lay imbedded in the ground.—Wm. Jones, inf'n, 1905.
Ah-kuh'-ne-näk.—Morgan, Anc. Soc., 170, 1877 (given as the Bone gens).

**Akutan.** An Aleut village on a small island of the same name adjacent to Unalaska, Alaska; pop. 65 in 1880, 80 in 1890.
Akutanskoe.—Veniaminoff, Zapiski, II, 203, 1840.

**Akvetskoe** ('lake town'). A summer village of the Huna division of the Koluschan family, on Lituya bay, Alaska; pop. 200 in 1835.—Veniaminoff, Zapiski, II, pt. 3, 29, 1840.
Ahkvaystkie.—Elliott, Cond. Aff. Alaska, 227, 1875 (from Veniaminoff). Akwetz.—Holmberg, Ethnol. Skizz., map, 1855.

**Akwech.** A Wichita subtribe.—J. O. Dorsey, inf'n, 1892.

**Ala** ('horn'). A phratry of the Hopi, consisting of the Horn, Deer, Antelope, Elk, and probably other clans. They claim to have come from a place in s. Utah called Tokonabi, and after their arrival in Tusayan joined the Lengya (Flute) phratry, forming the Ala-Lengya group.—Fewkes in 19th Rep. B. A. E., 583, 587, 1901.

**Ala.** The Horn clan of the Hopi.—Fewkes in 19th Rep. B. A. E., 583, 1901.
Áaltu.—Voth, Trad. of the Hopi, 38, 1905.—Ala wiñwû.—Fewkes, op. cit. (wiñwâ=clan).

**Alabaster.** See *Gypsum.*

**Alachua.** A former Seminole town in what is now Alachua co., Fla. It was settled by Creeks from Oconee, on Oconee r., Ga., about 1710. The name was subsequently extended so as to cover other small villages in the district, which collectively are frequently mentioned as a tribe, whose principal town was Cuscowilla. The Alachua Indians offered lively resistance to the encroachments of the white colonists in 1812–18 and took a prominent part in the Seminole war of 1835–42. (A. S. G. H. W. H.)
Alachees.—Schoolcraft, Ind. Tribes, II, 32, 1852. A-lack-a-way-talofa.—Bell in Morse, Rep. to Sec. War, 306, 1822. Alacua.—Romans, Florida, I, 280, 1775. Aulochawan Indians.—Hawkins (1812) in Am. State Papers, Ind. Aff., I, 813, 1832. Au-lot-che-wau.—Hawkins (1799), Sketch, 25, 1848. Lach-aways.—Seagrove (1793) in Am. State Pap., Ind. Aff., I, 378, 1832. Lackaway.—Brown (1793), ibid., 374. Latchione.—Brinton, Florida Penin., 145, 1859. Latchivue.—Penière in Morse, Rep. to Sec. War, 311, 1822. Lotchnoay.—Schoolcraft, Ind. Tribes, VI, 360, 1857. Lotchway towns.—Flint, Ind. Wars, 173, 1833. Sotchaway.—Seagrove, op. cit., 380.

**Alacranes** (Span.: 'scorpions'). A part of the Apache formerly living in Sonora, Mexico, but according to Taylor (Cal.

Farmer, June 13, 1862) roaming, with other bands from Texas, to the Rio Colorado and N. of Gila r. in Ariz. and N. Mex. They were apparently a part of the Chiricahua.

**Alacupusyuen.** A former Chumashan village near Purísima mission, Santa Barbara co., Cal.—Taylor in Cal. Farmer, Oct. 18, 1861.

**Alafiers** (*ala*='buckeye tree'). A Seminole town near Alafia r., an affluent of Tampa bay, Fla. Its inhabitants, few in number, appear to have been led by Chief Alligator, and the "Alligators" may have been the same people. They took part in the Seminole war of 1835–42. (H. W. H.)
Alafia.—Drake, Ind. Chron., 209, 1836. Alafiers.—Drake, Bk. of Inds., bk. 4, 77, 1848.

**Alaganik.** An Ahtena and Ugalakmiut village near the mouth of Copper r., Alaska. Pop. in 1880, with Eyak, 117; in 1890, 48. Serebrenikof visited the village in 1848, but Allen in 1885 found it on what he supposed to be a new site.
Alaganik.—Dall in Cont. N. A. Ethnol., I, map, 1877. Alaganuk.—Petroff, 10th Census, Alaska, 29, 1884. Alagnak.—Serebrenikof quoted by Baker, Geog. Dict. Alaska, 1901. Anahanuk.—Allen, ibid. Lookta-ek.—11th Census, Alaska, 161, 1893.

**Alaho-ateuna** ('those of the southernmost'). A phratry embracing the Tonashi (Badger) and Aiyaho (Red-topped-shrub) clans of the Zuñi.—Cushing, inf'n, 1891.

**Alahulapas.** A former Chumashan village near Santa Inés mission, Santa Barbara co., Cal.—Gatschet in Chief Eng. Rep., pt. 3, 553, 1876.

**Ala-Lengya** ('horn-flute'). A phratral group of the Hopi, consisting of the Ala (Horn) and Lengya (Flute) clans.
Ala-Leñya.—Fewkes in 19th Rep. B. A. E., 583, 1901.

**Alali.** A former Chumashan village on Santa Cruz id., off the coast of California.
A-la'-li.—Henshaw, Buenaventura MS. vocab., B. A. E., 1884.

**Alameda** (Span.: 'cottonwood grove'). A ruined pueblo on the E. side of the Rio Grande, about 10 m. above Albuquerque, Bernalillo co., N. Mex. It was occupied by the Tigua until 1681, and was formerly on the bank of the river, but is now a mile from it, owing to changes in the course of the stream (Bandelier in Arch. Inst. Rep., V, 88, 1884). It was the seat of a Spanish mission, with 300 inhabitants about 1660–68, and a church dedicated to Santa Ana which was doubtless destroyed in the Pueblo revolt of 1680–96 (Vetancurt (1697), Teatro Mex., III, 311, 1871). The settlement was afterward reestablished as a mission visita of Albuquerque. (F. W. H.)
Alamada.—Abert in Emory, Recon., map, 1848. Alameda de Mora.—Villa Señor, Theatro Am., pt. 2, 415, 1748. Alameda.—Abert in Emory Recon., 464, 1848. Alemeda.—Gallegas (1844) misquoted, ibid., 479.

**Alamillo.** (Span.: 'little cottonwood'). A former pueblo of the Piros on the Rio Grande about 12 m. N. of Socorro, N. Mex.,

the seat of a Franciscan mission, established early in the 17th century, which contained a church dedicated to Santa Ana. The inhabitants did not participate in the Pueblo revolt of 1680, and most of them joined the Spaniards in their flight to El Paso, Chihuahua. In the following year, however, on the return of Gov. Otermin, the remaining inhabitants of the pueblo fled, whereupon the village was destroyed by the Spaniards. The population in 1680 was 300. See Vetancurt (1697), Teatro Mex., III, 310, repr. 1871; Bandelier in Arch. Inst. Papers, IV, 239, 1892. (F. W. H.)

**Alamingo.** A village of hostile Delawares(?) in 1754, probably on Susquehanna r., Pa.; possibly the people of Allemoebi, the "king" of the Delawares, who lived at Shamokin about 1750 (Drake Trag. Wild., 153, 1841).

**Alamo.** See *San Antonio de Valero.*

**Alamo Bonito** (Span.: 'beautiful cottonwood'). A small settlement of Mission Indians on Torres res., 75 m. from Mission Tule River agency, s. Cal.
Alimo Bonita.—Ind. Aff. Rep., 170, 1904. Alimo Bonito.—Ibid., 175, 1902.

**Alamos** (Span.: 'cottonwoods'). A pueblo of the Eudeve division of the Opata, the seat of a Spanish mission established in 1629; situated on a small tributary of the Rio Sonora, in Sonora, Mexico. Pop. 165 in 1678, 45 in 1730 (Rivera quoted by Bancroft, Mex. No. States, I, 513, 1884).
Asuncion Álamos.—Zapata (1678) quoted by Bancroft, op. cit., 246. Los Alamos.—Orozco y Berra, Geog., 344, 1864.

**Alamos.** A former rancheria, probably of the Sobaipuri, on Rio Santa Cruz, s. Ariz.; visited and so named by Father Kino about 1697.—Bernal (1697) quoted by Bancroft, Ariz. and N. Mex., 356, 1889.

**Alamucha.** A former Choctaw town in Kemper co., Miss., 10 m. from Succarnooche cr., an affluent of Tombigbee r.
Allamutcha Old Town.—Gatschet, Creek Migr Leg., I, 109, 1884.

**Alapaha.** A former Seminole town in Hamilton co., Fla., on Allapaha r. It was once under Chief Okmulgee, who died before 1820. (H. W. H.)
A-la-pa-ha-tolafa.—Bell in Morse, Rep. to Sec. War, 306, 1822.

**Alaskaite.** A mineral, according to Dana (Text-book Mineral., 420, 1888), so called from having been found in the Alaska mine, Poughkeepsie gulch, Colo.; primarily from *Alaska*, the name of the territory of the United States, and the English suffix *-ite*. Alaska, according to Dall, is derived from *Alákshak*, or *Aláyeksa*, signifying 'mainland,' the term by which the Eskimo of Unalaska id. designated the continental land of N. w. America. (A. F. C.)

**Alawahku.** The Elk clan of the Pecos tribe of New Mexico.—Hewett in Am. Anthrop., VI, 431, 1904.

**Alberdozia.** A province of Florida, probably Timuquanan.—Linschoten, Descr. de l'Am., 6, 1638.

**Albivi.** Given by Vater (Mith., pt. 3, sec. 3, 347, 1816) as a division of the Illinois, but that is doubtful. The name is wrongfully attributed to Hervas.

**Alcalde** (Span.: a mayor of a town who also administers justice). A Papago village, probably in Pima co., s. Ariz.; pop. 250 in 1860.—Poston in Ind. Aff. Rep. 1863, 385, 1864.

**Alcash.** A former Chumashan village at La Goleta, or, as stated by a Santa Barbara Indian, on Moore's ranch, near Santa Barbara, Cal.
Alcax.—Taylor in Cal. Farmer, Apr. 24, 1863. Al-kă-ă'c.—Henshaw, Buenaventura MS. vocab., B. A. E., 1884.

**Alchedoma.** A former Yuman tribe which, according to Father Garcés, spoke the same language as the Yuma proper, and hence belonged to the same closely related Yuman division as the Yuma, Maricopa, and Mohave. As early as 1604–05 Juan de Oñate found them in 8 rancherias (the northernmost with 2,000 people in 160 houses) below the mouth of the Gila on the Rio Colorado, but by 1762 (Rudo Ensayo, 130, 1894) they occupied the left bank of the Colorado between the Gila and Bill Williams fork, and by Garcés' time (1776) their rancherias were scattered along the Colorado in Arizona and California, beginning about 38 m. below Bill Williams fork and extending the same distance downstream (Garcés, Diary, 423–428, 450, 1900). At the latter date they were said to number 2,500, and while well disposed toward other surrounding tribes, regarded the Yuma and Mohave as enemies. Garcés says of them: "These Jalchedun [Alchedoma] Indians are the least dressed, not only in such goods as they themselves possess, but also in such as they trade with the Jamajabs [Mohave], Genigueches [Serranos], Cocomaricopas [Maricopa], Yabipais [Yavapai], and Moquis [Hopi], obtaining from these last mantas, girdles, and a coarse kind of cloth (sayal), in exchange for cotton." This statement is doubtless an error, as the Alchedoma raised no cotton, while the Hopi were the chief cultivators of this plant in the entire S. W. According to Kroeber the Alchedoma were absorbed by the Maricopa, whom they joined before fleeing from the Rio Colorado before the Mohave. Asumpcion, Lagrimas de San Pedro, San Antonio, and Santa Coleta have been mentioned as rancherias. (F. W. H.)
Achedomas.—Venegas, Hist. Cal., II, 185, 1759. Alchedomes.—Taylor in Cal. Farmer, Dec. 6, 1861. Alchedum.—Garcés (1775-6), Diary, 488, 1900. Alchedumas.—Consag (1746) quoted by Bancroft, Nat. Races, I, 588, 1882. Alchidomas.—Alcedo, Dic. Geog., I, 48, 1786. Algodomes.—Heintzelman (1853) in H. R., Ex. Doc. 76, 34th Cong., 42, 1857 (seems to be local name here). Algodones.—Blake in Pac. R. R. Rep., v, 112, 1856. Algodon-

nes.—Derby, Colorado R., map, 1852. Chidumas.—Garcés (after Escalante, 1775), Diary (1775–76), 474, 1900. Halchedoma.—Zarate-Salmeron (ca. 1629), Rel., in Land of Sunshine, 106, Jan., 1900. Halchedumas.—Bancroft, Ariz. and N. Mex., 156, 348, 1889. Halchidhoma.—A. L. Kroeber, inf'n, 1905 (Mohave name). Hudcoadamas.—Rudo Ensayo (1762), 24, 1863 (probably the same). Hudcoadan.—Rudo Ensayo (1762), Guiteras transl., 130, 1894. Hudcoadanes.—Orozco y Berra, Geog., 59, 353, 1864. Jakechedunes.—Hinton, Handbook to Ariz., 28, 1878. Jalchedon.—Arricivita (1792) quoted by Bandelier in Arch. Inst. Papers, v, 100, 1890. Jalchedum.—Orozco y Berra, Geog., 38, 1864, (misquoting Garcés). Jalchedunes.—Garcés (1775–76), Diary, 308, 1900. Talchedon.—Forbes, Hist. Cal., 162, 1839 (misprint). Talchedums.—Domenech, Deserts, I, 444, 1860. Yalchedunes.—Pac. R. R. Rep., III, pt. 3, 124, 1856.

**Alcoz.** A former village of the Kalindaruk division of the Costanoan family in California.—Taylor in Cal. Farmer, Apr. 20, 1860.

**Aleksashkina.** A former Kaniagmiut Eskimo settlement on Wood id. in St. Paul harbor, Kodiak id., Alaska.
Aleksashkina.—Tebenkof quoted by Baker, Geog. Dict. Alaska, 1901 (called a Chiniak settlement). Tanignag-miut.—Russ. Am. Co. map quoted by Baker, ibid. (called an Aleut settlement).

**Aleta.** A former village, presumably Costanoan, connected with Dolores mission, San Francisco, Cal.—Taylor in Cal. Farmer, Oct. 18, 1861.
Aleytac.—Ibid.

**Aleut.** A branch of the Esquimauan family inhabiting the Aleutian ids. and the N. side of Alaska pen., w. of Ugashik r. The origin of the term is obscure. A reasonable supposition is given by Engel (quoted by Dall in Smithson. Contrib., XXII, 1878) that Aliut is identical with the Chukchi word aliat, 'island.' The early Russian explorers of Kamchatka heard from the Chukchi of islanders, aliuit, beyond the main Asian shore, by which the Chukchi meant the Diomede islanders; but when the Russians found people on the Aleutian ids. they supposed them to be those referred to by the Chukchi and called them by the Chukchi name, and the Chukchi often adopt the Russian name, Aleut, for themselves, though asserting that it is not their own. According to Dall, Ūnŭng'ŭn, 'people,' is the generic term which the Aleut apply to themselves, it being probably a form of the Eskimo Innuin, plural of Inung, Inuk.

It is stated by various authorities that the Aleut differ markedly from the Eskimo in character and mental ability as well as in many practices. According to Dall the Aleut possess greater intellectual capacity than the Eskimo, but are far inferior in personal independence, and while the Aleuts' physiognomy differs somewhat from that of the typical Eskimo, individuals are often seen who can not be distinguished from ordinary Innuit. Notwithstanding the differences, there is no doubt that the Aleut are an aberrant offshoot from the great Esquimauan stock, and that however great their distinguishing traits these have resulted in the lapse of time from their insular position and peculiar environment. Dall considers the evidence from the shell heaps conclusive as to the identity with the continental Eskimo of the early inhabitants of the islands as regards implements and weapons. The testimony afforded by language seems to be equally conclusive, though perhaps less evident. The Aleut language, though differing greatly from the dialects of the mainland, possesses many words whose roots are common to the Eskimo tongues. The Aleut are divided, chiefly on dialectal grounds, into Unalaskans, who inhabit the Fox ids., the w. part of Alaska pen., and the Shumagin ids., and Atkans who inhabit the Andreanof, Rat, and Near ids. When first visited by the Russians the Aleutian ids. had a much larger population than at present. As compared with the mainland Eskimo and the Indians the Aleut are now unwarlike and docile, though they fought well when first discovered, but had only darts against the Russian firearms and were consequently soon overpowered, and they speedily came under the absolute power of the Russian traders, who treated them with great cruelty and brutality. This treatment had the effect of reducing them, it is said, to 10 per cent of their original number, and the survivors were held in a condition of slavery. Later, in 1794–1818, the Russian Government interfered to regulate the relations between traders and natives with the result of somewhat ameliorating their condition. In 1824 the missionary Veniaminoff began his labors, and to hm is largely due most of the improvement, moral and mental. Through his exertions and those of his colaborers of the Greek church all the Aleut were Christianized and to some extent educated.

The population of the Aleutian ids., which before the arrival of the Russians was by their own tradition 25,000 (which estimate, judging by the great number of their village sites, Dall does not think excessive), in 1834, according to Veniaminoff, was 2,247, of whom 1,497 belonged to the E. or Unalaskan division and 750 to the w. or Atkan division. According to Father Shaiesnekov there were about 1,400 on the Aleutian ids. in 1848. After the epidemic of smallpox in that year some 900 were left. In 1874 Dall estimated the population at 2,005, including mixed bloods. According to the census of 1890 there were 968 Aleut and 734 mixed-bloods, total 1,702; in 1900 the statistics of the previous decade were repeated.

The following are Aleut villages: Aku-tan, Attu, Avatanak, Belkofski, Biorka, Chernofski, Eider, Iliuliuk, Kashiga, Korovinski, Makushin, Mashik, Morzhovoi, Nateekin, Nazan, Nikolaief, Nikolski, Pavlof, Pogromni, Popof, St George, St Paul, Sannak, Unga, Vossnessenski. The following villages no longer exist: Agulok, Akun, Alitak, Artelnof, Beaver, Chaliuknak, Ikolga, Imagnee, Itchadak, Kalekhta, Kutchlok, Riechesni, Seredka, Sisaguk, Takamitka, Tigalda, Totchikala, Tulik, Ugamitzi, Uknodok, Unalga, Veselofski. The following ruined places have been discovered on a single island, Agattu, now uninhabited: Agonakagna, Atkulik, Atkigyin, Hachimuk, Hamnulik, Hanilik, Hapkug, Higtiguk, Hilksuk, Ibin, Imik, Iptugik, Isituchi, Kakuguk, Kamuksusik, Kaslukug, Kigsitatok, Kikchik, Kikun, Kimituk, Kitak, Kuptagok, Magtok, Mukugnuk, Navisok, Riechesni, Siksatok, Sunik, Ugiatok, Ugtikun, Ugtumuk, Ukashik.

Aléouteans.—Drake, Bk. of Inds., bk. I, 16, 1848. Aleuten.—Holmberg, Ethnol. Skizz., 7, 1855. Aleuts.—Dall in Proc. Cal. Acad. Sci., IV, 35, 1873. Aleyut.—Coxe, Russ. Disc., 219, 1787. Allayume.—Powell in Cont. N. A. Ethnol., III, 553, 1877 (Olamentke name). Cagatsky.—Mahoney (1869) in Senate Ex. Doc. 68, 41st Cong., 2d sess., 19, 1870 ('easterners': Russianized form of Aleut name). Kagataya-Koung'ns.—Humboldt, New Spain, II, 346, 1822 (own name: 'men of the east'; refers only to the Aleut living E. of Umnak str. in contradistinction to the tribes w. of it.—Dall, inf'n, 1905). Kataghayekiki.—Coxe, Russ. Disc., I, 219, 1787. Khāgān'-tāyā-khūn'-khin.—Dall in Cont. N. A. Ethnol., I, 22, 1877 (sig. 'eastern people'). Kχagantaiahounhin.—Pinart in Mém. Soc. Ethnol. Paris, XI, 157, 1872 (name of natives of Shumagin ids. and of Aleut of Alaska pen: 'men of the east'). Oonángan.—Veniaminoff quoted by Petroff, 10th Census, Alaska, 146, 1884. Taiahounhins.—Pinart in Mém. Soc. Ethnol. Paris, XI, 158, 1872 (own name: 'men'). Takhayuna.—Petroff, 10th Census, Alaska, 146, 1884 (Knaiakhotana name). Taxeju-na.—Davidof in Radloff, Wörterb., d. Kinai-Spr., 29, 1874. Täxēmna.—Doroschin in Radloff, Wörterb., d. Kinai-Spr., 29, 1874 (Knaiakhotana name). Tiyakh'unin.—Pinart, op. cit. Unangan.—Applegate in 11th Census, Alaska, 85, 1893. Ū-nŭng'ŭn.—Dall in Cont. N. A. Ethnol., I, 22, 1877 (own national name).

**Alexandrovsk.** A Kaniagmiut village and trading post on Graham harbor, Alaska; pop. 88 in 1880, 107 in 1890. Alexandrousk.—Post route map, 1903. Alexandrovsk.—Petroff, 10th Census, Alaska, 29, 1884. English Bay.—11th Census, Alaska, 163, 1893. Port Graham.—Ibid., 68.

**Alexeief.** A Chnagmiut village in the Yukon delta, Alaska; pop. 16 in 1880. Alexeief's Odinotchka.—Petroff, 10th Census, Alaska, 12, 1884 ('Alexeief's trading post').

**Algic.** A term applied by H. R. Schoolcraft to the Algonquian tribes and languages, and used occasionally by other writers since his time. *Algique* is employed by some Canadian French essayists. Schoolcraft himself (Ind. Tribes, V, 536, 1855) includes the term in his list of words of Indian origin. The word seems to be formed arbitrarily from *Alg*, a part of Algonkin, and the English adjectival termination *ic*.   (A. F. C.)

**Algonkian.** A geological term used to designate an important series of rocks lying between the Archean and the Paleozoic systems. These rocks are most prominent in the region of L. Superior, a characteristic territory of the Indians of the Algonquian family, whence the name. Geologists speak of the "Algonkian period." (A. F. C.)

**Algonkin** (a name hitherto variously and erroneously interpreted, but Hewitt suggests that it is probably from (Micmac) *algoomeaking*, or *algoomaking*, 'at the place of spearing fish and eels [from the bow of a canoe]'). A term applied originally to the Weskarini, a small Algonquian tribe formerly living on the present Gatineau r., a tributary of Ottawa r., E. of the present city of Ottawa, in Quebec. Later the name was used to include also the Amikwa, Kichesipirini, Keinouche, Kishkakon, Maskasinik, Matawachkirini, Missisauga, Michacondibi, Nikikouek, Ononchataronon, Oskemanitigou, Ouasouarini, Outaouakamigouk, Outchougai, Pawating, Sagaiguninini, and Sagnitaouigama. French writers sometimes called the Montagnais encountered along the lower St Lawrence the Lower Algonquins, because they spoke the same language; and the ethnic stock and family of languages has been named from the Algonkin, who formed a close alliance with the French at the first settlement of Canada and received their help against the Iroquois. The latter, however, afterward procured firearms and soon forced the Algonkin to abandon the St Lawrence region. Some of the bands on Ottawa r. fled w. to Mackinaw and into Michigan, where they consolidated and became known under the modern name of Ottawa. The others fled to the N. and E., beyond reach of the Iroquois, but gradually found their way back and reoccupied the country. Their chief gathering place and mission station was at Three Rivers in Quebec. Nothing is known of their social organization. The bands now recognized as Algonkin, with their population in 1900, are as follows. In Ottawa: Golden Lake, 86; North Renfrew, 286; Gibson (Iroquois in part), 123. In Quebec: River Desert, 393; Temiscaming, 203; Lake of Two Mountains (Iroquois in part), 447; total, 1,536. As late as 1894 the Canadian Indian Office included as Algonkin also 1,679 "stragglers" in Pontiac, Ottawa co., Champlain, and St Maurice, in Quebec, but these are omitted from subsequent reports. In 1884 there were 3,874 Algonkin in Quebec province and in E. Ontario, including the Temiscaming. Following are the Algonkin villages, so far as they are known to have been recorded: Cape Magdalen, Egan, Hartwell, Isle aux Tourtes (Kichesipirini

and Nipissing), Rouge River, Tangouaen (Algonkin and Huron). (J. M.   C. T.)

**Abnaki.**—For forms of this word as applied to the Algonkin, see *Abnaki*. **Akwanake.**—Brebœuf quoted by Schoolcraft, Ind. Tribes, IV, 207, 1854. **Alagonkins.**—Croghan (1765) in Monthly Am. Jour. Geol., 272, 1831. **Algokin.**—McKenzie quoted by Tanner, Narr., 332, 1830. **Algomeequin.**—Schoolcraft, Ind. Tribes, I, 306, 1851. **Algomequins.**—Ibid., V, 38, 1855. **Algommequin.**—Champlain (1632), Œuv., pt. 2, 193, 1870. **Algomquins.**—Sagard (1636), Canada, I, 247, 1866. **Algoncains.**—Hennepin, New Disc., 95, 1698. **Algongins.**—Tracy (1667) in N. Y. Doc. Col. Hist., III, 153, 1853. **Algonguin.**—Morse, N. Am., 238, 1776. **Algonic Indians.**—Schoolcraft, Ind. Tribes, I, 38, 1851. **Algonkins.**—Hennepin (1683) in Harris, Voy. and Trav., II, 916, 1705. **Algonméquin.**—Martin in Bressani, Rel. Abrégée, 319, 1653. **Algonovins.**—Alcedo, Dic. Geog., V, 120, 1789. **Algonquains.**—Jes. Rel. 1653, 3, 1858. **Algonquens.**—Schoolcraft, Ind. Tribes, II, 358, 1852. **Algonquin.**—Jes. Rel. 1632, 14, 1858. **Algoomenquini.**—Keane in Stanford, Compend., 500, 1878. **Algoquins.**—Lewis and Clark, Trav., I, map, 1817. **Algoquins.**—Audouard, Far West, 207, 1869. **Algouinquins.**—Gorges (1658) in Me. Hist. Soc. Coll., II, 67, 1847. **Algoumekins.**—Gallatin in Trans. Am. Antiq. Soc., II, 24, 1836. **Algoumequini.**—De Laet (1633) quoted by Vater, Mithridates, pt. 3, sec. 3, 404, 1816. **Algoumequins.**—Champlain (1603), Œuv., II, 8, 1870. **Algumenquini.**—Kingsley, Standard Nat. Hist., pt. 6, 147, 1883. **Alinconguins.**—Nicolls (1666) in N. Y. Doc. Col. Hist., I-I, 147, 1853. **Alkonkins.**—Hutchins (1778) quoted by Jefferson, Notes, 141, 1825. **Alquequin.**—Lloyd in Jour. Anthrop. Inst. G. B., IV, 44, 1875. **Altenkins.**—Clinton (1745) in N. Y. Doc. Col. Hist., VI, 281, 1855 (misprint). **Attenkins.**—Clinton (1745), ibid., 276.

**Algonquian Family** (adapted from the name of the Algonkin tribe). A linguistic stock which formerly occupied a more extended area than any other in North America. Their territory reached from the E. shore of Newfoundland to the Rocky mts. and from Churchill r. to Pamlico sd. The E. parts of this territory were separated by an area occupied by Iroquoian tribes. On the E. Algonquian tribes skirted the Atlantic coast from Newfoundland to Neuse r.; on the s. they touched on the territories of the eastern Siouan, southern Iroquoian, and the Muskhogean families; on the w. they bordered on the Siouan area; on the N. w. on the Kitunahan and Athapascan; in Labrador they came into contact with the Eskimo; in Newfoundland they surrounded on three sides the Beothuk. The Cheyenne and Arapaho moved from the main body and drifted out into the plains. Although there is a general agreement as to the peoples which should be included in this family, information in regard to the numerous dialects is too limited to justify an attempt to give a strict linguistic classification; the data are in fact so meager in many instances as to leave it doubtful whether certain bodies were confederacies, tribes, bands, or clans, especially bodies which have become extinct or can not be identified, since early writers have frequently designated settlements or bands of the same tribe as distinct tribes. As in the case of all Indians, travelers, observing part of a tribe settled at one place and part at another, have frequently taken them for different peoples, and have dignified single villages, settlements, or bands with the title "tribe" or "nation," named from the locality or the chief. It is generally impossible to discriminate between tribes and villages throughout the greater part of New England and along the Atlantic coast, for the Indians there seem to have been grouped into small communities, each taking its name from the principal village of the group or from a neighboring stream or other natural feature. Whether these were subordinate to some real tribal authority or of equal rank and interdependent, although still allied, it is impossible in many instances to determine. Since true tribal organization is found among the better known branches and can be traced in several instances in the eastern division, it is presumed that it was general. A geographic classification of the Algonquian tribes follows:

Western division, comprising three groups dwelling along the E. slope of the Rocky mts: Blackfoot confederacy, composed of the Siksika, Kainah, and Piegan; Arapaho and Cheyenne.

Northern division, the most extensive one, stretching from the extreme N. w. of the Algonquian area to the extreme E., chiefly N. of the St Lawrence and the great lakes, including several groups which, on account of insufficient knowledge of their linguistic relations, can only partially be outlined: Chippewa group, embracing the Cree (?), Ottawa, Chippewa, and Missisauga; Algonkin group, comprising the Nipissing, Temiscaming, Abittibi, and Algonkin.

Northeastern division, embracing the tribes inhabiting E. Quebec, the Maritime Provinces, and E. Maine: the Montagnais group, composed of the Nascapee, Montagnais, Mistassin, Bersiamite, and Papinachois; Abnaki group, comprising the Micmac, Malecite, Passamaquoddy, Arosaguntacook, Sokoki, Penobscot, and Norridgewock.

Central division, including groups that resided in Wisconsin, Illinois, Indiana, Michigan, and Ohio: Menominee; the Sauk group, including the Sauk, Fox, and Kickapoo; Mascouten; Potawatomi; Illinois branch of the Miami group, comprising the Peoria, Kaskaskia, Cahokia, Tamaroa, and Michigamea; Miami branch, composed of the Miami, Piankashaw, and Wea.

Eastern division, embracing all the Algonquian tribes that lived along the Atlantic coast s. of the Abnaki and including several confederacies and groups, as the Pennacook, Massachuset, Wampanoag, Narraganset, Nipmuc, Montauk, Mohegan, Mahican, Wappinger, Delawares, Shawnee, Nanticoke, Conoy, Powhatan, and Pamlico.

As the early settlements of the French, Dutch, and English were all within the territory of the eastern members of the family, they were the first aborigines N. of the Gulf of Mexico to feel the blighting effect of contact with a superior race. As a rule the relations of the French with the Algonquian tribes were friendly, the Foxes being the only tribe against whom they waged war. The English settlements were often engaged in border wars with their Algonquian neighbors, who, continually pressed farther toward the interior by the advancing white immigration, kept up for a time a futile struggle for the possession of their territory. The eastern tribes, from Maine to Carolina, were defeated and their tribal organization was broken up. Some withdrew to Canada, others crossed the mountains into the Ohio valley, while a few bands were located on reservations by the whites only to dwindle and ultimately become extinct. Of many of the smaller tribes of New England, Virginia, and other eastern states there are no living representatives. Even the languages of some are known only by a few words mentioned by early historians, while some tribes are known only by name. The Abnaki and others who fled into Canada settled along the St Lawrence under the protection of the French, whose active allies they became in all the subsequent wars with the English down to the fall of the French power in Canada. Those who crossed the Allegheny mts. into the Ohio valley, together with the Wyandot and the native Algonquian tribes of that region, formed themselves into a loose confederacy, allied first with the French and afterward with the English against the advancing settlements with the declared purpose of preserving the Ohio r. as the Indian boundary. Wayne's victory in 1794 put an end to the struggle, and at the treaty of Greenville in 1795 the Indians acknowledged their defeat and made the first cession of land w. of the Ohio. Tecumseh and his brother, Ellskwatawa, instigated by British intriguers, again aroused the western tribes against the United States a few years later, but the disastrous defeat at Tippecanoe in 1811 and the death of their leader broke the spirit of the Indians. In 1815 those who had taken part against the United States during the War of 1812 made peace with the Government; then began the series of treaties by which, within thirty years, most of the Indians of this region ceded their lands and removed w. of the Mississippi.

A factor which contributed greatly to the decline of the Algonquian ascendency was the power of the Iroquoian confederacy, which by the beginning of the 17th century had developed a power destined to make them the scourge of the other Indian population from the Atlantic to the Mississippi and from Ottawa r. in Canada to the Tennessee. After destroying the Huron and the Erie, they turned their power chiefly against the Algonquian tribes, and ere long Ohio and Indiana were nearly deserted, only a few villages of Miami remaining here and there in the northern portion. The region s. and w. they made a desert, clearing of native inhabitants the whole country within 500 m. of their seats. The Algonquian tribes fled before them to the region of the upper lakes and the banks of the Mississippi, and only when the French had guaranteed them protection against their deadly foes did they venture to turn back toward the E.

The central Algonquians are tall, averaging about 173 cm.; they have the typical Indian nose, heavy and prominent, somewhat hooked in men, flatter in women; their cheek bones are heavy; the head among the tribes of the great lakes is very large and almost brachycephalic, but showing considerable variation; the face is very large. The type of the Atlantic coast Algonquians can hardly be determined from living individuals, as no full-bloods survive, but skulls found in old burial grounds show that they were tall, their faces not quite so broad, the heads much more elongate and remarkably high, resembling in this respect the Eskimo and suggesting the possibility that on the New England coast there may have been some mixture with that type. The Cheyenne and Arapaho are even taller than the central Algonquians; their faces are larger, their heads more elongate. It is worthy of remark that in the region in which the mound builders' remains are found, rounded heads prevailed, and the present population of the region are also more round-headed, perhaps suggesting fusion of blood (Boas, inf'n, 1905). See *Anatomy, Physiology*.

The religious beliefs of the eastern Algonquian tribes were similar in their leading features. Their myths are numerous. Their deities, or *manitus*, including objects animate and inanimate, were many, but the chief culture hero, he to whom the creation and control of the world were ascribed, was substantially the same in character, although known by various names, among different tribes. As Manibozho, or Michabo, among the Chippewa and other lake tribes, he was usually identified as a fabulous great rabbit, bearing some relation to the sun; and this identification with the great rabbit appears to have prevailed among other

tribes, being found as far s. as Maryland. Brinton (Hero Myths, 1882) believes this mythological animal to have been merely a symbol of light, adopted because of the similarity between the Algonquian words for rabbit and light. Among the Siksika this chief beneficent deity was known as Napiw, among the Abnaki as Ketchiniwesk, among the New England tribes as Kiehtan, Woonand, Cautantowit, etc. He it was who created the world by magic power, peopled it with game and the other animals, taught his favorite people the arts of the chase, and gave them corn and beans. But this deity was distinguished more for his magical powers and his ability to overcome opposition by trickery, deception, and falsehood than for benevolent qualities. The objects of nature were deities to them, as the sun, the moon, fire, trees, lakes, and the various animals. Respect was also paid to the four cardinal points. There was a general belief in a soul, shade, or immortal spiritual nature not only in man but in animals and all other things, and in a spiritual abode to which this soul went after the death of the body, and in which the occupations and enjoyments were supposed to be similar to those of this life. Priests, or conjurers, called by the whites medicine-men, played an important part in their social, political, and religious systems. They were supposed to possess influence with spirits or other agencies, which they could bring to their aid in prying into the future, inflicting or curing disease, etc.

Among the tribes from s. New England to Carolina, including especially the Mohegan, Delawares, the people of the Powhatan confederacy, and the Chippewa, descent was reckoned in the female line; among the Potawatomi, Abnaki, Blackfeet, and probably most of the northern tribes, in the male line. Within recent times descent has been paternal also among the Menominee, Sauk and Fox, Illinois, Kickapoo, and Shawnee, and, although it has been stated that it was anciently maternal, there is no satisfactory proof of this. The Cree, Arapaho, and Cheyenne are without clans or gentes. The gens or clan was usually governed by a chief, who in some cases was installed by the heads of other clans or gentes. The tribe also had its chief, usually selected from a particular clan or gens, though the manner of choosing a chief and the authority vested in him varied somewhat in the different tribes. This was the peace chief, whose authority was not absolute, and who had no part in the declaration of war or in carrying it on, the leader in the campaign being one who had acquired a right to the position by noted deeds and skill. In some tribes the title of chief was hereditary, and the distinction between a peace chief and a war chief was not observed. The chief's powers among some tribes, as the Miami, were greater than in others. The government was directed in weighty matters by a council, consisting of the chiefs of the clans or gentes of the tribe. It was by their authority that tribal war was undertaken, peace concluded, territory sold, etc.

The Algonquian tribes were mainly sedentary and agricultural, probably the only exceptions being those of the cold regions of Canada and the Siksika of the plains. The Chippewa did not formerly cultivate the soil. Maize was the staple Indian food product, but the tribes of the region of the great lakes, particularly the Menominee, made extensive use of wild rice. The Powhatan tribes raised enough maize to supply not only their own wants but those of the Virginia colonists for some years after the founding of Jamestown, and the New England colonists were more than once relieved from hunger by corn raised by the natives. In 1792 Wayne's army found a continuous plantation along the entire length of the Maumee from Ft Wayne to L. Erie. Although depending chiefly on hunting and fishing for subsistence, the New England tribes cultivated large quantities of maize, beans, pumpkins, and tobacco. It is said they understood the advantage of fertilizing, using fish, shells, and ashes for this purpose. The tools they used in preparing the ground and in cultivation were usually wooden spades or hoes, the latter being made by fastening to a stick, as a handle, a shell, the shoulder blade of an animal, or a tortoise shell. It was from the Algonquian tribes that the whites first learned to make hominy, succotash, samp, maple sugar, johnnycake, etc. Gookin, in 1674, thus describes the method of preparing food among the Indians of Massachusetts: "Their food is generally boiled maize, or Indian corn, mixed with kidney beans, or sometimes without. Also, they frequently boil in this pottage fish and flesh of all sorts, either new taken or dried, as shad, eels, alewives, or a kind of herring, or any other sort of fish. But they dry mostly those sorts before mentioned. These they cut in pieces, bones and all, and boil them in the aforesaid pottage. I have wondered many times that they were not in danger of being choked with fish bones; but they are so dexterous in separating the bones from the fish in their eating thereof that they are in no hazard. Also, they boil in this frumenty all sorts of flesh they take in hunting, as venison, beaver, bear's flesh, moose, otters, raccoons, etc., cutting this flesh in small pieces and boiling it as aforesaid. Also, they mix with the said pottage several sorts of roots, as Jerusalem artichokes, and groundnuts, and other roots, and pompions, and squashes, and also several sorts of nuts or masts, as oak acorns, chestnuts, and walnuts; these husked and dried and powdered, they thicken their pottage therewith. Also, sometimes, they beat their maize into meal and sift it through a basket made for that purpose. With this meal they make bread, baking it in the ashes, covering the dough with leaves. Sometimes they make of their meal a small sort of cakes and boil them. They make also a certain sort of meal of parched maize. This meal they call 'nokake.'" Their pots were made of clay, somewhat egg-shaped; their dishes, spoons, and ladles of wood; their water pails of birch bark, doubled up so as to make them four-cornered, with a handle. They also had baskets of various sizes in which they placed their provisions; these were made of rushes, stalks, corn husks, grass, and bark, often ornamented with colored figures of animals. Mats woven of bark and rushes, dressed deerskins, feather garments, and utensils of wood, stone, and horn are mentioned by explorers. Fish were taken with hooks, spears, and nets, in canoes and along the shore, on the sea and in the ponds and rivers. They captured without much trouble all the smaller kinds of fish, and, in their canoes, often dragged sturgeon with nets stoutly made of Canada hemp (De Forest, Hist. Inds. Conn., 1853). Canoes used for fishing were of two kinds—one of birch bark, very light, but liable to overset; the other made from the trunk of a large tree. Their clothing was composed chiefly of the skins of animals, tanned until soft and pliable, and was sometimes ornamented with paint and beads made from shells. Occasionally they decked themselves with mantles made of feathers overlapping each other as on the back of the fowl. The dress of the women consisted usually of two articles, a leather shirt, or undergarment, ornamented with fringe, and a skirt of the same material fastened round the waist with a belt and reaching nearly to the feet. The legs were protected, especially in the winter, with leggings, and the feet with moccasins of soft dressed leather, often embroidered with wampum. The men usually covered the lower part of the body with a breech-cloth, and often wore a skin mantle thrown over one shoulder. The women dressed their hair in a thick heavy plait which fell down the neck, and sometimes ornamented their heads with bands decorated with wampum or with a small cap. Higginson (New England's Plantation, 1629) says: "Their hair is usually cut before, leaving one lock longer than the rest." The men went bareheaded, with their hair fantastically trimmed, each according to his own fancy. One would shave it on one side and leave it long on the other; another left an unshaved strip, 2 or 3 in. wide, running from the forehead to the nape of the neck.

The typical Algonquian lodge of the woods and lakes was oval, and the conical lodge, made of sheets of birch-bark, also occurred. The Mohegan, and to some extent the Virginia Indians, constructed long communal houses which accommodated a number of families. The dwellings in the N. were sometimes built of logs, while those in the S. and parts of the W. were constructed of saplings fixed in the ground, bent over at the top, and covered with movable matting, thus forming a long, round-roofed house. The Delawares and some other eastern tribes, preferring to live separately, built smaller dwellings. The manner of construction among the Delawares is thus described by Zeisberger: "They peel trees, abounding with sap, such as lime trees, etc., then cutting the bark into pieces of 2 or 3 yards in length, they lay heavy stones upon them, that they may become flat and even in drying. The frame of the hut is made by driving poles into the ground and strengthening them by cross beams. This framework is covered, both within and without, with the above-mentioned pieces of bark, fastened very tight with bast or twigs of hickory, which are remarkably tough. The roof runs up to a ridge, and is covered in the same manner. These huts have one opening in the roof to let out the smoke and one in the side for an entrance. The door is made of a large piece of bark without either bolt or lock, a stick leaning against the outside being a sign that nobody is at home. The light enters by small openings furnished with sliding shutters." The covering was sometimes rushes or long reed grass. The houses of the Illinois are described by Hennepin as being "made like long arbors" and covered with double mats of flat flags. Those of the Chippewa and the Plains tribes were circular or conical, a framework covered with bark among the former, a frame of movable poles covered with dressed skins among the latter. The villages, especially along the Atlantic coast, were frequently surrounded with stockades of tall, stout stakes firmly set in the ground. A number of the western Algonquian towns are described by early explorers as fortified or as surrounded with palisades.

In no other tribes N. of Mexico was picture writing developed to the advanced stage that it reached among the Delawares and the Chippewa. The figures were scratched or painted on pieces of bark or on slabs of wood. Some of the tribes, especially the Ottawa, were great traders, acting as chief middlemen between the more distant Indians and the early French settlements. Some of the interior tribes of Illinois and Wisconsin made but little use of the canoe, traveling almost always afoot; while others who lived along the upper lakes and the Atlantic coast were expert canoemen. The canoes of the upper lakes were of birch-bark, strengthened on the inside with ribs or knees. The more solid and substantial boat of Virginia and the western rivers was the dugout, made from the trunk of a large tree. The manufacture of pottery, though the product was small, except in one or two tribes, was widespread. Judged by the number of vessels found in the graves of the regions occupied by the Shawnee, this tribe carried on the manufacture to a greater extent than any other. The usual method of burial was in graves, each clan or gens having its own cemetery. The mortuary ceremonies among the eastern and central tribes were substantially as described by Zeisberger. Immediately after death the corpse was arrayed in the deceased's best clothing and decked with the chief ornaments worn in life, sometimes having the face and shirt painted red, then laid on a mat or skin in the middle of the hut, and the arms and personal effects were placed about it. After sunset, and also before daybreak, the female relations and friends assembled around the body to mourn over it. The grave was dug generally by old women; inside it was lined with bark, and when the corpse was placed in it 4 sticks were laid across, and a covering of bark was placed over these; then the grave was filled with earth. An earlier custom was to place in the grave the personal effects or those indicative of the character and occupation of the deceased, as well as food, cooking utensils, etc. Usually the body was placed horizontally, though among some of the western tribes, as the Foxes, it was sometimes buried in a sitting posture. It was the custom of probably most of the tribes to light fires on the grave for four nights after burial. The Illinois, Chippewa, and some of the extreme western tribes frequently practised tree or scaffold burial. The bodies of the chiefs of the Powhatan confederacy were stripped of the flesh and the skeletons were placed on scaffolds in a charnel house. The Ottawa usually placed the body for a short time on a scaffold near the grave previous to burial. The Shawnee, and possibly one or more of the southern Illinois tribes, were accustomed to bury their dead in box-shaped sepulchers made of undressed stone slabs. The Nanticoke, and some of the western tribes, after temporary burial in the ground or exposure on scaffolds, removed the flesh and reinterred the skeletons.

The eastern Algonquian tribes probably equaled the Iroquois in bravery, intelligence, and physical powers, but lacked their constancy, solidity of character, and capability of organization, and do not appear to have appreciated the power and influence they might have wielded by combination. The alliances between tribes were generally temporary and without real cohesion. There seems, indeed, to have been some element in their character which rendered them incapable of combining in large bodies, even against a common enemy. Some of their great chieftains, as Philip, Pontiac, and Tecumseh, attempted at different periods to unite the kindred tribes in an effort to resist the advance of the white race; but each in turn found that a single great defeat disheartened his followers and rendered all his efforts fruitless, and the former two fell by the hands of deserters from their own ranks. The Virginia tribes, under the able guidance of Powhatan and Opechancanough, formed an exception to the general rule. They presented a united front to the whites, and resisted for years every step of their advance until the Indians were practically exterminated. From the close of the Revolution to the treaty of Greenville (1795) the tribes of the Ohio valley also made a desperate stand against the Americans, but in this they had the encouragement, if not the more active support, of the British in Canada as well as of other Indians. In individual character many of the Algonquian chiefs rank high, and Tecumseh stands out prominently as one of the noblest figures in Indian history.

The present number of the Algonquian family is about 90,000, of whom about 40,000 are in the United States and 50,000 in Canada. The largest tribes are the Chippewa and the Cree. (J. M. C. T.)

>**Algonkin-Lenape.**—Gallatin in Trans. Am. Antiq. Soc., II, 23, 305, 1836. Berghaus (1845), Physik. Atlas, map 17, 1848. Ibid., 1852. >**Algonquin.**—Bancroft, Hist. U. S., III, 237, 1840. Prichard, Phys. Hist. Mankind, v, 381, 1847 (follows Gallatin). >**Algonkins.**—Gallatin in Trans. Am. Ethnol. Soc., II, pt. 1, xcix, 77, 1848. Gallatin in Schoolcraft, Ind. Tribes, III, 401, 1853. >**Algonkin.**—Turner in Pac. R. R. Rep., III, pt. 3, 55, 1856. Hayden, Ethnog. and Philol. Mo. Val., 232, 1862 (treats only of Crees, Blackfeet, Shyennes). Hale in Am. Antiq., 112, April, 1883 (treated with reference to migration). <**Algonkin.**—Latham in Trans. Philol. Soc. Lond., 1856 (adds to Gallatin's list of 1836 the Bethuck, Shyenne, Blackfoot, and Arapaho). Latham, Opuscula, 327, 1860 (as in preceding). Latham, Elem. Comp. Philol., 447, 1862. <**Algonquin.**—Keane in Stanford, Compend., Cent. and S. Am., 460, 465, 1878 (list includes the Maquas, an Iroquois tribe). >**Saskatschwainer.**—Berghaus, Physik. Atlas, map 17, 1848 (probably designates the Arapaho). >**Arapahoes.**—Berghaus, Physik. Atlas, map 17, 1852.

×**Algonkin und Beothuk.**—Berghaus, Physik. Atlas, map 72, 1887.

**Algonquins of Portage de Prairie.** A Chippewa band formerly living near L. of the Woods and E. of it in Manitoba. They removed before 1804 to the Red r. country through persuasions of the traders.—Lewis and Clark, Disc., 55, 1806.

**Alibamu** (said to be from the Choctaw *alba ayamule*, 'I open or clear the thicket'). A Muskhogean tribe of the Creek confederacy that formerly dwelt in s. Alabama. It is clear that the Alibamu and Koasati were closely related, the language of the two being practically identical. When first found by the whites the home of the tribe was on Alabama r. a short distance below the junction of the Coosa and Tallapoosa. Their early history, owing to confusion in the use of the name, is uncertain, but according to tradition they had migrated from a westerly locality. In the Creek legend, as given by Gatschet, they are mentioned, under the name Atilamas, as one of 4 tribes contending for the honor of being considered the most ancient and valorous. The chroniclers of De Soto's expedition in 1541 locate the "province" or "town" of Alibamo a short distance N. w. of the Chicasa, in N. w. or central Mississippi. According to the Gentleman of Elvas they found a strongly fortified town, named Ullibahali, on Alabama or lower Coosa r. Coxe (French, Hist. Coll. La., II, 235, 1850) says that below the Coza, or Coussa, on the same river, are the Ullibalies, or Olibahalies, according to the French the Allibamons. The identification with the Ullibahali would be complete if this statement could be accepted, but Gatschet is inclined to doubt its correctness. The history of the tribe recommences with the appearance of the French in Mobile bay in 1701–02. Bienville found "on the banks and many adjacent islands, places abandoned by the savages on account of war with the Conchaques [Conshac] and Alibamons" (Hamilton, Colon. Mobile, 41, 1897). The French soon became involved in war with the tribe, who, joining the Cherokee, Abihka, and Catawba in 1708, descended Alabama r. to attack Ft Louis and the Mobile Indians in that vicinity, but retired after burning some villages. In 1713 the French established Ft Toulouse in their country to hold them in check and to protect French traders. The site of the fort was occupied in 1812 by Ft Jackson. After the cession in 1763 by France to Great Britain the fort was abandoned, and at that time a part of the tribe removed to the banks of the Mississippi and established a village 60 m. above New Orleans. This band numbered about 120, including 30 warriors. Subsequently the tribe removed to w. Louisiana, and in 1890 some were still living in Calcasieu parish, others in the Creek Nation in Indian T., and a party of about 200 in Polk co., Tex.

Little has been recorded in regard to the character and customs of the Alibamu, but that they were warlike in disposition is evident from their early history. One singular custom mentioned by Pénicaut seems to apply to the Alibamu as well as to the Mobile Indians. They caused their children, both boys and girls, to pass in array at a certain festival and receive a flogging of such severity as to draw blood, after which they were lectured by one or more of the elders. Hawkins states: "They did not conform to the customs of the Creeks, and the Creek law for the punishment of adultery was not known among them. They cultivated the soil to some extent and had some hogs, horses, and cattle. Though hospitable, it was their custom when a white person visited them, as soon as he had eaten, what was left was thrown away and everything which had been used [by the white person] was washed." The 4 Alibamu towns situated on Alabama r. are given by Hawkins (Sketch of Creek country, 1799) as Kanchati, Tawosa, Pawokti, and Atagi. Others give Nitahauritz as one of the four. (A. S. G.    C. T.)

Aibamos.—Barcia, Ensayo, 313, 1723. Ala.—H. R. Ex. Doc. 276, 24th Cong., 310, 1836 (probably an abbreviation.) Alabama.—Bartram, Travels, 463, 1791. Ala Bamer.—Weatherford (1793) in Am. State Pap., Ind. Aff., I, 385, 1832. Albamas.—N. C. Col. Records (1721), II, 422, 1886. Alebamah.—Charlevoix, New France, VI, 25, 1872. Alebamons.—Boudinot, Star in West, 125, 1816. Alibam.—McKenney and Hall, Ind. Tribes, III, 80, 1854. Alibamas.—Nuttall, Journal, 287, 1821. Alibamies.—Schermerhorn (1812) in Mass. Hist. Coll., 2d s., 152, 1814. Alibamo.—French, Hist. Coll. La., II, 104, 1850. Alibamons.—Dumont, La., I, 134, 1753. Alibamous.—Smyth, Tour in U. S., I, 348, 1784. Alibamus.—Brackenridge, Views of La., 82, 1814. Alibanio.—Smith, Coll. Docs. Hist. Florida, I, 56, 1857. Alibanons.—N. Y. Doc. Col. Hist., X, 156, 1858. Alimamu.—Gentleman of Elvas (1539) in Hakluyt Soc. Pubs., IX, 87, 1851. Allibama.—Drake, Bk. Inds., VI, 1848. Allibamis.—Sibley, Hist. Sketches, 81, 1806. Allibamons.—Bossu (1758), Travels La., I, 219, 1771. Allibamous.—Coxe, Carolana, 24, 1741. Atilamas.—Gatschet, Creek Migr. Leg., II, 13, 1888 (Creek name). Aybamos.—Barcia, Ensayo, 333, 1723. Ewemalas.—Coxe, Carolana, 25, 1741. Habbamalas.—Spotswood (1720) in N. C. Col. Records, II, 383, 1886. Halbama.—Vaugondy, map of America, Nancy, 1778. Holbamas.—Rivers, Early Hist. So. Car., 97, 1874. Limanu.—Ranjel (1541) in Bourne, Narr. De Soto, II, 136, 1904. Ma'-mo aⁿ-ya-di.—Dorsey, Biloxi MS. Dict., B. A. E., 1892 (Biloxi name). Ma'-mo haⁿ-ya. Ibid. (another Biloxi name). Ma'-mo ha-yaⁿ-di'.—Ibid. (another Biloxi name). Oke-choy-atte.—Schoolcraft, Ind. Tribes, I, 266, 1851. Olibahalies.—Coxe, Carolana, 24, 1741. (See *Ullibahali*.)

**Alibamu.** A town of the Creek Nation, on the N. fork of Canadian r., Ind. T.—Gatschet, Creek Migr. Leg., II, 185, 1888.

**Alican.** A former Chumashan village at Cañada Maria Ignacio, near Santa Barbara, Cal.—Taylor in Cal. Farmer, Apr. 24, 1863.

**Alimacani.** A Timuquanan village on the Florida coast, N. of St Johns r., in 1565.
Alimacani.—Fontaneda in Ternaux-Compans, Voy., XX, 24, 1863. Alimacany.—French, Hist. Coll. La., 2d s., 264, 1875. Allicamany.—Bassanier, Histoire Notable, 57, 1586. Allimacany.—Laudonnière in French, Hist. Coll. La., n. s., 257, 1869. Halianacani.—Gourgues quoted in French, Hist. Coll. La., 2d s., 275, 1875. Halmacanir.—Laudonnière, ibid., n. s., 349, 1869.

**Alimibegouek** (probably cognate with the Chippewa *Ûnimîbigog*, 'they that live by the river'.—Wm. Jones). Mentioned as one of the four divisions of the Cree, living on L. Alimibeg (Nipigon?), which discharges into L. Superior, Ontario. Creuxius places them immediately N. of the lake, near the s. end of Hudson bay. What part of the Cree of modern times these include is not determinable. (J. M.    C. T.)
Alimibegoueci.—Creuxius, map New France, 1664. Kilistinons Alimibegouek.—Jes. Rel. 1658, 21, 1858.

**Alipconk** ('place of elms'). A village of the Wecquaesgeeks on the site of Tarrytown, Westchester co., N. Y. It was burned by the Dutch in 1644.
Alipconck.—Ruttenber, Tribes Hudson R., 78, 1872 ('place of elms'). Alipkonok.—Von der Donck (1656) quoted, ibid., 72.

**Alipoti.** Apparently a pueblo of the Queres in New Mexico in 1598.—Oñate (1598) in Doc. Inéd., XVI, 114, 1871.

**Alizway.** A former Chumashan village near Santa Inés mission, Santa Barbara co., Cal.—Taylor in Cal. Farmer, Oct. 18, 1861.

**Alkali Lake.** A Shuswap village or band near Fraser r. and opposite the mouth of Chilcotin r., Brit. Col.; pop. 158 in 1902.
Alkakalilkes.—Brit. Col. Map, Ind. Aff., Victoria, 1872 (probably identical). Alkali Lake.—Can. Ind. Aff., 269, 1902.

**Alkehatchee.** A former Upper Creek town on Tallapoosa r., Ala.
Alkehatchee.—Brahm (18th cent.) quoted by Gatschet, Creek Migr. Leg., II, 214, 1888. Elkatcha.—Robin, Voy., II, map, 1888.

**Alki.** The motto on the official seal of the State of Washington, taken from *alki* in the Chinook jargon, which signifies 'by-and-by', 'in the future', 'soon'. The word came into the jargon from the Chinook proper, a dialect of the Chinookan stock, in which it has a like meaning. (A. F. C.)

**Alkunwea** (*A'lk'unwēE*, 'lower corner'). A subdivision of the Laalaksentaio, a Kwakiutl gens.—Boas in Rep. Nat. Mus. 1895, 332, 1897.

**Allagasomeda.** A Chimmesyan village on upper Skeena r., British Columbia.—Downie in Jour. Roy. Geog. Soc., XXXI, 253, 1861.

**Allakaweah** (*Al-la-kā'-we-āh*, 'Paunch Indians'). The name applied by a tribe which Lewis and Clark (Trav., 25, Lond., 1807) located on Yellowstone and Bighorn rs., Mont., with 800 warriors and 2,300 souls. This is exactly the country occupied at the same time by the Crows, and although these latter are mentioned as distinct, it is probable that they were meant, or perhaps a Crow band, more particularly as the Crows are known to their cousins, the Hidatsa, q. v., as the "people who refused the paunch." The name seems not to have reference to the Grosventres, q. v.　(J. M.)

**Al-la-kâ-we-âh.**—Lewis (1805) quoted by Coues, Lewis and Clark Exped., I, 199, 1893. **Gens de Panse.**—Ibid. (given as their French name). **Panneh.**—Drake, Bk. Inds., bk. x, 1848 (misprint for Paunch). **Paunch (Indians).**—Lewis quoted by Coues, op. cit., I, 199, 1893. **Ponch Indians.**—Prescott quoted by Schoolcraft, Ind. Tribes, III, 251, 1853.

**Allapata.** An unidentified town formerly on Hillsboro r., E. Fla.—Brion de la Tour, War map, 1782.

**Allaquippa.** A Delaware woman sachem of this name lived in 1755 near the mouth of Youghiogheny r., Allegheny co., Pa., and there may have been there a small Delaware settlement known by her name.　(J. M.)

**Allaquippas.**—La Tour, map, 1779. **Alleguipes.**—Esnauts and Rapilly, map, 1777. **Allequippe.**—Lattré, U. S. map, 1784.

**Alle.** A pueblo of New Mexico in 1598, doubtless situated in the Salinas in the vicinity of Abo, and evidently occupied by the Tigua or the Piros.—Oñate (1598) in Doc. Inéd., XVI, 114, 1871.

**Alleghany Indians.** A geographical group, comprising Delawares and Shawnee, residing on Alleghany r. in the 18th century.—Rupp (1756), Northampton, etc., 106, 1845.

**Allegany Indians.**—Post (1758), Journ., 147, repr. 1867. **Alleghany.**—Lotter, map, about 1770. **Alligany.**—Homann Heirs, map, 1756. **Attegheny.**—Esnauts and Rapilly, map, 1777 (misprint).

**Allh.** A body of Salish E. of Chemanis lake, Vancouver id.—Brit. Col. map, Ind. Aff., Victoria, 1872.

**Alligator.** A former Seminole town in Suwannee co., Fla.

**Alligator Hole.**—Bartram, Voy., I, map, 1799. **Alligator Indians.**—Schoolcraft, Ind. Tribes, VI, 360, 1857.

**Alloc.** A Chumashan village w. of Pueblo de las Canoas (San Buenaventura), Ventura co., Cal., in 1542 (Cabrillo, Narr., 1542, in Smith, Coll. Doc., 181, 1857). Placed by Taylor on the rancho Orteaga, near the beach.

**Alloouloanshaw.** A town on the headwaters of Pearl r., Neosho co., Miss., occupied by the Oklafalaya Choctaw.—West Fla. map, ca. 1772.

**Allu.** The Antelope clan of the Pecos tribe of New Mexico.—Hewett in Am. Anthrop., VI, 431, 1904.

**Almotu.** A Paloos village on the N. bank of Snake r., about 30 m. above the mouth of Palouse r., Wash.—Mooney in 14th Rep. B. A. E., 735, 1896.

**Alouko.** A former Seminole town on the E. side of St Marks r., 20 m. N. of St Marks, Wakulla co., Fla.—H. R. Ex. Doc. 74 (1823), 19th Cong., 27, 1826.

**Alpincha.** A former Chumashan village near the center of the present town of Santa Barbara, Cal.

**Al-pĭn-tcä.**—Henshaw, Santa Barbara MS. vocab., B. A. E, 1884.

**Alpowna.** A former Nez Percé village at the mouth of a creek that flows into Snake r. from the N., below Lewiston, Idaho. At this point the people mixed with the Paloos, hence more than one language was spoken in the village. (A. C. F.)

**Alpawa.**—Gatschet, Nez Percé MS., B. A. E., 1878 (given as the village name, but really the name of the creek). **Elpawawe.**—Ibid.

**Alsea** (corruption of *Alsi'*, the aboriginal name). A Yakonan tribe formerly occupying a small territory at and about the mouth of Alsea r., w. Oreg. Little is known of the early history of the tribe, of which there are now only a dozen survivors on the Siletz res., Oreg. According to Dorsey (Jour. Am. Folk-lore, III, 229, 1890) the following are the former Alsea villages: Kutaŭwa, Kyamaisu, Tachuwit, Kaukhwan, Yukhais, Kakhtshanwaish, Shiuwauk, Khlokhwaiyutslu, Mekumtk, N. of Alsea r.; Yahach, Chiink, Kauhuk, Kwulisit, Kwamk, Skhakhwaiyutslu, Khlimkwaish, Kalbusht, Panit, Thlekushauk, and Thlekuhweyuk, on the s. side of the river. Milhau (in letter to Gibbs) gave Neahumtuk as an Alsea village at the mouth of Alsea r., which has not been identified. See Farrand in Am. Anthrop., III, 240, 1901. (L. F.)

**Alcea.**—Sikes in Ind. Aff. Rep., 215, 1860. **Aleya.**—Gairdner (1835) in Jour. Geog. Soc. Lond., XI, 255, 1841. **Alsea.**—Dorsey in Jour. Am. Folk-lore, III, 229, 1890. **Alseya.**—Duflot de Mofras, Explor., II, 104, 1844. **Äl-si'.**—Dorsey in Jour. Am. Folk-lore, III, 229, 1890 (own name). **Alsiias.**—Duflot de Mofras, Explor., II, 335, 1844. **Älsi'-me ɉûnnĕ.**—Dorsey, MS. Naltûnne tûnnĕ vocab., B. A. E., 1884 (Naltunne name). **Alsiya.**—Ind. Aff. Rep., 253, 1877. **Kû-nis' ɉûnnĕ.**—Dorsey, MS. Chasta Costa vocab., B. A. E., 1884 (Chastacosta name). **Päifan amím.**—Gatschet, Lakmiut MS., B. A. E., 105 (Lakmiut name). **Si ni'-tĕ-lĭ tûnnĕ.**—Dorsey, MS. Naltûnne tûnnĕ vocab., B. A. E., 1884 ('flatheads': Naltunne name). **Tcha yáχo amín.**—Gatschet, op. cit. (Lakmiut name). **Tĕhayesátlu.**—Gatschet, MS. Nestucca vocab., B. A. E. (Nestucca name). **Ulseah.**—Lewis and Clark, Exped., II, 118, 1814.

**Altahmo.** A division of the Costanoan family formerly living on San Francisco bay, Cal., and connected with Dolores mission, San Francisco.

**Al-tah-mos.**—Schoolcraft, Ind. Tribes, II, 506, 1852. **Altajumi.**—Taylor in Cal. Farmer, Oct. 18, 1861. **Altajumo.**—Bancroft, Nat. Races, I, 452, 1874. **Altatmos.**—Latham in Trans. Philol. Soc. Lond., 82, 1856.

**Altamaha.** A "province" in E. Georgia in 1540, mentioned in the narratives of De Soto's expedition. The name is preserved in Altamaha r. The word seems to be of Timucua origin, the last part, -*paha*, signifying 'town,' 'home.' (J. M.)

**Alatamahas.**—Baudry des Lozières, Voy. La., 241, 1802. **Altamaca.**—Gentleman of Elvas in Hakluyt Soc. Pubs., IX, 49, 1851. **Altamaha.**—La Harpe (1707) in French, Hist. Coll. La., III, 36, 1851. **Altapaha,**—

Biedma (1540) in Smith, Coll. Doc. Fla., 50, 1857. **Attapaha.**—Biedma (1544) in French, Hist. Coll. La., II, 100, 1850. **Ilatamaa.**—De l'Isle, map (1707) in Winsor, Hist. America, II, 294, 1886.

**Altar.** Using the term in its broadest sense, an altar, on which sacrifices were made or offerings laid or around which some other act of worship was performed, was a feature of the performance of every ceremony of the American Indians. Some of these altars are so simple that their nature is not easily apprehended: an excavation in the earth, a pile of rocks, a

SIA ALTAR. (M. C. STEVENSON)

fire, a buffalo skull serving the purpose. Others, presenting a complex assemblage of parts, are definitely recognizable as altars and in some cases resemble in form the altars of civilized people, for example, those of the Hopi and the Sia. The altar, on account of its universal distribution, thus renders important aid to the comparative study of religions. The effect of the altar is to localize the worship and to furnish a place where the worshiper can convey to the deity his offering and prayers. Altar-shrines are often placed by springs, rivers, caves, rocks, or trees on mountains and near spots which certain deities are supposed to inhabit, in the belief that the roads of these deities extend from these localities. In pursuance of a like idea the Haida deposit certain offerings in the sea, and many tribes throw offerings into springs, lakes, and rivers. Some of the temporary altars of the eastern and southern Indians, so far as may be learned from the illustrations of early writers, consisted of an oval or circular palisade of carved stakes surrounding an area in the center of which was a fire or a mat on which were laid various symbolic cult apparatus. Lafitau (Mœurs des Sauvages, II, 327, 1724) regards as a fire altar the pipe in the calumet ceremony of the Illinois described by Marquette. Such altars are more primitive than the temporary altars erected for the celebration of a ritual or a portion of a ritual, and the distinction should

be noted. In this connection the cloud-blowing tubes and pipes of the ancient and modern Pueblos may also be mentioned. The widespread connection of fire with the altar is an important fact. The disposition of logs in cruciform pattern for the kindling of new fire by the Creeks suggests an altar. Interesting examples of the use of fire in ceremony are the Iroquois white-dog rite and the night chant of the Navaho. Among the Siksika every tent contains an altar—a small excavation in the earth—where sweet gum is burned daily (Wissler). Prehistoric altars consisting of blocks of fire-hardened clay or, in rare cases, boxes of stone form the essential characteristic of many mounds and belong to the class of fire altars (Thomas, Putnam, Moorehead, Mills, Fowke). Among the altars that survive in the ceremonies of tribes of the United States may be cited the fire altar of the Kwakiutl cannibal ceremony (Boas in Rep. Nat. Mus. for 1895); the holy place of the Pawnee Hako ceremony (Fletcher in 22d Rep. B. A. E., 36, 1904); the altars of the Sioux (Fletcher in 16th Rep. Peabody Mus., 1883); the sun-dance altar of the Arapaho (Dorsey in Field Columb. Mus. Pub., no. 75, pl. lxi, 1903); and altars of various ceremonies of the Navaho (Matthews in 5th Rep. B. A. E., 1887; Stevenson in 8th Rep. B. A. E., 1891), the Zuñi (Stevenson in 23d Rep. B. A. E., 1905), and the Hopi (Fewkes in recent reports B. A. E., and articles in Am. Anthrop. and Jour. Am. Folk-lore; Dorsey and Voth in Field Col. Mus. Pubs.). Temporary altars are characteristic of the Pueblos and consist, as in the flute ceremony, for example, of a reredos formed of one horizontal and two vertical slats painted with symbols of rain and clouds, lightning, corn, cult figures,

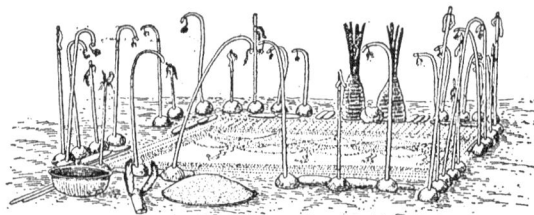

HOPI ALTAR. (FEWKES)

animals, etc. In front of the reredos stand figurines, sticks representing corn, the tiponi, or palladium bundle, flower mounds, netted gourds, ears of corn, figures of birds, and a row of eagle feathers. Connected with the altar are bowls, baskets, rattles, prayer-sticks, pipes, stone implements, and other paraphernalia, and a characteristic feature of some of them is the dry-painting. During the progress of some ceremonies a direction altar, or cloud altar, consisting of a medicine bowl surrounded with ears of corn pointed toward the cardinal points, is temporarily used. The construction of the altar, the rites performed before it, and its destruction form interesting features of Hopi ceremonies and date back to ancient times. Numerous shrine altars are mentioned, some near, others distant from, the present pueblos, and many have been observed which were the worshiping places of inhabitants of the ancient pueblos. (w. h.)

**Altinin** (from *Altau*, the native name of a place in their territory). A Yokuts tribe formerly living near the upper end of the Tulare basin, Cal. They are said to have ranged as far s. as Kern r. A few survivors now reside on Tule River res. They may be the same as the Paleuyami. (A. L. K.)

**Aluenchi.** A former village, presumably Costanoan, connected with Dolores mission, San Francisco, Cal.—Taylor in Cal. Farmer, Oct. 18, 1861.

**Aluik.** A former Eskimo village on the E. coast of Greenland, about lat. 64° 15′; pop. 130 in 1829.—Graah, Exped., map, 1837.

**Aluk.** An Eskimo settlement in s. E. Greenland, lat. 60° 10′.—Meddelelser om Grönland, XXV, map, 1902.

**Alwathalama.** A former Chumashan village at the marsh of Goleta, near Santa Barbara, Cal.—Taylor in Cal. Farmer, Apr. 24, 1863.
Allvatalama.—Bancroft, Nat. Races, I, 459, 1874. Alwaththalam.—Taylor in Cal. Farmer, May 4, 1860. Aswalthatans.—Gatschet in Chief Eng. Rep., pt. 3, 553, 1876.

**Alyeupkigna.** A former Gabrieleño rancheria in Los Angeles co., Cal., at a place later called Santa Anita.
Aleupkigna.—Ried (1852) quoted by Taylor in Cal. Farmer, Jan. 11, 1861. Almpquig-na.—Ried misquoted by Hoffman in Bull. Essex Inst., XVII, 2, 1885.

**Amacahuri.** Mentioned as a clan of the Apohola phratry of the Timucua.—Pareja (ca. 1612) quoted by Gatschet in Am. Philos. Soc. Proc., XVII, 492, 1878.

**Amahami** (*ama* 'land,' *khami* 'broken': 'mountainous country'). A former distinct Siouan tribe, long since incorporated with the Hidatsa; also the name of their village. Along with the Hidasta they claimed to have formerly constituted one tribe with the Crows. Their language, however, indicated closest affinity with the Hidatsa, differing but slightly from it, although they occupied a separate village and long maintained separate tribal organization. They were recognized as a distinct tribe by Lewis and Clark in 1804, but had practically lost their identity 30 years later. In Lewis and Clark's time their village was at the mouth of Knife r., N. Dak., and was one of three, the other two being Hidatsa, which for many years stood on the banks of that stream. Their

strength was estimated at 50 warriors. After the epidemic of 1837 all or the greater part of the survivors joined the Hidatsa and were merged with that tribe. Lewis and Clark state that they had been a numerous and prosperous agricultural tribe which once divided the upper Missouri valley, w. of the Dakota group, with the Arikara, Mandan, and Hidatsa, the remains of the old towns of these four tribes being visible on every prairie terrace along the river for 600 miles. The remnants of all four were found by Matthews (Ethnog. Hidatsa, 13, 1877) at Fort Berthold, numbering fewer than 2,500.
Ahahawa.—Schoolcraft, Ind. Tribes, III, 522, 1853. Ahahaway.—Ibid., 250. Ahnahaways.—Lewis and Clark, Exped., I, 115, 1814. Ahwahawas.—Brown, West. Gaz., 212, 1817. Ahwahaways.—Lewis and Clark, Exped., II, 452, 1814. Ah-wâh-hâway.—Lewis and Clark, Disc., 25, 1806. Amahami.—Matthews, Ethnog. Hidatsa, 15, 1877. Amasi.—Ibid., 36 ('earthen lodges': Crow name). A-ma'-te-wat-se'.—Hayden, Ethnog. and Philol. Mo. Val., 402, 1862. Ä ma tîhä mi.—Matthews, Ethnog. Hidatsa, 133, 1877. Anhawas.—McKenney and Hall, Ind. Tribes, III, 80, 1854. Annahawas.—Gallatin in Trans. Am. Antiq. Soc., II, 125, 1836. Arwacahwas.—Lewis and Clark, Exped., I, 120, 1814. Arwâchaon.—Ibid., map. Awachâwi.—Maximilian, Travels, 178, 1843. A-wa-ha-was.—Schermerhorn in Mass. Hist. Coll., 2d s., II, 35, 1814. A-waha-ways.—Brackenridge, Views of La., 85, 1815. Corneille.—Balbi, Atlas Ethnog., 56, 1826. Gens des Soulier.—Lewis and Clark, Disc., 25, 1806. Les Souliers.—Maximilian, Travels, 323, 1843. Mahaha.—Lewis and Clark, Exped., I, 130, 1814. Maharhar.—Lewis and Clark, Coues ed., I, 183, 1893. Mahawha.—Maximilian, Travels, 335, 1843. Mattasoons.—Keane in Stanford, Compend., 521, 1878. Sauliers.—Schermerhorn (1812) in Mass. Hist. Coll., 2d s., II, 35, 1814 (misprint). Shoe Indians.—Lewis and Clark, Exped., I, 130, 1814. Soulier Noir.—Ibid. (French: 'black shoe'). Watasoons.—Gass, Journal, 59, 1807. Watersoons.—Orig. Jour. Lewis and Clark, I, 220, 1904. Wattasoons.—Lewis and Clark, Exped., I, 130, 1814 (so called by the Mandan). Weetersoon.—Lewis and Clark, Exped., Coues ed., I, 204, note, 1893.

**Amaikiara.** A former Karok village on the w. bank of Klamath r., at the rapids a mile or two below the mouth of Salmon r., N. w. Cal. Though not a large village, it was of importance because an annual salmon ceremony and the jumping dance were held here. Together with most of the villages near the mouth of the Salmon it was burned by the whites in the summer of 1852. (A. L. K.)
A-mi-ke-ar-rum.—Taylor in Cal. Farmer, Mar. 23, 1860. Eh-nek.—Gibbs (1851) in Schoolcraft, Ind. Tribes, III, 151, 1853. Enek.—Kroeber, inf'n, 1903 (Yurok name of the lower part of the village). Ihnek.—Meyer, Nach dem Sacramento, 236, 1855. In-neck.—McKee (1851) in Sen. Ex. Doc. 4, 32d Cong., spec. sess., 164, 1853. Mik-iára.—Gibbs, MS. Misc., B. A. E., 1852. Tumitl.—Kroeber, inf'n, 1903 (Yurok name for the upper part of the village).

**Amakalli.** A former Lower Creek town established by Indians from Chiaha town on Amakalli cr., the main branch of Kitchofuni cr., an affluent of Flint r., Ga. It had 60 warriors in 1799. (A. S. G.)
Au-muc-cul-le.—Hawkins (1799), Sketch, 64, 1848.

**Amalahta.** A Chickasaw town in N. Mississippi, which, according to Adair

(Hist. Inds., 354, 1775), stood at some distance from the other Chickasaw towns. They met the French there in a sanguinary battle during the first Chickasaw war of 1736. (A. S. G.)

Melattaw.—Romans, East and West Fla., 63, 1775.

**Amalgua** ('island of the mists'). An island off the w. coast of Lower California, about lat. 30°, on which was a Cochimí rancheria.—Venegas, Hist. Cal., II, 437, 1757.

Huamalgua.—Clavigero quoted by Taylor in Cal. Farmer, Jan. 17, 1862.

**Amani-ini** ('mescal corner'). A rancheria, probably Cochimí, connected with Purísima mission, Lower California, in the 18th century.

Amani iní.—Doc. Hist. Mex., 4th s., V, 189, 1857.

**Amaseconti** ('abundance of small fish' [herring]). A small division of the Abnaki formerly residing in part at Farmington falls, on Sandy r., Franklin co., Me., and partly near the present New Sharon, a few miles distant. They took part with the other Abnaki in the early Indian wars against the English and joined in the treaty made at Portsmouth, N. H., in 1713. Some of them lingered in their old homes until about 1797, when the last family removed to St Francis, lower Canada, where they retained their distinctive name until 1809. (J. M.)

Amasaconticook.—Ballard in U. S. Coast Surv. Rep., 251, 1871 (given as the correct name of Sandy r.). Amasacontoog.—Portsmouth treaty (1713) in Me. Hist. Soc. Coll., VI, 250, 1859. Amasaguanteg.—Gyles (1726), ibid., III, 357, 1853. Amasconly.—Niles (1761?) in Mass. Hist. Soc. Coll., 3d s., VI, 247, 1837. Amascontie.—Niles (1761?), ibid., 4th s., V, 335, 1861. Amasconty.—Penhallow (1726) in N. H. Hist. Soc. Coll., I, 21, 1824. Amasecontee.—Ibid., 82. Amassacanty.—Niles (1761?) in Mass. Hist. Soc. Coll., 3d s., VI, 246, 1837. Amassaconty.—Penhallow, op. cit. Amosequonty.—Map of 1719 cited by Ballard in U. S. Coast Survey Rep., 251, 1871. Añmesoukkanti.—Rasles quoted by Ballard, ibid. Anmessukkantti.—Rasles (1722) quoted by Vetromile, Abnakis, 23–27, 1866. Anmiss8kanti.—Abnaki letter (1721) in Mass. Hist. Soc. Coll., 2d s., VIII, 262–3, 1819. Aumesoukkantti.—Rasles in Me. Hist. Soc. Coll., IV, 102, 1856. Meesee Contee.—Allen, ibid., 31 (trans. 'herring place'). Meesucontu.—Willis, ibid., 105.

**Amatidatahi.** A former Hidatsa village on or near Knife r., N. Dak.

Ă má ti dá ta hi.—Matthews, Ethnog. Hidatsa, 133, 1877. Ă ma ti natahi.—Ibid.

**Amatiha.** A former Hidatsa village on the s. bank of Knife r., half a mile above its mouth, in N. Dak.

Amatiha.—Matthews, Ethnog. and Philol., 35, 38, 1877. Awatichaï-Echpou.—Maximilian, Voy. dans l'Int. de l'Am., III, 2, 1843. Awatichay.—Maximilian, Trav., 178, 1843.

**Amatpan.** A former Chitimacha village on Bayou Gris, in St Marys parish, La., 3 m. E. of Charenton, on the shore of Grand lake.

Amátpan námu.—Gatschet in Trans. Anthrop. Soc. Wash., II, 151, 1883 (námu='village').

**Amaxa.** A pueblo of New Mexico in 1598, doubtless situated in the Salinas in the vicinity of Abo, and evidently occupied by Tigua or Piros.—Oñate (1598) in Doc. Inéd., XVI, 114, 1871.

**Amaye.** A town and province visited by the De Soto expedition in 1542; situated probably in extreme s. w. Arkansas.—Gentl. of Elvas (1557) in French, Hist. Coll. La., II, 195, 1850.

Amay.—Harris, Voy. and Trav., I, 810, 1705.

**Amber.** A fossilized vegetable resin occurring in small quantities in the more recent geological formations in many parts of the continent. So far as known it was little used by the aborigines, excepting the Eskimo of Alaska, who valued it for beads and other small ornaments. These people obtained it from the alluvium of the Yukon delta and from the Tertiary formations of the Fox ids. Murdoch (9th Rep. B. A. E., 1892) illustrates a string of four small amber beads obtained from the Pt Barrow Eskimo. See also Kunz, Gems and Precious Stones, 1890. (W. H. H.)

AMBER BEADS, ALASKA (1-2)

**Amdowapuskiyapi** ('those who lay meat on their shoulders to dry it during the hunt'). A Sisseton band or subtribe.—Dorsey in 15th Rep. B. A. E., 217, 1897.

**Amediche.** A tribe, probably Caddoan, that lived about 68 leagues w. of Natchitoches, in E. Texas. La Harpe stated that in 1714–16 they were at war with the Natchitoches, and that the Spaniards had established a settlement among them a few years previously, but soon abandoned it. (A. C. F.)

Amedichez.—La Harpe (1719) in Margry, Déc., VI, 266, 1886.

**Amen** (A'men). A village or a group of 3 adjacent villages of the Yurok on the coast 6 m. N. of the mouth of Klamath r., Cal., their northernmost habitation. (A. L. K.)

**Amerdlok** ('the smaller one,' referring generally to a bay near a larger one). An Eskimo village in w. Greenland, lat. 67°.—Nansen, First Crossing, map, 1890.

**American Horse.** An Oglala Sioux chief, known in his tribe as Wasechun-tashunka. He was probably the son or nephew of the American Horse who went out with Sitting Bull in the Sioux war and was killed at Slim buttes, S. Dak., Sept. 29, 1875. As speaker for the tribe he signed the treaty secured by the Crook commission in 1887, by which the Sioux reservation in Dakota was reduced by one-half. Nearly half the tribe objected to the cession, alleging that the promises of the commissioners could not be depended on, and the malcontents, excited by the messianic craze that had recently reached the Sioux and by the killing of Sitting Bull, its chief exponent among them, in 1890, withdrew from the council and prepared to fight the Government. The expected benefits of the treaty proved illusory.

While the tribe were gathered at the agency to treat with the commissioners, their great herds of cattle destroyed their growing crops and were subsequently stolen. The signers expected that the rations of beef that had been cut off by the Government would be restored, and the agent began to issue the extra rations. In the following year, when drought had ruined the new crop, authority to increase the rations having been withheld, they were reduced at the most unseasonable time. The Sioux were actually starving when the malcontents took their arms and went out to the bad-lands to dance themselves into the exalted state necessary for the final struggle with the whites. American Horse and other friendlies induced them to submit, and the episode would have been concluded without further bloodshed had not a collision occurred between some raw troops and Big Foot's band after its surrender. In 1891 American Horse headed the delegation from Pine Ridge to Washington, composed of leaders of both the friendly and the lately hostile party, and the conferences resulted in the issue of living rations and in fairer treatment of the Sioux. (F. H.)

**Amerind.** A word composed of the first syllables of "American Indian," suggested in 1899 by an American lexicographer as a substitute for the inappropriate terms used to designate the race of man inhabiting the New World before its occupancy by Europeans. The convenience of such derivatives as Amerindic, Amerindize, Amerindian, proto-Amerind, pre-Amerindic, pseudo-Amerind, etc., argues in favor of the new word. The introduction of "Amerind" was urged by the late Maj. J. W. Powell, and it has the support of several anthropologists. A plea by Dr W J McGee for its general adoption appeared in 1900 in the Journal of the Anthropological Institute of Great Britain. The use of "Amerind" at the International Congress of Americanists in New York, Oct., 1902, occasioned a discussion (Science, n. s., XVI, 892, 1902) in which it was supported by some and attacked by others. The name, nevertheless, has found its way into both scientific and popular literature. (A. F. C.)

**Ametzilhacaamanc** ('mouth of the sandy arroyo'). A rancheria, probably Cochimi, connected with Purísima mission, Lower California, in the 18th century.—Doc. Hist. Mex., 4th s., v, 190, 1857.

**Amicoa.** Mentioned by Coxe (Carolana, 14, 1741) as a tribe on the Honabanou, an imaginary river entering the Mississippi from the w., 15 leagues above the mouth of the Ohio. It is probably an imaginary tribe.

**Amikwa** (from *amik*, 'beaver'). An Algonquian tribe found by the French on the N. shore of L. Huron, opposite Manitoulin id., where they were located in the Jesuit Relations at various dates up to 1672. Bacqueville de la Potherie (Hist. Am. Sept., 1753) says that they and the Nipissing once inhabited the shores of L. Nipissing, and that they rendered themselves masters of all the other nations in those quarters until disease made great havoc among them and the Iroquois compelled the remainder of the tribe to betake themselves, some to the French settlements, others to L. Superior and to Green bay of L. Michigan. In 1740 a remnant had retired to Manitoulin id. Chauvignerie, writing in 1736, says of the Nipissing: "The armorial bearings of this nation are, the heron for the Achagué or Heron tribe, the beaver for the Ameko8es [Amikwa], the birch for the Bark tribe." The reference may possibly be to a gens only of the Nipissing and not to the Amikwa tribe, yet the evidently close relation between the latter and the Nipissing justifies the belief that the writer alluded to the Amikwa as known to history. They claimed in 1673 to be allies of the Nipissing. (J. M. C. T.)

Amehouest.—Heriot, Travels, 197, 1807. **Ameko8es.**—Chauvignerie (1736) in N. Y. Doc. Col. Hist., IX, 1053, 1855. **Amicawaes.**—Boyd, Ind. Local Names, 3, 1885. **Amicois.**—Doc. of 1693 in N.Y. Doc. Col. Hist., IX, 566, 1855. **Amicouës.**—Jes. Rel. 1671, 25, 1858. **Amicoures.**—Jes. Rel. 1670, 79, 1858. **Amicours.**—Heriot, Trav., 194, 1807. **Amic-ways.**—Boyd, Ind. Local Names, 3, 1885. **Amihouis.**—Colden (1727), Five Nations, 86, 1747. **Amikois.**—N.Y. Doc. Col. Hist., IX, 722, 1855. **Amikones.**—McKenney and Hall, Ind. Tribes, III, 81, 1854. **Amiköüai.**—Jes. Rel. 1640, 34, 1858. **Amiköüas.**—Perrot (*ca.* 1700), Mém., 20, 1864. **Amikouek.**—Jes. Rel. 1648, 62, 1858. **Amiköües.**—Gallinee (1669-70) in Margry, Déc., I, 162, 1875. **à Mikouest.**—La Potherie, Hist. l'Amér., II, 48, 1753 (misprint). **Amikouest.**—Ibid., 58. **Amiköüets.**—Neill in Minn. Hist. Soc. Coll., v, 403, 1885. **Amikouis.**—Jefferys, Fr. Doms., pt. 1, 47, 1761. **Amikouys.**—Charlevoix (1743), Voy., II, 47, 1761. **Beaver (Indians).**—Shea, Catholic Missions, 366, 1855. **Castor.**—McKenney and Hall, Ind. Tribes, III, 81, 1854. **Naiz Percez.**—Jes. Rel. 1636, 92, 1858. **Nation du Castor.**—Ibid. **Nation of the Beaver.**—Jefferys, French Doms. Am., pt, 1, 47, 1761. **Nedspercez.**—Jes. Rel. 1657, 11, 1858. **Nez-Percés.**—Charlevoix, Hist. New France, Shea ed., III, 130, 1872. **Nez Percez.**—Ibid., 119. **Omikoues.**—Rasles (*ca.* 1723) in Mass. Hist. Soc. Coll., 2d s., VIII, 251, 1819. **Ounikanes.**—Chauvignerie (1736) quoted by Schoolcraft, Ind. Tribes, III, 554, 1853 (misprint.)

**Amilcou.** Mentioned by Iberville in connection with the Biloxi, Moctobi, Huma, Paskagula, etc., as a small tribe E. of the lower Mississippi in 1699 (Margry, Déc., IV, 155, 1880); not identified.

**Aminoya.** A province or village, possibly Siouan, situated in 1542 on the w. bank of the Mississippi, probably a short distance below the mouth of Arkansas r. It was here the remnant of De Soto's followers, under the leadership of Moscoso, embarked for Mexico (Garcilasso de la Vega, Florida, 222, 1723). The people were probably related to the Natchez or the Tunica.

**Aminoia.**—La Salle (1679) in Margry, Déc., II, 41, 1877. **Daminoia.**—Hennepin (1683), Shea trans., 163, 1880. **Minoia.**—Coxe, Carolana, 22, 1741. **Minoya.**—Gentleman of Elvas (1557) in French, Hist. Coll. La., II, 206, 1850.

**Amitok** ('narrow'). A winter settlement of the Amitormiut on the E. coast of Melville peninsula.

**Amitigoke.**—Gilder, Schwatka's Search, 181, 1881. **Amitioke.**—Parry, Second Voy., 206, 1824. **Amittioke.**—Ibid., map, 197. **Amitoq.**—Boas in 6th Rep. B. A. E., map, 1888. **Amityook.**—Lyon, Private Jour., 406, 1825.

**Amitormiut** ('inhabitants of the narrow place.'—Boas). An Eskimo tribe on the E. coast of Melville penin. Their principal village is Amitok, from which they take their name.—Gilder, Schwatka's Search, 181, 1881.

**Amivik.** An Angmagsalingmiut settlement on Angmagsalik fiord, E. Greenland.—Holm, Ethnol. Skizze af Angmagsalikerne, 14, 1887.

**Ammoncongan.** A village, probably belonging to the Abnaki, on the N. E. side of Presumpscot r., at Saccarappa falls, Cumberland co., Me.—Deed of 1657 in Me. Hist. Soc. Coll., I, 118, 1865.

**Aumoughcawgen.**—Smith (1616) in Mass. Hist. Soc. Coll., 3d s., VI, 97, 1837. **Aumuckcawgen.**—Ibid., 117. **Aumughcawgen.**—Smith (1631), ibid., III, 22, 1833.

**Amo.** A pueblo of the province of Atripuy in the region of the lower part of the Rio Grande, N. Mex., in 1598.—Oñate (1598) in Doc. Inéd., XVI, 115, 1871.

**Amolomol** (*Amŏ′lomŏl*). A former Chumashan village at the old wharf at Santa Barbara, Cal.—Henshaw, Buenaventura MS. vocab., B. A. E., 1884.

**Amonces.** A tribe or division, presumably of the Yokuts, said to have lived on San Joaquin r., Cal., in 1854.—Henley in Ind. Aff. Rep., 512, 1854.

**Amonokoa.** A band of the Illinois about 1680.—Hennepin, New Disc., 310, 1698.

**Amanakoa.**—La Salle (1680) quoted in Hist. Mag., 1st s., V, 197, 1861.

**Amoque.** A former Maricopa rancheria on Gila r., s. Ariz.—Sedelmair (1744) quoted by Bancroft, Ariz. and N. Mex., 366, 1889.

**Amoskeag** (*namos* 'small fish,' *kkig* 'to take': 'one takes small fish'). A small tribe or band of the Pennacook confederacy, living about 1675 in a village of the same name at Amoskeag falls, on Merrimac r., in Hillsboro co., N. H. This village was the residence of Wannalanset, head chief of the Pennacook confederacy, son of Passaconnaway.

**Amoskeag.**—Hubbard (1680) in Mass. Hist. Soc. Coll., 2d s., V, 32, 1815. **Naamhok.**—Gookin (1677) in Trans. Am. Antiq. Soc., II, 462, 1836. **Naamkeeks.**—Gookin (1674) in Mass. Hist. Soc. Coll., 1st s., I, 149, 1806. **Namaoskeags.**—Schoolcraft, Ind. Tribes, V, 221, 1855. **Namaschaug.**—Owaneco (1700) in N. Y. Doc. Col. Hist., IV, 614, 1854. **Namaske.**—Eliot (*ca.* 1650) in Mass. Hist. Soc. Coll., 3d s., IV, 123, 1834. **Namekeake.**—Gookin (1677) quoted by Drake, Bk. Inds., bk. 2, 115, 1848 (near Chelmsford, Mass.; same?). **Namkeake**—Gookin (1677) in Trans. Am. Antiq. Soc., II, 518, 1836 (same?).

**Ampalamuyu.** A Lakmiut band near Luckiamute r., Oreg.—Gatschet, Lakmiut MS. vocab., B. A. E., 1877.

**Ampishtna.** The Lakmiut name of a band of the Calapooya proper, residing E. of upper Willamette r., Oreg.—Gatschet, Lakmiut MS., B. A. E., 1877.

**Amu** (*Amü′*). The Ant clan of the Pecos tribe of New Mexico.—Hodge, field notes, B. A. E., 1895.

**Amulet.** See *Fetish*.

**Amusaya.** Mentioned as a Timucua clan of the Apohola phratry.—Pareja (*ca.* 1612) quoted by Gatschet in Am. Philos. Soc. Proc., XVII, 492, 1878.

**Amusements.** When not bound down by stern necessity, the Indian at home was occupied much of the time with dancing, feasting, gaming, and story-telling. Though most of the dances were religious or otherwise ceremonial in character, there were some which had no other purpose than that of social pleasure. They might take place in the day or the night, be general or confined to particular societies, and usually were accompanied with the drum or other musical instrument to accentuate the song. The rattle was perhaps invariably used only in ceremonial dances. Many dances were of pantomimic or dramatic character, and the Eskimo had regular pantomime plays, though evidently due to Indian influence. The giving of presents was often a feature of the dance, as was betting of all athletic contests and ordinary games. The amusements of the Eskimo and extreme northern tribes were chiefly athletic, such as racing, wrestling, throwing of heavy stones, and tossing in a blanket. From Hudson bay to the Gulf of Mexico, and from the Atlantic to the border of the plains, the great athletic game was the ball play, now adopted among civilized games under the name of *lacrosse*. In the N. it was played with one racket, and in the S. with two. Athletes were regularly trained for this game, and competitions were frequently intertribal. The wheel-and-stick game in one form or another was well-nigh universal. As played in the E. one gamester rolled forward a stone disk, or wheel, while his opponent slid after it a stick curved at one end in such a way that the wheel, when it fell to the ground, rested within the crook of the stick. On the plains and in the S. W. a wooden wheel, frequently netted, took the place of the stone disk. Like most Indian institutions, the game often had a symbolic significance in connection with a sun myth. A sacred variant of the game was played by the priests for divinatory purposes, or even as a sort of votive ceremony to procure the recovery of a patient. Target practice with arrows, knives, or hatchets, thrown from the hand, as well as with the bow or rifle, was also universal among the warriors and boys of the various tribes. The gaming arrows were of special design and ornamentation, and the game itself had often a symbolic purpose. Horse races, frequently intertribal, were prominent amusements, especially on the plains, during the warm season, and foot races, often elaborately ceremonial in character, were common among the sedentary agricultural tribes, particularly the Pueblos and the Wichita.

Games resembling dice and hunt-the-button were found everywhere and were played by both sexes alike, particularly in the tipi or the wigwam during the long winter nights. The dice, or their equivalents, were of stone, bone, fruit seeds, shell, wood, or reed, variously shaped and marked. They were thrown from the hand or from a small basket or wooden bowl. One form, the awl game, confined to the women, was played around a blanket, which had various tally marks along the border for marking the progress of the game. The hunt-the-button games were usually accompanied with songs and rhythmic movements of the hands and body, intended to confuse the parties whose task was to guess the location of the button. Investigations by Culin show a close correspondence between these Indian games and those of China, Japan, Korea, and northern Asia.

Special women's games were shinny, football, and the deer-foot game, besides the awl game already noted. In football the main object was to keep the ball in the air as long as possible by kicking it upward. The deer-foot game was played, sometimes also by men, with a number of perforated bones from a deer's foot, strung upon a beaded cord, having a needle at one end. The purpose was to toss the bones in such a way as to catch a particular one upon the end of the needle.

Among the children there were target shooting, stilts, slings, and tops for the boys, and buckskin dolls and playing-house for the girls, with "wolf" or "catcher," and various forfeit plays, including a breath-holding test. Cats'-cradles, or string figures, as well as shuttle-cocks and buzzes, were common. As among civilized nations, the children found the greatest delight in imitating the occupations of the elders. Numerous references to amusements among the various tribes may be found throughout the annual reports of the Bureau of American Ethnology. Consult especially Games of the American Indians, by Stewart Culin, 24th Rep. B. A. E., 1905. See *Ball play*, *Dance*, *Games*. (J. M.)

**Amushungkwa.** A former pueblo of the Jemez on a mesa w. of the Hot Springs, about 12 m. N. of Jemez pueblo, N. Mex. It was abandoned prior to the revolt of 1680. See *Patoqua*.
Amo-shium-qua.—Bandelier in Arch. Inst. Papers, III, pt. 1, 127, 1890. Amo-xium-qua.—Bandelier (1888) in Proc. Internat. Cong. Am., VII, 452, 1890. Amoxunqua.—Zárate-Salmeron (ca. 1629) in Land of Sunshine, 183, Feb., 1900. Amoxunque.—Bandelier in Arch. Inst. Papers, III, pt. 1, 127, 1890. Amúshungkwa.—Hodge, field-notes, B. A. E., 1895.

**Amutaja.** A former village, presumably Costanoan, connected with Dolores mission, San Francisco, Cal.—Taylor in Cal. Farmer, Oct. 18, 1861.

**Ana.** The Tobacco clan of the Zuñi.
Ána-kwe.—Cushing in 13th Rep. B. A. E., 368, 1896 (*kwe*='people').

**Ana.** A village of 70 Papago in 1865, probably in Pima co., s. Ariz.—Ind. Aff. Rep., 135, 1865.

**Anacbuc.** A Chumashan village w. of Pueblo de las Canoas (San Buenaventura), Ventura co., Cal., in 1542.—Cabrillo (1542) in Smith, Coll. Doc. Fla., 181, 1857.
Anacarck.—Cabrillo quoted by Taylor in Cal. Farmer, Apr. 17, 1863. Anacbue.—Ibid.

**Anacharaqua.** A village in Florida, subject to Utina, chief of the Timucua, in 1564. The De Bry map places it E. of lower St Johns r.
Anacharaqua.—Laudonnière (1564) in French, Hist. Coll. La., n. s., 243, 1869. Anachatagua.—Barcia, Ensayo, 48, 1723. Onachaquara.—De Bry, map (1591) in Le Moyne, Narr., Appleton trans., 1875 (transposed?).

**Anachorema.** A village visited by La Salle in 1687. According to Douay (Shea, Discov. Miss., 210, 1852) it was on the "first Cane r." N. E. of La Salle's Ft St Louis on St Bernard (Matagorda) bay, Texas. Thwaites (Hennepin, New Discov., II, 420, 1903) regards the stream as probably the Rio Colorado of Texas.

**Anacoac.** A Chumashan village between Goleta and Pt Conception, Cal., in 1542.—Cabrillo (1542) in Smith, Coll. Doc. Fla., 189, 1857.
Almacoac.—Taylor in Cal. Farmer, Apr. 17, 1863.—Anacoat.—Cabrillo, op. cit., 183.

**Anacot.** A Chumashan village between Goleta and Pt Conception, Cal., in 1542 (Cabrillo (1542) in Smith, Coll. Doc., 183, 1857); evidently distinct from Anacoat.

**Anadarko** (from *Nädä'ko*, their own name). A tribe of the Caddo confederacy whose dialect was spoken by the Kadohadacho, Hainai, and Adai. The earliest mention of the people is in the relation of Biedma (1544), who writes that Moscoso in 1542 led his men during their southward march through a province that lay E. of the Anadarko. The territory occupied by the tribe was s. w. of the Kadohadacho. Their villages were scattered along Trinity and Brazos rs., Tex., higher up than those of the Hainai, and do not seem to have been visited so early as theirs by the French. A Spanish mission was established among the Anadarko early in the 18th century, but was soon abandoned. La Harpe reached an Anadarko village in 1719, and was kindly received. The people shared in the general friendliness for the French. During the contentions of the latter with the Spaniards and later with the English, throughout the 18th century, the Anadarko suffered greatly. They became embroiled in tribal wars; their villages were abandoned; and those who survived the havoc of war and the new diseases brought into the country by the white people were forced to seek shelter and safety with their kindred toward the N. E. In 1812 a village of 40 men and 200 souls was reported on Sabine r. The Anadarko lived in villages, having fixed habitations similar to those of the other tribes of the Caddo confederacy, to whom they were evidently also similar in customs, beliefs, and clan organization. Nothing is known definitely of the subdivisions of the tribe, but that such existed is probable from the fact that the people were scattered over a considerable territory and lived in a number of villages. They are now incorporated with the Caddo on the allotted Wichita res. in Oklahoma. The town of Anadarko perpetuates the tribal name. (A. C. F.)

Ah mau dah kas.—Parker (1855) quoted by Schoolcraft, Ind. Tribes, v, 682, 1855. Ah-nan-dah-kas.—Parker, Texas, 213, 1856. Ahnaudahkas.—Schoolcraft, Ind. Tribes, v, 712, 1855. Ahnauda-kas.—Keane in Stanford, Comp., 499, 1878. Amandaicoes.—Neighbors in H. R. Doc. 100, 29th Cong., 2d sess., 3, 1847. Ana-da-ca.—Sen., Ex. Conf. Doc. 13, 29th Cong., 2d sess., 1, 1846. Anadaghcoes.—Alvord in Sen. Ex. Doc. 18, 40th Cong., 3d sess., 7, 1869. Anadahcoe.—Ind. Aff. Rep. 1856, 184, 1857. An-a-dah-has.—Schoolcraft, Ind. Tribes, I, 518, 1851. An-a-dah-kas.—Ind. Aff. Rep., 28, 1848. Anadahkoes.—Ibid., 177. Anadahkos.—Ibid., 1856, 14, 1857. Anadakas.—Schoolcraft, Ind. Tribes, vi, 686, 1857. An-a-dak-has.—Marcy quoted by Schoolcraft, ibid., v, 712, 1855. Anadakkas.—Ibid. Anadáko.—Gatschet, Creek Migr. Leg., I, 43, 1884. Anadako's.—ten Kate, Reizen in N. Am., 460, 1885 (name of agency). Anadaku.—Gatschet, Caddo and Yatassi MS., 42, B. A. E. Anadarcos.—Bollaert in Ethnol. Soc. Lond. Journ., II, 283, 1850. Anadarko.—Dorsey, Caddo MS., B. A. E., 1882. Anadarko's.—ten Kate, Reizen in N. Am., 460, 1885. Anadogheos.—Alvord in Sen. Ex. Doc. 18, 40th Cong., 3d sess., 6, 1869. Anadorkoes.—H. R. Rep. 82, 44th Cong., 2d sess., 2, 1877. An-ah-dah-koes.—Ind. Aff. Rep. 1859, 267, 1860. An-ah-dah-kos.—Ibid., 310. Anahdakas.—Marcy, Army Life, 171, 1866. Anandarkoes.—Smithson. Misc. Coll., II, 49, 1862. Andaicos.—Ind. Aff. Rep., 261, 1851. Andarcos.—Latham, Essays, 401, 1860. And-daicoes.—Ind. Aff. Rep., 263, 1851. Anduico.—Schoolcraft, Ind. Tribes, III, 403, 1853. Annadahkoes.—Ind. Aff. Rep. 1854, 367, 1855. Anna-darcoes.—Ibid., 1849, 33, 1850. Anndggho's.—Alvord (1868) in Sen. Ex. Doc. 18, 40th Cong., 3d sess., 9, 1869. An-no-dar-coes.—Butler and Lewis (1846) in H. R. Doc. 76, 29th Cong., 2d sess., 7, 1847. Madaha.—Schoolcraft, Ind. Tribes, vi, 686, 1857. Mondaque.—Philippeaux, Map of Eng. Col., 1781 (misprint). Nadaco.—Joutel (1687) in Margry, Déc., II, 410, 1878. Nadacoc.—Jefferys (1763), Am. Atlas, map 5, 1776. Nadacoe.—De l'Isle, map in Winsor, Hist. Am., II, 294, 1886. Nadacogs.—Mezières (1778) quoted by Bancroft, No. Mex. States. I, 661, 1886. Nadaho.—Joutel (1687) in Margry, Déc., III, 409, 1878. Nädä'ko.—Mooney, MS. Caddo notes, B. A. E., 1891.

Nadáko's.—ten Kate, Reizen in N. Am., 374, 1885. Nadáku.—Gatschet, Caddo and Yatassi MS., 65, B. A. E. Nadáku hayánu.—Gatschet, Caddo MS., III, B. A. E. (Caddo name). Nadatcho.—Joutel (1687) in Margry, Déc., III, 409, 1878 (probably the Anadarko). Nadocogs.—Morfi quoted by Charlevoix, New Fr., IV, 80, 1870. Nandacaho.—Biedma in Hakluyt Soc. Pubs., 197, 1851. Nandako.—Latham, Essays, 402, 1860. Nandakoes.—Pénicaut (1701) in French, Hist. Coll. La., n. s., I, 73, 1869. Nandaquees.—Schermerhorn (1812) in Mass. Hist. Coll., 2d s., II, 24, 1814. Nandaquies.—Brown, W. Gaz., 214, 1817. Nandoquies.—Ibid., 215. Naráko's.—ten Kate, Reizen in N. Am., 374, 1885. Naudacho.—Biedma (1544) in French, Hist. Coll. La., II, 108, 1850. Nau-do-ques.—Brackenridge, Views of La., 81, 1815. Nondacao.—Gentl. of Elvas (1539) in Hakluyt Soc. Pubs., IX, 135, 1851. Nondaco.—Joutel (1687) in Margry, Déc., III, 409, 1878. Nondaque.—Jefferys (1763), Am. Atlas, map 5, 1776. Onadahkos.—Ind. Aff. Rep., 903, 1846. Onadaicas.—Butler and Lewis (1846) in H. R. Doc. 76, 29th Cong., 2d sess., 4, 1847. Onadakoes.—Ind. Aff. Rep., 894, 1846. Unatagua.—Latham, Varieties of Man, 350, 1850. Unataguous.—Le Branche (1839) in Sen. Ex. Doc. 14, 32d Cong., 2d sess., 27, 1853. Unataquas.—Bonnell, Texas, 140, 1840.

**Anagnak.** An Eskimo village of the Nushegagmiut on Wood r., Alaska; pop. 87 in 1880.—Nelson in 18th Rep. B. A. E., map, 1899.
Anaknak.—Petroff, Rep. on Alaska, 47, 1884.

**Anagok.** An Eskimo village of the Kuskwogmiut tribe, Alaska, on the coast near C. Avinof; pop. 75 in 1880.
Anogogmute.—Nelson in 18th Rep. B. A. E., map, 1899. Anogokmute.—Petroff, Rep. on Alaska, 54, 1884.

**Anaham.** A band of the Tsilkotin, numbering 216 in 1901, occupying a valley near Chilcotin r., 60 m. from its mouth in British Columbia.—Can. Ind. Aff., 162, 1902.
Amahim.—Can. Ind. Aff., 271, 1889. Anahem.—Ibid., 415, 1898. Anahim.—Ibid., 314, 1892. Anahim's tribe.—Ibid., 190, 1884.

**Anakwaikona.** An outcast element formerly existing among the Zuñi who were the servants, if not in many cases the slaves, of the intramural or city population.—Cushing in Proc. Internat. Cong. Am., VII, 176, 1890.
Á-wa-na-kwai-k'ya-ko-na.—Cushing, ibid.

**Analao.** A tribe, possibly Caddoan, formerly residing on Washita r., Ark. Deputies from the Analao and Tanico (Tonica) came to the village of Cahaynohoua in 1687, when Joutel and the other survivors of La Salle's party were there while on their way from the Red r. of Louisiana to the Mississippi. See Joutel in French, Hist. Coll. La., I, 172, 1846; Douay quoted by Shea, Discov. Miss. Val., 223, 1903. (A. C. F.)
Analac.—Coxe, Carolana, map, 1741.

**Analco.** A prehistoric pueblo of the Tewa at the place where there is now the so-called "oldest house," adjacent to San Miguel chapel, in Santa Fé, N. Mex. According to Bandelier this name was first applied in the 18th century. Ritch (N. Mex., 153, 196, 1885) asserts that the house referred to formed part of the old pueblo, and that two of the old women then living therein claimed to be lineal descendants of the original occupants (p. 113). Bandelier, however, inclines to the opinion (Arch. Inst. Papers, I, 19, 1881; IV, 89, 1892) that the structure dates from Spanish times, a belief substantiated by E. L. Hewett, in 1902, when the building was partly dismantled and found to be of Spanish construction, excepting about 18 inches of the foundation walls which were of Pueblo work.

**Anamas.** A former village, presumably Costanoan, connected with Dolores mission, San Francisco, Cal.—Taylor in Cal. Farmer, Oct. 18, 1861.

**Anamic.** A former rancheria, probably Papago, visited by Father Kino in 1701; situated in N. W. Sonora, Mexico, between Busanic and Sonoita. See *Bibiana.*
Sta Ana Anamic.—Kino (1701) quoted by Bancroft, No. Mex. States, I, 497, 1884.

**Anamiewatigong** ('at the tree of prayer,' i. e., the cross, from a large wooden cross planted by one of the early missionaries on the bluff where the village now stands.—Kelton). An Ottawa village in Emmet co., lower Michigan. It is called La Croix by the French, and Cross Village by the Americans, both conveying the same idea as the Indian name.
Cross Village.—Detroit treaty (1855) in U. S. Ind. Treaties, 614, 1873. La Croix.—Shea, Cath. Miss., 390, 1855.

**Anamis.** A village visited by La Salle in 1686 on his first journey from Ft St Louis, on Matagorda bay, Tex., to search overland for the Mississippi, and again in 1687 on his last journey northward. The people seem to have lived in the vicinity of the Caddoan tribes, but their ethnic relationship is uncertain. See Cavelier in Shea, Early Voy., 40, 1861. Cf. *Aranama, Cotonam.*                    (A. C. F.)
Anames.—Rivera, Diario, leg. 2,602, 1736.

**Anamon.** A former village, presumably Costanoan, connected with Dolores mission, San Francisco, Cal.—Taylor in Cal. Farmer, Oct. 18, 1861.

**Anarnisok** ('having smell [of walrus dung]'; old dialect). A former Eskimo village in E. Greenland, about lat. 63° 10′; pop. 20 in 1829.—Graah, Exped., map, 1837.

**Anarnitung** ('having smell [of walrus dung]'). A winter village of the Kingua branch of Okomiut in Baffin land at the head of Cumberland sd. (Boas in 6th Rep. B. A. E., map, 1888); pop. 43 in 1883.
Annanatook.—Howgate, Cruise of Florence, 33, 1877. Annanetoote.—Wareham in Jour. Geog. Soc. Lond., XII, 24, 1842.

**Anasitch.** A Kusan village or tribe on the s. side of Coos bay, coast of Oregon.—Milhau, MS. Coos Bay vocab., B. A. E.
Hau-nay-setch.—Milhau, MS. Letter to Gibbs, B. A. E. (Haunaysetch and Melukitz are names given to Coos bay).

**Anaskenoans.** A village of the Powhatan confederacy of Virginia, situated in 1608 on Rappahannock r., in the present Caroline co.—Smith (1629), Virginia, map, repr. 1819.

**Anatichapko** (*Anáti-chápko* 'long thicket'). A former Creek village on a N. tributary of Hillabee cr., a branch of Tallapoosa r., Ala. A battle occurred there during the Creek or Red Stick war, Jan. 24, 1814.—Gatschet, Creek Migr. Leg., I, 126, 1884.
Anáti tchápko.—Gatschet, op. cit., I, 126, 1884. Au-net-te chap-co.—Hawkins (1799), Sketch, 43, 1848. Enitachopko.—Pickett, Hist. Ala., II, 330, 1851. Enotochopco.—Schoolcraft, Ind. Tribes, VI, 371, 1857. Enotochopko.—Drake, Bk. Inds., bk. 4, 59, 1848. Long Swamp.—Gatschet, op. cit.

**Anatomy.** While the American Indians show many minor and even some important physical variations, and can be separated into several physical types, they present throughout the continent so many features in common that they may properly be regarded as one great race, admitting of a general anatomical description. The Eskimo form a distinct sub-race of the Mongolo-Malay and must be treated separately.

The Indian, in many of his anatomical characters, stands between the white and the negro. His skin is of various shades of brown, tinged in youth, particularly in the cheeks, with the red of the circulating blood. The term "red Indian" is a misnomer. Very dark individuals of a hue approaching chocolate or even the color of some negroes are found in more primitive tribes, especially in the S. and among the old men, who often went nearly naked. Most women and school children or others who wear clothing and live a more civilized life are lighter in color. Prolonged exposure to the elements tends, as with whites, to darken the skin. The darkest parts of the skin are ordinarily the back of the hands, wrists, and neck, the axilæ, nipples, perineal regions, and the exposed parts of the feet. A newborn infant is of varying degrees of dusky red.

The color of the hair is generally black, with the luster and slight bluish or brownish tinge that occurs among whites, not the dull grayish black of the African negro. With many individuals of all ages above early childhood who go much with bare head the hair becomes partly bleached, especially superficially, turning to a rusty hue.

The color of the eyes varies from hazel-brown to dark brown. The sclera in the young is bluish; in adults, especially the old, dirty-yellowish. The iris is often surrounded with a narrow but clearly marked ring.

The skin appears to be slightly thicker than that of the whites. The normal corrugations on the back of the hand and wrist are from childhood decidedly more pronounced in Indians of both sexes.

The hair of the head is straight, almost circular in cross-section, slightly coarser than in the average white, rather abundant and long. The range of variation in natural length is from 40 to 100 cm., or 18 in. to 36 in. Most male Indians would have a slight to moderate mustache and some beard on the chin if they allowed the hair to grow; but side whiskers in many are absent, or nearly so. Both mustache and chin beard are scarcer and coarser than with the whites, straight, of the same black as the hair, and in length 4 to 7 cm., or 1½ in. to 2½ in. The hair in the axillæ and on the pubis is moderate in quantity, in some instances nearly absent, and on the rest of the body hairs are shorter and less abundant than with the average white person. The nails are dull bluish in hue and moderately tough.

The face is well rounded and agreeable in childhood, interesting and occasionally handsome during adolescence and earlier adult life, and agreeable but much wrinkled in old age. The forehead in adults with undeformed skulls is somewhat low and in males slopes slightly backward. The eyebrows, where not plucked, are frequently connected by sparser hair above the nose. The eyelashes are moderately thick and long. The apertures of the eyes are slightly oblique, the outer canthi, especially the right one, being the higher. In children the fold called Mongolic is general, but not excessive. The root of the nose is usually depressed, as in most whites. The size and shape of the nose vary much, but it is commonly slightly shorter at the base and relatively wider than in whites, with an aquiline bridge predominating in men. In many men the point of the nose is lower than the base of the septum, the distal length exceeding the proximal. This peculiarity is especially frequent in some tribes. In women the nasal depression is wider and oftener shallower, and the bridge lower. Thin noses are not found. The lips are well formed and, barring individual exceptions, about as thick as in average whites. Prognathism is greater than in whites. The malars are in both sexes somewhat large and prominent; this becomes especially apparent in old age when much of the adipose tissue below them is gone. The chin often appears less prominent than in whites, but this effect is due to the greater alveolar protrusion. The ears are well formed and of good size, occasionally somewhat thick. The neck is of fair dimensions, never very long or thin.

The body as a rule is of good proportions, symmetrical, and, except in old age, straight and well nourished. The chest is of ample size, especially in men. The abdomen, which in children is often rather large, retains but slight fulness in later life. The pelvis, on account of the ample chest, appears somewhat small, but is not so by actual measurement. The spinal curves are only moderate, as are the size and prominence of the buttocks. The thighs are rather shapely; the calves are usually smaller than in whites. The upper limbs are of good shape and medium musculature. The feet and hands are well molded and in many tribes smaller than they ordinarily are in whites. The toes are rather short, and, where the people walk much barefoot or in sandals, show more or less separation. The proximal parts of the second and third toes are often confluent. In the more sedentary tribes the women, and occasionally also the men, are inclined to corpulence. The breasts of women are of medium size; in the childless the conical form predominates; the nipple and areola are more pronounced than in whites; in later life the breasts become small and flaccid. The genital organs do not differ essentially from those of the whites.

The Indian skull is, on the average, slightly smaller than that of whites of equal height. Cranial capacity in men ranges from 1,300 to 1,500 c. c.; in women from about 1,150 to 1,350 c. c. The frontal region in men is often low and sloping, the sagittal region elevated, the occipital region marked with moderate ridges and, in the dolichocephalic, protruding. Sutures are mostly less serrated than in whites; metopism, except in some localities, is rare, and occipital division is uncommon, while malar division is very rare and parietal division extremely so. Intercalated bones are few in undeformed crania; in deformed crania they are more numerous. The glabella, supraorbital ridges, and mastoids in male skulls are well-developed and sometimes heavy; in women they are small or of medium size. The nasal bridge is occasionally low, the nasal spine smaller than in whites; the lower borders of the nasal aperture are not often sharp, but nasal gutters are rare; subnasal fossæ are rather common. Orbits are of fair volume, approaching the quadrilateral, with angles rounded. Malars are often large, submalar depressions medium or shallow. The upper alveolar process, and occasionally also the lower, shows in both sexes a degree of prognathism greater than the average in whites, but less than in the negro. The protrusion on the whole is somewhat greater in the females. The face is meso- or ortho-gnathic. The lower jaw varies greatly. The chin is of moderate prominence, occasionally high, sometimes square in form. The prominence of the angles in full-grown males is not infrequently pronounced.

As to base structures, the foramen magnum is seldom large, and its position and inclination are very nearly the same as in whites; the styloid process is mostly smaller than in whites and not infrequently rudimentary; petrous portions on the average are less depressed below the level of neighboring parts than in whites; anterior lacerated foramina are smaller; the palate is well formed and fairly spacious, mostly parabolic, occasionally U-shaped.

The teeth are of moderate size; upper incisors are ventrally concave, shovel-shaped; canines not excessive; molars much as in whites; third molars rarely absent when adult life is reached. The usual cuspidory formula, though variations are numerous, is 4, 4, 3, above; 5, 5, irregular, below. A supernumerary conical dental element appears with some frequency in the upper jaw between, in front of, or behind the middle permanent incisors.

The bones of the vertebral column, the ribs, sternum, clavicles, and the smaller bones of the upper and lower limbs present many marks of minor importance. The pelvis is well formed, moderately spacious, approaching the European in shape. The humerus is rather flat, at times very much so; the fossa in 31 per cent is perforated; but vestiges of a supracondyloid process are much rarer than in whites. The humero-radial index of maximum frequency in adult males is 77 to 80 (in whites 71 to 75); humero-femoral index, 71 to 75 (in whites 70 to 74). The femur is quite flat below the tuberosities; the tibia, often flat (platycnemic).

Of the brain and other soft organs but little is known. Two adult male Apache brains, collected by Dr W. Matthews and now preserved in the U. S. National Museum, weighed after removal 1,191 and 1,304 grams, respectively. Both show good gyration.

The Eskimo differs anatomically from the Indian in many important features. His hair and eyes are similar in shade, though the eyes are more obliquely set; but his skin color on the whole is lighter, being yellowish or light brown, with a pronounced redness of the face. The Eskimo skull is high, normally scaphoid, and usually spacious. The face is large and flat, and the nasal bones are narrower than in any other people. The bones of the body are usually strong. There is less flattening of the shaft of the humerus, of the upper part of the shaft of the femur, and of the tibia. The superior border of the scapula shows often an angular instead of a curved outline.

In anthropometric differentiation the native tribes N. of Mexico are primarily separable into Indians and Eskimo. Some of the adjacent Indian tribes show Eskimo admixture.

The Indians among themselves vary considerably in stature, in form of the head and face, and of the orbits, the nose, and the nasal aperture. Low stature, from 160 to 165 cm. in males, is found among some of the Californian tribes (as the Yuki of Round Valley agency), many of the Pueblos, and some of the tribes of the N. W. coast, as the Salish of Harrison lake and Thompson r., and others. Among the Tigua, Tewa, Apache, Navaho, Comanche, northern Ute, Paiute, and Shoshoni, among the majority of California, Washington, and Oregon tribes, and among the eastern Cherokee, Chickasaw, Kiowa, and Iowa the height in male adults ranges between 165 and 170 cm., while among the Yuma, Mohave, Maricopa, Pima, Nez Percés, Sioux, Crows, Winnebago, Cheyenne, Arapaho, Iroquois, Osage, Chippewa, and eastern Algonquians the prevalent stature of adult men is from 170 to 175 cm. The range of variation in the majority of tribes and in both sexes is within 30 cm. The stature does not regularly follow the geographic or climatic features, nor does it agree wholly with the distribution of the other principal physical characteristics. The women are on the average about 12.5 cm. shorter than the men; the difference is greater among the tall than among the short tribes.

The distribution of the Indians according to cephalic index is of much interest. Excluding tribes that are known to be much mixed, there are found in the territory N. of Mexico all the three principal classes of cranial form, namely, dolicho-, brachy-, and meso-cephalic. Among the extremely dolichocephalic were the Delawares and the southern Utah cliff-dwellers. Moderate dolichocephaly, with occasional extreme forms, was and is very prevalent, being found in the Algonquian and the majority of the Siouan and Plains tribes and among the Siksika, Shoshoni, some Pueblos (e. g., Taos), and the Pima. Pure brachycephaly existed in Florida, and prevailed in the mound region and among the ancient Pueblos. It is best represented to-day among the Apache, Walapai, Havasupai, Nez Percés, Harrison lake Salish, Osage, and Wichita, and in a less degree among the Hopi, Zuñi, most of the Rio Grande Pueblos, Navaho, Mohave, Yuma, California Mission Indians, Comanche, Winnebago, many of the northwestern tribes, and Seminole. Mesocephaly existed principally among the California Indians, the Cherokee, and some of the Sioux and Iroquois. There are numerous tribes in North America about whose cephalic form there is still much uncertainty on account of the prevailing head deformation. As to the height of the head, which must naturally be considered in connection with the cephalic index, fair uniformity is found. In the Apache the head is rather low, among most other tribes it is moderate.

The form of the face is generally allied, as among other peoples, to the form of the head, being relatively narrow in narrow heads and broad in the brachycephalic. Orbits show variations, but the prevalent form is mesoseme. The nose and the nasal aperture are generally mesorhinic; the principal exception to this is found on the w. coast, especially in California, where a relatively narrow nose (leptorhinic) was common. The projection of the upper alveolar region is almost uniformly mesognathic.

The Eskimo range in height from short to medium, with long and high head, relatively broad flat face, high orbits, and narrow nose, showing alveolar prognathism like the Indians.

Consult Morton, (1) Crania Americana, 1839, (2) Distinctive characteristics, 1844; Retzius, Om foramen af hufvudets benstomme, 1847; Meigs, Observations, 1866; Gould, Investigations, 1869; Wyman, (1) Observations on crania, 1871, (2) Fresh water shell mounds, 1875; Verneau, Le bassin suivant les sexes, 1875; Eleventh and Twelfth Reps. Peabody Museum, 1878; Quatrefages and Hamy, Crania ethnica, 1878–79; Flower, Catalogue of specimens, 1879; Carr, (1) Observations on crania from Tennessee, 1878, (2) Measurements of crania from California, 1880, (3) Observations on crania from Santa Barbara Ids., 1879, (4) Notes on crania of New England Indians, 1880; Otis, List of specimens, 1880; Langdon, Madisonville prehistoric cemetery, 1881; Chudzinsky, Sur les trois encéphales des Esquimaux, 1881; Virchow (1) in Beiträge zur Craniologie der Insulaner von der Westküste Nordamerikas, 1889, (2) Crania Ethnica Americana, 1892; ten Kate, Somatological Observations, 1892; Matthews and Wortman, Human bones of Hemenway collection, 1891; Boas, (1) Zur anthropologie der nordamerikanischen Indianer, 1895, (2) A. J. Stone's measurements of natives of the N. W., 1901, (3) Anthropometrical observations on Mission Indians, 1896; Boas and Farrand, Physical characteristics of tribes of British Columbia, 1899; Allen, Crania from mounds of St. John's r., Fla., 1896; Sergi, Crani esquimesi, 1901; Duckworth, Contribution to Eskimo craniology, 1900; Hrdlicka, (1) An Eskimo brain, 1901, (2) The crania of Tren-

ton, N. J., 1902, (3) The Lansing skeleton, 1903, (4) Notes on the Indians of Sonora, 1904, (5) Contributions to physical anthropology of Cal., 1905; Spitzka, Contributions to encephalic anatomy of races, 1902; Tocher, Note on measurements of Eskimo, 1902; Matiegka, Schädel und Skelette von Santa Rosa, 1904. See *Artificial head deformation, Physiology.* (A. H.)

**Anawan.** See *Annawan.*

**Ançalagresses.** A small tribe mentioned by Milfort (Mémoire, 106, 1802) as residing w. of Mississippi r. and near the Kakias (Cahokia) in 1782.

**Ancavistis.** A division of the Faraon Apache.—Orozco y Berra, Geog., 59, 1864.

**Ancestor worship.** See *Mythology, Religion.*

**Anchguhlsu** ('town they abandoned'). The chief town of the Auk, situated opposite the N. end of Douglas id., Alaska.—Swanton, field notes, 1904.
Āk!ān.—Swanton, op. cit.('lake town'). Ak'ăn.—Krause, Tlinkit Ind., 116, 1885. Āntɔgɛłtsu.—Swanton, op. cit.

**Anchin.** A former village, presumably Costanoan, connected with Dolores mission, San Francisco, Cal.—Taylor in Cal. Farmer, Oct. 18, 1861.

**Anchor stones.** The native tribes N. of Mexico used bark and skin boats, dugouts, and, in the extreme S. W. and on the California coast, balsas; and in the use of these frail craft for purposes of travel, transportation, fishing, hunting, and warfare, the necessity for some means of anchorage was felt. In shallow waters with soft bottoms poles were often used; but of most general availability were stones that could be secured with a line and dropped from the vessel at any point. Commonly the stones thus used were simply bowlders or fragments of rock of proper weight, but in some cases the form was modified to facilitate attachment of the cord. A simple encircling groove, mere notches in the margins, or a rude perforation, sufficed for the purpose; the

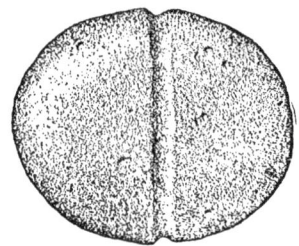

ANCHOR STONE, ILLINOIS RIVER
(DIAMETER 12 IN.)

former treatment gave to the utensil the appearance of a grooved hammer. Indeed, it probably often happened that these anchor stones were used as hammers or as mauls or sledges for heavy work when occasion required. It is observed also that some specimens have served as mortars or anvil stones, and no doubt also for grinding and shaping implements of stone. Stones of all available varieties were used, and the weight, so far as observed, rarely exceeds 40 or 50 pounds. The grooves or marginal notches were usually rudely pecked or chipped; but some show careful treatment, and in a number of cases a part or the whole of the surface of the stone has been worked down, probably for safety and convenience in handling, and in some cases as a result of the habit of reducing articles in common use to symmetrical and somewhat artistic shapes. Snyder records one case of the discovery of an anchor stone in an Indian grave. These stones are still used by Indians as well as by white people. Consult Snyder in Smithson. Rep. 1887, 1889; Rau in Smithson. Cont., XXV, 1884. (W. H. H.)

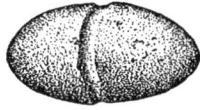

ANCHOR STONE IN USE BY CHIPPEWA (12 1-2 IN. LONG)

**Anchu.** A Cochimi rancheria of San Juan de Londo mission, Lower California.—Picolo in Stöcklein, Neue Welt-Bott, no. 72, 36, 1792.

**Andacaminos** (Span.: 'wanderers,' probably referring to their roving character). One of the tribes of w. Texas, some at least of whose people were neophytes of the mission of San José y San Miguel de Aguayo.—Texas State Archives, Nov., 1790.

**Andeguale.** A Niska town inhabited by two Chimmesyan families, the Lakseel of the Raven clan and the Gitgigenih of the Wolf clan.—Boas in 10th Rep. N. W. Tribes, 48–49, 1895.

**Anderson Lake.** A band of Upper Lillooet on a lake of the same name in British Columbia (Can. Ind. Aff., 415, 1898.); pop. 66 in 1902.

**Anderson's Town.** A former Delaware village on the s. side of White r., about the present Anderson, Madison co., Ind. (Hough, map in Ind. Geol. Rep., 1883). Named from the principal chief of the Delawares of Indiana about 1810–20.

**Andesite.** An eruptive rock, varying from light gray of several hues to black, belonging to the Tertiary and post-Tertiary lavas, and much used by the Indians for implements and utensils. It was shaped mainly by the pecking and grinding processes. Its distribution is very wide, especially in the W. (W. H. H.)

**Andiata.** A former Huron village in Ontario.—Jes. Rel. of 1636, III, 1858.
Andiatae.—Jes. Rel. of 1637, 134, 1858.

**Andreafski.** A Chnagmiut village on the N. bank of the Yukon, Alaska, 5 m. above the former redoubt of that name, for the murder of whose inmates in 1855 the Russians wreaked such vengeance that the river natives never again molested the whites. Pop. 14 in 1880; 10 in 1890. Andréaffsky.—Dall, Alaska, 119, 1870. Andreafsky.—Baker, Geog. Dict. Alaska, 1901. Andreievsky.—Petroff, 10th Census, Alaska, map, 1884. Andreivsky.—Nelson in 18th Rep. B. A. E., map, 1899.

**Andshankualth.** The Lakmiut name of a Yamel band on a w. tributary of the Willamette, in Oregon.—Gatschet, Calapooya MS., B. A. E., 1877.

**Andshimmampak.** The Lakmiut name of a Yamel band on Yamhill cr., Oregon.—Gatschet, Calapooya MS., B. A. E., 1877.

**Anegado** (Span. 'overflowed,' referring to the country). A tribe of which Cabeza de Vaca heard while in Texas in 1529–34. They lived not far from the Yguases. Anagados.—Cabeza de Vaca, Smith trans., 66, 1851. Anegados.—Ibid., 114, ed. 1871. Lanegados.—Ibid., 112.

**Anejue.** A former Chumashan village near Santa Barbara, Cal.—Taylor in Cal. Farmer, Apr. 24, 1863. Anijue.—Bancroft, Nat. Races, I, 459, 1874.

**Anektettim** (*Anɛxtĕ′t′tĭm*, 'stony little hollow'). A village of the Lytton band of Ntlakyapamuk, situate on the E. side of Fraser r., 3 m. above Lytton, British Columbia.—Teit in Mem. Am. Mus. Nat. Hist., II, 172, 1900.

**Anelo.** A Kaviagmiut Eskimo settlement at Port Clarence, Alaska.—11th Census, Alaska, 162, 1893.

**Anemuk.** An Unaligmiut Eskimo village on Anvik r., Alaska.—Sen. Ex. Doc. 12, 42d Cong., 1st sess., 25, 1871.

**Anepo** ('buffalo rising up.'—Hayden). A division of the Kainah tribe of the Siksika. A-ne′-po.—Morgan, Anc. Soc., 171, 1878 (said to be the name of an extinct animal). I-ni′-po-i.—Hayden, Ethnog. and Philol. Mo. Val., 264, 1862.

**Angakok.** A magician or conjurer among the Eskimo, the word for shaman in the eastern Eskimo dialects, now much used especially in American anthropological literature. (A. F. C.)

**Angmagsalingmiut** ('with-capelins people.'—Boas). A tribe of Eskimo on the E. coast of Greenland, between lat. 65° and 68°, inhabiting the fiords of Angmagsalik, Sermilik, and Sermiligak. According to Rink the total population was 413 in 1886. A Danish mission and commercial station on Angmagsalic fiord is the most northerly inhabited place on the E. coast. Each Angmagsalingmiut village consists of a single house, which has room for 8 or 10 families. Holm (Ethnol. Skizz. af Anmagsalikerne, 1887) names 8 villages on the fiord, with a total population of 225. Notwithstanding their isolation the people, according to Nansen (First Crossing of Greenland, I, 211, 1890), are among the most vigorous of the Eskimo. Angmagsalink.—Rink in Geog. Blätt., VIII, 350, 1886.

**Angmalook** (Eskimo name). A species of salmon (*Salmo nitidus*) found in the lakes of Boothia.—Rep. U. S. Fish Com., 122, 1872–73.

**Angmalortuk** ('the round one'). A Netchilirmiut winter village on the w. coast of Boothia bay, Canada. Angmalortoq.—Boas in 6th Rep. B. A. E., map, 1888.

**Angnovchak.** An Eskimo village in the Nushagak district, Alaska; pop. 16 in 1890.
Angnovchamiut.—11th Census, Alaska, 164, 1893.

**Angoutenc.** A former Huron village situated between Wenrio and Ossossane, about 2 m. from the latter place, in Ontario.
Angoutenc.—Jes. Rel. for 1638, 34, 1858. Ang8iens —Ibid., 1636, 116 (misprint). Ang8tenc.—Ibid., 35.

**Angun.** A Hutsnuwu village N. of Hood bay, Admiralty id., Alaska; pop. 420 in 1880. The greater part of the people have since removed to Killisnoo, a fishing village established by the whites.
Angoon.—Emmons in Mem. Am. Mus. Nat. Hist., III, pl. vii, 1903. Angun.—Krause, Tlinkit Ind., 105, 1885. Augoon.—Petroff, Tenth Census, Alaska, 32, 1884.

**Angwassag.** A Chippewa village near St Charles, Saginaw co., Mich., with perhaps 50 inhabitants in 1894.
Angwassag.—Smith quoted by Mason in Nat. Mus. Rep. 1902, 385, 1904. Angwasŭg.—Wm. Jones, inf'n, 1905 (sig. 'snags floating in the water').

**Angwusi.** The Raven clan of the Kachina phratry of the Hopi.
Ang-wush-a.—Dorsey and Voth, Mishongnovi Ceremonies, 175, 1902 (Crow clan). Añwuci wiñwû.—Fewkes in 19th Rep. B. A. E., 584, 1900 (wiñwû='clan'). Añ-wu'-si wüñ-wü.—Fewkes in Am. Anthrop., VII, 404, 1894 (wüñ-wü='clan'). Uñ-wu'-si.—Stephen in 8th Rep. B. A. E., 39, 1891.

**Anibiminanisibiwininiwak.** ('Pembina (cranberry) river men,' from nibimina 'high-bush cranberry,' sibiw 'river,' ininiwak 'men'). A Chippewa band living on Pembina r. in extreme N. Minnesota and the adjacent part of Manitoba. They removed from Sandy lake, Minn., to that region about 1807, at the solicitation of the Northwest Fur Company.—Gatschet, Ojibwa MS., B. A. E.
Chippewas of Pembena River.—Lewis, Travels, 178, 1809. Pembina band.—Events in Ind. Hist., suppl., 613, 1841.

**Anicam.** A Papago rancheria, probably in Pima co., s. Ariz.; pop. 96 in 1858.—Bailey in Ind. Aff. Rep., 208, 1858.

**Anilco.** A village, probably Quapaw, presumably on the s. side of Arkansas r., and said to contain 5,000 people when visited by De Soto's army in 1542.
Anicoyanque.—Biedma (1544) in French, Hist. Coll. La., II, 107, 1850. Anilco.—Garcilasso de la Vega, Florida, 201, 1723. Anileos.—Rafinesque, introd. Marshall, Ky., I, 34, 1824. Ilicos.—Ibid., 36. Nilco.—Gentleman of Elvas (1557) quoted by French, Hist. Coll. La., II, 184, 1850.

**Anilukhtakpak.** A Kaiyuhkhotana village on Innoko r., Alaska; pop. 170 in 1844.
Anilukhtakkak.—Zagoskin, Desc. Russ. Poss. Am., map, 1844.

**Animas** (Span. 'souls'). An Apache settlement, apparently near Gila r., Ariz., in 1769.—Anza in Doc. Hist. Mex., 4th s., II, 114, 1856.

**Animikite.** An impure massive mineral, according to Dana (Text-book Mineral., 420, 1888) supposed to be a silver antimonide, found at Silver islet, L. Superior; derived from Animiki, a local place name which in the Chippewa and closely re-

lated Algonquian dialects signifies 'thunder.' (A. F. C.)

**Animism.** See Religion.

**Animpayamo.** A former village of the Kalindaruk, a division of the Costanoan Indians, connected with San Carlos mission, Cal.—Taylor in Cal. Farmer, Apr. 20, 1860.

**Aniyak.** A village of the Nunatogmiut Eskimo on the Arctic coast just N. of Kotzebue sd., Alaska; pop. 25 in 1880.
Aniyak.—Baker, Geog. Dict. Alaska, 1901. Aniyakh.—Petroff, Rep. on Alaska, 4, 1884.

**Ankachagmiut.** A local subdivision of the Chnagmiut Eskimo living on Yukon r. above Andreafski, Alaska.
Angechag'emūt.—Dall in Cont. N. A. Ethnol., I, 17, 1877.

**Ankachak.** A Chnagmiut village, the home of the Ankachagmiut, on the right bank of the lower Yukon, Alaska; perhaps identical with Kenunimik.
Ankachagamuk.—Raymond in Sen. Ex. Doc. 12, 42d Cong., 1st sess., 25, 1871. Ankatchag-miout.—Zagoskin in Nouv. Ann. Voy., 5th ser., XXI, map, 1850. Ankatschagmiut.—Holmberg. Ethnol. Skizz., map, 1855. Ankochagamuk.—Post route map, 1903.

**Ankakehittan** ('people of the house in the middle of the valley'). A Koluschan division at Killisnoo, Alaska, belonging to the Raven clan; they are said to have separated from the Deshitan on account of some domestic trouble.
Am-khark-hit-ton.—Emmons in Mem. Am. Mus. Nat. Hist., III, pl. vii, 1903. Anq!a'ke hît tān.—Swanton, field notes. B. A. E., 1904. Nanchágetan.—Krause, Tlinkit Ind., 118, 1885. Q!a'ketan.—Swanton, op. cit.

**Anlik.** A Kaviagmiut village on Golofnin bay, Alaska.
Anlygmjuten.—Holmberg, Ethnol. Skizz., 6, 1855.

**Annaooka.** A Tuscarora town in North Carolina at the beginning of the 18th century.
Anna Ooka.—Lawson (ca. 1701), Hist. Car., 383, 1860.

**Annapolis.** One of the 7 districts of the territory of the Micmac, as recognized by themselves. It includes the s. w. part of Nova Scotia.—Rand, First Micmac Reading Book, 81, 1875.

**Annas.** An unidentified tribe mentioned by Rivera (Diario y Derrotero, leg. 2, 602, 1736) as living in s. Tex.

**Annawan.** A Wampanoag sachem, the chief captain and counselor of Philip, who under that chief's father had won a reputation for prowess in wars with many different tribes. When King Philip fell Annawan rallied the warriors and safely extricated them from the swamp where they were surrounded. Afterward he ranged through the woods, harrying the settlers of Swansea and Plymouth, until Capt. Benjamin Church raised a new expedition to hunt the Indians as long as there was one of them in the woods. Some were captured by Capt. Church's Indian scouts, but Annawan eluded pursuit, never camping twice in the same spot. Having learned from a captive where the old chief was, Church went with his Indian soldiers and only one white companion to capture him. When he reached the retreat, a rocky hill in the middle of a swamp, he sent the captives forward to divert the attention of Annawan's people. Church and his scouts then stole up, the noise they made being drowned by the sound of a pestle with which a woman was pounding corn, and jumped to the place where the arms were stacked. Annawan and his chief counselors, thus surprised and ignorant of the fewness of their assailants, gave themselves up and were bound. The fighting men, who were encamped near by, surrendered when they were told that the place was surrounded by English soldiers. Annawan brought the wampum belts and other regalia of King Philip, which he gave to Capt. Church as his conqueror, who had now overcome the last company that stood out against the English. Annawan's captor interceded to have his life spared, but the authorities at Plymouth, extracting from him a confession that he had put to death several English prisoners, some of them with torture, beheaded him in 1676 while Capt. Church was absent. (F. H.)

**Anne.** See *Queen Anne.*

**Annugamok.** A Nushagagmiut village on an E. tributary of Nushagak r., Alaska; pop. 214 in 1880.

Annugannok.—Petroff, 10th Census, Alaska, 17, 1884. Annuganok.—Nelson in 18th Rep. B. A. E., map, 1899. Anoogamok.—Petroff, Rep. on Alaska, 49, 1884.

**Annuities.** See *Agency System.*

**Anoatok** ('windy'). An Ita settlement at C. Inglefield, N. Greenland, the northernmost human habitation, lat. 78° 31'.

Anatoak.—Markham in Trans. Ethnol. Soc. Lond., 129, 1866. Anoretŏ'.—Stein in Petermann's Mittheil., IX, map, 1902. Aunatok.—Kane, Arctic Explor., II, 107, 1856. Rensselaer Harbor.—Ibid., I, 12.

**Anoginajin** (*anog* 'on both sides,' *i-* prefix, *na-* 'with feet,' *zing* 'to stand erect': 'he stands on both sides'). A band of the Wakpaatonwedan division of the Mdewakanton, named from its chief.

A-nog-i-na jin.—Neill, Hist. Minn., 144, note, 1858. He-stands-both-sides.—Ibid.

**Anoixi.** A village or division, probably of a southern Caddoan tribe, formerly situated near the Hot Springs country of Arkansas. Through this region De Soto's troops passed in the winter of 1541 on their way toward the place where De Soto later met his death. See Gentleman of Elvas (1557) in French, Hist. Coll. La., II, 182, 1850. Cf. Annocchy, a synonym of *Biloxi.* (A. C. F.)

**Anonatea.** A Huron village situated a league from Ihonatiria, in Ontario in 1637.—Jesuit Relation for 1637, 143, 1858.

Anenatea.—Ibid., 141. Anonatra.—Ibid., 166 (misprint).

**Anoritok** ('without wind'). An Eskimo settlement in E. Greenland, lat. 61° 45'.—Meddelelser om Grönland, XXV, 23, 1902.

Aneretek.—Ausland, 162, 1886.

**Anouala.** According to Le Moyne (De Bry, map, 1591) a village in 1564 on a w. branch of St Johns r., Fla., in the territory occupied generally by tribes of the Timuquanan family.

Novola.—Jeffreys, Am. Atlas, 24, 1776.

**Anovok.** A Magemiut Eskimo village on a small river N. of Kuskokwim bay, Alaska; pop. 15 in 1890.

Annovokhamiut.—11th Census, Alaska, 109, 1893.

**Anpanenikashika** ('those who became human beings by the aid of the elk'). A Quapaw division.

Aⁿ'paⁿ e'nikaci'ꭓa.—Dorsey in 15th Rep. B. A. E., 230, 1897. Elk gens.—Ibid, 229. Oⁿphŭⁿ enikaciꭓa.—Ibid.

**Ansactoy.** A village, probably of a part of the Patwin division of the Copehan family which formerly lived in Napa and Yolo cos., Cal. It concluded a treaty of peace with Gov. Vallejo in 1836.—Bancroft, Hist. Cal., IV, 71, 1886.

**Ansaime.** A village, said to have been Costanoan, in California; situated in the mountains 25 m. E. of the Mutsun, whom the inhabitants of this village attacked in 1799–1800.—Engelhardt, Franciscans in Cal., 397, 1897.

Absayme.—Taylor in Cal. Farmer, Nov. 23, 1860. Ansaimas.—Ibid.

**Anskowinis** (*Anskówĭnĭs*, 'narrow nosebridge'). A local band of the Cheyenne, taking its name from a former chief. (J. M.)

**Antap.** A former Chumashan village at the mill near San Pedro, Ventura co., Cal.—Henshaw, Buenaventura MS. vocab., B. A. E., 1884.

**Antigonishe.** Mentioned as an Indian settlement on a river of the same name which rises in a lake near the coast of the Strait of Canso, in "the province and colony of New Scotland." It was probably on or near the site of the present Antigonishe, in Antigonishe co., Nova Scotia, and perhaps belonged to the Micmac.

Artigoniche.—Alcedo, Dic. Geog., I, 161, 1786.

**Antiquity.** The antiquity of man on the American continent is a subject of interest to the student of the aborigines as well as to the historian of the human race, and the various problems that arise with respect to it in the region N. of Mexico are receiving much scientific attention. As the tribes were without a system of writing available to scholars, knowledge of events that transpired before the Columbian discovery is limited to the rather indefinite testimony furnished by tradition, by the more definite but as yet fragmentary evidences of archeology, and by the internal evidence of general ethnological phenomena. The fact that the American Indians have acquired such marked physical characteristics as to be regarded as a separate race of very considerable homogeneity from Alaska to Patagonia, is regarded as indicating a long and complete separation from their parental peoples. Similarly, the existence in America of numerous culture groups, measurably distinct one from another in language, social customs, religion, technology, and esthetics, is thought to indicate a long and more or less exclusive occupancy of independent areas. But as a criterion of age the testimony thus furnished lacks definiteness, since to one mind it may signify a short time, while to another it may suggest a very long period. Native historical records of even the most advanced tribes are hardly more to be relied on than tradition, and they prove of little service in determining the duration of occupancy of the continent by the race, or even in tracing the more recent course of events connected with the historic peoples. No one can speak with assurance, on the authority of either tradition or history, of events dating farther back than a few hundred years. Archeology, however, can furnish definite data with respect to antiquity; and, aided by geology and biology, this science is furnishing results of great value, although some of the greater problems encountered remain still unsolved, and must so remain indefinitely. During the first centuries of European occupancy of the continent, belief in the derivation of the native tribes from some Old World people in comparatively recent times was very general, and indeed the fallacy has not yet been entirely extinguished. This view was based on the apparently solid foundation of the Mosaic record and chronology as determined by Usher, and many works have been written in the attempt to determine the particular people from which the American tribes sprang. (See *Popular Fallacies*, and for various references consult Bancroft, Native Races, v, 1886; Winsor, Narrative and Critical History, I, 1884). The results of researches into the prehistoric archeology of the eastern continent during the last century, however, have cleared away the Usherian interpretation of events and established the fact of the great antiquity of man in the world. Later, investigations in America were taken up, and the conclusion was reached that the course of primitive history had been about the same on both continents. Observations that seemed to substantiate this conclusion were soon forthcoming and were readily accepted; but a more critical examination of the testimony shows its shortcomings and tends to hold final determinations in abeyance. It is clear that traces of early man are not so

plentiful in America as in Europe, and investigations have proceeded with painful slowness and much halting along the various lines of research. Attempts have been made to establish a chronology of events in various ways, but without definite result. The magnitude of the work accomplished in the building of mounds and other earthworks has been emphasized, the time requisite for the growth and decay upon these works of a succession of forests has been computed (see *Mounds*). The vast accumulations of midden deposits and the fact that the strata composing them seem to indicate a succession of occupancies by tribes of gradually advancing culture, beginning in savagery and ending in well-advanced barbarism, have impressed themselves on chronologists (see *Shell-heaps*). Striking physiographic mutations, such as changes of level and the consequent retreat or advance of the sea and changes in river courses since man began to dwell along their shores, have been carefully considered. Modifications of particular species of mollusks between the time of their first use on the shell-heap sites and the present time, and the development in one or more cases of new varieties, suggest very considerable antiquity. But the highest estimate of elapsed time based on these evidences does not exceed a few thousand years. Dall, after carefully weighing the evidence collected by himself in Alaska, reached the conclusion that the earliest midden deposits of the Aleutian ids. are probably as much as 3,000 years old. Going beyond this limit, the geological chronology must be appealed to, and we find no criteria by means of which calculations can be made in years until we reach the close of the Glacial epoch, which, according to those who venture to make estimates based on the erosion of river channels, was, in the states that border the St Lawrence basin, not more than 8,000 or 10,000 years ago (Winchell). Within this period, which in middle North America may properly be designated post-Glacial, there have been reported numerous traces of man so associated with the deposits of that time as to make them measurably valuable in chronological studies; but these evidences come within the province of the geologist rather than of the archeologist, and findings not subjected to critical examination by geologists having special training in the particular field may well be placed in the doubtful category.

Post-Glacial rivers, in cutting their channels through the various deposits to their present level, have in some cases left a succession of flood-plain terraces in which remains of man and his works are embedded. These terraces afford rather imperfect means of subdividing post-Glacial time, but under discriminating observation may be expected to furnish valuable data to the chronologist. The river terraces at Trenton, N. J., for example, formed largely of gravel accumulated at the period when the southern margin of the ice sheet was retreating northward beyond the Delaware valley, have been the subject of careful and prolonged investigation. At the points where traces of man have been reported the section of these deposits shows generally beneath the soil a few feet of superficial sands of uncertain age, passing down rather abruptly into a more or less uniform deposit of coarse gravel that reaches in places a depth of 30 feet or more. On and near the surface are found village sites and other traces of occupancy by the Indian tribes. Beneath the soil, extending throughout the sand layers, stone implements and the refuse of implement-making occur; but the testimony of these finds can have little value in chronology, since the age of the deposits inclosing them remains in doubt. From the Glacial gravels proper there has been recovered a single object to which weight as evidence of human presence during their accumulation is attached; this is a tubular bone, regarded as part of a human femur and said to show glacial striæ and traces of human workmanship, found at a depth of 21 feet. On this object the claim for the Glacial antiquity of man in the Delaware valley and on the Atlantic slope practically rests (Putnam, Mercer, Wright, Abbott, Hrdlicka, Holmes). Other finds E. of the Alleghenies lacking scientific verification furnish no reliable index of time. In a post-Glacial terrace on the s. shore of Lake Ontario the remains of a hearth were discovered at a depth of 22 feet by Mr Tomlinson in digging a well, apparently indicating early aboriginal occupancy of the St Lawrence basin (Gilbert). From the Glacial or immediately post-Glacial deposits of Ohio a number of articles of human workmanship have been reported: A grooved ax from a well 22 feet beneath the surface, near New London (Claypole); a chipped object of waster type at Newcomerstown, at a depth of 16 feet in Glacial gravels (Wright, Holmes); chipped stones in gravels, one at Madisonville at a depth of 8 feet, and another at Loveland at a depth of 30 feet (Metz, Putnam, Wright, Holmes). At Little Falls, Minn., floodplain deposits of sand and gravel are found to contain many artificial objects of quartz. This flood plain is believed by some to have been finally abandoned by the Mississippi well back toward the close of the Glacial period in the valley (Brower, Winchell, Upham), but that

these finds warrant definite conclusions as to time is seriously questioned by Chamberlin. In a Missouri r. bench near Lansing, Kans., portions of a human skeleton were recently found at a depth of 20 feet, but geologists are not agreed as to the age of the formation (see *Lansing Man*). At Clayton, Mo., in a deposit believed to belong to the loess, at a depth of 14 feet, a well-finished grooved ax was found (Peterson). In the Basin Range region between the Rocky mts. and the Sierras, two discoveries that seem to bear on the antiquity of human occupancy have been reported: In a silt deposit in Walker r. valley, Nev., believed to be of Glacial age, an obsidian implement was obtained at a depth of 25 feet (McGee); at Nampa, Idaho, a clay image is reported to have been brought up by a sand pump from a depth of 320 feet in alternating beds of clay and quicksand underlying a lava flow of late Tertiary or early Glacial age (Wright, Emmons; see *Nampa Image*). Questions are raised by a number of geologists respecting the value of these finds (McGee). The most extraordinary discoveries of human remains in connection with geological formations are those from the auriferous gravels of California (Whitney, Holmes). These finds are numerous and are reported from many localities and from deposits covering a wide range of time. So convincing did the evidence appear to Whitney, state geologist of California from 1860 to 1874, that he accepted without hesitation the conclusion that man had occupied the auriferous gravel region during pre-Glacial time, and other students of the subject still regard the testimony as convincing; but consideration of the extraordinary nature of the conclusions dependent on this evidence should cause even the most sanguine advocate of great human antiquity in America to hesitate (see *Calaveras Man*). Geologists are practically agreed that the gravels from which some at least of the relics of man are said to come are of Tertiary age. These relics represent a polished-stone culture corresponding closely to that of the modern tribes of the Pacific slope. Thus, man in America must have passed through the savage and well into the barbarous stage while the hypothetical earliest representative of the human race in the Old World, *Pithecanthropus erectus* of Dubois, was still running wild in the forests of Java, a half-regenerate Simian. Furthermore, the acceptance of the auriferous-gravel testimony makes it necessary to place the presence of man in America far back toward the beginning of the Tertiary age, a period to be reckoned not in tens but in hundreds of thousands of years. (See Smithson. Rep. for 1899.) These and other equally striking considerations suggest the wisdom of formulating conclusions with the utmost caution.

Caves and rock shelters representing various periods and offering dwelling places to the tribes that have come and gone, may reasonably be expected to contain traces of the peoples of all periods of occupancy; but the deposits forming their floors, with few exceptions, have not been very fully examined, and up to the present time have furnished no very tangible evidence of the presence of men beyond the limited period of the American Indian as known to us. The University of California has conducted excavations in a cave in the N. part of the state, and the discovery of bones that appear to have been shaped by human hands, associated with fossil fauna that probably represent early Glacial times, has been reported (Sinclair); but the result is not decisive. The apparent absence or dearth of ancient human remains in the caves of the country furnishes one of the strongest reasons for critically examining all testimony bearing on antiquity about which reasonable doubt can be raised. It is incredible that primitive man should have inhabited a country of caverns for ages without resorting at some period to their hospitable shelter; but research in this field is hardly begun, and evidence of a more conclusive nature may yet be forthcoming.

In view of the extent of the researches carried on in various fields with the object of adducing evidence on which to base a scheme of human chronology in America, decisive results are surprisingly meager, and the finds so far made, reputed to represent a vast period of time stretching forward from the middle Tertiary to the present, are characterized by so many defects of observation and record and so many apparent incongruities, biological, geological, and cultural, that the task of the chronologist is still largely before him.

For archeological investigations and scientific discussion relating to the antiquity of man within the limits of the United States, see Abbott (1) in Proc. Boston Soc. Nat. Hist., XXIII, 1888, (2) in Proc. A. A. A. S., XXXVII, 1888; Allen, Prehist. World, 1885; Bancroft, Native Races, IV, 1882; Becker in Bull. Geol. Soc. Am., II, 1891; Blake in Jour. Geol., VII, no. 7, 1899; Brower, Memoirs, V, 1902; Chamberlin (1) in Jour. Geol., X, no. 7, 1902, (2) in The Dial, 1892; Claypole in Am. Geol., XVIII, 1896; Dall (1) in Proc. Acad. Nat. Sci. Phila., 1899, (2) in Cont. N. Am. Ethnol., I, 1877; Emmons in Proc. Boston Soc. Nat. Hist., XXIV, 1889; Farrand, Basis of Am. Hist., 1904; Foster, Prehist. Races, 1878; Fowke, Archeol. Hist. Ohio, 1902; Gilbert in Am. Anthrop., II, 1889; Haynes in Winsor,

Narr. and Crit. Hist. Am., I, 1889; Holmes (1) in Rep. Smithson. Inst. 1899, 1901, (2) ibid. 1902, 1903, (3) in Jour. Geol., I, nos. 1, 2, 1893, (4) in Am. Geol., XI, no. 4, 1893, (5) in Science, Nov. 25, 1892, and Jan. 25, 1893; Hrdlicka (1) in Am. Anthrop., n. s., V, no. 2, 1903, (2) in Bull. Am. Mus. Nat. Hist., XVI, 1902; Kummel in Proc. A. A. A. S., XLVI, 1897; Lapham in Smithson. Cont., VII, 1855; Lewis, ibid., XXIX, 1880; McGee (1) in Am. Anthrop., II, no. 4, 1889; V, no. 4, 1892; VI, no. 1, 1893, (2) in Pop. Sci. Mo., Nov., 1888, (3) in Am. Antiq., XIII, no. 7, 1891; Mercer (1) in Proc. A. A. A. S., XLVI, 1897, (2) in Am. Nat., XXVII, 1893, (3) in Pubs. Univ. of Pa., VI, 1897; Morse in Proc. A. A. A. S., XXXIII, 1884; Munro, Archæol. and False Antiq., 1905; Nadaillac, Prehist. America, 1884; Peterson in Records of Past, II, pt. 1, 1903; Powell in The Forum, 1890; Putnam (1) in Proc. Boston Soc. Nat. Hist., XXI, 1881–83; XXIII, 1885–88, (2) in Peabody Mus. Reps., IX–XXXVII, 1876–1904, (3) in Proc. A. A. A. S., XLVI, 1897, (4) in Rep. Am. Mus. Nat. Hist. 1899, 1900; Salisbury (1) in Proc. A. A. A. S., XLVI, 1897, (2) in Science, Dec. 31, 1897; Shaler in Peabody Mus. Rep., II, no. 1, 1877; Sinclair in Pub. Univ. Cal., II, no. 1, 1904; Skertchley in Jour. Anthrop. Inst., XVII, 1888; Squier and Davis, Smithson. Cont., I, 1848; Thomas (1) Hist. N. Am., II, 1904, (2) in 12th Rep. B. A. E., 1894, (3) Introd. Study of N. Am. Arch., 1903; Upham in Science, Aug., 1902; Whitney, Auriferous Gravels of the Sierra Nevada, 1879; Williston in Science, Aug., 1902; Winchell (1) in Am. Geol., Sept., 1902, (2) in Bull. Geol. Soc. Am., XIV, 1903; Wright, (1) Man and the Glacial Period, 1895, (2) Ice Age, 1889, (3) in Pop. Sci. Mo., May, 1893, (4) in Proc. Boston Soc. Nat. Hist., XXIII, 1888, (5) in Rec. of the Past, II, 1903; IV, 1905; Wyman in Mem. Peabody Acad. Sci., I, no. 4, 1875.

The progress of opinion and research relating to the origin, antiquity, and early history of the American tribes is recorded in a vast body of literature fully cited, until within recent years, by Bancroft in Native Races, IV, 1882, and Haynes in Winsor's Narrative and Critical History, I, 1884. (w. h. h.)

**Antler.** See *Bone-work*.

**Anu.** The Red-ant clan of the Ala (Horn) phratry of the Hopi.

**Án-ñamu.**—Voth, Traditions of the Hopi, 37, 1905. **A'-nü wüñ-wü.**—Fewkes in Am. Anthrop., VII, 401, 1894 (*wüñ-wü*='clan').

**Anuenes** (*Anuē'nes*). A gens of the Nanaimo.—Boas in 5th Rep. N. W. Tribes, 32, 1889.

**Anvik.** A Kaiyuhkhotana village at the junction of Anvik and Yukon rs., Alaska. Pop. in 1844, 120; in 1880, 95;

in 1890, 100 natives and 91 whites; in 1900, 166. An Episcopal mission and school were established there in 1887. **Anvic.**—Whymper, Alaska, 265, 1869. **Anvig.**—Zagoskin quoted by Petroff, 10th Census, Alaska, 37, 1884. **Anvik.**—Petroff, ibid., 12.

**Anvils.** Primitive workers in metal were dependent on anvil stones in shaping their implements, utensils, and ornaments. Anvils were probably not especially shaped for the purpose, but consisted of bowlders or other natural masses of stone, fixed or movable, selected according to their fitness for the particular purpose for which they were employed. Few of these utensils have been identified, however, and the types most utilized by the tribes are left to conjecture. The worker in stone also sometimes used a solid rock body on which to break and roughly shape masses of flint and other stone. These are found on many sites where stone was quarried and wholly or partially worked into shape, the upper surface showing the marks of rough usage, while fragments of stone left by the workmen are scattered about. (w. h. h.)

**Anyukwinu.** A ruined pueblo of the Jemez, situated N. of the present Jemez pueblo, N. central N. Mex.
**Añu-quil-i-gui.**—Bandelier in Arch. Inst. Papers, IV, pt. 2, 207, 1892. **Anyúkwinu.**—Hodge, field notes, B. A. E., 1895.

**Aogitunai** (ᵍ*Ao-gitAnā'-i*, 'Masset inlet gituns'). A Masset subdivision residing in the town of Yaku, opposite North id., and deriving their name from Masset inlet, Queen Charlotte ids., British Columbia.—Swanton, Cont. Haida, 275, 1905.

**Aogni.** A former Chumashan village in Ventura co., Cal.—Taylor in Cal. Farmer, July 24, 1863.

**Aokeawai** (ᵍ*Ao-qē'awa-i*, 'those born in the inlet'). A division of the Raven clan of the Skittagetan family which received its name from Masset inlet, Queen Charlotte ids., British Columbia, where these people formerly lived. Part of them, at least, were settled for a time at Dadens, whence all finally went to Alaska. There were two subdivisions: Hlingwainaashadai and Taolnaashadai.—Swanton, Cont. Haida, 272, 1905.
**Kào-kē'-owai.**—Boas, 12th Rep. N. W. Tribes, 22, 1898. **Kēo Hāadē.**—Harrison in Trans. Roy. Soc. Can., sec. II, 125, 1895.

**Aondironon.** A branch of the Neutrals whose territory bordered on that of the Huron in w. Ontario. In 1648, owing to an alleged breach of neutrality, the chief town of this tribe was sacked by 300 Iroquois, mainly Seneca, who killed a large number of its inhabitants and carried away many others in captivity.—Jes. Rel. for 1640, 35, 1858.
**Ahondihronnons.**—Jes. Rel. for 1656, 34, 1858. **Aondironnons.**—Jes. Rel. for 1648, 49, 1858. **Ondironon.**—Ibid., III, index, 1858.

**Aopomue.** A former Maricopa rancheria on Rio Gila, s. w. Arizona.—Sedel-

mair (1744) quoted by Bancroft, Ariz. and N. Mex., 366, 1889.

**Aoreachic** ('where there is mountain cedar'). A small rancheria of the Tarahumare, not far from Norogachic, Chihuahua, Mexico. Also called Agorichic; distinct from Aboreachic.—Lumholtz, inf'n, 1894.

**Aostlanlnagai** (ᵍ*Ao sL!an lnagā'i*, 'Masset inlet rear-town people'). A local subdivision of the Raven clan of the Skittagetan family. Masset inlet gave them the separate name.—Swanton, Cont. Haida, 271, 1905.
**Stl'ᴇɴɢᴇ lā' nas.**—Boas, 12th Rep. N. W. Tribes, 22, 1898.

**Aoyakulnagai** (ᵍ*Ao yā' ku lnagā' i*, 'middle town people of Masset inlet'). A branch of the Yakulanas division of the Raven clan of the Skittagetan family, which received the name from Masset inlet, where its town stood.—Swanton, Cont. Haida, 271, 1905.
**G·anyakoîlnagai.**—Boas, 12th Rep. N. W. Tribes, 23, 1898 (probably a misprint for G·auyakoîlnagai, its name in the Skidegate dialect). **Ou yākū Ilnigē.**—Harrison in Trans. Roy. Soc. Can., 125, 1895.

**Apache** (probably from *ápachu*, 'enemy,' the Zuñi name for the Navaho, who were designated "Apaches de Nabaju" by the early Spaniards in New Mexico). A number of tribes forming the most southerly group of the Athapascan family. The name has been applied also to some unrelated Yuman tribes, as the Apache Mohave (Yavapai) and Apache Yuma. The Apache call themselves *N'de*, *Dinë*, *Tinde*, or *Inde*, 'people.' (See *Athapascan*.)

They were evidently not so numerous about the beginning of the 17th century as in recent times, their numbers apparently having been increased by captives from other tribes, particularly the Pueblos, Pima, Papago, and other peaceful Indians, as well as from the settlements of northern Mexico that were gradually established within the territory raided by them, although recent measurements by Hrdlicka seem to indicate unusual freedom from foreign admixture. They were first mentioned as Apaches by Oñate in 1598, although Coronado, in 1541, met the Querechos (the Vaqueros of Benavides, and probably the Jicarillas and Mescaleros of modern times) on the plains of E. N. Mex. and w. Tex.; but there is no evidence that the Apache reached so far w. as Arizona until after the middle of the 16th century. From the time of the Spanish colonization of New Mexico until within twenty years they have been noted for their warlike disposition, raiding white and Indian settlements alike, extending their depredations as far southward as Jalisco, Mexico. No group of tribes has caused greater confusion to writers, from the fact that the popular names of the tribes are derived from some local or temporary habitat, owing to their shifting propensities, or were given by the Spaniards on account of some tribal characteristic; hence some of the common names of apparently different Apache tribes or bands are synonymous, or practically so; again, as employed by some writers, a name may include much more or much less than when employed by others. Although most of the Apache have been hostile since they have been known to history, the most serious modern outbreaks have been attributed to mismanagement on the part of civil authorities. The most important recent hostilities were those of the Chiricahua under Cochise, and later Victorio, who, together with 500 Mimbreños, Mogollones, and Mescaleros, were assigned, about 1870, to the Ojo Caliente reserve in w. N. Mex. Cochise, who had repeatedly refused to be confined within reservation limits, fled with his band, but returned in 1871, at which time 1,200 to 1,900 Apache were on the reservation. Complaints from neighboring settlers caused their removal to Tularosa, 60 m. to the N. w., but 1,000 fled to the Mescalero reserve on Pecos r., while Cochise went out on another raid. Efforts of the military agent in 1873 to compel the restoration of some stolen cattle caused the rest, numbering 700, again to decamp, but they were soon captured. In compliance with the wishes of the Indians, they were returned to Ojo Caliente in 1874. Soon afterward Cochise died, and the Indians began to show such interest in agriculture that by 1875 there were 1,700 Apache at Ojo Caliente, and no depredations were reported. In the following year the Chiricahua res. in Arizona was abolished, and 325 of the Indians were removed to the San Carlos agency; others joined their kindred at Ojo Caliente, while some either remained on the mountains of their old reservation or fled across the Mexican border. This removal of Indians from their ancestral homes was in pursuance of a policy of concentration, which was tested in the Chiricahua removal in Arizona. In April, 1877, Geronimo and other chiefs, with the remnant of the band left on the old reservation, and evidently the Mexican refugees, began depredations in s. Arizona and N. Chihuahua, but in May 433 were captured and returned to San Carlos. At the same time the policy was applied to the Ojo Caliente Apache of New Mexico, who were making good progress in civilized pursuits; but when the plan was put in action only 450 of 2,000 Indians were found, the remainder forming into predatory bands under Victorio. In September 300 Chiricahua, mainly of the Ojo Caliente band, escaped from San Carlos, but surrendered after many engagements. These were returned to Ojo Caliente, but they soon ran off again. In February, 1878, Victorio surrendered in the hope that he and his people might remain on their former reservation, but another attempt was made to force the Indians to go to San Carlos, with the same result. In June the fugitives again appeared at the Mescalero agency, and arrangements were at last made for them to settle there; but, as the local authorities found indictments against Victorio and others, charging them with murder and robbery, this chief, with his few immediate followers and some Mescaleros, fled from the reservation and resumed marauding. A call was made for an increased force of military, but in the skirmishes in which they were engaged the Chiricahua met with remarkable success, while 70 settlers were murdered during a single raid. Victorio was joined before April, 1880, by 350 Mescaleros and Chiricahua refugees from Mexico, and the repeated raids which followed struck terror to the inhabitants of New Mexico, Arizona, and Chihuahua. On April 13 1,000 troops arrived, and their number was later greatly augmented. Victorio's band was frequently encountered by superior forces, and although supported during most of the time by only 250 or 300 fighting men, this warrior usually inflicted severer punishment than he suffered. In these raids 200 citizens of New Mexico, and as many more of Mexico, were killed. At one time the band was virtually surrounded by a force of more than 2,000 cavalry and several hundred Indian scouts, but Victorio eluded capture and fled across the Mexican border, where he continued his bloody campaign. Pressed on both sides of the international boundary, and at times harassed by United States and Mexican troops combined, Victorio finally suffered severe losses and his band became divided. In October, 1880, Mexican troops encountered Victorio's party, comprising 100 warriors, with 400 women and children, at Tres Castillos; the Indians were surrounded and attacked in the evening, the fight continuing throughout the night; in the morning the ammunition of the Indians became exhausted, but although rapidly losing strength, the remnant refused to surrender until Victorio, who had been wounded several times, finally fell dead. This disaster to the Indians did not quell their hostility. Victorio was succeeded by Nana, who collected the divided force, received reenforcements from the Mescaleros and the San

Carlos Chiricahua, and between July, 1881, and April, 1882, continued the raids across the border until he was again driven back in Chihuahua. While these hostilities were in progress in New Mexico and Chihuahua the Chiricahua of San Carlos were striking terror to the settlements of Arizona. In 1880 Juh and Geronimo with 108 followers were captured and returned to San Carlos. In 1881 trouble arose among the White Mountain Coyoteros on Cibicu cr., owing to a medicine-man named Nakaidoklini (q.v.), who pretended power to revive the dead. After paying him liberally for his services, his adherents awaited the resurrection until August, when Nakaidoklini avowed that his incantations failed because of the presence of whites. Since affairs were assuming a serious aspect, the arrest of the prophet was ordered; he surrendered quietly, but as the troops were making camp the scouts and other Indians opened fire on them. After a sharp fight Nakaidoklini was killed and his adherents were repulsed. Skirmishes continued the next day, but the troops were reenforced, and the Indians soon surrendered in small bands. Two chiefs, known as George and Bonito, who had not been engaged in the White Mountain troubles, surrendered to Gen. Wilcox on Sept. 25 at Camp Thomas, but were paroled. On Sept. 30 Col. Riddle was sent to bring these chiefs and their bands back to Camp Thomas, but they became alarmed and fled to the Chiricahua, 74 of whom left the reserve, and, crossing the Mexican border, took refuge with the late Victorio's band in Chihuahua. In the same year Nana made one of his bloody raids across the line, and in September Juh and Nahchi, with a party of Chiricahua, again fled from the reservation, and were forced by the troops into Mexico, where, in April, 1882, they were joined by Geronimo and the rest of the hostile Chiricahua of San Carlos, with Loco and his Ojo Caliente band. The depredations committed in N. Chihuahua under Geronimo and other leaders were perhaps even more serious than those within the limits of the United States. In March, 1883, Chato with 26 followers made a dash into New Mexico, murdering a dozen persons. Meanwhile the white settlers on the upper Gila consumed so much of the water of that stream as to threaten the Indian crops; then coal was discovered on the reservation, which brought an influx of miners, and an investigation by the Federal grand jury of Arizona on Oct. 24, 1882, charged the mismanagement of Indian affairs on San Carlos res. to local civil authorities.

Gen. G. H. Crook having been reassigned to the command, in 1882 induced about 1,500 of the hostiles to return to the reservation and subsist by their own exertions. The others, about three-fourths of the tribe, refused to settle down to reservation life and repeatedly went on the warpath; when promptly followed by Crook they would surrender and agree to peace, but would soon break their promises. To this officer had been assigned the task of bringing the raiding Apache to terms in cooperating with the Mexican troops of Sonora and Chihuahua. In May, 1883, Crook crossed the boundary to the headwaters of the Rio Yaqui with 50 troops and 163 Apache scouts; on the 13th the camp of Chato and Bonito was discovered and attacked with some loss to the Indians. Through two captives employed as emissaries, communication was soon had with the others, and by May 29 354 Chiricahua had surrendered. On July 7 the War Department assumed police control of the San Carlos res., and on Sept. 1 the Apache were placed under the sole charge of Crook, who began to train them in the ways of civilization, with such success that in 1884 over 4,000 tons of grain, vegetables, and fruits were harvested. In Feb., 1885, Crook's powers were curtailed, an act that led to conflict of authority between the civil and military officers, and before matters could be adjusted half the Chiricahua left the reservation in May and fled to their favorite haunts. Troops and Apache scouts were again sent forward, and many skirmishes took place, but the Indians were wary, and again Arizona and New Mexico were thrown into a state of excitement and dread by raids across the American border, resulting in the murder of 73 white people and many friendly Apache. In Jan., 1886, the American camp under Capt. Crawford was attacked through misunderstanding by Mexican irregular Indian troops, resulting in Crawford's death. By the following March the Apache became tired of the war and asked for a parley, which Crook granted as formerly, but before the time for the actual surrender of the entire force arrived the wily Geronimo changed his mind and with his immediate band again fled beyond reach. His escape led to censure of Crook's policy; he was consequently relieved at his own request in April, and to Gen. Nelson A. Miles was assigned the completion of the task. Geronimo and his band finally surrendered Sept. 4, 1886, and with numerous friendly Apache were sent to Florida as prisoners. They were later taken to Mt Vernon, Ala., thence to Ft Sill, Okla., where they have made progress toward civilization. Some of the hostiles were never captured, but remained in the mountains, and as late as Nov., 1900, manifested their hostile character by an attack on Mormon settlers in Chihuahua. Apache hostility in Arizona and New Mexico, however, has entirely ceased. (See Hodge in Encyc. Brit., "Indians," 1902.)

Being a nomadic people, the Apache practised agriculture only to a limited extent before their permanent establishment on reservations. They subsisted chiefly on the products of the chase and on roots (especially that of the maguey) and berries. Although fish and bear were found in abundance in their country they were not eaten, being tabued as food. They had few arts, but the women attained high skill in making baskets. Their dwellings were shelters of brush, which were easily erected by the women and were well adapted to their arid environment and constant shifting. In physical appearance the Apache vary greatly, but are rather above the medium height. They are good talkers, are not readily deceived, and are honest in protecting property placed in their care, although they formerly obtained their chief support from plunder seized in their forays.

The Apache are divided into a number of tribal groups which have been so differently named and defined that it is sometimes difficult to determine to which branch writers refer. The most commonly accepted divisions are the Querechos or Vaqueros, consisting of the Mescaleros, Jicarillas, Faraones, Llaneros, and probably the Lipan; the Chiricahua; the Pinaleños; the Coyoteros, comprising the White Mountain and Pinal divisions; the Arivaipa; the Gila Apache, including the Gileños, Mimbreños, and Mogollones; and the Tontos. The present official designation of the divisions, with their population in 1903, is as follows: White Mountain Apache (comprising the Arivaipa, Tsiltaden or Chilion, Chiricahua, Coyoteros, Mimbreños, Mogollones, Pinals, "San Carlos," and Tontos), under Ft Apache agency, 2,058; Apache consisting of the same divisions as above, under San Carlos agency, 2,275; Apache at Angora, Ariz., 38; Jicarillas under school superintendent in New Mexico, 782; Mescaleros under Mescalero agency, N. Mex., 464; Chiricahua at Ft Sill, Okla., 298; Kiowa Apache, under Kiowa agency, Okla., 156. Besides these there were 19 Lipan in N. w. Chihuahua, some of the survivors of a tribe which, owing to their hostility, was almost destroyed, chiefly by Mexican Kickapoo cooperating with Mexican troops. This remnant was removed from Zaragoza, Coahuila, to Chihuahua in Oct., 1903, and a year later were brought to the U. S. and placed under the Mescalero agency in New Mexico. Until 1904 there lived with the

Apache of Arizona a number of Indians of Yuman stock, particularly "Mohave Apache," or Yavapai, but these are now mostly established at old Camp McDowell. The forays and conquests of the Apache resulted in the absorption of a large foreign element, Piman, Yuman, and Spanish, although captives were treated with disrespect and marriages with them broke clan ties. The Pinal Coyoteros, and evidently also the Jicarillas, had some admixture of Pueblo blood. The Tontos (q. v.) were largely of mixed blood according to Corbusier, but Hrdlicka's observations show them to be pure Apache. Tribes or bands known or supposed to be Apache, but not otherwise identifiable, are the following: Alacranes, Animas, Bissarhar, Chafalote, Cocoyes, Colina, Doestoe, Goolkizzen, Janos, Jocomes, Tejua, Tremblers, Zillgaw.

The Apache are divided into many clans which, however, are not totemic and they usually take their names from the natural features of localities, never from animals. Like clans of different Apache tribes recognize their affiliation. The Juniper clan found by Bourke among the White Mountain Apache at San Carlos agency and Ft Apache (Jour. Am. Folklore, III, 112, 1890), called by them Yogoyekayden, reappears as Chokonni among the Chiricahua and as Yagoyecayn among the Pinal Coyoteros. The White Mountain Apache have a clan called Destchin (Red Paint), which is correlated to the Chie clan of the Chiricahua and appears to have separated from the Satchin (Red Rock) clan, both being represented among the Navaho by the Dhestshini (Red Streak). The Carrizo clan, Klokadakaydn, of San Carlos agency and Ft Apache is the Klugaducayn (Arrow Reed) of the Pinal Coyoteros. Tutzose, the Water clan of the Pinal Coyoteros, is found also among the White Mountain Apache, who have a Walnut clan, called Chiltneyadnaye, as the Pinal Coyotero have one called Chisnedinadinaye. Natootzuzn (Point of Mountain), a clan at San Carlos agency, corresponds to Nagosugn, a Pinal Coyotero clan. Tizsessinaye (Little Cottonwood Jungle of the former) seems to have divided into the clans Titsessinaye of the Pinal Coyotero, of the same signification, and Destchetinaye (Tree in a Spring of Water). Kayhatin is the name of the Willow clan among both, and the Navaho have one, called Kai. Tzisequittzillan (Twin Peaks) of the White Mountain Apache, Tziltadin (Mountain Slope) of the Pinal Coyotero, and Navaho Dsilanothilni (Encircled Mountain), and Tsayiskidhni (Sage-brush Hill), are supposed by Bourke to have had a common origin. And there are many others traceable in the various Apache divisions and in the Navaho.

**Ai-a′-ta.**—Henshaw, MS. vocab., B. A. E., 1883 (Panamint name). **Apacci.**—Clavijero, Storia della Cal., I, 29, 1789. **Apachas.**—Hardy, Trav. in Mex., 438, 1829. **Apache.**—Benavides, Memorial, 50, 1630. **Apacherian.**—Bigelow in Pac. R. R. Rep., IV, 7, 1856. **Apaches.**—Oñate (1598) in Doc. Inéd., XVI, 114, 1871. **Apachis.**—Humboldt, Kingd. N. Sp., II, 271, 1811. **Apachu.**—N. Y. Nation, XLII, 397, May 13, 1886. **Apaci.**—Clavigero, Storia della Cal., map, 1789. **Apades.**—Oñate (1598) in Doc. Inéd., XVI, 114, 303, 1871 (misprint). **Apaehe.**—Beckwith in Pac. R. R. Rep., II, 28, 1855 (misprint). **A-pa-huache.**—Thomas, Yuma vocab., B. A. E., 1868 (Yuma name). **Apatch.**—Latham (1853) in Proc. Ethnol. Soc. Lond., VI, 74, 1854. **Apátches.**—Derbanne (1717) in Margry, Déc., VI, 206, 1886. **Apáts.**—Gatschet, MS., B. A. E. (Seri name). **Apatschees.**—Bancroft, Nat. Races, V, 641, 1882. **Apatsh.**—Latham in Trans. Philol. Soc. Lond., 105, 1856. **Apedes.**—Columbus Mem. Vol., 155, 1893 (misprint). **Apiches.**—Oñate (1599) in Doc. Inéd., XVI, 308, 1871 (misprint). **Apichi.**—Espejo misquoted by Bourke, On the Border with Crook, 122, 1891. **Apoches.**—Perea, Segunda Rel., 4, 1633. **Appaches.**—Ind. Aff. Rep., 1837. **Appaches.**—Sibley, Hist. Sketches, 110, 1806. **Appeches.**—Schermerhorn in Mass. Hist. Coll., II, 29, 1814. **A-pwa′-tci.**—Dorsey, MS. Kansa vocab., B. A. E., 1883 (Kansa form). **Atokúwe.**—ten Kate, Synonymie, 10, 1884 (Kiowa name). **Awátch.**—Ibid., 8 (Ute name). **Awátche.**—Ibid. **Áwp.**—Grossman, Pima and Papago vocab., B. A. E., 1871 (Pima name). **Chah′-shm.**—Whipple, Pac. R. R. Rep., III, pt. 3, 89, 1856 (Santo Domingo Keres name). **Chïshyë′.**—Hodge, field notes, B. A. E., 1895 (Laguna name). **Ha-ma-kaba-mitc kwa-dig.**—Corbusier, MS. Mojave vocab., B. A. E., 1885 (Mohave name: 'faraway Mohaves'). **H'iwana.**—Hodge, field notes, B.A.E., 1895 (Taos name: 'filthy people'). **Igihua′-a.**—Gatschet, Yuma-Spr., III, 86, 1886 (Havasupai name). **Inde.**—Bourke in Jour. Am. Folk-lore, II, 181, 1889 (own name). **Jarosoma.**—Kino (1700) in Doc. Hist. Mex., 4th ser., I, 346, 1856 (Pima name). **Mountain Comanche.**—Yoakum, Hist. Texas, I, map, 1855. **Muχtsuhintan.**—Gatschet, MS. Cheyenne vocab., B. A. E. (Cheyenne name). **N'day.**—Bandelier in Arch. Inst. Papers, III, 175, 1890 (original tribal name). **'Ndé.**—ten Kate, Reizen in N. Am., 196, 1885 (a form of Tinneh: 'people'). **N'De.**—Bandelier in Arch. Inst. Papers, III, 259, 1890. **Oop.**—ten Kate, Reizen in N. Am., 26, 1885 (Papago name). **Op.**—Gatschet, Yuma-Spr., III, 86, 1886 (Pima name). **Orp.**—Whipple, Pac. R. R. Rep., III, pt. 3, 94, 1856 (Pima name). **Paches.**—Parker, Jour., 32, 1840. **Patchisági.**—Gatschet, Shawnee MS., B. A. E. (Shawnee name). **Petchisági.**—Ibid. (alternative Shawnee form). **Póanïn.**—Hodge, field notes, B. A. E., 1895 (Sandia and Isleta name). **P'ónin.**—Gatschet, MS. Isleta vocab. (Isleta name). **Red Apaches.**—Vargas (1692) transliterated by Davis, Span. Conq. N. Mex., 371, 1869. **Shis-Inday.**—Cremony, Life among Apaches, 243, 1868 ('men of the woods': so called by themselves because their winter quarters are always located amidst forests). **Tá-ashi.**—Gatschet, Comanche MS., B. A. E. (Comanche name for Apache in general: 'turned up,' referring to their moccasins). **Tagúi.**—Mooney in 14th Rep. B. A. E., 1081, 1896 (old Kiowa name). **Tágukerésh.**—Hodge, Pueblo MS. notes, B. A. E., 1895 (Pecos name; see *Querecho*). **Tashïn.**—Mooney in 17th Rep., B. A. E., 245, 1898 (Comanche name). **Taχkáhe.**—Gatschet, MS. Arapaho vocab. (Arapaho name; cf. *Tha′kahine′na*, 'saw-fiddle men,' under *Kiowa Apache*). **Thaĥ-a-i-nin′.**—Hayden, Ethnog. and Philol. Mo. Val., 326, 1862 ('people who play on bone instruments,' that is, a pair of buffalo ribs, one notched, over which the other is rubbed: Arapaho name). **Tinde.**—Bourke in Jour. Am. Folk-lore, II, 181, 1889 ('people': own name). **Tinnä′-ash.**—Gatschet, MS. Wichita vocab., B. A. E., (Wichita name; cf. *Gïnä′s* under *Kiowa Apache*). **Tokúwe.**—ten Kate, Synonymie,

10,1884 (Kiowa name). **Tshishé.**—Ibid., 7 (Laguna name). **Utce-oí-nyu-mûh.**—Fewkes in Jour. Am. Folk-lore, V, 33, 1892 (Hopi name). **Útsaamu—**Voth, Traditions of the Hopi, 59, 1905 (Hopi name). **Xa-hë′-ta-ño′.**—Gatschet, inf'n, 1891 (Cheyenne name: 'those who tie their hair back'). **Yapaches.**—Robin, Voy. à la Louisiane, III, 14, 1807. **Yostjéemé.**—ten Kate, Reizen in N. Am., 259, 1885 (Hopi name). **Yotché-eme.**—ten Kate, Synonymie, 7, 1884 (Hopi name). **Yuíttcemo.**—Stephen in 8th Rep. B. A. E., 35, 1891 (Hopi name). **Yúte-shay.**—Bourke, Moquis of Ariz., 118, 1884 (Hopi name).

**Apaches del Perrillo** (Span.: 'Apaches of the little dog'). A band of Apache occupying, in the 16th and 17th centuries, the region of the Jornada del Muerto, near the Rio Grande, in s. N. Mex., where a spring was found by a dog, thus saving the Spaniards much suffering from thirst. They were probably a part of the Mescaleros or of the Mimbreños of later date. (F. W. H.)

**Apaches del perillo.**—De l'Isle, map Am. Sept., 1700. **Apaches del Perrillo.**—Benavides, Memorial, 14, 1630. **Apaches de Peryllo.**—Linschoten, Desc. de l'Am., map 1, 1638.

**Apaches del Quartelejo.** A band of Jicarillas which in the 17th and 18th centuries resided in the valley of Beaver cr., Scott co., Kans. The district was called Quartelejo by Juan Uribarri, who on taking possession in 1706 named it the province of San Luis, giving the name Santo Domingo to the Indian rancheria. See *Quartelejo.* (F. W. H.)

**Apaches del Cuartelejo.**—Bandelier in Arch. Inst. Papers, III, 181, 1890. **Apaches del Quartelejo.**—Rivera (1736), quoted by Bandelier, op. cit., V, 184, 1890. **Apaches of Cuartelejo.**—Bancroft, Ariz. and N. Mex., 236, 1889.

**Apaches Mansos** (Span.: 'tame Apaches'). An Apache band of Arizona consisting of 100 persons (Browne, Apache Country, 291, 1869). Apparently so called by the Mexicans in contradistinction to the more warlike Apache.

**Apahiachak.** A Kuskwogmiut Eskimo village in the Kuskokwim district, Alaska; pop. 91 in 1890.

**Apahiachamiut.**—11th Census, Alaska, 164, 1893 (here referring to the inhabitants).

**Apalache.** One of the principal native tribes of Florida, formerly holding the region N. of the bay now called by the name, from about the neighborhood of Pensacola E. to Ocilla r. The chief towns were about the present Tallahassee and St Marks. They were of Muskhogean stock, and linguistically more nearly related to the Choctaw than to the Creeks. The name is of uncertain etymology, but is believed by Gatschet to be from the Choctaw *A'palachi*, signifying '(people) on the other side.' The Apalachee were visited by the expeditions under Narvaez in 1528 and DeSoto in 1539, and the latter made their country his winter headquarters on account of its abundant resources for subsistence. The people were agricultural, industrious and prosperous, and noted above all the surrounding tribes for their fighting qualities, of which the Spanish adventurers had good proof. They continued resistance to the Spanish occupancy until after the year 1600, but were finally subdued and Christianized, their country becoming the most important center of missionary effort in Florida next to the St Augustine (Timucua) district. In 1655 they had 8 considerable towns, each with a Franciscan mission, besides smaller settlements, and a total population of 6,000 to 8,000. Their prosperity continued until about the year 1700, when they began to suffer from the raids by the wild Creek tribes to the N., instigated by the English government of Carolina, the Apalachee themselves being strongly in the Spanish interest. These attacks culminated in the year 1703, when a powerful expedition under Gov. Moore of Carolina, consisting of a company of white troops with a thousand armed savage allies of various tribes, invaded the Apalachee country, destroyed the towns and missions, with their fields and orange groves, killed the Spanish garrison commander and more than 200 Apalachee warriors, and carried off 1,400 of the tribe into slavery. Another expedition about a year later ravaged the neighboring territory and completed the destruction. The remnants of the Apalachee became fugitives among the friendly tribes or fled for protection to the French at Mobile, and although an effort was made by one of the Christian chiefs in 1718 to gather some of them into new mission villages (Soledad and San Luis) near Pensacola, the result was only temporarily successful. A part of the deported Apalachee were colonized by the Carolina government on Savannah r., at a settlement known as Palachoocla (Palachi-okla), or Apalachicola, but were finally merged into the Creeks. Those who settled under French protection near Mobile crossed the Mississippi into Louisiana after the cession of Florida to England in 1763, and continued to preserve their name and identity as late, at least, as 1804, when 14 families were still living on Bayou Rapide. Among the principal Apalachee towns or mission settlements of certain identification are Apalachee (1528–39 and later, believed to have been near the present Tallahassee), Ayavalla, Ivitachuco, San Marcos, San Juan, Santa Cruz, San Luis (1718), and Nuestra Señora de la Soledad (1718). Consult Barcia, Ensayo, 1723; Sibley, Hist. Sketches, 1806; Shea, Catholic Missions, 1855; Gatschet, Creek Migr. Legend, I, 1884. (J. M.)

Abalache.—Fontaneda (ca. 1559) in Doc. Inéd., v, 537, 1866. Abalachi.—Fontaneda in Ternaux Compans, xx, 19, 1841. Abolachi.—French, Hist. Coll., II, 256, 1875. Apahlahche.—Brinton, Florida, 92, 1859. Apalaccium.—Morelli, Fasti Novi Orbis, 20, 1776. Apalacha.—Quesada (1792) in Am. State Pap., Ind. Aff., I, 303, 1832. Apalache.—Biedma (1544) in Smith, Colec. Doc. Fla., 47, 1857. Apalachen.—Cabeza de Vaca (1528), Smith trans., 35, 1871. Apalachia.—Linschoten, Description de l'Amér., 6, 1638. Apalachians.—Harris, Voy. and Trav., II, 275, 1706. Apalachias.—McKenney and Hall, Ind. Tribes, III, 80, 1854. Apalachinos.—Barcia, Ensayo, 329, 1723. Apalachins.—Jefferys, Fr. Doms. Am., pt. 1, 161, 1761. Apalachis.—Rafinesque, introd. to Marshall, Ky., I, 23, 1824. Apalachita.—Hervas, Idea dell' Universo, XVII, 90, 1784 (name of language). Apalachites.—Oldmixon, Brit. Emp., II, 229, 1708. Apalans.—Rafinesque, introd. to Marshall, Ky., I, 23, 1824 (general term, used for several unrelated tribes). Apalatchees.—Rivers, Hist. S. C., 94, 1856. Apalatchia.—Carroll, Hist. Coll. S. C., II, 575, 1836. Apalatchy.—Coxe, Carolana, 22, 1741. Apalatci.—De Bry, Brev. Narr., II, map, 1591. Apalchen.—Mercator, map (1569), quoted in Maine Hist. Coll., I, 392, 1869. Apalehen.—Rafinesque in introd. to Marshall, Ky., I, 23, 1824. Apallachian Indians.—Mills, S. C., 222, 1826. Apelash.—Woodward, Reminiscences, 79, 1859. Apeolatei.—Brinton, Florida, 92, 1859. Apilaches.—Woodward, op. cit., 25. Apilashs.—Ibid., 39. Apolacka.—Holden (1707) in N. C. Col. Records, I, 664, 1886. Apolashe.—Schoolcraft, Ind. Tribes, III, 585, 1853. Appalaches.—Dumont, La., I, 134, 1753. Appalachians.—Mills, S. C., 107, 1826. Appalachites.—Schoolcraft in N. Y. Hist. Soc. Coll., 79, 1844. Appalachos.—Boudinot, Star in West, 125, 1816. Appallatcy.—French, Hist. Coll., II, 256, 1875. Appallatta.—Brinton, Florida, 92, 1859. Appelathas.—Moll, map in Humphreys, Hist. Acct., 1730. Appellachee.—Humphreys, Hist. Acct., 98, 1730. Asphalashe.—Clarke and Cass in H. R. Ex. Doc. 117, 20th Cong., 100, 1829. Palache.—Cabeza de Vaca (1527), Smith trans., 25, 1871. Palachees.—Coxe, Carolana, 22, map, 1741. Palatcy.—French, Hist. Coll., II, 256, 1875. Palaxy.—Brinton, Florida, 92, 1859. Peluches.—N. Y. Doc. Col. Hist., VII, 641, 1856. Tlapans.—Rafinesque, introd. to Marshall, Ky., I, 23, 1824 (given as an "Apalahan" province). Valachi.—Fontaneda in Doc. Inéd., v, 538, 1866.

Apalachicola (possibly 'people on the other side'). A Hitchiti town formerly situate on the w. bank of lower Chattahoochee r., Ala., a short distance below Chiaha, nearly opposite the present Columbus, Ga. Formerly one of the most important Hitchiti settlements, it had lost its importance by 1799. It was a peace town and received the name *Talua-hlako*, 'great town.' Bartram states that about 1750 it was moved up the river, and that the people spoke the Hitchiti dialect. In the abbreviated form Palatchukla the name is applied to part of Chattahoochee r. below the junction with Flint r. Hodgson (introd. to Hawkins, Sketch) states that "Palachookla," the capital of the confederacy, was a very ancient Uchee town, but this statement may be due to confusion with the later Apalachicola (q. v.) on Savannah r., S. C. The name Apalachicola was also frequently used by both Spaniards and French in the 18th century to include all the Lower Creeks then settled on Chattahoochee r. (J. M.)

Apalachecolo.—Barcia (1718), Ensayo Cron., 336, 1723. Apalachicoloes.—Archdale in Carroll, Hist. Coll. S. C., II, 107, 1707. Apalachicoly.—Iberville (1701) in Margry, Déc., IV, 594, 1880. Apalachicoulys.—Ibid., 551. Apalachoocla.—U. S. Ind. Treat. (1814), 162, 1837. Apalachucla.—Bartram, Travels, 387, 1791. Apalatchúkla.—Gatschet, Creek Migr. Leg., I, 68, 1884. Apalatchy-Cola.—Coxe, Carolana, 29, 1741. Appalachicolas.—Gallatin, Arch. Am., 96,

1836. **Conchaques.**—Iberville in Margry, Déc., IV, 594, 1880. **English Indians.**—Archdale in Carroll, Hist. Coll. S. C., II, 107, 1707. **Itálua 'láko.**—Gatschet, Creek Migr. Leg., I, 145, 1884 ('great town': popular Creek name). **Pahlachocolo.**—Schoolcraft, Ind. Tribes, IV, 578, 1854. **Pah-lo-cho-kó-los.**—Drake, Bk. Inds., IV, 94, 1848. **Palachicolas.**—Jefferys, French Dom., map, 134, 1761. **Palachocalas.**—Stevens, Hist. Ga., 117, 1847. **Palachoocla.**—Hodgson in Hawkins, Sketch (1799), 17, 1848. **Pā-lā-chooc-le.**—Hawkins, ibid., 65. **Palachuckolas.**—McCall, Hist. Georgia, I, 363, 1811. **Palachuola.**—Swan (1791) in Schoolcraft, Ind. Tribes, V, 262, 1855. **Parachuctaus.**—Boudinot, Star in West, 128, 1816. **Paracpoocla.**—Hodgson in Hawkins, Sketch, 17, 1848. **Polachucolas.**—Drake, Bk. of Inds., 29, 1848. **Poollachuchlaw.**—Moll, map in Humphreys, Hist. Acct., 1730. **Tallawa Thlucco.**—U. S. Ind. Treat. (1827), 420, 1837. **Tal-lo-wau thlucco.**—Hawkins, Sketch (1799), 65, 1848. **Tálua 'láko.**—Gatschet, Creek Migr. Leg., I, 145, 1884. **Tolowarch.**—H. R. Ex. Doc. 276, 24th Cong. 308, 1836. **Tolowar thlocco.**—Schoolcraft, Ind. Tribes, IV, 578, 1854.

**Apalachicola.** A town on Savannah r., in what is now Hampton co., S. C., where was settled a remnant of the Apalachee from the towns about Apalachee bay, which were carried thither as captives when the tribe was destroyed by Gov. Moore in 1703. (A. S. G.)

**Apalou.** An unidentified village near the mouth of St Johns r., Fla., in 1564.—Laudonnière in French, Hist. Coll. La., n. s., 315, 1869.
**Appalou.**—De Bry, Brev. Nar., map, 1591.

**Apangasi.** A former Miwok village on Tuolumne r., Tuolumne co., Cal.
**Apangape.**—McKee et al. (1851) in Sen. Ex. Doc. 4, 32d Cong., spec. sess., 74, 1853 (misprint). **Apangasi.**—Latham in Trans. Philol. Soc. Lond., 81, 1856. **Apangasse.**—Barbour et al. (1851) in Sen. Ex. Doc. 4, 32d Cong., spec. sess., 70, 1853. **A-pang-assi.**—Johnston (1851) in Sen. Ex. Doc. 61, 32d Cong., 1st sess., 22, 1852. **Apoung-o-sse.**—Ind. Aff. Rep., 222, 1851. **Ap-yang-ape.**—Barbour (1852) in Sen. Ex. Doc. 4, 32d Cong., spec. sess., 252, 1853 (misprint).

**Apannow.** See *Epanow.*

**Apap** (*A'pap*). A social division of the Pima, belonging to the Stoamohimal, or White Ants, phratral group.—Russell, Pima MS., B. A. E., 313, 1903.

**Apaqssos** ('deer'). A subphratry or gens of the Menominee.—Hoffman in 14th Rep. B. A. E., pt. 1, 42, 1896.

**Apatai** ('a covering,' from *apatayas*, 'I cover'). A former subordinate village of the Lower Creek town Kasihta, on a creek 20 m. E. of Chattahoochee r., Ga., probably on the site of the present town of Upatoie, on a creek of the same name in Muscogee co., Ga.
**Au-put-tau-e.**—Hawkins, Sketch (1799), 59, 1848.

**Apatsiltlizhihi** ('black [*tlizhi*] Apache'). A division of the Jicarilla Apache who claim the district of Mora, N. Mex., as their former home. (J. M.)
**Äpä'tsil-tlĭ-zhi'hi.**—Mooney, field notes, B. A. E., 1897.

**Apeche.** A Luiseño village w. of San Luis Rey mission, San Diego co., Cal.
**Apeche.**—Jackson and Kinney, Rep. Miss. Ind., 29, 1883. **La Piche.**—Ind. Aff. Rep. 1902, 175, 1903.

**Apena.** A pueblo of New Mexico in 1598; doubtless situated in the Salinas, in the vicinity of Abo, and occupied by the Tigua or the Piros.—Oñate (1598) in Doc. Inéd., XVI, 114, 1871.

**Aperger.** The Yurok name of a Karok village on the w. bank of Klamath r., several miles below Orleans Bar, said to consist of 10 houses in 1852. (A. L. K.)
**Sogorem.**—Kroeber, inf'n, 1903 (said to be the Karok name).

**Apewantanka** (*ape* 'leaf,' 'fin,' *apehin* 'mane,' *tangka* 'large': 'large manes [of horses]'). A division of the Brulé Sioux.
**Apewan tanka.**—Dorsey in 15th Rep. B. A. E., 218, 1897. **Apewan-tañka.**—Ibid.

**Apichi.** A "family" or division of the Cuyuhasomi phratry of the Timucua.—Pareja (*ca.* 1612) quoted by Gatschet in Am. Philos. Soc. Proc., XVII, 492, 1878.

**Apikaiyiks** ('skunks'). A division of the Kainah and of the Piegan.
**Ah-pe-ki'.**—Morgan, Anc. Soc., 171, 1877 (Kainah). **Ah-pe-ki'-e.**—Ibid. (Piegan). **Ap'-i-kai-yiks.**—Grinnell, Blackfoot Lodge Tales, 209, 1892 (Kainah and Piegan). **A-pi-kai'-yĭks.**—Hayden, Ethnog. and Philol. Mo. Val., 264, 1862 (Piegan).

**Apil.** A Costanoan village, containing neophytes in 1819 according to Friar Olbez; situated near the mission of Santa Cruz, Cal.—Taylor in Cal. Farmer, Apr. 5, 1860.

**Apish, Apisha.** See *Pishaug.*

**Apishamore.** A saddle blanket, made of buffalo-calf skins, used on the great prairies (Bartlett, Dict. Americanisms, 15, 1877). An impossible derivation of this word from the French *empêchement* has been suggested. Meaning and form make it evident that the term is a corruption of *apishimon*, which in the Chippewa and closely related dialects of Algonquian signifies 'anything to lie down upon.' (A. F. C.)

**Apishaug.** See *Pishaug.*

**Apistonga.** An unidentified tribe apparently in N. Ala.; marked on Marquette's map of 1673 (Shea, Discov., 268, 1852).

**Aplache.** Given as the name of a band and its village on upper Tuolumne r., Tuolumne co., Cal., in 1850. According to Adam Johnson (Schoolcraft, Ind. Tribes, IV, 407, 1854) the people could not speak the Miwok language; nevertheless, judging by their location and the bands with which they are mentioned, it is probable that they belonged to the Moquelumnan family.
**Ap-la-che.**—Barbour (1852) in Sen. Ex. Doc. 4, 32d Cong., spec. sess., 252, 1853.

**Apohola** ('buzzard'). A Timucua phratry which included the Nuculaha, Nuculahaqus, Nuculaharuqui, Chorofa, Usinaca, Ayahanisino, Napoya, Amacahuri, Hauenayo, and Amusaya clans. They were prohibited from marrying among themselves.—Pareja (*ca.* 1612) quoted by Gatschet in Proc. Am. Philos. Soc., XVII, 492, 1878.

**Apoholythas.** A Creek town in Indian Ter., 10 m. from the N. fork of Canadian r.—Raines (1838) in H. R. Doc. 219, 27th Cong., 3d sess., 110, 1843.

**Apokak.** A Kuskwogmiut Eskimo village near the mouth of Kuskokwim r., Alaska; pop. 94 in 1880, 210 in 1890.
Ahpokagamiut.—11th Census, Alaska, 164, 1893. Apokachamute.—Hallock in Nat. Geog. Mag., 88, 1898. Apokagmute.—Petroff, 10th Census, Alaska, 153, 1884.

**Aponitre.** A pueblo of the province of Atripuy in the region of the lower Rio Grande, N. Mex., in 1598.—Oñate (1598) in Doc. Inéd., XVI, 115, 1871.

**Apontigoumy.** An Ottawa village, attacked by the Seneca in 1670.—Courcelles (1670) in N. Y. Doc. Col. Hist., IX, 788, 1855.

**Apoon.** A Chnagmiut village on Apoon pass, the N. mouth of Yukon r., Alaska.
Aphoon.—Post-route map, 1903.

**Aposon.** See *Opossum.*

**Apoya.** The extinct Sky clan of the Zuñi.
Ápoya-kwe.—Cushing in 13th Rep. B. A. E., 368, 1896 (kwe=‘people’).

**Apozolco.** A former pueblo of the Colotlan division of the Cora and the seat of a mission, situated on the Rio Colotlan, a tributary of the Rio Grande de Santiago, Jalisco, Mexico.—Orozco y Berra, Geog., 280, 1864.

**Appeelatat.** A Montagnais village on the s. coast of Labrador.—Stearns, Labrador, 271, 1884.

**Appoans.** See *Pone.*

**Appocant.** A village of the Powhatan confederacy in 1608 on the N. bank of Chickahominy r., New Kent co., Va.—Smith (1629), Virginia, map, repr. 1819.

**Appomattoc.** A tribe of the Powhatan confederacy formerly living on lower Appomattox r., Va. They had 60 warriors in 1608, and were of some importance as late as 1671, but were extinct by 1722. Their principal village, which bore the same name and was on the site of Bermuda Hundred, Prince George co., was burned by the English in 1611. Appomatox was also one of the terms applied to the Matchotic, a later combination of remnants of the same confederacy.
(J. M.)
Apamatica.—Percy in Purchas, Pilgrimes, IV, 1,688, 1626. Apamaticks.—Lawson (1701), Hist. Carolina, 163, 1860. Apamatuck.—Smith quoted by Drake, Bk. Inds., bk. 4, 10, 1848. Apamatuk.—Smith (1629), Virginia, II, 12, repr. 1819. Apomatock.—Batts (1671) in N. Y. Doc. Col. Hist., III, 193, 1853. Appamatox.—Beverly, Virginia, 199, 1722. Appamattocs.—Jefferson, Notes, 179, 1801. Appamattucks.—Strachey (1612 ?), Virginia, VI, 35, 1849. Appamatucks.—Smith (1629), Virginia, I, 116, repr. 1819. Appomatocks.—Macauley, N. Y., II, 166, 1829. Appomattake.—Doc. of 1643 in N. C. Col. Rec., I, 17, 1886. Appomatuck.—Doc. of 1728, ibid., II, 784, 1886. Appomotacks.—Boudinot, Star in the West, 125, 1816.

**Apukasasocha** (apoka=‘settlement’). A former Seminole town of which Enehemathlochee was chief in 1823, situated 20 m. w. of the head of St Johns r., central Fla.—H. R. Ex. Doc. 74, 19th Cong., 27, 1826.

**Apuki** (A′pŭkĭ). A social divison of the Pima, belonging to the Stoamohimal, or White Ants, phratral group.—Russell, Pima MS., B. A. E., 313, 1903.

**Aputitek.** A ruined Eskimo village in E. Greenland, lat. 67° 47′.—Meddelelser om Grönland, XXVII, map, 1902.

**Aputosikainah** (‘northern Bloods’). A band of the Kainah division of the Siksika.
Ap-ut′-o-si-kai-nah.—Grinnell, Blackfoot Lodge Tales, 209, 1892.

**Apyu.** The Yurok name of the northern part of the important Karok village of Katimin, on Klamath r., Cal., a mile above the mouth of the Salmon. (A.L.K.)

**Aqbirsiarbing** (‘a lookout for whales’). A winter settlement of Nugumiut at C. True, Baffin land.—Boas in 6th Rep. B. A. E., 422, 1888.

**Aquacalecuen.** A Timuquanan village near Suwannee r., N. w. Fla., visited by De Soto in 1539.—Biedma (1544) in French, Hist. Coll. La., II, 98, 1850.
Caliquen.—Gentl. of Elvas (1557) in French, op. cit., 131.

**Aquackanonk** (from ach-quoa-k-kannonk, ‘a place in a rapid stream where fishing is done with a bush-net.’—Nelson). A division of the Unami Delawares which occupied lands on Passaic r., N. J., and a considerable territory in the interior, including the tract known as Dundee, in Passaic, just below the Dundee dam, in 1678. In 1679 the name was used to describe a tract in Saddle River township, Bergen co., as well as to designate "the old territory, which included all of Paterson s. of the Passaic r., and the city of Paterson." The Aquackanonk sold lands in 1676 and 1679. See Nelson and Ruttenber, below.
Achquegenonck.—Doc. of 1714 quoted by Nelson, Inds. N. J., 122, 1894. Achquickenough.—Doc. of 1696, ibid. Achquickenunck.—Doc. of 1698, ibid. Achquickenunk.—Doc. of 1696, ibid. Achquikanuncque.—Doc. of 1698, ibid. Ackquekenon.—Doc. of 1679, ibid. Acquackanonk.—Ruttenber, Tribes Hudson R., 91, 1872. Acquicanunck.—Doc. of 1692 quoted by Nelson, op. cit. Acquiggenonck.—Doc. of 1693, ibid. Acquikanong.—Doc. of 1706, ibid. Amakaraongky.—De Laet (ca. 1633) in N. Y. Hist. Soc. Coll., 2d s., I, 315, 1841 (same?). Aquachonongue.—Doc. of 1696 quoted by Nelson, op. cit. Aquackanonks.—De Laet, op. cit. Aquaninoncke.—Doc. of 1683 quoted by Nelson, op. cit. Aquaquanuncke.—Doc. of 1684, ibid. Aqueckenonge.—Doc. of 1696, ibid. Aqueckkonunque.—Doc. of 1698, ibid. Aquegnonke.—Doc. of 1679, ibid. Aqueyquinunke.—Doc. of 1682, ibid. Aquickanucke.—Doc. of 1678, ibid. Aquickanunke.—Doc. of 1685, ibid. Aquoechononque.—Doc. of 1698, ibid. Hackquickanon.—Doc. of 1694, ibid. Hacquickenunk.—Doc. of 1696, ibid. Haghquagenonck.—Doc. of 1736, ibid. Haquequenunck.—De Laet, op. cit. Haquicqueenock.—Doc. of 1678, ibid. Hockquackanonk.—Doc. of 1707, ibid. Hockquackonong.—Ibid. Hockquecanung.—Doc. of 1683, ibid. Hockquekanung.—Doc. of 1680, ibid. Hockquickanon.—Doc. of 1693, ibid.

**Aquadocta.** The dwelling place of "a tribe of Indians" in 1690, living westward from Casco and Saco, Me., and seemingly allied with the Abnaki.—Niles (*ca.* 1761) in Mass. Hist. Soc. Coll.,3d s., VI, 217, 1837.

**Aquascogoc.** An Algonquian village on the coast of Hyde co., N. C., at the time of the first visit of the English. It was burned by them in 1585.

Agnascoga.—Martin, N. C., I, 30, 1829. Aguasco-sack.—Bozman, Maryland, I, 60, 1837. Aquasco-goc.—Lane (1586) in Smith (1629), Virginia, I, 86, repr. 1819. Aquascogoke.—Strachey (*ca.* 1612), Virginia, 145, 1849. Aquoscojos.—Schoolcraft, Ind. Tribes, VI, 93, 1857. Aqusoogock.—Dutch map (1621) in N. Y. Doc. Col. Hist., I, 1856.

**Aquebogue** (the word suggests the Chippewa *ä'kupiyag*, a locative term referring to the place where land and water meet; it has the meaning 'shore,' but the specific use is for 'the edge of the water,' the point of view being from the land; *ä'ku* refers to the 'end,' 'edge,' *pi* to 'water.'—Wm. Jones). A village, probably of the Corchaug, about the year 1650, on a creek entering the N. side of Great Peconic bay, Long Island (Ruttenber; Thompson). In 1905 R. N. Penny (in Rec. of Past, IV, 223, 1905) discovered the remains of an ancient village "of 12-wigwam size" in a thick wood near Aquebogue, inland from Peconic bay, w. of the w. branch of Steeple Church cr. and between that stream and a large tributary of Peconic r. These may be the remains of the ancient Aquebogue.

Accopogue.—Ruttenber, Tribes Hudson R., 365, 1872. Aquebogue.—Thompson, Long Id.,181,1839.

**Aquetnet** (*aquetn-et*, 'at an island.'—Trumbull). A village in 1655 at Skauton neck, Sandwich tp., Barnstable co., Mass., under chief Ackanootus, in the territory of the Nauset. The word seems to be the same as Aquidneck (Quidnick), R. I., which Trumbull thinks means 'place at the end of the hill,' compounded from *ukque-adene-auke;* or possibly 'place beyond the hill,' *ogque-adene-auke.* Mentioned by a writer of 1815 in Mass. Hist. Soc. Coll., 2d s., IV, 293, 1816. (J. M.)

**Aqui.** A former Maricopa rancheria on the Rio Gila, s. w. Ariz.—Sedelmair (1744) quoted by Bancroft, Ariz. and N. Mex., 366, 1889.

**Aquicabo.** A pueblo of the province of Atripuy in the region of the lower Rio Grande, N. Mex., in 1598.—Oñate (1598) in Doc. Inéd., XVI, 115, 1871.

Aquicato.—Oñate misquoted by Bancroft, Ariz. and N. Mex., 135, 1889.

**Aquile.** A village in N. w. Fla. on the border of the Apalachee territory, visited by De Soto in 1539.—Biedma (1544) in French, Hist. Coll., II, 98, 1850.

**Aquimundurech.** A former Maricopa rancheria on the Rio Gila, s. w. Ariz.—Sedelmair (1744) quoted by Bancroft, Ariz. and N. Mex., 366, 1889.

**Aquimuri** (probably from Pima *akimurl,* 'river'). A rancheria of one of the

Piman tribes, probably Papago, visited by Father Kino about 1700; situated in Sonora, on the headwaters of the Rio Altar, just s. of the Arizona boundary. It was later a visita of the mission of Guevavi. Consult Rudo Ensayo (1763), 150, 1863; Kino, map (1701) in Bancroft, Ariz. and N. Mex., 360, 1889.

Akimuri.—Kino, map (1701) in Stöcklein, Neue Welt-Bott, 74, 1726. Aquimuricuca.—Cancio (1768) in Doc. Hist. Mex., 4th s., II, 270, 1856. S. Bernardo Aquimuri.—Kino quoted by Bancroft, No. Mex. States, I, 501, 1884.

**Aquinsa.** Mentioned by Oñate in 1598 as one of 6 villages occupied by the Zuñi in New Mexico. In the opinion of Bandelier (Arch. Inst. Papers, IV, 338, 1892) it is identical with Pinawan, a now ruined pueblo 1½ m. s. w. of Zuñi pueblo. Cushing (in Millstone, IX, 55, 1884) regarded Ketchina, 15 m. s. w. of Zuñi, as the probable Aquinsa of the Spaniards, and in 1888 (Internat. Cong. Amer., VII, 156, 1890) the same authority gave Kwakina in connection with Pinawan as the pueblo to which Oñate referred.

**Aquitun** (*Akuchiny*, 'creek mouth'—Russell). A former Pima rancheria 5 m. w. of Picacho, on the border of the sink of Rio Santa Cruz, s. Ariz., visited by Father Garcés in 1775. It was abandoned about the beginning of the 19th century. A few Mexican families have occupied its vicinity for many years. The present Pima claim that it was a village of their forefathers.

Akútciny.—Russell, Pima MS., B. A. E., 16, 1902 (Pima name; *tc=ch*). Aquitun.—Arricivita, Crón. Seráf., II, 416, 1792. Bajio de Aquituno.—Anza and Font (1780) quoted by Bancroft, Ariz. and N. Mex., 392, 1889. Equituni.—Garcés (1776), Diary, 65, 1900.

**Aquixo.** A town visited by De Soto's army in 1541, situated on the w. bank of the Mississippi, not far from the mouth of St Francis r., Ark., and perhaps belonging to the Quapaw. (Gentl. of Elvas, 1557, quoted in French, Hist. Coll. La., II, 169, 1850.)

**Aquouena.** An unidentified town w. of upper St Johns r., Fla., in 1565.—De Bry, Brev. Nar., II, map, 1591.

**Aracuchi.** An unidentified village apparently in N. w. S. C., visited by Juan Pardo in 1565.—Vandera (1567) in Smith, Colec. Docs. Fla., I, 17, 1857.

Arauchi.—Vandera, op. cit.

**Aragaritka.** The name given by the Iroquois to the tribes, including the Huron and Tionontati, which they drove out from the peninsula between L. Huron and L. Erie and from lower Michigan.—Iroquois deed (1701) in N. Y. Doc. Col. Hist., IV, 908, 1854.

**Arahasomi** ('bear gens,' from *ara* 'black bear,' *hasomi* 'family'). A Timucua clan of the Chulufichi phratry.—Pareja (*ca.* 1612) quoted by Gatschet in Proc. Am. Philos. Soc., XVII, 492, 1878.

**Aramay.** A former village, presumably Costanoan, connected with Dolores mission, San Francisco, Cal.—Taylor in Cal. Farmer, Oct. 18, 1861.

**Aranama.** A small agricultural tribe formerly living on and near the s. coast of Texas; later they were settled for a time at the mission of Espiritu Santo de Zúñiga, opposite the present Goliad, where some Karankawa Indians were also neophytes. It is reported that they had previously suffered from an attack by the Karankawa. Morse located them in 1822 on San Antonio r. and estimated them at 125 souls. In 1834 Escudero (Not. Estad. de Chihuahua, 231) spoke of them as follows: "The same coast and its islands are inhabited by the Curancahuases and Jaranames Indians, fugitives from the missions. The larger portion have lately settled in the new mission of Nuestra Señora del Refugio, and to-day very few rebellious families remain, so that the injuries caused by these cowardly but cruel Indians have ceased." As a tribe the Aranama were extinct by 1843. (A. C. F.)

**Anames.**—Rivera, Diario y Derrot., leg. 2,602, 1736. **Aranamas.**—Thrall, Hist. Texas, 446, 1879. **Aranâmes.**—Rivera, op. cit. **Arrenamuses.**—Morse, Rep. to Sec. War, 374, 1822. **Aurananeans.**—Boudinot, Star in the West, 125, 1816. **Hazanames.**—Robin, Voy. à la Louisiane, III, 14, 1807. **Jaranames.**—Escudero, Not. Estad. de Chihuahua, 231, 1834. **Juranames.**—Morfi quoted by Bancroft, No. Mex. States, I, 631, 1886. **Xaramenes.**—Bollaert in Ethnol. Soc. Lond. Jour., II, 265, 280, 1850. **Xaranames.**—Texas State Archives, MS. no. 83, 1791- 92.

**Aranca.** The name of two Pima villages in s. Ariz., one with 208 inhabitants in 1858, the other with 991.—Bailey in Ind. Aff. Rep., 208, 1858.

**Aranimokw.** The Yurok name of a Karok village near Red Cap cr., an affluent of Klamath r., Cal. (A. L. K.)

**Arapaho.** An important Plains tribe of the great Algonquian family, closely associated with the Cheyenne for at least a century past. They call themselves *Inuñaina*, about equivalent to 'our people.' The name by which they are commonly known is of uncertain derivation, but it may possibly be, as Dunbar suggests, from the Pawnee *tirapihu* or *larapihu*, 'trader.' By the Sioux and Cheyenne they are called "Blue-sky men" or "Cloud men," the reason for which is unknown.

According to the tradition of the Arapaho they were once a sedentary, agricultural people, living far to the N. E. of their more recent habitat, apparently about the Red r. valley of N. Minn. From this point they moved s. w. across the Missouri, apparently about the same time that the Cheyenne (q. v.) moved out from Minnesota, although the date of the formation of the permanent alliance between the two tribes is uncertain.

The Atsina (q. v.), afterward associated with the Siksika, appear to have separated from the parent tribe and moved off toward the N. after their emergence into the plains. The division into Northern and Southern Arapaho is largely geographic, originating within the last century, and made permanent by the placing of the two bands on different reservations. The Northern Arapaho, in Wyoming, are considered the nucleus or mother tribe and retain the sacred tribal articles, viz, a tubular pipe, one ear of corn, and a turtle figurine, all of stone.

Since they crossed the Missouri the drift of the Arapaho, as of the Cheyenne and Sioux, has been w. and s., the Northern Arapaho making lodges on the edge of

ARAPAHO MAN

the mountains about the head of the North Platte, while the Southern Arapaho continued down toward the Arkansas. About the year 1840 they made peace with the Sioux, Kiowa, and Comanche, but were always at war with the Shoshoni, Ute, and Pawnee until they were confined upon reservations, while generally maintaining a friendly attitude toward the whites. By the treaty of Medicine Lodge in 1867 the Southern Arapaho, together with the Southern Cheyenne, were placed upon a reservation in Oklahoma, which was thrown open to white settlement in 1892, the Indians at the same time receiving allotments in severalty, with the rights of American citizenship. The Northern Arapaho were assigned to their present reservation on Wind r. in Wyoming in 1876, after having made peace with their hereditary enemies, the Shoshoni, living upon the same reservation. The Atsina division, usually regarded as a distinct tribe, is associated with the Assiniboin on Ft Belknap res. in Montana. They numbered, respectively, 889, 859, and 535 in 1904, a total of 2,283, as against a total of 2,638 ten years earlier.

As a people the Arapaho are brave, but kindly and accommodating, and much given to ceremonial observances. The annual sun dance is their greatest tribal ceremony, and they were active propagators of the ghost-dance religion (q. v.) a few years ago. In arts and home life, until within a few years past, they were a typical Plains tribe. They bury their dead in the ground, unlike the Cheyenne and Sioux, who deposit them upon scaffolds or on the surface of the ground in boxes. They have the military organization common to most of the Plains tribes (see *Military societies*), and have no trace of the clan system.

They recognize among themselves five main divisions, each speaking a different dialect and apparently representing as many originally distinct but cognate tribes, viz:

(1) Nákasině′na, Báachiněna, or Northern Arapaho. Nakasiněna, 'sagebrush men,' is the name used by themselves. Baachiněna, 'red willow men (?),' is the name by which they were commonly known to the rest of the tribe. The Kiowa distinguished them as Tägyäko, 'sagebrush people,' a translation of their proper name. They keep the sacred tribal articles, and are considered the nucleus or mother tribe of the Arapaho, being indicated in the sign language (q. v.) by the sign for "mother people."

(2) Náwuněna, 'southern men,' or Southern Arapaho, called Nawathíněha, 'southerners,' by the Northern Arapaho. The Kiowa know them as Ähayädal, the (plural) name given to the wild plum. The sign for them is made by rubbing the index finger against the side of the nose.

(3) Aä′niněna, Hitúněna, Atsina, or Gros Ventres of the Prairie. The first name, said to mean 'white clay people,' is that by which they call themselves. Hitúněna, or Hituněnina, 'begging men,' 'beggars,' or more exactly 'spongers,' is the name by which they are called by the other Arapaho. The same idea is intended to be conveyed by the tribal sign, which has commonly been interpreted as 'big bellies,' whence the name Gros Ventres applied to them by the French Canadians. In this way they have been by some writers confused with the Hidatsa, the Gros Ventres of the Missouri. See *Atsina*.

(4) Bäsawuněna, 'wood-lodge people,' or, possibly, 'big lodge people.' These, according to tradition, were formerly a distinct tribe and at war with the Arapaho, but have been incorporated for at least 150 years. Their dialect is said to have differed considerably from the other Arapaho dialects. There are still about 50 of this lineage among the Northern Arapaho, and perhaps a few with the other two main divisions.

(5) Hánahawuněna ('rock men'— Kroeber) or Aanû′nhawă. These, like the Bäsawuněna, lived with the Northern Arapaho, but are now practically extinct.

The two main divisions, Northern and Southern, are subdivided into several local bands, as follows: (a) Forks of the River Men, (b) Bad Pipes, and (c) Greasy Faces, among the Northern Arapaho; (d) Wáquithi, bad faces, (e) Aqáthině′na, pleasant men, (f) Gawuněna, Blackfeet, said to be of Siksika admixture; (g) Háqihana, wolves, (h) Säsábäithi, looking up, or looking around, i. e., watchers.

Consult Mooney, Ghost Dance Religion, in 14th Rep. B. A. E., II, 1896; Clark, Ind. Sign Language, 1885; Hayden, Ethnog. and Philol. Mo. Val., 1862; Kroeber, The Arapaho, Bull. Am. Mus. Nat. Hist., XVIII, 1900; Dorsey and Kroeber, Traditions of the Arapaho, Field Columb. Mus. Pubs., Anthrop. ser., V, 1903; Dorsey, Arapaho Sun Dance, ibid., IV, 1903.

(J. M.)

**Aarapahoes.**—Blackmore, quoting Whitfield (1855) in Jour. Ethnol. Soc. Lond., I, 315, 1869. **Ähyä′to.**—Mooney in 14th Rep. B. A. E., 953, 1896 (Kiowa name). **Anapaho.**—Garrard, Wahtoyah, 119, 1850 (given as Cheyenne form). **A′nipahu.**—Gatschet, Kaw vocab., B. A. E., 1878 (Kansa name). **Ano′s-anyotskano.**—Mooney in 14th Rep. B. A. E., 953, 1896 (Kichai name). **Arapahas.**—Drake, Bk. Inds., vi, 1848. **Arapahays.**—Ross, Adventures, 232, 1849. **Arapaho.**—Ruxton, Adventures, 220, 1818. **Arapahoos.**—Mitchell in Ind. Aff. Rep., 59, 1842. **Äräpakäta.**—Mooney in 14th Rep. B. A. E., 953, 1896 (Crow name, from 'Arapaho'). **Araphahoe.**—Wyeth in Schoolcraft, Ind. Tribes, I, 219, 1851. **Araphas.**—Bollaert in Jour. Ethnol. Soc. Lond., II, 279, 1850. **Araphoes.**—Ibid. **Arophaes.**—Audouard, Far West, 182, 1869. **Arapoho.**—Hayden, Ethnog. and Philol. Mo. Val., 321, 1862. **Arapohose.**—Ibid., 402 (Crow name). **Arbapaoes.**—Orozco y Berra, Geog., 40, 1864. **Arepahas.**—Cass (1834) in Schoolcraft, Ind. Tribes, III, 609, 1853. **Aripahoes.**—Hildreth, Dragoon Campaigns, 153, 1836. **Aripohoes.**—Ind. Aff. Rep., app., 241, 1846. **Ar-rah-pa-hoo.**—Lewis and Clark, Travels, 15, 1807 (wrongly applied by them to a body of Pawnee). **Arrapahas.**—Ind. Aff. Rep., 594, 1837. **Arrapaho.**—Long, Exp. Rocky Mts., II, 192, 1823. **Arrapahoes.**—Dougherty (1837) in H. R. Doc. 276, 25th Cong., 2d sess., 16, 1838. **Arrapaoes.**—Gallatin in Trans. Am. Ethnol. Soc., II, cix, 1848. **Arraphas.**—Am. Pioneer, I, 257, 1842. **Arraphoes.**—Bollaert in Jour. Ethnol. Soc. Lond., II, 265, 1850. **Arrapohoes.**—Cumming in H. R. Ex. Doc. 65, 34th Cong., 1st sess., 13, 1856. **Arrepahas.**—Porter (1829) in Schoolcraft, Ind. Tribes, III, 596, 1853. **Arripahoes.**—Fitzpatrick in Ind. Aff. Rep., 74, 1851. **Arspahas.**—Ind. Aff. Rep., 425, 1842. **A′-ya-to.**—ten Kate, Synonymie, 10, 1884 (Kiowa name). **Bětiděě.**—Mooney in 14th Rep. B. A. E., 953, 1896 (Kiowa Apache name). **Big Bead.**—Bradbury, Travels, 124, 1817.

**Chariticas.**—Doc. of 1828 in Soc. Geogr. Mex., 265, 1870 (see *Sarĕtika*, below). **Detseka'yaa.**—Mooney in 14th Rep. B. A. E., 953, 1896 (Caddo name: 'dog eaters'). **Dog-eaters.**—Kingsley, Stand. Nat. Lib., pt. 6, 153, 1883. **Eiriohtih-Aruohpahga.**—Maximilian, op. cit., II, 213 (Hidatsa name, German form). **E-tah-leh.**—Long, Exp. Rocky Mts., II, 192, 1823 (Hidatsa name: 'bison-path Indians' [cf. *adi*, path; *mite*, bison—Matthews']). **Gens des vach.**—Clark (1804) in Lewis and Clark Journals, I, 190, 1904 (given as synonymous with "Kun na-nar-wesh"; the name is the French for 'buffalo people'). **Hitäniwo'ĭv.**—Mooney in 14th Rep. B. A. E., 953, 1896 (Cheyenne name: 'cloud men' or 'sky men'). **Hi-tă-ng-wo'-i-e.**—ten Kate, Synonymie, 8, 1884 (Cheyenne name: 'people with teats,' peuple aux tetons, mistaking the 'mother' sign; the name means 'cloud men'). **Inûna-ina.**—Mooney in 14th Rep. B. A. E., 953, 1896 (tribal name: 'our people'). **Ita-Iddi.**—Maximilian, Travels, II, 284, 1839–1841 (Hidatsa name). **I-tun-i-wo.**—Hayden, Ethnog. and Philol. Mo. Val., 290, 1860 (Cheyenne name: 'shy-men', for 'sky men'). **Kaninahoic.**—Mooney in 14th Rep. B. A. E., 953, 1896 (Chippewa name). **Kaninahoich.**—Senate Ex. Doc. no. 72, 20th Cong., 104, 1829. **Kanină'-vish.**—Mooney in 14th Rep. B. A. E., 953, 1896. **Komséka-Ki'ñahyup.**—Ibid., 954 ('men of the worn-out leggings': former Kiowa name). **Kun na-nar-wesh.**—Clark (1804) in Lewis and Clark Journals, I, 190, 1904 (given as synonymous with "Gens des vach"). **Lapahógi.**—Gatschet, MS. Shawnee vocab., B. A. E., 1879–80 (Shawnee name; singular, Lapaho). **Maḣpíyato.**—Riggs, Dakota Dict., 2d ed., 305, 1890 (Sioux name). **Maŋḣpi-yato.**—Cook, MS. Yankton vocab., B. A. E., 1882 (Yankton name). **Maqpi'ăto.**—Mooney in 14th Rep. B. A. E., 954, 1896 ('blue cloud': Sioux name). **Niă'rharĭ's-kûrikiwă'shûski.**—Ibid. (Wichita name). **Rapahos.**—De Smet, Missions, 253, 1848 (Garrard, Wahtoyah, 120, 1850, gives this as the Spanish name for them). **Rappaho.**—Long, Exp. Rocky Mts., II, 192, 1823. **Sani'ti'ka.**—Mooney in 14th Rep. B. A. E., 954, 1896 (Pawnee name, from the Comanche name). **Särĕtĭka.**—Ibid. ('dog eaters': Comanche and Shoshoni name). **Sarĕ-tika.**—Ibid. (Wichita name, from the Comanche name). **Saritch-ka-e.**—ten Kate, Synonymie, 8, 1884 (Southern Ute name). **Sa-ritc'-ká-e.**—Ibid. (Ute name). **Sá-ri-te'-ka.**—Ibid., 9 (Comanche and Caddo name). **Sarritehca.**—Rejon quoted in Pimentel, Cuadro Descr., II, 347, 1865 (given as Comanche division). **Schahä'.**—Maximilian, Travels, II, 247, 1841 (Arikara name, German form; seemingly an error for Cheyenne). **Seraticks.**—Burnet (1847) in Schoolcraft, Ind. Tribes, I, 239, 1853. **Seratics.**—Bollaert in Jour. Ethnol. Soc. Lond., II, 265, 1850. **Sharetikeh.**—Burton, City of the Saints, 176, 1861 (Shoshoni name). **Tocani-nambiches.**—Perrin du Lac, Voy. Louisianes, 260, 1805 (seemingly the Arapaho).

**Araste.** An Iroquoian village in 1535 on or near St Lawrence r., below the site of Quebec.—Cartier (1545), Bref Récit, 32, 1863.

**Arathcoon.** See *Raccoon*.

**Arawakan Colony.** In addition to the many proofs of constant communication between the tribes of Florida and those of the West Indian ids. from the earliest period, it is definitely known that a colony of Indians from Cuba, in quest of the same mythic fountain of youth for which Ponce de Leon afterward searched, landed on the s. w. coast of Florida, within the territory of the Calusa (q. v.), about the period of the discovery of America, and that they were held as prisoners by the chief of that tribe and formed into a settlement whose people kept their separate identity as late at least as 1570. This tradition of a wonderful spring or stream

upon the mainland of Florida or on one of the adjacent Bahama ids. was common to all the tribes of the larger islands as far south as Porto Rico, and it is probable that more than one party of islanders made a similar attempt. According to Brinton and other investigators the Indians of Cuba, as well as of the Bahamas and the larger islands, were of the great Arawakan stock, which extends in South America as far as s. Brazil and Bolivia. For the Cuban settlement in Florida see Fontaneda, Memoir, Smith trans, 1854; Barcia, Ensayo, introd., 1723; Herrera, Hist. Gen., I, 1720. (J. M.)

**Arbadaos.** A tribe that Cabeza de Vaca (Smith trans., 76, 1851) met during his sojourn in Texas (1527–34) in the vicinity of the Avavares. He describes the people as "lank and weak," owing to scarcity of food; and although they seem to have lived in a fertile country they did not cultivate the soil. Their ethnic relations are not known.

**Acubadaos.**—Cabeza de Vaca, Smith trans., 84, 1851. **Arbadaos.**—Ibid., 76. **Arbadoes.**—Harris, Voy. and Trav., I, 803, 1705.

**Arbaktung.** A subdivision of the Akudnirmiut; they winter generally on C. Bisson, Home bay, Baffin land.—Boas in Deutsche Geog. Blätt., VIII, 34, 1885.

**Archeology.** Archeological researches are applied to the elucidation of three principal departments of inquiry: (1) The history of the race and the sub-races; (2) the history of the separate families, tribes, and inferior social groups; (3) the history of culture in its multifarious forms. Questions of origin and antiquity are necessarily considered in connection with investigations in each of these departments. In the present article all that can be included is a brief review of the salient features of the archeology of northern America.

In no part of America are there remains of man or his works clearly indicating the presence of peoples distinct from the Indian and the Eskimo, or having culture markedly different in kind and degree from those characterizing the aborigines of historic times. Archeological researches serve to carry the story of the tribes and their culture back indefinitely into the past, although the record furnished by the various classes of remains grows rapidly less legible as we pass beyond the few well-illumined pages of the historic period. It is now known that the sedentary condition prevailed among the aborigines to a much larger extent than has been generally supposed. The more advanced nations of Middle and South America have been practically stationary for long periods, as indicated by the magnitude of their architectural achievements, and even such primitive groups as the Iroquois, Algonquians, and others of northern America have occupied their general historic habitat for unnumbered generations. The prehistoric remains of the various regions thus pertain in large measure to the ancestors of the historic occupants, and the record is thus much more simple than that of prehistoric Europe.

Within the area of the United States pre-Columbian progress was greatest in two principal regions: (1) The Mississippi valley, including portions of the Southern states farther eastward, and (2) the Pueblo country, comprising New Mexico, Arizona, and parts of Colorado, Utah, and Texas. The first-mentioned area is characterized by remains of extensive fixed works, such as mounds and fortifications; the second by its ruined pueblos of stone and adobe. In the remainder of the area, as on the Atlantic and Pacific slopes and in the regions of the Great Lakes, the N. Rocky mts., and the Great Basin, there is comparatively little save minor movable relics and kitchen deposits to mark earlier occupancy. The fixed works which occur in the first-mentioned region are very numerous, and are extremely important to the student of native history. In the Mississippi valley and the Southern states these works consist of mounds of diversified shapes, built mainly of earth and devoted to a variety of purposes, such as dwelling, observation, defense, burial, and ceremony. Some of these are of great size, as the Cahokia mound (q. v.) in Illinois, and the Etowah mound (q. v.) in Georgia, which compare well 'in bulk with the great pyramids of middle America. There are also fortifications and inclosures of extremely varied form and, in many instances, of great extent. These are well illustrated by Ft Ancient (q. v.), Warren co., Ohio, and the earthworks at Newark, Ohio (q. v.). The animal-shaped mounds, occurring principally in the Ohio and upper Mississippi valleys, are a striking variety of these remains. Well-known examples are the Serpent mound (q. v.), Adams co., Ohio, and the so-called Elephant mound (q. v.), Grant co., Wis. The materials used in these structures include earth, clay, sand, and, along the coast, shells. Stone entered into the construction where it was readily available, but rarely as well-built walls or as masonry. These works indicate the former presence in the region of a numerous sedentary population relying mainly on agriculture for subsistence. It is now known, as a result of the more recent archeological investigations, that these people, often called the "Moundbuilders," were no other than Indians, and in some cases at least the ancestors of tribes occupying the general region within historic times. (See *Fortifications, Mounds.*)

In the Pueblo region the fixed works consist of villages and dwellings of stone, and, in the southern Pueblo area, of adobe. Of unusual interest are the cliff-dwellings, built of stone in rifts and shelters in the canyon walls and along the faces of the table-lands or excavated in friable cliffs. The advanced condition of the earlier occupants of the region is indicated not only by these remains but by the presence of traces of extensive irrigating ditches. A careful study of these various remains, including the skeletal parts, demonstrates the fact that they pertain in large measure to the ancestors of the present occupants of the Pueblo towns and that no antecedent distinct people or culture can be differentiated. (See *Casa Grande, Cliff-dwellings, Irrigation, Pueblos.*)

In the districts lying outside of the areas referred to above are encountered occasional burial mounds and earthworks, as well as countless refuse deposits marking occupied sites. The most notable of the latter are the shell mounds of the Atlantic and Pacific shore lines, which offer a rich reward for the labors of the archeologist. (See *Shell-heaps.*)

Among fixed works of somewhat wide distribution are the quarries where flint, soapstone, mica, quartzite, obsidian, and other varieties of stone were obtained for the manufacture of implements and utensils. Such are the extensive workings at Flint Ridge, Ohio; Hot Springs, Ark.; and Mill Creek, Ill., the sites being marked by numerous pittings surrounded with the refuse of manufacture. Their lesson is a most instructive one, demonstrating especially the great enterprise and perseverance of the tribes. There are also numerous copper mines in the L. Superior region, marked by excavations of no great depth but of surprising extent, indicating the fulness of the native awakening to the advantages of metal in the arts. (See *Mines and Quarries.*) Caverns formerly occupied by the tribes also contain deposits of refuse, and their walls display numerous examples of pictography. In connection with fixed works may also be mentioned the petroglyphs, or rock inscriptions, found in nearly every part of the country. These give little aid, however, to the study of aboriginal history, since they can not be interpreted, save in rare cases where tradition has kept the significance alive. (See *Pictographs.*)

Knowledge of native history in post-Columbian as well as in pre-Columbian times is greatly enhanced by a study of the minor remains and relics—the implements, utensils, ornaments, ceremonial and diversional objects and appliances—great numbers of which are now preserved in our museums. (See *Arts and Industries, Stone-work, Bone-work, Shell-*

*work, Wood-work, Metal-work, Pottery, Problematical Objects, Weaving.*)

A study of the archeological remains contained in the area N. of the Rio Grande as a whole supplements the knowledge gained by investigations among the living tribes in such a way as to enable us not only to prolong the vista of many tribal histories but to outline, tentatively at least, the native general history somewhat as follows: An occupancy of the various regions in very early times by tribes of low culture; a gradual advance in arts and industries, especially in favorable localities, resulting in many cases in fully sedentary habits, an artificial basis of subsistence, and the successful practice of many arts and industries, such as agriculture, architecture, sculpture, pottery, weaving, and metallurgy—accomplishments characterizing a well-advanced stage of barbarism, as defined by Morgan; while in the less favored regions, comprising perhaps three-fourths of the area of the United States and a larger proportion of the British possessions, the more primitive hunter-fisher stage mainly persisted down to historic times. (See *Agriculture, Arts and Industries, Fishing, Hunting.*)

Efforts have been made to distinguish definite stages of culture progress in America corresponding to those established in Europe, but there appears to be no very close correspondence. The use of stone was universal among the tribes, and chipped and polished implements appear to have been employed at all periods and by peoples of every stage of culture, although the polishing processes seem to have grown relatively more important with advancing culture, being capable of producing art works of the higher grades, while flaking processes are not. Some of the more advanced tribes of the S. were making marked headway in the use of metals, but the culture was everywhere essentially that of polished stone. (See *Stone-work, Metal-work.*)

The antiquity of man in America has been much discussed in recent years, but as yet it is not fully agreed that any great antiquity is established. Geological formations in the United States, reaching well back toward the close of the Glacial period, possibly ten thousand years, are found to include remains of man and his arts; but beyond this time the traces are so meager and elements of doubt so numerous that conservative students hesitate to accept the evidence as satisfactory. (See *Antiquity, Calaveras Man, Lansing Man, Caves and Rock-shelters.*)

The literature of the northern archeology is very extensive and can not be cited here save in outline. Worthy of particular mention are publications by (1) GOVERNMENT DEPARTMENTS. U. S. Interior Dept.: Reps. Survey of Territories, with papers by Bessels, Holmes, Jackson; Contributions to N. Am. Ethnology, papers by Dall, Powers, Rau, and others. U. S. War Dept.: Reps. of Surveys, papers by Abbott, Ewbank, Loew, Putnam, Schumacher, Yarrow, and others. Education Department, Toronto, Canada: Reps. of Minister of Education, papers by Boyle, Hunter, Laidlaw, and others. (2) INSTITUTIONS: Smithsonian Institution Annual Reports, Contributions to Knowledge, Miscellaneous Collections, containing articles by Abbott, Dall, Fewkes, Holmes, Jones, Lapham, Rau, Squier and Davis, Whittlesey, Wilson, and others (see published list); National Museum Reports, Proceedings, Bulletins, containing papers by Holmes, Hough, Mason, McGuire, Wilson, and others (see published list); Bureau of American Ethnology Reports, Bulletins, containing articles by Cushing, Dall, Fewkes, Fowke, Henshaw, Holmes, Mindeleff, Thomas, and others (see list under article *Bureau of American Ethnology*); Peabody Museum Reports, Memoirs, Archeol. and Ethnol. Papers, containing articles by Abbott, Putnam, Willoughby, Wyman, and others; American Museum of Natural History, Memoirs, Bulletins, containing articles by Hrdlicka, Smith, and others (see published list); Museum of Arts and Science University of Pennsylvania, Publications, containing articles by Abbott, Culin, Mercer, and others; Field Columbian Museum, Publications, containing papers by Dorsey, Phillips, and others; N. Y. State Museum Reports; University of the State of New York, Bulletins, containing papers by Beauchamp; University of California, Publications, containing papers by Sinclair and others. (3) ACADEMIES, SOCIETIES, AND ASSOCIATIONS: Academy of Natural Sciences of Phila., Journal, with numerous memoirs by Moore; American Ethnological Society, Transactions, with papers by Schoolcraft, Troost, and others; Davenport Academy of Science, Proceedings, with papers by Farquharson, Holmes, and others; American Association for the Advancement of Science, Proceedings, with numerous papers; Archæological Institute of America, Papers, containing articles by Bandelier and others; National History Society of New Brunswick, Bulletins; International Congress of Americanists; Washington Anthropological Society; Wyoming Historical and Geological Society; Ohio Archæological and Historical Society; Canadian Institute; American Antiquarian Society; Boston Society of Natural History. (4) PERIODICALS: American Geologist; American Journal of Science and Art; American An-

thropologist; American Antiquarian; The
Archeologist; Popular Science Monthly;
Science; American Journal of Science;
American Naturalist; Journal of Geology.
(5) SEPARATE INDIVIDUAL PUBLICATIONS:
Abbott, Primitive Industry, 1881; Allen,
Prehist. World, 1885; Bancroft, Native
Races, 1882; Brower, Memoirs of Explora-
tions, 1898–1903; Clark, Prehist. Remains,
1876; Dellenbaugh, North Americans of
Yesterday, 1901; Fewkes, Journal of
American Ethnology and Archeology,
I–IV, 1891–94; Foster, Prehist. Races, 1878;
Fowke, Archeol. Hist. Ohio, 1902; Jones,
(1) Monumental Remains of Georgia,
1861, (2) Antiquities of the Southern
Indians, 1873; McLean, Mound Builders,
1879; Moorehead, (1) Prehistoric Imple-
ments, 1900, (2) Fort Ancient, 1890, (3)
Primitive Man in Ohio, 1892; Morgan,
League of Iroquois, 1854, 1904; Munro,
Archeology and False Antiquities, 1905;
Nadaillac, Prehist. Am., 1884; Nordens-
kiöld, Cliff Dwellers of the Mesa Verde,
1893; Read and Whittlesey in Ohio Cen-
tennial Rep., 1877; Schoolcraft, Indian
Tribes, vols. I–IV, 1851–57; Short, North
Americans of Antiquity, 1880; Starr, First
Steps in Human Progress, 1895; Squier,
Antiquities of New York and the West,
1851; Terry, Sculp. Anthr. Ape Heads,
1891; Thruston, Antiq. of Tenn., 1897;
Warden, Recherches sur les antiquités
de l'Amér. Sept., 1827. Wilson, Prehis-
toric Man, 1862; Winsor, Narrative and
Critical History of America, I, 1884;
Wright, Man and the Glacial Period,
1895. For archeological bibliography of
Ontario, Canada, see 9th Archeological
Report of Minister of Education, Ontario,
1897. (W. H. H.)

**Architecture.** The simple constructions
of the tribes N. of Mexico, although almost exclusively practical in their purpose, serve to illustrate many of the initial steps in the evolution of architecture;
they are hence worthy of careful consideration by the student of culture history.
Various branches of the building arts are
treated separately under appropriate
heads (see *Adobe, Cliff-dwellings, Earth-
lodge, Fortifications, Grass-lodge, Habitations, Kivas, Mounds, Pile-dwellings, Pueblos, Tipis*), but as these topics are there
considered mainly in their ethnologic as-
pects, they will here be briefly treated as
products of environment and as illustrations of the manner in which beginnings
are made and the higher architectural
forms are evolved. The kind and character of the buildings in a given district
or region depend on a number of conditions, namely: (*a*) The capacity, habits,
and characteristics of the people; (*b*) the
cultural and especially the social status of
the particular peoples; (*c*) the influence
of neighboring cultures; (*d*) the physi-

ography of the district occupied; (*e*) the
resources, animal, vegetal, and mineral,
and especially the building materials
available within the area; (*f*) climate.
These in the main are the determining
factors in the art development of all peoples in all times, and may be referred to
somewhat at length.

(1) In these studies it is necessary that
the man himself and especially his mental capacities and characteristics should
be considered as essential elements of the
environment, since he is not only the
product, as is his culture, of present and
past environments, but is the primary
dynamic factor in all culture development.

(2) The culture status of the people—
the particular stage of their religious, social, technical, and esthetic development—
goes far toward determining the character of their buildings. The manner in
which social status determines the character of habitations is dwelt on by Morgan (Cont. N. A. Ethnol., IV, 1881), to the
apparent exclusion of other criteria.
Within the area N. of Mexico the various
phases characterizing the culture of numerous tribes and groups of tribes are
marked by more or less distinctive habitations. People of the lowest social
grade are content with nature's cano-
pies—the sky, the forest, and the overhanging rocks—or construct simple
shelters of brush or bark for protection against sun, wind, and rain. Some
build lodges of skins and mats, so
light that they may be carried from
place to place as the food quest or the
pressure of foes requires; while others,
higher in the scale, construct strong
houses of timber or build fortress-like
pueblos of hewn stone or adobe. Along
with the succession of steps in culture
progress there goes progressive differentiation of use. The less advanced tribes
have only the dwelling, while the more
cultured have, in addition, fortifications,
temples, civic structures, tombs, storage
houses, observation towers, dams, canals,
reservoirs, shelters for domestic animals,
and various constructions employed in
transportation. Social customs and religion play each a part in the results accomplished, the one acting on the habitation and the other giving rise to a separate and most important branch of the
building arts.

(3) The building arts of the tribes N.
of Mexico have been little affected by
outside influence. In the N. there is
only a limited contact with the Siberian
tribes, which have little to give; and in the
S. nearly a thousand miles separate the
tribes of our s. border from the semicivil-
ized Indians of central Mexico. So slowly
did intertribal influence act within the

area here included, and so fully does environment control culture, that in many cases where the conditions have remained reasonably stable distinct styles of building exist almost side by side, and have so existed from time immemorial.

(4) It is apparent at a glance that the physiographic characters of a country exercise strong influence on aboriginal building arts, and at the same time have much to do with the trend of culture in general and with results finally achieved in civilization. Dwellings on the open plains necessarily differ from those in the mountains, those of a country of forests from those of an arid region, and those of rich alluvial bottoms from those of the land of plateaus and cliffs. Even the characteristics of the particular site impress themselves strongly on the buildings and the building group.

(5) In any area the natural resources have much to do with determining the economic status of the people and, according as they are favorable or unfavorable, foster or discourage progress in the arts. The building materials available to a people exercise a profound influence on the building arts. The presence of plentiful, easily quarried stone, well adapted to building purposes, permits and encourages rapid development of these arts, while its absence may seriously retard their development, and in fact may be accountable for the backward condition of a people not only in this activity but in the whole range of its activities. The highest development is not possible without stone, which alone of the materials available to uncivilized man for building purposes is sufficiently permanent to permit the cumulative growth necessary to the evolution of the higher forms of the art of architecture.

(6) Climate is an element of the highest significance in the history of building. In warm, arid districts shelter is not often a necessity, and a primitive people may have no buildings worthy of the name; but in the far N. carefully constructed dwellings are essential to life. The habitations of an arid region naturally differ from those of a region where moisture prevails.

The conditions thus outlined have operated in the various culture areas N. of the Rio Grande to produce the diversified results observed; and these results may now be passed briefly in review. Among the most clearly defined and characteristic of these environments are (1) the Arctic area, (2) the North Pacific area, (3) the middle Pacific area, (4) the arid region of the S. W., (5) the Basin range and Rocky mtn. highlands, (6) the Mississippi lowlands and the middle S., (7) the woodlands of the N. and E., and

(8) the Gulf coast and Florida. Within some of these the conditions are practically uniform over vast areas, and the results are uniform in proportion, while in others conditions are greatly diversified, numerous more or less distinct styles of house construction having developed almost side by side. As with the larger areas, each inferior division displays re-

EARTH-COVERED HOUSE, WESTERN ESKIMO. (MURDOCH)

sults due to the local conditions. It may be observed that of the various conditioning agencies of environment one may dominate in one district and another in another district, but with our present imperfect knowledge of the facts in a majority of cases the full analysis of conditions and effects is not yet possible.

It is not to be expected that the build-

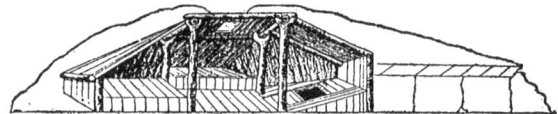

SECTION OF HOUSE, WESTERN ESKIMO. (MURDOCH)

ing arts can flourish within the Arctic circle. Along the many thousands of miles of N. shore line agriculture is out of the question. Wood is known only as it drifts from the s. along the icy shores, and save for the presence of oil-producing animals of the sea primitive man could not exist. Snow, ice, stone, bones of animals, and driftwood

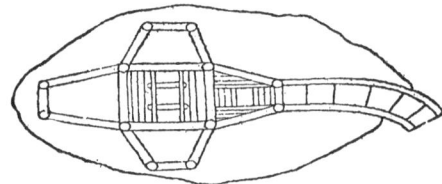

PLAN OF HOUSE, WESTERN ESKIMO. (MURDOCH)

are the materials available for building, and these are utilized for dwellings and storage places according to the requirements and capacities of the tribes. The house is depressed beneath the surface of the ground, partly, perhaps, better to withstand the cold, and partly, no doubt, because of the lack of necessary timbers to build walls and span the space required above ground. The large winter houses are entered by a long underground passage, the low walls of which are constructed of whale bones, stones, or timbers, while the house has a framework of timbers or whale-ribs covered with earth. The ground-plan and interior arrangement are simple, but well perfected, and remarkably uniform over the vast extent of the Arctic shore line. The snow house is particularly a product of the N. Snow and ice, available for the greater part of the year, are utilized in the construction of dwellings unique on the face of the earth. These are built of blocks of compacted snow held in position, not by utilizing any of the ordinary principles of construction, but by permitting the blocks to crystallize by freezing into a solid dome of ice—so solid that the key block may be omitted for a window or for the passage of smoke without danger to the structure. This house lasts during the winter, and in the summer

SNOW-HOUSE, HUDSON BAY ESKIMO. (TURNER)

melts away. The summer houses are mere shelters of driftwood or bones covered with skins. There is no opportunity for esthetic display in such houses as these, and clever as the Eskimo are in their minor art work, it is not likely that esthetic effect in their buildings, interior or exterior, ever received serious consideration. The people do not lack in ability and industry, but the environment restricts constructive effort to the barest necessities of existence and effectually blocks the way to higher development. Their place in the culture ladder is by no means at the lowest rung, but it is far from the highest.

The houses of the N. W. coast derive their character largely from the vast forests of yellow cedar, which the enterprising people were strong enough to master and utilize. They are substantial and roomy structures, and indicate on the part of the builders decided ability in planning and remarkable enterprise in execution. They mark the highest achievement of the native tribes in wood construction that has been observed. The genius of this people applied to building with stone in a stone environment might well have placed them

among the foremost builders in America. Vast labor was expended in getting out the huge trunks, in hewing the planks, posts, and beams, in carving the house and totem poles, and in erecting the

HOUSES OF NORTHWEST COAST TRIBES. HIGHEST EXAMPLES OF WOOD CONSTRUCTION. (NIBLACK)

massive structures. The façade, with its mythological paintings and huge heraldic columns, is distinctly impressive. In early days the fortified towns, described by Vancouver and other pioneer explorers, were striking and important

CLIFF HOUSE, MESA VERDE, COLORADO. HIGHEST TYPE OF STONE CONSTRUCTION

constructions. It is indeed a matter of regret that the genius of such a people should be expended upon a material of which no trace is left, save in museums, after the lapse of a few generations.

The contrast, due to differences in environment, between the buildings of the N. W. coast and those of the Pueblo region is most striking. With greater ability, perhaps, than the Pueblos, the northern peoples labored under the disadvantage of employing materials that rapidly decay, while with the Pueblos the results of the skill and effort of one generation were supplemented by those of the next, and the cumulative result was the great pueblo. The lot of the Pueblo tribes fell in the midst of a vast region

structures and embankments, and the cumulative growth gave massive and enduring results, but the superstructures were of materials difficult to utilize in an effective manner by a stone-age people and, being subject to rapid decay, were not cumulative. Had the environment furnished to this group of vigorous and talented tribes the materials for adobe cement or plentiful deposits of readily quarried stone, the results might have been very different: the mound-builders' culture

CAHOKIA MOUND, ILLINOIS.    TERRACED PYRAMID 1,180 FT. LONG, 100 FT. HIGH.   RESTORED

of cliffs and plateaus, where the means of subsistence admitted of the growth of large communities and where the ready-quarried stone, with scarcity of wood, led inevitably to the building of houses of masonry. The defensive motive being present, it directed the genius of the people toward continued and united effort, and the dwelling group became a great stronghold. Cumulative results encouraged cumulative effort; stronger and stronger walls were built, and story grew on story. The art of the stone mason was mastered, the stones were hewn and laid in diversified courses for effect, door and window openings were accurately and symmetrically framed with cut stone and spanned with lintels of stone and wood, and towers of picturesque outline in picturesque situations, now often in ruins, offer suggestions of the feudal castles of the Old World. (See *Cliff-dwellings, Pueblos.*)

Standing quite alone among the building achievements of the tribes N. of Mexico are the works of the ancient mound-building Indians of the Mississippi valley and the Southern states. Earthworks, grand in proportions and varied in character, remain as a partial and imperfect index of the extent and nature of the architecture of these people. The great embankments probably inclosed thriving villages, and the truncated pyramids must have supported temples or other important structures. But these, built no doubt of wood or bark, have wholly disappeared. The nearest approach to permanent house construction observed in E. United States is found in the clay-covered wattle-work walls of the more southerly tribes (Thomas; Adair). The people had acquired only partial mastery of the building materials within their environment. Earth, sand, and clay, indestructible and always at hand, were utilized for the sub-

and the mound-building people might have been no mean factor in the American nation to-day.

The primitive habitations of the Pacific slope from the Straits of Fuca to the Gulf of California afford a most instructive lesson. In the N. the vigorous tribes had risen to the task of utilizing the vast forests, but in the S. the improvident and enervated natives were little short of homeless wanderers. In the N. the roomy communal dwellings of the Columbia valley, described by Lewis and Clark, were found, while to the S. one passes through varied environments where timber and earth, rocks and caves, rushes, bark, grass, and brush in turn

MOKELUMNE CEREMONIAL HOUSE, CALIFORNIA.   (SANTA FE RY.)

played their part in the very primitive house-making achievements of the strangely diversified tribesmen.

In the highlands of the Great Divide and in the vast inland basins of the N. the building arts did not flourish, and houses of bark, grass, reeds, the skins of animals, and rough timbers covered with earth gave only necessary shelter from winter blasts. In the whole expanse of the forest-covered E. the palisaded fortress and the long-house of the Iroquois, in use at the beginning of the historical period, mark the highest limit in the building arts.    On the Gulf coast the

TIPI OF PLAINS TRIBES; SHOSHONI.    MADE OF SKINS OR CLOTH

simple pile dwellings set in the shallow waters were all that the conditions of existence in a mild climate required.

BARK HOUSE.    METHOD OF CONSTRUCTION OF THE IROQUOIS LONG-HOUSE

It is probably useless to speculate on what might have been in store for the native builders had they been permitted to continue unmolested throughout the ages.  The stone-builders had the most promising outlook, but they were still in the elementary stages of the arts of construction. They had not made the one essential step toward great building—the discovery of the means of covering large spaces without the use of wood. Although they were acquainted

GRASS LODGE, WICHITA.    EMBELLISHED CONSTRUCTION.    (MOONEY)

with many essential elements of construction, they had devised neither the offset span of stone nor the keystone arch.

In none of these areas had the tribes reached the stage in the building arts where constructive features or architec-

tural details are utilized freely for purposes of embellishment.    A people that could carve wood and stone and could decorate pottery and weave baskets of admirable pattern could not mold the unwieldy elements of the building into esthetic form.    But esthetic suggestions and features did not pass entirely unappreciated.    Some of the lower types of structures, such as the grass lodge and the mat house, partaking of textile technique, were characterized by elements of symmetry, grace, and rhythmic repetition of details.    The wooden house of

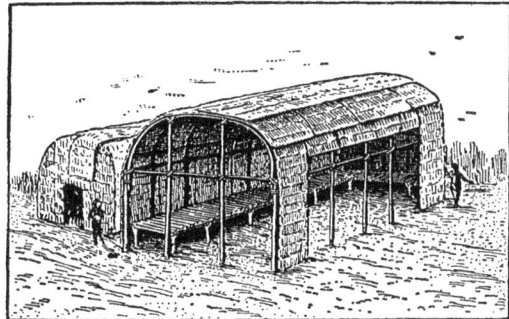

MAT HOUSE, CAROLINA INDIANS.    (AFTER JOHN WHITE, OF THE ROANOKE COLONY, 1585)

the N. W. had massiveness of form and boldness of outline, and the sculptured and painted details lent much esthetic interest; while in the arid region the stone-builders had introduced a number of features to relieve the monotony of walls and to add to the pleasing effect of the interiors.    In these things the native mind certainly took some pleasure, but probably little thought was given to architectural effect as this is known to the more civilized tribes, such as the Maya of Yucatan, who spent a vast amount of time and energy on the purely decorative features of their stone buildings.

Numerous authors dwell more or less on the buildings of the tribes N. of Mexico, but only the more important publications will here be cited. See Boas, Dorsey, Fewkes, Hoffman, the Mindeleffs, Nelson, Mrs Stevenson, Thomas, and Turner in various Reports, B. A. E.; Adair, Hist. Amer. Inds., 1775; Bandelier, various reports in Papers Arch. Inst. Am., 1881–92; Beauchamp, Iroquois

Trail, 1892; Boas in Rep. Nat. Mus. 1895, 1897; Catlin, N. Am. Inds., 1841, 1866; Dawson in Proc. and Trans. Royal Soc. Can., IX, 1891; De Bry, Collectiones Peregrinationum, 1590–1628; Dellenbaugh, North Americans of Yesterday, 1901; Du Pratz, Hist. Louisiane, III, 1758; Eells in Smithson. Rep. 1887, 1889; Foster, Prehist. Races, 1878; Goddard in Univ. Cal. Pubs., I, no. 1, 1903; Hariot, Narr. First Plant. Virginia, repr. 1893; Hrdlicka in Am. Anthrop., VII, no. 3, 1905; Jackson in Metropol. Mag., XXII, no. 3, 1905; Lewis and Clark, Exped. (1804–06), Coues ed., 1893; MacLean Mound Builders, 1879; Moore, various memoirs in Jour. Acad. Nat. Sci. Phila., 1894–1905; Morgan in Cont. N. Am. Ethnol., IV, 1881; Morice in Trans. Can. Inst., IV, 1895; Niblack in Nat. Mus.

N. w. of them. The women are supposed to be of ordinary stature. They hunt in kaiaks and provide for their husbands, who are covered with hair and are so tiny that they carry them about in their hoods.—Boas in 6th Rep. B. A. E., 640, 1888.

**Areitorae.** A Papago village s. of Sonorita, Sonora, Mexico.—Box, Adventures, 262, 1869.

**Arekw.** A Yurok village on the coast at the mouth of Redwood cr., N. w. Cal. The town of Orick, 2 m. up the stream, takes its name therefrom.    (A. L. K.)
Oruk.—Gibbs in Schoolcraft, Ind. Tribes, III, 139, 1853.

**Arenal** (Span.: 'sandy ground,' 'desert'). A village, presumably Piman, on the Pima and Maricopa res., Gila r., Ariz.; pop. 557 in 1860 (Taylor in Cal. Farmer,

MASONRY WALL, ANCIENT PUEBLO, NEW MEXICO.    ELEMENTARY EMBELLISHMENT

Rep. 1888, 1890; Nordenskiöld, Cliff Dwellers of the Mesa Verde, 1893; Powers in Cont. N. Am. Ethnol., III, 1877; Schoolcraft, Ind. Tribes, I–VI, 1851–57; Smith, Hist. Va., repr. 1819; Squier, Antiq. N. Y. and West, 1851; Squier and Davis in Smithson. Cont., I, 1848; Starr, First Steps in Human Progress, 1895; Swan in Smithson. Cont., XXI, 1874; Teit in Mem. Am. Mus. Nat. Hist., II, 1900; Thruston, Antiq. of Tenn., 1897. See *Habitations.*    (w. h. h.)

**Ardeco.** A small tribe or village, probably Caddoan, indefinitely described as on a s. w. branch of Arkansas r. in the 18th century.—La Harpe (1719) in Margry, Déc., VI, 299, 1886.
Adero.—La Harpe, op. cit. Ardeco.—Beaurain in Margry, op. cit. (mentioned with the Touacaro= Tawakoni).

**Ardnainiq.** A mythical people believed by the Central Eskimo to live far to the

June 19, 1863), and 616 in 1869 (Browne, Apache Country, 290, 1869).

**Arendahronon** ('rock people'). One of the four chief tribes of the Huron, having the most easterly situation and claiming to be the first allies of the French, who founded among them the missions of St Jean Baptiste, St Joachim, and Ste Elisabeth. In 1639 they were said to have been resident of the Huron country for about 50 years. In 1649, on the political destruction and expulsion of the Huron tribes by the Iroquois, the inhabitants of St Jean Baptiste submitted in a body to the Seneca, who adopted them. They constituted the Stone, or Rock, tribe of the Huron. See Jesuit Relation for 1639, 40, 1858.    (J. N. B. H.)
Ahrenda.—Shea, Cath. Miss., 182, 1855. Ahrendahronons.—Schoolcraft, Ind. Tribes, III, 522, 1853. Ahrendaronons.—Jes. Rel. for 1640, 61, 1858. Arenda.—Charlevoix (1635), New France, II, 72, 1872.

Arendacronons.—Jes. Rel. for 1641, 67, 1858. **Arendaehronons.**—Ibid., 83. **Arendaenhronons.**—Jes. Rel. for 1642, 82, 1858. **Arendarhononons.**—Jes. Rel. for 1635, 24, 1858. **Arendaronons.**—Jes. Rel. for 1644, 99, 1858. **Arendaronons.**—Jes. Rel. for 1640, 90, 1858. **Arendarrhonons.**—Jes. Rel. for 1637, 109, 1858. **Arendoronnon.**—Jes. Rel. for 1636, 123, 1858. **Avendahs.**—Kingsley, Stand. Nat. Hist., pt. 6, 154, 1883. **Enarhonon.**—Sagard, Gr. Voy., I, 79, 1865. **Nation d' Atironta.**—Ibid. **Nation de la Roche.**—Jes. Rel., III, index, 1858. **Nation du Rocher.**—Jes. Rel. for 1657, 23, 1858. **Renarhonon.**—Sagard, Hist. du Can., I, 234, 1865.

**Arendaonatia.** A Huron village in Ontario about 1640.—Jes. Rel. for 1637, 159, 1858.

Anendaonactia.—Ibid., 165.

**Arente.** A Huron village in Ontario about 1640.—Jes. Rel. for 1637, 150, 1858.

**Argillite** (slate). This material, which is much diversified in character, was in very general use by the tribes N. of Mexico for the manufacture of utensils, implements, and ornaments, and for carvings in general. The typical slates, characterized by their decided foliate structure, were used to some extent for implements; but the more massive varieties, such as the greenish striped slates of the Eastern states, the argillite of New Jersey, Pennsylvania, and the states to the s., and the black slate of the N. W. coast were usually preferred for polished implements and carvings. Argillite was much used by the tribes of the Delaware and Susquehanna valleys, and an ancient quarry of this material, situated at Point Pleasant, Pa., has been described by Mercer (see *Mines and Quarries*). Material from this and other quarries in the Appalachian region was used mainly for flaked implements, including leaf-shaped blades, knives, and arrow and spear heads, and these are widely distributed over the Middle Atlantic states. The fine-grained greenish and striped slates of the Eastern and Middle states and Canada were extensively used in the manufacture of several varieties of objects of somewhat problematic use, including so-called banner-stones, bird-stones, and perforated tablets. It is probable that, like the green agates and jadeites of Mexico, some varieties of this stone had special significance with the native tribes. The tribes of the N. W. coast employ a fine-grained slate in their very artistic carvings, which the Haida obtain chiefly from deposits on Slate cr., Queen Charlotte ids. This slate has the desirable qualities of being soft and easily carved when freshly quarried, and of growing harder with time. It is black and takes an excellent polish (Niblack). See *Sculpture and Carving, Totem-poles.*

References to the use of argillite and slate occur in many works relating to ethnologic and archeologic subjects, but are not sufficiently important to be given in full. Worthy of special mention are Abbott, Prim. Industry, 1881; Holmes in 15th Rep. B. A. E., 1897; Mercer in Pubs. Univ. Penn., VI, 1897; Niblack in Rep. Nat. Mus. 1888, 1890; Rau in Smithson. Rep. 1872, 1873; Squier and Davis in Smithson. Cont., I, 1848. (W. H. H.)

**Arhau.** A village or tribe formerly between Matagorda bay and Colorado r., Texas; mentioned to Joutel in 1687 by the Ebahamo Indians. The region was the domain of the Karankawan tribes, with whom the Arhau people were possibly affiliated. See Gatschet, Karankawa Inds., Peabody Mus. Papers, I, 35, 46, 1891. (A. C. F.)

Arhan.—Joutel (1687) in French, Hist. Coll. La., I, 137, 1846. **Arhau.**—Joutel (1687) in Margry, Déc. III, 288, 1878.

**Aribaiba.** A former rancheria of the Sobaipuri, on the Rio San Pedro, not far from its junction with the Gila, in s. Arizona. It was visited by Father Kino about 1697. See *Arivaipa.*

Aribabia.—De l'Isle, Map Am., 1703. **S. Pantaleon Aribaiba.**—Kino (1697) quoted by Bancroft, No. Mex. States, I, 265, 1884.

**Aridian.** A term applied to the early occupants of the desert region of the S. W., particularly of s. Arizona, whose culture, as exemplified by their art and other remains, was similar to that of the Zuñi.—Cushing in Proc. Int. Cong. Am., VII, 157, 1890. See *Pueblos.*

Original Pueblo.—Ibid. **Shiwian.**—Ibid. (so called from the similarity in the "Aridian" and the Shiwi or Zuñi cultures).

**Arikara** (Skidi: *ariki* 'horn,' referring to the former custom of wearing the hair with two pieces of bone standing up like horns on each side of the crest; *ra*, pl. ending). A tribe forming the northern group of the Caddoan linguistic family. In language they differ only dialectically from the Pawnee.

When the Arikara left the body of their kindred in the S. W. they were associated with the Skidi, one of the tribes of the Pawnee confederacy. Tradition and history indicate that at some point in the broad Missouri valley the Skidi and Arikara parted, the former settling on Loup r., Neb., the latter continuing N. E., building on the bluffs of the Missouri the villages of which traces have been noted nearly as far s. as Omaha. In their northward movement they encountered members of the Siouan family making their way westward. Wars ensued, with intervals of peace and even of alliance between the tribes. When the white race reached the Missouri they found the region inhabited by Siouan tribes, who said that the old village sites had once been occupied by the Arikara. In 1770 French traders established relations with the Arikara, below Cheyenne r., on the Missouri. Lewis and Clark met the tribe 35 years later, reduced in numbers and living in three villages between Grand and Cannonball rs., Dak. By 1851 they had moved up to the vicinity of Heart r. It is not probable that this rapid rate of movement obtained during migrations prior to the settlement of the Atlantic coast by the English. The steady westward pressure of the colonists, together with their policy of fomenting intertribal wars, caused the continual displacement of many native communities, a condition that bore heavily on the semisedentary tribes, like the Arikara, who lived in villages and cultivated the soil. Almost continuous warfare with aggressive tribes, together with the ravages of smallpox during the latter half of the

RUSHING BEAR—ARIKARA

18th and the beginning of the 19th centuries, nearly exterminated some of their villages. The weakened survivors consolidated to form new, necessarily composite villages, so that much of their ancient organization was greatly modified or ceased to exist. It was during this period of stress that the Arikara became close neighbors and, finally, allies of the Mandan and Hidatsa. In 1804, when Lewis and Clark visited the Arikara, they were disposed to be friendly to the United States, but, owing to intrigues incident to the rivalry between trading companies, which brought suffering to the Indians, they became hostile. In 1823 the Arikara attacked an American trader's boats, kill-

ing 13 men and wounding others. This led to a conflict with the United States, but peace was finally concluded. In consequence of these troubles and the failure of crops for 2 successive years the tribe abandoned their villages on the Missouri and joined the Skidi on Loup r., Neb., where they remained 2 years; but the animosity which the Arikara displayed toward the white race made them dangerous and unwelcome neighbors, so that they were requested to go back to the Missouri. They did so, and there they have remained ever since. Under their first treaty, in 1825, they acknowledged the supremacy of the National Government over the land and the people, agreed to trade only with American citizens, whose life and property they were pledged to protect, and to refer all difficulties for final settlement to the United States. After the close of the Mexican war a commission was sent by the Government to define the territories claimed by the tribes living N. of Mexico, between the Missouri and the Rocky mts. In the treaty made at Ft Laramie, in 1851, with the Arikara, Mandan, and Hidatsa, the land claimed by these tribes is described as lying w. of the Missouri, from Heart r., N. Dak., to the Yellowstone, and up the latter to the mouth of Powder r., Mont.; thence s. E. to the headwaters of the Little Missouri in Wyoming, and skirting the Black hills to the head of Heart r. and down that stream to its junction with the Missouri. Owing to the nonratification of this treaty, the landed rights of the Arikara remained unsettled until 1880, when, by Executive order, their present reservation was set apart; this includes the trading post, established in 1845, and named for Bartholomew Berthold, a Tyrolese, one of the founders of the American Fur Company. The Arikara, Mandan, and Hidatsa together share this land, and are frequently spoken of, from the name of their reservation, as Ft Berthold Indians. In accordance with the act of Feb. 8, 1887, the Arikara received allotments of land in severalty, and, on approval of the allotments by the Secretary of the Interior, July 10, 1900, they became citizens of the United States and subject to the laws of North Dakota. An industrial boarding school and 3 day schools are maintained by the Government on Ft Berthold res. A mission boarding school and a church are supported by the Congregational Board of Missions. In 1804 Lewis and Clark gave the population of the Arikara as 2,600, of whom more than 600 were warriors. In 1871 the tribe numbered 1,650; by 1888 they were reduced to 500, and the census of 1904 gives the population as 380. As far back as their traditions go the Arikara have cultivated the soil, depending for their staple food supply on crops of corn, beans, squashes, and pumpkins. In the sign language the Arikara are designated as "corn eaters," the movement of the hand simulating the act of gnawing the kernels of corn from the cob. They preserved the seed of a peculiar kind of small-eared corn, said to be very nutritious and much liked. It is also said that the seed corn was kept tied in a skin and hung up in the lodge near the fireplace, and when the time for planting came only those kernels showing signs of germination were used. The Arikara bartered corn with the Cheyenne and other tribes for buffalo robes, skins, and meat, and exchanged these with the traders for cloth, cooking utensils, guns, etc. Early dealings with the traders were carried on by the women. The Arikara hunted the buffalo in winter, returning to their village in the early spring, where they spent the time before planting in dressing the pelts. Their fish supply was obtained by means of basket traps. They were expert swimmers, and ventured to capture buffaloes that were disabled in the water as the herd was crossing the river. Their wood supply was obtained from the river; when the ice broke up in the spring the Indians leaped on the cakes, attached cords to the trees that were whirling down the rapid current, and hauled them ashore. Men, women, and the older children engaged in this exciting work, and although they sometimes fell and were swept downstream, their dexterity and courage generally prevented serious accident. Their boats were made of a single buffalo skin stretched, hair side in, over a frame of willows bent round like a basket and tied to a hoop 3 or 4 feet in diameter. The boat could easily be transported by a woman and, according to Hayden, "would carry 3 men across the Missouri with tolerable safety." Before the coming of traders the Arikara made their cooking utensils of pottery; mortars for pounding corn were made with much labor from stone; hoes were fashioned from the shoulder-blades of the buffalo and the elk; spoons were shaped from the horns of the buffalo and the mountain sheep; brooms and brushes were made of stiff, coarse grass; knives were chipped from flint, and spears and arrowheads from horn and flint; for splitting wood, wedges of horn were used. Whistles were constructed to imitate the bleat of the antelope or the call of the elk, and served as decoys; popguns and other toys were contrived for the children and flageolets for the amusement of young men. Garments were embroidered with dyed porcupine quills; dentalium shells from the Pacific were prized as ornaments. Matthews and

others mention the skill of the Arikara in melting glass and pouring it into molds to form ornaments; they disposed of the highly colored beads furnished by the traders in this manner. They have preserved in their basketry a weave that has been identified with one practised by former tribes in Louisiana—a probable survival of the method learned when with their kindred in the far S. W. The Arikara were equally tenacious of their language, although next-door neighbors of Siouan tribes for more than a century, living on terms of intimacy and intermarrying to a great extent. Matthews says that almost every member of each tribe understands the language of the other tribes, yet speaks his own most fluently, hence it is not uncommon to hear a dialogue carried on in two tongues. Until recently the Arikara adhered to their ancient form of dwellings, erecting, at the cost of great labor, earth lodges that were generally grouped about an open space in the center of the village, often quite close together, and usually occupied by 2 or 3 families. Each village generally contained a lodge of unusual size, in which ceremonies, dances, and other festivities took place. The religious ceremonies, in which each subtribe or village had its special part, bound the people together by common beliefs, traditions, teachings, and supplications that centered around the desire for long life, food, and safety. In 1835 Maximilian of Wied noticed that the hunters did not load on their horses the meat obtained by the chase, but carried it on their heads and backs, often so transporting it from a great distance. The man who could carry the heaviest burden sometimes gave his meat to the poor, in deference to their traditional teaching that "the Lord of life told the Arikara that if they gave to the poor in this manner, and laid burdens on themselves, they would be successful in all their undertakings." In the series of rites, which began in the early spring when the thunder first sounded, corn held a prominent place. The ear was used as an emblem and was addressed as "Mother." Some of these ceremonial ears of corn had been preserved for generations and were treasured with reverent care. Offerings were made, rituals sung, and feasts held when the ceremonies took place. Rites were observed when the maize was planted, at certain stages of its growth, and when it was harvested. Ceremonially associated with maize were other sacred objects, which were kept in a special case or shrine. Among these were the skins of certain birds of cosmic significance, also 7 gourd rattles that marked the movements of the seasons. Elaborate rituals and ceremonies attended the opening of this shrine and the exhibition of its contents, which were symbolic of the forces that make and keep all things alive and fruitful. Aside from these ceremonies there were other quasireligious gatherings in which feats of jugglery were performed, for the Arikara, like their kindred the Pawnee, were noted for their skill in legerdemain. The dead were placed in a sitting posture, wrapped in skins, and buried in mound graves. The property, except such personal belongings as were interred with the body, was distributed among the kindred, the family tracing descent through the mother. A collection of Arikara traditions, by G. A. Dorsey, has been published by the Carnegie Institution (1903).

The Arikara were a loosely organized confederacy of subtribes, each of which had its separate village and distinctive name. Few of these names have been preserved. Lewis and Clark (Exped., I, 97, 1814) mention Lahoocat, a village occupied in 1797, but abandoned about 1800. How many subtribes were included in the confederacy can not now be determined. Lewis and Clark speak of the Arikara as the remnant of 10 powerful Pawnee tribes, living in 1804 in 3 villages. The inroads of disease and war have so reduced the tribe that little now remains of their former divisions. The following names were noted during the middle of the last century: Hachepiriinu ('young dogs'), Hia ('band of Cree'), Hosukhaunu ('foolish dogs'), Hosukhaunukarerihu ('little foolish dogs'), Sukhutit ('black mouths'), Kaka ('band of Crows'), Okos ('band of bulls'), Paushuk ('band of cut-throats'). Some of these may refer to military and other societies; others seem to be nicknames, as "Cut-throats."

(A. C. F.)

Ă da ka′ da ho.—Matthews, Ethnog. Hidatsa, 125, 1877 (Hidatsa name). **Ah-pen-ope-say.**—Anon. MS. Crow vocab., B. A. E. (Crow name). **Ai-dĭk′-a-da-hu.**—Hoffman in Proc. Am. Philos. Soc., 294, 1886 (='people, of the flowing hair'). **Ankora.**—Ind. Aff.Rep.,63,1851. **A-pan-to′-pse.**—Hayden,Ethnog. and Philol. Mo. Val., 402, 1862 (Crow name). **Aracaris.**—Gass, Voy., 400, 1810. **Ă ra ka′da ho.**—Matthews, Ethnog. Hidatsa, 125, 1877 (Hidatsa name). **Archarees.**—Morgan in No. Am. Rev., 493, 1869. **Aricaras.**—Beaurain (ca. 1720) in Margry, Déc., VI, 289, 1886. **Aricarees.**—Saxton quoted by Stevens, Rep. on Pac. R. R., 239, 1854. **Aricarie.**—Schermerhorn in Mass. Hist. Coll., 2d s., II, 34, 1814. **Aricaris.**—Gass, Jour., 48, 1807. **Aricas.**—Carte des Poss. Ang., 1777. **Ariccarees.**—Culbertson in Smithson. Rep. 1850, 115, 1851. **Aricharay.**—Sen. Doc. 47, 16th Cong., 1st sess., 4, 1820. **Arichard.**—Sen. Ex. Doc. 90, 22d Cong., 1st sess., 63, 1832. **Arickara.**—Clark and Cass in H. R. Ex. Doc. 117, 20th Cong., 2d sess., 99, 1829. **A-rick-a-ra-one.**—Long, Exped. Rocky Mts., II, lxxxiv, 1823 (Hidatsa name). **Arickaraws.**—Sen. Ex. Doc. 94, 34th Cong., 1st sess., 13, 1856. **Arickare.**—Ind. Aff. Rep., 297, 1835. **Arickarees.**—Ind. Aff. Rep., 403, 1836. **Arickera.**—Ind. Aff. Rep. 245, 1846. **A-rĭk′-a-hŭ.**—Hoffman in Proc. Am. Philos. Soc., 294, 1886 (Hidatsa form). **Arĭkāra.**—Matthews, Ethnog. Hidatsa, 13, 1877 (Mandan

name). **A′-rĭ-kă′-ră.**—Hoffman in Proc. Am. Philos. Soc., 294, 1886 (abbreviation of the Mandan Ai-dĭk′-a-da-hu). **Arikare.**—Ind. Aff. Rep., 247, 1877. **Arĭk′-arĕ.**—Hoffman in Proc. Am. Philos. Soc., 294, 1886 (name of Hidatsa origin). **Arikarees.**—Keane in Stanford, Compend., 533, 1878. **Arikari.**—Burton, City of Saints, 119, 1861. **Arikera.**—Sen.Ex.Doc.90, 22d Cong., 1st sess., 29, 1832. **Arikkaras.**—Maximilian, Trav., 143, 1843. **Arrekaras.**—McCoy, Ann. Reg., 52, 1836. **Arricara.**—La Harpe (1719) in Margry, Déc., VI, 293, 1886. **Arricarees.**—Warren (1855), Nebr. and Dak., 50, 1875. **Arrickaraws.**—Dougherty (1837) in H. R. Doc. 276, 25th Cong., 2d sess., 16, 1838. **Arrickaree.**—Ind. Aff. Rep. 1856, 67, 1857. **Arrickora.**—Webb, Altowan, I, 83, 1846. **Arriekaris.**—Domenech, Des. N.Am., I, map, 1860. **Auricara.**—U. S. Ind. Treaties, 447, 1837. **Aurickarees.**—Schoolcraft, Ind. Tribes, I, 523, 1851. **Biccarees.**—Domenech, Des. N. Am., I, 431, 1860. **Black Pawnee.**—Prichard, Phys. Hist. Mankind, V, 408, 1847 (applying properly to the Wichita, the Black-bear Pawnee of the Omaha). **Corn Eaters.**—Culbertson in Smithson. Rep. 1850, 130, 1851 (given as their own name). **Eokoros.**—Lahontan, New Voy., I, 110, 1703. **Eskoros.**—Lahontan, misquoted by Schoolcraft,Trav.,viii, 1821. **Ka′-nan-in.**—Hayden, Ethnog. and Philol. Mo. Val., 326, 1862 (Arapaho name: 'people whose jaws break in pieces'). **Kees.**—Terry in Rep. Sec.War, pt 1, 35, 1869 (misprint). **Kicaras.**—Lewis, Trav., 15, 1809 (misprint). **la Ree.**—Lewis and Clark, Disc., 22, 1806. **Okoro.**—Lahontan, New Voy., I, 120, 1703. **O-no′-ni-o.**—Hayden, Ethnog. and Philol. Mo. Val., 290, 1862 (Cheyenne name). **Padani.**—For forms of this name as applied to the Arikara, see Pawnee. **Pa′ɸiⁿ-dĭza.**—Dorsey, MS. Ȼegiha Dict., B. A. E., 1878 (Omaha and Ponka name: 'Sand Pawnee'). **Panis ricaras.**—Jefferys, Fr. Dom. Am., pt. 1, 143, 1761. **Pányi púda.**—Dorsey, MS. Tciwere vocab., B. A. E., 1879 (Iowa, Oto, and Missouri name: 'Sand Pawnee'). **Pawnee-Rikasree.**—Nuttall, Jour., 81, 1821. **Pucaras.**—Alegre, Hist. Comp. Jesus, I, 336, 1841. **Racres.**—Lewis, Trav., 15, 1809. **Recars.**—Ibid. **Ree.**—Powell in 7th Rep. B. A. E., 60, 1891. **Re-ka-ras.**—Bonner, Life of Beckwourth, 255, 1856. **Re-ke-rahs.**—Ibid., 162. **Rhea.**—Hallam in Beach, Ind. Misc., 134, 1877. **Ric′-ârâs.**—Perrin du Lac, Voy. Louisiane, 257, 1850. **Ricaree.**—Snelling, Tales of Trav., 35, 1830. **Ricaries.**—Domenech, Des. N. Am., I, 443, 1860. **Ricaris.**—Gass, Jour., 82, 1810. **Ricars.**—Lewis and Clark, Disc., 24, 1806. **Ric-ca-ras.**—Hunter, Captivity, 87, 1823. **Riccaree.**—Boller, Among Inds. in the Far West, 210, 1868. **Riccarrees.**—Catlin, O-kee-pa, 40, 1867. **Richara.**—Sen. Ex. Doc. 90, 22d Cong., 1st sess., 12, 1832. **Rickaras.**—Lewis and Clark, Discov., 30, 1806. **Rickarees.**—Gass, Jour., 48, 1807. **Rickerees.**—Ibid., 53. **Rickrees.**—Ibid., 48. **Ricora.**—Boudinot, Star in West, 128, 1816. **Rikaras.**—Irving, Astoria, 199, 1849. **Rikkara.**—Maximilian, Trav., 167, 1843. **Ris.**—Ibid. (so called by the Canadians). **Sa-nish′.**—Hayden, Ethnog. and Philol. Mo. Val., 356, 1862. **Satrahe.**—Balbi, Atl. Ethnog., 54, 1826. **S′quĭes′-tshi.**—Hoffman in Proc. Am. Philos. Soc., 371, 1886 (Salish name). **Starrahe.**—Bradbury, Trav., iii, 1817. **Stâr-râh-he′.**—Lewis and Clark, Discov., 22, 1806 (own name). **Ta-nish′.**—Hayden, Ethnog. and Philol. Mo. Val., 356, 1862 ('the people': own name). **Tsa′-nish.**—Hoffman in Proc. Am. Philos. Soc., 294, 1886. **Wakinas.**—Hildreth, Dragoon Campaigns, 164. 1836 (probably the same). **Wa-zi′-ya-ta Pa-da′-niⁿ.**—Cook, MS. Yankton vocab., B. A. E., 184, 1882 ('northern Pawnee': Yankton name).

**Ariswaniski.** A Chnagmiut village on the right bank of the lower Yukon, Alaska.—Coast Surv. map, 1899.

**Aritutoc.** A former Maricopa rancheria on the N. side of Rio Gila at or near the present Oatman flat and the great bend of the river, in s. Arizona. It was visited by Father Sedelmair in 1744, and by Anza, Font, and Garcés in 1775.

**Aritoac.**—Garcés, Diary, 117, 1900. **Aritutoc.**—Sedelmair cited by Bancroft, Ariz. and N. Mex.,

366, 1889. **Rinconada.**—Anza and Font (1780), ibid., 392.

**Arivaca.** A former Piman village w. of Tubac, s. Ariz., dating from prior to 1733. It was abandoned during the Pima revolt of 1751, before which time it was a visita of the mission of Guevavi. (Bancroft, Ariz. and N. Mex., 385–6, 1889.)
**Aribac.**—Anon. rep. (1777) in Bancroft, Ariz. and N. Mex., 385, 1889. **Aribaca.**—Rudo Ensayo (1763), 161, 1863.

**Arivaipa** (Nevome Pima: *aarivapa*, 'girls,' possibly applied to these people on account of some unmanly act). An Apache tribe that formerly made its home in the canyon of Arivaipa cr., a tributary of the Rio San Pedro, s. Ariz., although like the Chiricahua and other Apache of Arizona they raided far southward and were reputed to have laid waste every town in N. Mexico as far as the Gila prior to the Gadsden purchase in 1853, and with having exterminated the Sobaipuri, a Piman tribe, in the latter part of the 18th century. In 1863 a company of California volunteers, aided by some friendly Apache, at Old Camp Grant, on the San Pedro, attacked an Arivaipa rancheria at the head of the canyon, killing 58 of the 70 inhabitants, men, women, and children—the women and children being slain by the friendly Indians, the men by the Californians—in revenge for their atrocities. After this loss they sued for peace, and their depredations practically ceased. About 1872 they were removed to San Carlos agency, where, with the Pinaleños, apparently their nearest kindred, they numbered 1,051 in 1874. Of this number, however, the Arivaipa formed a very small part. The remnant of the tribe is now under San Carlos and Ft Apache agencies on the White Mountain res., but its population is not separately enumerated. (F. W. H.)
**Apachè Arivapah.**—Hoffman in 10th Rep. Hayden Surv., 461, 1878. **Araivapa.**—White, MS. Hist. Apaches, B. A. E., 1875. **Aravaipa.**—Ind. Aff. Rep. 1873, 342, 1874. **Aravapa.**—Ind. Aff. Rep. 1871, 54, 1872. **Aravapai.**—Ind. Aff. Rep., 246, 1877. **Aravapa Piñals.**—Ind. Aff. Rep. 1871, 54, 1872. **Aravipais.**—Keane in Stanford, Compend., 501, 1878. **Aribaipa.**—Ind. Aff. Rep., 306, 1877. **Aribapais.**—Ind. Aff. Rep., 175, 1875. **Arivapa.**—Ind. Aff. Rep., 292, 1886. **Arivapa Apaches.**—Ind. Aff. Rep., 141, 1868. **Arivapais.**—Haines, Am. Ind., 135, 1888. **Arivaypa Apaches.**—Ind. Aff. Rep. 1871, 3, 1872. **Arrivapis.**—Colyer (1871) quoted in Ind. Aff. Rep., 299, 1886. **Avipa Apache.**—Palmer, Pinella and Avipa MS. vocab., B. A. E.

**Arivechi.** A pueblo of the Jova and the seat of a Spanish mission founded in 1627; situated in E. Sonora, Mexico, about lat. 29° 10′. Pop. 466 in 1678, 118 in 1730. It is no longer an Indian settlement.
**Aribechi.**—Bandelier in Arch. Inst. Papers, III, 56, 1890. **Arivetzi.**—Orozco y Berra, Geog., 345, 1864. **San Francisco Javier Arivechi.**—Zapata (1678) quoted by Bancroft, No. Mex. States, I, 245, 1884.

**Ariziochic.** A Tarahumare settlement on the E. bank of one of the upper tributaries of Rio Yaqui, lat. 28° 25′, long. 107°,

Chihuahua, Mexico.—Orozco y Berra, Geog., 323, 1864.

**Arizonac** (prob. 'small springs' or 'few springs'). Evidently a former Papago rancheria situated between Guevavi and Saric, in Sonora, Mexico, just below the present s. boundary of Arizona, not far from the site of Nogales. In 1736–41 the finding in its vicinity of some balls of native silver of fabulous size caused a large influx of treasure seekers, and through the fame that the place thus temporarily acquired, its name, in the form Arizona, was later applied to the entire country thereabout, and, when New Mexico was divided, was adopted as the name of the new Territory. In 1764–67 Arizonac was a visita of the mission of Saric, on the upper waters of Rio Altar, Sonora. See Bancroft, Ariz. and N. Mex., 362, 371, 1889. (F. W. H.)

**Arizpe** (according to Bandelier a corrupted abbreviation of *Huc-aritz-pa*, the native name, while Hardy says it is from the Opata *aripa*, 'the great congregation of ants'). A former Opata pueblo on Rio Sonora, about lat. 30° 25′, Sonora, Mexico. It became the seat of a Spanish mission in 1648, and was afterward the capital of the state, but its importance as a town decreased after the removal of the capital to Ures, in 1832, and subsequent Apache depredations. Arizpe is identical with the Arispa of Castañeda and the Ispa of Jaramillo, visited by Coronado in 1540. The population of the mission was 416 in 1678, 316 in 1730, and 359 in 1777 (Doc. Hist. Mex., 4th ser., I, 469, 1856, and authors quoted below). It is no longer an Indian town. There are ruins N. W. of the village. (F. W. H.)
**Aripa.**—Hardy, Trav. in Mex., 442, 1829 (Opata name: 'the great congregation of ants'). **Arispa.**—Castañeda (1540) in 14th Rep. B. A. E. 515, 1896. **Arispe.**—Kino (1696) in Doc. Hist. Mex., 4th ser., I, 265, 1856. **Asuncion Arizpe.**—Zapata (1678) quoted by Bancroft, No. Mex. States, I, 246, 1884. **Guagarispa.**—Castañeda (1540) in Ternaux-Compans, Voy., IX, 158, 1838. **Huc-aritz-pa.**—Bandelier, Gilded Man, 175, 1893 (Opata name). **Ispa.**—Jaramillo (1540) in 14th Rep. B. A. E., 585, 1896. **Nuestra Señora de la Asuncion Arizpe.**—Orozco y Berra, Geog., 343, 1864 (mission name).

**Arkansite.** A variety of the mineral brookite, so called from having been discovered at Magnet Cove, Ark. (Dana, Text-book Mineralogy, 278, 1888); from the place and ethnic name *Arkansas* and the English suffix -*ite*. (A. F. C.)

**Arkokisa.** A people formerly living in villages chiefly along lower Trinity r., Tex. The Spanish presidio of San Agustin de Ahumada was founded among them in 1756, and 50 Tlascaltec families from s. Mexico were settled there, but the post was abandoned in 1772. They were allied with the Aranama and the Attacapa, and were on friendly terms also with the Bidai, but their linguistic affinity is not known. According to Sibley they numbered about 80 men in 1760–70 and subsisted principally on shellfish and fruits, and in 1805 their principal town was on the w. side of Colorado r. of Texas, about 200 m. s. w. of Nacogdoches. They had another village N. of this, between the Neches and the Sabine, nearer the coast than the villages of the Adai. Sibley speaks of the Arkokisa as migratory, but they could not always have been entitled to that characterization. It is probable that, owing to the conditions incident to the intrusion of the white race, the people became demoralized; their tribal relations were broken up, their numbers decimated by disease, and the remnant of them was finally scattered and disorganized. Of their habits very little is known; their language seems to have been distinct from that of their neighbors, with whom they conversed by signs. (A. C. F.)

Accocesaws.—Lewis, Travels, 191, 1809. Accocke-saws.—Fisher, Int. Acc., 201, 1812. Accokesaus.—Brackenridge, Views of La., 81, 1814. Accoke-saws.—Sibley, Hist. Sketches, 71, 1806. Aco-ke-sas.—Brackenridge, op. cit., 87. Acossesaws.—Latham in Trans. Philol. Soc. Lond., 103, 1856. Arkokisa.—Yoakum, Hist. Tex., map, 1855. Enquisacoes.—Clarke in Tex. Hist. Assn. Quar., IX, 53, 1905. Horcaquisacs.—MS. of, 1770 quoted by Bancroft, No. Mex. States, I, 656, 1886. Horconcitos.—Bancroft, ibid., 643. Horcoquisa.—Tex. State archives, Aug. 26, 1756. Horcoquisaes.—Doc. of 1793 in Tex. State archives. Naquizcoza.—Gentl. of Elvas quoted by Shea, Early Voy., 149, 1861 (same?). Ocosaus.—Soc. Geog. Mex., Bul., 266, 1870. Orcoquisa.—Doc. of 1805 in Tex. State archives. Orcoquisacs.—Mezières (1778) quoted by Bancroft, No. Mex. States, I, 661, 1886. Orcoquizas.—Doc. of 1791 in Tex. State archives. Orquisaco.—Yoakum, Hist. Tex., I, 49, 1855. Oxquoquiras.—Robin, Voy. à la Louisiane, III, 14, 1807.

**Arksutite.** According to Dana (Textbook Mineralogy, 265, 1888) a fluorine mineral whose exact nature is not yet known, named from the Eskimo *Arksut*, a fiord in Greenland where it was discovered. (A. F. C.)

**Arlagnuk.** An Iglulirmiut Eskimo village near Melville pen., on Iglulik id., lat. 69° 11′ 33″.—Parry, Second Voy., 355, 1824.

**Arliaktung.** An Eskimo village of the Akudnirmiut, N. of Home bay, E. Baffin land.—Boas in Deutsch. Geog. Blätt., VIII, 34, 1885.

**Armor.** Shields and body armor appear to have been in more or less general use among the Indian tribes N. of Mexico. The Eskimo are said not to employ the shield, but it was in use among the tribes of the plains, the S. W., and British Columbia, and occasionally among the Iroquois and other eastern Indians. The Plains Indians made their shields of buffalo hide, covered with buckskin or elk skin; others used basketry (Pueblo), cedar rods (Navaho), osiers or bark (Virginia Indians, Iroquois). With the exception of a sort of oblong armor-shield 4 to 5 ft. long, made of elk hide by the Ntlakyapamuk (Teit in Mem. Am. Mus. Nat. Hist., Anthrop. ser., I, 1900), the Indian shield is circular. The decoration of the shield, the ceremonies connected with its acquisition, its use in ritual, etc., constitute important chapters in the art and religion of the aborigines. The shield ceremony of the Hopi and the heraldry of the shield among the Kiowa have respectively been specially studied by Dr J. Walter Fewkes and Mr James Mooney of the Bureau of American Ethnology. Helmets and head defenses are found among some of the tribes of the North Pacific coast, and are often ornamented with the crest of the owner. North of Mexico body armor presents at least five types: Rows of overlapping plates of ivory, bone, and, since contact with the whites, iron (Eskimo, Chukchi); twined wooden slats (N. W. coast, Shasta, Iroquois, Virginia Indians); twined wooden rods (Aleut, N. W. coast, Columbia r. tribes, Klamath, Hupa, Iroquois, Powhatan, etc.); bands of skin arranged in telescoping fashion (Chukchi); coats, etc., of hardened hide (Tlingit, Haida, Chinook, Hupa, Shoshoni, Navaho, Pawnee, Mohawk, etc.). The ivory plate armor is believed by Boas to be an imitation of the iron armor of the Chukchi, and the other plate armor may also be of N. E. Asiatic (Japanese) origin. The presence

BODY ARMOR OF WOOD; TLINGIT

of the buffalo in the Mississippi region, and of the elk, moose, etc., in other parts of the country, had much to do with the nature of armor. The data concerning armor among the Indians are summarized by Hough (Primitive American Armor, Rep. Nat. Mus. 1893, 625–651). One sort of defensive armor did the early English adventurers in Virginia good service on one occasion. At the suggestion of Mosco and the friendly Indians, Capt. John Smith, when fighting a tribe on the Chesapeake, made use of the "Massawomek targets," or shields (Smith, Va., I. 185, 1819; Holmes in 13th Rep. B. A. E., 18, 1896). These the English set "about the forepart of our Boat, like a forecastle, from whence we securely beat back the Salvages from off the plaine without any hurt." And so, protected by "these light Targets (which are made of little small sticks woven betwixt strings of their hempe, but so firmly that no arrow can possibly pierce them)," the English drove back the enemy. In general, it may be said that the shield and lance were used chiefly by the equestrian tribes of the open country, while body armor, with the knife and tomahawk, were more in favor with those of the timber and coast region. See *Shields*. (A. F. C.)

**Armouchiquois** (apparently a French cor-corruption of *Alemousiski*, 'land of the little dog,' from *allum* 'dog,' *ousis* diminutive, *ac* or *auk* 'land,' "for there were many little dogs in the prairies of this territory."—Maurault). The name given by the Abnaki to the country of the Indians of the New England coast s. of Saco r., Me. Williamson (Hist. Maine, I, 477, 1832) says they were the Marechites (Malecite) of St Johns r., but Champlain, who visited the Armouchiquois country, says that it lies beyond, that is, s. of, Choüacoet (Sokoki), and that the language differed from that of the Souriquois (Micmac) and the Etchimin. Laverdière affirms that "the French called Almouchiquois several peoples or tribes that the English included under the term Massachusetts." According to Parkman (Jesuits in N. Am., XXI, 1867) the term included the Algonquian tribes of New England—Mohegan, Pequot, Massachuset, Narraganset, and others "in a chronic state of war with the tribes of New Brunswick and Nova Scotia." (C. T.)

Allemouchicois.—Champlain (*ca.* 1635), Œuvres, V, pt., 2, 33, 1870. Almauchicois.—Vetromile, Abnakis, 50, 1866. Almonchiguois.—Champlain (1616), Œuvres, IV, 73, 1870. Almouchicoisen.—Dutch map of 1616 in N. Y. Col. Doc. I, 1856. Almouchiquois.—Maurault, Hist. Abenakis, 4, 1866. Almouchiquoise.—Champlain (1605), Œuvres, III, 62, 1870. Armouchicois.—Champlain (1603), ibid., II, 58, 1870. Armouchiquois.—Jes. Rel. for 1611, 33, 1858. Armucīceses.—Alcedo, Dic. Geog., I, 158, 1786.

**Arocoum.** See *Raccoon*.

**Arontaen** ('it is a lying log.'—Hewitt). A Huron village situated near Pt. Cockburn, on the N. shore of Nattawasaga bay, Ontario, in 1636.—Jesuit Relation for 1636, 133, 1858.

**Arosaguntacook.** A tribe of the Abnaki confederacy, formerly living in Androscoggin co., Me. Their village, which bore the same name, was on Androscoggin r., probably near Lewiston. The various names used indiscriminately for the tribe and the river may be resolved into the forms Ammoscoggin and Arosaguntacook, which have received different interpretations, all seeming to refer to the presence of fish in the stream. The name seems to have been used only for the part of the river in Androscoggin co. between the falls near Jay and those near Lewiston. The present name was obtained by changing the first part of the word to Andros in compliment to Gov. Andros. The Arosaguntacook lived on the edge of the first English settlements in Maine, and consequently suffered much in the various Indian wars, in which they took a prominent part from 1675 until their removal to Canada. Their town was burned by the English in 1690. As the settlements pushed into the interior the Wawenoc, at the mouth of the river, moved up and joined the Arosaguntacook, and at a later period the combined tribes moved still farther up and joined the Rocameca. These movements led to much confusion in the statements of writers, as the united tribes were commonly known by the name of the leading one, the Arosaguntacook or Androscoggin. These tribes, together with the Pigwacket, removed to St Francis, Canada, soon after the defeat of the Pequawket by Lovewell in 1725. Here the Arosaguntacook were still the principal tribe and their dialect (Abnaki) was adopted by all the inhabitants of the village, who were frequently known collectively as Arosaguntacook. (J. M.)

Adgecantehook.—Doc. of 1709 in N. Y. Doc. Col. Hist., V, 86, 1855. Alsigantégwi.—Gatschet, Penobscot MS., B. A. E., 1887 (Penobscot name for the St Francis Indians; pl. Alsigantégwiak). Amarascoggin.—Stoughton (1695) in N. Y. Doc. Col. Hist., IX, 613, 1855. Amarascogin.—La Potherie, Hist. Am., IV, 40, 1753. Amarescoggin.—Trumbull, Conn., II, 77, 1818. Amariscoggins.—Schoolcraft, Ind. Tribes, V, 223, 1855. Amaroscoggen.—Drake, Bk. Inds., bk. 3, 108, 1848. Amasagunticook.—True in N. Y. Hist. Mag., 238, 1864. Amerascogen.—Pike (1690) in Drake, Ind. Wars, 152, 1825. Amerescogin.—Douglass, Summary, I, 185, 1755. Ameriscoggins.—Gallatin in Trans. Am. Antiq. Soc., II, 32, 1836. Amerriscoggin.—Maine Hist. Soc. Coll., III, 357, 1853. Amircankanne.—Vaudreuil (1721) in N. Y. Doc. Col. Hist., IX, 904, 1855. Amireaneau.—Doc. of 1693 in N. Y. Doc. Col. Hist., IX, 571, 1855 (misprint). Ammarascogin.—Georgetown treaty (1717) in Maine Hist. Soc. Coll., VI, 261, 1859. Ammarescoggin.—Same in N. H. Hist. Soc. Coll., II, 242, 1827. Ammascoggen.—Church (1690) in Mass. Hist. Soc. Coll., 4th s., V, 271, 1861. Amonoscoggan.—Drake, Bk. Inds., bk. 3, 104, 1848. Amonoscoggin.—Mather, Magnalia (1702) quoted by Drake, Bk. Inds., bk. 3, 150, 1848. Amoscongen.—Sagadahoc treaty (1690) in Mass. Hist. Soc. Coll., 3d s., I, 113, 1825. Amresscoggin.—Casco conference (1727) in N. H. Hist. Soc. Coll., II, 261, 1827. Anasaguntacooks.—Sullivan in Mass. Hist. Soc. Coll., 1st s., IX, 210, 1804. Anasaguntakook.—Drake, Bk. Inds., vi, 1848. Anasaguntieooks.—Williamson in N. Y. Doc. Col. Hist., IX, 475, 1855. Anasuguntakook.—Schoolcraft, Ind. Tribes, III, 527, 1853. Androscoggins.—Sullivan in Mass. Hist. Soc. Coll., 1st s., IX, 210, 1804. Anmoughcawgen.—Smith (1629), Virginia, II, 177, repr. 1819. Annirkakan.—La Potherie, Hist. Am., III, 189, 1753. Aresaguntacooks.—Colman (1726) in Mass. Hist. Soc. Coll., 1st s., VI, 115, 1800. Arisaguntacooks.—Drake, Bk. Inds., bk. 3, 152, 1848. Arosagantakuk.—Keane in Stanford, Compend., 500, 1878. Arosaguntacook.—Drake, Trag. Wild., 144, 1841. Arosaguntakûk.—Vater, Mithridates, pt. 3, sec. 3, 390, 1816. Arouseguntecook.—Douglass, Summary, I, 185, 1755. Arrasaguntacook.—Falmouth conf. (1727) in Maine Hist. Soc. Coll., III, 438, 1853. Arreaguntecooks.—Falmouth treaty report (1726), ibid., 386. Arreguntenocks.—Penhallow (1726) in N. H. Hist. Soc. Coll., I, 129, 1824. Arreraguntecook.—Falmouth treaty report, op. cit. Arreruguntenocks.—Niles (*ca.* 1761) in Mass. Hist. Soc. Coll., 4th s., V, 365, 1861. Arresagontacook.—Casco conf. (1727) in N. H. Hist. Soc. Coll., II, 261, 1827. Arresaguntacooks.—Falmouth conf. report (1727) in Maine Hist. Soc. Coll., III, 413, 1853. Arresaguntecook.—Falmouth treaty report (1726), ibid., 386–390. Arreseguntecook.—Ibid. Arreseguntoocook.—Falmouth treaty journal (1749), ibid., IV, 157, 1856. Arresuguntoocooks.—Ibid., 155. Arseguntecokes.—Document of 1764 in N. Y. Doc. Col. Hist., VII, 641, 1856. Arsikanteg8.—

French letter (1721) in Mass. Hist. Soc. Coll., 2d s., VIII, 262, 1819. **Arunseguntekooks.**—La Tour, map, 1779. **Aruseguntekooks.**—Jefferys, French Dom., pt. 1, map, 1761. **Assagunticook.**—Record (1755) in Maine Hist. Soc. Coll., VII, 186, 1876. **Ersegontegog.**—Gyles (1726), ibid., III, 357, 1853. **Massakiga.**—Purchas (1625), ibid., v, 156, 1857.

**Aroughcond, Aroughcun.** See *Raccoon.*

**Arpik.** An Eskimo village in w. Greenland, lat. 73°.—Meddelelser om Grönland, VIII, map, 1889.

**Arrohattoc** (cf. Delaware *allahattek,* 'empty,' 'all gone.'—Heckewelder). A tribe of the Powhatan confederacy, formerly living in Henrico co., Va. They had 30 warriors in 1608. Their chief village, of the same name, was on James r., 12 m. below the falls at Richmond, on the spot where Henrico was built in 1611. (J. M.)
**Arrohateck.**—Smith (1629), Virginia, I, 142, repr. 1819. **Arrohattock.**—Drake, Bk. Inds., bk. 4, 7, 1848. **Arrowhatocks.**—Smith, op. cit., I, 116. **Arrowhatoes.**—Boudinot, Star in the West, 125, 1816. **Arsahattock.**—Smith, op. cit., II, 10. **Irrohatock.**—Ibid., I, 117.

**Arrowheads.** The separate tips or points of arrow-shafts. Among the Indian tribes

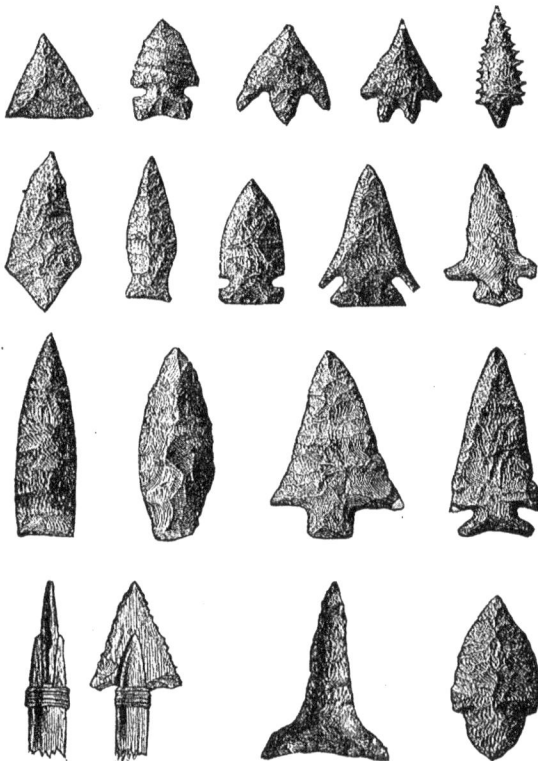

STONE ARROWHEADS, EASTERN FORMS. (ABOUT 1-2)

many were made of flint and other varieties of stone, as well as bone, horn, antler, shell, wood, and copper. Copper was much used by such tribes as were able to obtain a supply from the L. Superior region and to some extent by those of British Columbia and Alaska. Iron has largely taken the place of these materials since the coming of the whites. In stone implements of this class the only line of dis-

tinction between arrowheads and spearheads is that of size. Very few flint arrowheads are as much as 2 inches long, and these are quite slender; thick or strong ones are much shorter. Solid flesh, being almost as resistant as soft rubber, could not be penetrated by a large projectile unless it were propelled by greater power than can be obtained from a bow without artificial aid which is not at the command of a

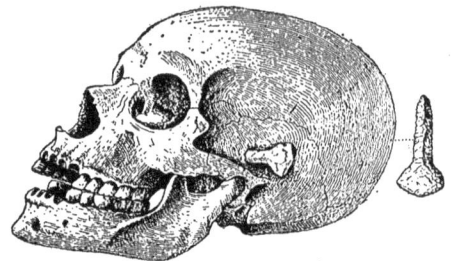

ARROWHEAD EMBEDDED IN A SKULL. (FROM A MOUND IN ILLINOIS)

savage. The shape of the stone arrowhead among the Indian tribes is usually triangular or pointed-oval, though some have very slender blades with expanding base. Many of them are notched. These were set in a slot in the end of the shaft and tied with sinew, rawhide, or cord, which passed through the notches. Those without notches were secured by the cord passing over and under the angle at the base in a figure-8 fashion. It is said that war arrows often had the head loosely attached, so that it would remain in the wound when the shaft was withdrawn, while the hunting point was firmly secured in order that the arrow might be recovered entire. Glue, gum, and cement were used in some sections for fixing the point or for rendering the fastening more secure. The accompanying diagram will explain the different

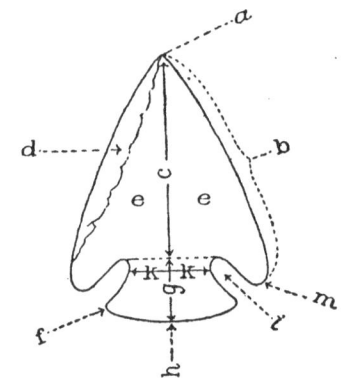

ARROWHEAD NOMENCLATURE. (*a*, POINT; *b*, EDGE; *c*, FACE; *d*, BEVEL; *e*, BLADE; *f*, TANG; *g*, STEM; *h*, BASE; *i*, NOTCH; *k*, NECK; *m*, BARB OR SHOULDER)

ent terms used with reference to the completed arrowhead. A specimen which has the end rounded or squared instead of pointed is known as a "bunt." As a rule both faces are worked off equally so as to bring the edge opposite the middle plane of the blade, though it is sometimes a little on one side. For the greater part these seem to be redressed ordinary spearheads, knives, or arrowheads whose points have been broken off, though some appear to have been originally made in this form. A few are smooth or polished at the ends, as if used for knives or scrapers; but most of them have no marks of use except occasionally such as would result from being shot or struck against a hard substance. It is probable that their purpose was to stun birds or small game, in order to secure the pelt or plumage free from cuts or blood stain. They are relatively few in number, though widely distributed in area. The Eskimo employ arrowheads of stone of usual forms.

Consult Abbott (1) Prim. Indus., 1881, (2) in Surv. W. 100th Merid., VII, 1879; Beauchamp in Bull. N. Y. State Mus., no. 16, 1897, and no. 50, 1902; Fowke in 13th Rep. B. A. E., 1896; Moorehead, Prehist. Impls., 1900; Morgan, League of the Iroquois, 1904; Nordenskiöld, Cliff Dwellers of Mesa Verde, 1893; Rau in Smithson. Cont., XXII, 1876; Wilson in Rep. Nat. Mus. 1897, 1899; the Reports of the Smithsonian Inst.; the Am. Anthropologist; the Am. Antiquarian; the Archæologist; the Antiquarian. (G. F. W. H. H.)

**Arrows, Bows, and Quivers.** The bow and arrow was the most useful and universal weapon and implement of the

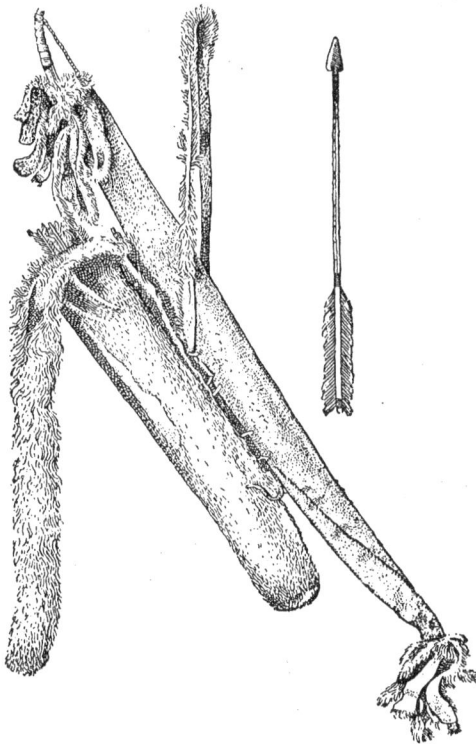

TYPICAL QUIVER; NAVAHO

chase possessed by the Indians N. of Mexico for striking or piercing distant objects.

ARROWS.—A complete Indian arrow is made up of six parts: Head, shaft, foreshaft, shaftment, feathering, and nock. These differ in material, form, measurement, decoration, and assemblage, according to individuals, locality, and tribe. Arrowheads have three parts: Body, tang, and barbs. There are two kinds of arrowheads, the blunt and the sharp. Blunt heads are for stunning, being top-shaped. The Ute, Paiute, and others tied short sticks crosswise on the end of the shafts of boys' arrows for killing birds. Sharp

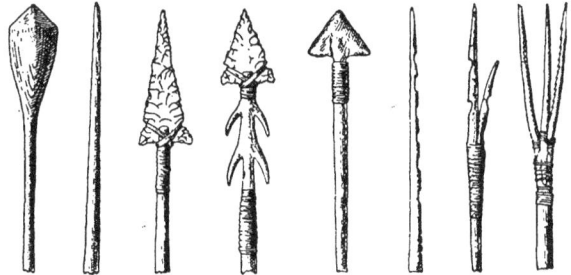

TYPES OF ARROWHEADS

arrowheads are of two classes, the lanceolate, which can be withdrawn, and the sagittate, intended for holding game or for rankling in the wound. The former are used on hunting, the latter on war or retrieving arrows. In the S. W. a sharpened foreshaft of hard wood serves for the head. Arctic and N. W. coast arrows have heads of ivory, bone, wood, or copper, as well as of stone; elsewhere they are more generally of stone, chipped or polished. Many of the arrowheads from those two areas are either two-pronged, three-pronged, or harpoon-shaped. The head is attached to the shaft or foreshaft by lashing with sinew, by riveting, or with gum. Among the Eskimo the barbed head of bone is stuck loosely into a socket on the shaft, so that this will come out and the head rankle in the wound. The barbs of the ordinary chipped head are usually alike on both sides, but in the long examples from ivory, bone, or wood the barbing is either bilateral or unilateral, one-barbed or many-barbed, alike on the two sides or different. In addition to their use in hunting and in war, arrows are commonly used in games and ceremonies. Among certain Hopi priesthoods arrowheads are tied to bandoleers as ornaments, and among the Zuñi they are frequently attached to fetishes.

Arrowshafts of the simplest kind are reeds, canes, or stems of wood. In the Arctic region they are made of driftwood or are bits of bone lashed together, and are rather short, owing to the scarcity of material. The foreshaft is a piece of ivory, bone, or heavy wood. Among the Eskimo foreshafts are of bone or ivory on wooden shafts; in California, of hard wood on shafts of pithy or other light wood; from California across the continent to Florida, of hard wood on cane shafts. The shaftments in most arrows are plain; but on the W. coast they are

USE OF ARROWSHAFT STRAIGHTENER; SHOSHONI (ELLIOTT)

painted with stripes for identification. The Plains Indians and the Jicarillas cut shallow grooves lengthwise down their arrowshafts, called "lightning marks," or "blood grooves," and also are said by Indians to keep the shaft from warping (Fletcher) or to direct the flight. The feathering is an important feature in the Indian arrow, differing in the species of birds, the kind and number of feathers and in their form, length, and manner of setting. As to the number of feathers, arrows are either without feathering, two-feathered, or three-feathered. As to form, feathers are

IVORY ARROWSHAFT STRAIGHT-
ENER; ESKIMO. (LENGTH,
3 IN.)

whole, as among most of the Eskimo and some S. W. tribes, or halved or notched on the edges. In length they vary from the very short feathering on S. W. arrows, with long reed shafts and heavy fore-shafts, to the long feathering on Plains arrows, with their short shafts of hard wood. The feathers are set on the shaftment either flat or radiating; the ends are lashed with sinew, straight or doubled under, and the middles are either free or glued down. In some arrows there is a slight rifling, due perhaps to the twist needed to make a tight fit, though it is not said that this feature is intentional. The nocks of arrows, the part containing the notch for the string, are, in the Arctic, flat; in the S., where reed shafts were employed, cylindrical; and in localities where the shafts were cut, bulbous. Besides its use as a piercing

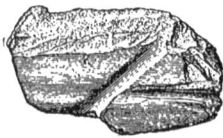

STONE ARROWSHAFT RUB-
BER; MASSACHUSETTS.
(LENGTH, 4 1-2 IN.)

or striking projectile, special forms of the arrow were employed as a toy, in gaming, in divining, in rain-making, in ceremony, in symbolism, and in miniature forms with prayer-sticks. The modulus in arrow-making was each man's arm. The manufacture of arrows was usually attended with much ceremony.

The utmost flight, the certainty of aim, and the piercing power of Indian arrows

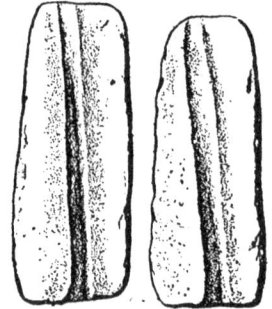

SANDSTONE ARROWSHAFT RUB-
BER; INDIAN GRAVE, BRITISH
COLUMBIA. (H. I. SMITH)

are not known, and stories about them are greatly exaggerated. The hunter or warrior got as near to his victim as possible. In shooting he drew his right hand to his ear. His bow register scarcely exceeded 60 pounds, yet arrows are said to have gone quite through the body of a buffalo (Wilson in Rep. Nat. Mus. for 1897, 811–988).

Bows.—The bows of the North Americans are quite as interesting as their arrows. The varied environments quickened the inventive faculty and produced several varieties. They are distinguished by the materials and the parts, which are known as back, belly, wings, grip, nocks, and string. The varieties are as follow: (1) Self-bow, made of one piece; (2) compound bow, of several pieces of wood, bone, or horn lashed together; (3) sinew-backed bow, a bow of driftwood or other brittle wood, reinforced with cord of sinew wrapped many times about it lengthwise, from wing to wing; (4) sinew-lined bow, a self-bow, the back of which is further strengthened with sinew glued on. In some cases bows were decorated in colors.

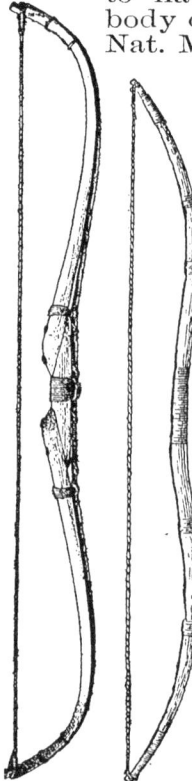

a      b
TYPES OF BOWS. a,
COMPOUND BOW,
EASTERN ESKIMO
(BOAS); b, SINEW-
LINED BOW, NAVAHO
(MASON)

The varieties characterizing the culture areas are distinguished as follow:

1. *Arctic.*—Compound bows in the E., very clumsy, owing to scarcity of material; the grip may be of wood, the wings of whale's ribs or bits of wood from whalers. In the W. excellent sinew-

backed bows were made on bodies of driftwood. Asiatic influence is apparent in them. (See Boas in 6th Rep. B. A. E., 399–669, 1884; Murdoch in 9th Rep. B. A. E., 133–617, 1887, and Rep. Nat. Mus. for 1884, 307–316.)

2. *Northern Athapascan.*—Long, straight bows of willow or birch, with wooden wrist-guards projecting from the belly.

3. *St Lawrence and Eastern United States.*—Self-bows of ash, second-growth hickory, osage orange (bois d'arc), oak, or other hard wood.

4. *Gulf States.*—Long bows, rectangular in section, of walnut or other hard wood.

5. *Rocky mts.*—(1) Self-bow of osage orange or other hard wood; (2) a compound bow of several strips of buffalo horn lashed together and strengthened.

6. *North Pacific coast.*—Bows with rounded grip and flat wings, usually made of yew or cedar.

7. *Fraser-Columbia region.*—Similar to No. 6, but with wings much shorter and the nocks curved sharply outward.

8. *Interior basin.*—A long slender stick of rude form; many are strengthened by means of a sinew lining on the back and cross wrappings.

9. *California.*—Like No. 7, but neatly lined with sinew and often prettily decorated.

10. *Southwest.*—Like No. 8, but seldom sinew-lined (Navaho). Small painted bows are used much in ceremony, especially by the Pueblos, who deposit them in shrines. In the s. part of this area long cottonwood bows with cross lashing are employed by Yuman and Piman tribes. The Jicarillas make a cupid's bow, strengthened with bands of sinew wrapping.

The bows E. of the Rockies have little distinction of parts, but the w. Eskimo and Pacific slope varieties have flat wings, and the former shows connection with Asia. The nocks are in some tribes alike, but among the Plains Indians the lower nock is cut in at one side only. Bow-strings are of sinew cord tied at one end and looped at the other.

WRIST-GUARD.—When the bowman's left arm was exposed he wore a wrist-guard of hide or other suitable material to break the blow of the released string. Wrist-guards were also decorated for ceremonial purposes.

ARROW RELEASE.—Arrow release is the way of holding the nock and letting loose the arrow in shooting. Morse describes four methods among the tribes N. of Mexico, the first three being Indian: (1) Primary release, in which the nock is held between the thumb and the first joint of the forefinger; (2) secondary release, in which the middle and the ring fingers are laid inside of the string; (3) tertiary release, in which the nock is held between the ends of the forefinger and the middle finger, while the first three fingers are hooked on the string; (4) the Mediterranean method, confined to the Eskimo, whose arrows have a flat nock, in which the string is drawn with the tips of the first, second, and third fingers, the nock being lightly held between the first and the second fingers. Morse finds

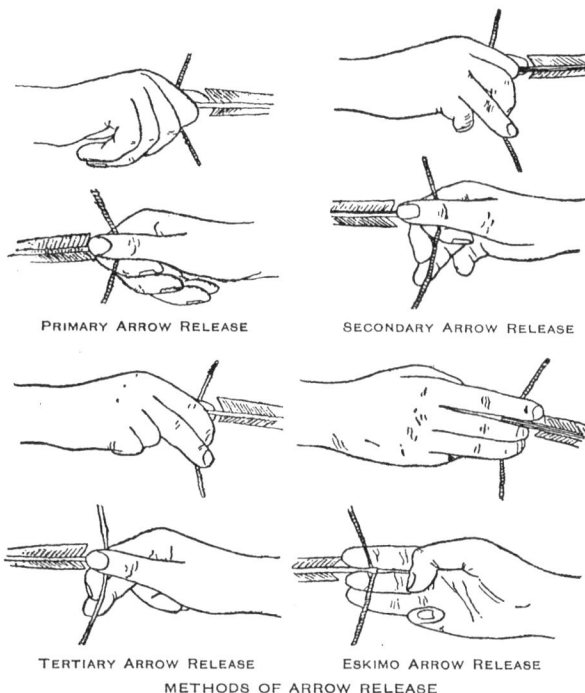

PRIMARY ARROW RELEASE    SECONDARY ARROW RELEASE

TERTIARY ARROW RELEASE    ESKIMO ARROW RELEASE
METHODS OF ARROW RELEASE

that among the North American tribes, the Navaho, Chippewa, Micmac, and Penobscot used the primary release; the Ottawa, Chippewa, and Zuñi the secondary; the Omaha, Arapaho, Cheyenne, Assiniboin, Comanche, Crows, Siksika, and some Navaho, the tertiary.

QUIVERS.—The form of the quiver depended on the size of the bow and arrows; the materials, determined by the region, are skin or wood. Sealskin quivers are used in the Arctic region; beautifully decorated examples of deerskin are common in Canada, also E. of the Rockies and in the Interior basin. On the Pacific coast cedar quivers are employed by the canoe-using tribes, and others make them of skins of the otter, mountain lion, or coyote.

In addition to the works cited under the subject *Arrowheads,* consult Cushing (1) in Proc. A. A. A. S., XLIV, 1896, (2) in Am. Anthrop., VIII, 1895; Culin, Am. Indian Games, 24th Rep. B. A. E., 1905; Mason, N. Am. Bows, Arrows, and Quivers, in Rep. Smithson. Inst. 1893, 1894; Murdoch, Study of Eskimo Bows, Rep. Nat. Mus. 1884, 1885; Morse, Arrow Release, in Bull. Essex Inst., 1885; Arrows and Arrow-makers, in Am. Anthrop., 45–74, 1891; also various Reports of the Bureau of American Ethnology. (O. T. M.)

**Arroyo Grande.** A Pima settlement in s. Arizona with 110 inhabitants in 1858.
Del Arroyo Grande.—Bailey in Ind. Aff. Rep., 208, 1858.

**Arseek.** A tribe living in 1608 in the vicinity of the Sarapinagh, Nause, and Nanticoke (Smith, Hist. Va., I, 175, repr. 1819). They are not noted on Smith's map, but the Nause and Nanticoke are, by which their location is indicated as on Nanticoke r., in Dorchester or Wicomico co., Md. (J. M.)
Aroeck.—Bozman, Maryland, I, 12, 1837 (misprint).
Arsek.—Purchas (1625), Pilgrimes, IV, 1713.

**Arsuk.** An Eskimo village in s. Greenland, w. of Cape Farewell, lat. 61°.—Nansen, First Crossing of Greenland, map, 1890.

**Art.** The term "art" is sometimes applied to the whole range of man's cultural activities, but as here employed it is intended to refer only to those elements of the arts which in the higher stages of culture come fully within the realm of taste and culminate in the ornamental and fine arts (see *Ornament*). Among primitive peoples many of these esthetic elements originate in religious symbolism. Among the tribes N. of Mexico such elements are exceedingly varied and important, and extend in some degree to all branches of the arts in which plastic, graphic, sculptural, constructional, and associative processes are applicable, as well as to the embellishment of the human person. These symbolic elements consist very largely of natural forms, especially of men and beasts, and of such natural phenomena as the sun, stars, lightning, and rain; and their introduction is probably due largely to the general belief that symbols carry with them something of the essence, something of the mystic influence of the beings and potencies which they are assumed to represent. In their introduction into art, however, these symbols are subject to esthetic influence and supervision, and are thus properly classed as embellishments. In use they are modified in form by the various conventionalizing agencies of technique, and a multitude of variants arise which connect with and shade into the great body of purely conventional decoration. Not infrequently, it is believed, the purely conventional designs originating in the esthetic impulse receive symbolic interpretations, giving rise to still greater complexity. Entering into the arts and subject to similar influences are also many ideographic signs and representations which contribute to embellishment and to the development of purely esthetic phases of art. These elements, largely pictographic, contribute not only to the growth of the fine art, painting, but equally to the development of the recording art, writing. The place occupied by the religious, ideographic, and simply esthetic elements in the various arts of the northern tribes may be briefly reviewed:

(1) The building arts, employed in constructing dwellings, places of worship, etc., as practised N. of Mexico, although generally primitive, embody various religious and esthetic elements in their nonessential elaborations. As a rule, these are not evolved from the constructive features of the art, nor are they expressed in terms of construction. The primitive builder of houses depends mainly on the arts of the sculptor and the painter for his embellishments. Among Pueblo tribes, for example, conventional figures and animals are painted on the walls of the kivas, and on their floors elaborate symbolic figures and religious personages are represented in dry-painting (q. v.); at the same time nonsignificant pictorial subjects, as well as purely decorative designs, occur now and then on the interior walls, and the latter are worked out in crude patterns in the stonework of the exterior. Though the buildings themselves present many interesting features of form and proportion, construction has not been brought to any considerable degree under the supervision of taste. The dwellings of primitive tribes in various parts of the country, constructed of reeds, grass, sod, bark, mats, and the like, are by no means devoid of that comeliness which results from careful construction, but they show few definite traces of the influence of either symbolism or the esthetic idea. The skin tipis of the Plains tribes present tempting surfaces to the artist, and are frequently tastefully adorned with heraldic and religious symbols and with graphic designs painted in brilliant colors, while the grass lodge is embellished by emphasizing certain constructive features in rhythmic order, after the manner of basketry. The houses of the N. W. coast tribes, built wholly of wood, are furnished within with carved and painted pillars, whose main function is practical, since they serve to support the roof, while the totem-poles and mortuary columns outside, still more elaborately embellished, are essentially emblematic. The walls both within and without are often covered with brilliantly colored designs embodying mythologic conceptions. Although these structures depend for their effect largely on the work of the sculptor and the painter, they show decided archi-

tectural promise, and suggest the possibilities of higher development and final esthetic control, as in the great architectural styles of the Old World. (See *Architecture, Dry-painting, Habitations.*)

(2) The art of sculpture, which includes also carving, had its birth, no doubt, in the fashioning of implements, utensils, ornaments, and sacred objects; and embellishments, symbolic and esthetic, which were at first entirely subordinate, were gradually introduced as culture advanced, and among some of the northern tribes acquired great prominence. The sculpture elaborations consist of life elements, such as men and beasts, executed in relief and in the round, and having an esthetic as well as a religious function. This strong sculptural tendency is well illustrated by the stone pipes, ornaments, and images of the mound-builders of the Mississippi valley, the carvings of the pile-dwellers of Florida, the masks, utensils, and totem poles of the N. W. coast tribes, and the spirited ivory carvings of the Eskimo. Sculpture, the fine art, is but a higher phase of these elementary manifestations of the esthetic. (See *Sculpture and Carving.*)

(3) The plastic art was practised with much skill by all the more advanced American tribes. North of Mexico the potter's art had made exceptional progress in two great specialization areas—the Pueblo country of the S. W. and the Mississippi valley—and symbolic elements, derived mainly from the animal kingdom, were freely introduced, not only as modifications of the fundamental shapes of vases, but as embellishments variously and tastefully applied. The supervision of taste extended also to the simple forms of vases, the outlines being in many cases highly pleasing even to persons of culture. (See *Pottery.*)

(4) Closely allied with the plastic art is the metallurgic art, which had made sufficient progress among the tribes N. of Mexico to display traces of the strong aboriginal bent for the esthetic. From the mounds of Ohio, especially from the Chillicothe district, many implements, ornaments, and symbolic objects of copper have been obtained, certain highly conventional ornamental figures in sheet-copper being especially noteworthy. From mounds of the Etowah group, in Georgia, numerous repoussé images executed in sheet-copper have been recovered which, as illustrations of artistic as well as of mechanical achievement, take precedence over most other aboriginal works N. of Mexico. (See *Copper, Metal-work.*)

(5) The textile art, which for present purposes may be regarded as including, besides weaving proper, the arts of basketry, needlework, beadwork, quillwork, featherwork, etc., as practised by the northern tribes, abounds in both symbolic and purely decorative elements of embellishment. The former have their origin, as in the other arts, in mythology, and the latter arise mainly from the technical features of the art itself. No branch of art practised by the primitive tribes calls so constantly for the exercise of taste as does this, and probably none has contributed so greatly to the development of the purely geometric phases of decorative art. Illustrations may be found in the weaving of the Pueblo and Navaho tribes of the arid region and the Chilkat of the N. W., in the basketry of numerous tribes of the far W. and S. W., and in the beadwork, quillwork, embroidery, and featherwork of tribes of the great plains, the upper Mississippi valley, and the region of the great lakes. (See *Basketry, Beadwork, Featherwork, Needlework, Quillwork, Weaving.*)

(6) Primitive phases of the art of painting and other related branches, such as engraving and tattooing, appear in the handiwork of all of the northern tribes. Colors were employed in decorating the human body, in embellishing manufactured articles of all kinds, and in ideographic delineations on bark, skins, rock surfaces, etc. A branch of much importance was, and is, the decoration of earthenware, as among the Pueblo tribes; and allied to this was the painting of masks and other carvings, as among the Haida and Kwakiutl of the N. W., and the painting of skins, as among the Plains tribes. In only a few cases had considerable progress been made in pictorial art; perspective, light and shade, and portraiture were unknown. Engraving and stamping were favorite means of decorating pottery among the ancient tribes of E. United States, and tattooing was common among many tribes. (See *Adornment, Dry-painting, Engraving, Painting, Pictographs, Pottery, Tattooing.*)

Besides those branches of art in which taste manifests itself in elaborations of color, form, proportion, and arrangement there are other arts coming less within the range of the practical and having a correspondingly greater proportion of the symbolic and esthetic elements, namely, music, poetry, and drama. All of these have their root deep down in the substrata of human culture, and they take a prominent place in the ceremonial and esthetic life of the primitive tribesmen. (See *Dramatic representations, Music, Poetry.*)

For papers dealing with the primitive art of the northern tribes, see various reports of the Bureau of American Ethnology, the U. S. National Museum, and the Smithsonian Institution; publications of the Peabody Museum, the American Museum of Natural History, the Field Columbian Museum, the University of California, and the Annual Archeological Reports of Ontario. Consult also the American Anthropologist; the American Antiquarian; the Journal of American Folk-lore; Balfour, Evolution of Decorative Art, 1893; Boas in Pop. Sci. Month., Oct., 1903; Haddon, Evolution of Art, 1895; Dellenbaugh, North Americans of Yesterday, 1901; and the various works cited under the articles above referred to. (W. H. H.)

**Artelnof.** A former Aleut village and Russian post on Akun id., Alaska; pop. 32 in 1834.
**Artaylnovskoi.**—Elliott, Cond. Aff. Alaska, 225, 1875. **Arteljnowskoje.**—Holmberg, Ethnol. Skizz., map, 142, 1855. **Artelnovskoe.**—Veniaminoff, Zapiski, II, 202, 1840.

**Arthur, Mark.** A full-blood Nez Percé, born in 1873. His mother being captured with Chief Joseph's band in 1877, Mark became a wanderer among strange tribes until about 1880, when he found his way back to the Nez Percé res., Idaho, where he entered the mission school of Miss McBeth and soon began to prepare for the ministry. When the Nez Percé captives sent to the Indian Territory were returned to their northern home, Mark found his mother among them and cared for her until her death. About 1900 he was ordained by the Walla Walla presbytery and became pastor, at Lapwai, Idaho, of the oldest Presbyterian church w. of the Rocky mts., in which charge he has met with excellent success. In 1905 he was elected delegate to represent both whites and Indians at the general assembly of the Presbyterian church. (A. C. F.)

**Artificial Head Deformation.** Deformations of the human head have been known since the writings of Herodotus. They are divisible into two main classes, those of pathological and those of mechanical or artificial origin. The latter, with which this article is alone concerned, are again divisible into unintentional and intentional deformations. One or the other of these varieties of mechanical deformation has been found among numerous primitive peoples, as the ancient Avars and Krimeans, some Turkomans, Malays, Africans, etc., as well as among some civilized peoples, as the French and Wends, in different parts of the Old World, and both varieties existed from prehistoric through historic time to the present among a number of Indian tribes throughout the Western hemisphere. Un-

CHINOOK WOMAN WITH CHILD IN HEAD-DEFORMING CRADLE. (CATLIN)

intentional mechanical deformations of the head present but one important, widely distributed form, that of occipital compression, which results from prolonged contact of the occiput of the infant with a resistant head support in the cradleboard.

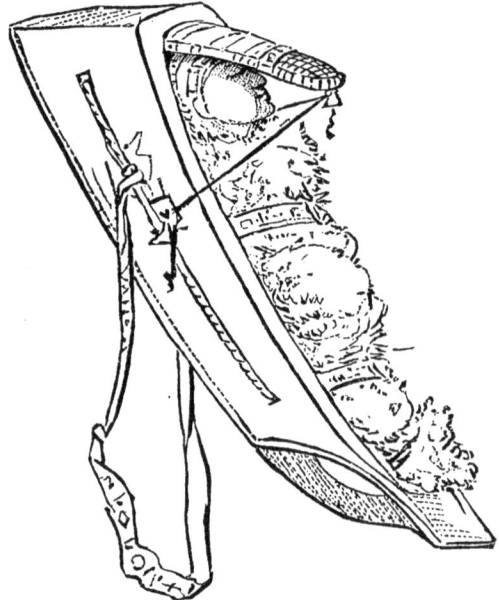
CHINOOK CRADLE WITH WICKER HEAD-BOARD. (CATLIN)

Intentional deformations, in all parts of the world and in all periods, present two important forms only. In the first of these, the flat-head form, the forehead is flattened by means of a board or a variety of cushion, while the parietes of the head undergo compensatory expansion. In the second form, known as macrocephalous, conical, Aymara, Toulousian, etc., the pressure of bandages, or of a series of small cushions, applied about the head, passing over the frontal region and under the occiput, produces a more or less conical, truncated, bag-like, or irregular deformity, characterized by low forehead, narrow parietes, often with a depression just behind the frontal bone, and a protruding occiput. All of these forms present numerous individual variations, some of which are sometimes improperly described as separate types of deformation.

Among the Indians N. of Mexico there are numerous tribes in which no head deformation exists and apparently has never existed. Among these are included many of the Athapascan and Californian peoples, all of the Algonquian, Shoshonean (except the Hopi), and Eskimo tribes, and most of the Indians of the great plains. Unintentional occipital compression is observable among nearly all the southwestern tribes, and it once extended over most of the United States (excepting Florida) s. of the range of the tribes above mentioned. It also exists in ancient skulls found in some parts of the N. W. coast.

Both forms of intentional deformation are found in North America. Their geographical distribution is well defined and limited, suggesting a comparatively late introduction from more southerly peoples. The flat-head variety existed in two widely separated foci, one among the Natchez and in a few other localities along the northeast coast of the Gulf of Mexico, and the other on the N. W. coast from s. Oregon as far N. as s. Vancouver id., but chiefly w. of the Cascades, along Columbia r. The Aymara variety existed, and still exists, only on and near the N. w. extremity of Vancouver id.

The motives of intentional deformation among the Indians, so far as known, are the same as those that lead to similar practices elsewhere; the custom has become fixed through long practice, hence is considered one of propriety and duty, and the result is regarded as a mark of distinction and superiority.

The effects of the various deformations on brain function and growth, as well as on the health of the individual, are apparently insignificant. The tribes that practise it show no indication of greater mortality at any age than those among which it does not exist, nor do they show a larger percentage of imbeciles, or of insane or neuropathic individuals. The deformation, once acquired, persists throughout life, the skull and brain compensating for the compression by augmented extension in directions of least resistance. No hereditary effect is perceptible. The custom of head deformation among the Indians, on the whole, is gradually decreasing, and the indications are that in a few generations it will have ceased to exist.

Consult Morton, Crania Americana, 1839; Gosse, Essai sur les déformations artificielles du crâne, 1855; Lunier, Déformations artificielles du crâne, Dict. de Médic. et de Chirurg., x, 1869; Broca, Sur la déformation Toulousaine du crâne, 1872; Lenhossek, Die künstlichen Schädelverbildungen, 1881; Topinard, Élém. d'anthrop. génér., 739, 1885; Bräss, Beiträge z. Kenntniss d. künstlichen Schädelverbildungen, 1887; Porter, Notes on Artificial Deformation of Children, Rep. Nat. Mus., 1889; Bancroft, Native Races, i, 180, 226, et seq., 1874; Hrdlicka, Head deformation among the Klamath, Am. Anthrop, vii, no. 2, 360, 1905; Catlin, North American Indians, i–ii, 1841. See *Flatheads.* (A. H.)

**Arts and Industries.** The arts and industries of the North American aborigines, including all artificial methods of making things or of doing work, were numerous and diversified, since they were not limited in purpose to the material conditions of life; a technic was developed to gratify the esthetic sense, and art was ancillary to social and ceremonial institutions and was employed in inscribing speech on hide, bark, or stone, in records of tribal lore, and in the service of religion. Many activities too, existed, not so much in the service of these for their own sake as for others. After the coming of the whites, arts and industries in places were greatly improved, multiplied in number, and rendered more complex by the introduction of metallurgy, domestic animals, mechanical devices, and more efficient engineering. Great difficulties embarrass the student in deciding whether some of the early crude inventions were aboriginal or introduced.

The arts and industries of the Indians were called forth and developed for utilizing the mineral, vegetal, and animal products of nature, and they were modified by the environmental wants and resources of every place. Gravity, buoyancy, and elasticity were employed mechanically, and the production of fire with the drill and by percussion was also practised. The preservation of fire and its utilization in many ways were also known. Dogs were made beasts of burden and of traction, but neither beast nor wind nor water turned a wheel N. of Mexico in pre-Columbian times. The savages were just on the borders of machinery, having the reciprocating two-hand drill, the bow and strap drills, and the continuous-motion spindle.

Industrial activities were of five kinds: (1) Going to nature for her bounty, the primary or exploiting arts and industries; (2) working up materials for use, the secondary or intermediary arts and industries, called also shaping arts or manufactures; (3) transporting or traveling devices; (4) the mechanism of exchange; (5) the using up or enjoyment of finished products, the ultimate arts and industries, or consumption. The products of one art or industry were often the material or apparatus of another, and many tools could be employed in more than one; for example, the flint arrowhead or blade could be used for both killing and skinning a buffalo. Some arts or industries were practised by men, some by women, others by both sexes. They had their seasons and their etiquette, their ceremonies and their tabus.

*Stone craft.*—This embraces all the operations, tools, and apparatus employed in gathering and quarrying minerals and working them into paints, tools, implements, and utensils, or into ornaments and sculptures, from the rudest to such as exhibit the best expressions in fine art. Another branch is the gathering of stone for building.

*Water industry.*—This includes activities and inventions concerned in finding, carrying, storing, and heating water, and in irrigation, also, far more important than any of these, the making of vessels for plying on the water, which was the mother of many arts. The absence of the larger beasts of burden and the accommodating waterways together stimulated the perfecting of various boats to suit particular regions.

*Earth work.*—To this belong gathering, carrying, and using the soil for construction purposes, excavating cellars, building sod and snow houses, and digging ditches. The Arctic permanent houses were made of earth and sod, the temporary ones of snow cut in blocks, which were laid in spiral courses to form low domes. The Eskimo were especially ingenious in solving the mechanical problems presented by their environment of ice. The St Lawrence, Atlantic, and Canadian tribes undertook no earth-building that required skill; but those of the Mississippi valley, the Gulf states, and the far S. W., in their mounds and earthworks developed engineering and coöperative ability of no mean order. In some cases millions of cubic feet of earth were built up into geometric forms, the material often having been borne long distances by men and women. The tribes of the Pacific coast lived in partly subterranean houses. The Pueblo tribes were skilful in laying out and digging irrigating ditches and in the builder's art, erecting houses and walls of stones, pisé, or adobe. Some remains of stone structures show much taste in arrangement.

*Ceramic art.*—This industry includes all operations in plastic materials. The Arctic tribes in the extreme W., which lack proper stone, kneaded with their fingers lumps of clay mixed with blood and hair into rude lamps and cooking vessels, but in the zone of intense cold besides the ruder form there was no pottery. The tribes of Canada and of the N. tier of states w. of L. Superior and those of the Pacific slope worked little in clay; but the Indians of the Atlantic slope, of the Mississippi valley, and especially of the S. W. knew how to gather and mix clay and form it into pottery, much of which has great artistic merit. This industry was quite generally woman's work, and each region shows separate types of form and decoration.

*Metal craft.*—This included mining, grinding of ores and paint, rubbing, cold-hammering, engraving, embossing, and overlaying with plates. The metals were copper, hematite and meteoric iron, lead in the form of galena, and nugget gold and mica. No smelting was done.

*Wood craft.*—Here belongs the felling of trees with stone axes and fire. The softest woods, such as pine, cedar, poplar, and cypress, were chosen for canoes, house frames, totem poles, and other large objects. The stems of smaller trees were used also for many purposes. Driftwood was wrought into bows by the Eskimo. As there were no saws, trunks were split and hewn into single planks on the N. Pacific coast. Immense communal dwellings of cedar were there erected, the timbers being moved by rude mechanical appliances and set in place with ropes and skids. The carving on house posts, totem poles, and household furniture was often admirable. In the S. W. underground stems were carved into objects of use and ceremony.

*Root craft.*—Practised for food, basketry, textiles, dyes, fish-poisoning, medicine, etc. Serving the purposes of wood, the roots of plants developed a number of special arts and industries.

*Fiber craft.*—Far more important than roots for textile purposes, the stems, leaves, and inner and outer bark of plants and the tissues of animals, having each its special qualities, engendered a whole series of arts. Some of these materials were used for siding and roofing houses; others yielded shredded fiber, yarn, string, and rope; and some were employed in furniture, clothing, food receptacles, and utensils. Cotton was extensively cultivated in the S. W.

*Seed craft.*—The harvesting of berries, acorns and other nuts, and grain and other seeds developed primitive methods of gathering, carrying, milling, storing, cooking, and serving, with innumerable observances of days and seasons, and multifarious ceremony and lore.

Not content with merely taking from the hand of nature, the Indians were primitive agriculturists. In gathering roots they first unconsciously stirred the soil and stimulated better growth. They planted gourds in favored places, and returned in autumn to harvest the crops. Maize was regularly planted on ground cleared with the help of fire and was cultivated with sharpened sticks and hoes of bone, shell, and stone. Tobacco was cultivated by many tribes, some of which planted nothing else.

*Animal industries.*—Arts and industries depending on the animal kingdom include primarily hunting, fishing, trapping, and domestication. (See *Hunting.*) The secondary arts involve cooking and otherwise preparing food; the butchering and skinning of animals, skin-dressing in all its forms; cutting garments, tents, boats, and hundreds of smaller articles and sewing them with sinew and other thread; working claws, horn, bone, teeth, and shell into things of use, ornaments, and money; and work in feathers, quills, and hair. These industries went far beyond the daily routine and drudgery connected with dress, costume, receptacles, and apparatus of travel and transportation. Pictographs were drawn on specially prepared hides; drums and other musical instruments were made of skins and membranes; for gorgeous headdresses and robes of ceremony the rarest and finest products of animals were requisite; embroiderers everywhere most skilfully used quills and feathers, and sometimes grass and roots.

*Evolution of arts.*—Much was gathered from nature for immediate use or consumption, but the North Americans were skilful in secondary arts, becoming manufacturers when nature did not supply their demands. They built a different kind of house in each environment—in one place snow domes and underground dwellings, in another houses of puncheons hewn from the giant cedar, and in other regions conical tents made of hides of animals, pole arbors covered with matting or with cane, and houses of sods or grass laid on a framework of logs. The invention of house furniture and utensils, such as cooking vessels of stone, pottery, or vegetal material, vessels of clay, basketry, worked bark or hide for serving food, and bedding, developed the tanner, the seamstress, the potter, the wood-worker, the painter, the dyer, and the stonecutter. The need of clothing the body also offered employment to some of these and gave rise to other industries. The methods of preparing food were baking in pits, roasting, and boiling; little invention was necessary therein, but utensils and apparatus for getting and transporting food materials had to be devised. These demands developed the canoe-maker and the sled-builder, the fabricator of weapons, the stone-worker, the wood-worker, the carvers of bone and ivory, the skilful basket-maker, the weaver, the netter, and the makers of rope and babiche. These arts were not finely specialized; one person would be skilful in several. The workshop was under the open sky, and the patterns of the industrial workers were carried in their minds.

The arts and industries associated with the use and consumption of industrial products were not specially differentiated. Tools, utensils, and implements were worn out in the using. There was also some going about, traffic, and luxury, and these developed demands for higher grades of industry. The Eskimo had fur suits that they would not wear in hunting;

all the deer-chasing tribes had their gala dress for festal occasions, ceremony, and worship, upon which much time and skill were expended; the southern and western tribes wove marvelously fine and elegant robes of hemp, goat's hair, rabbit skin in strips, and skins of birds. The artisans of both sexes were instinct with the esthetic impulse; in one region they were devoted to quillwork, those of the next area to carving wood and slate; the ones living across the mountains produced whole costumes adorned with beadwork; the tribes of the central area erected elaborate earthworks; workers on the Pacific coast made matchless basketry; those of the S. W. modeled and decorated pottery in an endless variety of shapes and colored designs. The Indians N. of Mexico were generally well advanced in the simpler handicrafts, but had nowhere attempted massive stone architecture.

Consult the Annual Reports and Bulletins of the Bureau of American Ethnology, which are replete with information regarding Indian arts and industries. See also Bancroft, Native Races, I–V, 1886; Boas in Bull. Am. Mus. Nat. Hist., XV, 1901; Dellenbaugh, North Americans of Yesterday, 1901; Goddard, Life and Culture of the Hupa, 1903; Hoffman in Nat. Mus. Rep. 1895, 739, 1897; Holmes (1) in Smithson. Rep. 1901, 501, 1903; (2) in Am. Anthrop., III, 684, 1901; Hough (1) in Nat. Mus. Rep. 1888, 531, 1890; (2) ibid., 1889, 395, 1891; McGuire, ibid., 1894, 623, 1896; Mason, (1) ibid., 1889, 553, 1891; (2) ibid., 1890, 411, 1891; (3) ibid., 1894, 237, 1896; (4) ibid., 1897, 725, 1901; (5) ibid., 1902, 171, 1904; (6) in Am. Anthrop., I, 45, 1899; Moore, McGuire, Willoughby, Moorehead, et al., ibid., V, 27, 1903; Niblack in Nat. Mus. Rep. 1888, 1890; Powers in Cont. N. A. Ethnol., III, 1877; Rau (1) in Smithson. Rep. 1863; (2) in Smithson. Cont. Knowl., XXV, 1885; Willoughby in Am. Anthrop., VII, nos. 3, 4, 1905; Wilson in Nat. Mus. Rep. 1897, 1899; Schoolcraft, Indian Tribes, I–VI, 1851–57; also the Memoirs and Bulletins of the American Museum of Natural History, and the Memoirs and Papers of the Peabody Museum. See also the articles on the subjects of the various individual arts and industries and the works thereunder cited. (O. T. M.)

**Arukhwa** ('cow buffalo'). A gens of the Oto and of the Iowa. The subgentes of the latter are Chedtokhanye, Chedtoyine, Cheposhkeyine, Cheyinye.

Ah'-ro-whä.—Morgan, Anc. Soc., 156, 1877 (Oto). A-rú-qwa.—Dorsey in 15th Rep. B. A. E., 240, 1897 (Oto). A'-ru-qwa.—Ibid., 239, (Iowa). **Cow Buffalo.**—Morgan, op. cit. (Oto).

**Asa** ('tansy mustard'). A phratral organization of the Hopi, comprising the Chakwaina (Black Earth kachina), Asa

(Tansy mustard), Kwingyap (Oak), Hosboa (Chapparal cock), Posiwu (Magpie), Chisro (Snow bunting), Puchkohu (Boomerang hunting-stick), and Pisha (Field-mouse) clans. In early days this people lived near Abiquiu, in the Chama r. region of New Mexico, at a village called Kaekibi, and stopped successively at the pueblos of Santo Domingo, Laguna, Acoma, and Zuñi before reaching Tusayan, some of their families remaining at each of these pueblos, except Acoma. At Zuñi their descendants form the Aiyaho clan. On reaching Tusayan the Posiwu, Puchkohu, and Pisha clans settled with the Hopi Badger clan at Awatobi, the remainder of the group continuing to and settling first at Coyote spring near the E. side of Walpi mesa, under the gap, and afterward on the mesa at the site of the modern Hano. This village the Asa afterward abandoned, on account of drought and disease, and went to Canyon de Chelly, about 70 m. N. E. of Walpi, in the territory of the Navaho, to which tribe many of their women were given, whose descendants constitute a numerous clan known among the Navaho as Kinaani (High-standing house). Here the Asa lost their language, and here they planted peach trees in the lowlands; but a quarrel with the Navaho caused their return to Hano, at which pueblo the Tewa, from the Rio Grande, in the meantime had settled. This was probably between 1700 and 1710. The Asa were taken to Walpi and given a strip of ground on the E. edge of the mesa, where they constructed their dwellings, but a number of them afterward removed with some of the Lizard and Bear people to Sichumovi. See the works cited below, also Fewkes in 19th Rep. B. A. E., 610, 1900; Mindeleff, ibid., 639. (F. W. H.)

Asa.—Stephen and Mindeleff in 8th Rep. B. A. E., 30–31, 1891. Asanyumu.—Ibid. (*nyu-mu* = 'phratry').—Tca'-kwai-na nyû-mû.—Fewkes in Am. Anthrop., VII, 404, 1894 (*nyû-mû* = 'phratry'; likewise called A'-sa-nyû-mû).

**Asa.** The Tansy Mustard clan of the Asa phratry of the Hopi.
A'-sa.—Stephen in 8th Rep. B. A. E., 39, 1891. As-wuñ-wu.—Fewkes in Am. Anthrop., VII, 404, 1894 (*wuñ-wu* = 'clan').

**Asahani.** One of the 7 clans of the Cherokee. The name can not be interpreted, but it may have archaic connection with *sa'kani, sa'kanigeĭ,* 'blue.' It does not refer to cutting of the ears, as has been asserted. (J. M.)

A-să-hâ'-nĭ.—Mooney, Cherokee MS. vocab., B. A. E., 1885 (Cherokee form; pl., A'-nĭ'-să-hâ'-nĭ). Nesonee.—Haywood, Tenn., 276, 1823.

**Asao.** An unidentified town, probably on Wassau id., Ga. A mission was established there about 1592 by Spanish Franciscans, but it was destroyed by the natives in their revolt against the mis-

sionaries in 1597. See Shea, Cath. Miss., 66, 1855.

**Asapalaga.** A former Seminole village located on some maps on the E. bank of St Marks r., Fla., below Yapalaga. Taylor's war map places it, probably correctly, on the E. bank of Apalachicola r., in Gadsden co., where Appalaga now is.
Asapalaga.—Jefferys, French Dom. Am., I, map, 135, 1761. Aspalaga.—Roberts, Fla., 14, 1763.

**Ascahcutoner.** Mentioned by Balbi (Atlas Ethnog., 33, 1826) as a tribe belonging to his Sioux-Osage family, apparently associating them with the Teton. Not identified. The final part of the term suggests Kutenai.

**Aseakum.** A Samish village in N. W. Washington.—Gibbs, Clallam and Lummi, 38, 1863.

**Aseik** (*Asē'ĭx*). One of the three Bellacoola towns of the Talio dîvision at the head of South Bentinck arm, British Columbia.—Boas in Mem. Am. Mus. Nat. Hist., II, 49, 1898.
A'sēQ.—Boas in 7th Rep. N. W. Tribes, 3, 1891.

**Asenane** (*AsE'nanē*). A former Bellacoola town on Bellacoola r., British Columbia.—Boas in 7th Rep. N. W. Tribes, 3, 1891.

**Ashamomuck.** Probably a Corchaug village whose name was later attached to a white settlement on its site in Suffolk co., Long id., N. Y.—Thompson, Long Id., 181, 1839.

**Ashbochia.** A band or division of the Crows.
Ash-bot-chee-ah.—Morgan, Anc. Soc., 159, 1877. Treacherous lodges.—Culbertson in Smithson. Rep. 1850, 144, 1851.

**Ashegen.** A Yurok village on the coast of California, 5 or 6 m. s. of the mouth of Klamath r. (A. L. K.)
Osse-gon.—Gibbs in Schoolcraft, Ind. Tribes, III, 133, 1859.

**Ashihi** ('salt'). A Navaho clan.
Ácihi.—Matthews in Jour. Am. Folk-lore, III, 104, 1890. Acihiḍine.—Ibid. Asihi.—Matthews, Navaho Legends, 30, 1897. Ásihiḍĭne'.—Ibid.

**Ashimuit** (from *ashim,* 'a spring,' in the Nauset dialect). A village in 1674 at a large spring in Barnstable co., Mass., near the junction of Falmouth, Mashpee, and Sandwich townships. It probably belonged to the Nauset. (J. M.)
Ashimuit.—Bourne (1674) in Mass. Hist. Soc. Coll., 1st ser., I, 197, 1806. Shumuit.—Ibid.

**Ashinadea** ('lost lodges'). A band or division of the Crows.
Ah-shin'-nä-de'-ah.—Morgan, Anc. Soc., 159, 1877.

**Ashipak** ('in the basket'). A Karok village on Klamath r., a few miles above the mouth of Salmon r., in Siskiyou co., N. W. Cal.
Hakh-kutsor.—Kroeber, inf'n, 1904 (Yurok name).

**Ashipoo.** An unidentified village on a stream between Edisto and Combahee r., S. C., about 12 m. from the coast.—Brion de la Tour, map U. S., 1784.

**Ashivak.** A Kaniagmiut village near C. Douglas, Alaska; pop. 46 in 1880.—Petroff, 10th Census, Alaska, 28, 1884.

**Ashkanena** ('Blackfoot lodges'). A band of the Crows.
Ash-kane'-na.—Morgan, Anc. Soc., 159, 1877.

**Ashkum.** A Potawatomi village, named from its chief, on the N. side of Eel r., about Denver, Miami co., Ind. The reservation, including the village, was sold in 1836. (J. M.)

**Ashnola.** A body of Okinagan in s. w. British Columbia; pop. 54 in 1901.—Can. Ind. Aff. for 1901, pt. 2, 166.

**Ashukhŭma** ('red grass'). A Chickasaw town mentioned by Romans (East and West Fla., 63, 1775). It was probably in Pontotoc or Dallas co., Miss.

**Asidahech.** A Wichita subtribe.—J. O. Dorsey, inf'n, 1881; Mooney, inf'n, 1902.
Ci-da'-hetc.—Dorsey, op. cit. (pron. Shi-da'-hetch, or She-dar'haitch).

**Asilao.** A Kelatl town on lower Fraser r., above Yale, British Columbia.
Asilā'o.—Boas in Rep. Brit. A. A. S., 454, 1894.

**Asimina.** The American papaw (*Asimina triloba*). In Louisianian and Canadian French the word *assiminier* or *asiminier*, papaw tree, first occurs in the latter part of the 17th century, and it is through this source that the term has entered English. The origin is from the Illinois or some closely related dialect of Algonquian. Trumbull (Am. Philol. Assoc., 25, 1872) considers that the "older form," *racemina*, used in 1712 by Father Marest, is etymologically more correct, representing the Illinois *rassimina*, from *rassi*, 'divided lengthwise in equal parts'; *mina*, plural of *min*, 'seed,' 'fruit,' 'berry.' (A. F. C.)

**Asimu.** A Chumashan village w. of Pueblo de las Canoas (San Buenaventura), Ventura co., Cal., in 1542.—Cabrillo (1542) in Smith, Colec. Doc., 181, 1857.

**Asisufuunuk.** A Karok village on Klamath r. at Happy Camp, at the mouth of Indian cr., N. w. Cal. (A. L. K.)
As-sif-soof-tish-e-ram.—Taylor in Cal. Farmer, Mar. 23, 1860.

**Asiuhuil.** A former Chumashan village near Santa Inés mission, Santa Barbara co., Cal.—Taylor in Cal. Farmer, Oct. 18, 1861.

**Askakep.** A village of the Powhatan confederacy in 1608, near Pamunkey r., in New Kent co., Va.—Smith (1629), Va., I, map, repr. 1819.

**Askimimkansen.** A village, perhaps connected with the Nanticoke, formerly on an upper E. branch of Pocomoke r., probably in Worcester co., Md.—Herrman, map (1670) in Rep. on Boundary Line between Va. and Md., 1873.

**Askinuk.** A Kaialigmiut Eskimo village on Hooper bay, near C. Romanzoff, Alaska; pop. 175 in 1880, 138 in 1890.
Askeenac.—Hooper, Cruise of Corwin, 6, 1880. Askinaghamiut.—11th Census Rep. on Alaska, 164, 1893. Askinak.—Petroff, 10th Census, Alaska, 54, 1884. Askinuk.—Nelson in 18th Rep. B. A. E., map, 1899.

**Asko.** An Ikogmiut village on the right bank of the Yukon, below Anvik, Alaska; pop. 30 in 1880.
Askhomute.—Nelson in 18th Rep. B. A. E., map, 1899 (the people).

**Asnela.** A small island in Penobscot r., Me., occupied by the Penobscot. The name is derived from that of an Indian called Assen or Ossen.—Gatschet, Penobscot MS., B. A. E., 1887.

**Asomoches.** A division of the New Jersey Delawares formerly living on the E. bank of Delaware r., between Salem and Camden. In 1648 they were estimated at 100 warriors.
Asomoches.—Evelin (1648) in Proud, Pa., I, 113, 1797. Asoomaches.—Sanford, U. S., cxlvi, 1819.

**Asopo.** A former village on the Georgia coast, possibly on St Catherines id., the site of a Spanish Franciscan mission destroyed in the Indian revolt of 1597.

**Aspasniagan.** A former village of the Chalones, of the Costanoan family, near Soledad mission, Monterey co., Cal.
Aspasniaga.—Taylor in Cal. Farmer, Apr. 20, 1860. Aspasniagan.—Ibid. Aspasniaquan.—Ibid. Aspasniaques.—Galiano, Relac. del Sutil y Mexicana, 164, 1802.

**Aspenquid.** An Abnaki of Agamenticus, Me., forming a curious figure in New England tradition. He is said to have been born toward the end of the 16th century and converted to Christianity, to have preached it to the Indians, traveled much, and died among his own people at the age of about 100 years. Up to 1775–76 Aspenquid's day was celebrated in Halifax, Nova Scotia, by a clam dinner. He is said to be buried on the slope of Mt Agamenticus, where he is reported to have appeared in 1682. He is thought by some to be identical with Passaconaway. In Drake's New England Legends there is a poem, "St Aspenquid," by John Albee. See Am. Notes and Queries, II, 1889. (A. F. C.)

**Asphaltum.** See *Cement*.

**Aspinet.** A sachem of Nauset on C. Cod, Mass. He was known to the Plymouth colonists as early as 1621, and is noted chiefly for his unwavering friendship for the English. He kindly treated and returned to his parents a white boy who had lost his way in the woods and was found by some of Aspinet's people. In the winter of 1622, when Thomas Weston's men saw famine staring them in the face, and the Plymouth people were but little better off, Aspinet and his people came to their relief with corn and beans. It was his firm stand in favor of peace with the colonists, and his self-restraint when provoked almost beyond forbearance by Standish's hasty temper, that preserved the friendly relations of the surrounding Indians with the Plymouth colony during its early years. He was, however, finally driven into the swamps by threats of attacks by the English, and died in his unhealthful hiding place probably in 1623. (c. t.)

**Assabaoch.** A band, probably of the Assiniboin or Chippewa, in the vicinity of Rainy lake, Ontario, in 1874; pop. 152.—Can. Ind. Rep., 85, 1875.

**Assacomoco.** A village about 1610, probably near Patuxent r., Md. (Pory in Smith (1629), Virginia, II, 63, repr. 1819). The name is Algonquian and contains the word *comoco*, 'house,' common in names of Virginia settlements.

**Assacombuit.** An Abnaki ("Tarratine") chief who appeared in history about 1696. He was a faithful adherent of the French and rendered important aid to Iberville and Montigny in the reduction of Ft St Johns, N. B., Nov. 30, 1696. With two other chiefs and a few French soldiers Assacombuit attacked the fort at Casco, Me., in 1703, then defended by Capt. March, which was saved by the timely arrival of an English vessel. He assisted the French in 1704–5 in their attempt to drive out the English who had established themselves in Newfoundland, and in 1706 visited France, where he became known to Charlevoix and was received by Louis XIV, who knighted him and presented him an elegant sword, after boasting that he had slain with his own hand 150 of the King's enemies in New England (Penhallow, Ind. Wars, 40, 1726). Assacombuit returned from France in 1707 and in the following year was present with the French in their attack on Haverhill, Mass. After leaving New England he was with the St. Francis Indians. He died in 1727. Assacombuit is sometimes mentioned under the name Nescambiouit, and in one instance as Old Escambuit. (c. t.)

**Assameekg.** A village in 1698, probably near Dartmouth, Bristol co., Mass., in Wampanoag territory. Mentioned in connection with Acushnet and Assawompset by Rawson and Danforth (1698) in Mass. Hist. Soc. Coll., 1st s., x, 129–134, 1809.

**Assaomeck.** A village of the Powhatan confederacy, in 1608, situated about Alexandria, Va.—Smith (1629), Virginia, I, map, repr. 1819.

**Assapan.** A dictionary name for the flying squirrel (*Sciuropterus volucella*), spelt also *assaphan*, evidently cognate with Chippewa *ä'sipŭn*, Sauk and Fox *ä'sepàn^a*, 'raccoon.' (A. F. C. W. J.)

**Assawompset.** A village existing as late as 1674 in Middleborough tp., Plymouth co., Mass, probably within Wampanoag territory.
Assawampsit.—Rawson and Danforth (1698) in Mass. Hist. Soc. Coll., 1st s., x, 129–134, 1809. Assawanupsit.—Ibid. Assoowamsoo.—Bourne (1674), ibid., I, 198, 1806. Assowamsett.—Records (1671) quoted by Drake, Bk. Inds., bk. 3, 20, 1848.

**Assegun** (probably from Chippewa *ŭ'shigŭn* 'black bass.'—W. J.). A traditional tribe said to have occupied the region about Mackinaw and Sault Ste Marie on the first coming of the Ottawa and Chippewa, and to have been driven by them southward through lower Michigan. They are said, and apparently correctly, to have been either connected with the Mascoutens or identical with that tribe, and to have made the bone deposits in N. Michigan. See *Mascoutens*. (J. M.)
Asseguns.—Schoolcraft, Ind. Tribes, VI, 202–4, 1857. Assigunaick.—Brinton, Lenape Legend, 228, 1885. Assigunaigs.—Schoolcraft, op. cit., I, 191, 1851. Bone Indians.—Ibid., 307.

**Asseheholar, Asseola.** See *Osceola*.

**Assilanapi** ('yellow or green leaf tree'). A former Creek town, a branch of Okchayi (q. v.), in Alabama. There is a township of the same name in the Creek Nation, Okla.—Gatschet, Creek Migr. Leg., I, 128, 1884.
Arselarnaby.—H. R. Ex. Doc. 276, 24th Cong., 250, 1836. Ossalonida.—Ibid., 325.

**Assi-luputski.** See *Black drink*.

**Assiminehkon.** By the treaty of Prairie du Chien in 1829 the Ottawa, Potawatomi, and Chippewa reserved "one section at the village of the As-sim-in-eh-Kon, or Paw-paw Grove." Probably a Potawatomi village in Lee co., Ill.—Prairie du Chien treaty (1829) in U. S. Ind. Treaties, 163, 1873.

**Assiminier.** See *Asimina*.

**Assinapi** (Chippewa: *ŭsi'nâpä*, 'stone person.'—W. J.). A people, mentioned in the *Walam Olum* (Brinton, Lenape, 190, 1885), with whom the Delawares fought during their migration toward the E.
Assinipi.—Rafinesque, Am. Nations, I, 146, 1836.

**Assiniboin** (Chippewa: *ŭ'sin^i* 'stone,' *ŭ'pwäw^a* 'he cooks by roasting': 'one who cooks by the use of stones.'—W. J.). A large Siouan tribe, originally constituting a part of the Yanktonai. Their separation from the parent stem, to judge by the slight dialectal difference in the language, could not have greatly preceded the appearance of the whites, but it must have taken place before 1640, as the Jesuit Relation for that year mentions the Assiniboin as distinct. The Relation of 1658 places them in the vicinity of L. Alimibeg, between L. Superior and Hudson bay. On Jefferys' map of 1762 this name is applied to L. Nipigon, and on De l'Isle's map of 1703 to Rainy lake. From a tradition found in the widely scattered bodies of the tribe and heard by the first Europeans who visited the Dakota, the Assiniboin appear to have separated from their ancestral stem while the latter resided somewhere in the region about the headwaters of the Mississippi, whence they moved northward and joined the Cree. It is probable that they first settled about Lake of the Woods, then drifted northwestward to the region about L. Winnipeg, where they were living as early as 1670, and were thus located on Lahontan's map of 1691. Chauvignerie (1736) place them in the same

RED DOG—ASSINIBOIN

region. Dobbs (Hudson Bay, 1744) located one division of the Assiniboin some distance N. W. of L. Winnipeg and the other immediately W. of an unidentified lake placed N. of L. Winnipeg. These divisions he distinguishes as Assiniboin of the Meadows and Assiniboin of the Woods. In 1775 Henry found the tribe scattered along Saskatchewan and Assiniboine rs., from the forest limit well up to the headwaters of the former, and this region, between the Sioux on the s. and the Siksika on the w., was the country over which they continued to range until gathered on reservations. Hayden (Ethnog. and Philol. Mo. Val., 1862) limits their range at that time as follows: "The Northern Assiniboins roam over the country from the w. banks of the Saskatchewan and Assiniboin rs., in a w. direction to the Woody mts., N. and w. amongst some of the small outliers of the Rocky mts. E. of the Missouri, and on the banks of the small lakes frequently met with on the plains in that district. They consist of 250 or 300 lodges. The remainder of the tribe, now [1856] reduced to 250 lodges, occupy the district defined as follows: Commencing at the mouth of the White Earth r. on the E., extending up that river to and as far beyond its source as the Grand Coulée and the head of La Rivière aux Souris,

thence N. W. along the Côteau de Prairie, or divide, as far as the beginning of the Cypress mts., on the N. fork of Milk r., down that river to its junction with the Missouri, thence down the Missouri to White Earth r., the starting point. Until the year 1838 the tribe still numbered from 1,000 to 1,200 lodges, trading on the Missouri, when the smallpox reduced them to less than 400 lodges. They were also surrounded by large and hostile tribes, who continually made war upon them, and in this way their number was diminished, though at the present time they are slowly on the increase."

From the time they separated from the parent stem and joined the Cree until brought under control of the whites, they were almost constantly at war with the Dakota. As they have lived since the appearance of the whites in the N. W. almost wholly on the plains, without permanent villages, moving from place to place in search of food, their history has been one of conflict with surrounding tribes.

Physically the Assiniboin do not differ materially from the other Sioux. The men dress their hair in various forms; it is seldom cut, but as it grows is twisted into small locks or tails, and frequently false hair is added to lengthen the twist. It sometimes reaches the ground, but is

ASSINIBOIN WOMAN

generally wound in a coil on top of the head. Their dress, tents, and customs generally are similar to those of the Plains Cree, but they observe more decorum in camp and are more cleanly, and their hospitality is noted by most traders who have visited them. Polygamy is common. While the buffalo abounded their principal occupation consisted in making pemmican, which they bartered to the whites for liquor, tobacco, powder, balls, knives, etc. Dogs are said to have been sacrificed to their deities. According to Alexander Henry, if death happened in winter at a distance from the burial ground of the family, the body was carried along during their journeying and placed on a scaffold, out of reach of dogs and beasts of prey, at their stopping places. Arrived at the burial place, the corpse was deposited in a sitting posture in a circular grave about 5 feet deep, lined with bark or skins; it was then covered with bark, over which logs were placed, and these in turn were covered with earth.

The names of their bands or divisions, as given by different writers, vary considerably, owing to the loose organization and wandering habit of the tribe. Lewis and Clark mention as divisions in 1805: (1) Menatopa (Otaopabinè of Maximilian), Gens de Feuilles [for *filles*] (Itscheabinè), Big Devils (Watopachnato), Oseegah, and another the name of which is not stated. The whole people were divided into the northern and southern and into the forest and prairie bands. Maximilian (Trav., 194, 1843) names their gentes as follows: (1) Itscheabinè (gens des filles); (2) Jatonabinè (gens des roches); (3) Otopachgnato (gens du large); (4) Otaopabinè (gens des canots); (5) Tschantoga (gens des bois); (6) Watopachnato (gens de l'age); (7) Tanintauei (gens des osayes); (8) Chabin (gens des montagnes). A band mentioned by Hayden (op. cit., 387), the Minishinakato, has not been identified with any named by Maximilian. Henry (Jour., ii, 522–523, 1897) enumerated 11 bands in 1808, of which the Red River, Rabbit, Eagle Hills, Saskatchewan, Foot, and Swampy Ground Assiniboin, and Those-who-have-water-for-themselves-only can not be positively identified. This last may be Hayden's Minishinakato. Other divisions mentioned, chiefly geographical, are: Assiniboin of the Meadows, Turtle Mountain Sioux, Wawaseeasson, and Assabaoch (?). The only Assiniboin village mentioned in print is Pasquayah.

Porter (1829) estimated the Assiniboin population at 8,000; Drake at 10,000 before the smallpox epidemic of 1836, during which 4,000 of them perished. Gallatin (1836) placed the number at 6,000; the U. S. Indian Report of 1843, at 7,000. In 1890 they numbered 3,008; in 1904, 2,600. The Assiniboin now (1904) living in

the United States are in Montana, 699 under Ft Belknap agency and 535 under Ft Peck agency; total, 1,234. In Canada there were in 1902 the Mosquito and Bears Heads' and Lean Man's bands at Battleford agency, 78; Joseph's band of 147, Paul's of 147, and 5 orphans at Edmonton agency; Carry-the-Kettle band under Assiniboin agency, 210; Pheasant Rump's band, originally 69, and Ocean Man's, 68 in number, at Moose mtn.; and the bands on Stony res., Alberta, 661; total, 1,371. See Powell in 7th Rep. B. A. E., 111, 1891; McGee, Siouan Indians, 15th Rep. B. A. E., 157, 1897; Dorsey, Siouan Sociology, ibid., 213; Hayden, Ethnog. and Philol. Mo. Val., 1862. (J. M. C. T.)

**Apinulboines.**—Lloyd in Jour. Anthrop. Inst., v, 246, 1876 (misprint). **Arsenipoitis.**—Barcia, Ensayo, 238, 1723. **Arsenipoits.**—McKenney and Hall, Ind. Tribes, iii, 80, 1854. **Asinbols.**—Trumbull, Ind. Wars, 185, 1851. **Asiniboels.**—Anville, Am. Sept. map, 1756. **Asiniboines.**—Morgan in N. Am. Rev., 44, Jan., 1870. **Asiʹ-ni-bwaⁿ.**—Am. Natur., 829, Oct., 1882 (wrongly given as Dorsey's spelling). **Asinibwanak.**—Cuoq, Lex. de la Langue Algonquine, 77, 1886. **A-si-ni-poiʹ-tuk.**—Hayden, Ethnog. and Philol., 381, 1862 (Cree and Chippewa name). **Asinipovales.**—Barcia, Ensayo, 176, 1723. **As-ne-boines.**—Bonner, Life of Beckwourth, 158, 1856. **Asseenaboine.**—Franklin, Journ. Polar Sea, 168, 1824. **Asseeneepoytuck.**—Ibid., 55 (Cree name). **Asselibois.**—Doc. of 1683 in N. Y. Doc. Col. Hist., ix, 798, 1855. **Assenepoils.**—Hennepin, New Discov., map, 1698. **Asseniboines.**—Perrin, Voy. dans les Louisianes, 263, 1805. **Asseniboualak.**—Du Lhut (1678) in Margry, Déc., vi, 21, 1886. **Assenipoëls.**—Chauvignerie (1736) in N. Y. Doc. Col. Hist., ix, 1055, 1855. **Assenipoils.**—Hennepin, New Discov., map, 1698. **Assenipoualacs.**—Hennepin quoted by Shea, Disc., 131, 1852 (trans. 'stone warriors'). **Assenipoualak.**—Shea, ibid., note. **Assenipouals.**—Radout (1710) in Margry, Déc., vi, 14, 1886. **Assenipouel.**—Ibid., 11. **Assenipoulacs.**—Hennepin misquoted by Neill, Hist. Minn., 134, 1858. **Assenipoulaes.**—Hennepin (1680) in French, Hist. Coll. La., i, 212, 1846. **Assenipoulaks.**—Du Lhut (1678) in Margry, Déc., vi, 22, 1886. **Assenipouvals.**—Coxe, Carolana, 43, 1741. **Assenipovals.**—Alcedo, Dict. Geog., iv, 557, 1788. **Assenniboins.**—Schoolcraft, Trav., 245, 1821. **Assenpoels.**—N. Y. Doc. Col. Hist., index, 289, 1861. **Assilibouels.**—Iberville (1702) in Margry, Déc., iv, 600, 1880. **Assimpouals.**—Lahontan, New Voy., i, 231, 1703. **Assinaboes.**—Smith, Bouquet's Exped., 69, 1766. **Assinaboil.**—Boudinot, Star in the West, 125, 1816. **Assinaboine.**—Ind. Aff. Rep., 498, 1839. **Assinaboins.**—Ibid., 297, 1835. **Assinabwoines.**—Schoolcraft, Ind. Tribes, v, 99, 1855. **Assineboes.**—Hutchins (1765), ibid., iii, 556, 1853. **Assineboin.**—Brackenridge, Views of La., 79, 1815. **Assineboines.**—Richardson, Arct. Exped., i, map, 1851. **Assinebwannuk.**—Jones, Ojebway Inds., 178, 1861. **Assinepoel.**—Chauvignerie (1736) quoted by Schoolcraft, Ind. Tribes, iii, 556, 1853. **Assinepoils.**—Hayden, Ethnog. and Philol. Mo. Valley, 380, 1862. **Assinepoins.**—Ramsey in Ind. Aff. Rep. 1849, 70, 1850. **Assinepotuc.**—Balbi, Atlas Ethnog., 55, 1826. **Assinepoualaos.**—Coxe, Carolana, 43, 1741. **Assiniboelle.**—Beauharnois and Hocquart (1731) in Margry, Déc., vi, 568, 1886. **Assiniboels.**—Frontenac (1695), ibid., v, 63, 1883. **Assiniboesi.**—Capellini, Ricordi, 185, 1867. **Assiniboile.**—Vaudreuil and Bégon (1716) in Margry, Déc., vi, 496, 1886. **Assiniboils.**—Carver, Travels, map, 1778. **Assiniboines.**—West, Jour., 86, 1824. **Assiniboins.**—Gass, Jour., 69, 1807. **Assinibois.**—Denonville (1685) in N. Y. Doc. Col. Hist., ix, 286, 1855. **Assiniboleses.**—Alcedo, Dicc. Geog., i, 165, 1786. **Assiniboualas.**—Perrot in Minn. Hist. Coll., ii, pt. 2, 24, 1864. **Assinibouane.**—Pachot (1722) in Margry

Déc., VI, 517, 1886. **Assinibouels.**—Vaudreuil (1720), ibid., 510. **Assinibouets.**—Du Chesneau (1681) in N. Y. Doc. Col. Hist., IX, 153, 1855. **Assiniboüles.**—Perrot, Mém., 91, 1864. **Assinib'wans.**—Ramsey in Ind. Aff. Rep. 1849, 77, 1850. **Assinipoals.**—Proc. verb. (1671) in Margry, Déc., I, 97, 1876. **Assinipools.**—Du Lhut (1678), ibid., VI, 19, 1886. **Assinipoile.**—Vaudreuil and Bégon (1716), ibid., 500. **Assinipoileu.**—Balbi, Atlas Ethnog., 55, 1826. **Assinipoils.**—Le Sueur (1700) in Margry, Déc., VI, 82, 1886. **Assiniponiels.**—Gallatin in Trans. Am. Antiq. Soc., II, 123, 1836. **Assinipotuc.**—Keane in Stanford, Compend., 501, 1878. **Assinipoual.**—Lahontan, New Voy., I, 207, 1703. **Assinipoüalac.**—Jes. Rel., 1667, III, 23, 1858. **Assinipoualaks.**—Ibid., 21, 1658. **Assinipoüars.**—Ibid., 1670, 92. **Assinipoulac.**—Du Lhut (1684) in Margry, Déc., VI, 51, 1886. **Assinipour.**—Le Jeune in Jes. Rel., 1640, III, 35, 1858. **Assinipovals.**—Harris, Coll. Voy. and Trav., II, map, 1705. **Assini-poytuk.**—Richardson, Arct. Exped., 51, 1851. **Assinipwanak.**—Gatschet, MS., B. A. E. (Chippewa name). **Assinnaboin.**—Drake, Bk. Inds., vi, 1848. **Assinnaboines.**—Ibid. **Assinneboin.**—Tanner, Nar., 50, 1830. **Assinnee-Poetuc.**—Me. Hist. Soc. Coll., VI, 270, 1859. **Assinnibains.**—Lewis and Clark, Disc., 23, 1806. **Assinniboan.**—Coues, Lewis and Clark Exped., I, 193, note, 1893 (Chippewa name). **Assinniboine.**—Hind, Labr. Pen., II, 148, 1863. **Assinniboine Sioux.**—Can. Ind. Rep., 77, 1880. **Assinniboins.**—Lewis and Clark, Disc., 30, 1806. **Assinopoils.**—La Harpe (1700) in French, Hist. Coll. La., III, 27, 1851. **Assinpouele.**—Anon. Carte de l'Am. Sépt., Paris, n. d. **Assinpoulac.**—Bowles, map of Am., after 1750. **Assinpouls.**—Lahontan, quoted by Ramsey in Ind. Aff. Rep., 72, 1849. **Ausinabwaun.**—Parker, Minn. Handb., 13, 1857. **Chiripinons.**—Perrot (1721) in Minn. Hist. Soc. Coll., II, pt. 2, 24, 1864. **Essinaboin.**—Ex. Doc. 90, 22d Cong., 1st sess., 64, 1832. **E-tans-ke-pa-se-qua.**—Long, Exped. Rocky Mts., II, lxxxiv, 1823 (Hidatsa name, from *i-ta-ha-tski*, 'long arrows'). **Fish-eaters.**—Hayden, Ethnog. and Philol. Mo. Val., 381, 1862 (Hohe or; Dakota name). **Guerriers de la Roche.**—Perrot, Mém., 232, 1864. **Guerriers de pierre.**—Jes. Rel., 1658, III, 21, 1858. **Haha.**—Coues, Pike's Exped., I, 348, 1895. **Ho-ha.**—Gallatin in Trans. Am. Antiq. Soc., II, 123, 1836 ('rebel': sometimes applied by other Sioux tribes). **Hohays.**—Snelling, Tales of N. W., 21, 1830. **Hohe.**—Dorsey in 15th Rep. B. A. E., 222, 1897 (Dakota name: 'rebels'). **Ho'-he.**—Hayden, Ethnog. and Philol. Mo. Val., 381, 1862 (trans. 'fish-eaters'). **Hoheh.**—Williamson in Minn. Hist. Soc. Coll., I, 296, 1872. **Ho-he'-i-o.**—Hayden, Ethnog. and Philol. Mo. Val., 290, 1862 (Cheyenne name). **Hoh-hays.**—Ramsey in Minn. Hist. Soc. Coll., I, 48, 1872. **Indiens-Pierre.**—Balbi, Atlas Ethnog., 55, 1826. **Issati.**—Henry, Travels, 286, 1809 (erroneous identification for Santee). **Left hand.**—Culbertson in Smithson. Rep, 1850, 143, 1851 (translation of the French name of their chief). **Mantopanatos.**—Keane in Stanford, Compend., 470, 1878. **Nacota.**—Maximilian, Trav., 193, 1843 (own name, same as Dakota: 'our people'). **Nation of the great Water.**—Dobbs, Hudson Bay, 20, 1744. **Osinipoilles.**—Henry, Trav., 273, 1809. **Ossineboine.**—Coues, Lewis and Clark Exped., I, 178, note 58, 1893. **Ossiniboine.**—Ibid., 59. **Ossnobians.**—Mass. Hist. Soc. Coll., III, 24, 1794. **Sioux of the Rocks.**—Ramsey in Ind. Aff. Rep., 77, 1850. **Stone.**—Keane in Stanford, Compend., 536, 1878. **Stone Indians.**—Fisher, New Trav., 172, 1812. **Stone Roasters.**—Tanner, Nar., 51, 1830. **Stone Sioux.**—Lewis and Clark, Disc., 46, 1806. **Stoney.**—Keane in Stanford, Compend., 536, 1878. **Stoney Indians.**—Can. Ind. Rep., 80, 1880. **Stonies.**—Inf'n of Chas. N. Bell, of Winnipeg, Manitoba, 1886 (the common name used by English in Canada). **Thickwood.**—Keane in Stanford, Compend., 536, 1878 (applied to the Assiniboin of the Rocky mts.). **Tlū'tlämā'Ekā.**—Chamberlain, inf'n, 1903 ('cutthroats': Kutenai name). **Ussinebwoinug.**—Tanner, Nar., 316, 1830 (Chippewa name). **Weepers.**—Henry, Trav., 286, 1809.

**Assiniboin of the Plains.** A division of the Assiniboin described by Dobbs (Hudson Bay, 35, 1744) as distinguished from that portion of the tribe living in the wooded country. On his map they are located w. of L. Winnipeg. De Smet (Miss. de l'Oregon, 104, 106, 1848) estimated them at 300 lodges, and in the English edition of his work (Oregon Miss., 156, 1847) the number given is 600 lodges. He says they hunt over the great plains between the Saskatchewan, Red, Missouri, and Yellowstone rs., and as compared with the Assiniboin of the woods "are more expert in thieving, greater topers, and are perpetually at war," but that in general the men are more robust and of commanding stature. They include the Itscheabine, Watopachnato, Otaopabine, and Jatonabine. **Assiniboels of the South.**—Jefferys, French Dom. in Am., pt. I, map, 1741. **Assiniboins des Plaines.**—Smet, Miss. de l'Oregon, 104, 1848. **Assinibouels of the Meadows.**—Dobbs, Hudson Bay, 35, 1744. **Plain Assineboins.**—Hind, Red River Exped., II, 152, 1860.

**Assonet.** A river and village in Bristol co., Mass., and probably the name of a former Indian village in the vicinity. Schoolcraft (Ind. Tribes, I, 117, 1851) uses the name "Assonets" to denote the probable Indian authors of the inscriptions on Dighton rock. (J. M.)

**Assuapmushan.** A Montagnais mission founded by the Jesuits in 1661 about 300 m. up Saguenay r., Quebec, probably at the entrance of Ashuapmouchouan r. into L. St John. A trading post of the same name was on that river in 1832.—Hind, Labrador, II, 25, 26, 38, 1863.

**Assumption.** A mission established in 1728 at the Wyandot village near the present city of Detroit, Mich., and removed soon afterward to the opposite shore. It continued until 1781.—Shea, Cath. Miss., 202, 1855.

**Assunpink** ('at the stone stream'). A division of the Delawares formerly on Stony cr., on the Delaware, near Trenton. Probably from the Indian name of Stony cr. (J. M.)
**Assanpinks.**—Boudinot, Star in the West, 125, 1816. **Asseinpinks.**—Sanford, U. S., cxlvii, 1819. **Assunpink.**—Proud, Pa., II, 294, 1798. **Stony Creek Indians.**—Ibid.

**Assunta.** A former village, presumably Costanoan, connected with Dolores mission, San Francisco, Cal.—Taylor in Cal. Farmer, Oct. 18, 1861.

**Assuti.** A small Nez Percé band formerly living on Assuti cr., Idaho. They joined Chief Joseph in the Nez Percé war of 1877.—Gatschet, MS., B. A. E., 1877.

**Assuweska.** A village of the Powhatan confederacy in 1608 on the N. bank of the Rappahannock, in King George co., Va.—Smith (1629), Va., I, map, repr. 1819.

**Astakiwi** (*es-ta-ke'*, 'hot spring.'—Powers). A Shastan village near Canby, in Warm Springs valley, Modoc co., Cal., whose people were described by Powers (Cont. N. A. Ethnol., III, 267, 1877) as most miserable and squalid, having been brutalized not only by their scanty and inferior diet, but also by the loss of their comeliest maidens and best young men, who were carried off into slavery by the Modoc.

**Astakaywas.**—Powers in Overland Mo., XII, 412, 1874. **Astakywich.**—Ibid. **Astaqkéwa.**—Curtin, MS. Ilmawi vocab., B. A. E., 1889. **Es-ta-ke'-wach.**—Powers in Cont. N. A. Ethnol., III, 267, 1877. **Hot Spring Valley Indians.**—Ibid. (includes also the Hantewa).

**Astialakwa.** A former pueblo of the Jemez, on the summit of a mesa that separates San Diego and Guadelupe canyons at their mouths. It was probably the seat of the Franciscan mission of San Juan, established early in the 17th century. Distinct from Ostyalakwa.

**Asht-ia-la-qua.**—Bandelier in Arch. Inst. Papers, III, 126, 1890. **Ash-tyal-a-qua.**—Ibid., IV, 206, 1890. **Asht-ya-laqua.**—Bandelier in Proc. Cong. Internat. Am., VII, 452, 1890. **Astialakwá.**—Hodge, field notes, B. A. E., 1895. **Ateyala-keokvá.**—Loew in Wheeler Survey Rep., VII, 343, 1879.

**Astina.** A village in N. Florida in 1564, subject to Utina, head chief of the Timucua (Laudonnière in French, Hist. Coll. La., n. s., 298, 1869). De Bry's map (1590) places it w. of St Johns r.

**Astouregamigoukh.** Mentioned as one of the small tribes N. of St Lawrence r. (Jes. Rel. 1643, III, 38, 1858). Probably a Montagnais band or settlement about the headwaters of Saguenay or St Maurice r.

**Asumpcion.** A group of Alchedoma rancherias on or near the Rio Colorado, in California, more than 50 m. below the mouth of Bill Williams fork. They were visited and so named by Fray Francisco Garcés in 1776.—Garcés, Diary, 426, 1900.

**Asystarca.** A former Costanoan village of central California attached to the mission of San Juan Bautista.—Engelhardt, Franciscans in Cal., 398, 1897.

**Ataakut.** A village of the Tolowa formerly situated on the coast of N. Cal.—Dorsey in Jour. Am. Folk-lore, III, 236, 1890.

**Ă'-ta-ă-kût'.**—Dorsey in Jour. Am. Folk-lore, III, 236, 1890 (Tutu name). **A'-ta-a-kût'-ti.**—Ibid. (Tutu name). **A-ta-ke-té tûn'-ně.**—Dorsey, MS. Chetco vocab., B. A. E., 1884. **Ni-yañk'-ta-ke'-te te'-ne.**—Dorsey, MS. Smith R. vocab., B. A. E., 1884. **Yah-nih-kahs.**—Hamilton, MS. Hay-narger vocab., B. A. E. **Yantuckets.**—Bancroft, Nat. Races, I, 445, 1874. **Yatuckets.**—Taylor in Cal. Farmer, June 8, 1860. **Yau-tuck-ets.**—Ibid., Apr. 12, 1861. **Yon-tooketts.**—Hamilton, MS. Hay-narger vocab., B. A. E.

**Ataakwe** ('seed people'). A people encountered by the Zuñi before reaching their final residing place at Zuñi, N. Mex. They joined the Seed clan of the Zuñi, whose descendants constitute the present Taakwe, or Corn clan, of that tribe.—Cushing in The Millstone, IX, 2, 23, 1884.
**A'-ta-a.**—Cushing, ibid.

**Ata-culculla.** See *Attakullakulla*.

**Atagi.** One of the 4 Alibamu towns formerly situated in what is now Autauga co.,

Ala., extending 2 m. along the w. bank of Alabama r., a short distance w. of the present Montgomery. Autaugaville, Autauga cr., and Autauga co. are named after it. Hawkins (1798) speaks of it as a small village 4 m. below Pawokti, and says that the people have little intercourse with the whites but are hospitable. Schooler (Schoolcraft, Ind. Tribes, IV, 578, 1854) states that it contained 54 families in 1832. (A. S. G.)

**At-tau-gee.**—Hawkins (1799), Sketch, 36, 1848. **Autallga.**—Sen. Ex. Doc. 425, 24th Cong., 1st sess., 331, 1836. **Autauga.**—Campbell (1836) in H. R. Doc. 274, 25th Cong., 2d sess., 20, 1838. **Autobas.**—Swan (1791) in Schoolcraft, Ind. Tribes, V, 262, 1855. **Dumplin Town.**—Woodward, Reminiscences, 12, 1859.

**Atalans.** An imaginary prehistoric civilized race of North America (Rafinesque, introd. to Marshall, Ky., I, 23, 1824); probably based on the Atlantis fable.

**Atamasco lily.** The name of a plant (*Amaryllis atamasco*), defined by Bartlett (Dict. of Americanisms, 20, 1877) "as a small one-flowered lily, held in like esteem, in Virginia and North Carolina, with the daisy in England." Parkinson (Paradisus, 87, 1629) says that "the Indians in Virginia do call it Attamusco." Gerard (*Sun*, N. Y., July 30, 1895) states that the word means 'stained with red,' in reference to the color of the flowers. In this case the chief component would be the Algonquian radical *misk*, signifying 'red.' (A. F. C.)

**Atana** (*Atá'na*). A Haida town on House, or Atana, id., E. coast of Moresby id., Queen Charlotte group, British Columbia. According to Skidegate legend, House id. was the second to appear above the waters of the flood. At that time there was sitting upon it a woman who became the ancestress of the Tadjilanas. The Kagialskegawai also considered her as their "grandmother," although saying that they were not descended directly from her but from some people who drifted ashore at the same place in a cockleshell. The town was occupied by the Tadjilanas. As the name does not occur in John Work's list, it would seem to have been abandoned prior to 1836–41.—Swanton, Cont. Haida, 277, 1905.

**Atanekerdluk.** An Eskimo settlement on Nugsuak pen., w. Greenland.—Peary, My Arct. Jour., 208, 1893.

**Atangime.** A settlement of Eskimo in E. Greenland.—Meddelelser om Grönland, XXV, 24, 1902.

**Atanumlema.** A small Shahaptian tribe living on Yakima res., on Atanum cr., Wash. They are said to speak a dialect closely related to the Yakima and Klikitat.—Mooney in 14th Rep. B. A. E., 738, 1896.

**Atanus** (*atá'nAs*, 'bilge-water'). A Skittagetan town, occupied by the Do-gitunai, on the N. E. coast of Hippa id., British Columbia—Swanton, Cont. Haida, 281, 1905.

**Ataronchronon.** One of the minor tribes of the Huron confederation, among whom the Jesuit mission of Sainte Marie was established.—Jes. Rel. for 1640, 61, 1858.

Andoouanchronon.—Jes. Rel. for 1640, 35, 1858. Andowanchronon.—Jes. Rel., index, 1858. Ataronchronons.—Jes. Rel. for 1637, 114, 1858. Ataronch.—Kingsley, Stand. Nat. Hist., pt. 6, 154, 1883.

**Atarpe.** A former village, presumably Costanoan, connected with Dolores mission, San Francisco, Cal.

Atarpe.—Taylor in Cal. Farmer, Oct. 18, 1861. Oturbe.—Ibid. Uturpe.—Ibid.

**Atasi** (Creek: *ă'tăssa*, 'warclub.'—Gatschet). An ancient Upper Creek town on the s. side of Tallapoosa r., in Macon co., Ala., adjoining Calibee cr., 5 m. above Huhliwahli town. In 1766 it contained about 43 warriors, and when seen by Hawkins, about 1799, it was a poor, miserable-looking place. On Nov. 29, 1813, a battle was fought there between the Creeks and Jackson's troops. The name was later applied to a town in the Creek Nation, Indian Ter., the people of which are called Atasálgi. See Jefferys, French Dom. Am., 135, map, 1761; Bartram, Trav., 454, 1791; Gatschet, Creek Migr. Leg., I, 128, 1884; II, 185, 1888.

Allasis.—Bartram, Voy., I, map, 1799 (erroneously placed on the Chattahoochee). Altasse.—Boudinot, Star in the West, 260, 1816. Atases.—Jefferys, French Dom., I, 134, map, 1761. Átasi.—Gatschet, Creek Migr. Legend, I, 128, 1884. Átassi.—Ibid. Atĕsi.—Ibid. (in Indian Ter.). Attases.—Roberts, Florida, 13, 1763. Attasis.—Phelipeau, Carte Générale, 1783. Attasse.—Bartram, Travels, 448, 1791. Autisees.—Woodward, Reminiscences, 24, 1859. Autossee.—Drake, Ind. Chron., 198, 1836. Aut-tos-se.—Hawkins (1799), Sketch, 31, 1848. Auttotsee.—Hawkins (1813) in Am. State Pap., Ind. Aff., I, 849, 1832. Citasees.—Romans, Florida, I, 280, 1775. Gitases.—Jefferys, French Dom. Am., I, 134, map, 1761 (mislocated, but probably the same). Olasse.—Bartram, Voy., I, map, 1799. Otasee.—Thomas (1793) in Am. State Pap., Ind. Aff., I, 407, 1832. Otasse.—Bartram, Travels, 394, 461, 1791. Otisee.—Carley (1835) in H. R. Doc. 452, 25th Cong., 2d sess., 75, 1838. Otissee.—Ibid., 31. Otoseen.—H. R. Ex. Doc. 276, 24th Cong., 1st sess., 131, 1836. Ottasees.—U. S. Ind. Treat. (1797), 70, 1837. Ottersea.—Sen. Ex. Doc. 425, 24th Cong., 1st sess., 152, 1836. Ottesa.—Campbell (1836) in H. R. Doc. 274, 25th Cong., 2d sess., 20, 1838. Ottessa.—Crawford (1836), ibid., 24. Ottisse.—Schoolcraft, Ind. Tribes, IV, 578, 1854. Ottissee.—Wyse (1836) in H. R. Doc. 63, 25th Cong., 2d sess., 63, 1838.

**Atastagonies.** An unidentified tribe mentioned by Rivera (Diario y Derrotero, leg. 2, 602, 1736) as formerly living in s. Texas.

**Atchaluk.** An Eskimo village in the Kuskokwim district, Alaska; pop. 39 in 1890.

Atchalugumiut.—11th Census, Alaska, 164, 1890 (the inhabitants).

**Atchatchakangouen** (from *atchitchak*, 'crane'). The principal division of the Miami. On account of the hostility of the Illinois they removed w. of the Mississippi, where they were attacked by the

Sioux, and they afterward settled near the Jesuit mission at Green Bay, and moved thence into Illinois and Indiana with the rest of the tribe. In 1736 Chauvignerie gave the crane as one of the two leading Miami totems. (J. M.)

Atchatchakangouen.—Perrot (*ca.* 1721) Mémoire, 222, 1864. Atchatchakangouen.—Jes. Rel., LVIII, 40, 1899. Chacakengua.—Coxe, Carolana, map, 1741. Chachakingua.—Ibid., 12. La Grue.—La Salle (1680) in Margry, Déc., II, 216, 1877. Miamis de la Grüe.—Perrot, op. cit., 154. Outichacouk.—Coxe, Carolana, map, 1741. Outitchakouk.—Jesuit Rel., 1658, 21, 1858. Tchatchakigoa.—La Salle (1680) in Margry, Déc., II, 216, 1877. Tchatchaking.—Ibid. (1683), 320. Tchidüakoüingoües.—Bacqueville de la Potherie, Hist. Am., II, 261, 1753. Tchiduakouongues.—Bacqueville de la Potherie misquoted by Shea in Wis. Hist. Soc. Coll., III, 134, 1856.

**Atchaterakangouen.** An Algonquian tribe or band living in the interior of Wisconsin in 1672, near the Mascouten and Kickapoo.

Atchaterakangouen.—Jes. Rel., LVIII, 40, 1899.

**Atchialgi** (*atchi* 'maize,' *álgi* 'people'). One of the twenty Creek clans.

Atchíalgi.—Gatschet, Creek Migr. Leg., I, 155, 1884.

**Atchinaalgi** ('cedar grove people'). A former small village of the Upper Creeks, on a tributary of Tallapoosa r., probably in Tallapoosa co., Ala. It was their northernmost settlement in the 18th century, and was destroyed by Gen. White, Nov. 13, 1813. (A. S. G.)

Atchina-álgi.—Gatschet, Creek Migr. Leg., I, 128, 1884. Au-che-nau-ul-gau.—Hawkins (1799), Sketch of Creek country, 47, 1848. Genalga.—Pickett, Hist. Ala., II, 299, 1851.

**Atchinahatchi** ('cedar creek'). A former branch settlement of the Upper Creek village of Kailaidshi, on a small stream of the same name, a tributary of the Tallapoosa, probably in Coosa co., Ala. (A. S. G.)

Ahcharalar.—H. R. Ex. Doc. 276, 24th Cong., 1st sess., 322, 1836 (a doubtful synonym). Atchina Hátchi.—Gatschet, Creek Migr. Leg., I, 128, 1884. Au-che-nau-hat-che.—Hawkins (1799), Sketch, 49, 1848.

**Atchitchiken** (*Atci'tcĭkEn*, sig. doubtful, or *Nkaitu'sus*, 'reaches the top of the brow or low steep,' because the trail here passes on top of a bench and enters Spapiam valley). A village of the Spences Bridge band of the Ntlakyapamuk on the N. side of Thompson r., 3 m. back in the mountains from Spences Bridge, British Columbia.—Teit in Mem. Am. Mus. Nat. Hist., II, 173, 1900.

**Ateacari.** A branch of the Cora division of the Piman family on the Rio de Nayarit, or Rio de San Pedro, in Jalisco, Mexico.

Ateacari.—Orozco y Berra, Geog., 59, 1864. Ateakari.—Pimentel, Lenguas de Mex., II, 83, 1865. Ateanaca.—Orozco y Berra, op. cit. (name of language).

**Atepua.** A pueblo of the province of Atripuy, in the region of the lower Rio Grande, N. Mex., in 1598.—Oñate (1598) in Doc. Inéd., XVI, 115, 1871.

Atepíra.—Bancroft, Ariz. and N. Mex., 135, 1889 (misprint).

**Atfalati** (*Atfálati*). A division of the Kalapooian family whose earliest seats, so far as can be ascertained, were the plains of the same name, the hills about Forest Grove, and the shores and vicinity of Wappato lake, Oreg.; and they are said to have extended as far as the site of Portland. They are now on Grande Ronde res. and number about 20. The Atfalati have long given up their native customs and little is known of their mode of life. Their language, however, has been studied by Gatschet, and our chief knowledge of the Kalapooian tongue is from this dialect. The following were the Atfalati bands as ascertained by Gatschet in 1877: Chachambitmanchal, Chachanim, Chachemewa, Chachif, Chachimahiyuk, Chachimewa, Chachokwith, Chagindueftei, Chahelim, Chakeipi, Chakutpaliu, Chalal, Chalawai, Chamampit, Chapanaghtin, Chapokele, Chapungathpi Chatagithl, Chatagshish, Chatakuin, Chatamnei, Chatilkuei, Chawayed. (L. F.)

Atfálati.—Gatschet in Jour. Am. Folk-lore, XII, 212, 1899. Fallatahs.—Slocum in H. R. Rep. 101, 25th Cong., 3d sess., 42, 1839. Fallatrahs.—Slocum in Sen. Doc. 24, 25th Cong., 2d sess., 15, 1838. Follaties.—Hale in U. S. Expl. Exped., VI, 569, 1846. Juálati.—Gatschet in Mag. Am. Hist., VIII, 256, 1882. Snalatine.—Lane (1849) in Sen. Ex. Doc. 52, 31st Cong., 1st sess., 172, 1850. Sualatine.—Lane in Ind. Aff. Rep., 160, 1850. Tuálati.—Gatschet in Jour. Am. Folk-lore, XII, 212, 1899. Tualatims.—Taylor in Sen. Ex. Doc. 4, 40th Cong., spec. sess., 27, 1867. Tualatin.—Palmer in Ind. Aff. Rep., 260, 1854. Tuality.—Tolmie in Trans. Oreg. Pion. Assn., 32, 1884. Tuhwalati.—Hale in U. S. Expl. Exped., VI, 569, 1846. Turlitan.—Huntington in Ind. Aff. Rep.1867, 62, 1868. Twalaties.—Ind. Aff. Rep., 221, 1861. Twalaty.—Pres. mess., Ex. Doc. 39, 32d Cong., 1st sess., 2, 1852. Twalites.—Ind. Aff. Rep. 1864, 503, 1865. Twallalty.—Ibid., 205, 1851. Twaltatines.—Meek in H. R. Ex. Doc. 76, 30th Cong., 1st sess., 10, 1848. Wapato Lake.—McClane in Ind. Aff. Rep., 184, 1887. Wapatu.—Gatschet in Jour. Am. Folk-lore, IV, 143, 1891. Wapatu Lake.—Gatschet in Cont. N. A. Ethnol., II, pt. 1, xlvi, 1890. Wapeto.—Ind. Aff. Rep., 492, 1897. Wapoto Lake.—McClane in Ind. Aff. Rep., 269, 1889. Wappato.—Smith in Ind. Aff. Rep., 56, 1875. Wappatoo.—Victor in Overland Mo., VII, 346, 1871. Wapto.—Meacham, Wigwam and Warpath, 117, 1875.

**Athabasca** (Forest Cree: *athap* 'in succession,' -*askaw* 'grass,' 'reeds'; hence 'grass or reeds here and there.'—Hewitt). A northern Athapascan tribe, from which the stock name is derived, residing around Athabasca lake, Northwest Ter., Canada. Ross (MS., B. A. E.) regards them as a part of the Chipewyan proper. They do not differ essentially from neighboring Athapascan tribes. In 1902 (Can. Ind. Aff., 84, 1902) 326 were enumerated at Ft Chipewyan.

Arabaskaw.—Lacombe, Dict. des Cris, 1874 ("Athabasca" Cree name). Athabaskans.—Petitot, Dict. Dènè-Dindjié, xx, 1876. Athapascow.—Drake, Bk. Inds., vi, 1848. Athapuscow.—Hearne, Journ. N. Ocean, 177, 1795. Ayabaskau.—Gatschet, MS., B. A. E. (Cree name). Kkρay-tρèlè-Ottinè.—Petitot, Autour du lac des Esclaves, 363, 1891 ('people of the willow floor,' i. e., of Ft Chipe-

wyan). Kkρest'aylé-kkè ottiné.—Petitot, Dict. Dènè-Dindjié, xx, 1876 ('people of the poplar floor'). Yéta-Ottinè.—Petitot, Autour, op. cit. ('people from above').

**Athapascan Family.** The most widely distributed of all the Indian linguistic families of North America, formerly extending over parts of the continent from the Arctic coast far into N. Mexico, from the Pacific to Hudson bay at the N., and from the Rio Colorado to the mouth of the Rio Grande at the S.—a territory extending for more than 40° of latitude and 75° of longitude.

The languages which compose the Athapascan family are plainly related to each other and, because of certain peculiarities, stand out from the other American languages with considerable distinctness. Phonetically they are rendered harsh and difficult for European ears because of series of guttural sounds, many continuants, and frequent checks and aspirations. Morphologically they are marked by a sentence verb of considerable complexity, due largely to many decayed prefixes and to various changes of the root to indicate the number and character of the subject and object. Between the various languages much regular phonetic change, especially of vowels, appears, and while certain words are found to be common, each language, independently of the others, has formed many nouns by composition and transformed the structure of its verbs. The wide differences in physical type and culture and the differences in language point to a long separation of the family, certainly covering many centuries. Geographically it consists of three divisions: Northern, Pacific, and Southern.

The Northern division, known as the Tinneh, or Déné, the name they apply to themselves, consists of three groups: The eastern, the northwestern, the southwestern. The eastern group occupies a vast extent of continuous territory, bounded on the E. by the Rocky mts. and lower Mackenzie r., on the s. by the watershed between the Athabasca and lower Peace rs., Athabasca lake, and Churchill r. To the E. and N. a narrow but continuous strip of Eskimo territory bars them from Hudson bay and the Arctic ocean. Their neighbors on the s. are members of the Algonquian family. This group seems to constitute a culture area of its own, rather uniform and somewhat limited on its material side. Very little is known of the folklore and religion of the people of this region. The principal tribes are the Tatsanottine or Yellowknives, E. of Yellowknife r., the Thlingchadinne or Dogribs, between Great Slave and Great Bear lakes; on Mackenzie r., beginning at the N., the Kawchodinneh or Hares, and the Etchaottine or Slaves; the Chipewyan on Slave r., the Tsattine or Beavers on Peace r.; and some 500 m. to the S. beyond the area outlined, the Sarsi, a small tribe allied with their Algonquian neighbors, the Siksika. The northwestern group occupies the interior of Alaska and adjacent portions of British territory as far as the Rocky mts. The shore lands to the N. and W. are held by the Eskimo, except at Cook inlet and Copper r. The people seem to have been too much occupied with the severe struggle with the elements for a bare existence to have developed much material culture. They are usually distinguished into three principal divisions: The Kutchin of Porcupine and Tanana rs., the middle course of the Yukon, and the lower Mackenzie (where they are often spoken of as Louchoux); the Ahtena of Copper r.; and the Khotana of the lower Yukon, Koyukuk r., and Cook inlet. The southwestern group occupies the mountainous interior of British America from the upper Yukon to lat. 51° 30′, with the Rocky mts. for their E. barrier, and with the Skittagetan, Koluschan, Chimmesyan, and Wakashan families between them and the Pacific. Their S. neighbors are the Salish. They are said to show considerable variety of physical appearance, culture, and language. The tribes composing this group are, according to Morice, beginning at the N., the Nahane; the Sekani; the Babine (Nataotin), on the shores of a lake bearing that name; the Carriers (Takulli), who occupy the territory from Stuart lake southward to Alexandria on Fraser r., and the Chilcotin (Tsilkotin), who live in the valley of the river to which they have given their name.

The Pacific division consisted formerly of a small band in Washington and of many villages in a strip of nearly continuous territory about 400 m. in length, beginning at the valley of Umpqua r. in Oregon and extending toward the S. along the coast and Coast Range mts. to the headwaters of Eel r. in California. Their territory was cut through at one point by the Yurok on Klamath r. These villages were in many cases separated by low but rugged mountains, and were surrounded by, and here and there surrounded, the small stocks characteristic of the region. The culture throughout this territory was by no means uniform, partly on account of the great differences between the conditions of life on the seacoast and those of inland mountain valleys, and partly because there was little intercourse between the river valleys of the region. For the greater part, in language there was a gradual transition through intermediate dialects from one end of the region to the other. There were probably 5 of these dialects which were mutually unintelligible. There were no tribes in this region, but groups of villages which sometimes joined in a raid against a common enemy and where the same dialect was spoken. The following dialectic groups made up this division: The Kwalhioqua in Washington; the Umpqua and Coquille (Mishikhwutmetunne), formerly on rivers of these names; the Taltushtuntude, Chastacosta, and Tututunne on Rogue r. and its tributaries, and the Chetco on Chetco r. in Oregon; the Tolowa on Smith r. and about Crescent City; the Hupa and Tlelding on the lower portion of Trinity r.; the Chilula and Whilkut on Redwood cr.; the Mattole on the river of that name; the Sinkyone, Lassik, and Kuneste in the valley of Eel r., in California. But few of the members of this division now remain. The Oregon portion has been on the Siletz and Grande Ronde res. for many years; those of California still reside near their ancient homes.

The Southern division held sway over a vast area in the S. W., including most of Arizona and New Mexico, the S. portion of Utah and Colorado, the W. borders of Kansas and Texas, and the N. part of Mexico to lat. 25°. Their principal neighbors were the members of the Shoshonean family and the various Pueblo tribes in the region. So far as is known the language and culture of this division are quite uniform. The peoples composing it are the Navaho s. of San Juan r. in N. E. Arizona and N. W. New Mexico, the Apache (really a group of tribes) on all sides of the Navaho except the N., and the Lipan formerly in W. Texas but now living with the Mescaleros in New Mexico.

Not included in the three divisions described above are the Kiowa Apache, a small band which has maintained its own language while living on intimate terms with the Kiowa. They seem never to have been connected with the Southern division, but appear to have come from the N. many years ago.

The tendency of the members of this family to adopt the culture of neighboring peoples is so marked that it is difficult to determine and describe any distinctive Athapascan culture or, indeed, to say whether such a culture ever existed. Thus, the tribes of the extreme N., especially in Alaska, had assimilated many of the customs and arts of the Eskimo, the Takulli had adopted the social organization and much of the mythology of the Tsimshian, the western Nahane had adopted the culture of the Tlingit, the Tsilkotin that of the Salish, while the Sarsi and Beavers possessed much in common with their Algonquian neighbors to the s. and E. Passing to the Pacific group, practically no difference is found between the culture which they presented and that of the surrounding tribes of other stocks, and it is evident that the social organization and many of the rites and ceremonies of the Navaho, and even of the Apache, were due to Pueblo influences. Although in this respect the Athapascan resembles the Salishan and Shoshonean families, its pliability and adaptability appear to have been much greater, a fact noted by missionaries among the northern Athapascans up to the present day.

If a true Athapascan culture may be said to have existed anywhere, it was among the eastern tribes of the Northern group, such as the Chipewyan, Kawchodinne, Stuichamukh, Tatsanottine, and Thlingchadinne, although differing comparatively little from that of the northernmost Algonquian tribes and the neighboring Eskimo. Although recognizing a certain individuality, these tribes had little coherence, and were subdivided into family groups or loose bands, without clans or gentes, which recognized a kind of patriarchal government and descent. Perhaps the strongest authority was that exercised by the leader of a hunting party, the difference between success and failure on such a quest being frequently the difference between the existence or extinction of a band.

Clothing was made of deerskins in the hair, and the lodges of deer or caribou skins, sometimes replaced by bark farther s. Their food consisted of caribou, deer, moose, musk-ox, and buffalo, together with smaller animals, such as the beaver and hare, various kinds of birds, and several varieties of fish found in the numerous lakes and rivers. They killed deer by driving them into an angle formed by two converging rows of stakes, where they were shot by hunters lying in wait. The man was complete master in his own lodge, his wife being entirely subservient and assuming the most laborious duties. Infanticide, especially of female children, was common, but had its excuse in the hard life these people were obliged to undergo. In summer transportation was effected in birch-bark canoes; in winter the dogs carried most of the household goods, except in so far as they were assisted by the women, and on the barren grounds they were provided with sledges. The bodies of the dead were placed on the ground, covered with bark and surrounded by palings, except in the case of noted men, whose bodies were placed in boxes on the branches of trees. Shamans existed, and their sayings were of much influence with some of the people, but

religion does not seem to have exerted as strong an influence as in most other parts of America. At the same time they had absolute faith in the necessity and efficacy of certain charms which they tied to their fishing hooks and nets. Nearly all have now been Christianized by Roman Catholic missionaries and seem to be devout converts. For an account of the culture of the remaining Athapascan tribes, see the special articles under the tribal names and articles dealing with other tribes in the same localities.

For the Northern division of Athapascans see Hearne, Travels, 1795; the numerous writings of Émile Petitot; Morice (1) in Trans. Roy. Soc. Canada, (2) Trans. Canadian Inst., and elsewhere; Richardson, Arct. Searching Exped., 1851; Bancroft, Native Races, I, 1886; Russell, Explor. Far North, 1898; Hardesty and Jones in Smithson. Rep., 1866, 1872. For the Pacific division: Powers in Cont. N. A. Ethnol., III, 1877; Goddard in Pubs. Univ. Cal., I, 1903. For the Southern division: Matthews (1) in 5th Rep. B. A. E., 1887, (2) Memoirs Am. Mus. Nat. Hist., VI, Anthrop. V, 1902, (3) Navaho Legends, 1897; Bourke (1) in Jour. Am. Folk-lore, III, 1890, (2) in 9th Rep. B. A. E., 1892.

In the synonymy which follows the names are not always to be accepted as true equivalents. The Northern Athapascan or Déné are usually meant.

(P. E. G. J. R. S.)

Adènè.—Petitot, Dict. Dènè-Dindjié, xix, 1876 (Kawchodinne name). Arabasca.—Petitot in Jour. Roy. Geog. Soc., 641, 1883. Arathapescoas.—Boudinot, Star in the West, 125, 1816. Athabasca.—Bancroft, Nat. Races, I, 38, 1874. Athabascan.—Richardson, Arct. Exped., II, 1, 1851. Athapaccas.—Gallatin in Schoolcraft, Ind. Tribes, III, 401, 1853. Athapaches.—Petitot, Autour du lac des Esclaves, 98, 1891. Athapascan.—Turner in Pac. R. R. Rep., III, pt. 3, 84, 1856. Athapascas.—Gallatin in Trans. Am. Antiq. Soc., II, 17, 1836. Athapasques.—Kingsley, Standard Nat. Hist., pt. 6, 147, 1883. Ayabasca.—Petitot in Jour. Roy. Geog. Soc., 641, 1883. Chepewyan.—Richardson, Arct. Exped., II, 1, 1851. Chepeyans.—Pritchard, Phys. Hist. Man., V, 375, 1847. Chippewyan.—Dall, Alaska, 428, 1870. Danè.—Petitot, Dict. Dènè-Dindjié, xix, 1876. Danites.—Petitot, Autour du lac des Esclaves, 99, 1891. Dendjyé.—Petitot, MS. B. A. E., 1865 (used by Kutchin). Dènè.—Petitot, Autour du lac des Esclaves, 363, 1891 (used by Chipewyan). Dènè-Dindjié.—Petitot, Dict. Langue Dènè-Dindjié, passim, 1876. Deneh-Dindschieh.—Kingsley, Stand. Nat. Hist., pt. 6, 143, 1883. Dinais.—Cox, Columbia R., II, 374, 1831. Dindjié.—Petitot, Dict. Dènè-Dindjié, xix, 1876 (used by Tukkuthkutchin). Dindjitch.—Ibid. (used by Kutchakutchin). Dinè.—Morice in Proc. Can. Inst., 3d s., VII, 113, 1889 (used by Etagottine). Dinné.—Keane in Stanford, Compend., 512, 1878. Dinnee.—Cox, Columbia R., II, 374, 1831. Dinneh.—Franklin, Nar., I, 241, 1824. Dinni.—Rafinesque, Am. Nations, I, 146, 1836. Dnainè.—Petitot, Dict. Dènè-Dindjié, xix, 1876 (used by Knaiakhotana). 'Dtinnè.—Richardson, Arct. Exped., II, 1, 1851. Dunè.—Morice in Proc. Can. Inst., 3d s., VII, 113, 1889 (used by Thlingchadinne). Gunana.—Swanton, inf'n (Tlingit name: 'strange people'). Irkρéléït'.—Petitot, Dict. Dènè-Dindjié, xix, 1876 (Eskimo name: 'larvæ of lice'). Itynai.—Dall in Cont. N. A. Ethnol., I, pt. 1, 25, 1877 (misprint). **Kenaians.**—Halleck (1868) quoted by Petroff, 10th Census, Alaska, 40, 1884. **Kenaizer.**—Holmberg quoted by Dall, Alaska, 428, 1870. **Northern.**—Schouler in Jour. Roy. Geog. Soc. Lond., XI, 218, 1841 (partial synonym). **Tanai.**—Zagoskin quoted by Dall in Cont. N. A. Ethnol., I, 25, 1877. **Tannai.**—Corbusier in Am. Antiq., 276, 1886. **Tede.**—Dorsey, MS. Applegate Cr. vocab., B. A. E., 1884 (used by Dakubetede). **Tene.**—Dorsey, MS. Smith R. vocab., B. A. E., 1884 (used by Tolowa). **Tennai.**—Corbusier in Am. Antiq., 276, 1886. **Thnaina.**—Holmberg quoted by Dall, Alaska, 428, 1870. **Thynné.**—Pinart in Rev. de Philol. et d'Ethnol., no. 2, 1, 1875. **Tinaï.**—Zagoskin in Nouv. Ann. Voy., 5th s., XXI, 226, 1850. **Tinnătte.**—Wilson in Rep. on N. W. Tribes Can., 11, 1888 (used by Sarsi). **Tinnè.**—Richardson, Arct. Exped., II, 1, 1851. **Tinneh.**—Hardisty in Smithson. Rep. 1866, 303, 1872. **Tinney.**—Keane in Stanford, Compend., 539, 1878. **Toené.**—Morice in Proc. Can. Inst., 3d s., VII, 113, 1889 (used by Takulli). **Toeni.**—Ibid. (used by Tsilkotin). **Ttynai.**—Zagoskin, quoted by Schott in Erman, Archiv., VII, 480, 1849. **Ttynai-chotana.**—Zagoskin quoted by Bancroft, Nat. Races, III, 589, 1882. **Ttynnaï.**—Zagoskin (1842) quoted by Petroff, 10th Census, Alaska, 37, 1884. **Tûde.**—Dorsey, MS. Galice Creek vocab., B. A. E., 1884 (used by Taltushtuntude). **Tumeh.**—Butler, Wild N. Land, 127, 1873. **Tûnně.**—Dorsey, MS. Tutu vocab., B. A. E., 1884 (used by Tututunne). **Wabasca.**—Petitot in Jour. Roy. Geog. Soc, 641, 1883.

**Ati.** A former Papago rancheria, visited by Kino about 1697–99, and the seat of a mission established about that date; situated on the w. bank of Rio Altar, between Uquitoa and Tubutama, just s. of the Arizona boundary. Pop. 56 in 1730. The mission was evidently abandoned within the following 40 years, as Garcés (Diary, 1775–76, 455, 1900) speaks of Ati as a favorable site for one. Not to be confounded with San Francisco Ati. (F. W. H.)
**Addi.**—Venegas, Hist. Cal., I, map, 1759. **At.**—Font, map (1777), in Coues, Garcés Diary, I, 1900. **Ati.**—Font, map (1777), in Bancroft, Ariz. and N. Mex., 393, 1889. **Atic.**—Orozco y Berra, Geog., 347, 1864. **Axi.**—Venegas, Hist. Cal., I, 303, 1759. **Siete Principes Atí.**—Rivera (1730) quoted by Bancroft, No. Mex. States, I, 514, 1884.

**Atiahigui.** A former Maricopa rancheria on the Rio Gila, s. w. Ariz.—Sedelmair (1744) quoted by Bancroft, Ariz. and N. Mex., 366, 1889.

**Atica.** An unidentified pueblo of New Mexico in 1598.—Oñate (1598) in Doc. Inéd., XVI, 103, 1871.

**Atiga.** A village formerly on the w. bank of Allegheny r., below French cr., according to Bellin's map, 1755. It may have belonged to the Delawares or the Mingo. Marked distinct from Attigua, q. v. (J. M.)

**Atisawaiân.** See *Savoyan*.

**Atka** (native name of the largest of the Andreanof ids., called Atchu by Coxe, Atchka by Cook in 1778, and by various writers Atchgi, Atchka, and Alcha, according to Baker, Geog. Dict. Alaska, 1901). One of the two dialectic divisions of the Aleut, occupying Andreanof, Rat, and Near ids. (Holmberg, Ethnol. Skizz., 1855). The Atka are great hunters of the sea otter, and the furs they sold during the Russian occupancy made them

wealthy. About half of them learned to read and write their own language, of which Russian missionaries made a grammar. With Christianity and civilization the Russians introduced alcohol, for which the natives developed an inordinate craving, making their own liquor, after the importation of spirits was forbidden, by fermenting sugar and flour. Their diet of fish and occasional waterfowl is supplemented by bread, tea, and other imported articles that have become indispensable. The native dress, consisting of a long tight-sleeved coat of fur or bird skins, overlapping boots that reached above the knee, has been generally discarded for European clothing, though they still wear in wet weather a waterproof shirt of intestines obtained from the sea-lion. All are now Christianized, and nearly all live in houses furnished with ordinary things of civilization.—Schwatka, Mil. Recon., Compil. of Explor. in Alaska, 358, 1900.
**Andrejanouschen Aleuten.**—Holmberg, Ethnol. Skizz., 8, 1855. **Atchaer.**—Ibid. **Atkan.**—Dall, Alaska, 386, 1870. **Atkhas.**—Keane in Stanford, Compend., 502, 1878. **Kighigufl.**—Coxe, Russian Disc., 219, 1787. **Kigikhkhun.**—Dall in Cont. N. A. Ethnol., I, 22, 1877 (sig. 'northernwestern people'). **Namikh'-hūn'.**—Ibid. (sig. 'western people'). **Nihouhins.**—Pinart in Mém. Soc. Ethnol. Paris, XI, 157, 1872. **Nikhū-khnin.**—Dall in Cont. N. A. Ethnol., op. cit.

**Atkigyin.** A former Aleut village on Agattu id., Alaska, one of the Near id. group of the Aleutians, now uninhabited.

**Atkulik.** A former Aleut village on Agattu id., Alaska, one of the Near id. group of the Aleutians, now uninhabited.

**Atlalko.** A Hahuamis village at the head of Wakeman sd., British Columbia.
**Ā-tl-al-ko.**—Dawson in Can. Geolog. Surv., map, 1888.

**Atlantis.** The theory of the lost island of Atlantis can be traced back to the Timæus of Plato. It was mentioned by many subsequent ancient historians, some of whom considered it a myth while others believed it to be true. The discovery of America revived interest in the subject, and by many theorists the continent itself was believed to be the lost island, while others, as the Abbé Brasseur de Bourbourg (Quatre Lettres sur le Méxique, 1868; Manuscrit Troano, I, 1869) held that Atlantis was the extension of America which stretched from Central America and Mexico far into the Atlantic, the Canaries, Madeiras, and Azores being the only remnants which were not submerged. Rafinesque (American Nations, 1836) devotes a chapter to the subject of the Atlantes. He finds three routes by which the ancient nations of the Eastern and Western hemispheres could communicate, namely, the northern, tropical, and southern paths, "without taking into account the probable connection of North America with Asia and

many islands in the Atlantic.'' His argument, if such it can be called, is incoherent and fantastic in the extreme. The theory is probably better known to Americans through the writings of Donnelly (Atlantis, the Antediluvian World), who undertakes to prove the case by modern scientific methods, and locates the Atlantis of Plato as an island opposite the mouth of the Mediterranean, a remnant of the lost continent. The mere statement of a few of the postulates which Donnelly endeavors to prove is a sufficient characterization, if not refutation, of his theory:
(1) That Atlantis was the region where man first rose from a state of barbarism to civilization. (2) That its inhabitants became, in the course of ages, a populous and mighty nation, from whose overflowings the shores of the Gulf of Mexico, the Mississippi r., the Amazon, the Pacific coast of South America, the Mediterranean, the w. coast of Europe and Africa, the Baltic, the Black sea, and the Caspian were populated by civilized nations. (3) That it was the true antediluvian world; the Garden of Eden; the Gardens of the Hesperides; the Elysian Fields; the Gardens of Alcinous; the Mesamphalos; the Olympos; the Asgard of the traditions of the ancient nations, representing a universal memory of a great land where early mankind dwelt for ages in peace and happiness. (4) That the oldest colony formed by the Atlanteans was probably in Egypt, whose civilization was a reproduction of that of the Atlantic island. (5) That the Phenician alphabet, parent of all European alphabets, was derived from an Atlantis alphabet, which was also conveyed from Atlantis to the Mayas of Central America. (6) That Atlantis was the original seat of the Aryan or Indo-European family of nations, as well as of the Semitic peoples, and possibly also of the Turanian races. (7) That Atlantis perished in a terrible convulsion of nature, in which the whole island sank into the ocean with nearly all its inhabitants. (8) That a few persons escaped in ships and on rafts, and carried to the nations E. and w. the tidings of the appalling catastrophe, which has survived to our own time in the Flood and Deluge legends of the different nations of the old and new worlds.

Among modern scholars there are very few who regard Atlantis in any other light than as a myth. See Winsor, Narrative and Critical History of America, I, 141, 1884, for an excellent summary of the subject and for many references to the literature. The term Atlantic (ocean) is not derived from Atlantis, but from the Atlas mts. in N. Africa. (H. W. H.)

**Atlatl.** See *Throwing stick.*

**Atlklaktl** (*Alqla'xL*). A Bellacoola village where the present mission is situated, on the N. side of Bellacoola r., near its mouth, British Columbia. It was one of the 8 villages called Nuhalk.—Boas in Mem. Am. Mus. Nat. Hist., II, 48, 1898.

**Atlkuma** (*Ā-tl-kuma*). A Tlauitsis village on the N. side of Cracroft id., Brit. Col.—Dawson in Can. Geol. Surv., map, 1887.

**Atnik.** A village of the Sidarumiut Eskimo near Pt Belcher, Alaska; pop. 34 in 1890.
Ataniek.—Tikhmenief (1861) quoted by Baker, Geog. Dict. Alaska, 1901. **Atinikq.**—Zagoskin, Descr. Russ. Poss. Am., pt. 1, 74, 1847. **Atnik.**—Baker, op. cit. **Attanak.**—11th Census, Alaska, map, 1893. **A'tûnĕ.**—Murdoch in 9th Rep. B. A. E., 44, 1892. **Kuik.**—Zagoskin, op. cit.

**Atnuk.** An Eskimo village of the Kaviagmiut tribe at Darby cape, Alaska; pop. 20 in 1880, 34 in 1890.
Atnikmioute.—Zagoskin in Nouv. Ann. Voy., 5th s., XXI, map, 1850. **Atnikmut.**—Zagoskin, Descr. Russ. Poss. Am., pt. I, 73, 1847. **Atnuk.**—Nelson in 18th Rep. B. A. E., map, 1899.

**Atoko.** The extinct Crane clan of the Chua (Snake) phratry of the Hopi.
A-tó-co.—Bourke, Snake Dance, 117, 1884. **Atoko wiñwû.**—Fewkes in 19th Rep. B. A. E., 583, 1901 (*wiñ-wû* = 'clan'). **A'-to-ko wuñ-wü.**—Fewkes in Am. Anthrop., VII, 403, 1894 (*wuñ-wü* = clan).

**Atotarho.** See *Wathatotarho.*

**Atotonilco** (from Nahuatl: *atl* 'water,' *totonilli* 'warm.'—Buelna). A former Tepehuane pueblo in lat. 25° 30′, long. 107°, E. Sinaloa, Mexico. It was the seat of the mission of San Juan.
San Juan Atotonilco.—Orozco y Berra, Geog., 324, 1864.

**Atotonilco.** A former Tepehuane pueblo in lat. 24° 35′, long. 104° 10′, s. E. Durango, Mexico. It was the seat of the mission of San Andrés.
San Andres Atotonilco.—Orozco y Berra, Geog., 318, 1864.

**Atquanachuke.** A tribe or band residing early in the 17th century in s. or central New Jersey. All references to them are indefinite. Smith, who did not visit them, says they were on the seacoast beyond the mountains northward from Chesapeake bay, and spoke a language different from that of the Powhatan, Conestoga, Tocwogh, and Cuscarawaoc. Most of the early authorities put them in the same general locality, but Shea, evidently misled by the order in which Smith associates this name with names of E. shore tribes, says they lived in 1633 on the E. shore of Maryland and were allies of the Conestoga. (J. M.)
Aquaauchuques.—Keane in Stanford, Compend., 501, 1878. **Aquamachukes.**—Map *ca.* 1614 in N. Y. Doc. Col. Hist., I, 1856. **Aquamachuques.**—De Laet, Novus Orbis, 72, 1633. **Aquanachukes.**—Dutch map (1621) in N. Y. Doc. Col. Hist., I, 1856. **Atquanachuck.**—Simons in Smith (1629), Virginia, I, 183, repr. 1819. **Atquanachukes.**—Ibid., 120. **Atquanachuks.**—Ibid., 183. **Atquanahuokes.**—De Laet, Hist. Nouv. Monde, 93, 1640. **Atquinachunks.**—Shea, Cath. Miss., 486, 1855.

**Atrakwaye** (probably 'at the place of the sun,' or 'south'). A palisaded town of the Conestoga, situated in 1608 on the

E. side of Susquehanna r., below the forks at Northumberland, in Northumberland co., Pa. Probably identical with the Quadroque of Smith's map of Virginia, whereon it is placed from information derived by Smith directly from the Susquehanna (Conestoga). The Journal of the Jesuits for 1651–52 states that during the winter of 1652 this town was taken by 1,000 Iroquois warriors who, with a loss of 130 men, carried away 500 or 600 captives, chiefly men. Atrakwayé was the seat of the Akhrakouaeronon, a division of the Conestoga. (J. N. B. H.)

Akrakwaé.—Jes. Rel., Thwaites' ed., XXXVI, 248, note, 49, 1899. Atra'K8ae.—Ibid., Jour. for 1650–51,140. Atra'kwae.—Ibid.,141. Atra'K8a,e.—Ibid., XXXVII, 110, 1899. Atra'kwa,e.—Ibid.,111. Quadroque.—Smith (ca. 1608), Va., map, repr. 1884.

**Atripuy.** Mentioned by Oñate (Doc. Inéd., XVI, 114–116, 1871) in 1598 as a province containing 42 pueblos in the region of the lower Rio Grande, N. Mex. The name was probably derived from that of a village of the N. branch of the Jumano. The first pueblo of this province, journeying northward, was Trenaquel; the second Qualacu, both of which Bandelier identifies as villages of the Piros who occupied the Rio Grande valley from below Isleta to San Marcial, N. Mex. It may therefore be inferred that Atripuy was the name applied to the country inhabited at that time by the Piros. (F. W. H.)

**Atripuy.** A large pueblo of the Jumano of New Mexico in 1598.—Oñate (1598) in Doc. Inéd., XVI, 114, 1871.

**Atselits.** An insignificant Chilliwack settlement in s. British Columbia, with only 2 adults in 1902.

Aitchelich.—Can. Ind. Aff., 357, 1895. Aitchelitz.—Ibid., 413, 1898. Assyletch.—Ibid., 78, 1878. Assylitch.—Ibid., 316, 1880. Assylitlh.—Brit. Col. Map, Ind. Aff., Victoria, 1872. Atchelity.—Can. Ind. Aff., 276, 1894. A'tsElits.—Hill-Tout in Ethnol. Surv. Can., 4, 1902.

**Atsep.** A Yurok village on lower Klamath r., 5 m. below the mouth of Trinity r., N. Cal.

**Atsepar.** The uppermost village of the Yurok on Klamath r., Cal., situated at the mouth of Bluff cr., 6 m. above the junction of Trinity r.

**Atshuk.** A Yaquina village on the s. side of Yaquina r., Oreg.

A'-touk.—Dorsey in Jour. Am. Folk-lore, X, 229, 1890.

**Atsina** (Blackfoot: ăt-se′-na, said to mean 'gut people.'—Grinnell. Cf. Aä′ninĕna, under *Arapaho*). A detached branch of the Arapaho (q. v.), at one time associated with the Blackfeet, but now with the Assiniboin under Ft Belknap agency, Mont., where in 1904 they numbered 535, steadily decreasing. They called themselves Aä′ninĕna, said to mean 'white clay people,' but are known to the other Arapaho as Hitúnĕna, 'beggars,' or 'spongers,' whence the tribal sign, commonly but incorrectly rendered

'belly people,' or 'big bellies,' the Gros Ventres of the French Canadians and now their popular name. The Atsina are not prominent in history, and in most respects are regarded by the Arapaho proper as inferior to them. They have been constantly confused with the Hidatsa, or Gros Ventres of the Missouri. (J. M.)

Aä′ninĕna.—Mooney in 14th Rep. B. A. E., 955, 1896. Acapatos.—Duflot de Mofras, Explor., II, 341, 1844 (a similar name is also applied to the Arapaho). Achena.—De Smet, Missions, 253, note, 1848. Ahahnelins.—Morgan, Systems of Consang., 226, 1871. Ahnenin.—Latham, Essays, 276, 1860. Ahni-ninn.—Maximilian, Travels, I, 530,1839. A-lân-sâr.—Lewis and Clark, Travels, 56, 1806. Alesar.—Keane in Stanford, Compend., 470, 1878. A-rĕ-tĕăr-ȯ-păn-gȧ.—Long, Exped. Rocky Mts., II, lxxxiv, 1823 (Hidatsa name). Ăt-sē′-nā.—Grinnell, inf'n, 1905 (Blackfoot name, said to mean 'gut people'). Atsina.—Latham in Proc. Philol. Soc. Lond., VI, 86, 1854. Azäna.—Maximilian, Travels, I, 530, 1839 (Siksika name, German form). Bahwetego-weninnewug.—Tanner, Narr., 63, 1830 ('fall people': Chippewa name). Bahwetig.—Ibid., 64. Bot-k'iñ'ago.—Mooney in 14th Rep. B. A. E., 955, 1896 ('belly men'). Bowwetegoweninnewug.—Tanner, op. cit., 315 (Ottawa name). Bowwetig.—Ibid., 83. E-tá-ni-o.—Hayden, Ethnog. and Philol. Mo. Val., 290, 1862 ('people:' one Cheyenne name for them, the other and more common being Histuitanio). Fall Indians.—Umfreville (1790) in Maine Hist. Soc. Coll., VI, 270, 1859. Gros ventre of the Fort prairie.—Long, Exped. Rocky Mts., II, lxxxiv, 1823. Gros Ventres.—See under that name. Gros Ventres des Plaines.—De Smet, Missions, 253, note, 1848. Gros Ventres des Prairies.—Schermerhorn (1812) in Mass. Hist. Soc. Coll., 2d s., II, 36, 1814 (French name). Gros Ventres of the Falls.—Latham in Trans. Philol. Soc. Lond., 62, 1856. Gros Ventres of the Prairie.—Brackenridge, Views of La., 79, 1815. Grosventres of the Prairie.—McCoy, Ann. Reg. Ind. Aff., 47, 1836. Hahtz-nai koon.—Henry, MS. vocab., 1808 (Siksika name). His-tu-i′-ta-ni-o.—Hayden, Ethnog. and Philol. Mo. Val., 290, 1862 (Cheyenne name: *etanio* = 'people'). Hitu′nĕna.—Mooney in 14th Rep. B. A. E., 955, 1896 ('begging men': Arapaho name). Hitunĕnina.—Ibid. Minetares of the Prairie.—Gallatin in Trans. Am. Ethnol. Soc., II, 21, 1848 (by confusion with "Gros Ventres"). Minitares of the Prairie.—Latham in Proc. Philol. Soc. Lond., VI, 85, 1854. Minnetarees of Fort de Prairie.—Lewis and Clark, Trav., I, 131, 1814. Minnetarees of the Plains.—Ibid. Minnetarees of the Prairie.—Hayden, Ethnog. and Philol. Mo. Val., 344, 1862. Minnitarees of Fort de Prairie.—Lewis and Clark, quoted by Hayden, ibid., 422. Pawaustic-eythin-yoowuc.—Franklin, Journ. Polar Sea, 169, 1824. Paw-is-tick I-e-ne-wuck.—Harmon, Jour., 78, 1820. Pawistucienemuk.—Drake, Bk. Inds., X, 1848. Pawistuck-Ienewuck.—Morse, Rep. to Sec. War, 332, 1822. Prairie Grossventres.—Gass, Jour., 245, 1807. Rapid Indians.—Harmon, Jour., 78, 1820. Sä′pani.—Mooney in 14th Rep. B. A. E., 955, 1896 ('bellies': Shoshoni name). Sku′tani.—Ibid. (Sioux name). To-i-nin′-a.—Hayden, Ethnog. and Philol. Mo. Val., 326, 1862 ('people that beg': Arapaho name for Hitúnĕna).

**Atsina-Algo.** An adjective invented by Schoolcraft (Ind. Tribes, I, 198, 1853) to describe the confederate Atsina and Siksika.

**Atsmitl** (Chihalis name for Shoalwater bay). Chinookan divisions living around Shoalwater bay, Wash.—Boas, field notes.

Arts-milsh.—Swan, N. W. Coast, 210, 1857. Karwee-wee.—Ibid. Shoalwater Bay Indians.—Ford in Ind. Aff. Rep. 1857, 341, 1858.

**Atsugewi.** A Shastan tribe formerly residing in Hat Creek, Burney, and Dixie valleys, Cal. Their language is quite divergent from that of the Achomawi, from whom they regard themselves as distinct. Very few of them survive. (R. B. D.)

Adwanuqdji.—Curtin, MS. Ilmawi vocab., B. A. E., 1889 (Ilmawi name). **Atsugei.**—Powell in 6th Rep. B. A. E., xxxvii, 1888. **Atsugē'wi.**—Dixon, inf'n, 1905. **Chenoya.**—Curtin, MS. vocab., B. A. E., 1885 (Yana name). **Chenoyana.**—Ibid. **Chunoiyana.**—Dixon, inf'n, 1903 (Yana name). **Hat Creek Indians.**—Hanson in Ind. Aff. Rep. 1862, 311, 1863. **Tcunoíyana.**—Dixon, inf'n, 1903 (Yana name; tc=ch).

**Attacapa** (Choctaw: *hatak* 'man,' *apa* 'eats,' hence 'cannibal': a name applied by the Choctaw and their congeners to different tribes inhabiting s. w. La. and s. and s. E. Tex.; see *Cannibalism*). A tribe forming the Attacapan linguistic family, a remnant of which early in the 19th century occupied as its chief habitat the Middle or Prien lake in Calcasieu parish, La. It is learned from Hutchins (Geog. U. S., 1784) that "the village de Skunnemoke or Tuckapas" stood on Vermilion r., and that their church was on the w. side of the Tage (Bayou Tèche). The Attacapa country extended formerly to the coast in s. w. Louisiana, and their primitive domain was outlined in the popular name of the Old Attacapa or Tuckapa country, still in use, which comprised St Landry, St Mary, Iberia, St Martin, Fayette, Vermilion, and, later, Calcasieu and Vernon parishes; in fact all the country between Red, Sabine, and Vermilion rs. and the Gulf (Dennett, Louisiana, 1876). Charlevoix states that in 1731 some Attacapa with some Hasinai and Spaniards aided the French commander, Saint Denys, against the Natchez. Pénicaut (Margry, Déc., v, 440) says that at the close of 1703 two of the three Frenchmen whom Bienville sent by way of the Madeline r. to discover what nations dwelt in that region, returned and reported that they had been more than 100 leagues inland and had found 7 different nations, and that among the last, one of their comrades had been killed and eaten by the savages, who were anthropophagous. This nation was called Attacapa. In notes accompanying his Attacapa vocabulary Duralde says that they speak of a deluge which engulfed men, animals, and the land, when only those who dwelt on a highland escaped; he also says that according to their law a man ceases to bear his own name as soon as his wife bears a child to him, after which he is called the father of such and such a child, but that if the child dies the father again assumes his own name. Duralde also asserts that the women alone were charged with the labors of the field and of the household, and that the mounds were erected by the women under the supervision of the chiefs for the purpose of giving their

lodges a higher situation than those of other chiefs. Milfort (Mém., 92, 1802), who visited St Bernard bay in 1784, believed that the tribe came originally from Mexico. He was hospitably received by a band which he found bucanning meat beside a lake, 4 days' march w. of the bay; and from the chief, who was not an Attacapa, but a Jesuit, speaking French, he learned that 180, nearly half the Attacapa tribe, were there, thus indicating that at that time the tribe numbered more than 360 persons; that they had a custom of dividing themselves into two or three bodies for the purpose of hunting buffalo, which in the spring went to the w. and in the autumn descended into these latitudes; that they killed them with bows and arrows, their youth being very skilful in this hunt; that these animals were in great numbers and as tame as domestic cattle, for "we have great care not to frighten them;" that when the buffaloes were on the prairie or in the forest the Attacapa camped near them "to accustom them to seeing us." Sibley (Hist. Sketches, 82, 1806) described their village as situated "about 20 m. w. of the Attakapa church, toward Quelqueshoe;" their men numbered about 50, but some Tonica and Huma who had intermarried with the Attacapa made them altogether about 80. Sibley adds: "They are peaceable and friendly to everybody; labor, occasionally for the white inhabitants; raise their own corn; have cattle and hogs. They were at or near where they now live, when that part of the country was first discovered by the French." In 1885 Gatschet visited the section formerly inhabited by the Attacapa, and after much search discovered one man and two women at Lake Charles, Calcasieu parish, La., and another woman living 10 m. to the s.; he also heard of 5 other women then scattered in w. Texas; these are thought to be the only survivors of the tribe. (J. N. B. H.)

Atacapas.—Berquin-Duvallon, Trav. in La. and Fla., 97, 1806. **Atac-Apas.**—Le Page du Pratz, Hist. Louisiane, II, 231, 1758. **Atacapaz.**—Mezières (1778) quoted by Bancroft, No. Mex. States, I, 661, 1886. **Atac-assas.**—Jefferys, French Dom., I, 163, 1761. **Atakapas.**—Robin, Voy., map, 1807. **Attacapacas.**—Keane in Stanford, Compend., 502, 1878. **Attacapas.**—Brown in West. Gazetteer, 152, 1817. **Attacappa.**—Hutchins, Hist. Nar., 43, 1784. **Attakapas.**—Pénicaut (1703) in French, Hist. Coll. La., n. s., 87, 1869. **Attakapo.**—Lewis, Trav., 193, 1809. **Attaquapas.**—Butel-Dumont, Mém. sur la Louisiane, I, 134, 1753. **Attencapas.**—Gallatin in Trans. Am. Ethnol. Soc., II, 76, 1848. **Attuckapas.**—Schoolcraft, Ind. Tribes, VI, 35, 1857. **Hattahappas.**—McKenney and Hall, Ind. Tribes, III, 81, 1854. **Hattakappas.**—Romans, Hist. Fla., I, 101, 1775. **Man eaters.**—Pénicaut (1703) in French, Hist. Coll. La., n. s,, 87, 1869. **Skunnemoke.**—Hutchins (1784) in Imlay, West. Ter., 421, 1797. **Tákapo ishak.**—Gatschet, Attakapa MS., B. A. E., (adopted from whites; with *ishak* 'people'). **Tuckapas.**—Hutchins (1784) in Imlay, West. Ter., 421, 1797. **Tuckapaus.**—Ker, Trav., 300, 1816. **Tûkpa'-haⁿ-ya-di.**—Dorsey, Biloxi MS. Dict., B. A. E.,

1892 (Biloxi name). **Yúk' hiti ishak.**—Gatschet, MS., B. A. E. (own name: 'our people').

**Attacapan Family.** A linguistic family consisting solely of the Attacapa tribe, although there is linguistic evidence of at least two dialects. Under this name were formerly comprised several bands settled in s. La. and N. E. Tex. Although this designation was given them by their Choctaw neighbors on the E., these bands, with one or two exceptions, do not appear in history under any other general name. Formerly the Karankawa and several other tribes were included with the Attacapa, but the vocabularies of Martin Duralde and of Gatschet show that the Attacapa language is distinct from all others. Investigations by Gatschet in Calcasieu parish, La., in 1885, show that there were at least two dialects of this family spoken at the beginning of the 19th century—an eastern dialect, represented in the vocabulary of Duralde, recorded in 1802, and a western dialect, spoken on the 3 lakes forming the outlet of Calcasieu r. See Powell in 7th Rep. B. A. E., 56, 1891.

**Attakullaculla** (*Ătă'-gŭl'kălŭ'*, from *ătă'* 'wood,' *gŭl'kălŭ'* a verb implying that something long is leaning, without sufficient support, against some other object; hence 'Leaningwood.'—Mooney). A noted Cherokee chief, born about 1700, known to the whites as Little Carpenter (Little Cornplanter, by mistake, in Haywood). The first notice of him is as one of the delegation taken to England by Sir Alexander Cumming in 1730. It is stated that he was made second in authority under Oconostota in 1738. He was present at the conference with Gov. Glenn, of South Carolina, in July, 1753, where he was the chief speaker in behalf of the Indians, but asserted that he had not supreme authority, the consent of Oconostota, the war chief, being necessary for final action. Through his influence a treaty of peace was arranged with Gov. Glenn in 1755, by which a large cession of territory was made to the King of England; and it was also through his instrumentality that Ft Dobbs was built, in the year following, about 20 m. w. of the present Salisbury, N. C. When Ft Loudon, on Little Tennessee r., Tenn., was captured by the Indians in 1760, and most of the garrison and refugees were massacred, Capt. Stuart, who had escaped the tomahawk, was escorted safely to Virginia by Attakullaculla, who purchased him from his Indian captor, giving to the latter, as ransom, his rifle, clothes, and everything he had with him. It was again through the influence of Attakullaculla that the treaty of Charleston was signed in 1761, and that Stuart, after peace had

been restored, was received by the Cherokee as the British agent for the southern tribes; yet notwithstanding his friendship for Stuart, who remained a steadfast loyalist in the Revolution, and the fact that a large majority of the Cherokee espoused the British cause, Attakullaculla raised a force of 500 native warriors which he offered to the Americans. He is described by William Bartram (Travels, 482, 1792), who visited him in 1776, as "a man of remarkably small stature, slender and of a delicate frame, the only instance I saw in the nation, but he is a man of superior abilities." Although he had become sedate, dignified, and somewhat taciturn in maturer years, Logan (Hist. Upper So. Car., I, 490, 515, 1859) says that in his younger days he was fond of the bottle and often inebriate. The date of his death has not been recorded, but it was probably about 1780. See Mooney in 19th Rep. B. A. E., 1900.

**Attamtuck.** A village of the Powhatan confederacy, in 1608, situated between the Chickahominy and Pamunkey rs., in New Kent co., Va.—Smith (1629), Virginia, I, map, repr. 1819.

**Attamusco.** See *Atamasco*.

**Attaock.** A Conestoga village existing in 1608 w. of Susquehanna r., probably in what is now York co., Pa.—Smith (1608), Virginia, I, map, repr. 1819.

**Attapulgas** (Creek: *atap'halgi*, 'dogwood grove'). A former Seminole town on a branch of Oklokonee or Yellowwater r., Fla. A town of the name is now in Decatur co., Ga.
**Taphulgee.**—Roberts, Florida, 1763. **Top-hulga.**—Bell in Morse, Rep. to Sec. War, 307, 1822. **Topkegalga.**—Ibid., 306. **Topkélaké.**—Penière, ibid. **Tuphulga.**—H. R. Ex. Doc. 74 (1823), 19th Cong., 27, 1826.

**Attenmiut.** A division of the Malemiut Eskimo whose chief village is Atten, near the source of Buckland r., Alaska.
**Attenmut.**—Dall, Alaska, 284, 1870. **At'tenmūt.**—Dall in Cont. N. A. Ethnol., I, 16, 1877.

**Attenok.** A Sidarumiut Eskimo village on Seahorse ids., Alaska.
**Attenokamiut.**—11th Census, Alaska, 162, 1893.

**Attignawantan** (Huron: *hati* 'they,' *annioñniĕⁿ* 'bear': 'bear people'). One of the largest tribes of the Huron confederacy, comprising about half the Huron population, formerly living on Nottawasaga bay, Ontario. In 1638 they were settled in 14 towns and villages (Jes. Rel. 1638, 38, 1858). The Jesuit missions of St Joseph and La Conception were established among them. (J. N. B. H.)
**Atignaoüantan.**—Jes. Rel. for 1642, 61, 1858. **Atingyahointan.**—Sagard (1632), Hist. Can., IV, 1866. **Atingyahoulan.**—Coxe, Carolana, map, 1741. **Atinniao8nten.**—Jes. Rel. for 1649, 12, 1858. **Atinnia8enten.**—Jes. Rel. for 1644, 77, 1858. **Atinouaentans.**—Champlain (1618), Œuvres, IV, 140, 1870. **Attignaoouentan.**—Kingsley, Stand. Nat. Hist., pt. 6, 154, 1883. **Attigna8antan.**—Jes. Rel. for 1639, 50,

1858. **Attignaouentan.**—Jes. Rel. for 1640, 61, 1858.
**Attigñawantan.**—Schoolcraft, Ind. Tribes, IV, 204, 1854. **Attignouaatitans.**—Champlain (1616), Œuvres, IV, 58, 1870. **Attigouantan.**—Ibid. (1632), V, pt. 1, 247, 1870. **Attigouantines.**—Alcedo, Dic. Geog., II, 174, 1786. **Attigouautan.**—Champlain (1615), op. cit., IV, 23, 1870. **Bear nation.**—Schoolcraft, Ind. Tribes, III, 544, 1853. **Nation de l'Ours.**—Jes. Rel. for 1632, 14, 1858. **Nation des Ours.**—Jes. Rel. for 1636, 81, 1858.

**Attigneenongnahac.** One of the four tribes of the Huron confederation, living on L. Simcoe, Ontario, s. E. of the others. In 1624 they were said to have 3 villages. The Jesuit mission of St Joseph was established among them.
**Altignenonghac.**—Jes. Rel. for 1636, 123, 1858. **Atigagnongueha.**—Sagard (1632), Hist. Can., IV, 234, 1866 (Huron name). **Atignenongach.**—Jes. Rel. for 1637, 127, 1858. **Atignenonghac.**—Ibid., 109. **Atingueennonnihak.**—Jes. Rel. for 1644, 87, 1858. **Attigneenongnahac.**—Jes. Rel. for 1639, 50, 1858. **Attigneenonguahac.**—Schoolcraft, Ind. Tribes, IV, 204, 1854. **Attigueenongnahac.**—Jes. Rel. for 1638, 42, 1858. **Attiguenongha.**—Jes. Rel. for 1635, 28, 1858. **Attingneenongnahac.**—Jes. Rel. for 1640, 73, 1858. **Attingueenongnahac.**—Jes. Rel. for 1641, 67, 1858. **Attinquenongnahac.**—Jes. Rel. for 1640, 61, 1858. **Attiquenongnah.**—Kingsley, Stand. Nat. Hist., pt. 6, 154, 1883. **Attiquenongnahai.**—Schoolcraft, Ind. Tribes, III, 544, 1853. **Nation d'Entauaque.**—Sagard, Gr. Voy., 79, 1865.

**Attikamegue** (Chippewa: *ŭdi‛k* 'caribou,' *mäg* 'fish': 'whitefish.'—W. J.). A band of the Montagnais residing, when first known, in Quebec province, N. of the St Maurice basin (Jes. Rel. 1636, 37, 1858), and accustomed to ascend the St Lawrence to trade with the French. Charlevoix says their chief residence was on a lake connected with the St Maurice. They were so harassed by the attacks of the Iroquois that a part at least fled to the vicinity of Tadoussac. They were so nearly destroyed by smallpox in 1670 that they became extinct as a tribe. They were esteemed by the missionaries as a quiet, inoffensive people, readily disposed to receive religious instruction. (J. M.)
**Altihamaguez.**—McKenney and Hall, Ind. Tribes, III, 81, 1854. **Altikamek.**—Hervas quoted by Vater, Mithridates, pt. 3, sec. 3, 347, 1816. **Altikameques.**—Charlevoix (1743), Voy., I, 152, 1766. **Atikamegues.**—Jes. Rel. for 1643, 8, 1858. **Attekamek.**—Richardson, Arct. Exped., II, 39, 1851. **Attibamegues.**—Boudinot, Star in the West, 125, 1816. **Atticameoets.**—La Tour, map, 1779. **Atticameouecs.**—Bellin, map, 1755. **Atticamiques.**—Keane in Stanford, Compend., 502, 1878. **Atticamoets.**—La Tour, map, 1784. **Attikamegouek.**—Jes. Rel. for 1643, 38, 1858. **Attikamegs.**—La Tour, map, 1784. **Attikameguekhi.**—Jes. Rel. 1636, 37, 1858. **Attikamegues.**—Jes. Rel. 1637, 82, 1858. **Attikamek.**—Lahontan, New Voy, I, 230, 1703. **Attikameques.**—Drake, Ind. Chron., 161, 1836. **Attikamigues.**—Drake, Bk. Inds., VI, 1848. **Attikouetz.**—Jefferys, French Doms., pt. I, map, 1761. **Outakouamiouek.**—Jes. Rel. 1640, 12, 1858. **Outakouamiwek.**—Jes. Rel., III, index, 1858. **Poissons blancs.**—Jes. Rel. 1639, 19, 1858. **White Fish Indians.**—Winsor, Cartier to Frontenac, 171, 1894.

**Attikiriniouetch** (*ŭdi‛kwininiwŭg* 'caribou people.'—W. J.). A Montagnais tribe formerly living northward from Manicouagan lake, Quebec.
**Attik Iriniouetchs.**—Bellin, map, 1755. **Attikou Iriniouetz.**—La Tour, map, 1779. **Gens du Caribon.**—La Tour, map, 1784 (misprint). **Gens du Caribou.**—Bellin, map, 1755. **Les Caribou.**—Lotter, map, ca. 1770.

**Attique.** A village, probably of the Seneca, that stood in 1749 on the present site of Kittanning, Pa.
**Attigné.**—Céloron (1749) in Margry, Déc., VI, 685, 1886. **Attigua.**—Bellin, map, 1755. **Attiqué.**—Céloron in Margry, op. cit., 693.

**Attoughcomoco** (Algonquian: *atǐk* 'deer,' *komoko* 'house,' hence 'deer enclosure'). An unidentified village of one of the Algonquian tribes, situated, about 1608, probably near Patuxent r., Md. Not given by Capt. John Smith nor marked on his map. Mentioned by Pory in Smith (1629), Virginia, II, 62, repr. 1819.

**Attu** (native name, variously written At, Atako, Ataka, Attak, Attou, and Otma by explorers). An Atka Aleut settlement at Chichagof harbor, Attu id., the westernmost of the Aleutians, 173° E. from Greenwich. Pop. 107 in 1880; 101 in 1890. Once very prosperous, the settlement has decayed owing to the gradual disappearance of the sea otter.
**Attoo.**—Elliott, Our Arct. Prov., 179, 1886. **Chichagov.**—Schwatka, Mil. Recon. Alaska, 359, 1900.

**Attucks, Crispus.** An Indian-negro halfblood of Framingham, Mass., near Boston, noted as the leader and first person slain in the Boston massacre of Mar. 5, 1770, the first hostile encounter between the Americans and the British troops, and therefore regarded by historians as the opening fight of the great Revolutionary struggle. In consequence of the resistance of the people of Boston to the enforcement of the recent tax laws a detachment of British troops had been stationed in the town, to the great irritation of the citizens. On Mar. 5 this feeling culminated in an attack on the troops, in front of the old State House, by a crowd made up largely of sailors, and said to have been led by Attucks, although this assertion has been denied by some. The troops retaliated by firing into the party, killing four men, of whom Attucks was the first to fall. A monument to his memory was erected in Boston Common by the commonwealth of Massachusetts in 1888. Although the facts in regard to his personality are disputed, the evidence goes to show that Attucks was a sailor, almost a giant in stature, the son of a negro father and an Indian mother of Framingham, or the neighboring village of Natick, formerly the principal Indian mission settlement of Massachusetts. The name Attucks, derived from his mother, appears to be the Natick (Massachuset) *ahtuk*, or *attuks*, 'small deer.' See G. Bancroft, Hist. U. S.; Appleton's Encyclop. Am. Biog.; Am. Hist. Rec., I, Nov., 1872. (J. M.)

**Atuami.** A Shastan tribe formerly living in Big valley, Lassen co., Cal.
**A-tu-a'-mih.**—Powers in Cont. N. A. Ethnol., III, 267, 1877. **Hamefcutellies.**—Powers in Overland Mo., XII, 412, 1874. **Ha-mef-kut'-tel-li.**—Powers in

Cont. N. A. Ethnol., III, 267, 1877. **Tuqtéumi.**—Curtin, MS. Ilmawi vocab., B. A. E., 1889 (Ilmawi name).

**Atuyama.** A pueblo of New Mexico in 1598; doubtless situated in the Salinas, in the vicinity of Abo, and evidently occupied by the Tigua or the Piros.—Oñate (1598) in Doc. Inéd., XVI, 114, 1871.

**Auarkat.** A settlement of East Greenland Eskimo, lat. 59°.—Meddelelser om Grönland, XXV, map, 1902.

**Aubbeenaubbee** (*Wȧbȧnȧbȧ*, 'morning person,' a mythic being.—W. J.). A Potawatomi chief of this name occupied a village, commonly known as Aubbeenaubbee's village, on a reservation in the present Aubbeenaubbee tp., in Fulton co., Ind. The tract was sold by the treaty of Tippecanoe r. in 1836. Other forms of the name are Aubbanaubba, Aubbanaubbee, Aubeenaubee, Aubinaubee. (J. M.)

**Aubomesk** (probably 'white beaver'). A village of the Powhatan confederacy, in 1608, on the N. bank of the Rappahannock, in Richmond co., Va.—Smith (1629), Virginia, I, map, repr. 1819.

**Aucheucaula.** A former Creek town situated on the E. bank of Coosa r., in the extreme N. w. corner of Coosa co., Ala.—Royce in 18th Rep. B. A. E., Ala. map, 1900.

**Aucocisco.** The name of the territory about Casco bay and Presumpscot r., in the area now included in Cumberland co., Me. It was also sometimes applied to those Abnaki Indians by whom it was occupied. Since the section was settled at an early date by the whites, the name soon dropped out of use as applied to the Indians, or rather it was changed to "Casco," but this was a mere local designation, not a tribal distinction, as the Indians referred to were Abnaki. The proper form of the word is given by Willis as Uh-kos-is-co, 'crane' or 'heron,' the first syllable being guttural. These birds still frequent the bay. It is said by Willis to have been the Indian name of Falmouth (Portland), Me.
**Ancocisco.**—Smith (1629), Virginia, II, 177, repr. 1819 (misprint). **Aucasisco.**—Schoolcraft, Ind. Tribes, III, 545, 1853. **Aucocisco.**—Smith (1629), Virginia, II, 193, repr. 1819. **Aucosisco.**—Drake, Bk. Inds., VI, 1848. **Casco.**—Sullivan in Mass. Hist. Soc. Coll., 1st s., IX, 210, 1804 ("Casco Indians"). **Quack.**—Levett (1628) in Mass. Hist. Soc. Coll., 3d s., VIII, 168, 1843 (same?). **Uh-kos-is-co.**—Willis in Me. Hist. Soc. Coll., I, 31, 1831, repr. 1858.

**Au Glaize.** Mentioned by Drake (Bk. Inds., bk. 5, 63, 1848) as if a Delaware village on the s. w. [s. E.] branch of the Miami of the Lake (Maumee r.), Ohio.

**Augpalartok** ('the red one,' designating a cliff.—Boas). An Eskimo village in w. Greenland, lat. 72° 53′.—Meddelelser om Grönland, VIII, map, 1889.

**Augustine.** A rancheria and reservation of 615 acres of desert land occupied by Mission Indians; situated 75 m. from the Mission Tule River agency, s. Cal.—Rep. Ind. Aff., 175, 1902.

**Auk.** A Koluschan tribe on Stephens passage, Douglas and Admiralty ids., Alaska; pop. 640 in 1880–81, 279 in 1890. Their chief town was called Anchguhlsu. The other settlements mentioned by Petroff were probably summer camps. One such camp was Tsantikihin, now called Juneau. The social divisions are Tlenedi and Wushketan. (J. R. S.)
**Ahkootskie.**—Elliott, Cond. Aff. Alaska, 227, 1875 (transliterated from Veniaminoff). **Ak-kŏn.**—Krause, Tlinkit Ind., 116, 1885. **Akutskoe.**—Veniaminoff, Zapiski, II, pt. 3, 30, 1840. **Armos.**—Scott in Ind. Aff. Rep., 309, 1868 (probably misprint for Awks). **Auke.**—Kane, Wand. in N. Am., app., 1859. **Auke-qwan.**—Emmons in Mem. Am. Mus. Nat. Hist., III, 233, 1903. **Awks.**—Halleck in Rep. Sec. War, pt. I, 38, 1868.

**Aukardneling.** A village of the Talirpingmiut division of the Okomiut Eskimo on the w. side of Cumberland sd.
**Auqardneling.**—Boas in 6th Rep. B. A. E., map, 1888.

**Aukpatuk** ('red'). A Suhinimiut Eskimo village on Ungava bay, Labrador.—Hind, Lab. Pen., II, map, 1863.

**Aukumbumsk.** A Pequot village in the center of their country and the residence of their chief before the coming of the English, in 1636; probably in New London co., Conn.
**Aukumbumsk.**—Trumbull, Ind. Names Conn., 7, 1881 (Mohegan form). **Awcumbucks.**—Ibid. (Narraganset form).

**Aulintac.** A Costanoan village at Santa Cruz mission, Cal. The name has been taken for a dialectic division of the Costanoan family.

**Aureuapeugh.** A village of the Powhatan confederacy, in 1608, on Rappahannock r., in Essex co., Va.—Smith (1629), Virginia, I, map, repr. 1819.

**Auriferous gravel man.** See *Calaveras Man.*

**Ausion.** A former Chumashan village near Purísima mission, Santa Barbara co., Cal.—Taylor in Cal. Farmer, Oct. 18, 1861.

**Aute.** An Apalachee (?) town on the coast of Apalachee bay, Fla., first visited by Narvaez in 1528. It has been identified in location with St Marks.
**Ante.**—French, Hist. Coll. La., II, 246, 1875 (misprint). **Aute.**—Cabeza de Vaca, Smith trans., 38, 1871 (Smith identifies it with Ochete). **Autia.**—Linschoten, Desc. de l'Amér., 6, 1638. **Haute.**—Gallatin in Trans. Am. Ethnol. Soc., II, lvi, 1848.

**Autiamque.** The town, possibly Caddoan, where De Soto's troops went into winter quarters in 1541–42. It had an abundance of maize and provisions, and lay on the same river as Cayas, apparently Arkansas r.
**Autiamque.**—Gentl. of Elvas (1557) in French, Hist. Coll. La., II, 181, 1850. **Utiangue.**—Rafinesque, introd. Marshall, Ky., I, 35, 1824. **Utianque.**—Shipp, De Soto and Fla., 683, 1881. **Vicanque.**—Biedma in French, op. cit., 107. **Viranque.**—Biedma in Smith, Collec. Docs. Fla., 61, 1857. **Vtiangue.**—Garcilasso de la Vega, Fla., 193, 1723.

**Avak.** A Yuit Eskimo village near Cape Chukotsky, N. E. Siberia; pop. 101 in 16 houses about 1895; 98 in 12 houses in 1901. The people are of the Aiwan division.

**Agvan.**—Nelson in 18th Rep. B. A. E., map, 1899. **A'vak.**—Bogoras, Chukchee, 29, 1904 (Eskimo name). **Awan.**—Krause in Deutsche Geog. Blätter, v, 80, map, 1882 (Chukchi name for Eskimo about Indian pt.). **Eu'nmun.**—Bogoras, op. cit. (Chukchi name).

**Avatanak.** An Aleut village on a small island of the same name, between Unalaska and Unimak ids., Alaska; pop. 19 in 1880.

**Aiaialgutak.**—Krenitzin and Levashef (1768), quoted by Baker, Geog. Dict. Alaska, 1901. **Avatanak.**—Petroff, 10th Census, Alaska, 22, 1884. **Avatanakskoi.**—Elliott, Cond. Aff. Alaska, 225, 1875. **Avatanovskoe.**—Veniaminoff, Zapiski, II, 203, 1840. **Awatanak.**—Holmberg, Ethnol. Skizz., map, 152, 1855.

**Avaudjelling.** A summer settlement of Akudnirmiut Eskimo at the N. end of Home bay, Baffin land.—Boas in 6th Rep. B. A. E., map, 1888.

**Avavares.** A former tribe of Texas, possibly Caddoan, which lived "behind" the Quintoles toward the interior, and to which Cabeza de Vaca, in 1527–34, fled from the Mariames. Their language was different from that of the Mariames, although they understood the latter. They bartered bones, which the Mariames ground and used for food, and also traded in bows. While staying with the Avavares Cabeza de Vaca and his companion became noted for their successful treatment of the sick. The people seem to have been kindly disposed and different in habits from the coast tribes. (A. C. F.)

**Ananares.**—Harris, Voy. and Trav., I, 803, 1705. **Anavares.**—Linschoten, Desc. de l'Amérique, 6, 1638. **Avaraes.**—Cabeza de Vaca (1534) quoted by Barcia, Ensayo, 13, 1723. **Avares.**—Herrera, Hist. Gen., dec. v, 94, 1725. **Avavares.**—Cabeza de Vaca, Smith trans., 58, 84, 1851. **Chavavares.**—Cabeza de Vaca, Smith trans., 137, 1871.

**Avendaughbough.** A former village, probably of the Sewee, in South Carolina in 1701.—Lawson, Hist. Car., 24, 1860.

**Avnulik.** A Chnagmiut village in the Yukon district, Alaska; pop. 30 in 1890. **Avnuligmiut.**—11th Census, Alaska, 165, 1893.

**Avolabac.** A rancheria, probably Cochimi, connected with Purísima mission, Lower California, about lat. 26° 20′.—Doc. Hist. Mex., 4th s., v, 189, 1857.

**Avoyelles** (probably 'people of the rocks'). A tribe spoken of in the 18th century as one of the nations of the Red r., having their villages near its mouth, within what is now Avoyelles parish, La. They probably belonged to the Natchez group of the Muskhogean family, representing a body that remained near the ancient habitat of its kindred. The country occupied by the Avoyelles was fertile and intersected by lakes and bayous, one of the latter being still called by their name. The tribe lived in villages, cultivated maize and vegetables, and practised the arts common to the tribes of the Gulf region. Nothing definite is known of their beliefs and ceremonies. Like their neighbors, they had come into possession of horses, which they bred, and later they obtained cattle, for Du Pratz mentions that they sold horses, cows, and oxen to the French settlers of Louisiana. During the general displacement of the tribes throughout the Gulf states, which began in the 18th century, the Avoyelles country proved to be attractive. The Biloxi settled there and other tribes entered and took possession. Under the influences incident to the advent of the white race the Avoyelles mingled with the newcomers, but through the ravages of wars and new diseases the tribe was soon reduced in numbers. Before the close of the century their villages and their tribal organization melted away, their language became extinct, and the few survivors were lost in the floating Indian population. In 1805, according to Sibley, the tribe had become reduced to two or three women. (A. C. F.)

**Ajouelles.**—Homann, Indiæ Occidentalis, map, ca. 1740. **Aouayeilles.**—Margry, Déc., VI, 230, 1886. **Avogall.**—Schermerhorn in Mass. Hist. Soc. Coll., 2d s., II, 26, 1812. **Avovelles.**—Jefferys, Am. Atlas, 5, 1776. **Avoyall.**—Brackenridge, Views of La., 83, 1814. **Avoyellas.**—Dumont, La., I, 134, 1753. **Avoyelles.**—Sibley (1805) in Am. State Papers, IV, 725, 1832. **Avoyels.**—Jefferys, French Dom. Am., I, 165, 1761.

**Awaitlala** ('those inside the inlet'). A Kwakiutl tribe on Knight inlet, Brit. Col. Their town is called Kwatsi.

**A'wa-iLala.**—Boas in Rep. Nat. Mus. 1895, 332, 1897. **Aˢwaē'LEla.**—Boas in Mem. Am. Mus. Nat. Hist., v, pt. 1, 122, 1902. **Oughtella.**—Brit. Col. map, Ind. Aff., Victoria, 1872 (given as name of town).

**Awalokaksaksi** ('at the little island'). A Klamath settlement on Williamson r., s. w. Oreg.—Gatschet in Cont. N. A. Ethnol., II, pt. 1, xxix, 1890.

**Awani.** A division of the Miwok living in Yosemite valley, Mariposa co., Cal. Powers states that the name Yosemite is a distorted form of the Miwok *uzumaiti*, 'grizzly bear,' a term never used by the Indians to designate the valley itself or any part of it. Awani, the name applied by the natives of the valley, was the principal village, which by extension was given to the whole valley and its inhabitants, who occupied it when snow permitted. The Awani had 9 villages, containing 450 people, when the whites first came, and they seem to have had a larger number at an earlier period. At present the population is unknown, but small. Their villages were Awani, Hokokwito, Kumaini, Lesamaiti, Macheto, Notomidula, and Wahaka. (H. W. H.)

**Ahwahnachee.**—Hittell, Yosemite, 42, 1868. **Ahwahnechee.**—Ibid., 35. **Awalache.**—Johnston (1851) in Sen. Ex. Doc. 61, 32d Cong., 1st sess., 22, 1852. **Awallache.**—McKee et al. (1851) in Sen. Ex. Doc. 4, 32d Cong., spec. sess., 74, 1853. **Awanee.**—Powers in Overland Monthly, X, 333, 1874. **Oosemite.**—Hittell, Yosemite, 35, 1868. **Oosoomite.**—Ibid., 36.

Sosemiteiz.—Lewis in Ind. Aff. Rep. 1857, 399, 1858. Sosemity.—Ibid., 252, 1856. Ya-seem-ne.— Barbour in Sen. Ex. Doc. 4, 32d Cong., spec. sess., 256, 1853. Yoamity.—Hittell, Yosemite, 42, 1868. Yohamite.—Ibid. Yosahmittis.—Taylor in Cal. Farmer, June 8, 1860. Yo-sem-a-te.—Wessells (1853) in H. R. Ex. Doc. 76, 34th Cong., 1st sess., 30, 1857. Yosemetos.—Barbour (1851) in Sen. Ex. Doc. 4, 32d Cong., spec. sess., 61, 1853. Yo-sem-ety.—Johnston in Schoolcraft, Ind. Tribes, IV, 222, 1854. Yosemites.—Taylor in Cal. Farmer, Dec. 7, 1860. Yosimities.—Ind. Com'rs (1851) in Sen. Ex. Doc. 4, 32d Cong., spec. sess., 88, 1853. Yosoomite.—Hittell, Yosemite, 36, 1868.

**Awash** ('buffalo'). A Tonkawa clan or gens.—Gatschet, MS., B. A. E., 1884.

**Awashlaurk.** A former Chumashan village near Santa Inés mission, Santa Barbara co., Cal.
A-wac-la'-ŭrk.—Henshaw, Santa Inez MS. vocab., B. A. E., 1884.

**Awashonks.** The woman chief of Seconet, R. I., whose fame obscured that of Tolony, her husband (Drake, Inds. of N. Am., 249, 1880). Her name is signed to the Plymouth agreement of 1671. She was drawn into King Philip's war in support of that chief, but afterward made her peace with the English. One of her sons is said to have studied Latin in preparation for college, but succumbed to the palsy. (A. F. C.)

**Awata.** The Bow clan of the Hopi.
Aoát.—Voth, Oraibi Summer Snake Ceremony, 283, 1903. A-wa'-ta.—Fewkes in Am. Anthrop., VII, 367, 1894. Awata wiñwû.—Fewkes in 19th Rep. B. A.E., 584, 1900 (wiñwû = 'clan'). A-wata wun-wu.—Fewkes in Am. Anthrop., VII, 404, 1894.

**Awatobi** ('high place of the bow,' referring to the Bow people). A former pueblo of the Hopi on a mesa about 9 m. S. E. of Walpi, N. E. Ariz. It was one of the original villages of the province of Tusayan of the early Spaniards, being visited by Tobar and Cardenas of Coronado's expedition in 1540, by Espejo in 1583, and by Oñate in 1598. It became the seat of the Franciscan mission of San Bernardino in 1629, under Father Porras, who was poisoned by the Hopi in 1633; but the endeavor to Christianize the Hopi at this and other pueblos was continued until 1680, when, in the Pueblo rebellion, which began in August, the Awatobi missionary, Father Figueroa, was murdered. At this time the Awatobi people numbered 800. Henceforward no Spanish priests were established among the Hopi, although in 1700 Father Garaycoechea visited Awatobi, where he baptized 73 natives, but was unsuccessful in his attempt to reestablish missions among them. In November of the same year, owing to the friendly feeling which the Awatobi are said to have had for the Spanish friars, their kindred, especially of Walpi and Mashongnovi, joined in an attack on Awatobi at night, setting fire to the pueblo, killing many of its inhabitants, including all the men, and carrying off women and children to the other pueblos, chiefly to Mashongnovi, Walpi, and Oraibi. Awatobi was never again inhabited. The walls of the old Spanish church are still partly standing. See Mindeleff in 8th Rep. B. A. E., 1891; Fewkes in Am. Anthrop., Oct., 1893; Fewkes in 17th Rep. B. A. E., 592 et seq., 1898. (F. W. H.)

RUINS OF AWATOBI AND ITS MISSION. (V. MINDELEFF)

Aguato.—Espejo (1583) in Doc. Inéd., XV, 120, 182, 1871. Aguatobi.—Doc. of 1584 cited by Bandelier in Arch. Inst. Papers, I, 15, 1881; Vetancurt (1693), Menolog. Fran., 275, 1871. Aguatubi.—Ayeta (1680) quoted by Bandelier in Arch. Inst. Papers, IV, 369, 1892. Aguatuby.—Jefferys, Am. Atlas, map 5, 1776. Aguatuví.—Buschmann, Neu-Mexico, 231, 1858. Aguatuya.—Bandelier in Jour. Am. Eth. and Arch., III, 85, 1892 (misquoting Oñate following). Aguatuybá.—Oñate (1598) in Doc. Inéd., XVI, 137, 1871 (erroneously given as name of chief). Aguitobi.—Bandelier in Arch. Inst. Papers, III, 115, 1890. Ahuato.—Hakluyt (1600), Voy., 470, 1810. Ahuatu.—Bandelier in Arch. Inst. Papers, III, 115, 135, 1890. Ahuatuyba.—Ibid., 109, and IV, 368, 1892. Ahuzto.—Hakluyt (1600), Voy., repr. 1891. Ahwat-tenna.—Bourke, Moquis of Ariz., 195, 1884. Aoátovi.—Voth, Traditions of the Hopi, 47, 1905. Aquatasi.—Walch, Charte America, 1805. Aquatubi.—Davis, Span. Conq. N. Mex., 368, 1869. Atabi-hogandi.—Bourke, Moquis of Ariz., 84, 1884 (Navaho name). Aua-tu-ui.—Bandelier in Arch. Inst. Papers, IV, 368, 1892. A-wa-te-u.—Cushing in Atl. Monthly, 367, Sept., 1882. A-wā'-to-bi.—Fewkes in Am. Anthrop., V, 10, 1892. Awatúbi.—

Bourke, op. cit., 91. **Á wat u i.**—Cushing in 4th Rep. B. A. E., 493, 1886. **Á wat u ians.**—Ibid., 494. **San Bernahdino de Ahuatobi.**—Bandelier in Arch. Inst. Papers, IV, 369, 1892 (misprint). **San Bernardino.**—Fewkes in Am. Anthrop., VI, 394, 1894. **San Bernardino de Aguatuvi.**—Bancroft, Ariz. and N. Mex., 349, 1889. **San Bernardino de Ahuatobi.**—Vetancurt (1693), Teatro Mex., III, 321, 1871. **S. Bernardo de Aguatuvi.**—Vargas (1692) quoted by Bancroft, Ariz. and N. Mex., 201, 1889. **Talla-Hogan.**—Mindeleff, quoted by Powell, 4th Rep. B. A. E., xxxix, 1886 ('singing house': Navaho name). **Talla-hogandi.**—Bandelier in Arch. Inst. Papers, IV, 368, 1892. **Tally-hogan.**—Powell, 3d Rep. B. A. E., xxi, 1884. **Tolli-Hogandi.**—Bourke, Moquis of Ariz., 84, 1884. **Zagnato.**—Brackenridge, Early Span. Discov., 19, 1857. **Zaguate.**—Prince, N. Mex., 34, 1883. **Zaguato.**—Espejo (1583) in Hakluyt, Voy., 463, 470, 1810. **Zuguato.**—Hinton, Handbook to Ariz., 388, 1878.

**Awausee** (*awasisi*, 'bullhead,' a fish). A Chippewa phratry or gens. According to Warren a phratry including all the fish gentes of the Chippewa. According to Morgan and Tomazin it is a gens in itself. Cf. *Ouasouarini.*
**Ah-wah-sis'-sa.**—Morgan, Anc. Soc., 166, 1877. **Ah-wa-sis-se.**—Tanner, Narr., 315, 1830 ('small catfish'; given by Tanner as a gens; he adds: "sometimes they call the people of this totem 'those who carry their young,' from the habits of the small catfish"). **Awassissin.**—Gatschet, Ojibwa MS., B. A. E., 1882. **A-waus-e.**—Warren in Minn. Hist. Soc. Coll., v, 44, 1885. **A-waus-e-wug.**—Ibid., 87. **A-waus-is-ee.**—Ramsey in Ind. Aff. Rep., 91, 1850.

**Awenanish.** See *Ouananiche.*

**Awhawhilashmu.** A former Chumashan village on the coast between Pt Conception and Santa Barbara, Cal., in the locality now called Punta Capitan.
**A-wha-whi-lac'-mu.**—Henshaw, Buenaventura MS. vocab., B. A. E., 1884.

**Awhut.** A Diegueño rancheria in N. Lower Cal. whose inhabitants spoke the Hataam dialect.—Gatschet, Yuma Spr., 107, 1886.

**Awighsaghroone.** A tribe, probably Algonquian, that lived about the upper great lakes and which sent a friendly message to the Seneca in 1715. Perhaps identical with the Assisagigroone, or Missisauga.
**Awighsaghroene.**—Livingston (1715) in N. Y. Doc. Col. Hist., v, 446, 1855. **Awighsaghroone.**—Ibid.

**Awigna.** A former Gabrieleño rancheria in Los Angeles co., Cal., at a place later called La Puenta.
**Awigna.**—Ried (1852) quoted by Taylor in Cal. Farmer, June 8, 1860. **Awiz-na.**—Ried quoted by Hoffman in Bull. Essex Inst., XVII, 2, 1885.

**Awls.** The aboriginal American awl is a sharpened stick, bone, stone, or piece of metal, used as a perforator in sewing. It was universal among Indians from the earliest times, and is one of the familiar archeologic objects recovered from excavations in prehistoric sites. For temporary use awls were improvised from splinters of flint, wood, and bone, cactus spines, agave needles, thorns, etc. Before the introduction of iron, bone was the most serviceable material. Rude awls, formed by grinding to a point a long-bone or sliver of bone, are frequently encountered in graves and on the sites of

early habitations, and with them may be found others that are elaborately finished and decorated with carving and etching. Perhaps most Indians preferred deer bone as a material for awls, but bear and turkey bones and antler were also extensively employed, those of turkey bone being especially common in New Mexico. The fibula of the deer merely needed sharpening to produce the tool, while the articular extremity formed a convenient and ornamental handle. Ivory from the walrus, narwhal, and fossil elephant was valued for making awls in regions where it could be procured. Awls of chipped or ground stone, shell, hard wood, and copper have been found on ancient sites. Awls of bone or of wood were not usually hafted, but stone and copper awls were often mounted and perhaps served also for drills (q. v.). The modern awl of iron is always hafted with wood, bone, dried tendon or gristle, or horn, and the hafts are often carved, painted, or otherwise decorated.

The awl was used to make perforations through which thread of sinew or other sewing material was passed when skins for moccasins, clothing, tents, etc., were sewed, and in quillwork, beadwork, and basketwork. Other uses for awls were for making holes for pegs in woodwork, as a gauge in canoe-making, for shredding sinew, for graving, etc. Various awl-like implements that were used by the Indians in weaving and making pottery, as pins for robes, as head-scratchers, pipe-picks, blood pins for closing wounds in game to save the blood, marrow-extractors, forks, corn-huskers, etc., have sometimes been classed as awls. The Alaskan Eskimo have an awl with a small barb near the end which was used like a crochet hook.

The awl was so indispensable in everyday work that it was usually carried on the person, and many kinds of sheaths and cases were made for holding it. These were formed from joints of cane or hollow bones, or wrought out of bone, wood, metal, or leather, and were ornamented by etching, carving, or painting, or with beadwork, quillwork, or other decorative devices. See *Drills and Drilling, Needles.*

Consult Stephen, The Navajo Shoemaker, Proc. Nat. Mus., XI, 131, 1888; papers in Reps. B. A. E. by Nelson, Murdoch, Boas, Turner, Hoffman, and Fewkes; and Mason, Basketry, Rep. Nat. Mus., 1902. (w. h.)

**Awluhl** (*á'lú'hl*). A clan of Taos pueblo, New Mexico. The meaning of the name is indefinite, but it is said to bear some reference to transformation from human beings into animals.—Hodge, field notes, B. A. E., 1899.

**Axacan.** A place in Virginia, somewhere w. from Chesapeake bay, at 37° or 37° 30′, in which the Spaniards attempted to establish a Jesuit mission in 1570. Through the treachery of their Indian guide, brother of the chief of the tribe, the entire party of missionaries, 7 in number, was massacred and the temporary mission building destroyed. Two years later Menendez revenged their death by hanging 8 of the principal murderers. (J. M.)

Aixacan.—Shipp, De Soto and Fla., 560, 1881. Axacan.—Barcia, Ensayo, 142, 1723.

**Axauti.** A pueblo of New Mexico in 1598; doubtless situated in the Salinas, in the vicinity of Abo, and evidently occupied by the Tigua or the Piros.—Oñate (1598) in Doc. Inéd., XVI, 114, 1871.

Axanti.—Columbus Memorial Vol., 155, 1893 (misprint).

**Axes.** The grooved ax takes a prominent place among the stone implements used by the northern tribes. The normal form is that of a thick wedge, with rounded angles and an encircling groove near the top for securing the handle; but there is great variation from the average. Usually the implement is made of some hard, tough stone, as trap, granite, syenite, greenstone, or hematite, where such can be procured; but when these are not available softer material is utilized, as sandstone or slate. Copper axes are of rare occurrence. Among the stone specimens there is a very wide range in size, the largest weighing upward of 30 pounds

AX WITH SIMPLE GROOVE; DISTRICT OF COLUMBIA (LENGTH, 7 IN.)

and the smallest scarcely an ounce. As these extreme sizes could serve no economic purpose, they were probably for ceremonial use; the smaller may have been amulets or talismans. The majority range from 1 pound to 6 pounds, which mark close to the limits of utility. As a rule the groove is at a right angle to the longer axis, though sometimes it is oblique, and it may extend entirely or only partially around the ax. In the latter case it is always one of the narrow sides that is left without a groove, and this is frequently flattened or hollowed to accommodate the handle better. Ordinarily the complete or entire groove is pecked in a ridge encircling the ax, leaving a protuberance above and below, while the partial groove is sunken in the body of the implement. Axes with two or more grooves are rare excepting in the Pueblo country, where multiple grooves are common. The haft was placed parallel with the blade and

was usually a withe doubled around the groove and fastened securely with cords or rawhide, but heavier T-shape sticks were sometimes used, the top of the T being set against the flattened or hollow side of the implement and firmly lashed. Axes with holes drilled for the insertion of a handle are common in Europe, but this method of hafting was of very rare occurrence among the American aborigines. When not made from bowlders closely approximating in shape the desired implement,

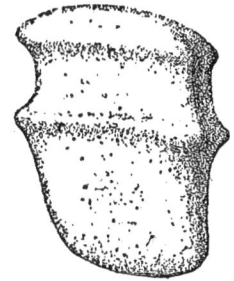

AX WITH DIAGONAL GROOVE AND LATERAL RIDGES; TENNESSEE

the ax was roughed out by chipping and was reduced to the desired shape by pecking with a hard stone and by grinding. Axes of rude shape, made by flaking a flattish bowlder along one end and breaking notches in the sides for hafting, are found in some sections. Axes are well distributed over the country wherever good material is readily available, excepting in the Pacific states, British Columbia, and Alaska, where specimens are exceedingly rare. Few are found in Florida, and although plentiful in the mound region are seldom found in mounds. The shapes vary with the different regions, examples from the Atlantic slope, for example, being quite unlike those of the Pueblo country.

It is probable that the ax served various purposes in the arts, and especially in war and in the chase. Numerous badly fractured specimens are found in the soapstone quarries of E. United States, where they were used for cutting out masses of this rock. The grooved ax is said to have been used in felling trees and in cutting them up, but it is manifestly not well suited for such work; it would serve, however, to assist in cutting wood in conjunction with charring. The hafted stone ax passed immediately out of use on the introduction by Europeans of the iron ax, which was the first and most obviously useful tool that the Indians saw in the hands of the white man.

See Abbott, Prim. Indust., 1881; Fowke (1) in 13th Rep. B. A. E., 1896, (2) Arch. Hist. Ohio, 1902; Holmes in 15th Rep. B. A. E., 1897; Jones, Antiq. So. Inds., 1873; Jones in Smithson. Cont., XXII, 1876; Moorehead, Prehist. Impls., 1900; Putnam in Surv. W. 100th Merid., VII, 1879; Squier and Davis in Smithson. Cont., I, 1848; Stevenson in 2d Rep. B. A. E., 1883; Thruston, Antiq. Tenn., 1897; Wilson in Smithson. Reps. 1887 and 1888. (G. F. W. H. H.)

**Axille.** A former fortified village of 50 houses in N. w. Florida., visited by De Soto in 1539. It was on a river, doubtless the one which still retains the name Ocilla. The same root may appear in the name of the province, Uzachil. It was on the frontier of the territory of the Apalachee tribe.

Asila.—French, Hist. Coll. La., 2d s., 255, 1875. Axille.—Gentl. of Elvas (1557) in French, Hist. Coll. La., II, 134, 1850. Ochile.—Garcilasso de la Vega, Florida, 51, 1723.

**Axion** ('the muddy place,' from *assiscu* 'mud'). A division of the New Jersey Delawares, formerly living on the E. bank of Delaware r., between Rancocas cr. and the present Trenton. In 1648 they were one of the largest tribes on the river, being estimated at 200 warriors. Brinton thinks the name may be a corruption of Assiscunk, the name of a creek above Burlington. See Evelin (1648) in Proud, Pa., I, 113, 1797.

**Axol.** A Tewa pueblo in New Mexico in 1598.—Oñate (1598) in Doc. Inéd., XVI, 116, 1871.

Axoytre.—Oñate, ibid., 102 (probably the same).

**Ayabaskawininiwug.** A division of the Cree (q. v.), commonly known as Wood Cree.

**Ayahanisino.** A clan of the Apohola phratry of the Timucua.—Pareja (*ca.* 1612) quoted by Gatschet in Am. Philos. Soc. Proc., XVII, 492, 1878.

**Ayak.** A Kaviagmiut Eskimo village on Sledge id., Alaska.

Ahyak.—11th Census, Alaska, 162, 1893.

**Ayanabi** ('ironwood'). A former Choctaw village on Yannubbee cr., 2 m. above its confluence with Petickfa, about 8 m. s. w. of Dekalb, Kemper co., Miss. According to tradition it was the scene of a conflict between the Creeks and the Choctaw in the 18th century, and being a neutral town was selected as the place for negotiating peace. In 1811 the town was visited by Ellskwatawa, the Shawnee Prophet, in the interest of Tecumtha, and 2 years later a band of about 30 of its warriors joined the Creeks in the British cause.

Aianabe.—Alcedo, Dic. Geog., I, 36, 1786. Ayanabe.—D'Anville, map (1732), in Miss. Hist. Soc. Pub., III, 367, 1900. Ayanabi.—West Fla. map, *ca.* 1772. Iyanabi.—Halbert in Miss. Hist. Soc. Pub., op. cit., 368 (given as proper Choctaw form). Yanabi.—Ibid. (alternative form). Yannubbee Town.—Halbert in Ala. Hist. Soc. Pub., 77, 1899. Yanubbee.—Ibid.

**Ayanamon.** A village formerly situated, according to old maps, on a lake about the sources of Tuscarawas r., Ohio.

Ayanamon.—Lattré, map, 1784. Ayououtou.—Esnauts and Rapilly, map, 1777.

**Ayanemo.** See *Ninigret*.

**Ayavalla.** An important Apalachee (or Timacua?) town and mission about 1700. It was destroyed by the English and their Indian allies under Gov. Moore in 1704, or, according to Shea, in the later invasion of 1706. Fairbanks locates it "near the St Mark's r.," w. Fla., while Shea incorrectly makes it a town of the Atimucas (Timucua) on Apalachicola r. (J. M.)

Ayavala.—Jefferys, French Dom. Am., map, 135, 1761. Ayavalla.—Shea, Cath. Miss., 74, 1855. Ayaville.—Carroll, Hist. Coll. S. C., II, 574, 1836.

**Aycate.** A former Maricopa rancheria on the Rio Gila, s. w. Ariz.—Sedelmair (1744) quoted by Bancroft, Ariz. and N. Mex., 366, 1889.

**Aychini.** An unidentified pueblo in New Mexico in 1598.—Oñate (1598) in Doc. Inéd., XVI, 103, 1871.

**Aymay.** A village in E. Georgia, visited by De Soto in 1540 and called by the Spaniards Socorro, 'Relief.'—Gentl. of Elvas (1557), Hakluyt trans., 54, 1851.

**Ayotl.** A Yurok village 1 m. above the mouth of Blue cr., on Klamath r., N. Cal.

Oiyotl.—Gibbs in Schoolcraft, Ind. Tribes, III, 138, 1853.

**Ayqui.** A pueblo of the province of Atripuy, in the region of the lower Rio Grande, N. Mex., in 1598 (Oñate, 1598, in Doc. Inéd., XVI, 115, 1871). Probably the same as the pueblo at Ayquiyn, attributed by the same authority (p. 102) to the "Trios."

Ayquiyu.—Bancroft, Ariz. and N. Mex., 136, 1889 (misprint).

**Azavay.** A former Timuquanan village on St Johns r., Fla., 50 or 60 leagues upstream.—Fontaneda (*ca.* 1570) in Ternaux-Compans, Voy., XX, 35, 1841.

**Azcapotzalco** (Nahuatl name). Probably an ancient settlement of the Tepecano or of a related tribe, but occupied since the early part of the 18th century by Tlaxcaltecs originally introduced by the Spaniards for defense against the Chichimecs; situated about 10 m. E. of Bolaños, in Jalisco, Mexico.—Hrdlicka in Am. Anthrop., V, 425, 1903.

**Aziagmiut.** The inhabitants of Sledge or Aziak id., Alaska, a subdivision of the Kaviagmiut, numbering 67 in 1890.—11th Census, Alaska, 154, 1893.

Aziagmut.—Zagoskin, Descr. Russ. Poss. Am., pt. I, 73, 1847.

**Aziak.** The village of the Aziagmiut on Sledge id., near C. Nome, Alaska; pop. 50 in 1880.—Petroff, 10th Census, Alaska, 11, 1884.

**Aziavik.** A town of the Chingigmiut Eskimo near C. Peirce, Alaska; pop. 90 in 1890.

Aziavigamut.—Nelson in 18th Rep. B. A. E., map, 1899. Aziavigamute.—Petroff, 10th Census, Alaska, VIII, map, 1884. Aziavigiokhamiut.—Schanz in 11th Census, Alaska, 93, 1893.

**Azqueltan** (Nahuatl: 'where there are small ants,' referring to the former numerous population). The most important Tepecano settlement, consisting of about 40 dwellings, situated on the Rio de Bolaños, about lat. 22° 12′, long. 104°, Jalisco, Mexico. In 1902 a Mexican trader was permitted to settle among them for the first time.

**Alquestan.**—Lumholtz, Unknown Mex., II, 16, map, 123, 1902 (popular name, properly pronounced Asqueltan). **Askeltan.**—Hrdlicka in Am. Anthrop., V, 387, 1903. **Kī-dagh-ra.**—Ibid., 420 (Tepecano name). **San Lorenzo.**—Ibid., 410 (early Spanish name). **Totonaltám.**—Lumholtz, op. cit. (Tepecano name: same meaning).

**Azucsagna.** A former Gabrieleño rancheria in Los Angeles co., Cal., at the locality now called Azusa.—Hoffman in Bull. Essex Inst., XVII, 2, 1885.

**Asucsagna.**—Ried (1852) quoted by Taylor in Cal. Farmer, June 8, 1860. **Azucsagna.**—Ried quoted by Hoffman in Bull. Essex Inst., XVII, 2, 1885.

**Baada.** A former Makah village on Neah bay, Wash. According to Swan it was abandoned in 1863, its inhabitants moving to Neah.

**Bäada.**—Swan in Smithson. Cont., XVI, 2, 1870. **Behda.**—Gibbs, MS. no. 248, B. A. E.

**Babacomero.** A former rancheria, probably of the Papago, on the w. branch of Rio San Pedro, between Tombstone and Camp Huachuca, s. Ariz.—Box, Adventures, 322, 1869.

**Babasaqui.** A ruined village, probably of the Papago, 3 m. above Imuris, between Cocospera and Magdalena, Sonora, Mexico.

**Babasaqui.**—Kino (1706) quoted by Bancroft, No. Mex. States, I, 501, 1884. **Babesagui.**—Box, Adventures, 278, 1869.

**Babbyduclone.** See *Nakaidoklini.*

**Babesakundiba, Babesigaundibay.** See *Curly Head.*

**Babiacora.** A pueblo of the Teguima Opata and the seat of a Spanish mission established in 1639; situated on the Rio Sonora, Sonora, Mexico, 110 m. s. of the Arizona boundary; pop. 445 in 1678, 294 in 1730.

**Babiacora.**—Kino, map (1702), in Stöcklein, Neue Welt-Bott, 74, 1726. **Babicori.**—Orozco y Berra, Geog., 343, 1864. **Batacora.**—Escudero, Noticias Sonora y Sinaloa, 101, 1849 (probably the same). **Batacosa.**—Cancio (1767) in Doc. Hist. Mex., 4th s., II, 224, 1856 (probably the same). **Baviácora.**—Davila, Sonora Hist., 317, 1894. **Concepcion Babiacora.**—Zapata (1678) quoted by Bancroft, No. Mex. States, I, 246, 1884. **Concepcion Babicora.**—Rivera (1730), ibid., 514. **Purísima de Babicora.**—Orozco y Berra, Geog., 343, 1864.

**Babiche.** A thong of skin, particularly of eel skin. The word is derived through Canadian French, in which the term is old, occurring in Hennepin (1688), from one of the eastern dialects of Algonquian. The original source is probably the old Micmac *ababich*, 'cord,' 'thread' (Lescarbot, Hist. Nouv. France, 666, 1612). A cognate word is the Chippewa *assababish*, 'thread.' For the manufacture and use of babiche, see *Rawhide.* (A. F. C.)

**Babine** ('big lips'). A branch of the Takulli comprising, according to Morice (Trans. Can. Inst., 27, 1893), the Nataotin, the Babine proper, and the Hwotsotenne tribes living about Babine lake, British Columbia, with a total population of 610 in 7 villages. The name was given to them by French Canadians from the custom of wearing labrets, copied from the Chimmesyan; and indeed their entire culture was greatly affected by that of the coast tribes.

**Babisi.** A former rancheria, probably of the Sobaipuri, at the s. boundary of Arizona, near Suamca, of which it was a visita.

**Sta Cruz Babisi.**—Bancroft, Ariz. and N. Mex., 371, 1889.

**Babispe** (from *babipa*, 'the point where the river takes a new course.'—Hardy). An Opata pueblo and the seat of a Spanish mission founded in 1645; situated on an E. branch of Rio de Babispe, in N. E. Sonora, Mexico, near the Chihuahua boundary. Pop. 402 in 1678, 566 in 1730. The town was destroyed by an earthquake in May, 1887. (F. W. H.)

**Babispe.**—Orozco y Berra, Geog., 343, 1864. **Bapispes.**—Ribas (1645) quoted in Arch. Inst. Papers, III, 58, 1890 (referring to the inhabitants). **S. Miguel Babispe.**—Zapata (1678) quoted by Bancroft, No. Mex. States, I, 246, 1884. **S. Miguel de Vavispe.**—Rivera, Diario, leg. 1,444, 1736.

**Baborigame.** A former Tepehuane pueblo, situated in a plain 1½ m. in diameter, in lat. 26° 40′, long. 107°, s. w. Chihuahua, Mexico. The settlement is now Mexicanized, but it is surrounded by Tepehuane rancherias.

**Baborigame.**—Orozco y Berra, Geog., 324, 1864. **Baborigami.**—Lumholtz in Scribner's Mag., XVI, 303, Sept., 1894. **Vāwúlile.**—Lumholtz, Unknown Mex., I, 420, 1902 ('where there is a large fig tree': native name).

**Babuyagui.** A pueblo founded in 1670 by Father Álvaro Flores de la Sierra with some converted Varohio of Yecarome; situated on or near the headwaters of the upper Rio Fuerte, in N. Sinaloa, Mexico. It was given a resident priest in 1673, but on the death of Sierra in that year it soon became a mere visita of the mission of Taro (Tara), whence many of the converts removed 3 years later.—Bancroft, No. Mex. States, 247, 1886.

**Baca** (abbr. of *bacapa*, 'reed grass.'—Buelna). A Mayo settlement near the E. bank of Rio del Fuerte, about lat. 26° 50′, in the northernmost corner of Sinaloa, Mexico.

**Báca.**—Hardy (1829) quoted by Bancroft, Nat. Races, I, 608, 1882. **Bacabachi.**—Hrdlicka in Am. Anthrop., VI, 59, 1904 (probably the same). **Vaca.**—Orozco y Berra, Geog., 332, 1864.

**Bacaburiachic.** A Tarahumare settlement of Chihuahua, Mexico; definite locality unknown.—Orozco y Berra, Geog., 323, 1864.

**Bacadeguachi.** A Coguinachi Opata pueblo and the seat of a Spanish mission founded in 1645; situated on the Rio de Batepito, or Babispe, in E. Sonora, Mexico; pop. 370 in 1678, 272 in 1730. In 1884, when visited by Bandelier, it contained about 500 Mexicans and Mexicanized Indians, but the town was much neglected and dilapidated on account of Apache depredations.

**Bacadeguachi.**—Rivera, Diario, leg. 1,444, 1736. **Bacadeguatzi.**—Ribas (1764) quoted by Bandelier in Arch. Inst. Papers, IV, 508, 1892. **Baca de Huachi.**—Hamilton, Mexican Handbook, 47, 1883.

**Bacatu de Guachi.**—Mange (*ca.* 1700) quoted by Bancroft, No. Mex. States, I, 233, 1884. **San Luis Bacadeguachi.**—Rivera (1730), ibid., 514. **San Luis Gonzaga de Bacadeguatzi.**—Doc. of 1764 quoted by Bandelier in Arch. Inst. Papers, III, 56, 1890. **S. Luis Gonzaga Bacadeguachi.**—Zapata (1678), ibid., 246.

**Bacanora.** A pueblo of the Eudeve division of the Opata and the seat of a Spanish mission founded in 1627; situated in E. Sonora, Mexico, on Rio Batepito, lat. 29° 10′, long. 109°. Pop. 253 in 1678, 116 in 1730.
**Bacanora.**—Rivera (1730) quoted by Bancroft, No. Mex. States, I, 513, 1884. **Basacora.**—Allegre quoted by Bancroft, ibid., 523 (probably the same). **S. Ignacio Bacanora.**—Zapata (1678), ibid., 245.

**Bacanuchi.** A rancheria, apparently of the Opata, on the E. bank of the Rio Sonora, Sonora, Mexico, in lat. 30° 40′. It was visited by Father Kino in Oct., 1706, and was the seat of a mission with 266 inhabitants in 1777 (Doc. Hist. Mex., 4th s., I, app., 1856). Distinct from Bacuachi.
**Bacanuchi.**—Kino, map (1702) in Stöcklein, Neue Welt-Bott, 74, 1726. **Real de Bacanuchi.**—Kino quoted by Bancroft, No. Mex. States, I, 501, 1884.

**Bacapa** (said by Buelna to signify 'reed grass' (*carrizo*), but the term *bac*, or *vac*, in Pima signifies 'house,' 'ruined house'). A Papago rancheria in N. w. Sonora, Mexico, located slightly s. E. of Carrizal on the map of Father Kino (1701), by whom it was visited in 1700, and by Anza and Font in 1776. Not to be confounded with Matape in any of its various forms, but identical with the later Quitobac in lat. 31° 40′, long. 112° 45′. (F. W. H.)
**Quitobac.**—Font, map (1777) in Bancroft, Ariz. and N. M., 393, 1889. **San Louis de Bacapa.**—Venegas, Hist. Cal., II, 176, 1759. **San Luis Bacupa.**—Bancroft, op. cit., 359. **San Luis Beltran de Bacapa.**—Bandelier in Arch. Inst. Papers, V, 123, 1890. **S. Ludlov de Bacapa.**—Kino, map (1702) in Stöcklein, Neue Welt-Bott, 74, 1726. **S. Luis Bacapa.**—Kino, map (1701) in Bancroft, op. cit., 360.—**S. Luis de Bacapa.**—Venegas, Hist. Cal., I, map, 1759. **S. Luis Quitobac.**—Anza and Font (1774) quoted by Bancroft, op. cit., 393. **St. Ludlovic de Vacapa.**—Bandelier, op. cit., 122.

**Bachipkwasi** (a species of lizard). A clan of the Lizard (Earth or Sand) phratry of the Hopi.
**Ba-tci′p-kwa-si.**—Stephen in 8th Rep. B. A. E., 39, 1891.

**Backhook.** One of the small tribes formerly living on lower Pedee r. and its branches in South Carolina. Almost nothing is known of it. With the Hook tribe they are mentioned by Lawson as foes of the Santee and as living in 1701 about the mouth of Winyah bay, S. C. (J. M.)
**Backhook.**—Lawson (1714), Hist. Car., 45, 1860. **Back Hook.**—Rivers, Hist. S. C., 35, 1856. **Black Hook.**—Ibid., 36.

**Bacoburito.** A rancheria, apparently occupied by one of the Cahita tribes of the Piman family, situated on the Rio Petatlan, or Rio Sinaloa, in lat. 26°, N. w. Sinaloa, Mexico. Christianized early in 17th century, the natives rebelled about 1604 and burned their church, but the up-

rising was soon quelled by Gov. Hurtaide who put the leading rebels to death and compelled the others to rebuild the edifice.—Bancroft, No. Mex. States, I, 213, 1886.

**Bacuachi.** A former pueblo of the Teguima Opata and the seat of a Spanish mission founded in 1650; situated on the headwaters of the Rio Sonora, in Sonora, Mexico, below latitude 31°. It still existed as a mission in 1777 (Doc. Hist. Mex., 4th s., I, app., 1856). Pop. 195 in 1678, and 51 in 1730, but Bartlett (Personal Narr., I, 278, 1854) found it almost depopulated in 1851.
**Bacatzi.**—Bandelier in Arch. Inst. Papers, IV, 530, 1892 (misprint). **Bacoachi.**—Orozco y Berra, Geog., 343, 1864. **Bacoaiz.**—Ibid. **Bacoatzi.**—Rudo Ensayo (1763), 160, 1863. **Bacouiz.**—Rivera (1730) quoted by Bancroft, No. Mex. States, 514, 1884. **Bacuachi.**—Kino, map (1702) in Stöcklein, Neue Welt-Bott, 74, 1726. **Biquache.**—Hrdlicka in Am. Anthrop., VI, 72, 1904. **S. Miguel Bacuachi.**—Zapata (1678) quoted by Bancroft, op. cit., 246.

**Bacuancos.** A Pima rancheria visited by Father Kino about 1697; situated 7 leagues s. of the mission of Guevavi in Pimeria Alta, N. w. Sonora, Mexico. Probably the later Buenavista. See *Quiquiborica*.
**Bacuancos.**—Bernal (1697) quoted by Bancroft, Ariz. and N. M., 356, 1889. **Bacuanos.**—Mange, ibid., 356. **S. Antonio(?).**—Ibid. **S. Luis Bacuancos.**—Ibid., 358.

**Bacum.** A Yaqui settlement on the s. bank of the lower Rio Yaqui, s. w. Sonora, Mexico, with an estimated population of 4,000 in 1849.
**Bacum.**—Velasco, Noticias de Sonora, 84, 1850. **Bahium.**—Orozco y Berra, Geog., 355, 1864. **Santa Cruz Bacum.**—Ibid.

**Bacuvia.** Mentioned as an early settlement apparently within the province of Apalachee, Fla.
**Bacutia.**—Barcia, Ensayo, 339, 1723. **Bacuvia.**—Ibid., 336.

**Bad Arms.** A Brulé band.—Culbertson in Smithson. Rep. 1850, 141, 1851.

**Badeuachi.** A former Opata village, now in ruins, a short distance w. of Rio Sonora, about lat. 30°, near Huepaca and Aconchi, N. central Sonora, Mexico.—Bandelier in Arch. Inst. Papers, III, 71, 1890.

**Badwisha.** A Mariposan tribe on Kaweah r., Cal., said to have lived near the Wikchamni. Mentioned by Hoffman in 1886 as formerly on Kaweah r., but then at Tule agency.
**Bâdwis′ha.**—Hoffman in Proc. Am. Philos. Soc., XXIII, 301, 1886. **Balwisha.**—Kroeber, inf'n, 1905. **Pal-wish-a.**—Barbour (1852) in Sen. Ex. Doc. 4, 32d Cong., spec. sess., 255, 1853. **Pat-wish-a.**—Johnston (1851) in Sen. Ex. Doc. 61, 32d Cong., 1st sess., 23, 1852. **Pol-we-sha.**—Wessells (1853) in H. R. Ex. Doc. 76, 34th Cong., 3d sess., 32, 1857.

**Bagaduce.** The name of the peninsula in Hancock co., Me., on which Castine is situated. Purchas mentions Chebegnadose (*n* should probably be *u*) as a town in 1602–1609 on Penobscot r. in Abnaki territory, with 30 houses and 90 men, which may be connected with the more modern name. It is also, according to Willis (Coll. Me. Hist. Soc., IV, 103, 1856), under the form Abagadusset (from a sachem of that name), the name of a tributary of the Kennebec. It is introduced here for the reason that Sullivan (Hist. Me., 95, 1795) applies the name, under the plural form Abagadusets, to a body of Indians which, in 1649, resided in this immediate section. Vetromile, however, says: "We are sure there was no Indian village at Castine, called at present Bagaduce, a corruption for *matchibignadusek*, 'water bad to drink.'" Ballard (Rep. U. S. Coast Surv., 1868, 248) gives as the full form *matche-be-gua-toos*, 'bad bay,' referring to a part of Castine harbor, and this is the meaning commonly given. Rasles gives *bagadassek* as meaning 'to shine.' Dr William Jones suggests that the Chippewa *pagŭdā-sink*, 'windward side,' may be a related term.

**Abagadusets.**—Sullivan, Hist. Maine, 95, 1795. **Chebegnadose.**—Purchas (1625) quoted in Maine Hist. Soc. Coll., V, 156, 1857.

**Bagiopa.** A tribe of whom Fray Francisco Garcés (Diary, 1900) heard in 1776, at which time they lived N. of the Rio Colorado, where they are located on Font's map of 1777. The fact that Padre Eusebio Kino, while near the mouth of the Rio Colorado in 1701, heard of them from other Indians and placed them on the gulf coast of Lower California on his map of that date, has created the impression that the Bagiopa were one of the Lower Colorado Yuman tribes; but because they were never actually seen in this locality by the Jesuit and Franciscan missionaries of the period, they are regarded as probably having belonged to the Shoshonean family. The name is apparently of Piman origin (*opa*, 'people'). (F. W. H.)

**Acquiora.**—Garcés (1775-6), Diary, 489, 1900 (apparently a misprint of Baquiova). **Bagiopas.**—Venegas, Hist. Cal., I, map, 1759. **Bagopas.**—Güssefeld, map, 1797. **Bajiopas.**—Venegas, Hist. Cal., II, 171, 1759. **Baquioba.**—Garcés (1776), Diary, 405-6, 1900. **Baquiova.**—Ibid., 444. **Raguapuis.**—Mayer, Mexico, II, 38, 1853 (possibly intended for Baguiopas).

**Bagoache.** Given by La Chesnaye in 1697 (Margry, Déc., VI, 6, 1886) as the name of a country about the N. shore of L. Superior, with a people of the same name numbering from 200 to 300 men.

**Bags and Pouches.** Many varieties of bags and pouches were made by the Indians of the United States and were used for a great number of purposes. The costume of the aborigines was universally destitute of pockets, and various pouches served in their stead. On occasion articles were tucked away in the clothing or were tied up in bits of cloth or skin. The blanket also served at times for a bag, and among the Eskimo the woman's coat was enlarged over the shoulders and at the back to form a pouch for carrying the baby. The pouch was a receptacle of flexible material for containing various objects and substances of personal use or ceremony, and was generally an adjunct of costume. The bag, larger and simpler, was used for the gathering, transportation, and storage of game and other food. The material was tawed leather of various kinds, tanned leather, rawhide, fur skins, skins of birds; the bladder, stomach or pericardium of animals; cord of babiche, buckskin or wool, hair, bark, fiber, grass, and the like; basketry, cloth, beadwork, etc. Rectangular or oval pouches were made with a flap or a gathering-string and with a thong, cord, or strap for attaching them at the shoulder or to the belt. The Eskimo had pouches with a flap that could be wrapped many times around and secured by means of a string and an ivory fastener. The Zuñi use, among others, crescent-shaped pouches into the horns of which objects are thrust through a central opening. Bags showed less variety of form. They were square or oblong, deep or shallow, flat or cylindrical. Many of these were provided with a shoulder band, many with a carrying-strap and a forehead band. The Eskimo bag was provided with an ivory handle, which was frequently decorated with etching. Small pouches were used for holding toilet articles, paint, medicine, tobacco, pipes, ammunition, trinkets, sewing tools, fetishes, sacred meal, etc. Large pouches or bags, such as the bandoleer pouch of the Chippewa, held smaller pouches and articles for personal use.

Bags were made for containing articles to be packed on horses, frequently joined together like saddlebags. The tribes of the far N. made use of large sleeping bags of fur. Most bags and pouches were ornamented, and in very few other belongings of the Indian were displayed such fertility of invention and such skill in the execution of the decorative and symbolic designs. Skin pouches, elaborately ornamented with beadwork, quillwork, pigments, and dyes, were made by various tribes. Decorated bags and wallets of skin are characteristic of the Aleut, Salish, Nez Percés, the northern Athapascan and Algonquian tribes, and the Plains Indians. Bags of textiles and basketry are similarly diversified. Especially noteworthy are the muskemoots of the Thlingchadinne, made of babiche, the bags of the Nez Percés, made of apocynum fiber and corn-husks, the woven hunting bags of northern woodland tribes, and the painted rawhide pouches and bags of the tribes of the great plains.

Consult Mason (1) Aboriginal American Basketry, Rep. Nat. Mus., 1902, 1904,

(2) Primitive Travel and Transportation, ibid., 1894, 1896; Boas, Holmes, Hoffman, Nelson, and Turner, in Reports of the B. A. E.; Kroeber, The Arapaho, Bull. Am. Mus. Nat. Hist., XVIII, 1902; Boas in Jour. Am. Mus. Nat. Hist., IV, no. 3, suppl., 1904; Willoughby in Am. Anthrop., VII, nos. 1, 4, 1905; Teit in Mem. Am. Mus. Nat. Hist., I, no. 4, 1900; Lumholtz, Unknown Mexico, 1902. (w. h.)

**Baguacat.** An unidentified pueblo of New Mexico in 1598.—Oñate (1598) in Doc. Inéd., XVI, 103, 1871.

**Baguiburisac.** A rancheria, probably Maricopa, visited by Kino and Mange in 1699; apparently near the Rio Gila in s. w. Ariz.—Mange (1699) quoted by Bancroft, Ariz. and N. Mex., 358, 1889.

**Bagwanageshig.** See *Hole-in-the-day*.

**Bahacecha.** A tribe visited by Oñate in 1604, at which time it resided on the Rio Colorado in Arizona, between Bill Williams fork and the Gila. Their language was described as being almost the same as that of the Mohave, whose territory adjoined theirs on the N. and with whom they were friendly. Their houses were low, of wood covered with earth. They are not identifiable with any present Yuman tribe, although they occupied in Oñate's time that part of the Rio Colorado valley inhabited by the Alchedoma in 1776. See Zarate-Salmeron (*ca.* 1629) in Land of Sunshine, 105, Jan., 1900; Garcés (1775–76), Diary, 1900; Bandelier in Arch. Inst. Papers, III, 110, 1890. (f. w. h.)

**Bahekhube.** A village occupied by the Kansa after they left the mouth of Big Blue r., near a mountain s. of Kansas r., Kans.
Bahĕ′qúbĕ.—Dorsey, MS. Kansas vocab., B. A. E., 1882.

**Bahohata** ('lodge'). A Hidatsa band. Matthews says it may be Maohati.
Bä-ho-häꞋ-ta.—Morgan, Anc. Soc., 159, 1877.

**Baicadeat.** A former rancheria, evidently of the Sobaipuri, on Rio San Pedro, s. Ariz.; it was visited by Father Kino about 1697, and became a visita of the mission of Suamca about 1760–67.
Baicadeat.—Mange (1697) quoted by Bancroft, Ariz. and N. Mex., 356, 1889. S. Pablo Baiboat.—Bancroft, ibid., 371.

**Baidarka.** The sealskin boat of the Alaskan Eskimo. The Russian adaptation of *paithak*, or *paithalik*, in the Kaniagmiut dialect, applied to a three-paddle boat of this kind. (a. f. c.)

**Baimena** (possibly from *bahime*, pl. of *bahi*, 'a species of locust,' *la* 'continuance,' 'habit,' hence 'a place where locusts habitually live.'—Buelna). A former small tribe and pueblo, evidently Piman, 6 leagues s. e. of San José del Toro, Sinaloa, Mexico. According to Zapata the people spoke a dialect related to that of the Zoe, who lived next to them on the

N. in 1678. These two tribes traditionally came with the Ahome from the N. They are now extinct.
Baimena.—Orozco y Berra, Geog., 336, 1864. Santa Catalina Baimena.—Ibid., 333. Santa Catalina de Baitrena.—Zapata (1678) in Doc. Hist. Mex., 4th s., III, 396, 1857.

**Baipia.** A former settlement of either the Soba or the Papago proper, situated slightly N. w. of Caborca, probably on the Rio Altar, N. w. Sonora, Mexico.
Aribaipia.—Anza (1774) quoted by Bancroft, Ariz. and N. Mex., 389, 1889. Aribayopia.—Font, map (1777), ibid., 393. Arivac.—Orozco y Berra, Geog., 347, 1864 (probably the same). Baipia.—Kino, map (1701), in Bancroft, Ariz. and N. Mex., 360, 1889. San Edvardo de Baipia.—Venegas, Hist. Cal., II, 176, 1759. S. Eduard de Baipia.—Kino, map (1702) in Stöcklein, Neue Welt-Bott, 74, 1726. S. Eduardo.—Bancroft, Ariz. and N. M., 359, 1889. S. Eduardo Baipia.—Kino (1701) quoted by Bancroft, No. Mex. States, I, 495, 1884. S. Eduardo de Aribaopía.—Anza and Font (1776) quoted by Bancroft, Ariz. and N. M., 393, 1889. S. Edward.—Venegas, Hist. Cal., I, map, 1759.

**Bajío** (Span.: 'shoal,' 'sand-bank'). A Papago settlement with 150 inhabitants in 1858.
Del Bajio.—Bailey in Ind. Aff. Rep., 208, 1858.

**Bakihon** ('gash themselves with knives'). A band of the Upper Yanktonai Sioux.
Bakihoⁿ.—Dorsey in 15th Rep. B. A. E., 218, 1897. Bakihoꞅ.—Ibid.

**Baking stones.** A name applied to a numerous class of prehistoric stone relics found principally on inhabited sites in s. California. They are flattish, often rudely rectangular or somewhat oval plates, sometimes convex beneath and slightly concave above, and rare specimens have obscure rims. Usually they

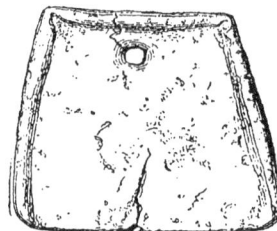
PREHISTORIC BAKING PLATE; CALIFORNIA (1-10)

are made of soapstone, and often show traces of use over fire. They rarely exceed a foot in length, are somewhat less in width, and perhaps an inch in average thickness. The characteristic feature of these plates is a roughly made perforation at the middle of one end, giving the appearance of a huge pendant ornament. This perforation served, no doubt, to aid in handling the plate while hot. Some of these objects may have been boiling stones to be heated in the fire and suspended in a pot or basket of water for cooking purposes. This utensil passes imperceptibly into certain ladle-like forms, and these again into dippers, cups, bowls, and globular ollas in turn, the whole group forming part of the culinary outfit. A remarkable ladle-like object of gray diorite was obtained from the auriferous gravels 16 feet below the surface in Placer co., Cal. It is superior in make to other kindred objects. The baking stones of the Pueblo Indians, employed in making the wafer bread, are smooth, oblong slabs set over the fireplace. See Abbott in Surveys West of the 100th Merid., VII,

HOPI BAKING STONE.   (MINDELEFF)

1879; Cushing, Zuñi Breadstuff, in Millstone, Nov. 1884; Holmes in Smithson. Rep. 1899, 1901; Mindeleff in 8th Rep. B. A. E., 1891.   (w. h. h.)

**Balcony House.** A cliff house, comprising about 25 rooms, situated in Ruin canyon, Mesa Verde, s. Colo. It derives its name from a shelf or balcony which extends along the front of two of the houses, resting on the projecting floor beams. See H. R. Rep. 3703, 58th Cong., 3d sess., 1905.

**Bald Eagle's Nest.** A Delaware (?) village, taking its name from the chief, Bald Eagle, formerly on the right bank of Bald Eagle cr., near the present Milesburg, Center co., Pa. It is marked on La Tour's map of 1784 and described by Day, Pennsylvania, 201, 1843.

**Ballokai Pomo** ('Oat valley people.'—Powers). A subtribe or division of the Pomo, formerly living in Potter valley, Mendocino co., Cal.

Bal-lo' Kai Pó-mo.—Powers in Cont. N. A. Ethnol., III,155,1877. Poam Pomo.—Ibid.,156. Poma poma.—Kroeber, inf'n, 1903. Poma pomo.—Ibid. Pomas.—McKee (1851) in Sen. Ex. Doc. 4, 32d Cong., spec. sess., 144, 1853. Pome Pomos.—Powers in Overland Mo., IX, 504, 1872. Pone Pomos.—Hittell, Hist. Cal., I, 730, 1885.

**Ball play.** The common designation of a man's game, formerly the favorite athletic game of all the eastern tribes from Hudson bay to the Gulf. It was found also in California and perhaps elsewhere on the Pacific coast, but was generally superseded in the W. by some form of shinny. It was played with a small ball of deerskin stuffed with hair or moss, or a spherical block of wood, and with 1 or 2 netted rackets, somewhat resembling tennis rackets. Two goals were set up at a distance of several hundred yards from each other, and the object of each party was to drive the ball under the goal of the opposing party by means of the racket without touching it with the hand. After picking up the ball with the racket, however, the player might run with it in his hand until he could throw it again. In the N. the ball was manipulated with a single racket, but in the S. the player used a pair, catching the ball between them. Two settlements or two tribes generally played against each other, the players numbering from 8 or 10 up to hundreds on a side, and high stakes were wagered on the result. Preceding and accompanying the game there was much ceremonial of dancing, fasting, bleeding, anointing, and prayer under the direction of the medicine-men. The allied tribes used this game as a stratagem to obtain entrance to Ft Mackinaw in 1764. Numerous places bearing the name of Ball Play give evidence of its old popularity among the former tribes of the Gulf states, who have carried it with them to their present homes in Indian Ter., where it is still kept up with the old ceremonial and enthusiasm. Shorn of its ceremonial accompaniments it has been adopted by the Canadians as their national game under the name of *la crosse*, and by the Louisiana French creoles as *raquette*. The Indians of many tribes played

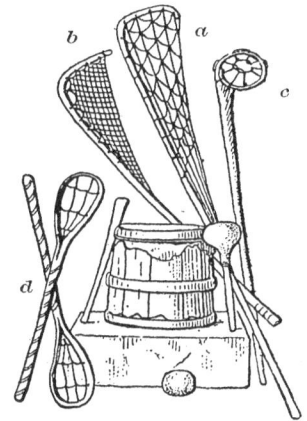

RACKETS, ETC., USED IN BALL PLAY. *a*, IROQUOIS; *b*, PASSAMAQUODDY; *c*, CHIPPEWA; *d*, CHEROKEE

other games of ball, noteworthy among which is the kicked ball of the Tarahumare, which, it is said, gave the name to the tribe. Consult Adair, Hist. Am. Inds., 1775; Bartram, Trav., 1792; Catlin, N. A. Inds., 1841; Mooney, Cherokee Ball Play, Am. Anthrop., III, 1890; Culin, Games of N. Am. Inds., in 24th Rep. B. A. E., 1905. Lumholtz, Unknown Mexico, 1902. See *Games*.   (j. m.)

**Balsa.** See *Boats*.

**Bamoa** (*ba* 'water,' *moa* 'ear' or 'spike' (of corn): 'spike in the water'; or preferably *ba*, and *maioa* 'bank': 'on the bank of the river.'—Buelna). According to Orozco y Berra, a pueblo "founded by the Pima who came with Cabeza de Vaca and his companions on that famous expedition which gave rise to the story of the Queen of Quivira and the Seven Cities. Settled on the shore of the river [Sinaloa], they received in after times a goodly number of their compatriots who, drawn by the fame of the missionaries before the latter reached their country, placed themselves in the way of receiving Christianity. They speak the Pima and generally the Mexican, being also well accustomed to the Castilian tongue."

**Bamoa.**—Cabeza de Vaca, Rel. (1529), Smith trans., 225, 1871. **Baymoa.**—Alegre, Hist. Comp. Jesus, I, 340, 1841. **La Concepcion Bamoa.**—Orozco y Berra, Geog., 333, 1864.

**Bamom** ('salt water'). A former Maidu village at the site of the present Shingle, Eldorado co., Cal. (R. B. D.)

**Banamichi.** A pueblo of the Teguima Opata and the seat of a Spanish mission in 1639; situated below Arizpe, on the Rio Sonora, Sonora, Mexico; pop. 338 in 1678, 127 in 1730. Not to be confounded with Remedios, q. v.

**Banamiche.**—Hrdlicka in Am. Anthrop., VI, 72, 1904. **Banamichi.**—Rivera (1730) quoted by Bancroft, No. Mex. States, I, 514, 1884. **Banamitzi.**—Orozco y Berra, Geog., 343, 1864. **Nuestra Señora de los Remedios de Beramitzi.**—Ibid. **Remedios Banamichi.**—Zapata (1678) in Doc. Hist. Mex., 4th s., III, 372, 1857.

**Band that Don't Cook.** A band of Yankton Sioux under Smutty Bear (Matosahitchiay).—Culbertson in Smithson. Rep. 1850, 141, 1851.

**Band that Eats no Geese.** A band of Yankton Sioux under Padaniapapi.—Culbertson in Smithson. Rep. 1850, 141, 1851.

**Band that Wishes the Life.** A band of Yanktonai Sioux of which Black Catfish was the principal chief in 1856.—H. R. Ex. Doc. 130, 34th Cong., 1st sess., 7, 1856.

**Bankalachi** (Yokuts name). A small Shoshonean tribe on upper Deer cr., which drains into Tulare lake, s. Cal. With the Tubatulabal they form one of the four major linguistic divisions of the family. Their own name is unknown. (A. L. K.)

**Boⁿgalaatshi.**—Hoffman in Proc. Am. Philos. Soc., XXIII, 301, 1886.

**Banner stones.** A name applied to a group of prehistoric objects of polished stone, which, for lack of definite information as to their use, are assigned to the problematical class (see *Problematical objects*). Their form is exceedingly varied, but certain fundamental features of their shape are practically unvarying, and are of such a nature as to suggest the use of the term "banner stones" in classifying them. These features are the axial perforations and the extension of the body or midrib into two wing-like projections. Of the various forms the most typical is that which suggests a two-bladed ax, the blades passing on the one hand from the type into pick-like points, and on the other into broad wings, suggesting those of the bird or butterfly. The name "butterfly stones" is sometimes applied to the latter variety. In some of their features these stones are

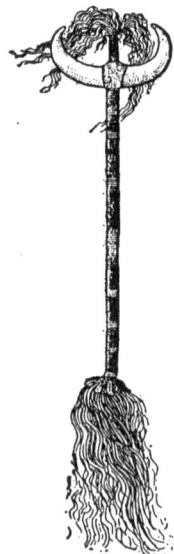

SIOUX CEREMONIAL WAND, SUGGESTING MANNER OF USING BANNER STONES. (MOONEY)

related to pierced tablets, and in others, respectively, to boat stones, bird stones, spade stones, tubes (see articles on these several topics), and platform pipes, and there can be little doubt that all of these classes of objects were related to one another in symbolism or use. Nothing is definitely known, however, of the particular significance attached to them, or of the manner of their use, save by inference from their form and the known customs of the tribes. It appears probable, from the presence of the perforations, that they

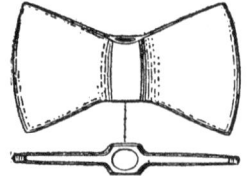

GREENSTONE; IOWA (1-6)

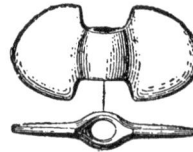

QUARTZITE; ILLINOIS (1-6)

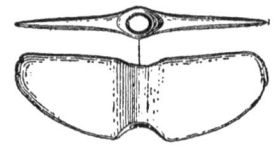

SYENITE; DISTRICT OF COLUMBIA (1-6)

were mounted for use on a staff, on a handle as a ceremonial weapon, or on the stem of a calumet, but the appearance of similar winged forms as parts of the head-

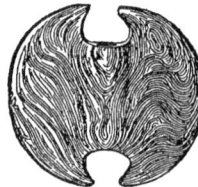

BANDED SLATE; OHIO (1-6)

BANDED SLATE; CANADA; 1-6. (BOYLE)

BANDED SLATE; OHIO (1-6)

dress in sheet-copper figures from Georgia mounds (see *Copper*) suggests connection with the headdress.

These objects are usually made of varieties of stone selected for their fine grain and pleasing color, and are carefully shaped and finished. In Florida, and perhaps elsewhere, examples made of shell are found. The perforation is cylindrical, and is bored with great precision longitudinally through the thick portion or midrib, which may symbolically represent the body of a bird. Numerous unfinished specimens are found, some of which, partly bored, show the depressed ring and elevated core that result from the use of the tubular drill. They are found in burial mounds and on formerly inhabited sites generally, and were probably as a class the outgrowth of the remarkable culture development which accompanied and resulted in the construction of the great earthworks of the Mississippi valley.

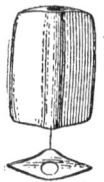

QUARTZITE; INDIANA (1-6)

For record of discovery and illustrations of banner stones see especially Boyle, Prim. Man in Ontario, 1895; Fowke (1) in 13th Rep. B. A. E., 1896, (2) Archæol. Hist. Ohio, 1902; Moore, various memoirs in Jour. Acad. Nat. Sci. Phila., 1894–1905; Moorehead, Prehist. Impls., 1900; Rau in Smithson. Cont., XII, 1876; Read, Rep. Ohio Centen. Managers, 1877; Squier and Davis in Smithson. Cont., I, 1848; Thomas in 12th Rep. B. A. E., 1894.    (W. H. H.)

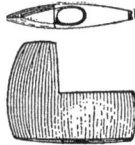

RELATED FORM WITH SINGLE WING AND OVAL PERFORATION. BANDED SLATE; MICHIGAN (1-6)

**Bannock** (from *Panaíti*, their own name). A Shoshonean tribe whose habitat previous to being gathered on reservations can not be definitely outlined. There were two geographic divisions, but references to the Bannock do not always note this distinction. The home of the chief division appears to have been S. E. Idaho, whence they ranged into W. Wyoming. The country actually claimed by the chief of this southern division, which seems to have been recognized by the treaty of Ft Bridger, July 3, 1868, lay between lat. 42° and 45°, and between long. 113° and the main chain of the Rocky mts. It separated the Wihinasht Shoshoni of W. Idaho from the so-called Washaki band of Shoshoni of W. Wyoming. They were found in this region in 1859, and they asserted that this had been their home in the past. Bridger (Ind. Aff. Rep., 363, 1859) had known them in this region as early as 1829. Bonneville

WASTAWANA—BANNOCK

found them in 1833 on Portneuf r., immediately N. of the present Ft Hall res. Many of this division affiliated with the Washaki Shoshoni, and by 1859 had extensively intermarried with them. Ft Hall res. was set apart by Executive order in 1869, and 600 Bannock, in addition to a large number of Shoshoni, consented to remain upon it. Most of them soon wandered away, however, and as late as 1874 an appropriation was made to enable the Bannock and Shoshoni scattered in S. E. Idaho to be moved to the reservation. The Bannock at Ft Hall were said to number 422 in 1885. The northern division was found by Gov. Stevens in 1853 (Pac. R. R. Rep., I, 329, 1855) living on Salmon r. in E. Idaho. Lewis and Clark, who passed through the country of this N. division in 1805, may have included them under the general term Shoshoni, unless, as is most likely, these are the Broken Moccasin Indians they mention (Expd., Coues ed., II, 523, 1893). In all probability these Salmon River Bannock had recently crossed the mountains from the eastward owing to pressure of the Siksika, since they claimed as their territory S. W. Montana, including the rich areas in which are situated Virginia City, Bozeman, and other towns (Ind. Aff. Rep., 289, 1869). Stevens (1853) states that they had been more than decimated by the ravages of smallpox and the inroads of the Siksika. It is probable that at no distant time in the past, perhaps before they had acquired horses, the various groups of the entire Bannock tribe were united in one locality in S. E. Idaho, where they were neighbors of the Shoshoni proper, but their language is divergent from the latter. The Bannock were a widely roving tribe, a characteristic which favored their dispersal and separation into groups. Both the men and the women are well developed; and although Shoshonean in language, in physical characters the Bannock resemble more closely the Shahaptian Nez Percés than other Shoshonean Indians. Kroeber reports that the language of the Fort Hall Bannock connects them closer with the Ute than with any other Shoshonean tribe. At the same time Powell and Mooney report that the tribes of W. Nevada consider the Bannock very nearly related to themselves.

The loss of hunting lands, the diminution of the bison herds, and the failure of the Government to render timely relief led to a Bannock outbreak in 1877–8, the trouble having been of long standing. During the exciting times of the Nez Percé war the Bannock were forced to remain on their inhospitable reservation, to face the continued encroachment of the whites, and to subsist on goods provided from an appropriation amounting to 2½ cents per capita per diem. During the summer a drunken Indian of the tribe shot and wounded two teamsters; the excitement and bitter feeling caused by his arrest, Nov. 23, 1877, resulted in the killing of an agency employee. Troops were called for, and the murderer was pursued, captured, tried, and executed. This episode so increased the excitement of the Indians that, fearing what was assumed to be threatening demonstrations, the troops surrounded and captured two Bannock camps in Jan., 1878; but most of the Indians were afterward released. On account of insufficient food the Bannock left the reservation in the spring and went to Camas prairie, where they killed several settlers. A vigorous campaign under Gen. Howard resulted in the capture of about 1,000 of them in August, and the outbreak came to an end after a fight on Sept. 5, at Clark's ford, where 20 Bannock lodges were attacked and all the women and children killed.

Bridger states that when he first knew them (about 1829) the southern Bannock numbered 1,200 lodges, indicating a population of about 8,000. In 1869 they were estimated as not exceeding 500, and this number was probably an overestimate as their lodges numbered but 50, indicating a population of about 350. In 1901 the tribe numbered 513, so intermixed, however, with the Shoshoni that no attempt is made to enumerate them separately. All the Bannock except 92 under Lemhi agency are gathered on Ft Hall res., Idaho. Practically nothing is known of the former organization of the Bannock or of their divisions. The names of four divisions were obtained by Hoffman, and a fifth is given by Schoolcraft. These are Kutshundika, or Buffalo-eaters; Penointikara, or Honey-eaters; Shohopanaiti, or Cottonwood Bannock; Yambadika, or Root-eaters; Waradika, or Rye-grass-seed-eaters. (H. W. H. C. T.)

Banac.—Smet, Letters, 129, 1843. Ban-acks.—Forney in Ind. Aff. Rep., 213, 1858. Banai'ti.—Hoffman in Proc. Am. Philos. Soc., XXIII, 298, 1886 (Shoshoni name). Banáni.—Gatschet, Chippewa MS., B. A. E. (Chippewa name). Ban-at-tees.—Ross, Fur Hunters, I, 249, 1855. Banax.—Mullan in Pac. R. R. Rep., I, 329, 1855. Bannach Snakes.—Wallen in H. R. Ex. Doc. 65, 36th Cong., 1st sess., 223, 1860. Bannacks.—Irving, Rocky Mts., I, 71, 1837. Banneck.—Ibid., 159. Ban'-ni-ta.—Stuart, Montana, 25, 1865. Bonacks.—Schoolcraft, Ind. Tribes, VI, 697, 1857. Bonak.—Farnham, Travels, 76, 1843. Bonarch Diggers.—Meek in H. R. Ex. Doc. 76, 30th Cong., 1st sess., 10, 1848. Bonarchs.—Ibid. Bonarks.—Sen. Ex. Doc. 1, 31st Cong., 2d sess., 198, 1850. Bonnacks.—Dennison in Ind. Aff. Rep., 371, 1857. Bonnaks.—Hale, Ethnog. and Philol., 218, 1846. Bonnax.—Parker, Jour., map, 1842. Bonochs.—Prichard, Phys. Hist., V, 430, 1847. Boonacks.—Irving, Astoria, map, 1849. Broken-Moccasin.—Lewis and Clark, Exped., I, 330, 1842 (probably the Bannock). Diggers.—Many authors. Moccasin-with-Holes.—Lewis and Clark, op. cit. Ogoize.—Giorda, Calispel Dict., I, 439, 1877 (Calispel name). Panack.—Townsend, Nar., 75, 1839.

Panai'ti.—Hoffman in Proc. Am. Philos. Soc., XXIII, 299, 1886 (own name). Panak.—Gebow, Snake Vocab., B. A. E. (Shoshoni name). Pán-asht.—Hale, op. cit. Pannacks.—Lander in Sen. Ex. Doc. 42, 36th Cong., 1st sess., 121, 1860. Pannah.—Ibid. Pannakees. — Ibid. Paunaques. — Wyeth (1848) in Schoolcraft, Ind. Tribes, I, 206, 1851. Pohas.—Robertson (1846) in H. R. Ex. Doc. 76, 30th Cong., 1st sess., 9, 1848. Ponacks.—Schoolcraft, Ind. Tribes, VI, 697, 1857. Ponashita.—Ibid., I, 521, 1853. Ponashta.—Lane (1849) in Sen. Ex. Doc. 52, 31st Cong., 1st sess., 169, 1850. Ponishta Bonacks.—Schoolcraft, op. cit., VI, 701, 1857. Pŭn-äsh.—Long, Exped. Rocky Mts., II, lxxix, 1823 (Shoshoni name). Punashly.—Fremont, Geog. Mem. Upper Cal., map, 1848. Pun-naks.—Bonner, Life of Beckwourth, 93, 1856. Robber Indians.—Ross, Fur Hunters, I, 249, 1855. Tannockes.—Audouard, Far West, 182, 1869. Ush-ke-we-ah.—Crow MS. vocab., B. A. E. (Crow name).

**Bantam.** According to Trumbull, a former village at Litchfield, Litchfield co., Conn. Part of the Indians there were converted by the Moravian missionaries about 1742–45, and followed them to Bethlehem, Pa., where many died, and the remnant returned to Scaticook, in Kent co., Conn.

Bantom.—Trumbull, Conn., II, 82, 1818.

**Bantas.** A village of the Cholovone E. of the San Joaquin and N. of the Tuolumne r., Cal.—Pinart, Cholovone MS., B. A. E., 1880.

**Baqueachic** (*bắkắ* 'bamboo reed,' *chik* 'place of.'—Lumholtz). A Tarahumare settlement on or near the Rio Conchos, lat. 27° 40′, long. 106° 50′, Chihuahua, Mexico.

Baqueachic.—Lumholtz, Unknown Mex., I, 320, 1902. Baquiachic.—Orozco y Berra, Geog., 323, 1864.

**Baquiarichic.** A Tarahumare settlement on or near a branch of the s. tributary of the Rio Conchos, lat. 26° 55′, long. 106° 30′, Chihuahua, Mexico.—Orozco y Berra, Geog., 322, 1864.

**Baquigopa** (*baqui-go* 'cane'; Buelna says the name means 'plain of the canes'). A former Opata village on the upper Yaqui, locally known as the Rio Babispe, E. of Guachinera, N. E. Sonora, Mexico. Its abandonment was the result of attacks by Indians of w. Chihuahua, the inhabitants finally settling at Guachinera. See *Batesopa*. (F. W. H.)

Bacayopa.—Buelna, Pereg. Aztecas, 123, 1892. Baquigopa.—Bandelier in Arch. Inst. Pap., III, 59, 64, 1890; IV, 518, 1892.

**Bar-du-de-clenny.** See *Nakaidoklini*.

**Bark.** Among the resources of nature utilized by the tribes of North America bark was of prime importance. It was stripped from trees at the right season by hacking all around and taking it off in sheets of desired length. The inner bark of cedar, elm, and other trees was in some localities torn into strips, shredded, twisted, and spun or woven. The bark of wild flax (Apocynum) and the Asclepias were made into soft textiles. Bark had a multitude of functions. In connection with the most important of wants, the necessity for food, it supplied many tribes with an article of diet in the spring, their period of greatest need. The name Adirondack, signifying 'they eat trees,' was applied by the Mohawk to certain Algonquian tribes of Canada in allusion to their custom of eating bark. The N. Pacific and some S. W. tribes made cakes of the soft inner bark of the hemlock and spruce; those living about the great lakes chewed that of the slippery elm, while many Indians chewed the gum that exuded from trees.

ESKIMO BARK BASKET WITH BUCKSKIN TOP AND DRAW-STRING.  (TURNER)

Drink was made from bark by the Arapaho, Winnebago, and Mescaleros. Willow bark and other kinds were smoked in pipes with or instead of tobacco, and the juices of barks were employed in medicine.

For gathering, carrying, garnering, preparing, and serving food, bark of birch, elm, pine, and other trees was so handy as to discourage the

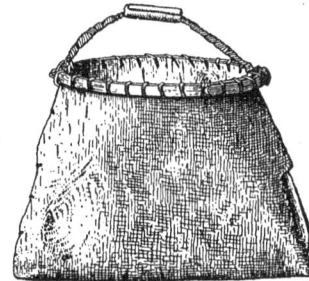

MENOMINEE BARK BUCKET.  (HOFFMAN)

potter's art among nonsedentary tribes. It was wrought into yarn, twine, rope, wallets, baskets, mats, canoes, cooking pots for hot stones, dishes for serving, vessels for storing, and many textile utensils connected with the consumption of food in ordinary and in social life. Both men and women were food gatherers, and thus both sexes were refined through this material; but preparing and serving were women's arts, and here bark aided in developing their skill and intelligence.

Habitations in Canada, E. United States, and s. E. Alaska often had roofs and sides of bark, whole or prepared. The conical house, near kin of the tipi, was frequently covered with this material. Matting was made use of for floors, beds, and

partitions. Trays and boxes, receptacles of myriad shapes, could be formed by merely bending large sheets and sewing or

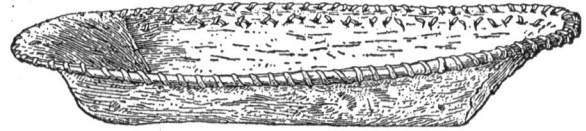

CHIPPEWA BIRCH-BARK WINNOWING TRAY.  (JENKS)

simply tying the joints. Bast could be pounded and woven into robes and blankets. The Canadian and Alaskan tribes

CHIPPEWA FETISH CASE OF BARK.  (HOFFMAN)

carried their children in cradles of birch bark, while on the Pacific coast infants were borne in wooden cradles or baskets of woven bark on beds of the bast shredded, their foreheads being often flattened by means of pads of the same material. In the S. W. the baby-board had a cover of matting. Among the Iroquois the dead were buried in coffins of bark. Clothing of bark was made chiefly from the inner portion, which was stripped into ribbons, as for petticoats in the S. W., shredded and fringed, as in the cedar-bark country, where it was also woven into garments, or twisted for the warp in weaving articles of dress, with woof from other materials. Dyes were derived from bark and certain

CEREMONIAL USE OF BARK COLLAR; KWAKIUTL.  (BOAS)

kinds also lent themselves to embroidery with quills and overlaying in basketry. Bark was also the material of slow-matches and torches, served as padding for the carrier's head and back and as his wrapping material, and furnished strings, ropes, and bags for his wooden canoes. The hunter made all sorts of apparatus from bark, even his bowstring. The fisher wrought implements out of it and poisoned fish with its juices. The beginnings of writing in some localities were favored by bark, and car-

CHIPPEWA BARK HOUSE.  (GILFILLAN)

tography, winter counts, medical formulas, and tribal history were inscribed thereon. Finally it comes into the service of ceremony and religion. Such a series of masks and dance regalia as Boas and others found among the Kwakiutl illustrates how obligingly bark lends itself to coöperative activities, whether in amusement, social functions, or adoration of the spirit world. There are also rites connected with gathering and working bark. See Boas in Nat. Mus. Rep. 1895, 1897; in Hoffman in 14th Rep. B. A. E., 1896; Holmes in 3d and 13th Reps. B. A. E., 1884, 1896; Jenks in 19th Rep. B. A. E., 1900; Jones in Smithson. Rep. 1867, 1872; Ma-

CEREMONIAL COLLAR OF BARK; KWAKIUTL. (BOAS)

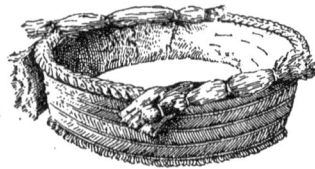

CEREMONIAL HEAD RINGS OF BARK; KWAKIUTL. (BOAS)

son (1) in Rep. Nat. Mus. 1887, 1889, (2) ibid., 1894, 1896, (3) ibid., 1902, 1904; Niblack, ibid, 1888, 1890; Turner in 11th Rep. B. A. E., 1894. (O. T. M.)

**Barnard.** See *Timpoochee Barnard.*

**Barrancas** (*Las Barrancas*, Span.: 'the ravines'). Formerly a small village, apparently of the Piros, on the Rio Grande, near Socorro, N. Mex; evidently abandoned during the Pueblo revolt of 1680. **La Barrancas.**—Kitchin, map N. A., 1787. **Las Barancas.**—D'Anville, map N. A., Bolton's ed., 1752. **Las Barrancas.**—Davis, Span. Conq. New Mex., 314, 1869.

**Basalt.** A widely variable class of lavas of a prevailing dark color and, in the compact varieties, with a dull conchoidal fracture. The rock is often more or less pumiceous and scoriaceous. The larger superficial flows of the W. are often known as "the lava beds." The basalts occur in large bodies in many parts of the country, especially in the far W., and were extensively used by the aborigines for implements and utensils. (W. H. H.)

**Basaseachic.** A Tarahumare settlement of Chihuahua, Mexico; definite locality unknown.—Orozco y Berra, Geog., 323, 1864.

**Basawunena** (*Bä'sawunĕ'na,* 'woodlodge men'). Formerly a distinct though cognate tribe that made war on the Arapaho (q. v.), but with whom they have been incorporated for 150 years. About 100 are still recognized in the northern and a few in the southern group.—Mooney in 14th Rep. B. A. E., 955, 1896.

**Basdecheshni** ('those who do not split the buffalo'). A band or division of the Sisseton Sioux. **Basdeće-śni.**—Dorsey in 15th Rep. B. A. E., 217, 1897. **Basdetce-cni.**—Ibid.

**Baserac** ('place where the water is seen,' because up to this point the river is so deep among the mountains that in most places it is invisible.—Rudo Ensayo). An Opata pueblo, and the seat of a Spanish mission founded in 1645, on an E. branch of Rio de Batepito, a tributary of the Yaqui, in N. E. Sonora, Mexico. Population 399 in 1678, 839 in 1730. There are many descendants of the Opata in the modern town, but only a few of them speak their native tongue. (F. W. H.) **Bacerac.**—Orozco y Berra, Geog., 343, 1864. **Baserac.**—Bandelier in Arch. Inst. Papers, IV, 527, 1892. **Baseraca.**—Mange (ca. 1700) quoted by Bancroft, No. Mex. States, I, 233, 1884. **Santa María Baceraca.**—Zapata (1678) in Doc. Hist. Mex., III, 366, 1857. **Santa Maria Vaseraca.**—Rudo Ensayo (1762), Guiteras transl., 217, 1894. **Sta Maria de Uasaraca.**—Rivera, Diario, leg. 1,444, 1736. **Vaceraca.**—Kino et al. in Doc. Hist. Mex., 4th s., I, 401, 1856.

**Basigochic** ('sand bank,' 'flat'). A Tarahumare rancheria near Achyarachki, Chihuahua, Mexico.—Cubas, Mexico, 74, 1876.

**Basiroa.** A Nevome division, doubtless in S. central Sonora, Mexico; definite locality unknown. The name is probably that of their settlement.—Orozco y Berra, Geog., 58, 1864.

**Basketry.** Basketry, including wattling, matting, and bagging, may be defined as the primitive textile art. Its materials include nearly the whole series of North American textile plants, and the Indian women explored the tribal habitat for the best. Constant digging in the same favorite spot for roots and

IROQUOIS WOMAN WEAVING A BASKET. (FROM LAFITAU)

the clearing away of useless plants about the chosen stems constituted a species of primitive agriculture. They knew the time and seasons for gathering, how to harvest, dry, preserve, and prepare the tough and pliable parts for use and to reject the brittle, and in what way to com-

bine different plants with a view to the union of beauty and strength in the product. The tools and apparatus of the basket maker, who was nearly always a woman, were most skilful fingers, aided by finger nails for gauge, teeth for a third hand or for nippers, a stone knife, a bone awl, and polishers of shell or gritty stone.

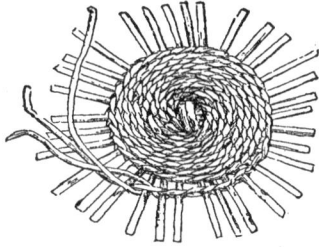

THREE-STRAND BRAIDING

She knew a multitude of dyes, and in some instances the bark was chewed and the splint drawn between the lips. In later

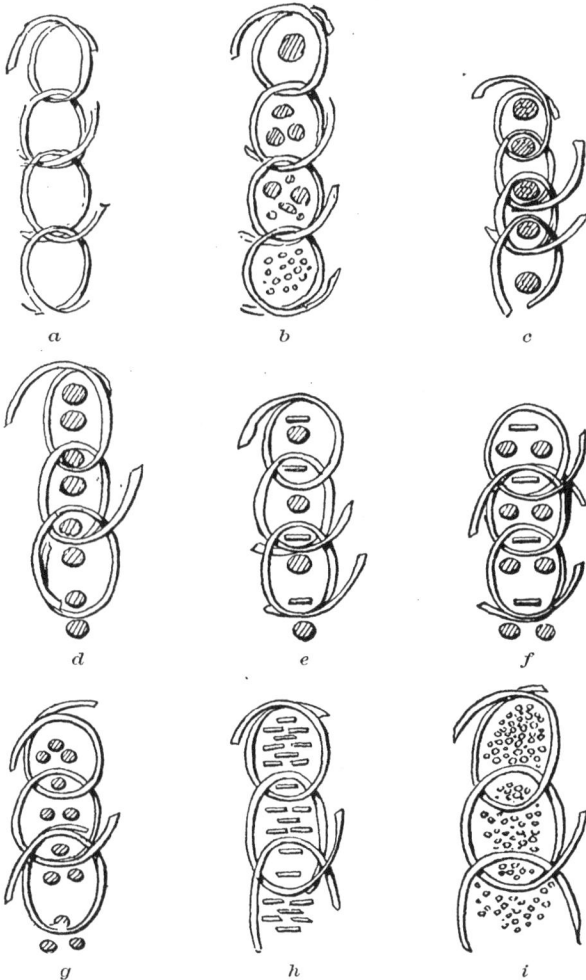

CROSS-SECTIONS OF VARIETIES OF COILED BASKETRY. *a*, COILED, WITHOUT FOUNDATION; *b*, SIMPLE INTERLOCKING COILS; *c*, SINGLE-ROD FOUNDATION; *d*, TWO-ROD FOUNDATION; *e*, ROD-AND-SPLINT FOUNDATION; *f*, TWO-ROD-AND-SPLINT FOUNDATION; *g*, THREE-ROD FOUNDATION; *h*, SPLINT FOUNDATION; *i*, GRASS-COIL FOUNDATION

times knives, awls, scissors, and other utensils and tools of steel were added. In its technic basketry is divided into two species—woven and coiled. Woven bas-

ketry has warp and weft, and leads up to loom work in softer materials. Of this species there are the following varieties: Checkerwork, in which the warp and weft pass over and under one another

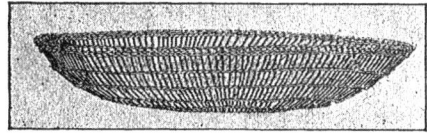

HUPA FOOD TRAY (1-9)

singly and are indistinguishable; twilled work, in which each element of the weft passes over and then under two or more warp elements, producing by varying width and color an endless variety of effects; wickerwork, in which the warp of one larger or two or more smaller elements is inflexible, and the bending is done in the weft;

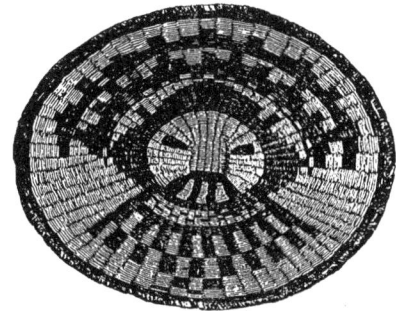

HOPI WILLOW TRAY (1-10)

wrapped work, wherein the warp is not flexed, and the weft in passing a warp element is wrapped once around it, varied by drawing both warp and weft tight so as to form half of a square knot; twined work, in which the warp is not bent and the weft is made up of two or more elements, one of them passing behind each warp element as the weaving progresses. Of this last variety

HUPA STORAGE BASKET (1-24)

there are many styles—plain twined, twilled twined, crossed or divided warp with twined work, wrapped, or bird-cage weaving, three-strand twining after several methods, and three-strand braid. Coiled basketry is not weaving, but sewing, and leads up to point lace. The work is done by sewing or whipping together, in

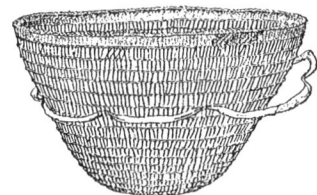

HUPA CARRYING BASKET (1-20)

a flat or ascending coil, a continuous foundation of rod, splint, shredded fiber, or grass, and it receives various names from the kinds of foundation employed and the manner of applying the stitches; or the sewing may form genuine lace work of interlocking stitches without foundation. In coiled work in which a foundation is used the interlocking stitches pass either above, through, or quite under the foundation. Of coiled basketry there are the following varieties: Coiled work without foundation; simple interlocking coils with foundation; single-rod foundation; two-rod foundation; rod-and-splint foundation; two-rod-and-splint foundation; three-rod foundation; splint foundation; grass-coil foundation; and Fuegian stitches, identical with the buttonhole stitch. By using choice materials, or by adding pitch or other resinous substance, baskets were

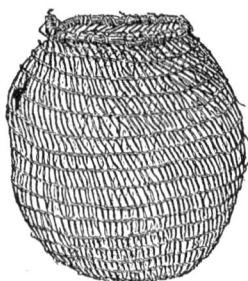

HUPA GATHERING BASKET, 16 INCHES HIGH

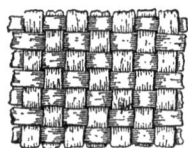

*a*

*b*

*c*

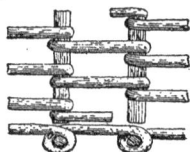

*d*

*e*

*f*

*g*

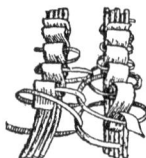

*h*

FORMS OF BASKETRY WEAVING. *a*, CHECKER; *b* TWILLED; *c*, WICKER; *d*, WRAPPED; *e*, TWINED; *f*, CROSS-WARP TWINED; *g*, WRAPPED TWINED; *h*, IMBRICATE

made water-tight for holding or carrying water for cooking.

The chief use of baskets is as receptacles, hence every activity of the Indians was associated with this art. Basket work was employed, moreover, in fences, game drives, weirs, houses, shields, cloth-

ing, cradles, for harvesting, and for the disposal of the dead. This art is interesting, not only on account of the technical processes employed, the great delicacy of technic, and the infinite number of purposes that it serves, but on account of the ornamentation, which is effected by dyeing, using materials of different colors, overlaying, beading, and plaiting, besides great variety in form and technic. This is always added in connection with the weaving or sewing, and is further increased with decorative beads, shells, and feathers. In forms basketry varies from flat wattling, as in gambling and bread plaques, through trays, bowls, pots, cones, jars, and cylinders, to the exquisite California art work. The

PAIUTE GATHERING BASKET (1-12)

geometric forms of decussations and stitches gave a mosaic or conventional appearance to all decoration. The motives in ornamentation were various. No doubt a sense for beauty in articles of use and a desire to awaken admiration and envy in others were uppermost. Imitation of pretty objects in nature, such as snake skins, and designs used by other tribes, were naturally suggested. Such designs pass over into the realms of symbolism and religion. This is now alive and in full vigor among the Hopi of Arizona. The Indian women have left the best witness of what they could do in handiwork and expression in their basketry. In E. United States almost all of the old-fashioned methods of basket making have passed away, but

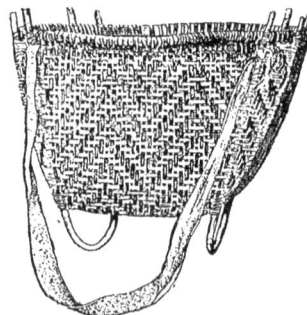

ARIKARA CARRYING BASKET (1-10)

by taking impressions of pottery Holmes has been able to reconstruct the ancient processes, showing that they did not differ in the least from those now extant in the tribes w. of the Rocky mts. In the southern states the existence of pliable cane made possible twilled weaving, which may still be found among the Cherokee and the tribes of Louisiana. The Athapascan tribes in the interior of Alaska made coiled basketry from the roots of evergreen trees. The Eskimo about Bering str. manufactured both woven mattings and wallets and coiled basketry of pliable grass. The Aleutian islanders are now among the most refined artisans in twined work. South of them the Tlingit and the Haida also practise twined work only. From British Columbia, beginning with the Salishan tribes, southward to the borders of Mexico, the greatest variety of basket making in every style of weaving is practised.

Consult Mason, Aboriginal American Basketry, Rep. Nat. Mus. 1902, 1904, and the bibliography therein; also

TWINED BASKET WITH DEER-SKIN TOP AND DRAW-STRING (1-4)

Barrett in Am. Anthrop., VII, no. 4, 1905; Dixon in Bull. Am. Mus. Nat. Hist., XVII, pt. I, 1902; Kroeber in Univ. Cal. Publ., II, 1905; Goddard, ibid; Willoughby in Am. Anthrop., VII, no. 1, 1905. See *Art, Arts and Industries, Weaving.* (O. T. M.)

**Basonopa.** A Tepehuane pueblo in the Sierra Madre, on the headwaters of the Rio del Fuerte, s. w. Chihuahua, Mexico.—Orozco y Berra, Geog., 324, 1864.

**Basosuma.** A rancheria, seemingly of the Sobaipuri, 12 Sp. leagues E. of the mission of Suamca, probably in the vicinity of the s. boundary of Arizona, s. of Ft Huachuca; visited by Kino and Mange in 1697.
San Joaquin de Basosuma.—Kino (1697) in Doc. Hist. Mex., 4th s., I, 276, 1856. S. Joaquin.—Bernal (1697) quoted by Bancroft, Ariz. and N. Mex., 356, 1889.

**Basotutcan.** Apparently a former rancheria of the Papago, visited by Kino in 1701; situated on the Rio Salado, 28 m. below Sonoita, N. w. Sonora, Mexico.
Basotucan.—Kino (1701) quoted by Bancroft, No. Mex. States, I, 495, 1886. J. José Ramos Ayodsudao.—Ibid.

**Basque influence.** The Basque fishermen who frequented the fishing grounds of the N. E. Atlantic in the 16th and 17th centuries influenced to some extent the Indians of New France and Acadia. But such influence was only of a temporary character, and the relations of the Indians with the Basques were only such as naturally came from the industry pursued by the latter. Lescarbot (Hist. Nouv. France, 695, 1612) states that a sort of jargon had arisen between the French and Basque fishermen and traders and the Indians, in which "a good deal of Basque was mixed," but does not give examples of it. (See Reade, The Basques in North America, in Trans. Roy. Soc. Canada, 1888, sec. II, pp. 21–39.) Attempts have been made to detect pre-Columbian influences through alleged lexical and other resemblances

between Basque and Indian languages, but without success. (A. F. C.)

**Bastita.** A Huichol rancheria and religious place, containing a temple; situated about 12 m. s. w. of San Andres Coamiata, q. v.—Lumholtz, Unknown Mex., III, 16, 72, map, 1902.

**Baston.** La Salle in 1681 speaks of the Indians of Baston, by which he means those adjacent to Boston and that part of New England.—La Salle (1681) in Margry, Déc., II, 148, 1877.

**Batacosa.** A Mayo settlement on a small independent stream w. of the Rio de los Cedros, an arm of the Rio Mayo, s. w. Sonora, Mexico.
San Bartolome Batacosa.—Orozco y Berra, Geog., 356, 1864.

**Batawat.** A division of the Wishosk formerly living about the lower course of Mad r., N. W. Cal. In 1851 McKee said of them: "This band has been permitted to live at their present rancheria only upon condition that they confine themselves to the immediate neighborhood of the mouth of the river, and not come into the town."
Mad river Indians.—McKee in Sen. Ex. Doc. 4, 32d Cong., spec. sess., 155, 1853. Pat-a-wat.—Powers in Cont. N. A. Ethnol., III, 96, 1877.

**Batepito** ('where the water turns' (Rudo Ensayo), doubtless in allusion to the bend of the river). An Opata pueblo in N. W. Sonora, Mexico, about lat. 31°, on the upper waters of the Rio Babispe, a tributary of the Rio Yaqui.
Batepito.—Orozco y Berra, Geog., 343, 1864. Vatepito.—Rudo Ensayo (1762), Guiteras trans., 219, 1894.

**Batequi** ('a well.'—Buelna). Apparently a rancheria of the Soba or the Papago proper; placed E. of the Rio Altar in N. W. Sonora, Mexico, on early Spanish maps, as that of Kino (1701) in Bancroft, No. Mex. States, I, 499, 1884. Not to be confounded with the Tadeo Baqui of the Maricopa, which bears also a similar name. (F. W. H.)

**Batesopa.** A former Opata village on the Rio Babispe, E. of Guachinera, in N. E. Sonora, Mexico. Repeatedly attacked by Indians from Chihuahua, it was abandoned, its inhabitants finally settling at Guachinera.—Bandelier in Arch. Inst. Pap., III, 59, 1890; IV, 519, 1892. See *Baquigopa.*

**Bat House.** A ruined pueblo of the Hopi, probably so named from its having been built and occupied by the Bat clan; situated on the N. W. side of Jeditoh valley, N. E. Ariz., on part of the mesa occupied by the Horn House. See 8th Rep. B. A. E., 52, 1891.

**Batista** (Span.: *Bautista*?) Mentioned as one of the former two principal villages of the Koasati, on lower Trinity r., Tex.—Bollaert in Jour. Ethnol. Soc. Lond., II, 282, 1850.

**Batni** (a gourd vessel in which sacred water is carried; also the name of a spring where sacrificial offerings are deposited.—Fewkes). According to Stephen the site of the first pueblo built by the Snake people of the Hopi; situated in Tusayan, N. E. Ariz., but the exact location is known only to the Indians. It is held as a place of votive offerings during the ceremony of the Snake dance.

Batni.—Stephen in 8th Rep. B. A. E., 18, 1891.

**Baton Rouge** (French transl. of Choctaw *itu-úma* 'red pole.'—Gatschet). A point on the high banks of the Mississippi, in Louisiana, at which the natives planted a painted pole to mark the boundary between the Bayogoula below and the Huma who extended for 30 leagues above. See Pénicaut in Margry, Déc., V, 395, 1883. The place is now occupied by the capital of Louisiana. See *Red Stick*.

**Batons.** As emblems of authority or rank, batons were in common use among

HAIDA BATON REPRESENTING EAGLE AND BEAVER. (NIBLACK)

the more advanced northern tribes, and probably the most conspicuous modern

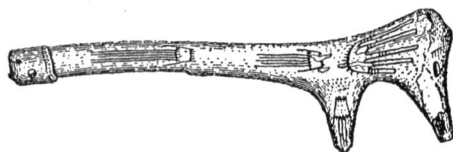
BATON OF DEERHORN, FROM AN OHIO MOUND; 1-7. (CROMER AND MACLEAN COLL.)

representatives are the carved wooden batons of the Haida and other northwestern tribes. Here they are carried in the hands of chiefs, shamans, and song leaders on state occasions, and are permitted only to such personages. Weapons of various kinds were similarly used and probably had kindred significance. In prehistoric times long knives of stone, masterpieces of the chipping art, seem to have been a favorite form of ceremonial weapon, and their use still continues among some of the Pacific slope tribes, especially in California. Batons used in marking time are probably without particular significance as emblems. Among the Kwakiutl and other tribes the club-shaped batons, carved to represent various animals, are used by the leaders in ceremonial dances and serve for beating time. Consult Boas in Rep. Nat. Mus. 1895, 1897; Goddard in Publ. Univ.

BATON OF FLINT, TENNESSEE (1-9). (THRUSTON)

Cal., I, no. I, 1903; Niblack in Rep. Nat. Mus. 1888, 1890; Powers in Cont. N. A.

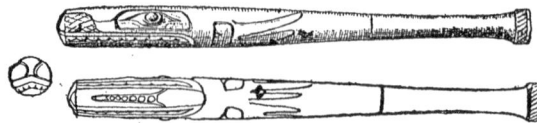
KWAKIUTL BATON REPRESENTING A SEA-LION. (BOAS)

Ethnol., III, 1877; Rust and Kroeber in Am. Anthrop., VII, no. 4, 1905. See *Clubs, Knives*. (W. H. H.)

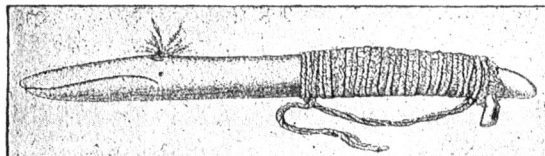
IVORY BATON FOR BEATING TIME ON A STICK; ESKIMO. (NELSON)

**Batture aux Fièvres** (French: 'Malarial flat'). One of four Dakota (probably Mdewakantonwan) villages near St Peters, Minn., in 1826.—Minn. Hist. Soc. Coll., I, 442, 1872.

**Batucari** (*batuhue* 'river,' *cari* 'house': 'houses in the river'; or *batui* 'dove,' and *cari*: 'dove houses.'—Buelna). A subdivision of the Cahita, speaking the Vacoregue dialect and formerly subsisting by hunting in the vicinity of a large lagoon 3 leagues from Ahome, N. Sinaloa, Mexico. They afterward united with the Ahome people under the Jesuit missionaries and abandoned their wandering life.—Orozco y Berra, Geog., 58, 322, 1864.

Batuearis.—Century Cyclopedia, 1894 (misprint).

**Batuco** ('shallow water.'—Och). A former pueblo of the Eudeve division of the Opata, on the Rio Oposura, a w. branch of the Rio Yaqui, a league N. of Santa María Batuco, about lat. 29° 30′, Sonora, Mexico. It became the seat of the Jesuit mission of San Javier about 1629. Pop. 480 in 1678, 188 in 1730.

San Jávier de Batuco.—Zapata (1678) in Doc. Hist. Mex., 4th s., III, 357, 1857. S. Francisco Javier Batuco.—Bancroft, No. Mex. States, I, 246, 1886. Vatuco.—Och (1756), Nachrichten, I, 72, 1809.

**Batuco.** A former pueblo of the Opata on the Rio Oposura, a w. tributary of the Yaqui, 8 leagues E. of San José Matape, in Sonora, Mexico. It was apparently the Batuco that was visited by Coronado's army in 1540–42, and was the seat of the Jesuit mission of Santa María founded in 1629. Population 428 in 1678, 212 in 1730.

Asuncion Batuco.—Bancroft, No. Mex. States, I, 246, 1884. Batuco.—Castañeda (1596) in 14th Rep. B. A. E., 537, 1896. Santa María Batuco.—Zapata (1678) in Doc. Hist. Mex., 4th s., III, 356, 1857. Sta María Tepuspe.—Doc. of 1730 cited by Bancroft, op. cit., 513 (same?).

**Batza.** A Koyukukhotana village on Batza r., Alaska, long. 154°.

Batzakákat.—Allen, Rep. on Alaska, 123, 1877.

**Batzulnetas.** An Ahtena village near upper Copper r., where the trail starts for Tanana r., Alaska; lat. 62° 58′, long. 145° 22′ (post route map, 1903). Pop. 31 men, 10 women, and 15 children in 1885.
Batzulneta's village.—Allen, Rep. on Alaska, 121, 1887.

**Bauka.** A former Maidu village on the right bank of Feather r., near Gridley, Butte co., Cal. (R. B. D.)
Bogas.—Ind. Aff. Rep., 124, 1850. **Bóka.**—Powers in Cont. N. A. Ethnol., III, 282, 1877. **Bookû.**—Curtin, MS. vocab., B. A. E. 1885.

**Bawiranachiki** ('red water place'). A Tarahumare rancheria in Chihuahua, Mexico.—Lumholtz, inf'n, 1894.

**Bayberry wax.** A product of the bayberry, or wax myrtle (*Myrica cerifera*), the method of extracting which was learned from the Indians by the New England colonists whose descendants probably still use it. It was esteemed for the manufacture of candles and tallow on account of its fragrance. See Rasles in Coll. Mass. Hist. Soc., 2d ser., VIII, 252, 1819; Alice Morse Earle, Customs and Fashions of Old New England, 126, 1893. (A. F. C.)

**Bay du Noc.** A Chippewa (?) band mentioned in the Detroit treaty of 1855 (U. S. Ind. Treaties, 614, 1873). They probably lived on Noquet bay of L. Michigan, in upper Michigan.

**Bayogoula** (Choctaw: *Báyuk-ókla* 'bayou people'). A Muskhogean tribe which in 1700 lived with the Mugulasha in a village on the w. bank of the Mississippi, about 64 leagues above its mouth and 30 leagues below the Huma town. Lemoyne d'Iberville (Margry, Déc., IV, 170–172, 1880) gives a brief description of their village, which he says contained 2 temples and 107 cabins; that a fire was kept constantly burning in the temples, and near the door were kept many figures of animals, as the bear, wolf, birds, and in particular the *choucoüacha*, or opossum, which appeared to be a chief deity or image to which offerings were made. At this time they numbered 200 to 250 men, probably including the Mugulasha. Not long after the Bayogoula almost exterminated the Mugulasha as the result of a dispute between the chiefs of the two tribes, but the former soon fell victims to a similar act of treachery, since having received the Tonica into their village in 1706, they were surprised and almost all massacred by their perfidious guests (La Harpe, Jour. Hist. La., 98, 1831). Smallpox destroyed most of the remainder, so that by 1721 not a family was known to exist. (A. S. G. C. T.)
Babayoulas.—Baudry des Lozières, Voy., 241, 1802. **Baiagoulas.**—de Sauvole (1700) in French, Hist. Coll. La., III, 224–240, 1851. **Baiougoula.**—Gravier (1701) in Shea, Early Voyages, 150, 159, 1861. **Bayagola.**—Coxe, Carolana, map, 1741. **Bayagoubas.**—Jefferys, French Dom. Am., I, 147, 1761. **Bayagoulas.**—d'Iberville in French, Hist. Coll. La.,

II, 67, 1875. **Baya-Ogoulas.**—Pénicaut (1703), ibid., n. s., I, 85, note, 1869. **Bayogola.**—Coxe, Carolana, 7, 1741. **Bayogoulas.**—d'Iberville in Margry, Déc., IV, 169, 1880. **Bayonne Ogoulas.**—Jefferys, French, Dom. Am., I, 164, 1761. **Bayouc Agoulas.**—McKenney and Hall, Ind. Tribes, III, 80, 1854. **Bayouc Ogoulas.**—Le Page du Pratz., La., I, 271, 1774. **Bayuglas.**—N. Y. Doc. Col. Hist., VII, 641, 1856.

**Bayou.** A sluggish stream forming the inlet or outlet of a lake or bay, or connecting two bodies of water or a branch of a river flowing through a delta. The generally accepted etymology from the French *boyau* 'gut', is wrong (Chamberlain in Nation, LIX, 381, 1894). According to Gatschet (Creek Migr., Leg., I, 113, 1884) the Choctaw word for a smaller river, or a river forming part of a delta, is *báyuk*, and the word comes into English through the French, from this or a closely related Muskhogean dialect. The same word appears in another form in the *bogue* of such Louisiana and Mississippi place-names as Boguechito, Boguefalala, Boguelusa, representing in a French form the contracted *bok*, from *báyuk*. (A. F. C.)

**Bayou Chicot** (Creole French: *chicot*, 'snag,' 'tree-stump'). A former Choctaw village s. of Cheneyville, St Landry parish, La.
Bayacchito.—d'Iberville (1699) in Margry, Déc., IV, 155, 1880. **Bayou Chico.**—Claiborne (1808) in Am. State Pap., Ind. Aff., I, 755, 1832.

**Bayu.** A former Maidu village at Sandy gulch, Butte co., Cal. It was located by Powers on Feather r., and there may possibly have been a second village of the same name at that place. (R. B. D.)
Bai'-yu.—Powers in Cont. N. A. Ethnol., III, 282, 1877. **Bayu.**—Powell in 7th Rep. B. A. E., 100, 1891. **Biyous.**—Powers in Overland Mo., XII, 420, 1874.

**Bazhi.** An Ikogmiut village on the Yukon at the upper mouth of Innoko r., Alaska.
Bazhigagat.—Tikhmenief (1861) quoted by Baker, Geog. Dict. Alaska, 1901.

**Beadwork.** Attractive and precious objects, perforated usually through the middle and strung for various purposes, constitute a class of ornaments universally esteemed, which the Indians of North America did not fail to develop. Akin to beads, and scarcely separable from them, were objects from the same materials called pendants. They were perforated near the end or edge and hung on the person or on garments. All were made from mineral, vegetal, or animal substances, and after the discovery the introduction of beads of glass and porcelain, as well as that of metal tools for making the old varieties, greatly multiplied their employment. Mineral substances showing pretty colored or brilliant surfaces, from which beads were made, were copper, hematite, all kinds of quartz, serpentine, magnetite, slate, soapstone, turquoise, encrinite sections, pottery, and, in later times, silver and other metals, porcelain, and glass. They were of many sizes and shapes. Among vegetal substances seeds and, especially along the southern tier of states from Florida to California, nuts were widely used for beads, and here and there stems and roots of pretty or scented plants were cut into sections for the same purpose. But far the largest share of beads were made from animal materials—shell, bone, horn, teeth, claws, and ivory. Beads of marine or fresh-water shells were made by grinding off the apex, as in the case of dentalium, or the unchanged shells of bivalves were merely perforated near the hinge. Pearls were bored through the middle, and shells were cut into disks, cylinders, spheres, spindles, etc. In places the columellæ of large conchs were removed and pierced through the long diameter for stringing. Bone beads were usually cylinders produced by cutting sections of various lengths from the thigh or other parts of

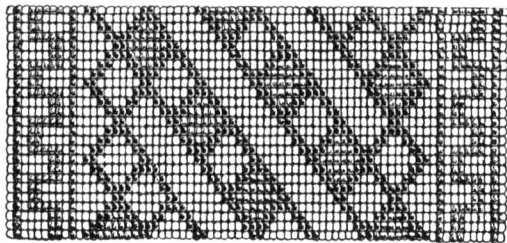

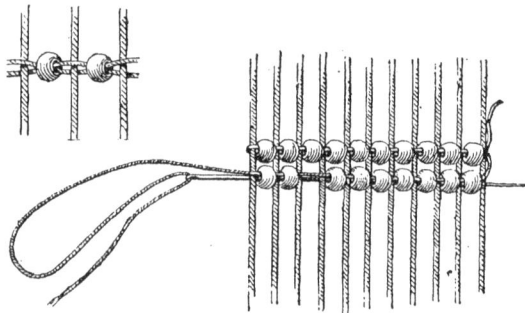

MENOMINEE BEADWORK.  (HOFFMAN)

vertebrate skeletons. When the wall of the bone was thick the ends were ground to give a spherical form. The milk teeth of the elk, the canine teeth of the bear, and the incisors of rodents were highly valued, and in later times the incisors of the horse were worn. The beaks of the puffin, the talons of rapacious birds, and bears' claws were wrought into ceremonial dress and paraphernalia. A great deal of taste and manual skill were developed in selecting the materials, and in cutting, grinding, and rolling them into shape and uniform size, as well as in polishing and perforating substances, some of them very hard, as jasper. Many of the cylinders are several inches long. The tribes of N. w. California wrap dentalia with snake skin glued on in strips, while the Pomo and their neighbors make large cylinders of a baked mineral (Kroeber).

The general uses to which beads were put are legion. They were tied in the hair, worn singly or in strings from the ears, on the neck, arms, wrist, waist, and lower limbs, or were attached to bark and wooden vessels, matting, basketry, and other textiles. They were woven into fabrics or wrought into network, their varied and bright colors not only enhancing beauty but lending themselves to heraldry. Glass beads thus woven produce effects like those of cathedral glass. Again, they were embroidered on every part of ceremonial costume, sometimes entirely covering headdress, coat, regalia, leggings, or moccasins, and on all sorts of receptacles. The old-time technic and designs of quillwork are closely imitated. They were largely employed as gifts and as money, also as tokens and in records of hunts or of important events, such as treaties. They were conspicuous accessories in the councils of war and peace, in the conventional expression of tribal symbolism, and in traditional story-telling, and were offered in worship. They were regarded as insignia of functions, and were buried, often in vast quantities, with the dead.

In each of the ethnic areas of North America nature provided tractable and attractive material to the bead-maker. In the Arctic region it was walrus ivory and the glossy teeth of mammals. They served not only for personal adornment, but were hung to all sorts of skin receptacles and inlaid upon the surfaces of those made of wood and soft stone. The Danes brought glass to the eastern Eskimo, the whalers to the central, and the Russians to the western tribes. In the St Lawrence-Atlantic area whole shells were strung, and cylinders, disks, and spindles were cut from the valves of the clam ( *Venus mercenaria* ). In Virginia a cheap kind, called roanoke, were made from oyster shells. In the N. small white and purple cylinders, called wampum, served for ornament and were used in elaborate treaty belts and as a money standard, also flat disks an inch or more in width being bored through their long diameters. The Cherokee name for beads and money is the same. Subsequently imitated by the colonists, these beads received a fixed value. The mound-builders and other tribes of the Mississippi valley and the Gulf states used pearls and beads of shell, seeds, and rolled copper. Canine teeth of the elk were most highly esteemed, recently being worth 50 cents to $1 each. They were carefully saved, and a garment covered with them was valued at as much as $600 or $800. The modern tribes also used the teeth of rodents, the claws of bears and carnivores, and the dewclaws of ruminants. Nuts and berries were universally strung and worn, and the Mandan and other Missouri r. tribes pounded and melted glass and molded it into beads. After the colonization cradles and articles of skin were profusely covered with beadwork replete with symbolism. The Yukon-Mackenzie tribes were most skilful in quillwork, but later decked their garments and other useful things with glass beads. All along the Pacific slope dentalium, abalone, and clam shells furnish the most valuable materials. The length of the wrought bead represented a certain amount of work and established the money value. The price of dentalium shells increased rapidly after a certain length was exceeded. These beads were decorated with grass, skin, and feathers to enhance their worth. The California coast tribes and the ancient peoples of Santa Barbara ids. were rich in the little flat-shell disks as well as the stone drill, and they knew how to reduce them to uniform diameter by rolling long strings of them between slabs or through grooves in sandstone. The tribes of the N. part of the interior basin were not well supplied with bead material, but early made the acquaintance of the trader. A series of Ute costumes made before the advent of glass shows much pretty decoration in dewclaws, bits of goat and sheep horn, and perforated seeds. The Pueblo Indians string the yellow capsules of Solanum, sections of woody stems of plants, seashells, turquoise and other varieties of bright-colored stones, of which they have great store. The Hyde Expedition found more than 30,000 turquoise beads in a single room at Pueblo Bonito, N. Mex. The Huichol, with colored beads of glass, using wax as an adhesive, make pretty mosaic figures on gourds, carved images of wood, etc.

Consult Beauchamp in Bull. N. Y. State Mus., no. 73, 1903; Catlin, N. A. Inds., 1841; Hoffman in 14th Rep. B. A. E., 1896; Mason in Rep. Nat. Mus. 1899, 485–510, 1901; Matthews, Ethnog. and Philol. Hidatsa, 18, 1877; Nelson in 18th Rep. B. A. E., 1899; Holmes, Annals, I, 271, 1829; Sumner, Hist. Am. Currency, 4, 8, 1874; Powers in Cont. N. A. Ethnol., III, 1877; Lumholtz, Unknown Mexico, 1902; Pepper in Am. Anthrop., VII, no. 2, 1905. See *Adornment, Art, Arts and Industries, Basketry, Copper, Quillwork, Shellwork, Turquoise, Wampum*, and articles on the various raw materials mentioned above as having been used for beads. (O. T. M.)

**Bear River.** A tribe mentioned by Lawson (N. C., 383, 1860) as living in North Carolina in 1701, and having then a single village, Raudauquaquank, with 50 warriors. According to Hawks (Hist. N. C., 1858–59) they lived in Craven co., probably on a branch of the Neuse.

**Beaubassin.** A (Micmac?) mission established by the French in the 17th century.—Shea, Discov. Miss. Val., 86, 1852.

**Beauport.** A village established in 1650 in Quebec co., Canada, by fugitive Huron, who removed in the next year to the island of Orleans.—Shea, Cath. Miss., 196, 1855.

**Beaver.** A former Aleut village on Unalaska, Aleutian ids.; pop. 41 in 1834. Bobrovo.—Sarichef (1792) quoted by Baker, Geog. Dict. Alaska, 1901 (= 'sea otter'). Bobrovskoe.—Veniaminoff, Zapiski, II, 202, 1840. Bobrovskoi.—Elliott, Cond. Aff. Alaska, 225, 1875. Uguiug.—Baker, op. cit. (native name).

**Beaver Island Indians.** A Chippewa band formerly residing on the Beaver ids. of Michigan, at the outlet of L. Michigan.—Washington treaty (1836) in U. S. Ind. Treaties, 607, 1873.

**Beaversville.** A Delaware settlement in 1856 near the junction of Boggy cr. and Canadian r. in Indian Territory.—Whipple, Pac. R. R. Rep., III, 18, 1856.

**Beavertown.** A mixed village, identical with Sawcunk (q. v.), situated in 1766 on the E. side of the extreme E. head branch of Hocking r., at or near the present Beavertown, in Morgan co., Ohio. Beaver, or King Beaver, was at that time chief of the Unami tribe of Delawares. See *Tamaque*. Beaver Town.—Hutchins map in Bouquet, Exped., 1766. King Beaver's Town.—Bouquet, ibid., 67.

**Bécancour.** A village on St Lawrence r., in Quebec province, settled by Abnaki who removed from Maine in 1713 when that state was ceded to England by the treaty of Utrecht. In 1736 they were estimated at about 300; in 1858 they numbered 172, with French admixture, and in 1884 they were reduced to 39, but in 1902 numbered 51. They are members of the Roman Catholic church.
(J. M.)
Băcāndēē.—King, Jour. to Arctic Ocean, I, 11, 1836 (incorrectly given as an Iroquois village at Lake of Two Mountains, but distinct from "Kănĕsătārkēē"). Beauancourt.—Vaudreuil (1710) in N. Y. Doc. Col. Hist., IX, 849, 1855. Beçancour.—Vaudreuil (1724) in Maine Hist. Soc. Coll., VI, 240, 1859. Becancourians.—Rasles (1724) trans. in Mass. Hist. Soc. Coll., 2d s., VIII, 246, 1819. Bécancourt.—Vaudreuil (1721) in N. Y. Doc. Col. Hist., IX, 904, 1855. Becquancourt.—La Tour, map, 1784. Becquencourt.—Ibid., 1782. Becuncourt.—Clinton (1745) in N. Y. Doc. Col. Hist., VI, 281, 1855. Bekancourt.—DeLancey (1754) in Ruttenber, Tribes Hudson R., 216, 1872. Besançon.—Chauvignerie (1736) quoted by Schoolcraft, Ind. Tribes, III, 553, 1853.

**Bece.** An abandoned village of the Koskimo, 6 m. E. of Koprino harbor, in N. Quatsino sd., Vancouver id. Bēce.—Dawson in Trans. Roy. Soc. Can., 7, 1888.

**Beds.** See *Furniture*.

**Beech Creek.** A former Seminole town on Beech cr., Fla., settled by Chiaha Indians from lower Chattahoochee r., Ga.; exact location unknown.—Bell in Morse, Rep. to Sec. War, 308, 1822.

**Bejuituuy** ('village of the rainbow'). A former pueblo of the Tigua near the s.

limit of their habitat, on the Rio Grande, at the present Los Lunas, N. Mex.

Be-jui Tu-uy.—Bandelier in Arch. Inst. Papers, III, 130, 1890. Be-juij Tu-aij.—Bandelier in Jour. Am. Eth. and Arch., III, 61, 1892. Be-Jui Tu-ay.—Bandelier in Arch. Inst. Papers, IV, 218, 1892. Be-juÿ Tu-aÿ.—Bandelier in Jour. Am. Eth. and Arch., op. cit. San Clemente.—Bandelier in Arch. Inst. Papers, IV, 219, 1892. Village of the Rainbow.—Bandelier in Jour. Am. Eth. and Arch., op. cit.

**Beku** (*Be'-ku*). Given by Powers (Cont. N. A. Ethnol., III, 393, 1877) as the name of a tribe related to the Paiute, but identified by Kroeber (inf'n, 1903) as a form of Békiu, the Yokuts name of a locality on Poso cr., Cal., within the territory of the Paleuyami Yokuts.

**Beldom.** A Missisauga village in Ontario in 1855.—Jones, Ojebway Inds., 229, 1861.

**Belen.** A village on the w. bank of the Rio Grande in Valencia co., N. Mex., and the seat of the Spanish mission of Nuestra Señora, with 107 inhabitants in 1805 and 133 in 1809. Like Abiquiu and Tome it was apparently established as a refuge for Genizaros, or redeemed captive Indians, of whom a few were at Belen in 1766. It is now a "Mexican" settlement. The ruins of the old Spanish church may still be traced. (F. W. H.)

Belem.—Alencaster (1805) quoted by Prince, N. Mex., 231, 1883. Belen.—Moïse in Kan. Cy. Rev., 481, Dec. 1881. Neustra Senora de Belem.—Alencaster (1805) quoted by Meline, Two Thousand Miles, 212, 1867 (misprint). N. S. de Belem.—Bancroft, Nat. Races, I, 599, 1882 (after Meline). N. S. de Belen.—Alencaster (1805) quoted by Prince, N. Mex., 37, 1883. Nuestra Señora de la Belen.—Ward in Ind. Aff. Rep. for 1867, 213, 1868. Belue.—Ibid., 210 (misprint).

**Belen.** A settlement of the Yaqui, including some members of the Seri and Guayma tribes, on the N. bank of Yaqui r., about 20 m. above its mouth, in s. Sonora, Mexico. It was the seat of an important mission founded about 1678, and in 1849 its population was estimated at 3,000.

Belem.—Velasco in Bol. Soc. Mex. Geog. Estad., VIII, 226, 1860. Belen.—Velasco, Noticias de Sonora, 84, 1850. Nuestra Señora de Belem.—Orozco y Berra, Geog., 355, 1864. Nuestra Señora de Belen.—Zapata (1678) in Doc. Hist. Mex., 4th s., III, 379, 1857.

**Belkofski** (Russian: *Bielkovskoie*, 'squirrel village'). An Aleut village near the end of Alaska pen.; pop. 102 in 1833, 268 in 1880, 185 in 1890, 147 in 1900.

Bailkovskoe.—Veniaminof, Zapiski, II, 203, 1840. Belkovsky.—Schwatka, Mil. Recon. Alaska, 116, 1885. Bellkovskoi.—Elliott, Cond. Aff., Alaska, 225, 1875. Bjelkowskoje.—Holmberg, Ethnol. Skizz., map, 142, 1855.

**Bellabella** (an Indian corruption of *Milbank* taken back into English). The popular name of an important Kwakiutl tribe living on Milbank sd., Brit. Col. Their septs or subtribes are Kokaitk, Oetlitk, and Oealitk. The following clans are given: Wikoktenok (Eagle), Koetenok (Raven), Halhaiktenok (Killerwhale). Pop. 330 in 1901.

The language spoken by this tribe and shared also by the Kitamat, Kitlope, China Hat, and Wikeno Indians is a peculiar dialect of Kwakiutl, called Heiltsuk from the native name of the Bella-

BELLABELLA MAN. (AM. MUS. NAT. HIST.)

bella. These tribes resemble each other furthermore in having a system of clans with descent through the mother—derived probably from their northern neigh-

BELLABELLA WOMAN. (AM. MUS. NAT HIST.)

bors—while the Bellacoola and Kwakiutl to the s. have paternal descent. Anciently the Bellabella were very warlike, a character largely attributable to the fact that they were flanked on one side by the Tsimshian of Kittizoo and on the other by the Bellacoola, while war parties of Haida from the Queen Charlotte ids. were constantly raiding their coasts. For this reason, perhaps, the peculiar secret societies of the N. W. coast, the most important of which evidently had their origin in war customs, first arose among them. When voyagers first began frequenting the N. Pacific coast, Milbank id., which offers one of the few good openings into the inner ship channel to Alaska, was often visited, and its inhabitants were therefore among the first to be modified by European contact. Together with the other Heiltsuk tribes they have now been Christianized by Protestant missionaries, and most of their ancient culture and ritual have been abandoned. (J. R. S.)

Belbellahs.—Dunn, Oregon Ter., 183, 1845. Bella-Bella.—Can. Ind. Aff., 361, 1897. Elk·la'sumH.—Boas in 5th Rep. N. W. Tribes Can., 9, 1889 (Bellacoola name). Haeeltruk,—Scouler in Jour. Geog. Soc. Lond., I, 224, 1841. Haeeltsuk.—Scouler in Jour. Ethnol. Soc. Lond., I, 233, 1848. Haeeltz.—Latham, ibid., 164. Haeeltzuk.—Scouler in Jour. Geog. Soc. Lond., I, 223, 1841. Haeetsuk.—Latham in Trans. Philol. Soc. Lond., 64, 1856. Haeltzuk.—Latham in Jour. Ethnol. Soc. Lond., I, 155, 1848. Hailtsa.—Hale in U. S. Expl. Expd., VI, 221, 1846. Hailtzuk.—Tolmie and Dawson, Vocabs. Brit. Col., 117B, 1884. Ha-iltzukh.—Gibbs in Cont. N. A. Ethnol., I, 145, 1877. Hē′iltsuk.—Boas in Petermanns Mitt., pt. 5, 130, 1887. Hē′iltsuq.—Boas in Rep. Nat. Mus. for 1895, 328 (own name). Hiletsuck.—Can. Ind. Aff., 252, 1891. Hiletsuk.—Ibid., 191, 1883. Iletsuck.—Powell, ibid., 122, 1880. Ilet Suck.—Ibid., 315. Millbank Indians.—Dunn, Hist. Oreg., 271, 1844. Millbank Sound Indians.—Ibid., 358. Witsta.—Tolmie and Dawson, op. cit. (Chimmesyan name). Wutsta′.—Boas in 5th Rep. N. W. Tribes Can., 9, 1889.

**Bellacoola** (*Bi′lxula*). A coast Salish tribe, or rather aggregation of tribes, on N. and S. Bentinck arm, Dean inlet, and Bellacoola r., Brit. Col. This name is that given them by the Kwakiutl, there being no native designation for the entire people. They form the northernmost division of the Salishan stock, from the remaining tribes of which they are separated by the Tsilkotin and the Kwakiutl. In the Canadian reports on Indian affairs the name is restricted by the separation of the Tallion (see *Talio*) and the Kinisquit (people of Dean inlet), the whole being called the Tallion nation. The population in 1902 was 311. The chief divisions mentioned are the Kinisquit, Noothlakimish, and Nuhalk. The gentes of the Bellacoola without reference to the tribal divisions are: Hamtsit, Ialostimot, Koökotlane, Smoen, Spatsatlt, Tlakaumoot, Tumkoaakyas. The following are mentioned as gentes of the Nuhalk division: Keltakkaua, Potlas, Siatlhelaak, Spukpukolemk, and Tokoaïs. The Bellacoola villages (chiefly after Boas) are: Aseik, Asenane, Atlklaktl, Koapk, Koatlna, Komkutis, Noutchaoff, Nuiku, Nukaakmats, Nukits, Nusatsem, Nuskek, Nus-

kelst, Nutltleik, Osmakmiketlp, Peisela, Sakta, Satsk, Selkuta, Senktl, Setlia, Slaaktl, Snutele, Snutlelatl, Sotstl, Stskeitl, Stuik, Talio, Tkeiktskune, Tskoakkane, Tsomootl. (J. R. S.)

Belhoola.—Gibbs in Cont. N. A. Ethnol., I, 267, 1877. Bellacoola.—Can. Ind. Aff., 315, 1880. Bellaghchoolas.—Dunn, Hist. Oregon, 267, 1844. Bellahoola.—Schoolcraft, Ind. Tribes, V, 488, 1855. Bell-houla.—Mayne, Brit. Col., 146, 1862. Bellichoola.—Scouler in Jour. Ethnol. Soc. Lond., I, 234, 1848. Bilhoola.—Tolmie and Dawson, Vocabs. Brit. Col., 122B, 1884. Billechoola.—Scouler in Jour. Roy. Geog. Soc., I, 224, 1841. Billikūla.—Gibbs quoted by Dall in Cont. N. A. Ethnol., I, 241, 1877. Bilqula.—7th Rep. N. W. Tribes of Can., 2, 1891. Bi′lxula.—Boas in Rep. Nat. Mus. for 1895, 320. Ilghi′mī.—Tolmie and Dawson, Vocabs. Brit. Col., 122B, 1884. Tallion Nation.—Can. Ind. Aff., 417, 1898.

**Bells.** Metal bells were in common use in middle America in pre-Columbian times, but they are rarely found N. of the Rio Grande, either in possession of the tribes or on ancient sites; but bells were certainly known to the Pueblos and possibly to the mound-builders before the arrival of the whites. The rattle made of shells of various kinds or modeled in clay passed naturally into the bell as soon as metal or other particularly resonant materials were available for their manufacture. Occasionally copper bells with stone tinklers are found on ancient sites in New Mexico and Arizona, where examples in baked clay are also found; these are usually quite small and are of the hawk-bell or sleigh-bell type, and doubtless served as pendant ornaments. Rare examples of copper bells have been collected in the southern states, but it is not certain that they were of local origin, since many specimens must have reached Florida from Mexico and Central America in early Columbian times; and it is well known that bells of copper or bronze were employed in trade with the tribes by the English colonists, numerous examples of which have been obtained from mounds and burial places.

Consult Fewkes (1) in 17th Rep. B. A. E., 1898, (2) in 22d Rep. B. A. E., 1903; Hough in Rep. Nat. Mus. 1901, 1903; Moore in Jour. Acad. Nat. Sci. Phila., 1894–1905; Thomas in 12th Rep. B. A. E., 1894. See *Copper*. (W. H. H.)

**Beothukan Family** (from the tribal or group name *Béothuk*, which probably signifies 'man,' or 'human being,' but was employed by Europeans to mean 'Indian,' or 'Red Indian'; in the latter case because the Beothuk colored themselves and tinted their utensils and arms with red ocher). So far as known only a single tribe, called Beothuk, which inhabited the island of Newfoundland when first discovered, constituted this family, although

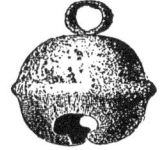

existing vocabularies indicate marked dialectic differences. At first the Beothuk were classified either as Eskimauan or as Algonquian, but now, largely through the researches of Gatschet, it is deemed best to regard them as constituting a distinct linguistic stock. It is probable that in 1497 Beothukan people were met by Sebastian Cabot when he discovered Newfoundland, as he states that he met people "painted with red ocher," which is a marked characteristic of the Beothuk of later observers. Whitbourne (Chappell, Voy. to Newfoundland, 1818), who visited Newfoundland in 1622, stated that the dwelling places of these Indians were in the N. and w. parts of the island, adding that "in war they use bows and arrows, spears, darts, clubs, and slings." The extinction of the Beothuk was due chiefly to the bitter hostility of the French and to Micmac invasion from Nova Scotia at the beginning of the 18th century, the Micmac settling in w. Newfoundland as hunters and fishermen. For a time these dwelt in amity with the Beothuk, but in 1770, quarrels having arisen, a destructive battle was fought between the two peoples at the N. end of Grand Pond. The Beothuk, however, lived on friendly terms with the Naskapi, or Labrador Montagnais, and the two peoples visited and traded with each other. Exasperated by the petty depredations of these tribes, the French, in the middle of the 18th century, offered a reward for every head of a Beothuk Indian. To gain this reward and to obtain the valuable furs they possessed, the more numerous Micmac hunted and gradually exterminated them as an independent people. The English treated the Beothuk with much less rigor; indeed, in 1810 Sir Thomas Duckworth issued a proclamation for their protection. The banks of the River of Exploits and its tributuaries appear to have been their last inhabited territory.

De Laet (Novus Orbis, 34, 1633) describes these Newfoundland Indians as follows: "The height of the body is medium, the hair black, the face broad, the nose flat, and the eyes large; all the males are beardless, and both sexes tint not only their skin but also their garments with a kind of red color. And they dwell in certain conical lodges and low huts of sticks set in a circle and joined together in the roof. Being nomadic, they frequently change their habitations. They had a kind of cake made with eggs and baked in the sun, and a sort of pudding, stuffed in gut, and composed of seal's fat, livers, eggs, and other ingredients." He describes also their peculiar crescent-shaped birch-bark canoes, which had sharp keels, requiring much ballast to keep them from overturning; these were not more than 20 feet in length and they

could bear at most 5 persons. Remains of their lodges, 30 to 40 feet in circumference and constructed by forming a slender frame of poles overspread with birch bark, are still traceable. They had both summer and winter dwellings, the latter often accommodating about 20 people each. Jukes (Excursions, 1842) describes their deer fences or deer stockades of trees, which often extended for 30 miles along a river. They employed pits or caches for storing food, and used the steam bath in huts covered with skins and heated with hot stones. Some of the characteristics in which the Beothuk differed from most other Indians were a marked lightness of skin color, the use of trenches in their lodges for sleeping berths, the peculiar form of their canoes, the non-domestication of the dog, and the dearth of evidence of pottery making. Bonnycastle (Newfoundland in 1842) states that the Beothuk used the inner bark of *Pinus balsamifera* as food, while Lloyd (Jour. Anthrop. Inst., IV, 1875) mentions the fact that they obtained fire by igniting the down of the bluejay from sparks produced by striking together two pieces of iron pyrites. Peyton, cited by Lloyd, declares that the sun was the chief object of their worship. Carmack's expedition, conducted in behalf of the Beothic Society for the Civilization of the Native Savages, in 1827, failed to find a single individual of this once prominent tribe, although the island was crossed centrally in the search. As they were on good terms with the Naskapi of Labrador, they perhaps crossed the strait of Belle Isle and became incorporated with them. (J. N. B. H.  A. S. G.)

**Beathook.**—Leigh quoted by Lloyd in Jour. Anthrop. Inst., IV, 38, 1875. **Béhathook.**—Gatschet in Proc. Am. Philos. Soc., 410, 1885 (quoting older form). **Beothics.**—Lloyd in Jour. Anthrop. Inst., IV, 33, 1875. **Beothik.**—Gatschet, op. cit. (quoting old form). **Beoths.**—Vetromile, Abnakis, 47, 1866. **Beothucs.**—Lloyd in Jour. Anthrop. Inst., IV, 21, 1875. **Beothues.**—Jour. Anthrop. Inst., IV, pl. facing p. 26, 1875. **Beothugs.**—Ibid., v, pl. facing p. 223, 1876. **Beothuk.**—Gatschet in Proc. Am. Philos. Soc., 408, 1885. **Bethuck.**—Latham in Trans. Philol. Soc. Lond., 58, 1856. **Bœothick.**—Mac Dougall in Trans. Canad. Inst., II, 98, 1890–91. **Boeothuk.**—Gatschet in Proc. Am. Philos. Soc., 410, 1885 (quoting older form). **Good-night Indians.**—Lloyd, following blunder of Latham, in Jour. Anthrop. Inst., v, 229, 1876. **Macquaejeet.**—Gatschet in Proc. Am. Philos. Soc., 410, Oct., 1885 (Micmac name: 'red man,' evidently a transl. of the European 'Red Indian'). **Red Indians of Newfoundland.**—Cartwright (1768) quoted by Lloyd in Jour. Anthrop. Inst., IV, 22, 1875. **Shawatharott.**—King quoted by Gatschet in Proc. Am. Philos. Soc., 410, 1885 (= 'Red Indian man'). **Shawdtharut.**—Ibid. **Ulnōbah.**—Latham quoted by Gatschet, ibid., 411 (Abnaki name). **Ulnŏ mequāegit.**—Ibid. (said to be the Micmac name, sig. 'red man,' but evidently a trader's or fisherman's rendering of the European 'Red Indians').

**Beowawa.** Incorrectly given as the name of a Hopi village; it seems to be the name of a man.
**Beowawa.**—Beadle, Western Wilds, 227, 1878. **Beowawe.**—Beadle, Undeveloped West, 576, 1873.

**Berlin tablet.** See *Notched plates.*

**Bersiamite.** One of the small Algonquian tribes composing the eastern group of the Montagnais, inhabiting the banks of Bersimis r., which enters St Lawrence r. near the gulf. These Indians became known to the French at an early date, and being of a peaceable and tractable disposition, were soon brought under the influence of the missionaries. They were accustomed to assemble once a year with cognate tribes at Tadoussac for the purpose of trade, but these have melted away under the influence of civilization. A trading post called Bersimis, at the mouth of Bersimis r., had in 1902 some 465 Indians attached to it, but whether any of them were Bersiamite is not stated.     (J. M.)

**Baisimetes.**—McKenney and Hall, Ind. Tribes, III, 79, 1854. **Bersamis.**—Stearns, Labrador, 263, 1884. **Bersiamites.**—Jes. Rel. for 1640, 34, 1858. **Bersiamits.**—Hind, Labrador Penin., I, 125, 1863. **Bersiamitts.**—McKenney and Hall, Ind. Tribes, III, 81, 1854. **Bertiamistes.**—Iroquois treaty (1665) in N. Y. Doc. Col. Hist., III, 122, 1853. **Bertiamites.**—Memoir of 1706, ibid., IX, 786, 1855. **Bethsiamits.**—Can. Ind. Aff. Rep., 38, 1880. **Betsiamites.**—Le Clercq quoted by Champlain (1632), Œuvres, IV, 105, 1870. **Betsiamits.**—Can. Ind. Aff. Rep. 1884, pt 1, 185, 1885. **Bussenmeus.**—McKenney and Hall, Ind. Tribes, III, 81, 1854. **Notre Dame de Betsiamits.**—Boucher in Can. Ind. Aff. Rep. for 1884, pt. 1, 36, 1885 (mission name). **Oubestamiouek.**—Jes. Rel. for 1643, 38, 1858. **Oumamiois.**—Albanel (1670) quoted by Hind, Labrador Penin., I, 126, 1863. **Oumamioucks.**—McKenney and Hall, Ind. Tribes, III, 79, 1854. **Oumamiwek.**—Hind, Labrador Penin., I, 224, 1863.

**Besheu** (*bĭjĭᵘ* 'lynx'). A gens of the Chippewa.

**Be-sheu.**—Warren in Minn. Hist. Soc. Coll., V, 44, 1885. **Pe-zhew.**—Tanner, Narrative, 315, 1830 (trans. 'wild cat'). **Pishiu.**—Gatschet, Ojibwa MS., B. A. E., 1882.

**Beshow.** The black candle-fish (*Anoplopoma fimbria*) of the Puget sd. region; from *bishowᵏ*, in the Makah dialect of the Wakashan stock.     (A. F. C.)

**Bethel.** An Eskimo mission, founded in 1886 by Moravian brethren from Pennsylvania, on Kuskokwim r., close to Mumtrelek, Alaska. Pop. 20 in 1890.

**Bethlehem.** A Moravian settlement established in 1740 at the present Bethlehem, Northampton co., Pa. Although a white settlement, the Moravians drew toward it many of the Indians, and in 1746 the Mahican converts from Shecomeco resided there for a short time before settling at Friedenshuetten.     (J. M.)

**Betonukeengainubejig** (*Pi'tona'kingkaĭnŭpĭchĭg*, 'they who live in the neighborhood of [L. Superior on the s.].'—W. J.). An important division of the Chippewa living in N. Wisconsin, between L. Superior and Mississippi r. The Munominikasheenhug, Wahsuahgunewininewug, and Lac Court Oreilles Chippewa are incorporated with them. Their principal villages were at Desert lake (Vieux Desert), Flambeau lake, Pelican lake, Lac Court Oreilles, Lac Chetec, Pukwaawun, and Mononimikau lake.     (J. M.)

**Be-ton-auk-an-ub-yig.**—Ramsey in Ind. Aff. Rep., 85, 1850. **Be-ton-uk-eeng-ain-ub-e-jig.**—Warren in Minn. Hist. Soc. Coll., V, 38 1885. **Pi'tōna'kingkāinapitcig.**—W. Jones, inf'n, 1905 (correct form).

**Betty's Neck.** A place in Middleboro, Plymouth co., Mass., where 8 Indian families lived in 1793, and took its name from an Indian woman (Drake, Bk. Inds., bk. 3, 10, 1848). The people seem to have been Nemasket and subject to the Wampanoag.     (J. M.)

**Biara.** A subdivision or settlement of the Tehueco, formerly on the lower Rio Fuerte or the Fuerte-Mayo divide, N. W. Sinaloa, Mexico.—Orozco y Berra, Geog., 58, 1864.

**Biauswah** (*payaswá*, 'dried,' as when meat is hung over fire until smoked and dried; it may also refer to meat hung on a pole to dry in the sun.—W. J.). A Chippewa chief, also known as Byianswa, son of Biauswah, a leading man of the Loon gens which resided on the s. shore of L. Superior, 40 m. w. of La Pointe, N. W. Wis. He was taken prisoner by the Fox Indians when a boy, but was saved from torture and death by his father, who became a voluntary substitute. After the death of his father he moved with his people to Fond du Lac. Being made chief he led the warriors of various bands in an expedition against the Sioux of Sandy lake and succeeded in driving the latter from their village, and later the Sioux were forced to abandon their villages on Cass and Winnipeg lakes and their stronghold on Leech lake, whence they moved westward to the headwaters of Minnesota r. The Chippewa under Biauswah were those who settled in the country of the upper Mississippi about 1768 (Minn. Hist. Coll., V, 222, 1885). The date of his death is not recorded, but it probably occurred not long after the date named.     (C. T.)

**Bibiana.** A former rancheria, probably of the Papago, in N. W. Sonora, Mexico, between Busanic and Sonoita, near (or possibly identical with) Anamic. It was visited by Kino in 1702.

**Sta Bibiana.**—Kino (1706) quoted by Bancroft, No. Mex. States, I, 502, 1886.

**Bible translations.** The Bible has been printed in part or in whole in 32 Indian languages N. of Mexico. In 18 one or more portions have been printed; in 9 others the New Testament or more has appeared; and in 5 languages, namely, the Massachuset, Cree, Labrador Eskimo, Santee Dakota, and Tukkuthkutchin, the whole Bible is in print.

The Norwegian missionaries, Hans and Paul Egede, were the first to translate any part of the Bible into Greenland Eskimo, their version of the New Testament being printed in part in 1744, and as a whole in 1766. A revision of this translation, by Otto Fabricius, was twice printed before the close of the 18th century; and in 1822 the Moravian Brethren brought out a new translation, which ran through several editions. Nearly three-quarters of the Old Testament was printed in the same language between 1822 and 1836, when the work was discontinued. In Labrador Eskimo the earliest printed Bible text was the Harmony of the Gospels, which appeared in 1800. This was followed by the Gospel of St John in 1810, the complete New Testament in 1840, and all of the Old Testament between 1834 and 1867. In other Eskimo languages there were printed: In Labrador Eskimo some New Testament extracts in 1878 and the Four Gospels in 1897, translated by E. J. Peck; in the Aleutian Unalaska dialect, with adaptation also to the Atka dialect, John Veniaminoff's translation of St Matthew's Gospel in 1848; and in Kaniagmiut, Elias Tishnoff's translation of the same Gospel, also in 1848.

Four languages of the Athapascan family have been provided with Bible translations. The Gospels were translated by Robert McDonald and printed in the Tukkuthkutchin language of Mackenzie r. in 1874, and the whole Bible in 1898. In the Chipewyan Archdeacon Kirkby's translation of the Gospels appeared in 1878 and the whole New Testament in 1881; in the Etchareottine, Kirkby's translation of St John's Gospel in 1870, and Bishop Bompas's of the New Testament between 1883 and 1891; and in the Tsattine, A. C. Garrioch's version of St Mark's Gospel in 1886.

Translations have been made into 13 languages of the Algonquian family. In the Cree, William Mason's work comprises several editions of the Gospel of St John made between 1851 and 1857, the complete New Testament in 1859, and the whole Bible in 1861-62. Archdeacon Hunter's version of three of the Gospels in the same language appeared in 1853-55 (reprinted in 1876-77). Bishop Horden's Four Gospels in Cree was printed in 1859, and his complete New Testament in 1876. In the Abnaki, St Mark's Gospel, translated by Wzokhilain, was printed in 1844; in the Micmac, beginning with the printing of St Matthew's Gospel in 1853, Mr Rand continued at work until the whole New Testament was published in 1871-75, besides the books of Genesis, Exodus, and the Psalms; and in the Malecite, St John's Gospel, also translated by Rand, came out in 1870. The Massachuset language, which comes next in geographical order, was the first North American Indian language into which any Bible translation was made; John Eliot began his

Natick version in 1653 and finished it in 1661-63, with a revised edition in 1680-85. In 1709 Experience Mayhew published his translation, in the Wampanoag dialect of Martha's Vineyard, of the Psalms and St John's Gospel. In the Delaware, Dencke's translation of the Epistles of St John was printed in 1818, Zeisberger's Harmony of the Gospels in 1821, and Luckenbach's Scripture Narratives in 1838. In Chippewa, the earliest translations were those of the Gospels of St Matthew and St John, by Peter and John Jones, printed in 1829-31. There are three complete translations of the New Testament in this language: One by Edwin James in 1833, another by Henry Blatchford in 1844 (reprinted in 1856 and 1875), and a third by F. A. O'Meara in 1854 (reprinted in 1874). O'Meara also translated the Psalms (1856) and the Pentateuch (1861), and McDonald translated the Twelve Minor Prophets (1874). In the Shawnee language, St Matthew's Gospel, by Johnston Lykins, was printed in 1836 and a revision in 1842, and St John's Gospel, by Francis Barker, in 1846. In the Ottawa, Meeker's translation of St Matthew and St John appeared in 1841-44; in the Potawatomi, St Matthew and the Acts, by Lykins, in 1844; in the Siksika, St Matthew, by Tims, in 1890; in the Arapaho, St Luke, by Roberts, in 1903; and in the Cheyenne, the Gospels of St Luke and St John by Petter, who has published also some other portions of the Bible.

Three languages of the Iroquoian family possess parts of the Bible. In Mohawk, extracts from the Bible were printed as early as 1715; the Gospel of St Mark, by Brant, in 1787; and St John, by Norton, in 1805. Between 1827 and 1836 the rest of the New Testament was translated by H. A. Hill, W. Hess, and J. A. Wilkes, and the whole was printed in successive parts. A new version of the Gospels, by Chief Onasakenrat, was printed in 1880. The only part of the Old Testament in Mohawk is Isaiah, printed in 1839. In the Seneca language, St Luke, by Harris, was printed in 1829, and the Four Gospels, by Asher Wright, in 1874. In the Cherokee language St Matthew's Gospel was translated by S. A. Worcester and printed in 1829, the other Gospels and the Epistles following, until the complete New Testament was issued in 1860. Genesis and Exodus, also by Worcester, were printed in 1856 and 1853, respectively, besides some portions of the Psalms, Proverbs, and Isaiah.

The two languages of the Muskhogean family that come into our record are the Choctaw and the Creek. In Choctaw, three of the Gospels, translated by Alfred Wright, were printed as early as 1831, and the complete New Testament, by Wright and Byington, in 1848. The Pentateuch, the historical books of the Old Testament, and the Psalms, by Wright, Byington, and Edwards, came out between 1852 and 1886. In Creek, St John's Gospel, translated by Davis and Lykins, was printed in 1835; another version, by Buckner, in 1860; and the whole New Testament, by Mrs Robertson and others, between 1875 and 1887; and Genesis and the Psalms, by the same, in 1893–96.

Only two languages of the Siouan family, the Santee Dakota and the Mandan, are represented in scriptural translations. Portions of the Bible were translated into the former by Renville and printed as early as 1839; the whole New Testament, by Riggs and others, was published in 1865; the Old Testament, by Williamson and Riggs, was finished in 1877; and a revised edition of the complete Bible was issued in 1880. A small volume of hymns and scriptural selections, translated into Mandan by Rev. C. F. Hall, was published in 1905.

The Caddoan language is represented by a small volume of Bible translations and hymns in Arikara, by Rev. C. F. Hall (1900; 2d ed., enlarged, 1905).

In the Nez Percé language, of the Shahaptian family, St Matthew's Gospel, by Spalding, was twice printed (in 1845 and 1871); and St John, by Ainslie, appeared in 1876. In the Kwakiutl language, of the Wakashan family, A. J. Hall's translation of the Gospels of St Matthew and St John came out in 1882–84 and the Acts in 1897. In the Tsimshian language, of the Chimmesyan family, the Four Gospels, translated by William Duncan, were printed in 1885–89; and in the Niska language J. B. McCullagh began work on the Gospels in 1894. In the Haida language, of the Skittagetan family, translations of three of the Gospels and of the Acts, by Charles Harrison and J. H. Keen, were printed in 1891–97.

Consult the various bibliographies of Indian languages, by J. C. Pilling, published as bulletins by the Bureau of American Ethnology. See *Books in Indian languages, Dictionaries, Eliot Bible, Periodicals.*                    (W. E.)

**Bicam.** A Yaqui settlement on the s. bank of the lower Rio Yaqui, s. w. Sonora, Mexico, with an estimated population of 9,000 in 1849.

Bicam.—Velasco, Noticias de Sonora, 84, 1850. Bican.—Mühlenpfordt quoted by Bancroft, Nat. Races, I, 608, 1882. Santísima Trinidad Vicam.—Orozco y Berra, Geog., 355, 1864 (or Bicam).

**Bichechic.** A Tarahumare settlement on the headwaters of the Rio Conchos, lat. 28° 10′, long. 107° 10′, Chihuahua, Mexico.—Orozco y Berra, Geog., 323, 1864.

**Bidai** (Caddo for 'brushwood,' probably referring to the peculiar growth characteristic of the region). An extinct tribe, supposed to have belonged to the Caddoan stock, whose villages were scattered over a wide territory, but principally about Trinity r., Texas, while some were as far N. as the Neches or beyond. A creek emptying into Trinity r. between Walker and Madison cos., Tex., bears the name of the tribe, as did also, according to La Harpe, a small bay on the coast N. of Matagorda bay. A number of geographic names derived from this tribe survive in the region. The tribal tradition of the Bidai is that they were the oldest inhabitants of the country where they dwelt. This belief may have strengthened tribal pride, for although the Bidai were surrounded by tribes belonging to the Caddo confederacy, the people long kept their independence. They were neighbors of the Arkokisa, who lived on lower Trinity r. and may have been their allies, for according to La Harpe (1721) they were on friendly terms with that tribe while they were at war with the people dwelling on Matagorda bay. During the latter part of the 18th century the Bidai were reported to be the chief intermediaries between the French and the Apache in the trade in firearms; later they suffered from the political disturbances incident to the controversy between the Spaniards and the French, as well as from intertribal wars and the introduction of new diseases. As a result remnants of different villages combined and the olden tribal organization was broken up. Little is known of their customs and beliefs. They lived in fixed habitations, cultivated the soil, hunted the buffalo, which ranged through their territory, and were said by Sibley in 1805 to have had "an excellent character for honesty and punctuality." At that time they numbered about 100, but in 1776–7 an epidemic carried off nearly half their number. About the middle of the 19th century a remnant of the Bidai were living in a small village 12 m. from Montgomery, Tex., cultivating maize, serving as cotton pickers, and bearing faithful allegiance to the Texans. The women were still skilled in basketry of "curious designs and great variety." They appear to have remained in Montgomery and Harris cos., Texas, until they died out.   (A. C. F.)

Badies.—Ker, Travels, 122, 1816. Beadeyes.—Edward, Hist. Tex., 92, 1836. Bedais.—French, Hist. Coll. La., II, 11, 1875. Beddies.—Brackenridge, Views of La., 81, 1815. Bedees.—Ibid., 87. Bedies.—Sibley (1805), Hist. Sketches, 71, 1806. Bidais.—Robin, Voy. Louisiane, III, 14, 1807. Bidaises.—Soc. Mex. Geog., 266, 1870. Biday.—Doc. of 1719–21 in Margry, Déc. VI, 341, 1886. Bidayes.—La Harpe (ca. 1721), ibid., 341. Bidias.—Latham in Trans.

Philol. Soc. Lond., 103, 1856. **Quasmigdo.**—Ker, Trav., 122, 1816 (given as their own name). **Redais.**—Foote, Texas, I, 299, 1841. **Spring Creeks.**— Ibid. **Vidaes.**—Mezières (1778) quoted by Bancroft, No. Mex. States, I, 661, 1886. **Vidais.**— French, Hist. Coll. La., II, 11, 1875. **Vidays.**—Doc. 503 (1791–92) in Texas State archives. **Vivais.**— Doc. of Aug. 26, 1756, ibid.

**Bidamarek.** An indefinite division of the Pomo of California, the name being applied by the Pomo of upper Clear lake to the inhabitants of the region w. of them on Russian r., as distinguished from the Danomarek, or hill people, of the same region. Gibbs, in 1851, mentioned the Bedahmarek as living with the Shanelkaya in a valley apparently at the source of the E. fork of Russian r.; and McKee, in the same year, gave the Medamarec, said to number 150, as inhabiting with the Chanetkai the hills dividing the waters of Clear lake from Eel (*sic*) r.   (A. L. K.) **Bedah-marek.**—Gibbs (1851) in Schoolcraft, Ind. Tribes, III, 109, 1853. **Me-dama-rec.**—McKee (1851) in Sen. Ex. Doc. 4, 32d Cong., spec. sess., 136, 1853.

**Big Bill.** A Paiute chief. He led the Indians who aided the notorious Mormon John D. Lee in the Mountain Meadow massacre in s. w. Utah on Sept. 11, 1857.

**Big Canoe.** A Kalispel war chief who acquired considerable notoriety as a leader in battle. He was born in 1799 and died in 1882 at the Flathead agency, Mont.       (C. T.)

**Big Chief.** An Osage village 4 m. from the Mission in Ind. T. in 1850; pop. 300. **Big-chief.**—Smet, West. Missions, 355, 1863.

**Big Cypress Swamp.** A Seminole settlement, with 73 inhabitants in 1880, situated in the "Devil's Garden" on the N. edge of Big Cypress swamp, 15 to 20 m. s. w. of L. Okeechobee, Monroe co., Fla.—MacCauley in 5th Rep. B. A. E., 478, 1887.

**Big Foot** (Si-tanka). A Hunkpapa Sioux chief, of the Cheyenne River res., S. Dak., leader of the band of about 300 men, women, and children who fled from the reservation after the killing of Sitting Bull in the autumn of 1890, intending to join the hostiles in the Bad-lands. They were intercepted by troops on Wounded Knee cr. and surrendered, but in attempting to disarm the Indians a conflict was precipitated, resulting in an engagement in which almost the entire band, including Big Foot, was exterminated, Dec. 29, 1890. See Mooney in 14th Rep. B. A. E., 1896.

**Big Hammock.** The most populous Seminole settlement in central Florida in 1821; situated N. of Tampa bay, probably in Hillsboro co.—Bell in Morse, Rep. to Sec. War, 307, 1822.

**Big-island** (translation of the native name *Ămăye'l-e'gwa*). A former Cherokee settlement on Little Tennessee r., at Big island, a short distance below the mouth of the Tellico, in Monroe co.,

Tenn.; not to be confounded with Longisland town below Chattanooga.—Mooney in 19th Rep. B. A. E., 508, 1900. **Ămăye'l-e'gwa.**—Mooney, op. cit. **Big Island.**— Royce in 5th Rep. B. A. E., map, 1887. **Mialaquo.**—Timberlake, Memoir, map, 1762. **Nilaque.**—Bartram, Travels, 372, 1792.

**Big Jim.** The popular name of a noted full-blood Shawnee leader, known among his people as Wapameepto, 'Gives light as he walks.' His English name was originally Dick Jim, corrupted into Big Jim. He was born on the Sabine res., Texas, in 1834, and in 1872 became chief of the Kispicotha band, commonly known as Big Jim's band of Absentee Shawnee. Big Jim was of illustrious lineage, his grandfather being Tecumseh and his father one of the signers of the "Sam

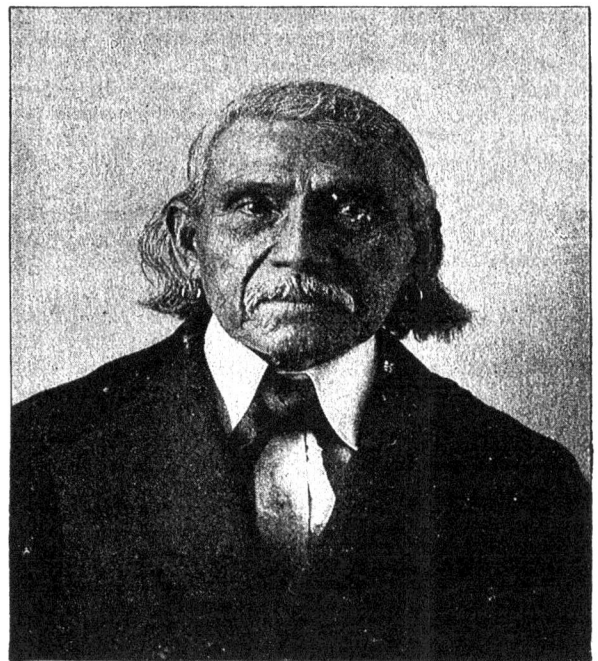

BIG JIM (SHAWNEE)

Houston treaty" between the Cherokee and affiliated tribes and the Republic of Texas, Feb. 23, 1836. He was probably the most conservative member of his tribe. In the full aboriginal belief that the earth was his mother and that she must not be wounded by tilling of the soil, he refused until the last to receive the allotments of land that had been forced upon his band in Oklahoma, and used every means to overcome the encroachments of civilization. For the purpose of finding a place where his people would be free from molestation, he went to Mexico in 1900, and while there was stricken with smallpox in August, and died. He was succeeded by his only son, Tonomo, who is now (1905) about 30 years of age.

**Big Kettle.** See *Sonojowauga*.

**Big Mouth.** A chief of the Brulé Sioux, though an Oglala by descent. A contemporary of Spotted Tail, and as highly regarded by his tribe for his manly and warlike qualities as the latter, though of less historical note. He is spoken of (Ind. Aff. Rep., 316, 1869) as one of the principal chiefs at Whetstone agency on the Missouri, where most of the Brulé and Oglala bands had gathered. The stand taken by Big Mouth in reference to the relations of the Sioux with the whites caused him to gain steadily in influence and power. Spotted Tail, having visited Washington and other cities, where he was much fêted, returned with changed views as to the Indian policy, a fact seized upon by Big Mouth to disparage his rival. Realizing that the tide was turning against him, Spotted Tail, in 1873 or 1874, called at the lodge of Big Mouth, who on appearing at the entrance was seized by two warriors and held by them while Spotted Tail shot him dead.     (C. T.)

**Big-mush.** A noted western Cherokee, known to the whites also as Hard-mush and among his people as Gatûñ'wa‘li ('bread made into balls or lumps'), killed by the Texans in 1839.—Mooney in 19th Rep. B. A. E., 1900. See *Bowl*.

**Big Neck.** See *Moanahonga*.

**Big Rock.** A point on Shiawassee r., in lower Michigan, at which in 1820 the Chippewa had a reservation.—Saginaw treaty (1820) in U. S. Ind. Treaties, 142, 1873.

**Big Swamp Indians.** A name applied to Seminole, principally of the Mikasuki division, near Miccosukee lake, Leon co., Fla.—McKenney and Hall, Ind. Tribes, II, 157, 1854.
Long Swamp Indians.—Ibid.

**Big Tree.** See *Adoeette*.

**Big White.** See *Shahaka*.

**Bihi Konlo.** One of the 5 hamlets composing the Choctaw town of Imongalasha.—Halbert in Miss. Hist. Soc. Publ., VI, 432, 1902.

**Biktasatetuse** ('very bad lodges': a Crow name). A subtribe or band of the Crows or of some neighboring tribe; apparently the same as Ashiapkawi.
A-shi-ap'-ka-wi.—Hayden, Ethnog. and Philol. Mo. Val., 402, 1862. Bik-ta'-sa-te-tu'-se.—Ibid.

**Biloxi** (a Muskhogean corruption of *Taneks*, their own name). A small Siouan tribe formerly living in s. Mississippi, now nearly or quite extinct. The Biloxi were supposed to belong to the Muskhogean stock until Gatschet visited the survivors of the tribe in Louisiana in 1886 and found that many of the words bore strong resemblance to those in Siouan languages, a determination fully substantiated in 1882 by J. Owen Dorsey. To what particular group of the Siouan family the tribe is to be assigned has not been determined; but it is probable that the closest affinity is with Dorsey's Dhegiha group, so called. The first direct notice of the Biloxi is that by Iberville, who found them in 1699 about Biloxi bay, on the gulf coast of Mississippi, in connection with two other small tribes, the Paskagula and Moctobi, the three together numbering only about 20 cabins (Margry, Déc., IV, 195, 1880). The Biloxi removed to the w. shore of Mobile bay in 1702. In 1761 Jefferys spoke of them as having been N. E. of Cat id., and of their subsequent removal to the N. w. of Pearl r. Hutchins, in 1784, mentions a Biloxi village on the w. side of the Mississippi, a little below the Paskagula, containing 30 warriors. According to Sibley (1805) a part of the Biloxi came with some French, from near Pensacola, about 1763, and settled first in Avoyelles parish, La., on Red r., whence they "moved higher up to Rapide Bayou, and from thence to the mouth of Rigula de Bondieu, a division of Red r., about 40 m. below Natchitoch, where they now live, and are reduced to about 30 in number." Berguin-Duvallon (1806) mentions them as in two villages, one on Red r., 19 leagues from the Mississippi, the other on a lake called Avoyelles. He also refers to some as being wanderers on Crocodile bayou. Schoolcraft said they numbered 55 in 1825. In 1828 (Bul. Soc. Mex. Geog., 1870) there were 20 families of the tribe on the E. bank of Neches r., Tex. Porter, in 1829 (Schoolcraft, Ind. Tribes, III, 596), gave the number as 65 living with the Caddo, Paskagula, and other small tribes on Red r., near the Texas frontier, and in 1846 Butler and Lewis found a Biloxi camp on Little r., a tributary of the Brazos in Texas, about two days' journey from the latter stream. After this little was heard of them until 1886. According to Gatschet there were in that year a few Biloxi among the Choctaw and Caddo, but he visited only those in Avoyelles parish, La. In 1892 Dorsey found about a dozen of the tribe near Lecompte, Rapides parish, La., but none remained at Avoyelles. From the terms they used and information obtained Dorsey concluded that prior to the coming of the whites the men wore the breechcloth, a belt, leggings, moccasins, and garters, and wrapped around the body a skin robe. Feather headdresses and necklaces of bone, and of the bills of a long-legged redbird (flamingo?) were worn, as also were nose-rings and earrings. The dwellings of the people resembled those found among the northern tribes of the same family, one kind similar to the low tent of the Osage and Winnebago, the other like the high tent of the Dakota, Omaha, and others. It is said they formerly made pottery.

They made wooden bowls, horn and bone implements, and baskets. Tattooing was practised to a limited extent. Descent was through the female line, and there was an elaborate system of kinship. The charge of cannibalism was made against them by one or two other tribes; this, however, is probably incorrect. Dorsey recorded the following clan names: Itaanyadi, Ontianyadi, and Nakhotodhanyadi. See Dorsey in Proc. A. A. A. S., XLII, 267, 1893; Mooney, Siouan Tribes of the East, Bull. 22, B. A. E., 1894; McGee in 15th Rep. B. A. E., 1897, and the authorities cited below.

**Ananis.**—Doc. of 1699 in French, Hist. Coll., II, 99, 1875. **Anaxis.**—Margry, Déc., IV, 113, 1880. **Annocchy.**—Iberville (1699) in Margry, Déc., IV, 172. 1880. **Baluxa.**—Brown, West. Gazett., 133, 1817, **Baluxie.**—Woodward, Remin., 25, 1859. **Belochy.**—Neill, Hist. Minn., 173, 1858. **Belocsé.**—Bull. Soc. Mex. Geog., 267, 1870. **Beloxi.**—Sen. Ex. Doc. 72, 20th Cong., 104, 1829. **Beluxis.**—Doc. of 1764 in N. Y. Doc. Col. Hist., VII, 641, 1856. **Beluxy.**—Biog. and Hist. Mem. N. W. La., 526, 1890. **Bilexes.**—Berquin-Duvallon, Trav. in La., 97, 1806. **Billoxie.**—Ex. Doc. 21, 18th Cong., 2d sess., 5, 1825. **Billoxis.**—Butel-Dumont, Louisiane, I, 134, 1753. **Bilocchi.**—Gravier (1701) in French, Hist. Coll., II, 88, 1875. **Bilocchy.**—Iberville (1699) in Margry, Déc., IV, 172, 1880. **Bilocci.**—Ibid., 473. **Biloccis.**—Ibid. **Bilochy.**—Ibid. 184. **Bilocohi.**—Coxe, Carolana, 31, 1741. **Bilocohy.**—Ibid., 30. **Biloui.**—Berquin-Duvallon, Trav. in La., 91, 1806. **Biloxi.**—Sauvole (1700) in Margry, Déc., IV, 451, 1880. **Biloxis.**—Penicaut (1699) in French, Hist. Coll., n. s., 38, 1869. **Biloxy.**—Iberville(1700) in Margry, Déc., IV, 425,1880. **Bilusi.**—Michler in Rep. Sec. War, 32, 1850. **Biluxi.**—Michler (1849) in H. R. Ex. Doc. 67, 31st Cong., 1st sess., 5, 1850. **Binuxsh.**—Gatschet, Caddo and Yatassi MS., B. A. E., 66 (Caddo name). **Binu'χshi.**—Ibid., 73. **Blu'-kci.**—Dorsey, inf'n, 1881 (Caddo name). **B'lúksi.**—Gatschet, MS., B. A. E., 1886 (Choctaw name). **Bolixes.**—Parker (1854) in Schoolcraft, Ind. Tribes, V, 702, 1855. **Bolixies.**—Schoolcraft, ibid., IV, 561, 1854. **Boluxas.**—Sibley, Hist. Sketches, 80, 1806. **Boluxes.**—Keane in Stanford, Compend., 503, 1878. **Boluxie.**—Butler and Lewis (1846) in H. R. Doc. 76, 29th Cong., 2d sess., 3, 1847. **Boluxies.**—Bonnell, Texas, 140, 1840. **Paluxies.**—Parker (1854) in Schoolcraft, Ind. Tribes, V, 702, 1855. **Paluxsies.**—Parker, Unexplored Texas, 221, 1856. **Polúksalgi.**—Gatschet, Creek MS., B. A. E. (Creek name). **Poutoucsis.**—Berquin-Duvallon, Trav. in La., 94, 1806 (misprint). **Tanĕksayⁿa.**—Dorsey in Proc. A. A. A. S., XLII, 267, 1893 (own name; varients are *Tanĕks anyadi*, *Tanĕks hanyadi*, 'first people').

**Biorka** (Swed.: *Björk Ö.* = Birch id.). An Aleut village on Biorka id. near Unalaska, Alaska. Pop. 44 in 1831, 140 in 1880, 57 in 1890.

**Borka.**—Petroff, 10th Census, Alaska, 20, 1884. **Saydankooskoi.**—Elliott, Cond. Aff. Alaska, 225, 1875 (from Siginak, written "Sithanak" by Sauer, quoted by Baker, Geog. Dict. Alaska, 1901; Aleut name of the island, sig. 'curled'). **Sedankovskoe.**—Veniaminof, Zapiski, II, 203, 1840. **Sidanak.**—Holmberg, Ethnol. Skizz., map, 1855. **Sidankin.**—Sauer quoted by Baker, Geog. Dict. Alaska, 1901. **Ugiú-ug.**—Veniaminof quoted by Baker, ibid. (own name).

**Birch River.** A local name applied to the Maskegon (Swampy Cree) res., near lower Saskatchewan r., Saskatchewan, Canada, and to the Indians gathered on it.—Can. Ind. Aff., passim.

**Bird-stones.** A name given to a class of prehistoric stone objects of undetermined purpose, usually resembling or remotely suggesting the form of a bird. In many cases the resemblance is so slight that without the aid of a series of specimens, grading downward from the more realistic bird representations through successive simplifications, the life form would not be suggested. In its simplest form the body is an almost featureless bar of polished stone. Again, the ends are curved upward, giving a saddle shape; but usually the head, tail, and eyes are differentiated, and in the more graphic forms the tail is expanded and turned upward to balance the head. The most remarkable feature is the pair of projecting knobs, often on rather slender stems, representing the eyes, giving somewhat the effect of a horned animal. These objects are most plentiful in the Ohio valley and around the great lakes, and occur sparingly in the S. and to the westward beyond the Mississippi. Although many kinds of stone were used in their manufacture, the favorite material was a banded slate which occurs over a wide area in the Northern states and in Canada. They are shaped with much care, being symmetrical and highly polished.

BIRD-SHAPED STONES. *a*, EPIDOTE; OHIO (1-3). *b*, BANDED SLATE; NEW YORK (1-4). *c*, BANDED SLATE; PENNSYLVANIA. *d*, ARGILLITE; OHIO (1-4). *e*, BANDED SLATE; ONTARIO (1-3). *f*, BARLIKE FORM; BANDED SLATE; OHIO (1-6)

The under side is flat or slightly concave, and there are two perforations at the extremities of the base intended to serve in attaching the figure to the surface of some object, as a tablet, a pipe stem, a flute, or a staff or baton, or to some part of the costume, or to the hair. There is good reason to believe that these and the various related objects—banner stones, boat-stones, etc.—had kindred uses in religious ceremony or magic (see *Problematical objects*). Gillman (Smithson Rep. 1873, 1874) was informed by an aged Chippewa " that in olden time these ornaments were worn on the heads of Indian women, but only after

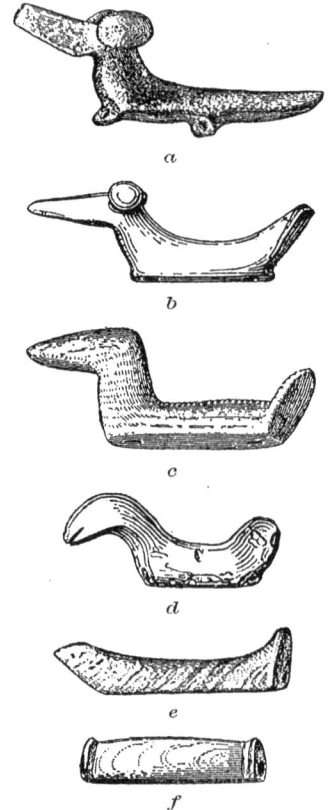

marriage," and suggests that the bird-stones may have symbolized the brooding bird. Abbott (Primitive Industry, 370) published a statement originating with Dr E. Stirling, of Cleveland, Ohio, that "such bird effigies, made of wood, have been noticed among the Ottawa of Grand Traverse bay, Mich., fastened to the top of the heads of women as an indication that they are pregnant." The probability, however, is that these bird-stones were used or worn by the men rather than by the women, and Cushing's theory that they were attached to a plate and fixed to the hair is plausible.

See Abbott, Primitive Industry, 1881; Beauchamp in Bull. N. Y. State Mus., 1897; Boyle in Rep. Minister of Education, Ontario, 1895; Fowke (1) in 13th Rep. B. A. E., 1896, (2) Archæol. Hist. Ohio, 1902; Gillman in Rep. Smithson. Inst. 1873, 1874; Moorehead, (1) Bird-stone Ceremonial, 1899; (2) Prehist. Impls., 1900, (3) in Am. Anthrop., II, 1900; Rau in Smithson. Cont., XXII, 1876; Schoolcraft, Ind. Tribes, I-VI, 1851–56; Squier and Davis in Smithson. Cont., I, 1848. (W. H. H.)

**Birdwoman.** See *Sacagawea.*

**Bis.** A Chumashan village w. of Pueblo de las Canoas (San Buenaventura), Ventura co., Cal., in 1542.—Cabrillo (1542) in Smith, Col. Docs. Fla., 181, 1857.

**Bisani.** A Pima settlement 8 leagues s. w. of Caborca, in the present Sonora, Mexico, of which it was a visita in Spanish colonial times. Pop. 178 in 1730.
Bisani.—Rudo Ensayo (1762), 152, 1863. **Jesus María Basani.**—Doc. of 1730 quoted by Bancroft, No. Mex. States, I, 514, 1886.

**Bishkon.** One of the towns forming the noted "Sixtowns" of the Choctaw, situated a few miles from the present Garlandsville, in the N. part of Jasper co., Miss.
Bishkon.—Gatschet, Creek Migr. Leg., I, 109, 1884. **Bishkun Tamaha.**—Halbert in Ala. Hist. Soc. Publ., I, 382, 1901.

**Bissarhar** ('Indians with many bridles'). A division of the Apache under chiefs Goodegoya and Santos in 1873–75.—White, Apache Names of Indian Tribes, MS., B. A. E.

**Bissasha** (*Bissa-asha*, 'blackberries are ripe there'). A former Choctaw town on the w. side of Little Rock cr., Newton co., Ga. Judging from the stone implements and other débris lying scattered over its site, the town covered an area of about 10 acres, making it a rather small town as Choctaw towns were generally built.—Brown in Miss. Hist. Soc. Publ., VI, 442, 1902.
Bishapa.—Romans, Florida, map, 1772 (probably identical).

**Bistchonigottine.** A division of the Etchaottine on Bistcho lake, Mackenzie Ter., Canada.

Bes-tchonhi-Gottinè.—Petitot, Autour du Lac des Esclaves, 339, 1891.

**Bithahotshi** (Navaho: 'red place on top,' referring to the color of the sandstone rocks; the second *h* = German *ch.*) The name of a mesa, and, by extension, of a valley in which a trading store is situated, about half-way between Holbrook and the Hopi villages in N. E. Arizona. The name is sometimes employed to designate a group of ancient pueblo ruins in and near the valley.
Biddahoochee.—Hough in Rep. Nat. Mus. 1901, 326, 1903. **Bǐtáhotsi.**—Matthews, Navaho Legends, 153, 1897 (correct Navaho name: *t* = th, *h* = German ch, *s* = sh).

**Bithani** ('folded arms'). A Navaho clan.
Biçá'ni.—Matthews in Jour. Am. Folk-lore, III, 103, 1890 (ç=th). **Bǐtá'ni.**—Matthews., Navaho Legends, 30, 1897 (*t*=th).

**Bitumen.** See *Boats, Cement.*

**Black Beaver.** A Delaware guide, born at the present site of Belleville, Ill., in 1806; died at Anadarko, Okla., May 8, 1880. He was present as interpreter at

BLACK BEAVER (DELAWARE)

the earliest conference with the Comanche, Kiowa, and Wichita tribes, held by Col. Richard Dodge on upper Red r. in 1834, and from then until the close of his days his services were constantly required by the Government and were invaluable to military and scientific explorers of the plains and the Rocky mts. In nearly every one of the early transcontinental expeditions he was the most intelligent and most trusted guide and scout.

**Blackbird.** A Chippewa village, commonly known as Black Bird's town from a chief of that name, which formerly existed on Tittibawassee r., Saginaw co., lower Michigan, on a reservation sold in 1837.                                (J. M.)

**Blackbird** (Mukatapenaise). A Potawatomi chief who lived in the early part of the 19th century. He was conspicuous at the massacre of the garrison at Ft Dearborn, Chicago, in Aug., 1812.

**Black Bob**. The chief of a Shawnee band, originally a part of the Hathawekela division of the Shawnee, q. v. About the year 1826 they separated from their kindred, then living in E. Missouri on land granted to them about 1793 by Baron Carondelet, near Cape Girardeau, then in Spanish territory, and removed to Kansas, where, by treaty with their chief, Black Bob, in 1854, they were given rights on the Shawnee res. in that state. Under Black Bob's leadership they refused to remove with the rest of the tribe to Indian Ter. in 1868, but are now incorporated with them, either in the Cherokee Nation or with the Absentee Shawnee. See *Shawnee*, and consult Halbert in Gulf States Hist. Mag., I, no. 6, 1903.                              (J. M.)

**Black Dog**. An Osage village, named from its chief, 60 m. from the Mission, in Indian Ter., in 1850; pop. 400.—Smet, West. Miss. and Missionaries, 355, 1863.

**Black drink** ("Carolina tea"; Catawba *yaupon;* Creek *ássi-lupútski*, 'small leaves,' commonly abbreviated *ássi*). A decoction, so named by British traders from its color, made by boiling leaves of the *Ilex cassine* in water. It was employed by the tribes of the Gulf states and adjacent region as "medicine" for ceremonial purification. It was a powerful agent for the production of the nervous state

PREPARING BLACK DRINK.   (LAFITAU, 1723)

and disordered imagination necessary to "spiritual" power. Hall (Rep. Nat. Mus., 218, 1885) says that among the Creeks the liquid was prepared and drank before councils in order, as they believed, to invigorate the mind and body and prepare for thought and debate. It was also used in the great "busk" or annual green-corn thanksgiving. The action of the drink in strong infusion is purgative, vomitive, and diuretic, and it was long thought that this was the only effect, but recent investigation has shown that the plant contains caffeine, the leaves yielding a beverage with stimulating qualities like tea and coffee, and that excessive indulgence

produces similar nervous disturbance. The plant was held in great esteem by the southern Indians, and the leaves were collected with care and formed an article of trade among the tribes (Griffith, Med. Bot., 1847). The leaves and tender shoots were gathered, dried, roasted, and stored in baskets until needed. According to Gatschet the Creeks made three potions from cassine of differing strength for different uses. In its preparation the leaves having been roasted in a pot, were added to water and boiled. Before drinking, the Indians agitated the tea to make it frothy. Tea made from the *Ilex cassine* is still sometimes used by white people in localities where the shrub grows. Personal names referring to the black-drink ceremony were very common, especially among the Creeks and Seminole. The name of Osceola (q. v.), the noted Seminole chief, is properly *Asi-yahóla*, 'Black-drink Singer.' The drink was called *ássi-lupútski* by the Creeks. C. C. Jones (Tomochichi, 118, 1868) calls the drink "foskey." See Gatschet, Creek Migr. Leg., II, 56, 1888, and works therein cited; Hale, Ilex Cassine, Bull. 14, Div. Botany, U. S. Dept. Agriculture, 1891; Speck in Am. Anthr., IX, 292, 1907.                             (W. H.)

**Black Fox** (*Inálï*). A principal chief of the Cherokee who, under the treaty of Jan. 7, 1806, by which the Cherokee ceded nearly 7,000 sq. m. of their lands in Tennessee and Alabama, was given a life annuity of $100. He was then an old man. In 1810, as a member of the national council of his tribe, he signed an enactment formally abolishing the custom of clan revenge hitherto universal among the tribes, thus taking an important step toward civilization.—Mooney in 19th Rep. B. A. E., 87, 1900.

**Black Hawk** (*Ma'katawimeshekā'kää*, from *ma'katäwi* 'it is black, *mishi* 'big,' *kā'kää* 'chest,' the name referring to the description of a bird, or sparrow hawk.—W. J.). A subordinate chief of the Sauk and Fox Indians and leader in the Black Hawk war of 1832. He was born at the Sauk village at the mouth of Rock r., Ill., in 1767, and belonged to the Thunder gens of the Sauk tribe. When only 15 years of age he distinguished himself in war; and before he was 17, at the head of a war party of young men, he attacked an Osage camp of 100 persons and came away safely with the scalp of a warrior. The next party that he led out, however, he brought to a deserted village, on account of which all except 5 of his party left him; but with these he kept on and brought away 2 scalps with which to efface his disgrace. At the age of 19 he led 200 Sauk and Foxes in a desperate engagement with an equal number of Osage, destroying half of his opponents, killing 5 men and a woman with his own hands. In a subsequent raid on the Cherokee his party killed 28, with a loss of but 7; but among the latter was his own father, who was guardian of the tribal medicine, hence Black Hawk refrained from war during the 5 years following and endeavored to acquire greater supernatural power. At the end of that time he went against the Osage, destroyed a camp of 40 lodges, with the exception of 2 women, and himself slew 9 persons. On a subsequent expedition against the Cherokee in revenge for his father's death he found only 5 enemies, 4 men and a woman. The latter he carried off, but the men he released, deeming it no honor to kill so few.

On the outbreak of the war of 1812 Black Hawk, with most of his people, joined the British and fought for them throughout, committing many depredations on the border settlements. Afterward, in opposition to the head chief, Keokuk, who cultivated American friendship, he was leader of the British sympathizers who traded at Malden in preference to St Louis.

By treaty of Nov. 3, 1804, concluded at St Louis, the Sauk and Foxes had agreed to surrender all their lands on the E. side of the Mississippi, but had been left undisturbed until the country should be thrown open to settlement. After the conclusion of the war of 1812, however, the stream of settlers pushed westward once more and began to pour into the old Sauk and Fox territory. Keokuk and the majority of his people, bowing to the inevitable, soon moved across the Mississippi into the present Iowa, but Black Hawk declined to leave, maintaining that when he had signed the treaty of St Louis he had been deceived regarding its terms. At the same time he entered into negotiations with the Winnebago, Potawatomi, and Kickapoo to enlist them in concerted opposition to the aggressions of the whites.

By the spring of 1831 so much friction had taken place between the settlers and Indians that Gov. Reynolds, of Illinois, was induced to call out the militia. Gen. Gaines, desiring to avoid the expense of a demonstration, summoned Black Hawk and his friends to a convention at Ft Armstrong, but a violent scene followed and the convention came to nothing. On June 15 the militia left their camp at Rushville and marched upon Black Hawk's village. Finding that Black Hawk and his people had effected their escape shortly before, they burned the lodges. Immediately afterward Gaines demanded that all the hostile warriors

should present themselves for a peace talk, and on June 30 Black Hawk and 27 of his followers signed a treaty with Gov. Reynolds by which they agreed to abstain from further hostilities and retire to the farther side of the Mississippi.

During the following winter Black Hawk, like his great Shawnee predecessor, Tecumseh, sent emissaries in all directions to win various tribes to his interest, and is said to have endeavored, though unsuccessfully, to destroy the authority of his own head chief, Keokuk, or commit him to a war against the whites. On Apr. 1, 1832, Gen. Atkinson received orders to demand from the Sauk and Foxes the chief members of a band who had massacred some Menominee the

BLACK HAWK.    (AFTER CATLIN)

year before. Arriving at the rapids of Des Moines r. on the 10th, he found that Black Hawk had recrossed the Mississippi 4 days previously at the head of a band estimated at 2,000, of whom more than 500 were warriors. Again the militia were called out, while Atkinson sent word to warn the settlers, and collected all the regular troops available.

Meantime Black Hawk proceeded up Rock r., expecting that he would be joined by the Winnebago and Potawatomi, but only a few small bands responded. Regiments of militia were by this time pushing up in pursuit of him, but they were poorly disciplined and unused to Indian warfare, while jealousy existed among the commanders. Two brigades under Isaiah Stillman, which had pushed on in close pursuit, were met by 3 Indians bearing a flag of truce; but, other Indians showing themselves near by, treachery was feared, and in the confusion one of the bearers of the flag was shot down. A general but disorderly pursuit of the remainder ensued, when the pursuers were suddenly fallen upon by Black Hawk at the head of 40 warriors and driven from the field (May 14, 1832) in a disgraceful rout. Black Hawk now let loose his followers against the frontier settlements, many of which were burned and their occupants slain, but although able to cut off small bands of Indians the militia and regulars were for some time able to do little in retaliation. On June 24 Black Hawk made an attack on Apple River fort, but was repulsed, and on the day following defeated Maj. Dement's battalion, though with heavy loss to his own side. On July 21, however, while trying to cross to the w. side of Wisconsin r. he was overtaken by volunteers under Gen. James D. Henry and crushingly defeated with a loss of 68 killed and many more wounded. With the remainder of his force he retreated to the Mississippi, which he reached at the mouth of Bad Axe r., and was about to cross when intercepted by the steamer *Warrior*, which shelled his camp. The following day, Aug. 3, the pursuing troops under Atkinson came up with his band and after a desperate struggle killed or drove into the river more than 150, while 40 were captured. Most of those who reached the other side were subsequently cut off by the Sioux. Black Hawk and his principal warrior, Nahpope, escaped, however, to the northward, whither they were followed and captured by some Winnebago. Black Hawk was then sent E. and confined for more than a month at Fortress Monroe, Va., when he was taken on tour through the principal E. cities, everywhere proving an object of the greatest interest. In 1837 he accompanied Keokuk on a second trip to the E., after which he settled on Des Moines r. near Iowaville, dying there Oct. 3, 1838. His remains, which had been placed upon the surface of the ground dressed in a military uniform presented by Gen. Jackson, accompanied by a sword also presented by Jackson, a cane given by Henry Clay, and medals from Jackson, John Quincy Adams, and the city of Boston, were stolen in July, 1839, and carried away to St Louis, where the body was cleaned and the bones sent to Quincy, Ill., for articulation. On protest being made by Gov. Lucas of the territory of Iowa, the bones were restored, but the sons of Black Hawk, being satisfied to let them stay in the governor's office, they remained there for some time and were later removed to the collections of the Burlington Geological and Historical Society, where they were destroyed in 1855 when the building containing them was burned. See Autobiography of Ma-ka-tai-me-she-kia-kiak, edited by J. B. Patterson, 1882, a life by Snelling, and The Black Hawk War, by Frank E. Stevens.        (J. R. S.)

**Black Hawk.** A village marked on Royce's map (First Rep. B. A. E., 1881) about Mount Auburn, Shelby co., Ind., on land sold in 1818. Probably a Delaware settlement.        (J. M.)

**Black Hoof.** See *Catahecassa*.

**Black Indians.** Mentioned by Bontemantel and Van Baerle in 1656 (N. Y. Doc. Col. Hist., I, 588, 1856). They and "the Southern Indians, called Minquas," are spoken of as bringing furs to trade with the Dutch on Schuylkill r. Possibly the Nanticoke, who were said to be darker than their neighbors.        (J. M.)

**Black Kettle.** An Onondaga chief, called by the French *Chaudière Noire*. When in the first French war the governor in Montreal sent one of his officers with 300 men to attack the Iroquois at Niagara, Black Kettle, with 80 warriors, gave the invaders a long running fight, from which the latter were the chief sufferers, although his force was in the end wiped out. In the following season he laid waste the French settlements in w. Canada. In 1691 the Iroquois planned the destruction of the French settlements and trading posts w. of Montreal. Their plans were revealed to the French commander by captive Indian women who escaped, and after the defeat of the expeditions the French destroyed parties that were encamped in their hereditary hunting grounds between the Ottawa and St Lawrence rs. Black Kettle retaliated by killing Indians who traded with Montreal and the French escort sent to guard them. On July 15, 1692, he attacked Montreal and carried off many prisoners, who were retaken by a pursuing party; and in the same season he attacked the party of de Lusignan and killed the leader. In 1697 he arranged a peace with the French, but before it was concluded he was murdered by some Algonkin while hunting near Cattaraugus, although he had notified the French commander at the fort of the peace negotiations.

**Black Kettle.** A Cheyenne chief and famous warrior whose village on Sand cr., Colo., was attacked by a force of Colorado militia under Col. Chivington in 1864 and a large number of innocent men, women, and children massacred and their bodies mutilated. Black Kettle had come in by direction of Gov. Evans, of Colorado, and surrendered to Maj. Wynkoop, U. S. A., who had promised him protection (Ind. Aff. Rep., 1865, and Condition of Indian Tribes, Rep. Joint Spec. Com., 1865). On Nov. 27, 1868,

United States troops under command of Gen. P. H. Sheridan attacked Black Kettle's village on the Washita, and destroyed it, Black Kettle being killed in the fight. He was a brother of Gentle Horse.    (G. B. G.)

**Black Leg's Village.** A former Iroquois settlement, situated on the N. bank of Conemaugh r., in S. E. Armstrong co., Pa.—Royce in 18th Rep. B. A. E., pl. clx, 1900.

**Black Lodges.** According to Grinnell (Soc. Org. Cheyennes, 144, 1905), a local designation for a part of the Northern Cheyenne.

**Black Muscogees.** A term applied to 40 to 60 Indians at Parras, Coahuila, Mexico, at the close of 1861. To what particular branch of the Creeks these refugees belonged is not known.—Rep. Mex. Bndy. Comm., 410, 1873.

**Blacksnake** (*Thaonawyuthe*, 'needle or awl breaker'). A chief, about the close of the 18th century, of the Seneca Indians, who lived on their reservation along the Alleghany r. in Cattaraugus co., N. Y. His residence was a mile above the village of Cold Spring. The date of his birth is not known, but is supposed to have been about 1760, as it is stated that in 1856 he had reached the age of 96 years. He was present on the English side at the battle of Oriskany, N. Y., in 1777, and it is said that he participated in the Wyoming massacre of 1778, but he fought on the American side in the battle of Ft George, N. Y., Aug. 17, 1813. He died in 1859,    (C. T.)

**Black-tailed Deers.** A Hidatsa band or secret order.—Culbertson in Smithson. Rep. 1850, 143, 1851.

**Black Thunder** (also called Makatananamaki, from *ma'katä* 'black,' *nenemekĩ<sup>a</sup>* 'thunder.'—W. J.). A Fox chief. He was the patriarch of the tribe when, at a council held at Portage, Wis., in July, 1815, he replied to charges of breach of treaties and of hostile intentions, made by the American commissioners, with a burst of indignant eloquence, claiming the protection of the Government for his tribe, that, having smoked the peace pipe, had remained faithful throughout the war, and respect also for their title to ancestral lands. He signed the treaty at St Louis on Sept. 14, 1815.—Drake, Bk. Inds., 631, 1880.

**Black Tiger.** A Dakota band of 22 lodges, named from its chief; one of the bands not brought into Ft Peck agency in 1872.—H. R. Ex. Doc. 96, 42d Cong., 3d sess., 15, 1873.

**Black Tortoise.** A mythical tribe alleged to have lived in the Mississippi valley and to have been conquered and driven away by the Elk Indians.—Pidgeon, Traditions of Decoodah, 162, 1858.

**Blaesedael** (Danish: 'windy valley'). An Eskimo village and Danish post on Disko bay, W. Greenland, containing 120 people.—Mrs Peary, Journ., 14, 1893.

**Blanchard's Fork.** By the treaty of Maumee Rapids, in 1819, a part of the Ottawa living in Ohio were given a reservation on Blanchard's fork of the Auglaize, in Ohio, and became known officially as the Ottawa of Blanchard's Fork. They sold their land in 1831 and removed to Kansas, and later to Indian Territory, where, with some others of the same tribe, they numbered 179 in 1904.

Ottawas of Blanchard's Creek.—Greenville treaty (1795) in U. S. Ind. Treat., 1033, 1873. Ottawas of Blanchard's Fork.—Present official name.

**Blankets.** In the popular mind the North American Indian is everywhere associated with the robe or the blanket. The former was the whole hide of a large mammal made soft and pliable by much dressing; or pelts of foxes, wolves, and such creatures were sewed together; or bird, rabbit, or other tender skins were cut into ribbons, which were twisted or woven. The latter were manufactured by basketry processes from wool, hair, fur, feathers, down, bark, cotton, etc., and had many and various functions. They were worn like a toga as protection from the weather, and, in the best examples, were conspicuous in wedding and other ceremonies; in the night they were both bed and covering; for the home they served for hangings, partitions, doors, awnings, or sunshades; the women dried fruit on them, made vehicles and cradles of them for their babies, and receptacles for a thousand things and burdens; they even then exhausted their patience and skill upon them, producing their finest art work in weaving and embroidery; finally, the blanket became a standard of value and a primitive mechanism of commerce.

In S. E. Alaska originated what is popularly called the Chilkat blanket—a marvel of spinning, weaving, fringing, and mythic designs. The apparatus for this seems inadequate. The woman hangs her warp of mountain goat's wool mixed with shredded cedar bast from a horizontal bar. The long ends are made into balls and covered with membrane to keep them clean. Weft is not even wound on a stick for shuttle, nor is there even the rudest harness or batten. The details of the great mythic design are carefully wrought in by the woman in twined weaving at the same time that a dainty lacework is produced on the selvage. The process ends with a long heavy fringe from the unused warp. Farther southward on the N. W. coast cedar bast finely shredded served for the weaving of soft blankets, which were neatly trimmed with fur.

The Nez Percés and other tribes in the Fraser-Columbia area were extremely skillful in producing a heavy and tastefully decorated blanket in twined weaving from mountain goat's hair with warp of vegetal fiber, and among the Atlantic and Pacific coast tribes generally soft barks, wild hemp, rabbit skins, the down of birds, and the plumes of feathers were put to the same use. Blankets of cords wound with feathers were produced, not only by the Pueblos and cliff-dwellers but quite extensively in the E. as well as in the N. W. These were all woven with the simplest possible apparatus and by purely aboriginal technical processes. They were the groundwork of great skill and taste and much mythology, and were decorated with strips of fur, fringes, tassels, pendants, beadwork, featherwork, and native money. After the advent of the whites the blanket leaped into sudden prominence with tribes that had no weaving and had previously worn robes, the preparation of which was most exhausting. The European was not slow in observing a widespread want and in supplying the demand. When furs became scarcer blankets were in greater demand everywhere as articles of trade and standards of value. Indeed, in 1831 a home plant was established in Buffalo for the manufacture of what was called the Mackinaw blanket. The delegations visiting Washington during the 19th century wore this article conspicuously, and in our system of educating them, those tribes that were unwilling to adopt modern dress were called "blanket Indians." In art the drapery and colors have had a fascination for portrait painters, while in citizen's garments the red man ceases to be picturesque.

In the S. W. the coming of Spaniards had a still more romantic association with the blanket. Perhaps as early as the 16th century the Navaho, in affiliation with certain Pueblo tribes, received sheep and looms from the conquerors. These were the promise of all that is wrapped in the words "Navaho blanket." The yarn for the finest was procured by unraveling the Spanish bayeta, a sort of baize, and the specimens from this material now command high prices. For coarser work the Navaho sheared their own sheep, washed the wool, colored it with their native dyes, and spun it on rude spindles consisting of a straight stick with a flat disk of wood for a flywheel. This coarse and uneven yarn was set up in their regular but primitive loom, with harness for shifting the warp, a straight rod for shuttle, a fork of wood for adjusting the weft, and a separate batten of the same material for beating it

home. Only the hands of the weaver managed all the parts of the operation with phenomenal patience and skill, producing those marvelous creations which are guarded among the most precious treasures of aboriginal workmanship. The popularity of this work proved its worst enemy. Through the influence of traders and greatly increased demands for blankets the art has deteriorated. Native products were imitated by machinery. To the Indians were brought modern dyes, cotton warp, factory yarns and worsted, and utterly depraved patterns, in place of native wool, bayeta, and their own designs so full of pathos and beauty. At present a reformation in such matters is being encouraged, both by the Government and by benevolent organizations, for the purpose of restoring the old art. In this connection should be mentioned the interesting variety of effects produced in the Indian blankets by simple native contrivances. There are all the technical styles of native handwork superadded to the machine work of the loom, including coiled, twined, and braided technic. Two-faced fabrics are produced, having intricate patterns entirely different on the two sides. Different Pueblos had their fancies in blankets. Among these must not be overlooked the white cotton wedding blanket of the Hopi, ceremonially woven by the groom for his bride, afterward embroidered with symbolic designs, and at death wrapped about her body in preparation for the last rites. In the same tribe large embroidered cotton blankets are worn by woman impersonators in several ceremonies; also a small shoulder blanket in white, dark blue, and red, forming part of woman's "full dress" as well as a ceremonial garment. From this list should not be omitted the great variety of Navaho products, commencing with the cheap and ubiquitous saddle paddings, personal wrappings, house furnishings, and ending in competitions with the world's artistry. There were also the dark embroidered and white embroidered blanket of Navaho legend. They also wove blankets with broad bars of white and black called "chief's pattern," to be worn by the head-men. The Zuñi, too, wove a blanket for their priest-chiefs. But they, as well as the Hopi, had plenty of the serviceable kinds, of cotton and of wool, which they made into skirts and tunics; coarse kinds likewise for domestic use, robes of rabbit skin, and finer work for ceremony. The Pima and Maricopa have abandoned the art lately, but their congeners—the Yaqui, Tarahumare, Mayo, and Opata—weave characteristic styles.

Consult Boas in Rep. Nat. Mus. 1895, 1897; Hodge in Am. Anthrop., VIII, no.

3, 1895; Holmes in 13th Rep. B. A. E., 1896; Matthews (1) in 3d Rep. B. A. E., 1884, (2) Navaho Legends, 1897; Pepper in Everybody's Mag., Jan. 1902; Stephen in Am. Anthrop., VI, no. 4, 1893; Voth in Am. Anthrop., II, no. 2, 1900. See *Adornment, Clothing, Dyes and Pigments, Receptacles, Weaving*. (O. T. M.  W. H.)

**Blewmouths.** Mentioned in a Georgia tract of 1740 (Force Tracts, I, 3, 1836) apparently as a tribe w. of the Choctaw. "According to the French Indians [Choctaw] there is a large city where a blue-lipped people live, of whom they have often heard it said that if any one tries to kill them he becomes insane" (Brinton, Nat. Leg. Chahta-Muskokee Tribes, 10, 1870). Nothing further is known of them.

**Bloody Knife.** A famous Arikara warrior and chief, who was long in the Government service. His father was a Hunkpapa Sioux and his mother an Arikara. He was born on the Hunkpapa res., N. Dak., but as he approached manhood his mother determined to return to her people and he accompanied her. Prior to the building of the Northern Pacific R. R. the mail for Ft Stevenson, N. Dak., and other Missouri r. points, was carried overland from Ft Totten. The high country E. of the Missouri was at that time a hunting ground for hostile Sioux who had been driven w. from Minnesota after the massacre of 1862, and so often were the mail carriers on this route killed that it became difficult to find anyone to carry the mails. Bloody Knife undertook the task, and traversing the country with Indian caution almost always got the mail through on time. Soon after the establishment of Ft Abraham Lincoln, N. Dak., a number of Arikara scouts were engaged for service at the post, and of these Bloody Knife was the chief. He was with Gen. Stanley on the Yellowstone expedition of 1873 and took part in the fighting of that trip; he also accompanied Custer to the Black-hills in 1874, and was one of the scouts with Custer and Terry's expedition in 1876. On the day of the Custer fight he was with the other scouts with Reno's command, took part in the effort made by them to check the Indians who were charging Reno's force while crossing Reno cr., and was killed there, fighting bravely. (G. B. G.)

**Blount Indians.** A Seminole band, numbering 43, under John Blunt, or Blount, for whom a reserve, 2 by 4 m. on Apalachicola r., Fla., was established in 1823 by the Moultrie Creek treaty (U. S. Ind. Treaties, 307, 1837). They went to lower Chattahoochee r., Ala., before the Seminole war of 1835–42, and after it removed with the Alibamu to Polk co., Tex., where 28 of them survived in 1870 (Ind. Aff. Rep., 327, 1870).

**Blunt Indians.**—Ibid.

**Blowgun.** A dart-shooting weapon, consisting of a long tube of cane or wood from which little darts are discharged by blowing with the mouth. The darts are slender splints or weed stems, pointed at one end and wrapped at the butt with cotton, thistle down, or other soft material. This implement was common in the more southerly parts of the United States, the habitat of the fishing cane of which it was made. The Cherokee, Iroquois, and Muskhogean tribes made use of it. In

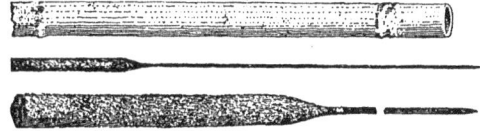

PORTION OF CANE BLOWGUN AND THISTLE-DOWN DART; CHEROKEE

the National Museum is an example from Louisiana made of four cane stems lashed together side by side. The Cherokee, who call the little darts by the same name as that of the thistle, gather the heads of thistles at the proper season and pack them together in the form of a wheel which they hang in their houses to be made into darts (Mooney). The northern Iroquois substituted elder stalks for cane (Hewitt). The Hopi, in certain ceremonies, blow feathers to the cardinal points through tubes of cane (Fewkes). (O. T. M.)

**Bluejacket** (*Weyapiersenwah*). An influential Shawnee chief, born probably about the middle of the 18th century. He was noted chiefly as the principal leader of the Indian forces in the battle with Gen. Wayne of Aug. 20, 1794, at Presque Isle, Ohio. In the fight with Gen. Harmer in 1790 he was associated in command with Little Turtle, but in the battle with Wayne Bluejacket assumed chief control, as Little Turtle was opposed to further warring and urged the acceptance of the offers of peace, but was overruled by Bluejacket. After the defeat of the Indians, Bluejacket was present at the conference at Greenville, Ohio, and signed the treaty of 1795 made with Wayne at that place. He also signed the treaty of Ft Industry, Ohio, July 4, 1805. It is probable that he died soon after this date, as there is no further notice of him. Later descendants of the same name continue to be influential leaders in the tribe in the W. (C. T.)

**Boalkea.** A Pomo village, speaking the northern dialect, in Scott valley, w. of upper Clear lake, Cal. Gibbs in 1851, gave them, under the name Moalkai, as one of the Clear lake groups, w. of the lake, with a population of 45. (A. L. K.)
Möal-kai.—Gibbs (1851) in Schoolcraft, Ind. Tribes, III, 109, 1853.

**Board of Indian Commissioners.** See *United States Board of Indian Commissioners.*

**Boat Harbor.** A Micmac village near Pictou, Nova Scotia.—Can. Ind. Aff. Rep. 1880, 46, 1881.

**Boats.** Under this general term are included various kinds of water craft used throughout North America wherever waters favored. The Eskimo have two forms—the man's boat (*kaiak*, Russian *baidarka*) and the woman's boat (*umiak*, Russian *baidarra*)—made by stretching a covering of seal hide over a framework of whale ribs or of driftwood. The

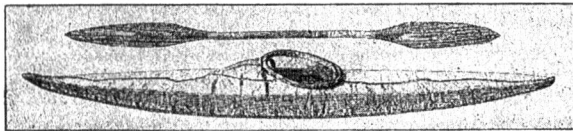

ESKIMO KAIAK. (MURDOCH)

umiak, or woman's boat, is an open scow with little modification of bow and stern, propelled with large oars and a sail made of intestines; but the man's boat is one of the most effective devices for water travel in the world. The man sits in a small hatch, and, in the lighter forms, when his water-tight jacket is lashed to the gunwale he is practically shut in, so that though the water may pass entirely over him, scarcely a drop enters the craft. He moves himself through the water by

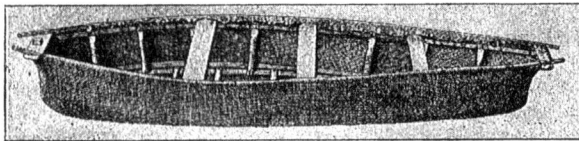

ESKIMO UMIAK. (TURNER)

means of a paddle, in most cases a double one.

Immediately in touch with the skin-boat countries all around the Arctic, from Labrador to Kodiak in Alaska and southward to the line of the white birch, eastward of the Rocky mts., and including the country of the great lakes, existed the birch-bark canoe. With framework of light spruce wood, the covering or sheathing of bits of tough bark sewed together

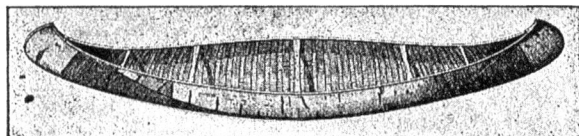

HUDSON BAY BIRCH-BARK CANOE. (TURNER)

and made water-tight by means of melted pitch, these boats are interesting subjects of study, as the exigencies of travel and portage, the quality of the material, and traditional ideas produce different forms

in different areas. Near the mouth of the Yukon, where the water is sometimes turbulent, the canoe is pointed at both ends and partly decked over. On the E. side of

CHIPPEWA DUGOUT. (HOFFMAN)

Canada the bow and the stern of the canoe are greatly rounded up. A curious form has been reported by travelers among the Beothuk of Newfoundland. On the Kootenai, and all over the plateaus of British Columbia and N. Washington, the Asiatic form, monitor-shaped, pointed at either end under the water, is made from pine bark instead of birch bark.

From the N. boundary of the United States, at least from the streams empty-

TLINGIT DUGOUT WITH PAINTED DESIGNS. (SWAN)

ing into the St Lawrence southward along the Atlantic slope, dugout canoes, or pirogues, were the instruments of navigation. On the Missouri r. and elsewhere a small tub-shaped craft of willow frame covered with rawhide, with no division of bow or stern, locally known as the bull-boat, was used by Sioux, Mandan, Arikara, and Hidatsa women for carrying their goods down or across the rivers. It was so light that when one was emptied a

BALSA OF TULE GRASS, PYRAMID LAKE, NEVADA. (POWERS)

woman could take it on her back and make her way across the land. On the w. coast, from Mt St Elias southward to Eel r., Cal., excellent dugout canoes were made from giant cedar and other light woods, some of them nearly 100 ft. long. The multitude of islands off the N. coast rendered it possible for the natives to pass from one to the other, and thus they were induced to invent seagoing canoes of fine quality. Here also from tribe to tribe the forms differ somewhat as to the shape of the bow and stern and the ornamentation. On the California coast and navigable streams N. of C. Mendocino, well-made wooden dugout canoes were used; wooden canoes, made chiefly of planks lashed together and calked, were used in the Santa Barbara id. region; both were important elements in influencing the culture of the people of these sections. Everywhere else in California, ·barring the occasional use of corracles and rafts of logs, transportation by water was conducted by means of balsas, consisting of rushes tied in bundles, generally, if not always, with more or less approximation to a boat of cigar shape.　In certain spots in California, as on Clear lake among the Pomo and Tulare lake among the Yokuts, these tule balsas were important factors in native life; elsewhere in the state much less so (Kroeber).　On the lower Rio Colorado and in s. central California the Indians made immense corracle-like baskets, called by the Spaniards *coritas*, which were coated with bitumen or other waterproofing and used for fording the streams, laden with both passengers and merchandise.

Consult Boas, The Central Eskimo, 6th Rep. B. A. E., 1888; Coues, Garcés Diary, 1900; Hoffman, The Menomini Indians, 14th Rep. B. A. E., 1896; Murdoch, Ethnological Results of the Point Barrow Expedition, 9th Rep. B. A. E., 1892; Nelson, The Eskimo about Bering Strait, 18th Rep. B. A. E., 1899; Niblack, The Coast Indians of Southern Alaska and Northern British Columbia, Rep. Nat. Mus., 1888; Powers in Cont. N. A. Ethnol., III, 1877; Simms in Am. Anthrop., VI, 191, 1904; Winship in 14th Rep. B. A. E., 407, 1896.　See *Commerce, Fur trade, Trails and Trade routes, Travel.*　(o. T. M.)

**Boat-stones.**　Prehistoric objects of polished stone having somewhat the shape of a canoe, the use of which is unknown. Some have straight parallel sides and square ends; in others the sides converge to a blunt point.　A vertical section cut lengthwise of either is approximately triangular, the long face is more or less hollow, and there is usually a perforation near each end; some have a groove

*a*

*b*

BOAT-STONE OF CHLORITE; TENNESSEE (1-3).　*a*, SIDE; *b*, BOTTOM

on the outer or convex side, apparently to receive a cord passed through the holes. Sometimes there is a keel-like projection in which this groove is cut.　It is surmised that they were employed as charms or talismans and carried about the person. They are found sparingly in most of the states E. of the Mississippi r. as well as in Canada.　Those in the Northern states are made principally of slate, in the S. and W. steatite is most common, but other varieties of stone were used. In form some of these objects approach the plummets (q. v.) and are perforated at one end for suspension; others approximate the cones and hemispheres (q. v.).　Analogous

BOAT-STONE OF SLATE (1-6)

objects are found on the Pacific coast, some of which are manifestly modeled after the native canoe while others resemble the boat-stones of the E., although often perforated at one end for suspension.　See *Problematical objects.*

Consult Fowke (1) in 13th Rep. B. A. E., 1896, (2) Archæol. Hist. Ohio, 1902; Moorehead (1) Prehist. Impls., 1902, (2) The Bird-stone Ceremonial, 1899; Moore, various memoirs in Jour. Acad. Nat. Sci. Phila., 1894–1905; Rau in Smithson. Cont., XXII, 1876.　(G. F. W. H. H.)

**Bobbydoklinny.**　See *Nakaidoklini.*

**Bocachee.**　See *Tomochichi.*

**Boca del Arroyo** (Span.: 'mouth of the gulch').　A Papago village, probably in Pima co., s. Ariz., with 70 inhabitants in 1858.

La Boco del Arroyo.—Bailey in Ind. Aff. Rep., 208, 1858.

**Bocherete.**　The name of a village given to Joutel in 1687 by an Ebahamo Indian and described as being N. or N. w. of the Maligne (Colorado) r., Tex.　The region designated was at that time occupied chiefly by Caddoan tribes.　The village can not be definitely classified.　See Gatschet, Karankawa Inds., 46, 1891.　(A. C. F.)

Bocrettes.—Joutel (1687) in French, Hist. Coll. La., I, 138, 1846.　Tserabocherete.—Joutel (1687) in Margry, Déc., III, 289, 1878 (= Tsera and Bocherete combined).　Tserabocretes.—Joutel (1687) in French, Hist. Coll. La., I, 152, 1846.

**Bocootawwonauke** ('fire people'?).　A tribe mentioned by Powhatan in 1607 as living N. w. of the falls of James r. at Richmond, Va., in the highland country, and as being workers of copper and other metals (Strachey, Hist. Va., 27, 1849).

Bocootawwanaukes.—Strachey, op. cit., 27.　Bocootawwonaukes.—Ibid.　Bocootawwonough.—Ibid., 49.　Bocootowwonocks.—Ibid., 27.　Pocoughtaonack.—Smith, Works, 25, 1884.　Pocoughtronack.—Ibid., 20.

**Bocoyna** (*ōcó* 'pine,' *ina* 'drips,' hence 'turpentine.'—Lumholtz).　A pueblo of civilized Tarahumare on the E. slope of the Sierra Madre, in lat. 28° 25′, long. 107° 15′, w. Chihuahua, Mexico.

Bocoyna.—Lumholtz in Scribner's Mag., XVI, 32, 1894.　Ocoina.—Lumholtz, Unknown Mex., I, 134, 1902 (aboriginal name).

**Bodkins.**　See *Awls, Needles.*

**Bœuf, Nation du.**　Mentioned in the Jesuit Relation of 1662 as a tribe against which the Iroquois that year sent out an expedition.　The name signifies 'Buffalo Nation,' but to what people it refers is unknown; it may have designated either the Buffalo clan or gens of some tribe or one of the buffalo-hunting tribes of the W. (J. M.)

**Bogan.** A marshy cove by a stream; called also *bogan hole* (Ganong in Proc. and Trans. Roy. Soc. Can., 209, 1896). In a letter (Apr. 8, 1903) Ganong says further: "A word very much used by guides and others who go into the New Brunswick woods is *bogan*, a still creek or bay branching from a stream. Exactly the same thing the Indians call a *pokologan*." He thinks *bogan*, like *logan*, probably the common name in Maine for the same thing, a corruption of *pokologan*. Both words, Ganong notes, are in good local use and occur in articles on sporting, etc. It is possible that "bogan hole" may be a folk etymologizing of *pokologan*. In the Chippewa language a marsh or bog is *tō'tōgŭn*.
(A. F. C.)

**Boguechito** ('big bayou'). A Choctaw band formerly residing in Neshoba co., Miss., in a district known by the same name.—Gatschet, Creek Migr. Leg., I, 108, 1884.
**Bogue Chittos.**—Claiborne (1843) in Sen. Doc. 168, 28th Cong., 1st sess., 91, 1844.

**Bogue Toocolo Chitto** (*Bok tuklo chitto* 'two big bayous'). A former Choctaw town, which derived its name from its location at the confluence of Running Tiger and Sukenatcha crs., about 4 m. N. w. of De Kalb, Kemper co., Miss.—Halbert in Miss. Hist. Soc. Publ., VI, 424, 1902.

**Bohnapobatin.** (*Bohnapo-batin*, 'western many houses'). The name applied by the Pomo living in the region of Clear lake, Cal., to those living along the upper course of Russian r.—Gibbs (1851) in Schoolcraft, Ind. Tribes, III, 110, 1853.

**Bokea.** A former Pomo village situated in what is known as Rancheria valley, on the headwaters of Navarro r., Mendocino co., Cal. (A. L. K. S. A. B.)
**Boch-heaf.**—Gibbs in Schoolcraft, Ind. Tribes, III, 112, 1853.

**Bokninuwad** (in part from *bok*, 'to find'). A Yokuts tribe formerly on Deer cr., Tulare co., Cal. They ceded lands to the United States by treaty of May 30, 1851, and went on a reservation on Kings r. (A. L. K.)
**Go-ke-nim-nons.**—Wessells (1853) in H. R. Ex. Doc. 76, 34th Cong., 32, 1857. **Noches Paginoas.**—Garcés (1776), Diary, 288, 1900. **Po-ken-well.**—Royce in 18th Rep. B. A. E., 782, 1900. **Po-ken-welle.**—Barbour in Sen. Ex. Doc. 4, 32d Cong., spec. sess., 255, 1853. **Pokoninos.**—Bancroft, Nat. Races, I, 456, 1874. **Po-kon-wel-lo.**—Johnston in Sen. Ex. Doc. 61, 32d Cong., 1st session, 23, 1852.

**Bokonghelas.** See *Buckongahelas*.

**Bolas.** Span.: 'balls'). A hunting weapon consisting of two or more balls of heavy material attached to the end of a cord by means of shorter cords. The type weapon is that used by the tribes of the pampas of South America to en-

tangle the legs of animals. The only weapon of this character found in North America is that used by the western Eskimo for hunting birds, especially waterfowl. It consists of from 4 to 10 blocks, or shaped pieces of bone or ivory, about the size of a walnut, each attached to a sinew or rawhide cord 24 to 30 in. long, and gathered and secured to a short handle made of grass stems or feathers, forming a grip. In throwing the bolas it is swung around the head once or twice, then released like a sling. During the first part of their course the balls remain bunched, but when they lose speed or come in contact with an object they diverge and entangle. In the hands of the Eskimo the weapon is effectual at 40 to 50 yds. The bolas is analogous to the slungshot, to the casse-tête of the Plains Indians, and to the cast-net of S. E. Asia. Zuñi children have a toy which resembles the bolas. Consult Murdoch in 9th Rep. B. A. E., 245, 1892; Nelson in 18th Rep. B. A. E., 134, 1899. (W. H.)

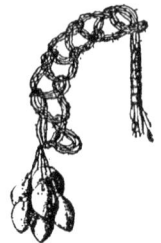

ESKIMO BIRD BOLAS. (MURDOCH)

**Bolbone.** A subdivision of the Cholovone, the northernmost group of the Mariposan family, residing E. of San Joaquin r. and N. of Tuolumne r., Cal. (A. L. K.)
**Bolbon.**—Taylor in Cal. Farmer, Oct. 18, 1861. **Bolbones.**—Chamisso in Kotzebue, Voy., III, 51, 1821. **Bulbones.**—Bancroft, Nat. Races, I, 453, 1874 (misquoted from Chamisso). **Pulpenes.**—Taylor in Cal. Farmer, Mar. 30, 1860. **Pulpones.**—Ibid. **Volvon.**—Ibid., Oct. 18, 1861.

**Boleck.**—See *Bowlegs*.

**Bolinas.** A name formerly applied to the people living in the region of Bolinas bay, S. of Pt Reyes, Marin co., Cal. Taylor (Cal. Farmer, Mar. 30, 1860) gives Bollanos, an incorrect spelling of Bolinas, as the name of a small division of the Olamentke (Moquelumnan stock) formerly "near Bollenos bay, Tamales bay, Punto de los Reyes, and probably as far up as Bodega bay." (S. A. B.)

**Bolshoigor.** A Koyukukhotana village on Yukon r., 25 m. above the mouth of Koyulsuk r., Alaska.—Petroff (1880), 10th Census, Alaska, map, 1884.
**Bolshoiger.**—Baker, Geog. Dict. Alaska, 1901 (after Petroff).

**Bomazeen.** A chief or sachem of the Kennebec tribe whose residence was at Norridgewock, Kennebec r., Me., the ancient capital or principal village of the tribe. He is mentioned as early as 1693 and is known to have died in 1724. He made a treaty with Gov. Phips in 1693; went to the fort at Pemaquid, Me., in 1694 under a flag of truce, and was treacherously seized and cast into prison in Boston. After his release he waged war for a time on the settlements, attacking

Chelmsford, Sudbury, and other towns in Massachusetts in 1706, and Saco, Me., in 1710. A treaty of peace to which his name was signed was made at Portsmouth, N. H., July 13, 1713. He was killed by a party under Capt. Moulton near Taconnet, Me., in 1724; about the same time his family at Norridgewock was fired upon, his daughter being killed and his wife taken prisoner.      (c. t.)

**Bones.** See *Anatomy*.

**Bone-work.** The use of bone and related materials, including antler, ivory, horn, whalebone, turtle-shell, and the teeth, hoofs, beaks, and claws of many creatures, was almost universal among Indian tribes. The hardness and toughness of these materials made them desirable for many kinds of implements and utensils, and their pleasing color and capacity for high polish caused them to be valued for personal ornaments. Since both man and beasts of various kinds have an important place in aboriginal mythology, it is to be expected that in numerous instances their bones had a special sacred significance and use, as when, for example, the skulls and paws of small animals were used for mixing medicine.

Not uncommonly the small bones, teeth, and claws of various animals, the beaks of birds, etc., were strung as beads, were perforated or grooved to be hung as pendant ornaments or rattles, or were sewed on garments or other objects of use. These uses are illustrated in the necklaces of crab claws and the puffin beak ceremonial armlets of the Eskimo, by the bear-tooth necklaces of many of the tribes, by the elk tusk embellishments of the buckskin costumes of the women among the Plains Indians, and by the small carved bone pendants attached to the edge of the garments of the ancient Beothuk (see *Adornment*). Teeth and small bones, such as the metacarpals of the deer, as well as worked bone disks and lozenges, were used as dice in playing games of chance, and gaming sticks of many varieties were made of bone. In precolonial times bone had to be cut, carved, and engraved with implements of stone, such as knives, scrapers, saws, gravers, drills, and grinding stones, and with some of the tribes the primitive methods still prevail. Although indispensable to primitive tribes everywhere, this material occupies a place of exceptional importance in the far N. beyond the limits of forest growth, where the only available wood is brought oversea from distant shores by winds and currents. The Eskimo have the bones of the whale, seal, walrus, bear, wolf, moose, reindeer, muskox, and a wild sheep, and the antlers of the moose and deer, the horns of the sheep and ox, the teeth of the bear, wolf,

and reindeer, the ivory of the walrus and narwhal, fossil ivory, the whalebone of the right-whale, and the bones of the smaller quadrupeds and various birds, and their skill in shaping them and adapting them to their needs in the rigorous arctic environment is truly remarkable. The larger bones, as the ribs of the whale, are employed in constructing houses, caches, and shelters; for ribs of boats, runners for sleds, and plates for armor (Nelson). Bone, ivory, and antler were utilized for bows, arrows, spears, harpoons, knives, scrapers, picks, flint-flaking implements, clubs, boxes, and a great variety of appliances and tackle employed in rigging boats, in fishing, in hunting, in transportation, in preparing the product of the chase for consumption; for weaving, netting, and sewing implements, household utensils, tobacco pipes, gaming implements, toys, dolls, fetishes, amulets, and artistic carvings of many kinds. Personal ornaments and toilet articles of bone and kindred materials are more numerous in Alaska, where beads, pendants, hairpins, combs, labrets, belt clasps, belt ornaments of reindeer teeth, etc., are largely made and ingeniously applied. The artistic work of these northern peoples is shown in their extremely clever carvings in ivory and their engravings of various ornamental and pictorial designs upon objects of use and ornament, but there seems to be sufficient ground for the opinion that these particular phases of their art are largely of recent development and are due to association with white men and as a result of the acquisition of metal tools and perhaps also to some extent to contact with Indian tribes which in their turn have been influenced by the whites. The wide range and vast numbers of the objects of art shaped from these materials by the arctic peoples of the present period will be more fully appreciated by reference to the works of Boas, Murdoch, Nelson, and Turner, in the annual reports of the Bureau of American Ethnology, and by a visit to the ethnologic museums.

Bone and the allied substances have been and are favorite materials with the tribes of the Pacific coast. The utensils, implements, ornaments, and totemic and symbolic carvings of the N. W. coast tribes are often admirable and display esthetic appreciation of a high order (Niblack, Boas). Their carvings in bone, ivory, and antler, often inlaid with abalone, and the graceful and elaborately carved cups, ladles, and spoons of horn, are especially noteworthy. The art of the tribes of the Frazer basin and the Pacific slope s. of Puget sd. is much more primitive, though bone was in general use for implements, utensils, musical instruments, gaming articles, and ornaments (Abbott, Goddard, Powers, Smith), great numbers being preserved in our museums. Many of the tribes of the arid region, the great divide, the Mississippi valley, and the E. still employ bone, horn, antler, and turtle-shell to a large extent, but metal has largely usurped their place, especially for implements, hence finds from village sites, cemeteries, and burial mounds must be depended on largely for knowledge of the aboriginal bone-work of these regions. The ancient Pueblos inlaid some of their implements and ornaments of bone with bits of turquoise and other bright stones (Fewkes, Pepper). Among the tribes of many sections bones of deer and the larger birds were used for flutes and whistles, and shells of turtles for rattles, and the latter were often made also of beaks of birds and hoofs and dewclaws of deer and other animals, or by attaching these articles to parts of the costume, or to bands for the wrists and ankles. Champlain illustrates a game drive in which the drivers appear to be beating with bones upon clavicles of some large animal, and among the Plains tribes and the Pueblos a sort of saw-fiddle in which sometimes a scapula is drawn over a notched stick, or over another scapula, for keeping time in ceremonial dances, is employed. The mounds of the Mississippi and Ohio valleys and the Southern states have yielded a wide range of objects, both useful and ornamental. Of the former class, awls, fish-hooks, pins, arrow-points, cutting tools made of beaver teeth, and scraping tools are the most important. Of the latter class, beads, pendants, gorgets, pins, wristlets, etc., are worthy of note. There are also bone whistles and flutes, engraved batons, and various carvings that would seem rather to be totemic and symbolic than simply useful or ornamental; horns of the buffalo and mountain sheep were made into dippers and cups, and were also, as were the antlers of deer, utilized in headdresses by the ancient as well as by the present peoples. The scapulæ of large animals formed convenient hoe blades and as such were probably universally employed by the native agriculturists. A novel use of bones is that of plating them with copper, illustrated by the plated jawbone of a wolf obtained by Moore from a Florida mound. In the wonderful collection of objects from the Hopewell mound, near Chillicothe, Ohio, is a human femur engraved with intricate and finely executed symbolic figures (Putnam and Willoughby).

The literature of this topic is voluminous, though much scattered, and is embodied mainly in reports on field researches published by the Smithsonian Institution, the National Museum, the Bureau of American Ethnology, the Reports of the Minister of Education, Ontario, the leading museums and academies, and in works of a more general nature, such as Moorehead's Prehistoric Implements and Fowke's Archæological History of Ohio.        (W. H. H.)

**Bonfouca.** A former Muskhogean settlement, a short distance N. of L. Pontchartrain, La.
Bonifoucas.—Baudry des Lozières, Voy. Louisiane, 241, 1802.

**Bonne Espérance.** A Montagnais settlement on the islands and mainland at the mouth of Esquimaux r., on the s. coast of Labrador. Some Nascapee are probably there also.—Stearns, Labrador, 264, 293, 1884.

**Bonostac.** Mentioned as a Pima settlement on the upper Rio Santa Cruz, below Tucson, Ariz., in 1764; but from the location it would seem more likely that it was a Papago rancheria.
Bonostac. — Orozco y Berra, Geog., 347, 1864. Bonostac.—Bandelier in Arch. Inst. Papers, IV, 472, 1892.

**Booadasha** ('fish-catchers'). A band of the Crows.
Boo-a-dă′-sha.—Morgan, Anc. Soc., 159, 1877.

**Booctolooee.** A former Choctaw village pertaining to the "Sixtowns," situated on Boguetulukusi cr., a w. affluent of Chicasawhay r., probably in Jasper co., Miss.—W. Fla. map, ca. 1775.

**Books in Indian languages.** In addition to dictionaries, versions of the Bible and the Prayer Book, whole and in part, Bible stories complete and summarized, catechisms, and cognate works, the literature translated into Indian languages embraces some interesting volumes. In Greenlandic Eskimo there is an abridged version of Stoud-Platon's Geography, by E. A. Wandall (1848); a translation of Thomas à Kempis' Imitation of Christ, by Paul Egede (1787, revised 1824); a History of the World, by C. E. Janssen (1861), and another by S. P. Kleinschmidt (1859). Peter Kragh's translations of Ingemann's Voices in the Wilderness, and The High Game, Krummacher's Parables and Feast Book, the Life of Hans Egede, and other books circulated in manuscript. In the Labrador dialect a geography, by A. F. Elsner, was published in 1880. Under the title *Mahpiya ekta oicimani ya*, 'Sky to traveling he went,' Rev. S. R. Riggs published in 1857 a translation of Bunyan's Pilgrim's Progress into the Dakota language of the Siouan stock. This same book was translated into Cree by Archbishop Vincent (1886), and into Cheyenne by Rev. R. Petter (1904). In 1879 Rev. D. W. Hemans published a Santee version of Rev. R. Newton's The King's Highway. Into the Massachuset dialect of the Algonquian stock Rev. John Eliot translated in 1664 Baxter's Call to the Unconverted, in 1665 Bayly's Practice of Piety, about 1687 the Rev. W. Perkins' Six Principles of Religion, and in 1689 Shepard's Sincere Convert. A Geography for Beginners was published in Chippewa in 1840, and in Santee Dakota in 1876. In 1839 the Rev. C. A. Goodrich's Child's Book of the Creation was translated into Choctaw by the Rev. L. S. Williams. The civilized tribes of Indian Territory, with the aid of the Cherokee and adapted alphabets, have published many laws, text-books, etc., in the native languages.

Exclusive of occasional texts, more or less brief, in native languages, to be found in the periodical literature of anthropology, in ethnological and linguistic monographs, books of travel and description, etc., there is accumulating a considerable literature of texts by accredited men of science and other competent observers. The Chimmesyan stock is represented by Boas' Tsimshian Texts (Bull. 27, B. A. E., 1902); the Chinookan by Boas' Chinook Texts (Bull. 20, B. A. E., 1904), and Kathlamet Texts (Bull. 26, 1901); the Salishan by Teit and Boas' Traditions of the Thompson River Indians (1898); the Wakashan (Kwakiutl-Nootka) by Boas and Hunt's Kwakiutl Texts (Mem. Am. Mus. Nat. Hist., 1902–05); the Skittagetan by Swanton's Haida Texts (Bull. 29, B. A. E., 1905); the Athapascan by Goddard's Hupa Texts (Publ. Univ. Cal., Am. Archæol. and Ethnol., I, 1904), and his Morphology of the Hupa Language (1905) perhaps belongs here also, likewise Matthews' Navaho Legends (1897) and The Night Chant (1902); the Siouan by Riggs' Dakota Grammar, Texts, and Ethnography (Cont. N. A. Ethnol., IX, 1893), Dorsey's Çegiha Language (Cont. N. A. Ethnol., VI, 1890), Omaha and Ponka Letters (Bull. 11, B. A. E., 1891), and Osage Traditions (6th Rep. B. A. E., 1888); the Iroquoian by Mooney's Sacred Formulas of the Cherokee (7th Rep. B. A. E., 1891), Hewitt's Iroquoian Cosmology (21st Rep. B. A. E., 1903), and Hale's Iroquois Book of Rites (1883)—the second records cosmologic myths, the last the great national ritual of the northern Iroquois. The Algonquian is represented by scattered texts rather than by books, although there are to be mentioned Brinton's Lenape and Their Legends (1885), which contains the text of the Walum Olum, and the Cree and Siksika Legends in Petitot's Traditions Indiennes du Canada Nord-ouest (1887), the scattered texts in the works of Schoolcraft, Hoffman, etc.; the Eskimo best by the texts in Boas' Eskimo of Baffin Land and

Hudson Bay (Bull. Am. Mus. Nat. Hist., XV, 1901), and other writings on the Eskimo, Thalbitzer's Phonetical Study of the Eskimo Language (1904), and Barnum's Grammatical Fundamentals of the Innuit Language (1901), the last relating to the Tununa dialect of Alaska. The monographs of Miss Alice C. Fletcher on the ceremonies of the Pawnee (22d Rep. B. A. E., 1903), of James Mooney on the Ghost Dance Religion (14th Rep. B. A. E., 1896), the numerous monographs of Dr Franz Boas on the Bellacoola, the Kwakiutl, etc., contain much textual material. The manuscript collection of the Bureau of American Ethnology is rich in texts of myths, legends, etc. As a whole, the body of linguistic material, here briefly noticed, is of increasing magnitude and value. The literature in the Chinook jargon also furnishes some titles, e. g., the stenographic periodical *Kamloops Wawa*, by Father Le Jeune, who is also the author of several pamphlets. Worthy of mention is Rev. Myron Eells' Hymns in the Chinook Jargon Language (1878–89), which is not merely a translation of English verse. See *Bible translations, Dictionaries, Periodicals.*

(A. F. C.)

**Boomerangs.** See *Rabbit sticks.*

**Boothroyd.** A body of Ntlakyapamuk Indians of Salishan stock on Fraser r., Brit. Col. The name seems to have been employed to include the towns of Spain, Kimus, Tzaumuk, Suk, and Nkattsim. Pop. 159 in 1902 (Can. Ind. Aff. for 1902, 238).

**Borego** ('sheep'). An ancient settlement of the Tepecano, now in ruins, situated on the E. bank of the Rio de Bolaños, approachable from Monte Escobedo, in Jalisco, Mexico. There is a native tradition that its people warred against those of Azqueltan after the first coming of the Spaniards.—Hrdlicka in Am. Anthrop., V. 409, 1903.

**Boring.** See *Drills and Drilling, Shell-work, Stone-work.*

**Borrados** (Span.: 'painted in stripes or blotches'). A tribe which, according to Orozco y Berra (Geog., 300, 308, 1864), formerly resided in Tamaulipas, Nuevo Leon, and Coahuila, N. Mexico. There is evidence that the tribe or a portion of it lived at one time in Texas, as the same authority (p. 382) says that the country of the lower Lipan Indians joined on the E. that of the Karankawa and Borrados in the province of Texas. The relationship of this tribe to the Coahuiltecan group is expressly affirmed by Bartolome Garcia.

**Bosomworth, Mary.** A noted Creek Indian woman, also known as Mary Mathews and Mary Musgrove, who created much trouble for the Georgia colonial government about 1752, nearly rousing the Creek confederacy to war against the English. She seems to have been of high standing among her own people, being closely related to leading chiefs both of the Upper and Lower Creeks, possessed of unusual intelligence and knowledge of English, for which reason, and to secure her good will, Oglethorpe, the founder of the colony, made her his interpreter and negotiator with the Indians at a salary of $500 per year. About 1749 she married her third white husband, the Rev. Thomas Bosomworth, who, by reason of his Indian marriage, was given a commission from the colony of South Carolina as agent among the Creeks, and within a few months had nearly precipitated civil war among the Indians and rebellion among the licensed traders. Being deeply in debt, he instigated his wife to assume the title of "Empress of the Creek Nation," and to make personal claim, first to the islands of Ossabaw, St Catharine, and Sapelo, on the Georgia coast, and afterward to a large territory on the mainland. Notifying Gov. Oglethorpe that she was coming to claim her own, she raised a large body of armed Creeks and marched against Savannah. The town was put in position for defense and a troop of cavalry met the Indians outside and obliged them to lay down their arms before entering. The procession was headed by Bosomworth in full canonical robes, with his "queen" by his side, followed by the chiefs in order of rank, with their warriors. They were received with a military salute and a council followed, lasting several days, during which the Indians managed to regain possession of their arms, and a massacre seemed imminent, which was averted by the seizure of Mary and her husband, who were held in prison until they made suitable apologies and promises of good behavior, the troops and citizens remaining under arms until the danger was over, when the Indians were dismissed with presents. Nothing is recorded of her later career. See Appleton's Cyclopædia of Am. Biog.; various histories of Georgia; Bosomworth's MS. Jour., 1752, in archives B. A. E.    (J. M.)

**Boston Indian Citizenship Committee.** An association for the protection of the rights of Indians; organized in 1879 on the occasion of the forcible removal of the Ponca. The tribe returned to their old home in South Dakota from the reservation in Indian Territory. Chief Standing Bear, released on a writ of habeas corpus, went to Boston, and, on the plea that most of the signatures in favor of removal were fraudulent, enlisted the sympathy of Hon. John D. Long, then governor of Massachusetts, and other organizers of this committee, who finally

secured the rescission of the edict and the restoration of the Dakota reservation. The committee undertook next to secure citizenship for Indians on the basis of the payment of taxes, a principle that was finally denied by the United States Supreme Court. When the Dawes bill granting land in severalty and citizenship was enacted, the committee devoted its attention to securing honest allotment. Since the organization of the Indian Rights Association in Philadelphia the Boston committee has confined itself to securing fair allotments of fertile lands, with adequate water supply, protecting homesteads, and especially to defending and generally promoting the interests of the more progressive bands of tribes that were backward in taking allotments. To safeguard the rights of such and prevent the sale or lease of the best Indian lands to whites at nominal prices, the committee has sought to obtain the dismissal of corrupt Government agents and inspectors whenever such were detected. Joshua W. Davis is chairman and J. S. Lockwood secretary (43 Federal st., Boston, Mass.).

**Bottles.** See *Pottery, Receptacles.*

**Boucfouca.** A former Choctaw town on the headwaters of Pearl r., Miss.
Bouc-fouca.—Jefferys, French Dom. Am., I, 135, map, 1761. **Bouc-fuca.**—Lattré, map U. S., 1784. **Bouk-fuka.**—Schoolcraft, Ind. Tribes, IV, 562, 1854.

**Boudinot, Elias** (native name *Gălă-gi′na*, 'male deer' or 'turkey'). A Cherokee Indian, educated in the foreign mission school at Cornwall, Conn., founded by the American Board of Commissioners for Foreign Missions, which he entered with two other Cherokee youths in 1818 at the instance of the philanthropist whose name he was allowed to adopt. In 1827 the Cherokee council formally resolved to establish a national paper, and the following year the *Cherokee Phœnix* appeared under Boudinot's editorship. After a precarious existence of 6 years, however, the paper was discontinued, and not resumed until after the removal of the Cherokee to Indian Ter., when its place was finally taken by the *Cherokee Advocate*, established in 1844. In 1833 Boudinot wrote "Poor Sarah; or, the Indian Woman," in Cherokee characters, published at New Echota by the United Brethren's Missionary Society, another edition of which was printed at Park Hill in 1843; and from 1823 to the time of his death he was joint translator with Rev. S. A. Worcester of a number of the Gospels, some of which passed through several editions. Boudinot joined an insignificant minority of his people in support of the Ridge treaty and the subsequent treaty of New Echota, by the terms of which the Cherokee Nation surrendered its lands and removed to Indian Ter. This attitude made him so unpopular that on June 22, 1839, he was set upon and murdered, although not with the knowledge or connivance of the tribal officers. See Mooney in 19th Rep. B. A. E., 1900; Pilling, Bibliography of the Iroquoian Languages, Bull. B. A. E., 1888.

**Bouscoutton.** The northernmost division of the Cree, living in 1658-71 about the s. shores of Hudson bay. According to Dr William Jones the Chippewa refer to the northernmost dwelling place of the Cree as Ininiwitōskwŭning, 'at the man's elbow,' and Ăntăwăt-otōskwŭning, 'they dwell at the elbow.' This *ăntăwăt* is probably the term usually prefixed, in one form or another, to the name Bouscoutton.

**Ataouabouscatouek.**—Jes. Rel., 1658, 21, 1858. **Outaouoisbouscottous.**—Tailhan, Perrot, 293, note, 1864. **Outaouois, Bouscouttous.**—Prise de possession (1671) in Margry, Déc., I, 97, 1875 (comma evidently inserted by mistake).

**Boutté Station.** A village in St Charles parish, La., at which lived a camp of Choctaw who manufactured cane basketry and gathered the okra which was ground into gumbo filé.—Harris, La. Products, 203, 1881.

**Bowl, The** (a translation of his native name, *Diwa'ʼlĭ*), also called Col. Bowles. A noted Cherokee chief and leader of one of the first bands to establish themselves permanently on the w. side of the Mississippi. At the head of some hostile Cherokee from the Chickamauga towns he massacred all of the male members of a party of emigrants at Muscle shoals in Tennessee r. in 1794, after which he retired up St. Francis r. on the w. side of the Mississippi, and, his act being disowned by the Cherokee council, who offered to assist in his arrest, he remained in that region until after the cession of Louisiana Territory to the United States. About 1824 so much dissatisfaction was caused by delay in adjusting the boundaries of the territory of the Western Cherokee in Arkansas and the withholding of their annuities that a party headed by Bowl crossed Sabine r. into Texas, where they were joined by bodies of refugees from a number of other eastern tribes and began negotiations with the Mexican government for a tract of land on Angelina, Neches, and Trinity rs., but were interrupted by the outbreak of the Texan war for independence in 1835. Houston, who had long been a friend of the Cherokee, entered into a treaty to assign them certain lands along Angelina r., but it was rejected by the Texas senate in 1837, and Houston's successor, Lamar, declared his intention to drive all the Indians from Texas. On the plea that they were entering into a conspiracy with the Mexican inhabitants, a commission,

supported by several regiments of troops, was sent to the Cherokee town on Angelina r. to demand that they remove at once across the border. On their refusal they were attacked, July 15-16, 1839, and defeated in two engagements, Bowl and his assistant chief, Hard-mush, being among the many killed. See Mooney in 19th Rep. B. A. E., 1900.          (J. R. S.)

**Bowlder outlines.** Certain outline surface figures, probably of Siouan origin, usually formed of bowlders a foot or less in diameter, though a few consisted of buffalo bones. The name "bowlder mosaics" was first applied to them by Todd. According to Lewis, structures of this type have been found from w. Iowa and Nebraska to Manitoba, and from w. Minnesota through North and South Dakota to Montana; but they appear to be, or rather to have been, more frequent in South Dakota than in any

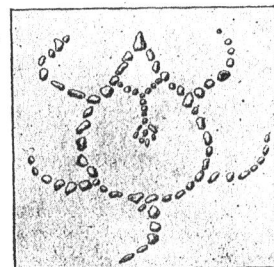

BOWLDER OUTLINE REPRESENTING A QUADRUPED; SOUTH DAKOTA; LENGTH 15 FT.  (THOMAS)

other section. These remains consist of animal, human, and other figures outlined upon the surface of the ground, usually on elevated sites, the human, turtle, and serpent figures being by far the most numerous. In Dakota the outlines are generally accompanied with small stone circles, known to be old tipi sites. In some instances long lines of bowlders or buffalo bones and small stone cairns have been found associated with them or occurring in their immediate neighborhood. Like the bowlder circles these are more or less embedded in the ground, but this does not necessarily indicate great antiquity; indeed, their frequent association with tipi circles seems to denote that they are comparatively recent. The accompanying turtle figure illustrates the type. Among the Crows of Montana a bowlder outline figure is made in the form of a woman to commemorate the unfaithfulness of a wife.

Consult Lewis in Am. Anthrop., II, Apr., 1889, III, July, 1890; Simms, ibid., n. s., v, 374, 1903; Thomas in 12th Rep. B. A. E., 534, 1894; Todd in Am. Naturalist, Jan., 1884.          (C. T.)

**Bowlegs** (probably corrupted from *Bolek*). An inferior Seminole chief who was brought temporarily into notice in 1812 during the Indian war on the Georgia frontier. When early in that year King Paine, also a Seminole chief, at the head of sundry bands of Seminole and negroes, started on a mission of blood and plunder, Bowlegs joined him. A small force under Capt. Williams was met and defeated Sept. 11. Their force being considerably increased, they soon thereafter marched from the Alachua towns to attack Gen. Neuman, who had been sent against them with orders to destroy their towns. After 4 severe charges in which King Paine was killed and Bowlegs wounded, the Indians were driven back. With this occurrence Bowlegs drops from history, though he probably lived several years longer. In a document exhibited in the trial of Arbuthnott and Ambrister his name is signed Boleck. (c. t.)

**Bowlegs Town.** A former Seminole town on Suwannee r., w. Fla.; named after an influential Seminole chief early in the 19th century.—Woodward, Reminiscences, 153, 1859.

**Bowles, Colonel,** see *Bowl, The.*

**Bowls.** With the Indian the bowl serves a multitude of purposes: it is associated with the supply of his simplest needs as well as with his religion. The materials employed in making bowls are stone, especially soapstone, horn, bone, shell, skin, wood, and bark. Bowls are often adapted natural forms, as shells, gourds, and concretions, either unmodified or more or less fully remodeled; and basket bowls are used by many tribes. The use of bowls in the preparation and serving of food is treated under *Dishes* (q. v.). Bowls are also used in primitive agriculture for gathering, winnowing, drying, and roasting seeds, and in connection with milling. With many tribes bowls are made from large knots, being hollowed out with fire and the knife. In Texas and Indian Territory plate-like bowls were made from the wood of the pecan tree, while poplar, oak, and other woods furnished others. Some bowls designed for practical use are no larger than drinking cups, while others, made by or for children as toys, are not much larger than a thimble. Some of the smaller ones, used for mixing medicine, had a small projection from the edge which served as a handle, while the typical Pueblo medicine bowl has terraced edges symbolizing rain clouds, a basket-like handle, and painted figures of sacred water animals, such as the tadpole and the frog. The most ancient permanent cooking utensil of the Plains tribes was a bowl made by hollowing out a stone. The Blackfeet and Cheyenne say that in very early times they boiled their meat in bowls made of some kind of soft stone. The Omaha and others had excellent wooden bowls, the standard of beauty being symmetry of outline and the grain of the gnarled roots from which they were made. Among many Indians bowls were used in games of chance and divination. In certain ceremonies of the Wahpeton

and Sisseton Sioux and of other tribes a game was played with plum-stone dice thrown from a wooden bowl, in the making of which great skill and care were exercised. In some cases the kind of wood was prescribed. Bowls that had been long in use for these games acquired a polish and color unattainable by art, and were prized as tribal possessions. The Micmac accorded supernatural powers to certain of their bowls, and thought that water standing over night in gaming bowls would reveal by its appearance past, present, and future events. Some bowls were supposed to have mysterious powers which would affect the person eating or drinking from them. Bowls and trays of basketry were used by the Sioux, Cheyenne, Arapaho, and other Plains tribes, though not by the Siksika, in the familiar seed game. These appear to be the only baskets made by these tribes (Grinnell).

Among the Pueblo tribes the pottery bowl, like the basket-bowl drum of the Navaho and the Panamint, is frequently a cult vessel employed in religious ceremonies, the medicine bowl with its nature symbols and the sacred meal bowl furnishing familiar examples. Such vessels are sacrificed to springs or are deposited in shrines and caves. The ancient Hopi evidently regarded the concave of the bowl as the vault of the sky, and pictured on it stars, birds, and celestial beings. The food bowls in animal forms, like those of the N. W. coast, were apparently associated primarily with the nourishment derived from animals. Wooden bowls used for religious purposes were often decorated by the Plains tribes with incised figures of sacred animals, whose supposed spiritual power had relation to the uses of the vessel; and like explanation may be made of the life-form decorations sculptured and modeled in relief and engraved and painted on bowls of many tribes, ancient and modern. See *Basketry, Dishes, Food, Games, Pottery, Receptacles.*

**Bows.** See *Arrows.*

**Boxelder Indians.** A branch of the Shoshoni formerly in n. w. Utah.—Lynde in Sen. Ex. Doc. 42, 36th Cong., 1st sess., 38, 1860.

**Boxes and Chests.** The distribution of tribes using boxes and chests illustrates in a striking manner the effect of environment on arts and customs. Thus woodland tribes made boxes of suitable timber, and the culmination of their manufacture is found among the tribes of the N. W. coast. The Eskimo had a great variety of small boxes of bone, wood, whalebone, and ivory, and displayed extraordinary skill and inventiveness in their manufacture. This was in large measure due to their damp and freezing environment, in which, though wood was scarce, boxes were better than pouches for keeping the contents dry. It appears that to the introduction of tobacco, percussion caps, and powder is due the great number of small boxes manufactured by the Eskimo, although they had previously many boxes for trinkets, lanceheads, tinder, etc. Eskimo boxes are provided with cords for fastening them to the person to prevent loss in the snow.

IVORY BOX FOR SMALL ARTICLES; ESKIMO; 1-3. (MURDOCH)

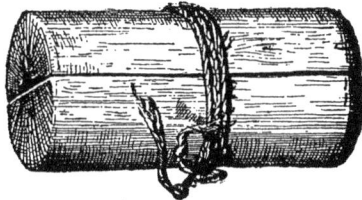

Boxes and chests, being difficult of transportation even on water, must be looked for chiefly among sedentary tribes living in a wooded country. Tribes that moved freely about stored and transported their goods in bags, rawhide cases, and basket wallets. Boxes and chests of wood are practically unknown among the Plains tribes, which had abundant skins of large animals out of which to make receptacles for their posses-

WOODEN BOX FOR WHALING AMULET; ESKIMO; 1-2. (MURDOCH)

sions, and the horse and the dog as pack and draft animals. Some of the Plains tribes, however, made box-like cases or trunks of rawhide similar in shape to the birch-bark boxes of the eastern tribes,

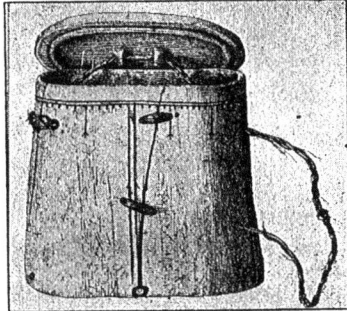

HOUSEHOLD CHESTS WITH CARVED AND PAINTED DESIGNS; HAIDA; 1-18. (NIBLACK)

and the Sioux made plume boxes of wood. Objects and materials that could be injured by crushing or by dampness usually required a box, the most widespread use of which was for the storing of feathers. The Plains tribes and some others made parfleches, or cases of rawhide, almost as rigid as a wooden box, for headdresses, arrows, etc.; the Pima, Papago, and Mohave made basket cases for feathers; and the Pueblos employed a box, usually excavated from a single piece of cottonwood, solely for holding the feathers used in ceremonies. The Yurok of California made a cylindrical wooden box in two sections for storing valuables. The eastern woodland tribes made boxes of birch bark. The N. W. coast tribes as far s. as Washington made large chests of wood for storing food, clothing, etc.; for cooking, for ripening salmon eggs, for the interment of the dead, for drums and other

WOODEN BOX FOR FEATHERS; HOPI; 1-15. (J. STEVENSON)

uses, and these were usually decorated with carving or painting, or both. These tribes also made long boxes as quivers for arrows, but smaller boxes were not so common among them as among the Eskimo.

Consult Boas, Decorative Art of the Indians of the North Pacific Coast, Bull. Am. Mus. Nat. Hist., IX, no. 10, 1897; Kroeber in Bull. Am. Mus. Nat. Hist., XVIII, pt. 1, 1902; Nelson, Eskimo about Bering Strait, 18th Rep. B. A. E., 1899; Niblack, Coast Indians, Rep. Nat. Mus. 1888, 1890; Stevenson in 2d Rep. B. A. E., 1883; Swan, Indians of Cape Flattery, Smithson. Cont., XVI, 1870; Swanton in Mem. Am. Mus. Nat. Hist., V, pt. 1, 1905. See *Bags and pouches, Basketry, Parfleche, Receptacles, Wood-work,* etc.　　(w. h.)

**Brain.** See *Anatomy.*

**Brant, Joseph.** See *Thayendanegea.*

**Breastworks.** See *Fortifications.*

**Brèche-dent.** See *Broken Tooth.*

**Breech-cloth.** See *Child life, Clothing.*

**Bridge River Indians.** A band of Upper Lillooet occupying the village of Kanlax, on Bridge r., which flows into the upper Fraser above Lillooet, Brit. Col.; pop. 108 in 1902.—Can. Ind. Aff., pt. II, 72, 1902.

**Briertown.** A former Cherokee settlement on Nantahala r., about the mouth of Briertown cr., in Macon co., N. C.—Mooney in 19th Rep. B. A. E., 524, 1900.
Kănu′gûʼlâyĭ.—Mooney, ibid. ('brier place').
Kănu′gûʼlûñʼyĭ.—Ibid. See *Nantahala.*

**Bright Eyes.** True name, Susette La Flesche. The eldest child of Eshtamaza, or Joseph La Flesche, a former head-chief of the Omaha. She was born in Nebraska about 1850 and attended the Presbyterian mission school on the Omaha res. Through the interest of one of her teachers, Susette was sent to a private school in Elizabeth, N. J., where she made rapid progress in her studies. After her return home she taught in a Government day school on the Omaha res. and exercised a stimulating influence on the young people of the tribe. In 1877–78 the Ponca were forcibly removed to Indian Territory from their home on Niobrara r., S. Dak. Not long afterward Susette accompanied her father to Indian Territory, where he went to render such help as he could to his sick and dying relatives among the Ponca. The heroic determination of the Ponca chief, Standing Bear, to lead his band back to their northern home; their sufferings during their march of more than 600 m.; his arrest and imprisonment; and, after a sharp legal struggle, his release by *habeas corpus*, in accordance with Judge Dundy's decision that "an Indian is a person" (U. S. *v.* Crook, 5 Dillon, 453), led to steps being taken by a committee of citizens to bring the matter of Indian removals before the public. Arrangements were made to have Standing Bear, accompanied by Susette La Flesche and her brother, visit the principal cities of the United States under the direction of Mr T. H. Tibbles, and tell the story of the Ponca removal. The name "Bright Eyes" was given Susette, and under that cognomen she entered upon her public work. Her clear exposition of the case, her eloquent appeals for humanity toward her race, her grace and dignity of diction and bearing aroused the interest of the thousands who listened to her. As a result, a request was urged on the Government that there be no more removals of tribes, and this request has been respected when practicable. In 1881 Bright Eyes married Mr T. H. Tibbles. Later she and her husband visited England and Scotland, where she made a number of addresses. After her return to this country she lived in Lincoln, Neb., and maintained activity with her pen until her death in 1902.          (A. C. F.)

**British Band.** A former band of the Sauk and Foxes. See *Sauk.*

**Broken Arrows.** A hunting band of Sioux found on the Platte by Sage (Scenes in Rocky Mts., 68, 1846); possibly the Cazazhita.

**Broken Tooth.** The son of Biauswah and chief of the Sandy Lake Chippewa, also referred to as Kadewabedas and Catawatabeta (strictly Ma‘kadēwâbidis, from *ma‘kadē* 'black,' *wâbidis* 'tooth'), and by the French Brèche-dent. He is spoken of as a little boy in 1763, and is mentioned in 1805 by Lieut. Z. M. Pike, who bestowed on him a medal and a flag, and according to whom his band at that time numbered but 45 men. Broken Tooth was one of the signers of the treaty of Prairie du Chien, Aug. 19, 1825; his death occurred in 1828. His daughter was the wife of Ermatinger, a British trader.          (C. T.)

**Brotherton.** The name of two distinct bands, each formed of remnants of various Algonquian tribes. The best-known band was composed of individuals of the Ma-

hican, Wappinger, Mohegan, Pequot, Narraganset, etc., of Connecticut and Rhode Island, and of the Montauk and others from Long Island, who settled in 1788 on land given them by the Oneida at the present Marshall, Oneida co., N. Y., near the settlement then occupied by the Stockbridges. Those of New England were mainly from Farmington, Stonington, Groton, Mohegan, and Niantic (Lyme), in Connecticut, and from Charlestown in Rhode Island. They all went under the leadership of Samson Occum, the Indian minister, and on arriving in Oneida co. called their settlement Brotherton. As their dialects were different they adopted the English language. They numbered 250 in 1791. In 1833 they removed to Wisconsin with the Oneida and Stockbridges and settled on the E. side of Winnebago lake, in Calumet co., where they soon after abandoned their tribal relations and became citizens, together with the other emigrant tribes settled near Green Bay. They are called Wapanachki, "eastern people," by the neighboring Algonquian tribes.

The other band of that name was composed of Raritan and other divisions of the Delawares who, according to Ruttenber (Tribes Hudson River, 293, 1872), occupied a reservation called Brotherton, in Burlington co., N. J., until 1802, when they accepted an invitation to unite with the Stockbridges and Brothertons then living in Oneida co., N. Y. In 1832 they sold their last rights in New Jersey. They were then reduced to about 40 souls and were officially recognized as Delawares and claimed territory s. of the Raritan as their ancient home. Their descendants are probably to be found among the Stockbridges in Wisconsin.          (J. M.)

Brotherton.—Ft Schuyler treaty (1788) quoted by Hall, N. W. States, 66, 1849. **Brothertown.**—Kirkland (1795) in Mass. Hist. Soc. Coll., 1st s., IV, 67–93, 1795. **Niĕn′tkĕn.**—J. N. B. Hewitt, inf'n, 1886 ('they two are brothers': Tuscarora name). **Wapanachki.**—See *Abnaki.*

**Brownstown.** A former Wyandot village in Wayne co., Mich., included in a reservation of about 2,000 acres granted to the Wyandot, Feb. 28, 1809, and ceded to the United States by treaty of Sept. 20, 1818.

**Brulé** ('burned,' the French translation of *Sichángxu*, 'burnt thighs,' their own name, of indefinite origin). A subtribe of the Teton division of the great Dakota tribe. They are mentioned by Lewis and Clark (1804) as the Tetons of the Burnt Woods, numbering about 300 men, "who rove on both sides of the Missouri, White, and Teton rs." In 1806 they were on the E. side of the Missouri from the mouth of the White to Teton r. Hayden (Ethnog. and Philol. Mo. Valley, 372, 1862) describes the country inhabited by them in 1856 as on the headwaters of the White and Niobrara, extending down these rivers about half their length, Teton r. forming the N. limit.   He also says they were for a number of years headed by a chief named

TWO STRIKES—BRULÉ SIOUX

Makatozaza, very friendly to the whites, who by uniformly good management and just government kept his people in order, regulated their hunts, and usually avoided placing them in the starving situations incident to bands led by less judicious chiefs.   They were good hunters, usually well clothed and supplied with meat, and had comfortable lodges and a large number of horses.   They varied their occupations by hunting buffalo, catching wild horses, and making war expeditions against the Arikara, then stationed on the Platte, or the Pawnee, lower down on that river.   Every summer excursions were made by the young men into the Platte and Arkansas country in quest of wild horses, which abounded there at that time.   After emigrants to California and Oregon began to pass through the Dakota country, the Brulés suffered more from diseases introduced by them than any other division of the tribe, being nearest

to the trail.   The treaty of Apr. 29, 1868, between the Sioux bands and the Government was in a large degree brought about through the exertions of Swift Bear, a Brulé chief.   Nevertheless, it was about this time or shortly after that a band of Brulés took part in the attack on Maj. Forsyth on Republican r.   Hayden gives 150 as the number of their lodges in 1856.   In 1890 the Upper Brulés on Rosebud res., S. Dak., numbered 3,245; the Lower Brulés at Crowcreek and Lower Brulé agency, S. Dak., 1,026.   Their present number as distinct from the other Teton is not given.

The group is divided geographically into the Kheyatawichasha or Upper Brulés, the Kutawichasha or Lower Brulés, and the Brulés of the Platte.

WIFE OF SPOTTED TAIL—BRULÉ SIOUX

The subdivisions are given by different authorities as follows:

Lewis and Clark (Discov., 34, 1806): 1 Esahateaketarpar (Isanyati?), 2 Warchinktarhe, 3 Choketartowomb (Chokatowela), 4 Ozash (see *Wazhazha*), 5 Menesharne (see *Minisala*).

In 1880 Tatankawakan, a Brulé, gave to J. O. Dorsey the names of 13 bands of the Brulés, Upper and Lower: 1 Iyakoza, 2

Chokatowela, 3 Shiyotanka, 4 Homna, 5 Shiyosubula, 6 Kanghiyuha, 7 Pispizawichasha, 8 Waleghaunwohan, 9 Wacheunpa, 10 Shawala, 11 Ihanktonwan, 12 Nakhpakhpa, 13 Apewantanka.

Rev. W. J. Cleveland (MS. list, 1884) enumerates the modern divisions as: 1 Sichanghu, 2 Kakegha, 3 (a) Hinhanshunwapa, (b) Shungkahanapin, 4 Hihakanhanhanwin, 5 Hunkuwanicha, 6 Miniskuyakichun, 7 (a) Kiyuksa, (b) Tiglabu, 8 Wacheunpa, 9 Waglukhe, 10 Isanyati, 11 Wagmezayuha, 12 (a) Waleghaonwohan, (b) Wakhna, 13 Oglalaichichagha, 14 Tiyochesli, 15 Wazhazha, 16 Ieskachincha, 17 Ohenonpa, 18 Okaghawichasha.

The Brulés of the Platte, not included in the above lists, are a part of the Brulés (Stanley in Poole, Among the Sioux, 232, 1881) formerly connected with Whetstone agency, S. Dak.        (J. O. D. C. T.)

Babarole.—Gass, Jour., 49, 1807. Bois brûle'.—Lewis and Clark, Discov., 21, 1806 (name applied by the French and commonly used by the whites; sig. 'burnt wood'). bois Ruley.—Clark, MS. codex, quoted by Coues, Lewis and Clark Exped., I, 101, note, 1893. Broule Sioux.—Schoolcraft, Ind. Tribes, V, 494, 1855. Brucellares.—Ind. Aff. Rep., 296, 1846 (probably the Brulés). Brulé Dakotas.—Hayden, Ethnog. and Philol. Mo. Val., map, 1862. Brulees.—Ind. Aff. Rep. 1854, 295, 1855. Brulé-Sioux.—Smithson. Misc. Col., XIV, 19, 1878. Brulies.—Hoffman (1854) in H. R. Doc. 36, 33d Cong., 2d sess., 3, 1855. Burned.—Smet, Letters, 37, 1843. Burnt Hip Brulé.—Robinson, Letter to Dorsey, B. A. E., 1879. Burnt Thighs.—Hayden, Ethnog. and Philol. Mo. Val., 290, 1862. Burnt-woods.—Ruxton, Life in Far West, 111, 1849. Ceetshongos.—Corliss, Dak. vocab., 106, 1874. Checher Ree.—Clark, MS. codex, quoted by Coues, Lewis and Clark Exped., I, 101, note, 1893. Ishango.—Brackett in Smithson. Rep., 466, 1876. Se-čang'-ŏos.—Hayden, Ethnog. and Philol. Mo. Val., 371, 1862. Siðaŋgu.—Riggs, Dakota Gram. and Dict., xvi, 1852 ('burnt thighs': own name). Sicaugu.—Hind, Red River Exped., II, 154, 1860. Sichangus.—Warren, Dacota Country, 16, 1856. Si-chankoo.—Jackson (1877) quoted by Donaldson in Nat. Mus. Rep. 1885, 62, 1886. Sitcan-xu.—Coues, Lewis and Clark Exped., I, 130, 1893. Tetans of the Burnt Woods.—Ramsey in Ind. Aff. Rep. 1849, 85, 1850. Teton (Bois brûle).—Lewis and Clark, Discov., 34, 1806. Teton (Bois rûle).—Amer. St. Paps., IV, 714, 1832. Tetons (Bois brûle').—Lewis and Clark, Discov., 21, 1806. Tetons Brules.—Farnham, Trav., 32, 1843. Tetons of the Boise Brule.—Lewis and Clark, Exped., I, 146, 1814. Tetons of the Burnedwood.—M'Vickar, Hist. Exped. Lewis and Clark, I, 148, 1842. Tetons of the Burnt-Wood.—Lewis and Clark, Exped., I, map, 1814. Wo-ni-to'-na-his.—Hayden, Ethnog. and Philol. Mo. Val., 290, 1862 (Cheyenne name). Yankton.—Clark, MS. codex, quoted by Coues, Lewis and Clark Exped., I, 101, note, 1893.

**Brulés of the Platte.** A part of the Brulé Sioux formerly connected with Whetstone agency, S. Dak. Stanley in Poole, Among the Sioux, app., 232, 1881.

**Bruneau Shoshoni.** A band of Wihinasht Shoshoni formerly living on Bruneau cr., S. E. Idaho; pop. 300 in 1868.—Powell in Ind. Aff. Rep., 201, 1868.

**Bruno's Village.** A former village in San Diego co., Cal., said to be Luiseño, but possibly Diegueño or Agua Caliente.—Hayes quoted by Bancroft, Nat. Races, I, 460, 1882.

**Brushes.** See *Painting*.

**Buckaloon.** A former Iroquois village on the N. side of Allegheny r., Warren co., Pa., above the mouth of Oil cr., near the site of the present town of Irvine. It was destroyed by Col. Brodhead of the Continental troops in 1779.
Baccaloons.—Güssefeld, map, 1784. Baccatoons.—Esnauts and Rapilly, map, 1777. Baccatous.—Lattré, U. S. map, 1784. Buckaloon.—Day, Penn., 653, 1843. Buckaloons.—Butterfield, Washington-Irvine Corr., 43, 1882. Buffaloons.—Lotter, map, ca.1770. Buffler's Town.—Homann Heirs' map, 1756. Gachimantiagon.—Bellin, map, 1755. Kachuidagon.—Marshall in Mag. Am. Hist., II, 139 (= 'cut or broken reed'). Kachiriodagon.—Joncaire (1749) in Margry, Déc., VI, 675, 1886. Paille Coupée.—Ibid.

**Bucker Woman's Town.** A former Seminole settlement E. of Big Hammock town, near Long swamp, central Fla.—Bell in Morse, Rep. to Sec. War, 307, 1822.

**Buckongahelas** ('breaker in pieces'). A Delaware chief who lived during the Revolutionary period; born in the first half of the 18th century. He was the son of Wewandochwalend, apparently a chief of a Delaware band in Ohio. Buckongahelas became the head warrior of all the Delaware Indians then residing on Miami and White rs. Although he took part with the English against the colonists, he does not appear to have been cruel to noncombatants; and Drake (Biog. and Hist. Inds., 63, 1837) says he was not only a great, but a noble warrior, who took no delight in shedding blood. The conduct of the English at the battle of Presque Isle, Ohio, in 1794, so disgusted him that his sympathies were diverted to the United States. He was present at Ft McIntosh, where Beaver, Pa., now stands, when the treaty of 1785 was made, but his name is not among the signers. He was a signer, however, of the treaty of Greenville, Ohio, Aug. 3, 1795; of Ft. Wayne, Ind., June 7, 1803, and of Vincennes, Ind., Aug. 18, 1804. Soon after signing the last his death occurred, probably in the same year. His name appears in print in various forms.        (C. T.)

**Buckskin.** See *Skin-dressing*.

**Buckstown.** A Delaware (?) village marked on Royce's map (1st Rep. B. A. E., 1881) as on the S. E. side of White r., about 3 m. E. of Anderson, Madison co., Ind., on land sold in 1818. See *Kiktheswemud*.

**Buena Vista** (Span.: 'pleasant view'). A descriptive name applied to one or more Shoshonean or Mariposan tribes living on Buena Vista lake, in the lower Kern r. drainage, California. By treaty of June 10, 1851, these tribes reserved a tract between Tejon pass and Kern r. and ceded the remainder of their land to the United States. See Barbour (1852) in Sen. Ex. Doc. 4, 32d Cong., spec. sess., 256, 1853.

**Buena Vista.** A prehistoric pueblo ruin on a high bluff near Solomonsville, on Gila r., a few miles N. E. of San José, Graham co., s. E. Ariz. It is probably the ruin which gave the name Pueblo Viejo (q. v.) to this part of Gila valley.—Fewkes in 22d Rep. B. A. E., 172, 1904.

**Pueblo Viejo.**—Bandelier quoted in Arch. Inst. Rep., v, 44, 1884.

**Buena Vista.** A pueblo of the Nevome on the Rio Yaqui, about lat. 28°, in Sonora, Mexico.—Orozco y Berra, Geog., 351, 1864.

**Buesanet.** Mentioned in connection with Choinóc (Choinok) as a rancheria N. of Kern r., Cal., in 1775–76. It evidently belonged to the Mariposan family and lay in the vicinity of Visalia, Tulare co. See Garcés, Diary, 289, 1900.

**Buffalo.** Remains of the early species of the bison are found from Alaska to Georgia, but the range of the present type (*Bison americanus*) was chiefly between the Rocky and Allegheny mts. While traces of the buffalo have been found as far E. as Cavetown, Md., and there is documentary evidence that the animal ranged almost if not quite to the Georgia coast, the lack of remains in the shell-heaps of the Atlantic shore seems to indicate its absence generally from that region, although it was not unknown to some of the tribes living on the rivers. The first authentic knowledge of the bison or buffalo by a European was that gained about 1530 by Alvar Nuñez Cabeza de Vaca, who described the animal living in freedom on the plains of Texas. At that time the herds ranged from below the Rio Grande in Mexico N. W. through what is now E. New Mexico, Utah, Oregon, Washington, and British Columbia; thence crossing the mountains to Great Slave lake they roamed the valleys of Saskatchewan and Red rs., keeping to the w. of L. Winnipeg and L. Superior and s. of L. Michigan and L. Erie to the vicinity of Niagara; there turning southward to w. Pennsylvania and crossing the Alleghenies they spread over the w. portion of Maryland, Virginia, North Carolina, South Carolina, Georgia, and N. Mississippi and Louisiana. All the tribes within this range depended largely on the buffalo for food and clothing, and this dependence, with the influence of

THE BUFFALO OF GOMARA, 1554

the habits of the animal, profoundly affected tribal customs and religious rites. This is more clearly seen in the tribes w. of the Mississippi, where the people were in constant contact with the buffalo during the summer and winter migrations of the great northern and southern herds. These great herds were composed of innumerable smaller ones of a few thousand each, for the buffalo was never solitary except by accident. This habit affected the manner of hunting and led to the organization of hunting parties under a leader and to the establishment of rules to insure an equal chance to every member of the party.

Early writers say that among the tribes E. of the Missouri the hunting party, dividing into four parts, closed the selected herd in a square, then, firing the prairie grass, pressed in upon the herd, which, being hedged by flame, was slaughtered. The accuracy of this statement is questioned by Indians, for, they say, the only time the grass would burn well was in the autumn, and at that time the animal was hunted for the pelt as much as for food, and fire would injure the fur. Fire was sometimes used in the autumn to drive the deer from the prairie into the woods.

In the N. pens were built of tree trunks lashed together and braced on the outside, into which the herds were driven and there killed. Sometimes, as on the upper Mississippi, a hunter disguised in a buffalo skin acted as a decoy, leading the herd to a precipice where many were killed by the headlong plunge. Upon the plains of Kansas and Nebraska the hunters formed a circle around the herd and then, rushing in, shot the animals with arrows.

The annual summer hunting party generally consisted of the entire tribe. As the main supply of meat and pelts was to be obtained, religious rites were observed throughout the time. "Still hunting" was forbidden under penalty of flogging, and if a man slipped away to hunt for himself, thereby scattering a herd and causing loss to the tribe, he was punished, sometimes even to death. These severe regulations were in force during the tribal or ceremonial hunt. This hunt occurred in June, July, and August, when the animals were fat and the hair thin, the flesh being then in the best condition for food and the pelts easiest to dress on both sides for the making of clothing, shields, packs, bags, ropes, snowshoes, tent and boat covers. The meat was cut into thin sheets and strips and hung upon a framework of poles to dry in the sun. When fully "jerked" it was folded up and put into parfleche packs to keep for winter use. A cow was estimated to yield about 45 pounds of dried meat and 50 pounds of pemmican, besides the marrow, which was preserved in bladder skins, and the tallow, which was poured into skin bags. The sinew of the animal furnished bowstrings, thread for sewing, and fiber for ropes. The horns were made into spoons and drinking vessels, and the tips were used for cupping purposes; the buffalo horn was also worn as insignia of office. The hair of the buffalo was woven into reatas, belts, and personal ornaments. The dried droppings of the animal, known among plainsmen as "buffalo chips," were valuable as fuel.

Tribal regulations controlled the cutting up of the animal and the distribution of the parts. The skin and certain parts of the carcass belonged to the man who had slain the buffalo; the remainder was divided according to fixed rules among the helpers, which afforded an opportunity to the poor and disabled to procure food. Butchering was generally done by men on the field, each man's portion being taken to his tent and given to the women as their property.

The buffalo was hunted in the winter by small, independent but organized parties, not subject to the ceremonial exactions of the tribal hunt. The pelts secured at this time were for bedding and for garments of extra weight and warmth. The texture of the buffalo hide did not admit of fine dressing, hence was used for coarse clothing, moccasins, tent covers, parfleche cases, and other articles. The hide of the heifer killed in the fall or early winter made the finest robe.

The buffalo was supposed to be the instructor of doctors who dealt with the treatment of wounds, teaching them in dreams where to find healing plants and the manner of their use. The multifarious benefits derived from the animal brought the buffalo into close touch with the people: It figured as a gentile totem, its appearance and movements were referred to in gentile names, its habits gave designations to the months, and it became the symbol of the leader and the type of long life and plenty; ceremonies were held in its honor, myths recounted its creation, and its folktales delighted old and

young. The practical extinction of the buffalo with the last quarter of the 19th century gave a deathblow to the ancient culture of the tribes living within its range.

Consult Allen in Mem. Geol. Survey of Kentucky, I, pt. II, 1876; Chittenden, Fur Trade, 1902; Hornaday in Rep. Nat. Mus. 1887, 1889; Relation of Alvar Nuñez Cabeça de Vaca, B. Smith trans., 1871; Winship, Coronado Expedition, 14th Rep. B. A. E., 1896.        (A. C. F.)

**Bukongehelas.** See *Buckongahelas.*

**Buldam.** A former Pomo village on the N. bank of Big r. and E. of Mendocino, Mendocino co., Cal.        (S. A. B.)
Bul'-dam Po'-mo.—Powers in Cont. N. A. Ethnol., III, 155, 1877.

**Buli.** The Butterfly clan of the Hopi.
Bôli.—Bourke, Snake Dance, 117, 1884. Buli wiñ-wû.—Fewkes in 19th Rep. B. A. E., 581, 1900 (*wiñ-wû*='clan'). Bu'-li wün-wü.—Fewkes in Am. Anthrop., VII, 405, 1894. Póvoli.—Voth, Hopi Proper Names, 102, 1905.

**Buli.** The Butterfly phratry of the Hopi.
Bu-li'-nya-mû.—Fewkes in Am. Anthrop., VI, 367, 1893 (*nya-mû*='people').

**Buliso.** The Evening Primrose clan of the Honani (Badger) phratry of the Hopi.
Bu-li'-so.—Stephen in 8th Rep. B. A. E., 39, 1891.

**Bulitzequa.** A former pueblo of the Jemez, in New Mexico, the exact site of which is not known.—Bandelier in Arch. Inst. Papers, IV, 207, 1892.

**Bull Dog Sioux.** A Teton Dakota division on Rosebud res., S. Dak.—Donaldson in Nat. Mus. Rep. 1885, 63, 1886.

**Bullets Town.** Marked on Hutchin's map in Bouquet's Exped., 1766, as in Coshocton co., Ohio, on both sides of Muskingum r., about half way between Walhonding r. and Tomstown. Probably a Delaware village.

**Bullroarer.** An instrument for producing rhythmic sound, consisting of a narrow, usually rectangular slat of wood, from about 6 in. to 2 ft. long and ½ in. to 2 in. wide, suspended by one end to a cord, the latter often being provided with a wooden handle. The bullroarer, which is often painted with symbolic designs, is whirled rapidly with a uniform motion about the head, and the pulsation of the air against the slat gives a characteristic whizzing or roaring sound. The instrument has also been called whizzer, whizzing stick, lightning stick, and rhombus, and its use was quite general. In North America it has been found among the Eskimo, Kwakiutl, Arapaho, and most western tribes, including the Navaho, Apache, Ute, the central Californian tribes (where, among the Pomo, it is nearly 2 ft. long), Pueblos, and in the ancient cliff-dwellings. The Hopi, who regard the bullroarer as a prayer-stick of the thunder and its whizzing noise as representing the wind that accompanies thunderstorms, make the tablet portion from a piece of lightning-riven wood and measure the length of the string from the heart to the tips of the fingers of the outstretched right hand (Fewkes). The Navaho make the bullroarer of the same material, but regard it as representing the voice of the thunderbird, whose figure they often paint upon it, the eyes being indicated by inset pieces of turquoise (Culin). Bourke was led to believe that the rhombus of the Apache was made by the medicine men from the wood of pine or fir that had been struck by lightning on the mountain tops. Apache, Hopi, and Zuñi bullroarers bear lightning symbols, and while in the semi-arid region the

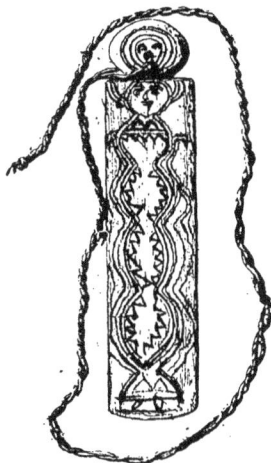

APACHE BULLROARER; LENGTH 7 INCHES. (BOURKE)

implement is used to invoke clouds, lightning, and rain, and to warn the initiated that rites are being performed, in the humid area it is used to implore the wind to bring fair weather. The bullroarer is a sacred implement, associated with rain, wind, and lightning, and among the Kwakiutl, according to Boas, with ghosts. By some tribes it retains this sacred character, but among others it has degenerated into a child's toy, for which use its European antitype also survives among civilized nations.

Consult Bourke, Medicine-men of the Apache, 9th Rep. B. A. E., 1892; Fewkes, Tusayan Snake Ceremonies, 16th Rep. B. A. E., 1897; Haddon, Study of Man, 219, 1898; Lang, Custom and Myth, 39, 1885; Mooney, Ghost Dance Religion, 14th Rep. B. A. E., 1896; Murdoch in 9th Rep. B. A. E., 1892; Schmeltz in Verh. d. Vereins f. naturw. Unterhaltung zu Hamburg, IX, 92, 1896.     (W. H.)

**Bulls.** A Hidatsa band or society; mentioned by Culbertson (Smithson. Rep. 1850, 143, 1851) as a clan. For a similar society among the Piegan, see *Stumiks*.

**Bulltown.** A Shawnee or Mingo village of 5 families on Little Kanawha r., W. Va.; destroyed by whites in 1772.—Kaufmann, W. Penn., 180, 1851.

**Buokongahelas.** See *Buckongahelas*.

**Buquibava.** A former Pima rancheria of Sonora, Mexico, visited by Kino about 1697–99; situated on San Ignacio r., below San Ignacio (of which mission it was subsequently a visita), at the site of the present town of Magdalena. Pop. 63 in 1730, probably including some Tepoca.

(F. W. H.)

Magdalena.—Doc. of 1730 quoted by Bancroft, No. Mex. States, I, 494, 514, 1884. Magdalena de Buvuibava.—Bancroft, Ariz. and N. M., 358, 1889 (quoting Mange, 1699). Santa Madaléna.—Hardy, Travels, 422, 1829. Santa Magdalena de Buquibava.—Kino (1694) in Doc. Hist. Mex., 4th ser., I, 248, 1856. S[anta] M[aria] Magdalen.—Venegas, Hist. Cal., I, map, 1759. S. Magdalena.—Kino, map (1701) in Bancroft, Ariz. and N. M., 360, 1889.

**Bureau of American Ethnology.** The Bureau of (American) Ethnology was organized in 1879 and was placed by Congress under the supervision of the Smithsonian Institution. It was directed that all the archives, records, and materials relating to the Indian tribes collected by the Survey of the Rocky Mountain Region under the auspices of the Interior Department should be transferred to the Institution for use by the Bureau. Prof. Spencer F. Baird, Secretary of the Institution, recognizing the great value of Maj. J. W. Powell's services in initiating researches among the western tribes, selected him as the person best qualified to organize and conduct the work.

The National Government had already recognized the importance of researches among the tribes. As early as 1795 the Secretary of War appointed Leonard S. Shaw deputy agent to the Cherokee with instructions to study their language and home life and to collect materials for an Indian history. President Jefferson, who planned the Lewis and Clark expedition of 1804–06, "for the purpose of extending the internal commerce of the United States," especially stipulated, in his instructions to Lewis, the observations on the native tribes that should be made by the expedition for the use of the Government. These were to include their names and numbers; the extent and limits of their possessions; their relations with other tribes or nations; their language, traditions, and monuments; their ordinary occupations in agriculture, fishing, hunting, war, arts, and the implements for these; their food, clothing, and domestic accommodations; the diseases prevalent among them and the remedies they use; moral and physical circumstances which distinguish them from known tribes; peculiarities in their laws, customs, and dispositions; and articles of commerce they may need or furnish, and to what extent; "and considering the interest which every nation has in extending and strengthening the authority of reason and justice among the people around them, it will be useful to acquire what knowledge you can of the state of morality, religion, and information among them, as it may better enable those who endeavor to civilize and instruct them to adapt their measures to the existing notions and practices of those on whom they are to operate." During much of his life Jefferson, like Albert

Gallatin later on, manifested his deep interest in the ethnology of the American tribes by publishing accounts of his observations that are of extreme value to-day. In 1820 Rev. Jedidiah Morse was commissioned by the President to make a tour for the purpose of "ascertaining, for the use of the Government, the actual state of the Indian tribes of our country." The Government also aided the publication of Schoolcraft's voluminous work on the Indians. The various War Department expeditions and surveys had reported on the tribes and monuments encountered in the W.; the Hayden Survey of the Territories had examined and described many of the cliff-dwellings and pueblos, and had published papers on the tribes of the Mississippi valley, and Maj. Powell, as chief of the Survey of the Rocky Mountain Region, had accomplished important work among the tribes of the Rio Colorado drainage in connection with his geological and geographical researches, and had commenced a series of publications known as Contributions to North American Ethnology. The Smithsonian Institution had also taken an active part in the publication of the results of researches undertaken by private students. The first volume of its Contributions to Knowledge is The Ancient Monuments of the Mississippi Valley, by Squier and Davis, and up to the founding of the Bureau of Ethnology the Institution had issued upward of 600 papers on ethnology and archeology. These early researches had taken a wide range, but in a somewhat unsystematic way, and Maj. Powell, on taking charge of the Bureau, began the task of classifying the subject-matter of the entire aboriginal field and the

selection of those subjects that seemed to require immediate attention. There were numerous problems of a practical nature to be dealt with, and at the same time many less strictly practical but none the less important problems to be considered. Some of the practical questions were readily approached, but in the main they were so involved with the more strictly scientific questions that the two could not be considered separately.

From its inception the Government has had before it problems arising from the presence within its domain, as dependent wards, of more than 300,000 aborigines. In the main the difficulties encountered in solving these problems arose from a lack of knowledge of the distribution, numbers, relationships, and languages of the tribes, and a real appreciation of their character, culture status, needs, and possibilities. It was recognized that a knowledge of these elements lies at the very foundation of intelligent administration, and thus one of the important objects in organizing the Bureau of Ethnology was that of obtaining such knowledge of the tribes as would enable the several branches of the Government to know and appreciate the aboriginal population, and that at the same time would enable the people generally to give intelligent administration sympathetic support. An essential step in this great work was that of locating the tribes and classifying them in such manner as to make it possible to assemble them in harmonious groups, based on relationship of blood, language, customs, beliefs, and grades of culture. It was found that within the area with which the nation has to deal there are spoken some 500 Indian languages, as distinct from one another as French is from English, and

J. W. POWELL, FOUNDER AND DIRECTOR OF THE BUREAU OF AMERICAN ETHNOLOGY

that these languages are grouped in more than 50 linguistic families. It was found, further, that in connection with the differences in language there are many other distinctions requiring attention. Tribes allied in language are often allied also in capacity, habits, tastes, social organization, religion, arts, and industries, and it was plain that a satisfactory investigation of the tribes required a systematic study of all of these conditions. It was not attempted, however, to cover the whole field in detail. When sufficient progress had been made in the classification of the tribes, certain groups were selected as types, and investigations among them were so pursued as to yield results applicable in large measure to all. Up to the present time much progress has been made and a deeper insight has been gained into the inner life and character of the native people, and thus, in a large sense, of primitive peoples generally, than had been reached before in the world's history. Many of the results of these researches have already been published and are in the hands of all civilized nations.

Some of the more directly practical results accomplished may be briefly mentioned: (1) A study of the relations, location, and numbers of the tribes, and their classification into groups or families, based on affinity in language—a necessary basis for dealing with the tribes practically or scientifically; (2) a study of the numerous sociologic, religious, and industrial problems involved, an acquaintance with which is essential to the intelligent management of the tribes in adjusting them to the requirements of civilization; (3) a history of the relations of the Indian and white races embodied in a volume on land cessions; (4) investigations into the physiology, medical practices, and sanitation of a people who suffer keenly from imperfect adaptation to the new conditions imposed on them; (5) the preparation of bibliographies embodying all works relating to the tribes; (6) a study of their industrial and economic resources; (7) a study of the antiquities of the country with a view to their record and preservation; and (8) a handbook of the tribes, embodying, in condensed form, the accumulated information of many years.

The more strictly scientific results relate to every department of anthropologic research—physical, psychological, linguistic, sociologic, religious, technic, and esthetic—and are embodied in numerous papers published in the reports, contributions, and bulletins; and the general results in each of these departments, compiled and collated by the highest available authorities, have now begun to appear in the form of handbooks.

Maj. Powell, director, died Sept. 23, 1902, and on Oct. 11 W. H. Holmes was appointed to succeed him, with the title of chief. In addition to the chief the scientific staff of the Bureau comprises (1906) 7 ethnologists, an illustrator, an editor, a librarian, and 7 other employees. Besides the regular scientific members of the Bureau there are numerous associates or collaborators, including many of the best-known ethnologists of the country, who contribute papers or who engage at intervals in research work under the Bureau's auspices. The library contains about 12,000 volumes and 7,000 pamphlets, accumulated largely through exchange of publications. There are about 1,600 linguistic manuscripts, and 15,000 photographic negatives illustrating the aborigines and their activities.

The publications consist of Contributions to North American Ethnology, Annual Reports, Bulletins, Introductions, and Miscellaneous Publications. The series of contributions was begun by the Survey of the Rocky Mountain Region before the organization of the Bureau, 3 volumes having been completed, and was discontinued after 8 volumes had been issued. Twenty-three annual reports, comprising 28 volumes, 30 bulletins (including the present Handbook), 4 introductions, and 6 miscellaneous publications have appeared. The present edition of the annual reports and bulletins is 9,850 copies, of which the Senate receives 1,500, the House of Representatives 3,000, and the Bureau 3,500 copies. Of the Bureau edition 500 are distributed by the Smithsonian Institution. From the remaining 1,850 copies are drawn the personal copies of members of Congress, and 500 for distribution to Government libraries and other libraries throughout the country, as designated by Congress; the remainder are sold by the Superintendent of Documents, Government Printing Office. With the exception of the few disposed of by the Superintendent of Documents, the publications are distributed free of charge; the popular demand for them is so great, however, that the editions are soon exhausted. The quota allowed the Bureau is distributed to libraries, to institutions of learning, and to collaborators and others engaged in anthropologic research or in teaching. The publications are as follows:

CONTRIBUTIONS TO NORTH AMERICAN ETHNOLOGY.—Published in part under the auspices of the Department of the Interior, U. S. Geographical and Geological Survey of the Rocky Mountain Region, J. W. Powell in charge. Vols. I–VII and IX.

Vol. I, 1877:
Part I.—Tribes of the extreme Northwest, by W. H. Dall.
On the distribution and nomenclature of the native tribes of Alaska and the adjacent territory.
On succession in the shell-heaps of the Aleutian islands.
On the origin of the Innuit.
Appendix to part I. Linguistics.
Notes on the natives of Alaska, by J. Furuhelm.
Terms of relationship used by the Innuit: a series obtained from natives of Cumberland inlet, by W. H. Dall.
Vocabularies, by George Gibbs and W. H. Dall.
Note on the use of numerals among the T'sim si-an', by George Gibbs.
Part II. Tribes of western Washington and northwestern Oregon, by George Gibbs.
Appendix to part II. Linguistics.
Vocabularies, by George Gibbs, Wm. F. Tolmie, and G. Mengarini.
Dictionary of the Niskwalli, by George Gibbs.
Vol. II, 1890:
The Klamath Indians of southwestern Oregon, by Albert Samuel Gatschet. Two parts.
Vol. III, 1877:
Tribes of California, by Stephen Powers.
Appendix. Linguistics, edited by J. W. Powell.
Vol. IV, 1881:
Houses and house-life of the American aborigines, by Lewis H. Morgan.
Vol. V, 1882:
Observations on cup-shaped and other lapidarian sculptures in the Old World and in America, by Charles Rau.
On prehistoric trephining and cranial amulets, by Robert Fletcher.
A study of the manuscript Troano, by Cyrus Thomas, with an introduction by D. G. Brinton.
Vol. VI, 1890:
The Çegiha language, by J. Owen Dorsey.
Vol. VII, 1890:
A Dakota-English dictionary, by Stephen R. Riggs, edited by J. Owen Dorsey.
Vol. VIII:
[Not issued].
Vol. IX, 1893:
Dakota grammar, texts, and ethnography, by Stephen R. Riggs, edited by J. Owen Dorsey.
ANNUAL REPORTS OF THE BUREAU OF (AMERICAN) ETHNOLOGY TO THE SECRETARY OF THE SMITHSONIAN INSTITUTION. 23 vols. roy. 8°.
First Report (1879–80), 1881.
Report of the Director.
On the evolution of language, as exhibited in the specialization of the grammatic processes; the differentiation of the parts of speech, and the integration of the sentence; from a study of Indian languages, by J. W. Powell.
Sketch of the mythology of the North American Indians, by J. W. Powell.
Wyandot government: A short study of tribal society, by J. W. Powell.
On limitations to the use of some anthropologic data, by J. W. Powell.
A further contribution to the study of the mortuary customs of the North American Indians, by H. C. Yarrow.
Studies in Central American picture-writing, by Edward S. Holden.
Cessions of land by Indian tribes to the United States: Illustrated by those in the State of Indiana, by C. C. Royce.
Sign language among North American Indians, compared with that among other peoples and deaf-mutes, by Garrick Mallery.
Catalogue of linguistic manuscripts in the library of the Bureau of Ethnology, by J. C. Pilling.
Illustration of the method of recording Indian languages. From the manuscripts of J. Owen Dorsey, A. S. Gatschet, and S. R. Riggs.

Second Report (1880–81), 1883.
Report of the Director.
Zuñi fetiches, by F. H. Cushing.
Myths of the Iroquois, by Erminnie A. Smith.
Animal carvings from mounds of the Mississippi valley, by H. W. Henshaw.
Navajo silversmiths, by Washington Matthews.
Art in shell of the ancient Americans, by W. H. Holmes.
Illustrated catalogue of the collections obtained from the Indians of New Mexico and Arizona in 1879, by James Stevenson.
Illustrated catalogue of the collections obtained from the Indians of New Mexico in 1880, by James Stevenson.
Third Report (1881–82), 1884.
Report of the Director (including On activital similarities).
Notes on certain Maya and Mexican manuscripts, by Cyrus Thomas.
On masks, labrets, and certain aboriginal customs, by W. H. Dall.
Omaha sociology, by J. Owen Dorsey.
Navajo weavers, by Washington Matthews.
Prehistoric textile fabrics of the United States, derived from impressions on pottery, by W. H. Holmes.
Illustrated catalogue of a portion of the collections made by the Bureau of Ethnology during the field season of 1881, by W. H. Holmes.
Illustrated catalogue of the collections obtained from the pueblos of Zuñi, N. Mex., and Wolpi, Ariz., in 1881, by James Stevenson.
Fourth Report (1882–83), 1886.
Report of the Director.
Pictographs of the North American Indians. A preliminary paper, by Garrick Mallery.
Pottery of the ancient Pueblos, by W. H. Holmes.
Ancient pottery of the Mississippi valley, by W. H. Holmes.
Origin and development of form and ornament in ceramic art, by W. H. Holmes.
A study of Pueblo pottery as illustrative of Zuñi culture growth, by F. H. Cushing.
Fifth Report (1883–84), 1887.
Report of the Director.
Burial mounds of the northern sections of the United States, by Cyrus Thomas.
The Cherokee Nation of Indians: A narrative of their official relations with the Colonial and Federal Governments, by C. C. Royce.
The mountain chant: A Navajo ceremony, by Washington Matthews.
The Seminole Indians of Florida, by Clay MacCauley.
The religious life of the Zuñi child, by Matilda C. Stevenson.
Sixth Report (1884–85), 1888.
Report of the Director.
Ancient art of the province of Chiriqui, Colombia, by W. H. Holmes.
A study of the textile art in its relation to the development of form and ornament, by W. H. Holmes.
Aids to the study of the Maya codices, by Cyrus Thomas.
Osage traditions, by J. Owen Dorsey.
The central Eskimo, by Franz Boas.
Seventh Report (1885–86), 1891.
Report of the Director.
Indian linguistic families of America north of Mexico, by J. W. Powell.
The Midē'wiwin or "grand medicine society" of the Ojibwa, by W. J. Hoffman.
The sacred formulas of the Cherokees, by James Mooney.
Eighth Report (1886–87), 1891.
Report of the Director.
A study of Pueblo architecture: Tusayan and Cibola, by Victor Mindeleff.
Ceremonial of Hasjelti Dailjis and mythical sand painting of the Navajo Indians, by James Stevenson.
Ninth Report (1887–88) 1892.
Report of the Director.
Ethnological results of the Point Barrow expedition, by John Murdoch.

The medicine-men of the Apache, by John G. Bourke.

**Tenth Report** (1888–89), 1893.
Report of the Director.
Picture writing of the American Indians, by Garrick Mallery.

**Eleventh Report** (1889–90), 1894.
Report of the Director.
The Sia, by Matilda C. Stevenson.
Ethnology of the Ungava district, Hudson bay territory, by Lucien M. Turner.
A study of Siouan cults, by J. Owen Dorsey.

**Twelfth Report** (1890–91), 1894.
Report of the Director.
Report on the mound explorations of the Bureau of Ethnology, by Cyrus Thomas.

**Thirteenth Report** (1891–92), 1896.
Report of the Director.
Prehistoric textile art of eastern United States, by W. H. Holmes.
Stone art, by Gerard Fowke.
Aboriginal remains in Verde valley, Arizona, by Cosmos Mindeleff.
Omaha dwellings, furniture, and implements, by J. Owen Dorsey.
Casa Grande ruin, by Cosmos Mindeleff.
Outlines of Zuñi creation myths, by F. H. Cushing.

**Fourteenth Report** (1892–93), 1896.
Report of the Director.
The Menomini Indians, by Walter J. Hoffman.
The Coronado expedition, 1540–42, by G. P. Winship.
The Ghost-dance religion and the Sioux outbreak of 1890, by James Mooney.

**Fifteenth Report** (1893–94), 1897.
Report of the Director (including On regimentation).
Stone implements of the Potomac-Chesapeake tidewater province, by W. H. Holmes.
The Siouan Indians: A preliminary sketch, by W J McGee.
Siouan sociology: A posthumous paper, by J. Owen Dorsey.
Tusayan katcinas, by J. Walter Fewkes.
The repair of Casa Grande ruin, Arizona, in 1891, by Cosmos Mindeleff.

**Sixteenth Report** (1894–95), 1897.
Report of the Director, and list of publications of the Bureau of American Ethnology.
Primitive trephining in Peru, by M. A. Muñiz and W J McGee.
The cliff ruins of Canyon de Chelly, Arizona, by Cosmos Mindeleff.
Day symbols of the Maya year, by Cyrus Thomas.
Tusayan snake ceremonies, by J. Walter Fewkes.

**Seventeenth Report** (1895–96), 1898.
Report of the Director, and list of publications of the Bureau of American Ethnology.
The Seri Indians, by W J McGee, with Comparative lexicology, by J. N. B. Hewitt.
Calendar history of the Kiowa Indians, by James Mooney.
Navaho houses, by Cosmos Mindeleff.
Archeological expedition to Arizona in 1895, by J. Walter Fewkes.

**Eighteenth Report** (1896–97), 1899.
Report of the Director.
The Eskimo about Bering strait, by E. W. Nelson.
Indian land cessions in the United States, compiled by C. C. Royce, with an introduction by Cyrus Thomas.

**Nineteenth Report** (1897–98), 1900.
Report of the Director (including Esthetology, or the science of activities designed to give pleasure).
Myths of the Cherokee, by James Mooney.
Tusayan migration traditions, by J. Walter Fewkes.
Localization of Tusayan clans, by Cosmos Mindeleff.
Mounds in northern Honduras, by Thomas Gann.
Mayan calendar systems, by Cyrus Thomas.
Primitive numbers, by W J McGee.
Numeral systems of Mexico and Central America, by Cyrus Thomas.

Tusayan flute and snake ceremonies, by J. Walter Fewkes.
The wild-rice gatherers of the upper lakes, a study in American primitive economics, by A. E. Jenks.

**Twentieth Report** (1898–99) 1903.
Report of the Director (including Technology, or the science of industries; Sociology, or the science of institutions; Philology, or the science of activities designed for expression; Sophiology, or the science of activities designed to give instruction; List of publications of the Bureau of American Ethnology).
Aboriginal pottery of the eastern United States, by W. H. Holmes.

**Twenty-first Report** (1899–1900), 1903.
Report of the Director.
Hopi katcinas, drawn by native artists, by J. Walter Fewkes.
Iroquois cosmogony, by J. N. B. Hewitt.

**Twenty-second Report** (1900–01), 1903.
Report of the Acting Director.
Two summers' work in pueblo ruins, by J. Walter Fewkes.
Mayan calendar systems—II, by Cyrus Thomas.
The Hako, a Pawnee ceremony, by Alice C. Fletcher.

**Twenty-third Report** (1901–02), 1904.
Report of the Acting Director.
The Zuñi Indians, by Matilda C. Stevenson.

**Twenty-fourth Report** (1902–03), 1905.
Report of the Chief.
American Indian games, by Stewart Culin.
BULLETINS.—Thirty volumes, 8°.
(1) Bibliography of the Eskimo language, by J. C. Pilling, 1887.
(2) Perforated stones from California, by H. W. Henshaw, 1887.
(3) The use of gold and other metals among the ancient inhabitants of Chiriqui, Isthmus of Darien, by W. H. Holmes, 1887.
(4) Work in mound exploration of the Bureau of Ethnology, by Cyrus Thomas, 1887.
(5) Bibliography of the Siouan languages, by J. C. Pilling, 1887.
(6) Bibliography of the Iroquoian languages, by J. C. Pilling, 1888.
(7) Textile fabrics of ancient Peru, by W. H. Holmes, 1889.
(8) The problem of the Ohio mounds, by Cyrus Thomas, 1889.
(9) Bibliography of the Muskhogean languages, by J. C. Pilling, 1889.
(10) The circular, square, and octagonal earthworks of Ohio, by Cyrus Thomas, 1889.
(11) Omaha and Ponka letters, by J. Owen Dorsey, 1891.
(12) Catalogue of prehistoric works east of the Rocky mountains, by Cyrus Thomas, 1891.
(13) Bibliography of the Algonquian languages, by J. C. Pilling, 1891.
(14) Bibliography of the Athapascan languages, by J. C. Pilling, 1892.
(15) Bibliography of the Chinookan languages (including the Chinook jargon), by J. C. Pilling, 1893.
(16) Bibliography of the Salishan languages, by J. C. Pilling, 1893.
(17) The Pamunkey Indians of Virginia, by J. G. Pollard, 1894.
(18) The Maya year, by Cyrus Thomas, 1894.
(19) Bibliography of the Wakashan languages, by J. C. Pilling, 1894.
(20) Chinook texts, by Franz Boas, 1894.
(21) An ancient quarry in Indian Territory, by W. H. Holmes, 1894.
(22) The Siouan tribes of the East, by James Mooney, 1894.
(23) Archeologic investigations in James and Potomac valleys, by Gerard Fowke, 1894.
(24) List of the publications of the Bureau of Ethnology with index to authors and subjects, by F. W. Hodge, 1894.
(25) Natick dictionary, by J. H. Trumbull, 1903.
(26) Kathlamet texts, by Franz Boas, 1901.
(27) Tsimshian texts, by Franz Boas, 1902.
(28) Mexican and Central American antiquities and calendar systems, twenty-nine papers, by

Eduard Seler, E. Förstemann, Paul Schellhas, Carl Sapper, and E. P. Dieseldorff, translated from the German under the supervision of Charles P. Bowditch.

(29) Haida texts and myths, Skidegate dialect, by J. R. Swanton.

(30) Handbook of the Indians north of Mexico, Parts I and II.

INTRODUCTIONS.—Four volumes, 4°.

(1) Introduction to the study of Indian languages, by J. W. Powell, 1877.

(2) Introduction to the study of Indian languages, 2d edition, by J. W. Powell, 1880.

(3) Introduction to the study of sign language among the North American Indians, by Garrick Mallery, 1880.

(4) Introduction to the study of mortuary customs among the North American Indians, by H. C. Yarrow, 1880.

MISCELLANEOUS PUBLICATIONS:

(1) A collection of gesture-signs and signals of the North American Indians, by Garrick Mallery, 1880.

(2) Proof-sheets of a bibliography of the languages of the North American Indians, by J. C. Pilling, 1885.

(3) Linguistic families of the Indian tribes north of Mexico [by James Mooney, 1885].

(4) Map of linguistic stocks of American Indians north of Mexico, by J. W. Powell, 1891.

(5) Tribes of North America, with synonymy: Skittagetan family [by Henry W. Henshaw, 1890].

(6) Dictionary of American Indians north of Mexico [advance pages], 1903.

(W. H. H.)

**Bureau of Indian Affairs.**—See *Office of Indian Affairs.*

**Burges' Town.** A Seminole town, the exact location of which is unknown, but it was probably on or near Flint or St Marys r., s. w. Ga.—Connell (1793) in Am. State Papers, Ind. Aff., I, 384, 1832.

**Burial.** See *Mortuary customs, Urn burial.*

**Burnt Woods Chippewa.** A former Chippewa band on Bois Brulé r., near the w. end of L. Superior, N. Wis.
Chippeways of the Burnt Woods.—Schoolcraft, Travels, 321, 1821.

**Burrard Inlet No. 3 Reserve.** The name given by the Canadian Department of Indian Affairs to one of 6 divisions of the Squawmish, q. v.; pop. 30 in 1902.

**Burrard Saw Mills Indians.** The local name for a body of Squawmish of Fraser River agency, Brit. Col.; noted only in 1884, when their number was given as 232.—Can. Ind. Aff., 187, 1884.

**Busac.** A former rancheria, probably of the Sobaipuri, visited by Kino about 1697; situated, apparently, on Arivaipa cr., a tributary of the San Pedro, E. of old Camp Grant, s. Ariz., although Bernal (Bancroft, Ariz. and N. Mex., 356, 1889) states that the settlement was on a creek flowing E.

**Busanic.** A Pima settlement s. w. of Guevavi, near the Arizona-Sonora boundary, in lat. 31° 10′, long. 111° 10′, visited by Kino in 1694 and by Kino and Mange in 1699. It was made a visita of Guevavi mission at an early date; pop. 253 in 1730, 41 in 1764. See Kino (1694) in Doc. Hist. Mex., 4th s., I, 252, 1856; Rudo Ensayo (1763), 150, 1863; Mange quoted by Bancroft, Ariz. and N. Mex., 358, 1889.
Bisanig.—Bancroft, No. Mex. States, I, 524, 1884. Busani.—Villa-Señor, Theatro Am., pt. 2, 408, 1748. Busanic.—Kino, op. cit. Busnio.—Venegas, Hist. Cal., I, map, 1759. Busona.—Box, Adventures, 270, 1869. Bussani.—Orozco y Berra, Geog., 347, 1864. Cinco Señores Busanic.—Sonora materiales (1730) quoted by Bancroft, No. Mex. States, I, 514, 1884. Ruzany.—Land Office map, U. S., 1881. S. Ambrosio Busanic.—Kino (1699) quoted by Bancroft, No. Mex. States, I, 270, 1884. San Ambrosio de Busanio.—Venegas, Hist. Cal., I, 300, 1759. Susanna.—Kino, map (1702) in Stöcklein, Neue Welt-Bott, 74, 1726 (misprint).

**Bushamul.** A Nishinam village formerly existing in the valley of Bear r., Cal.
Bashonees.—Taylor in Cal. Farmer, June 8, 1860. Booshamool.—Powers in Overland Mo., XII, 22, 1874. Bu'-sha-mūl.—Powers in Cont. N. A. Ethnol., III, 316, 1877. Bushones.—Bancroft, Nat. Races, I, 450, 1874. Bushumnes.—Hale, Ethnog. and Philol., 631, 1846.

**Bushy Head.** See *Unaduti.*

**Businausee** ('echo maker,' from *buswawag*, 'echo,' referring to the *achichak*, crane). A phratry of the Chippewa.
Bus-in-as-see.—Warren in Minn. Hist. Soc. Coll., V, 46, 1885. Bus-in-aus-e.—Ibid., 44. Bus-in-aus-e-wug.—Ibid., 88 (plural).

**Busk** (Creek: *puskita*, 'a fast'). A festival of the Creeks, by some early writers termed the green-corn dance. According to Gatschet (Creek Migr. Leg., I, 177, 1884) the solemn annual festival held by the Creek people of ancient and modern days. As this authority points out, the celebration of the *puskita* was an occasion of amnesty, forgiveness, and absolution of crime, injury, and hatred, a season of change of mind, symbolized in various ways.

The day of beginning of the celebration of the *puskita*, which took place chiefly in the "town square," was determined by the *miko*, or chief, and his council; and the ceremony itself, which had local variations, lasted for 4 days in the towns of less note and for 8 days in the more important. Hawkins (Sketch, 75, 1848) has left a description of the busk, or "boos-ke-tau," as it was carried out in the white or peace town of Kasihta in 1798–99. The chief points are as follows:

First day: The yard of the square is cleaned in the morning and sprinkled with white sand, while the black drink is being prepared. The fire maker, specially appointed, kindles new fire by friction, the 4 logs for the fire being arranged crosswise with reference to the cardinal points. The women of the Turkey clan dance the turkey dance, while the very strong emetic called *passa* is being brewed; this is drunk from about noon to the middle of the afternoon. Then comes the tadpole dance, performed by 4 men and 4 women known as "tadpoles." From evening until dawn the dance of the *hiniha* is performed by the men. The "old men's tobacco" is also prepared on the first day.

Second day: At about 10 o'clock the women perform the gun dance, so called from the men firing guns during its continuance. At noon the men approach the new fire, rub some of its ashes on the chin, neck, and belly, and jump headforemost into the river, and then return to the square. Meantime the women busy themselves with the preparation of new maize for the feast. Before the feast begins, the men as they arrive rub some of the maize between their hands and then on the face and chest.

Third day: The men sit in the square.

Fourth day: The women, who have risen early for this purpose, obtain some of the new fire, with which they kindle a similarly constructed pile of logs on their own hearths, which have previously been cleaned and sprinkled with sand. A ceremony of ash rubbing, plunging into water, etc., is then performed by them, after which they taste some salt and dance the "long dance."

Fifth day: The 4 logs of the fire, which last only 4 days, having been consumed, 4 other logs are similarly arranged, and the fire kindled as before, after which the men drink the black drink.

Sixth and seventh days: During this period the men remain in the town square.

Eighth day: In the square and outside of it impressive ceremonies are carried on. A medical mixture concocted by stirring and beating in water 14 kinds of plants (the modern Creeks use 15), supposed to have virtue as physic, is used by the men to drink, to rub over their joints, etc., after the priests have blown into it through a small reed. Another curious mixture, composed chiefly of the ashes of old corncobs and pine boughs, mixed with water, and stirred by 4 girls who have not reached puberty, is prepared in a pot, and 2 pans of a mixture of white clay and water are likewise prepared afterward by the men. The chief and the warriors rub themselves with some of both these mixtures. After this 2 men, who are specially appointed, bring flowers of old men's tobacco to the chief's house, and each person present receives a portion. Then the chief and his counselors walk 4 times around the burning logs, throwing some of the old men's tobacco into the fire each time they face the E, and then stop while facing the w. When this is concluded the warriors do the same. The next ceremony is as follows:

At the miko's cabin a cane having 2 white feathers on its end is stuck out. At the moment when the sun sets a man of the Fish clan takes it down and walks, followed by all spectators, toward

the river. Having gone half way, he utters the death-whoop, and repeats it 4 times before reaching the water's edge. After the crowd has thickly congregated at the bank each person places a grain of old men's tobacco on the head and others in each ear. Then at a signal repeated four times they throw some of it into the river, and every man at a like signal plunges into the water to pick up 4 stones from the bottom. With these they cross themselves on their breasts 4 times, each time throwing 1 of the stones back into the river and uttering the death whoop. They then wash themselves, take up the cane with the feathers, return to the square, where they stick it up, then walk through the town visiting. After nightfall comes the mad dance, which concludes the *púskita*.

The 4 days' busk, as performed at Odshiapofa (Little Talasse), as witnessed by Swan, whose account seems to have been really made up by McGillivray (Gatschet, Creek Migr. Leg., I, 181, 1884), adds some details concerning the dress of the fire maker, the throwing of maize and the black drink into the fire, the preparation and use of the black drink, and the interesting addition that any provisions left over are given to the fire maker. Other travelers and historians, as Adair, Bartram, and Milfort, furnish other items concerning the ceremony. Bartram says: "When a town celebrates the busk, having previously provided themselves with new clothes, new pots, pans, and other household utensils and furniture, they collect all their worn-out clothes and other despicable things, sweep and cleanse their houses, squares, and the whole town, of their filth, which with all the remaining grain and other old provisions, they cast together into one common heap and consume it with fire. After having taken medicine, and fasted for 3 days, all the fire in the town is extinguished. During this fast they abstain from the gratification of every appetite and passion whatever. A general amnesty is proclaimed, all malefactors may return to their town, and they are absolved from their crimes, which are now forgotten, and they are restored to favor." According to Gatschet (op. cit., 182) it appears that the busk is not a solstitial celebration, but a rejoicing over the first fruits of the year. The new year begins with the busk, which is celebrated in August, or late in July. Every town celebrated its busk at a period independent from that of the other towns, whenever their crops had come to maturity. In connection with the busk the women broke to pieces all the household utensils of the previous year and replaced them with new ones; the men refitted all their property so as to look new. Indeed the new fire meant the new life, physical and moral, which had to begin with the new year. Everything had to be new or renewed—even the garments hitherto worn. Taken altogether, the busk was one of the most remarkable ceremonial institutions of the American Indians. (A. F. C.)

**Butterfly-stones.** See *Banner stones.*

**Buzzard Roost.** A Creek town "where Tom's path crosses Flint r.," Ga.; exact locality not known. There was another Creek town of this name on upper Chattahoochee r., w. of Atlanta. See Urquhart (1793) in Am. State Papers, Ind. Aff., II, 370, 1832.

**Byainswa.** See *Biauswah.*

**Byengeahtein.** A Nanticoke village in 1707, probably in Dauphin or Lancaster co., Pa.—Evans (1707) in Day, Penn., 361, 1843.

**Caacat.** A Chumashan village between Goleta and Pt Concepcion, Cal., in 1542. Caacac.—Cabrillo, Narr., in Smith, Coll. Doc., 189, 1857. Caacat.—Ibid. Cacat.—Taylor in Cal. Farmer, Apr. 17, 1863. Cuncaae.—Ibid.

**Caamancijup** ('narrows of the arroyos'). A rancheria, probably Cochimi, connected with Purísima (Cadegomo) mission, Lower California, in the 18th century.—Doc. Hist. Mex., 4th s., v, 189, 1857.

**Cabbasagunti.** A small body of Indians dwelling in 1807 in the village of "Saint-Francais," on St Francis r., Quebec, in which they were named Cabbassaguntiac, i. e., 'people of Cabassaguntiquoke,' signifying 'the place where sturgeon abound.' The form Cobbisseconteag has been replaced by the modern Cobbosseecontee as the name of what formerly was Winthrop pond and outlet which flows into Kennebec r., in Kennebec co., Me. These Indians, it is reported by Kendall, regarded themselves not only as inhabitants of Cabbassaguntiquoke, but also as true *cabassas*, or sturgeons, because one of their ancestors, having declared that he was a sturgeon, leaped into this stream and never returned in human form. They related a tale that below the falls of Cobbosseecontee r. the rock was hewn by the ax of a mighty manito. (J. N. B. H.) Cabbassaguntiac.—Kendall, Travels, III, 124, 1809. Cabbassaguntiquoke.—Ibid. (their former place of settlement).

**Cabea Hoola.** Given by Romans as a former Choctaw village on the headwaters of Chickasawhay cr., probably in Lauderdale co., Miss. Cabea Hoala.—West Florida map., ca 1775. Cabea Hoola.—Romans, Florida, 1772.

**Caborca.** A rancheria of the Soba division of the Papago and the seat of a mission established by Kino about 1687; situated on the s. bank of the Rio Asuncion, lat. 30° 30′, long. 112°, Sonora, Mexico. It had 4 subordinate villages in 1721 (Venegas, II, 177, 285, 1759) and a population of

223 in 1730, but it was totally destroyed in the Pima rebellion of 1751. It is now a white Mexican village. (F. W. H.) Cabetka.—Kino, map (1702) in Stöcklein, Neüe Welt-Bott, 76, 1726. Cabona.—Box, Adventures, 267, 1869. Caborca.—Kino (1696) in Doc. Hist. Mex., 4th s., I, 267, 1856. Cabórea.—Hardy, Travels, 422, 1829. Concepcion Caborca.—Rivera (1730) quoted by Bancroft, No. Mex. States, I, 514, 1884. Concepcion de Caborca.—Venegas, Hist. Cal., I, 285, 1759. Concepcion del Cabetca.—Kino, map (1701) in Bancroft, Ariz. and N. Mex., 360, 1889 (misprint). Concepcion del Caborca.—Kino (1694) in Doc. Hist. Mex., 4th s., I, 243, 1856. Concepcion del Cabotea.—Writer of 1702?, ibid., v, 139, 1857.

**Caborh.** A former Maricopa rancheria on the Rio Gila, s. Ariz. (Sedelmair, 1744, quoted by Bancroft, Ariz. and N. Mex., 366, 1889). Mentioned as distinct from the following.

**Caborica.** A former Maricopa rancheria on the Rio Gila, s. Ariz.—Sedelmair (1744) quoted by Bancroft, Ariz. and N. Mex., 366, 1889.

**Cabusto** (possibly from *oka* 'water,' *ishto* 'great.'—Halbert). A town, probably of the Chickasaw, in N. E. Mississippi, visited by De Soto in 1540; situated between Taliepatava and Chicaça, and 5 days' march from the latter, near a great river, possibly the Tombigbee.—Gentleman of Elvas (1557) in French, Hist. Coll. La., II, 160, 1850; Halbert in Trans. Ala. Hist. Soc., III, 67, 1899.

**Caca Chimir.** A Papago village, probably in Pima co., s. Ariz., with a population of 70 in 1858, and 90 in 1865. Caca Chimir.—Davidson in Ind. Aff. Rep., 135, 1865. Del Caca.—Bailey in Ind. Aff. Rep., 208, 1858.

**Cacaria.** A former Tepehuane pueblo on the upper waters of the Rio San Pedro, central Durango, Mexico.—Orozco y Berra, Geog., 319, 1864.

**Cachanegtac.** A former village, presumably Costanoan, connected with Dolores mission, San Francisco, Cal.—Taylor in Cal. Farmer, Oct. 18, 1861.

**Cachanila.** A village, probably Pima, on the Pima and Maricopa res., Gila r., Ariz.; pop. 503 in 1860 (Taylor in Cal. Farmer, June 19, 1863), 438 in 1869 (Browne). Cachunilla.—Browne, Apache Country, 290, 1869.

**Cachaymon.** A village or tribe, possibly Caddoan, mentioned by Iberville (Margry, Déc., IV, 178, 1880), in the account of his voyage up the Mississippi in 1699, as being on or near Red r. of Louisiana. Possibly identical with Cahinnio.

**Cache disks and blades.** The term cache is applied to certain forms of storage of property (see *Storage*), and in archeology it is employed to designate more especially certain deposits of implements and other objects, mainly of stone and metal, the most noteworthy consisting of flaked flint blades and disks. These caches occur in the mound region of the Mississippi valley and generally throughout the Atlantic states. Very often they are associated with burials in mounds, but in some cases they seem merely to have been buried in the ground or hidden among rocks. The largest deposit recorded contained upward of 8,000 flint disks (Moorehead), a few exceed 5,000, while those containing a smaller number are very numerous. It is probable that many of these caches of flaked stones are accumulations of incipient implements roughed out at the quarries and carried away for further specialization and use. But their occurrence with burials, the uni-

DISCOIDAL FLINT BLADE FROM A CACHE OF 110 SPECIMENS; ILLINOIS. (1-6)

formity of their shape, and the absence of more than the most meager traces of their utilization as implements or for the making of implements, give rise to the conjecture that they were assembled and deposited for reasons dictated by superstition, that they were intended as memorials of important events, as monuments to departed chieftains, as provision for requirements in the future world, or as offerings to the mysterious powers or gods requiring this particular kind of sacrifice. If in the nature of a sacrifice they certainly fulfilled all re-

CACHE OF LANCEOLATE FLINT BLADES

quirements, for only those familiar with such work can know the vast labor involved in quarrying the stone from the massive strata, in shaping the refractory material, and in transporting the product to far distant points. In the Hopewell mound in Ohio large numbers of beautiful blades of obsidian, obtained probably from Mexico, had been cast upon a sacrificial altar and partially destroyed by the great heat; usually, however, the deposits do not seem to have been subjected to the altar fires. See *Mines and Quarries*, *Problematical objects*, *Stone-work*.

Consult Holmes in 15th Rep. B. A. E., 1897; Moorehead (1) Primitive Man in Ohio, pp. 190, 192, 1892, (2) in The Antiquarian, I, 158, 1897; Seever, ibid., 142; Smith, ibid., 30; Snyder (1) in Smithson. Rep 1876, 1877, (2) in Proc. A. A. A. S.,

XLII, 1894, (3) in The Archæologist, I, no. 10, 1893, (4) ibid., III, pp. 109–113, 1895; Squier and Davis in Smithson. Cont., I, 1848; Wilson in Nat. Mus. Rep. 1897, 1899; and various brief notices in the archeological journals.          (W. H. H.)

**Caches.**—See *Receptacles*, *Storage and Caches*.

**Cachopostales.** Mentioned by Orozco y Berra (Geog., 304, 1864), from a manuscript source, as a tribe living near the Pampopa who resided on Nueces r., Tex. They were possibly Coahuiltecan.

Cachapostate.—Powell in 7th Rep. B. A. E., 69, 1891.

**Caddehi** ('head of the reedy place'). A rancheria, probably Cochimi, connected with Purísima (Cadegomo) mission, Lower California, in the 18th century.—Doc. Hist. Mex., 4th s., v, 190, 1857.

**Caddo** (contracted from *Kä'dohädä'cho*, 'Caddo proper,' 'real Caddo,' a leading tribe in the Caddo confederacy, extended by the whites to include the confederacy). A confederacy of tribes belonging to the southern group of the Caddoan linguistic family. Their own name is Hasínai, 'our own folk.' See *Kadohadacho*.

*History.*—According to tribal traditions the lower Red r. of Louisiana was the early home of the Caddo, from which they spread to the N., W., and S. Several of the lakes and streams connected with this river bear Caddo names, as do some of the counties and some of the towns which cover ancient village sites. Cabeza de Vaca and his companions in 1535–36 traversed a portion of the territory occupied by the Caddo, and De Soto's expedition encountered some of the tribes of the confederacy in 1540–41, but the people did not become known until they were met by La Salle and his followers in 1687. At that time the Caddo villages were scattered along Red r. and its tributaries in what are now Louisiana and Arkansas, and also on the banks of the Sabine, Neches, Trinity, Brazos, and Colorado rs. in E. Texas. The Caddo were not the only occupants of this wide territory; other confederacies belonging to the same linguistic family also resided there. There were also fragments of still older confederacies of the same family, some of which still maintained their separate existence, while others had joined the then powerful Hasinai. These various tribes and confederacies were alternately allies and enemies of the Caddo. The native population was so divided that at no time could it successfully resist the intruding white race. At an early date the Caddo obtained horses from the Spaniards through intermediate tribes; they learned to rear these animals, and traded with them as far N. as Illinois r. (Shea, Cath. Ch. in Col. Days, 559, 1855).

During the 18th century wars in Europe led to contention between the Spaniards and the French for the territory occupied by the Caddo. The brunt of these contentions fell upon the Indians; the trails between their villages became routes for armed forces, while the villages were transformed into garrisoned posts. The Caddo were friendly to the French and rendered valuable service, but they suffered greatly from contact with the white race. Tribal wars were fomented, villages were abandoned, new diseases spread havoc among the people, and by the close of the century the welcoming attitude of the Indians during its early years had changed to one of defense and distrust. Several tribes were practically extinct, others seriously reduced in numbers, and

ANTELOPE, A CADDO

a once thrifty and numerous people had become demoralized and were more or less wanderers in their native land. Franciscan missions had been established among some of the tribes early in the century, those designed for the Caddo, or Asinais, as they were called by the Spaniards, being Purísima Concepción de los Asinais and (for the Hainai) San Francisco de los Tejas (q. v.). The segregation policy of the missionaries tended to weaken tribal relations and unfitted the people to cope with the new difficulties which confronted them. These missions were transferred to the Rio San Antonio in 1731. With the acquisition of Louisiana by the United States immigration increased and the Caddo were pushed from their old haunts. Under their first

treaty, in 1835, they ceded all their land and agreed to move at their own expense beyond the boundaries of the United States, never to return and settle as a tribe. The tribes living in Louisiana, being thus forced to leave their old home, moved s. w. toward their kindred living in Texas. At that time the people of Texas were contending for independence, and no tribe could live at peace with both opposing forces. Public opinion was divided as to the treatment of the Indians; one party demanded a policy of extermination, the other advocated conciliatory methods. In 1843 the governor of the Republic of Texas sent a commission to the tribes of its N. part to fix a line between them and the white settlers and to establish three trading posts; but, as the land laws of the republic did not recognize the Indian's right of occupancy, there was no power which could prevent a settler from taking land that had been cultivated by an Indian. This condition led to continual difficulties, and these did not diminish after the annexation of Texas to the United States, as Texas retained control and jurisdiction over all its public domain. Much suffering ensued; the fields of peaceable Indians were taken and the natives were hunted down. The more warlike tribes made reprisals, and bitter feelings were engendered. Immigration increased, and the inroads on the buffalo herds by the newcomers made scarce the food of the Indians. Appeals were sent to the Federal Government, and in 1855 a tract near Brazos r. was secured and a number of Caddo and other Indians were induced to colonize under the supervision of Agent Robert S. Neighbours. The Indians built houses, tilled fields, raised cattle, sent their children to school—lived quiet and orderly lives. The Comanche to the w. continued to raid upon the settlers, some of whom turned indiscriminately upon all Indians. The Caddo were the chief sufferers, although they helped the state troops to bring the raiders to justice. In 1859 a company of white settlers fixed a date for the massacre of all the reservation Indians. The Federal Government was again appealed to, and through the strenuous efforts of Neighbours the Caddo made a forced march for 15 days in the heat of July; men, women, and children, with the loss of more than half of their stock and possessions, reached safely the banks of Washita r. in Oklahoma, where a reservation was set apart for them. Neighbours, their friend and agent, was killed shortly afterward as a penalty for his unswerving friendship to the Indians (Ind. Aff. Rep. 1859, 333, 1860). During the civil war the Caddo remained loyal to the Government, taking refuge in Kansas, while some went even as far w. as Colorado. In 1872 the boundaries of their reservation were defined, and in 1902 every man, woman, and child received an allotment of land under the provisions of the severalty act of 1887, by which they became citizens of the United States and subject to the laws of Oklahoma. In 1904 they numbered 535.

Missions were started by the Baptists soon after the reservation was established, and are still maintained. Thomas C. Battey, a Quaker, performed missionary work among them in 1872. The Episcopalians opened a mission in 1881, the Roman Catholics in 1894.

*Customs and beliefs.*—In the legend which recounts the coming of the Caddo from the underworld it is related: "First an old man climbed up, carrying in one hand fire and a pipe, and in the other a drum; next came his wife with corn and pumpkin seeds." The traditions of the people do not go back to a time when they were not cultivators of the soil; their fields surrounded their villages and furnished their staple food; they were semisedentary in their habits and lived in fixed habitations. Their dwellings were conical in shape, made of a framework of poles covered with a thatch of grass, and were grouped about an open space which served for social and ceremonial gatherings. Couches covered with mats were ranged around the walls inside the house to serve as seats by day and beds by night. The fire was built in the center. Food was cooked in vessels of pottery, and baskets of varying sizes were skilfully made. Vegetal fibers were woven, and the cloth was made into garments; their mantles, when adorned with feathers, were very attractive to the early French visitors. Living in the country of the buffalo, that animal and others were hunted and the pelts dressed and made into clothing for winter use. Besides having the usual ornaments for the arms, neck, and ears, the Caddo bored the nasal septum and inserted a ring as a face decoration— a custom noted in the name, meaning "pierced nose," given the Caddo by the Kiowa and other unrelated tribes, and designated in the sign language of the plains. Tattooing was practised. Descent was traced through the mother. Chieftainship was hereditary, as was the custody of certain sacred articles used in religious ceremonies. These ceremonies were connected with the cultivation of maize, the seeking of game, and the desire for long life, health, peace, and prosperity, and were conducted by priests who were versed in the rites and who led the accompanying rituals and songs. According to Caddo belief all natural forms were animate and capable of rendering assistance to man. Fasting, prayer, and occasional sacrifices were observed; life was thought to continue after death, and kinship groups were supposed to be reunited in the spirit world. Truthfulness, honesty, and hospitality were inculcated, and just dealing was esteemed a virtue. There is evidence that cannibalism was ceremonially practised in connection with captives.

*Divisions and totems.*—How many tribes were formerly included in the Caddo confederacy can not now be determined. Owing to the vicissitudes of the last 3 centuries only a remnant of the Caddo survive, and the memory of much of their organization is lost. In 1699 Iberville obtained from his Taensa Indian guide a list of 8 divisions; Linares in 1716 gave the names of 11; Gatschet (Creek Migr. Leg., I, 43, 1884) procured from a Caddo Indian in 1882 the names of 12 divisions, and the list was revised in 1896, by Mooney, as follows: (1) Kadohadacho, (2) Hainai, (3) Anadarko, (4) Nabedache, (5) Nacogdoches, (6) Natchitoches, (7) Yatasi, (8) Adai, (9) Eyeish, (10) Nakanawan, (11) Imaha, a small band of Kwapa, (12) Yowani, a band of Choctaw (Mooney in 14th Rep. B. A. E., 1092, 1896). Of these names the first 9 are found under varying forms in the lists of 1699 and 1716. The native name of the confederacy, Hasinai, is said to belong more properly to the first 3 divisions, which may be significant of their prominence at the time when the confederacy was overlapping and absorbing members of older organizations, and as these divisions speak similar dialects, the name may be that which designated a still older organization. The following tribes, now extinct, probably belonged to the Caddo confederacy: Doustionis, Nacaniche, Nanatsoho, and Nasoni (?). The villages of Campti, Choye, and Natasi were probably occupied by subdivisions of the confederated tribes.

Each division of the confederacy was subdivided, and each of these subtribes had its totem, its village, its hereditary chieftain, its priests and ceremonies, and its part in the ceremonies common to the confederacy. The present clans, according to Mooney, are recognized as belonging equally to the whole Caddo people and in old times were probably the chief bond that held the confederacy together. See *Nasoni.*                     (A. C. F.)

Acinay.—Tex. St. Arch., Nov. 17, 1763. Ascanis.— La Harpe (1719) in Margry, Déc., VI, 289, 1886. Asenys.—Iberville (1699), ibid., IV, 316, 1880. A-Simaes.—French, Hist. Coll., II, 11, note, 1875. Asimais.—Kennedy, Repub. Texas, I, 217, 1841. A-Simais.—Yoakum, Hist. Texas, I, 28, note, 1855. Asinaes.—Kennedy, Repub. Texas, I, 217, 1841. Asinais.—Mézières (1778) quoted by Bancroft, No. Mex. States, I, 661, 1886. Asinay.—Teran (1691), ibid., 391. Asoni.—Barcia, Ensayo, 278, 1723. Asseni.—Charlevoix, New France, IV, 78, 1870. Assinais.—Pénicaut (1712) in Margry, Déc., v, 499, 1883. **Assinay.**—La Harpe (*ca.* 1717) in French, Hist. Coll. La., III, 48, 1851. **Assine.**—Gatschet, Creek Migr. Leg., I, 43, 1884. **Assinnis.**—Boudinot, Star in the West, 125, 1816. **Assoni.**—Joutel (1687) in Margry, Déc., III, 311, 1878. **Assony.**—Joutel, ibid., I, 147, 1846. **Assynais.**—Pénicaut (1716) in Margry, Déc., v, 539, 1883. **Ceneseans.**—Boudinot, Star in the West, 126, 1816. **Cenesians.**—Hennepin, New Discov., pt. 2, 25, 1698. **Cenis.**—Joutel (1687) in French, Hist. Coll. La., I, 148, 1851. **Cenys.**—Joutel (1687) in Margry, Déc., III, 266, 1878. **Ceries Assonys.**—French, Hist. Coll. La., II, 11, note, 1875. **Cneis.**—Drake, Bk. Inds., vii, 1848. **Coeni.**—Hennepin, New Discov., map, 1698. **Coenis.**—De l'Isle, map, 1700. **Couis.**—Morse, N. Am., map, 1776 (misprint). **Hasinai.**—ten Kate, Reizen in N. Am., 374, 1885 (own name). **Iscanis.**—Bull. Soc. Geog. Mex., 504, 1869. **Nasoni.**—For forms of this name, see *Nasoni*. **Senis.**—Cavelier (1687) quoted by Shea, Early Voy., 31, 1861. **Tiddoes.**—Keane in Stanford, Compend., Cent. and So. Am., 539, 1878 (same?). **Yscanes.**—Tex. State Arch., Nov. 15, 1785. **Yscanis.**—Census of Nacogdoches urisdiction, ibid., 1790.

**Caddoan Family.** A linguistic family, first classified by Gallatin (Trans. and Coll. Am. Antiq. Soc., II, 116, 1836), who regarded the Caddo and Pawnee languages as distinct, hence both names appear in his treatise as family designations. Although now regarded as belonging to the same linguistic stock, there is a possibility that future investigation may prove their distinctness. The Caddoans may be treated in three geographic groups: The Northern, represented by the Arikara in North Dakota; the Middle, comprising the Pawnee confederacy formerly living on Platte r., Neb., and to the w. and s. w. thereof; and the Southern group, including among others the Caddo, Kichai, and Wichita (Powell in 7th Rep. B. A. E., 58, 1891). The tribes included in the Southern group were scattered throughout the region of the Red r. of Louisiana and its tributaries, in Arkansas and s. Oklahoma, where their names survive in the Washita r., the Wichita mountains and river, Waco city, Kichai hills, etc.; they also spread along the Sabine, Neches, Trinity, and Brazos rs. of Texas, and in part controlled the territory as far as the Colorado r. of Texas and the Gulf of Mexico.

From cultural and other evidence the Caddoan tribes seem to have moved eastward from the S. W. The advance guard was probably the Caddo proper, who, when first met by the white race, had dwelt so long in the region of the Red r. of Louisiana as to regard it as their original home or birthplace. Other branches of the Caddoan family followed, settling along the rivers of N. E. Texas. Whether they drove earlier occupants of the region to the Gulf or at a later day were forced back from the coast by intrusive tribes is not clear, but that some displacement had occurred seems probable, as early Spanish and French travelers found tribes of different families on the Gulf coast, while the Caddoans held the rivers but were acquainted with the coast

and visited the bays of Galveston and Matagorda. The last group to migrate was probably the Pawnee, who kept to the N. and N. E. and settled in a part of what is now Kansas and Nebraska.

The tribes of N. E. Texas being in the territory over which the Spaniards, French, and English contended for supremacy, were the first to succumb to contact with the white race and the inroads of wars and new diseases. Those dwelling farther inland escaped for a time, but all suffered great diminution in numbers; the thousands of 2 centuries ago are now represented by only a few hundreds. The survivors to-day live on allotted lands in Oklahoma and North Dakota, as citizens of the United States, and their children are being educated in the language and the industries of the country.

From the earliest records and from traditions the Caddoan tribes seem to have been cultivators of the soil as well as hunters, and practised the arts of pottery making, weaving, skin dressing, etc. Tattooing the face and body was common among those of the Southern group. Two distinct types of dwellings were used—the conical straw house among the Southern group and the earth lodge among the Pawnee and Arikara. Their elaborate religious ceremonies pertained to the quest of long life, health, and food supply, and embodied a recognition of cosmic forces and the heavenly bodies. By their supernatural and social power these ceremonies bound the people together. The tribes were generally loosely confederated; a few stood alone. The tribe was subdivided, and each one of these subdivisions had its own village, bearing a distinctive name and sometimes occupying a definite relative position to each of the other villages of the tribe. A village could be spoken of in three ways: (1) By its proper name, which was generally mythic in its significance or referred to the share or part taken by it in the religious rites, wherein all the villages of the tribe had a place; (2) by its secular name, which was often descriptive of its locality; (3) by the name of its chief. The people sometimes spoke of themselves by one of the names of their village, or by that of their tribe, or by the name of the confederacy to which they belonged. This custom led to the recording, by the early travelers, of a multiplicity of names, several of which might represent one community. This confusion was augmented when not all the tribes of a confederacy spoke the same language; in such cases a mispronunciation or a translation caused a new name to be recorded. For instance, the native name of the Caddo confederacy, Hasinai, 'our own people,' was translated by the Yatasi, and "Texas" is a modification of the word they gave. Owing to the fact that a large proportion of the tribes mentioned by the writers of the last 3 centuries, together with their languages, are now extinct, a correct classification of the recorded names is no longer possible. The following list of confederacies, tribes, and villages is divided into 4 groups: (1) Those undoubtedly Caddoan; (2) those probably so; (3) those possibly so; (4) those which appear to have been within the Caddoan country.

(1) Arikara, Bidai, Caddo, Campti, Choye, Kichai, Nacaniche, Nacisi, Nanatsoho, Nasoni (=Asinai=Caddo?), Natasi, Pawnee, Wichita.

(2) Aguacay, Akasquy, Amediche, Anoixi, Ardeco, Avoyelles, Cahinnio, Capiche, Chacacants, Chaguate, Chaquantie, Chavite, Chilano, Coligoa, Colima, Doustioni, Dulchioni, Harahey, Palaquesson, Penoy, Tareque.

(3) Analao, Autiamque, Avavares, Cachaymon, Guaycones, Haqui, Irrupiens, Kannehouan, Naansi, Nabiri, Toxo.

(4) Acubadoas, Anamis, Andacaminos, Arkokisa, Bocherete, Coyabegux, Judosa, Kuasse, Mallopeme, Mulatos, Onapiem, Orcan, Palomas, Panequo, Peinhoum, Peissaquo, Petao, Piechar, Pehir, Salapaque, Taraha, Teao, Tohaka, Tohau, Tsepcoen, Tsera, Tutelpinco, Tyacappan.

(A. C. F.)

>**Caddoes.**—Gallatin in Trans. Am. Antiq. Soc., II, 116, 306, 1836 (based on Caddo alone); Prichard, Phys. Hist. Mankind, v, 406, 1847; Gallatin in Schoolcraft, Ind. Tribes, III, 402, 1853 [gives as languages Caddo, Red River (Nandakoes, Tachies, Nabedaches)]. >**Caddokies.**—Gallatin in Trans. Am. Antiq. Soc., II, 116, 1836 (same as his Caddoes); Prichard, Phys. Hist. Mankind, v, 406, 1847. >**Caddo.**—Latham in Trans. Philol. Soc. Lond., II, 31, 1846 (indicates affinity with Iroquois, Muskoge, Catawba, Pawnee); Gallatin in Trans. Am. Ethnol. Soc., II, pt. 1, xcix, 77, 1848 (Caddo only); Berghaus (1845), Physik. Atlas, map 17, 1848 (Caddo, etc.); ibid., 1852; Latham, Nat. Hist. Man, 338, 1850 (between the Mississippi and Sabine); Latham in Trans. Philol. Soc., Lond., 101, 1856; Turner in Pac. R. R. Rep., III, pt. 3, 55, 70, 1856 (finds resemblances to Pawnee, but keeps them separate); Buschmann, Spuren der aztek. Sprache, 426, 448, 1859; Latham, Opuscula, 290, 366, 1860. >**Caddo.**—Latham, Elem. Comp. Philol., 470, 1862 (includes Pawni and Riccari). >**Pawnees.**—Gallatin in Trans. Am. Antiq. Soc., II, 128, 306, 1836 (two nations: Pawnees proper and Ricaras or Black Pawnees); Prichard, Phys. Hist. Mankind, v, 408, 1847 (follows Gallatin); Gallatin in Trans. Am. Ethnol. Soc., II, pt. 1, xcix, 1848; Latham, Nat. Hist. Man, 344, 1850 (or Panis; includes Loup and Republican Pawnees); Gallatin in Schoolcraft, Ind. Tribes, III, 402, 1853 (gives as languages: Pawnees, Ricaras, Tawakeroes, Towekas, Wachos?); Hayden, Ethnog. and Philol. Mo. Val., 232, 345, 1862 (includes Pawnee and Arikara). >**Panis.**—Gallatin in Trans. Am. Antiq. Soc., II, 117, 128, 1836 (of Red river of Texas; mention of villages; doubtfully indicated as of Pawnee family); Prichard, Phys. Hist. Mankind, v, 407, 1847 (supposed from name to be of same race with Pawnee of the Arkansa); Latham, Nat. Hist. Man, 344, 1850 (Pawnees or); Gallatin in Schoolcraft, Ind. Tribes, III, 402, 1853 (here kept separate from Pawnee family). >**Pawnies.**—Gallatin in Trans. Am. Ethnol. Soc., II, pt. 1, 77, 1848 (see Pawnee above). >**Pahnies.**—Berghaus (1845), Physik. Atlas, map 17, 1848; ibid., 1852. >**Pawnee(?).**—Turner in Pac. R. R. Rep., III, pt. 3, 55, 65, 1856 (Kichai and Hueco vocabularies). =**Pawnee.**—Keane in Stanford, Compend., Cent. and So. Am., 478, 1878 (gives four groups: Pawnees proper; Arickarees; Wichitas; Caddoes). =**Pani.**—Gatschet, Creek Migr. Leg., I, 42, 1884; Berghaus, Physik. Atlas, map 72, 1887. >**Towiaches.**—Gallatin in Trans. Am. Antiq. Soc., II, 116, 128, 1836 (same as Panis above); Prichard, Phys. Hist. Mankind, v, 407, 1847. >**Towiachs.**—Latham, Nat. Hist. Man, 349, 1850 (includes Towiach, Tawakenoes, Towecas?, Wacos). >**Towiacks.**—Gallatin in Schoolcraft, Ind. Tribes, III, 402, 1853. >**Natchitoches.**—Gallatin in Trans. Am. Antiq. Soc., II, 116, 1836 (stated by Sibley to speak a language different from any other); Latham, Nat. Hist. Man, 342, 1850; Prichard, Phys. Hist. Mankind, v, 406, 1847 (after Gallatin); Gallatin in Schoolcraft, Ind. Tribes, III, 402, 1853 (a single tribe only). >**Aliche.**—Latham, Nat. Hist. Man, 349, 1850 (near Nacogdoches; not classified). >**Yatassees.**—Gallatin in Trans. Am. Antiq. Soc., II, 116, 1836 (the single tribe; said by Sibley to be different from any other; referred to as a family). >**Riccarees.**—Latham, Nat. Hist. Man, 344, 1850 (kept distinct from Pawnee family). >**Washita.**—Latham in Trans. Philol. Soc. Lond., 103, 1856; Buschmann, Spuren der aztek. Sprache, 441, 1859 (revokes previous opinion of its distinctness and refers it to Pawnee family). >**Witchitas.**—Buschmann, ibid. (same as his Washita). =**Caddoan.**—Powell in 7th Rep. B. A. E., 58, 1891.

**Cadecha.** A former Timuquanan tribe in the Utina confederacy of middle Florida.—Laudonnière (1564) in French, Hist. Coll. La., n. s., 243, 1869.

**Cadica.**—De Bry, Brev. Nar., II, map, 1591. **Cardecha.**—Fontaneda in French, op. cit., 2d ser., 264, 1875. **Chadeca.**—Barcia, Ensayo, 48, 1723.

**Cadecuijtnipa** ('over the lava mesas'). A rancheria, probably Cochimi, connected with Purísima (Cadegomo) mission, Lower California, in the 18th century.—Doc. Hist. Mex., 4th s., v, 188, 1857.

**Cadegomo** ('reedy arroyo'). A Cochimi settlement in lat. 26° 10′, not far from the Pacific coast of Lower California, at which the Jesuit mission of La Purísima Concepcion was established by Father Tamaral in 1718. It contained 130 neophytes in 1767, and in 1745 had 6 dependent villages within 8 leagues. From a statement by Venegas (Hist. Cal., II, 23, 1759) that he "hoped at La Purísima to find greater conveniences both for corn and pasture than at Cadigomo," it would seem that the Indian village and the mission did not occupy the same site.

**Cadegomo.**—Clavigero (1789), Hist. Baja Cal., 63, 1852. **Cadigomo.**—Venegas, Hist. Cal., I, 420; II, 23, 1759. **La Purissima Conception.**—Ibid., II, 23, 198. **Purísima Concepcion.**—Clavigero, op. cit., 109.

**Cadeudebet** ('reeds, or the reedy country, ends here'). A rancheria, probably of the Cochimi, under Purísima (Cadegomo) mission, from which it lay about 10 leagues distant, in central Lower California, in the 18th century.—Doc. Hist. Mex., 4th s., v, 188, 1857.

**Cadeudebet.**—Doc. Hist. Mex., op. cit.

**Cagnaguet.** A Laimon tribe which,

with the Adac and Kadakaman, formerly lived between San Fernando and Muleje, near San Francisco Borja, w. side of Lower California, lat. 29°.

Cagnaguet.—Taylor in Browne, Res. Pac. Slope, app., 54, 1869. Cagnajuet.—Taylor in Cal. Farmer, Jan. 17, 1862.

**Cahawba Old Towns.** A former group of Choctaw settlements in Perry co., Ala., probably on Cahawba r.—Pickett, Ala., II, 326, 1851; Halbert in Ala. Hist. Soc. Trans., III, 66, 1899.

**Cahelca** ('deep pool'). A rancheria, probably Cochimi, connected with Purísima (Cadegomo) mission, Lower California, in the 18th century.—Doc. Hist. Mex., 4th s., v, 189, 1857.

**Cahelejyu** ('brackish water'). A rancheria, probably Cochimi, connected with Purísima (Cadegomo) mission, Lower California, in the 18th century.—Doc. Hist. Mex., 4th s., v, 189, 1857.

Cahelijyu.—Ibid., 190. Cahelixyu.—Ibid., 186.

**Cahelembil** ('junction of waters'). A rancheria, probably Cochimi, connected with Purísima (Cadegomo) mission, Lower California, in the 18th century; it lay a league from the Pacific coast.—Doc. Hist. Mex., 4th s., v, 189, 1857.

**Cahelmet** ('water and earth'). A rancheria, probably Cochimi, connected with Purísima (Cadegomo) mission, Lower California, in the 18th century.—Doc. Hist. Mex., 4th s., v, 189, 1857.

**Cahiague.** A Huron village in Ontario, where the Jesuits had the mission of St John the Baptist in 1640.

Cahiagué.—Champlain (1615), Œuvres, IV, 29, 1870. S. Iean Baptiste.—Jes. Rel. for 1640, 90, 1858.

**Cahinnio.** A tribe visited by Cavelier de la Salle on his return from Texas in 1687, at which time they probably resided in s. w. Arkansas, near Red r. They were possibly more closely allied to the northern tribes of the Caddo confederacy (the Kadohadacho, Natchitoches, Yatasi, etc.) than to the southern tribes, with whom, according to Joutel, they were at enmity. During the vicissitudes of the 18th century the tribe moved N. w., and in 1763 were on upper Arkansas r., near their old allies, the Mento. By the close of the 18th century they were extinct as a tribe. (A. C. F.)

Cabinoios.—McKenney and Hall, Ind. Tribes, III, 81, 1854. Cahainihoua.—Joutel (1687) in French. Hist. Coll. La., I, 169, 1846. Cahainohoua.—Joutel (1687) in Margry, Déc., III, 413, 1878. Cahaynohoua.—Joutel in French, Hist. Coll. La., I, 172, 1846. Cahinnio.—Le Clercq (1691), First Estab. Faith, II, 265, 1881. Cahinoa.—Carver, Trav., map, 1778. Cahirmois.—Boudinot, Star in the West, 126, 1816. Cakainikova.—Barcia, Ensayo, 279, 1723. Chininoas.—McKenney and Hall, Ind. Tribes, III, 81, 1854. Cohainihoua.—Joutel in French, Hist. Coll. La., I, 169, 1846. Cohainotoas.—Barcia, Ensayo, 279, 1723. Kahinoa.—Jefferys (1763), Am. Atlas, map, 5, 1776.

**Cahita.** A group of tribes of the Piman family, consisting chiefly of the Yaqui and the Mayo, dwelling in s. w. Sonora and N. w. Sinaloa, Mexico, principally in the middle and lower portions of the valleys of the Rio Yaqui, Rio Mayo,

MAYO (CAHITA) MAN.    (HRDLICKA)

and Rio Fuerte, and extending from the Gulf of California to the Sierra Madre. Physically the men are usually large and

MAYO (CAHITA) WOMAN AND CHILD.    (HRDLICKA)

well formed; their complexion is of medium brown, and their features, though somewhat coarse, are not unpleasant. The dress of both sexes is coarse and simple, that of the men consisting of a short cotton shirt, trousers, straw hat, and leather sandals, the women wearing the typical cotton camisa and gown. The native blanket and sash are now rarely seen. The Yaqui formerly tattooed the chin and arms. Owing to the semitropical climate their typical dwellings were of canes and boughs, covered with palm leaves, but these have been largely superseded by huts of brush and adobe. Although belonging to the same division of the Piman stock and showing no marked difference in culture, the Mayo and Yaqui tribes have not been friendly; indeed the former waged war against the Yaqui until they themselves were finally conquered, when the Yaqui compelled them to pay tribute and to furnish warriors to aid the Yaqui in their almost incessant hostility first toward Spain, afterward against Mexico. They now hold aloof from each other, and while the Yaqui are habitually on the warpath, the Mayo are entirely pacific. In the fertile valleys along the streams respectively occupied by the tribes of this group, they engage in raising corn, cotton, calabashes, beans, and tobacco, and also in cultivating the mezcal-producing agave. They hunted in the neighboring Sierra Madre and fished in the streams that supplied the water to irrigate their fields, as well as on the coast, where the Yaqui still obtain salt for sale, principally in Guaymas. It has been said that neither the Mayo nor the Yaqui had a tribal chief, each tribe being settled in a number of autonomous villages which combined only in case of warfare; but there appears to have been a village ruler or kind of cacique. In the first half of the 17th century the Mayo and Yaqui together probably numbered between 50,000 and 60,000. There are now about 40,000, equally divided between the tribes, but like most of the southern tribes of the Piman family, these have largely become Hispanized, except in language. The Yaqui particularly are naturally industrious and are employed as cattlemen, teamsters, farmers, and sailors; they are also good miners, are expert in pearl diving, and are employed for all manual labor in preference to any others. They exhibit an unusual talent for music and adhere more or less to the performance of their primitive dances (now somewhat varied by civilization), engaged in principally on feast days, particularly during the harvest festival of San Juan and at the celebration of the Passover. The chief vices of the Yaqui, it is said, are an immoderate indulgence in intoxicants, gambling, and stealing, while conjugal fidelity is scarcely known to them. There is some uncertainty in regard to the tribal divisions of the Cahita

group. Pimentel (Lenguas, I, 453) and Buelna (Arte Lengua Cahita, x) divide it into three dialects, the Yaqui, Mayo, and Tehueco, but the latter, in his Peregrinacion de los Aztecas (21, 1892), mentions the Sinaloa, Tehueco, and Zuaque as distinct groups. Orozco y Berra (Geog., 58) gives Yaqui, Mayo, Tehueco, and Vacoregue. It appears that there was in fact a Sinaloa tribe which later lost its identity through absorption by the Tehueco, while the Zuaque were apparently identical with the latter. For the present condition of the Yaqui and the Mayo see Hrdlicka in Am. Anthrop., n. s., VI, 51, 1904.                                    (F. W. H.)

**Cahita.**—Orozco y Berra, Geog., 58, 1864. **Caita.**—Doc. of 1678 quoted by Bandelier in Arch. Inst. Papers, III, 53, 1890. **Cinaloa.**—Orozco y Berra, op. cit. **Sinaloa.**—Ibid.

**Cahlahtel Pomo.** An unidentifiable band of Pomo, said to have lived in Mendocino co., Cal.—Wiley in Ind. Aff. Rep. 1864, 119, 1865.

**Cahokia.** A tribe of the Illinois confederacy, usually noted as associated with the kindred Tamaroa. Like all the confederate Illinois tribes they were of roving habit until they and the Tamaroa were gathered into a mission settlement about the year 1698 by the Jesuit Pinet. This mission, first known as Tamaroa, but later as Cahokia, was about the site of the present Cahokia, Ill., on the E. bank of the Mississippi, nearly opposite the present St Louis. In 1721 it was the second town among the Illinois in importance. On the withdrawal of the Jesuits the tribe declined rapidly, chiefly from the demoralizing influence of the neighboring French garrison, and was nearly extinct by 1800. With the other remnant tribes of the confederacy they removed, about 1820, to the W., where the name was kept up until very recently, but the whole body is now officially consolidated under the name Peoria, q. v.            (J. M.)

**Caeuquias.**—De l'Isle, map (*ca.* 1705) in Neill, Hist. Minn., 1858. **Cahakies.**—Carver, Travels, map, 1778. **Cahau.**—Marain (1753) in Margry, Déc., VI, 654, 1886. **Cahoki.**—Gale, Upper Miss., 174, 1867. **Cahokia.**—Coxe, Carolana, map, 1741. **Cahokiams.**—Keane in Stanford, Compend., 504, 1878. **Cahokies.**—Esnauts and Rapilly, map, 1777. **Cahoqui.**—Alcedo, Dic. Geog., I, 302, 1786. **Cahoquias.**—Keane in Stanford, Compend., 504, 1878. **Cankia.**—Hennepin, New Discov., 310, 1698 (same? The "Caokia" are named as another Illinois band). **Caokia.**—Allouez (1680) in Margry, Déc., II, 96, 1877. **Caoquias.**—Perkins and Peck, Annals of the West, 680, 1850. **Caouquias.**—Du Pratz, La., II, 227, 1758. **Carrechias.**—St Cosme (1699) in Shea, Early Voy., 62, 1861. **Caskoukia.**—Moll, map, in Salmon, Modern Hist., 3d ed., III, 602, 1746. **Catiokia.**—Morse, N. Am., 255, 1776. **Catokiah.**—Nourse (1820) in Schoolcraft, Ind. Tribes, II, 588, 1852. **Cayaughkias.**—Stone, Life of Brant, II, 566, 1864. **Cohakias.**—Schermerhorn (1812) in Mass. Hist. Soc. Coll., 2d s., II, 8, 1814. **Cohakies.**—Am. Pioneer, I, 408, 1842. **Kahokias.**—Homann Heirs' map, 1756. **Kahoquias.**—Nuttall, Journal, 250, 1821. **Kakias.**—Milfort, Mémoire, 106, 1802 (same?). **Kaockhia.**—La Salle (1682) in Margry, Déc., II, 201, 1877. **Kaokia.**—Gravier (1701?) in Perrot, Mémoire, 221, 1864. **Kiokies.**—Lattré, map, 1784. **Kaoquias.**—

Perkins and Peck, Annals of the West, 69, 1850. **Kaouechias.**—Force, Inds. of Ohio, 21, 1879. **Kaoükia.**—Gravier (1701) in Shea, Early Voy., 118, 1861. **Kaßkias.**—Shea, ibid., 60. **Kavvachias.**—Shea, Rel. Miss. du Mississippi, 36, 1861. **Kavvchias.**—St Cosme (1699) in Shea, Early Voy., 67, 1861. **Kavvechias.**—Ibid., 66. **Kavvkias.**—Ibid., 60. **Kawkias.**—Ibid., 61. **Kerokias.**—Chauvignerie (1736) in Schoolcraft, Ind. Tribes, III, 555, 1853. **Koakias.**—Bos-u, Travels through La., 131, 1771. **Ooukia.**—Allouez (1680) in Margry, Déc., II, 96, 1877. **Tahokias.**—Browne in Beach, Ind. Miscel., 119, 1877.

**Cahokia Mound.** The largest prehistoric artificial earthwork in the United States, situated in Madison co., Ill., in what is known as the American bottom, about 6 m. E. of St Louis, Mo., and in plain view of the railroads entering that city from the E. Before their partial destruction by the plow the principal mound was surrounded by an extensive mound group, numbering, according to Brackenridge (Views La., 187, 1814), who visited the place in 1811, "45 mounds or pyramids, besides a great number of small artificial elevations." The name Cahokia is that of a tribe which formerly occupied a neighboring village of the same name. In form the tumulus is a quadrangular pyramid, with an apron, or terrace, extending from the s. side. The dimensions as given by McAdams (Antiq. of Cahokia or Monk's Mound, 2, 1883) are as follows: The base N. and S., 998 ft.; E. to w., 721 ft.; height, 99 ft.; height of lower terrace, 30 ft.; outward extent of terrace about 200 ft.; width about 500 ft. The area of the base of the mound is estimated at about 16 acres. On the w. side, some 30 ft. above the first terrace, there was a second slight terrace, now scarcely distinguishable. Patrick, who studied the mound and its surroundings, and prepared a model which was cast in iron (now in the Peabody Museum at Cambridge, Mass.), represented a small level area or terrace some 3 or 4 ft. below the level top. Omitting the lower terrace and counting the diameters of the base as 721 and 798 ft., and the height as 99 ft., without regard to the upper level, the contents somewhat exceed 18,690,000 cu. ft. Adding the terrace, 3,000,000 cu. ft., the total contents amount to 21,690,000 cu. ft. The wall of Ft Ancient, Ohio, has been frequently referred to as one of the most extensive ancient works of the United States, yet the contents of the Cahokia

mound would form a wall of the same base and height exceeding 17 m. in length, or more than five times the length of the wall of Ft Ancient, and would have required, according to the usual method of calculation, the labor of 1,000 persons for 4¾ years, with the means that prehistoric Indians had at hand. The places from which the earth was taken are apparent from the depressions surrounding the Cahokia mound. In 1811, when visited by Brackenridge, the largest terrace was used by a colony of Trappists (whence sometimes the name Monk's Mound), who resided in several small cabins on one of the smaller mounds, which latter was cultivated as a kitchen garden. See Brackenridge, op. cit.; Bushnell, Cahokia and Surrounding Mound Group, Peabody Mus. Publ., 1904; Conant, Footprints of Vanished Races, 1879; McAdams (1) Records of Ancient Races, 1887, (2) Antiquities of Cahokia, or Monk's Mound, 1883. (c. t.)

**Cahuabi.** A Papago village in Arizona, near the Sonora border, with 350 inhabitants in 1863 and 80 familes in 1871. Cf. *Guevavi.*

**Cahuabi.**—Wilbur in Ind. Aff. Rep. 1871, 365, 1872. **Cahuabia.**—Poston in Ind. Aff. Rep. 1863, 385, 1864. **Cahuavi.**—Taylor in Cal. Farmer, June 19, 1863. **Ousbabi.**—Browne, Apache Country, 291, 1869 (misprint from Poston).

**Cahuenga.** A former Gabrieleño rancheria in Los Angeles co., Cal.
**Cabeugna.**—Ried (1852) quoted by Taylor in Cal. Farmer, June 8, 1860. **Cabuenga.**—Hoffman in Bull. Essex Inst., XVII, 2, 1885.

**Cahunghage.** A former Iroquois village on the s. side of Oneida lake, N. Y.
**Cahunghage.**—Esnauts and Rapilly, map, 1777. **Cahung-Hage.**—Alcedo, Dic. Geog., I, 303, 1786. **Catumghage.**—Lattré, map, 1784.

**Caiasban.** An unidentified village or tribe mentioned in 1687 to Joutel (Margry, Déc., III, 409, 1878), while he was staying with the Kadohadacho on Red r., of Louisiana, by the chief of that tribe as being among his enemies.

**Caicaches.** A tribe said to have lived on the coast of Texas, but to have been extinct by 1850.—Bollaert in Jour. Ethnol. Soc. Lond., II, 265, 280, 1850.

**Caiman.** A former Tepehuane pueblo in Jalisco, Mexico.
**San Francisco.**—Lumholtz, Unknown Mex., I, 469, 1902 (probably the same). **S. Francisco del Caiman.**—Orozco y Berra, Geog., 281, 1864.

**Caitsodammo.** An unidentified village

CAHOKIA MOUND, ILLINOIS; HEIGHT, AS MEASURED BY McADAMS, 99 FT.; GREATEST LENGTH, 998 FT.

or tribe mentioned to Joutel in 1687 (Margry, Déc., III, 409, 1878), while he was staying with the Kadohadacho on Red r. of Louisiana, by the chief of that tribe as being among his enemies.

**Cajats.** A former Chumashan village near Santa Barbara, Cal.—Taylor in Cal. Farmer, Apr. 24, 1863.
Cojats.—Bancroft, Nat. Races, I, 459, 1874 (misquoted from Taylor).

**Cajon** (Span.: 'box' canyon). A Diegueño settlement about 1850, so called after a mountain pass about 10 m. N. E. of San Diego harbor, s. Cal.—Hayes MS. cited by Bancroft, Nat. Races, I, 458, 1882.

**Cajpilili.** A former Chumashan village near Santa Barbara, Cal.—Taylor in Cal. Farmer, Apr. 24, 1863.

**Cajuenche.** A Yuman tribe speaking the Cocopa dialect and residing in 1775–76 on the E. bank of the Rio Colorado below the mouth of the Gila, next to the Quigyuma, their rancherias extending s. to about lat. 32° 33′ and into central s. California, about lat. 33° 08′, where they met the Comeya. At the date named the Cajuenche are said to have numbered 3,000 and to have been enemies of the Cocopa (Garcés, Diary, 443, 1900). Of the disappearance of the tribe practically nothing is known, but if they are identical with the Cawina, or Quo-kim, as they seem to be, they had become reduced to a mere remnant by 1851, owing to constant wars with the Yuma. At this date Bartlett reported only 10 survivors living with the Pima and Maricopa, only one of whom understood his native language, which was said to differ from the Pima and Maricopa. Merced, San Jacome, and San Sebastian(?) have been mentioned as Cajuenche rancherias.          (F. W. H.)
Cafuenchi.—Escudero, Noticias Estadisticas de Chihuahua, 228, 1834. Cajuenche.—Garcés (1776), Diary, 434, 1900. Carjuenché.—Forbes, Hist. Cal., 162, 1839. Cawina.—Bartlett, Pers. Narr., II, 251, 1854. Cojuenchis.—Pike, Expeditions, 3d map, 1810. Kakhuana.—Kroeber, inf'n, 1905 (Mohave name). Kokhuene.—Ibid. Oajuenches.—Hinton, Handbook to Arizona, 28, 1878 (misprint). Quo-kim.—Thomas, MS. Yuma vocab., B. A. E., 1868.

**Cajurachic.** A Tarahumare settlement in Chihuahua, Mexico; definite locality unknown.—Orozco y Berra, Geog., 323, 1864.

**Calabashes.** See *Gourds*.

**Calabazas** (Span.: 'calabashes'). Formerly a Sobaipuri (?) rancheria, dating from the early part of the 18th century; situated on the Rio Santa Cruz, below Tubac, in s. Arizona. It was a visita of Guevavi until that mission was abandoned prior to 1784. A church and a house for the priest were erected in 1797, before which date Calabazas was probably a visita of Tubac. It had 116 neophytes in 1760–64, and 64 in 1772, but it was described as being only a rancho in 1828. When visited by Bartlett (Pers. Narr., I, 391, 1854), in

1851, it was in ruins, and seemed to have been abandoned many years before.                              (F. W. H.)
Colabazas.—Font, map (1777) in Bancroft, Ariz. and N. Mex., 393, 1889 (misprint). San Cayetano de Calabazas.—Bancroft, ibid., 369, 385. S. Cajetanus.—Kino, map (1702) in Stöcklein, Neue Welt-Bott, 74, 1726. S. Gaetan.—Kino, map (1701) in Bancroft, op. cit., 360.

**Calagnujuet.**—A place in N. Lower California, 8 m. above Borja, at which a Jesuit mission was established in Oct., 1766, but owing to the barrenness of the soil and the alkaline water it was moved in May, 1767, to a site 50 m. away, where new buildings were erected and where, under the name Santa María, it soon became somewhat prosperous. It was the last of the mission establishments of the Jesuits in Lower California, as they were expelled in the year last named. See Bancroft, No. Mex. States, I, 473, 1886.

**Calahuasa.** The mission of Santa Inés, or perhaps a Chumashan village formerly at or near its site.
Calahuasa.—Taylor in Cal. Farmer, Apr. 24, 1863. Calla Wassa.—Bancroft, Nat. Races, I, 459, 1874. Kalahuasa.—Taylor, op. cit., Oct. 18, 1861.

**Calany.** A former Timuquanan tribe or settlement of the Utina confederacy in middle or N. Florida.—Laudonnière (1564) in French, Hist. Coll. La., n. s., 243, 1869.
Calanay.—De Bry, Brev. Nar., II, map, 1591 (town on an E. tributary of middle St Johns r.) Cal-anio.—Barcia, Ensayo, 48, 1723.

**Calaobe.** A Calusa village on the s. w. coast of Florida, about 1570.—Fontaneda Mem. (ca. 1575), Smith trans., 19, 1854.
Calaboe.—Fontaneda as quoted in Doc. Inéd., v, 539, 1866.

**Calapooya.** The name, properly speaking, of a division of the Kalapooian family formerly occupying the watershed between Willamette and Umpqua rs., Oreg. The term as usually employed, however, includes all the bands speaking dialects of the Kalapooian language and is made synonymous with the family name. This double use of the term, coupled with the scanty information regarding the division, has wrought confusion in the classification of the bands which can not be rectified. The following were ascertained by Gatschet to have been bands of this division: Ampishtna, Tsanchifin, Tsanklightemifa, Tsankupi, and Tsawokot.     (L. F.)
Calahpoewah.—Lewis and Clark, Exped., II, 227, 1814. Calapooa.—Parker, Journal, 415, 1846. Calapooah.—Ibid., 173, 1840. Calapoogas.—Lea in Ind. Aff. Rep., 270, 1851. Calapooias.—U. S. Stat. at Large, X, 674, 1854. Calapoolia.—Lyman in Oreg. Hist. Soc. Quar., I, 325, 1900. Calapoosas.—Miller in Ind. Aff. Rep. 1859, 430, 1860. Calapooyas.—Lee and Frost, Oregon, 90, 1844. Calapuaya.—McClane in Ind. Aff. Rep. 203, 1888. Calapuyas.—Hale in U. S. Expl. Exped., VI, 198, 1846. Calipoa.—Lane (1849) in Sen. Ex. Doc. 52, 31st Cong., 1st sess., 172, 1850. Calipooias.—Ind. Aff. Rep., 260, 1854. Calipooya.—Bissell, Umpkwa MS. vocab., B. A. E. Calipoyas.—Gallatin in Trans. Am. Antiq. Soc., II, map, 1836. Calipuyowes.—Henry-Thompson Jour., Coues ed., 814, 1897. Cal-lah-po-e-ouah.—Nouv. Ann. Voy., 1e s., XII,

map, 1821. **Callahpoewah.**—Kelley, Oregon, 68, 1830. **Cal-lah-po-e-wah.**—Lewis and Clark, Exped., I, map, 1814. **Callapipas.**—McKenney and Hall, Ind. Tribes, III, 80, 1854. **Callapooahs.**—Parker, Journal, 239, 1840. **Callapoohas.**—Robertson (1846) in H. R. Ex. Doc. 76, 30th Cong., 1st sess., 8, 1848. **Callapooiales.**—Howison in H. R. Misc. Doc. 29, 30th Cong., 1st sess., 26, 1848. **Callapooias.**—Taylor in Sen. Ex. Doc. 4, 40th Cong., spec. sess., 25, 1867. **Callapootos.**—Kingsley, Stand. Nat. Hist., VI, 141, 1883. **Callapooya.**—Pres. Mess., Ex. Doc. 39, 32d Cong., 1st sess., 2, 1852. **Callapooyahs.**—Hale in U. S. Expl. Exped., VI, 217, 1846. **Calla puyas.**—Wilkes, ibid., IV, 368, 1845. **Callapuyes.**—Medill in H. R. Ex. Doc. 76, 30th Cong., 1st sess., 6, 1848. **Call-law-poh-yea-as.**—Ross, Fur Hunters, 108, 1855. **Cathlapooya.**—Drake, Bk. Inds., vi, 1848. **Cathlapouyeas.**—Stuart in Nouv. Ann. Voy., x, 117, 1821. **Col-lap-poh-yea-ass.**—Ross, Adventures, 235, 1847. **Kait-ka.**—Bissell, Umpkwa MS. vocab., B. A. E., 1881 (Umpkwa name). **Kalapooiah.**—Scouler in Jour. Geog. Soc. Lond., XI, 225, 1841. **Kalapooya.**—Tolmie and Dawson, Comp. Vocab., 11, 1884. **Kalapooyahs.**—Townsend, Narr., 175, 1839. **Kalapouyas.**—De Smet, Letters, 230, 1843. **Kalapuaya.**—Ind. Aff. Rep., 232, 1883. **Kalapuya.**—Hale in U. S. Expl. Exped., VI, 217, 1846. **Kallapooeas.**—Meek in H. R. Ex. Doc. 76, 30th Cong., 1st sess., 10, 1848. **Kallapooyah.**—Slocum (1835) in H. R. Rep. 101, 25th Cong., 3d sess., 42, 1839. **Kallapugas.**—Farnham, Travels, 112, 1843. **Kallapüia.**—Gibbs in Cont. N. A. Ethnol., I, 212, 1877. **Kallapuiah.**—Ludewig, Am. Aborig. Lang., 202, 1858. **Tsänh-alokual amim.**—Gatschet, Lakmiut MS., B. A. E., 1877 (Lakmiut name). **Vule Pugas.**—Warre and Vavasour in Martin, Hudson Bay Terr., 80, 1849.

**Calaveras Man.** During the early days of gold mining in California many relics of man and his implements and utensils were found embedded in the ancient river gravels from which the gold was washed. These remains were especially plentiful in Calaveras co., whence the name "Calaveras man," here employed. The gold-bearing gravels are largely of Tertiary age, although the conditions have been such that in places accumulations uniform in character with the older deposits have continued to the present time. Owing to this fact expert geologic discrimination is necessary in considering questions of age. The evidences of great antiquity, in many cases apparently almost conclusive, were accepted as satisfactory by J. D. Whitney, formerly state geologist of California; but the lack of expert observation or of actual record of the various finds reported makes extreme caution advisable, especially since the acceptance of the evidence necessitates conclusions widely at variance with the usual conception of the history of man, not only in America but throughout the world. The need of conservatism in dealing with this evidence is further emphasized by the fact that the human crania of the auriferous gravels are practically identical with the crania of the present California Indians, and

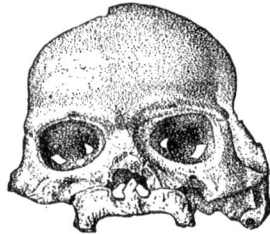

FRONTAL VIEW OF THE FRAGMENTARY CALAVERAS SKULL

it is also observed that the artifacts—the mortars and pestles, the implements and ornaments—found in the same connection correspond closely with those of the historic inhabitants of the Pacific slope. It is held by many students of human history that man already existed in some parts of the world in the late Tertiary—a period believed by conservative geologists to have closed hundreds of thousands of years ago. But few are ready to accept the conclusion, made necessary if the California testimony is fully sustained, that man had then reached the stage of culture characterized by the use of implements and ornaments of polished stone. In view of the somewhat defective nature of the testimony furnished, as well as the vast importance of the deductions depending on it, it is perhaps wise to suspend judgment until more systematic investigations can be made. The "Calaveras skull," which has had exceptional prominence in the discussion of this subject, is preserved in the Peabody Museum of Archæology and Ethnology, at Cambridge, Mass. Notwithstanding the well-fortified statements of early writers to the effect that this relic came from the gravels of Bald mtn. at a depth of about 130 feet, there are good reasons for suspecting that it may have been derived from one of the limestone caves so numerous in the Calaveras region. It thus appears that the importance of this specimen, as a feature of the evidence, has probably been greatly overestimated.

For details relating to the auriferous-gravel testimony consult Becker in Bull. Geol. Soc. Am., II, 1891; Blake in Jour. of Geol., Oct.–Nov., 1899; Dall in Proc. Acad. Nat. Sci. Phila., 1899; Foster, Prehist. Races, 1878; Hanks, Deep Lying Gravels of Table Mtn., 1901; Holmes in Smithson. Rep. 1899, 1901; Lindgren and Knowlton in Jour. of Geol., IV, 1896; Putnam in University of Cal. Publ., Dept. of Anthrop., 1905; Skertchley in Jour. Anthrop. Inst., May, 1888; Whitney in Mem. Mus. Comp. Zool., Harvard, VI, no. 1, 1879; Wright, Man and the Glacial Period, 1895. See *Antiquity, Archeology*.                    (w. h. h.)

**Calcefar.** A division of the New Jersey Delawares formerly living in the interior between Rancocas cr. and the present Trenton. In 1648 they were estimated at 150 men.
**Calafars.**—Sanford, U. S., 1819. **Calcefar.**—Evelin (1648) quoted by Proud, Penn., I, 113, 1797.

**Calchufines.** A band of Jicarilla Apache living in 1719 on Arkansas r., in the present s. E. Colorado.—Villa-Señor y Sanchez, Theatro Am., pt. 2, 412, 1748.
**Apaches Calchufines.**—Valverde y Costo (1719) quoted by Bancroft, Ariz. and N. Mex., 236, 1889.

**Calciati.** A pueblo of the province of

Atripuy in the region of the lower Rio Grande, N. Mex., in 1598.—Oñate (1598) in Doc. Inéd., XVI, 115, 1871.

**Calcite.**—Carbonate of calcium, the essential constitutent of chalk and limestone, when pure, colorless, and transparent, though sometimes yellow and red and even black. The crystals, which are so soft as to be readily shaped with primitive knives and scrapers, are of general occurrence and were employed by the Indians in the manufacture of ornaments and minor sculptures. See *Stone-work.*                    (w. h. h.)

**Caldrons.** See *Receptacles.*

**Caldwell, Billy.** See *Sagaunash.*

**Calendar.** Although the methods of computing time had been carried to an advanced stage among the cultured tribes of Mexico and Central America, the Indians N. of Mexico had not brought them beyond the simplest stage. The alternation of day and night and the changes of the moon and the seasons formed the bases of their systems. The budding, blooming, leafing, and fruiting of vegetation, the springing forth, growth, and decay of annuals, and the molting, migration, pairing, etc., of animals and birds were used to denote the progress of the seasons. The divisions of the day differed, many tribes recognizing 4 diurnal periods—the rising and setting of the sun, noon, and midnight—while full days were usually counted as so many nights or sleeps. The years were generally reckoned, especially in the far N., as so many winters or so many snows; but in the Gulf states, where snow is rare and the heat of summer the dominant feature, the term for year had some reference to this season or to the heat of the sun. As a rule the four seasons—spring, summer, autumn, and winter—were recognized and specific names applied to them, but the natural phenomena by which they were determined, and from which their names were derived, varied according to latitude and environment, and as to whether the tribe was in the agricultural or the hunter state. Some authorities state that the Indians of Virginia divided the year into five seasons: (1) The budding of spring; (2) the earing of corn, or roasting-ear time; (3) summer, or highest sun; (4) corn-gathering, or fall of the leaf; and (5) winter (*cohonk*). According to Mooney the Cherokee and most of the southeastern tribes also divided the year into five seasons. Swanton and Boas state that some of the tribes of the N. W. coast divided the year into two equal parts, with 6 months or moons to each part, the summer period extending from April to September, the winter period from October to March. Many tribes began the year with the vernal equinox;

others began it in the fall, the Kiowa about Oct. 1, the Hopi with the "new fire" in November, the Takulli in January, etc. The most important time division to the Indians N. of Mexico was the moon, or month, their count of this period beginning with the new moon. So far as can be ascertained, it was not universal in the past to correlate the moons with the year; where correlation was attempted, in order that the moons should bear a fixed relation to the seasons, 12 was the number usually reckoned; but some of the tribes, as those of New England, the Cree, and some others counted 13. The Kiowa system, although counting 12 moons to the year, presents the peculiarity of half a moon in one of the unequal four seasons, and the other half in the following season, thus beginning the year with the last half of a moon. Among the Zuñi half the months are "nameless," the other half "named." The year is called a "passage of time," the seasons the "steps" of the year, and the months "crescents," probably because each begins with a new moon. The new year is termed "mid-journey of the sun," i. e., the middle of the solar trip between one summer solstice and another, and occurring about the 19th of December usually initiates a short season of great religious activity. The first six months have definite and appropriate names, the others, while called the "nameless" months, are designated, in ritualistic speech, Yellow, Blue, Red, White, Variegated, and Black, after the colors of the prayer-sticks sacrificed in rotation at the full of each moon to the gods of the north, west, south, east, zenith, and nadir, respectively represented by those colors (Cushing in Millstone, IX, 58, Apr. 1884). There appears to have been an attempt on the part of some tribes to compensate for the surplus days in the solar year. Carver (Trav., 160, 1796), speaking of the Sioux or the Chippewa, says that when thirty moons have waned they add a supernumerary one, which they term the lost moon. The Haida formerly intercalated what they called a "between month," because between the two periods into which they divided the year, and it is likely that this was sometimes omitted to correct the calendar (Swanton in Am. Anthrop., v, 331, 1903). The Creeks counted 12½ moons to the year, adding a moon at the end of every second year, half counted in the preceding and half in the following year, somewhat as did the Kiowa. The Indians generally calculated their ages by some remarkable event or phenomenon which had taken place within their remembrance; but few Indians of mature years could possibly tell their age before learning the white man's way of counting time. Sticks were sometimes notched by the Indians as an aid in time counts. The oldest of these among the Pima (Russell in Am. Anthrop., v, 76, 1903) dates from the meteoric shower of 1833, a notable tally date in Indian time reckoning. Some of the northern tribes kept records of events by means of symbolic figures or pictographs. One of these is an extended calendar history, called the "Lone-dog

Those along the coast s. of San Francisco were brought under Spanish missionary influence in the latter part of the 18th and the beginning of the 19th centuries. Some tribes, however, were not known even by name until after the discovery of gold and the settlement of the country in 1849 and subsequently. The Californians were among the least warlike tribes of the continent and offered but little resistance, and that always ineffectual, to

LINGUISTIC FAMILIES OF CALIFORNIA

winter count," said to have been painted originally on a buffalo robe, found among the Dakota, the figures of which cover a period of 71 years from 1800 (Mallery in 10th Rep. B. A. E.). Another series is the calendar history of the Kiowa, described by Mooney in 17th Rep. B. A. E. See *Measures*, *Numeral systems*. (c. t.)

**California, Indians of.** The Indians of California are among the least known groups of natives of North America.

the seizure of their territory by the whites. Comparatively few of them are now on reservations. The majority live as squatters on the land of white owners or of the Government, or in some cases on land allotted them by the Government or even bought by themselves from white owners. Their number has decreased very rapidly and is now probably about 15,000, as compared with perhaps 150,000 before the arrival of the whites.

Physically, the California Indians, like other tribes of the Pacific coast, are rather shorter than the majority of those in eastern North America. In many cases they incline to be stout. Along the coast, and especially in the s., they are unusually dark. The most southern tribes approximate those of the Colorado r. in physical type and are tall and short-headed. The native population of California was broken up into a great number of small groups. These were often somewhat unsettled in habitation, but always within very limited territories, and were never nomadic. The dialects of almost all of these groups were different and belonged to as many as 21 distinct linguistic families, being a fourth of the total number found in all North America, and, as compared with the area of the state, so large that California must probably be regarded as the region of the greatest aboriginal linguistic diversity in the world. Three larger stocks have found their way into California: the Athapascan in the N. and the Shoshonean and Yuman in the s. The remainder are all small and purely Californian.

This diversity is accompanied by a corresponding stability of population. While there have undoubtedly been shiftings of tribes within the state, they do not appear to have extended very far territorially. The Indians themselves in no part of the state except the extreme s. have any tradition of migrations and uniformly believe themselves to have originated at the spot where they live. The groups in which they live are very loose, being defined and held together by language and the topography of the country much more than by any political or social organization; distinct tribes, as they occur in many other parts of America, do not really exist. The small village is the most common unit of organization among these people.

Culturally, the California Indians are probably as simple and rude as any large group of Indians in North America. Their arts (excepting that of basket making, which they possessed in a high form) were undeveloped; pottery was practically unknown, and in the greater part of the state the carving or working of wood was carried on only to a limited extent. Houses were often of grass, tule, or brush, or of bark, sometimes covered with earth. Only in the N. w. part of the state were small houses of planks in use. In this region, as well as on the Santa Barbara ids., wooden canoes were also made, but over the greater part of the state a raft of tules was the only means of navigation. Agriculture was nowhere practised. Deer and small game were hunted, and there was

considerable fishing; but the bulk of the food was vegetable. The main reliance was placed on numerous varieties of acorns, and next to these, on seeds, especially of grasses and herbs. Roots and berries were less used.

Both totemism and a true gentile organization were totally lacking in all parts of the state. The mythology of the Californians was characterized by unusually well-developed and consistent creation myths, and by the complete lack not only of migration but of ancestor traditions. Their ceremonies were numerous and elaborate as compared with the prevailing simplicity of life, but they lacked almost totally the rigid ritualism and extensive symbolism that pervade the ceremonies of most of America. One set of ceremonies was usually connected with a secret religious society; another, often spectacular, was held in remembrance of the dead.

With constant differences from group to group, these characteristics held with a general underlying uniformity over the greater part of California. In the extreme N. w. portion of the state, however, a somewhat more highly developed and specialized culture existed, which showed in several respects similarities to that of the N. Pacific coast, as is indicated by a greater advance in technology, a social organization largely upon a property basis, and a system of mythology that is suggestive of those farther N. The Santa Barbara islanders, now extinct, appear also to have been considerably specialized from the great body of Californian tribes, both in their arts and their mode of life. The Indians of s. California, finally, especially those of the interior, living under geographic conditions very different from those of the main portion of the state, resemble in certain respects of culture the Indians of Arizona and New Mexico. See *Mission Indians* and the articles on the individual linguistic families noted on the accompanying map.　　　　(A. L. K.)

**Caloucha.** A tribe on a river flowing into the Atlantic N. of St Augustine, Fla. (De Isle, map, 1707); possibly an erroneous location of Calusa, otherwise unidentifiable.

**Calumet** (Norman-French form of literary French *chalumet*, a parallel of *chalumeau* for *chalemeau*, Old French *chalemel*, Provençal *caramel*, a tube, pipe, reed, flute, especially a shepherd's pipe; Spanish *caramillo*, a flute; English, *shawm;* Low Latin, *calamellus*, diminutive of Latin *calamus*, reed). Either one of 2 highly symbolic shafts of reed or wood about 2 in. broad, ¼ in. thick, and 18 in. to 4 ft. long, the one representing the male, the other the female shaft, usually perforated for a pathway for the breath or spirit, painted with diverse symbolic colors and adorned with various symbolic objects, and which may or may not have a pipe bowl to contain tobacco for making a sacred offering of its benevolent smoke to the gods. In modern usage the term usually includes the pipe. Its coloring and degree of adornment varied somewhat from tribe to tribe and were largely governed by the occasion for which the calumet was used. From the meager descriptions of the calumet and its uses it would seem that it has a ceremonially symbolic history independent of that of the pipe; and that when the pipe became an altar, by its employment for burning sacrificial tobacco to the gods, convenience and convention united the already highly symbolic calumet shafts and the sacrificial tobacco altar, the pipe-bowl; hence it became one of the most profoundly sacred objects known to the Indians of northern America. As the colors and the other adornments on the shaft represent symbolically various dominant gods of the Indian polytheon, it follows that the symbolism of the calumet and pipe represented a veritable executive council of the gods. Moreover, in some of the elaborate ceremonies in which it was necessary to portray this symbolism the employment of the two shafts became necessary, because the one with its colors and accessory adornments represented the procreative male power and his aids, and was denominated the male, the fatherhood of nature; and the other with its colors and necessary adornments represented the reproductive female power and her aids, and was denominated the female, the motherhood of nature.

The calumet was employed by ambassadors and travelers as a passport; it was used in ceremonies designed to conciliate foreign and hostile nations and to conclude lasting peace; to ratify the alliance of friendly tribes; to secure favorable weather for journeys; to bring needed rain; and to attest contracts and treaties which could not be violated without incurring the wrath of the gods. The use of the calumet was inculcated by religious precept and example. A chant and a dance have become known as the chant and the dance of the calumet; together they were employed as an invocation to one or more of the gods. By naming in the chant the souls of those against whom war must be waged, such persons were doomed to die at the hands of the person so naming them. The dance and the chant were rather in honor of the calumet than with the calumet. To smoke it was prohibited to a man whose

wife was with child, lest he perish and she die in childbirth. The calumet was employed also in banishing evil and for obtaining good. Some, in order to obtain favor of the gods, sacrificed some animals in spirit to them, and, as the visible food was not consumed visibly by the gods, they ate the food and chanted and danced for the calumet.

J. O. Dorsey asserts that the Omaha and cognate names for this dance and chant signify "to make a sacred kinship," but not "to dance." This is a key to the esoteric significance of the use of the calumet. The one for whom the dance for the calumet was performed became thereby the adopted son of the performer. One might ask another to dance the calumet dance for him, or one might offer to perform this dance for another, but in either case the offer or invitation could be declined. The dancing party consisted of 2 leaders and sometimes as many as 20 or 30 adherents. In the lodge wherein the dance for the calumet was to be held the 2 *niniba weawan*, or calumet pipes, were placed on a forked support driven into the virgin soil in the rear part of the lodge. Each *weawan* has, instead of a pipe-bowl, the head and neck of a green-neck duck. Next on the staff are the yellowish feathers of the great owl, extending about 6 in.; next are the long wing-feathers of the war eagle, riven and stuck on lengthwise in 3 places; at the end a bit of horsehair, tinted red, is wrapped around the staff and bound on with sinew, and over this is fastened some fur of the white rabbit, strips of which dangle about 6 in.; below the rabbit fur the horsehair extends fully 6 in. The horsehair is wrapped around the staff in 2 other places and secured in a similar manner; the 3 tufts are equidistant, about 6 in. apart. Close to the last tuft is the head of the *wajiñ'gada* (?) woodcock, having the bill faced toward the mouthpiece. There may be, according to La Flesche, as many as 6 heads on 1 pipe. No part of the neck appears, and the lower mandible is removed. The head, or the heads, in case of a plurality, was secured to the shaft by means of a deer or antelope skin. Next to this are suspended 2 eagle plumes, symbolizing 2 eggs, typifying that the adopted person is still an immature child, and serving as a thinly veiled symbol suggestive of the source of life. Next are a number of eagle feathers secured to the shaft by means of 2 cords or thongs of deer or antelope skin. On one shaft the eagle feathers are white, being those of a male eagle, and the shaft is dark green. On the other shaft the feathers are spotted black and white, being those of the female eagle, and the shaft is dark blue. Two symbolically painted gourd rattles are also employed, 1 for each calumet.

When these shafts are set against the 2 forked sticks the heads of the ducks are placed next to the ground. Close to these shafts are 2 sticks connected with a sacred ear of corn, which must be in perfect condition; ears containing rough or shriveled or otherwise imperfect grains are rejected. All the people use corn for food, hence it is regarded as a mother. These sticks are tinted with Indian red. The longer stick, which stands nearer the calumet shafts, is driven about 4 in. into the earth and projects several inches above the ear of corn, the top end of it being on a level with that of the ear of corn, while the lower end hangs a short distance below the lower end of the ear of corn, but does not reach the ground. The ear of corn is fastened to the sticks by wrapping around the 3 a band braided from hair from the head of a buffalo. To the top of the smaller stick an eagle plume is secured with sinew. The lower part of the ear of corn is white; the upper part is painted green.

In this dance, lasting an hour, the movements of the war eagle are closely imitated, accompanied by a constant waving of the calumets. After the delivery of presents, the 2 calumets are given to the family to which the adopted child belongs. Such are, according to Dorsey, the Omaha calumets with their use in a ceremony for making a sacred kinship in the adoption of a child, who for this purpose must be less than 10 years of age. The Ponka use only 1 calumet, although they are well acquainted with the Omaha use of 2, and it may be a higher development of the intention of the symbolism.

From Dorsey's account of the Omaha calumets it is evident that they are together the most highly organized emblems known to religious observances anywhere, and it is further in evidence that the pipe is an accessory rather than the dominant or chief object in this highly complex synthetic symbol of the source, reproduction, and conservation of life.

For the purpose of comparison, the following description of the calumet by Hennepin may be given: "The quill, which is commonly two foot and a half long, is made of a pretty strong reed or cane, adorned with feathers of all colors, interlaced with locks of women's hair. They tie to it two wings of the most curious birds they find, which makes their calumet not much unlike Mercury's wand, or that staff ambassadors did formerly carry when they went to treat of peace. They sheath that reed into the

neck of birds they call huars [loons], which are as big as our geese and spotted with black and white; or else of a sort of ducks who make their nests upon trees, though water be their natural element, and whose feathers are of many different colours. However, every nation adorns the calumet as they think fit, according to their own genius and the birds they have in their own country."

In her description of the Hako ceremonial of the Pawnee, Miss Fletcher has set forth these conceptions with great sympathy and detail. Among this people two ash saplings are cut and brought with due ceremony; they are then warmed and straightened over a newly kindled sacred fire, and are cut the required length, "four spans from the thumb to the third finger." They are then peeled and the pith removed to permit the passage of the breath. A straight groove is cut the entire length of each shaft, and after the litter thus made is cast into the fire, the shafts are passed through the flames, "the word of the fire." Thereupon one of the shafts, with the exception of the groove, is painted blue with ceremonially prepared color to symbolize the sky, and while this is being done there is intoned a song in which a prayer is made that life be given to this symbol of the dwelling place of the chief deity. Then the shaft is placed in the hands of the chief shaman, whose function it is to paint the groove red, typifying the pathway of the spirits, represented by the objects placed later upon this ashen shaft, for their going forth to aid man in this ceremony; and, furthermore, the red color here employed typifies the passageways of the body, through which the breath of man—his life—comes and departs, and the sun is red, and also straight—like unto this—is the pathway on which the sun shines. In similar fashion is the other shaft painted green and its groove red, the latter color having the same significance it has on the other shaft, and the green color is employed to symbolize vegetation, the living covering of mother earth. In the accompanying song a prayer is made that life be breathed into the symbol to make it efficient in the approaching ceremonies and that living power may abide where this symbol shall be placed. Then the shaman, after anointing his hands with a sacred ointment, consisting of red clay and the fat of a deer or buffalo that has been consecrated to the chief deity, binds the symbolic objects separately on the two shafts. Splitting long feathers from the wings of an eagle, he glues them with pine pitch on the shaft, as in feathering an arrow. These feathers signify that the eagle soars near the abode of the chief deity. About the mouthpiece of the shaft soft blue feathers are fastened, symbolizing the sky wherein the powers abide. Then a woodpecker's head, with the mandible turned back upon the red crest, is bound to the shaft near the mouthpiece, indicating that the bird may not be angry; the inner side of the mandible thus exposed is painted blue, showing that the chief deity is looking down on it as the bird's spirit moves along the groove to reach the people; then about the middle of the shaft feathers from the owl are bound and the undecorated end of the shaft is thrust through the breast, throat, and mouth of the duck, the breast reaching the feathers of the owl. The end of the shaft projects a little from the duck's mouth, that a pipe may be fitted to the shaft. The duck's head, therefore, always faces downward toward the earth and water. Then 10 tail-feathers of the brown eagle, made sacred by sacrifice to the chief deity, are prepared for binding on one of the stems; a buckskin thong is threaded through a hole made in the quill midway of its length and another thong is passed through a hole near the end of the quill in such manner that the feathers may be expanded like a fan on these two thongs. The two little balls of white down from inside the thigh of the white male eagle, representing reproductive power, are secured to the ends of these thongs and this fan-like wing is secured to the side of the blue-colored shaft in such way that it may swing when the shaft is waved to simulate the movements of an eagle. Such is the female shaft, representing the night, the moon, the north, as well as kindness and gentleness; it cares for the people; it is the mother. Every bird represented on these shafts is a leader, a chief, a god; the eagle, the owl, the woodpecker, and the duck are chiefs, respectively, of the day, the night, the trees, and the water. Then 7 tail-feathers from the white eagle, prepared in similar fashion, are secured to the green-colored shaft; but while these are being prepared no song is sung, because the white eagle is not sacred, never being a sacrificial victim, and having less power than the brown eagle, for it is warlike and inclined to injure, and so can not lead, but must follow. Hence the green-colored shaft, the male, is prepared, painted, and decorated after the other.

From Charlevoix (1721) it is learned that the calumet is strictly the stem or shaft of what is commonly called the calumet pipe; that in those designed for public ceremonial purposes this shaft is very long, and "is of light wood, painted with different colors, and adorned with the heads, tails, wings, and feathers of the most beautiful birds," which he believed were "only for ornament" rather than for symbolic expression; that among those nations among which the calumet is in use it is as sacred as are the wampum belts and strands among the nations among whom these things are in use; that Pawnee tradition asserts that the calumet is a gift from the sun; that the calumet is in use more among the southern and western nations than among the eastern and northern, and it is more frequently employed for peace than for war. He says that if the calumet is offered and accepted it is the custom to smoke in the calumet, and the engagements contracted are held sacred and inviolable, in just so far as such human things are inviolable. Perrot also says that the Indians believe that the sun gave the calumet to the Pawnee. The Indians profess that the violation of such an engagement never escapes just punishment. In the heat of battle, if an adversary offer the calumet to his opponent and he accept it, the weapons on both sides are at once laid down; but to accept or to refuse the offer of the calumet is optional. There are calumets for various kinds of public engagements, and when such bargains are made an exchange of calumets is usual, in this manner rendering the contract or bargain sacred.

When war is contemplated, not only the shaft but the feathers with which it is dressed are colored red, but the feathers only on one side may be red, and it is claimed that from the disposition of the feathers in some instances it is possible to know to what nation the calumet is to be presented. By smoking together in the calumet the contracting parties intend to invoke the sun and the other gods as witnesses to the mutual obligations assumed by the parties, and as a guaranty the one to the other that they shall be fulfilled. This is accomplished by blowing the smoke toward the sky, the four world-quarters, and the earth, with a suitable invocation. The size and ornaments of the calumets which are presented to persons of distinction on occasions of moment are suited to the requirements of the case. When the calumet is designed to be employed in a treaty of alliance against a third tribe, a serpent may be painted on the shaft, and perhaps some other device indicating the motive of the alliance.

There were calumets for commerce and trade and for other social and political purposes; but the most important were those designed for war and those for peace and brotherhood. It was vitally necessary, however, that they should be distinguishable at once, lest through ignorance and inattention one should become the victim of treachery. The Indians in general chose not or dared not to violate openly the faith attested by the calumet, and sought to deceive an intended victim by the use of a false calumet of peace in an endeavor to make the victim in some measure responsible for the consequences. On one occasion a band of Sioux, seeking to destroy some Indians and their protectors, a French officer and his men, presented, in the guise of friendship, 12 calumets, apparently of peace; but the officer, who was versed in such matters and whose suspicion was aroused by the number offered, consulted an astute Indian attached to his force, who caused him to see that among the 12 one of the calumet shafts was not matted with hair like the others, and that on the shaft was graven the figure of a viper, coiled around it. The officer was made to understand that this was the sign of covert treachery, thus frustrating the intended Sioux plot.

The use of the calumet, sometimes called "peace-pipe" and "war pipe," was widespread in the Mississippi valley generally. It has been found among the Potawatomi, Cheyenne, Shoshoni, Pawnee Loups, Piegan, Santee, Yanktonais, Sihasapa, Kansa, Siksika, Crows, Cree, Skitswish, Nez Percés, Illinois, Chickasaw, Choctaw, Chitimacha, Chippewa, Winnebago, and Natchez. In the Ohio and St Lawrence valleys and southward its use is not so definitely shown.

For more detailed information consult Charlevoix, Journal, 1761; Dorsey in 3d Rep. B. A. E., 1885; Fletcher in 22d Rep. B. A. E., 1904; Jesuit Relations and Allied Documents, Thwaites ed., I–LXXIII, 1896–1901; Lafitau, Mœurs des Sauvages, 1724; Le Page du Pratz, Hist. de la Louisiane, 1758; Lesueur, La Danse du Calumet, in Les Soirées Canadiennes, IV, 1864; McGuire in Rep. Nat. Mus. 1897, 1899; Perrot, Mémoire, 1864; Relations des Jesuites, I–III, 1858. See *Catlinite, Ceremony, Dance, Pipes, Tobacco.*     (J. N. B. H.)

**Calumet.** A former Menominee village on the E. shore of L. Winnebago, Wis., with 150 inhabitants in 1817.—Starrow in Wis. Hist. Soc. Coll., VI, 171, 1872; Royce in 18th Rep. B. A. E., pl. clxxi, 1899.

**Calusa.** An important tribe of Florida, formerly holding the s. w. coast from about Tampa bay to C. Sable and C. Florida, together with all the outlying keys, and extending inland to L. Okeechobee. They claimed more or less authority also over the tribes of the E. coast, N. to about C. Cañaveral. The name, which can not be interpreted, appears as Calos or Carlos (province) in the early Spanish and French records, Caloosa and Coloosa in later English authors, and survives in Caloosa village, Caloosahatchee r., and Charlotte (for Carlos)

harbor within their old territory. They cultivated the ground to a limited extent, but were better noted as expert fishers, daring seamen, and fierce and determined fighters, keeping up their resistance to the Spanish arms and missionary advances after all the rest of Florida had submitted. Their men went nearly naked. They seem to have practised human sacrifice of captives upon a wholesale scale, scalped and dismembered their slain enemies, and have repeatedly been accused of being cannibals. Although this charge is denied by Adair (1775), who was in position to know, the evidence of the mounds indicates that it was true in the earlier period.

Their history begins in 1513 when, with a fleet of 80 canoes they boldly attacked Ponce de León, who was about to land on their coast, and after an all-day fight compelled him to withdraw. Even at this early date they were already noted among the tribes for the golden wealth which they had accumulated from the numerous Spanish wrecks cast away upon the keys in passage from the s., and two centuries later they were regarded as veritable pirates, plundering and killing without mercy the crews of all vessels, excepting Spanish, so unfortunate as to be stranded in their neighborhood. In 1567 the Spaniards established a mission and fortified post among them, but both seem to have been discontinued soon after, although the tribe came later under Spanish influence. About this time, according to Fontaneda, a captive among them, they numbered nearly 50 villages, including one occupied by the descendants of an Arawakan colony (q.v.) from Cuba. From one of these villages the modern Tampa takes its name. Another, Muspa, existed up to about 1750. About the year 1600 they carried on a regular trade, by canoe, with Havana in fish, skins, and amber. By the constant invasions of the Creeks and other Indian allies of the English in the 18th century they were at last driven from the mainland and forced to take refuge on the keys, particularly Key West, Key Vaccas, and the Matacumbe keys. One of their latest recorded exploits was the massacre of an entire French crew wrecked upon the islands. Romans states that in 1763, on the transfer of Florida from Spain to England, the last remnant of the tribe, numbering then 80 families, or perhaps 350 souls, was removed to Havana. This, however, is only partially correct, as a considerable band under the name of Muspa Indians, or simply Spanish Indians, maintained their distinct existence and language in their ancient territory up to the close of the second Seminole war.

Nothing is known of the linguistic affinity of the Calusa or their immediate neighbors, as no vocabulary or other specimen of the language is known to exist beyond the town names and one or two other words given by Fontaneda, none of which affords basis for serious interpretation. Gatschet, the best authority on the Florida languages, says: "The languages spoken by the Calusa and by the people next in order, the Tequesta, are unknown to us. . . . They were regarded as people distinct from the Timucua and the tribes of Maskoki origin" (Creek Migr. Leg., I, 13, 1884). There is a possibility that some fragments of the language may yet come to light, as boys of this tribe were among the pupils at the mission school in Havana in the 16th century, and the Jesuit Rogel and an assistant spent a winter in studying the language and recording it in vocabulary form.

Fontaneda names the following among about 50 Calusa villages existing about 1570: Calaobe, Casitoa, Cayovea, Comachica, Cuchiyaga, Cutespa, Enempa, Estame, Guacata, Guarungunve, Guevu, Jutun, Metamapo, Muspa, Ño (explained as meaning 'town beloved'), Quisiyove, Sacaspada, Sinaesta, Sinapa, Soco, Tampa (distinguished as 'a large town'), Tatesta, Tavaguemue, Tequemapo, Tomo, Tomsobe, Tuchi, Yagua. Of these, Cuchiyaga and Guarungunve were upon the keys.                                    (J. M.)

Calloosas.—Bartram, Trav., 378, 1792. Callos.—Brinton, Floridian Penin., 112, 1859 (given as one of the French forms). Caloosa.—Romans, Fla., 291, 1775. Calos.—De Bry, Brevis Narratio, II, Le Moyne map, 1591 ("province" and "chief": early French form as used by Le Moyne and Laudonnière). Calusas.—Rafinesque, introd. Marshall, Ky., I, 25, 1824. Cape Florida Indians.—Adair, Hist. Am. Inds., 152, 1775. Carlin.—Davies, Caribby Ids., 332, 1666 ("chief"). Carlos.—Barcia, Ensayo, 95, 1723 ("province" and "chief"; oldest Spanish form as used in León narrative, 1513, Fontaneda, 1575, etc). Coloosas.—Romans, Fla., app., xxxiv, 1775. Kaloosas.—Morse, Rep. to Sec. War, 364, 1822. Kalusa.—Gatschet, Creek Migr. Leg., I, map, 1884.

**Calusahatchee.** A former Seminole town on Calusahatchee r., s. w. Fla.
Caloosahatche.—Bartram, Travels, 462, 1791. Colooshatchie.—Drake, Bk. Inds., IV, 149, 1848. Culloo-sau hat-che.—Hawkins (1799), Sketch, 25, 1848.

**Calusi.** An unidentified province apparently in E. Ark., N. of Arkansas r. and w. of the St Francis, visited by De Soto in 1541.
Caluç.—Biedma in Smith, Coll. Doc. Fla., I, 60, 1857. Caluça.—Gentl. of Elvas (1557) in French, Hist. Coll. La., II, 175, 1850. Calusi.—Biedma, ibid., 106.

**Camajal.** A Diegueño rancheria represented in the treaty of 1852 at Santa Isabel, Cal.—H. R. Ex. Doc. 76, 34th Cong., 132, 1857.

**Camanc-nac-cooya** (probably 'round field of cactus'). A rancheria, probably Cochimi, connected with Purísima (Cadegomo) mission, Lower California, in the 18th century.—Doc. Hist. Mex., 4th s., v, 189, 1857.

**Camani.** A rancheria, probably of the Sobaipuri, on the Rio Gila not far from Casa Grande, s. Ariz.; visited by Anza and Font in 1775.—Bancroft, Ariz. and N. Mex., 392, 1889.
Laguna del Hospital.—Ibid.  La Laguna.—Ibid.

**Camano-ca-caamano** (probably 'arroyo of the great cord'). A rancheria, probably Cochimi, connected with Purísima mission, Lower California, in the 18th century.—Doc. Hist. Mex., 4th s., v, 188, 1857.

**Camas.** Any species of plant belonging to the genus *Quamasia* (*Camassia* of some later authors), especially *Quamasia quamash;* also the edible bulb of these plants. Camas is usually blue-flowered and in other respects also much resembles the hyacinth, to which it is botanically related. It is sometimes called wild hyacinth, and in Canadian French, but improperly, pomme blanche and pomme des prairies. The bulbs, which were a staple food of several N. W. coast tribes, and are still much used, are prepared for food by prolonged steaming. Camas is found from w. Washington and Oregon to N. California and British Columbia, and eastward to the northern Rocky mts. It was most extensively utilized in the valleys of the upper Columbia r. watershed. The word, spelled also *camass, quamash, kamass, quamish,* and in other ways, came into English through the Chinook jargon. Its ultimate source is *chamas,* signifying 'sweet' in the Nootka language of Vancouver id. The camas prairies of the w. slopes of the Rocky mts. were long famous. From its habit of feeding on this root the camas rat received its name. From *camas* have also been named villages in Fremont co., Idaho; Missoula co., Mont.; and Clarke co., Wash.; likewise a Camas valley in Douglas co., Oreg., and a town, Kamas, in Summit co., Utah. The Latin name of the plant also preserves the Indian appellation. See *Roots.*                    (A. F. C.  F. V. C.)

**Cambujos.** An imaginary Indian "province" E. of Quivira, which the abbess María de Jesus, of Agreda, Spain, claimed to have miraculously visited in the 17th century.
Aburcos.—Zarate-Salmeron (ca. 1629), Relacion, in Land of Sunshine, 187, Feb., 1900. Caburcos.—Maria de Jesus (1631) in Palou, Relacion Hist., 337, 1787. Cambujos.—Benavides (1631) in Palou, op. cit., 336. Jambujos.—Vetancurt (1693), Teatro Am., III, 303, 1871.

**Camiltpaw** ('people of Kamilt'; so named from their chief). A band of the Pisquows, formerly living on the E. side of Columbia r. One of the original treaty tribes of 1855, classed with the Yakima but really Salishan. They are now on Yakima res., Wash.
Kah-milt-pah.—Treaty of 1855 in U. S. Stat., 951, 1863. Kamilt-pah.—Ind. Aff. Rep., 302, 1877. Qamïl-'lĕma.—Mooney in 14th Rep. B. A. E., 736, 1896.

**Camitria.** A ruined pueblo of the Tewa,

situated in Rio Arriba co., N. Mex. (Bandelier in Ritch, N. Mex., 201, 1885). First mentioned by Oñate in 1598 (Doc. Inéd., XVI, 102, 116, 1871) as an inhabited village and assigned both to the Tewa and the "Chiguas" (Tigua).

Camitre.—Oñate, op. cit., 102. Comitría.—Bandelier in Arch. Inst. Papers, I, 19, 1881 (misprint).

**Camoa.** A Mayo settlement on the Rio Mayo, 70 m. from the coast, in s. Sonora, Mexico.

Camóa.—Hardv, Travels, 390, 1829. Canamoo.—Kino, map (1702) in Stöcklein, Neue Welt-Bott, 1726. Santa Catalina Cayamoa.—Orozco y Berra, Geog., 356, 1864.

**Camoles.** A tribe formerly living on the Texas coast "in front" of the Como; mentioned by Cabeza de Vaca (Smith transl., 137, 1871) in the account of his sojourn in Texas, 1527–34. They cannot be identified with any later historical tribe.

Camones.—Cabeza de Vaca, op. cit., 113.

**Camping and Camp circles.** Each North American tribe claimed a certain locality as its habitat and dwelt in communities or villages about which stretched its hunting grounds. As all the inland people depended for food largely on the gathering of acorns, seeds, and roots, the catching of salmon when ascending the streams, or on hunting for meat and skin clothing, they camped in makeshift shelters or portable dwellings during a considerable part of the year. These dwellings were brush shelters, the mat house and birch-bark lodge of the forest tribes, and the skin tent of the plains. The rush mats of different sizes, woven by the women, were rolled into a long bundle when a party was traveling. The oblong frame was made of saplings tied together with bark fiber. The longest and widest mats were fastened outside the frame to form the walls, and smaller ones were overlapped to make a rain-proof roof, an opening being left in the middle for the escape of the smoke from the central fire. For the skin tent, 10 to 20 poles were cut and trimmed by the men and preserved from year to year. To tan, cut, fit, and sew the skin cover and to set up the tent was the special work of women. Dogs formerly transported the long tent poles by means of travois, but in later years they were dragged by ponies.

Hunting, visiting, or war parties were more or less organized. The leader was generally the head of a family or of a kindred group, or he was appointed to his office with certain ceremonies. He decided the length of a day's journey and where the camp should be made at night. As all property, save a man's personal clothing, weapons, and riding horses, belonged to the woman, its care during a journey fell upon her. On the tribal hunt the old men, the women and children, and the laden ponies formed the body of the slowly moving procession, protected on either side by the warriors, who walked or rode, encumbered only by their weapons. The details of the camp were controlled by the women, except with war parties, when men did the work.

When a camping place was reached the mat houses were erected as most convenient for the family group, but the skin tents were set up in a circle, near of kin being neighbors. If danger from enemies was apprehended, the ponies and other valuable possessions were kept within the space inclosed by the circle of tents. Long journeys were frequently undertaken for friendly visits or for intertribal ceremonies. When traveling and camping the people kept well together under their leader, but when near their destination, the party halted and dispatched one or two young men in gala dress with the little packet of tobacco to apprise the leading men of the village of their approach. While the messengers were gone the prairie became a vast dressing room, and men, women, and children shook off the dust of travel, painted their faces, and donned their best garments to be ready to receive the escort which was always sent to welcome the guests.

When the tribes of the buffalo country went on their annual hunt, ceremonies attended every stage, from the initial rites, when the leader was chosen, throughout the journeyings, to the thanksgiving ceremony which closed the expedition. The long procession was escorted by warriors selected by the leader and the chiefs for their trustiness and valor. They acted as a police guard to prevent any straggling that might result in personal or tribal danger, and they prevented any private hunting, as it might stampede a herd that might be in the vicinity. When on the annual hunt the tribe camped in a circle and preserved its political divisions, and the circle was often a quarter of a mile or more in diameter. Sometimes the camp was in concentric circles, each circle representing a political group of kindred. The Dakota call themselves the "seven council fires," and say that they formerly camped in two divisions or groups, one composed of 4 and the other of 3 concentric circles. The Omaha and close cognates, when on the annual buffalo hunt and during the great tribal ceremonies camped in a circle. Each of the 10 Omaha gentes had its unchangeable place in the line. The women of each gens knew where their tents belonged, and when a camping ground was reached each drove her ponies to the proper place, so that when the tents of the tribe were all up each gens was in the position to which it was entitled by the regulations that were connected with ancient beliefs and customs. For particular ceremonies, especially the great annual sun dance (q. v.), the Kiowa, Cheyenne, and others camped in a circle made up of the different political divisions in fixed and regular order.

The tribal circle, each segment composed of a clan, gens, or band, made a living picture of tribal organization and responsibilities. It impressed upon the beholder the relative position of kinship groups and their interdependence, both for the maintenance of order and government within and for defense against enemies from without, while the opening to the E. and the position of the ceremonial tents recalled the religious rites and obligations by which the many parts were held together in a compact whole.

See Dorsey in 3d and 15th Reps. B. A. E.; Fletcher in Publ. Peabody Mus.; Matthews in 5th Rep. B. A. E.; Mooney in 14th and 17th Reps. B. A. E.   (A. C. F.)

**Campo** (Span.: 'field', 'camp'). A settlement and reservation of 18 Diegueños, 170 m. from Mission Tule River agency, Cal. The land, comprising 280 acres, is a waterless, unproductive tract for which a patent has been issued.—Ind. Aff. Rep., 175, 1902.

**Campti.** A village, probably of the Natchitoches, formerly on Red r. of Louisiana, about 20 m. above Natchitoches. In his report to President Jefferson in 1805, Sibley (Hist. Sketches, 1806) says the town was inhabited by the French, the Indians having left it on account of sickness in 1792.   (A. C. F.)

**Canaake.** Mentioned as the name of an ancient Florida tribe, of which a remnant still existed in 1821. The general context of the reference indicates that the form is a bad misprint for Calusa, q. v.

Canaacké.—Penière (1821) in Morse, Rep. to Sec. War, app., 311, 1822. Oana ake.—Ibid., 149.

**Canada.** (Huron: *kanáda*, 'village,' 'settlement.'—Cartier). A term used to designate all the Indians of Canada, and also by early writers in a more restricted sense. Cartier designates the chief of Stadaconé (Quebec) as the king of Canada, and applies the name Canada to the country immediately adjacent. His vocabularies indicate an Iroquoian (Huron) people living there. The early French writers used the term Canadiens to designate the Algonquian tribes on or near the St Lawrence, especially the Nascapee and the Montagnais tribes below the Saguenay, as distinguished from the Algonkin and Micmac. The New England writers sometimes designated as Canada Indians those Abnaki who had removed from

Maine to St Francis and Bécancour.     (J. M.)

Canada.—Cartier, Brief Recit, title, 1545. Canadacoa.—Lescarbot (1609) quoted by Charlevoix, New France, II, 237, 1866. Canadenses.—Lescarbot quoted by Tanner, Nar., 1830 (Latin form). Canadese.—Dobbs, Hudson Bay, 26, 1744. Canadiains.—Dutch map (1621) in N. Y. Doc. Col. Hist., I, 1856 (located north of Chaleur bay). Canadiens.—Jesr Rel. 1632, 14, 1858. Canide Indianes.—Gardne· (1662) in N. Y. Doc. Col. Hist., XIII, 225, 1881.

**Canadasaga** (*Gă-nă-dă-se'′-ge*, ' at the new town'). A former Seneca town near the present Geneva, N. Y. On account of its size it was for a time considered one of the chief towns of the tribe. In 1700 it was situated 1½ m. s. e. of Geneva, but in 1732, on account of the ravages of smallpox, the inhabitants removed 2 or 3 m. s. w., to the s. bank of Burrell's (Slate Rock) cr. At the breaking out of the French and Indian war this site was also abandoned, and the inhabitants moved to Canadasaga brook, or Castle brook, s. w. of Geneva. Here, in 1756, a stockade was built for their protection by Sir William Johnson. The town became known as New Castle, and was destroyed by Sullivan in 1779.   (J. M.   J. N. B. H.)

Canadaasago.—Conover, Kanadasaga and Geneva MS., B. A. E. Canada-saga.—N. Y. Doc. Col. Hist., II, 1191, 1849. Canadasager.—Ibid. Canadasaggo.—Johnson (1763), ibid., VII, 550, 1856. Canadasago.—Conover. op. cit. Canadaseago.—Ibid. Canadasege.—Ibid. Canadasegy.—Ibid. Canadayager.—Ibid. Canadesago.—Pickering (1790) in Am. St. Pap., IV, 214, 1832. Canadesaque.—Conover, op. cit. Canadesego.—Ibid. Canadisega.—Conf. of 1763 in N. Y. Doc. Col. Hist., VII, 556, 1856. Canadosago.—Conover, op. cit. Canandesaga.—Nukerck (1779) quoted by Conover, ibid. Canasadauque.—Ibid. Canasadego.—Evans, map (1755) quoted by Conover, ibid. Canatasaga.—Ibid. Canedesaga.—Ibid. Canesadage.—Ibid. Canidesego.—Ibid. Canidisego.—Jones (1780) in N. Y. Doc. Col. Hist., VIII, 786, 1857. Cannadasago.—Conover, op. cit. Cannadesago.—Ibid. Cannadisago.—Ibid. Cannisdagua.—Ibid. Cannisdaque.—Ibid. Cannondesaga.—McKendry (1779) quoted by Conover, ibid. Canodasega.—Ibid. Canodosago.—Ibid. Canosedagui.—Doc. of 1726 in N. Y. Doc. Col. Hist., V, 797, 1855. Canosedogui.—Bancker (1727) quoted by Conover, op. cit. Canundasauga.—Ibid. Caundaisauque.—Ibid. Caundasaque.—Ibid. Conadasaga.—Ibid. Conadasego.—Ibid. Connadasaga.—Ibid. Connadasego.—Ibid. Connadesago.—Ibid. Connagasago.—Ibid. Conodosago.—Ibid. Cunnesedago.—Barton (1779) quoted by Conover, ibid. Gă-nă-dä-sá-ga.—Morgan, League Iroq., 424, 1851 (Cayuga and Onondaga form). Gä-nä-dä-sage.—Ibid. (Oneida and Mohawk form). Gä-nä-dă-se'′-ge.—Hewitt, inf'n (Seneca form). Ganadesaga.—Conover, op. cit. Ganechsatáge.—Ibid. Ganechstáge.—Zeisberger (1750) quoted by Conover, ibid. Ga-nun-dä-sá-gä.—Morgan, League Iroq., 424, 1851 (Seneca form). Kaënsatague.—Pouchot, map (1758) in N. Y. Doc. Col. Hist., X, 694, 1858. Kanadagago.—Conover, op. cit. Kanadaoeaga.—Ibid. Kanadaoegey.—Ibid. Kanadaragea.—Ibid. Kanadasaega.—Ibid. Kanadasagea.—Ibid. Kanadaseagea.—Ibid. Kanadaseago.—Drake, Bk. Inds., V, 111, 1848. Kanadaseegy.—Johnson (1763) in N. Y. Doc. Col. Hist., VII, 576, 1856. Kanadasgoa.—Conover, op. cit. Kanadasero.—Johnson (1763) quoted by Conover, ibid. Kanadasigea.—Conver, op. cit. Kanadesaga.—Ibid. Kanadesego.—Ibid. Kanadesero.—Ibid. Kánádesség'y.—Johnson (1763) in N. Y. Doc. Col. Hist., VII, 550, 1856. Kanadessigy.—Conver, op. cit. Kanadosega.—Ibid. Kanagago.—Livermore (1779) in N. H. Hist. Soc. Coll., VI, 326, 1850. Kanandasagea.—Nukerck (1779) quoted by Conover, op. cit. **Kanasadagea.**—Ibid. **Kanasedaga.**—Ibid. **Kanedasaga.**—Ibid. **Kanedesago.**—Machin (1779) quoted by Conover, ibid. **Kanesadago.**—Conover, ibid. **Kanesadakeh.**—Ibid. **Kanesedaga.**—Ibid. **Kannadasaga.**—Grant (1779) quoted by Conover, ibid. **Kannadesagea.**—Ibid. **Kannadeseys.**—Pemberton in Mass. Hist. Soc. Coll., 1st s., II, 176, 1816. **Kanodosegea.**—Conover, op. cit. **Kaunaudasage.**—Ibid. **Kennedaseage.**—Ibid. **Kennesedaga.**—Ibid. **Konasadagea.**—Ibid. **Konasoa.**—Jefferys, Fr. Dom., pt. 1, map, 1761. **Konassa.**—Mann Heirs' map, 1756. **Old Castle.**—Conover, op. cit.(so called after removal to Castle brook, subsequent to 1756). **Otä-nä-sä-ga.**—Morgan, League Iroq., 424, 1851 (Tuscarora form). **Seneca Castle.**—Machin (1779) quoted by Conover, op. cit.

**Canajoharie** (*Kă-nă-'djo'-'ha-re'*, 'it, the kettle, is fixed on the end of it'). An important Mohawk village, known as Upper Mohawk Castle, formerly situated on the E. bank of Otsquago cr., nearly opposite Ft Plain, Montgomery co., N. Y. The community of this name occupied both banks of Mohawk r. for some distance above and below the village. It was also once known as Middle Mohawk Castle.          (J. N. B. H.)

**Canadsiohare.**—Hansen (1713) in N. Y. Doc. Col. Hist., v, 372, 1855. **Canaedsishore.**—Hansen (1700), ibid., IV, 802, 1854. **Cänäjohä.**—Morgan, League Iroq., chart, 1851 (Seneca form).—Ibid., 416, 1851. **Cänajohä'ga.**—Ibid., chart (Onondaga form). **Can-ajo'har.**—Ibid. (Tuscarora form). **Canajoharies.**—Conference of 1754 in Mass. Hist. Soc. Coll., 3d s., v, 36, 1836. **Canajoherie.**—Albany conf. (1745) in N. Y. Doc. Col. Hist., VI, 302, 1855. **Canajora.**—Parkman, Frontenac, 93, 1883. **Canajorha.**—Greenhalgh (1677) in N. Y. Doc. Col. Hist., III, 250, 1853. **Canijoharie.**—Hansen (1700), ibid., IV, 802, 1854. **Cannatchocary.**—Doc. of 1758(?), ibid., x, 676, 1858. **Cannojoharys.**—Albany conf. (1754), ibid., VI, 877, 1855 (the band). **Canojoharrie.**—Schuyler (1711), ibid., v, 245, 1855. **Caunaujohhaury.**—Edwards (1751) in Mass. Hist. Soc. Coll., 1st s., x, 143, 1809. **Chonoghoheere.**—Wraxall (1754) in N. Y. Doc. Col. Hist., VI, 857, 1855. **Conagohary.**—Murray (1782) in Vermont Hist. Soc. Coll., II, 357, 1871. **Conajoharees.**—Albany conf. (1747) in N. Y. Doc. Col. Hist., VI, 383, 1855. **Conajohary.**—Colden (1727), Five Nations, 164, 1747. **Conajorha.**—Greenhalgh (1677) in N. Y. Doc. Col. Hist., III, 250, 1853. **Conijoharre.**—Johnson (1775), ibid., VIII, 661, 1857. **Connajohary.**—Albany conf. (1754), ibid., VI, 868, 1855. **Connejories.**—Goldthwait (1766) in Mass. Hist. Soc. Coll., 1st s., x, 121, 1809 (the band). **Connojohary.**—Albany conf. (1754) in N. Y. Doc. Col. Hist., VI, 877, 1855. **Conojahary.**—N. Y. conf. (1753), ibid., VI, 784, 1855. **Conojoharie.**—Johnson (1749), ibid., VI, 512, 1855. **Gänäjohälä'-que.**—Morgan, League Iroq., chart, 1851 (Oneida form). **Gänäjoha'rla.**—Ibid. (Mohawk form). **Ganajohhore.**—Boyer (1710) quoted by Ruttenber, Tribes Hudson R., 188, 1872. **Gä-na-jo-hi'-e.**—Morgan, op. cit., 474, 1851 (Mohawk name). **Kǎ-nǎ-'djo'-'hǎ-re'.**—Hewitt, inf'n, 1886 (Mohawk name). **Kanajoharry.**—Hawley (1794) in Mass. Hist. Soc. Coll., 1st s., IV, 51, 1795. **Kǎ-nǎ'-tcǔ-hǎre'.**—Hewitt, inf'n, 1886 (Tuscarora name). **Middle Mohawk Cəstle.**—Morgan, League Iroq., 474, 1851 (common name). **Upper Castle.**—Colden (1727), Five Nations, 164, 1747.

**Canandaigua** (*Gǎ-nǎ-dǎ-ǎ'-gwän̄*, 'a village was formerly there'). An important Seneca town near the site of the present Canandaigua, N.Y., destroyed by Sullivan in 1779. There was another settlement not far distant, called New Canandaigua, which also was probably destroyed the same year.          (J. N. B. H.)

**Anandaque.**—Grant (1779) quoted by Conover, Kanadaga and Geneva MS., B. A. E. **Canadaqua.**—Doc. Hist. N. Y., II, 1191, 1849. **Cä-nä-dä'-quä.**—Doc. of 1792 in Mass. Hist. Soc. Coll., 1st ser., I, 285, 1806 (Onondaga form). **Canadauge.**—Onondaga conf. (1774) in N. Y. Doc. Col. Hist., VIII, 526, 1857. **Canadqua.**—Deed of 1789 in Am. St. Pap., IV, 211, 1832. **Canandaigua.**—Livermore (1779) in N. H. Hist. Soc. Coll., v, 327, 1850. **Canandaqua.**—Barton, New Views, xiii, 1798. **Canandarqua.**—Doc. Hist. N. Y., II, 1191, 1849. **Canandauqua.**—Chapin (1792) in Am. St. Pap., IV, 241, 1832. **Canandeugue.**—Dearborn (1779) quoted by Conover, Kanadaga and Geneva MS., B. A. E. **Cannandaquah.**—Norris (1779) quoted by Conover, ibid. **Cä'-tä-na-rä'-qua.**—Morgan, League Iroq., map, 1851 (Tuscarora name). **Connondaguah.**—Fellows (1779) quoted by Conover, op. cit. **Gä-nä-dä-ä'-gwän̄.**—Hewitt, inf'n, 1886 (Seneca name). **Gä-na-dä-gwa.**—Morgan, op. cit. (Cayuga name). **Gä-nä-dä-lo'-quä.**—Ibid., map, 1851 (Oneida name). **Gä-nä-tä-lä'-quä.**—Ibid. (Mohawk name). **Ganataqueh.**—Zeisberger, MS. (1750) quoted by Conover, op. cit. **Gä'nundä'gwa.**—Morgan, League Iroq., 469, 1851 (Seneca name). **Kanadaque.**—Grant (1779) quoted by Conover, op. cit. **Kanandagua.**—Nukerck (1779) quoted by Conover, ibid. **Kanandaigua.**—Burrows (1779) quoted by Conover, ibid. **Kanandalangua.**—Hubley (1779) quoted by Conover, ibid. **Kanandaque.**—Machin (1779) quoted by Conover, ibid. **Kanentage.**—Pouchot, map (1758) in N. Y. Doc. Col. Hist., x, 694, 1858. **Konnaudaugua.**—Pickering (1791) in Am. St. Pap., IV, 212, 1832. **Konondaigua.**—Treaty of 1794 quoted by Hall, N. W. States, 71, 1849. **Ono-dauger.**—Blanchard (1779) quoted by Conover, op. cit. **Shannondaque.**—Camfield (1779) quoted by Conover, ibid.

**Canarsee.** Formerly one of the leading tribes on Long Island, N. Y., occupying most of what is now Kings co. and the shores of Jamaica bay, with their center near Flatlands. According to Ruttenber they were subject to or connected with the Montauk; this, however, is doubtful, as the Indians of the w. end of the island appear to have been paying tribute, at the time of the Dutch settlement of New York, to the Iroquois. Their principal village, of the same name, was probably at Canarsee, near Flatlands, in addition to which they had others at Maspeth and apparently at Hempstead. They are important chiefly from the fact that the site of the city of Brooklyn was obtained from them. Having asserted their independence of the Mohawk, after the appearance of the Dutch, they were attacked by that tribe and nearly exterminated. They also suffered considerably during the war of the Long Island tribes with the Dutch. The last one of them died about 1800.          (J. M. C. T.)

**Canaresse.**—Document of 1656 in N. Y. Doc. Col. Hist., XIV, 340, 1883. **Canarise.**—Stuyvesant deed (1656) in Thompson, Long Id., 383, 1839. **Canarisse.**—Doc. of 1663 in N. Y. Doc. Col. Hist., XIV, 524, 1883. **Canarse.**—Wood quoted by Macauley, N. Y., II, 253, 1829. **Canarsees.**—Macauley, ibid., 164. **Canarsie.**—Nicolls (1666) in N. Y. Doc. Col. Hist., XIV, 586, 1883. **Cannarse.**—Document of 1650, ibid., I, 449, 1856. **Canorise.**—Dutch treaty (1656) in Ruttenber, Tribes Hudson River, 125, 1872. **Conarie See.**—Petition of 1656 in N. Y. Doc. Col. Hist., XIV, 339, 1883 (misprint). **Conarise.**—Map of 1666, ibid. **Conarsie.**—Ibid. (applied to river).

**Canasatego.** An Onondaga chief who played an important rôle in the proceedings of the council at Philadelphia in

1742. A dispute arose between the Delaware Indians and the government of Pennsylvania concerning a tract of land in the forks of Delaware r. It was on this occasion, evidently in accordance with a preconcerted arrangement between the governor of Pennsylvania and the Iroquois chief, that the latter, addressing the Delawares, made the memorable statement: "How came you to take upon you to sell land at all? We conquered you; we made women of you; you know you are women, and can no more sell land than women. We charge you to remove instantly; we don't give you liberty to think of it." The choice of Wyoming and Shamokin was granted, and the Delawares yielded. Little more is recorded regarding this chief. He died at Onondaga in 1750. His son, Hans Jacob, resided on the Ohio in 1758. (C. T.)

**Canasoragy.** A former Shawnee village on the w. branch of Susquehanna r., near the mouth of Canaserage cr. (now Muncy cr.), Lycoming co., Pa., about the site of the present Muncy. Conrad Weiser held a conference there in 1755, at which time it was occupied by 20 Shawnee and Chickasaw warriors, there being about 6 Chickasaw who had lived for many years among the Shawnee. During the Indian uprising in 1778–79 Capt. John Brady built a stockaded house, known as Ft Brady, near the mouth of Muncy cr. Brady was killed in the spring of 1779. Ft Muncy was built, about 4 m. from Muncy, in 1778. Both of these forts were the scenes of many historic events during the early days. See Frontier Forts of Pa., I, 387–392, 1895; Meginness, Otzinachson or History of the West Branch, 484, 1857; Egle, Hist. Pa., 919, 1883. (G. P. D.)
Canasoragy.—Weiser (1755) in Col. Rec. Pa., VI, 443, 1851.

**Canastigaone.** A former Mohawk village on the N. side of Mohawk r., just above Cohoes Falls, N. Y.
Canastigaone.—Tyron, map of Prov. N. Y., 1779. Canastigione.—Doc. Hist. N. Y., II, index, 1849. Connestigunes.—Macauley, N. Y., II, 295, 1829. Nistigione.—Doc. Hist. N. Y., II, 235, 1849.

**Canatlan** (*kan-at-lan′*). A former Tepehuane pueblo on the upper waters of the Rio San Pedro, central Durango, Mexico.—Orozco y Berra, Geog., 319, 1864.

**Candelaria.** See *Nuestra Señora de la Candelaria*.

**Caneadea** (*Gä-on′-hia′-di-on′*, 'it (sky) impinges on it'). A former Seneca village on the site of Caneadea, Allegany co., N. Y. Being the most distant southerly from the lower Genesee r. towns, and protected by mountains, it escaped destruction by Sullivan, in 1779, as he turned northward from Dayoitgao. Caneadea, which was a "castle" and for many years had a council lodge, was the point of departure of the Seneca on their war expeditions to the w. and s. w. (J. N. B. H.)

Canaseder.—Procter (1791) in Am. St. Papers, IV, 151, 1832. Caneadea.—Morgan, League Iroq., 467, 1851 (so called by whites). Caneadia.—Day, Penn., 248, 1843. Carrahadeer.—Procter (1791) in Am. St. Papers, IV, 158, 1832. Gäo′yadeo.—Morgan, League Iroq., 467, 1851. Kaounadeau.—Morris deed (1797) in Am. St. Papers, IV, 627, 1832. Karaghiyadirha.—Johnson map (ca. 1770) cited in N. Y. Doc. Col. Hist., VII, 723, 1856. Karathyadirs.—Johnson Hall conf. (1756), ibid.

**Canienga** ('at the place of the flint'). A former Mohawk castle situated at the distance of a bow-shot from the N. side of Mohawk r., N. Y. The Mohawk name for themselves is derived from this place. In 1677 it had a double palisade with 4 ports inclosing 24 lodges. (J. N. B. H.)
Agnié.—For forms of this name, see *Mohawk*. Agniée.—Jes. Rel. for 1656, 3, 1858. Agniegué.—Jes. Rel. for 1658, 3, 1858. Aniegué.—Ibid., 11. Aniené.—Jes. Rel. for 1652, 9, 1858. Cahaniaga.—Greenhalgh (1677) in N. Y. Doc. Col. Hist., III, 250, 1853. Decanohoge.—Hansen (1700), ibid., IV, 802, 1854. Dekanoge.—Livingston (1700), ibid., 655. Upper Mohawk Castle.—Morgan, League Iroq., 474, 1851 (common English name).

**Canjauda.** Mentioned as a former Creek town in Cherokee co., Ala.—Sen. Doc. 67, 26th Cong., 2d sess., 1, 1841.

**Cannel coal.** See *Jet*.

**Cannetquot.** Described by Thompson (Long Id., 293, 1839) as a semi-tribe or family occupying in 1683 the E. side of Connetquot r., about Patchogue, in Suffolk co., Long Island, N. Y. In another place he includes this territory as part of that belonging to the Patchoag. The name seems to be a dialectal form of Connecticut. (J. M.)

**Cannibalism.** In one form or another cannibalism has been practised among probably all peoples at some period of their tribal life. In America there are numerous recorded references to its occurrence within historic times among the Brazilians, Carib of northern South America, the Aztec and other Mexican tribes, and among many of the Indians N. of Mexico. The word itself, now more commonly used than the older term anthropophagy, is derived from *Carib* through Spanish corruption. Restricting treatment of the subject to the tribes N. of Mexico, many evidences of cannibalism in some form are found—from the ingestion, perhaps obligatory, of small quantities of human flesh, blood, brain, or marrow, as a matter of ceremony, to the consumption of such parts for food under stress of hunger, or even as a matter of taste. Among the tribes which practised it, in one or another of these forms, may be mentioned the Montagnais, and some of the tribes of Maine; the Algonkin, Armouchiquois, Micmac, and Iroquois; farther w. the Assiniboin, Cree, Foxes, Miami, Ottawa, Chippewa, Illinois, Kickapoo, Sioux, and Winnebago; in the s. the people who built the mounds in Florida (see *Calusa*), and the Tonkawa, Attacapa, Karankawa, Kiowa, Caddo, and Comanche(?); in the N. w. and w. parts of the continent, the Thlingchadinneh and other

Athapascan tribes, the Tlingit, Heiltsuk, Kwakiutl, Tsimshian, Nootka, Siksika, some of the Californian tribes, and the Ute. There is also a tradition of the practice among the Hopi, and allusions to the custom among other tribes of Arizona and New Mexico. The Mohawk, and the Attacapa, Tonkawa, and other Texas tribes were known to their neighbors as "man-eaters."

Taking all the evidence into consideration, it appears that cannibalism N. of the Mexican boundary existed in two chief forms. One of these was accidental, from necessity as a result of famine, and has been witnessed among the Hurons, Micmac, Chippewa, Etchareottine, and others. In most of such instances recourse was had to the bodies of those who had recently died, but cases are recorded in which individuals were killed to satisfy hunger. The second and prevalent form of cannibalism was a part of war custom and was based principally on the belief that bravery and other desirable qualities of an enemy would pass, through actual ingestion of a part of his body, into that of the consumer. Such qualities were supposed to have their special seat in the heart, hence this organ was chiefly sought, though blood, brain, marrow, and flesh were in many instances also swallowed. The parts were eaten either raw or cooked. The heart belonged usually to the warriors, but other parts were occasionally consumed by boys or even by women and children. In some cases a small portion of the heart or of some other part of an enemy might be eaten in order to free the eater from some tabu (Grinnell). The idea of eating any other human being than a brave enemy was to most Indians repulsive. One of the means of torture among the Indians of Canada and New York was the forcing of a prisoner to swallow pieces of his own flesh.

Among the Iroquois, according to one of the Jesuit fathers, the eating of captives was considered a religious duty. Among the Heiltsuk, and recently among the Tsimshian and Kwakiutl, cannibalism formed a part of one of their ceremonies. Several instances are recorded in which cannibalism was indulged in by individuals while in a frenzied state. Finally, it seems that among a few tribes, as the Tonkawa, Iroquois, and others, man-eating, though still with captives as the victims, was practised on a larger scale, and with the acquired taste for human flesh as one, if not the chief, incentive; yet the Tonkawa, as well as some men long associated with them, declared that the eating of human flesh by them was only ceremonial.

Indian mythology and beliefs are replete with references to man-eating giants, monsters, and deities, which point to the possibility that anthropophagy in some form was a practice with which the aborigines have long been acquainted.

Consult Bancroft, Native Races; Boas (1) in Jour. Am. Folk-lore, I, 58, 1888, (2) Rep. Nat. Mus., 1895; Gatschet, Karankawa Inds., 1891; Jesuit Relations, Thwaites ed.; Kohl, Kitchigami, 355, 1860; Letourneau in Bull. Soc. d'Anthrop. de Paris, X, 777, 1887, and XI, 27, 72, 123, 1888; Megapolensis (1644), Sketch of the Mohawk Inds., 1857; Mooney, Our Last Cannibal Tribe, 1901; Pénicaut (1712) in Margry, Découvertes, V. 504, 1883; Schaafhausen, Anthrop. Stud., 515, 1885; Somers in Pop. Sci. Mo., XLII, 203, 1892; Wyman (1) Human Remains in the Shell Heaps of St Johns r., (2) Fresh-water Shell Mounds, 1875.                    (A. H.)

**Canoa** (Span.; here doubtless referring to a trough or flume in which an irrigation ditch is conducted over broken ground). A former Papago rancheria between Tubac and San Xavier del Bac, on Rio Santa Cruz, s. Ariz.—Garcés (1775), Diary, 63, 74, 1900.
La Canoa.—Anza quoted by Bancroft, Ariz. and N. Mex., 392, 1889.

**Canoas, Pueblo de las** (Span.: 'village of the canoes'). A former Indian settlement on the California coast, about lat. 34° 27′, in what is within the Chumashan area. Its situation is regarded as having been at or near the present Ventura. See Heylyn, Cosmography, 969, 1703.

**Canocan.** A pueblo of the province of Atripuy in the region of the lower Rio Grande, N. Mex., in 1598.—Oñate (1598) in Doc. Inéd., XVI, 115, 1871.

**Canoe Creek.** A Shuswap village and band near upper Fraser r., Brit. Col., about 300 m. from its mouth; pop. 157 in 1902.—Can. Ind. Aff., 271, 1902.

**Canoe Lake Indians.** The local name for a body of Shuswap of Kamloops-Okanagan agency, Brit. Col.; pop. 129 in 1902, including the Chuckchuqualk, q. v.—Can. Ind. Aff. for 1879, 309.

**Canoes.** See *Boats*.

**Cañogacola** ('people'). An unidentified ancient tribe of N. w. Florida, mentioned by Fontaneda about 1575.
Cañegacola.—Ternaux-Compans, Voy., XX, 24, 1841. Cañogacola.—Fontaneda (ca. 1575), Mem., Smith trans., 20, 1854. Cañogacole.—Fontaneda in Doc. Inéd., V, 540, 1866.

**Canonchet.** See *Nanuntenoo*.

**Canonicus.** A chief of the Narraganset, who died in 1647, aged perhaps 80 years. Although in 1622 he sent to the people of Plymouth the customary Indian challenge to war, he early sought the friendship of the English. It was into the country of Canonicus that Roger Williams went, and from him he received the title to the land he afterward held. Canonicus was at war against the Wampanoag until in 1635, when the dispute was settled through the efforts of Williams. He never fully trusted the English, nor they him. Durfee, in his poem "What cheer?" calls Canonicus "cautious, wise, and old," and Roger Williams styles him a "prudent and peaceable prince." He is highly praised in John Lathrop's poem "The Speech of Canonicus," published at Boston in 1802. His name, which is spelled in a variety of ways, appears to have been changed, perhaps by contagion with the Latin *canonicus*, from Qunnoune (Drake, Inds. of N. Am., 118, 1880). He is not to be confused with Canonchet, a later Narraganset sachem.          (A. F. C.)

**Canopus.** The principal village of the Nochpeem, taking its name from their chief. It was situated in Canopus Hollow, Putnam co., N. Y.—Ruttenber, Tribes Hudson R., 80, 1872.

**Cant.** A former rancheria, probably of the Maricopa, not far below the mouth of Salt r., s. Ariz.; visited and so named by Kino and Mange in 1699.
San Mateo Cant.—Mange quoted by Bancroft, Ariz. and N. Mex., 357, 1889. S. Mateo Caut.—Mange quoted by Bancroft, No. Mex. States, I, 268, 1884 (misprint).

**Cantaunkack.** A village of the Powhatan confederacy in 1608, on York r., Gloucester co., Va. (Smith (1629), Va., I, map, repr. 1819). It apparently belonged to the Werowacomaco, although Strachey uses the name as that of a tribe having more than 100 warriors about the same time.          (J. M.)
Cantaunkank.—Strachey (*ca.* 1612), Va., map, 1849.

**Canteens.** See *Pottery, Receptacles.*

**Cantensapué.** A pueblo of the province of Atripuy, in the region of the lower Rio Grande, N. Mex., in 1598.—Oñate (1598) in Doc. Inéd., XVI, 115, 1871.

**Cantico.** This word, spelled also cantica, canticoy, kantico, kanticoy, kintacoy, kintecaw, kintecoy, kintekaye, kinticka, was in great use among the Dutch and English colonists in the region between New York and Virginia from the latter part of the 17th to the 19th century, nor is it yet entirely extinct in American English. In the literature of the 18th century it appears frequently, with the following meanings: (1) Dance, or dancing party. (2) Social gathering of a lively sort. (3) Jollification. The last signification still survives, in literature at least. In 1644 *kintekaye* was said to be a 'death dance,' but van der Donck (1653) wrote of the *kintecaw* as 'singing and dancing' of the young. Later on *kintekay* and *kinticoy* meant a noisy and demonstrative dance, with shouting and uproar. Dankers in 1679 defined *kintekay* as 'conjuring the devil,' and Denton (1670) called the *canticoy* 'a dancing match, a festival time.' Rev. Andrew Hesselius (Nelson, Inds. of N. J., 79, 1894), who

witnessed the first-fruits sacrifice of the New Jersey Indians, said: "This and other sacrifices of the Americans they call, from a native word of their own, *kinticka*, i. e., a festive gathering or a wedding." A word of the Delaware dialect of Algonquian is the source of *cantico* and its variants, namely, *gintkaan*, signifying 'to dance,' cognate with the Virginian *kantikanti*, ' to dance and sing.' The phrase 'to cut a cantico' was formerly in use. An absurd etymology from the Latin *canticare*, ' to sing,' was once proposed. According to Boas, New England whalers who visit Hudson bay use the term *antico*, or *anticoot*, to designate the performance of the *angekut* of the Eskimo, this form of the word probably being influenced by the Eskimo name.          (A. F. C.)

**Canuga** (*kănu'ga*, ' scratcher,' a sort of bone-toothed comb with which ball-players are ceremonially scratched). The name of two former Cherokee towns, one, a Lower Cherokee settlement, apparently on the waters of Keowee r., S. C., destroyed in 1761; the other a traditional settlement on Pigeon r., probably near the present Waynesville, Haywood co., N. C.—Mooney in 19th Rep. B. A. E., 479, 524, 1900.

**Canyon Butte.** The local name for a group of interesting prehistoric pueblo ruins near the N. escarpment of the chief basin of the Petrified forest, at the source of a wash that enters Little Colorado r. from the N. E. at Woodruff, near the Apache-Navajo - co. boundary, Arizona. The remains seem to indicate Zuñi origin.—Hough in Rep. Nat. Mus. 1901, 309, 1903.

**Capahnakes.** Possibly a misprint intended for the inhabitants of Capawac, or Marthas Vineyard, off the s. coast of Massachusetts. The form occurs in Boudinot, Star in the West, 129, 1816.

**Capahowasic.** A village of the Powhatan confederacy in 1608, about Cappahosic, Gloucester co., Va.
Capahowasick.—Smith (1629), Va., I, map, repr. 1819. Capahowosick.—Simons, ibid., 163. Capahowsick.—Drake, Bk. Inds., bk. 4, 10, 1848.

**Capasi.** A former village on the N. frontier of Florida and probably belonging to the Apalachee, visited by De Soto in 1539.—Garcilasso de la Vega, Fla., 74, 1723.

**Cape Breton.** One of the seven districts of the country of the Micmac, on Cape Breton id., N. of Nova Scotia. The chief of this district was the head chief of the tribe (Rand, First Micmac Reading Book, 1875). The name occurs in a list of 1760 as the location of a Micmac village or band.          (J. M.)

**Cape Fear Indians.** A small tribe, possibly Siouan, formerly living near the mouth of Cape Fear r., N. C. The proper name of the tribe is unknown, this local term being applied to them by the early colonists. They were first known to the English in 1661, when a colony from New England made a settlement near the mouth of the river, and soon incurred the ill will of the Indians by seizing their children and sending them away under pretense of instructing them in the ways of civilization, resulting in the colonists being finally driven from the country. In 1663 another party from Barbadoes purchased lands of Wat Coosa, head chief of the tribe, and made a settlement, which was abandoned a few years later. Necoes and other villages then existed on the lower part of the river. In 1665 another colony settled at the mouth of Oldtown cr. in Brunswick co., on the s. side of the river, on land bought of the Indians, but soon abandoned it, though the Indians were friendly. The next mention of them is by the colonial governor, Col. Johnson, in a letter of Jan. 12, 1719 (Rivers, Early Hist. So. Car., 94, 1874), which gives a table of Indian tribes in Carolina in 1715, when their population is given as 206 in 5 villages. They probably took part in the Yamasi war of that and the following year, and suffered proportionately in consequence. They are last noticed in 1751 in the record of the Albany Conference (N. Y. Doc. Col. Hist., vi, 721, 1855) as one of the small friendly tribes with which the South Carolina government desired the Iroquois to be at peace. See Mooney, Siouan Tribes of the East, Bull. B. A. E., 1894.

Cape Fears.—Rivers, Early Hist. S. C., 94, 1874.

**Cape Magdalen.** An Algonkin mission established on the St Lawrence in 1670, 3 leagues below Three Rivers, Quebec, by Indians who removed from the latter place on account of smallpox. It was abandoned before 1760.—Jefferys, Fr. Dom. Am., pt. I, 10, 110, 1761.

**Cape Sable Indians.** A name applied by early New England writers to those Micmac living near C. Sable, in s. Nova Scotia. The term is used by Hubbard as early as 1680. They were especially active in the wars on the New England settlements. (J. M.)

**Capiche.** A village, probably of one of the southern Caddoan tribes, near Red r. of Louisiana, "20 leagues inland from the Mississippi," visited by Tonti in 1690.

Capiché.—Tonti (1690) in French, Hist. Coll. La., I, 72, 1846. Capichis.—Coxe, Carolana, map, 1741. Capiga.—McKenney and Hall, Ind. Tribes, III, 79, 1854.

**Capinans.** A small tribe or band noted by Iberville, in 1699, together with the Biloxi and Pascagoula, in Mississippi. The three tribes then numbered 100 families. Judging by the association of names, the Capinans may be identical with the Moctobi, q. v.

Capiná.—De l'Isle, map, 1703. Capinans.—Iberville (1699) in Margry, Déc., IV, 602, 1880. Capinas.—De l'Isle, map, 1707.

**Capitan Grande** (Span.: 'great captain or chief'). A Diegueño village in a canyon of upper San Diego r., s. Cal. The tract, comprising 10,253 acres, now forms a reservation of patented land, largely desert. Pop. about 60 in 1883, 118 in 1902. The occupants, classed as Mission Indians, are under the Mission Tule River agency, 130 m. away.—Jackson and Kinney, Rep. Miss. Ind., 27, 1883; Ind. Aff. Rep., 175, 1902.

**Capola.** A former Seminole village E. of St Marks r., in Jefferson co., Fla.—Bartram, Travels, 223, 1791.

**Capote** ('mountain people.'—Hrdlicka). A division of the Ute, formerly living in the Tierra Amarilla and Rio Chama country, N. W. N. Mex. They are now under the jurisdiction of the Southern Ute school in s. w. Colo., and numbered 180 in 1904.

Capates.—Collins in Ind. Aff. Rep., 125, 1861 (misprint). Capotes.—Graves, ibid., 386, 1854. Capuchies.—Duro, Peñalosa, 67, 1882. Kapoti.—Ind. Aff. Rep., 246, 1877.

**Capoutoucha.** Marked on De l'Isle's map of 1707 as an Indian settlement on St Johns r., Fla.

Capeutoucha.—De l'Isle map (1707) in Winsor, Hist. Am., II, 294, 1886.

**Caprup.** A former village, presumably Costanoan, connected with Dolores mission, San Francisco, Cal.—Taylor in Cal. Farmer, Oct. 18, 1861.

**Captain Jack.** See *Kintpuash.*

**Captives.** The treatment accorded captives was governed by those limited ethical concepts which went hand in hand with clan, gentile, and other consanguineal organizations of Indian society. From the members of his own consanguineal group, or what was considered such, certain ethical duties were exacted of an Indian which could not be neglected without destroying the fabric of society or outlawing the transgressor. Toward other clans, gentes, or bands of the same tribe his actions were also governed by well recognized customs and usages which had grown up during ages of intercourse, but with remote bands or tribes good relations were assured only by some formal peace-making ceremony. A peace of this kind was very tenuous, however, especially where there had been a long-standing feud, and might be broken in an instant. Toward a person belonging to some tribe with which there was neither war nor peace, the attitude was governed largely by the interest of the moment. In such cases the virtues of the clan or gentile organizations as peace-making factors made themselves evident, for if the stranger belonged to a clan or gens represented in the tribe he was among, the members of that clan or gens usually greeted him as a brother and extended their protection over him. Another defense for the stranger was—what with civilized people is one of the best guaranties against war—the fear of disturbing or deflecting trade. If he brought among them certain much-desired commodities, the first impulse might be to take these from him by force and seize or destroy his person, but it would quickly be seen by wiser heads that the source of further supplies of this kind might thereby be imperiled, if not entirely cut off. If nothing were to be had from the stranger, he might be entirely ignored. And finally, the existence of a higher ethical feeling toward strangers, even when there was apparently no self-interest to be served in extending hospitality, is often in evidence. There are not wanting stories of great misfortune overtaking one who refused hospitality to a person in distress, and of great good fortune accruing to him who offered succor.

At the same time the attitude assumed toward a person thrown among Indians too far from his own people to be protected by any ulterior hopes or fears on the part of his captors was usually that of master to slave. This was particularly the case on the N. Pacific coast, where slavery was an institution. Thus John Jewitt, at the beginning of the 19th century, was preserved as a slave by the Nootka chief Maquinna, because he was an ironworker and would be valuable property. Most of the other whites who fell into the hands of Indians on this coast were treated in a similar manner.

The majority of captives, however, were those taken in war. These were considered to have forfeited their lives and to have been actually dead as to their previous existence. It was often thought that the captive's supernatural helper had been destroyed or made to submit to that of the captor, though where not put to death with torture to satisfy the victor's desire for revenge and to give the captive an opportunity to show his fortitude, he might in a way be reborn by undergoing a form of adoption.

It is learned from the numerous accounts of white persons who had been taken by Indians that the principal immediate hardships they endured were due to the rapid movements of their captors in order to escape pursuers, and the continual threats to which they were subjected. These threats were not usually carried out, however, unless they attempted escape or were unable to keep up with the band, or unless the band was pursued too hotly. Each person taken was considered the property of the one who first laid hands on him, and the character of this individual had much to do in determining the extent of his hardships. When two or more claimed a prisoner he was sometimes kept by all conjointly, but sometimes they settled the controversy by torturing him to death on the spot. The rapid retreat of a war party bore particularly hard upon women and children, yet a certain amount of consideration was often shown them. Sometimes the male captives were allowed to help them along, sometimes they were drawn on an improvised sledge or travois, and, if there were horses in the party these might be placed at their disposal, while one instance is recorded in which the child of a female captive was carried by her master for several days. It is worthy of remark that the honor of a white woman was almost always respected by her captors among the tribes E. of the Mississippi; but w. of that limit, on the plains, in the Columbia r. region, and in the S. W., the contrary was often the case.

Among the eastern tribes, on arriving at the village a dance was held, at which the captives were expected to play a conspicuous part. They were often placed in the center of a circle of dancers, were sometimes compelled to sing and dance also, and a few were usually subjected to revolting tortures and finally burned at the stake. Instances of cannibalism are recorded in connection with these dances after the return from war, and among some of the Texas and Louisiana tribes this disposition of the bodies of captives appears to have been something more than occasional. The Iroquois, some Algonquians, and several western tribes forced prisoners to run between two lines of people armed with clubs, tomahawks, and other weapons, and spared, at least temporarily, those who reached the chief's house, a certain post, or some other goal. Among many other tribes an escaped captive who reached the chief's house was regarded as safe, while the Creek peace towns also secured immunity from pursuit to the persons who entered them. Offering food to a visitor was usually equivalent to extending the host's protection over him.

From the experiences of the Spaniard Juan Ortiz, taken prisoner by the Florida chief Ucita, in 1528, as well as those of other whites, it would appear that captives were sometimes held in a sort of bondage elsewhere than on the N. Pacific coast, but usually where their lives were spared they were held for ransom or adopted into the tribe. J. O. Dorsey says of some Siouan tribes, however, that their captives were allowed either to go home or settle among themselves, but were neither tortured nor regularly adopted. Although the custom among the eastern Indians of holding white prisoners for ransom dates from early times, it is questionable whether it was founded on aboriginal usage. The ransoming or sale of captives, however, was common among the Plains and S. W. tribes, while the custom of ransoming slaves on the N. Pacific coast was certainly pre-Columbian. In most of North America, however, it was probably a rare procedure, especially since many tribes are said to have disowned any person who once had been taken prisoner. Doubtless it became common in dealing with white captives owing to the difficulty of reconciling adult whites to Indian life and customs, while captives taken from another tribe no doubt settled down into their new relationships and surroundings very contentedly.

The usual object in thus adopting a prisoner was that he might fill the place of someone who had died, and it is affirmed by one writer that, whatever his own character, he was treated exactly as if he possessed the character of his predecessor. John Gyles, who was captured by the Abnaki in 1689, informs us that a prisoner was brought out to be beaten and tortured during the war dances unless his master paid over a certain amount of property. Women and children were generally preserved and adopted, though there are instances in which white women were tortured to death, and it is said of the Ute that female captives from other Indian tribes were given over to the women to be tortured, while male prisoners who had distinguished themselves were sometimes dismissed unhurt. Among tribes possessing clans the adoption of captured women was of special importance, as it often resulted in the formation of a new clan from their descendants. Such, no doubt, was the origin of the Zuñi and Mexican clans of the Navaho. The Ute clan of the latter was recruited by a systematic capture and purchase of Ute girls undertaken with the object of supplying the tribe with good basket makers (Culin). Among the Plains tribes captives, especially children, were sometimes taken for the express purpose of being trained to the performance of certain ceremonial duties. Besides the numbers of white persons carried away by Indians and subsequently ransomed, it is evident from all the accounts that have reached us that many of English, French, and Spanish descent were taken into the tribe of their captors and, either because carried off when very young or because they developed a taste for their new life, never returned. Some of these even rose to high positions, as in the case of a Frenchman who became chief of the

Attacapa, of a Mexican who is recorded as the most prominent and successful war chief of the Comanche in 1855, and of another Mexican still a man of influence among the Zuñi. The present chief of the Comanche, Quanah Parker (q. v.), is the son of a captive American woman. The confederated tribes of Comanche, Kiowa, and Kiowa Apache still hold at least 50 adopted white captives, and it is probable that fully one-third of the whole population have a traceable percentage of captive blood. The same is probably true in nearly equal measure of the Apache of Arizona.

From Oregon to s. Alaska a different treatment of captives was brought about by the existence of a slave class. Since slaves were the most valuable property a man could have, the lives of those taken in war were always spared unless such captives had committed some great injury to the victorious tribe that prompted immediate revenge. After this they might be killed at any moment by their masters; but such a fate seldom overtook them until they grew too old to work, unless their masters became involved in a property contest, or the people of the town from which they had been taken had committed depredations. Among the Tlingit, however, slaves were killed during mortuary feasts, and bodies of slaves were thrown into the holes dug for the posts of a new house. Slave women, especially if they were known to be of noble descent, sometimes married their captors and became free. Four prominent Haida clans and one clan among the Tsimshian are said to have originated from marriages of this kind, while another prominent Haida clan was called "the Slaves," though it is impossible to say whether they were descended from slaves or whether the term is applied ironically. Whether male slaves ever rose to a high position is doubtful, owing to the strong caste system that here prevailed. Instead of receiving commendation, a slave who had escaped suffered a certain opprobrium which could be removed only by the expenditure of a great amount of property. At the same time it is related of the greatest Skidegate chief that he had been enslaved in his youth.

Consult Baker, True Stories of New England Captives, 1897; Drake, Indian Captivities, 1851; Gentl. of Elvas. in Hakluyt Soc. Publ., IX, 1851; Harris, Life of Horatio Jones, 1903; Herrick, Indian Narr., 1854; Hunter, Captivity among the Indians, 1823 (of questionable authenticity); Johnston, Incidents attending the Capture, etc., of Charles Johnston, 1827; Kelly, Narr. of Captivity among the Sioux, 1880; Larimer, Capture and Escape, or Life among the Sioux,

1870; Mooney in 17th Rep. B. A. E., 1898; Relacion of Alvar Nuñez Cabeça de Vaca, B. Smith transl., 1871; Narr. of Captivity of Mary Rowlandson, 1791, repr. 1856; Severance (ed.), Captivity of Benj. Gilbert, 1904; Spears (ed.), Dangers and Sufferings of Robert Eastburn, 1904; Spencer, Indian Captivity, 1834; Stratton, Captivity of the Oatman Girls, 1857; Tanner, Narr. of Captivity, 1830. See *Adoption, Cannibalism, Genizaros, Ordeals, Slavery, War and War discipline*.

(J. R. S.)

**Carantouan** ('it is a large tree'). One of the chief palisaded towns of the Conestoga, which in 1615 was situated 3 short days' journey from the fort of the Iroquois attacked by Champlain in that year. It was probably on the site of the present Waverly, N. Y., and the palisade attacked was at Nichols Pond, Madison co.

**Carapoa** (possibly a contraction of *carapohoua*, from *carami* 'raft,' *po* 'in,' *houa* 'house' = 'house on rafts'; or *carapohueye* 'to go into rafts.'—Buelna). An ancient settlement, apparently of the Tehueco or the Cahita, situated near El Fuerte, which is on the E. bank of the Rio Fuerte, N. Sinaloa, Mexico.—Orozco y Berra, Geog., 332, 1864.

**Carascan.** A former village, presumably Costanoan, connected with Dolores mission, San Francisco, Cal.—Taylor in Cal. Farmer, Oct. 18, 1861.

**Carcajou.** The Canadian French form of the Algonquian (Montagnais *kar-ka-joo*) name for the wolverene (*Gulo luscus*). The Chippewa *gwingwaage* (Baraga), *gwin-gwaw-ah-ga* (Tanner), the Cree *quiquakatch* (Mackenzie), *kikkwăhăkês* (Lacombe), *queequehatch* (Dobbs), the Algonkin *qwin-gwaage* (Cuoq), and *quickhatch, quiquihatch*, etc., of various authors, are parallels. By a freak of popular etymology this animal received the name of "glutton." Its Finnish name is *fjæl-frass*, 'dweller among rocks,' corrupted by the Germans into *vielfrass*, 'glutton.' The name *carcajou* has been incorrectly applied to several animals. For instance, Charlevoix, in describing one of the enemies of the deer, says the most cruel is "the carcajou or quincajou, a kind of cat, with a tail so long that it twists it several times around his body," a description taken evidently not from nature, but from the Algonquian myth of the fire-dragon. Among the Canadian French *diable des bois* is also a name of this little beast. (J. N. B. H.)

**Cardinal points.** See *Color symbolism, Cross, Orientation*.

**Carfaray.** An ancient pueblo of the Tigua, reference to which is made in the folk-tales of that people. Supposed to have been situated E. of the Rio Grande in New Mexico, beyond the saline lakes.—Bandelier (after Lummis) in Arch. Inst. Papers, IV, 255, 1892.
Car-far-ay.—Ibid.

**Carhagouha** ('in the forest.'—Hewitt). A Huron village in Tiny tp., about 2 m. N. W. of La Fontaine, Ontario, about 1640.
Carhagoua.—Champlain (1615), Œuvres, IV, 28, 1870. Carragouha.—Shea, Cath. Miss., 166, 1855. Cartagoua.—Doc. of 1637 in Margry, Déc., I, 3, 1878.

**Caribou.** The common name of the American reindeer, of which there are two chief species, the woodland caribou (*Rangifer caribou*) and the barren-ground caribou (*R. arcticus*). The word came into English from the French of Canada, in which it is old, Sagard-Théodat using it in 1632. Josselyn has the Quinnipiac form *maccarib* and the synonym *pohano*. The origin of the word is seen in the cognate Micmac χalibu and the Passamaquoddy *megal'ip*, the name of this animal in these eastern Algonquian dialects. According to Gatschet (Bull. Free Mus. Sci. and Art, Phila., II, 191, 1900) these words signify 'pawer' or 'scratcher,' the animal being so called from its habit of shoveling the snow with its forelegs to find the food covered by snow. In Micmac χalibu' mul-χadéget means 'the caribou is scratching or shoveling.' Formerly the word was often spelled cariboo, which gave name to the Cariboo district in British Columbia, famous for its gold mines, and other places in Canada and the United States. (A. F. C.)

**Caribous.** Wood, in 1769 (Hawkins, Missions, 361, 1845), speaks of the "Micmacs, Marashites [Malecite], and Carribous, the three tribes of New Brunswick," as all understanding the Micmac language. Probably the Abnaki or a part of them, as one of their gentes is the Maguⁿleboo, or Caribou.

**Carichic** (*garichic*, 'where there are houses.'—Lumholtz). A former Tarahumare settlement E. of Rio Nonoava, the upper fork of Rio Conchos, lat. 27° 50', long. 107°, about 72 m. s. of Chihuahua, Mexico. Although often visited by the Tarahumare, the place is now thoroughly Mexicanized. In the neighborhood are numerous Tarahumare burial caves. (A. H.)
Carichic.—Orozco y Berra, Geog., 323, 1864. Guanicarichic.—Zapata (1678) in Doc. Hist. Mex., 4th s., III, 329, 1857. Jesus Carichic.—Ibid., 324.

**Carises** (probably Span. *carrizo*, 'reed grass'). One of a number of tribes formerly occupying the country from Buena Vista and Carises lakes and Kern r. to the Sierra Nevada and Coast range, Cal. By treaty of June 10, 1851, they reserved a tract between Tejon pass and Kern r., and ceded the remainder of their lands to the United States. Native name unknown. Judging by locality and associations they were probably Mariposan, though possibly Shoshonean. See Barbour (1852) in Sen. Ex. Doc. 4, 32d Cong., spec. sess., 256, 1853; Royce in 18th Rep. B. A. E., 782, 1899.

**Carlanes** (so called from Carlana, their chief). A band of Jicarilla who in 1719–24 were on Arkansas r., N. E. of Santa Fe, N. Mex. (Bandelier in Arch. Inst. Papers, v, 191, 197, note, 1890; Bancroft, Ariz. and N. Mex., 236, 1889). Orozco y Berra (Geog., 59, 1864) classes them as a part of the Faraon Apache.

Apaches Carlanes.—Bandelier in Arch. Inst. Papers, v, 197, note, 1890.

**Carlisle School.** The first nonreservation school established by the Government was that of Carlisle, Pa., which had its inception in the efforts of Gen. R. H. Pratt, U. S. A., when a lieutenant in charge of Indian prisoners of war at St Augustine, Fla., from May 11, 1875, to Apr. 14, 1878. When the release of these prisoners was ordered, 22 of the young men were led to ask for further education, agreeing to remain in the E. 3 years longer if they could attend school. These were placed in school at Hampton, Va., and several other places. On Sept. 6, 1879, an order was issued transferring the Carlisle Barracks, Pa., comprising 27 acres, from the War Department to the Department of the Interior for Indian school purposes, pending action by Congress on a bill to establish such an institution. The bill became a law July 31, 1882.

On Sept. 6, 1879, having been ordered to report to the Secretary of the Interior, Lieut. Pratt was directed to establish a school at Carlisle and also to proceed to Dakota and Indian Ter. for the purpose of obtaining pupils. By the end of October he had gathered 136 Indians from the Rosebud, Pine Ridge, and other agencies, and, with 11 of the former Florida prisoners from Hampton, the school was formally opened Nov. 1, 1879.

Year after year since this modest beginning the school has steadily progressed, until its present (1905) enrollment is 1,000 pupils. Since the foundation of the school nearly every tribe in the United States has had representatives on its rolls, and at the present time pupils from the following tribes are in attendance: Apache, Arapaho, Arikara, Assiniboin, Bannock, Caddo, Catawba, Cayuga, Cherokee, Cayuse, Cheyenne, Chinook, Chippewa, Choctaw, Clallam, Comanche, Crow, Dalles, Delaware, "Digger," "Grosventre," Iroquois, Kickapoo, Klamath, Mandan, Mashpee, Menominee, Mission, Mohawk, Miami, Nez Percé, Okinagan, Omaha, Oneida, Onondaga, Osage, Ottawa, Paiute, Papago, Pawnee, Penobscot, Piegan, Peoria, Pit River, Pima, Potawatomi, Pueblo, Sauk and Fox, Sanpoil, Seneca, Shawnee, Shivwits, Shoshoni, Siletz, Sioux, Stockbridge, St Regis, Tonawanda, Tuscarora, Umpqua, Ute, Wallawalla, Wichita, Winnebago, Wyandot, Wailaki, Yokaia Pomo, Yuma, and Zuñi. There are also in attendance 68 Alaskans of various tribes.

In the words of Gen. Pratt, the aim of the school "has been to teach English and give a primary education and a knowledge of some common and practical industry and means of self-support among civilized people. To this end regular shops and farms were provided, where the principal mechanical arts and farming are taught the boys, and the girls taught cooking, sewing, laundry, and housework." In pursuance of this policy every inducement was offered to retain pupils, to prevent their return to reservation life, and to aid them to make for themselves a place among the people of the E. In his first annual report on the conduct of the school, Lieut. Pratt announced that 2 boys and 1 girl had been placed in the families of prosperous citizens of Massachusetts, and subsequently that 5 girls and 16 boys had found homes with white families in the vicinity of Carlisle during the summer months, thus enabling them by direct example and association to learn the ways of civilization. This was the commencement of the "outing system" that has come to be a distinctive civilizing feature not only of the Carlisle school but of the Indian school service generally. While thus employed the pupils attend the public schools whenever possible, and by association with white pupils in classes and games also acquire an acquaintance with civilized ways. In addition to these advantages the outing pupil is paid a stipulated sum for his labor, which tends to make him self-reliant and impresses on him the value of time and work. Of the thousand pupils at Carlisle at least half are placed at "outing" during different periods and for varying terms. An outing agent is employed, who visits the pupils at intervals in their temporary homes, observes their conduct and progress, and looks after their welfare. Frequent reports are required by the school management from both employer and pupil, thus keeping each in close touch with the school. The extent and success of the "outing system" since its inception is shown in the following table:

| | |
|---|---|
| Admitted during 25 years................ | 5,170 |
| Discharged during 25 years.............. | 4,210 |
| On rolls during fiscal year 1904......... | 1,087 |
| Outings, fiscal year 1904: Girls, 426; boys, 498...................................... | 924 |
| Outings during 21 years: Girls, 3,214; boys, 5,118.............................. | 8,332 |
| Students' earnings, 1904................. | $34,970 |
| Students' earnings during last 15 years.. | $352,951 |

Supplementing the outing system, the school conducts a bank, with which each student has an account that may be drawn upon under proper supervision. By this means practical instruction in finance is given.

Notwithstanding the efforts of the school to induce its graduates to remain in the E. instead of returning to their reservation homes, the plan has not been successful and has therefore necessitated a change in harmony with the conditions. Training suited to mechanical pursuits is given all male pupils who give promise of becoming efficient workers at the different trades, and a plan is in progress to train girls as professional nurses, several graduates having already adopted this occupation as a means of livelihood.

From its organization the aim of the school has been to give Indian youth a practical productive training. Farm work for the boys and housework for the girls under the outing system are the best types, but the school goes farther, and its curriculum is based on the plan of giving that productive training which is best adapted to the abilities of the individual pupils. At the school itself there are two large farms, and well-equipped shops in which regular trades are taught by competent instructors. All the clothing of the school is manufactured by the boys in the tailor shop, while in its adjunct, the sewing room, the girls are taught needlework. The carpenter shop furnishes the opportunity to learn the use of tools, which is practically demonstrated in the erection of buildings and in making repairs by the boys assigned to this trade. The blacksmith and wagon-making shops not only do the school work, but manufacture superior wagons, etc., which are furnished to other schools and agencies, while the harness shop is engaged in similar work and production. The shoe shop, tin shop, paint shop, and engineering department attend to the needs of the school in their respective branches. While the productive labors of the students are mainly for the school, yet all surplus finds a ready market outside, including other schools and agencies. The work of these branches is systematized into a department under the control of a superintendent of industries.

The literary curriculum of Carlisle stops at that point where the student may enter the higher grades of the public schools. The policy is to give a broad common school education, leaving to the individual and his own resources any further development of his intellectual faculties. The literary and industrial curricula are so correlated that when graduated the average student is as fully

equipped as the average white boy to take up the struggle for a livelihood.

During the 26 years of its existence the Carlisle School has graduated a large number of pupils, many of whom are filling responsible positions in the business world and especially in the Indian service, in which, during the fiscal year 1903, 101 were employed in various capacities from teachers to laborers, drawing a total of $46,300 in salaries. Others who have returned to their homes retain a fair portion of the civilization acquired at the school.

Physical training indoor and out for boys and girls is part of the life of the school, and a large gymnasium furnishes ample facilities for both sexes. In athletics and sports the Indian possesses decided capacity, and baseball, basketball, and football teams are regularly organized, the last of which has held its own in many warmly contested games with representative teams of the principal colleges and universities. The Carlisle football team now has a national reputation for its successes and for clean, skillful playing.

The Carlisle School band is an interesting feature of the school. Its members are selected from the various tribes in attendance, and under the leadership of Dennison and James Wheelock, Oneida Indians, was considered among the best. The former was not only a leader but a composer, and his compositions were rendered by his Indian musicians in a manner that has delighted large audiences in the principal American cities.

The Carlisle School produced the first paper printed by Indian boys. The printery was early established and became a potent factor in the industrial development of the students. *The Indian Helper*, a small leaflet, was first published, and afterward a larger journal, *The Red Man*, was issued. These were later consolidated under the title *Red Man and Helper*, and reflected the life and policies of the school. The new management has continued the publication as a weekly under the name of *The Arrow*. The school printery is well equipped with presses and materials, and under competent supervision the boys produce a large amount of job and pamphlet work that is a credit to their taste and industry.

The buildings of the plant, although consisting of portions of the old military barracks, have furnished adequate accommodations for the thousands of pupils who have been enrolled. Besides the superintendent, the school has 75 instructors, clerks, and other employees.

General Pratt remained in charge of the school from its organization until his retirement from the superintendency,

June 30, 1904, when he was succeeded by Maj. (then Capt.) William A. Mercer, U. S. A.  See *Education*.    (J. H. D.)

**Carmanah.** A Nitinat village near Bonilla pt., s. w. coast of Vancouver id.; pop. 46 in 1902.—Can. Ind. Aff., 264, 1902.

**Carmel.** A Moravian mission at the mouth of Nushagak r., Alaska (Bruce, Alaska, map, 1885); pop. 189 in 1890, 381 in 1900. See *Kanulik*.

**Carolina tea.** See *Black drink*.

**Caromanie** ('walking turtle'). An unidentified Winnebago gens.—McKenney and Hall, Ind. Tribes, I, 315; II, 289, 1854.

**Carrizo** (Span.: 'reed grass,' *Phragmites communis*). A small band of Apache, probably the clan Klokadakaydn, 'Carrizo or Arrow-reed people,' q. v. The name is also applied to a Navaho locality and to those Indians living about Carrizo mts., N. E. Ariz. (Cortez, 1799, in Pac. R. R. Rep., III, pt. 3, 119, 1856). In the latter case it has no ethnic significance.
Cariso.—Bollaert in Jour. Ethnol. Soc. Lond., II, 265, 1850 (misprint). Carrizalleños.—Hamilton, Mexican Handbook, 48, 1883 (probably the same).

**Carrizo.** The Coahuiltecan Indians between Camargo and Matamoras and along the Gulf coast in N. E. Tamaulipas, Mexico, including the remnants of the Comecrudo, Pinto or Pakawa, Tejon, Cotonam, and Casas Chiquitas tribes or bands, gathered about Charco Escondido; so called comprehensively by the white Mexicans in later years. Previous to 1886, according to Gatschet, who visited the region in that year, they used the Comecrudo and Mexican-Spanish languages, and he found that of the 30 or 35 then living scarcely 10 remembered anything of their native tongue. They repudiated the name Carrizo, calling themselves Comecrudo. It is probable that the Comecrudo was the ruling tribe represented in the group. The last chief elected by them was Marcelino, who died before 1856. This explains the later use of the name, but Orozco y Berra (Geog., 294, 308, 1864) and Mota Padilla (Hist. de la Conq., 1742, lxix, 1870) mention them as a distinct tribe, the former stating that they were common to Coahuila and Tamaulipas. It appears, however, that the name Carrizo was applied to the Comecrudo (q. v.) at this earlier date, and that it has generally been used as synonymous therewith. The Carrizos are known to the Kiowa and the Tonkawa as the 'shoeless people,' because they wore sandals instead of moccasins. Some Carrizo captives still live among the Kiowa.
Comecrudos.—Uhde, Die Länder, 120, 185, 1861. Dohe′ñko.—Mooney in 17th Rep. B. A. E., 400, 1898 ('shoeless people': Kiowa name). Kaéso.—Gatschet, Tonkawa MS., B. A. E., 1884 (Tonkawa name). Kä′nhe′ñko.—Mooney, op. cit. (another Kiowa name, same meaning). Napuat.—Pimen-

tel, Cuadro Descr., II, 347, 1865 (given as a Comanche division, but really the Comanche name for the Carrizo: 'shoeless people.'—J. M.). Quetahtore.—Ibid. Yi′ätä′teñko.—Mooney, op. cit. (another Kiowa name, same meaning).

**Caruana.** A tribe of 96 individuals, mentioned as on Ft Tejon res., s. central Cal., in 1862. They were probably Shoshonean or Mariposan.—Wentworth in Ind. Aff. Rep., 324, 1862.
Sierra.—Wentworth, ibid.

**Carving.** See *Art, Sculpture, Wood-work*.

**Casa Blanca** (Span.: 'white house'). Formerly a summer village of the Laguna tribe, but now permanently inhabited; situated 4½ m. w. of Laguna pueblo, Valencia co., N. Mex.
Casa Blanco.—Donaldson, Moqui Pueblo Inds., 123, 1893 (misprint). Pŭr-tyi-tyí-ya.—Hodge, field notes, B. A. E., 1895 (proper name: 'edge of the hill on the west'). Pu-sit-yit-cho.—Hodge (fide Pradt) in Am. Anthrop., IV, 346, 1891.

**Casa Blanca** (so called on account of a pueblo ruin in the vicinity; see *Casa Montezuma*). A Pima village consisting of about 50 scattered houses on Gila r., s. Ariz. It contained 535 inhabitants in 1858 and 315 in 1869.
Casa Blanca.—Bailey in Ind. Aff. Rep., 208, 1858. Va′-aki.—Russell, Pima MS., B. A. E., 18, 1902 (Pima name: 'ancient house'). Va Vak.—Stout in Ind. Aff. Rep. 1871, 59, 1872 (probably the same).

**Casa Blanca.** A ruined cliff pueblo in Canyon de Chelly, in the present Navaho country, N. E. Ariz.—Wheeler Survey Rep., VII, 373, 1879.

**Casa Chiquita** (Span.: 'small house'). A small ruined pueblo 1½ m. w. of Pueblo Bonito, on the N. side of the arroyo, against the mesa wall, in Chaco canyon, N. W. N. Mex. It is in the form of a solid parallelogram, 78 by 63 ft. A considerable part of the building was occupied by 2 large circular kivas. The rooms on the ground floor were mostly about 5 by 8 ft. in dimension. The pueblo was originally 4 stories high, but is now in a very ruinous condition, although such walls as remain standing display excellent workmanship, a well-preserved corner being found true to the square and plummet.    (E. L. H.)

**Casa del Eco** (Span.: 'house of the echo'). A large cliff village in San Juan canyon, s. Utah, 12 m. below the mouth of Montezuma canyon. Described by Gannett in Pop. Sci. Mo., 671, Mar., 1880; Hardacre in Scribner's Mag., 274, Dec., 1878; Jackson in 10th Rep. Hayden Survey, 420, 1879.

**Casa Grande** (Span.: 'great house'). The principal structure of an extensive prehistoric ruined pueblo ½ m. s. of Gila r., 9 m. s. w. from Florence, Pinal co., Ariz. It was first mentioned by the Jesuit Father Eusebio Kino, or Kuehne, who said mass within its walls in Nov., 1694, and who again visited it in 1697 and 1699. In Kino's time the great house was of 4 stories but roofless, and its condition was much the same about 1762, when seen by the author of the anonymous Rudo Ensayo. Its construction is of the *pisé* type, i. e., the walls, 3 to 5 ft. thick, consist of huge blocks of adobe mortar and gravel molded in place and allowed to dry hard, then smoothed on the inner surface. The present height of the outer walls is 20 to 25 ft., accommodating 2 stories, while the central part or tower, forming an additional story, is 28 to 30 ft. above the ground. The house measures 43 by 59 ft., with 5 rooms in its ground plan. Casa Grande was also visited Oct. 31, 1775, by Father Pedro Font, who wrote an excellent description of its appearance and mentions the outlying structures, then fairly preserved. Font remarks that the Casa Grande itself measured 50 by 70 ft., and infers that its beams (4 or 5 in. thick), apparently of pine, must have been carried 20 m., while the water supply for the settlement was conveyed from the river by means of a canal. At this date the building was of 3 stories, though the neighboring Pima informed Font that there had been 4. The celebrated ruins were visited 77 years later (July 12, 1852) by J. R. Bartlett, whose description indicates little change in the main structure since the time of Font, although all but 2 of the outlying buildings had been reduced to mounds. By act of Congress of Mar. 2, 1889, $2,000 was appropriated for the repair of the building, and the work was performed under the direction of the Secretary of the Interior. By Executive order of June 22, 1892, under the provisions of the same act, a tract of about ¾ sq. m., surrounding the ruin, was reserved from sale or settlement, and a custodian appointed. The origin of this and of other prehistoric pueblo groups in s. Arizona and N. Chihuahua is unknown. It has long been reputed to have been one of the places of sojourn of the Nahua or Aztec in their migration from the N. to the valley of Mexico (whence the name 'Casa de Montezuma'), and it has been mistakenly regarded by some writers as the Chichilticalli, or 'Red House,' of the

CASA GRANDE RUIN, ARIZONA. (MINDELEFF)

GROUND-PLAN OF CASA GRANDE RUIN. (MINDELEFF)

chroniclers of Coronado's expedition in 1540–42. The Pima, who have occupied the region from time immemorial, preserve a legend that it was constructed by one of their chiefs or deities named Civano, hence the name Civanoki, 'house of Civano,' which they apply to it. This has led to the general belief that these structures are the work of the ancestors of the Pima tribe, notwithstanding their historical habitations are of an entirely different character, being circular huts of grass or reeds, while their pottery is far inferior in quality and decoration to that found in the Casa Grande region. It would seem more probable that these remains are due to some of the clans of the present Hopi or Zuñi pueblos, one at least of the former tribe tracing its origin to the "land of the giant cactus"—a plant characteristic of the Gila valley Before its woodwork was taken away by relic hunters, Casa Grande showed evidences of having been burned.

Consult Apostolicos Afanes, 252 et seq., 1754; Bandelier in Arch. Inst. Rep., v, 66, 1890, and Arch. Inst. Papers, IV, 439, 1892; Bartlett, Pers. Narr., II, 272–280, 1854; Coues, Garcés Diary, I, 89–101, 1900; Doc. Hist. Mex., 4th s., I, 274–291, 1856; Emory, Recon., 83, 1848; Fewkes in Jour. Am. Eth. and Arch., II, 177–193, 1892; Mindeleff in 13th Rep. B. A. E., 289, 1896, and 15th Rep. B. A. E., 321, 1897; Rudo Ensayo (1762), 1863, also Guiteras transl., 124, 1894; Schoolcraft, Ind. Tribes, III, 301, 1853; Ternaux-Compans, Voy., IX, 383, 1838. (F. W. H.)

**Cara de Montezuma.**—Johnston in Emory, Reconnoissance, 596, 1848 (misprint). **Casa Granda.**—Browne, Apache Country, 116, 1869. **Casa Grande.**—Bernal (1697) quoted by Bancroft, Ariz. and N. Mex., 356, 1889. **Casagrande.**—Jefferys, Am. Atlas, map 5, 1776. **Casas Grandas.**—Hardacre in Scribner's Monthly, 270, Dec., 1878. **Casas Grandes.**—Mange (1697) quoted by Coues, Garcés Diary, I, 92, 1900. **Case grandi.**—Clavigero, Storia della Cal., map, 1789. **Chivano-ki.**—Bandelier in Mag. West. Hist., 667, Sept., 1886 ('house of Civano': Pima name). **Civano Ki.**—Bandelier in Arch. Inst. Papers, III, 255, 1890 (Pima name). **Ci-vano-Qi.**—Bandelier in Revue d'Ethnog., 129, 1886. **Ci-vă-nŏ-qi.**—Bandelier in Arch. Inst. Rep., v, 80, 1884 (='Civănŏ's house'). **Grande Maison Dite de Mooctecuzoma.**—Ternaux-Compans, Voy., IX, 383, 1838. **Great Houses.**—Bartlett, Pers. Narr., II, 272, 1854. **Hall of Montezuma.**—Hughes, Doniphan's Exped., 219, 1848. **Huis van Montezuma.**—ten Kate, Reizen in N. A., 162, 1885 (Dutch form: 'House of Montezuma'). **Maison Moctecuzoma.**—Ternaux-Compans, Voy., IX, 383, 1838 (French form). **Maison Moteczuma.**—Font (1775), ibid., 383 (French form). **Moctesuma.**—Rudo Ensayo (1762), B. Smith's transl., 18, 1863. **Mission Montezuma.**—Fewkes in Jour. Am. Eth. and Arch., 180 (locally so called). **Siwannoki.**—ten Kate quoted in Arch. Inst. Papers, V, 132, 1890 (from Siwanki, 'house of Siwanno'). **Văt-qi.**—Bandelier in Arch. Inst. Rep., V, 80, 1884 (='ruin,' another Pima name). **Wak.**—ten Rate, Reizen in N. A., 160, 1885 (also Wakh and Wahki = 'ruin': Pima name).

**Casa Grande.** A ruined pueblo, measuring 68 by 220 ft., situated a little below the junction of the Verde and Salt rs., Maricopa co., s. Ariz.—Bell, New Tracks, I, 199, 1869.

**Casalic.** A Chumashan village given in Cabrillo's narrative as near Pueblo de las Canoas (San Buenaventura), Cal., in 1542. It was placed by Taylor at Refugio, near Santa Barbara, and was also so located by the San Buenaventura Indians in 1884. Cf. *Cascel.*
**Casalic.**—Cabrillo, Narr., in Smith, Col. Doc., 181, 1857. **Casaliu.**—Taylor in Cal. Farmer, Apr. 17, 1863. **Cascile.**—Ibid., Apr. 24, 1863. **Kasi'l.**—Henshaw, Buenaventura MS. vocab., B. A. E., 1884.

**Casa Montezuma** (Span.: 'Montezuma house,' also called Casa Blanca, 'white house'). A prehistoric ruin near the Pima villages on the Gila, s. Ariz. Not to be confounded with Casa Grande nor with any other ruin, although the same name has been indiscriminately applied to various cliff-dwellings, ancient pueblos, etc., in s. w. United States and N. w. Mexico, because of their supposed ancient occupancy by the Aztec. (F. W. H.)
**A-vuc-hoo-mar-lish.**—Pac. R. R. Rep., III, pt. 3, 100, 1856 (Maricopa name). **Casa Blanca.**—Bell in Jour. Ethnol. Soc. Lond., N. s., I, 250, 1869. **Casa Montezuma.**—Ibid. **Ho-ho-qŏm.**—Bandelier in Arch. Inst. Rep., V, 80, 1884 (Pima name). **Huch-oo-la-chook-vaché.**—Pac. R. R. Rep., op. cit., 94 (Pima name). **Vĭ-pĭ-sĕt.**—Bandelier, op. cit. ('great grandparents': another Pima name).

**Casa Morena** (Span.: 'brown house'). An ancient pueblo ruin of considerable importance, situated near the top of the continental divide in N. w. New Mexico. It is usually assigned to the Chaco canyon group, but this is assumed without evidence except as to outward appearance. No excavations have been made and the ruin has not been described. It is built of sandstone after the manner of the Chaco canyon pueblos. It is in the midst of the desert, far from water, and not near any of the main trails. (E. L. H.)
**Kinahzin.**—Hewett, inf'n, 1905 (Navaho name).

**Casa Rinconada** (Span.: 'corner house'). A small pueblo ruin 500 yds. s. E. of Pueblo Bonito, s. of the arroyo, at the foot of the wall of Chaco canyon, n. w. N. Mex. The building did not contain more than 50 rooms. Its most interesting feature is an enormous double-walled kiva, the largest in the Chaco canyon group, measuring 72 ft. in diameter, the rooms of the pueblo being built partially around it. The 2 walls

were about 30 in. thick, and portions still stand from 10 to 12 ft. above the surrounding débris. Probably three-fourths of the kiva wall are still standing, being of fine, well-selected sandstone, smoothly laid. Thirty-two niches, 16 by 22 in., 14 in. deep, smoothly finished and plastered, extend around the interior of the kiva wall at regular intervals. The outer wall of the kiva is 8 ft. from the inner, the space between being divided into rooms. The indications are that the building was devoted to ceremonial rather than to domiciliary use. (E. L. H.)

**Casas Chiquitas** (Span.: 'small houses'). A tribe supposed to have been once affiliated with the Carrizo, a Coahuiltecan tribe, but which in 1887 was said to be extinct. (A. S. G.)

**Casas Grandes.** A name applied to the ruins of the Franciscan mission of Concepcion, founded in 1780 by Fray Francisco Garcés, near Yuma, Ariz.—Hardy, Travels in Mex., 355, 1829.

**Casca** (prob. Span. *casco*, 'potsherd'). A Papago village, probably in Pima co., s. Ariz., with 80 families in 1865.—Davidson in Ind. Aff. Rep., 135, 1865.

**Cascarba** (trans. 'white man'). An unidentified Dakota tribe that lived 35 leagues up St. Peters r. in 1804.—Orig. Jour. Lewis and Clark, I, 133, 1904.

**Cascel.** A former Chumashan village near Santa Inés mission, Santa Barbara co., Cal. Cf. *Casalic.*
**Cascel.**—Taylor in Cal. Farmer, Oct. 18, 1861. **Cascellis.**—Gatschet in Chief Eng. Rep., pt. III, 553, 1876. **Cascen.**—Taylor in Cal. Farmer, May 4, 1860. **Cascil.**—Ibid., Oct. 18, 1861. **Kusil.**—Ibid., Oct. 18, 1861.

**Cases.** See *Boxes, Receptacles.*

**Cashaw.** A name of the crook-neck squash, a species of pumpkin. Bartlett (Dict. Americanisms, 104, 1877) has "*cashaw*, sometimes spelt *kershaw* (Algonkin), a pumpkin." The word occurs in Hariot (1590) as *ecushaw*; in Beverley (1705) as *cashaw, cushaw*, etc. The latter uses it as synonymous with *macock*. The untruncated form, *ecushaw*, represents *escushaw*, from a Virginian dialect of Algonquian corresponding to the Cree *askisiw* and the Delaware *askasqueu*, which signify 'it is raw or green.' According to Dr William Jones *kasha* is an old Chippewa term for 'hard shell.' (A. F. C.)

**Cashiehtunk.** A village, probably belonging to the Munsee, situated in 1738 on Delaware r., near the junction of the N. New Jersey state line.—Colden (1738) in N. Y. Doc. Col. Hist., VI, 124, 1855.

**Cashong.** A small Seneca village situated in 1779 about 7 m. s. of the present site of Geneva, N. Y.—Clark in Sullivan (1779), Ind. Exped., 130, note, 1887.

**Cashwah.** A former Chumashan village at La Sinaguita (Cieneguita), about 3 m.

N. E. of Santa Barbara mission, Cal. It was still inhabited in 1876, according to Grinnell (inf'n, 1905).
Cashwah.—Father Timeno (1856) quoted by Taylor in Cal. Farmer, May 4, 1860. Cieneguita.—Gatschet in Chief Eng. Rep., 550, 1876. Kasua.—Ibid.

**Casio berry.** An old name, always used in combination with the word "bush," for *Viburnum obovatum* (*lævigatum*), the leaves of which, as well as those of *V. cassinoides* and *V. prunifolium*, were formerly, if not at present, used on the coast of the Carolinas as tea. Since the leaves of the *yopon* (*Ilex cassine*) were employed for the same purpose, the *Ilex* and *Viburnum* were early confused under the same name. See *Black drink*.
(W. R. G.)

**Casitoa.** A Calusa village on the s. w. coast of Florida, about 1570.—Fontaneda Memoir (*ca.* 1575), Smith trans., 19, 1854.

**Casnahacmo.** A former Chumashan village at Santa Clara rancho, Ventura co., Cal.—Taylor in Cal. Farmer, May 4, 1860.

**Casqui.** An unidentified province and town, probably on lower St Francis r., E. Ark., visited by De Soto's army immediately after crossing the Mississippi in 1541. It is possibly cognate with Akaⁿze, a name for the Quapaw.
Cascia.—La Salle (1680), from De Soto Narr., in Margry, Déc., II, 96, 1877. Cascin.—Hennepin, New Discov., 311, 1698. Casque.—Schoolcraft, Ind. Tribes, III, 48, 1853. Casqui.—Gentl. of Elvas (1557) in French, Hist. Coll. La., 169, 1850. Casquia.—Margry, Déc., I, 470, 1875. Casquin.—Garcilasso de la Vega, Fla., 179, 1723. Icasque.—Biedma in Smith, Col. Doc. Fla., I, 59, 1857. Ycasqui.—Biedma in Hakluyt Soc. Publ., IX, 190, 1851.

**Cassapecock.** Mentioned by Strachey (Va., 62, 1849) as a Powhatan tribe living on York or Pamunkey r., about 1612, and having 100 warriors. Not mentioned by Smith under this name, but probably one of the tribes alluded to by him under another designation.
(J. M.)

**Casse-tête.** See *Clubs*.

**Castahana.** A hunting tribe of 5,000 souls in 500 lodges, mentioned by Clark as a Snake band, and by Lewis and Clark also as speaking the Minitari (Atsina) language. They lived on Yellowstone and Loup rs., and roamed also on the Bighorn. Called also Gens des Vache, a name given to the Arapaho, with whom they are seemingly identical.
Castabanas.—M'Vickar, Hist. Exped. Lewis and Clark, I, map, 1842. Castahamas.—Warden, Acc. U. S. A., III, 562, 1819. Cas-ta-ha'-na.—Lewis and Clark, Discov., 23, 40, 1806. Castapanas.—Ibid., 36. Pastannownas.—Sanford, U. S., clxvi, 1819. Pastanow-na.—Brackenridge, Views of La., 86, 1814.

**Castake.** One of several tribes formerly occupying "the country from Buena Vista and Carises [Kern] lakes and Kern r. to the Sierra Nevada and Coast range," Cal. By treaty of June 10, 1851, these tribes reserved a tract between Tejon pass and Kern r. and ceded the remainder of their lands to the United States. In 1862 they were reported to number 162 on Ft Tejon res. The tribe belonged to the Chumashan family. Castac lake, in the Tejon

pass region, derives its name from this tribe and affords a further clue to its former habitat.
Cartaka.—Wentworth in Ind. Aff. Rep., 325, 1862. Cas-take.—Barbour (1852) in Sen. Ex. Doc. 4, 32d Cong., spec. sess., 256, 1853. Catagos.—Taylor in Cal. Farmer, June 26, 1862 (mentioned as in E. Nevada; same?). Curtakas.—Taylor in Cal. Farmer, May 8, 1863. Surrillos.—Wentworth in Ind. Aff. Rep., 325, 1862.

**Casti.** A former Timuquanan settlement on the w. bank of St Johns r., Fla., not far from the mouth.—Laudonnière (1564) in French, Hist. Coll. La., n. s., 306, 1869.

**Castildavid.** An unidentified pueblo on the Rio Grande in New Mexico in 1582; situated s. of Sia (?), but definite locality unknown.—Bustamente and Gallegos (1582) in Doc. Inéd., xv, 85, 1871.

**Casunalmo.** A former Chumashan village at Rafael Gonzales rancho, Ventura co., Cal.—Taylor in Cal. Farmer, May 4, 1860.

**Catahecassa** (Black Hoof, probably from *ma'ka-täwikashä*—W. J.). A principal chief of the Shawnee, born about 1740, near the present Winchester, Ky. He was one of the greatest captains of this warlike tribe throughout the period when they were dreaded by the whites. He was present at Braddock's defeat in 1755, and in the battle with the Virginian militia under Gen. Andrew Lewis at Point Pleasant, W. Va., in 1774 he bore a prominent part. He was an active leader of the Shawnee in their resistance to the advance of the white settlements w. of the Allegheny mts., and fought the troops of Harmar and St Clair. When the victory of Gen. Anthony Wayne broke the power of the Indian confederation and peace was signed on Aug. 3, 1795, Catahecassa's fighting days came to an end, but not his career as an orator and counselor. When finally convinced of the hopelessness of struggling against the encroachment of the whites, he used his great influence to preserve peace. He was a persuasive and convincing speaker and was thoroughly versed in the traditions of the tribe as well as in the history of their relations with the whites, in which he had himself borne a conspicuous part. As head chief of the Shawnee he kept the majority of the tribe in restraint when British agents endeavored to stir them into rebellion against the American government and succeeded in seducing Tecumseh and some of the younger warriors. He died at Wapakoneta, Ohio, in 1831.

**Catahoula** ('lake village,' from Choctaw *ak'hátaχ* 'lake,' *ougoula*, French form of *ókla* 'village'). A tribe of unknown affinity formerly living on Catahoula cr. in Catahoula parish, La.; mentioned in 1805 by Sibley (Hist. Sketches, 121, 1806) as extinct. Whether this tribe was a remnant or the Taensa village of Coutahaougoula is uncertain.
(A. S. G.)

Cataoulou.—Rafinesque, introd. Marshall, Ky., I, 43, 1824.

**Catalpa.** Any tree of the genus *Catalpa* belonging to the family Bignoniaceæ. The two species native in the United States are the common catalpa, bean-tree, Indian bean, or candle-tree (*Catalpa catalpa*); and the western catalpa, larger Indian bean, or Shawnee wood (*C. speciosa*). Both species are extensively planted as ornamental and shade trees. The second species is also called catawba tree, which name was applied earlier to the first. Britton and Brown (Flora of North. U. S., 201, 1896) say that catalpa is the American Indian name of the first species. In Chambers' Encyclopedia (II, 826, 1888) it is stated that "the genus was named by Catesby, probably from the Catawba r., where he first found them in 1726." It is generally thought to be identical with the tribal and river name Catawba, but W. R. Gerard (Gard. and For., IX, 262, 1896) says that catalpa is derived from *kutuhlpa*, signifying 'winged head,' in reference to its flowers, in the Creek language. (A. F. C.)

**Catalte.** The first province reached by Moscoso after the death of De Soto in 1542. It lay w. of the Mississippi, probably in E. Arkansas, s. of Arkansas r.—Gentl. of Elvas (1557) in French, Hist. Coll. La., II, 193, 1850.

**Catamaya.** A town w. of the Mississippi r., visited by the De Soto expedition in 1542 and mentioned as two days' journey from Anoixi, perhaps in s. w. Arkansas.—Gentl. of Elvas (1557) in French, Hist. Coll. La., II, 182, 1850.

**Catatoga** (corruption of *Gatu'gitse'yĭ*, 'new settlement place'). A former Cherokee settlement on Cartoogaja cr., to which it gave its name, a tributary of Little Tennessee r., above Franklin, in Macon co., N. C.—Mooney in 19th Rep. B. A. E., 519, 1900.
Cartoogaja.—Mooney, ibid. Gatu'gitse'.—Ibid. (abbreviation of Indian term).

**Cataumut.** A village formerly in Falmouth township, Barnstable co., Mass., probably near Canaumut neck. In 1674 there were some Praying Indians in it, and there were still a few mixed bloods there in 1792. It was in the territory of the Nauset. (J. M.)
Cataumut.—Freeman (1792) in Mass. Hist. Soc. Coll., 1st s., I, 230, 1806. Codtanmut.—Bourne (1674), ibid., 197.

**Catawatabeta.** See *Broken Tooth*.

**Catawaweshink.** A former village, probably of the Delawares, on or near Susquehanna r., near Big Island, Pa.—Post (1758) in Kauffman, West. Pa., app., 96, 1851.

**Catawba** (probably from Choctaw *katápa*, 'divided,' 'separated,' 'a division.'—Gatschet). The most important of the eastern Siouan tribes. It is said that Lynche cr., S. C., E. of the Catawba

territory, was anciently known as Kadapau; and from the fact that Lawson applies this name to a small band met by him s. E. of the main body, which he calls Esaw, it is possible that it was originally given to this people by some tribe living in E. South Carolina, from whom the first colonists obtained it. The Cherokee, having no *b* in their language, changed the name to Atakwa, plural Anitakwa. The Shawnee and other tribes of the Ohio valley made the word Cuttawa. From the earliest period the Catawba have also been known as

D. A. HARRIS, A CATAWBA

Esaw, or Issa (Catawba *iswă'*, 'river'), from their residence on the principal stream of the region, Iswa being their only name for the Catawba and Wateree rs. They were frequently included by the Iroquois under the general term Totiri, or Toderichroone, another form of which is Tutelo, applied to all the southern Siouan tribes collectively. They were classed by Gallatin (1836) as a distinct stock, and were so regarded until Gatschet visited them in 1881 and obtained a large vocabulary showing numerous Siouan correspondences. Further investigations by Hale, Gatschet, Mooney, and Dorsey proved that several other tribes of the same region were also of Siouan stock, while the linguistic forms and traditional evidence all point to this E. region as the original home of the Siouan tribes. The alleged tradition which brings the Catawba from the N., as refugees from the French and their

Indian allies about the year 1660, does not agree in any of its main points with the known facts of history, and, if genuine at all, refers rather to some local incident than to a tribal movement. It is well known that the Catawba were in a chronic state of warfare with the northern tribes, whose raiding parties they sometimes followed, even across the Ohio.

The first notice of the Catawba seems to be that of Vandera in 1579, who calls

BENJAMIN P. HARRIS, A CATAWBA

them Issa in his narrative of Pardo's expedition. Nearly a century later, in 1670, they are mentioned as Ushery by Lederer, who claims to have visited them, but this is doubtful.

Lawson, who passed through their territory in 1701, speaks of them as a "powerful nation" and states that their villages were very thick. He calls the two divisions, which were living a short distance apart, by different names; one the Kadapau and the other the Esaw, un-

aware of the fact that the two were synonyms. From all accounts they were formerly the most populous and most important tribe in the Carolinas, excepting the Cherokee. Virginia traders were already among them at the time of Lawson's visit. Adair, 75 years later, says that one of the ancient cleared fields of the tribe extended 7 m., besides which they had several smaller village sites. In 1728 they still had 6 villages, all on Catawba r., within a stretch of 20 m., the most N. being named Nauvasa. Their principal village was formerly on the w. side of the river, in what is now York co., S. C., opposite the mouth of Sugar cr. The known history of the tribe till about 1760 is chiefly a record of petty warfare between themselves and the Iroquois and other northern tribes, throughout which the colonial government tried to induce the Indians to stop killing one another and go to killing the French. With the single exception of their alliance with the hostile Yamasi, in 1715, they were uniformly friendly toward the English, and afterward kept peace with the United States, but were constantly at war with the Iroquois, Shawnee, Delawares, and other tribes of the Ohio valley, as well as with the Cherokee. The Iroquois and the Lake tribes made long journeys into South Carolina, and the Catawba retaliated by sending small scalping parties into Ohio and Pennsylvania. Their losses from ceaseless attacks of their enemies reduced their numbers steadily, while disease and debauchery introduced by the whites, especially several epidemics of smallpox, accelerated their destruction, so that before the close of the 18th century the great nation was reduced to a pitiful remnant. They sent a large force to help the colonists in the Tuscarora war of 1711–13, and also aided in expeditions against the French and their Indian allies at Ft Du Quesne and elsewhere during the French and Indian war. Later it was proposed to use them and the Cherokee against the Lake tribes under Pontiac in 1763. They assisted the Americans also during the Revolution in the defense of South Carolina against the British, as well as in Williamson's expedition against the Cherokee. In 1738 smallpox raged in South Carolina and worked great destruction, not only among the whites, but also among the Catawba and smaller tribes. In 1759 it appeared again, and this time destroyed nearly half the tribe. At a conference at Albany, attended by delegates from the Six Nations and the Catawba, under the auspices of the colonial governments, a treaty of peace was made between these two tribes. This peace was probably final as regards the Iroquois, but the western tribes continued their warfare against the Catawba, who were now so reduced that they could make little effectual resistance. In 1762 a small party of Shawnee killed the noted chief of the tribe, King Haiglar, near his own village. From this time the Catawba ceased to be of importance except in conjunction with the whites. In 1763 they had confirmed to them a reservation, assigned a few years before, of 15 m. square, on both sides of Catawba r., within the present York and Lancaster cos., S. C. On the approach of the British troops in 1780 the Catawba withdrew temporarily into Virginia, but returned after the battle of Guilford Court House, and established themselves in 2 villages on the reservation, known respectively as Newton, the principal village, and Turkey Head, on opposite sides of Catawba r. In 1826 nearly the whole of their reservation was leased to whites for a few thousand dollars, on which the few survivors chiefly depended. About 1841 they sold to the state all but a single square mile, on which they now reside. About the same time a number of the Catawba, dissatisfied with their condition among the whites, removed to the eastern Cherokee in w. North Carolina, but finding their position among their old enemies equally unpleasant, all but one or two soon went back again. An old woman, the last survivor of this emigration, died among the Cherokee in 1889. A few other Cherokee are now intermarried with that tribe. At a later period some Catawba removed to the Choctaw Nation in Indian Ter. and settled near Scullyville, but are said to be now extinct. About 1884 several became converts of Mormon missionaries in South Carolina and went with them to Salt Lake City, Utah.

The Catawba were sedentary agriculturists, and seem to have differed but little in general customs from their neighbors. Their men were respected, brave, and honest, but lacking in energy. They were good hunters, while their women were noted makers of pottery and baskets, arts which they still preserve. They seem to have practised the custom of head-flattening to a limited extent, as did several of the neighboring tribes. By reason of their dominant position they gradually absorbed the broken tribes of South Carolina, to the number, according to Adair, of perhaps 20.

In the early settlement of South Carolina, about 1682, they were estimated at 1,500 warriors, or about 4,600 souls; in 1728 at 400 warriors, or about 1,400 persons. In 1738 they suffered from smallpox; and in 1743, after incorporating several small tribes, numbered less than 400 warriors. In 1759 they again suffered from small-

pox, and in 1761 had some 300 warriors, or about 1,000 people. The number was reduced in 1775 to 400 souls; in 1780 it was 490; and in 1784 only 250 were reported. The number given in 1822 is 450, and Mills gives the population in 1826 as only 110. In 1881 Gatschet found 85 on the reservation, which, including 35 employed on neighboring farms, made a total of 120. The present number is given as 60, but as this apparently refers only to those attached to the reservation, the total may be about 100.

See Lawson, History of Carolina, 1714 and 1860; Gatschet, Creek Migration Legend, I–II, 1884–88; Mooney (1) Siouan Tribes of the East, Bull. 22, B. A. E., 1894, (2) in 19th Rep. B. A. E., 1900; H. Lewis Scaife, History and Condition of the Catawba Indians, 1896. (J. M.)

Ani'ta'guǎ.—Mooney in 19th Rep. B. A. E., 509, 1900 (Cherokee name, pl). Atakwa.—Mooney, Siouan Tribes, 67, 1894 (Cherokee form, sing.). Cadapouces.—Pénicaut (1708) in Margry, Déc., v, 477, 1883. Calabaws.—Humphreys, Acct., 98, 1730 (misprint). Calipoas.—Census of 1857 in Schoolcraft, Ind. Tribes, VI, 686, 1857. Canapouces.—Pénicaut (1708) in Margry, Déc., v, 547, 1883. Catabans.—Rafinesque, int. Marshall, Ky., I, 24, 1824. Catabas.—George Washington (1770) quoted by Kauffmann, West Penn., 396, 1851. Catabaw.—Doc. of 1738 in N. Y. Doc. Col. Hist., VI, 137, 1855. Catabaws.—Niles (1760) in Mass. Hist. Coll., 4th s., v, 549, 1861. Catapaw.—Map of N. Am. and W. Ind., 1720. Catapaws.—Gov. Johnson quoted by Rivers, Early Hist. So. Car., 94, 1874. Catauba.—Filson, Hist. of Ky., 84, 1793. Cataubos.—War map, 1711–15, in Winsor, Hist. Am., v, 346, 1887. Cataupa.—Potter (1768) in Mass. Hist. Soc. Coll., 1st s., x, 120, 1809. Catawba.—Albany conf. (1717) in N. Y. Doc. Col. Hist., v, 490, 1855. Catawbau.—Hist. Coll. So. Car., II, 199, 1836. Catawbaw.—Mandrillon, Spectateur Américain, 1785. Cattabas.—Doc. of 1715 in N. C. Records, II, 252, 1886. Cattabaws.—Albany conf. (1717) in N. Y. Doc. Col. Hist., v, 490, 1855. Cattawbas.—Clarke (1741), ibid., VI, 208, 1855. Cattoways.—Stobo (1754) in The Olden Time, I, 72, 1846 (incorrectly named as distinct from Catawbas). Cautawba.—Clinton (1751) in N. Y. Doc. Col. Hist., VI, 716, 1855. Chatabas.—Buchhanan, N. Am. Inds., 155, 1824. Contaubas.—Oglethorpe (1743) in N. Y. Doc. Col. Hist., VI, 243, 1855. Cotappos.—Doc. of 1776 in Hist. Mag., 2d s., II, 216, 1867. Cotawpees.—Rogers, N. Am., 136, 1765. Cotobers.—Doc. of 1728 in Va. St. Pap., I, 215, 1875. Cuttambas.—German map of British colony, ca. 1750. Cuttawa.—Vaugondy, map Partie de l'Am. Sept., 1755. Cuttaws.—Schoolcraft, Ind. Tribes, III, 292, 1853. Ea-tau-bau.—Hawkins (1799), Sketch, 62, 1848 (misprint). Elaws.—Craven (1712) in N. C. Records, I, 898, 1886 (misprint). Esau.—Martin, Hist. N. C., I, 194, 1829. Esaws.—Lawson (1714), Hist. Carolina, 73, 1860. Flatheads.—Albany conf. (1715) in N. Y. Doc. Col. Hist., v, 437, 1855. Issa.—Juan de la Vandera (1569) in French, Hist. Coll., II, 291, 1875. Kadapau.—Lawson (1714), Hist. Carolina, 76, 1860. Kadapaw.—Mills, Stat. of S. C., 109, 1826. Kaddepaw.—Ibid., 770. Kaddipeaw.—Ibid., 638. Katabas.—Jour. (1758) in N. Y. Doc. Col. Hist., x, 843, 1858. Katahba.—Adair, Hist. Am. Inds., 223, 1775. Kataubahs.—Drake, Bk. Inds., bk. 4, 25, 1848. Kattarbe.—Ibid., 27. Kattaupa.—De l'Isle, map, in Winsor, Hist. Am., II, 295, 1886. Kershaws.—Schoolcraft, Ind. Tribes, II, 344, 1853. Ojadagochrœhne.—Albany conf. (1720) in N. Y. Doc. Col. Hist., v, 567, 1855. Oyadagahrœnes.—Doc. of 1713, ibid., note, 386. Tadirighrones.—Albany conf. (1722), ibid., 660. Taguǎ.—Mooney in 19th Rep. B. A. E., 509, 1900 (Cherokee form, sing.; also Ata'gwǎ). Toderichroone.—Albany conf. (1717) in N. Y. Doc. Col. Hist., v, 491, 1855. Totiris.—Chauvignerie (1736), ibid., IX, 1057, 1855. **Usheree.**—Byrd (1728), Hist. of Dividing Line, I, 181, 1866. **Usherie.**—Lederer (1670), Discov., 27, 1672 (from *iswahere*, 'river down here'). **Usherys.**—Ibid., 17.

**Catawba.**—A grape, or the wine produced from it, made famous by Longfellow in one of his poems. This grape is a cultivated variety of the northern foxgrape (*Vitis labrusca*) and is said to have been named by Maj. Adlum, in 1825, after the Catawba tribe and r. of North Carolina.                    (A. F. C.)

**Catawissa.**—Probably a Conoy village, as Conyngham (Day, Penn., 243, 1843) says the Conoy "had a wigwam on the Catawese at Catawese, now Catawissa," in Columbia co., Pa. The name is probably derived from Piscatawese, a later designation for the Conoy.
**Catawese.**—Conyngham, op. cit.

**Catfish Lake.** A Seminole settlement, with 28 inhabitants in 1880, on a small lake in Polk co., Fla., nearly midway between L. Pierce and L. Rosalie, toward the headwaters of Kissimmee r.—MacCauley in 5th Rep. B. A. E., 478, 1887.

**Catfish Village.** A former settlement, probably of the Delawares, on Catfish run, a short distance N. of the site of Washington, Washington co., Pa.; so called, according to Day (Penn., 666, 1843), from a half-blood who settled there about the middle of the 18th century. See Royce in 18th Rep. B. A. E., pl. clx., 1900.

**Catherine's Town.** A former Seneca village situated about the site of the present Catherine, N. Y., or, according to Conover, at Havana Glen. It took its name from Catherine Montour, a Canadian woman who was taken by the Iroquois and afterward became the chief matron in her clan. It was destroyed by Sullivan in 1779.                    (J. N. B. H.)
**Catharine Town.**—Jones (1780) in N. Y. Doc. Col. Hist., VIII, 785, 1857. **Catherine Town.**—Pemberton (*ca.* 1792) in Mass. Hist. Soc. Coll., 1st s., II, 177, 1810. **French Catharinestown.**—Machin (1779) quoted by Conover, Kanesadaga and Geneva MS., B. A. E. **French Catherines town.**—Livermore (1779) in N. H. Hist. Soc. Coll., VI, 325, 1850.

**Cathlacomatup.** A Chinookan tribe residing in 1806, according to Lewis and Clark (Exped., II, 226, 1814), on the s. side of Sauvies id., in the present Multnomah co., Oreg., on a slough of Willamette r. Their estimated number was 170.
**Cathlacommatups.**—Lewis and Clark, op. cit., 473. **Cath-lah-com-mah-tup.**—Lewis and Clark Exped., Coues ed., 931, note, 1893.

**Cathlacumup.** A Chinookan tribe formerly living on the w. bank of the lower mouth of Willamette r., near the Columbia, claiming as their territory the bank of the latter stream from this point to Deer id., Oreg. Lewis and Clark estimated their number at 450 in 1806. They are mentioned in 1850 by Lane as being associated with the Namoit and Katlaminimim. See *Kasenos.*                    (L. F.)
**Cathlacumups.**—Lewis and Clark, Exped., II, 212, 1814. **Cathlahcumups.**—Coues, Lewis and Clark Exped., 915, 1893. **Cathlakamaps.**—Drake, Bk. Inds., vi, 1848. **Wacamuc.**—Farrand, communication (name of their chief village, used to designate the tribe). **Wa-come-app.**—Ross, Advent., 236, 1849. **Wakamass.**—Framboise quoted by Gairdner in Jour. Geog. Soc. Lond., XI, 255, 1841. **Wakamucks.**—Lane in Ind. Aff. Rep., 161, 1850. **Willamette tribe.**—Coues, Henry and Thompson Jour., 797, 1897.

**Cathlakaheckit.** A Chinookan tribe living at the cascades of Columbia r. in 1812, when their number was estimated at 900.
**Cath-lâk-a-heckits.**—Stuart in Nouv. Ann. Voy., XII, 23, 1821. **Cathlakahikits.**—Morse, Rep. to Sec. War, 368, 1822. **Cathlayackty.**—Coues, Jour. Henry and Thompson, 803, 1897 (in 3 villages just above cascades; probably identical).

**Cathlamet.** A Chinookan tribe formerly residing on the s. bank of Columbia r. near its mouth, in Oregon. They adjoined the Clatsop and claimed the

CATHLAMET WOMAN. (AM. MUS. NAT. HIST.)

territory from Tongue pt. to the neighborhood of Puget id. In 1806 Lewis and Clark estimated their number at 300. In 1849 Lane reported 58 still living, but they are now extinct. They seem to have had but one village, also known as Cathlamet. As a dialect, Cathlamet was spoken by a number of Chinookan tribes on both sides of the Columbia, extending up the river as far as Rainier. It is regarded as belonging to the upper Chinook division of the family. See Boas, Kathlamet Texts, Bull. 26, B. A. E., 1901.
                    (L. F.)
**Catelamet.**—Lane in Sen. Ex. Doc. 52, 31st Cong., 1st sess., 172, 1850. **Cath Camettes.**—Raymond in Ind. Aff. Rep. 1857, 354, 1858. **Cathelametts.**—Minto in Oregon Hist. Soc. Quar., I, 311, 1900.

**Cathlamah.**—Lewis and Clark, Exped., I, map; II, 473, 1814. **Cathlamaks.**—Domenech, Deserts N. Am., II, 16, 1860. **Cath-la-mas.**—Gass, Jour., 189, 1807. **Cathlamats.**—Stuart in Nouv. Ann. Voy., x, 23, 1821. **Cathlamet.**—Hale in U. S. Expl. Exped., VI, 215, 1846. **Cathlamuts.**—Scouler in Jour. Ethnol. Soc. Lond., I, 237, 1848. **Cathlamux.**—Ross, Adventures, 87, 1849. **Cathlawah.** — Lewis and Clark, Exped., II, 109, 1817. **Cathlumet.**—Medill in H. R. Ex. Doc. 76, 30th Cong., 1st sess., 7, 1848. **Catlahmas.**—Snelling, Tales of Travel, 78, 1830. **Cuthlamuhs.**—Robertson, Oregon, 129, 1846. **Cuthlamuks.**—Robertson in H. R. Ex. Doc. 76, 30th Cong., 1st sess., 9, 1848. **Guasámas.** — Gatschet, MS., B. A. E. (Clackama name). **Guithlameth¹.**—Ibid. **Kathlamet.**—Schoolcraft, Ind. Tribes, I, 521, 1853. **Kat-hlámet.**—Gibbs, Chinook vocab., 4, 1863. **Kathlamit.**—Lane in Ind. Aff. Rep., 162, 1850. **Kathlamut.**—Latham, Nat. Hist. Man., 317, 1850. **Kathlemit.**—Lane in Sen. Ex. Doc. 52, 31st Cong., 1st sess., 174, 1850. **Katlamak.**—Framboise quoted by Gairdner (1835) in Jour. Geog. Soc. Lond., XI, 255, 1841. **Katlāmat.**—Hale in U. S. Expl. Exped., VI, 215, 1846. **Katlammets.**—Townsend, Narr., 175, 1839. **Kwillu'chinl.**—Gibbs, MS., B. A. E. (Chinook name).

**Cathlanahquiah** ('people of the r. Naqoaix'). A Chinookan tribe living in 1806, according to Lewis and Clark, on the s. w. side of Wappatoo, now Sauvies id., Multnomah co., Oreg., and numbering 400 souls.

**Cath-lah-nah-quiah.**—Lewis and Clark Exped., Coues ed., 931, 1893. **Cathlanahquiah.**—Lewis and Clark, Exped., II, 226, 1814. **Cathlanaquiah.**—Drake, Bk. Inds., VI, 1848. **GaꞮā'naqoa-ix.**—Boas, inf'n, 1904. **Gatlánakoa-iq.**—Lewis and Clark Exped., Coues ed., 931, note, 1893 (Cathlamet name). **Nekuaiχ.**—Gatschet MS., B. A. E., 1877 (Clackama name).

**Cathlapotle** ('people of Lewis [*Nā'p!ōʟx·*] r.'). A Chinookan tribe formerly living on the lower part of Lewis r. and on the s. E. side of Columbia r., in Clarke co., Wash. In 1806 Lewis and Clark estimated their number at 900 in 14 large wooden houses. Their main village was Nahpooitle.                         (L. F.)

**Cath-lah-poh-tle.**—Orig. Jour. Lewis and Clark, IV, 214, 1905. **Cathlapootle.**—Morse, Rep. to Sec. War, 368, 1822. **Cathlapoutles.**—Stuart in Nouv. Ann. Voy., x, 115, 1821. **Cathlapouttes.**—Ibid., 29. **Catlipoh.**—Coues, Jour. Henry and Thompson, 821, 1897. **Catlipoks.**—Ibid., 798. **Cattleputles.**—Ross, Advent., 87, 1849. **Gā'Lap!ōʟx.**—Boas, inf'n, 1904. **Gā'tlap'otlh.**—Lewis and Clark Exped., Coues ed., 914, note, 1893 (Cathlamet name). **Guathla'-payak.**—Gatschet, MS., B. A. E., 1877 (Clackama name). **Kathlapootle.**—Franchère, Narr., 111, 1854. **Katlaportl.**—Framboise quoted by Gairdner in Jour. Geog. Soc. Lond., XI, 255, 1841. **Nah-pooitle.**—Lyman in Oreg. Hist. Soc. Quar., I, 322, 1900. **Quathlapohtle.**—Orig. Jour. Lewis and Clark, IV, 212, 1905. **Quathlahpothle.**—Kelly, Oreg., 68, 1830. **Quathlahpotle.**—Lewis and Clark, Exped., II, 469, 1814. **Quathlapohtle.**—Oreg. Jour. Lewis and Clark, VI, 68, 1905.

**Cathlathlalas.** A Chinookan tribe living on both sides of Columbia r., just below the cascades, in 1812. Their number was placed at 500. See *Clahclellah.*

**Cath-lath-la-las.**—Stuart in Nouv. Ann. Voy., XII, 23, 1821. **Cathlathlaly.**—Coues, Jour. Henry and Thompson, 801, 1897. **Cathlathlas.**—Morse, Rep. to Sec. War, 368, 1822.

**Catlinite** (red pipestone). Smoking was a custom of great moment among the aborigines of northern America, and much time and labor were expended in the manufacture and decoration of the tobacco pipe, which is often referred to as "the sacred calumet," because of its important place in the ceremonial affairs of the people. A favorite material for these pipes was the red claystone called catlinite, obtained from a quarry in s. w. Minnesota, and so named because it was first brought to the attention of mineralogists by George Catlin, the noted traveler and painter of Indians. Stone of closely analogous characters, save in the matter of color, is found in many localities and has been used by the Indians for the manufacture of pipes and other articles, but so far as known to us it has not been quarried to any considerable extent. Catlinite is a very handsome stone, the color varying from a pale grayish-red to a dark red, the tints being sometimes so broken and distributed as to give a mottled effect. It is a fine-grained, argillaceous sediment, and when freshly quarried is so soft as to be readily carved with stone knives and drilled with primitive hand drills. The analysis made by Dr Charles F. Jackson, of Boston, who gave the mineral its name, is as follows: Silica, 48.20; alumina, 28.20; ferric oxide, 5; carbonate of lime, 2.60; manganous oxide, 0.60; magnesia, 6; water, 8.40; loss, 1.

The deposit of catlinite occurs in a broad, shallow, prairie valley, on the margin of which is situated the town of Pipestone, county seat of Pipestone co. The outcrop was probably discovered by the natives where it had been slightly exposed in the bed of the small stream now called Pipestone cr., which descends into the valley on the E. in a fall 18 ft. in height, and traverses the basin, passing out to the N. W. So far as exposed, the stratum of pipestone varies from 10 to 20 in. in thickness, the band of pure, fine-grained stone available for the manufacture of pipes rarely measuring more than 3 or 4 in. in thickness. This stratum is embedded between massive layers of compact quartzite which dip slightly to the eastward, so that in working it the overlying quartzite had to be broken up and removed, the difficulty of this task increasing with every foot of advance. With the stone implements in use in early times the process was a very tedious one, and the excavations were consequently quite shallow. The ledge which crosses the stream approximately at right angles had been followed to the right and left by the quarrymen until the line of pittings, rather conventionally shown in Catlin's plate 151, was nearly a mile in length. These ancient diggings have been almost obliterated by the more recent operations, which since the advent of the whites have been greatly accelerated by the introduction of steel sledges, picks, shovels, and crowbars. It is said that with the aid of the whites blasting has been occasionally resorted to. Some of the present excavations are as much as 10 ft. in depth, and have advanced 20 ft. or more along the dip of the strata to the E. The usual section now exposed in the deeper excavations, beginning above, shows from 2 to 4 ft. of soil and from 5 to 8 ft. of quartzite resting on the thin stratum of pipestone, beneath which, again forming the bed of the quarry, are compact quartzites. Numerous hammers of hard stone, some roughly grooved to facilitate hafting, have been found about the older pits, and the prairie in the vicinity is dotted with camp sites and tent rings about which are strewn bits of pipestone and other refuse of manufacture (see *Mines and Quarries*).

There is a general impression among those who have written on the subject that the discovery and use of the red pipestone by the tribes is of comparatively recent date, and this is no doubt correct; but it is equally certain that it was in use before the arrival of the whites in the N. W. This is made clear not only by history and tradition but by the appearance of the ancient quarry excavations, and especially by the occurrence of pipes and other objects made of it by aboriginal methods in mounds in various sections of the country. (See *Pipes.*) This quarry is usually referred to as the sacred pipestone quarry. According to statements by Catlin and others, the site was held in much superstitious regard by the aborigines. Traditions of very general distribution lead to the belief that it was, in the words of Catlin, "held and owned in common, and as neutral ground amongst the different tribes who met here to renew their pipes, under some superstition which stayed the tomahawk of natural foes always raised in deadly hate and vengeance in other places" (N. Am. Indians, II, 201, 1844). Nicollet states (1838) that Indians of the surrounding nations made an annual pilgrimage to the quarry unless prevented by wars or dissensions. Since the earliest visits of the

INDIAN QUARRYMAN OF TO-DAY. THE PIPESTONE LEDGE APPEARS AT THE BASE OF THE WALL. (BENNETT, COLL.)

white man to the Côteau des Prairies, however, the site has been occupied exclusively by the Sioux, and Catlin met with strong opposition from them when he attempted to visit the quarry about 1837.

The following facts regarding the historic occupancy and ownership of the Pipestone quarry are extracted from a statement furnished by Mr Charles H. Bennett, of Pipestone: On Apr. 30, 1803, the region was acquired by the United States through the Louisiana purchase. On July 23, 1851, the lands, including the quarry, were relinquished to the United States by the Sisseton and Wahpeton Sioux, and on August 5 they were relinquished by the Mdewakanton and Wahpekute Sioux, and 64 chiefs and head warriors who had also a claim. A treaty with the Yankton Sioux, ratified Apr. 19, 1858, specifies that "the said Yancton Indians shall be secured in the free and unrestricted use of the red pipestone quarry, or so much thereof as they have been accustomed to frequent and use for the purpose of procuring stone for pipes; and the United States hereby stipulate and agree to be caused to be surveyed and marked so much thereof as shall be necessary and proper for that purpose, and retain the same and keep it open and free to the Indians to visit and procure stone for pipes, so long as they shall desire." In 1859, 1 sq. m., including the quarry, was surveyed as a reservation, and in 1892 Congress appropriated $25,000 for the establishment of an industrial school, which is now (1905) being successfully conducted, with several stone buildings and some 200 pupils. It is situated on the highland overlooking the pipestone quarries on the E. The Sioux have no other legal claim upon the quarry site than that of quarrying the pipestone, a privilege of which they yearly take advantage to a limited extent. The Yankton Sioux, sometimes accompanied by their friends, the Flandreau Sioux, continue to visit the quarry and dig pipestone, coming usually in

June or July. They establish their tents on the reservation near the excavations, and stay from 1 to 2 weeks, procuring the pipestone which they manufacture into pipes and trinkets of great variety.

The Indians sell much of the stone to the whites, who have taken up the manufacture of pipes and various trinkets, using lathes to aid in the work, and in a letter written by Mr Bennett in 1892 it is stated that not 1 percent of the pipes then made and disposed of were of Indian manufacture. White traders began the manufacture of pipes from the pipestone many years ago, and according to Hayden these were used by the fur companies in trade with the Indians of the N. W. At a meeting of the American Philosophical Society in 1866 Hayden stated that in the two years just passed the Northwestern Fur Company had manufactured nearly 2,000 pipes and traded them with the tribes of the upper Missouri. An important feature of the quarry site is a group of large granite bowlders, brought from the far N. by glacial ice, about the base of which, engraved on the glaciated floor of red quartzite, were formerly a number of petroglyphs no doubt representing mythological beings associated with the locality. These have been taken up and are now in possession of Mr Bennett. Additional interest attaches to the locality on account of an inscription left by the Nicollet exploring party in 1838. The name of Nicollet and the initials of 5 other persons, including those of John C. Frémont [C. F. only], are cut in the flinty quartzite rock face near the "leaping rock" at the falls. According to a letter written to Mr Bennett by Gen. Frémont several years ago, he at that time named the two small lakes adjoining the quarry, one after his wife, the other after his son.

The following publications will afford additional details: Barber in Am. Nat., XVII, 1883; Carver, Trav. Through N. Am., 1778; Catlin (1) in Am. Jour. Sci. and Arts, 1st s., XXXVIII, 1840, (2) No. Am. Inds., II, 1844; Donaldson in Rep. Nat. Mus. 1885, 1886; Hayden (1) in Am. Jour. Sci. and Arts, 2d s., XLIII, 1867, (2) in Proc. Am. Philos. Soc., X, 1865–68; Hoffman in 14th Rep. B. A. E., 1896; Holmes in Proc. A. A. A. S., XLI, 1892; Nicollet in Sen. Doc. 237, 26th Cong., 2d sess., 1841; Norris, Calumet of the Coteau, 1883; Rau in Rep. Smithson. Inst. 1872, 1873; White in Am. Nat., II, 1868; Winchell in Geol. Surv. Minn., I, 1884. (W. H. H.)

**Catoking.** A village, probably belonging to the Chowanoc, situated about Gatesville, Gates co., N. C., in 1585.—Smith (1629), Va., I, map, repr. 1819.

**Catouinayos.** An unidentified village or tribe mentioned to Joutel in 1687 (Margry, Déc., III, 409, 1878), while he was staying with the Kadohadacho on Red r. of Louisiana, by the chief of that tribe as being among his enemies.

**Catróo.** Mentioned in 1598 as a pueblo of the Jemez (q.v.) Not identified with the present native name of any of the ruined pueblos in the vicinity of Jemez. Caatri.—Oñate (1598) in Doc. Inéd., XVI, 102, 1871. Catróo.—Ibid., 114.

**Catskill.** A division of the Munsee formerly living on Catskill cr., w. of the Hudson, in Greene co., N. Y. They were one of the Esopus tribes, and were known to the French as Mahingans (or Loups) of Taracton, but this name may have included other bands in that region. The name Catskill is Dutch, and was first applied to the stream as descriptive of the totem of the band, which was really the wolf. Catkils.—Salisbury (1678) in N. Y. Doc. Col. Hist., XIII, 524, 1881. Catskil.—Document of 1659(?), ibid., 119. Catskills.—Smith (1660), ibid., 161. Catskill.—Cregier (1663), ibid., 325. Katskil.—Lease of 1650, ibid., 26. Katskill.—Schuyler (1691), ibid., III, 801, 1853. Taracton.—Frontenac (1674), ibid., IX, 117, 1855. Taractou.—Ibid., 793. Taraktons.—Bruyas (1678), ibid., XIII, 523, 1881. Taraktons.—Brockholst (1678), ibid., 527.

**Cattachiptico.** A village of the Powhatan confederacy on Pamunkey r., in King William co., Va., in 1608.—Smith (1629), Va., I, map, repr. 1819.

**Cattahecassa.** See *Catahecassa*.

**Cattaraugus** (*Gä'-dä-gäns'-geon*, 'where oozed mud roils.'—Hewitt). A Seneca settlement on a branch of Cattaraugus cr., Cattaraugus co., N. Y. In 1903 there were 1,272 Seneca and 182 Cayuga and Onondaga on the reserve, which contains 21,680 acres, 14,800 of which are under cultivation. Cataraugos.—Genesee treaty (1797) in Hall, N. W. States, 74, 1849. Cattaragus.—Procter (1791) in Am. St. Pap., IV, 155, 1832. Cattaraugus.—Buffalo Creek treaty (1802) in Hall, N. W. States, 76, 1849. Catteranga.—Keane in Stanford, Compend., 535, 1878. Gä'-dä-gäns'-geon.—Hewitt, inf'n, 1886 (Seneca form). Gadä'gesgao.—Morgan, League Iroq., 466, 1851. Kä-'tä-rä'-kräⱣ.—Hewitt, inf'n, 1886 (Tuscarora form).

**Caucus.** This word, defined by Bartlett (Dict. of Americanisms, 106, 1877) as "a private meeting of the leading politicians of a party, to agree upon the plans to be pursued in an approaching election," and by Norton (Polit. Americanisms, 28, 1890) as "a meeting of partisans, congressional or otherwise, to decide upon the action to be taken by the party," has now a legal signification. In Massachusetts it is defined as "any public meeting of the voters of a ward of a city, or of a town, or of a representative district, held for the nomination of a candidate for election, for the election of a political committee, or of delegates to a political convention." The origin of the word is not clear. Trumbull (Trans. Am. Philol. Assoc.,

30, 1872) suggested a derivation from *caw-cawaassough*, a word in the Virginian dialect of Algonquian, perhaps identical with *cockarouse*. It signifies 'one who advises, urges, encourages, pushes on.' Related words in other Algonquian dialects are the Abnaki *kakesoman*, 'to encourage, incite, arouse, speak to,' and the Chippewa *gagansoma*. From *caucus*, which is used both as a noun and a verb, are derived *caucuser*, *caucusing*, etc. (A. F. C.)

**Caughnawaga** (*Gă-hnă-wă'-ge*, 'at the rapids'). An Iroquois settlement on the Sault St Louis on St Lawrence r., Quebec. When the hostility of the pagan Iroquois to the missions established in their territory frustrated the object of the French to attach the former to their interests, the Jesuits determined to draw their converts from the confederacy and to establish them in a new mission village near the French settlements on the St Lawrence, in accordance with which plan these Indians were finally induced to settle at La Prairie, near Montreal, in 1668. These converts were usually called "French Praying Indians" or "French Mohawks" by the English settlers, in contradistinction to the Iroquois who adhered to their own customs and to the English interests. In 1676 they were removed from this place to Sault St Louis, where Caughnawaga and the Jesuit mission of St François du Sault were founded. The village has been removed several times within a limited area. The majority of the emigrants came from the Oneida and Mohawk, and the Mohawk tongue, somewhat modified, became the speech of the whole body of this village. The Iroquois made several unsuccessful efforts to induce the converts to return to the confederacy, and finally renounced them in 1684, from which time Caughnawaga became an important auxiliary of the French in their wars with the English and the Iroquois. After the peace of Paris, in 1763, many of them left their village on the Sault St Louis and took up their residence in the valley of Ohio r., principally about Sandusky and Scioto rs., where they numbered 200 at the outbreak of the American Revolution. From their contact with the wilder tribes of that region many of them relapsed into paganism, although they still retained their French allegiance and maintained connection with their brethren on the St Lawrence. About 1755 a colony from Caughnawaga formed a new settlement at St Regis, some distance farther up the St Lawrence. As the fur traders pushed their way westward from the great lakes they were accompanied by Caughnawaga hunters. As early as 1820 a considerable number of this tribe was incorporated with the Salish, while others found their

way about the same period down to the mouth of Columbia r. in Oregon, and N. even as far as Peace r. in Athabasca. In the W. they are commonly known as Iroquois. Some of the Indians from St Regis also undertook these distant wanderings. In 1884 Caughnawaga had a population of 1,485, while St Regis (in Canada and New York) had about 2,075, and there were besides a considerable number from the 2 towns who were scattered throughout the W. In 1902 there were 2,017 on the Caughnawaga res. and 1,386 at St Regis, besides 1,208 on the St Regis reserve, N. Y. (J. N. B. H.)

Cagnawage.—Doc. of 1695 in N. Y. Doc. Col. Hist., IV, 120, 1854. Cagnawagees.—Johnson (1750), ibid., VI, 592, 1855. Cagnawauga.—Hawley (1794) in Mass. Hist. Soc. Coll., 1st s., IV, 51, 1795. Cagnawaugen.—Stevens (1749) in N. H. Hist. Soc. Coll., V, 204, 1837. Cagnawaugon.—Stevens (1749), ibid., 200. Cagnewage.—Doc. of 1695 in N. Y. Doc. Col. Hist., IV, 120, 1854. Cagnowages.—Schuyler (1724) quoted in Hist. Mag., 1st s., X, 115, 1866. Cagnuagas.—Oneida letter (1776) in N. Y. Doc. Col. Hist., VIII, 689, 1857. Cahgnawaga.—N. H. Hist. Soc. Coll., III, 104, 1832. Cahnawaas.—Colden (1727), Five Nat., 55, 1747. Cahnawaga.—Hoyt, Ant. Res., 194, 1824. Cahnuaga.—Barton, New Views, xl, 1798. Caknawage.—Lydius (1750) in N. Y. Doc. Col. Hist., VI, 569, 1855. Canawahrunas.—French trader (1764) quoted by Schoolcraft, Ind. Tribes, III, 553, 1853. Caughnawaga.—Johnson Hall conf. (1763) in N. Y. Doc. Col. Hist., VII, 553, 1856. Caughnawageys.—Doc. of 1763, ibid., 544. Caughnawanga.—Lloyd in Jour. Anthrop. Inst. G. B., IV, 44, 1875. Caughnewaga.—Schuyler (1689) quoted by Drake, Bk. Inds., I, 32, 1848. Caughnewago.—Smith (1799) quoted by Drake, Trag. Wild., 186, 1841. Caynawagas.—Knox (1792) in Am. St. Pap., IV, 235, 1832. Cochenawagoes.—Keane in Stanford, Compend., 509, 1878. Cochnawagah.—Stoddert (1750) in N. Y. Doc. Col. Hist., VI, 582, 1855. Cochnewagos.—Bouquet (1764) quoted by Kauffman, W. Penn., app., 156, 1851. Cochnewakee.—Barton, New Views, 8, app., 1798. Cochnowagoes.—Vater, Mith., pt. 3, sec. 3, 319, 1816. Cocknawagas.—Lindesay (1749) in N. Y. Doc. Col. Hist., VI, 538, 1855. Cocknawagees.—Johnson (1749), ibid., 525. Cocknewagos.—Clarke (1741), ibid., 207. Coehnawaghas.—Doc. of 1747, ibid., 620. Coghnawagees.—Johnson (1747), ibid., 359. Coghnawages.—Johnson (1755), ibid., 946. Coghnawagoes.—Johnson (1747), ibid., 362. Coghnawayees.—Johnson (1747), ibid., 359. Coghnewagoes.—Croghan (1765) quoted in Am. Jour. Geol., 272, 1831. Cognahwaghah.—Doc. of 1798 in Williams, Vt., II, 283, 1809. Cognawagees.—Johnson (1747) in N. Y. Doc. Col. Hist., VI, 359, 1855. Cognawago.—Peters (1760) in Mass. Hist. Soc. Coll., 4th s., IX, 270, 1871. Cohnawaga.—Washington (1796) in Am. St. Pap., IV, 585, 1832. Cohnawagey.—Johnson (1763) in N. Y. Doc. Col. Hist., VII, 542, 1856. Cohnawahgans.—Carver, Trav., 173, 1778. Cohnewago.—Eastburn (1758) quoted by Drake, Trag. Wild., 272, 1841. Cohnawagus.—Imlay, W. Ter., 291, 1797. Cohunnawgoes.—Macauley, N. Y., II, 187, 1829. Cohunnegagoes.—Thompson quoted by Jefferson, Notes, 282, 1825. Cohunnewagoes. — Bouquet (1764) quoted, ibid., 141. Conawaghrunas. — French trader quoted by Smith, Bouquet's Exped., 69, 1766. Conaway Crunas.—Buchanan, N. Am. Inds., 156, 1824. Conwahago.—Mercer (1759) quoted by Kauffman, W. Penn., 129, 1851. Coughnawagas.—Goldthwait (1766) in Mass. Hist. Soc. Coll., 1st s., X, 121, 1809. Cunniwagoes.—Croghan (1757) in N. Y. Doc. Col. Hist., VII, 285, 1856. French Mohawks.—Penhallow (1726) in N. H. Hist. Soc. Coll., I, 57, 1824. Iroquois du Sault.—Bacqueville de la Potherie, III, 67, 1753. Iroquois of the Sault.—La Barre (1684) in N. Y. Doc. Col. Hist., IX, 241, 1855. Jernaistes.—Doc. of 1694, ibid., IV, 92, 1854. Kachanuage. —Schuyler (1700), ibid., 747.

Kachanuge.—Livingston (1700), ibid., 695. **Kachnauage.** — Schuyler (1700), ibid., 747. **Kachnuage.**— Livingston (1700), ibid., 696. **Kagnawage.**—Freerman (1704), ibid., 1163. **Ka'hnráwage lúnuak.**—Gatschet, Penobscot MS., B. A. E., 1887 (Penobscot name). **Kahnuages.**—Douglass, Summ., I, 186, 1755. **Kanatakwenke.**—Cuoq, Lex., 163, 1882. **Kǎnǎwǎrkǎ.**—King, Arct. Ocean, I, 9, 1836. **Kannaogau.**—Bleeker (1701) in N. Y. Doc. Col. Hist., IV, 920, 1854. **Kannawagogh.**—Mercer (1759) quoted by Kauffman, W. Penn., 129, 1851. **Kanungé-ono.**—Gatschet, Seneca MS., B. A. E., 1882 (Seneca name). **Kaughnawaugas.**—Pickering (1794) in Am. St. Pap., IV, 546, 1832. **Konuaga.**—Colden (1724) in N. Y. Doc. Col. Hist., V, 732, 1855. **Osault St Louis.**—Stoddert (1750), ibid., VI, 582, 1855 (for au Sault St Louis, 'at St Louis fall'). **St François Xavier du Sault.**—Shea, Cath. Miss., 304, 1855. **Saint Peter's.**—Ibid., 270. **Sault Indians.**—Doc. of 1695 in N. Y. Doc. Col. Hist., IX, 629, 1855. **Saut Indians.**—Doc. of 1698, ibid., 686.

**Caughnawaga.** The ancient capital of the Mohawk tribe, situated in 1667 on Mohawk r., near the present site of Auriesville, N. Y. The Jesuits maintained there for a time the mission of St Pierre. The town was destroyed by the French in 1693.

**Asserué.**—Megapolensis (1644) quoted by Parkman, Jes., 222, note, 1883. **Cachanuage.**—Livingston (1691) in N. Y. Doc. Col. Hist., III, 782, 1853. **Cachenuage.**—Hansen (1700), ibid., IV, 803, 1854. **Cachnawage.**—Doc. of 1709, ibid., V, 85, 1855. **Cachnewagas.**—Bouquet (1764) quoted by Kauffman, W. Penn., 165, 1851. **Cachnewago.**—Bouquet, ibid. **Cachnuagas.**—Pownall (1754) in N. Y. Doc. Col. Hist., VI, 896, 1855. **Cacknawages.**—Clinton (1745), ibid., 276. **Cacnawagees.**—Fox (1756), ibid., VII, 77, 1856. **Caghnawagah.**—Butler (1750), ibid., VI, 591, 1855. **Caghnawagos.**—Croghan (1756) quoted by Kauffman, W. Penn, 116, 1851. **Caghnenewaga.**—Morse quoted by Barton, New Views, app., 8, 1798. **Caghnewagos.**—Thompson quoted by Jefferson, Notes, 282, 1825. **Caghnuage.**—Bleeker (1701) in N. Y. Doc. Col. Hist., IV, 895, 1854. **Cagnawaga.**—De Lancey (1754), ibid., VI, 909, 1855. **Canoomakers.**—Dutch map (1616), ibid., I, 1856 (m = w). **Gǎ-'hnǎ-wǎ'-ge.**—Hewitt, inf'n, 1886 (Mohawk form). **Gandaoüagué.**—Jes. Rel. for 1670, 23, 1858. **Gandaouaqué.**—Bacqueville de la Potherie, Hist. de l'Am. Sépt., I, 353, 1753. **Gandaougue.**—Ruttenber, Tribes Hudson R., 97, 1872. **Gandawagué.**—Shea, Cath. Miss., 216, 1855. **Ganeganaga.**—Morgan (1851) quoted by Parkman, Jesuits, 222, note, 1883. **Gannaouagué.**—De l'Isle (1718) in N. Y. Doc. Col. Hist., III, 250, 1853. **Ga-nó-wau-ga.**—Morgan, League Iroq., 419, 1855. **Kaghenewagé.**—Conf. of 1674 in N. Y. Doc. Col. Hist., II, 712, 1858. **Kaghnawage.**—Burnet (1726), ibid., V, 813, 1855. **Kaghnewage.**—Ruttenber, Tribes Hudson R., 283, 1872 (Dutch form). **Kaghnuwagé.**—N. Y. Doc. Col. Hist., III, 250, 1853. **Lower Mohawk castle.**—Ruttenber, Tribes Hudson R., 97, 1872. **Onengioure.**—Ruttenber, Tribes Hudson R., 283, 1872. **Oneugi8ré.**—Jes. Rél. for 1646, 15, 1858. **Onewyiure.**—Shea, Cath. Miss., 215, 1855. **Ossernenon.**—Jogues (1643) in N. Y. Doc. Col. Hist., XIII, 580, 1881 (misprint). **Osserrïon.**—Jes. Rel. for 1646, 15, 1858. **Osseruenon.**—Parkman, Jesuits, 222, note, 1883.

**Causac.** A former ranchería of the Sobaipuri, on the Rio San Pedro, s. Ariz., visited by Father Kino about 1697.—Doc. Hist. Mex., 4th s., I, 279, 1856.

**Cavate dwellings.** See *Cliff-dwellings.*

**Caves and Rock shelters.** The native tribes N. of Mexico have been cave-dwellers to a less extent, apparently, than were the primitive peoples of Europe, and there is no period in American prehistory which can be referred to as a "Cave period." Vast areas of limestone

rocks of varying age occur in the middle E. sections of the United States, in which there are countless caves, the great caverns of Virginia, Kentucky, Indiana, and Missouri being well-known examples; and caves also occur in many parts of the far W., especially in Arizona and California. It is observed that in general these caverns have existed for a long period, extending back well beyond the time when man is assumed to have appeared on the continent. Few of the caverns have been explored, save in a most superficial manner, and as a rule where serious work has been undertaken the finds have been such as to discourage investigation by archeologists—not that meager traces of man are encountered, but because the osseous remains and works of art found represent the Indian tribes merely. The substrata of the cavern floors, which would naturally contain traces of very early occupants, are apparently barren of human remains, a condition that is difficult to understand if, as some suppose, the continent was occupied by man throughout all post-Tertiary time. Human remains occur along with the fossil fauna of the present period, but are not with certainty associated as original deposits with the older forms. Very considerable age is indicated, however, by the condition of the human bones, some of which, found in California caves, seem to be completely fossilized, the animal matter having disappeared, while in Arkansas and elsewhere the bones are deeply embedded in deposits of stalagmite. The length of time required for fossilization is not well known, however, and calcareous accumulations may be slow or rapid, so that these phenomena have no very definite value in determining age.

The American caves were occupied by the aborigines for a number of purposes, including burial, ceremony, and refuge. In a few cases chert, outcropping in the walls, was quarried for the manufacture of implements. Generally only the outer and more accessible chambers of deep caverns were occupied as dwelling places, and in these evidence of occupancy is often abundant. The floors are covered with deposits of ashes, in which are embedded various implements and utensils and the refuse of feasting, very much as with ordinary dwelling sites. The deeper chambers were sometimes used as temporary retreats in time

SECTION OF CAVERN

of danger and for the performance of religious rites. In numerous cases deposits of sacrificial offerings are found, and the walls are covered with symbolic or other paintings or engravings. The Zuñi employ caverns as shrines and as depositories for images of their gods and the painted bones of animals, and caves have an important place in the genesis myths of many tribes. Burial in caves was common, and chambers of various depths from the surface were used. Pits and crevices in the rocks were also repositories for the dead.

Far better adapted to man's use as dwellings than the deep caves are the rock recesses or shelters which owe their origin not to the action of underground waters, but to undercutting by the waters of the sea or lakes and ordinary streams or to disintegration of portions of steep rock faces aided by wind action. These recesses often have somewhat level floors and arched roofs, formed by hard layers of rock, which expand toward the front, thus forming roomy and well-lighted dwelling places. They are nowhere so numerous as in the plateau region of the Colorado and Rio Grande valleys, where the well-exposed rock faces in a multitude of cases are deeply undercut by the gnawing agencies of disintegration aided by the winds. In this region man was not content with the natural shelters so abundantly furnished, but the recesses were enlarged, and in places where the rock was massive and easily worked great numbers of chambers were excavated for dwellings. See *Archeology, Antiquity, Cliff-dwellings.*

SECTION OF ROCK SHELTER

Consult Andrews in 11th Rep. Peabody Mus., 1878; Dall (1) in Cont. N. A. Ethnol., I, 1877, (2) in Smithson. Cont., XXII, 1878; Haywood, Nat. and Aborig. Hist. Tenn., 1823; Holmes in Am. Anthrop., III, no. 3, 1890; Jones in Smithson. Cont., XXII, 1876; Mercer (1) in Jour. Acad. Nat. Sci. Phila., XI, pt 2, 1896; (2) in Proc. Am. Philos. Soc., XXXIV, no. 149, 1895; (3) in Pubs. Univ. Pa., VI, 1897; Mitchell in Trans. Am. Antiq. Soc., I, 1820; Palmer in 11th Rep. Peabody Mus., 1878; Peabody in Am. Anthrop., VII, no. 3, 1905; Peabody and Moorehead, Bull. 1, Dept. Archæol., Phillips Acad., 1904; Putnam in Peabody Mus. Reps.; Sinclair in Univ. Cal. Publ., Am. Archæol. and Ethnol., II, no. 1, 1904; Stevenson in 23d Rep. B. A. E., 1905; Yarrow in 1st Rep. B. A. E., 1881.
(W. H. H.)

**Cawasumseuck.** Given by Williams in 1643 as the name by which some tribe, settlement, or band of New England Indians called themselves (Mass. Hist. Soc. Coll., 1st s., III, 205, 1794). To what Indians he refers is unknown, but it is possibly to some then living on Cawsumsett Neck, near Pawtucket r., R. I.

**Cawruuoc.** A village in 1585, perhaps belonging to the Neusiok, and seemingly situated on the N. side of Neuse r., in the present Craven co., N. C.
Cawruuoc.—Smith (1629), Va., I, map, repr. 1819. Cwarenuock.—Dutch map (1621) in N. Y. Doc. Col. Hist., I, 1856.

**Cawwontoll.**—A village of the Powhatan confederacy in 1608, on the N. bank of the Rappahannock, in Richmond co., Va.—Smith (1629), Va., I, map, repr. 1819.

**Cayahasomi.** The Partridge clan of the Acheha phratry of the ancient Timucua tribe of Florida. — Pareja (*ca.* 1612) quoted by Gatschet in Proc. Am. Philos. Soc., XVII, 492, 1878.

**Cayahoga** (*Kaya'ha'ge'*, 'the fork of the stream.'—Hewitt). A village, perhaps belonging to the Wyandot, formerly situated on the N. E. side of Cuyahoga r., near Akron, Ohio.
Cajocka.—Stoddart (1753) in N. Y. Doc. Col. Hist., VI, 779, 1855. Cajuhaga.—Clinton (1750), ibid., 548. Caniahaga.—Albany conf. (1751), ibid., 720. Cauahogué.—Esnauts and Rapilly, map, 1777. Cayahagah.—Lindesay (1751) in N. Y. Doc. Col. Hist., VI, 706, 1855. Cayahoga.—Hutchins, map (1764) in Smith, Boquet Exped., 1766. Cwahago.—Esnauts and Rapilly, map, 1777. Gwahago.—Lotter, map, *ca.* 1770. Kaya'ha'ge'.—Hewitt, inf'n, 1903. Kichaga.—Doc. of 1747 in N. Y. Doc. Col. Hist., VI, 391, 1855. Kyahagah.—Lindesay (1751), ibid., 706.

**Cayas.** A tribe visited by the De Soto expedition in 1542, apparently in w. Arkansas. Schoolcraft's identification of the name with Kansa is of very doubtful value.
Cayas.—Ranjel (1543) in Smith, Col. Doc. Fla., I, 60, 1857. Cayase.—Ranjel (1543) quoted by Bourne, Narr. De Soto, II, 147, 1904.

**Cayeguas.** A former Chumashan village on the Cayeguas ranch, Ventura co., Cal.
Cayeguas.—Taylor in Cal. Farmer, July 24, 1863. Cayuguis.—Ibid., May 4, 1860 (located at Punta Alamo). Ka-yö'-wöc.—Henshaw, Buenaventura vocab., B. A. E., 1884 (c=sh).

**Caymus.** A former Yukian Wappo village on the site of the present Yountville, in Napa valley, Cal. (s. A. B.)
Caymas.—Bartlett, Pers. Narr., II, 20–21, 1854. Caymus.—Revere, Tour of Duty, 91–93, 1849.

**Cayomulgi.** An ancient Upper Creek town on a stream which joins Coosa r. at Coussa (Kusa) town, Ala. Possibly for Okmulgee, an ancient Creek town in E. Georgia.
Cayomugi.—Bartram, Voy., I, map, 1799. Cayomulgi.—Philippeaux, map of Engl. Col., 1781.

**Cayoosh Creek.** A local name for two bodies of Upper Lillooet Indians of Salishan stock near the junction of Bridge and Fraser rs., Brit. Col. Population of

one of the bodies in 1902, 34; of the other, also called Pashilqua, 15.—Can. Ind. Aff. for 1901, pt. II, 72.
**Cayoush.**—Survey map, Hydr. Office, U. S. N., 1882. **Kayuse Creek.**—Can. Ind. Aff. for 1878, 74. **Pashilquia.**—Can. Ind. Aff. for 1891, 251. **Pashilqua.**—Ibid., 1884, 190.

**Cayovea.** A Calusa village on the s. w. coast of Florida, about 1570.—Fontaneda Memoir (*ca.* 1575), Smith trans., 19, 1854.

**Cayuga** (*Kwĕñio'gwĕnᶜ*, 'the place where locusts were taken out.'—Hewitt). A tribe of the Iroquois confederation, formerly occupying the shores of Cayuga lake, N. Y. Its local council was composed of 4 clan phratries, and this form became the pattern, tradition says, of that of the confederation of the Five

CAYUGA.    (HOJIAGEDE, FISH-CARRIER)

Nations of the Iroquois, in which the Cayuga had 10 delegates. In 1660 they were estimated to number 1,500, and in 1778, 1,100. At the beginning of the American Revolution a large part of the tribe removed to Canada and never returned, while the rest were scattered among the other tribes of the confederacy. Soon after the Revolution these latter sold their lands in New York; some went to Ohio, where they joined other Iroquois and became known as the Seneca of the Sandusky. These are now in Indian Ter.; others are with the Oneida in Wisconsin; 175 are with the Iroquois still in New York, while the majority, numbering 700 or 800, are on the Grand River

res., Ontario. In 1670 they had three villages—Goiogouen, Kiohero, and Onnontare. Gayagaanha was their chief village in modern times. Their other villages of the modern period according to Morgan, were Ganogeh, Gewauga, and Neodakheat. Others were Chonodote, Gandaseteiagon, Kawauka, Kente, Nuquiage, Ondachoe, Owego, Onugareclury, St Joseph, Sannio, Skannayutenate, and Swahyawanah. Their clans were those common to the Iroquois. (J. M. J. N. B. H.)
**Caeŭjes.**—Andros (1690) in N.Y. Doc. Col. Hist., III, 722, 1853. **Căhŭgăs.**—Marshe (1744) in Mass. Hist. Soc. Coll., 1st s., VII, 189, 1801. **Caijougas.**—Ft Johnson conf. (1756) in N. Y. Doc. Col. Hist., VII, 55, 1856. **Caijouges.**—Wessels (1693), ibid., IV, 60, 1854. **Caiouga.**—Greenhalgh (1677) quoted by Conover, Kanadaga and Geneva MS., B. A. E. **Caiougues.**—Livingston (1698) in N. Y. Doc. Col. Hist., IV, 342, 1854. **Caiougos.**—Greenhalgh (1677), ibid., III, 251, 1853. **Caiuges.**—Andros (1690) in R. I. Col. Rec., III, 281, 1858. **Caiyougas.**—Ft Johnson conf. (1756) in N. Y. Doc. Col. Hist., VII, 67, 1856. **Cajoegers.**—Dellius (1697), ibid., IV, 279, 1854. **Cajougas.**—Wessels (1698), ibid., 372. **Cajouges.**—Maryland treaty (1682), ibid., III, 323, 1853. **Cajugas.**—Weiser (1748) quoted by Kauffman, W. Penn., app., 22, 1851. **Cajuger.**—Schuyler (1699) in N. Y. Doc. Col. Hist., IV, 563, 1854. **Cajuges.**—Ibid. **Cajugu.**—Barton, New Views, app., 7, 1798. **Cajukas.**—Weiser (1748) quoted by Kauffman, W. Penn., app., 22, 1851. **Cajyougas.**—Johnson Hall conf. (1765) in N. Y. Doc. Col. Hist., VII, 724, 1856. **Cajyugas.**—Ibid., 719. **Caujuckos.**—Weiser (1736) quoted by Schoolcraft, Ind. Tribes, IV, 339, 1854. **Cayagas.**—Crepy, map, *ca.* 1755. **Cayagoes.**—Bellomont (1698) in N. Y. Doc. Col. Hist., IV, 370, 1854. **Cayauga.**—Ft Johnson conf. (1756), ibid., VII, 186, 1856. **Cayauge.**—Livingston (1700), ibid., IV, 650, 1854. **Caycuges.**—Albany conf. (1737), ibid., VI, 99, 1855. **Cayeuges.**—Albany conf. (1744), ibid., 262. **Cayeugoes.**—Ingoldsby (1691), ibid., III, 797, 1853. **Cayhuga.**—Guy Park conf. (1775), ibid., VIII, 534, 1857. **Caynga.**—La Tour, map, 1779 (misprint). **Cayogas.**—Phelps deed (1788) in Am. St. Pap., IV, 210, 1832. **Cayonges.**—Penhallow (1726) in N. H. Hist. Soc. Coll., I, 41, 1824. **Cayoogoes.**—Conestoga treaty (1721) in Proud, Penn., II, 132, 1798. **Cayougas.**—Hunter (1714) in N. Y. Doc. Col. Hist., V, 384, 1855. **Cayouges.**—Doc. of 1684, ibid., III, 347, 1853. **Cayougues.**—Doc. of 1688, ibid., 548. **Cayounges.**—Teller (1698), ibid., IV, 352, 1854. **Cayowges.**—Bellomont (1698), ibid., 369. **Cayuaga.**—Doc. of 1792 in Mass. Hist. Soc. Coll., 1st s., I, 285, 1806. **Cayugas.**—Doc. of 1676 in N. Y. Doc. Col. Hist., XIII, 500, 1881. **Cayuges.**—Albany conf. (1737), ibid., VI, 103, 1855. **Cayukers.**—Barton, New Views, app., 7, 1798. **Cayungas.**—Vetch (1719) in N. Y. Doc. Col. Hist., V, 531, 1855. **Chingas.**—Albany conf. (1751), ibid., VI, 719, 1855 (misprint). **Chiugas.**—Dwight and Partridge (1754) in Mass. Hist. Soc. Coll., 1st s., V, 120, 1816. **Chuijugers.**—Dongan (1688) in N. Y. Doc. Col. Hist., III, 532, 1853. **Coiejues.**—Vaillant (1688), ibid., 527. **Coiejues.**—Leisler (1690), ibid., 732. **Cojages.**—Maryland treaty (1682), ibid., 321. **Cojoges.**—Goldthwait (1766) in Mass. Hist. Soc. Coll., 1st s., X, 121, 1809. **Coujougas.**—Albany conf. (1746) in N. Y. Doc. Col. Hist., VI, 317, 1855. **Coyougers.**—Jamison (1697), ibid., IV, 294, 1854. **Coyouges.**—Doc. *ca.* 1700 in Hist. Mag., 2d s., I, 300, 1867. **Cuiukguos.**—Drake, Bk. Inds., V, 4, 1848. **Cuyahuga.**—Iroquois deed (1789) in Am. St. Pap., IV, 211, 1832. **Gacheos.**—Proud, Penn., II, 295, 1798. **Gachoi.**—Map of 1616 in N. Y. Doc. Col. Hist., I, 1856. **Gachoos.**—Map, *ca.* 1614, ibid. **Gachpas.**—Loskiel, Miss. Unit. Breth., pt. 3, 16, 1794. **Gaiuckers.**—Weiser (1736) quoted by Schoolcraft, Ind. Tribes, IV, 332, 1854. **Gajuka.**—Zeisberger (1750) quoted by Conover, Kanadaga and Geneva MS., B. A. E. (German form). **Gajuquas.**—Barton, New Views, app., 7, 1798. **Gakaos.**—Boudinot, Star in the West, 126,

1816. **Gä-u'-gweh.**—Morgan, League Iroq., 159, 1851. **Gayuga.**—Pyrlæus (*ca.* 1750) quoted in Am. Antiq., IV, 75, 1881. **Gogouins.**—Chauvignerie (1736) quoted by Schoolcraft, Ind. Tribes, III 555, 1853. **Goiogoüens.**—Jes. Rel. for 1670, 75, 1858. **Goiogouioronons.**—Courcelles (*ca.* 1670) in Margry, Déc., I, 178, 1875. **Gojogoüen.**—Jes. Rel. for 1671, 3, 1858. **Gooiogouen.**—Lotter, map, *ca.* 1770. **Goyagouins.**—Bacqueville de la Potherie, Hist. Am., III, 3, 1753. **Goyogans.**—La Hontan (1703) quoted by Vater, Mith., pt. 3, sec. 3, 313, 1816. **Goyogoans.**—La Hontan, New Voy., I, map, 1703. **Goyogoin.**—Pouchot (1758) in N. Y. Doc. Col. Hist., X, 694, 1858. **Goyogouans.**—La Hontan, New Voy., I, 39, 1703. **Goyogouens.**—Louis XIV (1699) in N. Y. Doc. Col. Hist., IX, 698, 1855. **Goyogoüin.**—Bacqueville de la Potherie, Hist. Am., III, 27, 1753. **Goyoguans.**—La Hontan, New Voy., I, 231, 1703. **Goyoguen.**—Bellin, map, 1755. **Goyoguin.**—Jes. Rel., III, index, 1858. **Goyoguoain.**—Denonville (1685) in N. Y. Doc. Col. Hist., IX, 282, 1855. **Go-yo-gwĕⁿ'.**—Hewitt, MS. Mohawk vocab., B. A. E., 1882 (Mohawk name). **Guigouins.**—Jefferys, Fr. Dom., pt. 1, 117, 1761. **Gwaugueh.**—Morgan, League Iroq., map, 1851. **Gwe-u-gweh-o-no'.**—Ibid., 51 ('people of the mucky land': own name). **Honosuguaχtu-wáne.**—Gatschet, Seneca MS., B. A. E., 1882 ('big pipes': Seneca ceremonial name). **Kanáwa.**—Gatschet, Shawnee MS., B. A. E., 1879 (Shawnee name). **Kayowgaws.**—Homann Heirs' map, 1756. **Kayúgue-ónoⁿ.**—Gatschet, Seneca MS., B. A. E., 1882 (Seneca name). **Kei-u-gues.**—Dudley (1721) in Mass. Hist. Soc. Coll., 2d s., VIII, 244, 1819. **Ko-'se-a-ʒe'-nyoⁿ.**—Hewitt, Cayuga MS. vocab., B. A. E., 1884 (another Cayuga name). **Ko-yo-konk-ha-ka.**—Hewitt, Mohawk MS. vocab., B. A. E., 1882 (a Mohawk name). **Kuenyúgu-háka.**—Gatschet, Tuscarora MS., B. A. E., 1882 ('Tuscarora name). **Kuyúku-hága.**—Gatschet, Mohawk MS., B. A. E., 1879 (Mohawk name). **Oïogoen.**—Jes. Rel. for 1656, 20, 1858. **Oiogoenhronnons.**—Ibid., 29. **Oïogouan.**—Jes. Rel. for 1657, 15, 1858. **Oiogouanronnon.**—Ibid. **Oiogouen.**—La Salle (1679) in Margry, Déc., I, 504, 1875. **Oïogouenronnon.**—Jes. Rel. for 1657, 18, 1858. **Oiogouin.**—La Barre (1683) in Margry, Déc., II, 330, 1877. **Oiougovenes.**—Barcia, Ensayo, 225, 1723. **Ojongoveres.**—Ibid., 220. **Onionenhronnons.**—Jes. Rel. for 1653 (misprint). **Oniouenhronon.**—Jes. Rel. for 1640, 35, 1858 (misprint). **Orongouens.**—Hennepin, Cont. of New Disc., 93, 1698. **Oüioenrhonons.**—Jes. Rel. for 1635, 34, 1858. **Ouiouenronnons.**—Jes. Rel. for 1647, 46, 1858. **Oyogouins.**—La Barre (1683) in Margry, Déc., II, 332, 1877. **Petuneurs.**—Greenhalgh (1677) in N. Y. Doc. Col. Hist., III, 252, 1853 (French name). **Queyugwe.**—Macauley, N. Y., II, 176, 1829. **Queyugwehaughga.**—Ibid., 185. **Quingoes.**—Coursey (1682) in N. Y. Doc. Col. Hist., XIII, 558, 1881 (misprint). **Quiquogas.**—Stone, Life of Brant, I, 401, 1864. **Quiuquuhs.**—Edwards (1751) in Mass. Hist. Soc. Coll., 1st s., X, 146, 1809. **Sanonawantowane.**—Gatschet in Am. Antiq., IV, 75, 1881. **Shoneanawetowah.**—Macauley, N. Y., II, 185, 1829. **Shononowendos.**—Ibid. **S'ho-ti-noñ-nă-wäⁿ-tŏ'-nă.**—Hewitt, from Tuscarora informant, 1886 ('they are great pipes': council name). **So-nus'-ho-gwä-to-war.**—Morgan, League Iroq., 423, 1851 ('great pipe': council name). **Soon-noo-daugh-we-no-wenda.**—Macauley, N. Y., II, 185, 1829.

**Cayuse.** A Waiilatpuan tribe formerly occupying the territory about the heads of Wallawalla, Umatilla, and Grande Ronde rs. and from the Blue mts. to Deschutes r. in Washington and Oregon. The tribe has always been closely associated with the neighboring Nez Percés and Wallawalla, and was regarded by the early explorers and writers as belonging to the same stock. So far as the available evidence goes, however, they must be considered linguistically independent. The Cayuse have always been noted for their bravery, and owing largely to their constant struggles with the Snake and other tribes, have been numerically weak. According to Gibbs there were few pure-blood Cayuse left in 1851, intermarriage, particularly with the Nez Percés, having been so prevalent that even the language was falling into disuse. In 1855 the Cayuse joined in the treaty by which the Umatilla res. was formed, and since that time have resided within its limits. Their number is officially reported as 404 in 1904; but this figure is misleading,

CAYUSE. (PAUL SHOWEWAY, CHIEF)

as careful inquiry in 1902 failed to discover a single one of pure blood on the reservation and the language is practically extinct. The tribe acquired wide notoriety in the early days of the white settlement of the territory. In 1838 a mission was established among the Cayuse by Marcus Whitman at the site of the present town of Whitman, Wallawalla co., Wash. In 1847 smallpox carried off a large part of the tribe. The Cayuse, believing the missionaries to be the cause, attacked them, murdered Whitman and a number of others, and destroyed the mission. Owing to the confusion in the early accounts it is difficult to differentiate the Cayuse from the Nez Percés and Wallawalla, but there is no reason to suppose that in habits and customs they differed markedly from those tribes.       (L. F.)

**Caäguas.**—Palmer, Trav. Rocky Mts., 53, 1852. **Cailloux.**—Hale, Ethnog. and Philol., 214, 1846. **Cajouses.**—Ross, Advent., 127, 1849. **Cayoose.**—

Scouler in Jour. Ethnol. Soc. Lond., I, 237, 1848. **Cayouses.**—Wyeth (1848) in Schoolcraft, Ind. Tribes, I, 221, 1851. **Cayoux.**—Grant in Jour. Roy. Geog. Soc., 211, 1861. **Cayús.**—Latham in Trans. Philol. Soc. Lond., 74, 1856. **Cayuse.**—Parker, Jour., 131, 1840. **Conguses.**—Cain in Ind. Aff. Rep. 1855, 193, 1856. **Cuyuse.**—Stevens, Life of I. I. Stevens, II, 36, 1901. **Cyuse.**—Brown in Proc. Roy. Geog. Soc., 90, 1867. **Haí'luntchi.**—Gatschet, Mollalla MS., 27, B. A. E. (Molalla name). **Hains.**—Whitman in Mowry, Marcus Whitman, 272, 1901. **Kagouse.**—Dunn, Oregon, 218, 1845. **Kaijous.**—Smet, Letters, 230, 1843. **Kayouse.**—Townsend, Narr., 245, 1889. **Kayul.**—Coke, Ride over Rocky Mts., 305, 1852. **Kayuses.**—Smet, Letters, 220, 1843. **Kayuxes.**—Coke, op. cit., 282. **Keyuses.**—White in Ind. Aff. Rep., 450, 1843. **Kieoux.**—Meek in H. R. Ex. Doc. **76**, 30th Cong. 1st sess., 10, 1848. **Kinse.**—Lee and Frost, Oregon, 163, 1844. **Kioose.**—Palmer, Trav. Rocky Mts., 53, note, 1852. **Kiuses.**—Wilkes, Hist. Oregon, 92, 1845. **Kiwaw.**—Palmer, Trav. Rocky Mts., 53, note, 1852. **Kiyuse.**—Wilkes, Hist. Oregon, 44, 1845. **Kye-use.**—Kane, Wand. of an Artist, 280, 1859. **Kyoose.**—Lord, Natur. in Brit. Col., 245, 1866. **Nez Perce Kayuses.**—Smet, Oregon Miss., 104, 1847. **Rayouse.**—Gairdner (1835) in Jour. Geog. Soc. Lond., XI, 257, 1841 (misprint). **Skiuses.**—Wyeth, Corresp. and Jour., 142, 1899. **Skynses.**—Irving, Bonneville's Advent., 300, 1850. **Skyuse.**—Farnham, Trav. W. Prairies, 81, 1843. **Wailatpu.**—Hale, Ethnog. and Philol., 214, 1846. **Wailatpu.**—Gibbs in Pac. R. R. Rep., I, 416, 1855. **Waĭ'lĕtma.**—Mooney in 14th Rep. B. A. E., 744, 1896 (Yakima name.) **Wailĕtpu.**—Ibid. (own name). **Waillatpus.**—Armstrong, Oregon, 112, 1857. **Waitlat-pu.**—Stevens in Ind. Aff. Rep., 252, 1854. **Waulapta.**—Dart in Ind. Aff. Rep., 476, 1851. **Waulatpas.**—Ibid., 216. **Waulatpus.**—Lane (1850) in Schoolcraft, Ind. Tribes, III, 632, 1853. **Wi'alĕtpûm.**—Mooney in 14th Rep. B. A. E., 744, 1896 (another Yakima name). **Willetpos.**—Lewis and Clark, Exped., II, 309, 1814. **Wy-eilat.**—Lord, Natur. in Brit. Col., 245, 1866. **Yeletpo.**—Lewis and Clark, Exped., II, 471, 1814.

**Cayuse.** An Indian pony; from the name of a Waiilatpuan tribe. The horses, after the Indians had come into contact with the whites, were bred by the Cayuse, and from a merely local use the word has attained an extended currency in the N. w. Pacific states.                (A. F. C.)

**Cazazhita** (said to mean 'bad arrowpoints,' and so, perhaps, from *kaza* 'to pick to pieces,' *shicha* 'bad'; but arrowpoint is *waⁿhiⁿ*). A Dakota division, under chief Shonka, or Dog; probably a part of the Teton, or perhaps the same as Broken Arrows and Wannawega.
**Ca-za-zhee-ta.**—Catlin, N. A. Inds., I, 233, 1844.

**Cazopo.** A former village, presumably Costanoan, connected with Dolores mission, San Francisco, Cal.—Taylor in Cal. Farmer, Oct. 18, 1861.

**Cebolleta** (Span.: 'tender onion'). A place on Pojuate r., in the N. E. corner of Valencia co., N. Mex., at which, in 1746, a temporary settlement of 400 or 500 Navaho was made by Father Juan M. Menchero. A mission was established there in 1749, but in the following year the Navaho grew tired of sedentary life, and Cebolleta, together with Encinal, which was established at the same time, was abandoned. In 1804 a request from the Navaho to resettle at Cebolleta was refused by the Spanish authorities. It is now a white Mexican town. Cebolleta

mtn. and the Cebolleta land grant take their name from the settlement.
                (F. W. H. )
**Ceballeta.**—Hughes, Doniphan's Exped., 126, 1848. **Cebellitita.**—Parke, map New Mexico, 1851. **Ceboleta.**—Hughes, Doniphan's Exped., map, 1848. **Cebolleta.**—Ibid., 146. **Cebolletta.**—Buschmann, Neu-Mexico, 247, 1858 (misquoting Abert). **Cevolleta.**—Brevoort, New Mexico, 22, 1874. **Cevolleto.**—Domenech, Deserts of N. A., II, 7, 1860. **Cibaleta.**—Buschmann, Neu-Mexico, 247, 1858. **Cibaletta.**—Ibid., 247. **Ciboletta.**—Am. Ethnol. Soc. Trans., II, map, 1848. **Cibolleta.**—Abert in Emory, Reconnoissance, 468, 1848. **Cibolletta.**—Ibid., 465; Johnston, ibid., 589. **Seboyeta.**—U. S. Land Off. map, 1903. **Sevolleta.**—Cortez (1799) in Pac. R. R. Rep., III, pt. 3, 119, 1856. **Sibolletta.**—Folsom, Mexico, map, 1842.

**Ceca.** Mentioned by Oñate (Doc. Inéd., XVI, 114, 1871) as a pueblo of the Jemez in New Mexico in 1598. The name can not be identified with the present native name of any ruined settlement in the vicinity. **Leeca.**—Oñate, op. cit., 102.

**Celts.** Ungrooved axes or hatchets of stone, metal, or other hard material. It is uncertain whether the name is de-

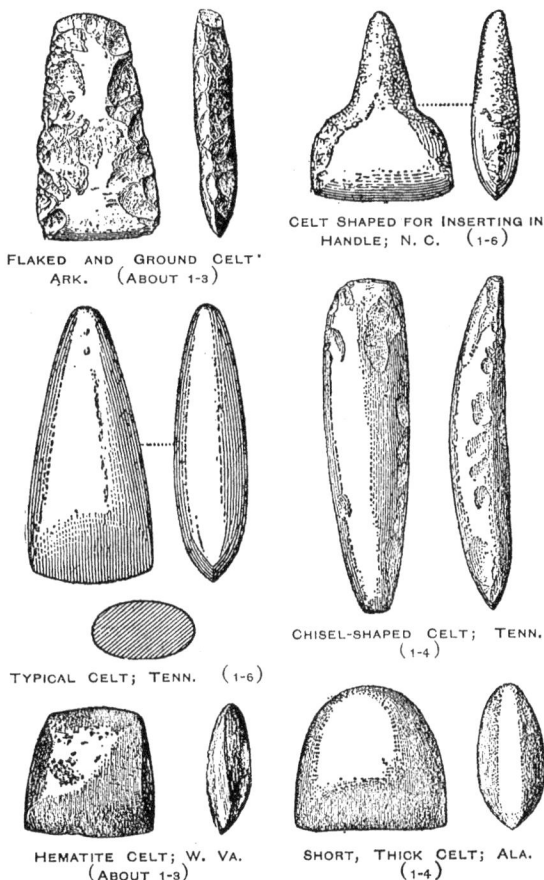

FLAKED AND GROUND CELT; ARK. (ABOUT 1-3)

CELT SHAPED FOR INSERTING IN HANDLE; N. C. (1-6)

TYPICAL CELT; TENN. (1-6)

CHISEL-SHAPED CELT; TENN. (1-4)

HEMATITE CELT; W. VA. (ABOUT 1-3)

SHORT, THICK CELT; ALA. (1-4)

rived from the Latin *celtis*, 'chisel,' to which the implement bears some resemblance, or from the Welsh *cellt*, 'a flint stone.' The celts range in weight from less than half an ounce to more than 20 pounds, while the diversity of form is very great. Their distribution is more general than that of the grooved ax. The primary purpose was probably that of a hatchet, but in one shape or another they served as adzes, chisels, scrapers, skinning knives, meat cutters, and weapons. Many have the surface roughened by pecking at the top, which was inserted in a cavity cut in a wooden club and secured with gum or glue; in others, this roughening was around the middle, to give a firmer grip to a withe handle; still others, wrapped perhaps in a piece of buckskin or some such substance to prevent slipping, were held in the hand. Some specimens were set in the end of a short piece of bone or antler, which, in turn, acting as a buffer, was attached to a handle of wood in the fashion of a hatchet, an adz, or a plane. The smallest specimens, especially those made of hematite, which usually have the scraper-form edge, were similarly set in the end of a longer piece of bone or antler, and used as knives or scrapers. Celts, in their various patterns, were among the most important implements known to primitive man.

Celts made of flint, jasper, and other brittle stone are shaped mainly by flaking. In most, the edge is more or less sharpened by grinding, and sometimes the entire implement is partially smoothed in the same way. They are common along the Atlantic coast, where argillite and rhyolite are easily procured; and the same is true of the Kanawha valley, where the black flint outcrops so abundantly. Along the Mississippi r., in Arkansas and Mississippi, are found numerous specimens which have been chipped from yellow jasper and then ground until the angles formed by the facets are nearly obliterated and the lower part of the blade attains a high degree of polish. These are mostly small, and approach more closely the European celts with rectangular section than any others found in America. They are sometimes classed with chisels. See *Adzes, Axes, Chisels, Copper, Hatchets, Stone-work, Tomahawks.*

Celts are described or briefly referred to and illustrated in numerous works on archeologic subjects. Among these are Abbott, Prim. Indus., 1881; Fowke (1) Archæol. Hist. Ohio, 1902, (2) in 13th Rep. B. A. E., 1896; Holmes in 15th Rep. B. A. E., 1897; Jones, Antiq. So. Inds., 1873; Moore, various memoirs in Jour. Acad. Nat. Sci. Phila., 1894–1905; Moorehead, Prehist. Impls., 1900; Rau in Smithson. Cont., XXII, 1876; Thruston, Antiq. Tenn., 1897.                    (G. F.    W. H. H.)

**Cements.**—The Indians used cements of animal, vegetal, and mineral origin, and sometimes combined two of these or added mineral substances for coloring. Animal cement was obtained by the Yokuts of California by boiling the joints of various animals and combining the product with pitch (Powers, Tribes of Cal., 373, 1877). The Hupa boiled the gland of the lower jaw and nose of the sturgeon and dried the products in balls (Ray in Smithson. Rep., 229, 1886). Capt. John Smith states that with sinew of deer and the tops of deer horns boiled to a jelly the Virginia Indians made glue that would not dissolve in cold water. The Plains tribes boiled the skin of the head of animals until it was softened into glue, which they dried in masses on sticks. Such glue-sticks formed a part of the equipment of the bow-and-arrow maker, and the horn arrow-straighteners of the S. W. tribes are often filled with resin. Sometimes one end of the hearth of the fire-drill bears a mass of resin, as a convenient way to carry this substance, which may readily be melted at the fire and applied to various uses. Wax and albumen from eggs had a limited use, and the Eskimo used blood mixed with soot. The chief use of animal cement was in the manufacture of bows and arrows, and, among the Plains tribes, in joining the stems of certain kinds of pipes. The only mineral cement known to the tribes was bitumen, which was used by the Indians of s. Arizona and California. Vegetal cements were numerous, and chief among these was the exudation from coniferous trees, employed by northern tribes for pitching the seams of bark canoes, baskets, etc.; by S. W. tribes for rendering basketry, water vessels, and the like water tight; by the Hopi for varnishing pottery, and by many tribes for mending, joining, inlaying, etc. The tribes of the S. W. made a strong cement of the gum resin of the mesquite and the gum of the greasewood, which was used to set the heads of arrows and for many other purposes. The Pima made a strong cement from a gum of parasitic origin on the *Covillea tridentata.* The Indians of Mendocino co., Cal., made a glue from the bulb of the soap plant (*Chlorogalum pomeridianum*) for fastening feathers on arrows.                    (W. H.)

**Cenyowpreskel.** A former village of either the Diegueños or Luiseños in the neighborhood of San Luis Rey mission, s. Cal.—Taylor in Cal. Farmer, May 11, 1860.

**Cepowig.** A village in 1608, perhaps belonging to the Conestoga, located by Guss in or near York co., Pa.—Smith (1629), Va., I, map, 1819.

**Ceremonials.** See *Problematical objects.*

**Ceremony.** A ceremony is the performance in a prescribed order of a series of formal acts often constituting a drama which has an ultimate object. Ceremonies spring from many diverse tendencies, which are the expression of some phase of religious emotion. Many features of the culture of the North American

Indians are regarded as ceremonies, such as the rites which pertain to birth, puberty, marriage, death, war, etc., but in the arbitrarily restricted sense in which the term is here used a ceremony is understood to be a religious performance of at least one day's duration. These ceremonies generally refer to one or the other of the solstices, to the germination or ripening of a crop, or to the most important food supply. There are ceremonies of less importance that are connected with the practices of medicine-men or are the property of cult societies. Ceremonies may be divided into those in which the whole tribe participates and those which are the exclusive property of a society, generally a secret one, or of a group of men of special rank, such as chiefs or medicine-men, or of an individual. Practically all ceremonies of extended duration contain many rites in common. An examination of these rites, as they are successively performed, reveals the fact that they follow one another in prescribed order, as do the events or episodes of the ritual.

The ritual, or that part of the ceremony which is spoken or sung, predominates among some tribes, as the Pawnee; among others, as the Hopi, it is greatly subordinated to the drama.

In enumerating the rites of the ceremonies it may be noted, first, that they may be divided into secret and public, the secret rites being proprietary, and, as a rule, occupying the major part of the time of the ceremony. The rites of the public performance may be considered as the actual play or drama. The secret rites are almost invariably performed in a specially constructed lodge, room, or chamber, into which none but the priests or initiated may enter, and which is generally indicated in such a manner that the public may not mistake it. Early in point of time in the secret rites is the procession of the priests for objects or raw material to be used in the preparation of an altar, which may be either secret or public, or to be used for paraphernalia or otherwise in the public performance. This procession of priests is generally symbolic, and the uninitiated may not accompany them. The remaining secret performances include such rites as smoking, which may be either fraternal or direct offerings in the nature of a sacrifice to the gods; thurification, similar in origin to the rite of smoking, in which the smoke of some sweet-smelling herb is offered direct to the deity, or the priest bathes his body, or some object of a special ceremonial nature, in the smoke of the incense; sweat-lodge purification; a ceremonial feast, preceded or followed by a

sacrifice of food; the offering of prayers, which may be in the form of a direct appeal to the gods or through the instrumentality of material prayer offerings, upon which, or into which, the prayer has been breathed; and the manufacture or redecoration of ceremonial masks and garments to be worn during the public performance, either by the priests exclusively or by all those taking part in the ceremony.

Occupying in point of time a period between the exclusively secret performances and the public presentation of the drama may be certain semi-public performances, which take place in the open but which are undertaken by priests exclusively. Such is the preparation of the site of the public performance, or the erection of a bower or lodge within which it is to take place. Either within this inclosure, or lodge, or within the secret lodge of preparation, an altar may be erected. This is especially the case with the ceremonies of the Pueblos and of the Plains tribes (see *Altars*), among which it is always symbolic, and its explanation must generally be sought in the ritual. It often symbolizes, as a whole, the earth or the heavens, or some god or the home of a god or the gods. The most prominent feature of the altar is a palladium, which may consist of a buffalo skull, an ear of corn, a flint knife, or some other object of supposed efficacious nature, within which is supposed to reside or which is typical or symbolic of the spirit or deity. On the altar, also, is generally found a recognition in one form or another of the gods of the four or six world-quarters, of the rainbow, of the lightning, of vegetation, etc. Falling within this semi-public period is often a contest, generally a foot race, the winner being favored by the gods or receiving some tangible object which possesses magic potency.

The public performance is usually ushered in by a stately procession of priests, the singing of traditional songs, rites of smoking, sacrifice of food, and offerings of prayer. The most prominent feature is the dance, which, as a rule, is of a dignified and stately nature, the dancers being appropriately costumed and otherwise adorned. The costume worn in public is often supplemented with paint upon the body or by masks over the face. The dancer, thus arrayed, generally represents a minor deity, or he places himself, by virtue of the character of his costume, in an attitude of defiance to the deity and thus opposes his magic power to that of the supernatural. Following the dance, which may vary in duration from a few minutes to several days, is generally a ceremonial removal of the costume, whereupon the dancers undergo a purification rite, often in the form of a powerful emetic. This may be followed by an act of self-inflicted torture, which, however, often forms an intrinsic part of the public performance. During the entire ceremony, as a rule, certain tabus are enforced, the most common being a prohibition of the presence of women during menstruation.

The time of the performance of ceremonies varies. Some are held annually, or biennially, at stated periods; such are the solstitial or seasonal ceremonies, for which no special provision is necessarily made. Some are held during certain seasons within the year, but are dependent on the will of an individual who may have pledged or taken a vow to perform the ceremony. Others are held at any season, whenever occasion may demand; such are the ceremonies of the medicine-men.

Inasmuch as ceremonies form intrinsic features and may be regarded as only phases of culture, their special character depends on the state of culture of the people by which they are performed; hence there are at least as many kinds of ceremonies as there are phases of culture in North America. A few characteristic ceremonies may be considered for some of the better-defined areas:

Among the Plains tribes the most spectacular ceremony is the Sun dance, q. v. This varied from an annual performance, as among the Ponca and some other Siouan tribes, to a presentation only as the direct result of a vow, as among the Cheyenne, Arapaho, and Siksika. In the Sun dance of all tribes are found certain common features, such as the secret tipi or tipis of preparation; the manufacture of objects to be used on the public altar; the procession of priests in search of an object generally symbolic of spying out the world; the ceremonial erection of the great lodge, of which the center pole is the most prominent feature; the erection of the altar; and the characteristic dance lasting from 1 to 4 days. During the public performance the dancers are symbolically painted and otherwise so adorned that their evolutions are supposed to lead to a distinct result—the production of rain. While the Sun dance varies from tribe to tribe, not only in its symbolism but also in many important details, it seems primarily to have been a rain ceremony, and its ritual generally recounts the origin or the rebirth of mankind. The second group of ceremonies are those performed by cult societies, generally four or more in number. Each society has its special esoteric songs, its own paraphernalia, and often distinct gradations in rank. The membership is generally exclusively male, although a limited number of maidens are admitted into the societies of the Cheyenne, while the Arapaho have a society which belongs exclusively to the women, of which there are several gradations of rank. The third group comprises the performances of cult societies in which the warrior element does not predominate; these are often spoken of as dances, although they are, strictly speaking, ceremonies. Among the best known of these are the Buffalo, the Bear, and the Elk. The basis is usually the acquisition and perpetuation of magic power which, primarily, was derived from the animal after which the society takes its name and from which it is supposed to have originated. A fourth group comprises those of the medicine-men, and are either ceremonies in which one or more medicine-men perform for the benefit of the sick, or, more often, in which all the medicine-men of the tribe join in a performance to make public demonstration of magic power through sleight-of-hand. The last group of Plains ceremonies includes those connected with the planting and reaping of the maize, or the first killing of game in the hunting season, or the first coming of the fish—all, it may be noted, connected with the gift of food for the sustenance of life.

The Pueblo tribes of the S. W. are especially noted for their extended ceremonies, which among the Hopi number no fewer than 13, each of 9 days' duration. The secret rites are almost always held in an underground chamber called a kiva (q. v.), or estufa, in which, in addition to the performances, an elaborate altar is erected. During the initiation of candidates into the brotherhood of these societies, dry-paintings (q. v.) are laid on the floor of the kiva in front of the altar. The symbolism both of these and of the altar itself is generally very elaborate, but with a strong predominance of symbols in which reference is made to rain clouds. During certain of these ceremonies masked dancers appear, the symbolism of the mask being distinctive. The most notable of the Hopi are: The Soyal, a winter solstice ceremony; the Powamu, a February bean-planting ceremony; a New Fire ceremony, in early spring; the Niman, or the departure of the masked personages, a ceremony of early summer; the Snake-Antelope, of the summer, alternating each year with that of the Flute ceremonies; those of the women in the autumn comprising the Lagon, the Oaqöl, and the Marau. In addition to these the Hopi have a large number of minor ones, generally of one day's duration. Such are the Katcina or masked dances, and various others of a social nature

Among the non-Pueblo tribes of the S. W., especially among the Navaho and Apache, the extended ceremonies are almost entirely the property of the medicine-men, and must be regarded as medicine dances. Many of these are of an elaborate and complicated nature, but all are designed for the restoration of the sick. In these ceremonies masks are often worn and complicated and elaborate dry-pictures are made, both these features probably having been borrowed from the Pueblo tribes.

In California ceremonies of extended duration are not found; they partake rather of the nature of tribal mourning, sometimes spoken of as dances of the dead, or initiation rites into cult societies. These, generally lasting but a single day, are marked by the lack of symbolism, by the almost total want of fetishes such as abound on the altars of the Pueblos, and by the marked absence of rituals such as are found among certain Plains tribes. The costume of the dancers is generally restricted to profuse feather ornaments. In nearly all ceremonies of this region there is afforded an opportunity for the display of individual wealth.

Of the ceremonies of the tribes of the Great Basin, but little is known. The eastern Shoshonean tribes, such as the Shoshoni and the Ute, perform the Sun dance, presumably borrowed from the tribes of the Plains.

On the N. Pacific coast, extending from Columbia r. to s. Alaska, ceremonies of from 1 to 4 days' duration abound. These are performances of cult societies, generally secret, or of chiefs or lesser individuals who make it an opportunity to display personal wealth. In the ceremonies of the cult societies masks are worn. Those of the Kwakiutl of this region are held in winter, at which time the cult societies replace the gentile organization which prevails in summer. Membership into the society is acquired by marriage or through war. The object of the winter ceremony is "to bring back the youth who is supposed to stay with the supernatural being who is the protector of his society, and then, when he has returned in a state of ecstasy, to exorcise the spirit which possesses him and to restore him from his holy madness. These objects are attained by songs and dances." During the performance of these ceremonies special paraphernalia are worn in which the mask, substantially made of wood, predominates, the remainder consisting largely of rings of cedar bark (see Bark) which constitute the badges of the ceremony. The tribes to the N. have

societies and winter ceremonies similar to those of the Kwakiutl, from whom they are probably mainly derived.

Among the Eskimo extended ceremonies, such as prevail over a large part of North America, are not found. They are rather to be characterized as dances or festivals. These are generally held in winter and are of short duration. The most important of these are the Feasts to the Dead; others among the Alaskan Eskimo are the Asking festival, the Bladder feast, and the performances of the medicine-men. In some of the festivals wooden masks, representing supernatural or superhuman beings, are worn.

As stated at the outset the root of ceremonies may be discovered only by taking into consideration universal human tendencies which develop along certain lines according to historic or geographic environment. It may therefore be noted that the need for them among the Indians of North America varied in accordance with the character of their life. Thus it is found that in those tribes or in those areas extended forms abound where there exists a sessile population or a strong form of tribal government. Hence the greatest number of extended and complicated ceremonies are formed among the Pueblo people of the S. W. and in the village communities of the N. Pacific coast. Second only in importance to the ceremonies of these two areas are those which are found among the tribes of the Plains among which ceremonies abound, in which the strongest system of government is found. As a ceremony of any extended duration makes great demands upon the tribe, and presupposes law and order, highly developed and extended ones are not possible among the Eskimo or the tribes of California. See Dance, Religion. (G. A. D.)

**Cerocahui.** A settlement of the Temoris branch of the Guazapar in lat. 27° 25′, long. 108° 25′, w. Chihuahua, Mexico.— Orozco y Berra, Geog., 324, map, 1864.

**Cerrito** (Span.: 'little mountain'). A settlement, probably of the Pima, on the Pima and Maricopa res., Gila r., s. Ariz.; pop. 258 in 1860.—Taylor in Cal. Farmer, June 19, 1863.

**Cerritos.** Apparently a former Yuma rancheria on the s. bank of Gila r., about 10½ m. above its mouth; visited by Anza and Font in 1775.
Los Cerritos.—Anza and Font quoted by Bancroft, Ariz. and N. Mex., 392, 1889.

**Cerro Cabezon** (Span.: 'big-head hill,' so named from its shape; also El Cabezon, or Cavezon). A prominent butte about 40 m. N. E. of the summit of Mt Taylor, or Mt San Mateo, N. Mex., which figures in Navaho tradition (Matthews, Navaho Leg., 116, 1897). From some points the rock is visible 50 m. away. Cortez (Pac. R. R. Rep., III, pt. 3, 119, 1856) mentioned it as a Navaho settlement in 1799.          (F. W. H.)

**Cerro Chato** (Span.: 'flat-topped hill'). Mentioned by Cortez in 1799 (Pac. R. R. Rep., III, pt. 3, 119, 1856) as a Navaho settlement, but it is probably only a geographic name.

**Cerro Chiquito** (Span.: 'little mountain'). A village, probably of the Pima, on the Pima and Maricopa res., Gila r., s. Ariz.; pop. 232 in 1860.—Taylor in Cal. Farmer, June 19, 1863.

**Cexeninuth.** A tribe or division about Queen Charlotte sd., Brit. Col.; possibly a Gyeksem gens of the Kwakiutl.
Cex-e-ni-nuth.—Kane, Wand. in N. Am., app., 1859. Ex e ni nuth.—Schoolcraft, Ind. Tribes, V, 488, 1855 (misspelt).

**Chaahl** (*Tc!ā'ał*). A former Haida town on the N. w. coast of Moresby id., Queen Charlotte ids., Brit. Col. This seems to have been the Kow-welth of John Work, who assigned to it 35 houses with 561 inhabitants in 1836–41. Old people recall the names of 28 houses, but many more are said to have existed before a great fire which destroyed a large part of the town. In later times the people moved to New Gold Harbor, on the E. end of Maude id., and thence into Skidegate.—Swanton, Cont. Haida, 280, 1905.
Cha-atl.—Dawson, Q. Charlotte Ids., 168B, 1880. Kaw-welth.—Kane, Wand. in N. Am., app., 1859 (probably the same; misprint from Work, 1836–41). Kow-welth.—Schoolcraft, Ind. Tribes, V, 489, 1855 (probably the same; from Work's table).

**Chaahl** (*Tc!ā'ał*). A former Haida town on the E. coast of North id., Queen Charlotte ids., Brit. Col. It was occupied by a family of the same name who afterward moved to Alaska and settled at Howkan.—Swanton, Cont. Haida, 281, 1905.

**Chaahl-lanas** (*Tc!ā'ał lā'nas*, 'Chaahl town people'). A Haida family of the Eagle clan, one of those which moved to Alaska and constituted the Kaigani. They are said to have branched off from the Kaiahl-lanas, but derived their name from the place on North id. where their town stood before they moved to Alaska. In the latter country they owned the town of Howkan. There are said to have been 4 subdivisions: Stulnaas-hadai, Lanagukunhlin-hadai, Skahene-hadai, and Hotagastlas-hadai.— Swanton, Cont. Haida, 276, 1905.
Ts'ātl lā'nas.—Boas, 5th Rep. N. W. Tribes Can., 26, 1889.

**Chabanakongkomun** ('boundary fishing place.'—Trumbull). A village of Praying Indians established about 1672 near Dudley, Worcester co., Mass. In 1674 it contained about 45 inhabitants. In later times the Indians about Dudley were

known as the Pegan tribe and continued to live there after the settlement of the town. Ten of them were still on a reservation in Dudley in 1793. They were classed as Nipmuc.          (J. M.)
Chabanakongkomun.—Gookin (1674) in Mass. Hist. Soc. Coll., 1st s., I, 189–190, 1806. Chanagongum.— Trumbull, Conn., I, 346, 1818. Chaubunakongkomuk.—Eliot (1668) quoted by Trumbull, Ind. Names Conn., 9, 1881. Chobonakonkon.—Gookin (1677) in Trans. Am. Antiq. Soc., II, 467, 1836. Chobone-Konhonom.—Ibid., 477. Chobonokonomum.—Ibid., 443. Pegans.—Drake, Bk. Inds., x, 1848.

**Chabin** (from *qe*, 'mountain'). A division of the Assiniboin.—Maximilian, Trav., 194, 1843. See *Mountain Assiniboin.*
Gens des Montagnes.—Ibid.

**Chacacants.** A village, possibly Caddoan, formerly on Red r., at the mouth of a N. affluent, in what is now Oklahoma.— De l'Isle, map (1707) in French, Hist. Coll. La., III, 1851.
Chacacantes.—Baudry des Lozières, Voyage à la La., 242, 1802. Chacakante.—De l'Isle, map of La. (1701?) in Winsor, Hist. Am., II, 294, 1886.

**Chacat.** Mentioned by Pike (Exped., 3d map, 1810) as a Navaho settlement. It is probably identical in name with that of Chaco canyon, N. w. N. Mex.

**Chachambitmanchal.** An Atfalati band formerly living 3½ m. N. of Forest Grove, Washington co., Oreg.
Tcha tchambit mantchal.—Gatschet, Atfalati MS., B. A. E., 1877.

**Chachanim.** An Atfalati band formerly living on Wapatoo Lake prairie, Washington co., Oreg.
Tcha tchannim.—Gatschet, Atfalati MS., B. A. E., 1877.

**Chachat.** A former village connected with San Carlos mission, Cal., and said to have been Esselen.—Taylor in Cal. Farmer, Apr. 20, 1860.

**Chachaubunkkakowok.** A village of Christian Indians in E. Massachusetts in 1684.—Eliot (1684) in Mass. Hist. Soc. Coll., 1st s., III, 185, 1794.

**Chachemewa.** An Atfalati band formerly residing at Forest Grove, 6 m. from Wapatoo lake, Yamhill co., Oreg.
Tcha-tchĕméwa.—Gatschet, Atfalati MS., B. A. E., 1877.

**Chachif.** An Atfalati band formerly living on Wapatoo lake, Yamhill co., Oreg.
Tch'atchif.—Gatschet, Atfalati MS., B. A. E., 1877.

**Chachimahiyuk** (refers to a swamp grass). An Atfalati band formerly living between Wapatoo lake and Willamette r., in Washington co., Oreg.
Tcha tchimmahíyuk.—Gatschet, Atfalati MS., B. A. E., 1877.

**Chachimewa.** An Atfalati band formerly living on or near Wapatoo lake, Yamhill co., Oreg.
Tcha tchmewa.—Gatschet, Atfalati MS., B. A. E., 1877.

**Chachokwith** (refers to a small shell). An Atfalati band formerly living at a place of the same name N. of Forest Grove, in Washington co., Oreg.
Tcha tchokuith.—Gatschet, Atfalati MS., B. A. E., 1877.

**Chactoo.** A body of Indians, possibly related to the Attacapa, mentioned in 1753 as living in Louisiana. In 1805 they were on Bayou Bœuf, about 10 m. s. of Bayou Rapide, toward Opelousas, and numbered 30 men. They were not Choctaw, and in addition to their own tongue they spoke the Mobilian trade language. (A. S. G.)

Chacchoux.—Dumont, La., I, 134, 1753. Chactoos.—Sibley, Hist. Sketches, 84, 1806. Chaetoos.—Schermerhorn in Mass. Hist. Soc. Coll., 2d s., II, 27, 1814. Chattoos.—Lewis and Clark, Jour, 156, 1840.

**Chafalote.** An Apache tribe or band of Sonora, Mexico, mentioned in connection with the Gileños and Faraones by Orozco y Berra (Geog., 59, 1864) and by Malte-Brun (Congrés Amér., II, 37, 1877); otherwise unknown.

**Chagee.** A former Cherokee settlement near the mouth of Chatooga cr., a tributary of Tugaloo r., at or near the site of the present Ft Madison, in the s. w. part of Oconee co., N. w. S. C. It was destroyed during the Revolutionary war. (J. M.)

**Chagindueftei.** An Atfalati band formerly living between Hillsboro and Sauvies id., Washington co., Oreg.

Tcha gī'nduefte-i.—Gatschet, Atfalati MS., B. A. E., 1877.

**Chagu** ('lungs'). A division of the Yankton Sioux.

Band of the lights.—Culbertson in Smithson. Rep. 1850, 141, 1851. Caġu.—Dorsey in 15th Rep. B. A. E., 217, 1897. Tcaxu.—Ibid.

**Chaguate.** A village, probably belonging to a division of a southern Caddoan tribe, formerly situated in the region of Washita r., Ark.; visited by Moscoso and his troops in the summer of 1542. See Gentleman of Elvas (1557) in French, Hist. Coll. La., II, 193, 1850.

**Chagunte.** A former village, presumably Costanoan, connected with Dolores mission, San Francisco, Cal.—Taylor in Cal. Farmer, Oct. 18, 1861.

**Chagvagchat.** A Kaiyuhkhotana village near the headwaters of Anvik r., Alaska.

Tchagvagtchatchachat.—Zagoskin in Nouv. Ann. Voy., 5th s., XXI, map, 1850.

**Chahelim** (helim='outdoors'). An Atfalati band formerly settled in Chehelim valley, 5 m. s. of Wapatoo lake, Yamhill co., Oreg.

Chehalim.—Lyman in Oreg. Hist. Soc. Quar., I, 323, 1900. Tcha helim.—Gatschet, Atfalati MS., B. A. E., 1877.

**Chahichic** (che-chen, a variety of mosquito; chik, or chiki, 'place of'). A Tarahumare rancheria near Palanquo, Chihuahua, Mexico.—Lumholtz, inf'n, 1894.

**Chahthulelpil.** A body of Salish of the old Victoria superintendency, Brit. Col.; pop. 104 in 1881.—Can. Ind. Aff., 258, 1882.

**Chaicclesaht** (To'ē'k·tlisath, 'large-cut-in-bay people'). A Nootka tribe on Ououkinsh and Nasparte inlets, w. coast of Vancouver id., numbering 105 in 1902. Acous is their principal town.

Chaic-cles-aht.—Can. Ind. Aff., 357, 1897. Chaykisaht.—Sproat, Sav. Life, 308, 1868. Checklesit.—Can. Ind. Aff., 158, 1901. Naspatl.—Jacob in Jour. Anthrop. Soc. Lond., xi, Feb., 1864. Naspatle.—Latham, Nat. Hist. Man, 301, 1850. Naspatte.—Scouler (1846) in Jour. Ethnol. Soc. Lond., I, 234, 1848. Nespods.—Grant in Jour. Roy. Geog. Soc., 293, 1857. To'ē'k·tlisath.—Boas, 6th Rep. N. W. Tribes Can., 1890.

**Chaik.** A Kaviagmiut village on the N. shore of Norton sd., Alaska.

Chaimut.—Zagoskin, Descr. Russ. Poss. in Am., pt. I, 73, 1847. Tchaïmuth.—Zagoskin in Nouv. Ann. Voy., 5th s., XXI, map, 1850.

**Chaikikarachada** ('those who call themselves the deer'). A Winnebago gens.

Chä'-rä.—Morgan, Anc. Soc., 157, 1877. Tca'i-ki'-ka-ra'-tca-da.—Dorsey in 15th Rep. B. A. E., 241, 1897.

**Chailkutkaituh.** A former Hupa village on or near Trinity r., Cal.

Chail'-kut-kai-tuh.—Powers in Cont. N. A. Ethnol., III, 73, 1877.

**Chainiki.** A Karok village on the s. bank of Klamath r., N. Cal., about midway between the Trinity and the Salmon.

Tshei-nik-kee.—Gibbs MS., B. A. E., 1852.

**Chainruk.** A Kaviagmiut village at Pt Clarence, Alaska.—11th Census, Alaska, 162, 1893.

**Chaizra.** The Elk clan of the Ala-Leng-ya phratral group of the Hopi.

Tcaizra wiñwû.—Fewkes in 19th Rep. B. A. E., 583, 1901 (tc=ch; wiñwû='clan'). Tcai'-zri-sa wün-wü.—Fewkes in Am. Anthrop., VII, 401, 1894.

**Chak** ('eagle'). A name given by the northern Tlingit to one of the two phratries into which they are divided.

Chethl'.—Dall, Alaska, 414, 1870. Tcāk!.—Swanton, field notes, B. A. E., 1904.

**Chakankni.** A Molala band formerly settled in the Cascade range, N. w. of upper Klamath lake, on the headwaters of Rogue r., Oreg. In 1881 they were rapidly becoming absorbed by the neighboring tribes and had practically given up their own language for that of the Klamath. (L. F.)

Tchakänkni.—Gatschet in Cont. N. A. Ethnol., II, 426, 1890. Tchakenikni.—Ibid. (Modoc name).

**Chakawech.** A Modoc camping place near Yaneks, on Sprague r., Klamath res., s. w. Oreg.

Tchakáwĕtch.—Gatschet in Cont. N. A. Ethnol., II, XXXI, 1890.

**Chakchiuma** (Choctaw: saktchi 'crawfish,' huma 'red,' probably referring to a clan totem). A tribe speaking a Choctaw-Chickasaw dialect, formerly living on Yazoo r, Miss., and, according to Iberville (Margry, Déc., IV, 180, 1880), between the Taposa below them and the Outapo or Ibitoupa above, in 1699. At that time they were probably the most populous of the Yazoo tribes, and spoke the Chickasaw language. They were an important tribe at the time of De Soto's expedition (1540–41) and lived in a walled town. During the 18th century they were included in the Chickasaw confederacy, and had the reputation of being warlike. Adair (Hist. Am. Inds., 66, 352, 1775) mentions a tradition that they came

to the E. side of the Mississippi with the Choctaw and Chickasaw and settled on the Tallahatchie, the lower part of which was called by their name. Jefferys (French Dom., I, 163, 1761) states that in his time they occupied 50 huts on the Yazoo r. (A. S. G. C. T.)
Cacchumas.—Jefferys, Am. Atlas, 5, 1776. Chacchooma.—Romans, Fla., 315, 1775. Chacchoumas.—La Harpe (1721) in French, Hist. Coll. La., III, 106, 1851. Chacchumas.—Lattré, map of U. S., 1784. Chacci Cumas.—Boudinot, Star in the West, 126, 1816. Chacci Oumas.—McKenney and Hall, Ind. Tribes, III, 80, 1854. Chacehoumas.—Jefferys, Am. Atlas, 7, 1776. Chachachouma.—McKenney and Hall, Ind. Tribes, III, 81, 1854. Chachoumas.—La Harpe (1721) in French, Hist. Coll. La., III, 110, 1851. Chachümas.—Hervas, Idea dell' Universo, XVII, 90, 1784. Chackchioomas.—Keane in Stanford, Compend., 506, 1878. Chacksihoomas.—Ibid. Chacoumas.—Tonti (1688) in French, Hist. Coll. La., I, 72, 1846. Chacoume.—Coxe, Carolana, map, 1741. Chacsihomas.—Hawkins (1799), Sketch, 15, 1848. Chacsihoomas.—Romans, Fla., 90, 1775. Chactchi-Oumas.—Du Pratz, La., II, 226, 1758. Chactioumas.—Jefferys, French Dom., I, 163, 1761. Chacxoumas.—Pénicaut (1722) in Margry, Déc., V, 575, 1883. Chaquesauma.—Iberville (1699), ibid., IV, 180, 1880. Chiachi-Oumos.—Schermerhorn in Mass. Hist. Coll., 2d s. II, 15, 1814. Chocchuma.—Durant (1843) in Sen. Doc. 168, 28th Cong., 1st sess., 135, 1844. Choccomaws.—Pickett, Hist. Ala., I, 134, 1851. Chokchoomah.—Adair, Hist. Am. Ind., 66, 352, 1775. Choquichoumans.—Iberville (1700) in Margry, Déc., IV, 430, 1880. Chouchoumas.—Tonti (1684), ibid., I, 604, 1875. Craw-fish band.—Catlin, N. A. Inds., 589, 1860. Ecrevisses rouges.—Du Pratz, La., II, 226, 1758. Red crayfish.—Boudinot, Star in the West, 126, 1816. Red lobsters.—Jefferys, French Dom. Am., 163, 1761. Saquechuma.—Gentleman of Elvas (1557) in French, Hist. Coll. La., II, 162, 1850. Tchaoumas.—Martin, Hist. La., I, 280, 1827. Tchouchoumas.—La Salle (ca. 1680) in Margry, Déc., II, 198, 1877.

**Chakeipi** (Tch'akeïpi, 'at the beaver place'). An Atfalati band that lived about 10 m. w. of Oregon City, Oreg., before the treaty of 1855.—Gatschet, Atfalati MS., B. A. E., 1877.

**Chakeletsiwish** (Klamath: 'running with blood'). A small Shoshonean settlement in Sprague River valley, Oreg.; so named from a spring of reddish water.
Tchä'kĕle Tsiwish.—Gatschet in Cont. N. A. Ethnol., II, pt. II, xxxi, 1890.

**Chakihlako.** A Creek town near the junction of Deep and North forks of Canadian r., Ind. Ter.
Tcháχki'láko.—Gatschet, Creek Migr. Leg., II, 186, 1888.

**Chakkai.** A Squawmish village community on the E. side of Howe sd., Brit. Col.
Tcākqai.—Hill-Tout in Rep. Brit. A. A. S., 474, 1900.

**Chakpahu** (Hopi: 'speaker spring,' or 'speaking spring'). A ruined pueblo on the rim of Antelope mesa, overlooking Jeditoh valley, in the Tusayan country, N. E. Arizona. It is regarded by the Hopi as one of three "Kawaika" pueblos—the others being Kawaika and Kokopki (?)—from which it may be assumed that it was built and occupied by Keresan people from New Mexico, the name Kawaika being the Hopi designation of the present Keresan pueblo of Laguna.

The ruin was first described and surveyed in 1885 by V. Mindeleff, of the Bureau of American Ethnology, and in 1893 James Mooney of that Bureau was present during the excavation by some Navaho of its main spring in which a sacrificial deposit of pottery vessels was uncovered. In ground-plan the ruin recalls those of the Rio Grande pueblos, well represented in the Payupki and Sikyatki ruins of Tusayan, but the Chakpahu pottery, noted for its excellence of texture and decoration, has little in common with that of Payupki, which was occupied within historic time, while it resembles closely the Sikyatki ware. This, coupled with the fact that one of the neighboring ruined Kawaika pueblos was traditionally occupied by Kokop clans, who lived also in Sikyatki, would indicate a connection between the Sikyatki and the Kawaika people, although the former are reputed to have come from Jemez. (J. W. F.)
Bat House.—Mindeleff in 8th Rep. B. A. E., 52, 1891. Chak-pahŭ.—Mooney in Am. Anthrop., VI, 284, 1893 (given as name of springs; transl. 'little water'). Chapkaku.—Hough in Rep. Nat. Mus. 1901, 336, 1903 (misprint). Kawaika.—Fewkes in 17th Rep. B. A. E., 590, 1898 (name of spring and ruin; see Kawaika). To-alchĭn'di.—Mooney, op. cit. (given as Navaho name of springs; same meaning; mistake).

**Chakutpaliu.** An Atfalati band formerly settled N. E. of Hillsboro, Washington co., Oreg.
Tcha kutpaliu.—Gatschet, Atfalati MS., B. A. E., 1877.

**Chakwaina.** The Black Earth Kachina clan of the Hopi.
Tca'-kwai-na.—Stephen in 8th Rep. B. A. E., 39, 1891. Chakwaina wiñwû.—Fewkes in 19th Rep. B. A. E., 584, 1900 (wiñwû='clan'). Tca'-kwai-na wüñ-wü.—Fewkes in Am. Anthrop., VII, 404, 1894.

**Chakwayalham** ('summer town'). A former Wahkiakum town near Pillar rock, Columbia r., Oreg.
Tcakwayā'lχam.—Boas, inf'n, 1905.

**Chala.** A tribe mentioned by Hutchins in 1764 as living on the St Lawrence in connection with the Abnaki, Micmac, and Malecite, and having 130 warriors.
Chalas.—Hutchins (1764) quoted by Schoolcraft, Ind. Tribes, III, 553, 1853. Chatas.—Smith (1785), ibid.

**Chalahume.** A Creek town of the 16th century, 3 days' journey westward from Chiaha, about the present Columbus, Ga., and 2 leagues from Satapo, probably within the present limits of Alabama (Vandera, 1567, in Smith, Col. Doc. Fla., I, 18, 1857). The termination hume may be the Choctaw huma, 'red.' (A. S. G.)

**Chalal.** An Atfalati band formerly settled near the outlet of Wapatoo lake, Yamhill co., Oreg.
Tcha lal.—Gatschet, Atfalati MS., B. A. E., 1877.

**Chalawai.** An Atfalati band that lived S. E. of Wapatoo lake, Yamhill co., Oreg. They became extinct probably about 1830.

Tcha lawai.—Gatschet, Atfalati MS., B. A. E., 1877.

**Chalcedony.** Under this head may be grouped a number of varieties of silica (see *Quartz*), including flint, chert, hornstone, jasper, agate, novaculite in part, onyx, carnelian, etc., most of which were used by the aborigines in the manufacture of flaked implements. The distinctions between these rocks have not been sharply drawn by mineralogists, and the archeologist must be content with grouping them according to their resemblance to recognized types. The term flint has come into somewhat general use among archeologists for the whole group, but this is not sanctioned by mineralogists. Chalcedony is a translucent and variously tinted indistinctly crystalline variety of silica. It is formed by infiltration in cavities in the older rocks, as a secondary product during decomposition of many rocks, and as accumulations of the siliceous residue from various organisms. It occurs as nodules distributed through sedimentary strata, as in the middle Mississippi valley; as thin, more or less interrupted layers, as in Wyandot cave, Indiana, and at Millcreek, Ill.; or as massive strata, as in Flint ridge, Ohio, and on the Peoria res., Ind. Ter. *Flint* (true flint), q. v., is formed as nodular segregations in chalky limestone, and is composed mainly of nearly amorphous silica and partially dissolved radiolaria and spicules of sponges. The colors are dark gray and brownish to nearly black, and somewhat translucent on thin edges. It occurs extensively in England, France, and N. W. Europe, and has recently been found in Arkansas and Texas, where it was used by the aborigines in making implements. *Chert*, as commonly recognized, differs from true flint in being lighter in color, as a rule, although variously tinted and less translucent. It occurs in the limestones of a wide range of geological formations. The best-known deposits utilized by the Indians are on the Peoria res., near Seneca, Mo., and at Millcreek, Ill. *Hornstone* is the term usually applied to varieties of chalcedony displaying peculiar horn-like characteristics of toughness and translucency. Much of the nodular chalcedony of the Ohio valley, extensively employed by the aborigines in the manufacture of implements and the blades and disks deposited in caches, has been known under this name. *Jasper* (q. v.) is a ferruginous variety of chalcedony, of red, yellow, and brownish tints. The greenish varieties are known as *prase*, and these when marked with red are called *bloodstone*. Numerous aboriginal quarries of jasper occur in E. Pennsylvania. *Agate* is a banded variety of chalcedony found mainly in cavities in igneous rocks. The natural colors are white to gray, passing into various delicate tints. *Onyx* is a banded variety of agate, but owing to fancied similarities the name has been applied to certain calcareous deposits, as the so-called Mexican onyx.

Consult Dana, System of Mineralogy, 1892; Merrill, Rocks, Rock-weathering and Soils, 1897. See *Mines and Quarries, Stone-work.*  (W. H. H.  G. P. M.)

**Chalichiki** (*chali* 'blue corn', *chíki* 'place of' : 'field of blue corn'). A Tarahumare rancheria near Palanquo, Chihuahua, Mexico.—Lumholtz, inf'n, 1894.

**Chalit.** A Magemiut Eskimo village near Kuguklik r., Alaska; pop. 60 in 1880, 358 in 1890.
Chalitmiut.—Nelson in 18th Rep. B. A. E., map, 1899.  Chalitmute.—Petroff, Rep. on Alaska, 54, 1884.

**Chaliuknak.** A former Aleut village on Beaver bay, Unalaska id., Alaska.—Baker, Geog. Dict. Alaska, 1901.

**Chalkunts.** A Squawmish village community on Gambier id., Brit. Col.
Tcā′lkunts.—Hill-Tout in Rep. Brit. A. A. S., 474, 1900.

**Chalone.** A division of the Costanoan family of California which resided E. of Soledad mission, with which they were connected. Chalone villages are mentioned as follows: Aspasniagan, Chulare, Ekgiagan, Eslanagan, Goatcharones, Ichenta, and Yumanagan. Eslanagan, however, may be Esselen; the Goatcharones are undoubtedly the Wacharones of San Juan Bautista, and the Yumanagan are probably the Ymunacam of San Carlos mission, who are also ascribed to the Kalindaruk division, so that the constitution and limits of the Chalone are uncertain. Chalone peak and creek are named from them.  (H. W. H.)
Chalones.—Taylor in Cal. Farmer, Apr. 20, 1860.

**Chalosas.** A former Chumashan village on Santa Cruz id., Cal.—Taylor in Cal. Farmer, Apr. 24, 1863.
Tcâ-lâ-cuc.—Henshaw, Buenaventura MS. vocab., B. A. E., 1884.

**Chalowe.** A former pueblo of the Zuñi, 1½ m. N. W. of Hawikuh. The ruins form a widely scattered series of dwelling clusters, which traditionally belonged to one people, known by the general name of Chalowe. It is said to have been inhabited at the time of the first arrival of the Spaniards. The general character and arrangement of the pueblo, however, are so different from the prevailing type in this region that it seems hardly probable that it belonged to the same people and to the same age as the other ruins.—Mindeleff in 8th Rep. B. A. E., 83, 1891.
Chall-o-wha.—Fewkes in Jour. Am. Ethnol. and Archæol., I, 101, 1891.

**Chalumu.** A Costanoan village formerly situated a mile N. W. of Santa Cruz mission, Cal.—Taylor in Cal. Farmer, Apr. 5, 1860.

**Chamada.** A former rancheria of the Jova division of the Opata, near the Sonora-Chihuahua boundary, about lat. 29°, Mexico. It appears to have been abandoned after 1690, the inhabitants finally moving to Sahuaripa.—Doc. of 18th century quoted by Bandelier in Arch. Inst. Papers, IV, 511, 1892.

**Chamampit.** An Atfalati band which lived on Wapatoo cr., at the E. end of Wapatoo lake, Yamhill co., Oreg.
Tcha mámpit.—Gatschet, Atfalati MS., B. A. E., 1877.

**Chamblee.** See *Shabonee.*

**Chamhallach.** A former village on French prairie, Marion co., Oreg., probably belonging to the Ahantchuyuk.—Lyman in Oreg. Hist. Soc. Quar., I, 323, 1900.

**Chamifu.** The Lakmiut name of a Santiam band on Yamhill cr., a w. tributary of Willamette r., Oreg.
Tch'ammífu.—Gatschet, Calapooya MS., B. A. E., 1877.

**Chamifu.** A Yamel band formerly living between the forks of Yamhill r., Yamhill co., Oreg.
Tcha mifu amim.—Gatschet, Atfalati MS., B. A. E., 1877.

**Chamisso.** A village of the Malemiut Eskimo on Chamisso id., in Eschscholtz bay, Alaska.—Nelson in 18th Rep. B. A. E., map, 1899.
E-ow-ick.—Beechey (1827) quoted by Baker, Geog. Dict. Alaska, 1901 (native name).

**Chamiwi.** The Lakmiut name of a Yamel band on Yamhill cr., a w. tributary of Willamette r., and near Independence, Oreg.
Tch'ammíwi.—Gatschet, Calapooya MS., B. A. E., 1877.

**Chamkhai.** The name, in the upper Clear lake dialect, of a Pomo band or village on the E. fork of Russian r., Cal. (A. L. K.)

**Champikle.** A Yamel band on Dallas (La Creole) cr., a w. tributary of Willamette r., Oreg.
Tch'ampiklĕ ami'm.—Gatschet, Lakmiut MS., B. A. E., 1877.

**Champoeg.** A Kalapooian village between Chemeketa and Willamette falls, Oreg. It is not known to which division of the family it belonged.
Champoeg.—Rees in Trans. Oreg. Pion. Assn., 25, 1879. Champoicho.—Slocum (1837) in Sen. Doc. 24, 25th Cong., 2d sess., 15, 1838 (misprint). Champoicks.—Slocum (1835) in H. Rep. 101, 25th Cong., 3d sess., 42, 1839.

**Chananagi** ('ridge of land,' or 'hill ridge'). A former Upper Creek town E. of the site of Montgomery, Ala.
Chanahuniege.—Güssefeld, map of U. S., 1784. Chanahunrege.—Jefferys, French Dom. Am., I, 134, map, 1761. Cheurkany.—H. R. Ex. Doc. 276, 24th Cong., 310, 1836.

**Chanatya.** The extinct "Pegwood" (?) clan of the Keresan pueblo of Sia, N. Mex.
Chánatya-háno.—Hodge in Am. Anthrop., IX, 351, 1896 (*háno* = 'people').

**Chanchampenau.** The Lakmiut name of a Santiam band formerly living E. of Willamette r., Oreg.
Tchantchámpĕnau amím.—Gatschet, Lakmiut MS., B. A. E., 1877.

**Chanchantu.** The Lakmiut name of a former Santiam band in Oregon.
Tchän-tchäntu amim.—Gatschet, Lakmiut MS., B. A. E., 1877.

**Chanco.** A Powhatan Indian of Virginia who gave timely warning to the English of the intended massacre by Opechancanough, in Mar., 1622, thus preserving a number of lives.—Drake, Bk. Inds., 361, 1880.

**Chanech.** A Costanoan village formerly situated near the mission of Santa Cruz, Cal., as stated by Friar Olbez in 1819.—Taylor in Cal. Farmer, Apr. 5, 1860.

**Chaneleghatchee.** Probably a former Creek town in Alabama, between Tallapoosa and Chattahoochee rs. (Robin, Voy., II, map, 1807.) Not identifiable.

**Chanigtac.** A former village, presumably Costanoan, connected with Dolores mission, San Francisco, Cal.—Taylor in Cal. Farmer, Oct. 18, 1861.

**Chankaghaotina** ('dwellers in logs' [i. e., log huts?]). A division of the Wahpeton Sioux.
Ċan-kaġa-otina.—Dorsey (after Ashley) in 15th Rep. B. A. E., 216, 1897. Tcaⁿ-kaxa-otina.—Ibid.

**Chankaokhan** ('sore back,' referring to horses). A Hunkpapa division of the Teton Sioux.
Ċaŋ-ho-ham'-pa.—Hayden, Ethnog. and Philol. Mo. Val., 376, 1862. Ċaŋka oĥan.—Dorsey in 15th Rep. B. A. E., 221, 1897. Sore backs.—Culbertson in Smithson. Rep. 1850, 141, 1851. Tcañka-oqaⁿ.—Dorsey in 15th Rep. B. A. E., 221, 1897.

**Chankute** ('shoot in the woods among the deciduous trees'; a name of derision). A division of the Sisseton Sioux.
Ċaŋ kute.—Dorsey in 15th Rep. B. A. E., 217, 1897. Tcaⁿ-kute.—Dorsey in Jour. Am. Folk-lore, IV, 260, 1891.

**Chankute.** A division of the Yankton Sioux.
Barbarole.—Gass, Journal, 49, 1807. Ċaŋ kute.—Dorsey in 15th Rep. B. A. E., 217, 1897.—Jonkta.—Gass, op. cit. (told by an Indian that he belonged to the Jonkta or Barbarole people). Tcaⁿ-kute.—Dorsey, op. cit.

**Chanona** ('shoot at trees'). A division of the Upper Yanktonai Sioux, from which sprang the Hohe or Assiniboin.
Ċaŋ ona.—Dorsey in 15th Rep. B. A. E., 218, 1897. Tcaⁿ-ona.—Ibid. Wazi-kute.—Ibid. ('shooters among the pines').

**Chanshdachikana** (from the name of the chief, otherwise known as Istahba, Sleepy Eyes). A division of the Sisseton Sioux. One of the Dakota bands below L. Traverse, Minn., formerly considered a part of the Kahmiatonwan.
Ċaŋsdaċikana.—S. R. Riggs, letter to Dorsey, 1882. Sleepy Eyes band.—Ind. Aff. Rep. 1859, 60, 102, 1860.

**Chanshushka** ('box elder'). An unidentified division of the Dakota.

Chan-shu'-shka.—Boyd, Ind. Local Names, 1885.

**Chantapeta's Band.** A Dakota division, probably a part or all of the Hunkpapa, so called from their chief, commonly known as Fire Heart.—H. R. Ex. Doc. 117, 19th Cong., 1st sess., 6, 1826.

Arrapapas.—Sen. Ex. Doc. 90, 22d Cong., 1st sess., 63, 1832. Fire Heart's band.—Ibid.

**Chantkaip.** The Lakmiut name of a Santiam band formerly living below the junction of the Santiam forks, Oreg.

Tchän tkäíp.—Gatschet, Lakmiut MS., B. A E., 1877.

**Chants.** A Squawmish village community on Burrard inlet, Brit. Col.

Tcänts.—Hill-Tout in Rep. Brit. A. A. S., 475, 1900.

**Chaolgakhasdi.** One of the stopping places of the Tsejinkini and Tsehtlani clans of the Navaho, where, according to their genesis myth, they lived long and cultivated corn.

Tca'olgáqasdi.—Matthews in Jour. Am. Folk-lore, III, 91, 1890.

**Chaouacha.** A small tribe living, when first known, on Bayou La Fourche, a short distance below the present New Orleans, La. Although they had aided the French in their Indian wars, they fell under suspicion after the Natchez war, and in consequence were attacked and a number of the people massacred, in 1730, by negro slaves acting under orders from the French governor, who had in view the double purpose of weakening the power of the Indians and of overcoming any projected combination between them and the negroes. Subsequently they seem to have removed to the w. side of the Mississippi, a little above their former position.   (J. M.)

Chaouachas.—Pénicaut (1703) in French, Hist. Coll. La., n. s., I, 85, 1869. Chaouchas.—Boudinot, Star in the West, 126, 1816. Chawachas.—Jefferys, French Dom. Am., I, 150, 1761. Chorouachas.—Pénicaut (1713) in Margry, Déc., v, 506, 1883. Chouacas.—B. des Lozières, Voy. à la La., 242, 1802. Chouachas.—Dumont in French, Hist. Coll. La., v, 101, 1853. Tchaouachas.—Pénicaut (1703) in French, Hist. Coll. La., n. s., I, 85, 1869. Tehacoachas.—Lattré, map U. S., 1784.

**Chaoucoula.** One of the 7 villages or tribes formerly constituting the Taensa confederacy.—Iberville in Margry, Déc., IV, 179, 1880.

**Chapana.** A former village of Costanoan Indians of central California, connected with the mission San Juan Bautista. — Engelhardt, Franciscans in California, 398, 1897.

**Chapanaghtin.** An Atfalati band formerly living N. of Hillsboro, Washington co., Oreg.

Tcha panaχtin.—Gatschet, Atfalati MS., B. A. E., 1877.

**Chapokele.** An Atfalati band formerly residing 4 m. w. of Wapatoo lake, Yamhill co., Oreg.

Tcapókele.—Gatschet, Atfalati MS., B. A. E., 1877.

**Chapticon.** A tribe formerly living in St Mary or Charles co., Md., probably on Chaptico r. They were displaced in 1652 by the whites and with other tribes were assigned a tract at the head of Wicomico r.   (J. M.)

Chapticons.—Bozman, Maryland, II, 421, 1837. Choptico.—Ibid., 468 (incorrectly (?) made synonymous with Porto-Back [Potapaco]). Chopticons.—Davis, Daystar, 196, 1855.

**Chapugtac.** A former village, presumably Costanoan, connected with Dolores mission, San Francisco, Cal.—Taylor in Cal. Farmer, Oct. 18, 1861.

**Chapungathpi.** An Atfalati band formerly residing at Forest Grove, Washington co., Oreg., and on Wapatoo lake.

Tcha púngathpi.—Gatschet, Atfalati MS., B. A. E., 1877.

**Chaquantie.** A tribe in 1700, described by Bienville (Margry, Déc. IV, 442, 1880), on Indian information, as living on Red r. of Louisiana 4 days' travel above the Kadohadacho, which would place them apparently in the N. E. corner of Texas. They have not been identified, but may have been of Caddo affinity and alliance.

**Charac.** A Tehueco settlement on the Rio del Fuerte, about lat. 26° 15′, N. W. Sinaloa, Mexico. Hardy mentions it as a Mayo pueblo, which is improbable, although it may have contained some people of that tribe.

Charác.—Hardy, Travels in Mexico, 438, 1829. Charai.—Ibid., map. Charay.—Orozco y Berra, Geog., map, 1864. San José Charay.—Ibid., 332. Tscharai.—Kino, map (1702), in Stöcklein, Neue Welt-Bott, 1726.

**Charco** (Span.: 'pool'). A Papago village in s. Arizona with 50 inhabitants in 1858; probably identical with Chioro.

Del Charco.—Bailey in Ind. Aff. Rep., 208, 1858.

**Charco Escondido** ('hidden pool'). A locality about 9 leagues s. w. of Reynosa, between Matamoros and Victoria, in Tamaulipas, Mexico, one of the sections occupied by the Carrizo.

**Charcowa.** A band, probably of the Chinookan tribe of Clowwewalla, found in 1806 on the w. bank of Willamette r., Oreg., just above the falls. Their number was estimated at 200.

Chahcowahs.—Lewis and Clark Exped., Coues ed., 932, 1893. Charcawah.—Kelley, Oregon, 68, 1830. Charcowah.—Lewis and Clark, Exped., II, 474, 1814.

**Charity.** See *Hospitality.*

**Charlestown.** A township in Washington co., R. I., where a few mixed bloods, the remnants of the Narraganset and Nehantic, still live.   (J. M.)

**Charms.** See *Fetishes, Problematical objects.*

**Charnrokruit.** A Sidarumiut Eskimo village on Seahorse ids., Arctic coast, Alaska.—11th Census, Alaska, 162, 1893.

**Chartierstown.** An Iroquois village, before 1748, on the Ohio r., about 60 m. by water above Logstown, probably near Kittanning, Armstrong co., Pa. Peter Chartier was an influential Shawnee halfbreed about that period.   (J. M.)

Charretièr's band.—Vaudreuil (1760) in N. Y. Doc. Col. Hist., x, 1092, 1858. Chartiers.—Alcedo,

Dic. Geog., I, 476, 1786. **Chartiers Old-Town.**— Weiser (1748) in Kauffman, W. Penn., app., 14, 1851. **Chartiers - Town.**—Ibid. **Old Showonese Town.**—Ibid.

**Chaskpe.** A tribe or people mentioned by La Salle in 1683 (Margry, Déc., II, 314, 1877) as having come in company with the Shawnee and Ouabano at his solicitation to Ft St Louis, Ill., his desire being to draw them away from trade with the Spaniards. It is not known to what Indians the name refers, but from the fact that La Salle speaks of them as allies of the Chickasaw, it is probable that their home was s. of the present Illinois.
(J. M.    C. T.)

**Chasmuna** ('sandy'). An unidentified Dakota division.
**Chasmu'na.**—Boyd., Local Ind. Names, 7, 1885.

**Chasta.** A tribe, probably Athapascan, residing on Siletz res., Oreg., in 1867, with the Skoton and Umpqua, of which latter they were then said to have formed a part. The Chasta, Skoton, and Umpqua were distinct tribes which concluded a treaty Nov. 18, 1854. The Chasta were divided into the Kwilsieton and Nahelta, both residing on Rogue r. J. O. Dorsey thought these may have been identical with Kushetunne and Nakatkhetunne of the Tututunne. Kane, in 1859, located them near Umpqua r. In 1867 the Chasta, the Scoton, and the Umpqua together, at Siletz agency, numbered 49 males and 74 females, total 123. They may be identical with the Chastacosta or form a part of the Takilma. They do not seem to have any connection with the Shasta, who did not extend down Rogue r. below Table Rock, and who were generally bitterly at war with their Athapascan neighbors.
**Chastà.**—Parker, Jour., 257, 1840. **Chasta band of Rogue Rivers.**—Palmer in Rep. Ind. Aff., 464, 1854. **Chastay.**—Kane, Wand. in N. Am., 182, 1859. **Haw-quo-e-hov-took.**—Palmer in Rep. Ind. Aff., 464, 1854. **Illinois Creek bands.**—Ibid.

**Chastacosta** (*Shista kwŭsta*, their name for themselves, meaning unknown). A group of Athapascan villages formerly situated along Rogue r., Oreg., mostly on its N. bank from its junction with Illinois r. nearly to the mouth of Applegate cr. The Tututunne, who did not differ from them in customs or language, were to the w. of them; the Coquille, differing slightly in language, were N. of them; and the Gallice (Tattushtuntude), with the same customs but a quite different dialect, to the E. The Takilma, an independent stock, were their s. neighbors, living on the s. bank of Rogue r. and on its s. tributaries. In the summer of 1856, after a few months of severe fighting with the whites, 153 of them, consisting of 53 men, 61 women, 23 boys, 16 girls (Parrish in Ind. Aff. Rep. 1857, 357, 1858) were taken to Siletz res., Oreg., where now there are but a few individuals left.

It is practically certain that nearly all the inhabitants of these villages were removed at this time. Considering the number of the villages—33 according to Dorsey (Jour. Am. Folk-lore, III, 234, 1890), 19 according to an aged Gallice informant—this number is surprisingly small. The names of the villages, as given by Dorsey, usually referring to the people (*-tun*, *-tunne*) thereof, are Chetuttunne, Chunarghuttunne, Chunsetunneta, Chunsetunnetun, Chushtarghasuttun, Chusterghutmunnetun, Chuttushshunche, Khloshlekhwuche, Khotltacheche, Khtalutlitunne, Kthelutlitunne, Kushletata, Mekichuntun, Musme, Natkhwunche, Nishtuwekulsushtun, Sechukhtun, Senestun, Setaaye, Setsurgheake, Sheethltunne, Silkhkemechetatun, Sinarghutlitun, Skurghut, Sukechunetunne, Surghustesthitun, Tachikhwutme, Takasichekhwut, Talsunme, Tatsunye, Thethlkhuttunne, Tisattunne, Tsetaame, Tsetutkhlalenitun, Tukulitlatun, Tukwilisitunne, Tuslatunne. The following villages may be synonymous with ones in the list: Klothchetunne, Sekhatsatunne, Tasunmatunne.
(P. E. G.)
**Atchàshti amē'nmei.**—Gatschet, Kalapuya MS., B. A. E., 31 (Atfalati name). **Atchashti ámmim.**—Ibid. (Kalapuya name). **Càs-tä-k'o'-stä těné.**—Everette, MS. Tutu vocab., B. A. E., 1883 (trans.: 'people by the hills'). **Chasta Costa.**—Newcomb in Ind. Aff. Rep., 162, 1861. **Ci'-stă kqwŭs'-tä.**—Dorsey, Chasta Costa MS. vocab., B. A. E., 1884 (own name). **Ci'-stă qwŭs'-ta ɉŭnně.**—Dorsey, Chetco MS. vocab., B. A. E., 1884. **Cistocootes.**—Palmer in Ind. Aff. Rep. 1856, 216, 1857. **Katuku.**—Gatschet, MS., B. A. E. (Shasta name). **Shastacosta.**—Metcalfe in Ind. Aff. Rep. 1857, 357, 1858. **Shasta Costa.**—Abbott, MS. Coquille census, B. A. E., 1858. **Shis-tah-cos-tahs.**—Kautz, MS. Toutouten census, B. A. E., 1855. **Shis-tah-koastah.**—Ibid. **Shis-ta-koos-tee.**—Parrish in Ind. Aff. Rep. 1854, 495, 1855. **Shis-ta-kū-sta.**—Schumacher in Bull. U. S. Geol. Surv., III, 31, 1877. **Sisticoosta.**—Schoolcraft, Ind. Tribes, VI, 702, 1857. **Wálamskni.**—Gatschet, MS., B. A. E. (Klamath name). **Wálamswash.**—Gatschet, MS., B. A. E. (Modoc name).

**Chasta-Skoton.** A tribe or two tribes (Chasta and Skoton) formerly living on or near Rogue r., Oreg., perhaps the Chastacosta or (Dorsey in Jour. Am. Folk-lore, III, 235, 1890) the Sestikustun. There were 36 on Grande Ronde res. and 166 on Siletz res., Oreg., in 1875.
**Chasta-Scotans.**—Ind. Aff. Rep., 62, 1872. **Chasta Scoten.**—Taylor in Cal. Farmer, June 12, 1863. **Chasta Scoton.**—U. S. Stat. at Large, x, 675, 1854. **Shasta Scoton.**—Ind. Aff. Rep., 495, 1854. **Skoton-Shasta.**—Ind. Aff. Rep., 253, 1877.

**Chatagihl** (*atágihl*='firewood bark'). An Atfalati settlement at the upper end of Wapatoo lake, Yamhill co., Oreg.
**Tch atági'l.**—Gatschet, Atfalati MS., B. A. E., 1877.

**Chatagithl.** An Atfalati band formerly settled a mile s. w. of Wapatoo lake, Yamhill co., Oreg. Its last chief lived on Grande Ronde res. in 1878.
**Tch tágithl.**—Gatschet, Atfalati MS., B. A. E., 1877.

**Chatagshish.** A small Atfalati band formerly living in Washington co., Oreg.

Tcha tägshish.—Gatschet, Atfalati MS., B. A. E., 1877.

**Chatakuin** (*atakuin* refers to a tree). A former Atfalati settlement 7 m. N. of Hillsboro, Washington co., Oreg.
Tch' atakuin.—Gatschet, Atfalati MS., B. A. E., 1877.

**Chatamnei.** An Atfalati band, long extinct, that lived 10 m. N. of Wapatoo lake, in Washington co., Oreg.
Tcha támnei.—Gatschet, Atfalati MS., B. A. E., 1877.

**Chatchini.** A camping place not far from the Haida town of Kasaan, s. w. Alaska. As John Work gives it as the name of a town, the people of Kasaan may have had a permanent settlement there at one time. In 1836–41 it contained 249 inhabitants and 18 houses.—Swanton, field notes, 1900–01.
Chal-chu-nie.—Kane, Wand. N. A., app., 1859 (after Work, 1836–41). Chasinskoe.—Veniaminoff, Zapiski, II, pt. 3, 30, 1840. Chatcheeni.—Dawson, Queen Charlotte Ids., 173B, 1880 (simplified from Work). Chat-chee-nie.—Schoolcraft, Ind. Tribes, V, 489, 1855 (after Work). Chatounic.—Can. Ind. Aff., 8, 1872. Chatsinahs.—Scott in Ind. Aff. Rep., 312, 1868. Tcatcī'nî.—Swanton, Cont. Haida, 282, 1905.

**Chatelaw** (said to mean ' copper town '). A former Chickasaw town in N. Mississippi.—Romans, Fla., 63, 1775.

**Chatelech** ('outside water'). The present town of the Seechelt Indians on Trail bay, at the neck of Seechelt penin., Brit. Col. As a permanent settlement it dates only from Bishop Durien's time (*ca.* 1890), not having been occupied before for fear of the Lekwiltok.
TcatElētc.—Hill-Tout in Jour. Anthrop. Inst., 21, 1904.

**Chatilkuei.** An Atfalati band formerly residing 5 m. w. of Wapatoo lake, in Yamhill co., Oreg.
Tcha tilkuei.—Gatschet, Atfalati MS., B. A. E., 1877.

**Chatinak.** A Chnagmiut Eskimo village near the mouth of Yukon r., Alaska; pop. 40 in 1880. Petroff, 10th Census, Alaska, 12, 1884.
Catinakh.—Elliot, Our Arct. Prov., map, 1886. Chatinak.—Petroff, 10th Census, Alaska, 12, 1884. Chatinakh.—Nelson in 18th Rep. B. A. E., map, 1899.

**Chatoksofki** (*Chát aksúfki*, 'rock bluff'). A former Upper Creek town in Talladega co., Ala., with 143 families in 1833. Chatoksofki, Abikudshi, Niuyaka, and Oakfuskee were anciently considered one town whose people met at one place for their annual busk, q. v. In former times these were the greatest ball players of the Creeks. The few survivors are consolidated with the Eufaula in the Creek Nation, Ind. Ter., where a modern town known as Chatoksofki now exists. (A. S. G.)
Chattoesofkar.—H. R. Ex. Doc. 276, 24th Cong., 140, 1836. Chattofsofker.—Crawford (1836) in H. R. Doc. 274, 25th Cong., 2d sess., 24, 1838. Chat-tok-sof-ke.—Wyse, ibid., 61. Chattoksofker.—Jones et al., ibid., 101. Chattossofkins.—Campbell, ibid., 20. Chotoksaufk.—Taylor, ibid., 71. Old Merrawnaytown.—H. R. Ex. Doc. 276, 24th Cong., 333, 1836.

**Chatot.** A tribe or band which the French settled s. of Ft St Louis, on Mobile bay, Ala., in 1709. Bienville, wishing to change his settlement, "selected a place where the nation of the Chatots were residing, and gave them in exchange for it a piece of territory fronting on Dog r., 2 leagues farther down" (Pénicaut, 1709, in French, Hist. Coll. La., I, 103, 1869). According to Baudry des Lozières (Voy., 1794) the Chatot and Tohome tribes were related to the Choctaw and spoke the French and Choctaw languages.
Chactots.—Jefferys, French, Dom. Am., 162, 1761.

**Chats-hadai** (*Tcāts xā'da-i*, 'Tcats river people'). A subdivision of the Koetas, a Haida family belonging to the Kaigani group. They were probably so named from a camping place.—Swanton, Cont. Haida, 272, 1905.

**Chattahoochee** (Creek: *chátu* 'rock,' *hutchas* 'mark, design': 'pictured rocks'). A former Lower Creek town on the upper waters of Chattahoochee r., to which it gave its name; seemingly in the present Harris co., Ga. So called from some pictured rocks found at that point. The town was above Huthlitaiga, or War-ford, and it had probably been abandoned prior to Hawkins' time (1798–99), as he alludes to it as the "old town Chattohoche," not as an occupied village. (A. S. G.)
Catahouche.—Güssefeld, map of U. S., 1784. Catohoche.—Jefferys, French Dom. Am., 134, map, 1761. Cattagochee.—Lattré, map U. S., 1784. Chatahoochas.—Romans, Florida, I, 280, 1775. Chatahoosie.—Swan (1791) in Schoolcraft, Ind. Tribes, V, 262, 1855. Chatahouchi.—Alcedo, Dic. Geog., I, 477, 1786. Chata Uche.—Bartram, Travels, 462, 1792. Chat-to-ho-che.—Hawkins (1798–99), Sketch, 52, 1848. Katahooche.—Jefferys, Am. Atlas, 5, 1776. Tchattaouchi.—De l'Isle, map, in Winsor, Hist. Am., II, 295, 1886.

**Chattanooga** (Cherokee: *Tsatănu'gĭ*, meaning unknown.) The Cherokee name for a point on the creek entering Tennessee r. at the city of Chattanooga, Tenn. The ancient name for the site of the present city of Chattanooga was A'tlă'nuwă, from *tlă'nuwă* '(hawk) hole.' So far as is known there was no Cherokee settlement at the place, although some prominent men of the tribe lived in the vicinity.—Mooney in 19th Rep. B. A. E., 412, 413, 1900.

**Chattooka.** A village of the Neuse Indians, formerly on the site of Newbern, N. C. Graffenried bought the tract from the owners in 1710 and planted a German colony on it, the Indians withdrawing probably to the Tuscarora, with whom they were on intimate terms. (J. M.)
Chatoueka.—Graffenried (1711) in N. C. Rec., I, 978, 1886. Chattauqua.—Du Four (1885), ibid. Chattawka.—Graffenreid (1711), ibid., 910. Chattoka.—Lawson, map (1710) in Hawks, N. C., II, 1858. Chattoocka.—Graffenried, op. cit., 933. Chattooka.—Lawson (1710), Hist. N. C., 384, 1860.

**Chatuga** (also Chattooga, a corruption of the Cherokee *Tsatu'gĭ*, possibly meaning 'he drank by sips,' or 'he has crossed the stream and come out upon the other side,' but more likely of foreign origin). The name of three Cherokee settlements: (1) An ancient village on Chattooga r., a headstream of Savannah r., on the boundary between South Carolina and Georgia; (2) probably situated on upper Tellico r., in Monroe co., Tenn.; (3) perhaps on Chattooga r., a tributary of the Coosa, in N. W. Georgia.—Mooney in 19th Rep. B. A. E., 536, 1900.

Chatuga.—Bartram, Travels, 371, 1792. Chatugee.—Doc. of 1755 cited by Royce in 5th Rep. B. A. E., 142, 1887.

**Chatukchufaula.** An Upper Creek town on Tallapoosa r., Ala., probably in Chambers co., settled apparently by the Talasse.

Chalaacpauley.—Swan (1791) in Schoolcraft, Ind. Tribes, V, 262, 1855. Chattukchufaule.—Hawkins (1813) in Am. State Pap., Ind. Aff., I, 852, 1832. Chetocchefaula.—Woodward, Reminis., 35, 1859 (a branch of the Talasse).

**Chaubaqueduck.** A former village on Martha's Vineyard, Mass., or on Chappaquiddick id., just E. of it. In 1698 it had about 138 inhabitants. Boyd derives the word from *chippi-aquidne*, 'separated island.'

Chappaquidgick.—Mass. Hist. Soc. Coll., 1st s., I, 204, 1806. Chaubaqueduck.—Report of 1698, ibid., X, 131, 1809.

**Chaubatick.** A village of the Narraganset or Nehantic in 1651, probably within a few miles of Providence, R. I.—Williams (1651) in Mass. Hist. Soc. Coll. 3d s., IX, 292, 1846.

**Chaudière Noire.** See *Black Kettle*.

**Chaui** ('in the middle.'—Grinnell). A tribe of the Pawnee confederacy, spoken of by the French as Grand Pawnee. In the positions maintained by the 4 tribes of the Pawnee confederacy the villages of the Chaui were always between those of the Pitahauerat on the E. and Kitkehahki on the W. In the council of the confederacy the Chaui held a prominent place, their head chiefs outranking all others, and being accepted as representative of the Pawnee, although without power to dominate all the tribes. Little that is distinctive is known of this tribe. In 1833 they ceded to the United States their lands S. of Platte r., Nebr., and in 1857 all lands on the N. side of that stream, when the Pawnee res. on Loup r. was established. This land was ceded in 1876 and their reservation in Oklahoma set apart. Here they now live. Having taken their lands in severalty, in 1892 they became citizens of the United States. They were included in the missions established among the Pawnee. In customs and beliefs the Chaui did not differ from their congeners. They possessed many interesting ceremonies, of which that connected with the calumet (q. v.) has been preserved entire and gives evidence of their well-defined cosmogony and religious system. The divisions and totems

are not known. See Dunbar in Mag. Am. Hist., IV, V, VIII, 1880–82; Fletcher, The Hako, 22d Rep. B. A. E., II, 1904; Grinnell, Pawnee Hero Stories, 1889.
(A. C. F.)

Chä'-ne.—Morgan in Smithson. Cont., XVII, 196, 1871 (misprint.) Chau-i.—Grinnell, Pawnee Hero Stories, 215, 1889. Chä'-we.—Morgan, op. cit., 286. Chowees.—Ind. Aff. Rep., 213, 1861. Grand Pans.—Gregg, Com. of Prairies, II, 301, 1850 (so called by Canadians). Grand Par.—Lewis and Clark, Discov., 17, 1806. Grand Paunee.—H. R. Ex. Doc. 117, 19th Cong., 1st sess., 7, 1826. Grand Pawnee.—Pike, Exped., 143, 1810. Grands.—Ind. Aff. Rep., 213, 1861. Grands Panis.—Du Lac, Voy. Louisianes, vij, 1805. Great Pawnee.—Lewis and Clark, Exped., I, map, 1814. Panai Proper.—Lewis and Clark, Trav. in Amer., 38, 1807. Pânee.—Lewis and Clark, Discov., 17, 1806. Pania Proper.—Ibid., 62. Panias proper.—Ibid., 19. Panias propres.—Gass, Voyage, 417, 1810. Payiⁿ'qtci.—Dorsey, Kansa MS. vocab., B. A. E., 1882 (Kansa name). Páyiⁿqtsi.—Dorsey, Osage MS. vocab., B. A. E., 1883 (Osage name). Tcami'.—Dorsey, Kansa MS. vocab., B. A. E., 1882 (another Kansa name). Tcawi.—Dorsey, Çegiha MS. Dict., B. A. E., 1878–80 (own name and Omaha name). Tchắ-wè.—Long, Exped. Rocky Mts., II, lxxxv, 1823. Tsa'-u-i.—Gatschet, Pawnee MS. vocab., B. A. E. (own name). Tsáwi.—Ibid. χau'-i.—Dunbar in Mag. Am. Hist., IV, 251, 1880.

**Chaunis Temoatan** (*Chaun-istem-oatan*, 'salt-making village.'—Tooker). A country situated, in 1586, indefinitely westward from the English settlement on Roanoke id., N. C. Ralph Lane, from misinterpreted Indian information, believed it to have been a copper-producing region, and that it was situated "vp that riuer Moratoc [Roanoke]," 20 days' journey overland from the Mangoaks (Nottoway), who then dwelt about 160 m. above the Roanoke settlement. Lane's version of the Indian report shows that the Indians referred to salt making rather than copper mining. By Bozman, Bancroft, and others, this Indian report, as given by Lane, has been regarded as a fiction devised by a crafty Indian to lure the English to destruction; but Reynolds says that N. Georgia "corresponds as nearly as possible to the province of Chaunis Temoatan, described by distance and direction in Lane's account," while Tooker places it in the vicinity of Shawneetown, Gallatin co., Ill. In view of what Lane said of the Moratoc r. itself, the Indians probably referred to salt springs of the Kanawha and Little Kanawha valleys of West Virginia, or in the slopes and foothills of the Blue Ridge and Cumberland mts. "And for that not only Menatonon," says Lane, "but also the sauages of Moratoc themselves doe report strange things of the head of that riuer, and that from Moratoc itself, which is a principal towne upon that River, it is thirtie dayes as some of them say, and some say fourtie dayes voyage to the head thereof, which head they say springeth out of a maine rocke in that abundance; that forthwith it maketh a most violent stream; and further, that this huge rock standeth so neere unto a sea, that many times in stormes (the winds coming outwardly from the sea) the waues thereof are beaten into the said fresh streame, so that the fresh water for a certaine space, groweth salt and brackish." From this it would appear that even the sources of the Roanoke were reputed to be 30 or 40 days' journey from Moratoc town.

Consult Lane in Hakluyt, Voy., III, 1810. Reynolds in Am. Anthrop., I, Oct., 1888; Tooker in Am. Antiq., Jan., 1895. (J. N. B. H.)

**Chaushila.** A Yokuts (Mariposan) tribe in central California, N. of Fresno r., probably on lower Chowchilla r., in the plains and lowest foothills, their neighbors on the N. being of Moquelumnan stock. As a tribe they are now extinct. They are confused with, but are distinct from, the Chowchilla, under which name the synonymy of both is given.

Chaushila.—A. L. Kroeber, inf'n, 1905 (so pronounced by the Indians).

**Chautauqua.** (Seneca: *T'kĕñ chiată''kwĕⁿ*, 'one has taken out fish there,' referring to L. Chautauqua.—Hewitt). A system of popular education by means of lectures, reading circles, etc.; so called from Chautauqua, a village and lake in w. New York, where the Chautauqua Assembly (1874) and the Chautauqua Literary and Scientific Circle (1878) were founded under the auspices of Bishop Vincent of the Methodist Episcopal Church, by whom also a history of "The Chautauqua Movement" has been published. (A. F. C.)

**Chavite.** A province w. of the Mississippi and near Washita r., Ark., which probably took its name from a tribe of the southern Caddoan group. De Soto's troops passed through this country during the summer of 1542, and found the people making salt. See Biedma (1544) in French, Hist. Coll. La., II, 107, 1850.

**Chawagis-stustae** (*Tcawā'gĭs stAstā'-i*, 'the Stustas from Low-tide r.'). A subdivision of the Stustas, a great Haida family of the Eagle clan. The creek where they camped and which gave them the name is on the coast a short distance s. of Naikun or Rose spit, Graham id., Brit. Col.—Swanton, Cont. Haida, 276, 1905.

Tsiquā'gis stastaai'.—Boas, 12th Rep. N. W. Tribes Can., 23, 1898.

**Chawakli.** An ancient Lower Creek town on Apalachicola r., 12 m. below Ocheese Bluff, probably in Calhoun co., Fla. Its people were merged with the Eufaula.

Ehawho-ka-les.—Morse, Rep. to Sec. War, 364, 1822.

**Chawakoni.** A former Karok village on Klamath r., N. Cal.; exact location unknown.

Cha-ma-ko-neo.—McKee (1851) in Sen. Ex. Doc. 4, 32d Cong., spec. sess., 161, 1853. Cha-ma-ko-nees.—Ibid., 215 (given as a Hupa division). Cham-ma-ko-neo.—Ibid., 194. Tscha-wa-co-nihs.—Meyer, Nach dem Sacramento, 282, 1855.

**Chawayed.** An Atfalati band formerly living w. of Forest Grove, in Washington co., Oreg.

Tcha waye'd.—Gatschet, Atfalati MS., B. A. E., 1877.

**Chawopo.** A village of the Powhatan confederacy, in 1608, at the mouth of Chipoak cr., Surry co., Va.

Chawopo.—Smith (1629), Va., I, map, repr. 1819. Chawopoweanock.—Pots in Smith, ibid., 204 (incorrect combination of Chawopo and Weanock).

**Chawulktit.** The Lakmiut name of a camping place of the Calapooya on the forks of Yamhill r., a w. affluent of Willamette r., Oreg.

Tcha wúlktit.—Gatschet, Lakmiut MS., B. A. E., 1877.

**Chayen.** A former village, presumably Costanoan, connected with Dolores mission, San Francisco, Cal.—Taylor in Cal. Farmer, Oct. 18, 1861.

**Chayopin.** One of the tribes named by Garcia (Manual, title, 1760) as living at the missions about Rio San Antonio and Rio Grande in Texas, and identified by Mooney as a division of the Tonkawa. In 1785 there was a rancheria called Chayopin, with 8 inhabitants, near the presidio of La Bahía (the present Goliad) and the mission of Espíritu Santo de Zúñiga, on the lower San Antonio (Bancroft, No. Mex. States, I, 659, 1886).

Chapopines.—Taylor in Cal. Farmer, Apr. 17, 1863 (misprint).

**Cheálo.** A province of New Mexico in 1598, supposed to have been situated E. of the Rio Grande in the vicinity of the Salinas (Oñate, 1598, in Doc. Inéd., XVI, 118, 1871). It evidently pertained to the Tigua or the Piros. See *Salineros*.

**Cheam.** A town said to belong to the Pilalt, a Cowichan tribe of lower Chilliwack r., Brit. Col., but evidently containing representatives of other tribes as well; pop. 100 in 1902.

Che-ahm.—Brit. Col. map, Victoria, 1872. Cheam.—Can. Ind. Aff., pt. II, 158, 1901. Tcē'iām.—Boas in Rep. Brit. A. A. S., 454, 1894.

**Chebacco.** A sort of boat, thus defined by Bartlett (Dict. of Americanisms, 111, 1877): "*Chebacco* boat. A description of fishing vessel employed in the Newfoundland fisheries. So called from *Chebacco* parish, Ipswich, Mass., where many were fitted out. They are also called pinksterns, and sometimes tobacco-boats." The last name is probably a corruption of the first. Dr Murray, in the Oxford Dictionary, inclines to believe that the place may have been named from the boat, in which case *Chebacco* would be related to *Xebec*, etc. But it is probably from the Massachuset dialect of Algonquian. (A. F. C.)

**Chebog.** A name of the menhaden, from one of the eastern dialects of the

Algonquian stock, probably Narraganset or Massachuset. (A. F. C.)

**Chebontes.** A tribe mentioned in 1853 (Wessells in H. R. Ex. Doc. 76, 34th Cong., 3d sess., 32, 1857) as living s. E. of Tulare lake, Cal. Supposed from the location and association to be Mariposan, though possibly Shoshonean.

**Cheboygan** (*Kichibwagan*, 'a large pipe.'—Hewitt). An Ottawa band formerly living on Cheboygan r., Cheboygan co., Mich. By treaty of July 31, 1855, they were granted 2 townships about Burts lake; subsequently lands were allotted to them in severalty and the surplus restored to the public domain by acts of Congress of June 10, 1872, and May 23, 1876.
Cheboigan band.—Schoolcraft, Ind. Tribes, I, 478, 1853. Cheboygan.—Detroit treaty (1855) in U. S. Ind. Treat., 615, 1873. Cībaiigan.—W. Jones, inf'n, 1905.

**Chechawkose** (diminutive of *chi'-chăk*, crane: 'Little Crane.'—Dunn). A Potawotami chief who lived at a village commonly called "Chechawkose's village," on the s. side of Tippecanoe r., about Harrison tp., Kosciusko co., Ind. The reserve was sold in 1836. Also spelled Cheechawkose and Chitchakos. (J. M.)

**Chechelmen.** A Squawmish village community on Burrard inlet, Brit. Col.
Tcetcē'lmen.—Hill-Tout in Rep. Brit. A. A. S., 474, 1900.

**Chechilkok.** A Squawmish village community at Seymour cr., Burrard inlet, Brit. Col.; pop. 44 in 1902.
Creek.—Seymour in Can. Ind. Aff., pt. II, 160, 1900. Tcētcilqōk.—Hill-Tout in Rep. Brit. A. A. S., 475, 1900.

**Chechinquamin.** See *Chinquapin*.

**Checopissowo.** A village of the Powhatan confederacy, in 1608, on Rappahannock r., above Tobacco cr., in Caroline co., Va.—Smith (1629), Virginia, I, map, repr. 1819.

**Checout.** See *Chickwit*.

**Chedtokhanye** ('big buffalo bull'). A subgens of the Arukhwa, the Buffalo gens of the Iowa.
Tce-ʒo' qaⁿ'-ye.—Dorsey in 15th Rep. B. A. E., 239, 1897.

**Chedtoyine** ('young buffalo bull'). A subgens of the Arukhwa, the Buffalo gens of the Iowa.
Tce-ʒo yiñ'-e.—Dorsey in 15th Rep. B. A. E., 239, 1897.

**Chedunga** ('buffalo bull,' or 'buffalo with dark hair'). A Kansa gens, the 6th on the Yata side of the tribal circle. Its subgentes are Chedunga and Yukhe.
Buffalo.—Morgan, Anc. Soc., 156, 1877. Buffalo bull.—Dorsey in Am. Natural., 671, July, 1885. Che-dong-ga.—Stubbs, Kaw MS. vocab., B. A. E., 1877. Mo-é-kwe-ah-hä.—Morgan, Anc. Soc., 156, 1877. Si-tañga.—Dorsey, Kansa MS. vocab., B. A. E., 1882 (sig. 'big foot'). Tcedŭñga.—Dorsey in Am. Natural., 671, July, 1885. Wadjúta tañga.—Dorsey, Kansa MS. vocab., B. A. E., 1882 (sig. 'big quadruped').

**Chedunga.** A subgens of the Chedunga gens of the Kansa.
Tcedŭñga.—Dorsey in 15th Rep. B. A. E., 232, 1897.

**Cheechawkose.** See *Chechawkose*.

**Cheerno.** A body of Songish at Beecher bay, s. E. end of Vancouver id. It perhaps includes the Kekayaken gens. Pop. 48 in 1902.
Cheerno.—Can. Ind. Aff., 66, 1902. Tche-a-nook.—Can. Ind. Aff., 308, 1879 (probably the same).

**Cheeshateaumuck, Caleb.** The only New England Indian in early days who completed his studies at Harvard College, taking his degree in 1666. He died of consumption. (A. F. C.)

**Cheesoheha.** A former Cherokee settlement on a branch of Savannah r., in upper South Carolina; destroyed during the Revolutionary war. (J. M.)

**Cheewack.** A body of Salish under Williams Lake agency, Brit. Col.; pop. 9 in 1891, when the name last appears.
Chawack.—Can. Ind. Aff. 78, 1878. Cheewack.—Ibid., 251, 1891.

**Chefixico's Old Town.** A Seminole settlement formerly on the s. side of Old Tallahassee lake, 5 m. E. of Tallahassee, Fla.—Roberts, Florida, 1763.

**Chefoklak.** A Chnagmiut village near the head of the Yukon delta, Alaska; pop. 26 in 1880.
Chefokhlagamute.—Petroff, 10th Census, Alaska, 54, 1884.

**Cheghita** ('eagle'). A Missouri gens with the Wakanta, Khra, Kretan, and Momi subgentes.—Dorsey in 15th Rep. B. A. E., 240, 1897.
Eagle people.—Dorsey, Tciwere MS. vocab., B. A. E., 1879. Tce'xi-ta.—Dorsey in 15th Rep. B. A. E., 240, 1897. Thunder-bird.—Dorsey, Tciwere MS. vocab., B. A. E., 1879. Wakanta.—Ibid.

**Cheghita.** An Oto gens.
Eagle.—Morgan, Anc. Soc., 156, 1877. Kĥa'-ă.—Ibid. (='eagle'[?]; cf. *Khra*). Tce'-xi-ta.—Dorsey in 15th Rep. B. A. E., 240, 1897.

**Cheghita.** An Iowa gens. Its subgentes are Nachiche, Khrahune, Khrakreye, and Khrapathan.
Cheh'-he-tä.—Morgan, Anc. Soc., 156, 1877. Eagle.—Ibid. Tce'-xi-ta.—Dorsey in 15th Rep. B. A. E., 238, 1897.

**Cheghulin** ('village on the open prairie'). A former Kansa village on the s. side of Kansas r., Kans.
Tcexúliⁿ.—Dorsey, Kansa MS. vocab., B. A. E., 1882.

**Cheghulin.** A Kansa village, evidently named after the earlier settlement of that name; situated on a tributary of Kansas r., on the N. side, E. of Blue r., Kans.
Tcexúliⁿ.—Dorsey, Kansa MS. vocab., B. A. E., 1882.

**Chegnakeokisela** ('half breechcloth'). A division of the Hunkpapa Teton Sioux.
Born in the middle.—Culbertson in Smithson. Rep. 1850, 141, 1851. Cegnake-okisela.—Dorsey in 15th Rep. B. A. E., 221, 1897. Ce'-ĥa-na-ka'.—Hayden, Ethnog. and Philol. Mo. Valley, 376, 1862 ('three-cornered cloth'). Half breech clout people.—Culbertson, op. cit. Tcegnake-okisela.—Dorsey, op. cit.

**Chegoli.** A former town on the E. bank of Tallapoosa r., Ala. (Bartram, Trav., I, map, 1799). Not identified, but probably Creek.

**Chegwalis** ('spotted frog'). A gens of the Abnaki.

**Chehalis.** A collective name for several Salishan tribes on Chehalis r. and its affluents, and on Grays harbor, Wash. Gibbs states that it belongs strictly to a village at the entrance of Grays harbor, and signifies 'sand.' There were 5 principal villages on the river, and 7 on the N. and 8 on the S. side of the bay; there were also a few villages on the N. end of Shoalwater bay. By many writers they are divided into Upper Chehalis or Kwaiailk (q. v.), dwelling above Satsop r., and the Lower Chehalis from that point down. The following subdivisions are mentioned, some of which were single villages, while others probably embraced people living in several: Chiklisilkh, Cloquallum, Hoquiam, Hooshkal, Humptulips, Kishkallen, Klimmim, Klumaitumsh, Koalekt, Nickomin, Nooachhummilh, Noohooultch, Nookalthu, Noosiatsks, Nooskoh, Satsop, Wenatchi, Whiskah. The Satsop speak a dialect distinct from the others. In 1806 Lewis and Clark assigned to them a population of 700 in 38 lodges. In 1904 there were 147 Chehalis and 21 Humptulips under the Puyallup school superintendent, Wash.    (H. W. H.    J. R. S.)

Atchiχe'lish.—Gatschet, Calapooya MS. vocab., 31, B. A. E. (Calapooya name).    Chachelis.—Framboise quoted by Gairdner in Jour. Geog. Soc. Lond., XI, 255, 1841.    Chealis.—Taylor in Cal. Farmer, June 12, 1863.    Chebaylis.—Lane in Ind. Aff. Rep., 162, 1850.    Checaldish.—Lee and Frost, Ten Years in Oregon, 99, 1844.    Checalish.—Ibid., 103.    Chechili.—Latham in Trans. Philol. Soc. Lond., 71, 1856.    Cheehales.—Dart in Ind. Aff. Rep., 215, 1851.    Cheenales.—Schoolcraft, Ind. Tribes, III, map, 200, 1853.    Chehalis.—Mooney in 14th Rep. B. A. E., pl. lxxxviii, 1896.    Chehaylis.—Lane (1849) in Sen. Ex. Doc. 52, 31st Cong., 1st sess., 174, 1850.    Chekalis.—Townsend, Narr., 175, 1839.    Chekilis.—Duflot de Mofras, Expl. de l'Orég., II, 335, 1844.    Chick-a-lees.—Starling in Ind. Aff. Rep., 172, 1852.    Chickeeles.—Wilkes, West. Am., 88, 1849.    Chickelis.—Ross, Adventures, 87, 1849.    Chihales.—Starling in Ind. Aff. Rep., 447, 1854.    Chihalis.—Gibbs in Pac. R. R. Rep., I, 435, 1855.    Chiheelees.—Scouler (1846) in Jour. Ethnol. Soc. Lond., I, 249, 1848.    Chiheeleesh—Drake, Book Inds., vii, 1848.    Chihelish.—Morse, Rep. to Sec. War, 368, 1822.    Chikailish.—Hale in U. S. Expl. Exped., VI, 211, 1846.    Chikalish.—Gallatin in Trans. Am. Ethnol. Soc., II, 20, 1848.    Chikeelis.—Scouler (1846) in Jour. Ethnol. Soc. Lond., I, 235, 1848.    Chikelis.—Farnham, Travels, 112, 1843.    Tcheheles.—Chikilishes.—Domenech, Deserts, II, 56, 1860.    Chikoilish.—Hale in U. S. Expl. Exped., VI, 198, 1846.    Chillates.—Schoolcraft, Ind. Tribes, III, 571, 1853.    Chilts.—Lewis and Clark, Exped., I, map, 1814.    Chiltz.—Gass, Jour., 189, 1807.    Ehihalis.—Schoolcraft, Ind. Tribes, V, 490, 1853.    Ilgát.—Gatschet, B. A. E., 1877 (Nestucca name).    Staq-túbc.—McCaw, Puyallup MS. vocab., B. A. E., 1885 (Puyallup name: 'inland people').    Tcheheles.—De Smet, Letters, 231, 1843.    Tchikeylis.—Franchère, Narr., 124, 1854.    Tcïts-hets.—Eells in letter of Feb., 1886 (own name).    Tsehalish.—Gray, Letter to Gibbs, B. A. E., 1869.    Tsheheilis.—Tolmie and Dawson, Vocabs., B. C., 121B, 1884.    Tsihaili-Selish.—Hale in U. S. Expl. Exped., VI, 211, 1846.    Tsihailish.—Ibid.    Tsihalis.—Gibbs in Cont. N. A. Ethnol., I, 171, 1877.    Tsi-he-lis.—Eells in letter of Feb., 1886.

**Chehalis** (*StsEē'lis*). A Cowichan tribe living along the middle course of Harrison r., Brit. Col. Chehalis and Koalekt were their villages. Pop. (of tribe or village) 112 in 1902.

Chehales.—Can. Ind. Aff. for 1880, 317.    Chehalis.—Ibid., 1901, pt. II, 158.    Saelis.—Brit. Col. map, Ind. Aff., Victoria, 1872.    StsEē'lis.—Boas in Rep. Brit. A. A. S., 454, 1899 (the village).

**Chehelu.** A clan of the Acheha phratry of the ancient Timucua in Florida.—Pareja (*ca.* 1612) quoted by Gatschet in Am. Philos. Soc. Proc., 492, 1878.

**Cheikikarachada** ('they call themselves after a buffalo'). A Winnebago gens.

Buffalo.—Morgan, Anc. Soc., 157, 1877.    Cha'-rä.—Ibid.    Tcéi-ki'-ka-ra'-tca-da.—Dorsey in 15th Rep. B. A. E. 240, 1897.

**Chein.** Mentioned by Oñate (Doc. Inéd., XVI, 114, 1871) as a pueblo of New Mexico in 1598; doubtless situated in the Salinas, in the vicinity of Abo, and in all probability occupied by the Tigua or the Piros.

**Cheindekhotding** ('place where he was dug up'). A Hupa village on Trinity r., Cal.

Chan-ta-kó-da.—Powers in Cont. N. A. Ethnol., III, 73, 1877.    Tceïndeqotdiñ.—Goddard, Hupa, 13, 1903.

**Chekase's Village.** A former Potawatomi village on the W. side of Tippecanoe r., between Warsaw and Monoquet, Kosciusko co., Ind. The reserve on which it was situated was sold in 1836. The name, which is also spelled Checose and Chicase (*cha'kosi*, 'short of stature'), is that of a chief who formerly resided there.    (J. M.)

**Chekhuhaton** ('kettle with legs'). A band of the Oglala Teton Sioux.

Çeh-huha-toɳ.—Dorsey (after Cleveland) in 15th Rep. B. A. E., 220, 1897.    Tceq-huha-toɳ.—Ibid.

**Chekilli** (from *achikilläs*, 'making a short step backward.'—Gatschet). The principal chief of the Creek confederacy at the period of the settlement of the Georgia colony in 1733, having succeeded the "Emperor Bream" on the death of the latter. He appears to have been one of the Creeks who visited England with Tomochichi in that year. In 1735, as "Emperor of the Upper and Lower Creeks," he headed a delegation in a council with the English at Savannah, on which occasion he recited the national legend of the Creeks, as recorded in pictographs upon a buffalo skin, which was delivered to the commissioners and afterward hung up in the London office of the colony. It is now lost, but the translation has been preserved, and has been made the subject of a brief paper by Brinton and an extended notice by Gatschet. In 1752 Chekilli was residing at Coweta, and although still regarded as principal ruler of the confederacy had delegated his active authority to Malatche, the war chief, a younger man. The name appears also as Chiggilli and Tchikilli. See Bosomworth, MS. Jour., 1752, copy in B. A. E.; Brinton, Nat. Leg. Chahta-

Muskokee Tribes, in Hist. Mag., Feb., 1870; Gatschet, Creek Migr. Leg., I, II, 1884, 1888.                    (J. M.)

**Chekoalch.** A Squawmish village community on Burrard inlet, Brit. Col.
Tcekō'altc.—Hill-Tout in Rep. Brit. A. A. S., 474, 1900.

**Chekwa** (prob. from *ching'wǎ*, 'thunder rolls'). Given by Morgan (Anc. Soc., 167, 1878) as the Thunder gens of the Potawatomi.

**Chelamela.** A small division of the Kalapooian family formerly living on Long Tom cr., a w. tributary of Willamette r., Oreg. They were included in the Dayton treaty of 1855. Nothing is known of their customs, and they are now extinct.
Chelamela.—U. S. Ind. Treat. (1855), 19, 1873. La-malle.— Ross, Adventures, 236, 1849. Long Tom.—U. S. Ind. Treat. (1855), 19, 1873.

**Cheli.** The Spruce clan of the Tewa pueblo of Hano, Ariz.
Ca'-la-bi.—Stephen in 8th Rep. B. A. E., 39, 1891 (Hopi name). Tce'-li.—Ibid. (own name). Ts'-co.—Ibid. (Navaho name).

**Chelly** (pron. *shay-ee*, frequently *shay*, Spanish corruption of Navaho *Tsé'gi*, or *Tséyi*, 'among the cliffs.'—Matthews). A canyon on the Navaho res., N. E. Ariz., in which are numerous ancient cliff-dwellings. Cortéz in 1799 (Pac. R. R. Rep., III, pt. 3, 119, 1856) gave the name (Chellé) to a Navaho settlement, but this is true only in so far as the canyon contains numerous scattered hogans or huts.

**Chemanis.** A Cowichan settlement on the E. coast of Vancouver id., presumably on the bay of the same name.
Chemainis.—Can. Ind. Aff. for 1891, map. Chemanis.—Brit. Col. map, Victoria, 1872.

**Chemapho.** Mentioned in the Dayton treaty of 1855 as a Kalapooian band.
Chem-a-pho.—U. S. Ind. Treat. (1855), 19, 1873. Maddy Band.—Ibid.

**Chemehuevi.** A Shoshonean tribe, apparently an offshoot of the Paiute, formerly inhabiting the E. bank of the Rio Colorado from Bill Williams fork to the Needles and extending westward as far as Providence mts., Cal., their chief seat being Chemehuevi valley, which stretches for 5 m. along the Colorado and nearly as far on either side. When or how they acquired possession of what appears to have been Yuman territory is not known. They may possibly have been seen by Alarcon, who navigated the Rio Colorado in 1540; but if so, they are not mentioned by name. Probably the first definite reference to the Chemehuevi is that by Fray Francisco Garcés, who passed through their country in journeying from the Yuma to the Mohave, and again from lower Kern r. to the latter tribe on his way to the pueblo of Oraibi in N. E. Arizona in 1775–76. Among the Indians whom Garcés saw, or of whom he heard, are the Chemegué, Chemegué Cuajála, Chemegué Sevinta, and Che-

meguaba, the first and last mentioned being apparently the Chemehuevi, while the others are the Virgin River Paiute and Shivwits, respectively, "Chemegué" here being used somewhat in the sense of denoting Shoshonean affinity. In passing down the Colorado from the Mohave rancherias Garcés does not mention any Chemehuevi or other Indians in Chemehuevi valley or elsewhere on the river until the Yuman Alchedoma ("Jalchedunes"), some distance below, were reached. He found the Chemehuevi in the desert immediately s. w., w., and N. w. of the Mohave. The same observer remarks that they wore Apache moccasins, antelope-skin shirts, and a white headdress like a cap, ornamented with the crest feathers of a bird, probably the roadrunner. They were very swift of foot, were friends of the Ute (Paiute?), Yavapai Tejua, and Mohave, and when the latter "break their weapons" (keep the peace), so do they also. It is said that they occupied at this time the country between the Beñemé (Panamint and Serrano) and the Colorado "on the N. side" as far as the Ute, and extending to another river, N. of the Colorado, where they had their fields. They made baskets, and those whom Garcés saw "all carried a crook besides their weapons," which was used for pulling gophers, rabbits, etc., from their burrows. Their language was noted as distinct from that of the other Rio Colorado tribes, as in fact it is, these being Yuman (see Garcés, Diary, Coues ed., op.cit., 1900; Heintzelman (1853) in H. R. Ex. Doc. 76, 34th Cong., 3d sess., 1857; Pacific R. R. Rep., III, pt. 3, 1856). Physically the Chemehuevi appear to have been inferior to the Yuma and Mohave. Ives properly credits them with being a wandering people, traveling "great distances on hunting and predatory excursions," and although they did live mainly on the natural products of the desert, they farmed on ɩ small scale where possible. Like the other Colorado r. tribes, they had no canoes, but used rafts made of bundles of reeds. Their number was estimated by Leroux about 1853 at 1,500, probably an excessive estimate for the whole tribe; in 1866 Thomas estimated their population at 750. In 1903 there were 300 on the Colorado River res. and probably a few under the Moapa agency. It is also likely that a few are not under any agent but roam as Paiute. Of the organization of the Chemehuevi nothing positive is known. Palonies is mentioned by Hoffman (Bull. Essex Inst., XVII, 28, 1885) as a subdivision.    (H. W. H. A. L. K.)
Ah'alakát.—ten Kate, Reizen in N. Am., 160, 1885 ('small bows': Pima name). Che-ma-hua-vas.— Thomas, Yuma MS. vocab., B. A. E., 1868. Che-ma-wa-was.—Heintzelman (1853) in H. R.

Ex. Doc. 76, 34th Cong., 3d sess., 1857. **Chemchuevis.**—Shipp, De Soto and Florida, 131, 1881 (misprint). **Chemebet.**—Garcés (1775–76), Diary, 219, 1900. **Chemegerabas.**—Simpson in Rep. Sec. War, 57, 1850 (misquoted from Ruxton). **Chemeguaba.**—Garcés (1775–76), Diary, 353, 1900. **Chemeguava.**—Escudero, Not. Estad. de Chihuahua, 228, 1834. **Chemegue.**—Garcés (1775–76), Diary, 444, 1900 (mentioned separately from "Chemeguaba," but doubtless the same). **Chemehnevis.**—Haines, Am. Ind., 139, 1888 (misprint). **Chemehuevas.**—Cushing in Atl. Mo., 544, Oct., 1882.—**Chem-e-húe-vis.**—Whipple, Pac. R. R. Rep., III, pt. 3, 16, 1856. **Chemehuevis.**—Ives, Col. Riv., 54, 1861 (misprint). **Chem-e-hue-vitz.**—Ibid. **Chemehuewas.**—Jones in Ind. Aff. Rep. 1869, 215, 1870. **Chemeonahas.**—Mayer, Mexico, II, 38, 1854. **Chemequaba.**—Cortez (1799) quoted in Pac. R. R. Rep., III, pt. 3, 126, 1856. **Chemeque.**—Ibid. (see *Chemegue* above). **Chemiguabos.**—Bollaert in Jour. Ethnol. Soc. Lond., II, 276, 1850 (misquoting Ruxton). **Chemiheavis.**—Ind. Aff. Rep., 578, 1865. **Chemihuahua.**—Gibbs, MS. letter to Higgins, B. A. E., 1866. **Chemihuaras.**—Maltby in Ind. Aff. Rep., 94, 1866. **Chemihuaves.**—Gibbs, MS., B. A. E., 1866. **Chemihuevas.**—Antisell in Pac. R. R. Rep., VII, pt. 4, 104, 1854. **Chemihuevis.**—Taylor in Cal. Farmer, June 12, 1863. **Cheminares.**—Maltby in Ind. Aff. Rep., 94, 1866. **Chimawava.**—Adams in H. R. Misc. Doc. 12, 41st Cong., 3d sess., 12, 1870. **Chimchinves.**—Maltby in Ind. Aff. Rep., 102, 1866. **Chimehuevas.**—Ehrenberg in Ind. Aff. Rep., 139, 1865. **Chimehueve.**—Kingsley, Stand. Nat. Hist., pt. 6, 189, 1883. **Chimehwhuebes.**—Mollhausen, Pacific, II, 274, 1858. **Chimewawas of Arizona.**—Ingalls in H. R. Ex. Doc. 66, 42d Cong., 3d sess., 2, 1873. **Chimhuevas.**—Ind. Aff. Rep., 175, 1875. **Chi-mi-huahua.**—Heintzelman in H. R. Ex. Doc. 76, 34th Cong., 3d sess., 44, 1857. **Chimohueois.**—Bourke, Moquis of Ariz., 228, 1884. **Chim-ue-hue-vas.**—Hodge, Arizona, 159, 1877. **Chim-woy-os.**—Whipple, Exped., 17, 1851. **Eche-mo-hua-vas.**—Thomas, Yuma MS. vocab, B. A. E., 1868. **Echi-mo-hua-vas.**—Ibid. **Itchi-mehueves.**—Gatschet, MS., B.A.E. (Mohave and Walapai name). **Kemahwivi.**—Ind. Aff. Rep., 246, 1877. **Mat-hat-e-vátch.**—Whipple, Pac. R. R. Rep., III, pt. 3, 16, map, 1856 (Yuma name ['northerners']). **Mat-jus.**—Heintzelman in H. R. Ex. Doc. 76, 34th Cong., 3d sess., 44, 1857. **Simojueves.**—Froebel, Seven Years' Trav., 511, 1859. **Tantawait.**—Ind. Aff. Rep., 251, 1877. **Tä'n-tá'wats.**—Powell, MS., B. A. E ('southern men': own name). **Tontewaits.**—ten Kate, Reizen in N. Am., 122, 1885.

**Chemeketas.** Supposed to have been one of the Kalapooian bands formerly near Salem, Oreg.—Ingersoll in Harper's Mag., 769, Oct., 1882.

**Chemetunne** ('people on the ocean coast'). A Tututunne village or group of villages formerly at the mouth of Rogue r., Oreg. The people were taken to Siletz res., Oreg., in June, 1856. A few individuals are still to be found on that reservation, where they are officially known as Joshuas, a corruption of *Ya'-shu*, their Alsea name; and a few others still live near their old home.
**I-ă'cu-we těné.**—Everette, MS. Tutu vocab., B. A. E., 1883 (trans.: 'people by the mossy swamp'). **Joshua.**—Newcomb in Ind. Aff. Rep., 162, 1861. **Joshuta.**—Taylor in Cal. Farmer, Mar. 22, 1861. **Joshuts.**—Palmer in Ind. Aff. Rep. 1856, 219, 1857. **Tcê'-mê.**—Dorsey, MS. Tutu vocab., B. A. E., 1884 ('on the coast of the ocean': Tututunne name). **Tce-me' těné.**—Everette, MS. Tutu vocab., B. A. E., 1883 (trans.: 'people by the mossy water'). **Tcê-me' ʒûnně.**—Dorsey in Jour. Am. Folk-lore, III, 233, 1890. **Tcê-mê' tûnně.**—Dorsey, Coquille MS. vocab., B. A. E., 1884 (Coquille name). **Ya'-cu.**—Dorsey, Alsea MS. vocab., B. A. E., 1884 (pron. *Ya'-shu*, Alsea name, the term from which "Joshua" is derived). **Ya'-cu-me' ʒûnně.**—Dorsey, Chetco MS. vocab., B. A. E., 1884 (Chetco

name). **Yah-shoots.**—Gibbs, MS. on coast tribes Oregon, B. A. E., 1856. **Yahshutes.**—Ind. Aff. Rep. 1854, 496, 1855. **Yash-ue.**—Abbott, MS. Coquille census, B. A. E., 1858. **Ya-su-chah.**—Pres. Mess., Ex. Doc. 39, 32d Cong., 1st sess., 2, 1852. **Yasuchaha.**—Domenech, Deserts N. Am., I, map, 1860. **Yasuchan.**—Schoolcraft, Ind. Tribes, III, maps, 96, 200, 1853. **Ya-sūt.**—Schumacher in Bull. G. and G. Surv., III, 31, 1877. **Yoshuway.**—Everette, MS. Tutu vocab., B. A. E., 1883.

**Chemisez** (apparently from Spanish *chamizo*, a species of small cane). A Pima village on the Rio Gila in Arizona; pop. 312 in 1858.—Bailey in Ind. Aff. Rep., 208, 1858.

**Chemung.** An Iroquois village, probably of the Seneca, formerly on or near the site of the present Chemung, N. Y. It was destroyed by Sullivan in 1779. An older village of the name stood about 3 m. farther down Chemung r. (J. M.)
**Chemeney.**—Pemberton (*ca.* 1792) in Mass. Hist. Soc. Coll., 1st sess., II, 176, 1810. **Chemong.**—Jones (1780) in N. Y. Doc. Col. Hist., VIII, 785, 1857. **Chemung.**—Livermore (1779) in N. H. Hist. Soc. Coll., VI, 321, 1850.

**Chenachaath**(*Tc'ē'natc'aath*). A division of the Toquart, a Nootka tribe.—Boas in 6th Rep. N. W. Tribes Can., 32, 1890.

**Chenango**(Seneca: *Ochenango*, 'large bull thistles.'—Hewitt). A former village on the river of the same name, about Binghamton, Broome co., N. Y. It was settled in 1748 by the Nanticoke from Maryland, under Iroquois protection. Soon thereafter they were joined by a part of the Shawnee, together with remnants of the Mahican and Wappinger tribes. The whole body moved w. about the beginning of the French and Indian war in 1754, and were mostly incorporated with the Delawares. (J. M.)
**Chenango.**—Guy Park conf. (1775) in N. Y. Doc. Col. Hist., VIII, 560, 1857. **Chenengo.**—Brown in Mass. Hist. Soc. Coll., 1st s., IX, 120, 1804. **Ochenäng.**—Morgan, League Iroq., 473, 1851 (Oneida name of Chenango r. and Binghamton). **Osewingo.**—Homann Heirs' map, 1756. **Oswingo.**—Mandrillon, Spectateur Américain, map, 1785. **Otseningo.**—Ft Johnson conf. (1756) in N. Y. Doc. Col. Hist., VII, 67, 1856. **Otsiningo.**—Johnson (1756), ibid., 141. **Otsininko.**—Ft Johnson conf. (1757), ibid., 253. **Schenenk.**—Pyrlaeus (*ca.* 1750) quoted by Barton, New Views, app. 4, 1798. **Shenengo.**—Ibid. **Utsanango.**—Croghan (1765) in Monthly Am. Jour. Geol., 271, 1831.

**Chenco, Chenko.** See *Chunkey*.

**Chenlin.** A former settlement of mixed Yuit Eskimo and Chukchi, between Acon and Wuteen, N. E. Siberia. The greater part of its inhabitants perished by famine in 1880; the remainder turned to reindeer breeding or emigrated to Cherinak and St Lawrence id.
**Če'nlin.**—Bogoras, Chukchee, 29, 1904.

**Chenposel** ('dwelling below'). A tribe of the Patwin division of the Copehan family, formerly living on lower Cache cr., Yolo co., Cal.—Powers in Cont. N. A. Ethnol., III, 219, 1877.

**Chentansitzan.**—A Yukonikhotana village on the N. bank of Yukon r., 30 m. below the mouth of Melozi r., Alaska.

**Chentsithala.** A Naskotin village on Fraser r., Brit. Col., at the mouth of Quesnelle r.

Chichula.—Brit. Col. map, Victoria, 1872. **Quesnel.**—Morice, Notes on W. Dénés, 24, 1893. **Quesnelle Mouth.**—Tolmie and Dawson, Vocabs. Brit. Col. map, 1884. **Tcentsithal'a.**—Morice in Trans. Roy. Soc. Can., x, sec. 2, 109, 1892.

**Cheokhba** ('sleepy kettle'). A division of the Hunkpapa Teton Sioux.

Ce-oḣba.—Dorsey in 15th Rep. B. A. E., 221, 1897. Ċi-o-ho'-pa.—Hayden, Ethnog. and Philol. Mo. Val., 376. 1862. **Sleepy kettle band.**—Culbertson in Smithson. Rep. 1850, 141, 1851 (under White Feet. O-jah-ska-ska). **Tce-oqba.**—Dorsey in 15th Rep. B. A. E., 221, 1897.

**Chepanoc** (Renape *tchĕpanok*, or *tchäpanok*, 'people separated'.—Gerard). A village of the Weapomeioc in 1586 on Albemarle sd., in Perquimans co., N. C.

Chapanun.—Dutch map (1621) in N. Y. Doc. Col. Hist., I, 1856. **Chepanoc.**—Lane (1586) in Smith (1629), Virginia, I, 87, repr. 1819. **Chepanu.**—Smith, ibid., I, map, 112. **Chepanuu.**—De Bry, map (*ca.* 1590), in Hawks, N. C., I, 1859. **Chepawy.**—Martin, N. C., I, 13, 1829. **Chippanum.**—Lane (1586) in Smith, op. cit., I, 90.

**Chepenafa.** A Kalapooian tribe, sometimes regarded as a subdivision of the Lakmiut, formerly residing at the forks of St Marys cr., near Corvallis, Oreg. They are now on Grande Ronde res., being officially known as Marys River Indians, and number about 25. (L. F.)

Api'nefu.—Gatschet, Calapooya MS., B. A. E., 1877 (so called by the other Calapooya). **Chepen-a-pho.**—U. S. Ind. Treat., 19, 1873. **Mary River.**—Smith in Ind. Aff. Rep., 56, 1875. **Mary's River.**—Victor in Overland Month., VII, 346, 1871. **Marysville.**—Taylor in Cal. Farmer, June 12, 1863. **Pineifu.**—Gatschet in Jour. Am. Folklore, XII, 213, 1899. **Tsa mpi'nefa ami'm.**—Gatschet, Calapooya MS., B. A. E., 1877 (Calapooya name).

**Cheponta's Village.** A former Choctaw village on the w. bank of Tombigbee r., in extreme s. E. Choctaw co., Ala.

Cheponta's Village.—Royce in 18th Rep. B. A. E., Ala. map, 1900. **Fuketcheepoonta.**—Treaty of 1805 in Am. State Papers, Ind. Aff., I, 749, 1832.

**Cheposhkeyine** ('swelled young buffalo bull'). A subgens of the Arukhwa, the Buffalo gens of the Iowa.

Tce p'o-cke yin'-e.—Dorsey in 15th Rep. B. A. E., 239, 1897.

**Chepoussa.** A name applied by La Salle and Allouez to a band of Illinois Indians, probably from a chief or leader of a portion of those collected at Kaskaskia by La Salle's invitation; on the other hand it may have been given to those Indians from a river (apparently Kaskaskia r.), in s. w. Illinois, to which the name Chepoussa was sometimes applied by early explorers. These people were probably connected with the Michigamea.

Cheponssea.—La Salle (1680) in Hist. Mag., 1st s., V, 197, 1861. **Chepontia.**—Procés Verbal (1682) in Margry, Déc., II, 189, 1877. **Chepousca.**—La Salle (1681), ibid., 134. **Chepoussa.**—Allouez (1680), ibid., 96. **Chepoussea.**—La Salle (1682), ibid., 201. **Chipoussa.**—Tonti (*ca.* 1680) in French, Hist. Coll. La., I, 82, 1846. **Choponsca.**—Hennepin, New Discov., 310, 1698.

**Chequet, Chequit.** See *Chickwit.*

**Cheraw.** An important tribe, very probably of Siouan stock, formerly ranging in central Carolina, E. of the Blue ridge, from about the present Danville, Va., southward to the neighborhood of Cheraw, S. C., which takes its name from them. In numbers they may have stood next to the Tuscarora among the North Carolina tribes, but are less prominent in history by reason of their almost complete destruction before the white settlements had reached their territory. They are mentioned first in the De Soto narrative for 1540, under the name Xuala, a corruption of Suali, the name by which they are traditionally known to the Cherokee, who remember them as having anciently lived beyond the Blue ridge from Asheville. In the earlier Carolina and Virginia records they are commonly known as Saraw, and at a later period as Cheraw. We first hear of "Xuala province" in 1540, apparently in the mountain country southward from Asheville. In 1672, Lederer, from Indian information, located them in the same general region, or possibly somewhat farther N. E., "where the mountains bend to the west," and says that this portion of the main ridge was called "Sualy mountain" from the tribe. This agrees with Cherokee tradition. Some years later, but previous to 1700, they settled on Dan r. near the s. line of Virginia, where the marks of their fields were found extending for several miles along the river by Byrd, in 1728, when running the dividing line between the 2 colonies. There seem to have been 2 villages, as on a map of 1760 we find this place designated as "Lower Saura Town," while about 30 m. above, on the s. side of the Dan and between it and Town fork, is another place marked "Upper Saura Town." They are also alluded to by J. F. D. Smyth (Tour in U. S., 1784), who says the upper town was insignificant. About the year 1710, being harassed by the Iroquois, they abandoned their home on the Dan and moving s. E. joined the Keyauwee. The colonists of North Carolina being dissatisfied at the proximity of these and other tribes, Gov. Eden declared war against the Cheraw, and applied to Virginia for assistance. This Gov. Spotswood refused, as he believed the people of Carolina were the aggressors; nevertheless the war was carried on against them and their allies by the Carolinas until the defeat and expulsion of the Yamasi in 1716. During this period complaint was made against the Cheraw, who were declared to be responsible for most of the mischief done N. of Santee r., and of endeavoring to draw into their alliance the smaller coast tribes. It was asserted by the Carolinians that arms were supplied them from Virginia. At the close of the Yamasi war the Cheraw were dwelling on the upper Pedee near the line between the Carolinas, where their name is perpetuated in the town of Cheraw, S. C. Their number in 1715, according to Rivers, was 510, but this estimate probably included the Keyauwee. Being still subject to attack by the Iroquois, they finally—between 1726 and 1739—became incorporated with the Catawba, with whom at an earlier date they had been at enmity. They are mentioned as with the Catawba but speaking their own distinct dialect as late as 1743 (Adair). In 1759 a party of 45 "Charraws," some of whom were under their chief, "King Johnny," joined the English in the expedition against Ft Du Quesne. The last notice of them is in 1768, when their remnant, reduced by war and disease to 50 or 60, were still living with the Catawba. (J. M.)

Ani'-Suwa'lĭ.—Mooney in 19th Rep. B. A. E., 509, 1900 (Cherokee name; also *Ani'-Suwa'la*). Characks.—N. Y. Doc. Col. Hist., v, 793, 1855. Charah.—Adair, Hist. Inds., 24, 1775. Charraws.—Gregg, Hist. Old Cheraws, 12, 1867. Charrows.—Ibid., 1. Chawraw.—Smyth, Tour in U. S., I, 207, 1784. Cheraws.—S. C. Gazette (1739) quoted by Gregg, Hist. Old Cheraws, 9, 1867. Chouala.—De l'Isle, map, *ca.* 1700. Chovala.—Shipp, De Soto and Florida, 366, 1881 (misprint). Joara.—Vandera (1567) in Smith, Colec. Doc. Fla., 15, 1857. Lower Sauratown.—Güssefeld, map U. S., 1784. Saras.—Lederer, Discoveries, 2, 1672. Saraus.—War map of 1711–15 in Winsor, Hist. America, v, 346, 1887. Sarau town.—Jefferys, Fr. Dom. Am., I, map, 134, 1761. Saraws.—Virginia Council (1716) in N. C. Records, II, 247, 1886. Saraw Town.—Lattré, map of U. S., 1784. Sarraws.—Doc. of 1715, ibid., 251. Sasa.—Lederer, Discoveries, 2, 1672. Saura.—Vaugondy, map Partie de l'Amérique Sept., 1755. Sauro.—Byrd (1728), Hist. Dividing Line, I, 20, repr. 1866. Sawara.—Gallatin in Trans. Am. Antiq. Soc., II, 86, 1836. Sawras.—Doc. of 1716 in N. C. Records, II, 246, 1886. Sawraw.—Ibid., 243. Sawro.—Byrd, Hist. Dividing Line, I, 113, 1866. Sawro's.—Ibid. Sharawas.—N. Y. Doc. Col. Hist., v, 793, 1855. Suali.—Mooney, Siouan Tribes of the East, 57, 1894 (Cherokee form). Sualy.—Lederer, Discoveries, 2, 1672. Swali.—Mooney, Siouan Tribes of the East, 57, 1894 (Cherokee form). Upper Sauratown.—Smyth, Tour in U. S., 253–259, 1784. Xuala.—Garcilasso de la Vega (1540), Fla., 135, 1723. Xualla.—Gentl. of Elvas (1540) quoted by Shipp, De Soto and Fla., 366, 1881.

**Cherinak.** An Eskimo village near C. Ulakhpen, N. E. Siberia; pop. 77 in 14 houses about 1895; 58 in 8 houses in 1901. They are regarded as so seamanlike and hardy that they might easily have come from the Alaskan shores.

Čeṛi'nak.—Bogoras, Chukchee, 29, 1904. Wute'-elit.—Ibid., 20 (Chukchi name of people). Wute'en.—Ibid., 29. Wu'turen.—Ibid.

**Cherkhu.** The westernmost Chilula village on Redwood cr., N. W. Cal.

Cherr'h-quuh.—Gibbs in Schoolcraft, Ind. Tribes, III, 139, 1853 (Yurok name).

**Chernofski.** An Aleut village on Unalaska, Aleutian ids., Alaska; pop. 44 in 1833 according to Veniaminoff; 70 in 1874 according to Shiesnekov; in 1880, 101; in 1890, 78.

Chernofski.—Sarichef (1792) quoted by Baker, Geog. Dict. Alaska, 1901. Chernovskoe.—Veniam-

inoff, Zapiski, II, 202, 1840. Chernovskoi.—Elliott, Cond. Aff. Alaska, 225, 1875.—Chernovsky.—Petroff, 10th Census, Alaska, 23, 1884. Tschernowskoje.—Holmberg, Ethnol. Skizz., map, 1855.

**Cherokee.** A powerful detached tribe of the Iroquoian family, formerly holding the whole mountain region of the s. Alleghenies, in s. w. Virginia, w. North Car-

CHEROKEE MAN. (BALL PLAYER)

olina and South Carolina, N. Georgia, E. Tennessee, and N. E. Alabama, and claiming even to the Ohio r. The tribal name is a corruption of Tsálăgĭ or Tsárăgĭ, the name by which they commonly called themselves, and which may be derived from the Choctaw *chiluk-ki*, 'cave people', in allusion to the numerous caves in their mountain country. They sometimes also call themselves *Ani'-Yûñ'-wiyâ'*, 'real people,' or *Ani'-Kĭtu'hwagĭ*, 'people of Kituhwa,' one of their most important ancient settlements. Their northern kinsmen, the Iroquois, called them *Oyata'ge'ronoñ'*, 'inhabitants of the cave country' (Hewitt), and the Delawares and connected tribes called them *Kittuwa*, from the settlement already noted. They seem to be identical with the Rickohockans, who invaded central Virginia in 1658, and with the ancient Talligewi, of Delaware tradition, who were represented to have been driven southward from the upper Ohio r. region by the combined forces of the Iroquois and Delawares.

The language has three principal dialects: (1) *Elatĭ*, or Lower, spoken on the

CHEROKEE GIRL

heads of Savannah r., in South Carolina and Georgia; (2) Middle, spoken chiefly on the waters of Tuckasegee r., in w. North Carolina, and now the prevailing dialect on the East Cherokee res.; (3) *Â'tălĭ*, Mountain or Upper, spoken throughout most of upper Georgia, E. Tennessee, and extreme w. North Carolina. The lower dialect was the only one which had the *r* sound, and is now extinct. The upper dialect is that which has been exclusively used in the native literature of the tribe.

Traditional, linguistic, and archeologic evidence shows that the Cherokee originated in the N., but they were found in possession of the s. Allegheny region

when first encountered by De Soto in 1540. Their relations with the Carolina colonies began 150 years later. In 1736 the Jesuit (?) Priber started the first mission among them, and attempted to organize their government on a civilized basis. In 1759, under the leadership of Â'ganstâ'ta (Oconostota), they began war with the English of Carolina. In the Revolution they took sides against the Americans, and continued the struggle almost without interval until 1794. During this period parties of the Cherokee pushed down Tennessee r. and formed new settlements at Chickamauga and other points about the Tennessee-Alabama line. Shortly after 1800, missionary and educational work was established among them, and in 1820 they adopted a regular form of government modeled on that of the United States. In the meantime large numbers of the more conservative Cherokee, wearied by the encroachments of the whites, had crossed the Mississippi and made new homes in the wilderness in what is now Arkansas. A year or two later Sequoya (q. v.), a mixed-blood, invented the alphabet, which at once raised them to the rank of a literary people.

At the height of their prosperity gold was discovered near the present Dahlonega, Ga., within the limits of the Cherokee Nation, and at once a powerful agitation was begun for the removal of the Indians. After years of hopeless struggle under the leadership of their great chief, John Ross, they were compelled to submit to the inevitable, and by the treaty of New Echota, Dec. 29, 1835, the Cherokee sold their entire remaining territory and agreed to remove beyond the Mississippi to a country there to be set apart for them—the present (1905) Cherokee Nation in Indian Ter. The removal was accomplished in the winter of 1838-39, after considerable hardship and the loss of nearly one-fourth of their number, the unwilling Indians being driven out by military force and making the long journey on foot. On reaching their destination they reorganized their national government, with their capital at Tahlequah, admitting to equal privileges the earlier emigrants, known as "old settlers." A part of the Arkansas Cherokee had previously gone down into Texas, where they had obtained a grant of land in the E. part of the state from the Mexican government. The later Texan revolutionists refused to recognize their rights, and in spite of the efforts of Gen. Sam Houston, who defended the Indian claim, a conflict was precipitated, resulting, in 1839, in the killing of the Cherokee chief, Bowl (q. v.), with a large number of his men, by the Texan troops, and the expulsion of the Cherokee from Texas.

When the main body of the tribe was removed to the W., several hundred fugitives escaped to the mountains, where they lived as refugees for a time, until, in 1842, through the efforts of Wm. H. Thomas, an influential trader, they received permission to remain on lands set apart for their use in w. North Carolina. They constitute the present eastern band of Cherokee, residing chiefly on the Qualla res. in Swain and Jackson cos., with several outlying settlements.

The Cherokee in the Cherokee Nation were for years divided into two hostile factions, those who had favored and those who had opposed the treaty of removal. Hardly had these differences been adjusted when the civil war burst upon them. Being slave owners and surrounded by southern influences, a large part of each of the Five Civilized Tribes of the territory enlisted in the service of the Confederacy, while others adhered to the National Government. The territory of the Cherokee was overrun in turn by both armies, and the close of the war found them prostrated. By treaty in 1866 they were readmitted to the protection of the United States, but obliged to liberate their negro slaves and admit them to equal citizenship. In 1867 and 1870 the Delawares and Shawnee, respectively, numbering together about 1,750, were admitted from Kansas and incorporated with the Nation. In 1889 the Cherokee Commission (see *Commission*) was created for the purpose of abolishing the tribal governments and opening the territories to white settlement, with the result that after 15 years of negotiation an agreement was made by which the government of the Cherokee Nation came to a final end Mar. 3, 1906; the Indian lands were divided, and the Cherokee Indians, native and adopted, became citizens of the United States.

The Cherokee have 7 clans, viz: Ani'-wa'ʿya (Wolf), Ani'-Kawĭ' (Deer), Ani'-Tsi'skwa (Bird), Ani'-wâ'dĭ (Paint), Ani'-Sahâ'ni, Ani'-Ga'tâgéwĭ, Ani'-Gilâ'hĭ. The names of the last 3 can not be translated with certainty. There is evidence that there were anciently 14, which by extinction or absorption have been reduced to their present number. The Wolf clan is the largest and most important. The "seven clans" are frequently mentioned in the ritual prayers and even in the printed laws of the tribe. They seem to have had a connection with the "seven mother towns" of the Cherokee, described by Cuming in 1730 as having each a chief, whose office was hereditary in the female line.

The Cherokee are probably about as numerous now as at any period in their history. With the exception of an estimate in 1730, which placed them at about 20,000, most of those up to a recent period gave them 12,000 or 14,000, and in 1758 they were computed at only 7,500. The majority of the earlier estimates are probably too low, as the Cherokee occupied so extensive a territory that only a part of them came in contact with the whites. In 1708 Gov. Johnson estimated them at 60 villages and "at least 500 men" (Rivers, So. Car., 238, 1856). In 1715 they were officially reported to number 11,210 (Upper, 2,760; Middle, 6,350; Lower, 2,100), including 4,000 warriors, and living in 60 villages (Upper, 19; Middle, 30; Lower, 11). In 1720 they were estimated to have been reduced to about 10,000, and again in the same year reported at about 11,500, including about 3,800 warriors (Gov. Johnson's Rep. in Rivers, op. cit., 93, 94, 103, 1874). In 1729 they were estimated at 20,000, with at least 6,000 warriors and 64 towns and villages (Stevens, Hist. Ga., I, 48, 1847). They are said to have lost 1,000 warriors in 1739 from smallpox and rum, and they suffered a steady decrease during their wars with the whites, extending from 1760 until after the close of the Revolution. Those in their original homes had again increased to 16,542 at the time of their forced removal to the W. in 1838, but lost nearly one-fourth on the journey, 311 perishing in a steamboat accident on the Mississippi. Those already in the W., before the removal, were estimated at about 6,000. The civil war in 1861–65 again checked their progress, but they recovered from its effects in a remarkably short time, and in 1885 numbered about 19,000, of whom about 17,000 were in Indian Ter., together with about 6,000 adopted whites, negroes, Delawares, and Shawnee, while the remaining 2,000 were still in their ancient homes in the E. Of this eastern band, 1,376 were on Qualla res., in Swain and Jackson cos., N. C.; about 300 are on Cheowah r., in Graham co., N. C., while the remainder, all of mixed blood, are scattered over E. Tennessee, N. Georgia, and Alabama. The eastern band lost about 300 by smallpox at the close of the civil war. In 1902 there were officially reported 28,016 persons of Cherokee blood, including all degrees of admixture, in the Cherokee Nation in the Territory, but this includes several thousand individuals formerly repudiated by the tribal courts. There were also living in the nation about 3,000 adopted negro freedmen, more than 2,000 adopted whites, and about 1,700 adopted Delaware, Shawnee, and other Indians. The tribe has a larger proportion of white admixture than any other of the Five Civilized Tribes. See Mooney, Myths of the Cherokee, 19th Rep. B. A. E., 1902; Royce, Cherokee Nation, 5th Rep. B. A. E., 1887.

The following were Cherokee settlements: Aguaquiri (?), Amahyaski, Amakalali, Amohi, Anisgayayi, Anuyi, Aquohee, Aracuchi, Atsiniyi, Aumuchee, Ayahliyi, Big-island, Briertown, Broomtown, Brown's Village, Buffalo Fish, Canuga, Catatoga, Chagee, Chattanooga, Chatuga, Cheesoheha, Chewase, Chicherohe, Chickamauga, Chilhowee, Conisca, Conontoroy, Conoross, Coongaleés(?), Cooweescoowee (district), Cotocanahut, Cowee, Coweeshee, Coyatee, Crayfish Town, Creek Path, Crowmocker, Crow Town, Cuclon, Cusawatee, Dulastunyi, Dustayalunyi, Echota, Ecochee, Elakulsi, Ellijay, Estatoee, Etowah, Fightingtown, Frogtown, Galley, Guhlaniyi, Gusti, Gwalgahi, Halfway Town, Hemptown, Hickory Log, High Tower Forks, Hiwassee, Ikatikunahita, Itseyi, Ivy Log, Johnstown, Jore, Kalanunyi, Kanastunyi, Kansaki, Kanutaluhi, Kawanuyi, Keowee, Kituhwa, Kuhlahi, Kulahiyi, Kulsetsiyi, Leatherwood, Long Island, Lookout Mountain, Naguchee, Nanatlugunyi, Nantahala, Natuhli, Nayuhi, Nickajack, Niowe, Noewe, Nowe, Nucassee, Nununyi, Ocoee, Oconaluftee, Oconee, Olagatano, Ooltewah, Oothcaloga, Paint Town, Pine Log, Quacoshatchee, Qualatchee, Qualla, Quanusee, Quinahaqui, Rabbit Trap, Red Bank, Red Clay, Running Water, Sanderstown, Selikwayi, Seneca, Setsi, Sitiku, Skeinah, Soquee, Spike Bucktown, Spring Place, Standing Peach Tree, Stikayi, Sutali, Suwanee, Tagwahi, Tahlasi, Takwashnaw, Talahi, Talaniyi, Talking Rock, Tallulah, Tamali, Tanasqui (?), Tasetsi, Taskigi, Tausitu, Tawsee, Tekanitli, Tellico, Tennessee, Tessuntee, Tikaleyasuni, Tikwalitsi, Tlanusiyi, Tocax, Tomassee, Toquo, Torsalla, Toxaway, Tricentee, Tsilaluhi, Tsiskwahi, Tsistetsiyi, Tsistuyi, Tsiyahi, Tsudinuntiyi, Tucharechee, Tuckaseegee, Tugaloo, Turkeytown, Turniptown, Turtletown, Tusquittah, Two Runs, Ustanali, Ustisti, Valleytown, Wahyahi, Wasasa, Watauga, Willstown, and Yunsawi. (J. M.)

Achalaque.—Garcilasso de la Vega, Florida, III, 1723. Allegans.—Colden, map (1727) quoted by Schoolcraft, Ind. Tribes, III, 525, 1853. Allegewe.—Hind, Labrador Penin., II, 7, 1863. Allegewi.—Schoolcraft, Ind. Tribes, v, 133, 1855. Allegewe.—Ibid., II, 37, 1852. Alleghans.—Hall, N. W. States, 29, 1849. Alleghanys.—Rafinesque, introd. to Marshall, Ky., I, 34, 1824. Allegwi.—Squier in Beach, Ind. Misc., 26, 1877. Alligewi.—Heckewelder (1819) quoted by Schoolcraft, Ind. Tribes, III, 525, 1853. Allighewis.—Keane in Stanford, Compend., 500, 1878. Bäniatho.—Gatschet, Arapaho MS., B. A. E., 1880 (Arapaho name). Caáxi.—Dorsey, Osage MS. vocab., B. A. E., 1883 (Osage name). Callageheahs.—McKenney and Hall, Ind. Tribes, I, 186, 1854. Cayaki.—Dorsey, Kansa MS. vocab., B. A. E., 1882 (Kansa name). Chalakee.—Nuttall, Jour., 124, 1821. Chalaque.—Gentleman of Elvas (1540) in Hakluyt Soc., Florida, 60, 1851. Chalaquies.—Barcia, Ensayo, 335, 1723 (Spanish

name). Charakees.—Homann Heirs' map, 1756. Charakeys.—Homann Heirs' map, ca. 1730. Charikees.—Doc. of 1718 quoted by Rivers, So. Car., 55, 1856. Charokees.—Johnson (1720) quoted, ibid., 93, 1874. Cheelake.—Barton, New Views, xliv, 1798 (Upper Cherokee form). Cheerake.—Adair, Am. Inds., 226, 1775. Cheerakee.—Ibid., 137. Cheeraque.—Moore (1704) quoted by Carroll, Hist. Coll. S. C., II, 576, 1836. Cheerokee.—Ross (ca. 1776) quoted in Hist. Mag., 2d s., II, 218, 1867. Chĕl-à-kĕ.—Long, Exped. Rocky Mts., II, lxx, 1823. Chelakes.—Gallatin in Trans. Am. Antiq. Soc., II, 90, 1836. Chelaques.—Nuttall, Jour., 247, 1821. Chelekee.—Keane in Stanford, Compend., 506, 1878. Chellokee.—Schoolcraft, Ind. Tribes, II, 204, 1852. Cheloculgee.—White, Stat. Ga., 28, 1849 (Creek name; singular, Che-lo-kee). Chelokees.—Gallatin in Trans. Am. Antiq. Soc., II, 104, 1836. Cheokees.—Johnson (1772) in N. Y. Doc. Col. Hist., VIII, 314, 1857 (misprint). Cheraguees.—Coxe, Carolana, 11, 1741. Cherahes.—Brickell (1737) quoted by Haywood, Tenn., 224, 1823. Cherakees.—Coxe, Carolana, map, 1741. Cherakis.—Chauvignerie (1736) quoted by Schoolcraft, Ind. Tribes, III, 555, 1853. Cheraquees.—Coxe, Carolana, 13, 1741. Cheraquis.—Pénicaut (1699) in Margry, Déc., v, 404, 1883. Cherickees.—Clarke (1739) in N. Y., Doc. Col. Hist., vi, 148, 1855. Cherikee.—Albany conf. (1742), ibid., 218. Cherokee.—Johnson (1708) quoted by Rivers, So. Car., 238, 1856. Cherokis.—Rafinesque, Am. Nat., I, 140, 1836. Cherookees.—Croghan (1760) in Mass. Hist. Soc. Coll., 4th s., IX, 372, 1871. Cheroquees.—Campbell (1761), ibid., 416. Cherrackees.—Evans (1755) quoted by Gregg, Old Cheraws, 15, 1867. Cherrokees.—Treaty of 1722 in Drake, Bk. Inds., IV, 32, 1848. Cherrykees.—Weiser (1748) quoted by Kauffman, W. Penn., app., 18, 1851. Chilukki.—Hewitt in Am. Anthrop., II, 592, 1900 (original Choctaw form). Chirakues.—Randolph (1699) in Rivers, So. Car., 449, 1856. Chirokys.—Doc. (ca. 1825) in Ann. de la Prop. de la Foi, II, 384, 1841. Chorakis.—Doc. of 1748 in N. Y. Doc. Col. Hist., X, 143, 1858. Chreokees.—Pike, Trav., 173, 1811 (misprint). Chulukki.—Hewitt in Am. Anthrop., II, 592, 1900 (alternative Choctaw form). Dog tribe.—Vaudreuil (1760) in N. Y. Doc. Col. Hist., X, 1094, 1858. Entari ronnon.—Potier, Huron MS. Gram., 1751 (a Wyandot name: 'mountain people'). Gatohuá.—Barton quoted by Gatschet, Creek Migr. Leg., I, 28, 1884. Gattóchwa.—Heckewelder quoted by Barton, New Views, app., 8, 1798 (Delaware name, German form). Isallanic race.—Schoolcraft in Ind. Aff. Rep. 73, 1850. Katowa.—Gatschet, Creek Migr. Leg., I, 28, 1884 (Shawnee form). Ketawaugas.—Haywood, Nat. and Aborig. Tenn., 234, 1823. Kittuwa.—Brinton, Lenape Leg., 16, 1885. Kĭtúhwagĭ'.—Mooney in 19th Rep. B. A. E., pt. I, 15, 1902 (originally the name of a Cherokee band, but used by Algonquian tribes to designate the whole tribe). Kuttoowauw.—Apaumut (1791) quoted by Brinton, Lenape Leg., 16, 1885 (Mahican name). Mâⁿtĕrâ'ⁿ.—Gatschet, Catawba MS., B. A. E., 1881 (Catawba name: 'coming out of the ground'). Nation du Chien.—Picquet (1752) quoted by Parkman, Montcalm and Wolfe, II, 417, 1884. Ochie'tari-ronnon.—Potier, Huron MS. Gram., 1751 (one of the Wyandot names). Ojadagoehroene.—Livingston (1720) in N. Y. Doc. Col. Hist., v, 567, 1855. Ondadeonwas.—Bleeker (1701), ibid., IV, 918, 1854. Oyadackuchraono.—Weiser (1753), ibid., vi, 795, 1855. Oyadagahroenes.—Letter of 1713, ibid., v, 386, 1855. Oyadage'-ono.—Gatschet, Seneca MS., B. A. E., 1882 (Seneca name: 'cave people,' from oyanduga-i 'cave,' ono 'people'). O-ya-dä'-go-o-no.—Morgan, League Iroq., 337, 1851 (Iroquois name). Oyata'ge'ronón'.—Hewitt, inf'n (Iroquois name: 'inhabitants of the cave country'). Oyaudah.—Schoolcraft, Notes on Iroq., 448, 1847 (Seneca name). Rechahecrians.—Drake, Bk. Inds., bk. IV, 22, 1848 (name given by the Virginians in 1656 to an invading mountain tribe; probably the Cherokee). Rechecrians.—Rafinesque in Marshall, Ky., I, 36, 1824. Rickohockans.—Lederer (1669) quoted by Hawks, No. Car., II, 48, 1858 (probably the Cherokee, as called by the Powhatan tribes; Hewitt gives the meaning as 'cavelanders'). **Shánaki.**—Gatschet, Caddo MS. vocab., B. A. E., 1882 (Caddo name). **Shannack.**—Marcy, Red R., 273, 1854 (Wichita form). **Shánnakiak.**—Gatschet, Fox MS., B. A. E., 1882 (Fox name; sing. Shannaki). **Sháyăge.**—Gatschet, Kaw MS., B. A. E., 1878 (Kansa name). **Sulluggoes.**—Coxe, Carolana, 22, 1741. **Talagans.**—Rafinesque in Marshall, Ky., I, 28, 1824. **Talegans.**—Ibid., 34. **Talegawes.**—Ibid. **Tallagewy.**—Schoolcraft, Ind. Tribes, II, 36, 1852. **Tallegwi.**—Rafinesque (ca. 1824) quoted by Mercer, Lenape Stone, 90, 1885. **Talligeŭ.**—Heckewelder (1819), ibid., 40. **Talligewi.**—Walam Olum (1833) in Brinton, Lenape Leg., 200, 1885. **Talliké.**—Brinton, ibid., 230 (given as singular form of Talligewi; Zeisberger translates *talegán*, plural *talegáwak*, as 'crane' in the Delaware language). **Toálke.**—Gatschet, Tonkawa MS., B. A. E., 1882 (Tonkawa name). **Tcerokiéco.**—Gatschet, Wichita MS., B. A. E., 1882 (Wichita name). **Tchatakés.**—La Salle (1682) in Margry, Déc., II, 197, 1877. **Tsálagi.**—Gatschet, Creek Migr. Leg., I, 25, 1884. **Tsálăgĭ'.**—Mooney in 19th Rep., B. A. E., I, 15, 1902 (Upper Cherokee form; plural, Aní-Tsálăgĭ', abbreviated to Aní-Tsálăk). **Tsalakies.**—Gallatin in Trans. Am. Antiq. Soc., II, 90, 1836. **Tsä-lókee.** Morgan, Anc. Soc., 113, 1877. **Tsárăgĭ'.**—Mooney in 19th Rep., B. A. E., I, 15, 1902 (Lower Cherokee form; plural, Aní-Tsárăgĭ'). **Tschirokesen.**—Wrangell, Ethnol. Nachr., XXIII, 1839. **Tsûlakkĭ.**—Grayson, MS. Creek vocab., B. A. E., 1885 (Creek name). **Tzulukis.**—Rafinesque, Am. Nations, I, 123, 1836. **Uwatáyo-róno.**—Gatschet, Creek Migr. Leg., I, 28, 1884 ('cave people': Wyandot name). **Uyáda.**—Ibid. (Seneca name). **Zolucans.**—Rafinesque in Marshall, Ky., I, 23, 1824. **Zulocans.**—Ibid.

**Chert.** See *Chalcedony.*

**Chesakawon.** A village of the Powhatan confederacy, in 1608, about the mouth of Corotoman r., Lancaster co., Va.—Smith (1629), Virginia, I, map, repr. 1819.

**Chesapeake.** (Algonquian: *K'che-sepiack*, 'country on a great river.'—Tooker). Little more is known in regard to the name than that it designated also a small Powhatan tribe residing in Princess Anne or Norfolk co., Va., in 1608, and also their principal village, situated, according to Jefferson (Notes, 138, 1809), on Linnhaven r., in Princess Anne co., a small stream, according to his map, flowing N. into Chesapeake bay. Stith says they were seated on the river now called Elizabeth, which falls into Chesapeake bay below Norfolk. Linnhaven, on Jefferson's map, is distinct from and is located E. of Elizabeth r. White's map (Hariot, Narr., Quaritch repr., 1893), drawn in 1585, locates them under the name Ehesepiooc, apparently on the stream indicated by Jefferson. In 1607 they were estimated at 100 warriors, equivalent to perhaps 350 inhabitants; by 1669 they had entirely disappeared as a distinct people. On the application of the name Chesapeake see Tooker, Algonquian Series, III, 1901. (J. M.) **Chesapeacks.**—Lane (1586) in Smith (1629), Virginia, I, 87, repr. 1819. **Chesapeakes.**—Bozman, Maryland, I, 61, 1837. **Chesapeians.**—Strachey (ca. 1612), Virginia, 35, 1849. **Chesepians.**—Harris, Voy. and Trav., I, 815, 1705. **Chesepioock.**—Dutch map (1621) in N. Y. Doc. Col. Hist., I, 1856. **Chisapeack.**—Smith (1629), Va., I, map, repr. 1819. **Chisapeans.**—Lane (1586) in Smith, ibid., I, 91. **Chi-sapiack.**—Tyndall, chart (1608) in Brown, Genesis

U. S., 184, 1890. **Ehesepiooc.**—White's map in Hariot, Narrative, Quaritch repr., 1893 (misprint?).

**Cheshish.** The principal village of the Muchalat, situated back of Bligh id., Nootka sd., Vancouver id.—Can. Ind. Aff., 264, 1902.

**Chesthltishtun.** A gens or village of the Tolowa, formerly on the coast of N. California, s. of Smith r.
Tc'ĕs-ǫlt'ĭc'-tûn.—Dorsey in Jour. Am. Folk-lore, III, 236, 1890.

**Chests.** See *Boxes and Chests, Receptacles.*

**Chetac Lake.** A Chippewa village, named from the lake on which it is situated, in Sawyer co., N. W. Wis.
Lac Shatac.—Warren (1852) in Minn. Hist. Soc. Coll., V, 191, 1885.

**Chetawe.** A village of the Ntlakyapamuk, on the E. side of Fraser r., about 16½ m. above Yale, Brit. Col. Pop. 16 in 1897, the last time it was separately enumerated.
Chataway.—Can. Ind. Aff. for 1884, 230. Chatowe.—Brit. Col. map, Ind. Aff., Victoria, 1872. Tca'tūā.—Hill-Tout in Rep. on Ethnol. Surv. Can. for Brit. A. A. S., 5, 1899. Tcê'tawe.—Teit in Mem. Am. Mus. Nat. Hist., II, 169, 1900.

**Chetco** (from *Cheti*, 'close to the mouth of the stream': own name.—J. O. Dorsey). A group of former Athapascan villages situated on each side of the mouth of and about 14 m. up Chetco r., Oreg. There were 9 villages, those at the mouth of the river containing 42 houses, which were destroyed by the whites in 1853, after which the Chetco were removed to Siletz res., Tillamook co., Oreg. In 1854 they numbered 117 men, 83 women, and 41 children; total, 241. In 1861 they numbered 62 men, 96 women, 104 children; total, 262. In 1877 only 63 resided on Siletz res. These villagers were closely allied to the Tolowa of California, from whom they differed but slightly in language and customs. The villages as recorded by Dorsey were Chettanne, Chettannene, Khuniliikhwut, Nakwutthume, Nukhwuchutun, Setthatun, Siskhaslitun, Tachukhaslitun, and Thlcharghilitun.
Cha-ta.—Abbott, MS. Coquille census, B. A. E., 1858. Cheahtoc.—Taylor in Cal. Farmer, June 8, 1860. Che-at-tee.—Parrish in Ind. Aff. Rep. for 1854, 495, 1855. Chetcas.—Palmer, ibid., 467. Chetcoe.—Newcomb, ibid., 162, 1861. Chetcoes.—Victor in Overland Mo., VII, 317, 1871. Chetcoos.—Palmer in Ind. Aff. Rep. 1856, 217, 1857. Chetkoe.—Wells in Harper's Mag., XIII, 588, 1856. Chit-co.—Abbott, MS. Coquille census, B. A. E., 1858. Chitcoes.—Buchanan in Ind. Aff. Rep. 1856, 222, 1856. Chitko.—Gibbs MS. on coast tribes, B. A. E., 1856. Tced'i'-tĕ-ne'.—Everette, MS. Tututene vocab., B. A. E., 1883 (trans.: 'people by the Mouse r.'). Tce'-ti.—Dorsey in Jour. Am. Folklore, III, 236, 1890 (own name: 'close to the mouth of the stream'). Tcê'-ʒi ʒûn-ne',—Ibid. (own name: 'people close to the mouth of the stream') Tci'-i-tĭ.—Dorsey, Smith R. vocab., B. A. E., 1888 (Khaamotene name).

**Chetleschantunne** ('people among the big rocks'). A division of the Tututunne formerly living on Pistol r., Oreg., and the coast from the headlands 6 m. s. of

Rogue r. Their villages were at Macks Arch, the great rock from which they took their name, at Crooks pt. at the eddy of Pistol r., and on the N. side of the mouth of that stream. In 1854 they numbered 51. The survivors, if there are any, are on the Siletz res., Oreg.

Chĕtl-ĕ-shĭn.—Schumacher in Bull. G. and G. Surv., III, 31, 1877. Chetlessentan.—Schoolcraft, Ind. Tribes, VI, 702, 1857. Chetlessenten.—Taylor in Cal. Farmer, June 8, 1860. Chet-less-en-tun.—Parrish in Ind. Aff. Rep. for 1854, 495, 1855. Chet-less-in-gen.—Gibbs, MS. on coast tribes of Oregon, B. A. E., 1856. Chit-les-sen-ten.—Abbott, MS. Coquille census, B. A. E., 1858. Pistol Rivers.—Buchanan in Ind. Aff. Rep. 1856, 222, 1857. Tcĕt-lĕs'-tcan ʒûn'nĕ.—Dorsey in Jour. Am. Folklore, III, 236, 1890. Tcût-lĕs-tcûn' tĕne'.—Everette, MS. Tutu vocab., B. A. E., 1883 (trans.: 'people by the flat rocks'). Tc'ût-lĕs'-tcûn-ʒûn.—Dorsey, Naltûnneʒûnnĕ MS. vocab., B. A. E., 1884 (Naltunne name).

**Chetlesiyetunne** ('people of the bursted rock'). A village of the Tututunne, located by Dorsey (Jour. Am. Folk-lore, III, 233, 1890) on the N. side of Rogue r., Oreg.

T'a-rxi'-li-i' ʒûnnĕ.—Dorsey in Jour. Am. Folklore, III, 233, 1890 ('people distant from the forks': Naltunne name). Tcĕt-lĕs'-i-ye' ʒûnnĕ'.—Ibid. (own name). Tc'ût'-lĕs-ye' ʒûnnĕ'.—Ibid. (Naltunne name).

**Chets** (*Tcĕts*). A Haida town, formerly occupied by the Chets-gitunai and Djushade, on an island at the mouth of Tsooskahli, Masset inlet, Brit. Col.—Swanton, Cont. Haida, 281, 1905.

**Chetsgitunai** (*Tcĕts-gĭtΛnā'-i,* 'Gituns of Chets id.'). A Haida family of the Eagle clan, so named from an island in the upper expansion of Masset inlet, Brit. Col., at the mouth of Tsooskahli, where they once lived. Afterward they moved to the mouth of Masset inlet. They formed one group with the Widjagitunai, Tohlka-gitunai, and Djushade.—Swanton, Cont. Haida, 275, 1905.

Chĭchkitone.—Harrison in Proc. Roy. Soc. Can., sec. II, 124, 1895. Tsĕts gyit'inai'.—Boas, 12th Rep. N. W. Tribes Can., 23, 1898.

**Chettanne.** A former village of the Chetco on the S. side of Chetco r., Oreg., at its mouth.

Tcĕt-tan'-nĕ.—Dorsey in Jour. Am. Folk-lore, III, 236, 1890.

**Chettannene.** A former village of the Chetco on the N. side of Chetco r., Oreg., at its mouth.

Tcĕt-tan' ne'-ne.—Dorsey in Jour. Am. Folk-lore, III, 236, 1890.

**Chettrokettle** ('Rain pueblo' in one of the New Mexican Indian languages). One of the most important ruins of the Chaco canyon group in N. w. New Mexico. It is less than ¼ m. E. of Pueblo Bonito, on the N. side of the arroyo near the base of the canyon wall. Its exterior dimensions are 440 by 250 ft. It incloses 3 sides of a parallelogram, the extremities of the wings being connected by a semicircular double wall, the space between being divided into apartments. There are 9 kivas within the space inclosed by the wings of the structure, 2 being in the

court and 7 wholly or in part embraced within the walls. The walls still stand in places to a height of 30 ft. The building was not less than 4 stories high, probably 5. Many timbers are yet in place and well preserved. The masonry, which is exceptionally good, is of fine-grained grayish-yellow sandstone, broken into small tabular pieces and laid in thin mortar; in places courses of heavier stone are laid in parallel at intervals, giving an ornamental effect and probably adding to the stability of the walls. The walls are finished alike on both sides. Jackson estimated that there were originally in the building not less than 315,000 cu. ft. of masonry. See Jackson (1875) in 10th Rep. Hayden Surv., 438, 1879, and the authors cited below.　　　　(E. L. H.)

Chetho Kette.—Bell in Jour. Ethnol. Soc. Lond., n. s., I, 247, 1869. Chetro Ketle.—Domenech, Deserts N. Am., I, 200, 1860. Chetro Kettle.—Lummis in Land of Sunshine, XV, 426, 1901. Chettro-Kettle.—Simpson, Exped. Navajo Country, 79, 1850. Rain Pueblo.—Ibid.

**Chetuckota.** A former Seminole village on the w. bank of Pease cr., below Pease lake, w. central Fla.—H. R. Doc. 78, 25th Cong., 2d sess., map, 768–769, 1838.

**Chetuttunne** ('people where the road crosses a stream'). A former village of the Chastacosta on the N. side of Rogue r., Oreg.

Tce-tût' ʒûnnĕ'.—Dorsey in Jour. Am. Folk-lore, III, 234, 1890.

**Cheucunsene.** See *Dragging-canoe.*

**Cheuek.** A village of the Ntlakyapamuk on Fraser r., above Lytton, Brit. Col.

TcEue'q.—Hill-Tout in Rep. Ethnol. Surv. Can. for Brit. A. A. A. S., 4, 1899.

**Chewagh.** A name of the Pacific red-spotted salmon trout, or Dolly Varden trout (*Salmo campbelli*), from *chiwakh*, in the Nisqualli and closely related dialects of the Salishan stock, signifying 'salmon trout.'　　　　(A. F. C.)

**Chewas.** A Squawmish village on the w. side of Howe sd., Brit. Col.

Tcē'was.—Hill-Tout in Rep. Brit. A. A. S., 474, 1900.

**Chewase.** One of the 5 "inland" towns of the Cherokee on a branch of Tennessee r., in E. Tennessee, in the latter part of the 18th century.—Bartram, Travels, 371, 1792.

**Chewing-gum.** See *Food.*

**Cheyenne** (from the Sioux name *Sha-hi'yena, Shai-ena,* or (Teton) *Shai-ela,* 'people of alien speech,' from *sha'ia,* 'to speak a strange language'). An important Plains tribe of the great Algonquian family. They call themselves Dzĭ'tsĭístäs, apparently nearly equivalent to 'people alike,' i. e. 'our people,' from *ĭtsĭstau,* 'alike' or 'like this' (animate); (*ehĭstă,* 'he is from, or of, the same kind'—Petter); by a slight change of accent it might also mean 'gashed ones', from *éhĭstăĭ,* 'he is gashed' (Petter), or possibly 'tall people.' The tribal form as here given is in the third person plural.

The popular name has no connection with the French *chien*, 'dog,' as has sometimes erroneously been supposed. In the sign language they are indicated by a gesture which has often been interpreted to mean 'cut arms' or 'cut fingers'—being made by drawing the right index finger several times rapidly across the left—but which appears really to indicate 'striped arrows,' by which name they are known to the Hidatsa, Shoshoni, Comanche, Caddo, and probably other tribes, in allusion to their old-time preference for turkey feathers for winging arrows.

The earliest authenticated habitat of the Cheyenne, before the year 1700, seems to have been that part of Minnesota bounded roughly by the Mississippi, Minnesota, and upper Red rs. The Sioux, living at that period more immediately on the Mississippi, to the E. and S. E., came in contact with the French as early as 1667, but the Cheyenne are first mentioned in 1680, under the name of Chaa, when a party of that tribe, described as living on the head of the great river, i. e., the Mississippi, visited La Salle's fort on Illinois r. to invite the French to come to their country, which they represented as abounding in beaver and other fur animals. The veteran Sioux missionary, Williamson, says that according to concurrent and reliable Sioux tradition the Cheyenne preceded the Sioux in the occupancy of the upper Mississippi region, and were found by them already established on the Minnesota. At a later period they moved over to the Cheyenne branch of Red r., N. Dak., which thus acquired its name, being known to the Sioux as "the place where the Cheyenne plant," showing that the latter were still an agricultural people (Williamson). This westward movement was due to pressure from the Sioux, who were themselves retiring before the Chippewa, then already in possession of guns from the E. Driven out by the Sioux, the Cheyenne moved w. toward Missouri r., where their further progress was opposed by the Sutaio—the Staitan of Lewis and Clark—a people speaking a closely cognate dialect, who had preceded them to the w. and were then apparently living between the river and the Black-hills. After a period of hostility the two tribes made an alliance, some time after which the Cheyenne crossed the Missouri below the entrance of the Cannonball, and later took refuge in the Black-hills about the heads of Cheyenne r. of South Dakota, where Lewis and Clark found them in 1804, since which time their drift was constantly w. and s. until confined to reservations. Up to the time of Lewis and Clark they carried on

desultory war with the Mandan and Hidatsa, who probably helped to drive them from Missouri r. They seem, however, to have kept on good terms with the Arikara. According to their own story, the Cheyenne, while living in Minnesota and on Missouri r., occupied fixed villages, practised agriculture, and made pottery, but lost these arts on being driven out into the plains to become roving buffalo hunters. On the Missouri, and perhaps also farther E., they occupied earth-covered log houses. Grinnell states that some Cheyenne had cultivated fields on Little Missouri r. as late as 1850. This was probably a recent settlement, as they are not mentioned in

YELLOW BEAR—CHEYENNE MAN

that locality by Lewis and Clark. At least one man among them still understands the art of making beads and figurines from pounded glass, as formerly practised by the Mandan. In a sacred tradition recited only by the priestly keeper, they still tell how they "lost the corn" after leaving the eastern country. One of the starting points in this tradition is a great fall, apparently St Anthony's falls on the Mississippi, and a stream known as the "river of turtles," which may be the Turtle r. tributary of Red r., or possibly the St Croix, entering the Mississippi below the mouth of the Minnesota, and anciently known by a similar name. Consult for early habitat and migrations: Carver, Travels, 1796; Clark, Ind. Sign Lang., 1885; Comfort in Smithson. Rep. for 1871; La Salle in Margry, Découvertes, II, 1877; Lewis and Clark, Travels, I, ed. 1842; Mooney in 14th Rep. B. A. E., 1896; Williamson in Minn. Hist. Soc. Coll., I, 1872.

Although the alliance between the Sutaio and the Cheyenne dates from the crossing of the Missouri r. by the latter,

CHEYENNE WOMAN AND CHILD

the actual incorporation of the Sutaio into the Cheyenne camp-circle probably occurred within the last hundred years, as the two tribes were regarded as distinct by Lewis and Clark. There is no good reason for supposing the Sutaio to have been a detached band of Siksika drifted down directly from the n., as has been suggested, as the Cheyenne expressly state that the Sutaio spoke "a Cheyenne language," i. e. a dialect fairly intelligible to the Cheyenne, and that they lived s. w. of the original Cheyenne country. The linguistic researches of Rev. Rudolph

Petter, our best authority on the Cheyenne language, confirm the statement that the difference was only dialectic, which probably helps to account for the complete assimilation of the two tribes. The Cheyenne say also that they obtained the Sun dance and the Buffalo-head medicine from the Sutaio, but claim the Medicine-arrow ceremony as their own from the beginning. Up to 1835, and probably until reduced by the cholera of 1849, the Sutaio retained their distinctive dialect, dress, and ceremonies, and camped apart from the Cheyenne. In 1851 they were still to some extent a distinct people, but exist now only as one of the component divisions of the (Southern) Cheyenne tribe, in no respect different from the others. Under the name Staitan (a contraction of Sŭtai-hitän, pl. Sŭtai-hitänio, 'Sŭtai men') they are mentioned by Lewis and Clark in 1804 as a small and savage tribe roving w. of the Black-hills. There is some doubt as to when or where the Cheyenne first met the Arapaho, with whom they have long been confederated; neither do they appear to have any clear idea as to the date of the alliance between the two tribes, which continues unbroken to the present day. Their connection with the Arapaho is a simple alliance, without assimilation, while the Sutaio have been incorporated bodily.

Their modern history may be said to begin with the expedition of Lewis and Clark in 1804. Constantly pressed farther into the plains by the hostile Sioux in their rear they established themselves next on the upper branches of the Platte, driving the Kiowa in their turn farther to the s. They made their first treaty with the Government in 1825 at the mouth of Teton (Bad) r., on the Missouri, about the present Pierre, S. Dak. In consequence of the building of Bent's Fort on the upper Arkansas, in Colorado, in 1832, a large part of the tribe decided to move down and make permanent headquarters on the Arkansas, while the rest continued to rove about the headwaters of North Platte and Yellowstone rs. This separation was made permanent by the treaty of Ft Laramie in 1851, the two sections being now known respectively as Southern and Northern Cheyenne, but the distinction is purely geographic, although it has served to hasten the destruction of their former compact tribal organization. The Southern Cheyenne are known in the tribe as Sówonĭă, 'southerners,' while the Northern Cheyenne are commonly designated as O'mĭ'sĭs eaters,' from the division most numerously represented among them. Their advent upon the Arkansas brought them into constant collision with the Kiowa, who, with the Comanche, claimed the territory to the southward. The old men of both tribes tell of numerous encounters during the next few years, chief among these being a battle on an upper branch of Red r. in 1837, in which the Kiowa massacred an entire party of 48 Cheyenne warriors of the Bowstring society after a stout defense, and a notable battle in the following summer of 1838, in which the Cheyenne and Arapaho attacked the Kiowa and Comanche on Wolf cr., N. W. Okla., with considerable loss on both sides. About 1840 the Cheyenne made peace with the Kiowa in the s., having already made peace with the Sioux in the N., since which time all these tribes, together with the Arapaho, Kiowa, Kiowa Apache, and Comanche have usually acted as allies in the wars with other tribes and with the whites. For a long time the Cheyenne have mingled much with the western Sioux, from whom they have patterned in many details of dress and ceremony. They seem not to have suffered greatly from the small-pox of 1837–39, having been warned in time to escape to the mountains, but in common with other prairie tribes they suffered terribly from the cholera in 1849, several of their bands being nearly exterminated. Culbertson, writing a year later, states that they had lost about 200 lodges, estimated at 2,000 souls, or about two-thirds of their whole number before the epidemic. Their peace with the Kiowa enabled them to extend their incursions farther to the s., and in 1853 they made their first raid into Mexico, but with disastrous result, losing all but 3 men in a fight with Mexican lancers. From 1860 to 1878 they were prominent in border warfare, acting with the Sioux in the N. and with the Kiowa and Comanche in the s., and have probably lost more in conflict with the whites than any other tribe of the plains, in proportion to their number. In 1864 the southern band suffered a severe blow by the notorious Chivington massacre in Colorado, and again in 1868 at the hands of Custer in the battle of the Washita. They took a leading part in the general outbreak of the southern tribes in 1874–75. The Northern Cheyenne joined with the Sioux in the Sitting Bull war in 1876 and were active participants in the Custer massacre. Later in the year they received such a severe blow from Mackenzie as to compel their surrender. In the winter of 1878–79 a band of Northern Cheyenne under Dull Knife, Wild Hog, and Little Wolf, who had been brought down as prisoners to Fort Reno to be colonized with the southern portion of the tribe in the present Oklahoma, made a desperate attempt at escape. Of an estimated 89 men and 146 women and children who broke

away on the night of Sept. 9, about 75, including Dull Knife and most of the warriors, were killed in the pursuit which continued to the Dakota border, in the course of which about 50 whites lost their lives. Thirty-two of the Cheyenne slain were killed in a second break for liberty from Ft Robinson, Nebr., where the captured fugitives had been confined. Little Wolf, with about 60 followers, got through in safety to the N. At a later period the Northern Cheyenne were assigned to the present reservation in Montana. The Southern Cheyenne were assigned to a reservation in w. Oklahoma by treaty of 1867, but refused to remain upon it until after the surrender of 1875, when a number of the most prominent hostiles were deported to Florida for a term of 3 years. In 1891–92 the lands of the Southern Cheyenne were allotted in severalty and the Indians are now American citizens. Those in the N. seem to hold their own in population, while those of the s. are steadily decreasing. They numbered in 1904—Southern Cheyenne, 1,903; Northern Cheyenne, 1,409, a total of 3,312. Although originally an agricultural people of the timber country, the Cheyenne for generations have been a typical prairie tribe, living in skin tipis, following the buffalo over great areas, traveling and fighting on horseback. They commonly buried their dead in trees or on scaffolds, but occasionally in caves or in the ground. In character they are proud, contentious, and brave to desperation, with an exceptionally high standard for woman. Polygamy was permitted, as usual with the prairie tribes. Under their old system, before the division of the tribe, they had a council of 44 elective chiefs, of whom 4 constituted a higher body, with power to elect one of their own number as head chief of the tribe. In all councils that concerned the relations of the Cheyenne with other tribes, one member of the council was appointed to argue as the proxy or "devil's advocate" for the alien people. This council of 44 is still symbolized by a bundle of 44 invitation sticks, kept with the sacred medicine-arrows, and formerly sent around when occasion arose to convene the assembly.

This set of 4 medicine-arrows, each of different color, constitutes the tribal palladium which they claim to have had from the beginning of the world, and is exposed with appropriate rites once a year if previously "pledged," and on those rare occasions when a Cheyenne has been killed by one of his own tribe, the purpose of the ceremony being to wipe away from the murderer the stain of a brother's blood. The rite did not die with the final separation of the two sections of the tribe in 1851, as has been stated, but the bundle is still religiously preserved by the Southern Cheyenne, by whom the public ceremony was performed as late as 1904. Besides the public tribal ceremony there is also a rite spoken of as "fixing" the arrows, at shorter intervals, which concerns the arrow priests alone. The public ceremony is always attended by delegates from the northern body. No woman, white man, or even mixed blood of the tribe has ever been allowed to come near the sacred arrows.

Their great tribal ceremony for generations has been the Sun dance (q. v.), which they themselves say came to them from the Sutaio, after emerging from the timber region into the open plains. So far as known, this ceremony belongs exclusively to the tribes of the plains or to those in close contact with them. The Buffalo-head ceremony, which was formerly connected with the Sun dance but has been obsolete for many years, also came from the Sutaio. The modern Ghost-dance religion (q. v.) was enthusiastically taken up by the tribe at its first appearance, about 1890, and the Peyote rite (q. v.) is now becoming popular with the younger men. They also had until lately a Fire dance, something like that credited to the Navaho, in which the initiated performers danced over a fire of blazing coals until they extinguished it with their bare feet. In priestly dignity the keepers of the Medicine-arrow (Cheyenne) and Sun dance (Sutaio) rites stood first and equal.

At the Sun dance, and on other occasions where the whole tribe was assembled, they formed their camp circle in 11 (?) sections, occupied by as many recognized tribal divisions. As one of these was really an incorporated tribe, and several others have originated by segregation within the memory of old men still living (1905), the ancient number did not exceed 7. One authority claims these divisions as true clans, but the testimony is not conclusive. The wandering habit—each band commonly apart from the others, with only one regular tribal reunion in the year—would make it almost impossible to keep up an exogamic system. While it is quite probable that the Cheyenne may have had the clan system in ancient times while still a sedentary people, it is almost as certain that it disappeared so long ago as to be no longer even a memory. The present divisions seem to have had an entirely different genesis, and may represent original village settlements in their old homes, a surmise rendered more probable by survivals of marked dialectic differences. As it is now some 70 years since the whole tribe camped together, the social struc-

ture having become further demoralized in the meantime by cholera, wars, and intermixture with the Sioux, the exact number and order of these divisions is a matter of dispute, even among their own old men, although all agree on the principal names.

The list given below, although subject to correction, is based on the best consensus of opinion of the southern chiefs in 1904 as to the names and order of the divisions in the circle, from the E. entrance around by S., W., and N. to the starting point. The name forms vary considerably as given by different individuals, probably in accordance with former dialectic differences. It is evident that in some instances the divisions are older than their existing names:

(1) *Hevĭqs'-nĭ'pahĭs* (sing., Hevĭqs'-nĭ'pa), 'aortas closed, by burning.' All authorities agree that this was an important division and came first in the circle. The name is said to have originated from several of the band in an emergency, having once made the aorta of a buffalo do duty as a pipe. Grinnell gives this story, and also an alternative one, which renders it 'small windpipes,' from a choking sickness sent as a punishment for offending a medicine beaver. The name, however, in its etymology, indicates something closed or shriveled by burning, although it is also true that the band has a beaver tabu. The name is sometimes contracted to *Hevĭ'qsin*, for which *Wee hee skeu* of Lewis and Clark's Journals (Clark, 1804, ibid., I, 190, 1904) seems to be a bad misprint.

(2) *Mŏĭséyu* (sing., Mŏĭs), 'flint people,' from *mŏĭso* 'flint', apparently having reference to an arrowpoint (Petter), possibly to the sacred medicine-arrows. Formerly a large division said to have been the nucleus of the Cheyenne tribe, and hence the Dzĭtsĭstäs proper. The Arrow-men of G. A. Dorsey. Now nearly extinct.

(3) *Wŭ'tapĭu* (sing., Wŭ'tap), a Sioux word (*wŏtap*) meaning 'eaters,' or 'eat'. A small division, perhaps of Sioux admixture (cf. *O'-mĭ'sĭs*). Some authorities claim this division as an offshoot from the Hévhaitä'nio.

(4) *Hévhaitä'nio* (sing., Hévhaitän), 'hair men,' i. e. 'fur men'; so called because in early days they ranged farthest to the S. W., remote from the traders on the Missouri, and continued to wear fur robes for every-day use after the other bands had adopted strouding and calicoes. A probable explanation, advanced by Grinnell, is that the name refers to ropes which they twisted from the long hair of the buffalo for use in capturing ponies from the tribes farther S. They formed the advance of the emigration to the Arkansas about 1835, hence the name is

frequently used as synonymous with Southern Cheyenne.

(5) *Oi'vimána* ( sing., Oi'vimán ), 'scabby people'; *oi'vi* 'scabby,' *mana* 'band,' 'people' (Petter); according to another authority, 'hive people.' An offshoot of the Hévhaitä'nio (no. 4). The name originated about 1840, when a band of the Hévhaitä'nio, under a chief known as Blue Horse, became infected from having used a mangy buffalo hide for a saddle blanket. They became later an important division. According to Grinnell (Social Organization, 1905) the name is also applied as a nickname to a part of the Northern Cheyenne on lower Tongue r., "because, it is said, Badger, a principal man among them, had a skin disease."

(6) *Hísiometä'nio* (sing., Hísiometä'n), 'ridge men,' referring to the ridge or long slope of a hill. Another offshoot from the Hévhaitä'nio. The name is said to have originated from their preference for camping upon ridges, but more probably from having formerly ranged chiefly N. of the upper Arkansas, in that portion of Colorado known to the Cheyenne as the "ridge country," or, according to another authority, from habitually ranging upon the Staked plain, in association with the Comanche. They were said to have originated from some Hévhaitä'nio who intermarried with the Sutaio before the regular incorporation of that tribe.

(7) (?) *Sutáio* (sing., Su'tai), meaning unknown. Formerly a distinct tribe, but incorporated. According to their own statement the people of this division occupied the w. of the Cheyenne circle, but others put them s., N. W., or N., the discrepancy probably arising from the fact that they had originally no place in the circle at all and were not admitted until the old system had fallen into decay. The w. side of the Cheyenne circle, as of the interior of the tipi, being the place of honor, they would naturally claim it for themselves, although it is extremely unlikely that the Cheyenne would grant it. Their true position seems to have been in the N. W. part of the circle.

(8) *Oqtógǔnǎ* (sing., Oqtógón), 'bare shins' (?).

(9) *Hó'nowǎ* (sing., Hó'nów), 'poor people.' A small division, an offshoot from the Oqtógǔnǎ.

(10) *Mǎsǐ'kotǎ* (sing., Mǎsǐ'kot), of doubtful meaning, interpreted by Grinnell as 'corpse from a scaffold,' or possibly 'ghost head,' i. e. gray hair, but more probably (Mooney) from a root denoting 'wrinkled' or 'drawn up,' as applied to old tipi skins or old buckskin dresses; from this root comes *masiskot*, 'cricket,' referring to the doubling up of the legs; the same idea of 'skin drawn

up' may underlie the interpretation 'corpse from a scaffold.' For some reason, apparently between 70 and 80 years ago, all the men of this division joined in a body the Hotámitä'nio warrior society, so that the two names became practically synonymous until the society name supplanted the division name, which is now obsolete, the Hotámitä'nio, with their families, being considered owners of that part of the circle originally occupied by the Mǎsǐ'kotǎ, viz, next to the last section, adjoining the O'mǐ'sǐs (no. 11), who camped immediately N. of the entrance.

(11) *O'mǐ'sis* (sing., O'mǐ'sǐsts), 'eaters'; the meaning of the name is plain, but its origin is disputed, some authorities claiming it as the name of an early chief of the division. Cf. *Wǔ'tapiu*, no. 3. This was the largest and most important division in the tribe and now constitutes the majority of the Northern Cheyenne, for which portion the name is therefore frequently used as a synonym. Before the tribe was divided they occupied that portion of the tribal circle immediately N. of the E. entrance, thus completing the circle. After the separation their next neighbors in the circle, the Masǐ'kotǎ, alias Hotámitä'nio, were considered as the last division in order.

Other names, not commonly recognized as divisional names, are:

(a) *Moqtávhaitä'niu*, 'black men,' i. e. 'Ute' (sing., Moqtávhaitän). To the Cheyenne and most other Plains tribes the Ute are known as 'Black men' or 'Black people.' A small band, apparently not a recognized division, of the same name is still represented among the Southern Cheyenne, and, according to Grinnell, also among the Northern Cheyenne. They may be descended from Ute captives and perhaps constituted a regular tribal division.

(b) *Ná'kuimána*, 'bear people'; a small band among the Southern Cheyenne, taking its name from a former chief and not recognized as properly constituting a division.

(c) *Anskówǐnǐs*, 'narrow nose-bridge,' a band of Sioux admixture and of recent origin, taking its name from a chief, properly named Broken Dish, but nicknamed Anskówǐnǐs. They separated from the O'mǐ'sǐs on account of a quarrel, probably, as Grinnell states, a dispute as to the guardianship of the sacred buffalohead cap, a stolen horn from which is now in possession of one of the band in the S. They are represented among both the Northern and the Southern Cheyenne.

(d) *Pǐ'nǎtgǔ'* 'Pe'nätĕ'ka' (Comanche). This is not properly a divisional or even a band name, but was the contemptuous name given by the hostile Cheyenne in 1874–75 to the "friendlies," under Whirlwind, who remained passive near the agency at Darlington, in allusion to the well-known readiness of the Penateka Comanche to sell their services as scouts against their own tribesmen on the plains.

(e) *Máhoyum*, 'red tipi ; this name, in the form Miayuma, 'red lodges,' is erroneously given in the Clarke MS., in possession of Grinnell, as the name of a band or division, but is really only the name of a heraldic tipi belonging by heredity to a family of the Hó'nowa division, now living with the Southern Cheyenne.

(f) *Wóopotsĭ't* (Wóhkpotsīt, Grinnell), 'white wolf' (?) A numerous family group taking its name from a noted common ancestor, in the southern branch of the tribe, who died about 1845. The name literally implies something having a white and frosty appearance, as hide-scrapings or a leaf covered with frost.

(g) *Totoimana* (Tūtoimanáh, Grinnell), 'backward or shy clan,' a modern nickname applied by the Northern Cheyenne to a band on Tongue r., "because they prefer to camp by themselves" (Grinnell). From the same root comes *toto*, 'crawfish,' referring to its going backward (Petter).

(h) *Black Lodges*. A local designation or nickname for those Northern Cheyenne living in the neighborhood of Lame Deer "because they are on friendly terms with the band of Crows known as Black Lodges" (Grinnell, ibid.).

(i) *Ree band*. A local designation or nickname for those Northern Cheyenne living about Rosebud cr., "because among them there are several men who are related to the Rees" (Grinnell, ibid.).

(j) *Yellow Wolf band* (Culbertson, Jour., 1850). From another reference this is seen to be only a temporary band designation from a chief of that name.

(k) *Half-breed band* (Culbertson, Jour., 1850). Probably only a temporary local designation, perhaps from a chief of that name (Mooney).

The Warrior Organization (*Nŭ'tqiu*, 'warriors,' 'soldiers'; sing., Nŭtaq) of the Cheyenne is practically the same as found among the Arapaho, Kiowa, and most other Plains tribes (see *Military Societies*), and consists of the following 6 societies, with possibly one or more extinct: (1) Hotámitä'nio, 'dog men'; (2) Woksíhitänio, '(kit) fox men,' alias Mótsónitänio, 'flint men'; (3) Hĭ'moiyóqĭs 'pointed-lance men' (Petter) or Oómi-nŭtqiu, 'coyote warriors'; (4) Máhohĭvás, 'red shield,' alias Hotóanŭ'tqiu, 'buffalo bull warriors'; (5) Himátanóhis, 'bowstring (men)'; (6) Hotam-ĭmsáw', 'crazy dogs.' This last society is of modern origin. Besides these the members of the council of 44 chiefs were sometimes considered to constitute in themselves another society, the Vĭ'hiyo, 'chiefs.' The equivalent list given by Clark (Ind. Sign Lang.), omitting No. 6, is Dog, Fox, Medicine Lance, Bull, Bowstring, and Chief. There seems to have been no fixed rule of precedence, but the Hotámitä'niu, or "Dog soldiers" as they came to be known to the whites, acquired most prominence and distinctive character from the fact that by the accession of the entire warrior force of the Masĭ''kota division, as already noted, they, with their families, took on the character of a regular tribal division with a place in the tribal circle. From subsequent incorporation by intermarriage of numerous Sioux, Arapaho, and other alien elements their connection with their own tribe was correspondingly weakened, and they formed the habit of camping apart from the others and acting with the Sioux or as an independent body. They were known as the most aggressive of the hostiles until defeated, with the loss of their chief, Tall Bull, by Gen. Carr's forces in 1869.

Consult Clark, Ind. Sign Lang. (articles, Cheyenne and Soldier), 1885; Culbertson in Smithson. Rep. 1850, 1851; Dorsey, The Cheyenne, Field Columb. Mus. Publ., Anthrop. ser., IX, nos. 1 and 2, 1905; Grinnell, various letters and published papers, notably Social Org. of the Cheyennes, in Proc. Internat. Cong. Americanists for 1902, 1905; Hayden, Ethnog. and Philol. Mo. Val., 1862; Indian Treaties, eds. 1837, 1873; Lewis and Clark, Exped., various editions; Margry, Découvertes, II, 1877; Maximilian, Travels, 1843; Mooney (1) Ghost Dance Religion, 14th Rep. B. A. E., 1896, (2) Calendar Hist. of the Kiowa, 17th Rep. B. A. E., 1898, (3) Cheyenne MS., B. A. E.; Reports of the Commissioner of Indian Affairs; War Dept. Rec. of Engagements with Hostile Inds., 1882; Williamson in Minn. Hist. Soc. Coll. I, 1872.　　　　　　　　　　(J. M.)

à-wǎs-shě-tǎn-quǎ. — Long, Exped. Rocky Mts., II, lxxxiv, 1823 (Hidatsa name). **Báhakosin.**—Mooney in 14th Rep. B. A. E., 1023, 1896 ('striped arrows': Caddo name). **Black-arms.**—Long, op. cit., I, 465, 1823 (evidently an error for 'cut-arms,' one of the renedrings of the tribal sign). **Caȼáni.**—Dorsey, Osage MS., vocab., B. A. E., 1883 (Osage name. c=sh, ȼ=dh, i. e. Shadháni). **Cáhieȼa.**—Dorsey, Ȼegiha MS. Dict., B. A. E. (Omaha and Ponka name; pron. Sháhiédha). **Cayáni.** — Dorsey, Kansa MS. vocab., B. A. E., 1882 (Kansa name; pron. Shayáni). **Chaa.**—La Salle (1680) in Margry, Déc., II, 54, 1877. **Chaguyennes.**—Perrin du Lac, Voy., 307, 1805. **Chaienne.**—Williamson in Minn. Hist. Soc. Coll., I, 296, 1872 (given as a French form). **Chaoenne.**—Lewis, Travels, 15, 1809. **Chawas.**—Schoolcraft, Ind. Tribes, I, 198, 1851. **Chayenne.**—Clark (1804) in Lewis and Clark Jour., I, 175, 1904. **Cheyennes.**—Cass (1834) in Schoolcraft, Ind. Tribes, III, 609, 1853. **Chians.**—Sen. Ex. Doc. 90, 22d Cong., 1st sess., 31, 1832. **Chien.**—Lewis and Clark, Travels, 35, 1806

(French name). **Chiennes.**—Brackenridge, Views of La., 77, 1815. **Choaenne.**—Fisher, New Travels, 26, 1812. **Chyannes.**—Lewis and Clark, Jour., 135, 1840. **Chyans.**—Dougherty (1837) in H. R. Doc. 276, 25th Cong., 2d sess., 20, 1838. **Chyennes.**—Lewis and Clark, Travels, 35, 1806. **Chynnes.**—Am. St. Papers, IV, 710, 1832. **Cien.**—Clark (1804) in Lewis and Clark Jour., I, 230, 1904. **Cut wrists.**—Burton, City of Saints, 151, 1861 (intended as an interpretation of the tribal sign). **Dog Indians.**—Clark (1804) in Lewis and Clark Jour., I, 175, 1904 (on p. 189 he speaks of "the Chien (Cheyenne) or Dog Inds.," from confusion with the French *chien*, 'dog'). **Dog nation.**—Gass, Jour., 63, 1807. **Dzĭtsĭ′stäs.** — Mooney in 14th Rep. B. A. E., 1023, 1896 (proper tribal name). **Gatsalghi.**—Ibid. (Kiowa Apache name). **Hĭtäsi′na.**—Ibid. ('scarred people': Arapaho name, sing., Hĭ′täsi). **I-sŏnsh′-pu-she.**—Hayden, Ethnog. and Philol. Mo. Val., 402, 1862 (Crow name). **Itah-Ischipahji.**—Maximilian, Travels, II, 234, 1839–41 (Hidatsa name). **ĭt-ȧnsĕ-pŏ-ṭjĕ.**—Long, Exped. Rocky Mts., II, lxxxiv, 1823 (Hidatsa name). **Ĭtäsi′nä.**—Mooney, Cheyenne MS., B. A. E., 1904 ('scarred people'; also *Hĭtäsi′na*, Arapaho name; sing., Ĭtäsi′). **I-tá-su-pu-zi.**—Matthews, Ethnog. and Philol. Hidatsa, 160, 1877 ('spotted arrow quills': from *itasu*, arrow quills; *puzi*, spotted: Hidatsa name; *s*=sh). **It-us-shi′-na.**—Hayden Ethnog. and Philol. Mo. Val., 326, 1862 ('scarred people'; Arapaho name). **Ka′neaheȧwastsĭk.**--Grinnell quoted by Mooney in 14th Rep. B. A. E., 1023, 1896 ('people with a language somewhat like Cree'; Cree name; cf. *Kaninavish*, the Arapaho). **Nanonĭ′ks-karo′nĭki.**—Mooney, ibid. (Kichai name). **Niere′rikwats-kûni′ki.**—Ibid. (Wichita name). **Päcarabó.**—Pimentel, Lenguas, II, 347, 1865 (given as a Comanche division, but evidently intended for Pägänävo). **Pägänävo.**—Mooney in 14th Rep. B. A. E., 1023, 1896 (Shoshoni and Comanche name: 'striped arrows,' from *päga* 'arrow,' *nävo* 'striped'). **Pah-kah-nah-vo.**—Gebow, Snake or Shoshonay Vocab., 9, 1868 (Shoshoni name). **Paikanavos.**—Burton, City of Saints, 151, 1861 (erroneously interpreted from the tribal sign as 'cut wrists'). **Paikandoos.**—Blackmore in Jour. Ethnol. Soc. Lond., I, 307, 1869 (for Pägänävo, and erroneously interpreted from the tribal sign as 'cut wrists'). **Pá ka na vo.**—ten Kate, Synonymie, 9, 1884 ('flèches peintes,' so called by the Comanche, who know them also as Si′-a-na-vo). **Pá-ka-na-wa.**—Ibid., 8 (Ute name). **Sa-hi′-ye-na.**—Riggs-Dorsey in Cont. N. A. Ethnol., VII, 440, 1890 (Yankton Sioux name, indicating a 'people speaking an alien language,' from *sá-i-a*, *sáiwaa*, 'to speak a strange language,' *sá-i-a-pi*, 'a foreign or unknown language'; *s*=sh; *na* is a diminutive suffix, which becomes *la* in the Teton and *dañ* in the Santee dialect). **Sa+k'o+t.**—ten Kate, op. cit., 10 (Kiowa name). **Säk'o′ta.**—Mooney in 14th Rep. B. A. E., 1023, 1896 (Kiowa name; sing., Säk'ódäl). **Saoyns.**—De Smet, Missions, 264, 1848. **Sa-Sis-e-tas.**—Clark, Ind. Sign Lang., 99, 1885 (given as their own name, properly Dzĭtsĭ′stäs). **Sayenagi.**--Gatschet, Shawnee MS., B. A. E., 1879 (Shawnee name; sing., Sáyen). **Scarred-Arms.**—Sage, Scenes in Rocky Mts., 92, 1846 (from misinterpretation of the tribal sign). **Scheyenne.**—Domenech, Deserts, II, 355, 1860. **Schianese.**—Carver, Trav., 50, 1796 (improperly noted as a Sioux band and distinct from the "Schians"). **Schiannesse.**—Williamson in Minn. Hist. Soc. Coll., I, 297, 1872 (misquoting Carver). **Schians.**—Carver, op. cit. (improperly noted as a Sioux band and distinct from the "Schianese"). **Shá-en.**—Gatschet, Kaw MS. vocab., B. A. E., 1878 (one Kansa name). **Shagen.**—Culbertson in Smithson. Rep. 1850, 96, 1851 (misprint for Shayen). **Sha-hō.**—Grinnell, inf'n, 1904 (Pawnee name). **Sha-i-a-pi.** — Williamson, op. cit., 299 (Santee Sioux name denoting a 'people speaking an alien language,' especially the Cheyenne, and equivalent to Sha-i-e-na, the Yankton Sioux form; *pi* =pl. suffix). **Shai-e′-la.**—Hayden, Ethnog. and Philol. Mo. Val., 274, 1862 (so called by some Sioux; this is the Teton Sioux form). **Sha-i-e-na.**—Williamson, op. cit., 299,

1872 (Yankton Sioux name, applied to people speaking an alien language, particularly the Cheyenne. Hayden, op. cit., 274, has Shai-en-a; Hodge, field notes, B. A. E., has Shaiena for their Taos Pueblo name). **Sharas.**—Hayden, op. cit., 274. **Shar′-ha.**—Lewis and Clark, Travels, 35, 1806 (incorrectly given as their own name, but properly from the Sioux form. Clark, 1804, has "Shârha (chien), the village on the other side; We hee skeu (chien) the villagers on this side," as though there were then two principal bands.—Lewis and Clark Journals, I, 190, 1904). **Sharshas.**--Hayden, op. cit., 274. **Shaways.**—De Smet, Letters, 33, 1843. **Shawhays.**—Brackenridge, Views of La., 299, 1815. **Shayén.**—Gatschet, Fox MS., B. A. E., 1882 (Fox name). **Sháyenna.**—Gatschet, Kaw MS. vocab., B. A. E., 1878 (another Kansa name). **Shéyen.**—Gatschet, Tonkawe MS., B. A. E., 1884 (Tonkawa name). **Sheyennes.**—De Smet, Letters, 13, 1843. **Shian.**—Irving, Ind. Sketches, II, 146, 1835. **Shiä′navo.**—Mooney in 14th Rep. B. A. E., 1023, 1896 (another Comanche name for the Cheyenne, probably a derivation from their common name). **Shiannes.**—Snelling, Tales of Travel, 100, 1830. **Shiárish.**—Gatschet, Wichita MS., B. A. E., 1879 (Wichita name). **Shiĕ′da.**—Mooney op. cit. (another Wichita name, probably a derivation from Cheyenne). **Shiene.** — Williamson in Minn. Hist. Soc. Coll., I, 296, 1872. **Shiennes.** — Maximilian, Travels, 389, 1843. **Shiens.**—Williamson, op. cit. **Shi-yä.**—Morgan in N. Am. Rev., 50, Jan., 1870 (given as Sioux name). **Shiyans.**—Ibid. (given as Sioux name). **Showays.**—Domenech, Deserts, II, 60, 1860 (for Shaway, etc.). **Shyennes.**—Gallatin in Trans. Am. Ethnol. Soc., II, 104, 1848. **Sianábone.** — Garcia Rejon in Pimentel, Lenguas, II, 347, 1865 (for Shiänavo). **Si′-a-na-vo.**—ten Kate, Synonymie, 9, 1884 (one of the names by which the Comanche know them, given as meaning 'plumes peintes,' but evidently another form of their popular name). **Tse-tis-tas′.**—Ibid., 8 (='nous, nous autres': their own name).

**Cheyenne, Northern.** The popular designation for that part of the Cheyenne which continued to range along the upper Platte after the rest of the tribe (Southern Cheyenne) had permanently moved down to Arkansas r., about 1835. They are now settled on a reservation in Montana. From the fact that the Omisis division (q. v.) is most numerous among them, the term is frequently used by the Southern Cheyenne as synonymous. (J. M.)
**Upper Cheyennes.**—Custer, Life on the Plains, 88, 1874.

**Cheyenne Sioux.** Possibly a loose expression for Cheyenne River Sioux, i. e., the Sioux on Cheyenne River res., S. Dak.; but more probably, considering the date, intended to designate those Sioux, chiefly of the Oglala division, who were accustomed to associate and intermarry with the Cheyenne. The term occurs in Ind. Aff. Rep. 41, 1856. (J. M.)

**Cheyenne, Southern.** That part of the Cheyenne which ranged in the s. portion of the tribal territory after 1835, now permanently settled in Oklahoma. They are commonly known as Sówoníä, 'southerners' (from *sowón*, 'south'), by the Northern Cheyenne, and sometimes as Hevhaitanio, from their most numerous division. (J. M.)
**Po-no-í-ta-ni-o.**—Hayden, Ethnog. and Philol. Mo. Val., 290, 1862 (evidently a misprint for Sowon′-itä′niu, 'southern men'). **So′wăniă.**—Mooney in 14th Rep. B. A. E., 1025, 1896.

**Cheyinye** ('buffalo calf'). A subgens of the Arukhwa, the Buffalo gens of the Iowa.

Tce yiñ′-ye.—Dorsey in 15th Rep. B. A. E., 239, 1897.

**Chiaha** (Chehaw). A common Creek town name. The earliest on record. Chiaha, visited by the De Soto expedition in 1540, was probably situated on Tennessee r., but may have been in N. Georgia or N. Alabama. A third town of the name was lower down on Flint r., and was considered a Seminole settlement. Still another of the name, belonging to the Upper Creeks, may have been on Upper Coosa r. in N. Georgia.

Achiha.—Jefferys, Am. Atlas, 7, 1776. Archieco.—U. S. Ind. Treat. (1827), 420, 1837. Big Chehaus.—Schoolcraft, Ind. Tribes, v, 263, 1855. Big Chehaws.—Barnard (1793) in Am. State Pap., Ind. Aff., I, 391, 1832 (on the Chattahoochee). Chahâh.—Adair, Am. Ind., 257, 1775. Che-anhun.—U. S. Ind. Treat. (1827), 420, 1837. Chearhau.—H. R. Ex. Doc. 276, 24th Cong., 327, 1836. Che-ar-haw.—Schoolcraft, Ind. Tribes, IV, 578, 1854. Che-au-hau.—Hawkins(1799),Sketch, 63, 1848. Checaws.—Harris, Coll. of Voyages, II, 335, 1705. Cheechaws.—Drake, Bk. Inds., bk. IV, 29, 1848 (on Flint r.; a small tribe destroyed in 1817 by Georgia militia). Cheehaws.—Morse, Rep. to Sec. War, 308, 1822. Chehau.—Swan (1791) in Schoolcraft, Ind. Tribes, v, 256, 1855. Chehawah.—Schoolcraft, ibid., IV, 578, 1854. Chehaws.—Barnard (1793) in Am. State Pap., Ind. Aff., I, 382, 1832. Chehawuseche.—Ibid., 309 (evident misprint for "Chehaw, Useche"). Chehew.—Crawford (1836) in H. R. Doc. 274, 25th Cong., 2d sess., 24, 1836. Chiaha.—Gentleman of Elvas (1557) in French, Hist. Coll. La., II, 145, 1850. Chiha.—Philippeaux, map of Engl. Col., 1781. China.—Biedma (1544), Hakluyt Soc. transl., 182, 1851. Ichiaha.—Garcilasso de la Vega, Fla., 139, 1723. Iciaha.—Shipp, De Soto and Florida, 370, 1881. Solameco.—Vandera (1569) in French, Hist. Coll. La., II, 247, 1875. Thiaha.—De Soto map (1543) in Harrisse, Discov. N. A., 644, 1892. Upper Cheehaws.—U. S. Ind. Treat. (1797), 69, 1837. Ychiaha.—Garcilasso de la Vega, Fla., 138, 1723.

**Chiaha.** A town of the Creek Nation, Ind. T., on Verdigris r., N. E. of Wealaka.—Gatschet, Creek Migr. Leg., II, 186, 1888.

Tchiaha.—Gatschet, ibid.

**Chiahudshi** (*Chiahu′dshi*, 'little Chiaha'). A former dependent settlement of the Chiaha, about 2 m. w. of Hitchiti town, E. Ala.

Che-au-hoo-che.—Hawkins (1799), Sketch, 64, 1848. Chiahū′dshi.—Gatschet, Creek Migr. Leg., I, 129, 1884. Little Chehaus.—Swan (1791) in Schoolcraft, Ind. Tribes, v, 263, 1855. Little Chíaha.—Gatschet, op. cit.

**Chiakamish.** A Squawmish village community on a creek of the same name, a tributary of Squawmisht r., Brit. Col.

Tcīā′kamic.—Hill-Tout in Rep. Brit. A. A. S., 474, 1900. Tcīā′qamic.—Boas MS., B. A. E., 1887.

**Chiakanessou.** Mentioned by a French trader as a tribe of 350 warriors, associated with the Alibamu, Caouikas (Kawita), Machecous (Creeks), and Souikilas (Sawokli). Possibly the Creeks of Chiaha, the ending being the misspelt Creek *isti*, 'people'; or, less likely, the Chickasaw. On the De l'Isle map of 1707 "Chiacante-

sou," which is probably the same, is located much farther N. W., within the Caddoan country. See Bouquet, Exped., Smith's ed., 70, 1766.     (A. S. G.)

Chenakisses.—McKenney and Hall, Ind. Tribes, III, 79, 1854. Chiacantefous.—B. des Lozières, Voyage à la La., 242, 1802. Chiahnessou.—Boudinot-Star in the West, 126, 1816. Chickanossous.—Schoolcraft, Ind. Tribes, III, 557, 1853.

**Chiaktel.** A Chilliwack village in S. Brit. Col.; pop. 43 in 1904.

Tcīā′ktE′l.—Hill-Tout in Ethnol. Surv. Can., 4, 1902. Tyeachten.—Can. Ind. Aff., pt. II, 160, 1901. Tzeachten.—Ibid., 224, 1902.

**Chiataina.** (*Chi′ä-tai′na*, 'knife people'). The Knife clan of the pueblo of Taos, N. Mex.     (F. W. H.)

**Chibaouinani** (*Shībā·u·naning*, 'passageway.—W. J.). A former Missisauga village, also known as La Cloche, on Cloche id., in L. Huron, N. of Manitoulin id.

Chibaouinani.—La Galissonière (1748) in N. Y. Doc. Col. Hist., x, 183, 1858. La Cloche.—Ibid.

**Chibukak.** A Yuit Eskimo village at Northwest cape, St Lawrence id., Bering sea.—Nelson in 18th Rep. B. A. E., map, 1899.

**Chicaça.** A chief town of the Chickasaw, situated, according to Halbert (Miss. Hist. Soc. Publ., VI, 452, 1902), 1 m. N. W. of Redland, in Pontotoc co., Miss., in the 16th century. This settlement was visited by the army of De Soto, who made it his headquarters during the winter of 1540–41, and whose chroniclers describe it as situated on a hill and consisting of thatch-roofed houses. In the following spring the Indians, after repeated attacks, succeeded in setting fire to the town, and, although finally repulsed, killed a number of Spaniards and horses. The day following this disaster the Spaniards moved to a spot a league away, where they built a temporary village which they called Chicacilla, i. e. 'Little Chicaça.'

Chicaça.—Ranjel (1546) quoted by Oviedo, Hist. Gen., I, 571, 1851. Great Village of the Chickasaws.—Jefferys, Am. Atlas, map 26, 1776. Sicacha.—Hennepin (1697), cited by Thwaites, Hennepin, II, 442, 1903.

**Chicago** (Sauk, Fox, and Kickapoo: *shĕkagua*, 'skunk', and *shĕkakohĕg i*, 'place of the skunk', an ancient name for the S. part of L. Michigan, due, it is said, to a large skunk that once lived along the S. shores and was killed in the lake by a party of fox hunters.—W. J.). A Miami village on the site of Chicago, Ill., at the period of the earliest explorations in that region, 1670–1700. A French document of 1695 makes it a Wea village at that time (N. Y. Doc. Col. Hist., IX, 619, 1855). Situated on one of the routes to the Mississippi, it was a place of importance from an early date. Marquette and Joliet passed by it on their return from their exploration of the Mississippi, and Marquette subsequently spent a winter there. Allouez took the same route in 1677, as did La Salle on his second journey, and Joutel and Cavelier were at Chicago in 1687–88, followed by La Hontan the following year. Chicago was also the name of a chief of the Illinois about 1725. See Hoffman in 14th Rep. B. A. E., 238.

Apkaw.—St Cosme (1699) in Shea, Early Voy., 52, 1861 (apparently intended for Chicago). **Checagou.**—Membré (1681) in Shea, Discov. Miss. R., 166, 1852. **Chégagou.**—Doc. of 1695 in N. Y. Doc. Col. Hist., IX, 619, 1855. **Chegakou.**—La Hontan (1703), New Voy., I, 231, 1735. **Chekakou.**—Ibid., I, 135, 1703. **Chicago.**—Iberville (1702) in Minn. Hist. Soc. Coll., I, 341, 1872. **Chicagou.**—Document of 1695 in N. Y. Doc. Col. Hist., IX, 627, 1855. **Chicag8.**—St Cosme (1699) in Shea, Early Voy., 56, 1861. **Chicags.**—Croghan (1765) in N. Y. Doc. Col. Hist., VII, 785, 1856. **Chicagu.**—St Cosme, op. cit., 51. **Chicagvv.**—Ibid., 59. **Chicaqw.**—Ibid., 54. **Chigagou.**—Ibid., 68. **Chikago.**—LaTour, map, 1784. **Chikagons.**—La Potherie, Hist. Amér., II, 346, 1753. **Chikagou.**—St Cosme (1699) in Shea, Early Voy., 55, 1861. **Chikagoüa.**—Gravier (1700), ibid., 116–117. **Chikagu.**—St Cosme, op. cit., 51. **Chikagvv.**—Shea, Rel. Mission de Miss., 22, 1861.

**Chicherohe.** A former Cherokee settlement on War Woman cr., in N. W. Rabun co., Ga.; destroyed in the Revolutionary war. (J. M.)

**Chichigoue** (seemingly cognate with Chippewa *shishikwe*, 'rattlesnake'.—W. J.). A tribe mentioned by La Chesnaye as living N. of L. Superior in 1697, and generally trading with the English on Hudson bay. They can not be identified with any known tribe, but they were evidently Algonquian. (J. M.)

Chichigoue.—La Chesnaye (1697) in Margry, Déc., VI, 7, 1886. **Chichigoueks.**—La Potherie, Hist. de l'Amér., II, 49, 1753.

**Chichilek.** A Squawmish village community on Burrard inlet, Brit. Col.

Tcitcilě′ɛk.—Hill-Tout in Rep. Brit. A. A. S., 475, 1900.

**Chichilticalli** (Nahuatl: *chichiltic* 'red,' *calli* 'house': 'red house'). A ruined pueblo visited by Coronado's army on its journey to Cibola (Zuñi) in 1540; apparently situated on the Gila, E. of the mouth of the San Pedro, S. Ariz., probably not far from Solomonsville. Owing to the glowing account of the place given by Fray Marcos de Niza in the preceding year, Coronado and his followers were "much affected by seeing that the fame of Chichilticalli was summed up in one tumble-down house without any roof, although it appeared to have been a strong place at some former time when it was inhabited, and it was very plain that it had been built by a civilized and warlike race of strangers who had come from a distance" (Castañeda). The same writer also states that it "was formerly inhabited by people who had separated from Cibola." Many writers have wrongly identified it with the present Casa Grande. See Bandelier in Arch. Inst. Papers, III, 178, 1890; Hodge, Coronado's March, 1899; Winship, Coronado Exped., 14th Rep. B. A. E., 1896. (F. W. H.)

Chichicticale.—Castañeda (1596) in Ternaux-Compans, Voy., IX, 12, 1838. **Chichillicale.**—Kern, map in Schoolcraft, Ind. Tribes, IV, 38, 1854. **Chichilte Calli.**—Jaramillo in Ternaux-Compans, Voy., IX, 365, 1838. **Chichilti.**—Gallatin in Trans. Am. Ethnol. Soc., II, lxxviii, 1848. **Chichilticah.**—Bandelier in Arch. Inst. Papers, I, 117, 1881 (misprint). **Chichilti-cal.**—Gallatin, op. cit., lxix. **Chichilticala.**—Ogilby, America, 299, 1671. **Chichilticale.**—Coronado (1540) in Hakluyt, Voy., 448, 1600. **Chichilticalen.**—De l'Isle, map Am. Sept., 1700. **Chichilticali.**—Mota-Padilla, Hist. de la Conquista, 113, 1742. **Chichilti-calli.**—Gallatin, op. cit., lx. **Chichiltic-Calli.**—Jaramillo in Ternaux-Compans, Voy., IX, 368, 1838. **Chichiltie.**—Jaramillo in Doc. Inéd., XIV, 307, 1870. **Chichiltie Allí.**—Jaramillo quoted by Bancroft, Ariz. and N. Mex., 40, 1889. **Chichiticala.**—Heylyn, Cosmography, 968, 1703. **Chichiticale.**—Coronado (1540) in Ramusio, Nav. et Viaggi, III, 362(F), 1565. **Chichitté Calli.**—Jaramillo in Doc. Inéd., XIV, 304, 1870. **Chiltcale.**—Beadle, Undeveloped West, 468, 1873. **Red House.**—Wallace in Atl. Monthly, 219, Aug., 1880 (or Chichiticale). **Red Town.**—Domenech, Deserts N. A., I, 175, 1860 (or Chichilticale). **Roode Huis.**—ten Kate, Reizen in N. A., 161, 1885 (Dutch form).

**Chichinak.** A Kaialigmiut Eskimo village on a small river flowing into Etolin str., Alaska; pop. 6 in 1880, 84 in 1890.

Chechinamiut.—11th Census, Alaska, 164, 1893. **Chichinagamute.**—Petroff, Rep. on Alaska, 54, 1884.

**Chichipé Outipé** (Chippewa has *Titipē′u′ntipē*, 'curly-head.'—W. J.). A large Potawatomi village in 1838 near South Bend, St Joseph co., Ind. (J. M.)

**Chichiveachic** (probably from the native term signifying 'peaks' + *chic* 'place of'). A Tarahumare rancheria in Chihuahua, Mexico.—Lumholtz, inf'n, 1894.

WILLIAM H. ADKINS, A CHICKAHOMINY

**Chickahominy** (from *K'chick-ahäm-min′-nough*, 'coarse-pounded corn people,' 'hominy people'—Tooker; or from *Tshikĕhämĕn*, a place name, meaning 'swept,' 'cleared,' and implying a clearing— Gerard). A tribe of the Powhatan confederacy, formerly living on Chickahominy r., Va. It was one of the most important tribes in Virginia, numbering 250 warriors, or perhaps 900 souls, in 1608, and was not so directly under the control of Powhatan as the other tribes over which he ruled. In 1613 they entered into an alliance with the English and assumed the name of Tassautessus (*sic*), or "Englishmen." In 1669 they were still estimated at 60 warriors, possibly 220 souls, but in 1722 were reported to number only about 80. Their last public notice occurs in this same year, when, in connection with the Pamunkey, they were named in the Albany conference with the Iroquois as among the Virginia tribes not to be molested by the

CHICKAHOMINY WOMAN.  (MOONEY)

latter. A mixed-blood band numbering about 220 still keeps up the name, but without regular tribal organization, on both sides of Chickahominy r. in New Kent and Charles City cos., Va., with Wm. H. Adkins as chief in 1905. They are on close terms of association with the neighboring bands of Pamunkey and Mattapony. On the origin and application of the name consult Tooker, Algonq. Ser., IX, 1900; Gerard in Am. Anthrop., VII, 224, 1905.          (J. M.)

Chechohomynies.—Smith, Works, Arber ed., lxxv, 1884. Checkahomanies.—Harris, Voy. and Trav., I, 839, 1705. Chekahomanies.—Ibid. Chicahamanias.— Smith (1629), Virginia, II, 16, repr. 1819. Chichominys.—Albany conference (1722) in N. Y. Doc. Col. Hist., v, 673, 1855. Chickahamanias.—Smith (1629), Virginia, II, 27, repr. 1819. Chickahamines.—Strachey (*ca.* 1612), Virginia, 51, 1849. Chickahomines.—Boudinot, Star in the West, 126,

1816. Chickahominys.—Spotswood (1712) in Va. Hist. Soc. Coll., n. s., I, 167, 1882. Chickahomones.— Jefferson (1781) in Schoolcraft, Ind. Tribes, v, 36, 1855. Chickahomonie.—Beverly, Virginia, 199, 1722. Chikahominy.—Martin, N. C., 1, 78, 1829. Tassautessus.—Smith (1624), Works, Arber ed., 515, 1884 ('strangers,' 'Englishmen,' an adopted name). Vttasantasough.—Simmonds (1612–24), ibid., 430.

**Chickamauga** (*Tsĭkăma'gĭ*, a word apparently of foreign origin and probably Shawnee, Creek, or Chickasaw). The name given to a band of Cherokee who espoused the English cause in the war of the Revolution and moved far down on Tennessee r., establishing new settlements on Chickamauga cr., in the neighborhood of the present Chattanooga. Under this name they soon became noted for their uncompromising and never-ceasing hostility. In 1782 their towns were destroyed by Sevier and Campbell, and they moved farther down the river, establishing what were afterward known as the "five lower towns," Running Water, Nickajack, Long Island, Crow Town, and Lookout Mountain Town. Here they were continually recruited by Creeks, Shawnee, and white Tories, until they were estimated to number a thousand warriors. They continued hostilities against the Tennessee settlements until 1794, when their towns were destroyed.—Mooney in 19th Rep. B. A. E., 54, 413, 537, 1900.

**Chickasaw.** An important Muskhogean tribe, closely related to the Choctaw in language and customs, although the two tribes were mutually hostile. Aside from tradition, the earliest habitat traceable for the Chickasaw is N. Mississippi. Their villages in the 18th century centered about Pontotoc and Union cos., where the headwaters of the Tombigbee meet those of Yazoo r. and its affluent, the Tallahatchie, about where the De Soto narratives place them in 1540, under the name Chicaza. Their main landing place on the Mississippi was at Chickasaw Bluffs, now the site of Memphis, Tenn., whence a trail more than 160 m. long led to their villages. They had two other landing places farther up the Mississippi. Adair, who for many years was a trader among the Chickasaw and gives a full and circumstantial account of them (Hist. Am. Inds., 352–373, 1775), states that in 1720 they had four contiguous settlements, and that the towns of one of these were Shatara, Chook'heereso, Hykehah, Tuskawillao, and Phalacheho. Two of the other settlements of which he gives the names were Yaneka, 6 m. long, and Chookka Pharáah (Chukafalaya), 4 m. long. Romans (Florida, 63, 1775), describing their country and villages, says that they "live nearly in the center of an uneven and large nitrous savannah; have in it 1 town, 1½ m. long, very narrow and irregular; this they divide into 7 [towns] by the names of Amalahta 'hat and feather,' Chatelaw 'copper town,' Chukafalaya 'long town,' Hikkihaw 'stand still,' Chucalissa 'great town,' Tuckahaw 'a cert'n weed,' Ashukhuma 'red grass.' Formerly the whole was inclosed in palisadoes.''

The warlike Chickasaw claimed other territory far beyond the narrow limits of their villages, and extending on the N. to the confluence of the Ohio with the Tennessee. They also claimed a large area N. of the Tennessee to the ridge between Duck r. and the Cumberland to the headwaters of Duck r. and s. to Chickasaw Old Fields on the Tennessee, thence along an indeterminate s. E. line to the Mississippi. This claim was admitted by the Cherokee. According to Haywood and other authorities an outlying colony of Chickasaw formerly dwelt on Savannah r. nearly opposite Augusta, Ga., but trouble with the Creeks drove them westward again. In 1795 the Chickasaw claimed payment from the United States for the land on the Savannah thus occupied.

The Chickasaw were noted from remote times for their bravery, independence, and warlike disposition. They were constantly fighting with the neighboring tribes; sometimes with the Choctaw and Creeks, then with the Cherokee, Illinois, Kickapoo, Shawnee, Mobilians, Osage, and Quapaw. In 1732 they cut to pieces a war party of Iroquois who had invaded their country. They were constant enemies of the French—a feeling intensified by the intrigues of British traders and their hatred of the Choctaw who had entered into friendly relations with the French colonists. The Chickasaw urged the Natchez to resist the French encroachments, and gave shelter to them when driven from their home. They defeated the French at Amalahta in 1736, at the Long House and other points, and baffled their attempts at conquest in the war of 1739–40. They combined with the Cherokee about 1715 and drove the Shawnee from their home on the Cumberland, and in 1769 utterly routed, at Chickasaw Old Fields, these former Cherokee allies.

Their relations with the United States began with the Hopewell treaty in 1786, when their boundary on the N. was fixed at the Ohio r. They began to emigrate w. of the Mississippi as early as 1822, and treaties for the removal of those who remained in their old seats were made in 1832 and 1834. By the treaty of 1855 their lands in Indian Ter. were definitely separated from those of the Choctaw, with which they had before been included.

In manners and customs they differed little from their congeners, the Choctaw, the principal difference being the more sedentary habits and greater devotion to agricultural pursuits by the Choctaw on the one hand, and the more turbulent, restless, and warlike disposition of the Chickasaw on the other. Their traditional origin is the same as that of the Creeks and Choctaw (q. v.), and is given in the so-called ''Creek migration legend'' (see *Creeks*). The Chickasaw appear to have sheltered and ultimately incorporated into their organization the small tribes along Yazoo r., who spoke substantially the same language. The Chickasaw language served as a medium of commercial and tribal intercourse for all the tribes along the lower Mississippi. Early estimates of population vary widely, those of the 18th century ranging from 2,000 to nearly 6,000. According to Adair (op. cit., 353) they had been much

CHICKASAW

more numerous than during his time (1744), one of the two divisions, the ''Long House,'' numbering not more than 450 warriors, indicating a population of 1,600 to 1,800 persons. He gives no estimate of the other division, but assuming it to have been about the same, the population of the entire tribe was between 3,000 and 4,000. Morse (Rep. to Sec. War, 364, 1822), though estimating the Choctaw at 25,000, gives the Chickasaw population as 3,625. In 1865 the estimated population was 4,500; in 1904 the official number was given as 4,826, including mixed bloods.

According to Morgan (Anc. Society, 163, 1878) the Chickasaw were divided into 12 gentes, arranged in 2 phratries, as follows:

I.—Koi, Panther: (1) Koinchush,

Wild cat; (2) Hatakfushi, Bird; (3) Nunni, Fish; (4) Issi, Deer. II.—Ishpanee, Spanish: (1) Shauee, Raccoon; (2) Ishpanee, Spanish; (3) Mingko, Royal; (4) Hushkoni, Skunk; (5) Funi, Squirrel; (6) Hochonchabba, Alligator; (7) Nashola, Wolf; (8) Chuhhla, Blackbird.

The list given by Gibbs (Gatschet, Creek Migr. Leg., I, 96, 1884) follows:

I.—Panther phratry, Koa: (1) Kointchush, Wild cat; (2) Fushi, Bird; (3) Nanni, Fish; (4) Issi, Deer. II.—Spanish phratry, Ishpani: (1) Shawi, Raccoon; (2) Ishpani, Spanish; (3) Mingo, Royal; (4) Huskoni; (5) Tunni, Squirrel; (6) Hotchon tchapa, Alligator; (7) Nashoba, Wolf; (8) Tchu'hla, Blackbird.

Mingos or chiefs could be chosen only from the "Spanish" gens, and were hereditary in the female line. The name must formerly have been different or this rule must have been established after the coming of the Spaniards.

The following are the old Chickasaw towns so far as recorded: Ackia, Amalahta, Ashukhuma, Chatelaw, Chucalissa, Chukafalaya, Chula, Hykehah, Latcha Hoa, Palacheho, Pontotoc, Shatara, Taposa, Tuckahaw, Tuskawillas, Yaneka. (A. S. G. C. T.)

Ani'-Tsĭ'ksû.—Mooney in 19th Rep. B. A. E., 509, 1900 (Cherokee name; sing., Tsĭ'ksû). Ceickasaw.—Simpson, Report, 11, 1850. Chekaihas.—Shea, Relat. Miss. on Miss. R., 28, 1861. Chekasaws.—Imlay, West. Terr., 290, 1797. Chiacasas.—Güssefeld, Map of U.S., 1784. Chicaça.—Gentl. of Elvas (1557) in Hakluyt Soc. Works, IX, 81, 1851. Chicachas.—La Salle (1682) in Margry, Déc., I, 553, 1875. Chicachos.—Chauvignerie (1736) in Schoolcraft, Ind. Tribes, III, 555, 1853. Chicaksaws.—Schoolcraft, ibid., 45. Chicasan.—Morse, Hist. Am., map, 1798. Chicasas.—Croghan (1759) in Proud, Penn., II, 297, 1798. Chicasauus.—Alcedo, Dic. Geog., I, 497, 1786. Chicasaws.—Barton, New Views, xlvii, 1798. Chicasou.—Mandrillon, Spect. Am., map, 1785. Chicàssas.—French, Hist. Coll. La., III, 237, 1851. Chicawchaws.—Perrin du Lac, Voy., 368, 1805. Chicaza.—Biedma (1545) in Smith, Col. Doc. Fla., I, 55, 1857. Chichacas.—Robin, Voy. à la Louisiane, I, 54, 1807. Chichasau.—Möllhausen, Reisen, I, 343, 1858. Chichasaws.—Imlay, West. Terr., 13, 1797. Chichashas.—Gamelin (1790) in Am. State Pap., Ind. Aff., I, 93, 1832. Chickasaws.—Niles (1760) in Mass. Hist. Coll., 4th s., V, 549, 1861. Chickassas.—Domenech, Deserts, I, 440, 1860. Chickesaw.—Frink (1764) in Hawkins, Missns., 101, 1845. Chicketaws.—Rogers, North America, 201, 1765. Chickisaw.—Bollaert in Jour. Ethnol. Soc. Lond., II, 280, 1850. Chickkasah.—Boudinot, Star in the West, 109, 1816. Chicksas.—Croghan (1759) in Kauffman, West. Pa., 146, 1851. Chicksaws.—Bossu (1751), Travels La., I, 92, 1771. Chicksha.—Penhallow (1726) in N. H. Hist. Coll., 1st s., 79, 1824. Chickshau.—Niles (1760) in Mass. Hist. Coll., 4th s., V, 333, 1861. Chigasaws.—Catesby, Nat. Hist. Car., II, x, 1743. Chikakas.—Vater, Mith., III, 245, 1816. Chikakas.—Shea, Relat. Miss. on Miss. R., 34, 1861. Chikasahs.—Prichard, Phys. Hist., V, 401, 1847. Chikasas.—Drake, Ind. Chron., 215, 1836. Chíkasha.—ten Kate, Reizen in N. A., 402, 1885. Chikitaws.—Rogers, North America, 149, 1765. Chikkasah.—Barton, New Views, xlvii, 1798. Chikkesah.—Boudinot, Star in the West, 231, 1816. Chiksah.—Tanner, Narr., 327, 1830. Chiquacha.—Hennepin (1680) in French, Hist. Coll. La., I, 206, 1846. Chixaxia.—French writer (1761) in Mass. Hist. Coll., 4th s., IX, 428, 1861. Chukesws.—Buchanan, N. Am. Inds., 155, 1824. Cicaca.—La Salle (1679) in Margry, Déc., II, 41, 1877. Cikaga.—Hennepin, New Discov., 141, 1698. Kasahá únûⁿ, inf'n (Yuchi name; abbreviated from Chikasahá únûⁿ). Ohikkasaw.—Latham, Opuscula, 278, 1860. Sicacas.—La Salle (1680) in Margry, Déc., I, 487, 1875. Sicacha.—Hennepin, New Discov., 152, 1698. Sicachia.—Ibid., 311. Sikacha.—Ibid., 152. Tchaktchán.—Gatschet, inf'n (Arapaho name). Tchicachas.—Bossu, Travels La., I, 92, 1771. Tchíkasa.—Gatschet, Creek Migr. Leg., II, 126, 1888 (Creek name, pl. Tchicasalgi). Tci'-ka-sa'.—Dorsey, Kansa MS. vocab., B. A. E., 1882 (Kansa name). Techichas.—Duquesne (1754) in N. Y. Doc. Col. Hist., x, 263, 1858. Ti-ka'- jă.—Dorsey, Kwapa MS. vocab., B. A. E., 1891 (Kwapa name). Tsi'-ka-cĕ.—Dorsey, Osage MS. vocab., B. A. E., 1883 (Osage name). Tsĭ'ksû.—Mooney in 19th Rep. B. A. E., 509, 1900 (Cherokee name, pl. Ani'-Tsĭ'ksû). Tsĭk-û-sû.—Grayson, Creek MS. vocab., B. A. E., 1885 (Creek name).

**Chickasaw Half Town.** Mentioned as a Choctaw town in the report of the Ft Adams conference in 1801.—Macomb in Am. State Pap., Ind. Aff., I, 661, 1832.

**Chickasawhay.** A former Choctaw town which stood, according to tradition, on the E. side of Chickasawhay r. about 3 m. below the present town of Enterprise, Clarke co., Ga. It also gave its name to a subdivision between Chickasawhay and Buckatunna rs.—Halbert in Rep. Ala. Hist. Soc., Misc. Coll., I, 379, 1901.

Chicasahay.—Romans, Florida, 86, 1775. Chickasawhays.—Ibid., 73. Chickasawka.—Ker, Travels, 331, 1816. Tchicachae.—Jefferys, French Dom. Am., 135, map, 1761. Tchikachaé. — D'Anville, map (ca. 1732) discussed by Halbert in Miss. Hist. Soc. Publ., III, 367, 370, 1902.

**Chickasaw Old Fields.** A place on the N. side of Tennessee r., opposite Chickasaw id., about 4 m. below Flint r., in S. E. Madison co., Ala.; claimed by the Chickasaw as one of their ancient village sites.—Treaty of 1805 in U. S. Ind. Treat., 116, 1837.

**Chickataubut** ('house afire'). A Massachuset sachem of the region about Weymouth, Mass., whose enmity against the English was early aroused by their depredations on the tribal cornfields and desecration of his mother's grave (Drake, Inds. N. Am., 107, 1880). In 1621, with several other chiefs, he submitted to the English authority, and in 1631 visited Gov. Winthrop at Boston, behaving "like an Englishman." In 1632 he served against the Pequot and died the next year of smallpox. He was a man of note and influence. (A. F. C.)

**Chickwit.** A name of the weakfish (*Labrus squeteague*) still used, according to Bartlett (Dict. of Americanisms, 112, 1877), in parts of Connecticut and Rhode Island. This word, spelled also *chickwick*, *chequet*, etc., is generally thought to be a further corruption of *squeteague*, another name of this fish. Trumbull (Natick Dict., 21, 1903) cites the forms *chequit* and *checout*, and suggests a derivation from *chohki*, signifying, 'spotted,' in the Massachuset dialect of Algonquian. (A. F. C.)

**Chicoli.** Mentioned as a Navaho settlement in 1799 (Cortez in Pac. R. R. Rep., III, pt. 3, 119, 1856); but as the Navaho are not villagers, it is probably only a geographical name.

**Chiconessex** (from *chiconesink*, 'place of small turkeys.'—Hewitt). A village of the Powhatan confederacy, formerly about Wiseville, Accomac co., Va. It was nearly extinct in 1722. (J. M.)
Chiconessex.—Beverly, Virginia, 199, 1722. **Chissenossick.**—Herrman map (1670) in Maps to Accompany the Rept. of the Comrs. on the Bdy. bet. Va. and Md., 1873.

**Chicora.** The name given by the Spaniards at the time of Ayllon's visit in 1521 to the coast region of South Carolina, s. of Edisto r., and to the Indians inhabiting it. The name Cusabo, subsequently applied, included most of the tribes of the same region. Gatschet suggests that the name Chicora is derived from the Catawba *Yuchi-kĕrĕ*, 'Yuchi are there, or over there,' but the connection is not very obvious. The French form of about the same period, Chigoula, has more the appearance of a Muskhogean word. Fontaneda, about 1570, makes Chicora and Orista (Edisto) equivalent. The tribes of this region were practically exterminated by Spanish and English slave hunters before the close of the 17th century. (J. M.)
Chicora.—Fontaneda (*ca.* 1570) in Ternaux-Compans, Voy., XX, 16, 1841. **Chicoria.**—Garcilasso de la Vega, Fla., 4, 1723. **Chicorie.**—Ayllon (*ca.* 1521) quoted by Shipp, De Soto and Florida, 240, 1881. **Chigoula.**—Laudonnière (1562) in French, Hist. Coll. La., n. s., 190, 1869. **Chiquola.**—Syms, Hist. S. C., 10, 1860.

**Chicoutimi.** The name of a locality, the end of smooth navigation of Saguenay r., Quebec, by which the Lake St John band of Montagnais was sometimes referred to (Jes. Rel. 1661, 13, 1858). The French formerly had a mission of the same name on the right bank of the Saguenay. In 1898 the Montagnais of L. St John numbered 404 and resided on a reservation at Pointe Bleue. (J. M.)
Checoutimi.—Jefferys, French Dom. Am., I, 18, 1761. **Checoutimiens.**—Ibid. **Chegoutimis.**—Jes. Rel. 1661, 14, 1858. **Chekoutimiens.**—Bellin, map, 1755. **Chekoutimis.**—La Tour, map, 1784. **Chicontami.**—Johnson (1764) in N. Y. Doc. Col. Hist., VII, 658, 1856 (misprint). **Chicoutime.**—Lords of Trade (1764), ibid., 635. **Chicoutimi.**—Jes. Rel. 1661, 13, 1858. **Chixoutimi.**—Johnson (1764) in N. Y. Doc. Col. Hist., VII, 664, 1856. **Montagnais of Lake St. John.**—Can. Ind. Aff. Rep. 1884, pt. I, 185, 1885.

**Chicuchatti** (probably Creek *chúka chati*, 'red houses,' referring to the custom of daubing the houses with red clay). A former Seminole town N. of Tampa bay, in the so-called Chocochatee savanna, Hernando co., Fla. According to Brinton it was one of the 7 bands into which the Seminole became divided after their separation from the Creeks.
Chickuchatty.—Lindsay (1836) in H. R. Doc. 78, 25th Cong., 2d sess., 149, 1838. **Chicuchatty.**—Drake, Ind. Chron., 209, 1836. **Chockechiatte.**—

Penière in Morse, Rep. to Sec. War, 311, 1822. **Chocochattee.**—Cowperwaite, Atlas, 1850. **Chokechatti.**—Brinton, Florida Penin., 145, 1859. **Chuku-chatta.**—Morse, op. cit., 307.

**Chicutae.** A former village, presumably Costanoan, connected with Dolores mission, San Francisco, Cal.—Taylor in Cal. Farmer, Apr. 5, 1860.

**Chie.** One of the two principal clans of the Chiricahua Apache, coördinate with the Destchin clan of San Carlos agency, Ariz.
Chi-e'.—Bourke in Jour. Am. Folk-lore, III, 115, 1890.

**Chief Joseph.** See *Joseph.*

**Chiefs.** Among the North American Indians a chief may be generally defined as a political officer whose distinctive functions are to execute the ascertained will of a definite group of persons united by the possession of a common territory or range and of certain exclusive rights, immunities, and obligations, and to conserve their customs, traditions, and religion. He exercises legislative, judicative, and executive powers delegated to him in accordance with custom for the conservation and promotion of the common weal.

The wandering band of men with their women and children contains the simplest type of chieftaincy found among the American Indians, for such a group has no permanently fixed territorial limits, and no definite social and political relations exist between it and any other body of persons. The clan or gens, the tribe, and the confederation present more complex forms of social and political organization. The clan or gens embraces several such chieftaincies, and has a more highly developed internal political structure with definite land boundaries. The tribe is constituted of several clans or gentes and the confederation of several tribes. Among the different Indian communities the social and political structure varied greatly. Many stages of social progress lay between the small band under a single chief and the intricate permanent confederation of highly organized tribes, with several kinds of officers and varying grades of councils of diverse but interrelated jurisdictions. With the advance in political organization political powers and functions were multiplied and diversified, and the multiplicity and diversity of duties and functions required different grades of officers to perform them; hence various kinds and grades of chiefs are found. There were in certain communities, as the Iroquois and Creeks, civil chiefs and subchiefs, chosen for personal merit, and permanent and temporary war chiefs. These several grades of chiefs bear distinctive titles, indicative of their diverse jurisdiction. The title to the dignity belongs to the community, usually to its women, not to the chief, who usually owes his nomination to the suffrages of his female constituents, but in most communities he is installed by some authority higher than that of his chieftaincy. Both in the lowest and the highest form of government the chiefs are the creatures of law, expressed in well-defined customs, rites, and traditions. Only where agriculture is wholly absent may the simplest type of chieftaincy be found.

Where the civil structure is permanent there exist permanent military chieftainships, as among the Iroquois. To reward personal merit and statesmanship the Iroquois instituted a class of chiefs whose office, upon the death of the holder, remained vacant. This latter provision was made to obviate a large representation and avoid a change in the established roll of chiefs. They were called "the solitary pine trees," and were installed in the same manner as the others. They could not be deposed, but merely ostracized, if they committed crimes rendering them unworthy of giving counsel.

Where the civil organization was of the simplest character the authority of the chiefs was most nearly despotic; even in some instances where the civil structure was complex, as among the Natchez, the rule of the chiefs at times became in a measure tyrannical, but this was due largely to the recognition of social castes and the domination of certain religious beliefs and considerations.

The chieftainship was usually hereditary in certain families of the community, although in some communities any person by virtue of the acquisition of wealth could proclaim himself a chief. Descent of blood, property, and official titles were generally traced through the mother. Early writers usually called the chief who acted as the chairman of the federal council the "head chief" and sometimes, when the tribe or confederation was powerful and important, "king" or "emperor," as in the case of Powhatan. In the Creek confederation and in that of the Iroquois, the most complex aboriginal government N. of Mexico, there was, in fact, no head chief. The first chief of the Onondaga federal roll acted as the chairman of the federal council, and by virtue of his office he called the federal council together. With this all preëminence over the other chiefs ended, for the governing power of the confederation was lodged in the federal council. The federal council was composed of the federal chiefs of the several component tribes; the tribal council consisted of the federal chiefs and subchiefs of the tribe.

Communities are formed on the basis of a union of interests and obligations.

By the union of several rudimentary communities for mutual aid and protection, in which each retained part of its original freedom and delegated certain social and political powers and jurisdiction to the united community, was evolved an assembly of representatives of the united bands in a tribal council having a definite jurisdiction. To these chiefs were sometimes added subchiefs, whose jurisdiction, though subordinate, was concurrent with that of the chiefs. The enlarged community constitutes a tribe. From tribes were organized confederations. There were therefore several grades of councils constituted. In the council of the Iroquois confederation the subchiefs had no voice or recognition.

Among the Plains tribes the chieftaincy seems to have been usually non-hereditary. Any ambitious and courageous warrior could apparently, in strict accordance with custom, make himself a chief by the acquisition of suitable property and through his own force of character. See *Social organization*.    (J. N. B. H.)

**Chifukluk.** A Magemiut Eskimo village on the left bank at the head of the Yukon delta, Alaska.
Chifukhlugumut.—Nelson in 18th Rep. B. A. E., map, 1899.

**Chiggilli.** See *Chekilli*.

**Chigilousa** (Choctaw: *lusa* 'black,' *chigi* 'houses'). A former tribe on the lower Mississippi, probably the same as the Chitimacha, w. of that river (La Tour, map, 1783); but possibly they were of Choctaw affinity.

**Chigmiut.** A subtribe of the Chugachugmiut Eskimo inhabiting Montague id., Prince William sd., Alaska.
Chigmut.—Dall in Cont. N. A. Ethnol., I, map, 1877.

**Chignecto** (from *sigunikt*, 'foot cloth'). A Micmac village in Nova Scotia in 1760.—Frye (1760) in Mass. Hist. Soc. Coll., 1st s., x, 115, 1809.

**Chiguau.** A former village, presumably Costanoan, connected with Dolores mission, San Francisco, Cal.—Taylor in Cal. Farmer, Oct. 18, 1861.

**Chihlakonini** (*chi'láko-nini*, 'horse-trail'). A former Lower Creek town on the upper waters of Chattahoochee r., seemingly in the present Harris Co., Ga. It was burned by the whites in Sept., 1793, at which date it consisted of 10 houses, but by 1799 the people had formed a new town on the left bank of Tallapoosa r., opposite Oakfuskee, Ala. The upper trail or war path crossed the latter stream by a horse ford at this place, about 60 m. above Kasihta town. It was probably identical with Okfuskinini.    (A. S. G.)
Cheolucca-ninne.—Bartram, Travels, 462, 1792. Che'láko Nini.—Gatschet, Creek Migr. Leg., I, 129, 1884. Che-luc-co ne-ne.—Hawkins (1799), Sketch, 45, 1848. Chelucconinny.—Swan (1791) in School-

craft, Ind. Tribes, v, 262, 1855. **Horse-Trail.**—Gatschet, Creek Migr. Leg., i, 129, 1884. **Little Oakfuskee.**—Knox (1793) in Am. State Pap., Ind. Aff., i, 362, 1832.

**Chihucchihui.** A former Chumashan village in Ventura co., Cal.—Taylor in Cal. Farmer, July 24, 1863.

**Chihupa** ('jawbone band'). A former Dakota band under Sishhola, or Barefoot. Úi-hu'-pa.—Hayden, Ethnog. and Philol. Mo. Val., 373, 1862.

**Chiink.** An Alsea village on the s. side of Alsea r., Oreg. Tci'-ink.—Dorsey in Jour. Am. Folk-lore, iii, 230, 1890.

**Chikak.** An Aglemiut village on Iliamna lake, Alaska; pop. 51 in 1880.—Petroff, 10th Census, Alaska, 17, 1884.

**Chikataubut.** See *Chickataubut.*

**Chikauach.** A Songish band at McNeill bay, s. end of Vancouver id., Brit. Col. Tcik·au'atc.—Boas in 6th Rep. on N. W. Tribes Can., 17, 1890.

**Chiklisilkh.** A Lower Chehalis settlement at Pt Leadbetter, the N. end of the land tongue at Shoalwater bay, Wash.—Gibbs, Chinook vocab., B. A. E., 23.

**Chikohoki** (from *Chikelaki; chíkeno* 'turkey,' *aki* 'land'). The former principal seat of the Unalachtigo Delawares, situated on the w. bank of Delaware r., near the present Wilmington, Del. Chichohocki.—Bozman, Maryland, i, 130, 1837. Chickahokin.—Smith (1629), Virginia, i, map, repr. 1819. Chihohocki.—Thompson quoted by Jefferson, Notes, 278, 1825. Chikahokin.—Brinton, Lenape Leg., 37, 1885. Chikelaki.—Ibid. Chikohocki.—Schermerhorn (1812) in Mass. Hist. Soc. Coll., 2d s., ii, 6, 1814. Chikolacki.—Brinton, op. cit.

**Chikohoki.** A former village, said to be of the Manta division of the Delawares, on the site of Burlington, Burlington co., N. J. According to Heckewelder it was the oldest village on Delaware r.
(J. M.)

**Chikonapi** (the Canadian Chippewa use the term *chikonāpä* for 'carpenter.'—W. J.). Mentioned in the Walam Olum of the Delawares as a people conquered or destroyed by the latter tribe (Brinton, Lenape Legends, 190, 1885). They can not be located with certainty.

**Chilano.** A village or tribe, probably Caddoan, visited by De Soto's troops under Moscoso toward the close of 1542, and at that time situated in N. E. Texas, near upper Sabine r. See Gentl. of Elvas (1557) in French, Hist. Coll. La., ii, 201, 1850.

**Chilchadilkloge** ('grassy-hill people'). An Apache band or clan at San Carlos agency and Ft Apache, Ariz., in 1881. Chilchadilklogue.—Bourke in Jour. Am. Folk-Lore, iii, 112, 1890.

**Child life.** The subject of Indian child life has been but very lightly treated by ethnologists, although the child is in fact the strongest bond of family life under a system which allowed polygamy and easy separation. Both parents alike were entirely devoted to their children, and bestowed upon them the fullest expression of affection and solicitude. The relation of parent to child brings out all the highest traits of Indian character.

Among some tribes, notably those of the plains, in anticipation of the new arrival the father prepares the wooden frame of the cradle which is to be its portable bed until it is able to walk. The body of the cradle, with its ornamentation of bead or quill design, fringes and bangles, is made either by the grandmother or by some woman noted in the tribe for her superior expertness. There were many well-marked varieties of cradle, differing with the tribe. Among the Choctaw, Catawba, and other former tribes of the Southern states, and among the Chinookan and Salishan tribes of the Columbia, there was used a special attachment which, by continued pressure upon the forehead while the bones were still soft, produced the so-called "flat head," esteemed with these tribes a point of beauty (see *Artificial Head Deformation*). One cradle was used for successive infants in the same family.

The newborn infant is commonly treated at once to a cold bath, and turned over to another matron to nurse until the mother's health is restored. Among the Hopi, ashes or sacred meal are rubbed on the newborn babe. Lactation is long continued, even for 2 years or more, and in rare cases much longer. With all the affection of the mother, the women are almost completely ignorant of ordinary sanitary rules as to feeding, exposure, etc., consequently the rate of infant mortality is very high in almost every tribe, many children being born, but only a small proportion coming to maturity, so that even in former times the tribal population remained almost stationary. The child sisters or cousins of the baby are its attendants, while the mother is occupied with other duties, and perform their work with the instinct of little mothers. The child is kept in its cradle usually only during a journey or while being carried about, and not, as is commonly supposed, during most of the time. At home it rolls about upon the grass or on the bed without restraint. Formerly, except in extreme weather, no clothing was worn during waking hours up to the age of from 5 to 10 years, according to the tribe and climate, and in some tribes this practice still prevails. The child may be named soon after birth, or not for a year or more after, this child name, like the first teeth, being discarded as the boy or girl grows up for another of more important significance (see *Names and Naming*). The child name is often bestowed by the grandparent. Among the Hopi the infant, when 20 days old, is given a name and is dedicated to the sun with much ceremony. With some tribes, as the Omaha, the hair is cut in a pattern to indicate the gens or band of the parent, and in some, as the Kiowa, to indicate the particular protecting medicine of the father.

Twins are usually regarded as uncanny, and are rather feared, as possessing occult power. With some Oregon and other coast tribes they were formerly regarded as abnormal and one or both were killed. There are well-authenticated instances of deformed children being put to death at birth. On the other hand children crippled by accident are treated by parents and companions with the greatest tenderness.

Among the Plains tribes the ceremonial boring of the ears for the insertion of pendants is often made the occasion of a more or less public celebration, while the investment of the boy with the breechcloth at the age of 9 or 10 years is observed with a quiet family rejoicing. The first tattooing and the first insertion of the labret are also celebrated among the tribes practising such customs. In many or most tribes the boys passed through an initiation ordeal at an early age, sometimes, as with the Zuñi, as young as 5 years (see *Ordeals*). With the Hopi and Zuñi the child is lightly whipped with yucca switches when initiated into the Kachina priesthood. With the Powhatan of Virginia, if we can believe the old chroniclers, the boys, who may have been about 10 years of age at the time, were actually rendered unconscious, the declared purpose being to take away the memory of childish things so that they should wake up as men (see *Huskanaw*). On the plains the boys at about the same age were formally enrolled into the first degree of the warrior society and put under regular instruction for their later responsibilities.

Children of both sexes have toys and games, the girls inclining to dolls and "playing house," while the boys turn to bows, riding, and marksmanship. Tops, skates of rib-bones, darts, hummers, balls, shinny, and hunt-the-button games are all favorites, and wherever it is possible nearly half the time in warm weather is spent in the water. They are very fond of pets, particularly puppies, which the little girls frequently dress and carry upon their backs like babies, in imitation of their mothers. Among the Zuñi and Hopi wooden figurines of the principal mythologic characters are distributed as dolls to the children at ceremonial performances, thus impressing the sacred traditions in tangible form (see *Amusements, Dolls, Games*).

Girls are their mothers' companions and are initiated at an early period into all the arts of home life—sewing, cooking, weaving, and whatever else may pertain to their later duties. The boys as naturally pattern from their fathers in hunting, riding, or boating. Boys and girls alike are carefully instructed by their elders, not only in household arts and hunting methods, but also in the code of ethics, the traditions, and the religious ideas pertaining to the tribe. The special ceremonial observances are in the keeping of the various societies. The prevalent idea that the Indian child grows up without instruction is entirely wrong, although it may be said that he grows up practically without restraint, as instruction and obedience are enforced by moral suasion alone, physical punishment very rarely going beyond a mere slap in a moment of anger. As aggressiveness and the idea of individual ownership are less strong with the Indian than with his white brother, so quarrels are less frequent among the children, and fighting is almost unknown. Everything is shared alike in the circle of playmates. The Indian child has to learn his language as other children learn theirs, lisping his words and confusing the grammatic distinctions at first; but with the precocity incident to a wild, free life, he usually acquires correct expression at an earlier age than the average white child.

At about 15 years of age in the old days, throughout the eastern and central region, the boy made solitary fast and vigil to obtain communication with the medicine spirit which was to be his protector through life; then, after the initiatory ordeal to which, in some tribes, he was subjected, the youth was competent to take his place as a man among the warriors. For a year or more before his admission to full manhood responsibilities the young man cultivated a degree of reserve amounting even to bashfulness in the presence of strangers. At about the same time, or perhaps a year or two earlier, his sister's friends gathered to celebrate her puberty dance, and thenceforth child life for both was at an end.

Consult Chamberlain, Child and Childhood in Folk Thought, 1896; Dorsey in 3d Rep. B. A. E., 1884; Eastman, Indian Boyhood (autobiographic), 1902; Fewkes (1) in Am. Anthrop., IV, 1902, (2) in 21st Rep. B. A. E., 1903; Fletcher in Jour. Am. Folk-lore, 1888; Gatschet, Creek Migr. Leg., I, 1884; La Flesche, The Middle Five, 1901 (autobiographic); Mason in Rep. Nat. Mus., 1887; Owens, Natal Ceremonies of the Hopi, 1892; Powers in Cont. N. A. Ethnol., III, 1877; Spencer, Education of the Pueblo Child, 1899; Stevenson in 5th Rep. B. A. E., 1887; and especially Jenks, Childhood of Jishib, the Ojibwa, 1900, a sympathetic sketch of the career of an Indian boy from birth to manhood.

(J. M.)

**Chilhowee** ( *Tsŭ'lŭñ we'i*, abbr. *Tsŭ'lŭñ'-we*, or *Tsŭla'wi*, possibly connected with *tsŭ'lŭ* 'kingfisher'). A former important Cherokee settlement on Tellico r., a branch of Tennessee r., in Monroe co., Tenn., near the North Carolina boundary. (J. M.)

Chelowe.—Bartram, Travels, 371, 1792. Chilhowee.—Royce in 5th Rep. B. A. E., map, 1887. Chilhowey.—Timberlake, Memoirs, 76, 1765. Chillhoway.—Census of 1755 cited by Royce, op. cit., 144.

**Chilili** ( *Chi-li-li'* ). A former Tigua pueblo on the w. side of the Arroyo de Chilili, about 30 m. s. e. of Albuquerque, N. Mex. It is inadvertently mentioned as a "captain" of a pueblo by Oñate in 1598, and is next referred to in 1630 as a mission with a church dedicated to Nuestra Señora de Navidad. In this church were interred the remains of Fray Alonzo Peinado, who went to New Mexico about 1608, and to whom was attributed the conversion of the inhabitants and the erection of the chapel. The village was abandoned, according to Bandelier, between 1669 and 1676 on account of the persistent hostility of the Apache, the inhabitants retiring mostly to the Tigua villages on the Rio Grande, but some joined the Mansos at El Paso. According to Vetancurt the pueblo contained 500 Piros in 1680, and Benavides referred to it as a Tompiros pueblo 50 years earlier; but Bandelier believes these statements to be in error, since the northern pueblos of the Salinas belonged to the Tigua. See the latter authority in Arch. Inst. Rep., v, 34, 1884; Arch. Inst. Papers, iii, 128–131, 1890; iv, 255–257, 1892. (F. W. H.)

Acolocú.—Oñate (1598) in Doc. Inéd., xvi, 118, 1871 (believed by Bandelier, Arch. Inst. Papers, iv, 113, 1892, to be probably Chilili). Chichilli.—Squier in Am. Rev., ii, 522, 1848. Chichiti.—Loew in Rep. Wheeler Surv., app. LL, 175, 1875. Chili.—Gallegas (1844) in Emory, Reconnoissance, 478, 1848. Chililé.—Bandelier, Gilded Man, 254, 1893 (misprint). Chilili.—Benavides, Memorial, 21, 1630. Chililí'.—Pac. R. R. Rep., iii, pt. 3, map 10, 1856. Chilily.—Jefferys, Am. Atlas, map 5, 1776. Chilili.—Squier in Am. Rev., ii, 522, 1848. Chititi.—Gallatin in Trans. Am. Ethnol. Soc., ii, xciv, 1848. Navidad de Nuestra Señora.—Vetancurt (1693), Teatro Mex., iii, 324, repr. 1871. Old Chilili.—Abert in Emory, Reconnoissance, 483, 1848.

**Chilili.** A former tribe or village of the Utina confederacy in N. Florida. On the De Bry map it is located e. of St Johns r.

Chilili.—Laudonnière (1565), Hist. Not. de la Floride, 90, 1853. Chililo.—Barcia, Ensayo, 48, 1723 (cacique's name). Chilily.—Laudonnière (1565) quoted by Shipp, De Soto and Fla., 525, 1881.

**Chilkat** (said to be from *tcĭl-xāt*, 'storehouses for salmon'). A Tlingit tribe about the head of Lynn canal, Alaska; noted for the manufacture of the famous blankets to which they have given their name (see *Adornment, Blankets*); pop. 988 in 1880, and 812 in 1890. Winter towns: Chilkoot, Katkwaahltu, Klukwan, Yendestake. Smaller towns: Deshu, Dyea, Skagway. Social divisions: Daktlawedi,
Ganahadi, Hlukahadi, Kagwantan, Nushekaayi, Takestina.

Cheelcat.—Anderson quoted by Gibbs in Hist. Mag., vii, 75, 1862. Cheelhaats.—Scouler in Jour. Ethnol. Soc. Lond., i, 242, 1848. Cheelkaats.—Ibid., 232. Chelkatskie.—Elliott, Cond. Aff. Alaska, 227, 1875. Chilcahs.—Scott in Ind. Aff. Rep., 314, 1868. Chilcales.—Ibid., 309. Chilcales.—Halleck in Rep. Sec. War, pt. 1, 38, 1868. Chilcat.—Kane, Wand. in N. A., app., 1859. Chilcates.—Halleck in Ind Aff. Rep. 1869, 562, 1870. Chilkäht-Kwăn.—Dall in Cont. N. A. Ethnol., i, 37, 1877. Chilkahts.—Halleck in Ind. Aff. Rep. 1869, 562, 1870. Chilkasts.—Dunn, Hist. Oreg., 288, 1844. Chilkat-qwan.—Emmons in Mem. Am. Mus. Nat. Hist., iii, 232, 1903. Chilkats.—Halleck in Rep. Sec. War, pt. 1, 38, 1868. Chilkatskoe.—Veniaminoff, Zapiski, ii, pt. 3, 30, 1840. Chilkhat.—Petroff in 10th Census, Alaska, 31, 1884. Chitl-kawt.—Jackson, Alaska, 242, 1880 (native pronunciation of name of Chilcat r.). Tchilcat.—Beardslee in Sen. Ex. Doc. 105, 46th Cong., 2d sess., 31, 1880. Tschilkat.—Wrangell, Ethnol. Nachr., 102, 1839. Tschĭlkāt-kŏn.—Krause, Tlinkit Ind., 116, 1885. Tschischlkhathkhoan.—Kingsley, Stand. Nat. Hist., pt. 6, 132, 1883. Tschischlkhath.—Holmberg, Ethnol. Skizz., map, 142, 1855. Tschischlkháthkhóan.—Ibid., 11–12.

**Chilkat.** According to Petroff (Comp. 10th Census, pt. 2, 1427, 1883) a Tlingit town or aggregation of towns, on Controller bay, e. of the mouth of Copper r., Alaska. It belonged to the Yakutat and had 170 inhabitants in 1880. Probably it was only a summer village.

**Chilkoot.** A Tlingit town on the n. e. arm of Lynn canal, Alaska. Pop. at Chilkoot mission in 1890, 106. These people are often regarded as a separate division of Koluschan, but are practically the same as the Chilkat.

Chilcoot.—Petroff in 10th Census, Alaska, 31, 1884. Chilkoot.—11th Census, Alaska, 3, 1893. Tschilkut.—Krause, Tlinkit Ind., 100, 1885.

**Chillescas.** An Indian province, e. of Quivira, which the abbess María de Jesus, of Agreda, Spain, claimed to have miraculously visited in the 17th century.—Benavides (1631) in Palou, Relacion Hist., 336, 1787.

**Chillicothe** (from *Chĭ-la-ka'-tha*). One of the four tribal divisions of the Shawnee. The division is still recognized in the tribe, but the meaning of the word is lost. The Chillicothe always occupied a village of the same name, and this village was regarded as the chief town of the tribe. As the Shawnee retreated w. before the whites, several villages of this name were successively occupied and abandoned. The old Lowertown, or Lower Shawnee Town, at the mouth of the Scioto, in Ohio, was probably called Chillicothe. Besides this, there were three other villages of that name in Ohio, viz:

(1) On Paint cr., on the site of Oldtown, near Chillicothe, in Ross co. This village may have been occupied by the Shawnee after removing from Lowertown. It was there as early as 1774, and was destroyed by the Kentuckians in 1787.

(2) On the Little Miami, about the site of Oldtown, in Greene co. The Shawnee

are said to have removed from Lowertown to this village, but it seems more probable that they went to the village on Paint cr. This village near Oldtown was frequently called Old Chillicothe, and Boone was a prisoner there in 1778. It was destroyed by Clark in 1780.

(3) On the (Great) Miami, at the present Piqua, in Miami co.; destroyed by Clark in 1782. (J. M.)

Chellicotheé.—Perrin du Lac, Voy. des Deux Louisianes, 146, 1805. Chilacoffee.—Brodhead (1779) in Penn. Archives, XII, 179, 1856. Chi-lah-cah-tha.—W. H. Shawnee in Gulf States Hist. Mag., I, 415, 1903 (name of division). Chilicothe.— Harmar (1790) in Kauffman, West Penn., app., 226, 1851. Chilikoffi.—Brodhead, op. cit., 181. Chillacothe.—Harmar, op. cit., app., 227. Chillicoffi.— Brodhead, op. cit., 258. Chillicothe.—Clark (1782) in Butterfield, Washington-Irvine Cor., 401, 1882. Chilocathe.—Lang and Taylor, Rep., 22, 1843. Paint Creek town.—Flint, Ind. Wars, 69, 1833 (in Ross co., on Paint cr.). Shillicoffy.—Brodhead, op. cit., 258. Tsalaχgásagi.—Gatschet, Shawnee MS., B. A. E., 1879 (correct plural form).

**Chilliwack.** A Salish tribe on a river of the same name in British Columbia, now speaking the Cowichan dialect, though anciently Nooksak according to Boas. Pop. 313 in 1902. Their villages, mainly on the authority of Hill-Tout, are Atselits, Chiaktel, Kokaia, Shlalki, Skaialo, Skaukel, Skway, Skwealets, Stlep, Thaltelich, Tsoowahlie, and Yukweakwioose. The Can. Ind. Aff. Reports give Koquapilt and Skwah (distinct from Skway), and Boas gives Keles, which are not identifiable with any of the above.

Chillwayhook.—Mayne, Brit. Col., 295, 1861. Chiloweyuk.—Gibbs, MS. vocab. 281, B. A. E. Chilukweyuk.—Wilson in Jour. Ethnol. Soc. Lond., I, 278, 1866. Squahalitch.—Ibid. Tc'ileQuē'uk·.—Boas in Rep. Brit. A. A. S., LXIV, 454, 1894. Tcil'-Qē'uk.—Hill-Tout in Rep. Ethnol. Surv. Can., 3, 1902. Tshithwyook.—Tolmie and Dawson, Vocabs. Brit. Col., 120B, 1884.

**Chilluckittequaw** ( *Chilú'ktkwa* ). A Chinookan tribe formerly living on the N. side of Columbia r. in Klickitat and Skamania cos., Wash., from about 10 m. below the Dalles to the neighborhood of the Cascades. In 1806 Lewis and Clark estimated their number at 2,400. According to Mooney a remnant of the tribe lived near the mouth of White Salmon r. until 1880, when they removed to the Cascades, where a few still resided in 1895. The Smackshop were a subtribe. (L. F.)

Chee-luck-kit-le-quaw.—Orig. Jour. Lewis and Clark, IV, 262, 1905. Che-luc-it-te-quaw.—Ibid., III, 164. Che-luok-kit-ti-quar.—Ibid., IV, 288. Chillokittequaws.—Wilkes, Hist. Oreg., 44, 1845. Chillo Kittequaws.—Robertson, Oreg., 129, 1846. Chilluckittequaw.—Lewis and Clark, Exped., II, 45, 1814. Chilluckkittequaws.—Orig. Jour. Lewis and Clark, op. cit., IV, 285. Chilluckkittaquaws.—Ibid., 295. Chil-luck-kit-tequaw.—Lewis and Clark, Exped., I, map, 1817. Chillukittequas.—Am. Pioneer, I, 408, 1842. Chillukittequaw.—Drake, Bk. Inds., vii, 1845. Chilluk-kit-e-quaw.—Gibbs in Pac. R. R. Rep., I, 417, 1855. Chil-luk-kit-te-quaw.—Lewis and Clark, Exped., I, map, 1814. Chilú'ktkwa.—Mooney in 14th Rep. B. A. E., 741, 1896.

**Chillychandize.** Mentioned as a small Kalapooian tribe on Willamette r., Oreg.

Otherwise not identifiable.—Ross, Adventures, 236, 1847.

**Chilocco Indian Industrial School.** A Government school for Indian children, conducted under the direction of the Commissioner of Indian Affairs; situated on a reserve of 13 sections of land (8,320 acres) along the Kansas boundary in Kay co., Okla., set aside by executive order of July 12, 1884. The school was opened Jan. 15, 1884, with 186 pupils. At that time only Indians living in Indian Ter. were permitted to enter; but through subsequent action by Congress all Indian children save those belonging to the Five Civilized Tribes are now admitted, although pupils are recruited chiefly from contiguous states and territories. The equipment of the school has increased from a single large building in 1884 to 35 buildings, principally of stone, with modern improvements for the health and convenience of the children and employees. The pupils now (1905) number more than 700. The corps consists of a superintendent, 51 principal employees, and 20 minor Indian assistants. The primary object of the Government in establishing the Chilocco school on such a large tract was to enable the allotment of small farms to Indian youth who had acquired knowledge of the theory of agriculture at the school, thus enabling them to learn farming in a practical and intelligent manner and to return to their homes and kindred well equipped for the struggle for a livelihood. In pursuance of this plan every department of the Chilocco school is now organized with the view of making it preëminently an institution for agriculture and the attendant industries, with the result that it has become the best-equipped institution in the Indian service for agricultural instruction. In 1904 800 acres of wheat and oats were harvested and threshed by the school force; there were also 60 acres in potatoes, 50 acres in garden truck, 350 acres in corn, 100 acres in cane, 80 acres in Kaffir corn, and 200 acres in meadow. In addition there have been planted 5,000 forest trees, more than 3,500 fruit trees, 4,000 grapevines, 6,000 strawberry plants, and a proportionately large number of other small fruits and vegetables. In addition to produce almost sufficient to supply the needs of the school, the nursery is largely drawn on to establish gardens and orchards at other Indian schools, and a surplus of hay, grain, garden and other seeds, and cattle, hogs, and poultry is annually sold for the school's benefit. Particular attention is paid to instruction of boys in the trades, especially those useful to the farmer, and include blacksmithing, horseshoeing, wagon making, shoe and harness making, carpentry, painting and paper hanging, tailoring, broom making, stonecutting, stone and brick laying, engineering, plumbing and steam fitting, and printing; while special instruction in sewing, baking, cooking, housekeeping, dairying, and along kindred lines is given the girls, who number about half the pupils enrolled. In addition to the industrial education every pupil is given a grammar-school training; religious instruction of a non-sectarian character also forms part of the school work, and the pupils are encouraged to form associations promotive of mutual strength and character. A printing office is in operation, the product, including a periodical, *The Indian School Journal*, being the work of Indian boys.    (J. H. D.)

**Chilohocki.** A village on Miami r., Ohio, in 1779 (Brodhead in Penn. Archives, XII, 177, 1856). Probably a Delaware village; the name seems to be connected with Chikohoki, q. v.    (J. M.)

**Chiltneyadnaye** ('walnut'). An Apache clan or band at San Carlos agency and Ft Apache, Ariz., in 1881; coördinate with the Chisnedinadinaye of the Pinal Coyoteros.—Bourke in Jour. Am. Folk-lore, III, 112, 1890.

**Chilula** (*Tsu-lu'-la*, from *Tsula*, the Yurok name for the Bald hills. A small Athapascan division which occupied the lower (N. W.) portion of the valley of Redwood cr., N. Cal., and Bald hills, dividing it from Klamath valley. They were shut off from the immediate coast by the Yurok, who inhabited villages at the mouth of Redwood cr. The name of the Chilula for themselves is not known; it is probable that like most of the Indians of the region they had none, other than the word for "people." Above them on Redwood cr. was the related Athapascan group known as Whilkut, or Xoilkut. The Yurok names of some of their villages are Cherkhu, Ona, Opa, Otshpeth, and Roktsho.    (A. L. K.)

Bald Hill.—Gibbs (1851) in Schoolcraft, Ind. Tribes, III, 139, 1853. Bald Hill Indians.—McKee (1851) in Sen. Ex. Doc. 4, 32d Cong., spec. sess., 160, 1853. Chalula.—Parker, Jour., 262, 1842. Chil-lú-la.—Powers in Cont. N. A. Ethnol., III, 87, 1877. Chillulahs.—Bancroft, Nat. Races, I, map, 322, 1882. Tcho-lo-lah.—Gibbs (1851) in Schoolcraft, Ind. Tribes, III, 139, 1853 ('Bald hill people': Yurok name). Tes'-wan.—Powers in Cont. N. A. Ethnol., III, 87, 1877 (Hupa name).

**Chimai.** A Squawmish village community on the left bank of Squawmisht r., Brit. Col.

Tcimai'.—Hill-Tout in Rep. Brit. A. A. S., 474, 1900.

**Chimakuan Family.** A linguistic family of the N. W. coast, now represented by one small tribe, the Quileute (q. v.), on the coast of Washington. There was formerly an eastern division of the family, the Chimakum, occupying the territory between Hood's canal and Port Townsend, which

is now probably extinct. The situation of these two tribes, as well as certain traditions, indicate that in former times the family may have been more powerful and occupied the entire region to the s. of the strait of Juan de Fuca from which they were driven out by the Clallam and Makah. This, however, is uncertain. Within historic times the stock has consisted solely of the two small branches mentioned above. They have borne a high reputation among their Indian neighbors for warlike qualities, but for the greater part have always been on friendly terms with the whites. In customs the Quileute, or eastern Chimakuan, resembled the Makah and Nootka; all were whalers. The Chimakum, on the other hand, resembled the Clallam in customs. The Chimakuan dialects have not been thoroughly studied, but the material collected shows the language to be quite independent, though with certain phonetic and morphologic relations to the Salish and Wakashan.    (L. F.)

=Chemakum.—Eells in Am. Antiq., 52, Oct., 1880 (considers language different from any of its neighbors). =Chimakuan.—Powell in 7th Rep. B. A. E., 62, 1891. =Chimakum.—Gibbs in Pac. R. R. Rep., I, 431, 1855 (family doubtful). <Nootka.—Bancroft, Native Races, III, 564, 1882 (contains Chimakum). <Puget Sound Group.—Keane in Stanford, Compend., Cent. and So. Am., 474, 1878 (Chinakum included in this group).

**Chimakum.** A Chimakuan tribe, now probably extinct, formerly occupying the peninsula between Hood's canal and Port Townsend, Wash. Little is known of their history except that they were at constant war with the Clallam and other Salish neighbors, and by reason of their inferiority in numbers suffered extremely at their hands. In 1855, according to Gibbs, they were reduced to 90 individuals. The Chimakum were included in the Point no Point treaty of 1855 and placed upon the Skokomish res., since which time they have gradually diminished in numbers. In 1890 Boas was able to learn of only three individuals who spoke the language, and even those but imperfectly. He obtained a small vocabulary and a few grammatical notes, published in part in Am. Anthrop., V, 37–44, 1892.    (L. F.)

Á-hwa-ki-lu.—Eells in Smithson. Rep. 1887, 606, 1889 (native name). Aqoχúlo.—Boas in Am. Anthrop., V, 37, 1892 (native name). Chema-keem.—Ross in Ind. Aff. Rep., 135, 1870. Chemakeum.—Eells in Am. Antiq., IX, 100, 1887. Chemakum.—Swan, N. W. Coast, 344, 1857. Chemicum.—Taylor in Cal. Farmer, June 12, 1863. Chim-a-kim.—Jones in H. R. Ex. Doc. 76, 34th Cong., 3d sess., 5, 1857. Chima-kum.—Gibbs in Pac. R. R. Rep., I, 431, 1855. Chimicum.—Simmons in Ind. Aff. Rep. 1859, 398, 1860. Chin-a-kum.—Starling, ibid., 170, 1852. Chine-a-kums.—Ibid., 172. Chumakums.—Morrow, ibid., 179, 1861. Clamakum.—Simmons, ibid., 1857, 333, 1858. Port Townsend.—Wilkes in Stevens' Rep. N. P. R. R., 463, 1854. Tsemakum.—Gibbs in Cont. N. A. Ethnol., I, 177, 1877.

**Chimalakwe.** Mentioned by Powers as an extinct tribe that once lived on New r.,

1. Cal., and included in his map, as by Powell (7th Rep. B. A. E., 63, 1891), with the Chimariko. The name Chimalakwe is undoubtedly only a variant of Chimariko, often pronounced Chimaliko. The Chimariko, however, did not occupy upper New r., which region, together with the adjacent territory about the headwaters of Salmon r., was held by a group of people belonging to the Shastan family, though markedly divergent from the Shasta proper in dialect. This Shastan group, the proper name of which is unknown, has been described by Dixon (Am. Anthrop., VII, 213, 1905) under the name of New River Shasta. In 1902 two aged women appeared to be the only survivors of this people. (A. L. K.)
Chi-mal'-a-kwe.—Powers in Cont. N. A. Ethnol., III, 91, 1877. Chimalaquays.—Powers in Overland Mo., IX, 156, 1872. Chimalquays.—Powers quoted by Bancroft, Nat. Races, I, 446, 1882. New River.—Dixon in Am. Anthrop., VII, 216, 1905.

**Chimaltitlan** (Nahuatl: 'where prayer-sticks are placed'). A former settlement of the Tepecano or of a related tribe, about 8 m. s. of Bolaños, in the valley of the Rio de Bolaños, Jalisco, Mexico.—Hrdlicka, inf'n, 1905.

**Chimarikan Family.** Established as a linguistic family on the language of the Chimariko, which was found to be distinct from that of any known tribe. All that is known in relation to the family, which is now nearly extinct, will be found under the tribal name Chimariko.
=Chimarikan.—Powell in 7th Rep. B. A. E., 63, 1891.
=Chim-a-ri'-ko.—Powell in Cont. N. A. Ethnol., III, 474, 1877; Gatschet in Mag. Am. Hist., 255, Apr., 1882 (stated to be a distinct family).

**Chimariko** (from *Djimaliko*, the name they apply to themselves; derived from *djimar* 'man'). A small tribe, comprising the Chimarikan family, formerly on Trinity r., near the mouth of New r., N. Cal., extending from Hawkins Bar to about Big Bar, and probably along lower New r.; they adjoined the Hupa downstream and the Wintun upstream. The Chimariko first became known to the whites on the influx of miners about 1850. They were then a small tribe, friendly with the Hupa and the neighboring Shastan tribes, but at war with the Wintun of Hay fork of Trinity r. In 1903 they numbered only 9 individuals, including mixed bloods, who lived scattered from Hupa up Trinity r., and on New r., among Indians of other tribes, and among the whites (Goddard, MS., Univ. Cal.). In general culture the Chimariko were much like their neighbors to the N. W., the Hupa, though they are said to have lacked canoes, and did not practise the deerskin dance of the Hupa and Yurok. They appear to have lived largely on salmon and eels caught in Trinity r., and on vegetal foods, especially acorns. Like the other tribes of N. W. California, they had no po-

litical organization or divisions other than villages, one of which was at or near Hawkins Bar, others at Burnt Ranch, Taylor's Flat, and Big Bar, and probably at other places, though their names for these settlements are not known with certainty. See *Chimalakwe*. (A. L. K.)
Djimaliko.—A. L. Kroeber, inf'n, 1903 (own name). Kwoshonipu.—Kroeber, inf'n, 1903 (name probably given them by the Shasta of Salmon r.). Me-em-ma.—McKee (1851) in Sen. Ex. Doc. 4, 32d Cong., spec. sess., 194, 1853. Meyemma.—Gibbs in Schoolcraft, Ind. Tribes, III, 139, 1853. Mi-em-ma.—Meyer in Nach dem Sacramento, 282, 1855.

**Chimbuiha.** A former settlement of the Molala on the headwaters of Santiam r., in the Cascade mts., Oreg. (A. S. G.)

**Chimiak.** A Kuskwogmiut village on Kuskokwim r., Alaska; pop. 71 in 1880, 40 in 1890.
Chim-e-kliág-a-mut.—Spurr and Post quoted by Baker, Geog. Dict. Alaska, 1901. Chimekliak.—Baker, ibid. Chimiagamute.—Petroff, 10th Census, Alaska, 17, 1884. Chimingyangamiut.—11th Census, Alaska, 164, 1893.

**Chimmesyan Family** (from *Tsimshian*, 'people of Skeena r.'). A small linguistic family on Nass and Skeena rs., N. Brit. Col., and the neighboring coast as far s. as Milbank sd. The 3 main divisions are the Tsimshian of lower Skeena r., the Kitksan of upper Skeena r., and the Niska of Nass r. The closest cultural affinities of these people are with the Haida of Queen Charlotte ids. and the Tlingit of the Alaskan coast, though their language is strikingly different and must be placed in a class by itself among the tongues of the N. W. According to their own traditions and those of neighboring tribes they have descended Nass and Skeena rs. in comparatively recent times to the coast, displacing the Tlingit.

In physical characters and social organization the Chimmesyan resemble the Haida and Tlingit, but the Kitksan, living farther inland, seem to have mixed with the Athapascan tribes, and more nearly approach their type. The Chimmesyan language is characterized by a very extensive use of adverbial prefixes principally signifying local relations, by an extreme use of reduplication, a great abundance of plural forms, and numerous temporal and modal particles (Boas). Like other coast tribes they obtain the largest part of their food from the sea and the rivers. The annual runs of salmon on the Skeena and of eulachon into the Nass furnish them with an abundance of provisions at certain seasons. Eulachon are a great source of revenue to the Niska, the oil being in great demand all along the coast, and indispensable for the great winter potlatches. Bear, mountain goats, and other wild animals are hunted, particularly by the interior tribes. The horns of mountain goats are carved into handles for spoons used at feasts and potlatches, and are sold to other tribes for the same purpose. Although good carvers and canoe builders, the Chimmesyan are surpassed by the Haida, from whom they still purchase canoes. Their houses were often huge structures made of immense cedar beams and planks, and accommodating from 20 to 30 people. Each was presided over by a house chief, while every family and every town had a superior chief; under him were the members of his household, his more distant clan relations, and the servants and slaves.

There were four clans or phrarties: Kanhada, Lakyebo ('On the Wolf'), Lakskiyek ('On the Eagle'), and Gyispawaduweda. Each of these clans comprised a great number of subdivisions, concerning which the information is more or less conflicting, some regarding them simply as names for the people of certain towns, while others treat them as family groups, not necessarily confined to one place. If their organization was anything like that of the Haida, the subdivisions were at one time local groups; but it is probable that many of them have been displaced from their ancient seats or have settled in more than one place. This view is corroborated by the account of the Niska tribes given by Boas (10th Rep. N. W. Tribes Can., 48, 49). Their names, as far as obtainable, will be found under the separate divisional headings. Descent is reckoned in the female line. While the present culture of the Chimmesyan tribes is similar to that of the neighboring coast peoples, there is some evidence of their recent assimilation. In most of the Tsimshian myths they appear primarily as an inland tribe that lived by hunting, and their ancestral home is described as on a prairie at the headwaters of Skeena r. This suggests an inland origin of the tribe, and the historical value of the traditional evidence is increased by the peculiar divergence of their mythological tales from those of neighboring tribes; the most characteristic tales of the Tsimshian being more like the animal tales of the w. plateaus and of the plains than like the tales of the N. coast tribes in which the human element plays an important part. The Chimmesyan tribes have also adopted customs of their s. neighbors on the coast, more particularly the winter ceremonial with its cannibal ceremonies, which they obtained from the Bellabella. In 1902 there were reported 3,389 Chimmesyan in British Columbia; and with the 952 enumerated as forming Mr Duncan's colony in Alaska in 1890, the total is about 4,341.　　　　　　　　　　(J. R. S.)

=**Chemmesyan.**—Scouler (1846) in Jour. Ethnol. Soc. Lond., I, 233, 1848. =**Chimmesyan.**—Schouler in Jour. Geog. Soc. Lond., I, 219, 1841. =**Chimsyans.**—Schoolcraft, Ind. Tribes, v, 487, 1855. =**Chymseyans.**—Kane, Wand. in N. A., app., 1859. ×**Haidah.**—

Scouler in Jour. Roy. Geog Soc. Lond., XI, 220, 1841. >**Hydahs.**—Keane in Stanford, Compend., 473, 1878 (includes other tribes). >**Naas.**—Gallatin in Trans. Am. Ethnol. Soc., II, pt. 1, c, 1848 (includes other tribes). >**Naass.**—Ibid., 77. >**Nass.**—Bancroft, Nat. Races, III, 564, 1882 (includes other tribes). =**Nasse.**—Dall in Cont. N. A. Ethnol., I, 36, 1877. ×**Northern.**—Scouler in Jour. Roy. Geog. Soc., XI, 220, 1841 (includes many other tribes). =**Tshimsian.**—Tolmie and Dawson, Vocabs. B. C., 114B, 1884. =**Tsimpsi-an'.**—Dall in Proc. A. A. A. S., 379, 1885.

**Chimnapum.** A small Shahaptian tribe located by Lewis and Clark in 1805 on the N. W. side of Columbia r. near the mouth of the Snake, and on lower Yakima r., Wash. They speak a dialect closely allied to the Paloos. By Lewis and Clark their population was estimated at 1,860, in 42 lodges. A remnant of the tribe is still living on the w. side of Columbia r., opposite Pasco, Wash.　　　　　　(L. F.)

**Chämnä'pûm.**—Mooney in 14th Rep. B. A. E., 739, 1896. **Chim-nah-pan.**—Stevens in Ind. Aff. Rep., 252, 1854. **Chim-nah-pum.**—Orig. Jour. Lewis and Clark, VI, 115, 1905. **Chim-nah-pun.**—Lewis and Clark, Exped., I, map, 1814. **Chimnapoos.**—Ibid., II 257, 1814. **Chimnapum.**—Ibid., II, 12. **Chimnâ-pum.**—Orig. Jour. Lewis and Clark, III, 123, 1905. **Chimnapuns.**—Wilkes, Hist. Oregon, 44, 1845. **Chinnahpum.**—Schoolcraft, Ind. Tribes, III, 570, 1853. **Chin-na-pum.**—Orig. Jour., op. cit., III, 184, 1905. **Chunnapuns.**—Nicolay, Oregon, 143, 1846. **Chym-nâh'-pos.**—Lewis and Clark, Exped., Coues ed., 973, note, 1893. **Chymnapoms.**—Orig. Jour., op. cit., IV, 339, 1905. **Chymnapums.**—Ibid., 73. **Cuimnapum.**—Lewis and Clark, Exped., II, 17, 1814.

**Chimuksaich.** A Siuslaw village on Siuslaw r., Oreg.

**Tcĭm'-mŭk-saitc'.**—Dorsey in Jour. Am. Folk-lore, III, 230, 1890.

**China Hat** (seemingly a corruption of *Xā'exaes*, their own name). A Kwakiutl tribe speaking the Heiltsuk dialect and residing on Tolmie channel and Mussel inlet, Brit. Col.; pop. 114 in 1901, 77 in 1904.

**Haihaish.**—Tolmie and Dawson, Vocabs. B. C., 117B, 1884. **Qē'qaes.**—Boas, 6th Rep. N. W. Tribes Can., 52, 1890. **Xā'exaes.**—Boas in Rep. Nat. Mus. 1895, 328 (own name).

**Chinakbi.** A former Choctaw town on the site of the present Garlandsville, Jasper co., Miss. It was one of the villages constituting the so-called Sixtowns, and gave its name to a small district along the N. side of Sooenlovie cr., partly in Newton co. and partly in Jasper co.—Halbert in Publ. Ala. Hist. Soc., Misc. Coll., I, 381–382, 1901.

**Chinokabi.**—Gatschet, Creek Migr. Leg., I, 109, 1884.

**Chinapa.** An Opata pueblo, and the seat of a Spanish mission founded in 1648, on the Rio Sonora, lat. 30° 30', Sonora, Mexico; pop. 393 in 1678, and 204 in 1730. It was burned by the Apache in 1836.

**Chinapa.**—Kino, map (1702) in Stöcklein, Neue Welt-Bott, 74, 1726. **Chinapi.**—Bartlett, Personal Narr., I, 279, 1854. **San José Chinapa.**—Zapata (1678) in Doc. Hist. Mex., 4th s., III, 370, 1857.

**Chinatu** (*Chi-na-tu'*, 'the hidden back of a mountain.'—Lumholtz). A pueblo, inhabited by both Tepehuane and Tarahumare, in the Sierra Madre, w. Chihuahua, Mexico.

**Chinatú.**—Orozco y Berra, Geog., 322, 1864. **Chismal.**—Ibid., 324.

**Chincapin.** See *Chinquapin.*

**Chinchal.** A Yamel band that formerly lived on Dallas cr., a w. tributary of Willamette r., Oreg.

**Tch'intchäl.**—Gatschet, Lakmiut MS., B. A. E., 1877.

**Chincomen.** See *Chinquapin.*

**Chincoteague** (*Chingua-tegwe,* 'large stream,' 'inlet.'—Hewitt). A village, probably belonging to the Accohanoc tribe of the Powhatan confederacy, formerly about Chincoteague inlet in Accomack co., Va. In 1722 the few remaining inhabitants had joined a Maryland tribe. Cf. *Cinquaeteck, Cinquoteck.*

**Chingoteacq.**—Herrman, map (1670) in Maps to Accompany Rept. of Comrs. on the Bdy. bet. Va. and Md., 1873. **Chingo-teagues.**—Bozman, Md., I, 102, 1837 (the villagers). **Gingo-teque.**—Beverly, Virginia, 199, 1722.

**Chingigmiut.** An Eskimo tribe inhabiting the region of C. Newenham and C. Peirce, Alaska. Their women wear birdskin parkas; the kaiaks have no hole through the bow like those of the Kuskwogmiut. The villages are Aziavik and Tzavahak.

**Chingigmut.**—Nelson in 18th Rep., B. A. E., map, 1899. **Tschinjagmjut.**—Holmberg, Ethnol. Skizz., map, 142, 1855.

**Chiniak.** A Kaniagmiut village at the E. end of Kodiak id., Alaska; pop. 24 in 1880.—Petroff, 10th Census, Alaska, map, 1884.

**Chinik.** A Kaviagmiut village and mission on Golofnin bay, Alaska; pop. 38 in 1890, 140 in 1900.

**Cheenik.**—Baker, Geog. Dict. Alaska, 1901. **Chillimiut.**—11th Census, Alaska, 162, 1893. **Chinigmut.**—Zagoskin, Descr. Russ. Poss. in Am., pt. I, 73, 1847. **Dexter.**—Baker, op. cit. **Ikaligvigmiut.**—Tikhmenief quoted by Baker, op. cit. **Ikaligwigmjut.**—Holmberg, Ethnol. Skizz., map, 1855. **Tchinimuth.**—Zagoskin in Nouv. Ann. Voy., 5th s., XXI, map, 1850.

**Chinik.** A Kaiyuhkhotana village on the E. bank of Yukon r., at the junction of Talbiksok.

**Tchinik.**—Zagoskin in Nouv. Ann. Voy., 5th s., XXI, map, 1850.

**Chinila.** A Knaiakhotana village of 15 persons in 1880, on the E. side of Cook inlet, Alaska, near the mouth of Kaknu r.

**Chernila.**—Petroff, 10th Census, Alaska, 29, 1884. **Chernilof.**—Ibid., map. **Chinila.**—Ibid., 29.

**Chinipa.** A term used in different senses by early Spanish authors; by some, as Ribas, the Chinipa are mentioned as a nation distinct from the Varohio, and by others it is applied to a group of villages. It is also used to designate a particular village on an upper affluent of the Rio del Fuerte, in Varohio territory, lat. 27° 30', long. 108° 30', in w. Chihuahua, Mexico, and by Hervas as that of a dialect of the Tarahumare. Curepo was a Chinipa rancheria in 1601.

**Chinipa.**—Hervas, Cat., I, 319, 1800. **Chinipas.**—Ribas, Hist. Triumphos, 255, 1645. **San Andres**

**Chinipas.**—Orozco y Berra, Geog., 324, 1864 (the settlement).

**Chinits.** A Karok village on the s. bank of Klamath r., just below Tsofkara, Humboldt co., Cal.

**Chee-nitch.**—Taylor in Cal. Farmer, Mar. 23, 1860. **T'cheh-nits.**—Gibbs, MS. Misc., B. A. E., 1852.

**Chinkapin.** See *Chinquapin.*

**Chinklacamoose** (possibly Delaware *Chingua-klakamoos,* 'large laughing moose.'—Hewitt). A former village of the Iroquois on the site of Clearfield, Clearfield co., Pa., before 1805. It probably took its name from a chief. The Seneca of Cornplanter's village also frequented the neighborhood.

**Chingleclamouche.**—Royce in 18th Rep. B. A. E., pl. clx, 1900. **Chingleolamolik.**—La Tour, map, 1784. **Chingleolamuk.**—Güssefeld, map, 1784. **Chinklacamoose.**—Day, Hist. Coll. Pa., 231, 1843. **Chinklacamoose's Oldtown.**—Ibid.

**Chinko.** A former division of the Illinois tribe.

**Chinko.**—Allouez (1680) in Margry, Déc., II, 96, 1877. **Chinkoa.**—La Salle (1681), ibid., 134.

**Chinkopin.** See *Chinquapin.*

**Chinlak.** A former village of the Tanotenne at the confluence of Nechaco and Stuart rs., Brit. Col., which had a flourishing population that the Tsilkotin practically annihilated in one night.

**Tcinlak.**—Morice, Notes on W. Dénés, 25, 1893.

**Chinnaby's Fort.** In 1813, at the time of the Creek rebellion, Chinnaby, a Creek chief friendly to the United States, had a "kind of fort" at Ten ids, on Coosa r., Ala.

**Chinnaby's Fort.**—Drake, Bk. Inds. IV, 55, 1848. **Ft Chinnabie.**—Royce in 18th Rep. B. A. E., Ala. map, 1900.

**Chinook** (from *Tsinúk,* their Chehalis name). The best-known tribe of the Chinookan family. They claimed the territory on the N. side of Columbia r., Wash., from the mouth to Grays bay, a distance of about 15 m., and N. along the seacoast as far as the N. part of Shoalwater bay, where they were met by the Chehalis, a Salish tribe. The Chinook were first described by Lewis and Clark, who visited them in 1805, though they had been known to traders for at least 12 years previously. Lewis and Clark estimated their number at 400, but referred only to those living on Columbia r. Swan placed their number at 112 in 1855, at which time they were much mixed with the Chehalis, with whom they have since completely fused, their language being now extinct. From their proximity to Astoria and their intimate relations with the early traders, the Chinook soon became well known, and their language formed the basis for the widely spread Chinook jargon, which was first used as a trade language and is now a medium of communication from California to Alaska. The portion of the tribe living around Shoalwater bay was called Atsmitl. The following divisions and villages have been recorded: Chinook, Gitlapshoi, Nakoaik, Nemah, Nisal, Palux, Wharhoots.    (L. F.)

Ala'dshūsh.—Gatschet, Nestucca MS. vocab., B. A. E. (Nestucca name). Cheenook.—Scouler in Jour. Ethnol. Soc. Lond., I, 236, 1848. Cheenooks.—Scouler in Jour. Geog. Soc. Lond., I, 224, 1841. Chenooks.—Parker, Jour., 142, 1842. Chenoux.—Meek in H. R. Ex. Doc. 76, 30th Cong., 1st sess., 10, 1848. Chenukes.—Hastings, Emigr. Guide to Oregon, 59, 1845. Chimook.—Emmons in Schoolcraft, Ind. Tribes, III, 224, 1853. Chin-hook.—Gass, Jour., 238, 1808. Chin-nooks.—Lewis and Clark, Exped., Coues ed., 755, 1893. Chinook.—Fitzpatrick in Ind. Aff. Rep., app., 245, 1847. Chin ook.—Gass, Jour., 176, 1807. Chinouks.—Smet, Oregon Miss., 33, 1847. Chinucs.—Rafinesque, introd. Marshall, Ky., I, 32, 1824. Chinúks.—Latham, Nat. Hist. Man., 317, 1850. Chonukes.—Hastings, Emigr. Guide to Oregon, 59, 1845. Flatheads.—Parker, Jour., 142, 1842. Nez Percés.—Ibid. Schinouks.—Smet, Letters, 220, 1843. Tchinooks.—Smet, Oregon Miss., 72, 1847. Tchinouks.—Duflot de Mofras, Explor. de l'Oregon, II, 125, 1844. Tchinoux.—Smet, Letters, 230, 1843. Tçinúk.—Hale in U. S. Expl. Exped., VI, 562, 1846. Tehenooks.—Smet, Letters, 152, 1843. Tetes-Plates.—Duflot de Mofras, Explor. de l'Oregon, II, 108, 1844. Thlála'h.—Gatschet, MS., B. A. E. (Clackama name). Tschinuk.—Latham in Trans. Philol. Soc. Lond., 73, 1856. Tshinuk.—Hale in U. S. Expl. Exped, VI, 214, 1846. Tsinuk.—Latham in Trans. Philol. Soc. Lond., 57, 1856. T'sinūk.—Gibbs in Cont. N. A. Ethnol., I, 241, 1877. Tsniuk.—Wickersham in Am. Antiq., XXI, 374, 1899.

CHINOOK MAN.    (AM. MUS. NAT. HIST.)

**Chinook.** The principal village of the Chinook, situated on Baker bay, Pacific co., Wash., near the mouth of Columbia r.

**Chinookan Family.** An important linguistic family, including those tribes formerly living on Columbia r., from The Dalles to its mouth (except a small strip occupied by the Athapascan Tlatskanai), and on the lower Willamette as far as the present site of Oregon City, Oreg. The family also extended a short distance along the coast on each side of the mouth of the Columbia, from Shoalwater bay on

the N. to Tillamook Head on the S. The family is named from the Chinook, the most important tribe. With the exception of a few traders near the mouth of the Columbia, Lewis and Clark were the first whites to visit these tribes, and their description still constitutes the main authority as to their early condition. The Chinookan villages were situated along the banks of the Columbia, near the mouths of its tributaries, and for the greater part on the N. side. The houses were of wood and very large, being occupied on the communal principle by 3 or 4 families and often containing 20 or more individuals. Their villages were thus fairly permanent, though there was much moving about in summer, owing to the nature of the food supply, which consisted chiefly of salmon, with the roots and berries indigenous to the region. The falls and Cascades of the Columbia and the falls of the Willamette were the chief points of gathering in the salmon season. The people were also noted traders, not only among themselves, but with the surrounding tribes of other stocks, and trips from the mouth of the Columbia to the Cascades for the purpose of barter were of frequent occurrence. They were extremely skilful in handling their canoes, which were well made, hollowed out of single logs, and often of great size. In disposition they are described as treacherous and deceitful, especially when their cupidity was aroused, and the making of portages at the Cascades and The Dalles by the early traders and settlers was always accompanied with much trouble and danger. Slaves were common among them and were usually obtained by barter from surrounding tribes, though occasionally in successful raids made for that purpose. Little is known of their particular social customs and beliefs, but there was no clan or gentile organization, and the village was the chief social unit. These villages varied greatly in size, but often consisted of only a few houses. There was always a headman or chief, who, by reason of personal qualities, might extend his influence over several neighboring villages, but in general each settlement was independent. Their most noteworthy historical character was Comcomly, q. v.

Physically the Chinookan people differed somewhat from the other coast tribes. They were taller, their faces wider and characterized by narrow and high noses; in this respect they resembled the Kwakiutl of Vancouver id. The custom of artificially deforming the head by fronto-occipital pressure was universal among them, a skull of natural form being regarded as a disgrace and permitted only to slaves. This custom later lost its force to some extent among the tribes of the upper Columbia.

Linguistically they were divided into 2 groups: (1) Lower Chinook, comprising two slightly different dialects, the Chinook proper and the Clatsop; (2) Upper Chinook, which included all the rest of the tribes, though with numerous slight dialectic differences. As a stock language the Chinookan is sharply differentiated from that of surrounding families. Its most striking feature is the high degree of pronominal incorporation, the phonetic slightness of verbal and pronominal stems, the occurrence of 3 genders, and the predominance of onomatopoetic processes. The dialects of Lower Chinook are now practically extinct. Upper Chinook is still spoken by considerable numbers.

The region occupied by Chinookan tribes seems to have been well populated in early times, Lewis and Clark estimating the total number at somewhat more than 16,000. In 1829, however, there occurred an epidemic of what was called ague fever, of unknown nature, which in a single summer swept away four-fifths of the entire native population. Whole villages disappeared, and others were so reduced that in some instances several were consolidated. The epidemic was most disastrous below the Cascades. In 1846 Hale estimated the number below the Cascades at 500, and between the Cascades and The Dalles at 800. In 1854 Gibbs gave the population of the former region as 120 and of the latter as 236. These were scattered along the river in several bands, all more or less mixed with neighboring stocks. In 1885 Powell estimated the total number at from 500 to 600, for the greater part on Warm Springs, Yakima, and Grande Ronde reservations, Oreg. The fusion on the reservations has been so great that no accurate estimate is now possible, but it is probable that 300 would cover all those who could properly be assigned to this family.

Most of the original Chinookan bands and divisions had no special tribal names, being designated simply as "those living at such a place." This fact, especially after the general disturbance caused by the epidemic of 1829, makes it impossible to identify all the tribes and villages mentioned by writers. The following list includes the different tribes, divisions, and the villages not listed under the separate tribes: Cathlacomatup, Cathlacumup, Cathlakaheckit, Cathlamet, Cathlanahquiah, Cathlapotle, Charcowa, Chilluckittequaw, Chinook, Chippanchickchick(?), Clackama, Clahclellah, Clahnaquah, Claninnatas, Clatacut, Clatsop, Clowwewalla, Cooniac, Cushook, Dalles Indians, Ithkyemamits, Kasenos,

Katlagulak, Katlaminimin, Killaxthokle, Klemiaksac, Knowilamowan, Ktlaeshatlkik, Lower Chinook, Multnomah, Namoit, Nayakaukaue, Nechacokee, Necootimeigh, Neerchokioon, Nemalquinner, Nenoothlect, Scaltalpe, Seamysty, Shahala, Shoto, Skilloot, Smackshop, Teiakhochoe, Thlakalama, Tlakatlala, Tlakluit, Tlakstak, Tlalegak, Tlashgenemaki, Tlegulak, Upper Chinook, Wahe, Wahkiacum, Wakanasisi, Wappatoo, Wasco, Watlala, Willopah, Wiltkwilluk, Yehuh. (L. F.)

>**Cheenook.**—Latham in Jour. Ethnol. Soc. Lond., I, 286, 1848. =**Chinook.**—Gatschet in Mag. Am. Hist., 167, 1877 (names and gives habitat of tribes). >**Chinook.**—Bancroft, Nat. Races, III, 565, 626–628, 1882 (enumerates Chinook, Wakiakum, Cathlamet, Clatsop, Multnomah, Skilloot, Watlala). =**Chinookan.**—Powell in 7th Rep. B. A. E., 65, 1891. >**Chinooks.**—Gallatin in Trans. Am. Antiq. Soc., II, 134, 306, 1836 (a single tribe at mouth of Columbia). =**Chinooks.**—Hale in U. S. Expl. Exped., VI, 198, 1846. <**Chinooks.**—Keane in Stanford, Compend., Cent. and So. Am., 474, 1878 (includes Skilloots, Watlalas, Lower Chinooks, Wakiakums, Cathlamets, Clatsops, Calapooyas, Clackamas, Killamooks, Yamkally, Chimook Jargon; of these Calapooyas and Yamkally are Kalapooian, Killamooks are Salishan). >**Chinuk.**—Latham, Nat Hist. Man, 317, 1850 (same as Tshinúk; includes Chinúks proper, Klatsops, Kathlamut, Wakáikam, Watlala, Nihaloitih). ×**Nootka-Columbian.**—Scouler in Jour. Roy. Geog. Soc. Lond., XI, 224, 1841 (includes Cheenooks and Cathlascons of present family). ×**Southern.**—Scouler, ibid., 224 (same as his Nootka-Columbian family above). =**Tschinuk.**—Berghaus (1851), Physik. Atlas, map 17, 1852. =**Tshinook.**—Gallatin in Schoolcraft, Ind. Tribes, III, 402, 1853 (Chinooks, Clatsops, and Watlala). =**Tshinuk.**—Hale in U. S. Expl. Exped., VI, 562, 569, 1846 (contains Watlala or Upper Chinook, including Watlala, Nihaloitih, or Echeloots; and Tshinuk, including Tshinuk, Tlatsap, Wakaikam). >**Tshinuk.**—Buschmann, Spuren der aztek. Sprache, 616, 1859 (same as his Chinuk). =**Tsinuk.**—Gallatin, after Hale, in Trans. Am. Ethnol. Soc., II, pt. 1, 15, 1848. =**T'sinūk.**—Dall, after Gibbs, in Cont. N. A. Ethnol., I, 241, 1877 (mere mention of family).

**Chinook jargon.** The Indian trade language of the Columbia r. region and the adjacent Pacific coast from California far up into Alaska. It was first brought to public notice in the early days of the Oregon fur trade, about 1810. In addition to the Indian elements it has now incorporated numerous words from various European languages, but there can be no doubt that the jargon existed as an intertribal medium of communication long before the advent of the whites, having its parallel in the so-called "Mobilian language" of the Gulf tribes and the sign language of the plains, all three being the outgrowth of an extensive aboriginal system of intertribal trade and travel. The Indian foundation of the jargon is the Chinook proper, with Nootka, Salish, and other languages, to which were added, after contact with the fur companies, corrupted English, French, and possibly Russian terms. Hale, in 1841, estimated the number of words in the jargon at 250; Gibbs, in 1863, recorded about 500; Eells, in 1894, counted 740 words actually in use, although his dictionary cites 1,402, 662 being obsolete, and 1,552 phrases, combinations of *mamook* ('do'), yielding 209. The following table shows the share of certain languages in the jargon as recorded at various periods of its existence, although there are great differences in the constituent elements of the jargon as spoken in different parts of the country:

| Words contributed | 1841 | 1863 | 1894 |
|---|---|---|---|
| Nootka | 18 | 24 | 23 |
| Chinook | 111 | 221 | 198 |
| English | 41 | 67 | 570 |
| French | 34 | 94 | 153 |
| Other languages | 48 | 79 | 138 |

There is much local variation in the way Chinook is spoken on the Pacific coast. While it tends to disappear in the country of its origin, it is taking on new life farther N., where it is evidently destined to live for many years; but in S. E. Alaska it is little used, being displaced by English or Tlingit. This jargon has been of great service to both the Indian and the white man, and its rôle in the development of intertribal and interracial relations on the N. Pacific coast has been important. For works bearing on the subject see Pilling, Bibliography of the Chinookan Languages, Bull. B. A. E., 1893. (A. F. C.)

Chee-Chinook.—Bulmer, MS., cited by Pilling, op. cit. **Chinook Jargon.**—Cox, Columbia R., II, 134, 1831. **Oregon jargon.**—McKee (1851) in Sen. Ex. Doc. 4, 32d Cong., spec. sess., 169, 1853. **Oregon Trade Language.**—Hale, Manual of Oregon Trade Lang., 1890.

**Chinook olives.** The name given by whites to an article of food of the Chinook in earlier days (Kane, Wanderings, 187, 1859), consisting of acorns ripened in a urine-soaked pit. (A. F. C.)

**Chinook salmon.** A name of the Columbia r. salmon (*Oncorhynchus chouicha*), more commonly known as the quinnat, and also called the tyee salmon. (A. F. C.)

**Chinook wind.** A name applied to certain winds of N. w. United States and British Columbia. According to Burrows (Yearbook Dept. Agric., 555, 1901) there are three different winds, each essentially a warm wind whose effect is most noticeable in winter, that are called chinooks. There is a wet chinook, a dry chinook, and a third wind of an intermediate sort. The term was first applied to a warm s. w. wind which blew from over the Chinook camp to the trading post established by the Hudson Bay Company at Astoria, Oreg. Under the influence of these chinook winds snow is melted with astonishing rapidity, and the weather soon becomes balmy and spring-like. The name is derived from Chinook,

the appellation of one of the Indian tribes of this region. (A. F. C.)

**Chinoshahgeh** ('at the bower' [?]). A Seneca village near Victor, N. Y., on or near the site of the earlier settlement called Kanagaro, that was broken up by the Denonville expedition.—Shea in Charlevoix, New Fr., III, 289, note, 1864.

Ga-o-sa-eh-ga-aah.—Marshall quoted by Conover, Kanadega and Geneva MS., B. A. E. (='the basswood bark lies there'). **Gäósâgäo.**—Morgan, League Iroq., 19, 1851 (='in the basswood country'). **Gä-o-ŭs-ä-gé-oⁿ.**—Hewitt, inf'n (Seneca form).

**Chinquapin.** A species of chestnut (*Castanea pumila*) common in the Middle and Southern states; spelled also chinkapin, chincapin, chinquepin, chinkopin. *Castanopsis chrysophylla* is called western chinquapin, and in California and Oregon chinquapin. Two species of oak (*Quercus acuminata* and *Q. prinoides*) are named chinquapin oak and dwarf chinquapin oak, respectively. A species of perch (*Pomoxys annularis*), known also as crappie, is called chinquapin or chinkapin perch. Such forms as chincomen and chechinquamin, found in early writings, make plausible the supposition that a *p* was later substituted for an *m* in the last syllable of the word, which would then represent the widespread Algonquian radical *min*, 'fruit,' 'seed.' The first component of the word, according to Hewitt, is probably cognate with the Delaware *chinqua*, 'large,' 'great.' (A. F. C.)

**Chintagottine** ('people of the woods'). A division of the Kawchodinneh, dwelling on Mackenzie r., Mackenzie Ter., Canada, N. of Ft Good Hope and between the river and Great Bear lake. Petitot often uses the term synonymously with Kawchodinneh.

Gāh-tau'-go ten'-ni.—Ross, MS. notes on Tinne, B. A. E. **Gāh-tŏw-gō tin'-nī.**—Kennicott, Hare Ind. MS. vocab., B. A. E. **Gens du Poil.**—Petitot, Expl. du grand lac des Ours, 349, 1893. **Ta-laottine.**—Petitot, MS., B. A. E., 1865 ('dwellers at the end of the pine trees'). **Tchin-t'a-gottinè.**—Petitot in Bull. Soc. Géog. Paris, chart, 1875. **Tchin-tpa-gottinè.**—Petitot, Autour du lac des Esclaves, 362, 1891. **Tcïn-tat' tĕne'.**—Everette, MS. Tutu vocab., B. A. E., 1883.

**Chinunga.** The extinct Thistle clan of the Chua (Snake) phratry of the Hopi.

Tci-nuña wuñ-wŭ.—Fewkes in Am. Anthrop., VII, 403, 1894 (*wuñ-wü*='clan').

**Chioro.** A village of 35 Papago, probably in Pima co., s. Ariz., in 1865 (Davidson in Ind. Aff. Rep., 135, 1865). Possibly identical with Charco.

**Chipewyan** ('pointed skins,' Cree *Chipwayanawok*, from *chipwa* 'pointed,' *weyanaw* 'skin,' *ok* plural sign: Cree name for the parkas, or shirts, of many northern Athapascan tribes, pointed and ornamented with tails before and behind; hence, the people who wear them). An Athapascan linguistic group, embracing the Desnedekenade and Athabasca, called the Chipewyan proper, the Thilanottine,

Etheneldeli, and Tatsanottine. The term was originally applied to the Chipewyan who assailed the Cree about L. Athabasca; subsequently the Cree and, following their example, the whites, extended it to include all Athapascan tribes known to them, the whites using it as a synonym of Tinneh, but it is now confined to the linguistic group above referred to, although the Tatsanottine, or Yellowknives, are generally separated in popular usage. The deerskin shirts worn by these people sometimes had the queue behind only, like a poncho, and the tales told by the early travelers of a race of people living in the far N., having a tail and being in a transition stage between animal and man, had their foundation in the misrepresentation of the descriptions given by other Indians of these people with the pointed shirts. Petitot (La Mer Glaciale, 303, 1887) characterized these people as innocent and natural in their lives and manners, imbued with a sense of justice, endowed with sound sense and judgment, and not devoid of originality. Ross (Notes on the Tinné, MS., B. A. E.) gave the habitat of the Chipewyan as Churchill r., and Athabasca and Great Slave lakes. Kennicot(MS., B. A. E.) said their territory extended as far N. as Ft Resolution on the s. shore of Great Slave lake, Brit. Col., and Drake (Bk. Inds., vii, 1848) noted that they claimed from lat. 60° to 65° and from long. 100° to 110°, and numbered 7,500 in 1812. In 1718, according to Petitot, the Chipewyan were living on Peace r., which they called Tsades, the river of beavers, the shores of L. Athabasca and the forests between it and Great Slave lake being then the domain of the Etchareottine. The Cree, after they had obtained guns from the French, attacked these latter and drove them from their hunting grounds, but were forced back again by the Chipewyan tribes. As a result of this contest the Thilanottine obtained for themselves the upper waters of Churchill r. about La Crosse lake, the Chipewyan proper the former domain of the Etchareottine, while a part went to live in the neighborhood of the English post of Ft Prince of Wales, newly established on Hudson bay at the mouth of Churchill r. for trade with the Eskimo, Maskegon, and Cree. These last became known as the Etheneldeli, 'eaters of reindeer meat,' or Theyeottine, 'stonehouse people,' the latter being the name that they gave their protectors, the English. In 1779 the French Canadians brought smallpox to the shores of La Crosse and Athabasca lakes. Cree and Chipewyan were decimated by the malady, and the former, already driven back to the s. shore of L. Athabasca by the martial attitude of the Chipewyan, were

now willing to conclude a lasting peace (Petitot, La Mer Glaciale, 297, 1887). There were 230 Cree at La Crosse lake in 1873, and 600 Thilanottine Chipewyan, many of whom were half-breeds bearing French names. The report of Canadian Indian Affairs for 1904 enumerates nearly 1,800 Indians as Chipewyan, including 219 Yellowknives (Tatsanottine).

**Athabasca.**—Bancroft, Nat. Races, I, 114, 1874. **Athapasca.**—Gallatin in Drake, Tecumseh, 20, 1852. **Che-pa-wy-an.**—Macauley, Hist. N. Y., II, 244, 1829. **Chepayan.**—Balbi, Atlas Ethnog., 58, 1826. **Chepé-ouyan.**—Ibid. **Chepewayan.**—Ross, MS. Notes on Tinne, B. A. E. **Chepewyan.**—Lewis, Travels, 143, 1809. **Chepeyan.**—Drake, Bk. Inds., vii, 1848. **Cheppewyan.**—Balbi, Atlas Ethnog., 58, 1826. **Cheppeyans.**—Gallatin in Trans. Am. Ethnol. Soc., II, 18, 1836. **Chipeouaïan.**—Duflot de Mofras, Oregon, II, 337, 1844. **Chipewan.**—Keane in Stanford, Compend., 508, 1878. **Chipeway.**—Harmon, Journal, 264, 1820. **Chipewayan.**—Kennicott, MS. vocab., B. A. E. **Chipewyan.**—Morse, System of Mod. Geog., I, 55, 1814. **Chipewyan Tinneys.**—Petitot in Can. Rec. Sci., I, 47, 1884. **Chipiouan.**—Balbi, Atlas Ethnog., 58, 1826. **Chippewayan.**—Howe, Hist. Coll., 380, 1851. **Chippewayanawok.**—Ibid. (Cree name). **Chippewayeen.**—Kane, Wanderings in N. A., 130, 1859. **Chippeweyan.**—McLean, Hudson's Bay, I, 224, 1849. **Chip-pe-wi-yan.**—Tanner, Nar., 390, 1830. **Chippewyan.**—Schermerhorn (1812) in Mass. Hist. Coll., 2d s., II, 42, 1814. **Chippowyen.**—Mackenzie misquoted by Brackenridge, Mexican Letters, 85, 1850. **Chipwayan.**—Can. Ind. Rep., 171, 1877. **Chipwayanawok.**—Kingsley, Stand. Nat. Hist., pt. 6, 143, 1883. **Chipweyan.**—Latham, Essays, 275, 1860. **Chip-wyan.**—Anderson, MS., B. A. E. **Chyppewan.**—Snelling, Tales of N. W., 195, 1830. **Dènè Tchippewayans.**—Petitot, Autour du lac des Esclaves, 289, 1891. **Gens des Montagnes.**—McLean, Hudson's Bay, II, 243, 1849. **Highlander.**—Petitot in Jour. Roy. Geog. Soc., 649, 1883. **Montagnais.**—Petitot, Dict. Dènè Dindjié, xx, 1876. **Montagnees.**—Smet, Oregon Miss., 193, 1847. **Montagnes.**—Belcourt in Minn. Hist. Coll., I, 227, 1872. **Montagnez.**—Henry, Trav. in Can., 173, note, 1809. **Mountains.**—Hooper, Tents of Tuski, 403, 1853. **Mountaineers.**—Ross, MS. notes on Tinne, B. A. E. **Mountain Indians.**—Franklin, 2d Exped. Polar Sea, 152, 1828. **Oochepayyan.**—McKeevor, Hudson's Bay, 73, 1819. **Ouachipuanes.**—Jefferys, French Dom. Am., Can. map, 1741. **Shepeweyan.**—Engl. writer (1786) in Mass. Hist. Coll., 1st s., III, 24, 1794. **Tckippewayan.**—Petitot, Expl. Grand lac des Ours, 363, 1893. **Tchipwayanawok.**—Petitot, Dict. Dènè-Dindjié, xix, 1876. **Wachipuanes.**—Jefferys, Am. Atlas, map 2, 1776. **Wetshipweyanah.**—Belcourt in Minn. Hist. Coll., I, 226, 1872.

**Chipiinuinge** (Tewa: 'house at the pointed peak'). A great ruined pueblo and cliff village occupying a small but high detached mesa between the Cañones and Polvadera cr., 4 m. s. of Rio Chama and about 14 m. s. w. of Abiquiu, Rio Arriba co., N. Mex. The site was doubtless selected on account of its defensible character, the pueblo being situated at least 800 ft. above the level of the creek and its walls built continuous with the edge of the precipice. The great Pedernal peak, from which the village takes its name, rises on the other side of the canyon about 2 m. to the s. w. The pueblo is inaccessible except by a single trail which winds up from the Polvadera and reaches the summit of the mesa at its s. end, passing thence through two strongly fortified gaps before the pueblo is reached. The site was impregnable to any form of attack possible to savage warfare. The commanding position was at the gateway to the Tewa country E. of the mountains, and, according to tradition, it was the function of Chipiinuinge to withstand as far as possible the fierce Navaho and Apache raids from the N. W. The pueblo was built entirely of stone and was of 3 stories, in places possibly 4. Portions of second-story walls are still standing and many cedar timbers are well preserved. The remains of 15 kivas, mostly circular, a few rectangular, are still traceable in and about the ruins; these were all mostly if not wholly subterranean, having been excavated in the rock surface on which the pueblo stands. The cliff-dwellings in the E. face of the mesa are all of the excavated type, and appear to have been used for mortuary quite as much as for domiciliary purposes. (E. L. H.)

**Chipisclin.** A former village, presumably Costanoan, connected with Dolores mission, San Francisco, Cal.—Taylor in Cal. Farmer, Oct. 18, 1861.

**Chipletac.** A former village, presumably Costanoan, connected with Dolores mission, San Francisco, Cal.—Taylor in Cal. Farmer, Oct. 18, 1861.

**Chipmunk.** The common name of the striped ground squirrel (*Tamias striatus*), of which the variants chipmonk, chipmuck, chitmunk, and others occur. The word has been usually derived from the "chipping" of the animal, but (Chamberlain in Am. Notes and Queries, III, 155, 1889) it is clearly of Algonquian origin. The word *chipmunk* is really identical with the *adjidaumo* ('tail-in-air') of Longfellow's Hiawatha, the Chippewa *atchitamon*, the name of the ordinary red squirrel (*Sciurus hudsonicus*). The Chippewa vocabulary of Long (1791) gives for squirrel *chetamon*, and Mrs Traill, in her Canadian Crusoes, 1854, writes the English word as *chitmunk*. By folk etymology, therefore, the Algonquian word represented by the Chippewa *atchitamon* has become, by way of *chitmunk*, our familiar *chipmunk*. The Chippewa word signifies 'head first', from *atchit* 'headlong,' *am* 'mouth,' from the animal's habit of descending trees. The Indian word applied originally to the common red squirrel and not to the chipmunk. (A. F. C.)

**Chippanchickchick.** A tribe or band of doubtful linguistic affinity, either Chinookan or Shahaptian, living in 1812 on Columbia r., in Klickitat co., Wash., nearly opposite The Dalles. Their number was estimated at 600.

Chippanchickchicks.—Morse in Rep. to Sec. War, 368, 1822. Tchipan-Tchick-Tchick.—Stuart in Nouv. Ann. Voy., XII, 26, 1821.

**Chipped implements.** See *Stonework*.

**Chippekawkay** (*Chĭp'-ka-kyun'-ge*, 'place of roots.'—Dunn, after Godfroy). A Piankishaw village, in 1712, on the site of Vincennes, Knox co., Ind.

Brushwood.—Baskin, Forster & Co.'s Hist. Atlas Ind., 249, 1876. Chih-kah-we-kay.—Hough in Ind. Geol. Rep., map, 1883. Chipcoke.—Baskin, Forster & Co., op. cit., 249, 1876. Chĭp'-kah-kyoon'-gay.—Dunn, after Godfroy, inf'n, 1908 ('place of roots': Miami name). Chipkawkay.—Baskin, Forster & Co., op. cit. Chip-pe-coke.—Hough, op. cit. Chippekawkay.—Ibid.

**Chippewa** (popular adaptation of *Ojibway*, 'to roast till puckered up,' referring to the puckered seam on their moccasins; from *ojib* 'to pucker up,' *ub-way* 'to roast'). One of the largest tribes N. of Mexico, whose range was formerly

CHIPPEWA MAN

along both shores of L. Huron and L. Superior, extending across Minnesota to Turtle mts., N. Dak. Although strong in numbers and occupying an extensive territory, the Chippewa were never prominent in history, owing to their remoteness from the frontier during the period of the colonial wars. According to tradition they are part of an Algonquian body, including the Ottawa and Potawatomi, which separated into divisions when it reached Mackinaw in its westward movement, having come from some point N. or N. E. of Mackinaw. Warren (Minn. Hist. Soc. Coll., V, 1885) asserts that they were settled in a large village at La Pointe, Wis., about the time of the discovery of America, and Verwyst (Missionary Labors, 1886) says that about 1612 they suddenly abandoned this locality, many of them going back to the Sault, while others settled at the w. end of L. Superior, where Father Allouez found them in 1665–67. There is nothing found to sustain the statement of Warren and Verwyst in regard to the early residence of the tribe at La Pointe. They were first noticed in the Jesuit Relation of 1640 under the name Baouichtigouin (probably Bāwaʿtigōwininiwŭg, 'people of the Sault'), as residing at the Sault, and it is possible that Nicollet met them in 1634 or 1639. In 1642 they were visited by Raymbaut and Jogues, who found them at the Sault and at war with a people to the w., doubtless the Sioux. A remnant or offshoot of the tribe resided N. of L. Superior after the main body moved s. to Sault Ste Marie, or when it had reached the vicinity of the Sault. The Marameg, a tribe closely related to if not an actual division of the Chippewa, who dwelt along the N. shore of the lake, were apparently incorporated with the latter while they were at the Sault, or at any rate prior to 1670 (Jesuit Rel., 1670). On the N. the Chippewa are so closely connected with the Cree and Maskegon that the three can be distinguished only by those intimately acquainted with their dialects and customs, while on the s. the Chippewa, Ottawa, and Potawatomi have always formed a sort of loose confederacy, frequently designated in the last century the Three Fires. It seems to be well established that some of the Chippewa have resided N. of L. Superior from time immemorial. These and the Marameg claimed the N. side of the lake as their country. According to Perrot some of the Chippewa living s. of L. Superior in 1670–99, although relying chiefly on the chase, cultivated some maize, and were then at peace with the neighboring Sioux. It is singular that this author omits to mention wild rice (*Zizania aquatica*) among their food supplies, since the possession of wild-rice fields was one of the chief causes of their wars with the Dakota, Foxes, and other nations, and according to Jenks (19th Rep. B. A. E., 1900) 10,000 Chippewa in the United States use it at the present time. About this period they first came into possession of firearms, and were pushing their way westward, alternately at peace and at war with the Sioux and in almost constant conflict with the Foxes. The French, in 1692, reëstablished a trading post at Shaugawaumikong, now La Pointe, Ashland co., W's., which became an important Chippewa settlement. In the

beginning of the 18th century the Chippewa succeeded in driving the Foxes, already reduced by a war with the French, from N. Wisconsin, compelling them to take refuge with the Sauk. They then turned against the Sioux, driving them across the Mississippi and s. to Minnesota r., and continued their westward march across Minnesota and North Dakota until they occupied the headwaters of Red r., and established their westernmost band in the Turtle mts. It was not until after 1736 that they obtained a foothold w. of L. Superior. While the main divisions of the tribe were thus extending their possessions in the w., others overran the peninsula between L. Huron and L. Erie, which had long been claimed by the Iroquois through conquest. The Iroquois were forced to withdraw, and the whole region was occupied by the Chippewa bands, most of whom are now known as Missisauga, although they still call themselves Ojibwa. The Chippewa took part with the other tribes of the N. W. in all the wars against the frontier settlements to the close of the war of 1812. Those living within the United States made a treaty with the Government in 1815, and have since remained peaceful, all residing on reservations or allotted lands within their original territory in Michigan, Wisconsin, Minnesota, and North Dakota, with the exception of the small band of Swan Creek and Black River Chippewa, who sold their lands in s. Michigan in 1836 and are now with the Munsee in Franklin co., Kans.

Schoolcraft, who was personally acquainted with the Chippewa and married a woman of the tribe, describes the Chippewa warriors as equaling in physical appearance the best formed of the N. W. Indians, with the possible exception of the Foxes. Their long and successful contest with the Sioux and Foxes exhibited their bravery and determination, yet they were uniformly friendly in their relations with the French. The Chippewa are a timber people. Although they have long been in friendly relations with the whites, Christianity has had but little effect on them, owing largely to the conservatism of the native medicine-men. It is affirmed by Warren, who is not disposed to accept any statement that tends to disparage the character of his people, that, according to tradition, the division of the tribe residing at La Pointe practised cannibalism, while Father Belcourt affirms that, although the Chippewa of Canada treated the vanquished with most horrible barbarity and at these times ate human flesh, they looked upon cannibalism, except under such conditions, with horror. According to Dr William Jones (inf'n, 1905), the Pillagers of Bear id.

assert that cannibalism was occasionally practised ceremonially by the Chippewa of Leech lake, and that since 1902 the eating of human flesh occurred on Rainy r. during stress of hunger. It was the custom of the Pillager band to allow a warrior who scalped an enemy to wear on his head two eagle feathers, and the act of capturing a wounded prisoner on the battlefield earned the distinction of wearing five. Like the Ottawa, they were expert in the use of the canoe, and in their early history depended largely on fish for food. There is abundant evidence that polygamy was common, and indeed it still occurs among the more wandering bands (Jones). Their wigwams were made of birch bark or of grass mats; poles were first planted in the ground in a circle, the tops bent together and tied, and the bark or mats thrown over them, leaving a smoke hole at the top. They imagined that the shade, after the death of the body, followed a wide beaten path, leading toward the w., finally arriving in a country abounding in everything the Indian desires. It is a general belief among the northern Chippewa that the spirit often returns to visit the grave, so long as the body is not reduced to dust. Their creation myth is that common among the northern Algonquians. Like most other tribes they believe that a mysterious power dwells in all objects, animate and inanimate. Such objects are *manitus*, which are ever wakeful and quick to hear everything in the summer, but in winter, after snow falls, are in a torpid state. The Chippewa regard dreams as revelations, and some object which appears therein is often chosen as a tutelary deity. The Medewiwin, or grand medicine society (see Hoffman, 7th Rep. B. A. E., 1891), was formerly a powerful organization of the Chippewa, which controlled the movements of the tribe and was a formidable obstacle to the introduction of Christianity. When a Chippewa died it was customary to place the body in a grave, sometimes in a sitting posture, or to scoop a shallow cavity in the earth and deposit the body therein on its back or side, covering it with earth so as to form a small mound, over which boards, poles, or birch bark were placed. According to McKenney (Tour to the Lakes, 1827); the Chippewa of Fond du Lac, Wis., practised scaffold burial in winter, the corpse being wrapped in birchbark. Mourning for a lost relative continued for a year, unless shortened by the *meda* or by certain exploits in war.

Authors differ as to the names and number of the Chippewa gentes, which range all the way from 11 to 23. Warren gives 21 gentes, of which the following are not included among those named by Morgan: Manᴊmaig (Catfish), Nebaunaubay (Merman), Besheu (Lynx), Mous (Moose), Nekah (Goose), Udekumaig (Whitefish), Gyaushk (Gull). Some of them, Warren says, have but few members and are not known to the tribe at large. The Maskegon sprang from the Reindeer, Lynx, and Pike (Pickerel) gentes, which went to the N. of L. Superior when the tribe moved w. from Sault Ste Marie. Among some of the Chippewa these gentes are associated in 5 phratries: the Awausee, Businausee, Ahahweh, Noka, and Mousonee. The Awausee phratry includes the Catfish, Merman, Sturgeon, Pike (Pickerel), Whitefish, and Sucker gentes—all the Fish gentes. The Businausee phratry includes the Crane and Eagle gentes, businausee, 'echo-maker,' being a name for the crane. The Ahahweh phratry includes the Loon, Goose, and Cormorant gentes, ahahweh being a name for the loon, though the Loon gens is called Mong. Morgan makes Ahahweh distinct and called them the 'Duck' gens. The Noka (No-'ke, Bear) phratry included the Bear gentes, of which there were formerly several named from different parts of the bear's body; but these are now consolidated and no differences are recognized excepting between the common and the grizzly bears. The Mousonee phratry includes the Marten, Moose, and Reindeer gentes. Mousonee seems to be the proper name of the phratry, though it is also called Waubishashe, from the important Marten gens which is said to have sprung from the incorporated remnant of the Mundua. Morgan (Anc. Soc., 166, 1877) names the following 23 gentes: Myeengun (Wolf), Makwa (Bear), Ahmik (Beaver), Mesheka (Mud turtle), Mikonoh (Snapping turtle), Meskwadare, (Little turtle), Ahdik (Reindeer), Chueskweskewa (Snipe), Ojeejok (Crane), Kakake (Pigeon hawk) [=Kagagi, Raven], Omegeeze (Bald eagle), Mong (Loon), Ahahweh (Duck), [=Wäᵉwäᵉ, Swan], Sheshebe (Duck), Kenabig (Snake), Wazhush (Muskrat), Wabezhaze (Marten), Mooshkaooze (Heron), Ahwahsissa (Bullhead), Namabin (Carp [Catfish]), Nama (Sturgeon), Kenozhe (Pike) [=Kinozhaⁿ, Pickerel]. Tanner gives also the Pepegewizzains (Sparrow-hawk), Mussundummo (Water snake), and the forked tree as totems among the Ottawa and Chippewa.

It is impossible to determine the past or present numbers of the Chippewa, as in former times only a small part of the tribe came in contact with the whites at any period, and they are now so mixed with other tribes in many quarters that no separate returns are given. The principal estimates are as follow: In 1764, about 25,000; 1783 and 1794, about 15,000; 1843, about 30,000; 1851, about 28,000. It is probable that most of these estimates take no account of more remote bands. In 1884 there were in Dakota 914; in Minnesota, 5,885; in Wisconsin, 3,656; in Michigan, 3,500 returned separately, and 6,000 Chippewa and Ottawa, of whom perhaps one-third are Chippewa; in Kansas, 76 Chippewa and Munsee. The entire number in the United States at this time was therefore about 16,000. In British America those of Ontario, including the Nipissing, numbered at the same time about 9,000, while in Manitoba and the Northwest Territories there were 17,129 Chippewa and Cree on reservations under the same agencies. The Chippewa now (1905) probably number 30,000 to 32,000—15,000 in British America and 14,144 in the United States, exclusive of about 3,000 in Michigan.

As the Chippewa were scattered over a region extending 1,000 m. from E. to W., they had a large number of villages, bands, and local divisions. Some of the bands bore the name of the village, lake, or river near which they resided, but these were grouped under larger divisions or subtribes which occupied certain fixed limits and were distinguished by marked differences. According to Warren there were 10 of these principal divisions: Kechegummewininewug, on the s. shore of L. Superior; Betonukeengainubejig, in N. Wisconsin; Munominikasheenhug, on the headwaters of St Croix r. in Wisconsin and Minnesota; Wahsuahgunewininewug, at the head of Wisconsin r.; Ottawa Lake Men, on Lac Court Oreilles, Wis.; Kitchisibiwininiwug, on the upper Mississippi in Minnesota; Mukmeduawininewug, or Pillagers, on Leech lake, Minn.; Sugwaundugahwininewug, N. of L. Superior; Kojejewininewug, on Rainy lake and r. about the N. boundary of Minnesota; and Wazhush, on the N. w. side of L. Superior at the Canadian border. Besides these general divisions the following collective or local names are recognized as belonging to various settlements, bands, or divisions of the tribe: Angwassag, Big Rock, Little Forks, Menitegow, Blackbird, Menoquet's Village, Ketchewaundaugenink, Kishkawbawee, Saginaw, Thunder Bay, Nagonabe, Ommunise, Shabwasing, Beaver Islands, Nabobish, Cheboygan, Otusson, Reaum's Village, and Wapisiwisibiwininiwak, in lower Michigan; Red Cedar Lake, Sukaauguning, Kechepukwaiwah, Long Lake, Chetac Lake, Turtle Portage, Rice Lake, Yellow Lake, Trout Lake, Pawating, Ontonagon, Wauswagiming, Lac Courte Oreilles, Shaugawaumikong, Burnt

Woods, Gatagetegauning, Bay du Noc, Wequadong, Mekadewagamitigweyawininiwak, Michilimackinac, St Francis Xavier, and Wiaquahhechegumeeng, in Wisconsin and upper Michigan; Grand Portage, Pokegama, Fond du Lac, Red Cliff, Crow Wing River, Gull Lake, Onepowesepewenenewak, Miskwagamiwisagaigan, Wabasemowenenewak(?), Wanamakewajenenik, Mikinakwadshiwininiwak, Misisagaikaniwininiwak, Oschekkamegawenenewak, Winnebegoshishiwininiwak, Gamiskwakokawininiwak, Gawababiganikak, Anibiminanisibiwininiwak, Kahmetahwungaguma, and Rabbit Lake, in Minnesota and the Dakotas; Oueschekgagamioulimy, Walpole Island, Obidgewong, Michipicoten, Doki's Band, Bagoache, Epinette (1744), Ouasouarini, Mishtawayawininiwak, Nopeming, and Nameuilni, in Ontario; Sagewenenewak, Mattawan, and Pic River in Manitoba; and Nibowisibiwininiwak in Saskatchewan.                    (J. M.  C. T.)

Achipoés.—Prise de Possession (1671) in Perrot, Mém., 293, 1864. Achipoué.—Neill in Minn. Hist. Soc. Coll., v, 398, 1885. Anchipawah.—Boudinot, Star in the West, 126, 1816. An-ish-in-aub-ag.—Warren in Minn. Hist. Soc. Coll., v, 45, 1885 ('spontaneous men'). A-wish-in-aub-ay.—Ibid., 37. Axshissayé-rúnu.—Gatschet, Wyandot MS., B. A. E., 1881 (Wyandot name). Baouichtigouin.—Jes. Rel. 1640, 34, 1858. Bawichtigouek.—Ibid., index. Bawichtigouin. — Ibid. Bedzaqetcha. — Petitot, Montagnais MS. vocab., B. A. E., 1869 ('long ears': Tsattine name). Bedzietcho.—Petitot, Hare MS. vocab., B. A. E., 1869 (Kawchodinne name). Bungees.—Henry, MS. vocab. (Bell copy, B. A. E.), 1812 (so called by Hudson Bay traders). Cabellos realzados.—Duro, Don Diego de Peñalosa, 43, 1882 (the Raised-hair tribe of Shea's Peñalosa; Cheveux-relevés of the French). Chebois.—Gass, Jour., 47, note, 1807. Chepawas.—Croghan (1759) quoted by Kauffman, West. Penn., 132, app., 1851. Chepeways.—Croghan (1760) in Mass. Hist. Soc. Coll., 4th s., IX, 287, 1871. Chepowas.—Croghan (1759) quoted by Proud, Penn., II, 296, 1798. Cheppewes.—Shirley (1755) in N. Y. Doc. Col. Hist., VI, 1027, 1855. Chiappawaws.—Loudon, Coll. Int. Nar., I, 34, 1808. Chibois.—Bouquet (1760) in Mass. Hist. Soc. Coll., 4th s., IX, 295, 1871. Chipawawas.—Goldthwait (1766) in Mass. Hist. Soc. Coll., 1st s., X, 122, 1809. Chipaways.—Croghan (1760), ibid., 4th s., IX, 250, 1871. Chipaweighs.—German Flats conf. (1770) in N. Y. Doc. Col. Hist., VIII, 229, 1857. Chipewas.—Lattré, map U. S., 1784. Chipéways.—Carver (1766) Trav., 19, 1778. Chipeweghs.—Johnson (1763) in N. Y. Doc. Col. Hist., VII, 526, 1856. Chipeweighs.—Johnson (1763), ibid., 583, 1856. Chipiwa.—Treaty of 1820, U. S. Ind. Treat., 369, 1873. Chipoës.—Prise de Possession (1671) in N. Y. Doc. Col. Hist., IX, 803, 1855. Chippawas.—Croghan (1759) quoted by Jefferson, Notes, 143, 1825. Chippawees.—Writer of 1756 in Mass. Hist. Soc. Coll., 1st s., VII, 123, 1801. Chippeouays.—Toussaint, map of Am., 1839. Chippewaes.—Johnson (1763) in N. Y. Doc. Col. Hist., VII, 525, 1856. Chippewais.—Perrot (ca. 1721) in Minn. Hist. Soc. Coll., II, pt. 2, 24, 1864. Chippewas.—Washington (1754) quoted by Kauffman, West. Penn., 67, 1851. Chippewaus.—Edwards (1788) in Mass. Hist. Soc. Coll., 1st s., IX, 92, 1804. Chippeways.—Chauvignerie (1736) quoted by Schoolcraft, Ind. Tribes, III, 556, 1853. Chippeweighs.—Johnson (1767) in N. Y. Doc. Col. Hist., VII, 969, 1856. Chippewyse.—Ft Johnson conf. (1755), ibid., VI, 975, 1855. Chippoways.—Washington (1754) in Mass. Hist. Soc. Coll., 1st s., VI, 140, 1800. Chippuwas.—Heckewelder quoted by Barton, New Views, app. 1, 1798. Chipwaes.—Croghan (1765) in N. Y. Doc. Col. Hist., VII, 782, 1856. Chipwas.—Bouquet (1760) in Mass. Hist. Soc. Coll., 4th s.,

IX, 321, 1871. **Chipways.**—Croghan (1765), op. cit. **Cypoways.**—Beltrami quoted by Neill, Minn., 350, 1858. **De-wă-kă-nhă'.**—Hewitt, Mohawk MS. vocab., B. A. E. (Mohawk name). **Dewoganna's.**—Bellomont (1698) in N. Y. Doc. Col. Hist., IV, 407, 1854. **Douaganhas.**—Cortland (1687), ibid., III, 434, 1853. **Douwaganhas.**—Ibid. **Dovaganhaes.**—Livingston (1691), ibid., 778. **Dowaganahs.**—Doc. of 1700, ibid., IV, 701, 1854. **Dowaganhas.**—Cortland (1687), ibid, III, 434, 1855. **Dowanganhaes.**—Doc. of 1691, ibid., 776. **Dshipowē-hága.**—Gatschet, Caughnawaga MS., B. A. E., 1882 (Caughnawaga name). **Dwă-kă-nĕⁿ.**—Hewitt, Onondaga MS. vocab., B. A. E. (Onondaga name). **Dwă-kă-nhă'.**—Hewitt, Seneca and Onondaga vocab., B. A. E., 1880 (Seneca and Onondaga name). **Eskiaeronnon.**—Jes. Rel. 1649, 27, 1858 (Huron name; Hewitt says it signifies 'people of the falls'). **Estiaghes.**—Albany conf. (1726) in N. Y. Doc. Col. Hist., V, 791, 1855. **Estiaghicks.**—Colden (1727), ibid., IV, 737, note, 1854. **Estjage.**—Livingston (1701), ibid., 899, 1854. **Etchipoës.**—Prise de possession (1671), ibid., IX, 808, 1855. **Gibbaways.**—Imlay, West Ter., 363, 1797. **Hāhatona.**—Featherstonhaugh, Canoe Voy., I, 300, 1847. **Ḣaḣatonwan.**—Iapi Oaye, XIII, no. 2, 6, Feb., 1884 (Sioux name). **Hahátoŋwaŋ.**—Riggs, Dakota Dict., 72, 1852 (Sioux name). **Ḣaḣatonway.**—Matthews, Hidatsa Inds., 150, 1877 (Sioux name). **Hă-hăt-tŏng.**—Long, Exped. Rocky Mts., II, lxxxiv, 1823 (Hidatsa name, incorrectly rendered 'leapers'). **Ha-há-tu-a.**—Matthews, Hidatsa Inds., 150, 1877 (Hidatsa name; h guttural). **Ha-ha-twawns.**—Neill, Minn., 113, 1858. **Hah-hah-ton-wah.**—Gale, Upper Miss., 265, 1867. **Hrah-hrah-twauns.**—Ramsey (ca. 1852) in Minn. Hist. Soc. Coll., I, 50, 1872. **Icbewas.**—Boudinot, Star in the West, 126, 1816 (misprint). **Jibewas.**—Smith (1799) quoted by Drake, Trag. Wild., 213, 1841. **Jumpers.**—Neill, Minn., 36, 1858 (incorrect translation of Saulteurs). **Khahkhahtons.**—Snelling, Tales of the Northwest, 137, 1830 (Sioux name). **Khakhatons.**—Ibid., 144. **Khakhatonwan.**—Williamson, Minn. Geol. Rep. for 1884, 107. **Kútaki.**—Gatschet, Fox MS., B. A. E., 1882 (Fox name). **Leapers.**—Hennepin, New Discov., 86, 1698 (incorrect rendering of Saulteurs). **Nation du Sault.**—Jogues and Raymbaut in Jes. Rel. 1642, II, 95, 1858. **Né-a-ya-og'.**—Hayden, Ethnog. and Philol. Mo. Val., 235, 1862 ('those speaking the same language': Cree name). **Ne-gá-tcĕ.**—St Cyr, oral inf'n, 1886 (Winnebago name; plural, Ne-gátc-hi-jáⁿ). **Ninniwas.**—Rafinesque, Am. Nations, I, 123, 1836. **Nwă'-kă.**—Hewitt, Tuscarora MS. vocab., B. A. E., 1880 (Tuscarora name). **Objibways.**—Kingsley, Stand. Nat. Hist., pt. 6, 143, 1883. **Ọ'chĕpĕ'wȧg.**—Long, Exped. St. Peter's R., II, 151, 1824. **Ochipawa.**—Umfreville (1790) in Me. Hist. Soc. Coll., VI, 270, 1859. **Ochipewa.**—Richardson, Arct. Exped., 71, 1851. **Ochipoy.**—York (1700) in N. Y. Doc. Col. Hist., IV, 749, 1854. **Ochippewais.**—Foster in Sen. Misc. Doc. 39, 42d Cong., 3d sess., 6, 1873. **Odchipewa.**—Hutchins (1770) quoted by Richardson, Arct. Exped., II, 38, 1851. **Odgiboweke.**—Perrot, Mém., 193, 1864. **Odjibewais.**—Ibid. **Od-jib-wäg.**—Schoolcraft quoted in Minn. Hist. Soc. Coll., V, 35, 1885. **Odjibwas.**—Schoolcraft, Ind. Tribes, I, 307, 1851. **Odjibwe.**—Kelton, Ft Mackinac, 153, 1884. **Odjibwek.**—Belcourt (1850?) in Minn. Hist. Soc. Coll., I, 227, 1872. **Ogibois.**—M'Lean Hudson Bay, II, 323, 1849. **O-je-bway.**—Jones, Ojebway Inds., 164, 1861. **Ojeebois.**—Henry, MS. vocab. (Bell copy, B. A. E.), 1812. **Ojibaway.**—Lewis and Clark, Trav., 53, 1806. **Ojibbewaig.**—Tanner, Narr., 315, 1830 (Ottawa name). **Ojibbeways.**—Ibid., 36. **Ojibboai.**—Hoffman, Winter in the Far West, II, 15, 1821. **Ojibeways.**—Perkins and Peck, Annals of the West, 1850. **Ojibois.**—Gunn in Smithson. Rep., 400, 1868. **Ojibua.**—Maximilian, Trav., 135, note, 1843. **O-jib-wage.**—Morgan, Consang. and Affin., 287, 1871. **Ojibwaig.**—Hale, Ethnog. and Philol. Mo. Val., 224, 1846. **Ojibwas.**—Ind. Aff. Rep., 454, 1838. **O-jib-wa-uk'.**—Morgan, Consang. and Affin., 287, 1871. **Ojibways.**—Am. Pioneer, II, 190, 1843. **Ojibway-ugs.**—Foster in Sen. Misc. Doc. 39, 42d Cong., 3d sess., 6, 1873. **Ojibwe.**—Burton, City of the Saints, 117, 1861. **Ontehibouse.**—Raymbaut

(1641) quoted in Ind. Aff. Rep. 1849, 70, 1850 (probably a misprint). **Oshibwek.**—Belcourt (1850?) in Minn. Hist. Soc. Coll., I, 227, 1872. **Ostiagaghroones.**—Canajoharie conf. (1759) in N. Y. Doc. Col. Hist., VII, 384, 1856. **Ostiagahoroones.**—Neill in Minn. Hist. Soc. Coll., V, 397, 1885 (Iroquois name). **Otchepóse.**—Proces verbal (1682) in French, Hist. Coll. La., II, 19, 1875. **Otchipoeses.**—La Salle (1682) in Margry, Déc., II, 187, 1877. **Otchipois.**—La Salle (1682) in French, Hist. Coll. La., I, 46, 1846. **Otchipoises.**—Hildreth, Pioneer Hist., 9, 1848. **Otchipwe.**—Baraga, Otchipwe Gram., title, 1878. **Otjibwek.**—Perrot, Mém., 193, 1864. **Ottapoas.**—Buchanan, N. Am. Inds., 156, 1824. **Oucahipoues.**—La Hontan (1703), New Voy., II, 87, 1735. **Ouchibois.**—Writer of 1761 in Mass. Hist. Soc. Coll., 4th s., IX, 428, 1871. **Ouchipawah.**—Pike (1806) quoted by Schoolcraft, Ind. Tribes, III, 563, 1853. **Ouchipöe.**—La Chesnaye (1697) in Margry, Déc., VI, 6, 1886. **Ouchipoves.**—Coxe, Carolana, map, 1741. **Outachepas.**—McKenney and Hall, Ind. Tribes, III, 79, 1854. **Outchibouec.**—Jes. Rel. 1667, 24, 1858. **Outchibous.**—Ibid., 1670, 79, 1858. **Outchipoue.**—Gallinèe (1669) in Margry, Déc., I, 163, 1875. **Outchipwais.**—Bell in Can. Med. and Surg. Jour., Mar. and Apr., 1886. **Outehipoues.**—La Hontan, New Voy., I, 230, 1703. **Paouichtigouin.**—Jes. Rel., III, index, 1858. **Paouitagoung.**—Ibid. **Paouitigoueieuhak.**—Ibid. **Paouitingouach-irini.**—Ibid. **Qa-qá-toⁿ-waⁿ.**—Dorsey, oral inf'n, 1886 (Sioux name). **Ra-ra-to-oans.**—Warren (1852) in Minn. Hist. Soc. Coll., V, 96, 1885. **Ra-ra-t'wans.**—Ramsey in Ind. Aff. Rep. 1849, 72, 1850 (Sioux name). **Salteur.**—Bacqueville de la Potherie, II, 48, 1753. **Santeaux.**—Brown, West. Gaz., 265, 1817 (misprint). **Santena.**—Gunn in Smithson. Rep. 1867, 400, 1868 (misprint). **Santeurs.**—Dobbs, Hudson Bay, 26, 1744 (misprint). **Saulteaux.**—Beauharnois (1745) in Minn. Hist. Soc. Coll., V, 432, 1885. **Saulteurs.**—Jes. Rel. 1670, 79, 1858. **Saulteuse.**—Belcourt (ca. 1850) in Minn. Hist. Soc. Coll., I, 228, 1872. **Saulteux.**—Gallinée (1669) in Margry, Déc., I, 163, 1875. **Sault Indians.**—Vaudreuil (1710) in N. Y. Doc. Col. Hist., IX, 843, 1855. **Sauteaux.**—Gamelin (1790) in Am. St. Papers, IV, 94, 1832. **Sauters.**—Schermerhorn (1812) in Mass. Hist. Soc. Coll., 2d s., II, 6, 1814. **Sauteurs.**—Jes. Rel. 1667, 24, 1858. **Sauteus.**—Cox, Columbia R., II, 270, 1831. **Sauteux.**—Vaudreuil (1719) in N. Y. Doc. Col. Hist., IX, 893, 1855. **Sautor.**—Carver (1766), Trav., 97, 1778. **Sautous.**—King, Journ. to Arct. Ocean, I, 32, 1836. **Sautoux.**—Ibid. **Schipuwe.**—Heckewelder quoted by Barton, New Views, app., 1, 1798 (German form). **Shepawees.**—Lindesay (1749) in N. Y. Doc. Col. Hist., VI, 538, 1855. **Shepewas.**—Bradstreet (ca. 1765), ibid., VII, 694, 1856. **Shepuway.**—Heckewelder quoted by Barton, New Views, app., 1, 1798. **Sothuze.**—Dalton (1783) in Mass. Hist. Soc. Coll., 1st s., X, 123, 1890. **Sotoes.**—Cox, Columbia R., II, 270, 1831. **Sotoos.**—Franklin, Journ. Polar Sea, 96, 1824. **Sotto.**—Kane, Wanderings in N. A., 438, 1859. **Soulteaux.**—Henry, MS. vocab. (Bell copy, B. A. E.), 1812. **Souteus.**—Chauvignerie (1736) quoted by Schoolcraft, Ind. Tribes, III, 556, 1853. **Souties.**—Am. Pioneer, II, 192, 1843. **Stiaggeghroano.**—Post (1758) quoted by Proud, Penn., II, app., 113, 1798. **Stiagigroone.**—Livingston (1700) in N. Y. Doc. Col. Hist., IV, 737, 1854. **Tcipu'.**—Dorsey, Kansas MS. vocab., B. A. E., 1882 (Kansa name). **Tschipeway.**—Wrangell, Ethnol. Nachr., 100, 1839. **Tschippiweer.**—Walch, map, 1805 (German form). **Tsipu'.**—Dorsey, Osage MS. vocab., B. A. E., 1883 (Osage name). **Twă-'kă'-nhă'.**—Smith, Cayuga and Oneida MS. vocabs., B. A. E., 1884 (Cayuga and Oneida name). **Uchipweys.**—Dalton (1783) in Mass. Hist. Soc. Coll., 1st s., X, 123, 1809. **Wahkah-towah.**—Tanner, Narr., 150, 1830 (Assiniboin name).

**Chippewa of Lake Nipegon.** A Chippewa band officially known by this name residing in the vicinity of L. Nipegon, N. of L. Superior, in Ontario. The "Christians," composing nearly one-half the entire band, occupy a village at the head of the lake near the Hudson Bay Company's post; the remainder live about 100 m.

farther inland. The aggregate number in 1884 was 426, and in 1901, 518. They are connected with the band at Red Rock on Nipegon bay.                    (J. M.)

Allenemipigons.—Denonville (1687), in Margry, Déc., VI, 52, 1886.

**Chippoy.** A former Potawatomi village on Big Shawnee cr., in Fountain co., Ind. It was settled after 1795, and the site was included in a tract sold in 1818 by the Miami.                    (J. M.)

Chipaille.—St Mary's treaty with Miamis (1818) in U. S. Ind. Treat., 493, 1873. **Chippoy.**—Harrison (1814) quoted by Drake, Tecumseh, 161, 1852.

**Chiputca.** A former village, presumably Costanoan, connected with Dolores mission, San Francisco, Cal.—Taylor in Cal. Farmer, Oct. 18, 1861.

**Chiricahua** (Apache: 'great mountain'). An important division of the Apache,

BEDAZ-ISHU—CHIRICAHUA APACHE

so called from their former mountain home in S. E. Arizona. Their own name is Aiáha. The Chiricahua were the most warlike of the Arizona Indians, their raids extending into New Mexico, S. Arizona, and N. Sonora, among their most noted leaders being Cochise, Victorio, Loco, Chato, Nachi, Bonito and Geronimo. Physically they do not differ materially from the other Apache. The men are well built, muscular, with well-developed chests, sound and regular teeth, and abundant hair. The women are even more vigorous and strongly built, with broad shoulders and hips and a tendency to corpulency in old age. They habitually wear a pleasant open expression of countenance, exhibiting uniform good nature, save when in

anger their face takes on a savage cast. White thought their manner of life, general physique, and mental disposition seemed conducive to long life. Their characteristic long-legged moccasins of deerskin have a stout sole turning up at the toes, and the legs of the moccasins, long enough to reach the thigh, are folded back below the knee, forming a pocket in which are carried paints and a knife. The women wore short skirts of buckskin, and the men used to display surplus skins folded about the waist. Their arrows were made of reed tipped with obsidian or iron, the shaft winged with three strips of feathers. They used in battle a long spear and a slung-shot made by inserting a stone into the green hide of a cow's tail, leaving a portion of the hair attached. They possessed no knowledge of weaving blankets. White (MS., B. A. E.) supposed that they had immigrated into Arizona from New Mexico three or four generations back. Their camps were located on the highlands in winter that they might catch the warm rays of the sun, and in summer near the water among stunted trees that sheltered them from its scorching glare. Their bands or clans were named from the nature of the ground about their chosen territory. Both men and women were fond of wearing necklaces and ear pendants of beads. The hair was worn long and flowing, with a turban, to which was attached a flap hanging down behind; they plucked out the hairs of the beard with tweezers of tin, and wore suspended from their necks a small round mirror which they used in painting their faces with stripes of brilliant colors. Strings of pieces of shell were highly prized. Their customary dwelling was a rude brush hut, circular or oval, with the earth scooped out to enlarge its capacity. In winter they huddled together for warmth and, if the hut was large, built a fire in the center. When they changed camp they burned their huts, which were always built close together. They subsisted on berries, nuts, and the fruit of various trees, mesquite beans, and acorns, of which they were particularly fond, and they ground the seeds of different grasses on a large flat stone and made a paste with water, drying it afterward in the sun. They relished the fruit of cacti and of the yucca, and made mescal from the root of the agave. Fish they would not eat, nor pork, but an unborn calf and the entrails of animals they regarded as delicacies, and horse and mule flesh was considered the best meat. Though selfish in most things, they were hospitable with food, which was free to anyone who was hungry. They were scrupulous in keeping accounts and paying debts.

Like many other Indians they would never speak their own names nor on any account speak of a dead member of the tribe. They tilled the ground a

LOCO—CHIRICAHUA CHIEF

little with wooden implements, obtaining corn and melon seeds from the Mexicans. In their clans all were equal. Bands, according to White, were formed of clans, and chiefs were chosen for their ability and courage, although there is evidence that chiefship was sometimes hereditary, as in the case of Cochise, son and successor of Nachi. Chiefs and old men were usually deferred to in council. They used the brain of the deer in dressing buckskin. It is said that they charged their arrows with a quick deadly poison, obtained by irritating a rattlesnake with a forked stick, causing it to bite into a deer's liver, which, when saturated with the venom, was allowed to putrefy. They stalked the deer and the antelope by covering their heads with the skull of the animal and imitating with their crouching body the movements of one grazing; and it was their custom to approach an enemy's camp at night in a similar manner, covering their heads with brush. They signaled war or peace by a great blaze or smoke made by burning cedar boughs or the inflammable spines on the giant cactus. Of their social organization very little is definitely known, and the statements of the two chief authorities are widely at variance. According to White, the children belong to the gens of the father, while Bourke asserts that the true clan system prevails. They married usually outside of the gens,

according to White, and never relatives nearer than a second cousin. A young warrior seeking a wife would first bargain with her parents and then take a horse to her dwelling. If she viewed his suit with favor she would feed and water the animal, and, seeing that, he would come and fetch his bride, and after going on a hunt for the honeymoon they would return to his people. When he took two horses to the camp of the bride and killed one of them it signified that her parents had given her over to him without regard to her consent. Youth was the quality most desired in a bride. After she became a mother the husband might take a second wife, and some had as many as five, two or more of them often being sisters. Married women were usually faithful and terribly jealous, so that single girls did not care to incur their rage. A woman in confinement went off to a hut by herself, attended by her women relatives. Children received their earliest names from something particularly noticeable at the time of their birth. As among the Navaho, a man never spoke to his mother-in-law, and treated his wife's father with distant respect; and his brothers were never familiar with his wife nor he with her sisters and brothers. Faithless wives were punished by whipping and cutting off a portion of the nose, after which they were cast off. Little

TSHAI-KLOGE—CHIRICAHUA WOMAN

girls were often purchased or adopted by men who kept them until they were old enough for them to marry. Often girls were married when only 10 or 11 years of age. Children of both sexes had perfect freedom, were not required to obey, and never were punished. The men engaged in pastimes every day, and boys in mock combats, hurling stones at each other with slings. Young wives and maidens did only light work, the heavy tasks being performed by the older women. People met and parted without any form of salute. Kissing was unknown. Except mineral vermilion, the colors with which they painted their faces and dyed grasses for baskets were of vegetal origin—yellow from beech and willow bark, red from the cactus. They would not kill the golden eagle, but would pluck its feathers, which they prized, and for the hawk and the bear they had a superstitious regard in a lesser degree. They made tizwin, an intoxicating drink, from corn, burying it until it sprouted, grinding it, and then allowing the mash diluted with water to ferment. The women carried heavy burdens on their backs, held by a strap passed over the forehead. Their basket work was impervious to water and ornamented with designs similar to those of the Pima, except that human figures frequently entered into the decorative motive. Baskets 2½ ft. in length and 18 in. wide at the mouth were used in collecting food, which was frequently brought from a great distance. When one of the tribe died, men carried the corpse, wrapped in the blankets of the deceased, with other trifling personal effects, to an obscure place in low ground and there buried it at once, piling stones over the grave to protect it from coyotes or other prowling beasts. No women were allowed to follow, and no Apache ever revisited the spot. Female relatives kept up their lamentations for a month, uttering loud wails at sunset. The hut in which a person died was always burned and often the camp was removed. Widows used to cut off their hair and paint their faces black for a year, during which time the mourner lived in the family of the husband's brother, whose wife she became at the expiry of the mourning. They had a number of dances, notably the "devil dance," with clowns, masks, headdresses, etc., in which the participants jumped over fire, and a spirited war dance, with weapons and shooting in time to a song. When anybody fell sick several fires were built in the camp, and while the rest lay around on the ground with solemn visages, the young men, their faces covered with paint, seized firebrands and ran around and through the fires and about the lodge of the sick person, whooping continually and flourishing the brands to drive away the evil spirit. They had a custom, when a girl arrived at puberty, of having the other young girls lightly tread on her

back as she lay face downward, the ceremony being followed by a dance.

In 1872 the Chiricahua were visited by a special commissioner, who concluded an agreement with Cochise, their chief, to cease hostilities and to use his influence with the other Apache to this end. By the autumn of this year more than 1,000 of the tribe were settled on the newly established Chiricahua res., s. E. Ariz. Cochise died in 1874, and was succeeded as chief by his son Taza, who remained friendly to the Government; but the killing of some settlers who had sold whisky to the Indians caused an intertribal broil, which, in connection with the proximity of the Chiricahua to the international boundary, resulted in the abolishment of the reservation against their will. Camp Apache agency was established in 1872, and in the year following 1,675 Indians were placed thereunder; but in 1875 this agency was discontinued and the Indians, much to their discontent, were transferred to San Carlos, where their enemies, the Yavapai, had also been removed. For further information regarding the dealings of the Chiricahua with the Government, see *Apache*.

The members of Geronimo's band, which was captured in 1886 and sent by the War Department in turn to Florida, Alabama, and Oklahoma, are now at Ft Sill, Okla., where they number 298. The remaining Chiricahua are included among the Apache under Ft Apache and San Carlos agencies, Ariz. The Pinaleño are that part of the Chiricahua formerly residing in the Pinal mts.

**Ai-ahá.**—ten Kate, Reizen in N. A., 197, 1885. **Aihá.**—Ibid. **Apaches Broncos.**—Steck in Cal. Farmer, June 5, 1863 (Span.: 'wild Apaches'). **Apaches Chiricaguis.**—Mayer, Mexico, II, 38, 1853. **Broncos.**—Taylor in Cal. Farmer, Feb. 14, 1862. **Cherecaquis.**—Simpson in Rep. Sec. War, 57, 1850. **Chericahui.**—Ind. Aff. Rep. 1869, 94, 1870. **Chicaraguis.**—Bonnycastle, Span. Am., 68, 1819. **Chiguicagui.**—Anza (1769) in Doc. Hist. Mex., 4th s., II, 114, 1856. **Chilcow.**—Ind. Aff. Rep. 1871, 3, 1872. **Chilecago.**—Ind. Aff. Rep., 122, 1861. **Chile Cowes.**—Ibid., 506, 1865. **Chilicagua.**—Ibid., 1859, 336, 1860. **Chiricaguis.**—Garcés (1769) in Doc. Hist. Mex., 4th s., II, 375, 1856. **Chirioahni.**—Ind. Aff. Rep. 1869, 223, 1870. **Chiricahua.**—White, MS. Hist. of Apaches, B. A. E., 1875. **Chir-i-ca-huans.**—Hodge, Arizona, 163, 1877. **Chiricahues.**—Escudero, Not. Estad. de Chihuahua, 212, 1834. **Chi-ri-ca-hui.**—Cremony, Life Among Apaches, 33, 1868. **Chiricaquis.**—Ruxton, Adventures, 194, 1848. **Chiricuagi.**—Stone in Hist. Mag., v, 166, 1861. **Chiriguais.**—Kingsley, Stand. Nat. Hist., pt. 6, 180, 1883. **Chirikahwa.**—Ind. Aff. Rep., 246, 1877. **Chiriquans.**—Smet, Letters, 135, 1843. **Chirocahue.**—Garcia in Soc. Mex. Geog. Boletin, v, 314, 1861. **Cohila Apache.**—Graves in Ind. Aff. Rep., 439, 1853. **Hayá-a.**—Gatschet, MS., B. A. E. **Hayáha.**—Ibid. ('live in the east': so called by the White Mountain Apache, because they formerly lived at Hot Springs, N. Mex.). **Heyá.**—Gatschet, Yuma-Spr., I, 370, 1883 (Apache name: 'below'). **Hi-ar.**—White, MS. Hist. of Apaches, B. A. E., 1875 (so called by other Apache; trans., 'lived away off'). **Pá 'lízen ab pónin.**—Gatschet, MS. Isleta vocab., B. A. E., 1885 (Isleta name). **Segatajenne.**—Orozco y Berra, Geog., 59, 1864. **Sagetaen-né.**—Escudero, Not. Estad. de Chihuahua, 212, 1834. **Southern**

**Chiricahua.**—Ind. Aff. Rep., 175, 1875. **Tchíshi dinné.**—Gatschet, Apache MS., B. A. E., 1883 (Navaho name).

**Chisca** (possibly from Cherokee *tsi'skwa* 'bird,' *tsiskwä'hï* 'bird place.'—Mooney). The mountainous northern region of the Cherokee in N. W. Georgia or N. E. Alabama, in search of which men were sent by De Soto in 1541 from the province of Chiaha to look for copper and gold. It seemingly received its name from a village of the same name on an island in the river of St Esprit (Coosa r.?), the inhabitants of which made a great deal of oil from nuts. De Soto's troops remained here 26 or 27 days. The Chisca of Garcilasso de la Vega (Florida, 175, 1723) is the Quizquiz of the other chroniclers of De Soto's expedition, situated in N. W. Mississippi, on Mississippi r. See Garcilasso de la Vega, Florida, 175, 1723; Biedma in French, Hist. Coll. La., pt. II, 101, 1850; Mooney in 19th Rep. B. A. E., 1900; Bourne, Narr. De Soto, I, 79, II, 110, 1904.
**Cheesca.**—Schoolcraft, Ind. Tribes, III, 47, 1853. **Chisca.**—Bourne, Narr. of De Soto, I, 79, 117; II, 110, 1904. **Cisca.**—La Salle (*ca.* 1680) in Margry, Déc., II, 196 et seq., 1877.

**Chisedec.** A Montagnais tribe, band, or settlement about the Bay of Seven Islands on the N. shore of St Lawrence r. where it enters the gulf. The name appears to have been applied to a locality and the people of that locality, as it is stated in the Jesuit Relation of 1645 that certain savages boasted of their warlike actions "at Chichedek, country of the Bersiamites, where they had killed 7 savages," probably Eskimo. In the Relation of 1640 it is stated that in ascending the St Lawrence, after passing the Eskimo, "we meet with the people of Chisedech and the Bersiamites, two small nations of which we have but slight knowledge." Lescarbot says that in his time (1609) the name of the river which enters into or near the Bay of Seven Islands was changed to Chi-sche-dec, an Indian appellation (Hind). A Dutch map of 1621 names the bay or locality Chichedec. It is possible, therefore, that the name applied to the Indians, who seem to have been closely connected with and possibly were a part of the Bersiamite tribe, was that of the river and referred only to a settlement. The name Ouakouiechidek, used in 1660 as that of a tribe in connection with the Outabitibek (Abittibi), if intended for the Chisedec would indicate a locality in the distant N. As the designation of a people the name dropped from history at an early date.    (C. T.)
**Chichedec.**—Dutch map (1621) in N. Y. Doc. Col. Hist., I, 1856. **Chichedek.**—Jes. Rel. 1645, 37, 1858. **Chisedech.**—Ibid., 1640, 34, 1858. **Ouak8iechidek.**—Ibid., 1660, 12, 1858, (same?). **Wakouiechiwek.**—Ibid., III, index, 1858.

**Chisels.** Long, slender, celt-like implements of stone or hard varieties of bone, with narrow cutting edge, and round, rectangular, elliptical, or half-elliptical in section. Those of stone, mainly prehistoric, are rarely more than a few inches in length. Some specimens are largest at the top, gradually tapering to the edge, but most of them decrease in size in each direction from near the middle. Some have hammer marks on the blunt end, others are polished at the top, while a few are sharp at both ends. It is probable that their primary intent was for woodworking, though they are numerous wherever steatite vessels were made, and the marks of their use are seen on the unfinished product and on the worked surfaces of the quarry face. These soapstone cutting tools have usually been flaked into the desired form, the edge only being carefully ground. In the lower Ohio valley and in the Southern states chisels are generally made of chert; toward the N., where glacial material is easily procured, they are of diorite, syenite, or other tough rock. Chisels of stone were in common use among the woodworking tribes of the N. W. coast, but these are now almost wholly superseded by chisels of metal. While not so abundant as celts (q. v.), from which they can not always be distinguished, they have practically the same distribution. See Fowke in 13th Rep. B. A. E., 1896; Holmes in 15th Rep. B. A. E., 1897; Rau in Smithson. Cont., XXII, 1876.
                            (W. H. H.   G. F.)

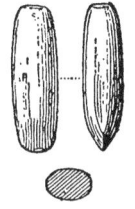

STONE CHISEL; ALA. (1-5)

**Chiserhonon.** A former Canadian tribe subordinate to the Ottawa.—Sagard (1632), Canada, IV, 1866.

**Chishafoka** ('among the post oaks'). A former Choctaw town on the site of the present city of Jackson, Miss.—Brown in Miss. Hist. Soc. Publ., IV, 445, 1902.

**Chishucks.** One of the 8 Tillamook villages at the mouth of Tillamook r., Oreg., in 1805.—Lewis and Clark, Exped., II, 117, 1814.

**Chisi.** A town in 1540 on a small river, between Toalli and Altamaca, in E. Georgia. The name seems to be intended for Ochisi, but not the town of that name on Chattahoochee r. It was entered by De Soto's army in Mar., 1540.
**Achese.**—Gentleman of Elvas (1557) in French, Hist. Coll. La., II, 138, 1850. **Chisi.**—Biedma (1544) in French, op. cit., 100.

**Chiskatalofa** (*chiski* 'post oak,' *talofa* 'town'). A former Creek town on the W. side of Chattahoochee r., 4 m. below Wikaihlako, in Henry co., Ala.
**Cheskitalowas.**—Morse, Rep. to Sec. War, 364, 1822. **Chuskee Tallafau.**—U. S. Ind. Treat. (1814), 163, 1837.

**Chiskelikbatcha.** A former Choctaw town belonging to the Sixtowns district, near Chicasawhay r., probably in

Jasper co., Miss. (West Fla. map, *ca.* 1775).

**Chiskiac.** A tribe of the Powhatan confederacy formerly living in York co., Va. They numbered about 200 in 1608. At that time their principal village, of the same name, was on the s. side of York r., about 10 m. below the junction of the Mattapony and Pamunkey.   (J. M.)

Chickiaes.—Boudinot, Star in the West, 126, 1816. Chiskaot.—Smith (1629), Virginia, II, 77, repr. 1819. Chiskiack.—Ibid., I, 117. Kiskiack.—Ibid., I, map. Kiskiak.—Strachey (*ca.* 1612), Virginia, 36, 1849.

**Chisnedinadinaye** ('walnut') A clan or band of the Pinal Coyoteros (Bourke in Jour. Am. Folk-lore, III, 112, 1890), coördinate with the Chiltneyadnaye clan of the White Mountain Apache.

**Chisro.** The Snow-bunting clan of the Hopi of Arizona.

Tcisro wiñwû.—Fewkes in 19th Rep. B. A. E., 584, 1900 (*wiñwû*='clan'). Tci'-sro wün-wû.—Fewkes in Am. Anthrop., VII, 405, 1894.

**Chitchakos.** See *Chechawkose.*

**Chithut.** Mentioned as a band associated with the Squaksin and Puyallup of Puget sd., Wash.; not to be confounded with Chitwout, a synonym of Similkameen.

Chit-hut.—Simmons in Ind. Aff. Rep., 226, 1858.

**Chitimacha** (Choctaw: *chúti* 'cooking pot,' *másha* 'they possess': 'they have cooking vessels'). A tribe, forming the Chitimachan linguistic family, whose earliest known habitat was the shores of Grand lake, formerly Lake of the Shetimasha, and the banks of Grand r., La. Some 16 or 18 of the tribe were living on Grand r. in 1881, but the majority, about 35, lived at Charenton, on the s. side of Bayou Tèche, in St Mary's parish, about 10 m. from the gulf. The remnant resides in the same district, but the present population is not known. The name of these Indians for themselves is Pántch-pinunkansh, 'men altogether red,' a designation apparently applied after the advent of the whites. The Chitimacha came into notice soon after the French settled Louisiana, through the murder by one of their men of the missionary St Cosme on the Mississippi in 1706. This was followed by protracted war with the French, who compelled them to sue for peace, which was granted by Bienville on condition that the head of the murderer be brought to him; this done, peace was concluded. The tribe then must have been reduced to a small number of warriors, though Le Page du Pratz, who was present at the final ceremony, says they arrived at the meeting place in many pirogues. Little is known in regard to their customs. Fish and the roots of native plants constituted their food, but later they planted maize and sweet potatoes. They were strict monogamists, and though the women appear to have had considerable authority in their government, there were no indications of

totems or the gentile system among them. The men wore their hair long, with a piece of lead at the end of the queue, and tattooed their arms, legs, and faces. The noonday sun is said to have been their principal deity. The dead were buried in graves, and after the flesh had decayed the bones were taken up and reinterred. Their villages or former settlements so far as known were: Amatpan, Grosse Tete Tcheti, Hipinimtch, Kamenakshtchat, Kushuh, Namukatsup, Nekunsisnis, Netpinunsh, Shoktangihanehetchinsh, Tchatikutingi, Tchatkasitunshki, Tsakhtsinshup. Chitimacha villages were situated also on the site of Donaldsonville, Ascension parish, on the w. bank of the Mississippi (here St Cosme was murdered in 1706), and at the mouth of Bayou Lafourche. See Trans. Anthrop. Soc. Wash., II, 148, 1883.   (A. S. G.)

Chetemachas.—Gallatin in Trans. Am. Ethnol. Soc., II, pt. 1, 77, 1848. Chetimachas.—Gallatin in Trans. Am. Antiq. Soc., II, 306, 1836. Chitimachas.—Ibid., 114. Pa'ntch pinunkansh.—Gatschet in Trans. Anthrop. Soc. Wash., II, 150, 1883. Shetimasha.—Ibid., 148. Shyoutémacha.—Ibid., 150 (early French form). Tchikěmahá.—Ibid. (Alibamu name). Tchitimachas.—Le Page du Pratz, Hist. de la Louisiane, I, 83, 1758. Tchoutymacha.—Gatschet, op. cit., 150 (early French form). Yachimichas.—Martin, Hist. La., I, 167, 1827 (mentioned with Chitimacha, but probably the same).

**Chitimachan Family.** A linguistic family consisting solely of the Chitimacha tribe (q. v.), from which it takes its name. See Powell in 7th Rep. B. A. E., 66, 1891.

**Chititiknewas** (Yokuts name). A former division of the Bankalachi that lived on upper Deer cr., s. E. of Tulare lake, Cal.   (A. L. K.)

Chetionewash.—Wessells (1853) in H. R. Ex. Doc. 76, 34th Cong., 3d sess., 32, 1857.

**Chitklin's Village.** A summer camp of one of the Taku chiefs (Koluschan family) named Tclītlĕn ('big *tclīt*,' a bird). 113 people were there in 1880.—Petroff in 10th Census, Alaska, 32, 1884.

**Chitlatamus.** A Kuitsh village on lower Umpqua r., Oreg.

Tci'-tlă-tă'-mus.—Dorsey in Jour. Am. Folk-lore, III, 231, 1890.

**Chitmunk.** See *Chipmunk.*

**Chitnak.** A Yuit Eskimo village on the s. shore of St Lawrence id., Bering sea.

Shetnak.—Elliott, Our Arct. Prov., map, 1886. Shitnak.—Nelson in 18th Rep. B. A. E., map, 1899.

**Chito** ('large' [people]). A Choctaw gens of the Watakihulata phratry.—Morgan, Anc. Soc., 162, 1878.

**Chitola.** The nearly extinct Rattlesnake clan of the Zuñi.

Chítola-kwe.—Cushing in 13th Rep. B. A. E., 368, 1896 (*kwe*='people').

**Chitsa** (refers to anything of a pale color; specifically, 'fair people'). One of the three classes or castes into which the Kutchakutchin are divided, the others being the Natesa and the Tangesatsa, faintly representing, respectively, "the aristocracy, the middle classes, and the poorer orders of civilized nations." Marriage was not allowed within the class or caste, however, and descent was in the female line.—Kirby in Smithson. Rep. 1864, 418, 1865; Hardisty, ibid., 1866, 315, 1872.

Chit-che-ah.—Jones in Smithson. Rep. 1866, 326, 1872. Chit-sa.—Kirby in Smithson. Rep. 1864, 418, 1865. Chitsah.—Hardisty in Smithson. Rep. 1866, 315, 1872. Chit-sangh.—Ibid. Etchian-Kρét.—Petitot, Trad. Ind. du Can. Nord-ouest, 14, 15, 1886. Tchit-che-ah.—Jones, ibid., 326.

**Chitto-Fanna-Chula.** See *Neamathla*.

**Chiuchin.** A former Chumashan village near Santa Barbara, Cal.—Taylor in Cal. Farmer, Apr. 24, 1863.

**Chiukak** ('pike village'). A Kaviagmiut village on the peninsula inclosing Golofnin bay, Alaska; pop. 15 in 1880.

Chiokuk.—Jackson, Reindeer in Alaska, map, 145, 1894. Chiookuk.—Petroff, 10th Census, Alaska, 11, 1884. Knecktakimut.—W. U. Tel. Exp., 1867, quoted by Baker, Geog. Dict. Alaska, 1901 (apparently the same). Scookuk.—Coast Surv. chart cited by Baker, ibid. Tchioukakmioute.—Zagoskin in Nouv. Ann. Voy., 5th s., XXI, map, 1850.

**Chiutaiina** (*Chiu-taína*). The Eagle clan of Taos pueblo, N. Mex. (F. W. H.)

**Chiwere** ('belonging to this place,' the home people). A term employed by J. O. Dorsey to designate a group of Siouan tribes, including the Oto, Iowa, and Missouri, for information regarding which, see under their respective names. Consult also Dorsey in 15th Rep. B. A. E., 1897; McGee, ibid., and the writings by Dorsey cited below.

'Ce'kiwere.—Dorsey in Bull. Philos. Soc. Wash., 128, 1880. 'Ciwere.—Ibid. Ookiwere.—Dorsey in Am. Antiq., 313, 1883 (misprint). Olwere.—Ibid. (misprint). Tcekiwere.—Dorsey in Am. Natur., 829, 1882. ɪoeɤiwere.—Dorsey in 3d Rep. B. A. E., 211, 1884. Tciwere.—Am. Natur., 829, 1882. Ti-re'-wi.—Dorsey in Am. Antiq., 168, 1879.

**Chizhu.** The 1st Ponka half-tribe, composed of 4 gentes.

Tciⁿju.—Dorsey in 15th Rep. B. A. E., 228, 1897.

**Chizhuwashtage** ('chizhu peacemaker'). The 15th Kansa gens, the 7th on the Yata side of the tribal circle.

Peacemaker.—Dorsey in Am. Natur., 671, July, 1885. Tciju Wactage.—Ibid.

**Chkungen.** A Songish band at McNeill bay, s. end of Vancouver id.

Tck'uñgē'n.—Boas in 6th Rep. N. W. Tribes Can., 17, 1890.

**Chlachaik.** Given by Krause as a Koluschan town occupied by the Tukdentan. Actually a summer camp on an island called Łā'xa, near Chichagof id., Alaska.

Chlachă-ĭk.—Krause, Tlinkit Ind., 118, 1885.

**Chlorite.**—A soft, greenish, often blackish, mineral, related to the micas, much used by the aborigines for ornaments, ceremonial objects, and pipes. When polished it is in many cases not readily distinguished from steatite or soapstone save by its somewhat greater hardness. It occurs as a secondary mineral resulting from alteration of other species, as biotite, pyroxene, amphibolite, etc. See *Stone-work*.                (W. H. H.)

**Chnagmiut** ('coast people'). An Alaskan Eskimo tribe occupying the shore of Pastol bay, the Yukon delta, and both banks of Yukon r. as far as Razboinski, Alaska. They hunt the seal and beluga, trap mink and muskrat, have fish in abundance, eggs, and berries, and no lack of driftwood; yet they often suffer privations, and their carelessly built villages are sometimes demolished by freshets. Subtribes are Ankachagmiut, Chukchagemiut, Koshkogemiut, Teletagmiut, and Ukagemiut. Their villages are Aiachagiuk, Aimgua, Alexief, Andreafski, Ankachak, Apoon, Ariswaniski, Avnulik, Chatinak, Chefoklak, Chukchuk, Claikehak, Fetkina, Ikuak, Ingichuk, Kanig, Kashutuk, Khaik, Kochkok, Komarof, Kotlik, Kusilvak, Kwiahok, Kwikak, Nigiklik, Ninvok, Nokrot, Nunapithlugak, Onuganuk, Pastoliak, Pastolik, Razboinski, Ribnaia, Staria Selenie, Starik, Takshak, Tiatiuk, Tlatek, and Uglovia. The tribe numbered 621 in 1890.

Agulmiut.—Worman quoted by Dall in Cont. N. A. Ethnol., I, 17, 1877. Kangjulit.—Erman quoted by Dall, ibid. Kaniulit.—Zagoskin quoted by Dall, ibid. Premorska.—Dall in Proc. A. A. A. S., 267, 1869 (Russian: 'people by the sea'). Premorski.—Dall in Cont. N. A. Ethnol., I, 17, 1877. Primoske.—Whymper, Trav. in Alaska, 235, 1868. Prinoski.—Raymond in Ind. Aff. Rep. 1869, 593, 1870. Tschnagmeuten.—Richardson, Arct. Exped., I, 370, 1851. Tschnagmjuten.—Holmberg, Ethnol. Skizz., 5, 1855. Tschnägmüten.—Wrangell, Ethnol. Nach., 122, 1839. Tsnagmyut.—Turner, MS. Unalit vocab., B. A. E. (= 'people of the outer edge, dwelling farthest seaward').

**Chobaabish.** A small band of Salish, subordinate to Skagit, on Swinomish res., Wash.; mentioned in Pt Elliott treaty of 1855; pop. 38 in 1870.

Che-baah-ah-bish.—Ross in Ind. Aff. Rep., 17, 1870. Cho-ba-abish.—Mallet in ibid., 198, 1877. Chobah-áh-bish.—U. S. Ind. Treat., 378, 1873.

**Chockrelatan** (*Thlcharghilii-tunne*, 'people away from the forks' of the stream). A former village of the Mishikhwutmetunne near the forks of Coquille r., Oreg. Their lands were drained by the waters of that stream, and the villagers were separated by mountain barriers from all neighbors except the Kusan, living on the coast.

Chak-re-le-a-ton.—Kautz, MS. Toutouten census, B. A. E., 1855. Chockrelatan.—Taylor in Cal. Farmer, June 8, 1860. Chockreletan.—Schoolcraft, Ind. Tribes, VI, 702, 1857. Choc-re-le-a-tan.—Parrish in Ind. Aff. Rep. 1854, 495, 1855. Çltc'a-rxi'-li-i' ʒûnně'.—Dorsey in Jour. Am. Folk-lore, III, 232, 1890 (= 'people away from the forks'). Okreletan.—Schoolcraft, Ind. Tribes, VI, 702, 1857.

**Choconikla.** A Seminole town, of about 60 warriors in 1820, on the w. side of Apalachicola r., contiguous to Ataphulga, on Little r., Decatur co., Ga. (A. S. G.)

Cho-co-nickla.—Bell in Morse, Rep. to Sec. War, 307, 1822.

**Chocorua.** The legendary last survivor of a small tribe of Indians who, previous to 1766, inhabited the region about the town of Burton, N. H. He was pursued by a white hunter to the mountain which bears his name and driven over the cliffs or shot to death. Before dying he is reported to have cursed the English and their cattle, and to this is attributed the fact that none of these animals thrive in Burton (Drake, Aboriginal Races, 285, 1880). It is possible that the chief has been conjured up to account for the name of the mountain.                    (A. F. C.)

**Choctaw** (from Choctaw *chah'ta*, of unknown meaning, but supposed to signify a separation—"separation from the Creeks and Seminole, who were once of one tribe."—Wright). An important tribe of the Muskhogean stock, formerly occupying middle and s. Mississippi, their territory extending, in their most flourishing days, E. of Tombigbee r., probably as far as Dallas co., Ga.

ALLEN WRIGHT—CHOCTAW

Ethnically they belong to the Choctaw branch of the Muskhogean family, which included the Choctaw, Chickasaw, Huma, and their allies, and some small tribes which formerly lived along Yazoo r. The dialects of the members of this branch are so closely related that they may be considered as practically identical (Gatschet, Creek Migr. Leg., I, 53, 1884). The earliest notice of these Indians is found in the De Soto narratives for 1540. The giant Tascalusa, whom he met in his march down Coosa valley and carried to Mauvila, was a Choctaw chieftain; and the natives who fought the Spaniards so fiercely at this town belonged to a closely related tribe. When the French, about the beginning of the 18th century, began to settle colonies at Mobile, Biloxi, and New Orleans, the Choctaw came early into friendly relations with them and were their allies in their wars against other Indian tribes. In the French war on the Natchez, in 1730, a large body of Choctaw warriors served under a French officer. They continued this friendship until the English traders succeeded in drawing over to the English interest some of the E. Choctaw towns. This brought on a war between them and the main body, who still adhered to the French, which continued until 1763. The tribe was constantly at war with the Creeks and Chickasaw. After the French had surrendered their American possessions to Great Britain, in 1763, and to some extent previously thereto, members of the tribe began to move across the Mississippi, where, in 1780, Milfort (Mémoire, 95, 1802) met some of their bands who were then at war with the Caddo. About 1809 a Choctaw village existed on Wichita r., and another on Bayou Chicot, Opelousas parish, La. Morse (1820) says there were 1,200 of them on the Sabine and Neches rs., and about 140 on Red r., near Pecan point (Rep. to Sec. War, 373, 1822). It is stated by some historians that this tribe, or parties of it, participated in the Creek war; this, however, is emphatically denied by Halbert (Creek War of 1813 and 1814, 124, 1895), who was informed in 1877 by some of the oldest members of the tribe that the Choctaw manifested no hostility toward the Americans during this conflict. A small band of perhaps 30 were probably the only Choctaw with the Creeks. The larger part of those in Mississippi began to migrate to Indian Ter. in 1832, having ceded most of their lands to the United States in various treaties (Royce, Indian Land Cessions, 18th Rep. B. A. E., 1899).

The Choctaw were preeminently the agriculturists of the southern Indians. Though brave, their wars in most instances were defensive. No mention is made of the "great house," or "the square," in Choctaw towns, as they existed in the Creek communities, nor of the busk (q. v.). The game of chunkey (q. v.), as well as the ball play (q. v.), was extensively practised by them. It was their custom to clean the bones of the dead before depositing them in boxes or baskets in the bone-houses, the work being performed by "certain old gentlemen with very long nails," who allowed their nails to grow long for this purpose. The people of this tribe also followed the custom of setting up poles around the new graves, on which they hung hoops, wreaths, etc., to aid the spirit in its ascent. They practised artificial head flattening and in consequence were sometimes called Flatheads.

The population of the tribe when it first came into relations with the French, about the year 1700, has been estimated at from 15,000 to 20,000. Their number in 1904 was 17,805, exclusive of 4,722 Choctaw freedmen (negroes). These are all under the Union agency, Ind. Ter. To these must be added a small number in Mississippi and Louisiana.

There are, or at least were formerly, several dialects spoken in different sections; these, however, differed so little that they have not been considered worthy of special mention. The small Muskhogean tribes known as Mobilian, Tohome or Tomez, Tawasa, Mugulasha, Acolapissa, Huma, and Conshac (q. v.), on the gulf coast of Mississippi and Alabama, are sometimes called Choctaw, but the Choctaw proper had their villages inland, on the upper courses of the Chickasawhay, Pearl, and Big Black rs. and the w. affluents of the Tombigbee. At least in later times they were distinguished into three sections, each under its mingo or chief. The western division was called Oklafalaya, 'the long people,' and consisted of small, scattered villages; the northeastern, Ahepatokla (Oypatukla), 'potato-eating people,' and the southeastern district came to be called Oklahannali, 'Sixtowns,' from the name of the dominant subdivision. The people of these two latter districts lived in large towns for mutual defense against their constant enemies the Creeks. Gatschet gives Cobb Indians as the name of those Choctaw settled w. of Pearl r.

According to Morgan (Ancient Society, 99, 162, 1877) the Choctaw were divided into two phratries, each including 4 gentes, as follows: A, Kushapokla (Divided people): 1, Kushiksa (Reed); 2, Lawokla; 3, Lulakiksa; 4, Linoklusha; B, Watakihulata (Beloved people): 1, Chufaniksa (Beloved people); 2, Iskutani (Small people); 3, Chito (Large people); 4, Shakchukla (Crayfish people). Besides these, mention is made of a gens named Urihesahe (Wright in Ind. Aff. Rep. 1843, 348), which has not been identified. Morgan's list is probably far from complete.

Following are names of Choctaw villages: Alamucha, Alloou Loanshaw, Ayanabi, Bayou Chicot, Bishkon, Bissasha, Bogue Toocola Chitto, Booctolooee, Boucfouca, Boutté Station, Cabea Hoola, Cahawba Old Towns, Cheponta's Village, Chicasawhay, Chinakbi, Chishafoka, Chiskelikbatcha, Chomontokali, Chooca Hoola, Chunkey, Chunkey Chitto, Coatraw, Coila, Concha, Conchachitou, Concha Consapa, Conchatikpi, Coosha, Couechitou, Cushtusha, Cutha Aimethaw, Cuthi Uckehaca, East Abeika, Ebita Poocolo Chitto, Ebita Poocolo Skatane, Es-

cooba, Etuck Chukke, Faluktabunnee, Haanka Ullah, Heitotowa, Hoola-tassa, Hopahka, Hushukwa, Hyukkeni, Ikatchiocata, Imongalasha, Imongalasha Skatane, Inkillis Tamaha, Kaffetalaya, Lukfa, Lushapa, Mahewala, Nashwaiya, Okaaltakala, Okachippo, Okacoopoly, Okahullo, Okakapassa, Okalusa, Okapoolo, Okatalaya, Okhatatalaya, Oktibbeha(?), Olitassa, Oony, Oskelagna, Osuktalaya, Otakshanabe, Panthe, Pineshuk, Pooscoostekale, Pooshapukanuk, Sapa Chitto, Sapeessa, Schekaha, Shanhaw, Shukhata, Shuqualak, Skanapa, Sukinatchi, Tala, Taliepataua, Talpahoka, Teeakhaily Ekutapa, Tombigbee, Tonicahaw, West Abeika, Wia Takali, Yagna Shoogawa, Yanatoe, Yazoo, Yazoo Skatane, Yowani. (J. R. S. C. T.)

**Ani'-Tsa'ta.** Mooney in 19th Rep. B. A. E., 509, 1900 (Cherokee name; sing. *Tsa'ta*). **ọa'-tă.**—Dorsey, Osage MS. vocab., B. A. E., 1883 (Osage name). **Chacatos.**—Barcia, Ensayo, 313, 1723. **Chacktaws.**—Jefferson (1781), Notes, 144, 1825. **Chactah.**—Rafinesque, Am. Nations, I, 241, 1836. **Chactanys.**—Ann. Propagation de la Foi, II, 380, 1841. **Chactas.**—Parraud, Hist. Kentucke, 111, 1785. **Chactaws.**—Jefferys, French Dom., I, 153, 1761. **Cha'hta.**—Gatschet in American Antiq., IV, 76, 1881-82. **Chaktaws.**—N. Y. Stat. at Large, Treaty of 1808, VII, 98, 1846. **Chaltas.**—Coxe, Carolana, map, 1741 (misprint). **Chaqueta.**—Iberville (1700) in Margry, Déc., IV, 463, 1880. **Chaquitas.** — Ibid., 419. **Chataw.** — Rogers, North America, 204, 1765. **Chat-Kas.**—Du Pratz, Hist. La., II, 216, 1758. **Chatkaws.**—Jefferys, French Dom., I, 165, 1761. **Chattaes.**—Coxe, Carolana, map, 1741. **Chattas.**—Ibid., 25. **Chattoes.**—Ibid., 22. **Chawetas.**—Perrin du Lac, Voy., 368, 1805. **Chectaws.**—Morse, N. Am., 218, 1776. **Chicktaws.**—Rogers, North America, 203, 1765. **Chictaws.**—Ibid., 238. **Chocataus.**—Disturnell, map Méjico, 1846. **Chocktaws.**—Ellicott, Jour., 35, 1797. **Chocta.**—Latham (1844) in Jour. Ethnol. Soc. Lond., I, 160, 1848. **Choctaughs.**—Catesby, Nat. Hist. Car., II, xi, 1743. **Choctaw.**—French writer (*ca.* 1727) in Shea, Cath. Missions, 429, 1855. **Choctos.**—Domenech, Deserts, II, 193, 1860. **Choktah.**—Barton, New Views, 1, 1798. **Choktaus.**—Am. Pioneer, I, 408, 1842. **Choktaw.**—Boudinot, Star in the West, 184, 1816. **Chouactas.**—Martin, Hist. of La., I, 249, 1827. **Chukaws.**—Boudinot, op. cit., 1826. **Flat Heads.**—Jefferys, French Dom., 135, map, 1761. **Flats.**—Bartram, Travels, 515, 1791. **Henne'sh.**—Gatschet, inf'n (Arapaho name). **Nabuggindebaig.**—Tanner, Narrative, 316, 1830, ('flat heads': the name given by the Ottawa to a tribe "said to have lived below the Illinois r."; probably Choctaw). **Sanakiwa.**—Gatschet, inf'n (Cheyenne name: 'feathers sticking up above the ears'). **Shacktaus.**—Penhallow (1726) in N. H. Hist. Coll., 1st s., 79, 1824. **Shocktaus.**—Niles (1760) in Mass. Hist. Coll., 4th s., 332, 1861. **Tá-qta.**—Dorsey, Kwapa MS. vocab., B. A. E., 1891 (Kwapa name). **Tca-qtá aⁿ-ya-dí.**—Dorsey, Biloxi MS. Dict., B. A. E., 1892 (one of the Biloxi names). **Tca-qtá haⁿ-ya.**—Ibid. (another Biloxi name). **Tca-tá.**—Ibid., Kansa MS. vocab., B. A. E., 1882 (Kansa name). **Tchactas.**—Charlevoix, Voy. to N. A., II, 210, 1766. **Tchataws.**—Margry, Déc., II, 197, 1877. **Tchiactas.**—Bienville (1708) in N. Y. Doc. Col. Hist., IX, 925, 1855. **Têtes Plates.**—Picquet letter (1752) in Parkman, Montcalm and Wolfe, II, 417, 1884. **Tsah-tû.**—Grayson, Creek MS. vocab., B. A. E., 1885 (Creek name). **Tsaꭓta.**—Müller, Grundriss der Sprachwissenschaft, II, pt. 1, 232, 1882. **Tschaktaer.**—Ally (1712), Historie der Reisen, xvi, 1758. **Tubbies.**—Am. Notes and Queries, VIII, 281, Apr. 16, 1892.

**Choctaw Capitale.** On a French map of 1777 this name appears on an affluent of Pascagoula r., Miss., E. of Yowani and Chicasawhay. On Philippeaux's map of the English colonies in 1781 it is located w. of Yowani. Possibly identifiable with Inkillis, q. v.

**Chaetaw Capitaleo.**—Bartram, Voy., I, map, 1799 (misprint).

**Chogset.** A New England name of the cunner, blue perch, or burgall (*Ctenolabrus cæruleus*). Gerard (Sun, N. Y., July 30, 1895) says the word means 'it is flabby', in Chippewa *shagosi*. Trumbull (Natick Dict., 30, 1903) derives *chogset*, in Pequot *cachauxet*, from *chohchohkesit* in the Massachuset dialect, signifying 'spotted' or 'striped,' which is a much preferable etymology.    (A. F. C.)

**Chohalaboohhulka.** A former Seminole town on the w. side of Suwanee r., above its junction with the Alapaha, in Hamilton co., Fla.—H. R. Ex. Doc. 74 (1823), 19th Cong., 27, 1826.

**Choinimni** (pl. Chuyenmani). A Mariposan tribe on Kings r., at or near the mouth of Mill cr., Cal. Powers calls them Chainimaini and says they lived downstream from the Tisechu and above the Iticha. Only a few families are left.

**Chai-nim'-ai-ni.**—Powers in Cont. N. A. Ethnol., III, 370, 1877. **Chewenee.**—Gatschet in Mag. Am. Hist., 158, 1877. **Choemimnees.**—Taylor in Cal. Farmer, June 8, 1860. **Cho-e-nem-nee.**—Royce in 18th Rep. B. A. E., 782, 1899. **Choe-nim-ne.**—Merriam in Science, XIX, 915, June 17, 1904. **Cho-e-nim-nees.**—Ind. Aff. Rep., 223, 1851. **Choe-wem-nes.**—Johnston (1851) in Sen. Ex. Doc. 61, 32d Cong., 1st sess., 23, 1852. **Choo-nemnes.**—Ibid., 22. **Chow-e-nim-ne.**—Wessells (1853) in H. R. Ex. Doc. 76, 34th Cong., 3d sess., 31, 1857. **Chunemmes.**—Henley in Ind. Aff. Rep., 511, 1854.

**Choinok.** A small Mariposan tribe, nearly extinct, which formerly inhabited the locality just s. of where the town of Visalia now stands, in Tulare co., Cal.

**Cho-e-nees.**—Barbour (1852) in Sen. Ex. Doc. 4, 32d Cong., spec. sess., 253, 1853. **Cho-e-nuco.**—Ibid., 254. **Choinóc.**—Garcés (1775–76), Diary, 289, 1900. **Choinook.**—Wessells (1853) in H. R. Ex. Doc. 76, 34th Cong., 3d sess., 32, 1857. **Choi-nuck.**—Royce in 18th Rep. B. A. E., 782, 1899. **Choinucks.**—Johnston (1851) in Sen. Ex. Doc. 61, 32d Cong., 1st sess., 22, 1852.

**Chokatowela** ('blue spot in the middle'). A band of the Brulé Teton Sioux.

**Choke-tar-to-womb.**—Lewis and Clark, Discov., 34, 1806 (probably synonymous). **Čoka-towela.**—Dorsey in 15th Rep. B. A. E., 218, 1897. **Tcoka-towela.**—Ibid.

**Chokishgna.** A former Gabrieleño rancheria in Los Angeles co., Cal., at a locality later called Jaboneria.

**Chokisgna.**—Taylor in Cal. Farmer, June 8, 1860. **Chokishgna.**—Ibid., June 11, 1861.

**Chokoukla.** A former Seminole town on the w. side of Apalachicola r., 4 m. below the forks, in Florida. Mulatto King was chief in 1823.—H. R. Ex. Doc. 74, 19th Cong., 27, 1826.

**Chokuyem.** The name probably applied originally to a single village somewhere in Petaluma valley, Sonoma co., Cal. It gained a wider significance, being used by Gibbs to designate all the Indians in the region from San Rafael mission N. to Santa Rosa and E. to Suscol, and by others

in a still broader sense as the name of a division of what they termed the Olamentke, and comprising all the Indians in Petaluma and Sonoma valleys. This latter broad significance is probably due to the association at Sonoma mission of the original Chokuyem people with those from various other villages.    (S. A. B.)

**Chocouyem.**—Latham (1853) in Proc. Philol. Soc. Lond., VI, 83, 1854. **Cho-kú-yen.**—Powers in Cont. N. A. Ethnol., III, 195, 1877. **Petaluma.**—Taylor in Cal. Farmer, Oct. 18, 1861. **Petlenum.**—Ibid. **Tcho-ko-yem.**—Gibbs in Schoolcraft, Ind. Tribes, III, 421, 1853. **Tshokoyem.**—Latham in Trans. Philol. Soc. Lond., 1856.

**Cholicus.** A former Chumashan village near Santa Inés mission, Cal.—Taylor in Cal. Farmer, Oct. 18, 1861.

**Cholocco Litabixee** (*Chu-'láko íli-tapíksi* 'horse's flat foot.'—A. S. G.). A former Upper Creek village on a bend of Tallapoosa r., Ala., in the river bottom, where, on Mar. 27, 1814, the defeat of the Redstick party took place at the battle of the Horseshoe.—Pickett, Hist. Ala., II, 341, 1851.

**Cholosoc.** A former Chumashan village near Santa Barbara, Cal.—Taylor in Cal. Farmer, Apr. 24, 1863.

**Cholovone.** A tribe or group of tribes constituting a portion of the Mariposan family, inhabiting San Joaquin valley, Cal., and occupying a strip of territory along the E. bank of San Joaquin r. in the vicinity of Stockton, from the Tuolumne to about Calaveras r. They were thus separated by Moquelumnan tribes from the main body of the family farther s. Little is known about them, and they are probably extinct. A Yokuts vocabulary (Powers in Cont. N. A. Ethnol., III, 571, 1877), from Takin or Dents Ferry on Stanislaus r., at the foot of the Sierra, may be from Cholovone territory. The following divisions or subtribes of the Cholovone are mentioned: Chupcan, Sawani, Yachikamni, Yachimese, and Yukolumni. The following are mentioned as Cholovone villages: Bantas, Heluta, Hosmite, Khulpuni, Mitutra, Pashashe, Takin, Tammakan, and Tawi. Somewhat doubtful are Lakisumne and Tuolumne, which may have been Moquelumnan.

**Cholobone.**—Pinart, Yokuts MS., B. A. E., 1880. **Cholovone.**—Ibid. **Tchalabones.**—Chamisso in Kotzebue Voy., III, 51, 1821. **Tcholoones.**—Bancroft, Nat. Races, I, 453, 1874 (misquoted from Chamisso). **Tcholovones.**—Chamisso, op. cit.

**Cholupaha.** A Timuquanan town in N. Florida, visited by De Soto's troops in Aug., 1539, before reaching Aquacalecuen. They spoke of it as a *villa farta*, a town of plenty, because they found an abundance of Indian corn there.—Gentl. of Elvas (1557) in French, Hist. Coll. La., II, 131, 1850.

**Chomaath** (*Tcŏ'māath*). A sept of the Toquart, a Nootka tribe.—Boas in 6th Rep. N. W. Tribes Can., 32, 1890.

**Chomchadila** ('pitch-pine'—Powers; or 'white-pine ridge'—Kroeber). A former Pomo village on the mesa s. w. of Calpella, Mendocino co., Cal.
Choam-Cha-di′-la Pómo.—Powers in Cont. N. A. Ethnol., III, 155, 1877.

**Chomonchouaniste.** A name given on several maps as that of a tribe formerly living N. w. of L. St John, Quebec. Probably a Montagnais band or settlement.
Chemonchovanistes.—Esnauts and Rapilly map, 1777. Chomonchouanistes.—Bellin map, 1755. Chomoncouanistes.—Lotter map, ca. 1755. Chomonehouanistes.—Lattré map, 1784.

**Chomontokali** (*shomo-takali*, 'hanging moss'). A former town of the Oypatukla or northeastern division of the Choctaw, consisting of 8 hamlets, with garden patches intervening, extending E. and w. about 2 m. and about ½ m. in width; situated between two head-streams of Black Water cr., in Kemper co., Miss. In 1830 the residence of Nita Homma, 'Red Bear,' was in the third hamlet from the w., and about 1,200 yds. s. of the site of his house is a mound about 12 ft. high. The town was on the trail that extended E. and w. from Imongolasha to Haankaulla.—Halbert in Miss. Hist. Soc. Publ., VI, 418, 1902.
Chomontakali.—Romans, Fla., map, 1775. Chomontokali.—West Fla. map, ca. 1775. Shomo Takali.—Halbert, op. cit.

**Chonacate.**—A Huichol settlement at the E. border of their territory, in the Sierra de los Huicholes, Jalisco, Mexico.—Lumholtz, Unknown Mex., II, 16, map, 1902.

**Chonakera.** The Black Bear gens of the Winnebago.
Bear.—Morgan, Anc. Soc., 157, 1877. Black bear.—Dorsey, MS. Winnebago vocab., B. A. E., 1878. Hone′-cha′-dä.—Morgan, Anc. Soc., 157, 1877. Honto′ i-ki′-ka-ra′-tca-da.—Dorsey in 15th Rep. B. A. E., 240, 1897 ('they who call themselves after the black bear'). Tco′-na-ke-rä.—Ibid. (archaic name).

**Chongasketon.** A division of the Sisseton Sioux, identified by Riggs as the Lac Traverse band; possibly the same as the Sisseton proper of Pike; applied by early writers to the whole tribe and interpreted Wolf or Dog nation, though now recognized as a form of the word Sisseton.
Chongaskabes.—Barcia, Ensayo, 238, 1723. Chongaskabion.—Hennepin quoted by Neill in Minn. Hist. Coll., I, 257, 1872. Chongaskethon.—Hennepin quoted by Shea, Early Voy. Miss., 111, 1861. Chongasketon.—Hennepin, New Discov., 185, 1698. Chongonsceton.—Neill, op. cit., 260 (misprint). Chongousceton.—Carver, Trav., 80, 1778. Chonkasketonwan.—Williamson quoted by Neill, op. cit., 260 (interpreted 'dwellers in a fort' and applied to the Sisseton of L. Traverse). Chonsgaskaby.—Hennepin, New Discov., map, 1698. Chougaskabees.—McKenney and Hall, Ind. Tribes, III, 80, 1854. Chougasketon.—La Salle (1679–81) in Margry, Déc., I, 481, 1876. Cnongasgaba.—Coxe, Carolana, map, 1741 (misprint). Conkasketonwan.—Riggs, Dakota Gram. and Dict., introd., ix, 1852.

**Chongyo.** The Pipe clan of the Piba (Tobacco) phratry of the Hopi.
Tcoñ-o.—Stephen in 8th Rep. B. A. E., 39, 1891. Tcoñ wüñ-wü.—Fewkes in Am. Anthrop., VII, 405, 1894 (*wüñ-wü* = 'clan').

**Chonodote** (perhaps *tyohnodote*,' 'where a spring issues.'—Hewitt). A former Cayuga settlement located on Machin's map of Sullivan's expedition (Conover, MS., B. A. E.) on the E. side of Cayuga lake, a few miles s. of the present Cayuga, N. Y. It was probably destroyed by Sullivan in 1779.

**Chonque.** Probably a Choctaw band on Yazoo r., Miss., below the Tioux, in the 17th century. See *Chunkey.*
Chenkus.—McKenney and Hall, Ind. Tribes, III, 80, 1854. Chongue.—Coxe, Carolana, 12, 1741. Chonque.—Tonti (1690) in French, Hist. Coll. La., 82, 1846.

**Chooahlitsh.** A former Samish settlement in the canoe passage E. of Hidalgo id., N. w. Wash.
Choo-áh-litsh.—Gibbs, MS. no. 248, B. A. E.

**Chooca Hoola** (*chúka* 'house,' 'lodge,' *hullo* 'beloved'). A former Choctaw settlement on the N. side of Sukenatcha cr., between the mouths of Running Tiger and Straight crs., in the N. part of Kemper Co., Miss.—Halbert in Miss. Hist. Soc. Publ., VI, 425, 1902.
Chooca Hoola.—Romans, Florida, map, 1775. Chooka-hoola.—Ibid., 310.

**Choppatee's Village.** A former Miami village on the w. bank of St Joseph r., a few miles from Ft Wayne, Allen co., Ind. Named after a chief who resided there. The tract was granted to J. B. Boure, an interpreter, by treaty of Oct. 23, 1826.

**Choptank.** Apparently a tribe consisting of 3 subtribes—the Ababco, Hutsawap, and Tequassimo—formerly living on Choptank r. in Maryland. In 1741 they were given a reserve near Secretary cr., on the s. side of Choptank r., in Dorchester co., on the Eastern shore, where a few of mixed Indian and negro blood still remained in 1837. See Bozman, Maryland, I, 115, 1837.

**Chorofa** ('bird'). A clan of the Apohola phratry of the ancient Timucua of Florida.—Pareja (1614) quoted by Gatschet in Proc. Am. Philos. Soc., XVII, 492, 1878.

**Choromi.** A Costanoan village formerly situated near Santa Cruz mission, Cal.—Taylor in Cal. Farmer, Apr. 5, 1860.

**Chorruco.** A tribe, formerly on the Texas coast, to whom Cabeza de Vaca fled from the Coaque with whom he had lived nearly a year after shipwreck on Malhado id. in 1528. The people, he said, took their name from the woods in which they lived. He stayed with this tribe about 6 years, traveling and trading with others in the vicinity and inland. The region was probably the home of the Karankawan family at that time. The Chorruco are now extinct. See Gatschet, Karankawa Indians, Peabody Museum Papers, I, 46, 1891.            (A. C. F.)
Carruco.—Harris, Voy. and Trav., I, 802, 1705. Charruco.—Cabeza de Vaca, Smith trans., 53, 1851.

**Chorruco.**—Ibid., 84. **Chorucco.**—Smith, Cabeza de Vaca, index, 1871. **Choruico.**—Latham, Elem. Comp. Philol., 466, 1862.

**Chosho.** A Chumashan village formerly on Santa Cruz id., Cal., probably E. of Prisoner's harbor.
**Toö-cö.**—Henshaw, Buenaventura MS. vocab., B. A. E., 1884.

**Chosro.** The Bluebird clan of the Hopi. **Choro.**—Dorsey and Voth, Mishongnovi Ceremonies, 175, 1902. **Chorzh.**—Voth, Oraibi Summer Snake Ceremony, 283, 1903. **Chórzh-ñamu.**—Voth, Trad. of the Hopi, 37, 1905. **Tco'-ro wüñ-wü.**—Fewkes in Am. Anthrop., VII, 404, 1894 (*wüñ-wü* =‘clan’). **Tcosro wiñwû.**—Fewkes in 19th Rep. B. A. E., 584, 1900. **Tco'-zir.**—Stephen in 8th Rep. B. A. E., 38, 1891 (given as the Jay clan).

**Chotanksofkee** (*tchat aksofka* ‘precipice’). A town situated 1 m. s. w. of Eufaula, in the Creek Nation, Ind. Ter. (H. R. Doc. 80, 27th Cong., 3d sess., 8, 1843). In the old Creek country there was formerly a settlement of the same name, probably near Abikudshi, E. of upper Coosa r., Ala.     (A. S. G.)

**Choupetoulas.** A village formerly on the left bank of the Mississippi, 2 or 3 leagues above New Orleans; spoken of by Pénicaut in 1718 as old and apparently abandoned. The name of the people, who were possibly of Choctaw affinity, is perpetuated in that of a street in New Orleans.     (A. S. G.)
**Chapitoulas.**—Dumont, La., I, 13, 1753. **Choupitoulas.**—Pénicaut (1718) in French, Hist. Coll. La., 141, 1869. **Tchoupitoulas.**—French, Hist. Coll. La., III, 59, note, 1851.

**Choutikwuchik** (Pima: *Tcóŭtĭk Wŭ'tcĭk*, ‘charcoal laying’). A former village of the Maricopa, in s. Arizona, which was abandoned by its inhabitants on their removal down the Gila to their present location below Gila crossing. It was then occupied by the Pima, who in turn abandoned it.—Russell, MS., B. A. E., 16, 1902.

**Chowanoc** (Algonquian: *shawŭni* ‘south’; *shawŭnogi* ‘they of the south,’ ‘southerners.’—W. J.). A tribe formerly living on Chowan r., N. E. N. C., about the junction of Meherrin and Nottoway rs. In 1584–85, when first known, they were the leading tribe in that region. Two of their villages at that time were Ohanoak and Maraton, and they probably occupied also Catoking and Metocaum. Ohanoak alone was said to have had 700 warriors. They gradually dwindled away before the whites, and in 1701 were reduced to a single village on Bennetts cr. They joined in the Tuscarora war against the whites in 1711–12, and at its close the remnant, estimated at about 240, were assigned a small reservation on Bennetts and Catherine crs. In 1820 they were supposed to be extinct. In addition to the settlements named, the Chowanoc also occupied Ramushonok.     (J. M.)
**Chawanook.**—Barlow (1584) in Smith (1629), Virginia, I, 84, repr. 1819. **Chawanook.**—Greenville (1585) in Hawks, N. C., I, 112, 1859. **Chawonacks.**—Mass. Hist. Soc. Coll., 4th s., IX, 15, 1871. **Chawonests.**—Lane (1586) in Smith (1629), Virginia, I, 88, repr. 1819. **Chawonoack.**—Ibid., 87, 90. **Chawonock.**—Ibid. **Chawonoks.**—Ibid. **Chawons.**—Dutch map (1621) in N. Y. Doc. Col. Hist., I, 1856. **Chawoon.**—Horne, map (1666) in Hawks, N. C., II, 1858. **Chawwonoocks.**—Smith (1629), op. cit., I, 75, repr. 1819. **Chawwonoke.**—Pots, ibid., 230. **Choan.**—Doc of 1653 in N. C. Rec., I, 17, 1886. **Choanists.**—Lane (1586) in Hakluyt, Voy., III, 314, repr.1810. **Chowah.**—Latham, Elem.Comp.Philol., 466, 1862. **Chowan.**—Doc. of 1663 in N. C. Rec., I, 54, 1886. **Chowane.**—Ibid., 55. **Chowanoake.**—Doc. of 1707, ibid., 657. **Chowanocs.**—Jefferson, Notes, 129, 1825. **Chowanok.**—Drake, Bk. Inds., vii, 1848. **Chowanooke.**—Strachey (*ca.* 1612), Virginia, 143, 1849. **Chowou.**—Lawson (1710), Hist. Car., 353, repr. 1860 (misprint for Chuwon). **Chuwon.**—Ibid., 383. **Shawan.**—Lederer (1670) in Hawks, N. C., II, 45, 1858 (used as a synonym for Roanoke r.)

**Chowchilla.** A name applied in various forms to two distinct divisions of California, one belonging to the Miwok (Moquelumnan family), the other to the Yokuts (Mariposan family). The former lived on the upper waters of Fresno and Chowchilla rs., and the latter, properly called Chaushila (q. v.), probably on lower Chowchilla r., in the plains and lowest foothills. Recorded under many forms of the same name from the time of the gold excitement, the two divisions have been inextricably confused. A treaty was made with them and numerous other tribes Apr. 29, 1851, by which a tract between Chowchilla and Kaweah rs. was reserved for their use. At this time the Yokuts Chowchilla, or Chaushila, together with the Howeches, Chukchansi, Pohoniche, and Nukchu were said to be under a single chief called Naiyakqua. The Miwok division, apparently, were considered the most powerful and warlike people of that region, and to them was attributed the greater part of the hostilities, murders, and robberies that had occurred, although this arraignment is probably due to nothing more than the defense by the Indians of themselves and their homes against the depredations of lawless whites. These numbered only 85 in 1857. The reservation was abandoned by 1859, and a smaller one, w. of Madera, was set aside; this, however, was seemingly never confirmed. There are some survivors of the Miwok Chowchilla living along the upper waters of the stream that bears their name.
**Chau-chil'-la.**—Powers in Cont. N. A. Ethnol., III, 349, 1877. **Chouchillas.**—Barbour et al. (1851) in Sen. Ex. Doc. 4, 32d Cong., spec. sess., 61, 1853. **Chouchille.**—Johnston (1851), ibid., 65. **Chou-chillies.**—McKee et al. (1851), ibid., 74. **Chow-chi-la.**—Wessells (1853) in H. R. Ex. Doc. 76, 34th Cong., 3d sess., 30, 1857. **Chow-chi-liers.**—Johnston in Sen. Ex. Doc. 61, 32d Cong., 1st sess., 22, 1852. **Chowchillas.**—Lewis in Ind. Aff. Rep. 1857, 399, 1858. **Chowchille.**—Johnston (1851) in Sen. Ex. Doc. 4, 32d Cong., spec. sess., 64, 1853. **Chow-chill-ies.**—McKee et al. in Ind. Aff. Rep., 223, 1851. **Chowclas.**—Henley in Ind. Aff. Rep., 512, 1854. **Cowchillas.**—Beale (1852) in Sen. Ex. Doc. 4, 32d Cong., spec. sess., 378, 1853.

**Chowigna.** A Gabrieleño rancheria formerly at Palos Verdes, Los Angeles co., Cal.—Ried (1852) quoted by Taylor in Cal. Farmer, June 8, 1860.

Unaungna.—Kroeber, inf'n, 1905 (Luiseño name).

**Choye.** A village, mentioned by Tonti (French, Hist. Coll. La., I, 72, 1846) in 1690, as near the settlements of the Yatasi on Red r., in the N. w. part of what is now Louisiana. The people were said to be hostile to the Kadohadacho, perhaps some passing quarrel. From its association with the Yatasi and Natasi, the village was probably inhabited by a subdivision of one of the Caddo tribes. The subsequent history of the settlement is not known; its inhabitants were probably scattered among their kindred during the contentions of the 18th century, later becoming extinct. (A. C. F.)

Chaye.—Margry, Déc., III, 409, 1878. Choye.—Tonti (1690) in French, Hist. Coll. La., I, 72, 1846.

**Choyopan** ('moving the eyelids or eyebrows'). A Tonkawa clan.

Tchóyopan.—Gatschet, Tonkawe vocab., B. A. E., 1884.

**Chozetta.** Mentioned in 1699 by Iberville (Margry, Déc., IV, 154, 193, 195, 311, 1880), who, after speaking of the "nation of the Annocchy and Moctobi" (q. v.), says: "They told me of a village of their neighbors, the Chozettas; they are on a river whose entrance is 9 leagues to the E., which they call Pascoboulas." In Gatschet's opinion the people of this village were Choctaw.

**Christanna Indians.** A group of Siouan tribes of Virginia, which were collected for a time in the early years of the 18th century at Ft Christanna, on Meherrin r., near the present Gholsonville, Va. Gov. Spotswood settled these tribes there about 1700 in the belief that they would form a barrier on that side against hostile Indians. The tribes were the Meipontsky, Occaneechi, Saponi, Stegaraki, and Tutelo. See Mooney, Siouan Tribes of the East, Bull. B. A. E., 1894.

Christanna Indians.—N. Y. Council minutes cited in N. Y. Doc. Col. Hist., V, 671, note, 1855. Christian Indians.—Albany conf. (1722), ibid., 671. Todirichroones.—Ibid., 673 (Iroquois name).

**Christianshaab.** A Moravian missionary station among the Eskimo near Spring bay, w. Greenland.—Crantz, Hist. Greenland, I, 13, 1820.

**Chua.** The Snake phratry of the Hopi, comprising the following clans: Chua (Snake), Tohouh (Puma), Huwi (Dove), Ushu (Columnar cactus), Puna (Cactus fruit), Yungyu (Opuntia), Nabowu (Opuntia frutescens), Pivwani (Marmot), Pihcha (Skunk), Kalashiauu (Raccoon). The Tubish (Sorrow), Patung (Squash), Atoko (Crane), Kele (Pigeonhawk), and Chinunga (Thistle) clans also belonged to this phratry, but are now extinct. According to tradition this people came from a place called Tokonabi, about the junction of San Juan and Colorado rs., and were the second migratory body to reach Tusayan. See Fewkes in Am. Anthrop., VII, 402, 1894, and in 19th Rep. B. A. E., 582, 1901.

Tcû'-a nyû-mu.—Fewkes in Am. Anthrop., VII, 402, 1894 (nyû-mu='phratry'). Tcuin nyumu.—Stephen in 8th Rep. B. A. E., 35, 1891.

**Chua.** The Rattlesnake clan of the Chua (Rattlesnake) phratry of the Hopi.

Chia.—Bourke, Snake Dance, 117, 1884. Tcû.—Voth, Oraibi Summer Snake Ceremony, 282, 1903. Tcu'-a.—Stephen in 8th Rep. B. A. E., 38, 1891. Tcûa.—Dorsey and Voth, Mishongnovi Ceremonies, 174, 1902. Tcüa wiñwû.—Fewkes in 19th Rep. B. A. E., 582, 1901 (wiñwû='clan'). Tcu'-a-wuñ-wü.—Fewkes in Am. Anthrop., VII, 402, 1894 (wuñ-wü='clan').

**Chuah.** A former Chumashan village at La Goleta, 6 m. from Santa Barbara mission, Cal.—Taylor in Cal. Farmer, May 4, 1860.

**Chuarlitilik.** A deserted Kuskwogmiut Eskimo village on Kanektok r., Alaska.—Spurr and Post quoted by Baker, Geog. Dict. Alaska, 1901.

**Chuba.** A Papago village in s. Arizona; pop. about 250 in 1863.—Ind. Aff. Rep., 385, 1863.

**Chubio.** The Antelope clan of the Ala (Horn) phratry of the Hopi.

To'ib-io.—Stephen in 8th Rep. B. A. E., 38, 1891. Tcübio wiñwû.—Fewkes in 19th Rep. B. A. E., 583, 1901. Tcüb'-i-yo wüñ-wü.—Fewkes in Am. Anthrop., VII, 401, 1894 (wüñ-wü='clan').

**Chubkwichalobi** (Hopi: 'antelope notch place'). A group of ruined pueblos on the hills above Chaves pass, 20 m. s. w. of Winslow, Ariz., claimed by the Hopi to have been built and occupied by some of their clans. Excavations by the Bureau of American Ethnology in 1897 revealed mortuary objects practically identical in character with those found in the valleys of the Verde and the Gila to the southward, thus indicating a common origin. See Fewkes in 22d Rep. B. A. E., 32, 1904.

Chaves Pass ruin.—Fewkes, ibid. Jettipehika.—Ibid. (Navaho name, with same meaning). Tcübkwitcalobi.—Ibid. (Hopi name).

**Chucalissa** ('great town'). One of the former Chickasaw settlements in N. Mississippi, probably in Pontotoc or Dallas co.

Chickalina.—West Fla. map, ca. 1775. Chook'heereso.—Adair, Am. Inds., 353, 1775. Chucalissa.—Romans, Florida, I, 63, 1775.

**Chuchictac.** A former village, presumably Costanoan, connected with Dolores mission, San Francisco, Cal.—Taylor in Cal. Farmer, Oct. 18, 1861.

**Chuchtononeda.** A Mohawk division formerly occupying the s. side of Mohawk r., N. Y., from Schenectady almost to Schoharie cr. (Macauley, N. Y., II, 295, 1829). Their principal village probably bore the same name.

**Chuchunayha.** A body of Okinagan, of the Similkameen group, in s. w. British Columbia; pop. 52 in 1901.

**Cheh-chewe-hem.**—Can. Ind. Aff. for 1883, 191. **Chuchunayha.**—Ibid., 1901, pt. II, 166. **Chuchuwayha.**—Ibid., 1894, 278.

**Chuckchuqualk** ('red place'). A Shuswap village on North Thompson r., Brit. Col.; pop. 129 in 1902.

**Chakchuqualk.**—Can. Ind. Aff. 1894, 277, 1895. **Chuchuqualk.**—Ibid., 244, 1902. **Chukchukualk.**—Ibid., 1892, 312, 1893. **Chuk-chu-quaeh-u.**—Ibid., 1885, 196, 1886. **Chukchuqualk.**—Ibid., 1886, 230, 1887. **North River.**—Ibid., 78, 1878. **North Thompson.**—Ibid., 74, 1878. **Tsuk-tsuk-kwālk'.**—Dawson in Trans. Roy. Soc. Can., sec. II, 44, 1891.

**Chucktin.** The southernmost Tillamook village on a creek emptying into Tillamook bay, N. W. Oreg., in 1805.

**Chucklin.**—Lewis and Clark, Exped., II, 148, 1817. **Chuck-tins.**—Orig. Jour. Lewis and Clark, VI, 71, 1905.

**Chueachiki** ('snouts'). A Tarahumare rancheria in Chihuahua, Mexico.—Lumholtz, inf'n, 1894.

**Chuemdu.** A Nishinam village formerly existing in the valley of Bear r., Cal.

**Che'-em-duh.**—Powers in Cont. N. A. Ethnol., III, 316, 1877.

**Chueskweskewa** ('snipe'). A gens of the Chippewa.       (J. M.)

**Chufaniksa** (*Chu-fan-ik'-sa*, 'beloved people'). A Choctaw clan of the Watakihulata phratry.—Morgan, Anc. Soc., 162, 1878.

**Chuga** (*Tc!ū'uga*, 'to go for cedar planks'). A Haida town of the Gunghetgitunai, near Houston Stewart channel and the abandoned town of Ninstints, Queen Charlotte ids., Brit. Col.—Swanton, Cont. Haida, 277, 1905.

**Chugachigmiut.** An Eskimo tribe occupying the territory extending from the w. extremity of Kenai penin. to the delta of Copper r., Alaska, and lying between the Kaniagmiut and Ugalakmiut. The Ugalakmiut have been almost absorbed by the Tlingit, who are encroaching on the Chugachigmiut also, who are now poor, although blubber, salmon, cod, halibut, ptarmigan, marmot, and bear are obtained in abundance, and occasionally a mountain sheep. The sea otter has become scarce, but silver fox and other fur-bearing animals are hunted and trapped, and the fish canneries afford employment. The hair seal is abundant, furnishing covers for the kaiaks as well as meat, blubber, and oil. The tribe numbered 433 in 1890. Their villages are Ingamatsha, Kanikluk, Kiniklik, Nuchek, and Tatitlek.

**Choogaks.**—Elliott, Cond. Aff. Alaska, 29, 1874. **Chuga.**—Dall in Cont. N. A. Ethnol., I, map, 1877. **Chugach.**—Petroff in Am. Nat., XVI, 568, 1882. **Chugachigmiut.**—11th Census, Alaska, 66, 1893. **Chūgăch'ig-mūt.**—Dall, op. cit., 20. **Chugachimute.**—Petroff, 10th Census, Alaska, 164, 1884. **Chugackimute.**—Ibid., map. **Chugatch.**—Petroff in Internat. Rev., XII, 113, 1882. **Tatliakhtana.**—Petroff, 10th Census, Alaska, 164, 1884 (so called by Kinai). **Tschugatschi.**—Humboldt, New Spain, II, 393, 1811. **Tschugazzes.**—Rink in Jour. Anthrop. Inst., XV, 240, 1885. **Tschugazzi.**—Prichard, Phys. Hist., V, 371, 1847. **Tshugazzi.**—Gallatin in Trans. Am. Antiq. Soc., II, 14, 1836.

**Chugita** ('edge of a precipice'). A Tarahumare rancheria of about 30 fami-

lies, not far from Norogachic, Chihuahua, Mexico.—Lumholtz, inf'n, 1894.

**Chugnut.** A small tribe living, about 1755, under Iroquois protection in a village of the same name on the s. side of Susquehanna r., opposite Binghamton, Broome co., N. Y. In 1758 they were on the Susquehanna with the Nanticoke, Conoy, and Tutelo. Choconut cr. takes its name from the tribe. Conoy, Mahican, Nanticoke, Shawnee, and probably Munsee bands also resided there, and the name may have been a local, not a tribal, designation.       (J. M.)

**Chaghnutt.**—Ft Johnson conf. (1756) in N. Y. Doc. Col. Hist., VII, 50, 1856. **Chagnet.**—Imlay, W. Ter., 291, 1797. **Chucknutts.**—Ft Johnson conf., op. cit., 172. **Chugants.**—Doc. of 1759 quoted by Rupp, Northampton Co., 50, 1845. **Chughnot.**—German Flats conf. (1770) in N. Y. Doc. Col. Hist., VIII, 243, 1857. **Chugnues.**—Macauley, N. Y., II, 166, 1829. **Chugnuts.**—Ruttenber, Tribes Hudson R., 201, 1872.

**Chuhhla** ('blackbird'). A Chickasaw clan of the Ishpanee phratry.

**Chuh-hlä.**—Morgan, Anc. Soc., 163, 1877. **Tchú'-hla.**—Gatschet, Creek Migr. Leg., I, 96, 1884.

**Chuhuirari** (*Chu-hwi'-ra-ri*, from a term meaning 'the dead ones'). A rancheria, with a cave dwelling containing a single Tarahumare family, not far from Norogachic, Chihuahua, Mexico.—Lumholtz, inf'n, 1894.

**Chuitna.** A Knaiakhotana village on Cook inlet, Alaska, at the mouth of Chuit r.

**Chuitna.**—Baker, Geog. Dict. Alaska, 1901. **Shuitna.**—Ibid.

**Chukafalaya** (*Chúkafaláya*, 'long town'). A former Chickasaw settlement, covering a district 4 m. long and a mile wide, in 1720, and forming one of the geographic divisions of the tribe. Adair states that it had more people in 1775 than the whole Chickasaw Nation in 1740. Several villages composed this settlement, which probably was in Pontotoc or Dallas co., Miss.       (A. S. G).

**Chattafallai.**—Hearrt in Trans. Am. Philos. Soc., III, 217, 1793. **Chookka Pharáah.**—Adair, Am. Ind., 353, 1775. **Chukafalaya.**—Romans, Fla., 63, 1775. **Long House Town.**—Adair, Am. Ind., 354, 1775. **Long Town.**—Blount (1792) in Am. State Pap., Ind. Aff., I, 288, 1832.

**Chukahlako** ('great house'). (1) A former Lower Creek town on Chattahoochee r., Ala. In 1799 the inhabitants had abandoned the place and moved to Oakfuskee, on the opposite side of Tallapoosa r. There is a Choccolocco post-office in Alabama on Choccolocco cr. (2) Mentioned in a census of 1832 as an Upper Creek town with 109 families.—Schoolcraft, Ind. Tribes, IV, 578, 1854.       (A. S. G.)

**Chau-kethluc-co.**—Hawkins (1799), Sketch, 45, 1848. **Chockalocha.**—H. R. Ex. Doc. 276, 24th Cong., 1st sess., 315, 1836. **Chockalook.**—Ibid., 312. **Chockeclucca.**—Bartram, Travels, 463, 1791. **Chockolocko.**—Sen. Ex. Doc. 425, 24th Cong., 1st sess., 220, 1836. **Tchúka 'láko.**—Gatschet, Creek Migr. Leg., I, 146, 1884. **Thlcocotcho.**—Gallatin in Archæol. Am., 112, 1836.

**Chukai.** The Mud clan of the Lizard (Earth or Sand) phratry of the Hopi.

**Tcu'-kai.**—Stephen in 8th Rep. B. A. E., 39, 1891.

**Chukaimina.** A Mariposan tribe formerly near Kings r., Cal. According to Powers (Cont. N. A. Ethnol., III, 370, 1877) they were in Squaw valley, Fresno co., and here Merriam found a few families in 1903.

Cho-co-men-as.—Johnston in Sen. Ex. Doc. 61, 32d Cong., 1st sess., 23, 1852. Cho-ke-me-nes.—Barbour in Sen. Ex. Doc. 4, 32d Cong., spec. sess., 252, 1853. Cho-ke-min-nah.—Wessells (1853) in H. R. Ex. Doc. 76, 34th Cong., 3d sess., 31, 1857. Cho-kem-nies.—Lewis in Ind. Aff. Rep. 1857, 399, 1858. Chokiamauves.—Bancroft, Nat. Races, I, 456, 1874 (misquoted from Taylor). Chokimauves.—Taylor in Cal. Farmer, June 8, 1860. Cho-ki-me-nas.—Ind. Aff. Rep., 223, 1851. Cho-ki'-min-ah.—Merriam in Science, XIX, 915, 1904. Chu-kai'-mi-na.—Powers in Cont. N. A. Ethnol., III, 370, 1877.

**Chukanedi** ('bush or grass people'). A clan among the Huna division of the Tlingit, belonging to the Wolf phratry. Anciently they are said to have stood low in the social scale. Their principal emblem was the porpoise.

Tcū'kAnedî.—Swanton, field notes, B. A. E., 1904. Tschūkanē'di.—Krause, Tlinkit Ind., 118, 1885.

**Chukchagemiut.** A subdivision of the Chnagmiut Eskimo whose chief village is Chukchuk, on the Yukon delta, Alaska.

Chŭkchăg'emūt.—Dall in Cont. N. A. Ethnol., I, 17, 1877 (the people). Chukchuk.—Baker, Geog. Dict. Alaska, 1901 (the village).

**Chukchansi.** A Mariposan tribe, forming one of the northern divisions of the family, the remnants of which now occupy the foothill country between Fresno cr. on the N. and San Joaquin r. on the s., from a little above Fresno Flat down to the site of old Millerton, Cal. (Merriam in Science, XIX, 915, June 17, 1904). In 1861 they were on Fresno reserve and numbered 240. Naiakawe, a noted prophet about 1854, was a member of this tribe, and Sloknich was chief about the same time. (A. L. K.)

Choocchanceys.—Lewis in Ind. Aff. Rep. 1856, 256, 1857. Chook-chan-cie.—Royce in 18th Rep. B. A. E., 822, 1899. Chook-chancy.—Johnston (1851) in Sen. Ex. Doc. 4, 32d Cong., spec. sess., 64, 1853. Chook-cha-nees.—Barbour (1852), ibid., 252. Chookchau-ces.—McKee et al. (1851), ibid., 74. Chookchaw-ces.—McKee et al. in Ind. Aff. Rep., 223, 1851. Chook-chuncy.—Savage (1851) in Sen. Ex. Doc. 4, 32d Cong., spec. sess., 231, 1853. Chootchancers.—Johnston (1851) in Sen. Ex. Doc. 61, 32d Cong., 1st sess., 22, 1852. Chuckehalins.—Barbour et al. (1851) in Sen. Ex. Doc. 4, 32d Cong., spec. sess., 61, 1853. Chuk-chan'-cy.—Merriam in Science, XIX, 915, June 17, 1904. Chŭk'-chan-si.—Powers in Cont. N. A. Ethnol., III, 370, 1877. Chu-ke-chan-se.—Wessells (1853) in H. R. Ex. Doc. 76, 34th Cong., 3d sess., 30, 1857. Cookchaneys.—Henley in Ind. Aff. Rep., 512, 1854. Cove-chances.—Ind. Aff. Rep., 219, 1861. Suksanchi.—Kroeber, inf'n, 1903 (Yaudanchi name).

**Chukchukts.** A Squawmish village community on the left bank of Squawmisht r., Brit. Col.

Tcuk·tcuk'ts.—Hill-Tout in Rep. Brit. A. A. S., 474, 1900.

**Chukela.** A Yuit Eskimo village in Siberia, w. of C. Chukoshki.—Jackson, Reindeer in Alaska, map, 145, 1894.

**Chukeu** (*Tcuq!e-ū'*, 'mouth of the tide'). A Haida town on the s. w. coast of Moresby id., N. w. Brit. Col., said to have been so named from an inlet in and out of which the tide rushes with great force. It was occupied by the Sakikegawai, a family of Ninstints.—Swanton, Cont. Haida, 277, 1905.

**Chukhuiyathl.** A Kuitsh village on lower Umpqua r., Oreg.

Tc'û-qu'-i-yǫl'.—Dorsey in Jour. Am. Folk-lore, III, 231, 1890.

**Chukkilissa.** One of five hamlets composing the former Choctaw town of Imongalasha, in the present Neshoba co., Miss.—Halbert in Miss. Hist. Soc. Publ., VI, 432, 1902.

**Chukotalgi** ('toad'). An extinct Creek clan, closely affiliated with the Toad or Sopaktalgi clan.

Tchukótalgi.—Gatschet, Creek Migr. Leg., I, 155, 1884. Tsuχódi.—Ibid.

**Chukubi.** A traditional settlement situated a mile N. E. of Shipaulovi, N. E. Arizona. It was occupied by the Squash, Sand, and other clans of the Hopi, who were afterward joined by the Spider clan. Being harassed by enemies, among them the Ute and the Apache, it was abandoned, its inhabitants joining those of old Mashongnovi in building the present Mashongnovi pueblo.

Chukubi.—Stephen and Mindeleff in 8th Rep. B. A. E., 25, 58, 1891; Fewkes in 17th Rep. B. A. E., 538, 1898. Chūkúvi.—Voth, Traditions of the Hopi, 40, 1905.

**Chukukh.** A Kuitsh village on lower Umpqua r., Oreg.

Tc'u-kŭkq'.—Dorsey in Jour. Am. Folk-lore, III, 231, 1890.

**Chula** ('fox'). A former Yazoo tribe, confederated with the Chickasaw, on or near the headwaters of Yazoo r., Miss. A village called Tchula is now in Holmes co., Miss.

Chola.—Gatschet, Creek Migr. Leg., I, 99, 1884. Choula.—La Harpe (1721) in French, Hist. Col. La., III, 106, 1851. Foxes.—Gatschet, op. cit. Tchúla.—Ibid.

**Chulare.** A former village of the Chalone division of the Costanoan family, situated in the vicinity of the present Guadalupe rancho, near Soledad mission, Cal. Chualar, a post-office in Salinas valley, is probably the same name.

Achulares.—Taylor in Cal. Farmer, Apr. 20, 1860. Chulares.—Ibid.

**Chulik.** A fishing station of the Nunivagmiut on Nunivak id., Alaska. Pop. 62 in 1890, comprising two villages called Chuligmiut and Upper Chuligmiut (11th Census, Alaska, 114).

**Chulithltiyu.** A Yaquina village on the s. side of Yaquina r., Oreg.

Tcŭl-liǫl'-ti-yu.—Dorsey in Jour. Am. Folk-lore, III, 229, 1890.

**Chulufichi.** A phratry of the ancient Timucua of Florida. Its clans were Arahasomi, Habachaca, and several others not recorded.—Pareja (1614) quoted by Gatschet in Proc. Am. Philos. Soc., XVII, 492, 1878.

**Chumash.** The Santa Rosa islanders, of the Chumashan family of California.—Bowers in Smithson. Rep., 316, 1877.

Tcumac.—Henshaw, Santa Rosa MS. vocab., B. A. E., 1884.

**Chumashan Family.** A linguistic family on the coast of s. California, known also as Santa Barbara Indians. Like most Californian aborigines, they appear to have lacked an appellation of general significance, and the term Chumash, the name of the Santa Rosa islanders, is arbitrarily chosen for convenience to designate the linguistic stock. Seven dialects of this family are known, those of San Luis Obispo, Purísima, Santa Inez, Santa Barbara, and San Buenaventura missions, and of Santa Rosa and Santa Cruz ids. These are fairly similar except the San Luis Obispo, which stands apart. It is probable that there were other dialects. The Chumashan languages show certain morphologic resemblances to the adjacent Shoshonean and Salinan, especially the latter, but constitute an independent family, as their stock of words is confined to themselves. The territorial limits of the Chumashan Indians are not accurately known. The area shown on Powell's map (7th Rep. B. A. E., 1891) includes the entire Santa Maria r. drainage, Santa Inez r., the lower half of the Santa Clara r. drainage, and Somis cr., the e. boundary line on the coast lying between Pt Dume and Santa Monica. Since the language of San Luis Obispo was Chumashan, this region n. of the Santa Maria and s. of the Salinas drainage must be added (see the linguistic maps accompanying the articles *California Indians* and *Linguistic Families*). The northern of the Santa Barbara ids. (Santa Cruz, Santa Rosa, and San Miguel) were inhabited by the Chumash, but the 3 southern islands of the group belonged to Shoshonean people.

The Chumashan Indians, both of the islands and of the coast, were visited by Europeans as early as 1542, when Cabrillo spent some time in their territory, meeting with an exceedingly friendly reception. Vizcayno in 1602 and Portola in 1769 also came in contact with them, and have left accounts of their visits. Five missions were established by the Franciscans among the Chumash; those of San Luis Obispo, San Buenaventura, Santa Barbara, Purísima, and Santa Inez, founded respectively in 1771, 1782, 1786, 1787, and 1804, the missionaries meeting with little opposition and no forcible resistance. The early friendship for the Spaniards soon changed to a sullen hatred under their rule, for in 1810 it was reported by a missionary that nearly all the Indian women at Purísima had for a time persistently practised abortion,

and in 1824 the Indians at Santa Barbara, Santa Inez, and Purísima revolted against the mission authority, which they succeeded in shaking off for a time, though the Spaniards apparently suffered no loss of life at their hands. Even during mission times the Chumash decreased greatly in numbers, and in 1884 Henshaw found only about 40 individuals. This number has been reduced to less than half, the few survivors being largely "Mexicanized," and the race is extinct on the islands.

In character and habits the Chumash differed considerably from the other Indians of California. All the early voyagers note their friendliness and hospitality, and their greater affluence and abundance of food as compared with their neighbors. They appear to have had a plentiful supply of sea food and to have depended on it rather than on the vegetal products which usually formed the subsistence of California Indians. With the islanders this was no doubt a necessity. Their houses were of grass or tule, dome-shaped, and often 50 ft. or more in diameter, accommodating as many as 50 people. Each was inhabited by several families, and they were grouped in villages. The Chumash were noted for their canoes, which were not dug out of a single log, but made of planks lashed together and calked. Most were built for only 2 or 3 men, but some carried 10 and even 13 persons. As no canoes were found anywhere else on the coast from C. San Lucas to C. Mendocino, even where suitable wood is abundant, rafts or tule balsas taking their place, the well-built canoes of the Chumash are evidence of some ethnographic specialization. The same may be said of their carved wooden dishes and of the figures painted on posts, described as erected over graves and at places of worship. On the Santa Barbara ids. stone killer-whale figurines have been found, though almost nowhere else in California are there traces of even attempted sculpture. An unusual variety of shell ornaments and of work in shell inlaid by means of asphaltum also characterize the archeologic discoveries made in Chumashan territory. Large stone jars similar to those in use among the neighboring Shoshoneans, and coiled baskets somewhat similar to those of their southern neighbors, were made by the Chumash. Their general culture has been extensively treated by Putnam (Wheeler, Survey Rep., VII, 1879). Of their religion very little is known, and nothing of their mythology. The gentile system was not recognized by them, marriage between individuals of the same village being allowed. On Santa Catalina id. birds which were called large crows by the Spaniards were kept and worshiped, agreeing with what Boscana tells of the Shoshonean condor cult of the adjacent coast. The medicine-men of one of the islands are said to have used stone pipes for smoking, sucking, and blowing to remove disease, dressing in a hair wig, with a belt of deer hoofs. This practice was similar to that which prevailed through Lower California. The dead among the Chumash were buried, not burned as in many other parts of California; property was hung on poles over their graves, and for chiefs painted planks were erected. The Franciscan missionaries, however, rightly declare that these Indians, like all others in California, were not idolaters.

True tribal divisions were unknown to the Chumash as to most other Indians of California, the only basis of social organization being the family, and of political, the village settlement. The names of village sites are given in great number from the time of the earliest voyage in the 16th century, but the majority can neither be located nor identified. The following is a list of the villages, most of the names being taken from the mission archives:

*Santa Inés Mission:* Achillimo, Aguama, Ahuamhoue, Akachumas, Akaitsuk, Alahulapas, Alizway, Asiuhuil, Awashlaurk, Calahuasa, Cascel, Cholicus, Chumuchu, Coloc, Geguep, Guaislac, Huhunata, Hunawurp, Ialamne, Ionata, Jonatas, Kalawashuk, Katahuac, Kolok, Kuyam, Matiliha, Mekewe, Mishtapawa, Nipoma, Nutonto, Sapelek, Saptuui, Sauchu, Shopeshno, Sikitipuc, Sisuchi, Situchi, Sotonoemu, Souscoc, Stucu, Suiesia, Suktanakamu, Tahijuas, Takuyumam, Talaxano, Tapanissilac, Tarkepsi, Tekep, Temesathi, Tequepis, Tinachi, Tsamala, Tujanisuissilac.

*San Miguel Island:* Nimoyoyo, Zaco.

*Santa Rosa Island:* Kshiwukciwu, Lilibeque, Muoc, Ninumu, Niquesesquelua, Niquipos, Patiquilid, Patiquiu, Pilidquay, Pisqueno. Poele, Siliwihi.

*Santa Cruz Island:* Alali, Chalosas, Chosho, Coycoy, Estocoloco, Hahas, Hitschowon, Klakaamu. Lacayamu, Liyam, Macamo, Maschal, Mishumac, Nanahuani, Niakla, Nichochi, Nilalhuyu, Nimatlala, Nimitapal, Nitel, Nomkolkol, Sasuagel, Xugua.

*San Buenaventura Mission:* Aguin, Alloc, **Anacbuc, Chihucchihui, Chumpache, Eshhulup, Kachyayakuch, Kanwaiakaku, Kinapuke, Lacayamu, Liam,** Lisichi, Lojos, Luupch, Mahow, Malahue, Malico, Matillija, Miguihui, Miscanaka, Piiru, Sespe, Shishalap, Simi, Sisa, Sisjulcioy, Sissabanonase, Somo, Tapo, Ypuc, Yxaulo.

*Purisima Mission:* Alacupusyuen, Aus- ion, Esmischue, Esnispele, Espiiluima,

Estait, Fax, Guaslaique, Huasna, Huenejel, Huenepel, Husistaic, Ialamma, Jlaacs, Kachisupal, Lajuchu, Lipook, Lisahuato, Lompoc, Nahuey, Naila, Ninyuelgual, Nocto, Omaxtux, Pacsiol, Paxpili, Sacsiol, Sacspili, Salachi, Sihimi, Silimastus, Silimi, Silino, Silisne, Sipuca, Sisolop, Sitolo, Stipu, Suntaho, Tutachro.

*Santa Barbara Mission:* Alcax, Alican, Alpincha, Alwathalama, Amolomol, Anejue, Awhawhilashmu, Cajats, Cajpilili, Casalic, Cashwah, Chiuchin, Cholosoc, Chuah, Cinihuay, Cuyamus, Eleunaxciay, Eljman, Eluaxcu, Estuc, Geliac, Gleuaxcuqu, Guainonost, Guima, Hanaya, Hello, Huelemin, Huililoc, Huixapapa, Humalija, Hunxapa, Inajalaihu, Inojey, Ipec, Ituc, Lagcay, Laycayamu, Lintja, Lisuchu, Lugups, Majalayghua, Mishtapalwa, Mistaughchewaugh, Numguelgar, Otenashmoo, Salpilel, Sayokinck, Sihuicom, Silpoponemew, Sinicon, Sisahiahut, Sisuch, Snihuax, Sopone, Taxlipu, Texmaw, Xalanaj, Xalou.

*Miscellaneous:* Anacoat, Anacot, Antap, Aogni, Asimu, Bis, Caacat, Casnahacmo, Casunalmo, Cayeguas, Chwaiyok, Cicacut, Ciucut, Ciyuktun, Elquis, Escumawash, Garomisopona, Gua, Helapoonuch, Honmoyaushu, Hueneme, Humkak, Immahal, Isha, Ishgua, Kamulas, Kasaktikat, Kashiwe, Kashtok, Kashtu, Kaso, Katstayot, Kaughii, Kesmali, Koiyo, Kuiyamu, Lohastahni, Mahahal, Malhokshe, Malito, Malulowoni, Maquinanoa, Masewuk, Mershom, Michiyu, Micoma, Misesopano, Mishpapsna, Misinagua, Mismatuk, Mispu, Mugu, Mupu, Nacbuc, Nipomo, Nocos, Ojai, Olesino, Onkot, Onomio, Opia, Opistopia, Paltatre, Partocac, Potoltuc, Pualnacatup, Quanmugua, Quelqueme, Quiman, Salnahakaisiku, San Emidio, Sapaquonil, Saticoy, Satwiwa, Shalawa, Shalikuwewich, Shalkahaan, Shishlaman, Shuku, Shup, Shushuchi, Shuwalashu, Simomo, Sisichii, Sitaptapa, Siuktun, Skonon, Spookow, Sulapin, Susuquey, Sweteti, Swino, Tallapoolina, Temeteti, Tocane, Topotopow, Tucumu, Tukachkach, Upop, Uva, Walekhe, Wihatset, Xabaagua, Xagua, Xocotoc, Yutum.      (H. W. H.   A. L. K.)

>**Santa Barbara.**—Latham in Trans. Philol. Soc. Lond., 85, 1856 (includes Santa Barbara, Santa Inez, San Luis Obispo languages); Buschmann, Spuren der aztek. Sprache, 531, 535, 538, 602, 1859; Latham, Opuscula, 351, 1860; Powell in Cont. N. A. Ethnol., III, 550, 567, 1877 (Kasuá, Santa Inez, id. of Santa Cruz, Santa Barbara); Gatschet in U. S. Geog. Surv. W. 100th Mer., VII, 419, 1879 (cites La Purisima, Santa Inez, Santa Barbara, Kasuá, Mugu, Santa Cruz id.). ×**Santa Barbara.**—Gatschet in Mag. Am. Hist., 156, 1877 (Santa Inez, Santa Barbara, Santa Cruz id., San Luis Obispo, San Antonio). =**Chumashan.**—Powell in 7th Rep. B. A. E., 67, 1891.

**Chumawi.** A former Shastan band or village in Big valley, Modoc co, Cal.

**Chu-mâ′-wa.**—Powers in Cont. N. A. Ethnol., III, 267, 1877.

**Chumidok.** A term used by Powers as a tribal name similar to Chumteya, q. v.

**Chimedocs.**—Powers in Overland Mo., x, 324, 1873. **Chim'-i-dok.**—Powers in Cont. N. A. Ethnol., III, 349, 1877. **Choomedocs.**—Powers in Overland Mo., x, 324, 1873. **Chu'-mi-dok.**—Powers in Cont. N. A. Ethnol., III, 349, 1877.

**Chumpache.** A former Chumashan village in Ventura co., Cal.—Taylor in Cal. Farmer, July 24, 1863.

**Chumteya.** A name meaning 'southerners,' and applied with dialectic variations by most Miwok (Moquelumnan) divisions to the divisions s. of them. In some cases the name or a form of it may have been the proper appellation of particular divisions, but on the whole it remained geographical rather than national or tribal; as explained by the Indians themselves, divisions called Chumteya by those N. of themselves applied the same term in turn to their southern neighbors, and so on. See also *Chumidok*, *Chumuch*, *Chumwit*. (A. L. K.)
**Chimteya.**—Powers in Cont. N. A. Ethnol., III, 353, 1877. **Choomtéyas.**—Powers in Overland Mo., x, 324, 1873. **Chúmĕto.**—Gatschet in Am. Antiq., V, 71, 1883. **Chūm-te'-ya.**—Powers in Cont. N. A. Ethnol., III, 349, 1877.

**Chumuch.** A term used by Powers as a tribal name similar to Chumteya, q. v.
**Choomuch.**—Powers in Overland Mo., x, 324, 1873. **Chu'-much.**—Powers in Cont. N. A. Ethnol., III, 349, 1877.

**Chumuchu.** Apparently 2 distinct Chumashan villages formerly near Santa Inés mission, Santa Barbara co., Cal.—Taylor in Cal. Farmer, Oct. 18, 1861.

**Chumwit.** A term used by Powers as a tribal name similar to Chumteya, q. v.
**Choomwits.**—Powers in Overland Mo., x, 324, 1873. **Chūm'-wit.**—Powers in Cont. N. A. Ethnol., III, 349, 1877.

**Chunacansti.** Mentioned by Alcedo (Dic. Geog., I, 565, 1786) as a pueblo of the province of South Carolina, on a swift river of the same name which flows S. E. to the sea. Unidentified.

**Chunaneets.** A Tuscarora village in North Carolina in 1701.—Lawson (1709), N. C., 383, 1860.

**Chunarghuttunne.** A former village of the Chastacosta on the N. side of Rogue r., E. of its junction with Applegate cr., Oreg.
**To'û-na'-rxût ɟûn'nĕ.**—Dorsey in Jour. Am. Folklore, III, 234, 1890.

**Chunkey.** The name commonly used by the early traders to designate a man's game formerly popular among the Gulf tribes and probably general in the S., E. of the Mississippi. It was played with a stone disk and a pole which had a crook at one end. The disk was rolled ahead, and the object was to slide the pole after it in such a way that the disk would rest in the curve of the crook when both came to a stop. It was usually played in the larger towns upon a piece of ground regularly prepared for the purpose, called by the traders the "chunkey yard," or "chunk yard," adjoining the town square, or central plaza, in which the most important public ceremonies were performed. In the W. a somewhat similar game was played with a netted wheel and a pair of throwing sticks. The name appears to come from the Catawba or some other language of Carolina, where Lawson, in 1701, mentions it under the name *chenco*. For diagrams of the Creek town square, with chunkey yard, see Gatschet, Creek Migr. Leg., II, 186, 1888, and Swan in Schoolcraft, Ind. Tribes, v, 264, 1855. See *Games, Discoidal stones*. (J. M.)

**Chunkey.** A former Choctaw town on the site of the modern village of Union, Newton co., Miss.—Brown in Miss. Hist. Soc. Publ., VI, 443, 1902.
**Chanki.**—Romans, Florida, map, 1775. **Chunky.**—Brown, op. cit.

**Chunkey Chitto** ('big Chunkey,' so called to distinguish it from Chunkey). A former Choctaw town on the w. bank of Chunky cr., about ½ m. below its confluence with Talasha cr., in Newton co., Miss. It was the southernmost town visited by Tecumseh in the fall of 1811.—Brown in Miss. Hist. Soc. Publ., VI, 443–444, 1902; Halbert and Ball, Creek War, 46, 1895.
**Chunky.**—Brown, op. cit.

**Chunsetunneta.** A former village of the Chastacosta on the N. side of Rogue r., Oreg.
**Tcûn-se'-tûn-ne'-ta.**—Dorsey in Jour. Am. Folklore, III, 234, 1890.

**Chunsetunnetun.** A former village of the Chastacosta on the N. side of Rogue r., Oreg.
**Tcûn-se'-tûn-ne'-tûn.**—Dorsey in Jour. Am. Folklore, III, 234, 1890.

**Chuntshataatunne** ('people of the large fallen tree'). A former village of the Mishikhwutmetunne on Coquille r., Oreg.
**Tcûn-tca'-tă-a' ɟûnnĕ.**—Dorsey in Jour. Am. Folklore, III, 232, 1890.

**Chunut** (pl. Chunotachi). A former important Yokuts tribe in the plains E. of Tulare lake, Cal. They were enemies of the Tadji at the N. end of the lake, but on friendly terms with the hill tribes. They lived in long communal houses of tule. Their dialect formed a group with the Tadji and Choinok. (A. L. K.)
**Cho-ho-nuts.**—Barbour (1852) in Sen. Ex. Doc. 4, 32d Cong., spec. sess., 256, 1853. **Choo-noot.**—Wessells (1853) in H. R. Ex. Doc. 76, 34th Cong., 3d sess., 32, 1857. **Chu'-nut.**—Powers in Cont. N. A. Ethnol., III, 370, 1877. **Chunute.**—Royce in 18th Rep. B. A. E., 782, 1899. **Chu-su-te.**—Barbour, op. cit. (mentioned as on Paint cr.).

**Chupatak** (*Tcüpatäk*, 'mortar stone'). A former Pima village in s. Arizona.—Russell, Pima MS., B. A. E., 16, 1902.

**Chupcan.** Mentioned as a village of the Cholovone on the E. bank of San Joaquin r., N. of the Tuolumne, Cal. The name may be another form of Chapposan, apparently a tribe on the San Joaquin, and also of the otherwise unidentifiable Chopee mentioned as on Fresno res. in 1861. (A. L. K.)

Chap-pah-seins.—Johnston (1851) in Sen. Ex. Doc. 61, 32d Cong., 1st sess., 20, 1852. Chap-po-sans.—Ryer (1851), ibid., 21. Chopees.—Ind. Aff. Rep., 219, 1861. Chupcan.—Taylor in Cal. Farmer, Oct. 18, 1861. Tchupukanes.—Kotzebue, New Voy., ii, 146, 1830.

**Chupichnushkuch.** A former Kuitsh village near lower Umpqua r., Oreg.
Tc'û'-pǐtc n'u' ckūtc.—Dorsey in Jour. Am. Folklore, iii, 231, 1890.

**Chupumni.** A former Miwok village not far s. of Cosumnes r., Cal.
Chupumnes.—Hale, Ethnog. and Philol., vi, 630, 1846.

**Churamuk.** A former village of the Iroquois on the E. side of Susquehanna r., 18 m. above Oswego, N. Y.; destroyed by Sullivan in 1779.—Livermore (1779) in N. H. Hist. Soc. Coll., vi, 322, 1850.

**Churan** ('red-eye people'). One of the two divisions or fraternities of Isleta pueblo, N. Mex. See *Shifunin*.
Chu-rän'.—Hodge, field notes, B. A. E., 1895. Shúren.—Gatschet, Isleta MS. vocab., B. A. E., 1885 (given as a clan).

**Churchcates.**—A small unidentified tribe mentioned by Gov. Archdale, of South Carolina, in the latter part of the 18th century, in a complaint that the Appalachicoloes, or English Indians, had attacked and killed 3 of them.—Carroll, Hist. Coll. S. C., ii, 107, 1836.

**Churchers.** A body of Indians living E. and N. E. of the white settlements in New England in 1634 (Wood, 1634, quoted by Barton, New Views, xviii, 1798). Not the Praying Indians, as the period is too early.

**Churehu.** The Mole clan of Isleta pueblo, N. Mex.
Chúrëhu-t'aínïn.—Lummis quoted by Hodge in Am. Anthrop., ix, 351, 1896 (*t'aínïn* = 'people').

**Churmutce.** A former village, presumably Costanoan, connected with Dolores mission, San Francisco, Cal.—Taylor in Cal. Farmer, Oct. 18, 1861.

**Churuptoy.** A tribe of the Patwin division of the Copehan family, formerly living in Yolo and perhaps in Napa co., Cal. It was one of the 7 which made peace with Gov. Vallejo in 1836.—Bancroft, Hist. Cal., iv, 71, 1886.

**Chusca.** The name (*Tsús-kai, Tsó-is-kai*) given by the Navaho to a prominent hill on the Navaho res., N. W. N. Mex. Geographers extend the name (Choiska) to the whole mountain mass from which the knoll rises. Cortez in 1779 (Pac. R. R. Rep., iii, pt. 3, 119, 1856) recorded it, with doubtful propriety, as the name of a Navaho settlement. In these mountains are the remains of breastworks and other evidences of a disastrous fight that took place before 1850, according to Navaho informants, between their warriors and Mexican troops. (W. M.)

**Chuscan.** A former village, presumably Costanoan, connected with Dolores mission, San Francisco, Cal.—Taylor in Cal. Farmer, Oct. 18, 1861.

**Chushtarghasuttun.** A former village of the Chastacosta on the N. side of Rogue r., Oreg.
Tc'uc'-ta-rxa-sût'-tûn.—Dorsey in Jour. Am. Folklore, iii, 234, 1890.

**Chusterghutmunnetun.** A former village of the Chastacosta, the highest on Rogue r., Oreg.
Tc'ûs-tê'-rxut-mûn-ne'-tûn.—Dorsey in Jour. Am. Folk-lore, iii, 234, 1890.

**Chutchin.** A former village, presumably Costanoan, connected with Dolores mission, San Francisco, Cal.—Taylor in Cal. Farmer, Oct. 18, 1861.

**Chutil** (named from a slough on which it was situated). A former village or camp of the Pilalt, a Cowichan tribe of lower Chilliwack r., Brit. Col.
Tcūtī'l.—Hill-Tout in Ethnol. Surv. Can., 48, 1902.

**Chuttusgelis.** The reputed site of Soledad mission, Cal.—Engelhardt, Franciscans in Cal., 380, 1897.

**Chuttushshunche.** A former village of the Chastacosta on the N. side of Rogue r., Oreg.
Tcût'-tûc-cûn-tcĕ.—Dorsey in Jour. Am. Folk-lore, iii, 234, 1890.

**Chuwutukawutuk** (*Tcü'wütükawütûk*, 'earth hill'). A former Pima village in s. Arizona.—Russell, Pima MS., B. A. E., 16, 1902.

**Chuyachic** ('the point of a ridge'). A small rancheria of the Tarahumare, not far from Norogachic, Chihuahua, Mexico.—Lumholtz, inf'n, 1894.

**Chwaiyok.** A former Chumashan village E. of San Buenaventura, Ventura co., Cal., a locality now called Los Pitos.
Tc'-wai-yök.—Henshaw, Buenaventura MS. vocab., B. A. E., 1884.

**Chynau.** A former village, presumably Costanoan, connected with Dolores mission, San Francisco, Cal.—Taylor in Cal. Farmer, Oct. 18, 1861.

**Cibolas** (Mexican Span.: 'buffaloes'). A term applied by early Spanish writers to any buffalo-hunting Indians. The name Vaqueros (see *Querecho*) was similarly applied to the Apache of the Texas plains in the 16th century.

**Cicacut.** A Chumashan village at Goleta, w. of Santa Barbara, Cal., in 1542.—Cabrillo in Smith, Colec. Doc., 181, 1857.
Cicauit.—Taylor in Cal. Farmer, Apr. 17, 1863. Pueblo de las Sardinas.—Cabrillo, op. cit.

**Cienega** (Span.: 'marsh,' 'moor,' and in s. w. U. S., 'meadow'; Tewa name, *Tziguma*, 'lone cottonwood tree'). A pueblo formerly occupied by the Tano, but apparently containing also some Queres, situated in the valley of Rio Santa Fe, 12 m. s. w. of Santa Fe, N. Mex. In the 17th century it was a visita of San Marcos mission. Of this pueblo Bandelier says: "It was abandoned at a time when the Pueblos were independent [between 1680 and 1692], and an effort to repeople it was made by Diego de Vargas after the pacification of New Mexico in 1695, but with little success. Tziguma was therefore a historic pueblo. Nevertheless, I am in doubt as to which stock its inhabitants belonged. They are mentioned as being Queres, . . . but the people of Cochiti do not regard them as having been of their own stock, but as belonging to the Puya-tye or Tanos. Until the question is decided by further researches among the Tanos of Santo Domingo, I shall hold that the pueblo was a Tanos village.'' It contained no Indians in 1782, and at no time did its population reach 1,000.—Arch. Inst. Papers, III, 125, 1890; IV, 91–92, 1892.

Alamo Solo.—Bandelier in Arch. Inst. Papers, IV, pt. 2, 92, 1892 (Spanish name of present village: 'Lone cottonwood tree'). Chi-mu-a.—Bandelier in Ritch, N. Mex., 201, 1885. Chiu-ma.—Ritch, ibid., 166. Ciénega de Carabajal.—Oñate (1598) in Doc. Inéd., XVI, 114, 1871. Cieneguilla.—Davis, Span. Conq. N. Mex.,333,1869. Cinega.—D'Anville, map N. A., Bolton's ed.,1752. La Cienega.—Bandelier in Arch. Inst. Papers, IV, 91, 1892. La Cienegia.—Davis, Span. Conq. N. Mex., 333, 1869. La Cienguilla.—Ibid., 350. Sienaguilla.—Ibid., map. Sienega.—Gallegas (1844) in Emory, Recon., 478, 1848. Tzi-gu-ma.—Bandelier in Arch. Inst. Papers, III, 125, 1890 (aboriginal name). Tzi-gu-may.—Ibid., IV, 91, 1892. Ziguma.—Ladd, N. Mex., 199, 1891.

**Cienega.** A large Cora rancheria in the Sierra de Nayarit, in the N. part of the territory of Tepic, Mexico.

Cienega.—Lumholtz, Unknown Mex., II, map, 16, 1902. La Cienega.—Ibid., I, 498.

**Cieneguilla** (Span.: 'little marsh'). A former village on the Potrero Viejo, above the present Cochiti pueblo, N. Mex., occupied almost continuously by the Cochiti between 1681 and 1694. It was burned in the latter year by Gov. Vargas during his reconquest of the country.—Bandelier in Arch. Inst. Papers, IV, 169, 1892.

Cienegui.—Escalante (1693?) quoted by Bandelier, ibid., 173, 1892. Cieneguilla.—Mendoza (1681), ibid., 169.

**Cincinnati Tablet.** See *Notched plates.*

**Cinco Llagas** (Span.: 'five wounds,' referring to the wounds of Christ). A Tepehuane village near the Cerro de Muinora, in the Sierra Madre, on the headwaters of the Rio del Fuerte, in the extreme s. w. part of Chihuahua, Mexico, the inhabitants of which are of pure blood, but speak Spanish.—Doc. Hist. Mex., 4th s., IV, 93, 1857; Lumholtz, Unknown Mexico, I, 429, 1902.

**Cinihuay.** A former Chumashan village at Los Gatos, near Santa Barbara, Cal.—Taylor in Cal. Farmer, Apr. 24, 1863.

**Cinnabar.** The sulphide of mercury, which supplies a brilliant red pigment used to a considerable extent by the native tribes. It is somewhat more brilliant in hue than the hematites, being

the basis of the vermilion of commerce. It occurs in pulverulent earthy forms and as a compact ore largely in connection with serpentines. It is found in California and Texas, and to a limited extent in Idaho, Utah, and Nevada. Yarrow found it associated with burials in s. California, and remarks that, used as a paint for the person, it might be expected to cause ''constitutional derangements of a serious nature'' (Surv. W. 100th Merid., VII, 1879), and Meredith (Moorehead, Prehist. Impls., 1900) even attributes the diseased bones so often obtained from native graves to the excessive use of this pigment.          (w. h. h.)

**Cinquack.** A village of the Powhatan confederacy near Smiths Pt on the Potomac, in Northumberland co., Va., in 1608.

Chinquack.—Doc. of 1638 in Bozman, Md., II, 73, 1837. Cinquack.—Smith (1629), Virginia, I, map, repr. 1819.

**Cinquaeteck.** A village on the Potomac, in the present Prince George co., Md., in 1608.—Smith (1629), Virginia, I, map, repr. 1819. Cf. *Chincoteague, Cinquoteck.*

**Cinquoteck.** A village of the Powhatan confederacy, probably of the Pamunkey tribe, in the fork of Mattapony and Pamunkey rs., King William co., Va., in 1608.—Smith (1629), Virginia, I, map, repr. 1819. Cf. *Chincoteague, Cinquaeteck.*

**Cisco.** A name applied to various species of fish found in the region of the great lakes, particularly the lake herring (*Coregonus artedi*) and the lake noon-eye (*C. hoyi*). The word is said to be taken from one of the Algonquian dialects of the region, but its origin is not clear. Perhaps it is a reduction of *ciscoette* or *siskowit*.          (A. F. C.)

**Cisco** (*Si'ska*, 'uncle'). A village of the Lytton band of Ntlakyapamuk on Fraser r., 8 m. below Lytton, Brit. Col.; pop. 32 in 1902.

Si'ska.—Teit in Mem. Am. Mus. Nat. Hist., II, 171, 1900. Siska Flat.—Can. Ind. Aff. for 1880, 317.

**Ciscoette.** A name of the lake herring (*Coregonus artedi*), seemingly a French diminutive in *ette* from *cisco*, but probably a French corruption of *siskowit*, q. v.          (A. F. C.)

**Ciscoquett, Ciscowet.** See *Siskowit.*

**Citisans.** One of the five tribes of which Badin, in 1830 (Ann. de la Prop. de la Foi, IV, 536, 1843), believed the Sioux nation to be composed. Possibly intended for Sisseton.

**Citizen Potawatomi.** A part of the Potawatomi who, while living in Kansas, withdrew from the rest of the tribe about 1861, took lands in severalty and became citizens, but afterward removed to Indian Ter. (now Oklahoma). They numbered 1,036 in 1890, but by 1900 had increased to 1,722, and in 1904 the number was given as 1,686.

**Ciucut.** A Chumashan village between Goleta and Pt Conception, Cal., in 1542.

Ciucut.—Cabrillo, Narr. (1542), in Smith, Colec. Doc. Fla., 183, 1857. **Cuicut.**—Taylor in Cal. Farmer, Apr. 17, 1863.

**Civilization.** To the aboriginal inhabitant of this continent civilization entails the overturning of his ancient form of government, the abolition of many of his social usages, the readjustment of his ideas of property and personal rights, and change of occupation. No community of natives was devoid of a social organization and a form of government. These varied, some tribes being much more highly organized than others (see *Clan and Gens*), but all possessed rules of conduct which must be obeyed, else punishment would follow. Native organization was based on kinship, which carried with it the obligation of mutual protection. The tribe, wherever it chanced to be, whether resting at home in the village, wandering on the plains in pursuit of game, or scattered in quest of fish on the rivers or sea, always preserved its organization and authority intact, whereas the organization which civilization imposes on the native is based on locality, those living within certain limits being, regardless of relationship, subject to common laws and having equal responsibilities; mere kinship warrants no claim, and the family is differently constituted. In the tribal family husband and wife very often must belong to different units. According to the custom of the particular tribe the children trace descent through their father and belong to his gens, or through their mother and are members of her clan. Modern civilization demands the abrogation of the clan or gens, and children must inherit from both parents and be subject to their authority, not that of a clan or gens.

Most of the common occupations of tribal life are wiped out by civilization. Intertribal wars have ceased, and war honors are no longer possible; the herds of buffalo and other animals are gone, and with them the hunter, and the makers of bows, arrows, spears, and other implements of the chase. The results of generations of training are of little avail to the civilized male Indian.

Under tribal conditions woman held, in many cases, a place in the management of tribal affairs. Upon her devolved partly the cultivation of the fields, the dressing of skins, the making of clothing, the production of pottery and baskets, the preparing of food, and all that went to conserve the home. Civilization puts an end to her outdoor work and consigns her to the kitchen and the washtub, while the white man's factories supply cloth, clothing, pots, pans, and baskets, for none of the native industries can survive in competition with machinery. Woman, moreover, loses her importance in public affairs and the independent ownership of property that was her right by tribal law. No group of peoples on the continent were destitute of religious beliefs or of rites and ceremonies expressive of them. These beliefs were based on the idea that man, in common with all created things, was endowed with life by some power that pervaded the universe. The methods of appealing to this power varied with the environment of the peoples, but the incentive was the desire for food, health, and long life, while the rites and ceremonies inculcated certain ethical relations between man and man. As among all races, priestcraft overlaid many of the higher thoughts and teachings of native religion and led to unworthy practices. Nevertheless the breaking down of the ancient forms of worship through the many changes and restrictions incident to the settlement of the country has caused the natives much distress and mental confusion. It is not surprising that it has been a slow and difficult process for the aborigines to accept and conform to such radical changes of organization, customs, and beliefs as are required by civilization. Yet many have done so, showing a grasp of mind, a power to apprehend the value of new ideals, and a willingness to accept the inevitable, and evincing a degree of courage, self-restraint, and strength of character that can not fail to win the admiration of thinking men. The younger generation, born under the new conditions, are spared the abrupt change through which their fathers had to struggle. Wherever the environment permits, the employments of the white race are now those of the Indian. In one branch of the Eskimo change has come through the introduction of the reindeer. Already the Indian is to be found tilling his farm, plying the trades, employed on the railroads, working in mines and logging camps, and holding positions of trust in banks and mercantile houses. Indians, of pure race or of mixed blood, are practising as lawyers, physicians, and clergymen; they have made their way in literature and art, and are serving the public in national and state offices, from that of road master to that of legislator. The school, the missionary, and the altered conditions of life are slowly but surely changing the Indian's mode of thought as well as his mode of living, and the old life of his tribe and race is becoming more and more a memory and a tradition. See *Agency system, Education, Government policy, Missions.* (A. C. F.)

**Ciyuktun.** A former Chumashan village near Santa Barbara, Cal.—Taylor in Cal. Farmer, May 4, 1860.

**Cizentetpi.** Mentioned by Oñate (Doc. Inéd., XVI, 114, 1871) as a pueblo of New Mexico in 1598. Doubtless situated in the Salinas, in the vicinity of Abo, E. of the Rio Grande, and in all probability formerly occupied by the Tigua or the Piros.

**Clackama.** A Chinookan tribe formerly occupying several villages on Clackamas r., in Clackamas co., Oreg. In 1806 Lewis and Clark estimated their number at 1,800; in 1851 their number was placed at 88, and at that time they claimed the country on the E. side of Willamette r. from a few miles above its mouth nearly to Oregon City and E. as far as the Cascade mts. This territory they ceded to the United States by the Dayton treaty of 1855, and later they were removed to the Grande Ronde res., Oreg., where they are said to number about 60. (L. F.)
A'kimmash.—Gatschet, Kalapuya MS., B. A. E. (Atfalati name.) Clackamas.—Dart in Ind. Aff. Rep., 214, 1851. Clackamis.—Palmer, Trav. Rocky Mts., 84, 1845. Clackamos.—Lewis and Clark, Exped., II, 219, 1814. Clackamurs.—Wilkes, Hist. Oregon, 44, 1845. Clack-a-mus.—Lewis and Clark, Exped., I, map, 1814. Clackanurs.—Robertson, Oregon, 129, 1846. Clackarners.—Robertson in H. R. Ex. Doc. 76, 30th Cong., 1st sess., 9, 1848. Clakamus.—Warre and Vavasour (1835) in Martin, Hudson Bay Ter., 80, 1849. Clakemas.—Duflot de Mofras, Explor. de l'Oregon, II, 335, 1844. Clarkamees.—Morse, Rep. to Sec. War, 372, 1822. Clarkames.—Drake, Bk. Inds., vii, 1848. Clarkamos.—Orig. Jour. Lewis and Clark (1806), IV, 255, 1905. Clarkamus.—Lewis and Clark, Exped., II, 474, 1814. Clukemus.—Coues, Henry-Thompson Jour., 811, 1897. Gitā'q¡ēmas.—Boas, Kathlamet Texts, 237, 1901 (Clatsop name). Guithla'kimas.—Gatschet, MS., B. A. E. (own name). Klackamas.—Hines, Oregon, 144, 1850. Klackamus.—Wilkes in U. S. Expl. Exped., IV, 368, 1845. Klackamuss.—Kane, Wand. in N. A., 196, 1859. Klakamat.—Gatschet in Beach, Ind. Miscel., 443, 1877. Klaki'mass.—Gairdner (1835) in Jour. Geog. Soc. Lond., XI, 256, 1841. Nsekau's.—Gatschet, Nestucca MS. vocab., B. A. E. (Nestucca name). Ns tiwat.—Ibid. (Nestucca name). Sehalatak.—Framboise quoted by Gairdner (1835) in Jour. Geog. Soc. Lond., XI, 256, 1841. Thlakeimas.—Tolmie and Dawson, Comp. Vocabs. Brit. Col., 11, 1884. Tlăkĭmĭsh.—Mooney, inf'n, 1904 (own name). Tlăkĭmĭsh-pûm.—Ibid. Tŭ'hŭ tane.—Gatschet, Umpqua MS. vocab., B. A. E., 1877 (Umpqua name).

**Clahclellah** (probably a variation of Watlala). A Chinookan tribe living in a single village of 7 houses near the foot of the Cascades of Columbia r., Oreg., in 1806.
Clahclallah.—Orig. Jour. Lewis and Clark, IV, 275, 1905. Clahclellah.—Ibid., 273. Clahclellars.—Ibid., 258.

**Clahnaquah.** A Chinookan tribe or division living in 1806 on Sauvies id., Multnomah co., Oreg., on Columbia r. below the upper mouth of the Willamette. Their estimated number was 130, in 4 houses.
Clahnahquah.—Lewis and Clark, Exped., II, 268, 1817. Clan-nah-quah.—Orig. Jour. Lewis and Clark, IV, 218, 1905. Clan-nah-queh's Tribe of Moltnomah's.—Ibid., VI, 116, 1905.

**Clahoose.** A Salish tribe on Toba inlet, Brit. Col., speaking the Comox dialect; pop. 73 in 1904.
Clahoose.—Mayne, Brit. Col., 243, 1862. Clayhoosh.—Whymper, Alaska, 49, 1869. Cle-Hure.—Kane, Wand. in N. A., app., 1859. Cle-Huse.—Schoolcraft, Ind. Tribes, v, 488, 1855. Klahoose.—Can. Ind. Aff. for 1874, 142. Klahose.—Ibid., 1891, map. Klahous.—Downie in Mayne, Brit. Col., app., 449, 1862 (name of inlet). Klashoose.—Can. Ind. Aff. for 1874, 144. Tlahoos.—Tolmie and Dawson, Vocabs. Brit. Col., 119B, 1884. Tlahū's.—Boas, MS., B. A. E., 1887.

**Claikahak.** A Chnagmiut village on the right bank of Yukon r., near Ukak, Alaska; perhaps identical with Khaik.
Claikahakamut.—Post-route map, 1903.

**Claikehak.** A Chnagmiut Eskimo village on the N. bank of Yukon r., above Tlatek, Alaska.
Claikehakamut.—Post route map, 1903.

**Clallam** ('strong people'). A Salish tribe living on the s. side of Puget sd., Wash., formerly extending from Port Discovery to Hoko r., being bounded at each end by the Chimakum and Makah. Subsequently they occupied Chimakum territory and established a village at Port Townsend. A comparatively small number found their way across to the s. end of Vancouver id., and, according to Kane, there was a large village on Victoria harbor. They are said to be more closely related to the Songish than to any other tribe. Their villages were: Elwha, Hoko, Huiauulch, Hunnint, Kahtai, Kaquaith, Klatlawas (extinct), Pistchin (extinct), Sequim, Stehtlum, Tsako, Tsewhitzen, Tsitsukwich, and Yennis. Eleven villages were enumerated by Eells in 1886, but only 3—Elwha, Pistchin, and Sequim—are spoken of under their native names. Pop. 800 in 1854, according to Gibbs. There were 336 on Puyallup res., Wash., in 1904—248 at Jamestown and 88 at Port Gamble. (J. R. S.)
Chalam.—Farnham, Travels, 111, 1843. Clalams.—Nicolay, Oregon, 143, 1846. Clallams.—Stevens in Ind. Aff. Rep., 450, 1854. Clallems.—Gallatin in Trans. Am. Ethnol. Soc., II, 19, 1848. Clal-lums Indians.—Kane, Wand. in N. A., 209, 1859 (referring to their village in Victoria harbor). Hueyang-uh.—Mackay quoted by Dawson in Trans. Roy. Soc. Can. for 1891, sec. II, 7 (own name: 'the people'). Khalams.—Smet, Letters, 231, 1843. Klalams.—Smet, Oregon Miss., 58, 1847. Klalanes.—Ibid., 56. Klallam.—Ind. Aff. Rep., 254, 1877. Noosdalum.—Scouler in Jour. Geog. Soc. Lond., I, 224, 1841 (Noos is a *prefixum gentilicium*). Nooselalum.—Lane (1849) in Sen. Ex. Doc. 52, 31st Cong., 1st sess., 173, 1850. Noostlalums.—Schoolcraft, Ind. Tribes, v, 700, 1855. Nostlalaim.—Tolmie and Dawson, Vocabs. Brit. Col., 120B, 1884. Nusdalum.—Latham in Trans., Philol. Soc. Lond., 71, 1856. Nu-sklaim.—Eells in letter, Feb., 1886 (own name: 'strong people'). Nūs-klāi-yūm.—Gibbs, Clallum and Lummi, v, 1863. S'calam.—Keane in Stanford, Compend., 534, 1878. Sclallum.—Jones (1853) in H. R. Ex. Doc. 76, 34th Cong., 3d sess., 5, 1857. Skal-lum.—Schoolcraft, Ind. Tribes, IV, 598, 1854. S'Klallams.—U. S. Ind. Treat., 800, 1873. S'Klallan.—Stevens in Ind. Aff. Rep., 450, 1854. SKlal-lum.—Starling, ibid., 170, 1852. Thwspā'-lûb.—McCaw, Puyallup MS. vocab., B. A. E., 1885. Tlalams.—Schoolcraft, Ind. Tribes, III, 96, map, 1853. Tla'lEm.—Boas in 5th Rep. N. W. Tribes Can., 10, 1889. Tlalum.—Tolmie and Dawson, Vocabs. Brit. Col., 120B, 1884. Tsclal-

lums.—Grant in Jour. Roy. Geog. Soc., 293, 1857.
**Wooselalim.**—Lane in Ind. Aff. Rep., 162, 1850.

**Clan and Gens.** An American Indian clan or gens is an intratribal exogamic group of persons either actually or theoretically consanguine, organized to promote their social and political welfare, the members being usually denoted by a common class name derived generally from some fact relating to the habitat of the group or to its usual tutelary being. In the clan lineal descent, inheritance of personal and common property, and the hereditary right to public office and trust are traced through the female line, while in the gens they devolve through the male line. Clan and gentile organizations are by no means universal among the North American tribes; and totemism, the possession or even the worship of personal or communal totems by individuals or groups of persons, is not an essential feature of clan and gentile organizations. The terms clan and gens as defined and employed by Powell denote useful discriminations in social and political organization, and, no better names having been proposed, they are used here practically as defined by Powell.

Consanguine kinship among the Iroquoian and Muskhogean tribes is traced through the blood of the woman only, and membership in a clan constitutes citizenship in the tribe, conferring certain social, political, and religious privileges, duties, and rights that are denied to aliens. By the legal fiction of adoption the blood of the alien might be changed into one of the strains of Iroquoian blood, and thus citizenship in the tribe could be conferred on a person of alien lineage. The primary unit of the social and political organization of Iroquoian and Muskhogean tribes is the *ohwachira*, a Mohawk term signifying the family, comprising all the male and female progeny of a woman and of all her female descendants in the female line and of such other persons as may be adopted into the *ohwachira*. An *ohwachira* never bears the name of a tutelary or other deity. Its head is usually the eldest woman in it. It may be composed of one or more firesides, and one or more *ohwachiras* may constitute a clan. The members of an *ohwachira* have (1) the right to the name of the clan of which their *ohwachira* is a member; (2) the right of inheriting property from deceased members; and (3) the right to take part in councils of the *ohwachira*. The titles of chief and subchief were the heritage of particular *ohwachiras*. In the development of a clan by the coalescence of two or more actually or theoretically related *ohwachiras* only certain *ohwachiras* obtained the inheritance and custody of the titles of and consequently the right to choose chief

and subchief. Very rarely were the offspring of an adopted alien constituted an *ohwachira* having chiefship or subchiefship titles. The married women of childbearing age of such an *ohwachira* had the right to hold a council for the purpose of choosing candidates for chief and subchief of the clan, the chief matron of one of the *ohwachiras* being the trustee of the titles, and the initial step in the deposition of a chief or subchief was taken by the women's council of the *ohwachira* to whom the title belongs. There were clans in which several *ohwachiras* possessed titles to chiefships. The Mohawk and Oneida tribes have only 3 clans, each of which, however, has 3 chiefships and 3 subchiefships. Every *ohwachira* of the Iroquois possessed and worshiped, in addition to those owned by individuals, one or more tutelary deities, called *oiaron* or *ochinagenda*, which were customarily the charge of wise women. An alien could be taken into the clan and into the tribe only through adoption into one of the *ohwachiras*. All the land of an *ohwachira* was the exclusive property of its women. The *ohwachira* was bound to purchase the life of a member who had forfeited it by the killing of a member of the tribe or of an allied tribe, and it possessed the right to spare or to take the life of prisoners made in its behalf or offered to it for adoption.

The clan among the Iroquoian and the Muskhogean peoples is generally constituted of one or more *ohwachiras*. It was developed apparently through the coalescence of two or more *ohwachiras* having a common abode. Amalgamation naturally resulted in a higher organization and an enlargement and multiplication of rights, privileges, and obligations. Where a single *ohwachira* represents a clan it was almost always due to the extinction of sister *ohwachiras*. In the event of the extinction of an *ohwachira* through death, one of the fundamental rules of the constitution of the League of the Iroquois provides for the preservation of the titles of chief and subchief of the *ohwachira*, by placing these titles in trust with a sister *ohwachira* of the same clan, if there be such, during the pleasure of the League council. The following are some of the characteristic rights and privileges of the approximately identical Iroquoian and Muskhogean clans: (1) The right to a common clan name, which is usually that of an animal, bird, reptile, or natural object that may formerly have been regarded as a guardian deity. (2) Representation in the council of the tribe. (3) Its share in the communal property of the tribe. (4) The right to have its elected chief and subchief of the clan confirmed and installed by the tribal council, among the

Iroquois in later times by the League council. (5) The right to the protection of the tribe. (6) The right to the titles of the chiefships and subchiefships hereditary in its *ohwachiras*. (7) The right to certain songs, chants, and religious observances. (8) The right of its men or women, or both together, to hold councils. (9) The right to certain personal names, to be bestowed upon its members. (10) The right to adopt aliens through the action of a constituent *ohwachira*. (11) The right to a common burial ground. (12) The right of the child-bearing women of the *ohwachiras* in which such titles are hereditary to elect the chief and subchief. (13) The right of such women to impeach and thus institute proceedings for the deposition of chiefs and subchiefs. (14) The right to share in the religious rites, ceremonies, and public festivals of the tribe. The duties incident to clan membership were the following: (1) The obligation not to marry within the clan, formerly not even within the phratry to which the clan belonged; the phratry being a brotherhood of clans, the male members of it mutually regarded themselves as brothers and the female members as sisters. (2) The joint obligation to purchase the life of a member of the clan which has been forfeited by the homicide of a member of the tribe or of an allied tribe. (3) The obligation to aid and defend fellow-members by supplying their needs, redressing their wrongs and injuries, and avenging their death. (4) The joint obligation to obtain prisoners or other persons to replace members lost or killed of any *ohwachira* of a clan to which they are related as father's clansmen, the matron of such *ohwachira* having the right to ask that this obligation be fulfilled. All these rights and obligations, however, are not always found together.

The clan or gentile name is not usually the common name of the animal or object after which the clan may be called, but denotes some salient feature or characteristic or the favorite haunt of it, or may be an archaic name of it. One of the Seneca clans is named from the deer, commonly called *neogĕⁿ*, 'cloven foot', while the clan name is *hadinioñgwaiiu*', 'those whose nostrils are large and fine-looking.' Another Seneca clan is named from the sandpiper, which has the onomatopoetic name *dowisdowi*', but the clan name is *hodi'nesiio*', 'those who come from the clean sand,' referring to the sandpiper's habit of running along the water's edge where the sand is washed by the waves. Still another clan is called after the turtle, commonly named *ha'n-owa* from its carapace, but the clan designation is *hadiniadéñ*', 'they have upright

necks.' The number of clans in the different Iroquois tribes varies. The smallest number is 3, found in the Mohawk and Oneida, while the Seneca have 9, the Onondaga 8, and the Wyandot 12.

Clans and gentes are generally organized into phratries and phratries into tribes. Usually only 2 phratries are found in the modern organization of tribes. The Huron and the Cayuga appear formerly to have had 4, but the Cayuga to-day assemble in 2 phratries. One or more clans may compose a phratry. The clans of the phratries are regarded as brothers one to another and cousins to the members of the other phratry, and are so addressed. The phratry has a certain allotted place in every assembly, usually the side of the fire opposite to that held by the other phratry. A clansman in speaking of a person of the opposite phratry may also say "He is my father's clansman," or "He is a child whom I have made," hence the obligation resting on members of a phratry to "find the word" of the dream of a child of the other phratry. The phratry is the unit of organization of the people for ceremonial and other assemblages and festivals, but as a phratry it has no officers; the chiefs and elders of the clans composing it serve as its directors.

The government of a clan or gens, when analytically studied, is seemingly a development from that of the *ohwachira*. The government of a tribe is developed from that of the clan or gens, and a confederation, such as the League of the Iroquois, is governed on the same principle.

The simpler unit of organization surrendered some of its autonomy to the higher unit so that the whole was closely interdependent and cohesive. The establishment of each higher unit necessarily produced new duties, rights, and privileges.

According to Boas the tribes of the N. W. coast, as the Tlingit, Haida, Tsimshian, Heiltsuk, and Kitamat, have animal totems, and a "maternal organization" in which the totem groups are exogamic. The Kwakiutl, however, although belonging to the same stock as the last two, do not have animal totems, because they are in "a peculiar transitional stage." The Kwakiutl is exogamic. In the N. part of this coast area a woman's rank and privileges always descend to her children. As the crest, or totemic emblem, descends in the female line through marriage among the Kwakiutl, a somewhat similar result has been brought about among them. Among the Haida and the Tlingit there are respectively 2 phratries; the Tsimshian have 4, the Heiltsuk 3, and the Kitamat 6. The tribes of the s. part of the coast, according to the same authority, are "purely paternally organized." Natives do not always consider themselves descendants of the totem, but rather of some ancestor of the clan who obtained the totem. An adopted remnant of a tribe may sometimes constitute a clan. See *Social organization.*                (J. N. B. H.)

**Claninnata.** A Chinookan tribe living in 1806 on the s. w. side of Sauvies id., Multnomah co., Oreg. Their estimated population was 200, in 5 houses.

Clah-in-nata.—Lewis and Clark Exped., Coues ed., 1249, note, 1893. Clâh-in-na-ta.—Orig. Jour. Lewis and Clark, IV, 213 et seq., 1905. Clanimatas.—Morse, Rep. to Sec. War, 371, 1822. Clan-in-na-ta's.—Orig. Jour., op. cit., VI, 116, 1905.

**Clatacut.** A former Chinookan village on the N. side of Columbia r., 10 m. below The Dalles, Oreg.—Lee and Frost, Oregon, 176, 1844.

**Clatchotin.** A division of the Tenankutchin on Tanana r., Alaska.

Bear Indians.—Dawson in Rep. Geol. Surv. Can. 1888, 203B, 1889. Clatochin.—Allen, Rep. on Alaska, 137, 1887. Sa-tshi-o-tin'.—Ibid.

**Clatsop.** (*Lā'kjēlak*, 'dried salmon.'— Boas). A Chinookan tribe formerly about C. Adams on the s. side of the Columbia r. and extending up the river as far as Tongue pt and s. along the coast to Tillamook Head, Oreg. In 1806 their number, according to Lewis and Clark, was 200, in 14 houses. In 1875 a few Clatsop were found living near Salmon r. and were removed to Grande Ronde res. in Oregon. The language is now practically extinct, and the remnant of the tribe has been almost wholly absorbed by neighboring groups. The villages of the Clatsop, so far as known, were Konope, Neacoxy, Neahkeluk, Niakewankih, Neahkstowt, and Necotat.         (L. F.)

Calt-sops.—Hunter, Captivity, 71, 1823. Chatsops.—Dart in Ind. Aff. Rep., 214, 1851. Cladsaps.—Scouler (1846) in Jour. Ethnol. Soc. Lond., I, 236, 1848. Clap-sott.—Clark (1805) in Orig. Jour. Lewis and Clark, III, 238, 1905. Clasaps.—Schoolcraft, Ind. Tribes, III, map, 96, 1853. Classops.—Smet, Letters, 220, 1843. Clastops.—Keane in Stanford, Compend., 509, 1878. Clatsaps.—Belcher, Voy., I, 307, 1843. Clât.sop's.—Orig. Jour. Lewis and Clark (1806), VI, 117, 1905. Clatstops.—Ibid. (1805), III, 241, 1905. Clatstops.—Farnham, Travels, 111, 1843. Clatsup.—Nesmith in Ind. Aff. Rep. 1857, 321, 1858. Clot sop.—Orig. Jour. Lewis and Clark (1805), III, 244, 1905. Klaat-sop.—Gibbs, MS., B. A. E. Klatraps.—Smet, Letters, 231, 1843. Klatsaps.—Townsend, Narr., 175, 1839. Klatsops.—Schoolcraft, Ind. Tribes, III, 201, 1853. Lā'kjēlak.—Boas, Chinook Texts, 277, 1894 (own name). Lā'kjēlaq.—Boas, field notes, (Upper Chinook name: 'dry salmon'). Latsop.—Ford in Ind. Aff. Rep., 250, 1858. Satchap.—Buschmann, Spuren der azt.-Spr., 632, 1859. Tlatsap.—Hale in U. S. Expl. Exped., VI, 215, 1846. Tschlahtsop-tschs.—Trans. Oregon Pion. Assn., 85, 887.

**Claushaven.** A former Eskimo missionary station on Disko bay, w. Greenland.

Claushaven.—Crantz, Hist. Greenland, I, 15, pl. 1. 1767. Claushavn.—Meddelelser om Grönland, XXV, map, 1902.

**Clay, Clay-work.** See *Adobe, Pottery.*
**Clay-eating.** See *Food.*

**Clayoquot.** A Nootka tribe living on Meares id. and Torfino inlet, Clayoquot sd., Vancouver id.; pop. 241 in 1904, having become reduced from about 1,100 in 60 years.

Claiakwat.—Swan, MS., B. A. E. Clao-qu-aht.—Can. Ind. Aff. Rep., 357, 1897. Claucuad.—Galiano, Relacion, 19, 1802. Clayoquot.—Mayne, Brit. Col., 251, 1862. Clayoquotoch.—Grant in Jour. Roy. Geog. Soc., 211, 1861. Clyoquot.—Bulfinch in H. R. Doc. 43, 26th Cong., 1st sess., 1, 1840. Clyquots.—Eells in Am. Antiq., 146, 1883. Ilaoquatsh.—Jacob in Jour. Anthrop. Soc. Lond., II, Feb., 1864. Klah-oh-quaht.—Sproat, Sav. Life, 308, 1868. Klahoquaht.—Ibid., 189. Kla-oo-qua-ahts.—Can. Ind. Aff., 52, 1875. Kla-oo-quates.—Jewitt, Narr., 37, 76, 1849. Klay quoit.—Findlay quoted by Taylor in Cal. Farmer, July 19, 1862. Tlaō'kwiath.—Boas in 6th Rep. N. W. Tribes Can., 31, 1890. Tlaoquatch.—Scouler in Jour. Geog. Soc. Lond., I, 224, 1841. Tlaoquatsh.—Latham, Elem. Comp. Philol., 403, 1862.

**Clear Lake Indians.** A collective name loosely applied to the Indians on Clear lake, N. Cal. The shores of this lake were occupied entirely by the Pomo except at the southernmost extremity of the southern arm, known as Lower lake, which for a few miles was controlled by Indians of the Moquelumnan family. See *Laguna.*                (S. A. B.)

Clear Lake Indians.—Wessells (1853) in H. R. Ex. Doc. 76, 34th Cong., 3d sess., 60, 1857. Lak.—Taylor in Cal. Farmer, Mar. 30, 1860. Lakamellos.—Ibid. Locollomillos.—Ibid. Lopillamillos.—Ibid. Lu-pa-yu-ma.—Gibbs (1851) in Schoolcraft, Ind. Tribes, III, 110, 1853 (so called by the Wintun Kope of Puta cr.). Lupilomis.—Taylor, op. cit. Lu-pi-yu-ma.—Wessells, op. cit. Socollomillos.—Bancroft, Nat. Races, I, 363, 1874.

**Clecksclocutsee.** A former village 12 m. inland from Clayoquot town, on the w. coast of Vancouver id.—Bulfinch in H. R. Doc. 43, 26th Cong., 1st sess., 2, 1840.

**Clelikitte.** An unidentified (Wakashan) tribe about Queen Charlotte sd., Brit. Col.

Cle-li-kit-te.—Kane, Wand. in N. Am., app., 1859.

**Clemclemalats.** A Salish tribe speaking the Cowichan dialect and residing in Cowichan valley, Vancouver id.; pop. 140 in 1904.

Clem-clem-a-lats.—Can. Ind. Aff. 1898, 417, 1899. Clem-clemalets.—Ibid., 1901, pt. II, 164. Clem-clem-a-lits.—Ibid., 308, 1879. Clymclymalats.—Brit. Col. Map, Ind. Aff., Victoria, 1872. Tlemtle'melets.—Boas, MS., B. A. E., 1887.

**Clickass.** Said to have been a former Kaigani village on Prince of Wales id. See *Klinkwan.*

Click-ass.—Work (1836) quoted by Dawson, Queen Charlotte Ids., 173B, 1880. Clict-ars.—Work (1836) quoted by Kane, Wand. in N. Am., app., 1859. Clict-ass.—Work (1836) quoted by Schoolcraft, Ind. Tribes, V, 489, 1855.

**Cliff-dwellings.** A term applied to designate the houses in the cliffs of the arid region, the former occupants of which belonged, at least in the main, to the group of tribes now known as the Pueblos. The plateau country of Arizona, New Mexico, Colorado, and Utah abounds in natural recesses and shallow caverns weathered in the faces of the cliffs; primitive tribes, on taking possession of the region, although by preference, no doubt, settling in the valleys along the running streams, in many cases naturally occupied the ready-made shelters for residence, storage, and burial, and for hiding and defense in time of danger. This

CASA BLANCA RUINS IN CANYON DE CHELLY, ARIZONA

occupancy led in time to the building of marginal walls for protection and houses within for dwelling, to the enlargement of the rooms by excavation when the formations permitted, and, probably later on, to the excavation of commodious dwellings, such as are now found in many sections of the arid region. Archeologists thus find it convenient to distinguish two general classes of cliff-dwellings, the cliff-house proper, constructed of masonry, and the cavate house, excavated in the cliffs.

It is commonly believed that the agricultural tribes of pre-Spanish times, who built large towns and developed an extensive irrigation system, resorted to the cliffs, not from choice, but because of the encroachment of warlike tribes, who were probably nonagricultural, having no well established place of abode. This must be true to some extent, for no people, unless urged by dire necessity, would resort to fastnesses in remote canyon walls or to the margins of barren and almost inaccessible plateaus and there establish their dwellings at enormous cost of time and labor; and it is equally certain that a people once forced to these retreats would, when the stress was removed, descend to the lowlands to reestablish their houses where water is convenient and in the immediate vicinity of arable lands. Although these motives of hiding and de-

fense should not be overlooked, it appears that many of the cliff sites were near streams and fields, and were occupied because they afforded shelter and were natural dwelling places. It is important to note also that many of the cliff-houses, both built and excavated, are mere storage places for corn and other property, while many others are outlooks from which the fields below could be watched and the approach of strangers observed. In some districts evidence of post-Spanish occupancy of some sites exists—walls of houses are built on deposits accumulated since sheep were introduced, and adobe bricks, which were not used in prehistoric times, appear in some cases. A well authenticated tradition exists among the Hopi that, about the middle of the 18th century a group of their clans, the Asa people, deserted their village on account of an epidemic and removed to the Canyon de Chelly, where they occupied the cliff-shelters for a considerable period, intermarrying with the Navaho.

The area in which the cliff-dwellings occur is practically coextensive with that in which are now found traces of town building and relics attributable to the Pueblo tribes. The most noteworthy of these groups of built dwellings are found in the canyons of the Mesa Verde in Colorado, in Hovenweep, McElmo, and

SQUARE TOWER IN CLIFF RUIN GROUP, McELMO CREEK, COLORADO

Montezuma canyons in Colorado and Utah, in Canyon de Chelly and its branches in N. E. Arizona, and, of the cavate variety, in the cliffs of the Jemez plateau facing the Rio Grande in New

Mexico, and in the Verde valley of Arizona. Although there are local differences in style of building, construction, plan, and finish, the chief characteristics are much the same everywhere. Corresponding differences with general likeness are observed in implements, utensils, and ornaments associated with the ruins— facts which go to show that in early periods, as now, numerous tribal groups were represented in the region, and that then, as now, there was a general community of culture, if not kinship in blood.

Owing to differences in the composition of the rocky strata, the natural shelters occupied by the cliff-dwellings are greatly varied in character. While many are mere horizontal crevices or isolated niches, large enough only for men to crawl into and build small stone lodges,

two, or more stories in height, or to the rocky roof, where this is low and overhanging. In the larger shelters the buildings are much diversified in plan and elevation, owing to irregularities in the conformation of the floor and walls. The first floor was the rock surface, or if that was uneven, of clay or flagstones, and upper floors were constructed of poles set in the masonry, often projecting through the walls and overlaid with smaller poles and willows, finished above with adobe cement. Some of the rooms in the larger buildings were round, corresponding in appearance and no doubt in purpose to the kivas, or ceremonial chambers, of the ordinary pueblos. The masonry is excellent, the rather small stones, gathered in many cases from distant sites, being laid in mortar. The stones were rarely

CLIFF VILLAGE (CLIFF PALACE), MESA VERDE, COLORADO.  (COURTESY OF SANTA FE RAILWAY)

there are extensive chambers, with comparatively level floors, and with roofs opening outward in great sweeps of solid rock surface, more imposing than any structure built by human hands. These latter are capable of accommodating not merely single households, but communities of considerable size. The niches occur at all levels in cliffs rising to the height of nearly a thousand feet, and are often approached with great difficulty from below or, in rare cases, from above. Where the way is very steep, niche stairways were cut in the rock face, making approach possible. Ladders of notched logs were also used. In the typical cliff-dwelling of this class, the entire floor of the niche is occupied, the doorway giving entrance through the outer wall, which is built up vertically from the brink of the rocky shelf and rises one,

dressed, but were carefully selected, so that the wall surface was even, and in some cases a decorative effect was given by alternating layers of smaller and larger pieces and by chinking the crevices with spalls. The walls were sometimes plastered inside and out and finished with clay paint. The doorways were small and squarish, and often did not extend to the floor, except an opening or square notch in the center for the passage of the feet. The lintels were stone slabs or consisted of a number of sticks or small timbers. Windows, or outlook apertures, were numerous and generally small.

Cliff-dwellings to which the term cavate is applied are not built but dug in the cliffs. Where the formations are friable or chalky, natural recesses or openings were enlarged by digging, and this led to the excavation of chambers and groups of chambers at points where no openings previously existed. In cases where the front opening was large, either originally or through the effects of weathering, it

TYPICAL CLIFF-HOUSE, MANCOS CANYON, COLORADO.
(HOLMES, JACKSON)

was walled up as in the ordinary cliff-dwelling, the doors and openings being of usual type; but the typical cavate dwelling is entered through a small hewn opening or doorway and consists of one

EXCAVATED DWELLINGS IN CLIFFS OF VERDE VALLEY, ARIZONA.
(FEWKES)

or more chambers, approximately rectangular or roundish in outline, adapted to the needs of the occupants. The floor is often below the level of the threshold,

and both floors and walls are sometimes plastered, and, in cases, a simple ornamental dado in one or more colors is carried around some of the principal rooms. Frequently crude fireplaces occur near the entrance, sometimes provided with smoke vents; and numerous niches, alcoves, and storage places are excavated at convenient points. In front of the excavated rooms, porches were sometimes built of poles, brush, and stones, holes cut in the cliff wall furnishing the posterior support for roof and floor beams. These cavate dwellings are most numerous on the E. side of the Jemez plateau, facing the Rio Grande, where almost every northern escarpment of the mesas between the mountains and the river is honeycombed with them (Bandelier, Hewett, Mindeleff). They are also numerous along the Rio San Juan and its N.

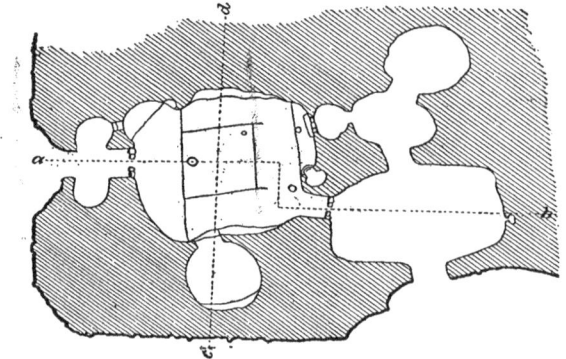

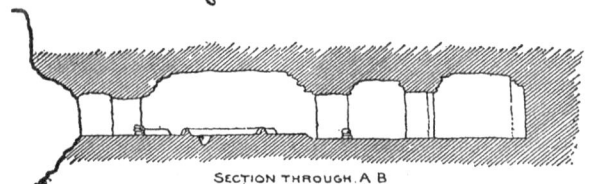

SECTION THROUGH A B

GROUND-PLAN AND SECTION OF EXCAVATED DWELLING, VERDE VALLEY, ARIZONA.   (C. MINDELEFF)

tributaries in New Mexico and Colorado (Holmes), and in the valley of the Rio Verde in Arizona (Fewkes, Mindeleff).

Belonging to the cavate class, yet measurably distinct from the dwellings last described, are certain rude habitations excavated in the slopes of cinder cones and in the steep faces of scoriaceous deposits in the vicinity of Flagstaff, Ariz. These are entered by doorways excavated in the steep slopes of cliffs, or by shafts descending obliquely or vertically where the slopes are gentle. The rooms are of moderate or small size and generally of rather irregular outline. The walls have been plastered in some cases, and not infrequently exterior chambers have been built of the rough scoriaceous rocks. The correspondence of these habitations and their accompanying artifacts with the architectural and minor remains of the general region make it clear that the occupants of these strange dwellings were a part of the great Pueblo family (Powell, Fewkes).

The minor works of art associated with the cliff-dwellings are in general closely analogous to similar remains from the ancient plateau and village sites of the same section. This applies to basketry, pottery, textile products, stone implements and utensils, and various kinds of weapons and ornaments. The presence of agricultural implements and of deposits of charred corn in many places indicates that the people depended largely on agriculture.

The antiquity of the cliff-dwellings can only be surmised. That many of them were occupied in comparatively recent times is apparent from their excellent state of preservation, but their great numbers and the extent of the work accomplished suggest very considerable antiquity. Just when the occupancy of the cliffs began, whether 500 or 5,000 years ago, must for the present remain a question. Some travelers have reported the occurrence of ancient stone houses overwhelmed and destroyed by flows of lava, and have inferred great age from this; but verification of these reports is wanting. Striking differences in the crania of earlier and later occupants of the cliff-dwellings are cited to prove early occupancy by a distinct race, but craniologists observe that equally striking differences exist between tribes living side by side at the present day. It may be safely said that to the present time no evidence of the former general occupancy of the region by peoples other than those now classed as Pueblo Indians or their neighbors to-day has been furnished. Among the more important examples of the cliff ruins are the so-called Cliff Palace in Walnut canyon and the Spruce Tree House in Navaho canyon, Mesa Verde, Colo. (Chapin, Nordenskiöld); Casa Blanca in Canyon de Chelly (Mindeleff); and the so-called Montezuma Castle on Beaver cr., Ariz. (Mearns). Intimately associated with these cliff-dwellings, and situated on the plateaus immediately above or at the base of the cliffs below, are ruins of pueblos in every way identical with the pueblos in the open country. See *Pueblos.*

In the canyons of the Piedras Verdes r., Chihuahua, Mexico, are cliff-dwellings corresponding in many respects with those of the Pueblo region. These are in ruins, but in other sections of the same state there are similar dwellings occupied to-day by the Tarahumare (Lumholtz). The most southerly cliff-dwellings thus far observed are in the state of Jalisco, central Mexico (Hrdlicka).

Quite distinct in type from the cliff-dwellings of the arid region are the picturesque and remarkable dwellings of the Eskimo fishermen of King id., near the N. margin of Bering sea. Here there are some 40 dwellings partly excavated in the side of the precipitous cliffs and partly built of stone and wood. The exterior portions are constructed of driftwood poles and covered with hides and earth. A low-covered passage, 10 to 15 ft. in length, leads under the center of the dwelling, which is entered by a small opening in the floor. In summer these caves sometimes become too damp for comfortable occupancy, and the people erect summer houses over them, which consist of a framework of wood covered with walrus hides, forming rooms from 10 to 15 ft. square. These houses are anchored to the rocks with ropes of rawhide which prevent their being blown into the sea (Jackson, Nelson). See *Pile-dwellings.*

Among works treating of the cliff-dwellings of the arid region are: Bandelier in Papers Arch. Inst. Am., III, 1890; IV, 1892; Birdsall in Bull. Am. Geog. Soc., XXIII, 1891; Chapin, Land of the Cliff Dwellers, 1892; Fewkes in 17th and 22d Reps. B. A. E., 1898, 1904; Hewett in Smithson. Rep. 1904, 1905; Holmes in Rep. U. S. Geol. Surv. of Terr. for 1876, 1879; Jackson, ibid., 1874, 1876; Lummis (1) Strange Corners, 1892, (2) Land of Poco Tiempo, 1893; Mearns in Pop. Sci. Mo., XXXVII, 1890; Mindeleff (V.) in 8th Rep. B. A. E., 1891; Mindeleff (C.) in 13th Rep. B. A. E., 1896; Nordenskiöld, Cliff Dwellings of the Mesa Verde, 1893; Powell in 7th Rep. B. A. E., XVIII, 1901; Prudden in Am. Anthrop., V, no. 2, 1903; Simpson, Exped. into Navajo Country, 1850; Stevenson in Bull. Am. Geog. Soc., XVIII, 1886. The Mexican cliff-houses are described by Lumholtz in Unknown Mexico, I, 1902, and by Hrdlicka in Am. Anthrop., V, 1903; and those of Alaska by Nelson in 18th Rep. B. A. E., 1899, and by Jackson in Metropol. Mag., Jan., 1905. See *Architecture, Habitations, Popular Fallacies, Pueblos.*　　　　　　　　(W. H. H.)

**Cliff Palace.** A celebrated ruined cliff-dwelling in Cliff canyon, Mesa Verde, s. Colo., 2 m. across the mesa, s. E. of the Spruce Tree House. It consists of a group of houses in a fair state of preservation, all connecting and opening one into another, the whole forming a crescent about 100 yds. from end to end. It contains ruins of 146 rooms, some of which are on a secondary ledge. The village contained 5 kivas or estufas. See H. R. Rep. 3703, 58th Cong., 3d sess., 1905, and consult Chapin and Nordenskiöld cited above under *Cliff-dwellings.*

**Clistowacka.** A Delaware village formerly near Bethlehem, Pa.—Loskiel (1742) in Day, Penn., 517, 1843.

**Clocktoot.** A body of Shuswap of Kamloops agency, Brit. Col.; pop. 194 in 1884. **Clock-toot.**—Can. Ind. Aff., pt. I, 188, 1884.

**Clo-oose.** A Nitinat village at the mouth of Suwany r., s. w. coast of Vancouver id.; pop. 80 in 1902.—Can. Ind. Aff., 264, 1902.

**Cloquallum.** A former subdivision and village of the Upper Chehalis on a river of the same name in w. Washington. **Clickquamish**-—Ford in Ind. Aff. Rep., 341, 1857 (called Lower Chehalis, but probably the same as the above.) **Kla-kwul-lum.**—Boas, inf'n, 1904. **Luqlu'lEm.**—Ibid.

**Clothing.** The tribes of northern America belong in general to the wholly clothed peoples, the exceptions being those inhabiting the warmer regions of s. United States and the Pacific coast, who

FLORIDA WAR CHIEF; SIXTEENTH CENTURY. (DE BRY)

were semiclothed. Tanned skin of the deer family was generally the material for clothing throughout the greater part of the country, and dressed fur skins and pelts of birds sewed together were invariably used by the Eskimo. The hide of the

buffalo was worn for robes by tribes of the plains, and even for dresses and leggings by older people, but the leather was too harsh for clothing generally, while elk or moose skin, although soft, was too thick. Fabrics of bark, hair, fur, mountain-sheep wool, and feathers were made in the N. Pacific, Pueblo, and southern regions, and cotton has been woven by the Hopi from ancient times. Climate, environment, elevation, and oceanic currents determined the materials used for clothing as well as the demand for clothing. Sinew from the tendons of the larger animals was the usual sewing material, but fibers of plants, especially the agave, were also employed. Bone awls were used in sewing; bone needles were rarely employed and

BOY'S COSTUME; WESTERN ESKIMO. (MURDOCH)

were too large for fine work. The older needlework is of exceptionally good character and shows great skill with the awl. Unlike many other arts, sewing was practised by both sexes, and each sex usually made its own clothing. The typical and more familiar costume of the Indian man was of tanned buckskin and consisted of a shirt, a breechcloth, leggings tied to a belt or waist-strap, and low moccasins. The shirt, which hung free over the hips, was provided with sleeves and was designed to be drawn over the head. The woman's costume differed from that of the man in the length of the shirt, which had short sleeves hanging loosely over the upper arm, and in the absence of the breechcloth. Women also wore the belt to confine the garment at the waist. Robes of skin, woven fabrics, or of feathers were also worn, but blankets(q.v.) were substituted for these later. The costume presented tribal differences in cut, color, and ornamentation. The free edges were generally fringed, and quill embroidery and beadwork, painting, scalp-locks, tails of animals, feathers, claws, hoofs, shells, etc., were applied

MAN'S COSTUME; WESTERN ESKIMO. (MURDOCH)

as ornaments or charms (see *Adornment*). The typical dress of the Pueblo Indians is generally similar to that of the Plains tribes, except that it is made largely of woven fabrics.

The Alaskan Eskimo costume also is quite similar, but the woman's coat is provided with a hood, and legging and moccasin are made into one garment, while the men wear breeches and boots. Besides the heavy fur outer clothing, under-coat, under-trousers, and stockings (the latter in s. Alaska of twined grass) are found necessary by the Eskimo as a protection from the cold. They also make waterproof coats of the intestines of seal and walrus, which are worn on hunting trips in the kaiak. In s. Alaska a long outer dress without hood, made of squirrel pelts, is worn, a costume indicating Russian influence. In general the Eskimo costume was more complete than that of any tribes within the United States. The British Columbia tribes made twined robes of frayed cedar bark and sagebrush bark, and bordered them with otter fur. The Chilkat of s. E. Alaska still weave remarkable ceremonial blankets of mountain-goat wool over a warp of twisted wool and bark.

Among the Pacific coast tribes, and those along the Mexican border, the Gulf, and the Atlantic coast, the customary garment of women was a fringe-like skirt of bark, cord, strung seeds, or peltry, worn around the loins. In certain seasons or during special occupations only the loin band was worn. For occasional

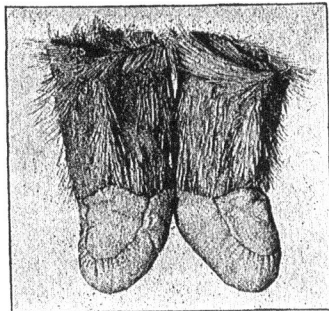

BOOTS OF HUDSON BAY ESKIMO. (TURNER)

WOMAN'S HOOD; WESTERN ESKIMO. (MURDOCH)

CHIEF'S COSTUME; HAIDA. (NIBLACK)

use in cooler weather a skin robe or cape was thrown about the shoulders, or, under exceptional conditions, a large robe woven

HUPA WOMAN'S CINCTURE. (MASON)

of strips of rabbit skin. Ceremonial costume was much more elaborate than that for ordinary wear. Moccasins and leggings were worn throughout much of this area, but in the warmer parts and in Cali-

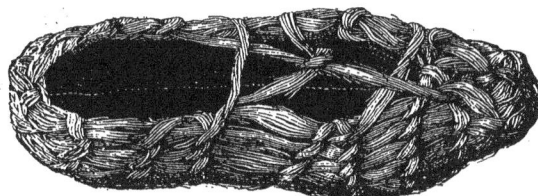

ANCIENT CLIFF-DWELLER'S SANDAL. (MASON)

fornia their use was unusual. Some tribes near the Mexican boundary wear sandals, and sandal-wearing tribes once ranged widely in the S. W. Those have also been found in Kentucky caverns.

ANCIENT SANDAL FROM A KENTUCKY CAVE. (HOLMES)

Hats, usually of basketry, were worn by many Pacific coast tribes. Mittens were used by the Eskimo and other tribes of the far N. Belts of various materials and ornamentation not only confined the clothing but supported pouches, trinket bags, paint bags, etc. Larger pouches and pipe bags of fur or deerskin, beaded or ornamented with quillwork, and of plain skin, netting, or woven stuff, were

BASKETRY HAT; HAIDA.   (NIBLACK)

slung from the shoulder. Necklaces, earrings, charms, and bracelets in infinite variety formed a part of the clothing, and the wrist-guard to protect the arm from the recoil of the bow-string was general.

Shortly after the advent of whites Indian costume was profoundly modified over a vast area of America by the copying of European dress and the use of traders' stuffs. Knowledge of prehistoric and early historic primitive textile fabrics has

BASKETRY HAT; HUPA.   (MASON)

been derived from impressions of fabrics on pottery and from fabrics themselves that have been preserved by charring in

MODERN BUCKSKIN COSTUMES; WOMAN AND CHILD; KIOWA.
(RUSSELL, PHOTO)

fire, contact with copper, or protection from the elements in caves.

A synopsis of the costumes worn by tribes living in the 11 geographical regions of northern America follows. The list is necessarily incomplete, for on account of the abandonment of tribal costumes the data are chiefly historical.

(1) ESKIMO (*Northern*). Men: Shirt-coat with hood, trousers, half or full boots, stockings, mittens. Women: Shirt-coat with large hood, trousers or legging-moccasins, belt and mittens, needle-case, workbag, etc. (*Southern*.) Men: Robe, gown, trousers, boots, hood on gown or cap.

(2) ATHAPASCAN (*Mackenzie* and *Yukon*). Men: Shirt-coat, legging-moccasins,

breechcloth, hat, and hood. Women: Long shirt-coat, legging-moccasins, belt.

(3) ALGONQUIAN-IROQUOIS (*Northern*). Men: Robe, shirt-coat, long coat, trousers, leggings, moccasins, breechcloth, turban. (*Virginia*.) Men and women: Cloak, waist garment, moccasins, sandals(?), breechcloth(?). (*Western*.) Men: Robe, long dress-shirt, long leggings, moccasins, bandoleer bag. Women: Long dress-shirt, short leggings, moccasins, belt. (*Arctic*.) Men: Long coat, open in front, short breeches, leggings, moccasins, gloves or mittens, cap or headdress. Women: Robe, shirt-dress, leggings, moccasins, belt, cap, and sometimes a shoulder mantle.

(4) SOUTHERN OR MUSKHOGEAN (*Seminole*). Men: Shirt, over-shirt, leggings, moccasins, breechcloth, belt, turban. Formerly the Gulf tribes wore robe, waist garment, and occasionally moccasins.

(5) PLAINS. Men: Buffalo robe, shirt to knees or longer, breechcloth, thigh-leggings, moccasins, headdress. Women: Long shirt-dress with short ample cape sleeves, belt, leggings to the knees, moccasins.

(6) NORTH PACIFIC (*Chilkat*). Men: Blanket or bark mat robe, shirt-coat (rare), legging-moccasins, basket hat. Women: Tanned skin shoulder-robe, shirt-dress with sleeves, fringed apron, leggings(?), moccasins, breechcloth(?).

(7) WASHINGTON-COLUMBIA (*Salish*). Men: Robe, headband, and, rarely, shirt-coat, leggings, moccasins, breechcloth. Women: Long shirt-dress, apron, and, rarely, leggings, breechcloth, moccasins.

(8) SHOSHONEAN. Same as the Plains tribes.

(9) CALIFORNIA-OREGON (*Hupa*). Men: Robe and waist garment on occasion, moccasins (rarely); men frequently and old men generally went entirely naked. Women: Waist garment and narrow aprons; occasionally robe-cape, like Pueblo, over shoulders or under arms, over breast; basket cap; sometimes moccasins. (*Central California*). Men: Usually naked; robe, network cap, moccasins and breechcloth occasionally. Women: Waist-skirt of vegetal fiber or buckskin, and basketry cap; robe and moccasins on occasion.

(10) SOUTHWESTERN (*Pueblo*). Men: Blanket or rabbit or feather robe, shirt with sleeves, short breeches partly open on outer sides, breechcloth, leggings to knees, moccasins, hair-tape, and headband. Women: Blanket fastened over one shoulder, extending to knees; small calico shawl over blanket thrown over shoulders; legging-moccasins, belt. Sandals formerly worn in this area. Snow

moccasins of fur sometimes worn in winter. (*Apache.*) Men: Same as on plains. Women: Same, except legging moccasins with shield toe. *Navaho*, now like Pueblo; formerly like Plains tribes.

(11) GILA-SONORA (*Cocopa* and *Mohave*). Men: Breechcloth, sandals, sometimes headband. Women: Waist garment, usually of fringed bark, front and rear. (*Pima.*) Same as Plains, formerly cotton robe, waist cloth, and sandals.

Consult the annual reports of the Bureau of American Ethnology; Bancroft, Native Races; Carr in Proc. Am. Antiq. Soc., 1897; Catlin, Manners and Customs N. Am. Inds., 1841; Dellenbaugh, North Americans of Yesterday, 1901; Goddard, The Hupa, Publ. Univ. of Cal., 1904; Hariot, Virginia, 1590, repr. 1871; Mason, Primitive Travel and Transportation, Rep. Nat. Mus., 1894; Schoolcraft, Indian Tribes, I–VI, 1851–57; Willoughby in Am. Anthrop., VII, nos. 1, 3, 4, 1905.
(W. H.)

**Clowwewalla.** A branch of the Chinookan family formerly residing at the falls of Willamette r., Oreg. They are said to have been originally a large and important tribe, but after the epidemic of 1829 were greatly reduced in numbers. In 1851 they numbered 13 and lived on the w. bank opposite Oregon City. They joined in the Dayton treaty of 1855, and later the remnant was removed to Grande Ronde res., Oreg. (L. F.)

**Claugh-e-wall-hah.**—Parker, Jour., 175, 1840. **Clough-e-wal-lah.**—Ibid., 178, 1846. **Clough-e-wall-hah.**—Ibid., 171, 1840. **Clowewallas.**—Coues, Henry-Thompson Jour., 811, 1897. **Clow-we-walla.**—U. S. Ind. Treat. (1855), 19, 1873. **Fall Indians.**—Meek quoted by Medill in H. R. Ex. Doc. 76, 30th Cong., 1st sess., 10, 1848. **GiLa′wēwalamt.**—Boas, field notes. **Gitlā′wē-walamt.**—Boas, MS., B. A. E. **Katlawewalla.**—Framboise quoted by Gairdner (1835) in Jour. Geog. Soc. Lond., XI, 256, 1841. **Keowewallahs.**—Slocum (1835) in H. R. Rep. 101, 25th Cong., 3d sess., 42, 1839. **Thlowiwalla.**—Tolmie and Dawson, Comp. Vocab. Brit. Col., 11, 1884. **Tla-we-wul-lo.**—Lyman in Oregon Hist. Soc. Quar., I, 323, 1900. **Tummewatas.**—Slocum (1835) in H. R. Rep. 101, 25th Cong., 3d sess., 42, 1839. **Tumwater.**—Dart in Ind. Aff. Rep., 214, 1851. **Wallamettes.**—Slocum (1835) in H. R. Rep. 101, 25th Cong., 3d sess., 42, 1839. **Willamette Falls Indians.**—Stanley in Smithson. Misc. Coll., II, 61, 1862. **Willammette Indians.**—Lane in Sen. Ex. Doc. 52, 31st Cong., 1st sess., 171, 1850. **Willamette Tum-water band.**—U. S. Ind. Treat. (1855), 19, 1873. **Willhametts.**—Slocum (1837) in Sen. Doc. 24, 25th Cong., 2d sess., 15, 1838.

**Clubs.** Every tribe in America used clubs, but after the adoption of more effectual weapons, as the bow and the lance, clubs became in many cases merely a part of the costume, or were relegated to ceremonial, domestic, and special functions. There was great variety in the forms of this weapon or implement. Most clubs were designed for warfare. Starting from the simple knobstick, the elaboration of the war-club may be followed in one line through the straight-shafted maul-headed club of the Zuñi, Pima, Mohave, Paiute,

Kickapoo, Kiowa, and Oto, to the slungshot club of other Pueblos, the Apache, Navaho, Ute, Oto, and Sioux, to the club with a fixed stone head of the Ute, Shoshoni, Comanche, Kiowa, and the Siouan tribes. Another line begins with the carved, often flattened, club of the typical pueblos, the Zuñi and Hopi (see *Rabbit sticks*), and includes the musket-shaped club of the northern Sioux, and the Sauk and Fox and other Algonquian tribes, and the flat, curved club with a knobbed head (Alg. *pogamoggan*, Fr. *casse-tête*) belonging to some Sioux, and to the Chippewa, Menominee, and other timber Algonquians. Clubs of this type are often set with spikes, lance-heads, knife-blades, or the like, and the elk horn with sharpened prongs belongs to this class.

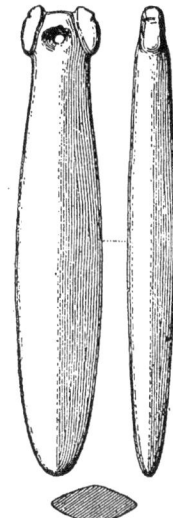

ANCIENT STONE CLUB; OREGON. (1-9)

ANCIENT COPPER CLUB; BRITISH COLUMBIA. (SMITH)

The Plains tribes and those of the N. forest country furnish many exam-

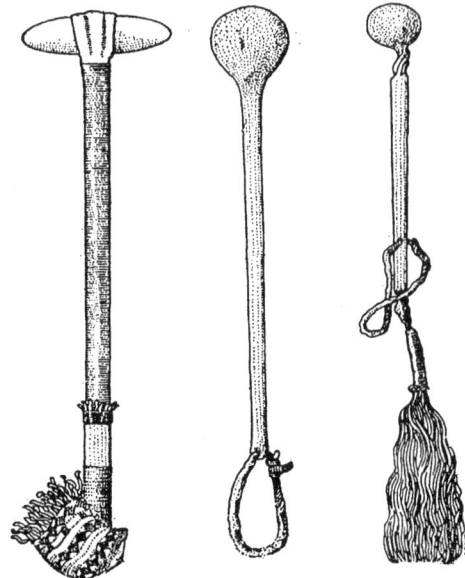

STONE-HEADED CLUBS OF THE PLAINS TRIBES

ples of dangerous-looking ceremonial clubs of this character. There is, however, archeologic evidence that rows of flint splinters or horn points were set in clubs by the Iroquois and the Indians of North Carolina, forming a weapon like the Aztec maquahuitl (Morgan, League of Iroquois, 359, 1851).

A series of interesting paddle-shaped clubs, ancient and modern, often with carved handles, are found in the culture area of the Salishan tribes. They are from 18 to 24 in. long, made of bone, stone, wood, and, rarely, copper. Shorter clubs, that could be concealed about the person, were also used. Le Moyne figures paddle-shaped clubs that were employed by Floridian tribes which in structure and function suggest a transition toward the sword.

Outside the Pueblos few missile clubs are found. Most Indian clubs are furnished with a thong for the wrist, and others have pendants, often a cow's tail, a bunch of hawk or owl feathers, or a single eagle feather.

The stone-headed clubs were usually made by paring thin the upper end of a wooden staff, bending it round the stone in the groove, and covering the withe part and the rest of the staff with wet rawhide, which shrank in drying and held all fast. In many cases, especially on the plains, the handle was inserted in a socket bored in the stone head, but this, it would seem, is a modern process. The head of the slung-shot club was a round or oval stone, entirely inclosed in rawhide, and the handle was so attached as to leave a pliable neck, 2 or

TSIMSHIAN WAR-CLUB OF WOOD; 1-12. (NIBLACK)

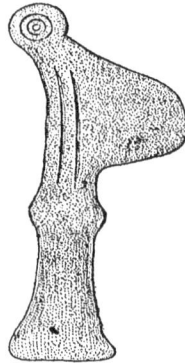

TLINGIT WAR-CLUB OF STONE; 1-7. (NIBLACK)

3 in. long, between the head and the upper end of the handle, also inclosed in rawhide.

The heads of the rigid clubs were of hard stone, grooved and otherwise worked into shape, in modern times often double-pointed and polished, catlinite being sometimes the material. The pemmican maul had only one working face, the other end of the stone being capped with rawhide. The hide-working maul followed the form of the typical club, but was usually much smaller.

The tribes of British Columbia and s. E. Alaska made a variety of clubs for killing slaves, enemies, salmon, seal, etc., and for ceremony. These clubs were usually handsomely carved, inlaid, and painted. The Eskimo did not make clubs for war, but a few club-like mallets of ivory and deer-horn in their domestic arts.

Mauls resembling clubs, and which could be used as such on occasion, were found among most tribes, the common form being a stone set on a short handle by means of rawhide, employed by women for driving stakes, beating bark and hide, and pounding pemmican.

Ceremonial clubs and batons (q. v.) were used, though few specimens of these now exist. The chief man of the Mohave carried a potato-masher-shaped club in battle, and clubs of similar shape have been found in caves in s. Arizona. The Zuñi employ in certain ceremonies huge batons made of agave flower stalks, as well as some of their ordinary club weapons, and in the New-fire ceremony of the Hopi a priest carries an agave-stalk club in the form of a plumed serpent (Fewkes). Batons were often carried as badges of office by certain officers of the Plains tribes and those of the N. W. coast. Captain John Smith describes clubs 3 ells long. The coup stick was often a ceremonial club. It is noteworthy that the parrying club was not

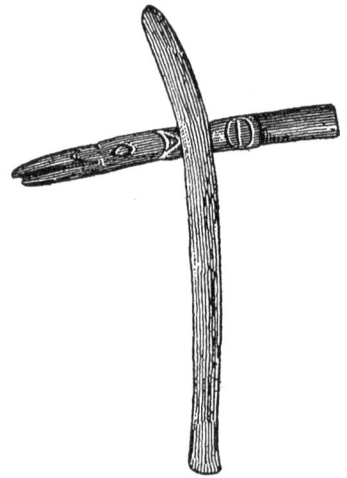

TLINGIT CLUB FOR KILLING SLAVES; 1-11. (NIBLACK)

known in America. See Batons, Hammers, Rabbit-sticks, Tomahawks.

Consult Boas in Rep. Nat. Mus. 1895, 1897; Knight, Savage Weapons at the Centennial, Smithson. Rep. 1879, 1880; Moorehead, Prehist. Impls., 1900; Morgan, League of the Iroquois, 1904; Niblack in Rep. Nat. Mus. 1888, 1890; Nelson in 18th Rep. B. A. E., 1899; Smith in Mem. Am. Mus. Nat. Hist., 1903.    (w. h.)

**Coahuiltecan.** A name adopted by Powell from the tribal name Coahuilteco used by Pimentel and Orozco y Berra to include a group of small, supposedly cognate tribes on both sides of the lower Rio Grande in Texas and Coahuila. The family is founded on a slender basis, and the name is geographic rather than ethnic, as it is not applied to any tribe of the group, while most of the tribes included therein are extinct, only meager remnants of some two or three dialects being preserved. Pimentel (Lenguas, II, 409, 1865)

says: "I call this language Tejano or Coahuilteco, because, according to the missionaries, it was the one most in use in the provinces of Coahuila and Texas, being spoken from La Candela to the Rio San Antonio." The tribes speaking this language were known under the names of Pajalates, Orejones, Pacaos, Pacoas, Tilijayos, Alasapas, Pausanes, Pacuaches, Mescales, Pampopas, Tacames, Venados, Pamaques, Pihuiques, Borrados, Sanipaos, and Manos de Perro. The only book known to treat of their language is the Manual para administrar los santos sacramentos, by Fray Bartholomé García, Mexico, 1760. Other names have been mentioned as possibly those of tribes belonging to the same family group, chiefly because they resided in the same general region: Aguastayas, Cachopostales, Carrizos (generic), Casas Chiquitas, Comecrudo, Cotonam, Pacaruja, Pakawa, Pastancoya, Patacal, Payaya, Pihuique, Tejones, and Tilijaes. In addition to these the following may possibly belong to the family, as the names where mentioned are given in connection with those of some of the preceding tribes: Mesquites, Parchinas, Pastias, Pelones, and Salinas. How many of the names given are applicable to distinct tribes and how many are synonyms is not known on account of the insufficiency of data. See Gatschet, Karankawa Inds., 1891. (A. S. G. C. T.)
=Coahuiltecan.—Powell in 7th Rep. B. A. E., 68, 1891. =Coahuilteco.—Orozco y Berra, Geog., map, 1864. =Tejano.—Pimentel, Lenguas, II, 409, 1865 (or Coahuilteco).

**Coama.** An Indian settlement of which Alarcon learned from natives of the Gulf of California region, and described as being in the vicinity of Cibola (Zuñi), but which was afterward found by him on his voyage up the Rio Colorado, or Buena Guia. See Alarcon (1540) in Hakluyt, Voy., III, 514, 1600; Ternaux-Compans, Voy., IX, 326, 1838.
Coana.—Ternaux-Compans, op. cit.

**Coanopa.** A tribe, apparently Yuman, residing probably on or in the vicinity of the lower Rio Colorado early in the 18th century. They visited Father Kino while he was among the Quigyuma and are mentioned by him in connection with the Cuchan (Yuma) and other tribes (Venegas, Hist. Cal., I, 308, 1759; Coues, Garcés Diary, 551, 1900). Possibly the Cocopa.

**Coapites.** An unidentified tribe or band formerly living in the coast region of the present State of Texas.—Rivera, Diario y Derrotero, leg. 2602, 1736.

**Coaque.** A tribe formerly living on Malhado id., off the coast of Texas, where Cabeza de Vaca suffered shipwreck in 1528. This was almost certainly Galveston id. Cabeza de Vaca found two tribes, each with its own language, living there—one

the Han, the other the Coaque. The people subsisted from October to March on a root taken from the shoal water and on fish which they caught in weirs; they visited the mainland for berries and oysters. They displayed much affection toward their children and greatly mourned their death. For a year after the loss of a son the parents wailed each day before sunrise, at noon, and at sunset. As soon as this cry was heard it was echoed by all the people of the tribe. At the end of the year a ceremony for the dead was held, after which "they wash and purify themselves from the stain of smoke." They did not lament for the aged. The dead were buried, all but those who had "practised medicine," who were burned. At the cremation a ceremonial dance was held, beginning when the fire was kindled and continuing until the bones were calcined. The ashes were preserved, and at the expiration of a year they were mixed with water and given to the relatives to drink. During the period of mourning the immediate family of a deceased person did not go after food, but had to depend on their kindred for means to live. When a marriage had been agreed on, custom forbade the man to address his future mother-in-law, nor could he do so after the marriage. According to Cabeza de Vaca this custom obtained among tribes "living 50 leagues inland." The houses of the Coaque were of mats and were set up on a "mass of oyster shells." The men wore a piece of cane, half a finger thick, inserted in the lower lip, and another piece two palms and a half long thrust through one or both nipples. Owing to the starvation which faced the Spaniards after their shipwreck, they were forced to eat their dead; this action gave the natives such great concern that "they thought to kill" the strangers, but were dissuaded by the Indian who had Cabeza de Vaca in charge.

Gatschet (Karankawa Inds., I, 34, 1891) is correct in identifying these Indians with the Cokés of Bollaert, but he is probably wrong in supposing the Cujanos are also the same. That the Coaques and the Cujanos or Cohani (q. v.) were distinct seems to be indicated by the statement of an early Texan settler (Texas Hist. Quar., VI, 1903) that "the Cokes and Cohannies" were "but fragments of the Carancawa tribe." Probably the latter are Cabeza de Vaca's Quevenes. That the Coaque spoke a dialect of Karankawa is indicated as well by Bollaert (Jour. Ethnol. Soc. Lond., II, 265, 1850), since he refers to them as a branch of the "Koronks," a variant of Karankawa. In 1778, according to Mezières, about 20 families of Mayeyes and Cocos lived between the Colorado and the Brazos, opposite the island of La Culebra. The mounds and graves found on the coast of Texas probably belonged to the Coaque and kindred tribes, which are now extinct.           (A. C. F.)

**Biscatronges.**—Barcia quoted by Gatschet, Karankawa Inds., 34, 1891 (='weepers'). **Biskatronge.**—Barcia, Ensayo, 263, 1723. **Cadoques.**—Davis, Span. Conq. N. Mex., 82, 1869. **Cahoques.**—Cabeça de Vaca (1529), Smith transl., 137, 1871. **Caoques.**—Ibid., 139. **Capoques.**—Ibid., 82. **Cayoques.**—Davis, op. cit. **Coaquis.**—Barcia, Ensayo, 259, 1723. **Cocos.**—Rivera, Diario, leg. 2602, 1736. **Cokés.**—Bollaert in Jour. Ethnol. Soc. Lond., II, 276, 1850. **Plañidores.**—Barcia, Ensayo, 264, 1723. **Pleureurs.**—Martin, Hist. La., I, 116. **Quoaquis.**—Douay (1687) quoted by Shea, Discov. Miss. Val., 207, 1852. **Weepers.**—Gatschet, Karankawa Inds., 34, 1891.

**Coassitt** ('at the pines.'—Hewitt). An Indian rendezvous during King Philip's war of 1675; situated about 56 m. above Hadley, Mass. (Appleton, 1675, in Barber, Mass. Hist. Coll., 294, 1839). Possibly Coosuc (q. v.).

**Coat.** A rancheria, probably of the Maricopa, visited by Kino and Mange in 1699.—Mange quoted by Bancroft, Ariz. and N. Mex., 358, 1889.

**Coatraw.** A former Choctaw town which probably stood about 4 m. w. of Newton, Newton co., Miss., where are several broad low mounds. The name is evidently greatly corrupted and can not be interpreted. See Romans, Florida, map, 1775; Brown in Miss. Hist. Soc. Publ., VI, 444, 1902.

**Coatuit.** A village of Praying Indians, probably belonging to the Nauset, near Osterville, Barnstable co., Mass., in 1674.—Bourne (1674) in Mass. Hist. Soc. Coll., 1st s., I, 197, 1806.

**Coaxet.** A village of Praying Indians formerly near Little Compton, Newport co., R. I., subject to the Wampanoag. As late as 1685 it contained about 100 adults. Acoakset r. preserves the name.

**Coaksett.**—Records (1664?) quoted by Drake, Bk. Inds., bk. 3, 10, 1848. **Coaxet.**—Drake, ibid., 14. **Cokesit.**—Rawson and Danforth (1698) in Mass. Hist. Soc. Coll., 1st s., X, 130, 1809. **Cooxet.**—Hinckley (1685), ibid., 4th s., V, 133, 1861. **Cooxitt.**—Ibid. **Coquitt.**—Cotton (1674), ibid., 1st s., I, 200, 1806. **Ooxit.**—Ibid.

**Coayos.** An unidentified tribe that lived near the Cutalchiches, Malicones, and Susolas, of whom Cabeza de Vaca (Smith trans., 72, 1851) heard during his stay with the Avavares in Texas in 1527–34.

**Cobardes.** Given by Dominguez and Escalante (Doc. Hist. Mex., 2d s., I, 537, 1854) as one of 5 divisions of the Ute in 1776, and subdivided into the Huascari, Parusi, Yubuincariri, Ytimpabichi, and Pagampache. Some of these appear to be Ute and some Paiute.

**Cobora.** An Opata village, now in ruins, near Guachinera, E. Sonora, Mexico.—Bandelier in Arch. Inst. Papers, IV, 517, 1892.

**Coca.** A former Papago village in s. Arizona.—Taylor in Cal. Farmer, June 19, 1863.

**Cocash.** A name of the red-stalk or purple-stem aster (*Aster puniceus*), known also as swan-weed, early purple aster, etc.; from one of the eastern dialects of the Algonquian language, signifying 'it is rough to the touch,' in reference to the stem of the plant.         (A. F. C.)

**Cochali.** Given by Coxe in 1741 as the name of one of 4 small islands in Tennessee r., 40 leagues above the Chickasaw, each occupied by a "nation" of the same name. The others were Kakick, Tahogale, and Tali (Little Talasse). The location was in N. Alabama, and the names may perhaps be Creek. They do not seem to be Cherokee, although Cochali may possibly be *kâtsălû'*, implying 'something in a sheath.'      (J. M.)

**Cochali.**—Coxe, Carolana, 14, 1741 (after Sauvole, 1701). **Cochaly.**—Ibid., map.

**Cochimi** (*ko-chi-mi'*). A term originally used to designate a Yuman dialect supposed to have been spoken from about lat. 26° to the N. limit of Lower California. It is doubtful, however, if any single dialect was spoken over such an extended area. It is here employed as a collective or divisional name embracing many former tribes of the Californian peninsula from lat. 31° southward to about lat. 26°, including the settlements around Loreto. The tribes of this division were the most populous in the peninsula, though it would be difficult now to define their limits to the N. and s. in a strictly ethnologic or linguistic sense. According to Hervas (Idea dell' Universo, XXI, 79–80, 1787) there existed in 1767 the following missions at which Cochimi dialects were spoken: San Xavier de Biaundo (pop. 485); San José Comondu (pop. 360); Santa Borja (1,500 neophytes); Santa Maria Magdalena (300 neophytes and 30 catechumens); La Purísima Concepcion (130 neophytes); Santa Rosalia de Mulege or Muleje (pop. 300); N. S. de Guadalupe (530 neophytes); San Ignacio (pop. 750), and Santa Gertrudis (pop. 1,000). A few of these Indians are said to survive. Duflot de Mofras (Expl., I, 227, 1844) states that in his time the Cora, Edu, Pericu, and Cochimi were no longer distinct from one another, but Buschmann regards this as doubtful.

The following are classed as Cochimi tribes or rancherias: Adac, Afegua, Aggavacaamanc, Amalgua, Amaniini, Ametzilhacaamanc, Anchu, Avolabac, Caamancijup, Caddehi, Cadecuijtnipa, Cadegomo, Cadeudebet, Cahelca, Cahelejyu, Cahelembil, Cahelmet, Camancnaccooya, Camanocacaamano, Cunitcacahel, Eguiannacahel, Gabacamanini, Gamacaamanc, Gamacaamancxa, Hualimea, Idelabuu, Idelibinaga, Ika, Jetti, Laimon, Liggige, Menchu, Mokaskel, Paviye, Paya, Piacaamanc, Piagadme, San Athanasio, San Benito de Aruy, San Francisco Borja, San Francisco Vellicata, San Ignacio de Kadakaman, San José de Comondu, San Juan, San Miguel, San Sabas, Santa Aguida, Santa Gertrudis, Santa Lucia, Santa Maria, Santa Marta, Santa Monica, Santa Nynfa, San Pedro y San Pablo, Santisima Trinidad, Tahuagabacahel, Temedegua, Uacazil, Vaba, Vabacahel, Vajademin, Vazacahel, Vinatacot. (H. W. H.)

**Cochiemes.**—Taylor in Cal. Farmer, May 18, 1860. **Cochimas.**—Mayer, Mexico, II, 38, 1853. **Cochime.**—Venegas, Hist. Cal., II, 340, 1759. **Cochimi.**—Hervas, Idea dell' Universo, XVII, 1784. **Cochimies.**—Clavijero, Hist Cal., 22, 1789, repr. 1852. **Cochimy.**—Venegas, Hist. Cal., II, 324, 1759. **Cochini.**—Ibid., 200. **Colimies.**—Humboldt, Atlas, carte 2, 1811. **Cotshimi.**—Baegert in Smithson. Rep., 1864, 393, 1865. **Cuchimies.**—Doc. Hist. Mex., 4th s., V, 53, 1857. **Cuchinu.**—Ibid., 80.

**Cochise.** A Chiricahua Apache chief, father and predecessor of Tazi Nachi. Although ever at feud with the Mexicans, he gave no trouble to the Americans until after he went, in 1861, under a flag of truce, to the camp of a party of soldiers to deny that his tribe had abducted a white child. The commanding officer was angered by this and ordered the visiting chiefs seized and bound because they would not confess. One was killed and four were caught, but Cochise, cutting through the side of a tent, made his escape with three bullets in his body and immediately began hostilities to avenge his companions, who were hanged by the Federal troops. The troops were forced to retreat, and white settlements in Arizona were laid waste. Soon afterward the military posts were abandoned, the troops being recalled to take part in the Civil war. This convinced the Apache that they need only to fight to prevent Americans from settling in their country. Cochise and Mangas Coloradas defended Apache pass in s. E. Arizona against the Californians, who marched under Gen. Carleton to reopen communication between the Pacific coast and the E. The howitzers of the California volunteers put the Apache to flight. When United States troops returned to resume the occupancy of the country after the close of the Civil war, a war of extermination was carried on against the Apache. Cochise did not surrender till Sept., 1871. When orders came to transfer his people from Cañada Alamosa to the new Tularosa res., in New Mexico, he escaped with a band of 200 in the spring of 1872, and his example was followed by 600 others. After the Chiricahua res. was established in Arizona, in the summer of 1872, he came in, and there died in peace June 8,

1874. He was succeeded as chief by his son Taza. The southeasternmost county of Arizona bears Cochise's name. See *Apache, Chiricahua.*

**Cochise Apache.**—A former band of Chiricahua Apache, named from their leader. **Cachees's band.**—Bell in Jour. Ethnol. Soc. Lond., I, 242, 1869. **Cachise Apaches.**—White, MS. Hist. Apaches, B. A. E., 1875. **Cachise Indians.**—Ibid. **Cochees.**—Ind. Aff. Rep., 141, 1868. **Cochise.**—Ind. Aff. Rep., 209, 1875. **Northern Chiricahua Apaches.**—Ibid.

**Cochiti** (*Ko-chi-ti'*). A Keresan tribe and its pueblo on the w. bank of the Rio Grande, 27 m. s. w. of Santa Fe, N. Mex. Before moving to their present location the inhabitants occupied the Tyuonyi, or Rito de los Frijoles, the Potrero de las Vacas, the pueblo of Haatze on Potrero San Miguel or Potrero del Capulin, and

FRANCISCO ARESO, A HEADMAN OF COCHITI

the pueblo of Kuapa in the Cañada de Cochiti. Up to this time, which was still before the earliest Spanish explorations, the ancestors of the present San Felipe inhabitants and those of Cochiti formed one tribe speaking a single dialect, but on account of the persistent hostility of their N. neighbors, the Tewa (to whom is attributed this gradual southerly movement and through whom they were compelled to abandon Kuapa), the tribe was divided, one branch going southward, where they built the pueblo of Katishtya (later called San Felipe), while the other took refuge on the Potrero Viejo, where they established at least a temporary pueblo known as Hanut Cochiti. On the abandonment of this village they retired 6 or 7 m. s. E. to the site of the present Cochiti, on the

Rio Grande, where they were found by Oñate in 1598. The Cochiti took an active part in the Pueblo revolt of 1680, but remained in their pueblo for 15 months after the outbreak, when, learning of the return of Gov. Otermin to reconquer New Mexico, they retreated with the Keresan tribes of San Felipe and Santo Domingo, reenforced by some Tewa from San Marcos and by Tigua from Taos and Picuris, to the Potrero Viejo, where they remained until about 1683, when it was reported that all the villages from San Felipe northward were inhabited. Between 1683 and 1692 the Cochiti, with their San Felipe and San Marcos allies, again took refuge on the Potrero Viejo. In the fall of the latter year they were visited in their fortified abode (known to the Spaniards as Cieneguilla) by Vargas, the reconqueror of New Mexico, who induced them to promise to return to their permanent villages on the Rio Grande. But only San Felipe proved sincere, for in 1692 the Cochiti returned to the Potrero, where they remained until early in the following year, when Vargas, with 70 soldiers, 20 colonists, and 100 warriors from the friendly villagers of San Felipe, Santa Ana, and Sia, assaulted the pueblo at midnight and forced the Cochiti to flee, the Indian allies leaving for the protection of their own homes. The force of Vargas being thus weakened, the Cochiti returned, surprised the Spaniards, and succeeded in liberating most of the Indian captives. Vargas remained a short time, then burned the pueblo and evacuated the Potrero, taking with him to Santa Fe a large quantity of corn and other booty and nearly 200 captive women. Cochiti was the seat of the Spanish mission of San Buenaventura, with 300 inhabitants in 1680, but it was reduced to a visita of Santo Domingo after 1782. These villagers recognize the following clans, those marked with an asterisk being extinct: Oshach (Sun), Tsits (Water), Itra (Cottonwood), Shuwhami (Turquoise), Mohkach (Mountain Lion), Kuhaia (Bear), Tanyi (Calabash), Shrutsuna (Coyote), Hapanyi (Oak), Yaka (Corn), Hakanyi (Fire), *Dyami (Eagle), *Tsin (Turkey), *Kuts (Antelope), *Shruhwi (Rattlesnake), *Washpa (Dance-kilt), *Kishqra (Reindeer?). In addition, Bandelier notes an Ivy and a Mexican Sage clan. Present population 300. The Cochiti people occupy a grant of 24,256 acres, allotted to them by the Spanish government and confirmed by United States patent in 1864. Consult Bandelier in Arch. Inst. Papers, IV, 139, 1892. See also *Keresan, Pueblos.*

(F. W. H.)

Cachiti.—Bandelier, Gilded Man, 216, 1893 (misprint). Chochité.—Barreiro, Ojeada Sobre N. Méx.,
15, 1832. Chochiti.—Oñate (1598) in Doc. Inéd., XVI, 114, 1871. Cocheli.—Vaugondy, map, Amérique, 1778. Cocheti.—Ind. Aff. Rep., 263, 1889. Cocheto.—Ibid., 264. Cochilis.—Meriwether (1856) in H. R. Ex. Doc. 37, 34th Cong., 3d sess., 146, 1857. Cochit.—Prince, N. Mex., 217, 1883. Coohite.—Zarate-Salmeron (ca. 1629) quoted by Bancroft, Nat. Races, I, 600, 1882. Co-chi-te-mi'.—Pac. R. R. Rep., III, pt. 3, 90, 1856 (given as own name). Cochiteños.—Lummis in Scribner's Mag., 92, 1893. Cochiteumi.—Cubas, Repub. of Mexico, 65, 1876. Cochiti.—Oñate (1598) in Doc. Inéd., XVI, 102, 1871. Cochitinos.—Bandelier in Arch. Inst. Bul., I, 26, 1883. Cochito.—Bancroft, Ariz. and N. Mex., map, 1889. Cochitti.—Vargas (1694) quoted by Bandelier in Arch. Inst. Papers, IV, 168, 1892. Cochity.—Ind. Aff. Rep. 1864, 194, 1865. Cocluti.—Curtis, Children of the Sun, 121, 1883. Cotchita.—Kingsley, Stand. Nat. Hist., VI, 183, 1885. Cotchiti.—Powell in Am. Nat., XIV, 604, Aug., 1880. Cuchili.—Simpson, Report Sec. War, map 4, 1850. Cuchin.—Abert, Report, map, 1848. Ko-cke.—Simpson, op. cit., 143 (proper name). Kótite.—Stephen in 8th Rep. B. A. E., 37, 1891 (Tewa name). Kot-ji-ti.—Bandelier in Arch. Inst. Papers, III, 260, 1890 (native name of pueblo). Kotŭ′tï.—Hodge, field notes, B. A. E., 1895 (Acoma name). Kotyit'.—Ibid. Ko-tyi-ti.—Bandelier in Arch. Inst. Papers, III, 126, 1890 (native name of pueblo). Oôtyı-ti.—Bandelier, Gilded Man, 216, 1893 (O=Q). Pa′hlaí.—Hodge, field notes, B. A. E., 1895 (Isleta and Sandia name; prob. sig. 'soapweed place'). Pá′l-āb.—Gatschet, Isleta MS. vocab., B. A. E., 1885 ('soapweed town': Isleta name). Pá′lahuide.—Ibid. (Isleta name for a Cochiti man). Qui′-me.—Pac. R. R. Rep., III, pt. 3, 90, 1856 (incorrectly given as Spanish name of the Cochitemi). St. Bartholomew.—Pike, Trav., 273, 1811 (evidently Cochiti; intended for San Buenaventura). San Bartolomeo.—Mühlenpfordt, Mejico, II, 533, 1844 (mistake). San Buena Ventura de Cochita.—Donaldson, Moqui Pueblo Inds., 91, 1893. San Buenaventura de Cochiti.—Ind. Aff. Rep. 1867, 213, 1868. San Buena Ventura de Cochiti.—Alencaster (1805) in Meline, Two Thousand Miles, 212, 1867. S. Buenaventura.—Bancroft, Ariz. and N. Mex., 281, 1889.

**Cockarouse.** A word, derived from the Algonquian dialect of Virginia, used by early writers in the sense of a person of distinction. In the 17th century the term, written also *cockerouse*, was applied to a member of the Provincial Council. Beverly, in 1705, stated that "a cockarouse is one that has the honor to be of the king's or queen's council." Capt. John Smith (Hist. Va., 38, 1624) couples the word with *werowance* as synonymous with "captain". Trumbull derives *cockarouse* from the Virginian *cawcawaassough*, 'adviser,' 'urger,' from which may be derived also *caucus.*                (A. F. C.)

**Cockenoe** (Algonq.: 'interpreter'). A Montauk, made captive in the Pequot war of 1637, who afterward became the interpreter of John Eliot, the missionary and Bible translator, and probably his first teacher in the Massachuset language. He died about the close of the 17th century, having rendered great service not only to individual settlers, but also to the authorities of New England and New York. Without him the Eliot Bible, in all probability, would never have been prepared. See Tooker, John Eliot's First Indian Teacher and Interpreter: Cockenoe de Long Island, 1896.                (A. F. C.)

**Cockerouse.** See *Cockarouse.*

**Cocoigui.** A former Maricopa rancheria on the Rio Gila, s. Ariz., visited by Father Sedelmair in 1744.—Bancroft, Ariz. and N. Mex., 366, 1889.

**Cocomorachic.** A Tarahumare settlement on the headwaters of the Rio Yaqui, lat. 28° 40′, long. 107° 40′, Chihuahua, Mexico.—Orozco y Berra, Geog., 323, 1864.

**Coconoon.** A Yokuts tribe of California, said by Johnston in 1851 (Schoolcraft, Ind. Tribes, IV, 413, 1854) to "live on the Merced r., with other bands, under their chief Nuella. There are the remnants of 3 distinct bands residing together, each originally speaking a different language. The aged of the people have difficulty in understanding each other." The vocabulary given by Johnston is Yokuts. Merced r. is, however, otherwise known to have been inhabited only by Moquelumnan tribes. The Coconoon are also mentioned by Royce (18th Rep. B. A. E., 780), together with 5 other tribes from Tuolumne and Merced rs. (all of which were undoubtedly Moquelumnan), as ceding all their lands, by treaty of Mar. 19, 1851, excepting a tract between the Tuolumne and the Merced. If these statements about the Coconoon are correct, they constituted a small detached division of the Mariposan family situated among Moquelumnan groups midway between the main body of the stock to the s. and the Cholovone to the N. w.
Co-co-noon.—Johnston (1851) in Sen. Ex. Doc. 61, 32d Cong., 1st sess., 23, 1852.

**Cocopa** (*ko′-ko-pa*). A division of the Yuman family which in 1604–05 lived in 9 rancherias on the Rio Colorado, 5 leagues above its mouth. At a later period they also extended into the mountains of Lower California, hence were confined almost exclusively to Mexico. According to Heintzelman, in 1856, the tribe was formerly strong in numbers and could muster 300 warriors; their total number was estimated by Fray Francisco Garcés in 1775–76 at 3,000, but there are now only 800 in N. Lower California, in the valley of the Rio Colorado. The Cocopa were reputed to be less hostile than the Yuma or the Mohave, who frequently raided their villages; nevertheless they were sufficiently warlike to retaliate when necessary. Garcés said of them in 1776 that they had always been enemies of the Papago, Jalliquamai (Quigyuma), and Cajuenche, but friendly toward the Cuñeil. Although spoken of as being physically inferior to the cognate tribes, the males are fully up to and in some cases rather above normal stature, and are well proportioned, while the females appear also to be of at least ordinary size and are also well developed. Heintzelman (H. R. Ex. Doc. 76, 34th Cong. 3d sess., 43, 1857) says "they so much

resemble the Cuchan (Yuma) in arms, dress, manners, and customs it is difficult to distinguish one from another." They depended for subsistence chiefly on corn, melons, pumpkins, and beans, which they cultivated, adding native grass seeds, roots, mesquite beans, etc. The Cocopa houses of recent time range in character from the brush arbor for summer use to

COCOPA MAN. (McGEE)

the wattled hut, plastered outside and inside with mud, for winter occupancy. Polygamy was formerly practised to some extent. They universally cremate their dead. The Cuculato are mentioned as a Cocopa division and Llagas as the name applied by the Spaniards to a former group of Cocopa rancherias. (F. W. H.)
Cacopas.—Ind. Aff. Rep., 390, 1863. Cacupas.—Schoolcraft, Ind. Tribes, III, 96, 1853. Cocapa.—

Ind. Aff. Rep., 361, 1859. **Cocapas.**—Zárate-Salmeron (*ca.* 1629) in Land of Sunshine, 106, Jan., 1900. **Cochopas.**—Stratton, Oatman Captivity, 175, 1857. **Co-co-pah.**—Schoolcraft, Ind. Tribes, II, 116, 1852. **Co-co-pas.**—Derby, Colorado River, 16, 1852. **Cucapa.**—Garcés (1776), Diary, 434, 1900. **Cucapachas.**—Mayer, Mexico, II, 38, 1853. **Cucassus.**—Hinton, Handbook to Ariz., 28, 1878. **Cucopa.**—Forbes, Hist. Cal., 162, 1839. **Cu-cu-pahs.**—Kern in Schoolcraft, Ind. Tribes, IV, 38, 1854. **Cuhanas.**—Orozco y Berra, Geog., 59, 1864 (Cucapá or; but Cuhana=Cuchan=Yuma). **Cupachas.**—Mayer,

COCOPA WOMAN

Mexico, II, 300, 1853. **Kokopa.**—Ind. Aff. Rep., 246, 1877. **Kukapa.**—A. L. Kroeber, infn., 1905 (Mohave name). **Kwikapa.**—Ibid. (Mohave name, alternative form).

**Cocori.** A former Yaqui settlement s. E. of the lower Rio Yaqui, Sonora, Mexico, with an estimated population of 4,000 in 1849. It is now a white Mexican town, the only Yaqui living there being those employed as laborers. See Escudero,

Not. Son. y Sin., 100, 1849; Velasco, Noticias de Sonora, 84, 1850.
**Cócori.**—Hardy, Trav. in Mexico, 438, 1829. **Cocorún.**—Mühlenpfordt, Mejico, II, pt. 2, 419, 1844. **Espíritu Santo de Cocorin.**—Orozco y Berra, Geog., 355, 1864.

**Cocospera** ('place of the dogs'). A former Pima settlement on the headwaters of Rio San Ignacio, lat. 31°, Sonora, Mexico; pop. 74 in 1730, 133 in 1760. The Apache compelled the abandonment of the village in 1845. See Bartlett, Pers. Narr., I, 417, 1854; Bancroft, No. Mex. States, I, 563, 1884.
**Cocospara.**—Kino, map (1702) in Stöcklein, Neue Welt-Bott, 74, 1726. **Cocospera.**—Kino (1696) in Doc. Hist. Mex., 4th s., I, 267, 1856. **Coespan.**—Rudo Ensayo (1762), 148, 1863. **Coscospera.**—Pineda (1769) in Doc. Hist. Mex., 4th s., II, 10, 1856. **Santiago.**—Bancroft, No. Mex. States, I, 563, 1884 (after early doc.). **Santiago Cocóspera.**—Rivera (1730), ibid., 514.

**Cocoueahra.** Indians who took part in the Santa Isabel treaty with the Diegueños of s. California in 1852. They may have been Yuman or Shoshonean, as some of the latter entered into the treaty. **Co-con-cah-ras.**—Wozencraft (1852) in Sen. Ex. Doc. 4, 32d Cong., spec. sess., 289, 1853. **Co-coueah-ra.**—Wozencraft (1852) in H. R. Ex. Doc 76, 34th Cong., 3d sess., 131, 1857.

**Cocoyes.** Mentioned in 1598 by Oñate (Doc. Inéd., XVI, 114, 303, 1871), in connection with the Apache, as a wild tribe of the New Mexican region. Judging from the name, it is possible that one of the Yuman tribes far to the w. was intended.

**Cocoyomes.** A mythical people, said to be regarded by some of the Tarahumare as their ancient enemies, by others as their ancestors; they are also spoken of as having been the first people. They were short of stature, lived in caves in the high cliffs, and subsisted chiefly on herbs, especially a small agave, and were also cannibals. According to one version, once when they were very bad the sun came down and burned most of them to death; the survivors escaped to 4 large caves at Zapuri, in which they built adobe houses, but the Tarahumare finally besieged the place for 8 days, when the Cocoyomes perished from hunger. Ancient ruins near Morelos, s. of Batopilas, in s. w. Chihuahua, Mexico, are also attributed to them by the Tarahumare, although according to Hrdlicka these are of Tepehuane origin. See Lumholtz, Unknown Mexico, I, 193, 441, 1902.

**Coe Hadjo's Town.** A former settlement of negro slaves affiliated with or belonging to the Seminole, w. of Oclawaha r., in Marion co., Fla. Perhaps identical with Oclawaha town (q. v.).
**Coe Hadjos Town.**—Taylor, War map of Fla., 1839. **King Heijah's.**—Bell in Morse, Rep. to Sec. War, 307, 1822.

**Coerntha.** A former town of the Tuscarora in North Carolina, situated on Neuse r., about 2 days' journey above the present Newbern, Craven co. (De Graffenried in N. C. Col. Rec., I, 927, 1886).

**Cofaqui.** A (Muskhogean?) settlement in E. Georgia, through which De Soto passed in Apr., 1540.

Cafaquj.—Map of 1597 in 5th Rep. B. A. E., 128, 1887. Cofachis.—Rafinesque, introd. to Marshall, Ky., I, 30, 1824. Cofaqui.—Garcilasso de la Vega, Florida, 113, 1723. Cofoque.—Biedma in French, Hist. Coll. La., II, 100, 1850. Cofoqui.—Biedma in Hakluyt Soc. Publ., IX, 179, 1851.

**Cofitachiqui.** A town and province of the Yuchi(?), situated on Savannah r.; visited by De Soto in 1540. According to Pickett (Inv. of Ala., 41, 1849) there was a tradition among the Indians about 1735 that the town stood on the E. bank at Silver Bluff, Barnwell co., S. C., and this view is taken by Jones (De Soto in Ga., 1880). On the other hand, the name of Vandera's Canos (Smith, Col. Doc. Fla., I, 16, 1857), identified with this place, is preserved in Cannouchee, a N. w. affluent of Ogechee r., Ga., while another place called Cannouchee is in Emanuel co., Ga. The province was governed at the time of De Soto's visit by a woman who was at war with the people of Ocute and Cofaqui. She gave the Spaniards a friendly reception and entertained them for several days. This friendship was ill requited by the Spanish leader, who carried her away with him a prisoner, but she managed to escape in the mountainous region of N. E. Georgia, returning to her village with a negro slave who had deserted the army. Her dominion extended along the river to about the present Habersham co., Ga., and westward probably across a third or more of the state. (C. T.)

Cafitachyque.—Biedma in Ternaux-Compans, Voy., XX, 63, 1841. Canos.—Vandera (1569) in French, Hist. Coll. La., II, 290, 1875. Canosi.—Ibid. Cofachiqui.—Garcilasso de la Vega, Florida, 105, 1723. Cofaciqui.—Shipp, De Soto and Florida, 337, 1881. Cofetaçque.—Vandera (1569) in French, op. cit. Cofitachyque.—Biedma in Hakluyt Soc. Publ., IX, 180, 1851. Cutifachiqui.—Gentl. of Elvas (1557) in French, op. cit., II, 143, 1850. Cutifiachiqua.—Stevens, Hist. Ga., 22, 1847.

**Cogoucoula** (prob. 'swan people,' from Choctaw ókok, 'swan'). One of the nine villages constituting the Natchez confederacy in 1699.—Iberville in Margry, Déc., IV, 179, 1880.

**Coguinachi.** Given by Velasco (Bol. Soc. Mex. Geog. Estad., 1ª s., X, 705, 1863) as one of the 4 divisions of the Opata, inhabiting principally the valley of the Rio Babispe, a tributary of the Yaqui, and adjacent small streams in E. Sonora, Mexico. Their villages, so far as known, were: Bacadeguachi, Guazavas, Matape (in part), Mochopa, Nacori, Oposura, Oputo, and Tonichi. As the division was based on neither linguistic nor ethnic characters, Coguinachi, Teguima, and Tegui were soon dropped as classificatory names.

Cagüinachi.—Davila, Sonora Hist., 317, 1894. Opatas cogüinachis.—Orozco y Berra, Geog., 344, 1864.

**Cohannet** (probably from quuneuet, or quuiunet, 'long'). A former Wampanoag village about Fowling Pond, near Taunton, Bristol co., Mass. King Philip often made it a hunting station. When John Eliot and others began their missionary work among the Indians, a part of those at Cohannet went to Natick, but the majority removed to Ponkapog about 1654. (J. M.)

Cohanat.—Forbes (1793) in Mass. Hist. Soc. Coll., 1st s., III, 166, 1794. Cohannet.—Mayhew (1653), ibid., 3d s., IV, 234, 1834.

**Cohas.** A tribe mentioned with the Chickasaw in 1748 as having been attacked by the Huron (N. Y. Doc. Col. Hist., X, 138, 1858). Possibly the Creeks.

**Cohatchie.** A former Upper Creek town on the left bank of Coosa r., in s. w. Talladega co., Ala.—Royce in 18th Rep. B. A. E., pl. cviii, 1899.

**Cohate.** A former Maricopa rancheria on the Rio Gila, s. Ariz., visited by Father Sedelmair in 1744 (Bancroft, Ariz. and N. Mex., 366, 1889). It was apparently distinct from Gohate.

**Cohes.** A division of Maidu in Sutter co., Cal., numerous in 1851.

Cohes.—Ind. Aff. Rep., 244, 1851. Cohias.—Wozencraft (1851) in Sen. Ex. Doc. 4, 32d Cong., spec. sess., 206, 1853.

**Cohog.** See *Quahog*.

**Cohosh.** The common name of several plants; written also cohush. Black cohosh is black snakeroot, or bugbane (*Cimicifuga racemosa*); blue cohosh is squawroot (*Caulophyllum thalictroides*); white cohosh is white baneberry (*Actæa alba*); red cohosh is red baneberry (*A. rubra*). The word comes from one of the E. dialects of Algonquian, probably derived from the root represented by the Massachuset *kushki* 'rough'. (A. F. C.)

**Cohoth.** A province of the s. coast of South Carolina, mentioned by Ayllon in 1520.—Barcia, Ensayo, 5, 1723.

**Cohowofooche.** A former Seminole town, of which Neamathla was chief, situated 23 m. N. w. of St Marks, Wakulla co., Fla.—H. R. Ex. Doc. 74 (1823), 19th Cong., 27, 1826.

**Cohush.** See *Cohosh*.

**Coila.** (*Koi-ai-vla*, 'panther comes there'). A former Indian town on a creek of the same name in Carroll co., Miss. This region may originally have been occupied by some of the Yazoo r. tribes, but in 1830, when Coila is referred to, it was probably occupied by Choctaw. See Halbert in Trans. Ala. Hist. Soc., III, 72, 1899.

Quiilla.—Records quoted by Halbert, op. cit.

**Coiracoentanon.** Mentioned by La Salle as a tribe or band of the Illinois living on a branch of Illinois r. about 1680. No Illinois tribe of this name is known.

**Caracontauon.**—Coxe, Carolana, 17, 1741. **Caracotanon.**—Ibid., map. **Coiracoentanon.**—La Salle (*ca.* 1680) in Margry, Déc., II, 201, 1877. **Koeracoenetanon.**—Ibid., 42. **Koracoonitonon.**—Hennepin, New Discov., 310, 1698. **Korakoenitanon.**—La Salle, op. cit., 96. **Kouivakouintanouas.**—Gravier (*ca.* 1700) in Tailhan, Perrot, 221, 1864.

**Coiracoitaga.** A tribe mentioned by La Salle (Margry, Déc., II, 149, 1877) in connection with the Mahican, Manhattan, Minnisink, and others in 1681.

**Cojate.** A Papago village of 103 families in 1865, in s. w. Pinal co., Ariz., near the present town of the same name. **Coajata.**—Ind. Aff. Rep., 135, 1865. **Cobota.**—Browne, Apache Country, 291, 1869 (misprint from Poston). **Cojate.**—Taylor in Cal. Farmer, June 19, 1863. **Cojota.**—Poston in Ind. Aff. Rep., 385, 1863. **Del Cojate.**—Bailey, ibid., 208, 1858.

**Cojoya.** An unidentified people, described by Fray Geronimo de Zarate-Salmeron, about 1629 (Land of Sunshine, 183, Feb., 1900), as living in a fertile and well-watered country "80 leagues before reaching New Mexico from the w. side, separated by 2 days of travel from the Rio del Norte [Rio Grande] and the King's highway." They raised cotton, corn, and other vegetables, and wove very fine, thin mantas. Their neighbors to the E. were the Gorretas (Mansos), and on the s. were their enemies, the Conchas, or Conchos, who lived about the junction of the Rio Conchas and the Rio Grande, in Chihuahua, Mexico. Zarate-Salmeron adds that the Cojoya had hitherto been believed to be the Guaguatu (q. v.). As here given their habitat coincides somewhat with that of the Jumano (q. v.), as given by Espejo in 1582.

**Cojuat.** A former Diegueño rancheria near San Diego, s. Cal.—Ortega quoted by Bancroft, Hist. Cal., I, 254, 1884.

**Cokah** ('eyes open'). A Cree band of 100 skin lodges on Lac Qu'apelle, Assiniboia, Canada, in 1856; named from their chief.—Hayden, Ethnog. and Philol. Mo. Val., 237, 1862.

**Colbert, William.** A Chickasaw chief. During the Revolutionary war he aided the Americans, and in the army of Gen. Arthur St Clair led the Chickasaw allies against the hostile tribes and was known as the great war-chief of his nation. In the war of 1812 he served 9 months in the regular infantry, then returned to lead his warriors against the hostile Creeks, whom he pursued from Pensacola almost to Apalachicola, killing many and bringing back 85 prisoners to Montgomery, Ala. He was styled a general when he visited Washington at the head of a Chickasaw delegation in 1816. In the treaties ceding Chickasaw lands to the United States the name of Gen. Colbert appears, except in the ones to which was signed the name Piomingo, which also was borne by a captain of the Chickasaw in the St Clair expedition, and was the pseudonym under which John Robertson, "a headman and warrior of the Muscogulgee nation," wrote *The Savage* (Phila., 1810).

**Colcene.** One of the 3 bands into which the Twana of N. w. Washington are divided. **Colcene.**—Eells in Smithson. Rep. 1887, 606, 1889 (name given by the whites). **Colcins.**—Ibid. **Colseed.**—Ibid. **Kolsids.**—Ibid. (own name). **Kolsins.**—Ibid. **Kwulseet.**—Gibbs in Cont. N. A. Ethnol., I, 178, 1877. **Quilcene.**—Eells, op. cit. (name given by the whites).

**Colchopa.** A body of Salish of Williams Lake agency, Brit. Col.; pop. 40 in 1889, the last time the name appears.—Can. Ind. Aff. for 1889, 271.

**Cold Country.** About 1756 some Indian allies of the French "of the tribe called the Cold Country," and armed with bows, attacked the English near Ft Edward, N. Y. They were recent allies of the French and sucked the blood of the slain. Mentioned by Niles (about 1761) in Mass. Hist. Soc. Coll., 4th s., v, 436, 1861. Probably some remote tribe toward Hudson bay.

**Colete.** One of the two principal villages of the Koasati on lower Trinity r., Tex.—Bollaert in Jour. Ethnol. Soc. Lond., II, 282, 1850.

**Coligoa.** A village visited by the De Soto expedition in 1542 and described as in a very fertile country, in which the troops made salt, "toward the mountains," and by a river at the foot of a hill; possibly in w. Arkansas or on the border of the Ozark mts. **Coligoa.**—Gentl. of Elvas in Hakluyt Soc. Publ., IX, 105, 1851. **Coligua.**—Biedma (1544) in French, Hist. Coll. La., II, 106, 1850. **Colima.**—Garcilasso de la Vega, La Florida, 188, 1723. **Province de Sel.**—Shipp, De Soto and Florida, 420, 1881. **Provincia de la Sal.**—Garcilasso de la Vega, op. cit., 189.

**Colina** ('small hill'). A wild tribe of New Mexico in the 18th century (VillaSeñor, Theatro Am., II, 412, 1748); not identified, but probably an Apache band.

**Collecting.** Trained observers, whose task is to bring together material and data on which accurate generalization may be based, play an important part in the development of the science of anthropology, in which minute detail and exact differentiation have increasing weight. The scientific value of an ethnologic collection depends particularly on the knowledge and skill of the collector.

*Archeology.*—In this branch there are for examination caves, rock-shelters, mounds, village and camp sites, shellheaps, refuse-heaps, mines and quarries, workshops, pueblos, cliff-ruins, cavate lodges, garden beds, irrigation works, forts, altars, shrines, springs, towers, stone mounds, cemeteries, camp sites, etc. While each of these requires individual treatment, depending on the conditions, and the judgment of the explorer may modify the methods, modern science requires that all data be reduced to measurement and graphic delineation. Thus the following points are essential: (1) Accurate location of the site on a map; (2) photographs of site; (3) plan, with measurement of areas to be worked; (4) stakes or datum marks placed; (5) removal of débris and location of specimens with reference to datum marks with the aid of camera and pencil; (6) field numbers on specimens and references to these numbers in the notebook; (7) care of specimens after collection.

Mounds are explored by means of trenches and then stripped of the upper part, which rarely contains anything of importance, but the contour of the mound is noted and one or more sections plotted. When the zone of deposits is reached a layer of earth is removed. The aspect of skeletons and other objects exposed is recorded and photographed and their position marked. Village sites near mounds are prolific in material illustrating the life of the former occupants. In the alluvial soil of the prairie states, wherever mounds abound such sites may be located by sounding the earth with an iron rod. The earth is then stripped off as in a mound, or it may be found preferable to excavate by "benching."

The top soil of a cave should be searched, calcareous deposits, if there be any, broken up and removed, and the underlying soil benched and thrown back, as in a mound. Specimens from different levels below the datum stakes or marks are kept separate. A preliminary exploration of the cave floor is sometimes made by means of test pits. It will be found usually that the front of a cave in the zone of illumination yields most material, and it is essential to examine the talus outside the mouth of a cave if any exists.

The site of an ancient pueblo is first searched for surface relics, and the cemetery is located. It is customary to ascertain the limits of the cemetery by test excavations and to work it by trenches, throwing the earth back and carefully examining it for small artifacts as the excavation progresses. On account of the unproductiveness of excavation in rooms and the great labor and expense required to remove the débris, no pueblos have been thoroughly explored. Generally a few living rooms and kivas only have been investigated.

No indication or object is insignificant. In turning up the soil around ancient habitations a decayed fragment of cloth, a wooden implement, or any relic of organic material may extend knowledge. The various offal of débris heaps, such as bones of animals, shells, and seeds, are secured, and an endeavor is made to observe, collect, and record everything that is brought to light. Every site under examination demands attention, not merely for what it may yield in tangible results; the environment, with its biological and geological resources, topography, and meteorology, requires to be studied. Notes and collections relating to this subject add much to the clearness of an appreciation of the conditions which aided or hampered the development of culture in a given locality. The relation of sites one to another, and the grouping or separation of sites in a locality, are necessary subjects of inquiry, as are the presence or absence in a neighborhood of springs, trails, shrines, detached houses, canals and reservoirs, and pictographs.

*Somatology.*—Human remains are frequently encountered in archeologic work, and such material is carefully collected, every bone being saved if possible. The surface of hard ground may be broken with a pick and the excavation continued with a shovel. As soon as any part of the human skeleton is reached, a short

METHOD OF EXHUMING A HUMAN SKELETON. (W. C. MILLS)

stick, a trowel, and a stiff brush are used for exposing the bones. Often the bones are fragile and should not be lifted out until the earth has been loosened around them. Exposure to sunlight and dry air usually hardens them. The bones of each skeleton should be marked with serial numbers, preferably with an aniline pencil, and packed in some light, elastic material. It is better to pack skulls apart from the rest of the bones. The collection of somatological data on the living requires familiarity with the use of instruments, a knowledge of anatomy and physiology, and some training in laboratory work.

*Ethnology.*—In this wide field it is necessary to specialize in order to produce effective results. Social organization, customs, language, arts, folklore, and religion each demands adequate time and the closest attention for its study. With the aid of a manual, like "Notes and Queries," used by the Anthropological Institute of Great Britain, the important data concerning a tribe may be sketched, giving material of value for comparative study as well as indicating subjects to be taken up by specialists. Ethnographic objects form the bulk of collections. Innumerable collectors gather material of this kind for various purposes, wittingly or unwittingly becoming contributors to the advance of anthropology. As a rule, however, striking objects only are acquired in desultory collecting. Common tools, appliances, and products do not attract the attention they merit.

The most obvious materials for collections among aboriginal tribes may be classed under the following headings: Aliment, habitations and appurtenances, vessels and utensils, clothing, adornment, implements, transportation, measuring and valuing, writing, games and pastimes, music, art, language, domestic life, social life, government, and religion. Physical man and his surroundings are prime objects of study. Collections will comprise specimens of implements, clothing, etc., actually or formerly in use, models carefully made, photographs and drawings, and descriptions of objects, customs, institutions of society, laws, beliefs, and forms of worship. A thorough investigation of a single tribe requires time and patience, but the result of painstaking work in one tribe renders easier the examination of other tribes. Wherever possible, photographs of Indians, front and profile views, should be taken. Casts of faces are desirable, and with a little instruction a collector can easily make them.

The field collector's outfit varies so much with circumstances and the work to be carried on that it is not possible to enumerate all the articles needed, yet a few desiderata of general utility may be indicated: String and stick tags, twine, glue, tissue paper, coarse muslin, cotton batting, small boxes, pencils, notebooks, quadrille paper, envelopes, and tape measure are essential. A 5 by 7 camera with glass plates is the most useful kind, though smaller film cameras are more convenient. The panorama camera is very useful for extended views or scenery. It is advantageous to take a film-developing machine, since by its means one may be sure of results.

For excavation, long-handled shovels, picks for rough work in hard soil, trowels, a long-bladed knife, and a whisk broom are sufficient. These tools, except trowels and brush, can nearly always be procured in the locality where the work is to be carried on. For work in dry, dusty caves, cheesecloth or sponge aspirators may be improvised, and acetylene lanterns or pocket electric lights used to furnish smokeless light, though the diffused light of candles sometimes gives more satisfactory results.

For work in somatology numerous accurate instruments are needed, which, with the methods, render essential a course of instruction in an anthropological laboratory. The instruments required are sliding calipers, open calipers, a wooden compass, a wooden standard graduated meter, a measuring rod, and a tape measure. A notebook ruled for recording data should be provided.

For casting, dental plaster, vaseline or other grease, soap, and cheesecloth are necessary.

Collections in ethno-botany are readily carried on in connection with other field work. For this purpose one may take 30 driers, with newspapers for inner sheets. The driers may be strapped to a board or between two boards of suitable dimensions; in camp, stones or other heavy objects placed on the package furnish the necessary pressure.

Consult Holmes and Mason, Instructions to Collectors of Historical and Anthropological Specimens, 1902; Hrdlicka, Directions for Collecting Information and Specimens for Physical Anthropology, 1904; Mason (1) Directions for Collecting Basketry, 1902, (2) Ethnological Directions Relative to the Indian Tribes of the United States, 1875; Mills, Explorations of the Gartner Mound and Village Site, 1904; Niblack, Instructions for taking Paper Molds of Inscriptions in Stone, Wood, Bronze, etc., 1883; Notes and Queries on Anthropology, 1899; Peabody and Moorehead, Explorations of Jacobs Cavern, 1904; Putnam, On Methods of Archæological Research in America, 1886; Thomas (1) Directions for Mound Explorations, 1884, (2) Mound Explorations, 1894; Willoughby, Prehistoric Burial Places in Maine, 1898. See *Preservation of Collections.*                    (w. h.)

**Coloc.** Apparently two Chumashan villages, one formerly near the Rincon or at Ortegas, near Santa Barbara, Cal., the other near Santa Inez mission.
Coloc.—Cabrillo (1542) in Smith, Colec. Doc. Fla., 181, 1857. Kolok.—Taylor in Cal. Farmer, May 4, 1860.

**Colomino.** (1) A town placed by Jefferys (French Dom. Am., pt. I, map, 134, 1761) on one of the head streams of Ocmulgee r., Ga. (2) A town on the w. bank of upper Altamaha or St George r., Ga. (Güssefeld, Map of U. S., 1784). Both places were within Muskhogean territory.

**Color.** See *Anatomy.*

**Coloradas.** A Tepehuane (?) village, apparently situated s. e. of Morelos, in the Sierra Madre, s. w. Chihuahua, Mexico.—Lumholtz, Unknown Mexico, I, 439, 1902.

**Colorado**. A White River Ute chief, leader in the outbreak of 1879. The Ute agent, N. C. Meeker, an enthusiast who believed that he could readily inure the Indians to labor, interested himself in the internal quarrels of the tribe and thus incurred the resentment of Colorado's faction. He removed the agency to their favorite pasture lands, but when he attempted to make a beginning of agricultural operations they stopped the plowing by force. They were hunters and did not care to learn farming. Troops under Maj. T. T. Thornburgh were dispatched at the request of Meeker, but after a parley the Indians understood that they would not enter the reservation. When they nevertheless advanced, Colorado, or Colorow, as he was popularly called, led one of the parties that ambushed the command and killed Thornburgh and many of his men on Sept. 29, 1879. Others then massacred employees of the agency and made captives of some of the women. The Ute head chief, Ouray, induced the Indians to cease hostilities before the arrival of reinforcements.

**Color symbolism**. The American Indians had extensive and elaborate systems of symbolism which was sometimes expressed by means of color. Perhaps the European and Asiatic races have systems as elaborate, but they are not generally employed, and knowledge of them is not so well diffused. The aborigines throughout the western continent either painted or tattooed their persons. In details they may have been governed to some extent by individual caprice, but there is good evidence that they usually followed established and rigid laws of symbolism, particularly in ceremonial decoration. There are records of such symbolic decoration among savage and barbarous peoples in all parts of the world, and the custom of tattooing, not always devoid of symbolism, remains among the most civilized. The four cardinal points are symbolized by color among many American tribes, and it is probable that at some time all had such a symbolism. In addition to the four horizontal points or regions of the universe, three others were sometimes recognized, which may be termed the vertical points or regions, namely, the upper, middle, and lower worlds. It is probable that the symbolism of the vertical regions was very extensive, but knowledge of it is meager. The following table shows a few of these systems of symbolism. The order in which the regions are placed is that of the Navaho:

| Tribe. | Authority. | East. | South. | West. | North. | Lower. | Middle. | Upper. |
|---|---|---|---|---|---|---|---|---|
| Apache | Gatschet | Black | White. | Yellow | Blue | | | |
| Cherokee | Mooney | Red | White. | Black | Blue | | | |
| Chippewa 1 | Hoffman | White | Green. | Red | Black | | | |
| Chippewa 2 | Hoffman | Red | Green. | White | Black | | | |
| Creek | Gatschet | White | Blue | Black | Red and yellow. | | | |
| Hopi 1 | Fewkes | White | Red | Blue | Yellow | Black | | All colors. |
| Isleta | Gatschet | White | Red | Blue | Black | | | |
| Navaho 1 | Matthews | White | Blue | Yellow | Black | White and black. | | Blue. |
| Navaho 2 | Matthews | Black | Blue | Yellow | White | | | |
| Omaha | | Red | Black | Yellow | Blue | | | |
| Sioux | Miss Fletcher. | Red | Black | Yellow | Blue | | | |
| Zuñi 1 | Mrs Stevenson | White | Red | Blue | Yellow | Black | | All colors. |
| Zuñi 2 | Cushing | White | Red | Blue | Yellow | Black | All colors. | Many colors. |

There are accounts of such symbolism among the Winnebago, Osage, and other tribes which do not give the orientation of the different colors.

Of the two schemes of color recorded for the Navaho the first is applied in all songs, ceremonies, prayers, and legends which pertain to the surface of the earth or to celestial regions, places of life and happiness; the second to songs, etc., which refer to the underground world, to the regions of danger, death, and witchcraft, where the goddess of witches and wizards dwells. In regard to other tribes where more than one system has been recorded there is a tendency among students to attribute this to an error on the part of narrator or recorder, but the Navaho afford evidence that more than one system may properly exist in the same tribe and cult. When the Hopi make dry-paintings the yellow (north) is first drawn, followed by green or blue (west), red (south), and white (east), in order, and the same sequence is observed in all cases where colors are employed (Fewkes).

The colors of the cardinal points have been used to convey something more than ideas of locality, but which may often have some connection in the mind with locality. J. Owen Dorsey tells us that the elements as conceived in Indian philosophy, viz, fire, wind, water, and earth, are among Siouan tribes symbolized by the colors of the cardinal points; and Cushing relates the same of the Zuñi. Mooney says that among the Cherokee red signifies success, triumph; blue, defeat, trouble; black, death; white, peace, happiness. In another connection he says: " Red is a sacred color with all Indians and is usually symbolic of strength and success, and for this reason is a favorite color in painting the face and body for the dance or warpath and for painting the war pony, the lance, etc." Likewise black was a sign of mourning and white of peace, while red was usually a sign of war.

There is a symbolism of sex among the Navaho that is based on that of the cardinal points. Where two things somewhat resemble each other but one is larger, more violent, noisy, or robust than the other, it is spoken of as the male, while the smaller, finer, or gentler is spoken of as female. Thus the supposedly turbulent San Juan r. is called " male water " and the placid Rio Grande " female water "; an electric storm is called " male rain," a gentle shower " female rain." So the land N. of the Navaho country, with giant snow peaks and violent winds, is regarded as the " male land," while the country to the s., devoid of very high mountains and sending forth warm, gentle breezes, is considered the " female land." For this reason, among the Navaho, black, the color of the N., belongs to the male in all things, and blue, the color of the s. to the female. Among the Arapaho white and yellow are the ceremonial colors for male and female respectively (Kroeber), while the Hopi associate red and yellow with the male, and white and blue or green with the female (Fewkes).

Many Indian personal names contain words denoting colors, often in relations which seem incongruous to us. It is probable that they generally have mystic meanings.

Implements used in games usually have different significant colors. Where there are two opposing sides the colors are often red and black, as they are in many of our games. Thus in the game of *nanzoz*, or hoop-and-pole, among the Navaho, one of the two long sticks is marked black at the base and the other red. In their game of *kesitse* the chip tossed up to determine which party shall first hide the stone in the moccasin is blackened on one side and left unpainted on the other. They say that this symbolizes night and day, and the game itself is based on a myth of the contest of night with day. Day is commonly symbolized by red and night by black among the Indians. The Hopi paint their prayer-sticks in prescribed colors; those for rain are green, for war **red**. Every *kachina* has a prayer-stick **painted** yellow, green, red, white, and black, indicative of the cardinal points (see the table). Hopi gods are also assigned special colors—the Sun god red, the Underworld god black, and the Fire god all colors (Fewkes). Many tribes do not distinguish by name between green and light blue, black and dark blue, or white and unpainted. (w. m.)

**Colotlan.** Classed by Orozco y Berra as a branch of the Cora division of the Piman stock inhabiting a N. tributary of the Rio Grande de Santiago (Rio Colotlan), between long. 104° and 105° and about lat. 22°, Jalisco, Mexico. The language was almost extinct by 1864. Among their towns were Comatlan and Apozolco, at which missions were established by the Spaniards. (F. W. H.)
Coloclan.—Orozco y Berra, Geog., map, 1864. Colotlan.—Ibid., 59, 280, 282.

**Columbians.** Applied by Bancroft (Nat. Races, I, 150, 1882) to the Indians of N. w. America dwelling between lat. 42° and 55°, and stated by him to be synonymous with the Nootka-Columbians of Scouler and others. The term Columbians, however, is evidently broader in its scope, as it includes all the tribes w. of the Rockies from the Skittagetan group, in the N., to the s. boundary of Oregon, while Scouler's term comprises a group of languages extending from the mouth of Salmon r. to the s. of Columbia r., now known to belong to several linguistic stocks.

**Colville.** A division of Salish between Kettle falls and Spokane r., E. Wash.; said by Gibbs to have been one of the largest of the Salish tribes. Lewis and Clark estimated their number at 2,500, in 130 houses, in 1806. There were 321 under the Colville agency in 1904.
**Basket People.**—Hale in U. S. Expl. Exped., IV, 444, 1845. **Cauldrons.**—Smet, Letters, 37, 1843. **Chaudiere.**—Cox, Columbia R., I, 189, 1831. **Chualpays.**—Kane, Wand. in N. Am., 309, 1859. **Collville.**—Dart (1851) in Schoolcraft, Ind. Tribes, III, 632, 1853. **Colville.**—Lane in Ind. Aff. Rep., 159, 1850. **Covilles.**—Stevens (1855) in H. R. Doc. 48, 34th Cong., 1st sess., 3, 1856. **Gens des Chaudières.**—Duflot de Mofras, Oregon, II, 335, 1844. **Hualpais.**—Petitot, Autour du Lac des Esclaves, 362, 1893. **Kettle Falls.**—Parker, Journal, 293, 1840. **Kettle Indians.**—Cox, Columbia R., II, 155, 1831. **KQoptlē'nik.**—Chamberlain, 8th Rep. on N. W. Tribes of Can., 8, 1892 ('people of the falls': Kutenai name). **Les Chaudières.**—Cox, op. cit., I, 358. **Quarlpi.**—Keane in Stanford, Compend., 532, 1878. **Quiarlpi.**—Hale in U. S. Expl. Exped., IV, 444, 1845. **Sälsχuyîlp.**—Gatschet, MS., B. A. E. (Okinagan name). **Schroo-yel-pi.**—Stevens in Ind. Aff. Rep., 428, 1854. **Schwo-gel-pi.**—Ibid., 445. **Schwoyelpi.**—Gibbs in Pac. R. R. Rep., I, 413, 1855. **Shuyelpees.**—Smet (1859) in H. R. Ex. Doc. 65, 36th Cong., 1st sess., 141, 1860. **Shuyelphi.**—Smet, Oregon Miss., 108, 1874. **Shuyelpi.**—Smet, Letters, 213, 1843. **Shwoi-el-pi.**—Stevens, Rep. on Pac. R. R., 94, 1854. **Sin-who-yelppe-took.**—Ross, Adventures, 290, 1849. **Siyélpa.**—Wilson in Jour. Ethnol. Soc. Lond., 292, 1866. **Skoiel-poi.**—Mayne, Brit. Col., 296, 1861. **Skuyélpi.**—Gatschet, MS., B. A. E. (so called by other

Salish tribes). **Soayalpi.**—Hale in U. S. Expl. Exped., VI, 205, 1846. **Squaw-a-tosh.**—Suckley in Pac. R. R. Rep., I, 300, 1855. **Squeer-yer-pe.**—Ibid. **Squiaelps.**—Lane in Ind. Aff. Rep., 159, 1850. **Sweielpa.**—Wilson in Jour. Ethnol. Soc. Lond., 292, 1866. **Swi-el-pree.**—Ross in Ind. Aff. Rep., 22, 1870. **Whe-el-po.**—Lewis and Clark, Exped., I, map, 1814. **Whe-el-poo.**—McVickar, Exped. Lewis and Clark, II, 385, 1842.

**Comac.** A former Pima rancheria, visited by Kino and Mange in 1699; situated on the Rio Gila, 3 leagues (miles?) below the mouth of Salt r., s. Ariz.

**S. Bartolomé Comac.**—Mange in Doc. Hist. Mex., 4th s., I, 306, 1856.

**Comachica.** A Calusa village on the s. w. coast of Florida, about 1570.—Fontaneda Memoir (*ca.* 1575), Smith transl., 19, 1854.

**Comanche.** One of the southern tribes of the Shoshonean stock, and the only one of that group living entirely on the plains. Their language and traditions show that they are a comparatively recent offshoot from the Shoshoni of Wyoming, both tribes speaking practically the same dialect and, until very recently, keeping up constant and friendly communication. Within the traditionary period the 2 tribes lived adjacent to each other in s. Wyoming, since which time the Shoshoni have been beaten back into the mountains by

ASAHABIT—PENATEKA COMMANCHE

the Sioux and other prairie tribes, while the Comanche have been driven steadily southward by the same pressure. In this southerly migration the Penateka seem to have preceded the rest of the tribe. The Kiowa say that when they themselves moved southward from the Black-hills region, the Arkansas was the N. boundary of the Comanche.

In 1719 the Comanche are mentioned under their Siouan name of Padouca as living in what now is w. Kansas. It must be remembered that from 500 to 800 m. was an ordinary range for a prairie tribe and that the Comanche were equally at home on the Platte and in the Bolson de Mapimi of Chihuahua. As late as 1805 the North Platte was still known as

COMANCHE WOMAN

Padouca fork. At that time they roamed over the country about the heads of the Arkansas, Red, Trinity, and Brazos rs., in Colorado, Kansas, Oklahoma, and Texas. For nearly 2 centuries they were at war with the Spaniards of Mexico and extended their raids far down into Durango. They were friendly to the Americans generally, but became bitter enemies of the Texans, by whom they were dispossessed of their best hunting grounds, and carried on a relentless war against them for nearly 40 years. They have been close confederates of the Kiowa since about 1795. In 1835 they made their first treaty with the Government, and by the treaty of Medicine Lodge in 1867 agreed to go on their assigned reservation between Washita and Red rs., s. w. Okla.; but it was not until after the last outbreak of the southern prairie tribes in 1874–75 that they and their allies, the Kiowa and Apache, finally settled on it. They were probably never a large tribe, although supposed to be populous on account of their wide range. Within the last 50 years they have been terribly wasted by war and disease. They numbered 1,400 in 1904, attached to the Kiowa agency, Okla.

The Comanche were nomad buffalo hunters, constantly on the move, cultivating little from the ground, and living in skin tipis. They were long noted as the finest horsemen of the plains and bore a reputation for dash and courage. They have a high sense of honor and hold themselves superior to the other tribes with which they are associated. In person they are well built and rather corpulent. Their language is the trade language of the region and is more or less understood by all the neighboring tribes. It is sonorous and flowing, its chief characteristic being a rolling *r*. The language has several dialects.

The gentile system seems to be unknown among the Comanche. They have, or still remember, 12 recognized divisions or bands and may have had others in former times. Of these all but 5 are practically extinct. The Kwahari and Penateka are the most important. Following, in alphabetic order, is the complete list as given by their leading chiefs: Detsanayuka or Nokoni; Ditsakana, Widyu, Yapa, or Yamparika; Kewatsana; Kotsai; Kotsoteka; Kwahari or Kwahadi; Motsai; Pagatsu; Penateka or Penande; Pohoi (adopted Shoshoni); Tanima; Tenawa or Tenahwit; Waaih. In addition to these the following have also been mentioned by writers as divisions of the Comanche: Guagejohe, Muvinabore, Nauniem, Parkeenaum. See *Dotame*.                                    (J. M.)

**Allebome.**—Lewis and Clark, Discov., 39, 1806 (so called by the French; see *Ne'-mo-sin*, below). **Bald Heads.**—Long, Exped. Rocky Mts., I, 155, 1823. **Bo'dălk'ĭñago.**—Mooney in 14th Rep. B. A. E., 1043, 1896 (Kiowa name: 'reptile people', 'snake men'). **Cadouca.**—Domenech, Deserts N. Am., II, 100, 1860 (misprint of Padouca). **Camanche.**—Pike, Trav., xiv, 214, note, 1811. **Camanchees.**—Pilcher in Sen. Doc. 198, 25th Cong., 2d sess., 23, 1838. **Camarsches.**—Morse, Rep. to Sec. War, 367, 1822. **Ċa'-tha.**—Hayden, Ethnog. and Philol. Mo. Val., 326, 1862 ('having many horses': Arapaho name). **Caumuches.**—La Harpe (1719) in Margry, Déc., VI, 289, 1886. **Caunouche.**—Beaurain, ibid. **Caw-mainsh.**—Gebow, Shoshonay Vocab., 8, 1868 (Shoshoni name). **Cemanlos.**—Escalante (1776) misquoted by Harry in Simpson, Explor. across Utah, 495, 1876. **Cintu-aluka.**—Corliss, Dacotah MS. vocab., B. A. E., 106, 1874 (Teton name). **Comances.**—Schoolcraft, Pers. Mem., 620, 1851. **Comancha.**—Barreiro, Ojeada, app., 9, 1832. **Comanchees.**—Abert in Emory, Recon., 470, 1848. **Comanchero.**—Gregg, Comm. Prairies, II, 56, 1844 (Spanish form). **Comanches.**—Sanchez (1757) in Doc. Hist. Mex., 4th s., I, 88, 1856. **Comanchos.**—Taylor in Cal. Farmer, Apr. 10, 1863. **Comandes.**—Maximilian, Trav., 510, 1843. **Comandus.**—Alegre, Hist. Comp. Jesus, I, 336, 1841. **Comanshima.**—Bourke, Moquis of Ariz., 118, 1884 (Hopi name). **Comantz.**—Gregg, Comm. Prairies, II, 34, 1844 (Comanche pronunciation). **Comauch.**—Morse, Rep. to Sec. War, 374, 1822 (misprint). **Cumanche.**—Doc. of 1720 quoted by Bandelier in Arch. Inst. Pap., V, 183, 1890. **Cumancias.**—Long, Exped. to Rocky Mts., I, 478, 1823. **Cumeehes.**—Schermerhorn in Mass. Hist. Coll., II, 29, 1812. **Dā'tsĕ-aⁿ.**—Gatschet, MS., B. A. E. (Kiowa Apache name). **Gyai'-ko.**—Mooney in 14th Rep. B. A. E., 1043, 1896 ('enemies': Kiowa name). **Idahi.**—Ibid. (Kiowa Apache name). **Ĭndá.**—Hodge, field notes, B. A. E., 1895 (Jicarilla name).

**Kă-män'-tci.**—Dorsey, MS. Biloxi Dict., B. A. E., 1892 (Biloxi name). **Kaumainsh.**—Burton, City of Saints, 75, note, 1861. **Kelamouches.**—Jefferys, Am. Atlas, map 5, 1776 (probably the same). **Komantsu.**—Ind. Aff. Rep., 248, 1877. **Komáts.**—ten Kate, Reizen in N. Am., 326, 1885 (Ute form). **Kú-man-i-a-kwe.**—Cushing, inf'n, 1891 (Zuñi form). **La Paddo.**—Lewis and Clark, Discov., 64, 1806 (French name; cf. *La Playes*, below). **La Plais.**—Long, Exped. Rocky Mts., I, 155, 1823 (French traders' name; perhaps corrupted from Tête Pelée). **La Play.**—Lewis and Clark, Discov., 17, 1806. **La Playes.**—Lewis and Clark, Trav., 177, 1809. **La'ri'hta.**—Gatschet, MS., B. A. E. (Pawnee name). **Le Plays.**—Lewis and Clark, Discov., 17, 1806. **Los Mecos.**—Bollaert in Jour. Ethnol. Soc. Lond., II, 265, 1850 (Mexican name). **Mahán.**—Hodge, field notes, B. A. E., 1895 (Isleta name). **Máhana.**—Ibid. (Taos name). **Memesoon.**—Lewis and Clark, Discov., 39, 1806 (see *Ne'-mo-sin*, below). **Na''lani.**—Mooney in 14th Rep. B. A. E., 1043, 1896 (Navaho name: 'many aliens,' or 'many enemies'; collective term for plains tribes). **Na'nita.**—Ibid. (Kichai name). **Nar-a-tah.**—Neighbors in Schoolcraft, Ind. Tribes, II, 126, 1852 (Waco name). **Na'tăa'.**—Mooney in 14th Rep. B. A. E., 1043, 1896 (Wichita name: 'snakes,' i. e. 'enemies' or 'dandies'). **Näüně.**—Schoolcraft, Ind. Tribes, II, ix, 1852. **Na-u-ni.**—Ibid., I, 518, 1851. **Nazanne.**—ten Kate, Reizen N. Am., 6, 1885 (Navaho name: 'rich ones'). **Nemausin.**—Schermerhorn in Mass. Hist. Coll., 2d s., II, 38, 1812 (see *Ne'-mo-sin*, below). **Néme' nē.**—Gatschet, MS., B. A. E. (own name). **Nemiseau.**—Brown, West. Gaz., 213, 1817. **Nemonsin.**—Am. State Papers, IV, 716, 1832. **Nemosen.**—Lewis and Clark, Discov., 23, 1806. **Ne'-mo-sin.**—Ibid., 39 (given as their own name; rove with Kiowa, Kiowa Apache, and others at heads of Platte and Cheyenne rs.; apparently a misprint of Néme'nē or Niměnim, the Comanche name for themselves). **Nemousin.**—Orig. Jour. Lewis and Clark, VI, 102, 1905. **Neum.**—Ind. Aff. Rep., 166, 1859 (own name). **Ne'-uma.**—Buschmann (1859) quoted by Gatschet, Karankawa Inds., 33, 1891. **Nĕ'-ume.**—Ibid. **Niménim.**—ten Kate, Reizen in N. Am., 382, 1885 (own name: 'people of people'). **Nimi-ou-sin.**—Orig. Jour. Lewis and Clark, VI, 102, 1905. **Ni'ⁿam.**—Hoffman in Proc. Am. Philos. Soc., XXIII, 300, 1886 (own name). **Niunas.**—Schoolcraft, Ind. Tribes, VI, 34, 1857. **Nóta-osh.**—Gatschet, MS., B. A. E. (Wichita name: 'snakes,' 'enemies'). **No-taw.**—Marcy, Explor. Red R., 273, 1854 (Wichita name). **Nŭma.**—Mooney in 14th Rep. B. A. E., 1043, 1896 (own name: 'people'). **Padacus.**—Lewis and Clark, Trav., 39, 1807 (misprint). **ɋadaṅka.**—Dorsey, MS., B. A. E., 1878 (Omaha and Ponka name). **Padaws.**—Perrin du Lac, Voy. La., 261, 1805. **Padducas.**—Pike, Trav., 347, 1811. **Padokas.**—Fabry (1741) in Margry, Déc., VI, 475, 1886. **Padoncas.**—Brackenridge, Views of La., 80, 1815. **Padonees.**—Morse, N. Am., map, 1776. **Padoo.**—Orig. Jour. Lewis and Clark, VI, 108, 1905 (Canadian French "nickname"). **Padoucahs.**—Hutchins (1764) quoted by Schoolcraft, Ind. Tribes, III, 557, 1853. **Padoucas.**—De l'Isle, map, 1712 (Siouan name; perhaps a contraction of Penateka.—Mooney). **Padoucee.**—McKenney and Hall, Ind. Tribes, III, 82, 1854. **Padoucies.**—Orig. Jour. Lewis and Clark, VI, 108, 1905. **Paduca.**—Clarke in Jour. Anthrop. Inst., IV, 152, 1875. **Paducahs.**—Kingsley, Stand. Nat. Hist., pt. 6, 186, 1883. **Paducas.**—Jefferys, Fr. Dom. Am., pt. 1, map, 1761. **Paduka.**—Dorsey, MS., B. A. E., 1882 (Kansa name). **Padüka.**—Hervas, Idea dell' Univ., XVII, 90, 1784. **Pah-to-cahs.**—Butler in H. R. Ex. Doc. 76, 29th Cong., 2d sess., 6, 1847. **Panaloga.**—McKenney and Hall, Ind. Tribes, III, 81, 1858. **Pandoga.**—Boudinot, Star in the West, 128, 1816. **Pandouca.**—Cass in Schoolcraft, Ind. Tribes, III, 596, 1853. **Paneloga.**—Douay (1687) in Shea, Miss. Valley, 222, 1852 (probably the same; there are many misprints and derivatives of this word, all probably being traceable to this source). **Panelogo.**—Hayden, Ethnog. and Philol. Mo. Val., 460, 1862. **Paneloza.**—Ibid., 346 (from Douay, 1687; misprint). **Panetoca.**—Harris, Coll. Voy. and

Trav., I, map, 685, 1705. **Panetonka.**—La Hontan, New Voy., I, 130, 1703. **Panoucas.**—Perkins and Peck, Ann. of West, 669, 1850. **Paoducas.**—Alcedo, Dicc. Geog., II, 630, 1787. **Par-too-ku.**—Neighbors in Schoolcraft, Ind. Tribes, II, 126, 1852. **Pa-tco'-χa.**—David St Cyr, inf'n (Winnebago name). **Pa-tco'-χă-jă.**—Ibid. **Patonca.**—Barcia, Ensayo, 298, 1723. **Pa-tŭh-kû.**—Grayson, MS. vocab., B. A. E., 1885 (Creek name). **Pa'-tu-kă.**—Dorsey, Kwapa MS. vocab., B. A. E., 1891 (Quapaw name). **Paχukă.**—Dorsey, MS., B. A. E., 1883 (Osage name). **Paχuñke.**—Ibid., 1881 (Iowa, Oto, and Missouri name). **Peducas.**—Perrin du Lac, Voy., 225, 1805. **Pen loca.**—Shea, Peñalosa, 21, note, 1882. **Sänko.**—Mooney in 14th Rep. B. A. E., 1043, 1896 (obsolete Kiowa name). **Sau'hto.**—Ibid. (Caddo name). **Sau'-tuχ.**—ten Kate, Synonymie, 10, 1884 (Caddo name). **Selakampóm.**—Gatschet, Comecrudo MS., B. A. E. (Comecrudo name for all warlike tribes, especially the Comanche). **Shishiniwotsítan.**—ten Kate, Reizen in N. Am., 361, 1885 (Cheyenne name: 'snake people'). **Shĭshino'wĭts-Itäniuw'.**—Mooney in 14th Rep. B. A. E., 1043, 1896 (Cheyenne name: 'snake people'). **Shĭ'shĭnówŭtz-hitä'neo.**—Mooney, inf'n, 1906 (correct Cheyenne name). **Snake Indians.**—Brackenridge, Views of La., 80, 1815 (see also under *Ietan*). **Sow-a-to.**—Neighbors in Schoolcraft, Ind. Tribes, II, 126, 1852 (Caddo name). **Tête Pelée.**—Mooney in 14th Rep. B. A. E., 1043, 1896 (French traders' name. "The identification is doubtful, as the Comanche cut their hair only when mourning"). **Têtes pelées.**—Perrin du Lac, Voy., 261, 1805. **Yampah.**—Stuart, Montana, 25, 1865 (Shoshoni name). **Yä'mpaini.**—Mooney in 14th Rep. B. A. E., 1045, 1896 (Shoshoni name: 'yampa people,' or 'yampa eaters'; cf. *Cawmainsh*, above). **Yämpairĭ'kani.**—Ibid.

**Comaquidam.** A former Papago rancheria visited by Kino and Mange in 1701; situated in N. w. Sonora, Mexico, on the Rio Salado, 10 m. below Sonoita.
**Anunciata.**—Bancroft, No. Mex. States, I, 495, 1884. **Comaquidam.**—Kino (1701) in Doc. Hist. Mex., 4th s., I, 328, 1856.

**Comarchdut.** A former Maricopa rancheria on the Rio Gila, s. Ariz.; visited by Father Sedelmair in 1744.—Bancroft, Ariz. and N. Mex., 366, 1889.

**Comarsuta.** A former Sobaipuri rancheria visited by Father Kino about 1697; situated on the Rio San Pedro, s. Ariz., between its mouth and the junction of Aravaipa cr.—Bernal (1697) quoted by Bancroft, Ariz. and N. Mex., 356, 1889.

**Comatlan.** A former pueblo of the Colotlan division of the Cora and the seat of a mission; situated on the Rio Colotlan, lat. 21° 50′, long. 104° 10′, Jalisco, Mexico.—Orozco y Berra, Geog., 280, 1864.

**Combahee.** A small tribe formerly living on Combahee r., S. C. Little is known of its history, as it early became extinct. See Rivers, Hist. S. C., 94, 1874.

**Comcomly.** A Chinook chief. He received the Lewis and Clark expedition hospitably when it emerged at the mouth of Columbia r. in 1805, and when the Astor expedition arrived to take possession of the country for the United States he cultivated close friendship with the pioneers, giving his daughter as wife to Duncan M'Dougal, the Canadian who was at their head. Yet he was probably an accomplice in a plot to massacre the garrison and seize the stores. When a British ship arrived in 1812 to capture the fort at Astoria, he offered to fight the enemy, with 800 warriors at his back. The American agents, however, had already made a peaceful transfer by bargain and sale, and gifts and promises from the new owners immediately made him their friend (Bancroft, N. W. Coast; Irving, Astoria). Writing in Aug., 1844, Father De Smet (Chittenden and Richardson, De Smet, II, 443, 1905) states that in the days of his glory Comcomly on his visits to Vancouver would be preceded by 300 slaves, "and he used to carpet the ground that he had to traverse, from the main entrance of the fort to the governor's door, several hundred feet, with beaver and otter skins."

**Comecrudo** ('eaters of raw meat'). One of the few tribes of the Coahuiltecan family that have been identified. The surviving remnant was visited in 1886 by Gatschet, who found only 8 or 10 old persons who could speak the dialect, living on the s. side of the Rio Grande, 2 of them at Las Prietas, Coahuila. Orozco y Berra (Geog., 293, map, 1864) placed them in Tamaulipas, Mexico, in the vicinity of the Tedexeños. They appear to have been known in later times as Carrizos, q. v.
**Estók pakaí peyáp.**—Gatschet, Comecrudo MS., B. A. E. (='Indians eaters raw'). **χaíma aranguás.**—Ibid. (='Indians of this locality': Cotonam name).

**Comeya.** Apparently a collective name indefinitely applied to the Yuman tribes from San Diego eastward to the lower Rio Colorado. By many authors it has been assumed to be synonymous with Diegueño, which doubtless it was in part. Just what tribes it included can not now be told, but the term is here applied only to interior tribes, the Diegueño about San Diego being excluded. (See *Cuñeil.*) When visited by Anza, Garcés, and Font, in 1775, the "Quemayá" wore sandals of maguey fiber and descended from their own territory (which began at the mountains, in lat. 33° 08′, some 100 m. to the N. w. of the mouth of New r. in N. E. Lower California, and extended as far as San Diego) to eat calabashes and other fruits of the river. They were described as "very dirty, on account of the much mezcal they eat; their idiom is foreign to those of the river" (Garcés, Diary, 1775, 165, 197, et seq., 1900). They were also visited in 1826 by Lieut. Hardy (Trav. in Mex., 368–372, 1829), who found them on the Colorado just above the mouth of the Gila, and who described them, under the name Axua (which, he says, is their tribal name), as being very numerous and filthy in their habits; to overcome vermin they coated their hair with mud, with which they also painted their bodies, and "on a hot day it is by no means uncommon to see them weltering in the mud like pigs." They were of medium stature, and were regarded by Hardy as excessively poor, having no animals except foxes, of which they had a few skins. The dress of the women in summer was a short bark skirt; the men appear to have been practically without clothing during this season. Both sexes practised facial painting, from which they were likened to the cobra de capello. The practice of selling children seemed to have been common. Their subsistence was fish, fruits, vegetables, and the seeds of grass, and many of the tribe were said to have been dreadfully scorbutic. Their weapons were bows, arrows, a few lances, and a short club like a round mallet. Whipple described the Comeya in 1849 (Schoolcraft, Ind. Tribes, ii, 116, 1852) as occupying the banks of New r., near Salt (Salton) lake, and as distinguishable from the Cuchan (Yuma) "by an oval contour of the face." The names of but few Comeya bands or rancherias are known. These are Hamechuwa, Hatawa, Hepowwoo, Itaywiy, Quathlmetha.

(H. W. H.   F. W. H.)

Axua.—Hardy, Trav. in Mexico, 368, 1829 (also Axúa). Camilya.—Bourke in Jour. Am. Folklore, ii, 176, 1889 (probably the same). Co-mái-yàh.—Whipple in Pac. R. R. Rep., iii, pt. 3, 16, 1856. Comedás.—Froebel, Seven Years' Travels, 511, 1859. Comeya.—Bartlett, Pers. Narr., ii, 7, 1854. Co-mo-yah.—Whipple (1849) in Schoolcraft, Ind. Tribes, ii, 116, 1852. Comoyàtz.—Whipple, Pac. R. R. Rep., iii, pt. 3, 16, map, 1856. Comoyeé.—Whipple, Exped. San Diego to the Colorado, 28, 1851. Co-mo-yei.—Whipple (1849) in Schoolcraft, op. cit. I'-um O'-otam.—Zeitschr. f. Ethnol., 86, 1886 (Pima name of Comeya and Diegueño). Kamia-akhwe.—Kroeber, inf'n, 1905 (='foreign Kamia,' i. e., foreign Diegueños; Mohave name for Yuman Inds. near head of gulf, who are not Diegueños; cf. Axua, above). New River Indians.—Heintzelman in H. R. Ex. Doc. 76, 34th Cong., 3d sess., 53, 1857 (Yum, or). Quathl-met-ha.—Thomas, Yuma MS. vocab., B. A. E., 1868 (on New r.). Quemayá.—Garcés (1775–76), Diary, 166, 450, 1900. Serranos.—Ibid., 196. Yum.—Heintzelman, op. cit., 42 (or New River Indians; cf. I'-um O'-otam, above).

**Comiakin** (*Qumiĕ'qEn*). A Salish tribe speaking the Cowichan dialect and inhabiting part of Cowichan valley, s. e. Vancouver id.; pop. 67 in 1904.

Comea-kin.—Can. Ind. Aff., 269, 1889. Comiaken.—Whymper, Alaska, 62, 1869. Comiakin.—Can. Ind. Aff., 417, 1898. Ko-ne-a kun.—Ibid., 1880, 316. Xumē'xẹn.—Boas, MS., B. A. E., 1887.

**Comitre.** Mentioned with San Felipe by Oñate in 1598 (Doc. Inéd., xvi, 114, 1871) as a pueblo of the "Castixes," which is identified with Katishtya, the aboriginal name of the inhabitants of San Felipe (q. v.), and, evidently through misunderstanding, given also as a "Trios" village. The name, according to Bandelier (Arch. Inst. Papers, iv, 189, 1892), is a corruption or misprint of Tamita, the name of the mesa at the base of which San Felipe stood, and not of the settlement itself.

**Commerce.** Evidences of widespread commerce and rude media of exchange in North America are found in ancient shell-heaps, mounds, and graves, the objects having passed from hand to hand often many times. Overland, this trade was done on foot, the only domestic animal for long-distance transportation being the dog, used as a pack beast and for the travois and the sled. In this respect the north temperate zone of America was in marvelous contrast with the same latitudes of the Old World, where most of the commercial animals originated.

The deficiency in the means of land commerce was made up by the waters. Natural conditions in the section of the New World along the Arctic circle and on Hudson bay, continuously inhabited by the homogeneous Eskimo, in the inlets of the Atlantic coast, in the neighboring Caribbean area, and in the archipelagoes of British Columbia and s. e. Alaska, encouraged and developed excellent water craft for commerce. Better still by far for the trader were the fresh-water rivers, navigable for canoes, of the Yukon-Mackenzie, St Lawrence, Atlantic, Mississippi, and Columbia systems, in which neighboring waters are connected for traffic by easy portages, a condition contrasting with that of Siberia, whose great rivers all end in frozen tundras and arctic wastes.

The North American continent is divided into culture areas in a way conducive to primitive commerce. Certain resources of particular areas were in universal demand, such as copper, jade, soapstone, obsidian, mica, paint stones, and shells for decoration and money, as dentalium, abalone, conus, olivella, and clam shells.

The Eskimo, to whom the Arctic area belonged, carried on extensive commerce among themselves and with the western Athapascan tribes and the Algonquian tribes to the e. They knew where soapstone for lamps, jade for blades, and driftwood for sleds and harpoons could be found, and used them for traffic. They lived beyond the timber line; hence the Athapascans brought vessels of wood and baskets to trade with them for oil and other arctic products.

The Mackenzie-Yukon tribes were in the lands of the reindeer and of soft fur-bearing animals. These they traded in every direction for supplies to satisfy their needs (see *Fur trade*). The Russians in Alaska and the Hudson's Bay Co. stimulated them to the utmost and taught them new means of capture, including the use of firearms. Remnants of Iroquois bands that were employed in the fur trade have been found on Rainy lake, on Red and Saskatchewan rs., even as far n. as the Polar sea and as far w. as the Siksika of the plains and the Takulli of British Columbia (Havard in Smithson. Rep., 318, 1879; Chamberlain in Am. Anthrop., vi, 459, 1904; Morice, N. Int. Brit. Col., 1904.) See *Caughnawaga*.

The Atlantic slope from Labrador to Georgia was the special home of Algonquian and Iroquoian tribes. Inland were found deer, bears, foxes, and turkeys. The salt-water bays and inlets not only supplied mollusks, crustaceans, fish, and aquatic birds in vast numbers, but stimulated easy transportation and commerce. The great lakes and the St Lawrence, moreover, placed the tribes about them in touch with the copper mines of L. Superior. Through this enlarging influence the Iroquois were ennobled and became the leading family of this area. A medium of exchange was invented in the shape of wampum, made from clam shells. The mounds of the s. portion of this slope reveal artifacts of copper, obsidian, and shell, which must have been transported commercially from afar along the water highways in birch-bark canoes and dugouts.

The Mississippi area was a vast receiving depot of commerce, having easy touch with other areas about it by means of portages between the headwaters of innumerable streams; with the Chesapeake bay, the great lakes, and the Mackenzie basins through the Ohio and the main stream; with the E. Rockies and Columbia r. through the Missouri and other great branches of the Mississippi in the w. Buffalo skins and horns were demanded by the Pueblos, while pemmican and beads enlivened trade. The mounds reveal dentalium shells from the Pacific, obsidian from the Rockies, copper from L. Superior, pipes of catlinite, and black steatite from Minnesota and Canada, and objects from the Atlantic.

The Gulf area includes the ancient home of the Muskhogean, the Caddoan, and a few smaller families. Commerce here was inland. Their coast was almost without islands and came in commercial touch with an outside world only through Mexico. The discoveries of Cushing in s. Florida reveal a colony in the southern Mexican or West Indian culture status. The shorter rivers of this area put its N. border in trade touch with Tennessee and the Carolinas, and its w. with Arkansas and Texas. The Mississippi lured its traders almost to the Canadian border. The Rio Grande was the commercial artery connecting the E. areas with the interior basin. The Rio Grande Pueblos still trade their paper-bread with the Kiowa and Comanche of Oklahoma. Coronado speaks of Pawnee and Wichita visitors among the Pueblos of the Rio Grande in 1540 (Winship in 14th Rep. B. A. E., 1896).

The Pacific coast tribes occupied two areas that present quite opposite conditions in regard to commercial activity. From Mt St Elias s. to California trade was active, transportation being effected in excellent dugout canoes; the waters and the lands offered natural products easy of access that stimulated barter. Copper, horn for spoons, eulachon, and Chilkat blankets were exchanged for abalone and dentalium shells, and baskets were bartered for other baskets and the teeth of a large southern shark, also for the furs of the interior Indians. The Haida regularly visited their Tsimshian neighbors to exchange canoes for eulachon oil, wood suitable for boxes, and mountain-goat horn, while the Tlingit were intermediaries in diffusing the copper that came from the N. On the Columbia r. camass and moose were articles of commerce. Farther s., in Oregon and California, whether from the islandless coast or the genius of the peoples, the spirit of commerce was less prominent. Among the N. w. California tribes, the Hupa and others, dentalia served for local money. In central California (Yuki, Pomo, Sacramento, and San Joaquin valleys, etc.) wampum of pierced disks almost exclusively served as a medium of exchange and standard of value. In s. California the inhabitants of the islands carried on a commerce in basketry, feathered wearing apparel, nets, vessels of steatite and serpentine, various implements of stone and bone, wampum, seashells and shell ornaments, and cured fish, which they bartered with the tribes of the mainland for basket materials, skins, nuts, prepared meats, and other articles which they did not have on the islands. The Indians of the mountains and the interior valleys of California constantly traveled to and fro for the purpose of barter, and the trails over the range to the coast are yet plainly visible, especially from the lower Tulare valley (A. L. Kroeber and C. P. Wilcomb, inf'n, 1905; Stearns in Nat. Mus. Rep., 297, 1887). From the early mariners we learn that the island Indians had canoes made of skins, some being very large and holding 20 persons. Vizcaino, the Spanish navigator, who made his voyage in 1602–3, mentions large boats of planks at Santa Catalina, Cal., and states that its natives engaged in trade, though not extensive, with those on the mainland (Hittell, Hist. Cal., i, 139, 1885). Hittell does not think that there were any voyages between the Santa Barbara ids. and Puget sd., though canoes may have drifted or have been carried by stress of weather over considerable distances.

The Interior basin, especially in the Pueblo country, had a lively home and distant commerce, the duration and extent of which are witnessed by the trails measuring in all many hundreds of miles in length. Pacific coast shells and copper bells of Mexican origin are encountered in the ancient ruins. The inland commerce was fostered by the two kinds of social life, pueblo and castral. After the advent of the Spaniards, this traffic was greatly quickened. The Hopi traded in cotton of their own cultivation with outside tribes, and are still the chief weavers and traders of ceremonial cotton blankets, sashes, and kilts in the S. W. The Zuñi and some of the Rio Grande pueblos use shell beads and turquoise, trading largely with the Navaho. The latter have a wide and varied commerce, trafficking with the Havasupai, Hopi, and Walapai for baskets and using their blankets and silver work as an exchange medium with neighboring tribes and with the whites.

Commerce was greatly stimulated through the coming of the whites by the introduction of domestic animals, especially horses, mules, donkeys, cattle, sheep, goats, poultry; by the vastly enlarged demand for skins of animals, ivory, fish, and native manufactures; by offering in exchange iron tools and implements, woven goods, and other European products desired by the Indians. The effects of this stimulated trade were profound, both for good and evil. Indians were drawn far from home. The Iroquois, for example, traveled with the fur traders into N. W. Canada.

Many kinds of Indian handiwork have entered into world commerce. Money is lavished on fine basketry, beadwork, wampum belts, ivory carvings, horn spoons, wooden dishes, silver work, costumes, feather and quill work, and especially Navaho blankets and Hopi and Zuñi textiles. In ancient times there were intertribal laws of commerce, and to its agents were guaranteed freedom and safety. See *Boats, Fur trade, Exchange, Horse, Trails and Trade-routes, Travel, Travois*, and the bibliographies thereunder; consult also Rau in Smithson. Rep., 271, 1872.          (O. T. M.)

**Commission to the Five Civilized Tribes.** A commission appointed by President Cleveland, under act of Congress of Mar. 3, 1893, and consisting of Henry L. Dawes of Massachusetts, chairman (1893–1903), Archibald S. McKennon of Arkansas (1893–98), and Meredith H. Kidd of Indiana (1893–95). It was increased to 5 members in 1895 and reduced to 4 in 1898. In addition to those named, it has included Frank C. Armstrong of the District of Columbia (1895–98), Thomas B. Cabaniss of Georgia (1895–97), Alexander B. Montgomery of Kentucky (1895–97), Tams Bixby of Minnesota (1897–1905), Thomas B. Needles of Illinois (1897–1905), Clifton R. Breckenridge of Arkansas (1898–1905), and William E. Standley of Kansas (1903–04). On the death of Mr Dawes, in Feb., 1903, Mr Bixby was appointed chairman. The work of the Commission being finished, it expired by law July 1, 1905. As the Indian governments did not dissolve until Mar. 4, 1906, all the remaining powers of the Commission were vested in the Secretary of the Interior during the interim.

The headquarters of the Commission were at Muscogee, Ind. Ter., except for short periods in 1895 and 1896 at South McAlester and Vinita, Ind. Ter., and at Fort Smith, Ark. Special headquarters have also been established temporarily when necessary in various towns of the Territory.

The Commission was instructed to negotiate with the Five Civilized Tribes for the extinguishment of the national or communal title to the land and its allotment in severalty, and for the dissolution of the tribal governments, looking toward their ultimate absorption into the United States as a territory or state. The Commission had no authority, but was directed to induce the Indians to consent to these changes on terms which should be just and equitable to all, and binding after due ratification both by the Indians and the United States.

The work of the Commission was required on account of conditions peculiar to the Indian Territory. When these tribes were removed from the E., they were given special titles to the land, in the form of patents, and their governments (modeled closely after those of the states) were recognized and established by treaties, under which they were required to hold the land in common for the use of the whole tribe and to secure its exclusive use to the Indians. To this end the United States guaranteed the title and the exclusive use of the land by the Indians. Their already advanced civilization was still further developed, but in time the Indians disregarded the treaties and invited white settlement, both by intermarriage and through commerce. A dominant class of mixed-bloods appropriated to their own benefit large tracts of land and other exclusive privileges through manipulation of the governments. The peculiar legal conditions encouraged great lawlessness. More than 250,000 white settlers had no control or protection of law whatever, as the United States courts had very little jurisdiction over the Indians and the Indian courts had no jurisdiction over the whites. Civilization was further obstructed in that 30,000 white children had no schools and no possibility thereof.

Immediately on its appointment the

Commission proceeded to request a hearing from each nation in turn, asking it to treat with the United States, and afterward made the same offer to a joint convention. The proposal was received with some favor, but persistent misinterpretation of the purpose and proposals of the United States by the favored class created prejudice among the ignorant Indians, and the overtures were refused. Private and public conferences were held and further proposals made. Whenever the purposes of the United States were understood a desire appeared for a friendly agreement, but adverse pressure of many kinds was constantly and successfully brought to bear. As the internal conditions grew worse the situation became a menace to the surrounding country. Accordingly the United States was compelled to resume its right of protection and control, hitherto held in abeyance. In June, 1898, Congress passed a law, generally known as the Curtis act, providing that in case no agreements could be reached the Indian courts should be abolished or curtailed in jurisdiction, and giving the Commission authority to allot the land and otherwise to proceed with the work for which it was created.

Agreements were made with the tribes at various times, but none of them was completed until after the passage of this act. As the land titles differed with each tribe, separate agreements were necessary. In the case of the Choctaw and Chickasaw the land was held in common, but agreements were necessary with each government. Two agreements were made with the Creeks in 1897, but failed of ratification. Many other vain attempts were made, but on Mar. 8, 1900, an agreement passed the Creek council which was ratified by Congress. Agreements with the Cherokee were made in 1899 and in 1900, but failed either in Congress or in the Cherokee council. Another agreement was sought by the Cherokee in Apr., 1901, but too late, and allotment proceeded under the Curtis act. An agreement made with the Choctaw and Chickasaw in Feb., 1901, failed to be ratified by the Chickasaw. Another in Mar., 1902, was ratified by both nations and by Congress. An agreement with the Seminole was made in Oct., 1899, and ratified by Congress. Several other agreements were made from time to time regarding the enrollment of citizens, or otherwise supplementary to the main agreements.

Allotment began among the Creeks in 1899, the Seminole in 1901, and in the other nations in 1903. Congress also provided that the Commission should make citizenship rolls for each tribe, containing lists of such Indians as were justly entitled to share in the division of the land. Of the 200,000 claims presented, about 90,000 were allowed. These decisions included the question of the rights of the Mississippi Choctaw, the care of the freedmen who had been owned as slaves by these Indians and after the Civil war granted citizenship, and several other difficult questions.

The Commission was required to allot the land according to its value. This differed greatly on account of the coal, asphalt, and other minerals, of the valuable timber, of its great agricultural possibilities, and of its large towns with flourishing business interests. It was therefore necessary to determine the value of each quarter section. The Commission surveyed the country, appraised these values, decided and carried out plans for the equitable and possible adjustment of the town sites, and made triplicate records of all these matters. This occupied a large clerical force, at one time amounting to 500, from 1898 to 1905.

In 1903 charges were made by the Indian Rights Association that the members and officers of the Commission had used their positions to advance their private interests. President Roosevelt appointed Hon. Charles J. Bonaparte and Mr Clinton R. Woodruff to investigate these charges. Their report, while advising circumspection in these particulars, exonerated the Commission from all malfeasance.

By the processes described, and by a large amount of other detailed work, 20,000,000 acres of land were justly distributed among 90,000 heirs; the interests of 600,000 other inhabitants were conserved, and an enormous amount of labor connected therewith was successfully carried on under difficult conditions of many kinds. The work of allotment occupied about 7 years and was accomplished at a cost equivalent to 10 cents an acre for the land allotted. Thus by the work of the Commission from 1893 to 1905 five governments with their executive, legislative, and judicial machinery were successfully transformed into a constituent part of the United States by transactions which secured all their just rights and promoted their highest welfare, as well as contributed to the best interests of the whole country.

See the Reports of the Commissioner of Indian Affairs, 1893–1905; Reports of the Commission to the Five Civilized Tribes, 1894–1905. (A. L. D.)

**Communipaw** ('good fishing.'—Jones, Ind. Bul., 15, 1867). The principal village of the Hackensack, about 1630, at the present Communipaw, Hudson co., N. J. (J. M.)
Communipau.—Ruttenber, Tribes Hudson R., 90, 1872. Gamoenapa.—Ibid. (Dutch form). Gamo-

enepa.—Doc. of 1665 in N. Y. Doc. Col. Hist., II, 463, 1858 (probably a Dutch settlement). **Gamonepa.**—Ibid., 466. **Gemoenepaen.**—Deed of 1654, ibid., XIII, 36, 1881. **Gemoenepaw.**—Deed of 1647, ibid., 22 (name of creek).

**Como.** An unidentified tribe that lived near the Susola, of whom Cabeza de Vaca (Smith trans., 84, 1851) heard while in Texas in 1527–34. The people seem to have been nearer the coast than the Susola, who, at the time Cabeza de Vaca heard of them, were at war with the Atayos (Adai).

**Comohuabi.** A Papago village in s. Ariz., on the border of Sonora; pop. 80 families in 1871.—Wilbur in Ind. Aff. Rep. 1871, 365, 1872.

**Comopori.** A warlike tribe of the Cahita group formerly inhabiting a peninsula 7 leagues from Ahome, N. w. Sinaloa, Mexico. They subsisted by fishing, and appear to have been related to the Vacoregue, speaking the same language.—Orozco y Berra, Geog., 58, 332, 1864.

**Comox.** An important coast Salish tribe on both sides of Discovery passage, between Chancellor channel and C. Mudge, Brit. Col. Their proper name, Çatlō′ltx, has been taken by Boas as the designation of one dialect of coast Salish, including, besides this, the Clahoose, Eeksen, Kakekt, Kaake, Klamatuk (?), Tatpoos, Homalko, and Sliammon. Pop. of the tribe 58 in 1904; of those speaking the dialect, about 300. (J. R. S.)
Çatlō′ltq.—Boas in 5th Rep. N. W. Tribes of Can., 10, 1889. **Commagsheak.**—Scouler (1846) in Jour. Ethnol. Soc. Lond., I, 234, 1848. **Co-moux.**—Schoolcraft, Ind. Tribes, v, 488, 1855. **Comox.**—Mayne, Brit. Col., 181, 1861. **Comuxes.**—Grant in Jour. Roy. Geog. Soc., 293, 1857. **K′ō′moks.**—Boas in 5th Rep. N. W. Tribes Can., 10, 1889. **Ko-mookhs.**—Gibbs in Cont. N. A. Ethnol., I, 269, 1877. **Komux.**—Sproat, Savage Life, 311, 1868. **Kowmook.**—Tolmie and Dawson, Vocabs. Brit. Col., 120B, 1884. **S'komook.**—Gibbs in Cont. N. A. Ethnol., I, 269, 1877 (Uguultas name). **S'tlaht-tohtlt-hu.**—Ibid. (own name). **Xōmoks.**—Boas, MS., B. A. E., 1887 (Lekwiltok name).

**Comoza.** A former Potawatomi village on Tippecanoe r., in Fulton co., Ind. The reserve on which it was situated was sold in 1834. The name was that of a chief. Also spelled Camoza.

**Comupatrico.** An Opata pueblo visited by Coronado in 1540. It was situated in the valley of the Rio Sonora, N. w. Mexico, doubtless in the vicinity of Arizpe. Possibly identical with a pueblo later known by another name.
Comupatrico.—Castañeda (1596) in 14th Rep. B. A. E., 515, 1896. **Upatrico.**—Castañeda in Ternaux-Compans, Voy., IX, 158, 1838.

**Cona.** A settlement of a semisedentary tribe called Teyas by the Spaniards, regarded as probably the Hainai, a Caddoan tribe. The place was visited by Coronado and his army in 1541, and described as situated 250 leagues (ca. 660 m.) from the Pueblo settlements of the Rio Grande and 40 days' journey s. of Quivira in E. central Kansas. See Casta-

ñeda (1596) in 14th Rep. B. A. E., 507, 1896.

**Conaliga.** A former Upper Creek band or settlement, probably near Tukabatchi, on Tallapoosa r., perhaps in Randolph co., Ala.—Woodward, Reminiscences, 37, 1859.

**Conauhkare.** A Tuscarora village in North Carolina in 1701.—Lawson (1709), N. C., 383, 1860.

**Concepción** (Spanish). A Tubar pueblo on the s. tributary of the Rio Fuerte, s. w. Chihuahua, Mexico.—Orozco y Berra, Geog., 323, 1864.

**Concepción.** A mission established among the Yuma by Fray Francisco Garcés, in 1780, on the w. bank of the Rio Colorado, in s. E. Cal., near the Arizona boundary, at the site of modern Ft Yuma. The mission was destroyed by the natives July 17–19, 1781, and about 50 Spaniards, including Garcés, 3 other friars, and Capt. Rivera y Moncada, were killed. See *San Pedro y San Pablo.*
Concepcion.—Taylor in Cal. Farmer, June 13, 1862; Bancroft, Ariz. and N. Mex., 397, 1889. **Immaculate Conception.**—Shea, Cath. Miss., 101, 1855. **Puerta de la Purísima Concepcion.**—Coues, Garcés Diary, 19, 1900.

**Concepción de Nuestra Señora.** A visitation town of (Cochimi?) Indians in 1745, situated 6 leagues s. of the parent mission, Nuestra Señora de Guadalupe, in lat. 27°, Lower California. Thirty-two rancherias were dependent on it.
Concepcion de Nuestra Señora.—Venegas, Hist. Cal., II, 198, 1759. **Purísima Conóepcion.**—Doc. Hist. Mex., 4th s., v, 186, 1857.

**Concha** (shortened from *Kunshak-boluktu*, 'round reed-brake'). A former important Choctaw town, named from its situation on the side of a circular reed-brake in the s. w. corner of Kemper co., Miss. It was at the junction of the lines which separated the three primary Choctaw divisions, although belonging itself to the N. E. division.—Halbert in Ala. Hist. Soc. Publ., I, 376, 1901; Miss. Hist. Soc. Publ., III, 370, 1900.
Concha.—Danville, map (1732) in Hamilton, Colonial Mobile, 158, 1897; Jefferys, French Dom. Am., 135, map, 1761. **Conshaques.**—LaHarpe (1715) in French, Hist. Coll. La., III, 44, 1851. **Coosak Baloagtaw.**—Romans, Florida, 311, 1775. **Couchas.**—Vaudreuil (1709) in N. Y. Doc. Col. Hist., x, 951, 1858.

**Conchachitou** (*Kunshak-chitto*, 'big reed-brake'). A former Choctaw town in Neshoba co., Miss., which extended from about 2 m. w. of Yazoo town almost to the vicinity of Schekaha. Often called West Congeto and West Cooncheto to distinguish it from another town of the same or a similar name. See *Couechitou*, and consult Halbert in Miss. Hist. Soc. Publ., VI, 427, 1902.
Conchachitou.—Philippeaux, Map of Engl. Col., 1781. **Conchàchitouu.**—Alcedo. Dicc. Geog., I, 638, 1786. **Quansheto.**—Adair, Am. Inds., 296, 1775. **West Congeta.**—Romans, Florida, 313, 1775. **West Congeto.**—Halbert, op. cit. **West Cooncheto.**—Ibid.

**Conchanty.** A town of the Creek Nation about the junction of Conchanti cr. with Arkansas r., Ind. Ter.

Conchanti.—Gatschet, Creek Migr. Leg., II, 185, 1888. Ikan'-tcháti.—Ibid. Kanshádi.—Ibid.

**Conchartimicco's Town.** A former town on Apalachicola r., Fla., evidently named from a chief called Conchart, or Concharti, and probably belonging to the Lower Creeks.

Conchaptimicco's town.—Jesup (1837) in H. R. Doc. 78, 25th Cong., 2d sess., 95, 1838. Conchartimicco's town.—Jesup (1837) in H. R. Doc. 225, 25th Cong., 3d sess., 65, 1839.

**Conchatikpi** (*Kuⁿshak-tikpi*, 'reed-brake knob'). A former Choctaw town on a creek of the same name, popularly called Coonshark, in the s. part of Neshoba co., Miss. It derived its name from the creek, which in turn was called after a prominent bluff near a reed-brake.—Halbert in Miss. Hist. Soc. Publ., VI, 430, 1902.

**Conchayon.** One of the 7 villages or tribes forming the Taensa confederacy in 1699.—Iberville in Margry, Déc., IV, 179, 1880.

**Conchi.** Mentioned by Garcia (Origen Inds., 293, 1729) as an Indian province of New Mexico, but more likely identifiable with the Conchas, or Conchos, a little-known tribe formerly living on a river of the same name in Chihuahua, Mexico.                        (F. W. H.)

**Concho** (Span.: 'conch'). The inhabitants of Concho bay, E. coast of Lower California, on which Loreto mission was established in 1697. The people spoke the Cochimi dialect.—Picolo (1702) in Lettres Edif., II, 63, 1841.

**Condawhaw.** A Seneca settlement, in 1779, on the site of the present North Hector, N. Y.—Doc. of 1779 quoted by Conover, Kanadesaga and Geneva MS., B. A. E.

**Conejeros** (Span.: 'rabbit men'). An unidentified Apache band, mentioned by Barcia (Ensayo Cronologico, 169, 1723): "In 1596 the Apaches called Conejeros destroyed a people they described as red and white who had come from Florida. The Spaniards could not ascertain of what nation they were nor find traces of their journey."

**Conejoholo** ('a kettle on a long upright object.'—Hewitt). A Conoy village, identical with the Dekanoagah of Evans, which Day locates on the E. bank of the Susquehanna, on or near the site of Bainbridge, Lancaster co., Pa. The Conoy removed to Conejoholo from their former home on the Potomac about 1700 and again removed farther up the Susquehanna before 1743.                    (J. M.)

Conejaghera.—Doc. of 1705 in Day, Penn., 390, 1843. Conejoholo.—Doc. of 1743 in Brinton, Lenape Leg., 26, 1885. Dekanoagah.—Evans (1707) in Day, op. cit., 389, 1843.

**Conejos** (Span.: 'rabbits'). A small Diegueño band on or near Capitan Grande res., at least 9 m. from San Diego, Cal.; pop. 80 in 1883.

**Conemaugh** (Delaware *kunamág*, 'long fishing place.'—Gerard). A former Delaware and Shawnee village on the site of the present Johnstown, Cambria co., Pa.

**Cones.** Small prehistoric objects of polished stone, the use of which is undetermined, and they are therefore classed with problematical objects (q. v.). They are usually made of hematite or other hard material, and occur most plentifully in the states E. of the Mississippi. The base often varies somewhat from a circle, and the apex is sometimes quite low. Occasionally the specimens are truncated or abruptly sloped above or grade into hemispheres (q. v.), and there are doubly conical and egg forms which grade into the typical plummets (q. v.), the top in cases being truncated or slightly hollowed out, as if to accommodate some kind of fastening. Some of the cones approximate in form the more conical boat-stones (q. v.). It is surmised that they were carried as charms or served as a part of the "medicine" kit of the shaman. It is possible, however, that they were employed in playing some game. It is observed that kindred objects of hematite of more or less irregular shape show facets, such as would result from rubbing them down for the red color which they somewhat readily yield. Similar conical objects of hematite are used by the Pueblos of to-day and were used by the ancient tribes in making sacred paint; a tablet of sandstone or shale served as the grinding plate, and the cone, which was the muller, also yielded the paint. See *Hemispheres*.

CONE OF HEMATITE; KENTUCKY. (1-3)

Cones are described and illustrated among others by Fowke (1) in 13th Rep. B. A. E., 1896, (2) Archæol. Hist. Ohio, 1902; Jones, Antiq. So. Inds., 1873; Moorehead, Prehist. Impls., 1900; Rau in Smithson. Cont., XXII, 6, 1872.

(W. H. H.    G. F.)

**Conestoga** (*Kanastóge*, 'at the place of the immersed pole'). An important Iroquoian tribe that formerly lived on Susquehanna r. and its branches. When first met by Capt. John Smith, in 1608, and until their conquest by the Iroquois confederacy in 1675, they were in alliance with the Algonquian tribes of the E. shore of Chesapeake bay and at war with those on the w. shore. They were described as warlike and as possessed of a physique far superior to that of all the other neighboring tribes. By conquest they claimed the lands on both sides of Chesapeake bay, from the Choptank and Patuxent N. to the territory of the Iroquois. In 1675, after their defeat, they established themselves on the E. bank of the Potomac, in Maryland, immediately N. of Piscataway cr., below which the Doag (Nanticoke) were then living. They formed a close alliance with the Dutch and Swedes, and with the English of Maryland. The Iroquois had carried on relentless war against them, with varying success, which finally reduced them from about 3,000 in 1608 to about 550 in 1648, while their allies brought the aggregate to about 1,250. Champlain says that in 1615 they had more than 20 villages, of which only 3 were at that time engaged in war with the Iroquois, and that their town of Carantouan alone could muster more than 800 warriors. The Iroquois of the N. drove the Conestoga down on the tribes to the S. and W., who were allies of the English, a movement involving the Conestoga in a war with Maryland and Virginia in 1675. Finding themselves surrounded by enemies on all sides, a portion of them abandoned their country and took refuge with the Occaneechi on Roanoke r., while the rest remained in Pennsylvania. A quarrel occurred soon with the Occaneechi, who made common cause with the whites against the fugitive Conestoga, who were compelled to return to Susquehanna r. and submit to the Iroquois. According to Colden they were all finally removed to the country of the Oneida, where they remained until they lost their language, when they were allowed to return to Conestoga, their ancient town. Here they rapidly wasted, until, at the close of the year 1763, the remnant, numbering only 20, were massacred by a party of rioters inflamed by the accounts of the Indian war then raging along the Pennsylvania frontier. About 1675 their stockade, where they were defeated by the Maryland forces, was on the E. side of Susquehanna r., 3 m. below Columbia, Pa. Herrman's map of 1676 located it at nearly the same point on the river, but on the w. bank. The Swedes and Dutch called them Minqua, from the Delaware name applied to all tribes of Iroquoian stock; the Powhatan tribes called them Susquehannock, a name signifying 'roily river,' which was adopted by the English of Virginia and Maryland. The names of their villages are Attaock, Carantouan, Cepowig, Oscalui, Quadroque, Sasquesahanough, Testnigh, and Utchowig. The Meherrin, on the river of that name in S. E. Virginia, were officially reported to be a band of the Conestoga driven s. by the Virginians during Bacon's rebellion in 1675–76. (J. N. B. H.)

Akhrakouaehronon.—Jes. Rel., III, index, 2, 1858. Akhrakvaeronon.—Jes. Rel. 1640, 35, 1858. Amdustez.—Boudinot, Star in the West, 125, 1816. Andaslaka.—Ibid. Andastaehronon.—Jes. Rel. for 1640, 35, 1858. Andastaeronnons.—Jes. Rel. for 1657, 11, 1858. Andastaes.—Treaty of 1666 in N. Y. Doc. Col. Hist., IX, 45, 1855. Andastagueus.—Coxe, Carolana, map, 1741. Andastaguez.—Parkman, Jes. in N. Am., xlvi, note, 1883. Andastakas.—Proud, Penn., II, 294, 1798. Andastes.—Raffeix (1672) quoted by Ruttenber, Tribes Hudson R., 52–53, 1872. Andastfs.—Alcedo, Dicc. Geog., I, 97, 1786 (misprint). Andastiguez.—Parkman, Conspiracy of Pontiac, I, 22, 1883. Andastiquez.—Keane in Stanford, Compend., 500, 1878. Andastoé.—Jes. Rel. for 1647, 58, 1858. Andasto'e'r.—Jes. Rel., Thwaites ed., XXXVII, 104, 1899. Andastoerhonon.—Jes. Rel. for 1637, 159, 1858. Andastoeronnon.—Jes. Rel. for 1646, 76, 1858. Andasto'e'ronnons.—Jes. Rel., Thwaites ed., XXXVII, 104, 1899. Andastoerrhcnons.—Jes. Rel. for 1635, 33, 1858. Andastognés.—Gale, Upper Miss., 49, 1867. Andastogué.—Jes. Rel. for 1663, 10, 1858. Andastoguehronnons.—Jes. Rel. for 1664, 35, 1858. Andastogueronnons.—Jes. Rel. for 1663, 10, 1858. Andastoguez.—Jes. Rel. for 1672, 24, 1858. Andastohé.—Jes. Rel. for 1647, 8, 1858. Andastonez.—McKenney and Hall, Ind. Tribes, III, 81, 1854. Andastoui.—Parkman, Jes. in N. Am., xlvi, note, 1883. Andastracronnons.—Ibid. Andosagués.—Memoir of 1681 in Margry, Déc., II, 270, 1877. Andostaguez.—Frontenac (1673) in N. Y. Doc. Col. Hist., IX, 110, 1855. Andostoues.—Gallineé (1669) in Margry, Déc., I, 130, 1875. Antastoez.—Ibid., 138. Antastogué.—Ibid., 124. Antasto8i.—Courcelles (1671) in N. Y. Doc. Col. Hist., IX, 84, 1855. Antastouais.—Gallineé (1669) in Margry, Déc., I, 124, 1875. Antastouez.—Courcelles (1670), ibid., I, 189, 1875. Atra'K8ae'r.—Jes. Rel., Thwaites ed., XXXVII, 104, 1899. Atra'kwae'ronnons.—Ibid., 105. Atrakwae.—Doc. of 1652 quoted by Schoolcraft, Ind. Tribes, VI, 137, 1857. Canastoga.—McKenney and Hall, Ind. Tribes, III, 79, 1854. Canastoge.—Zeisberger (1750) quoted by Conover, Kanadaga and Geneva MS., B. A. E. Canastogues.—Doc. of 1699 in N. Y. Doc. Col. Hist., IV, 579, 1854. Canestogas.—Barton, New Views, 97, 1798. Canestogo.—Colden (1727), Five Nations, app., 58, 1747. Canistage.—Livingston (1717) in N. Y. Doc. Col. Hist., V, 486, 1855. Canistoge.—Livingston (1717), ibid., 485. Canostogas.—Schoolcraft, Ind. Tribes, VI, 136, 1857. Carantouanis.—Champlain, Œuvres, V, pt. 2, 8, 1870. Carantouannais.—Ibib., IV, chart, 32, 1870. Carantouans.—Parkman, Pion. Fr., 337, 1883. Cinelas.—Peyton, Hist. Augusta Co., Va., 6, 1882. Conastagoe.—Peters (1764) in Mass. Hist. Soc. Coll., 4th s., x, 508, 1871. Conastoga.—Ft Johnson conf. (1756) in N. Y. Doc. Col. Hist., VII, 110, 1856. Conastogy.—Johnson (1747), ibid., VI, 390, 1855. Conestego.—Weyman (ca. 1719) quoted by Hawkins, Missions, 117, 1845. Conestoga.—Keith (1722) quoted by Day, Penn., 390, 1843. Conestogo.—Doc. of 1701, ibid. Conestogue.—Smith (ca. 1810) quoted by Day, Penn., 279. Conistogas.—Rupp, Northampton Co., 5, 1845. Connastago.—Peters (1764) in Mass. Hist. Soc. Coll., 4th s., x, 508, 1871. Conostogas.—Ft Stanwix treaty (1768) in N. Y. Doc. Col. Hist., VIII, 133, 1857. Endastes.—Denonville (1865), ibid., IX, 283, 1855. Gandastogués.—Jes. Rel. 1672, 26, 1858. Gandostogega.—La Salle (1682) in Margry, Déc., II, 237, 1877. Ganossetage.—Doc. of 1756 in Rupp, Northampton Co., 106, 1845. Guandastogues.—Gallatin in Trans. Am. Ethnol. Soc., 103, 1848. Guandostagues.—Schoolcraft, Ind. Tribes, III, 290, 1853. Guyandots.—Gallatin quoted in N. Y. Doc. Col. Hist., III, 125, note, 1853. Huskchanoes.—Carr (1664), ibid., 74. Kanneastoka-roneah.—Macauley, N. Y., II, 174, 1829. Machoeretini.—De Laet, Nov. Orb., 76, 1633. Minckus.—Holm (1702) in Mem., Hist. Soc. Pa., III, pt. 1, 157, 1834. Minquaas.—Dutch map (1616) in N. Y. Doc. Col. Hist., I, 1856. Minquaes.—Hendricksen (1616), ibid., 14. Minquaos.—Yong (1634) in Mass. Hist. Soc. Coll., 4th s., IX, 119, 1871. Minquas.—Dutch rec. (1649) quoted by Winfield, Hudson Co., 49, 1874. Minquase.—Hudde (1645) in N. Y. Doc. Col. Hist., XII, 30, 1877. Minquays.—Penn's treaty (1701) in Proud, Penn., I, 428, 1797. Minques.—Holm (1702) in Mem. Hist. Soc. Pa. III, pt. 1, 157, 1834. Minquinos.—Mitchell, map

(1755), quoted in Am. Antiq., I, 96, 1878. **Minquosy.**—De Laet, Nov. Orb., 76, 1633. **Mynckussar.**—Vater. Mith., pt. 3, sec. 3, 317, 1816. **Myncqueser.**—Ibid., 317. **Natio perticarum.**—Du Creux quoted by Schoolcraft, Ind. Tribes, VI, 137, 1857 (Lat.: 'Nation of the poles'). **Ogehage.**—Dutch map (1616) in N. Y. Doc. Col. Hist., I, 1856 (Mohawk name). **Ontastoes.**—Gallineé (1684) in Fernow, Ohio Val., 219, 1690. **Saskwihanang.**—Rafinesque, Am. Nations, I, 138, 1836. **Sasquahana.**—Herrman, map (1670) in Rep. on Boundary between Va. and Md., 1873. **Sasquahannahs.**—Doc. of 1726 in N. C. Rec., II, 643, 1886. **Sasquehannocks.**—Doc. ca. 1646 in Force, Hist. Tracts, II, 19, 1838. **Sasquesahanocks.**—Smith (1629), Va., I, 118, 1819. **Sasquesahanoughs.**—Ibid., 74. **Sasquesahanougs.**—Strachey (ca. 1612), Va., 39, 1849. **Sasquisahanoughes.**—Md. Rec. quoted in The Nation, 343, Apr. 22, 1886. **Sassquahana.**—Herrman, map (1670) in Rep. on Boundary between Va. and Md., 1873. **Sesquehanocks.**—Harris, Voy. and Trav., I, 843, 1705. **Sesquihanowes.**—Bozman, Md., I, 128, 1837. **Southern Minquas.**—Doc. of 1649 in N. Y. Doc. Col. Hist., XIII, 25, 1881. **Suscahannaes.**—Andros (1676), ibid., XII, 557, 1877. **Suscohannes.**—Andros, ibid., 556. **Susquahanna.**—Penn's treaty (1701) in Proud, Penn., I, 428, 1797. **Susquahannocks.**—Doc. of 1648, ibid., 114. **Susquehanas.**—Doc. of 1671 in N. Y. Doc. Col. Hist., XII, 488, 1877. **Susquehannagh.**—Penn. Rec. (1701) in Day, Penn., 390, 1843. **Susquehannah Minquays.**—Ibid. **Susquehanna's.**—Andros (1675) in N. Y. Doc. Col. Hist., XII, 543, 1877. **Susquehannocks.**—Doc. of 1648 in Proud, Penn., I, 114, 1797. **Susquehannoes.**—Doc. of 1642 quoted by White, Rel. Itin., 82, 1874. **Susquehannos.**—Doc. of 1677 in N. Y. Doc. Col. Hist., IX, 227, 1855. **Susquehanocks.**—Bozman, Md., I, 128, 1837. **Susquehanoes.**—White (ca. 1634), Rel. Itin., 37, 1874. **Susquhannok.**—Drake, Bk. Inds., xi, 1848. **Susquihanoughs.**—Doc. of 1638 in Bozman, Md., II, 62, 1837. **Takoulguehronnons.**—Jes. Rel., Thwaites ed., XXXVII, 104, 1899. **Trakouaehronnons.**—Jes. Rel., III, index, 1858. **Trak8aehronnons.**—Ibid, 1660, 7, 1858.

**Conestoga horse.** A heavy draft horse, said to have originated in Pennsylvania toward the close of the 18th century, from a cross of the Flemish cart horse with some English breed (Bartlett, Dict. Americanisms, 137, 1877). This horse was much in use before the era of railroads. (A. F. C.)

**Conestoga wagon.** A large white-topped wagon, to which 6 or more Conestoga horses were attached (Bartlett, Dict. Americanisms, 137, 1877). These horses and wagons "were a marked feature of the landscape of this state." The horse and the wagon were named from Conestoga, a village in Lancaster co., Pa., called after one of the Iroquoian peoples inhabiting this region in the 18th century. (A. F. C.)

**Confederation.** A political league for offense and defense was sometimes formed by two or more tribes, who entered into a compact or formal statement of principles to govern their separate and collective action. A looser, less formal, and less cohesive alliance of tribes was sometimes formed to meet some grave temporary emergency. The unit of a confederation is the organized tribe, just as the clan or gens is the unit of the tribe. The confederation has a supreme council composed of representatives from the several contracting tribes of which it is composed. The tribes forming a confederation surrendered to the league certain powers and

rights which they had exercised individually. The executive, legislative, and judicial functions of the confederation were exercised by the supreme council through instruments appointed in the compact or afterward devised. Every tribe of the confederation was generally entitled to representation in the supreme federal council. The chiefs of the federal council and the subchiefs of each tribe constituted the local council of the tribe. The confirmation of officials and their installation were functions delegated to the officers of the confederation. The supreme federal council had practically the same officers as a tribal council, namely, a speaker, fire-keeper, door-keeper, and wampum-keeper or annalist. In the Iroquoian confederation the original 5 tribes severally had a supreme war-chief, the name and the title of whom were hereditary in certain specified clans. The supreme federal council, sitting as a court without a jury, heard and determined causes in accordance with established principles and rules. The representation in the council of the Iroquois confederation was not based on the clan as its unit, for many clans had no representative in the federal council, while others had several. The supreme federal council of this confederation was organized on the basis of tribal phratries or brotherhoods of tribes, of which one phratry acted as do the presiding judges of a court sitting without a jury, having power to confirm, or on constitutional or other grounds to reject, the votes or conclusions of the two other phratries acting individually, but having no right to discuss any question beyond suggesting means to the other phratries for reaching an agreement or compromise, in the event that they offer differing votes or opinions, and at all times being jealously careful of the customs, rules, principles, and precedents of the council, requiring procedure strictly to conform to these where possible. The constituent tribes of the Iroquois confederation, the Mohawk, Oneida, Onondaga, Cayuga, and Seneca, constituted three tribal phratries, of which the Mohawk and Seneca formed the first, the Oneida and Cayuga the second, and the Onondaga the third; but in ceremonial and festal assemblies the last tribe affiliated with the Mohawk-Seneca phratry.

Among the looser confederations, properly alliances, may be mentioned that of the Chippewa, Ottawa, and Potawatomi; the 7 council fires of the Dakota; and the alliance of the tribes of Virginia and Maryland called the Powhatan confederacy. To these may be added the loose Caddo confederacy, which, like the others, was held together largely by religious affiliation. The records are insufficient to define with accuracy the political organization of these groups. See *Clan and Gens, Government, Social Organization, Tribe.*

(J. N. B. H.)

**Congaree.** A small tribe, supposed to be Siouan, formerly living in South Carolina. The grounds for including this tribe in the Siouan family are its location and its intimate relation with known Siouan tribes, especially the Catawba, with which it was ultimately incorporated; but according to Adair and Lawson the Congaree spoke a dialect different from that of the Catawba, which they preserved even after their incorporation. In 1693 the Cherokee complained that the Shawnee, Catawba, and Congaree took prisoners from among them and sold them as slaves in Charleston. They were visited in 1701 by Lawson, who found them on the N. E. bank of Santee r. below the junction of the Wateree. Their town consisted of not more than 12 houses, with plantations up and down the country. On a map of 1715 the village of the Congaree is placed on the s. bank of Congaree r., about opposite the site of Columbia. A fort bearing the tribal name was established near the village in 1718. They were a small tribe, having lost many by tribal feuds but more by smallpox. Lawson states that, although the several tribes visited by him were generally small and lived closely adjoining one another, they differed in features, disposition, and language, a fact which renders the assignment of these small tribes to the Siouan family conjectural. The Congaree, like their neighbors, took part in the Yamasi war in 1715, as a result of which they were so reduced that they were compelled to move up the country and join the Catawba, with whom they were still living in 1743. Moll's map of 1730 (Salmon, Modern History, III, 562, 1746) places their town or station on the N. bank of Congaree r., opposite which ran the trail to the Cherokee country. It was s. of lat. 34°, probably in Richland co. They were a friendly people, handsome and well built, the women being especially beautiful compared with those of other tribes. See Mooney, Siouan Tribes of the East, 1894.
Ani'-Gilĭ′.—Mooney in 19th Rep. B. A. E., 508, 1900 ('long-haired people,' a Cherokee clan, possibly originally Congaree). Canggaree.—Adair, Hist. Am. Inds., 225, 1775. Congarees.—Mills, Hist. S. C., 108, 1826. Congares.—Doc. of 1719 in Rivers, Hist. S. C., 93, 1874. Congerees.—Lawson, Hist. Carolina, 25, 1860. Congeres.—Moll, map of Carolina, 1720. Congrée.—La Tour, map of U. S., 1784. Conqerees.—War map of 1715 in Winsor, Hist. Am., v, 346, 1887.

**Congewichacha** (*wichacha*='man'). A Dakota division, possibly of the Teton. Cf. *Kanghiyuha.*
Conge-wee-cha-cha.—Corliss, MS. Lacotah vocab., B. A. E., 106, 1874 (Teton name).

**Conicari** (Nahuatl: *coni* 'crow,' 'raven', *cari* 'house': 'house of the raven.'— Buelna). A settlement of the Mayo, probably of the Tepahue division, on the Rio Mayo, 30 m. N. of Alamos, in lat. 27° 6′, S. E. Sonora, Mexico. It contained 200 families in 1645, and is still one of the most important Mayo settlements. For discussion as to its linguistic relations see Bandelier in Arch. Inst. Papers, III, 53, 1890.
Canicari.—Escudero, Noticias de Son. y Sin., 101, 1849. Conecáre.—Hardy, Travels in Mexico, 438, 1829. Conicare.—Kino, map (1702) in Stöcklein, Neue Welt-Bott, 1726. Conicari.—Rivera, Diario y Derrot., leg. 1179, 1736. San Andres Conicari.— Orozco y Berra, Geog., 356, 1864.

**Conisca** (seemingly from *kane′ska*, 'grass'). One of 4 Cherokee settlements mentioned by Bartram (Travels, 371, 1792) as situated on a branch of Tennessee r. about 1776.

**Conkhandeenrhonon.** An Iroquoian tribe living s. of St Lawrence r. in 1635.
Conkhandeenrhonons.—Brebeuf in Jes. Rel. for 1635, 33, 1858. Konkhandeenrhonon.—Jes. Rel. for 1640, 35, 1858.

**Conneaut.** A village composed of Onondaga and Missisauga and other Algonquian immigrants, situated on Conneaut lake, Pa., in the 18th century.
Coneyat.—Procter (1791) in Am. St. Pap., Ind. Aff., I, 163, 1832. Conyat.—Ellicot (1794), ibid., 516.

**Connecticut** (from the Mahican *quinnitukq-ut*, 'at the long tidal river'). Tribes living on Connecticut r., including the Scantie, Nawaas, and Podunk.
Conittekooks.—Van der Donck (1655) quoted by Ruttenber, Tribes Hudson R., 82, 1872. Connectacuts.—Wood (1639) quoted by Barton, New Views, xix, 1798. Connegticuts.—Russell (1682) in Mass. Hist. Soc. Coll., 4th s., VIII, 85, 1868. Quinticoock.— Williams (1643), ibid., 1st s., III, 205, 1794.

**Connewango** ('at the falls'). (1) A Seneca village that stood on the site of Warren, Pa., and was destroyed by Col. Brodhead in 1779. (2) A former Seneca village on the left bank of Alleghany r., above the site of Tionesta, Forest co., Pa. Both villages belonged to the division of the Seneca known as Cornplanter's band.
Cananouagan.—La Tour, map, 1779. Canaouagon.— Vaudreuil (1759) in N. Y. Doc. Col. Hist., x, 949, 1858. Canawagon.—Guy Park conf. (1775), ibid., VIII, 553, 1857. Canawagow.—Johnson Hall conf. (1774), ibid. Canawako.—Onondaga conf., ibid., 426. Canwagan.—Guy Park conf. (1774), ibid., 519. Cayantha.—Procter in Am. St. Pap., IV, 516, 1832. Conawago.—Royce in 18th Rep. B. A. E., pl. clx, 1899. Conewango.—Butterfield, Washington-Irvine Cor., 43, 1882. Conneogie.—Harris, Tour, map, 1805. Connewangoes.—Schoolcraft, Ind. Tribes, III, 288, 1853. Cornplanter's Town.—V. L. Thomas, letter, 1885. Kanaouagan.—Joncaire (1749) in Margry, Déc., VI, 675, 1886. Kanauagon.— Butterfield, op. cit. Kanoagoa.—Pouchot, map (1758) in N. Y. Doc. Col. Hist., x, 694, 1858. Kunoagon.—Doc. of 1759, ibid., 984.

**Conohasset.** A Massachuset village formerly about Cohasset, Norfolk co., Mass. The site was sold by the Indians in 1635.
Conohasset.—Flint (1821) in Mass. Hist. Soc. Coll., 3d s., II, 84–85, 1830. Quonahasit.—Smith (1629), Virginia, II, 194, repr. 1819. Quonahassit.—Smith (1616) in Mass. Hist. Soc. Coll., 3d s., VI, 108, 1837.

**Conontoroy.** Given as one of the "out towns" among the Cherokee in a document of 1755 (Royce in 5th Rep. B. A. E., 143, 1887). Not identified.

**Conop.** A former village, presumably Costanoan, connected with Dolores mission, San Francisco, Cal.—Taylor in Cal. Farmer, Oct. 18, 1861.

**Conoross** (corruption of *Kăwăn′-ură′-săñyĭ*, or *Kăwăn′-tsură′-săñyĭ*, 'where the duck fell off'). The supposed name of a Cherokee settlement on Conoross cr., which enters Keowee or Seneca r. from the w., in Anderson co., S. C.—Mooney in 19th Rep. B. A. E., 412, 1900.
**Conneross.**—Ibid.

**Conoy.** An Algonquian tribe, related to the Delawares, from whose ancestral stem they apparently sprang, but their closest relations were with the Nanticoke, with whom it is probable they were in late prehistoric times united, the two forming a single tribe, while their language is supposed to have been somewhat closely allied to that spoken in Virginia by the Powhatan. Heckewelder believed them to be identical with the Kanawha, who gave the name to the chief river of West Virginia. Although Brinton calls this "a loose guess," the names Conoy, Ganawese, etc., seem to be forms of Kanawha. The application of the same name to the Piscataway tribe of Maryland, and to the river, is difficult to explain by any other theory than that the former once lived on the banks of the Kanawha. In 1660 (Proc. Coun., 1636–67, Md. Archives, 403, 1885) the Piscataway applied to the governor of the colony to confirm their choice of an "emperor," and to his inquiry in regard to their custom in this respect, replied: "Long a goe there came a King from the Easterne Shoare who Comanded over all the Jndians now inhabiting within the bounds of this Province (nameing every towne severally) and also over the Patowmecks and Sasquehannoughs, whome for that he Did as it were imbrace and cover them all they called Vttapoingassinem this man dyeing without issue made his brother Quokonassaum King after him, after whome Succeeded his other brothers, after whose death they tooke a Sister's Sonn, and soe from Brother to Brother, and for want of such to a Sisters Sonne, the Governm^t descended for thirteene Generacōns without Jnterrupcōn vntill Kittamaquunds tyme who dyed without brother or Sister and apoynted his daughter to be Queene but that the Jndians withstood itt as being Contrary to their Custome, wherevpon they chose Weghucasso for their King who was descended from one of Vttapoingassinem brothers (But which of them they knowe not) and Weghucasso

at his death apoynted this other Vttapoingassinem to be King being descended from one of the first Kings this man they sayd was Jan Jan Wizous which in their language signifyes a true King. And would not suffer vs to call him Tawzin which is the Style they give to the sons of their Kings, who by their Custome are not to succeede in Rule, but his Brothers, or the Sons of his Sisters."

The order of descent in this extract gives it an impress of truth. It indicates close relation between the Nanticoke and the Conoy, though the inclusion of the Susquehanna (Conestoga) among the emperor's subjects must be rejected. One of the tribes of the E. shore from which this chief could have come was the Nanticoke. Thirteen generations would carry back the date of this first emperor to the beginning of the 16th century. Lord Baltimore's colonists in 1634 established a mission amongst them, and the "emperor" Chitomachen, otherwise known as Tayac, said to be ruler over a dominion extending 130 m. E. and w., was converted, with his family. They were, however, so harassed by the Conestoga that a few years later they abandoned their country and moved farther up the Potomac. They, then rapidly decreasing, were in 1673 assigned a tract on that stream, which Streeter (Hist. Mag., 1st s., I, 67, 1857) thinks may have been near the site of Washington, D. C. The Conestoga, when driven from their own country by the Iroquois in 1675, again invaded the territory of the Conoy and forced that tribe to retire up the Potomac and into Pennsylvania. This was a gradual migration, unless it took place at a much later period, for Baron Graffenried, while searching for a reported silver mine in 1711, found them on the Maryland side of the Potomac about 50 m. above Washington, and made a treaty of friendship with them. He calls them Canawest. About this time the Iroquois assigned them lands at Conejoholo on the Susquehanna, near the present Bainbridge, Pa., in the vicinity of the Nanticoke and Conestoga. Here they first began to be known as Conoy. Some of them were living with these tribes at Conestoga in 1742. They gradually made their way up the Susquehanna, stopping at Harrisburg, Shamokin, Catawissa, and Wyoming, and in 1765 were living in s. New York, at Owego, Chugnut, and Chenango, on the E. branch of the Susquehanna. At that time they numbered only about 150, and, with their associates, the Nanticoke and Mahican, were dependent on the Iroquois. They moved w. with the Mahican and Delawares, and soon became known only as a part of those tribes. In 1793 they attended a council near Detroit and used the turkey as their signature.

The customs and beliefs of the Conoy may best be given by the following quotation from White's Relatio Itineris, ca. 1635, although the author's interpretations of customs often go far astray: "The natives are very tall and well proportioned; their skin is naturally rather dark, and they make it uglier by staining it, generally with red paint mixed with oil, to keep off the mosquitoes, thinking more of their own comfort than of appearances. They disfigure their countenances with other colors, too, painting them in various and truly hideous and frightful ways, either a dark blue above the nose and red below, or the reverse. And as they live almost to extreme old age without having beards, they counterfeit them with paint, by drawing lines of various colors from the extremities of the lips to the ears. They generally have black hair, which they carry round in a knot to the left ear, and fasten with a band, adding some ornament which is in estimation among them. Some of them wear on their foreheads the figure of a fish made of copper. They adorn their necks with glass beads strung on a thread like necklaces, though these beads are getting to be less valued among them and less useful for trade. They are clothed for the most part in deerskins or some similar kind of covering, which hangs down behind like a cloak. They wear aprons round the middle, and leave the rest of the body naked. The young boys and girls go about with nothing on them. The soles of their feet are as hard as horn, and they tread on thorns and briers without being hurt. Their arms are bows, and arrows 3 ft. long, tipped with stag's horn, or a white flint sharpened at the end. They shoot these with such skill that they can stand off and hit a sparrow in the middle; and, in order to become expert by practice, they throw a spear up in the air and then send an arrow from the bow string and drive it into the spear before it falls. But since they do not string the bow very tight, they can not hit a mark at a great distance. They live by means of these weapons, and go out every day through the fields and woods to hunt squirrels, partridges, turkeys, and wild animals. For there is an abundance of all these, though we ourselves do not yet venture to procure food by hunting, for fear of ambushes. They live in houses built in an oblong, oval shape. Light is admitted into these through the roof, by a window a foot and a half long; this also serves to carry off the smoke, for they kindle the fire in the middle of the floor, and sleep around the fire. Their kings, however,

and chief men have private apartments, as it were, of their own, and beds, made by driving 4 posts into the ground, and arranging poles above them horizontally."

According to the same authority they acknowledged one god of heaven, yet paid him no outward worship, but strove in every way to appease a certain imaginary spirit, which they called Ochre, that he might not hurt them. They also worshiped corn and fire. The missionary probably here alludes to the use of corn and fire in certain religious ceremonies. The Conoy villages were Catawissa, Conedogwinit, Conejoholo, Conoytown, Kittamaquindi, Onuatuc, Opament, Peixtan.
(J. M.    C. T.)

**Arogisti.**—Colden (1727), Five Nations, 40, 1747 (given as the English name of the Cahnowas in 1679). **Cachnawayes.**—Maryland treaty (1682) in N. Y. Doc. Col. Hist., III, 323, 1853. **Cahnowas.**—Colden, op. cit. **Canagesse.**—Ibid., 38. **Canais.**—Heckewelder (1819) in Bozman, Md., I, 169, 1837 (given as the proper form). **Canavest.**—Graffenried (1711) in N. C. Rec., I, 958, 1886. **Canaways.**—Heckewelder, op. cit. **Canawese.**—Ibid. **Canawest.**—Graffenried, op. cit. **Canhaways.**—Drake, Bk. Inds., viii, 1848. **Canoise.**—Penn. Records (1707) in Day, Penn., 391, 1843. **Canowes.**—Maryland treaty (1682) in N. Y. Doc. Col. Hist., III, 322, 1853. **Canoyeas.**—McKenney and Hall, Ind. Tribes, III, 80, 1854. **Canoyias.**—Colden (1727), Five Nations, app., 58, 107, 1747. **Canoys.**—Doc. of 1764 in N. Y. Doc. Col. Hist., VII, 641, 1856. **Cochnewwasroonaw.**—McKenney and Hall, Ind. Tribes, III, 80, 1854. **Connays.**—Croghan (1757) in N. Y. Doc. Col. Hist., VII, 268, 1856. **Connoye.**—Johnson (1757), ibid., 329. **Connoys.**—Lincoln (1793) in Am. St. Papers, IV, 352, 1832. **Conoies.**—Imlay, West Terr., 291, 1797. **Conois.**—Heckewelder (1819) in Bozman, Md., I, 169–171, 1837. **Conoy.**—Colden (1727), Five Nations, app., 148, 1747. **Conoy-uch-such.**—Douglass, Summary, II, 315, 1755 (same?). **Conoyucksuchroona.**—McKenney and Hall, Ind. Tribes, III, 80, 1854 (same?). **Gachnawas-haga.**—Gatschet in Am. Antiq., IV, 75, 1881–82 (Mohawk name, according to Pyrlaeus). **Ganaway.**—Day, Penn., 398, 1843 (form used in treaties before 1744). **Ganawense.**—Ibid., 389. **Ganawese.**—Penn's treaty (1701) in Schoolcraft, Ind. Tribes, VI, 140, 1857. **Ganawoose.**—Boudinot, Star in the West, 126, 1816. **Ganawses.**—Domenech, Deserts, I, 441, 1860. **Gangawese.**—Conyngham in Day, Penn., 243, 1843. **Gannaouens.**—D'Heu (1708) in N. Y. Doc. Col. Hist., IX, 815, 1855. **Ganniessinga.**—Hennepin, New Discov., 59, 1698. **Guananesses.**—Domenech, Deserts, I, 441, 1860 (same?). **Kanaa.**—Worsley, View Am. Inds., 92, 1828. **Kanaai.**—Boudinot, Star in the West, 126, 1816. **Kanai.**—Worsley, op. cit. **Kanawhas.**—Brinton, Lenape Legends, 213, 1885 (Johnston, on Shawnee authority, renders this word, 'having whirlpools,' but Brinton thinks it but another form of Canai or Conoy). **Kanhawas.**—Heckewelder (1819) in Bozman, Md., I, 169–171, 1837. **Kanhaways.**—Drake, Bk. Inds., viii, 1848. **Kenhawas.**—Day, Penn., 243, 1843. **Kenowiki.**—Squier in Beach, Ind. Miscel., 34, 1877. **Konowiki.**—Rafinesque, Am. Nations, I, 139, 1836 (Delaware name). **Kuhnauwantheew.**—Aupaumut (1791) quoted by Brinton, Lenape Leg., 20, 1885 (Mahican name). **Pascatawaye.**—White (1634?), Relatio Itineris, 33, 1874. **Pascatoe.**—Ibid., 63. **Pascatoways.**—Brinton, Lenape Leg., 15, 1885. **Pascattawaye.**—Herrman, map (1670) in Maps to Accompany the Rep. of the Comrs. on the Bndry. Line bet. Va. and Md., 1873 (village about Piscataway cr., s. side). **Pascoticons.**—Spilman (ca. 1623) in Mass. Hist. Soc. Coll., 4th s., IX, 28, note, 1871. **Piscatawese.**—Conyngham in Day, Penn., 243, 1843. **Piscatoway.**—Maryland treaty (1682) in N. Y. Doc. Col. Hist., III, 322, 1853. **Piscatowayes.**—Ibid., 323. **Piscattawayes.**—Brockholls (1682), ibid., XIII, 561, 1881. **Piscatua.**—Doc. of 1743 quoted by Brinton, Lenape Leg., 25, 1885. **Pisscattaways.**—Brockholls, op. cit.

**Conoytown.** A Conoy village formerly on Susquehanna r. in Pennsylvania, between Conejoholo (Bainbridge) and Shamokin (Sunbury). In 1744 the Conoy abandoned it after but a short stay there and removed to the last-named place. — Brinton, Lenape Leg., 29, 1885.

**Conshac** ('cane', 'reed', 'reed-brake'). A name applied in three principal ways: (1) to the inhabitants of certain Choctaw towns (see *Concha, Conchachitou, Conchatikpi, Conshaconsapa, Coosha*); (2) to the Koasati, q. v.; (3) to a people living somewhere on Coosa r., not far from the Alibamu. Most of the later statements regarding these people seem to have been derived from Iberville (Margry, Déc., IV, 594–95, 602, 1880), who, in 1702, speaks of two distinct bands under this name, the one living with the Alibamu, the other some distance E. N. E. of them. The former were probably the Koasati, although it is possible that they were the people of Old Kusa, which was close by. The Conshac living higher up, 20 to 30 leagues beyond, Iberville states to have been called "Apalachicolys" by the Spaniards and to have moved into the district they then occupied from Apalachicola r. in order to trade with the English. Such a migration does not seem to have been noted by anyone else, however, and it is highly probable that these Conshac were the people of Kusa, the Upper Creek "capital." This is rendered more likely by the analogous case of the Choctaw Coosha, called Coosa by Romans, the name of which has been corrupted from the same word, and from the further consideration that Conshac and Kusa rarely occur on the same map. That the Conshac were an important tribe is attested by all early narratives and by the fact that Alabama r. was often called after them. If not identical with the people of Kusa specifically, the entire Muskogee tribe may be intended. (J. R. S.) **Conchaes.**—Du Pratz, Hist. de la Louisiane, II, 208, 1758. **Conchaes.**—Boudinot, Star in the West, 126, 1816. **Conchakus.**—McKenney and Hall, Ind. Tribes, III, 79, 1854. **Conchaques.**—Pénicaut (1708) in French, Hist. Coll. La., I, 101, 1869. **Conchas.**—French, ibid., III, 235, 1851. **Conchatez.**—De l'Isle, map (*ca.* 1710) in Winsor, Hist. Am., II, 294, 1886. **Conches.**—Keane in Stanford, Compend., 510, 1878. **Conshachs.**—Carroll, Hist. Coll. S. C., I, 190, 1836 (Coosas are also mentioned, but this is probably a duplication made in quoting earlier authorities). **Conshakis.**—Bossu (1759), Travels La., I, 229, 1771.

**Conshaconsapa** (corruption of *Kushakosapa*, 'reed-brake field'). A former Choctaw town E. of Imongalasha, Neshoba co., Miss.; exact location not known.—Halbert in Miss. Hist. Soc. Publ., VI, 431, 1902.

**Contahnah** ('a pine in the water.'—Hewitt). A Tuscarora village near the mouth of Neuse r., N. C., in 1701.

**Cau-ta-noh.**—Cusic (1825) quoted by Schoolcraft, Ind. Tribes, V, 636, 1855. **Contahnah.**—Lawson (1709), N. C., 383, 1860. **Kau-ta-noh.**—Cusic, op. cit. **Kautanohakau.**—Cusic, Six Nations, 24, 1828.

**Contarea.** One of the principal Huron villages in Ontario in the 17th century; situated near the present Lannigan's lake, Tiny township. See *Kontareahronon.* **Carmaron.**—Champlain (1615), Œuvres, IV, 27, 1870. **Contareia.**—Jes. Rel. for 1656, 10, 1858. **Contarrea.**—Jes. Rel. for 1636, 94, 1858. **Kontarea.**—Jes. Rel. for 1642, 74, 1858.

**Contla.** A branch of the Opata inhabiting the pueblo of Santa Cruz, Sonora, Mexico (Orozco y Berra, Geog., 344, 1864). The name is probably that applied by the natives to their town.

**Cooking.** See *Food.*

**Cook's Ferry.** A body of Ntlakyapamuk, probably belonging to the Nicola band, under the Fraser superintendency, Brit. Col.; pop. 282 in 1882, 204 in 1904.—Can. Ind. Aff. Reps.

**Coon.** See *Raccoon.*

**Coongaleés.** Given by Sauvole (French, Hist. Coll. La., 1st s., III, 238, 1851) as a village on Wabash (i. e. Ohio) r., above a Chickasaw village that was 140 leagues from the Mississippi in 1701. As it is represented as on the route to Carolina, Tennessee r. may have been intended. Perhaps a Cherokee town. **Tahogale.**—Coxe in French, Hist. Coll. La., II, 230, 1850.

**Cooniac.** A village of the Skilloot tribe of the Chinookan family at Oak point (from which the village was named), on the s. side of Columbia r., below the mouth of the Cowlitz, in Columbia co., Oreg. After 1830 the Cooniac people seem to have been the only surviving remnant of the Skilloot. (L. F.) **Cooniacs.**—Gibbs, Chinook Vocab., IV, 1863. **Kahnyak.**— Ibid. **Ketlakaniaks.** — Framboise (1835) quoted by Gairdner in Jour. Geog. Soc. Lond., XI, 255, 1841. **Konick.**—Lane (1849) in Sen. Ex. Doc. 52, 31st Cong., 1st sess., 174, 1850. **Konnaack.**—Pres. Mess., Ex. Doc. 39, 32d Cong., 1st sess., 2, 1852. **Kukhn-yak.**—Gibbs, Chinook Vocab., IV, 1863. **Ne-co-ni-ac.**—Lee and Frost, Oregon, 194, 1844. **Ne Coniacks.**—Ibid., 194. **Qā'niak.**—Boas, field notes (name for Oak point). **Whill Wetz.**—Ross, Adventures, 104, 1849.

**Coonti.** A cycadaceous plant (*Zamia integrifolia*), or the breadstuff obtained from it by the Seminole of Florida; spelled also *koontie, coontia*, etc. *Kunti* is the name of the "flour" in the Seminole dialect. (A. F. C.)

**Cooptee.** A Nootka winter village near the head of Nootka sd., w. coast of Vancouver id. **Coopte.**—Can. Ind. Aff. Rep. 1902, app., 83. **Cooptee.**—Jewitt, Narr., 104, 1849.

**Coos.** The term usually employed to denote the villages or tribes of the Kusan family formerly on Coos bay, Oreg. Lewis and Clark estimated their population at 1,500 in 1805. The name is often used as synonymous with the family name. Properly speaking there are 2 villages included under the term, Melukitz and Anasitch. (L. F.)

Cookkooooose.—Lewis and Clark, Exped., II, 118, 1814. Cookkoo-oose.—Drake, Bk. Inds., xi, 1848. Cookoose.—Bancroft, Nat. Races, I, 307, 1874. Coos.—Dorsey in Jour. Am. Folk-lore, III, 231, 1890. Coosas.—Ind. Aff. Rep., 62, 1872. Coos Bay.—Dorsey in Jour. Am. Folk-lore, III, 231, 1890. Co-ose.—Parrish in Ind. Aff. Rep. 1854, 495, 1855. Coose Bay.—Palmer in Ind. Aff. Rep. 1856, 218, 1857. Cooses.—Taylor in Sen. Ex. Doc. 4, 40th Cong., spec. sess., 5, 1867. Coose Taylors.—Dole in Ind. Aff. Rep., 220, 1861. Cowes.—Dorsey in Jour. Am. Folk-lore, III, 1890. Ha'tĕnĕ.—Everette, Tututĕne MS. vocab., B. A. E., 1883 (Tututunne name). Ha'ɹûnnĕ.—Dorsey, Chasta Costa MS. vocab., B. A. E., 1884 (Chastacosta name). Kaons.—Framboise (1835) quoted by Gairdner in Jour. Geog. Soc. Lond., XI, 256, 1841. Käüs.—Hale, Ethnog. and Philol., 221, 1846. Ko'-i-yäk'.—Bissell, Umpkwa MS. vocab., B. A. E. (Umpqua name). Ko-k'oc',—Dorsey, Alsea MS. vocab., B. A. E., 1884 (Alsea name). Kook-koo-oose.—Drake, Bk. Inds., viii, 1848. Kouse.—Armstrong, Oregon, 116, 1857. Kowes.—Drew (1855) in H. R. Ex. Doc. 93, 34th Cong., 1st sess., 94, 1856. Kowes Bay.—Ind. Aff. Rep. 1857, 359, 1858. K'qlo-qwec ɹûnnĕ.—Dorsey, Chasta Costa MS. vocab., B. A. E., 1884 (Chastacosta name). Kūs.—Dorsey in Jour. Am. Folk-lore, III, 231, 1890. Kusa.—Ind. Aff. Rep., 253, 1877. Kūs-me' ɹûnnĕ.—Dorsey, Chetco MS. vocab., B. A. E., 1884 (Chetco name). Kwokwöōs.—Hale, Ethnog. and Philol., 221, 1846. Mû-cĭn'-t'ă ɹûnnĕ.—Dorsey, Coquille MS. vocab., B. A. E., 1884 (Coquille (Athapascan) name). Sai-yu'-cle-me' ɹûnnĕ.—Dorsey, Tutu MS. vocab., B. A. E., 1884 (Tututunne name). Tcê'ɹûnnĕ.—Dorsey, Naltûnne ɹûnnĕ' MS. vocab., B. A. E., 1884 (Naltunne name).

**Coosa.** A small tribe, now extinct, which lived about the mouth of Edisto or Combahee r., South Carolina. Its name is preserved in Coosaw and Coosawhatchee rs. According to Rivers (Hist. S. C., 94, 1874) they lived N. E. of Combahee r., which separated them from the Combahee tribe. They appear to be identical with the Couexi of the Huguenot colonists (1562) and with the Coçao of Juan de la Vandera's narrative of 1569. They were hostile to the English in 1671; in 1675 the "great and lesser Casor" sold to the colonists a tract lying on Kiawah, Stono, and Edisto rs.; there is also record of a sale by the chief of "Kissah" in 1684. They are mentioned as Kussoes in the South Carolina trade regulations of 1707, and last appear in 1743, under the name Coosah, as one of the tribes incorporated with the Catawba but still preserving their own language. They were probably related to the Indians of the Creek confederacy. (J. M.)

Casor.—Deed of 1675 in Mills, S. C., app. 1, 1826. Coçao.—Vandera (1567) quoted by French, Hist. Coll. La., II, 290, 1875. Coosah.—Adair, Am. Inds., 225, 1775. Coosaw.—Rivers, Hist. S. C., 38, 1856. Cosah.—Mills, Stat. S. C., 107, 1826. Couexi.—Doc. cited by Mooney, Siouan Tribes of the East, 84, 1894. Cozao.—Vandera, op. cit. Kissah.—Mills, op. cit., 107, app. 1. Kussoe.—Doc. of 1671 quoted by Rivers, Hist. S. C., 372, 1856.

**Coosa.** Given as a Cherokee town in a document of 1799 (Royce in 5th Rep. B. A. E., 144, 1887). Unidentified, but perhaps on upper Coosa r., Ala. See *Kusa.*

**Coosada.** A former settlement of Koasati, from whom it received its name, established about 1784 on the left bank of Tennessee r. at what is now Larkin's Landing, Jackson co., Ala. From this village to the site of Guntersville there was an Indian trail.—Street in Ala. Hist. Soc. Publ., I, 417, 1901; Royce in 18th Rep. B. A. E., pl. cviii, 1899.

**Coosadi Hychoy.** A former Koasati settlement on Tombigbee r., in Choctaw and Marengo cos., Ala., about lat. 32° 35′.
Coosadi Hychoy.—West Fla. map, ca. 1775. Ochoy.—Romans, Florida, 327, 1775.

**Coosahatchi.** An Upper Creek town on Tallapoosa r., Ala., with 36 families in 1832.
Coosahatches.—Swan (1791) in Schoolcraft, Ind. Tribes, v, 262, 1855. Cubahatchee.—Hopoethle Yoholo (1836) in H. R. Ex. Doc. 80, 27th Cong., 3d sess., 36, 1843. Cube hatcha.—Schoolcraft, Ind. Tribes, IV, 578, 1854.

**Coosak-hattak-falaya** (Choctaw: 'long white cane'). Noted on Robin's map as an Indian town in 1807. Romans (Fla., 305, 1775) mentions it apparently as a settlement w. of lower Tombigbee r., Ala., in Muskhogean territory.
Coosak hattak.—Robin, Voy., I, map, 1807.

**Coosha** (*kushak,* or *kusha,* 'reed,' or 'reed-brake'). A former important Choctaw town on the N. side of a w. branch of Lost Horse cr., an affluent of Ponta cr., in Lauderdale co., Miss. (Halbert in Miss. Hist. Soc. Publ., VI, 416, 1902). Romans has transposed the location of this town and Panthe, q. v.
Coosa.—Romans, Florida, map, 1775 (misapplied). Coosahs.—Gatschet, Creek Migr. Leg., I, 108, 1884. Cusha.—Ibid. Konshaws.—Byington, Choctaw MS. Dict., B. A. E., ca. 1834.

**Coosuc** (from *koash* 'pine,' *ak* 'at:' 'at the pine'). A small band, probably of the Pennacook, formerly living about the junction of the Upper and Lower Ammonoosuc with the Connecticut, in Coos and Grafton cos., N. H. Their village, called Coos or Coosuc, seems to have been near the mouth of the Lower Ammonoosuc. They were driven off by the English in 1704 and joined the St Francis Indians, where they still kept up the name about 1809. (J. M.)
Cohâssiac.—Kendall, Travels, III, 191, 1809 (name still used for themselves by those at St Francis). Coos.—Macauley, N. Y., II, 162, 1829. Coosucks.—Schoolcraft, Ind. Tribes, v, 222, 1855. Cowasacks.—Kidder in Me. Hist. Soc. Coll., VI, 236, 1859. Cowassuck.—Penhallow (1726) quoted by Lyman in N. H. Hist. Soc. Coll., I, 36, 1824.

**Coot.** A Costanoan village situated in 1819 within 10 m. of Santa Cruz mission, Cal.—Taylor in Cal. Farmer, Apr. 5, 1860.

**Cooweescoowee** (*Gu'wisguwii'*, an onomatope for a large bird said to have been seen formerly at frequent intervals in the old Cherokee country, accompanying the migratory wild geese, and described as resembling a large snipe, with yellow legs and unwebbed feet). A district of the Cherokee Nation, Indian Ter., named in honor of the noted Cherokee chief so-called, better known as John Ross.— Mooney in 19th Rep. B. A. E., 285, 521, 1900.

**Cooxissett.** A village, probably in Plymouth co., Mass., having about 160 inhabitants in 1685. Mentioned by Hinckley (1685) in Mass. Hist. Soc. Coll., 4th s., v, 133, 1861.

**Copala.** A mythical province, about which the "Turk," apparently a Pawnee Indian, while among the Pueblos of the Rio Grande in New Mexico in 1540, endeavored to deceive Coronado and his army. It was said to have been situated in the direction of Florida and to have contained great wealth. See Winship in 14th Rep. B. A. E., 491, 1896. Cf. *Eyish, Iza, Quivira.*

**Copalis.** A division of Salish on Copalis r., 18 m. N. of Grays harbor, Wash. Lewis and Clark estimated their number at 200, in 10 houses, in 1805.
Copalis.—Swan, N. W. Coast, 210, 1857. **Pailishs.**—Domenech, Deserts, I, 443, 1860. **Pailsh.**—Lewis and Clark, Exped., II, 474, 1814. **Pailsk.**—Ibid., 119.

**Copeh** (from *kapai*, 'stream,' in the local dialect). A tribe of the Patwin division of the Copehan family formerly living on lower Puta cr., Yolo co., Cal.
Cop-éh.—Gibbs in Schoolcraft, Ind. Tribes, III, 428, 1853. **Ko-pe.**—Powell in Cont. N. A. Ethnol., III, 519, 1877. **Putos.**—Powers in Overland Mo., XIII, 543, 1874 (so called by the Spaniards "on account of their gross licentiousness").

**Copehan Family.** A linguistic stock formerly occupying a large territory in California, from Suisun and San Pablo bays on the s. to Mt Shasta and the country of the Shastan family on the N. Starting from the N., the E. boundary ran a few miles E. of McCloud r. to its junction with the Sacramento and thence to Redding, a large triangle E. of Sacramento r. belonging to the Copehan; and from Redding down the boundary was about 10 m. E. of Sacramento r., but s. of Chico it was confined to the w. bank. On the w. the summit of the Coast range formed the boundary, but from the headwaters of Cottonwood cr. northward it nearly reached the s. fork of the upper Trinity. The people of this family were among the most interesting of the California Indians, with a harmonious language and an interesting mythology. Their social and political system was like that of all California tribes: their largest unit was the village, more extensive combinations being for temporary purposes only. The people comprising this family have been divided by Powers (Cont. N. A. Ethnol., III, 1877) into 2 branches, the Patwin and the Wintun, differing considerably in language and customs. Following is a list of their villages:

Patwin subfamily: Aclutoy, Ansactoy, Chenposel, Churuptoy, Copeh, Guilitoy,

Korusi, Liwaito, Lolsel, Malaka, Napa, Olposel, Olulato, Suisun, Topaidisel, Tuluka, Waikosel, Wailaksel, Yodetabi, Yolo.

Wintun subfamily: Daupom, Noamlaki, Normuk, Nuimok, Nummuk, Puimem, Puimuk, Tientien, Waikenmuk, Winimem.

**Copper.** Copper had come into very general use among the tribes N. of Mexico before the arrival of the white race in the Mississippi valley and the region of the great lakes. The reign of stone, which in early times had been undisputed, was beginning to give way to the dominion of metal. It is probable that copper came into use in the N. as a result of the discovery of nuggets or small masses of the native metal among the débris deposited over a large area s. of the lakes by the sheets of glacial ice that swept from the N. across the fully exposed surface of the copper-bearing rocks of the L. Superior region (see *Mines and Quarries*). These pieces of copper were at first doubtless treated and used as were stones of similar size and shape, but the peculiar qualities of the metal must in time have impressed themselves upon the acute native mind, and implements were shaped by hammering instead of by pecking. At first the forms produced would be much the same as those of the stone implements of the same people, but after a while the celts, hatchets, awls, knives, drills, spearheads, etc., would take on new forms, suggested by the peculiar properties of the material, and other varieties of implements would be evolved. The metal was too soft to wholly supersede stone as a material for the manufacture of implements, but its pleasing color and its capacity for taking a high polish must have led at an early date to its use for personal ornaments, and on the arrival of the whites it was in great demand for this purpose over nearly the entire country.

A knowledge of the discovery of deposits of copper in the lake region passed in course of time beyond the local tribes, and it is not unlikely that it extended to Mexico, where the metallurgic arts had made remarkable headway and where the red metal was in great demand. That any extensive trade sprang up between the N. and the far S., however, seems improbable, since such communication would have led inevitably to the introduction of southern methods of manipulation among the more advanced tribes of the Mississippi valley and the Gulf coast and to the frequent presence of peculiarly Mexican artifacts in the burial mounds.

There can be no question that the supply of copper used by the tribes of E. United States came mainly from the L. Superior region, although native copper in small quantities is found in Virginia, North Carolina, Tennessee, Arizona, New Mexico, and Nova Scotia. It is not at all certain, however, that the natives utilized these latter sources of supply to any considerable extent before the coming of the whites. There seems to be little doubt that copper was somewhat extensively used in Alaska before the arrival of Europeans. It is possible that a small percentage of the copper found in mounds in the Southern states came from Cuba and Mexico, but there is no way of satisfactorily determining this point. The L. Superior copper can often be distinguished from other copper by the dissemination through it of minute particles of silver.

The processes employed in shaping copper (see *Metal-work*) were at first probably confined to cold hammering and grinding, but heat was employed to facilitate hammering and in annealing, and possibly rude forms of swedging in molds and even of casting were known, although little evidence to this effect has yet been obtained. It appears that in dealing with thin sheets of the metal, which were readily made by hammering with stone implements and by grinding, pressure with suitable tools was employed to produce repoussé effects, the sheet being laid for treatment on a mold of stone or wood, or on a pliable pad or a plastic surface. Certain objects of sheet copper with repoussé designs obtained from Indian mounds in Illinois, Ohio, Georgia, and Florida have attracted much attention on account of the very skilful treatment shown. That primitive methods of manipulation well within the reach of the aborigines are adequate to accomplish similar results is shown, however, by experiments conducted by Cushing.

The very considerable progress of the native metallurgist in copper working is well shown by examples of plating recovered from the mounds in Ohio and elsewhere. A headdress belonging to a personage of importance buried in one of the Hopewell mounds, near Chillicothe, Ohio, found by Moorehead, consists of a high frontal piece made of sheets of copper covered with indented figures, out of which rises a pair of antlers imitating those of a deer. The antlers are formed of wood and neatly covered or plated with sheet copper (Putnam). Other examples from the same source are spool-like objects, probably ear ornaments, formed of thin sheets of copper over a wood base, and most skilfully executed. Willoughby has very effectively imitated this work, using a bit of native copper with bowlders and pebbles from the beach as tools. Of the same kind of workmanship are numerous specimens obtained by Moore

from mounds on St Johns r., Fla., the most interesting being jaw-bones of wolves plated with thin sheets of copper. Other objects similarly treated are disks of limestone and beads of shell, bone, wood, and possibly other materials.

A popular belief exists that the Egyptians and other ancient nations, including the Mexicans and Peruvians, had a process for hardening copper, but there is no real foundation for this belief. The reputed hardened product is always an alloy. No specimen of pure copper has been found which has a greater degree of hardness than can be produced by hammering.

Although copper probably came into use among the northern tribes in comparatively recent times, considering the whole period of aboriginal occupancy, there can be no doubt of its extensive and widespread utilization before the coming of the whites. That the ancient mines of the L. Superior region are purely aboriginal is amply shown by their character and by the implements left on the ground; and the vast extent of the work warrants the conclusion that they had been operated hundreds of years before the white man set foot on American shores. It is true that the influence of French and English explorers and colonists was soon felt in the copper-producing districts, and led in time to modifications in the methods of shaping the metal and in the forms of the articles made from it, and that later foreign copper became an important article of trade, so that as a result it is now difficult to draw a very definite line between the aboriginal and the accultural phases of the art; but that most of the articles recovered from aboriginal sites are aboriginal and made of native metal can not be seriously questioned.

Considerable discussion has arisen regarding the origin and antiquity of certain objects of sheet copper, the most conspicuous of which are several human figures in elaborate repoussé work, from one of the Etowah mounds in Georgia, and a large number of objects of sheet copper cut in conventional patterns, found in a mound on Hopewell farm, Ross co., Ohio. Analysis of the metal in this and similar cases gives no encouragement to the theory of foreign origin (Moore). The evident antiquity of the mounds in which these objects were found and the absence in them of other objects open to the suspicion of foreign (European) origin or influence tend to confirm the belief in their American origin and pre-Columbian age.

The state of preservation of the implements, utensils, and ornaments found in mounds and other places of burial varies greatly, but many specimens are in perfect condition, some having retained the high surface polish acquired in long use. It happens that the presence of copper objects in association with more perishable objects of wood, bone, shell, and textile materials, has, through the action of the copper carbonates, resulted in the preservation of many precious things which otherwise would have entirely disappeared.

Of the various implements of copper, the celt, or chisel-like hatchet, has the widest distribution. The forms are greatly diversified, and the weight ranges from a few ounces to several pounds. The implement is never perforated for hafting, although hafts were undoubtedly used, portions of these having been preserved in a few cases. As with our own axes, the blade is sometimes widened toward the cutting edge, which is convex in outline. Many

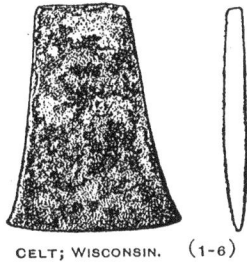

CELT; WISCONSIN. (1-6)

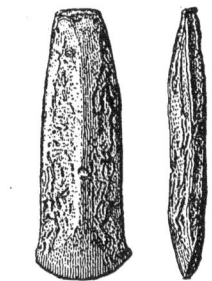

specimens, however, are nearly straight on the sides, while others are long and somewhat narrower toward the point. They could be hafted to serve as axes, adzes, or gouges. Some have one face flat and the other slightly ridged, suggesting the adz or gouge. The celt forms grade into other more slender shapes which have chisel edges, and these into drills and graver-like tools, while following in turn are needles and poniards, the latter being generally cylindrical, with long, tapering

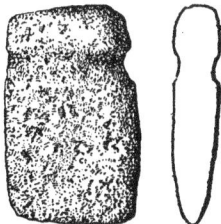

CELT; NEW YORK. (1-6)

GROOVED AX; MISSOURI; 1-4. (LONG COLLECTION)

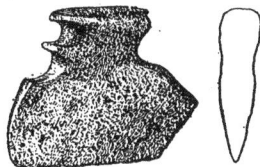

GROOVED AX; NEW MEXICO; 1-4. (LONG COLLECTION)

points, the largest examples being 2 or 3 ft. in length and weighing several pounds. The grooved ax is of rare occurrence, and where found appears to repeat the stone forms of the particular district. Squier and Davis illustrate a two-edged specimen with a hole through the middle of the blade from face to face, supposed to have been intended to aid in fixing the haft.

Related in general shape to the ax is another type of implement sometimes called a spud. Its distribution is limited to the district lying immediately s. of the great lakes. The socket is usually formed by hammering out lateral wings at the upper end of the implement and bending them inward. The purpose of this implement is not fully determined. With a long and straight handle it would serve as a spade or digging tool;

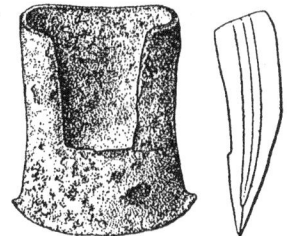

SPUD; MICHIGAN. (1-5)

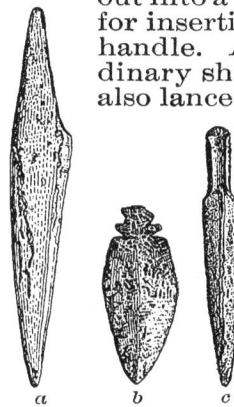

with the handle sharply bent near the point of insertion it would become a hatchet or an adz, according to the relative position of the blade and handle. The natives had already come to appreciate the value of copper for knives, and blades of various forms were in use; usually these are drawn out into a long point at the haft end for insertion into a wood or bone handle. Arrowheads of various ordinary shapes are common, as are also lance and spear heads, the latter being sometimes shaped for insertion into the end of the wooden shaft, but more frequently having a socket, made as in the spud, for the insertion of the handle. Drills, needles, pins, fishhooks, etc., occur in considerable numbers, especially in the Northern states.

a, KNIFE BLADE, WISCONSIN (1-6); b, SPEARHEAD OR KNIFE, WISCONSIN (1-6); c, SPEARHEAD, WISCONSIN (1-6)

Personal ornaments are of great variety, including beads, pendants, pins, eardisks, earrings, bracelets, gorgets, etc. The most interesting objects of copper do not come within either of the ordinary classes of ornaments, although they doubtless served in some way as adornments for the person, probably in connection with the ceremonial headdress. These are made of sheet copper, and certain of their features are suggestive of exotic, though not of European influence.

BRACELET FROM A MOUND. (1-3)

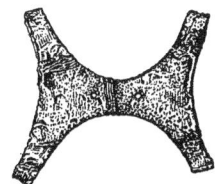

PIERCED TABLET; OHIO. (1-6)

The best examples are from one of the Etowah mounds in Georgia. Other remarkable objects found in mounds at Hopewell farm, Ross co., Ohio, appear to have been intended for some special

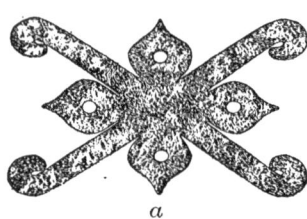

EAR ORNA-
MENT; TEN-
NESSEE.
(1-3)

symbolic use rather than for personal adornment, as usual means of attachment are not provided. The early voyagers, especially along the Atlantic coast, mention the use of tobacco pipes of copper. There is much evidence that implements as well as ornaments and other objects of copper were regarded as having exceptional virtues and magical powers, and certain early writers aver that

*a*　　　　　　　　　　*b*

some of the tribes of the great lakes held all copper as sacred, making no practical use of it whatever.

Copper was not extensively used within the area of the Pacific states, but was employed for various purposes by the tribes of the N. W., who are skilful metal workers, employing to some extent methods introduced by the whites. Formerly the na-

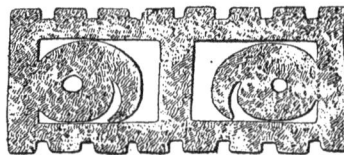

*c*

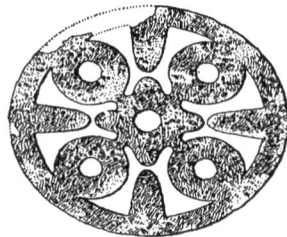

*d*

ORNAMENT—SYMBOLS; OHIO MOUND;
4 TO 12 INCHES IN GREATEST
DIMENSION. (MOOREHEAD)

tives obtained copper from the valley of Copper r. and elsewhere, but the market is now well supplied with the imported metal. It is used very largely for ornaments, for utensils, especially knives, and whistles, rattles, and masks are sometimes made of it. Perhaps the most noteworthy product is the unique, shield-like "coppers" made of sheet metal and

SHEET-COPPER EAGLE; ILLINOIS
MOUND; 1-6 (THOMAS)

highly esteemed as symbols of wealth or distinction. The origin of these "cop-

pers" and of their peculiar form and use is not known. The largest are about 3 ft. in length. The upper, wider portion,

SHEET-COPPER FIGURE; ETOWAH MOUND, GA. (ABOUT 1-5)

and in cases the lower part, or stem, are ornamented with designs representing mythic creatures (Niblack, Boas).

The literature of copper is extensive; the principal works, especially those contributing original material, are: Beauchamp in Bull. N. Y. State Mus., no. 73, 1903; Boas in Nat. Mus. Rep. 1895, 1897; Butler in Wis. Hist. Soc. Coll., VII, 1876; Cushing (1) in The Archæologist, II, no. 5, 1894, (2) in Am. Anthrop., VII, no. 1, 1894; Davis in Smithson. Rep. 1874, 1875; Farquharson in Proc. Davenport Acad., I, 1876; Foster, Prehist. Races, 1878; Foster and Whitney, Rep. on Geol. and Topog. L. Superior Land District (H. R. Doc. 69, 31st Cong., 1st sess., 1850); Fowke, Archæol. Hist. Ohio, 1902; Gillman in Smithson.

COPPER KNIFE;
HAIDA; LENGTH
9 1-2 INCHES.
(NIBLACK)

Rep. 1873, 1874; Hamilton in Wis. Archæol., I, no. 3, 1902; Hearne, Journey, 1796; Holmes in Am. Anthrop., III, 1901; Hoy in Trans. Wis. Acad. Sci., IV, 1878; Lapham, Antiq. of Wis., 1855; Lewis in Am. Antiq., XI, no. 5, 1889; McLean, Mound Builders, 1879; Mason in Proc. Nat. Mus., XVII, 1895; Mass. Hist. Soc. Coll., VIII, 1843; Moore, various memoirs in Jour. Acad. Nat. Sci. Phila., 1894–1905; Moore, McGuire, et al. in Am. Anthrop., n. s., v, no. 1, 1903; Moorehead (1) Prehist. Impl., 1900, (2) in

The Antiquarian, I, 1897; Nadaillac, Prehist. Amer., 1884; Niblack in Nat. Mus. Rep. 1888, 1890; Packard in Am. Antiq., xv, no. 2, 1893; Patterson in Nova Scotia Inst. of Sci., VII, 1888–89; Putnam (1) in Peabody Mus. Reps., xvI, 1884, (2) in Proc. A. A. A. S., XLIV, 1896; Rau (1) Archæol. Coll. Nat. Mus., 1876, (2) in Smithson. Rep. 1872, 1873; Reynolds in Am. Anthrop., I, no. 4, 1888; Schoolcraft, Ind. Tribes, I, 1851; Short, N. Am. of Antiquity, 1880; Slafter, Prehist. Copper Impl., 1879; Squier, Antiq. of N. Y. and the West, 1851; Squier and Davis, Ancient Monuments, 1848; Starr, First Steps in Human Progress, 1895; Strachey (1585), Hist. Va., Hakluyt Soc. Publ., VIII, 1843; Thomas in 12th Rep. B. A. E., 1894; Whittlesey, Ancient Mining on Lake Superior, Smithson. Cont., XIII, 1863; Willoughby in Am. Anthrop., v, no. 1, 1903; Wilson, Prehist. Man, 1862; Winchell in Engin. and Min. Jour., XXXII, Sept. 17, 1881.                    (w. H. H.)

KWAKIUTL CEREMONIAL COPPER; LENGTH 37 INCHES. (BOAS)

**Cops.** A former Papago rancheria visited by Kino and Mange in 1699; situated w. of the Rio San Pedro, probably in the vicinity of the present town of Arivaca, s. w. of Tubac, s. Ariz.

Cops.—Mange (1701) quoted by Bancroft, Ariz. and N. Mex., 358, 1889. **Humo.**—Mange, ibid.

**Copway, George** (*Kagĭgegabo*, 'he who stands forever.'—W. J.). A young Chippewa chief, born near the mouth of Trent r., Ontario, in the fall of 1818. His parents were Chippewa, and his father, until his conversion, was a medicine-man. George was educated in Illinois, and after acquiring considerable knowledge in English books returned to his people as a Wesleyan missionary. For many years he was connected with the press of New York city and lectured extensively in Europe and the United States, but he is noted chiefly as one of the few Indian authors. Among his published writings are: The Life, History, and Travels of Kah-ge-ga-gah-bowh (George Copway), Albany, 1847, and Philadelphia, 1847; The Life, Letters, and Speeches of Kah-ge-ga-gah-bowh, New York, 1850; The Traditional History and Characteristic Sketches of the Ojibway Nation, London and Dublin, 1850, and Boston, 1851; Recollections of a Forest Life, London, Edinburgh, and Dublin, 1851, and London, 1855; Indian Life and Indian History, Boston, 1858; The Ojibway Conquest, a Tale of the Northwest, New York,

1850; Organization of a New Indian Territory East of the Missouri River, New York, 1850; Running Sketches of Men and Places in England, France, Germany, Belgium and Scotland, New York, 1851. Copway also wrote a hymn in the Chippewa language (London, 1851) and co-operated with the Rev. Sherman Hall in the translation of the Gospel of St Luke (Boston, 1837) and the Acts of the Apostles (Boston, 1838). He died at Pontiac, Mich., about 1863.

**Coquilt.** One of the Diegueño rancherias represented in the treaty of 1852 at Santa Isabel, s. Cal.—H. R. Ex. Doc. 76, 34th Cong., 3d sess., 133, 1857.

**Coquite.** Mentioned by Mota Padilla (Historia, 164, 1742, repr. 1870) in connection with Jimena (Galisteo) and Zitos (Silos) as a pueblo which lay between Pecos and the Keresan villages of the Rio Grande in New Mexico when visited by Coronado in 1540–42. It was seemingly a Tano pueblo.

**Coquitlam.** A coast Salish tribe speaking the Cowichan dialect and inhabiting Fraser valley just above the delta, in British Columbia. They owned no land, being practically slaves of the Kwantlen. Pop. 25 in 1904.

Coquet-lane.—Can. Ind. Aff., pt. I, 268, 1889. **Coquetlum.**—Ibid., 309, 1879. **Coquilain.**—Trutch, Map Brit. Col., 1870. **Coquitlam.**—Can. Ind. Aff., 413, 1898. **Coquitlan.**—Ibid., 74, 79, 1878. **Coquitlane.**—Ibid., 276, 1894. **Coquitlum.**—Ibid., 316, 1880. **Koquitan.**—Brit. Col. Map, Victoria, 1872 (named as a town). **Kwĭkŏt/em.**—Boas, MS., B. A. E., 1887. **Kwĭ′kwitlεm.**—Hill-Tout in Ethnol. Surv. Can., 54, 1902.

**Cora.** A tribe or group of tribes belonging to the Piman family and occupying several villages and rancherias in the Sierra de Nayarit and on the Rio de Jesus María, Jalisco, Mexico. They were a brave and warlike people, living independently in the mountain glens and ravines until 1721–22 when they were subjugated by the Spaniards and missions established among them. According to José de Ortega (Vocab. Leng. Castil. y Cora, 1732, 7, repr. 1888) the Cora language consisted of 3 dialects: the Muutzizti, spoken in the middle of the sierra; the Teacuacueitzisti, spoken in the lower part of the sierra toward the w., and the Ateacari, spoken on the banks of the Rio Nayarit (Jesus María). Orozco y Berra (Geog., 59, 281, 1864) follows the same grouping and adds Colotlan as a dialect, while he quotes Alegre to the effect that the Cora are divided into the Cora (proper), the Nayarit, and the Tecualme or Gecualme. These are probably identical with Ortega's divisions. Nayari, or Nayariti, is the name by which the Cora are known among themselves. They still use their native language, which is guttural although quite musical, but all the men and most of the women also understand Spanish to some extent. They are proud of their Indian blood, and although they have largely adopted the clothing of the white Mexicans there is very little intermarriage between the two. The native costume of the men consists of buckskin trousers and a very short tunic of home-woven woolen material dyed dark blue. The Cora, especially those of the high sierra, possess an air of independence and manliness. In speech, religion, and customs they are akin to the Huichol, and while they trade with them for red paint, wax, and feathers, and the services of Huichol shamans are highly regarded by the Cora, there is no strong alliance between the two tribes. Most of the Cora men are slightly bearded, especially on the chin. The women weave belts and bags of cotton and wool, and the men manufacture fish-nets which are used in dragging the streams. Their houses are of stone with thatched roofs, with little ventilation. Their country, notwithstanding its altitude, is malarial, yet the Cora are said to attain remarkable longevity and their women are well preserved. In the valley a disease of the eyes prevails in summer. The waters of a crater lake E. of Santa Teresa are regarded as sacred, and necessary to the performance of every ceremony. An afternoon wind which prevails daily in the hot country is believed to be beneficial to the corn, and a tamal of ashes, 2 ft. long, is sacrificed to it. Easter is celebrated by a feast and a dance—a survival of missionary training—and the *mitote* is also danced for weeks in succession to bring needed rain. Connected with their puberty ceremonies is the drinking of home-made mescal. Fasting, sometimes conducted by shamans alone, is a ceremonial feature and is thought to be necessary to insure good crops. The morning star is the principal god and protecting genius, being characterized as a brother, a youth armed with bow and arrow who once shot the powerful sun at noontime on account of his intense heat. The moon is also a god—both man and woman—and there are many others, as everything is believed to be animate and powerful. In their sacred songs the musical bow, attached to a gourd, is played. At 15 years the Cora reach the marriageable age. Marriages are arranged by the parents of the boy, who on five occasions, every eighth day, go to ask for the bride they have selected. A new-born child was named after an uncle or an aunt, and at certain intervals during childhood feasts were prepared in its honor. It is said that on the spot where the relative of a Cora was killed in a fight a piece of

cloth was dipped in blood and kept as a remembrance until his death was avenged by killing the slayer or one of the males of his family. Some of the Cora still deposit the bodies of the dead in caves. The population is estimated at 2,500. The settlements pertaining to the various divisions of the Cora group are: Apozolco, Cienega, Comatlan, Corapa, Guasamota, Guaynamota, Ixtacan, Jesus María, Mesa del Nayarit, Nuestra Señora del Rosario, Peyotan, San Diego, San Francisco, San Juan Bautista, San Lucas, Santa Fé, Santa Rosa, Santa Teresa, and Tonati. See Lumholtz, Unknown Mexico, I, 1902.       (F. W. H.)

**Chora.**—Orozco y Berra, Geog., 59, 1864. **Chota.**—Ibid. **Hashi.**—Lumholtz, Unknown Mex., I, 492, 1902 ('crocodiles': Huichol name). **Nayaerita.**—Orozco y Berra, op. cit. **Nayari.**—Lumholtz, op. cit. (own name). **Nayarita.**—Orozco y Berra, op. cit. **Nayariti.**—Lumholtz, op. cit. (alternative form of their own name).

**Corapa.** A pueblo pertaining to the Cora division of the Piman stock and a visita of the mission of Nuestra Señora del Rosario. Probably situated on the Rio San Pedro, Jalisco, Mexico.

**S. Juan Corapa.**—Orozco y Berra, Geog., 280, 1864.

**Corazones** (Span.: 'hearts'). A pueblo of the Opata, determined by Hodge (Coronado's March, 35, 1899) to have been situated at or near the site of the present Ures, on the Rio Sonora, Sonora, Mexico. It was so named by Cabeza de Vaca in 1536 because the inhabitants presented to him more than 600 deer hearts. It was visited also by Coronado and his army in 1540, called by his chroniclers San Hieronimo de los Corazones, and described as being situated midway between Culiacan and Cibola (Zuñi). The houses were built of mats; the natives raised corn, beans, and melons, dressed in deerskins, and used poisoned arrows.       (F. W. H.)

**Coraçones.**—Barcía, Historiadores, I, 36, 1749. **Corazones.**—Cabeza da Vaca (1536), Smith trans., 172, 1871. **San Hieronimo.**—Castañeda (1596) in 14th Rep. B. A. E., 501, 1896. **San Hieronimo de los Corazones.**—Ibid., 484. **Villa de los Coraçones.**—Oviedo, Historia, III, 610, 1853.

**Corbitant.** A Massachuset sachem. He was a determined foe of the English, and when Massasoit entered into an alliance with them he strove to wrest the chieftaincy from the latter and form a league with the Narraganset to expel the intruders. He caught and tried to kill Squanto, whom he called the tongue of the English, and Hobomok, their spy and guide. With other hostile chiefs he signed a treaty of peace with the English in 1621.—Drake, Bk. Inds., 93, 1880.

**Corchaug.** A tribe or band formerly occupying Riverhead and Southold townships on Long id., N. Y., N. of Peconic bay, and extending w. to Wading r. Cutchogue, Mattituck, Ashamomuck, and Aquebogue were probably sites of their villages. The Yannococ Indians, N. of

Peconic r., must have been identical with the Corchaug tribe or a part of it.      (J. M.)

Chorchake.—Deed of 1648 in Thompson, Long Id., 181, 1839.  Corchaug.—Wood quoted by Macauley, N. Y., II, 252, 1829.  Corchongs.—Thompson, Long Id., I, 386, 1843 (misprint).  Corchougs.—Ibid., 238.  Yannacock.—Doc. of 1667 in N. Y. Doc. Col. Hist., XIV, 601, 1883.  Yannocock.—Ibid.  Yeannecock.—Ibid., 602.

**Coree.**   A tribe, possibly Algonquian, formerly occupying the peninsula s. of Neuse r., in Carteret and Craven cos., N. C.   They had been greatly reduced in a war with another tribe before 1696, and were described by Archdale as having been a bloody and barbarous people.  Lawson refers to them as Coranine Indians, but in another place calls them Connamox, and gives them two villages in 1701—Coranine and Raruta—with about 125 souls.   They engaged in the Tuscarora war of 1711, and in 1715 the remnants of the Coree and Machapunga were assigned a tract on Mattamuskeet lake, Hyde co., N. C., where they lived in one village, probably until they became extinct.                        (J. M.)

Caranine.—Oldmixon (1708) in Carroll, Hist. Coll. S. C., II, 459, 1836.  Connamox.—Lawson (1709), N. C., 383, 1860.  Coramine.—Archdale (ca. 1696) in Humphreys, Account, 282, 1730.  Coranine.—Archdale (1707) in Carroll, Hist. Coll. S. C., II, 89, 1836 (used by Lawson as the name both of the tribe and of one of its villages).  Corees.—Drake, Ind. Chron., 175, 1836.  Cores.—Williamson, N. C., I, 203, 1812.

**Coreorgonel.**   The chief Tutelo town in New York, settled in 1753; situated in 1779 on the w. side of Cayuga lake inlet and on the border of the great swamp, 3 m. from the s. end of Cayuga lake.   When destroyed by Dearborn in 1779 it contained 25 "elegantly built" houses.   Sir Wm. Johnson, in a conference with the Six Nations in July, 1753, said to the Cayuga: "It is agreeable news that you are about to strengthen your Castle by taking in the Tedarighroones [Tutelo], and shall give a pass to those of that Nation here among you that they and the rest of them may come and join your Castle unmolested" (N. Y. Doc. Col. Hist., VI, 811, 1855).   Three of these Tutelo were present at this meeting "to partake in the name of their Nation of the intended present."      (J. N. B. H.)

Coreargonell.—Norris in Jour. Mil. Exped. Maj. Gen. John Sullivan in 1779, 237, 1887.  Coreorgonel.—Dearborn, ibid., 77.  De Ho Riss Kanadia.—Grant, ibid., 118 (corruption of the Mohawk *Tehoterigh-kanada*, 'Tutelo town').  Kayeghtalagealat.—Map of 1779 cited by Hale, ibid.  Todevigh-rono.—Guy Johnson, map of 1771, cited by Hale, ibid.

**Cores.**   Small blocks of flint, obsidian, or other brittle stone from which flakes have been struck in such a manner as to leave them roughly cylindrical or conical in shape and with fluted sides.   There has been some discussion as to whether cores are really the wasters of flake making or were intended for some practical

use.   The sharp angle at the base in many of them would make an excellent edge for working a hard or tough substance, such as horn or bone; but few show the slightest marks of wear.   Wherever flint, obsidian, or other stone suitable for making flakes was worked, the cores also occur.   On Flint Ridge in Ohio they are more abundant than at any other known locality, many thousands of them lying around the flaking shop sites.   Although all are small, none being capable of yielding flakes more than 3 in. in length, there seems to be no reason for questioning the conclusion that they are the mere refuse of flake making.  The use to which the flakes derived from them were applied is problematical, but they would have served as knives or scrapers or for the making of small arrowpoints.   See *Stone-work*.   Consult Fowke in 13th Rep. B. A. E., 1896; Holmes (1) in Bull. 21, B. A. E., 1894, (2) in 15th Rep. B. A. E., 1897, (3) in Memoirs Internat. Cong. Anthrop., 1894; Rau in Smithson. Cont., XXII, 1876.      (G. F.)

CORE OF CHERT; IND. TER.   (1-4)

**Corn.**   See *Maize*.

**Corn Band.**   A band at Spotted Tail (later Rosebud) agency, S. Dak.; probably a part of the Teton.—Cleveland in Our Church Work, Dec. 4, 1875.   Cf. *Wagmezayuha*.

**Cornplanter** (*Kaiioñtwa''koⁿ*, 'by what one plants'—Hewitt; variously written Garganwahgah, Koeentwahka, etc.).   A Seneca chief, known also as John O'Bail, supposed to have been born between 1732 and 1740 at Ganawagus, on Genesee r., N. Y.   Drake (Biog. and Hist. Ind., 7th ed., 111, 1837) says he was a warrior at Braddock's defeat in 1755, which is evidently a mistake, though he may have been present as a boy of 12 or 15 years.   His father was a white trader named John O'Bail, or O'Beel, said by some to have been an Englishman, although Harris (Buffalo Hist. Soc. Pub., VI, 416, 1903) says he was a Dutchman, named Abeel, and Ruttenber (Tribes Hudson R., 317, 1872) also says he was a Dutch trader.   His mother was a full-blood Seneca.   All that is known of Cornplanter's early days is contained in a letter to the governor of Pennsylvania, in which he says he played with Indian boys who remarked the difference between the color of his skin and theirs; his mother informed him that his father resided at Albany.   He visited his father, who, it appears, treated him kindly but gave him nothing to carry back; "nor did he tell me," he adds, "that the United States were about to rebel against the Government of England."   He states that he was married before this visit.   He was one of the parties to the treaty of Ft Stanwix in 1784, when a large cession of land was made by the Indians; he also took part in the treaty of Ft Harmar in 1789, in which an extensive territory was conveyed to the United States (although his name is not among the signers); and he was a signer of the treaties of Sept. 15, 1797, and July 30, 1802. These acts rendered him so unpopular with his tribe that for a time his life was in danger. In 1790 he, together with Halftown, visited Philadelphia to lay before Gen. Washington the grievances complained of by their people. In 1816 he resided just within the limits of Pennsylvania on his grant 7 m. below the junction of the Connewango with the Allegheny, on the banks of the latter. He then owned 1,300

CORNPLANTER. (McKENNEY AND HALL)

acres, of which 640 formed a tract granted to him by Pennsylvania, Mar. 16, 1796, "for his many valuable services to the whites." It is said that in his old age he declared that the "Great Spirit" told him not to have anything more to do with the whites, nor even to preserve any mementos or relics they had given him. Impressed with this idea, he burned the belt and broke the elegant sword that had been given him. A favorite son (Henry Obeal), who had been carefully educated, became a drunkard, thus adding to the troubles of Cornplanter's last years. He received from the United States, for a time, a pension or grant of $250 per year. He was perhaps more than 90 years of age at the time of his death, Feb. 18, 1836. A monument erected to his memory on his reservation by the state of Pennsyl-

vania in 1866 bears the inscription "aged about 100 years."        (C. T.)

**Cornstalk.** A celebrated Shawnee chief (born about 1720, died in 1777) who held authority over those of the tribe then settled on the Scioto, in Ohio. He was brought most prominently into notice by his leadership of the Indians in the battle of Point Pleasant, at the mouth of Great Kanawha r., W. Va., Oct. 10, 1774. Although defeated in a battle lasting throughout the day, his prowess and generalship on this occasion—where his force, mostly Shawnee, numbering probably 1,000, was opposed to 1,100 Virginia volunteers—won the praise of the whites. After this battle he entered into a treaty of peace with Lord Dunmore in Nov., 1774, at Chillicothe, Ohio, although strenuously opposed by a part of his tribe, and faithfully kept it until 1777. In the latter year the Shawnee, being incited to renew hostilities, he went to Point Pleasant and notified the settlers that he might be forced into the war. The settlers detained him and his son as hostages, and they were soon after murdered by some infuriated soldiers in retaliation for the killing of a white settler by some roving Indians, thus arousing the vindictive spirit of the Shawnee, which was not broken until 1794. Cornstalk was not only a brave and energetic warrior, but a skilful general and an orator of considerable ability. A monument was erected to his memory in the court-house yard at Point Pleasant in 1896.

**Cornstalk's Town.** A Shawnee village on Scippo cr., opposite Squaw Town, Pickaway co., Ohio, nearly due s. from Circleville, in 1774.—Howe, Hist. Coll. Ohio, 402, 1896.

**Corn Village.** A former Natchez settlement.
Corn Village.—Gayarre, La., I, 411, 1851. **Flour Village.**—Dumont in French, Hist. Coll. La., V, 48, 1853.

**Corodeguachi.** A former Opata pueblo on the headwaters of the Rio Sonora, N. E. Sonora, Mexico, about 25 m. below the boundary of Arizona. It was the seat of the Spanish mission of Santa Rosa, founded in 1653, and of the presidio of Fronteras, established in 1690. In 1689 the mission was abandoned on account of the hostilities of the Jocome, Suma, Jano, and Apache; and owing to Apache depredations in more recent years the settlement was deserted by its inhabitants on several occasions, once as late as about 1847.        (F. W. H.)
Corodeguachi.—Bancroft, Ariz. and N. Mex., 354, 1889. **Santa Rosa Corodeguatzi.**—Doc. of 18th cent. quoted by Bandelier in Arch. Inst. Papers, IV, 529, 1892. **Santa Rosa de Coradeguatzi.**—Orozco y Berra, Geog., 343, 1854.

**Corral.** A ranchería of gentile Diegueños near San Diego, s. Cal., in 1775.

**El Corral.**—Ortega (1775) quoted by Bancroft, Hist. Cal., I, 254, 1884.

**Coruano.** One of 4 unidentified tribes, probably Shoshonean, formerly living E. of Tejon pass, s. Cal.—Taylor in Cal. Farmer, May 8, 1863.

**Cosaque** (probably from *konshak*, 'reed'). An unidentified town in N. E. Alabama, in the same region as Cossa (Kusa), visited by Juan Pardo in 1565.—Vandera (1567) in Smith, Colec. Doc. Fla., I, 18, 1857.

**Cosattuck.** A Pequot village in 1667, probably near Stonington, New London co., Conn.
Causattuck.—Noyes (1667) in Mass. Hist. Soc. Coll., 3d s., x, 67–68, 1849. Cosattuck.—Denison (1666), ibid., 64.

**Coshocton** (Heckewelder derives a similar name, Coshecton, from *gichiéchton* (German form), 'finished,' 'completed'). Formerly the chief town of the Turtle tribe of the Delawares, on the site of Coshocton, Coshocton co., Ohio. Destroyed by the whites in 1781. Cf. *Goshgoshunk.*
Cashictan.—Peters (1760) in Mass. Hist. Soc. Coll., 4th s., IX, 300, 1871. Coochocking.—Butterfield, Washington-Irvine Cor., 9, 1882. Cooshacking.—Ibid. Coshockton.—Rupp, West Penn., 201, 1846. Coshocton.—Heckewelder (1781) quoted by Butterfield, op. cit., 51. Goschachguenk.—Drake, Bk. Inds., bk. 5, 59, 1848. Goschaching.—Writer of 1784 in Harris, Tour, 214, 1805. Goschachking.—Heckewelder in Trans. Am. Philos. Soc., IV, 391, 1834. Goschochking.—Drake, Bk. Inds., bk. 5, 61, 1848. Goshachking.—Heckewelder, op. cit. Goshochking.—Ibid. Kushacton.—Pentecost (1782) in Butterfield, op. cit., 242. Kushocton.—Ibid., 241.

**Cosoy.** A Diegueño rancheria at which the mission of San Diego (q. v.) was established in 1769; situated at the present Old Town, on San Diego bay, s. Cal.

**Cossarl.** Marked by Jefferys (French Dom. Am., I, map, 134, 1761) as a native town on the extreme head of Yadkin r., in the mountains of N. w. North Carolina. Unidentified.

**Costanoan Family.** A linguistic family on the coast of central California. In 1877 Powell (Cont. N. A. Ethnol., III, 535) established a family which he called Mutsun, extending from San Francisco to Soledad and from the sea inland to the Sierras, and including an area in the Marin co. penin., N. of San Francisco bay, and gave vocabularies from various parts of this territory. In 1891 (7th Rep. B. A. E., 70, 92, map) Powell divided this area between two families, Moquelumnan and Costanoan. The Moquelumnan family occupied the portion of the old Mutsun territory E. of San Joaquin r. and N. of San Francisco bay.

The territory of the Costanoan family extended from the Pacific ocean to San Joaquin r., and from the Golden Gate and Suisun bay on the N. to Pt Sur on the coast and a point a short distance s. of Soledad in the Salinas valley on the s. Farther inland the s. boundary is uncertain, though it was probably near Big Panoche cr. The Costanoan Indians lived mainly on vegetal products, especially acorns and seeds, though they also obtained fish and mussels, and captured deer and smaller game. Their clothing was scant, the men going naked. Their houses were tule or grass huts, their boats balsas or rafts of tules. They made baskets, but no pottery, and appear to have been as primitive as most of the tribes of California. They burned the dead. The Rumsen of Monterey looked upon the eagle, the humming bird, and the coyote as the original inhabitants of the world, and they venerated the redwood. Their languages were simple and harmonious. Seven missions—San Carlos, Soledad, San Juan Bautista, Santa Cruz, Santa Clara, San José, and Dolores (San Francisco)—were established in Costanoan territory by the Franciscans subsequent to 1770, and continued until their confiscation by the Mexican government in 1834, when the Indians were scattered. The surviving individuals of Costanoan blood may number to-day 25 or 30, most of them "Mexican" in life and manners rather than Indian.

True tribes did not exist in Costanoan territory, the groups mentioned below being small and probably little more than village communities, without political connection or even a name other than that of the locality they inhabited.

The following divisions or settlements have been recognized: Ahwaste, Altahmo, Ansaime, Aulintac, Chalone, Costanos, Juichun, Kalindaruk, Karkin, Mutsun, Olhon, Romonan, Rumsen, Saclan, Thamien, Tulomo, and Wacharon (?).
=Costano.—Latham in Trans. Philol. Soc. Lond., 82, 1856 (includes the Ahwastes, Olhones or Costanos, Romonans, Tulomos, Altatmos); Latham, Opuscula, 348, 1860. <Mutsun.—Gatschet in Mag. Am. Hist., 157, 1877 (includes Ahwastes, Olhones, Altahmos, Romonans, Tulomos); Powell in Cont. N. A. Ethnol., III, 535, 1877 (includes under this family vocabs. of Costano, Mûtsûn, Santa Clara, Santa Cruz). Costanoan.—Powell in 7th Rep. B, A. E., 70, map, 1891.

**Costanos** (Span.: 'coastmen'). Certain tribes or groups belonging to the Costanoan family on San Francisco penin., connected with Dolores mission, Cal. The term has been applied to the Olhone, Ahwaste, Altahmo, Romonan, and Tulomo collectively; also to the Olhone and Ahwaste taken together; and to the Olhone alone. The term was chosen by Powell for the name of the Costanoan family, q.v.                    (A. L. K.)
Coast Indians.—Ind. Aff. Rep., 124, 1850. Coastmen.—Latham in Proc. Philol. Soc. Lond., VI, 79, 1854. Costanoes.—Ind. Aff. Rep., op. cit. Costanos.—Schoolcraft, Ind. Tribes, II, 506, 1852. Costeño.—Simeon, Dict. Nahuatl, xviii, 1885.

**Coste.** A province and town, apparently in Alabama, visited by De Soto in 1540. Biedma says the towns were built on islands in the river.
Acosta.—Shipp, De Soto and Florida, 373, 1881. Acoste.—Garcilasso de la Vega, La Florida, 141,

1723. **Costa.**—French, Hist. Coll. La., n. s., II, 247, 1875. **Coste.**—Gentleman of Elvas (1557), ibid., II, 149, 1850. **Costehe.**—Biedma (1544), ibid., 102.

**Cosumni.** A tribe, probably Moquelumnan, formerly residing on or near Cosumnes r., San Joaquin co., Cal. According to Rice (quoted by Mooney in Am. Anthrop., III, 259, 1890) these Indians went almost naked; their houses were of bark, sometimes thatched with grass and covered with earth: the bark was loosened from the trees by repeated blows with stone hatchets, the latter having the head fastened to the handle with deer sinew. Their ordinary weapons were bows and stone-tipped arrows. The women made finely woven conical baskets of grass, the smaller ones of which held water. Their amusements were chiefly dancing and football; the dances, however, were in some degree ceremonial. Their principal deity was the sun, and the women had a ceremony which resembled the sun dance of the tribes of the upper Missouri. Their dead were buried in graves in the earth. The tribe is now practically extinct.

**Cosemenes.**—Beechey, Narr., I, 366, 1831. **Cosumnes.**—Hale in U. S. Expl. Exped., VI, 631, 1846. **Cosumnies.**—Taylor in Cal. Farmer, June 8, 1860. **Kosumnès.**—Duflot de Mofras, Expl., II, 376, 1844.

**Cotan.** An Algonquian village in 1585 about Ransomville, Beaufort co., N. C.

**Cotam.**—Dutch map (1621) in N. Y. Doc. Col. Hist., I, 1856. **Cotan.**—Map in Smith (1629), Virginia, I, repr. 1819.

**Cotechney.** A town and palisade of the Tuscarora in North Carolina, which became noted in their war of 1711–18; situated, according to Hawks, on the site of Ft Barnwell, but according to Graffenried the town lay about 3 m. from the palisade, evidently on the opposite side of the Neuse, about the mouth of Contentnea cr., the name of which is probably a form of Cotechney. It was a large town, the residence of Hancock, one of the principal Tuscarora chiefs. Here Lawson and Graffenried were prisoners in 1711, and it was the scene of the execution of the former. On the outbreak of the Tuscarora war the inhabitants abandoned the town and intrenched themselves in the palisade, which was attacked by Barnwell, Jan. 28, 1712, when 400 of its defenders were killed or taken. Instead of completing his work, Barnwell, to save the lives of white prisoners held in the fort, made a worthless treaty with the remainder, who at once joined the other hostiles.　　　　(J. N. B. H.)

**Catohne.**—Pollock (1717) in N. C. Rec., II, 288, 1886. **Catechna.**—Graffenried (1711), ibid., I, 923, 1886. **Catechne.**—Pollock (1712), ibid., 882. **Catechnee.**—Pollock (1713), ibid., II, 39. **Catechneys.**—Pollock (1713), ibid., 38. **Contah-nah.**—Lawson (1710), Hist. N. C., 383, 1860. **Coteching.**—Pollock (1713) in N. C. Rec., II, 24, 1886. **Cotechnees.**—Pollock (1713), ibid., 62. **Cotechneys.**—Hawks, N. C., II, 547, 1858. **Hancock Fort.**—Hyde (1712) in N. C. Rec., I, 900, 1886. **Hencocks-Towne.**—Graffenried (1711), ibid., 927.

**Cotejen.** A Costanoan village formerly near San Francisco bay, Cal.—Mission book (1784) quoted by Taylor in Cal. Farmer, Oct. 18, 1861.

**Cotocanahut.** Given as one of the Cherokee "valley towns" in a document of 1755 (Royce in 5th Rep. B. A. E., 142, 1887). Not identified.

**Cotohautustennuggee.** A former Lower Creek town on the right bank of Upatoie cr., in Muscogee co., Ga.—Royce in 18th Rep. B. A. E., pl. cxxii, 1900.

**Cotonam.** A tribe affiliated with the Carrizos of the Coahuiltecan family and living in their vicinity, though their dialect differs largely from the Comecrudo language. The last of this tribe were at La Noria rancheria, in s. Hidalgo co., Tex., in 1886, and one man at Las Prietas was slightly acquainted with the native dialect. They call an Indian $\chi aima$, and are the Xaimame or Haname of the Texan tribes farther N. The Tonkawa say that the Cotonam were not cannibals and that they wore sandals instead of moccasins.　　　　(A. S. G.)

**Cotoplanemis.** Probably a division of the Moquelumnan family, living on a reserve between Stanislaus and Tuolumne rs., Cal., in 1851; but it is possible that they may have been a band of the Cholovone division of the Mariposan family.

**Co-ta-plane-mis.**—Johnston (1851) in Sen. Ex. Doc. 61, 32d Cong., 1st sess., 20, 1852. **Co-to-plane-mis.**—Ibid.

**Cotsjewaminck.** A former village on Long Island, N. Y., probably near the w. end.—Doc. of 1645 in N. Y. Doc. Col. Hist., XIV, 60, 1883.

**Cotton.** Judging from the lack of mention of it by early writers on the s. portion of the United States, cotton was not cultivated by the tribes of this section, notwithstanding the favorable soil and climate. The cotton blankets seen by De Soto's troops on the lower Mississippi were said to have been brought from the W., possibly from the far-off Pueblo country of New Mexico and Arizona. Although the latter section seems less favorable to its cultivation, cotton has been raised to a considerable extent by the Pueblos, especially the Hopi, from time immemorial, and cloth, cord, thread, and seed are commonly found in ancient deposits in caves, cliff-dwellings, and ruined pueblos throughout that region. The Hopi are now the only cultivators and weavers of cotton, their products, consisting chiefly of ceremonial robes, kilts, and scarfs, finding their way through trade to many other tribes who, like the Hopi, employ them in their religious performances. In the time of Coronado (1540–42) and of Espejo (1583) cotton was raised also by the people of

Acoma and the Rio Grande villages in New Mexico, and the Pima of s. Arizona also raised the plant until about 1850; but the introduction of cheap fabrics by traders has practically brought the industry to an end everywhere among the Indians, the Hopi alone adhering to the old custom of cultivating and weaving it, and that chiefly for ceremonial garments. In ancient Hopi and Zuñi mortuary rites raw cotton was placed over the face of the dead, and cotton seed was often deposited with food vessels and other accompaniments in the grave. Consult Bandelier in Arch. Inst. Papers, III, IV, 1890–92; Fewkes in 17th Rep. B. A. E., 1898; Holmes in 13th Rep. B. A. E., 1896; Hough in Rep. Nat. Mus., 1901; Winship in 14th Rep. B. A. E., 1896.          (w. h.)

**Couechitou.** A former important Choctaw town destroyed in the Choctaw civil war of 1764. Its location is in doubt, but it was traditionally placed in the neighborhood of Moscow, Kemper co., Miss. (Halbert in Miss. Hist. Soc. Publ., VI, 424, 1902). This name appears on Danville's map, ca. 1732, in which it seems to be translated "village of the great chief." In later times it was known by the same name as Conchachitou (q. v.), usually in the contracted form Congeto, or Cooncheto, and to distinguish it it was called East Congeto. Halbert assumes that the original name was Conchachitou and interprets it as 'big reed-brake,' like the other; but if such were indeed the case it is surprising that Danville, who locates and translates Conchachitou correctly, should have erred regarding this.          (J. R. S.)

Conachitow.—Lattré, map of U. S., 1784. Couetchiou.—Güssefeld, map of U. S., 1784. Coué-tchitou.—Danville map (1732) in Hamilton, Colonial Mobile, 158, 1897. Cowachitow.—Philippeaux, map, 1781. Cuoerchitou.—Bartram, Voy., I, map, 1799. East Congeata.—Romans, Florida, 310, 1775. East Congeeto.—West Fla. map, ca. 1775. East Coongeeto.—Romans, op. cit., 73.

**Couna.** Mentioned by Oñate (Doc. Inéd., XVI, 114, 1871) as a pueblo of New Mexico in 1598. Doubtless situated in the Salinas, in the vicinity of Abo, E. of the Rio Grande, and in all probability a Tigua or Piros village.

**Counting.** Two systems of counting were formerly in use among the Indians of North America, the decimal and the vigesimal. The latter, which was used in Mexico and Central America, was also in general use N. of Columbia r., on the Pacific slope, while between that area and the border of Mexico it was employed by only a few tribes, as the Pomo, Tuolumne, Konkau, Nishinam, and Achomawi. On the Atlantic side the decimal system was used by all except the Eskimo tribes. Both systems, based apparently on the finger and hand count, were as a rule fundamentally quinary. There are some

indications, however, of a more primitive count, with minor tribal differences. In Siouan and Algonquian the word for 2 is generally related to that for arms or hands, and in Athapascan dialects to the term for feet. In a few languages, the Siksika, Catawba, Gabrieleño, and some others, 3 is expressed by joining the words for 2 and 1. In many others the name for 4 signifies 2 and 2, or 2 times 2, as in most of the Shoshonean dialects, and in Catawba, Haida, Tlingit, and apparently Kiowa; the Pawnee formerly applied a name signifying 'all the fingers,' or 'the fingers of the hand,' thus excluding the thumb. Five has usually a distinct name, which in most cases refers to one hand or fist. The numbers from 6 to 9 are generally based on 5, thus, 6=5+1, 7=5+2, etc.; or the names refer to the fingers of the second hand as used in counting; thus, among the Eskimo of Pt Barrow 6 is 'to the other hand 1', 7 'to the other hand 2', and in many dialects 6='1 on the other hand.' There are exceptions to this rule, however; for example, 6 is 3 and 3 in Haida and some other dialects; in Bellacoola the name signifies 'second 1', and in Montagnais (Algonquian), '3 on each side.' Although 7 is usually 'the second finger on the second hand', in some cases it is based on 4, as among the Montagnais, who say '4 and 3.' Eight is generally expressed by 'the third finger on the second hand'; but the Montagnais say '4 on each side', and the Haida '4 and 4'; in Karankawa it signifies '2 fathers', and in the Kwakiutl and some other languages it is '2 from 10.' In a number of languages the name for 9 signifies 1 from 10, as with the Kwakiutl, the Eskimo of N. w. Alaska, the Pawnee, and the Heiltsuk.

The numbers from 11 to 19 are usually formed in both systems by adding 1, 2, 3, 4, etc., to 10; but in the vigesimal count the quinary count is carried out, 16 being 15+1, 17=15+2, etc., or, in some dialects, 17=10+5+2. Many of the Indians could count to 1,000, some by a regular system, while in a number of languages, as Tlingit, Cherokee, etc., its signification is 'great 100.' In Ottawa the meaning was 'one body'; in Abnaki, 'one box'; in Iroquois dialects, 'ten hand-claps,' that is, ten hundreds; in Kiowa, 'the whole hand hundred.' Baraga and Cuoq give terms for figures up to a million or more, but it is doubtful if such were actually in use before contact with Europeans.

The common Indian method of counting on the hands, as perhaps is usual with most savage or uncivilized peoples, was to "tell off" the fingers of the left hand, beginning with the little finger, the thumb being the fifth or 5; while in counting the right hand the order was usually reversed, the thumb being counted 6, the forefinger 7, and so on to the little finger, which would be 10. The movement was therefore sinistral. Although the order in counting the first 5 on the left hand was in most cases as given above, the order of counting the second 5 was subject to greater variation. It was a common habit to bend the fingers inward as counted, but there were several western tribes whose custom was to begin with the clenched hand, opening the fingers as the count proceeded, as among the Zuñi. Among the tribes using the vigesimal system, the count of the second 10 was practically or theoretically performed on the feet, the 20 making the "complete man," and often, as among the Eskimo and Tlingit, receiving names having reference to the feet. The Zuñi, however, counted the second 10 back on the knuckles.

Indians often made use of numeral classifiers in counting, that is, the number name was modified according to the articles counted; thus, in the Takulli dialect of Athapascan *tha* means 3 things; *thane*, 3 persons; *that*, 3 times; *thatsen*, in 3 places; *thauh*, in 3 ways; *thailtoh*, all 3 things, etc. Such classifiers are found in many dialects, and in some are quite numerous.

Certain numbers have been held as sacred by most tribes; thus 4, probably owing to the frequent reference to the cardinal points in ceremonies and religious acts, has become sacred or ceremonial. Among the Creeks, Cherokee, Zuñi, and most of the Plains tribes, 7 is also considered a sacred number. For the Zuñi, Cushing says it refers to the 4 cardinal points plus the zenith, nadir, and center or ego. Some of the Pacific coast Indians regard 5 as their sacred number. Although 13 appears in most of the calendar and ceremonial counts of the cultured nations of Mexico and Central America, its use as a sacred or ceremonial number among the Indians N. of Mexico was rare, the Pawnee, Hopi, and Zuñi being notable exceptions.

Consult Brinton, Origin of Sacred Numbers, Am. Anthrop., 1894; Conant, Number Concept, 1896; Cushing, Manual Concepts, Am. Anthrop., 1892; Hayden, Ethnog. and Philol. Mo. Val., 1862; McGee, Primitive Numbers, 19th Rep. B. A. E., 1900; Thomas, Numeral Systems of Mexico and Central America, ibid.; Trumbull, Numerals in American Indian Languages, Trans. Am. Philol. Ass'n, 1874; Wilson, Indian Numerals, Canad. Ind., I, 272, 1891. (c. t.)

**Coup** ('blow,' 'stroke'). The French-Canadian term adopted to designate the formal token or signal of victory in battle, as used among the Plains tribes.

Coups are usually "counted," as it was termed—that is, credit of victory was taken, for three brave deeds, viz, killing an enemy, scalping an enemy, or being first to strike an enemy either alive or dead. Each one of these entitled a man to rank as a warrior and to recount the exploit in public; but to be first to touch the enemy was regarded as the bravest deed of all, as it implied close approach during battle. Among the Cheyenne it was even a point of bravado for a single warrior to rush in among the enemy and strike one with quirt or gun before attempting to fire, thus doubly risking his own life. Three different coups might thus be counted by as many different persons upon the body of the same enemy, and in a few tribes 4 were allowed. The stealing of a horse from a hostile camp also carried the right to count coup. The stroke (coup) might be made with whatever was most convenient, even with the naked hand, the simple touch scoring the victory. In ceremonial parades and functions an ornamented quirt or rod was sometimes carried and used as a coup stick. The warrior who could strike a tipi of the enemy in a charge upon a home camp thus counted coup upon it and was entitled to reproduce its particular design upon the next new tipi which he made for his own use and to perpetuate the pattern in his family. In this way he was said to "capture" the tipi. Warriors who had made coups of distinguished bravery, such as striking an enemy within his own tipi or behind a breastwork, were selected to preside over the dedication of a new tipi. The noted Sioux chief Red Cloud stated in 1891 that he had counted coup 80 times. See *War and War discipline*.

(J. M.)

**Coups de Flèches.** An unidentified tribe mentioned as on the Texas border in connection with Tawakoni, Anadarko, Hainai, Tonkawa, etc., early in the 19th century.—Robin, Voy. Louisiana, III, 5, 1807.

**Cous.** See *Kouse*.

**Couth.** A Karok rancheria on Klamath r., Cal., in 1856.—Taylor in Cal. Farmer, Mar. 23, 1860.

**Couthaougoula** ('lake people'). One of the 7 villages or tribes forming the Taensa confederacy in 1699.—Iberville in Margry, Déc., IV, 179, 1880.

**Cowate.** A village of Praying Indians, in 1677, at the falls of Charles r., Middlesex co., Mass.—Gookin (1677) in Drake, Bk. Inds., bk. 2, 115, 1848.

**Cow Creek.** A Seminole settlement of 12 inhabitants in 1880, on a stream running southward, at a point about 15 m. N. E. of the entrance of Kissimmee r. into L. Okeechobee, Brevard co., Fla.—MacCauley in 5th Rep. B. A. E., 478, 1887.

**Cowee** (from *Kawi'*, abbreviated form of *Kawi'yĭ*, which is possibly a contraction of *Anĭ'-kawi'yĭ*, 'place of the Deer clan'). A former important Cherokee settlement about the mouth of Cowee cr. of Little Tennessee r., about 10 m. below Franklin, Macon co., N. C.—Mooney in 19th Rep. B. A. E., 525, 1900.

Cowe.—Bartram, Travels, 371, 1792.

**Coweeshee.** Given as a Cherokee town in the Keowee district, N. W. S. C.; exact locality uncertain.—Doc. of 1755 quoted by Royce in 5th Rep. B. A. E., 143, 1887.

**Coweset** ('place of small pine trees.'—Trumbull). A small tribe or band formerly living in N. Rhode Island, W. of Blackstone r. In 1637 they were subject to the Narraganset, but had thrown off the connection by 1660.                (J. M.)

Cawesitt.—Gookin (1674) in Mass. Hist. Soc. Coll., 1st s., I, 147, 1806. Corvesets.—Williams (1682), ibid., 2d s., VII, 76, 1818 (misprint). Cowesets.—Williams (1660) in R. I. Col. Rec., I, 460, 1856. Cowwesets.—Williams and Olney (1660), ibid., I, 39–41. Cowweseuck.—Williams (1643) in Mass. Hist. Soc. Coll., 1st s., III, 205, 1794 (name used by the tribe). Cowwesit.—Williams (1675), ibid., 4th s., VI, 300, 1863.

**Cowichan.** A group of Salish tribes speaking a single dialect and occupying the S. E. coast of Vancouver id. between Nonoos bay and Sanitch inlet, and the

COWICHAN MAN.    (AM. MUS. NAT. HIST.)

valley of lower Fraser r. nearly to Spuzzum, Brit. Col. The various bands and tribes belonging to this group aggregated 2,991 in 1902. The following list of Cowichan tribes is based on information obtained from Boas: On Vancouver id.—Clemclemalats, Comiakin, Hellelt, Kenipsim, Kilpanlus, Koksilah, Kulleets, Lil-

malche, Malakut, Nanaimo, Penelakut, Quamichan, Siccameen, Snonowas, Somenos, Tateke, and Yekolaos. On lower Fraser r.—Chehalis, Chilliwack, Coquitlam, Ewawoos, Katsey, Kelatl, Kwantlen, Matsqui, Musqueam, Nicomen, Ohamil, Pilalt, Popkum, Scowlitz, Siyita, Sewathen, Snonkweametl, Skwawalooks, Squawtits, Sumass, Tait, Tsakuam, and Tsenes.                (J. R. S.)

Caw-a-chim.—Jones (1853) in H. R. Ex. Doc. 76, 34th Cong., 5, 1857. Ca-witchans.—Anderson quoted by Gibbs in Hist. Mag., VII, 74, 1863. Cowegans.—Fitzhue in Ind. Aff. Rep. 1857, 329, 1858. Cowe-wa-chin.—Starling, ibid., 170, 1852. Cowichin.—Douglas in Jour. Roy. Geog. Soc., 246, 1854. Cowitchens.—Mayne, Brit. Col., 247, 1862. Cowitchins.—Kane, Wand. in N. Am., 220, 1859. Halkōmē'lEm.—Hill-Tout in Ethnol. Surv. Can., 54, 1902 (name of Fraser R. Cowichan for themselves). Hue-la-muh.—Mackay quoted by Dawson in Trans. Roy. Soc. Can. for 1891, sec. II, 7 ('the people': own name). Hum-a-luh.—Ibid. ('the people': name by which the Cowichan of Yale and Hope call themselves). Kauitchin.—Taylor in Cal. Farmer, July 19, 1862. K·au'itcin.—Boas in 5th Rep. N. W. Tribes Can., 10, 1889. Kawatskins.—Shea, Cath. Miss., 475, 1855. Kawichen.—Scouler (1846) in Jour. Ethnol. Soc. Lond., I, 234, 1848. Kawitchen.—Scouler in Jour. Geog. Soc. Lond., I, 224, 1841. Kawitshin.—in U. S. Expl. Exped., VI, 221, 1846. Kawitskins.—Smet, Oregon Miss., 59, 1847. Kowailchew.—Gibbs in Pac. R. R. Rep., I, 433, 1855. Kow-ait-chen.——Stevens in Ind. Aff. Rep., 455, 1854. Kowitchans.—Keane in Stanford, Compend., 578, 1878. Kowitsin.—Gibbs in Cont. N. A. Ethnol., I, 181, 1877. Qāūitcin.—Boas, MS., B. A. E., 1887. Quâmitchan.—Can. Ind. Aff. Rep., lx, 1877.

**Cowichan Lake.** A local name for Nootka Indians who in summer live on a reservation at the N. end of Cowichan lake, S. Vancouver id. There were only 2 there in 1904.—Can. Ind. Aff., 1902, 1904.

**Cowish.** See *Kouse*.

**Cowlitz.** A Salish tribe formerly on the river of the same name in s. w. Washington. Once numerous and powerful, they were said by Gibbs in 1853 to be insignificant, numbering with the Upper Chehalis, with whom they were mingled, not more than 165. About 1887 there were 127 on Puyallup res., Wash. They are no longer known by this name, being evidently officially classed as Chehalis. See *Sekwu*.                (J. R. S.)

Cawalitz.—Lee and Frost, Oregon, 99, 1844. Coneliskes.—Domenech, Deserts of N. A., 401, 1860. Cowelits.—Hale in U. S. Expl. Exped., VI, 211, 1846. Cowelitz.—Farnham, Travels, 112, 1843. Cow-ena-chino.—Starling in Ind. Aff. Rep., 171, 1852. Cowlitch.—Scouler (1846) in Jour. Ethnol. Soc. Lond., I, 235, 1848. Cowlits.—Meek in H. R. Ex. Doc. 76, 30th Cong., 1st sess., 10, 1848. Cowlitsick.—Drake, Book of Inds., vii, 1848. Cowlitsk.—Proc. Boston Soc. Nat. Hist., 84, 1851–54. Cowlitz.—Smet, Letters, 230, 1843. Kaoulis.—Duflot de Mofras, Oregon, II, 95, 1844. Kau'-lĭts.—McCaw, Puyallup MS. vocab., B. A. E., 1885 (Puyallup name). Kawelitsk.—Hale in U. S. Expl. Exped., VI, 211, 1846. Kowalitsks.—Townsend, Narr., 175, 1839. Kowelits—Latham in Trans. Philol. Soc. Lond., 71, 1856. Kowelitsk.—Gallatin in Trans. Am. Ethnol. Soc., II, 119, 1848. Kowlitz.—Gibbs in Cont. N. A. Ethnol., I, 164, 1877. Nū-so-lupsh.—Ibid., 172 (name given by Indians not on Sound to Upper Cowlitz and Upper Chehalis; refers to rapids).

**Cownantico.** A former division of the Skoton, living, according to the treaty of Nov. 18, 1854, on Rogue r., Oreg.

Cow-nan-ti-co.—U. S. Ind. Treaties, 23, 1873.

**Cowpens.** Given in a distribution roll of Cherokee annuities paid in 1799 as a Cherokee town. It may have been situated near the noted place of that name in Spartanburg co., S. C.—Royce in 5th Rep. B. A. E., 144, 1887.

**Cowsumpsit.** Mentioned in 1664 as if a village subject to the chief of the Wampanoag, in Rhode Island.—Deed of 1664 in Drake, Bk. Inds., bk. 3, 14, 1848.

**Cow Towns.** Mentioned with 9 other Upper Creek towns on Tallapoosa r., Ala.—Finnelson in Am. State Papers, Ind. Aff., I, 289, 1832.

**Coya.** A former village on or near middle St Johns r., Fla.

Choÿa.—De Bry, Brev. Nar., II, map, 1591. Coya.—Laudonnière (1564) in French, Hist. Coll. La., 287, 1869.

**Coyabegux.** A village or tribe, now extinct, mentioned by Joutel as being N. or N. w. of Maligne (Colorado) r., Tex., in 1687. This region was controlled chiefly by Caddoan tribes. The name seems to have been given Joutel by Ebahamo Indians, who were closely affiliated with the Karankawa. See Gatschet, Karankawa Indians, 35, 1891; Charlevoix, New France, IV, 78, 1870.

Cagabegux.—Joutel (1687) in French, Hist. Coll. La., I, 152, 1846. Coiaheguxes.—Barcia, Ensayo, 271, 1723. Coyabegux.—Joutel, op. cit., 136.

**Coyachic.** A Tarahumare settlement N. of the headwaters of the central arm of the Rio San Pedro, lat. 28° 20′, long. 106° 48′, Chihuahua, Mexico.—Orozco y Berra, Geog., 323, 1864.

**Coyatee.** A former Cherokee settlement on Little Tennessee r., about 10 m. below the Tellico, about the present Coytee, Loudon Co., Tenn. It was the scene of the treaty of Coyatee in 1786 between commissioners representing the state of Franklin, as Tennessee was then called, and the chiefs of the Overhill towns.—Mooney in 19th Rep. B. A. E., 63, 513, 1900.

Cawatie.—Mooney, op. cit. Coiatee.—Ibid. Coytee.—Ibid. Coytoy.—Ibid. Kai-a-tee.—Ibid.

**Coycoy.** A Chumashan village on one of the N. Santa Barbara ids., Cal., in 1542.—Cabrillo (1542) in Smith, Colec. Doc. Fla., 186, 1857.

**Coyoteros** (Span.: 'wolf-men'; so called in consequence, it is said, of their subsisting partly on coyotes or prairie wolves (Gregg, Com. Prairies, I, 290, 1844); but it seems more probable that the name was applied on account of their roving habit, living on the natural products of the desert rather than by agriculture or hunting). A division of the Apache, geographically divided into the Pinal Coyoteros and the White Mountain Coyoteros, whose principal home was the w. or s. w. part of the present White Mountain res., E. Ariz., between San Carlos cr. and Gila r., although they ranged almost throughout the limits of Arizona and w. New Mexico. The name has evidently been indiscriminately applied to various Apache bands, especially to the Pinal Coyoteros, who are but a part of the Coyoteros. They were said

COYOTERO APACHE MAN

to have numbered 310 under the San Carlos Agency in 1886, 647 in 1900, and 489 in 1904, but whether these figures include other Apache is not known. See *Apache, Tonto.* (F. W. H.)

Cayotes.—Emory, Recon., 70, 1848. Colloteros.—Bartlett, Pers. Narr., II, 601, 1854. Coyaheros.—H. R. Rep. 98, 42d Cong., 3d sess., 457, 1873. Coyatero.—Schoolcraft, Ind. Tribes, V, 203, 1855. Coyetero.—Cooke in Emory, Recon., map, 1848. Coyoleno.—Ind. Aff. Rep., 122, 1861. Coyotaro.—Emory, Recon., 96, 1848. Coyote.—Mayer, Mex., II, 122, 1853. Coyotens.—Lane (1854) in Schoolcraft, Ind. Tribes, V, 689, 1855. Coyotero Apaches.—Ind. Aff. Rep., 141, 1868. Coyotéros.—Hardy, Trav. in Mexico, 430, 1829. Coystero.—Simpson in Rep. Sec. War, 118, 1850 (misprint). Cyotlero.—Abert in Emory, Recon., 507, 1848. Eiotaro.—Pattie, Pers. Narr., 66, 1833 (misprint). Gilands.—Johnston in Emory, Recon., 587, 1848. Hilend's Gila Indians.—Ibid. ("or Kiataws, prairie wolves"). Kiataro.—Ibid. Kiataw.—Ibid. Kiateros.—Ibid., 591. Koiotero.—Ind. Aff. Rep., 246, 1877. Paláwi.—Gatschet, Yuma-Spr., I, 371, 1883 (Tonto name: 'they play cards'). Pawilkna.—Ibid., 411 (Tonto name). Quietaroes.—Ind. Aff. Rep., 506, 1865. Silká.—ten Kate, Synonymie, 6, 1884 ('on the mountain': Navaho name). Tzĕj-glá.—Ibid. Wilatsu'kwe.—Ibid., 7 (Zuñi name: 'lightning-shell people'). Wolf-Eaters.—Ruxton in Jour. Ethnol. Soc. Lond., II, 95, 1850 (Coyoteros or).

**Coyyo.** A village connected with the former San Carlos mission, Cal., and said to have been of the Esselen tribe.—Taylor in Cal. Farmer, Apr. 20, 1860.

**Cradles**. In North American ethnology, the device in which the infant was bound during the first months of life. It served

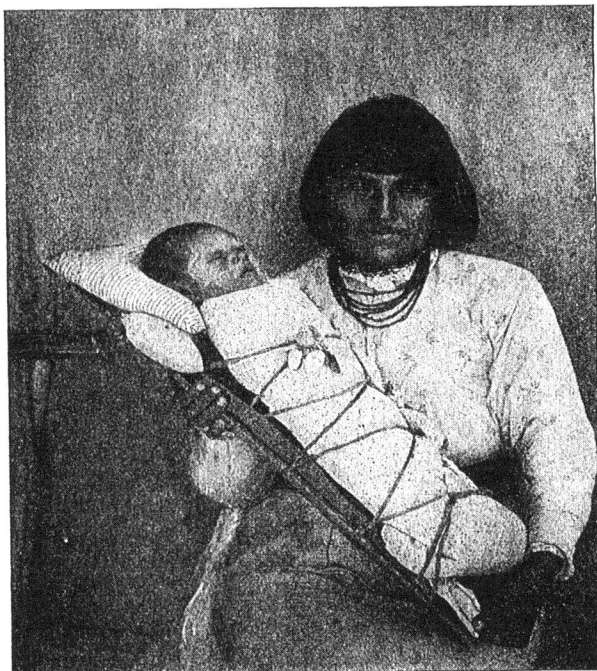

ACOMA WOMAN WITH CRADLE. (VROMAN, PHOTO.)

for both cradle and baby's carriage, more especially the latter. In the arctic region, where the extreme cold would have been fatal, cradles were not used, the infant being carried about in the hood of the mother's fur parka; the Mackenzie r. tribes put the baby in a bag of moss. In the warmer regions also, from the boundary of Mexico southward, frames were not universal, but the child, wearing little clothing, was in some way attached to the mother and borne on her hip, where it partly rode and partly clung, or rested in hammock-like swings. The territory between these extremes was the home of the cradle, which is found in great variety. The parts of a cradle are the body, the bed and covering, the pillow and other appliances for the head, including those for head flattening, the lashing, the foot rest, the bow, the awning, the devices for suspension, and the trinkets and amulets, such as dewclaws, serving for rattles and moving attractions as well as for keeping away evil spirits. Cradles differ in form, technic, and decoration. Materials and designs were often selected with great care and much ceremony, the former being those best adapted for the purpose that nature provided in each culture area, and they, quite as much as the wish of the maker, decided the form and decoration.

*Bark cradles.*—These were used in the interior of Alaska and in the Mackenzie

drainage basin. They were made of a single piece of birch or other bark, bent into the form of a trough, with a hood, and tastefully adorned with quill-work. The bed was of soft fur, the lashing of babiche. They were carried on the mother's back by means of a forehead band.

*Skin cradles.*—Adopted in the area of the buffalo and other great mammals. The hide with the hair on was rolled up, instead of bark, and in much the same way, to hold the infant; when composed of hide only they were seldom decorated.

SIOUX CRADLE

*Lattice cradles.*—On the plains, cradles made of dressed skins were lashed to a lattice of flat sticks, especially among

KIOWA CRADLE. (RUSSELL, PHOTO.)

the Kiowa, Comanche, and others; but all the tribes now borrow from one another. In these are to be seen the perfection of this device. The infant, wrapped in furs, was entirely encased. Over the face was bent a flat bow adorned with pendants or amulets and covered, in the best examples, with a costly hood. The whole upper surface of the hide was a field of beadwork, quillwork, or other decoration, in which symbolic and heraldic devices were wrought. The frame was supported and carried on the mother's back or swung from the pommel of a saddle by means of bands attached to the lattice frame in the rear. Among some tribes the upper ends of the frame projected upward and were decorated.

*Board cradles.*—Nearly akin to the last named is the form seen among the Iroquoian and Algonquian tribes of the E., in which a thin, rectangular board takes the place of the lattice. It was frequently carved and gorgeously painted, and had a projecting foot rest. The bow was also bent to a right angle and decorated. The infant, after swaddling, was laid upon the board and lashed fast by means of a long band. The tree for the Pawnee cradle-board was carefully selected, and the middle taken out so that the heart or life should be preserved, else the child would die. Equal care was taken that the head of the cradle should follow the grain. The spots on the wildcat skin used for a cover symbolized the stars, the bow the sky, and the crooked furrow cut thereon signified the lightning, whose power was typified by the arrows tied to the bow (Fletcher). All the parts were symbolic.

HUPA CRADLE OF WICKER

*Dugout cradles.*—On the N. Pacific coast the infant was placed in a little box of cedar. The region furnished material, and the adz habit, acquired in canoe excavation, made the manufacture easy. Interesting peculiarities of these cradles are the method of suspending them horizontally, as in Siberia, the pads of shredded bark for head flattening, and the relaxation of the child's body in place of straight lacing. Decorative features are almost wanting.

*Matting cradles.*—Closely allied to dugout cradles and similar in the arrangement of parts are those found in contiguous areas made from the bast of cedar.

*Basket cradles.*—On the Pacific slope and throughout the interior basin the basket cradle predominates and exists in great variety. Form, structure, and decoration are borrowed from contiguous regions. In British Columbia the dugout cradle is beautifully copied in coiled work and decorated with imbrications. The Salish have developed such variety in basketry technic that mixed types of cradles are not surprising. In the coast region of N. California and Oregon cradles are more like little chairs; the child's feet are free, and it sits in the basket as if getting ready for emancipation from restraint. The woman lavishes her skill upon this vehicle for the object of her affection. Trinkets, face protectors, and soft beds complete the outfit. Elsewhere in California the baby lies flat. In the interior basin the use of basketry in cradles is characteristic of the Shoshonean tribes. In certain pueblos of New Mexico wicker coverings are placed over them.

*Hurdle cradles.*—These consist of a number of rods or small canes or sticks arranged in a plane on an oblong hoop and held in place by lashing with splints or cords. The Yuman tribes and the Wichita so made them. The bed is of cottonwood bast, shredded, and the child is held in place in some examples by an artistic wrapping of colored woven belts. The Apache, Navaho, and Pueblo tribes combine the basket, the hurdle, and the board cradles, the Navaho covering the framework with drapery of the softest buckskin and loading it with ornaments. The ancient cliff-dwellers used both the board and the hurdle forms.

*Hammock cradles.*—Here and there were tribes that placed their infants in network or wooden hammocks suspended by the ends. In these the true function of the cradle as a sleeping place is better fulfilled, other varieties serving rather for carrying.

Among the San Carlos Apache at least the cradle is made after the baby is born, to fit the body; later on a larger one is prepared. The infant was not placed at once after birth into the cradle after the washing; a certain number of days elapsed before the act was performed with appropriate ceremonies. When the mother was working about the home the infant was not kept in the cradle, but was laid on a robe or mat and allowed free play of body and limbs. The final escape was gradual, the process taking a year or more. The cradle distorted the head by flattening the occiput as a natural consequence of contact between the resistant pillow and the immature bone, and among certain tribes this action was enhanced by pressure of pads. The Navaho are said to adjust the padding under the shoulders also. Hrdlicka finds skull deformations more pronounced and common in males than in females (see *Artificial head deformation*). In many tribes scented herbs were placed in the bedding. Among the Yuma difference was sometimes made in adorning boys' and girls' cradles, the former being much more costly. Some tribes make a new cradle for each child, but among the Pueblo tribes, particularly, the cradle was a sacred object, handed down in the family, and the number of children it had carried was frequently shown by notches on the frame. Its sale would, it is thought, result in the death of the child. If the infant died while in the helpless age, the cradle was either thrown away (Walapai and Tonto), broken up, burned, or placed on the grave (Navaho and Apache), or buried with the corpse, laced up inside as in life (cliff-dwellers, Kiowa). The grief of the mother on the death of an infant is intensely pathetic. The doll and the cradle were everywhere playthings of Indian girls. See *Child life, Moss-bag.*

Consult Fewkes in 15th Rep. B. A. E., 1897; Hrdlicka in Am. Anthrop., VII, nos. 2, 3, 1905; Mason in Rep. Nat. Mus., 161–212, 1887; Porter, ibid., 213–235.

(O. T. M.)

**Cranetown.** A former Wyandot village on the site of the present Royalton, Fairfield co., Ohio. It was known to the Indians as Tarhe, from the name of a chief in 1790, at which time it contained about 500 inhabitants in 100 wigwams built of bark.—Howe, Hist. Coll. Ohio, I, 588, 1898.

Tarhetown.—Ibid.

**Cranetown.** A former Wyandot village in Crawford co., Ohio, 8 or 10 m. N. E. of the present Upper Sandusky.—Royce in 18th Rep. B. A. E., pl. clvi, 1899.

**Craniology.** See *Anatomy, Artificial head deformation, Physiology.*

**Crayfish Town** (probably translated from Cherokee *Tsistûnă'yĭ*, 'crawfish place'). A former Cherokee settlement in upper Georgia about 1800. (J. M.)

**Crazy Horse.** An Oglala Sioux chief. He is said to have received this name because a wild pony dashed through the village when he was born. His bold, adventurous disposition made him a leader of the southern Sioux, who scorned reservation life and delighted to engage in raiding expeditions against the Crows or the Mandan, or to wreak vengeance on whites wherever they could safely attack them. When the Sioux went on the warpath in 1875, on account of the occupancy of the Black-hills and other grievances, Crazy Horse and Sitting Bull were the leaders of the hostiles. Gen. Reynolds, commanding a column of the army of Gen. Crook, in the winter of 1875 surprised Crazy Horse's camp and captured his horses, but the Indians succeeded in stampeding the herd in a blinding snowstorm. When Gen. Crook first encountered Crazy Horse's band on Rosebud r., Mont., the former was compelled to fall back after a sharp fight. The band at that time consisted of about 600 Minneconjou Sioux and Cheyenne. Later Crazy Horse was joined on Powder r. by warlike Sioux of various tribes on the reservation, others going to swell the band of Sitting Bull in Dakota. Both bands united and annihilated the column of Gen. George A. Custer on Little Bighorn r., Mont., June 25, 1876. When Gen. Nelson A. Miles pursued the Sioux in the following winter the two camps separated again s. of Yellowstone r., Crazy Horse taking his Cheyenne and Oglala and going back to Rosebud r. Gen. Mackenzie destroyed his camp on a stream that flows into Tongue r., losing several men in the engagement. Gen. Miles followed the band toward Bighorn mts. and had a sharp engagement in which the troops could scarcely have withstood the repeated assaults of double their number without their artillery, which exploded shells among the Indians with great effect. Crazy Horse surrendered in the spring with over 2,000 followers. He was suspected of stirring up another war and was placed under arrest on Sept. 7, 1877, but broke from the guard and was shot. See Miles, Pers. Recol., 193, 244, 1896.

**Creation myths.** See *Mythology, Religion.*

**Credit Indians.** A Missisauga band formerly living on Credit r., at the w. end of L. Ontario. About 1850 they removed to Tuscarora, on Grand r., Ontario, by invitation of the Iroquois.—Jones, Ojebway Inds., 211, 1861.

**Cree** (contracted from Kristinaux, French form of *Kenistenoag,* given as one of their own names). An important Algonquian tribe of British America whose former habitat was in Manitoba and Assiniboia, between Red and Saskatchewan rs. They ranged northeastward down Nelson r. to the vicinity of Hudson bay, and northwestward almost to Athabasca lake. When they first became known to the Jesuit missionaries a part of them resided in the region of James bay, as it is stated as early as 1640 that "they dwell on the rivers of the north sea where Nipissings go to trade with them"; but the Jesuit Relations of 1661 and 1667 indicate a region farther to the N. W. as the home of the larger part of the tribe. A portion of the Cree, as appears from the tradition given by Lacombe (Dict. Lang. Cris), inhabited for a time the region about Red r., intermingled with the Chippewa and Maskegon, but were attracted to the plains by the buffalo, the Cree like the Chippewa being essentially a forest people. Many bands of Cree were virtually nomads, their movements being governed largely by the food supply. The Cree are closely related, linguistically and otherwise, to the Chippewa. Hayden regarded them as an offshoot of the latter, and the Maskegon another division of the same ethnic group.

At some comparatively recent time the Assiniboin, a branch of the Sioux, in consequence of a quarrel, broke away from their brethren and sought alliance with the Cree. The latter received them cordially and granted them a home in their territory, thereby forming friendly relations that have continued to the present day. The united tribes attacked and drove southwestward the Siksika and allied tribes who formerly dwelt along the Saskatchewan. The enmity between these tribes and both the Siksika and the Sioux has ever since continued. After the Cree obtained firearms they made raids into the Athapascan country, even to the Rocky mts. and as far N. as Mackenzie r., but Churchill r. was accounted the extreme N. limit of their territory, and in their cessions of land to Canada they claimed nothing beyond this line. Mackenzie, speaking of the region of Churchill r., says the original people of this area, probably Slaves, were driven out by the Cree.

As the people of this tribe have been friendly from their first intercourse with both the English and the French, and until quite recently were left comparatively undisturbed in the enjoyment of their territory, there has been but little recorded in regard to their history. This consists almost wholly of their contests with neighboring tribes and their relations with the Hudson Bay Co. In 1786, according to Hind, these Indians, as well as those of surrounding tribes, were reduced to less than half their former numbers by smallpox. The same disease again swept off at least half the prairie tribes in 1838. They were thus reduced, according to Hind, to one-sixth or one-eighth of their former population. In more recent years, since game has become scarce, they have lived chiefly in scattered bands, depending largely on trade with the agents of the Hudson Bay Co. At present they are gathered chiefly in bands on various reserves in Manitoba, mostly with the Chippewa.

Their dispersion into bands subject to different conditions with regard to the supply and character of their food has resulted in varying physical characteristics; hence the varying descriptions given by explorers. Mackenzie, who describes the Cree comprehensively, says they are of moderate stature, well proportioned, and of great activity. Their complexion is copper-colored and their hair black, as is common among Indians. Their eyes are black, keen, and penetrating; their countenance open and agreeable. In regard to the women he says: "Of all the nations which I have seen on this continent, the Knisteneaux women are the most comely. Their figure is gener-

ally well proportioned, and the regularity of their features would be acknowledged by the more civilized people of Europe. Their complexion has less of that dark tinge which is common to those savages who have less cleanly habits." Umfreville, from whom Mackenzie appears to have copied in part what is here stated, says that they are more inclined to be lean of body than otherwise, a corpulent Indian being "a much greater curiosity than a sober one." Clark (Sign Language, 1885) describes the Cree seen by him as wretchedly poor and mentally and physically inferior to the Plains Indians; and Harmon says that those of the tribe who inhabit the plains are fairer and more cleanly than the others.

Their hair was cut in various fashions, according to the tribal divisions, and by some left in its natural state. Henry says the young men shaved off the hair except a small spot on the crown of the head. Their dress consisted of tight leggings, reaching nearly to the hip, a strip of cloth or leather about 1 ft. wide and 5 ft. long passing between the legs and under a belt around the waist, the ends being allowed to hang down in front and behind; a vest or shirt reaching to the hips; sometimes a cap for the head made of a piece of fur or a small skin, and sometimes a robe thrown over the dress. These articles, with moccasins and mittens, constituted their apparel. The dress of the women consisted of the same materials, but the shirt extended to the knees, being fastened over the shoulders with cords and at the waist with a belt, and having a flap at the shoulders; the arms were covered to the wrist with detached sleeves. Umfreville says that in trading, fraud, cunning, Indian finesse, and every concomitant vice was practised by them from the boy of 12 years to the octogenarian, but where trade was not concerned they were scrupulously honest. Mackenzie says that they were naturally mild and affable, as well as just in their dealings among themselves and with strangers; that any deviation from these traits is to be attributed to the influence of the white traders. He also describes them as generous, hospitable, and exceedingly good natured except when under the influence of spirituous liquor. Chastity was not considered a virtue among them, though infidelity of a wife was sometimes severely punished. Polygamy was common; and when a man's wife died it was considered his duty to marry her sister, if she had one. The arms and utensils used before trade articles were introduced by the whites were pots of stone, arrow-points, spearheads, hatchets, and other edged tools of flint, knives of buffalo rib, fishhooks made out of sturgeon bones, and awls from bones of the moose. The fibrous roots of the white pine were used as twine for sewing their bark canoes, and a kind of thread from a weed for making nets. Spoons and pans were fashioned from the horns of the moose (Hayden). They sometimes made fishhooks by inserting a piece of bone obliquely into a stick and sharpening the point. Their lines were either thongs fastened together or braided willow bark. Their skin tipis, like those of the N. Athapascans, were raised on poles set up in conical form, but were usually more commodious. They occasionally erect a larger structure of lattice work, covered with birch bark, in which 40 men or more can assemble for council, feasting, or religious rites.

The dead were usually buried in shallow graves, the body being covered with a pile of stones and earth to protect it from beasts of prey. The grave was lined with branches, some of the articles belonging to the deceased being placed in it, and in some sections a sort of canopy was erected over it. Where the deceased had distinguished himself in war his body was laid, according to Mackenzie, on a kind of scaffolding; but at a later date Hayden says they did not practise tree or scaffold burial. Tattooing was almost universal among the Cree before it was abandoned through the influence of the whites. The women were content with having a line or two drawn from the corners of the mouth toward the angles of the lower jaw; but some of the men covered their bodies with lines and figures. The Cree of the Woods are expert canoemen and the women lighten considerably their labors by the use of the canoe, especially where lakes and rivers abound. A double-head drum and a rattle are used in all religious ceremonies except those which take place in the sweat house. Their religious beliefs are generally similar to those of the Chippewa.

The gentile form of social organization appears to be wanting. On account of the uncertain application of the divisional names given by the Jesuit missionaries and other early writers it is impossible to identify them with those more modernly recognized. Richardson says: "It would, however, be an endless task to attempt to determine the precise people designated by the early French writers. Every small band, naming itself from its hunting grounds, was described as a different nation." The first notice of the Cree divisions is given in the Jesuit Relation of 1658, which states that they are composed of four nations or peoples, as follows: Alimibegouek, Kilistinons of the bay of Ataouabouscatouek, Kilistinons of the Nipisiriniens, and Nisibourounik. At least 3 of these divisions are erroneously located on the Creuxius map of 1660, and it is evident from the Relation that at least 3 of them were supposed by the writer to have been situated somewhere s. or s. w. of James bay. Nothing additional is heard of them in the subsequent notices of the tribe, which is otherwise divided into the Paskwawininiwug and Sakawininiwug (people of the plains and of the woods), the former subdivided into Sipiwininiwug and Mamikininiwug (river and lowland people), the latter into Sakittawawininiwug and Ayabaskawininiwug (those of Cross lake and those of Athabasca). In 1856 the Cree were divided, according to Hayden, into the following bands, all or nearly all taking their names from their chiefs: Apistekaihe, Cokah, Kiaskusis, Mataitaikeok, Muskwoikakenut, Muskwoikauepawit, Peisiekan, Piskakauakis, Shemaukan, and Wikyuwamkamusenaikata, besides several smaller bands and a considerable number around Cross lake, in the present Athabasca, who were not attached to any band. So far as now known the ethnic divisions, aside from the Cree proper, are the Maskegon and the Monsoni. Although these are treated as distinct tribes, they form, beyond doubt, integral parts of the Cree. It was to the Maskegon, according to Richardson, that the name Kilistenaux, in its many forms, was anciently applied, a conclusion with which Henry apparently agrees.

In 1776, before smallpox had greatly reduced them, the population of the Cree proper was estimated at about 15,000. Most of the estimates during the last century give them from 2,500 to 3,000. There are now about 10,000 in Manitoba (7,000 under agencies) and about 5,000 roving in Northwest Territory; total, 15,000.　　　　　　　　(J. M. C. T.)

**Ana.**—Petitot, Kutchin MS. vocab., B. A. E., 1869 ('foes': Kutchin name). **Annah.**—Mackenzie, Voy., 291, 1802 ('foes': Chipewyan name). **Ayis-iyiniwok.**—Petitot in Jour. Roy. Geog. Soc., 649, 1883 (name used by themselves). **Castanoe.**—Stanwix conf. (1759) in Rupp, West. Penn., app., 140, 1846. **Chahis.**—Maximilian, Trav., II, 234, 1841 (Hidatsa name). **Christaneaux.**—Buchanan, N. Am. Inds., 156, 1824. **Christenaux.**—Writer of 1719 in Minn. Hist. Soc. Coll., v, 424, 1885. **Christeneaux.**—Hutchins (1764) quoted by Schoolcraft, Ind. Tribes, III, 556, 1853. **Chris'-te-no.**—Lewis and Clark, Trav., 55, 1806. **Christenois.**—Ibid., 30. **Christianaux.**—La Harpe (1700), in French, Hist. Coll. La., III, 27, 1851. **Christianeaux.**—Gale, Upper Miss., map, 1867. **Christianux.**—Hutchins (1770) quoted by Richardson, Arct. Exped., II, 37, 1851. **Christinaux.**—Dobbs, Hudson Bay, 20, 1744. **Christineaux.**—French writer (1716) in Minn. Hist. Soc. Coll., v, 422, 1885. **Christinos.**—Proces verbal (1671) in Margry, Déc., I, 97, 1875. **Christinou.**—Hervas (ca. 1785) quoted by Vater, Mith., pt. 3, sec. 3, 348, 1816. **Chritenoes.**—Fisher, Interesting Acct., 190, 1812. **Cithinistinee.**—Writer of 1786 in Mass. Hist. Soc. Coll., 1st s., III, 24, 1794. **Clintinos.**—Ramsey in Ind. Aff. Rep., 72, 1850 (misprint). **Clistenos.**—Rafinesque, introd. to Marshall, Ky., I, 32, 1824. **Clistinos.**—La Hontan, New Voy., I, 231, 1703. **Cnistineaux.**—Neill, Minn., 111, 1858. **Crees.**—Harmon, Jour., 313, map, 1820. **Cries.**—Smet,

Missions, 109, 1848. **Criqs.**—Henry, Trav. in Can., 214, 1809. **Criques.**—Charlevoix (1667), New France, III, 107, 1868 (so called by Canadians). **Cris.**—Dobbs, Hudson Bay, map, 1744. **Cristeneaux.**—Chauvignerie (1736) quoted by Schoolcraft, Ind. Tribes, III, 556, 1853. **Cristinaux.**—Montreal treaty (1701) in N. Y. Doc. Col. Hist., IX, 722, 1855. **Cristineaux.**—Petitot in Jour. Roy. Geog. Soc., 649, 1883. **Cristinos.**—La Chesnaye (1697) in Margry, Déc., VI, 7, 1886. **Crists.**—Vaudreuil (1716), ibid., 496. **Crus.**—Gunn in Smithson. Rep., 399, 1867. **Cyininook.**—Kingsley, Stand. Nat. Hist., pt. 6, 148, 1883. **Eithinyook.**—Gallatin in Trans. Am. Antiq. Soc., II, 23, 1836. **Eithinyoowuc.**—Franklin, Jour. Polar Sea, 96, 1824 ('men': their own name). **Ennas.**—Petitot in Can. Rec. Sci., I, 49, 1884 ('strangers', 'enemies': Athapascan name). **Eta.**—Petitot, Hare MS. vocab., B. A. E., 1869 ('foe': Kawchodinne name). **Ethinu.**—Richardson, Arct. Exped., II, 1, 1851. **Ethinyu.**—Ibid., 34. **Eythinyuwuk.**—Ibid., 1 (own name). **Guilistinons.**—Jes. Rel. 1670, 79, 1858. **Gū'tskīā'wē.**—Chamberlain, inf'n, 1903 ('liars': Kutenai name). **Hillini-Lle'ni.**—Petitot in Jour. Roy. Geog. Soc., 650, 1883. **Ininyuwë-u.**—Richardson, Arct. Exped., II, 33, 1851. **Inninyu-wuk.**—Ibid., 70 (name used by themselves). **Iyiniwok.**—Petitot in Jour. Roy. Geog. Soc., 649, 1883 ('men': name used by themselves). **Ka-liste-no.**—Lewis and Clark quoted by Vater, Mith., pt. 3, sec. 3, 408, 1816. **Keiscatch-ewan.**—Hutchins (1770) quoted by Richardson, Arct. Exped., II, 37, 1851 ('people of Saskatchewan r.'). **Keiskatchewan.**—Ibid., 38. **Kelistenos.**—Schoolcraft, Ind. Tribes, VI, 33, 1857. **Ke-nish-té-no-wuk.**—Morgan, Consang. and Affin., 287, 1871. **Ke-nis-te-noag.**—Warren (1852) in Minn. Hist. Soc. Coll., V, 33, 1885 (Chippewa name). **Kenistenoo.**—Ind. Aff. Rep., 454, 1838. **Kenistenos.**—Burton, City of the Saints, 117, 1861. **Kilisteno.**—Prichard, Phys. Hist. Mankind, V, 410, 1847. **Kilistinaux.**—Jes. Rel. 1670, 92, 1858. **Kilistinon.**—Jes. Rel. 1658, 20, 1858. **Kilistinos.**—Du Lhut (1684) in Margry, Déc., VI, 51, 1886. **Kilistinous.**—Charlevoix quoted by Vater, Mith., pt. 3, sec. 3, 407, 1816. **Killestenos.**—Boudinot, Star in the West, 107, 1816. **Killini.**—Petitot in Jour. Roy. Geog. Soc., 650, 1883. **Killisteneaux.**—Army officer (1812) quoted by Schoolcraft, Ind. Tribes, III, 556, 1853. **Killistenoes.**—Mass. Hist. Soc. Coll., 2d s., X, 99, 1823. **Killistinaux.**—Henry, Trav. in Can., 247, 1809. **Killistini.**—Duponceau quoted by Petitot in Jour. Roy. Geog. Soc., 649, 1883. **Killistinoer.**—Vater, Mith., pt. 3, sec. 3, 257, 1816 (German form). **Killistinoes.**—Edwards (1788) in Mass. Hist. Soc. Coll., 1st s., IX, 92, 1804. **Killistinons.**—Henry, Trav. in Can., 247, 1809. **Killistinous.**—Jefferys, Fr. Doms., I, 44, 1760. **Killistins.**—Ibid., map. **Kinishtinak.**—Belcourt (before 1853) in Minn. Hist. Soc. Coll., I, 227, 1872 (trans.: 'being held by the winds'). **Kinishtino.**—Baraga, Eng.-Otch. Dict., 63, 1878 (Chippewa name). **Kinisteneaux.**—Mackenzie (1801) quoted by Kendall, Trav., II, 289, 1809. **Kinistinaux.**—Henry, Trav. in Can., 214, 1809. **Kinistineaux.**—Ibid., 247. **Kinistinoes.**—Harmon, Jour., 67, 1820. **Kinistinons.**—Jes. Rel. 1672, 54, 1858. **Kinistinuwok.**—Petitot in Jour. Roy. Geog. Soc., 649, 1883 (Chippewa name). **Kinstenaux.**—Lewis and Clark, Trav., 105, 1840. **Kinstinaux.**—Gallatin in Trans. Am. Ethnol. Soc., II, 104, 1848. **Kiristinon.**—Jes. Rel. 1640, 34, 1858. **Kislistinons.**—Du Chesneau (1681) in N. Y. Doc. Col. Hist., IX, 161, 1855. **Kistineaux.**—Ramsey in Ind. Aff. Rep., 71, 1850. **Klistinaux.**—Gallatin in Trans. Am. Antiq. Soc., II, 23, 1836. **Klistinons.**—Jes. Rel. (1671) quoted by Ramsey in Ind. Aff. Rep., 71, 1850. **Klistinos.**—Petitot in Jour. Roy. Geog. Soc., 649, 1883. **Kneestenoag.**—Tanner, Narr., 315, 1830 (Ottawa name). **Knisteaux.**—Howe, Hist. Coll., 357, 1851. **Knistenaus.**—Lewis and Clark, Trav., 45, 1806. **Knistenaux.**—Schermerhorn (1812) in Mass. Hist. Soc. Coll., 2d s., II, 11, 1814. **Knisteneau.**—Farnham, Trav., 32, 1843. **Knisteneaux.**—Gass, Jour., 42, note, 1807. **Knisteneux.**—Harmon, Jour., 313, 1820. **Knisteno.**—Wrangell, Ethnol. Nachr., 100, 1839. **Knistenoos.**—Brackenridge, Views of La., 86, 1815. **Knistinaux.**—Gallatin in Trans. Am. Antiq. Soc., II, 23, 1836. **Knistineaux.**—Shea, Cath. Miss., 141, 1855. **Knistinos.**—Kingsley, Stand. Nat. Hist., pt. 6, 148, 1883. **Krees.**—Henry, MS. vocab. (1812), Bell copy, B. A. E. **Kricqs.**—Bacqueville de la Potherie, Hist. Am., I, 170, 1753. **Kriés.**—Baudry des Lozières, Voy. a la Le., 242, 1802. **Kriqs.**—Lettres Édif., I, 645, 1695. **Kris.**—Jefferys, Fr. Doms., I, map, 1760. **Kristenaux.**—Kingsley, Stand. Nat. Hist., pt. 6, 148, 1883. **Kristeneaux.**—Franklin, Jour. to Polar Sea, 96, 1824. **Kristinaux.**—Gallatin in Trans. Am. Antiq. Soc., II, 23, 1836. **Kristino.**—Morse, Rep. to Sec. War, 34, 1822. **Kyristin8ns.**—Jes. Rel. 1641, 59, 1858. **Mehethawas.**—Keane in Stanford, Compend., 521, 1878. **Ministeneaux.**—Boudinot, Star in the West, 127, 1816 (misprint). **Naehiaok.**—Kingsley, Stand. Nat. Hist., pt. 6, 148, 1883. **Nahathaway.**—West, Jour., 19, 1824. **Naheawak.**—Long, Exped. St Peter's R., I, 376, 1824. **Nahhahwuk.**—Tanner, Narr., 315, 1830 (said to be their own name). **Nahiawah.**—Prichard, Phys. Hist. Mankind, V, 410, 1847. **Nahioak.**—Maximilian, Trav., I, 454, 1839. **Nakawawa.**—Hutchins (1770) quoted by Richardson, Arct. Exped., II, 38, 1851. **Naka-we-wuk.**—Ibid. **Nathehwy-within-yoowuc.**—Franklin, Journ. to Polar Sea, 96, 1824 ('southern men'). **Nathe'-wywithin-yu.**—Ibid., 71. **Nation du Grand-Rat.**—La Chesnaye (1697) in Margry, Déc., VI, 7, 1886. **Né-a-ya-óg.**—Hayden, Ethnol. and Philol. Mo. Val., 235, 1862 ('those who speak the same tongue': own name). **Ne-hetha-wa.**—Umfreville (1790) in Maine Hist. Soc. Coll., VI, 270, 1859. **Nehethé-wuk.**—Richardson, Arct. Exped., II, 36, 1851 ('exact men': own name). **Nehethowuck.**—Shea, note in Charlevoix, New Fr., III, 107, 1868. **Nehethwa.**—Umfreville (1790) quoted by Vater, Mith., pt. 3, sec. 3, 418, 1816. **Nehiyaw.**—Baraga, Ojibwa Dict., 1878 (Chippewa name). **Nehiyawok.**—Lacombe, Dict. des Cris, X, 1874 (own name; from *iyiniwok*,' those of the first race'). **Nenawehks.**—Keane in Stanford, Compend., 525, 1878. **Nenawewhk.**—Walch, map, 1805. **Nena Wewhok.**—Harmon, Jour., map, 1820. **Nithe-wuk.**—Hind, Lab. Penin., II, 10, 1863. **Northern Uttawawa.**—Hutchins (1770) quoted by Richardson, Arct. Exped., II, 38, 1851. **O'pimmitish Ininiwuc.**—Franklin, Journ. Polar Sea, 56, 1824 ('men of the woods'). **Quenistinos.**—Iberville (1702) in Minn. Hist. Soc. Coll., I, 342, 1872. **Queristinos.**—Iberville in Margry, Déc., IV, 600, 1880. **Re-nis-te-nos.**—Culbertson in Smithson. Rep. 1850, 122, 1851. **śa-hē'.**—Matthews, Hidatsa Inds., 200, 1877 (Hidatsa name). **Saie'kuŭn.**—Tims, Blackfoot Gram. and Dict., 124, 1889 (Siksika name; sing.). **Schahi.**—Maximilian, Trav., II, 234, 1841 (Hidatsa name). **sha-i-yé.**—Matthews, Hidatsa Inds., 200, 1877 (Assiniboin name). **Shi-e-á-la.**—Hayden, Ethnog. and Philol. Mo. Val., 235, 1862 (Sioux name). **Shi-é-ya.**—Ibid. (Assiniboin name: 'enemies,' 'strangers'). **Southern Indians.**—Dobbs, Hudson Bay, 95, 1744 (so called by the Hudson bay traders).

**Creek Path** (transl. of *Ku'să-nŭñnă'hǐ*). A former important Cherokee settlement, including also a number of Creeks and Shawnee, where the trail from the Ohio region to the Creek country crossed Tennessee r., at the present Guntersville, Marshall co., Ala. It was later known as Gunter's Landing, from a Cherokee mixed-blood named Gunter.—Mooney in 19th Rep. B. A. E., 526, 1900.

**Creeks.** A confederacy forming one of the largest divisions of the Muskhogean family. They received their name from the English on account of the numerous streams in their country. During early historic times the Creeks occupied the greater portion of Alabama and Georgia, residing chiefly on Coosa and Tallapoosa rs., the two largest tributaries of Alabama r., and on Flint and Chattahoochee rs. They claimed the territory on the E. from the Savannah to St Johns r. and all the islands, thence to Apalache bay, and from this line northward to the mountains. The s. portion of this territory was held by dispossession of the earlier Florida tribes. They sold to Great Britain at an early date their territory between Savannah and Ogeechee rs., all the coast to St Johns r., and all the islands up to tidewater, reserving for themselves St Catherine, Sapelo, and Ossabaw ids., and from Pipemakers bluff to Savannah (Morse, N. Am., 218, 1776). Thus occupying a leading position among the Muskhogean tribes the Creeks were sufficiently numerous and powerful to resist attacks from the northern tribes, as the Catawba, Iroquois, Shawnee, and Cherokee, after they had united in a confederacy, which they did at an early day. The dominating tribes at the time of the confederation seem to have been the Abihka, Kusa, Kasihta, Kawita, Wokokai, Hilibi, and Huhliwahli, and some other tribe or tribes at the junction of Coosa and Tallapoosa rs. Nothing certain can be said of their previous condition, or of the time when the confederacy was established, but it appears from the narratives of De Soto's expedition that leagues among several of these towns existed in 1540, over which head chiefs presided.

For more than a century before their removal to the W., between 1836 and 1840, the people of the Creek confederacy occupied some 50 towns, in which were spoken 7 distinct languages, viz, Muscogee, Hitchiti, Koasati, Alibamu, Natchez, Yuchi, and Shawnee. The first 5 were Muskhogean, the others were wholly alien incorporations. About half the confederacy spoke the Muscogee language, which thus constituted the ruling language and gave name to the confederacy. The meaning of the word is unknown. Although an attempt has been made to connect it with the Algonquian *maskeg*, 'swamp,' the probabilities seem to favor a southern origin. The people speaking the cognate Hitchiti and Koasati were contemptuously designated as "Stincards" by the dominant Muscogee. The Koasati spoke almost the same language as the Alibamu of central Alabama, while the Hitchiti, on lower Chattahoochee r., appear to have been the remnant of the ancient people of s. E. Georgia, and claimed to be of more ancient occupancy than the Muscogee. Geographically the towns were grouped as Upper Creek, on Coosa and Tallapoosa rs., Ala., and Lower Creek, on middle or Lower Chattahoochee r., on the Alabama-Georgia border. While the Seminole (q. v.) were still a small body confined to the extreme N. of Florida, they were frequently spoken of as Lower Creeks. To the Cherokee the Upper Creeks were known as *Ani-Kusa*, from their ancient town of Kusa, or

Coosa, while the Lower Creeks were called *Ani-Kawita*, from their principal town Kawita, or Coweta. The earlier Seminole emigrants were chiefly from the Lower Creek towns.

The history of the Creeks begins with the appearance of De Soto's army in their country in 1540. Tristan de Luna came in contact with part of the group in 1559, but the only important fact that can be drawn from the record is the deplorable condition into which the people of the sections penetrated by the Spaniards had been brought by their visit. Juan del Pardo passed through their country in 1567, but Juan de la Vandera, the chronicler of his expedition, has left little more than a list of unidentifiable names. The

CREEK MAN

Creeks came prominently into history as allies of the English in the Apalachee wars of 1703–08, and from that period continue almost uniformly as treaty allies of the South Carolina and Georgia colonies, while hostile to the Spaniards of Florida. The only serious revolt of the Creeks against the Americans took place in 1813–14—the well-known Creek war, in which Gen. Jackson took a prominent part. This ended in the complete defeat of the Indians and the submission of Weatherford, their leader, followed by the cession of the greater part of their lands to the United States. The extended and bloody contest in Florida, which lasted from 1835 to 1843 and is known as the Seminole war, secured permanent peace with the southern tribes. The removal of the larger part of the Creek and Seminole people and their negro slaves to the lands assigned them in Indian Ter. took place between 1836 and 1840.

The Creek woman was short in stature but well formed, while the warrior, according to Pickett (Hist. Ala., 87, ed. 1896), was "larger than the ordinary race of Europeans, often above 6 ft. in height, but was invariably well formed, erect in his carriage, and graceful in every movement. They were proud, haughty, and arrogant; brave and valiant in war." As a people they were more than usually devoted to decoration and ornament; they were fond of music, and ball play was their most important game. Exogamy, or marriage outside the clan, was the rule; adultery by the wife was punished by the relatives of the husband; descent was in the female line. Each town or small tribe (*tạlwạ*) was under an elected chief, or *miko*, who was advised by the council of the town in all important matters, while the council appointed the "great warrior" or *tustenuggi-hlako*. They usually buried their dead in a square pit under the bed where the deceased lay in his house. Certain towns were consecrated to peace ceremonies and were known as "white towns," while others set apart for war ceremonials were designated as "red towns." They had several orders of chiefly rank. Their great religious ceremony was the annual *puskita* (see *Busk*), of which the lighting of the new fire and the drinking of the black drink (q. v.) were important accompaniments.

The early statistics of Creek population are based on mere estimates. It is not known what numerical relation the mixed bloods hold to the full bloods and their former negro slaves, nor the number of their towns (having a square for annual festivities) and villages (having no square). In the last quarter of the 18th century the Creek population may have been about 20,000, occupying from 40 to 60 towns. Knox in 1789 (Am. State Pap., I, 1832) estimates them at 6,000 warriors, or a total of 24,000 inhabitants in 100 towns; but these evidently included the Seminole of Florida. Bartram, about 1775, credits the whole confederacy, exclusive of the Seminole, with 11,000 in 55 towns. Hawkins, in 1785, gave them 5,400 men, representing a total of about 19,000. Estimates made after the removal to Indian Ter. place the population between 15,000 and 20,000. In 1904 the "Creeks by blood" living in the Creek Nation, numbered 9,905, while Creek freedmen aggregated 5,473. The number of acres in their reserve in 1885 was 3,215,395, of which only a portion was tillable, and 90,000 were actually cultivated.

Some of the more important earlier treaties of the United States with the Creek Indians are: Hopewell, S. C., Nov. 28, 1785; New York, Aug. 7, 1790; Coleraine, Ga., June 29, 1796; Ft Jackson, Ala., Aug. 9, 1814; Creek agency on Flint r., Jan. 22, 1818; Indian Spring, Creek Nation, Jan. 8, 1821; Washington, D. C., Jan. 24, 1826, and Mar. 24, 1832; Ft Gibson, Ind. T., Nov. 23, 1838.

Until recently the Creek Nation in Oklahoma was divided into 49 townships ("towns"), of which 3 were inhabited solely by negroes. The capital was Okmulgee. Their legislature consisted of a House of Kings (corresponding to the Senate) and a House of Warriors (similar to the National House of Representatives), with a head chief as executive. Several volumes of their laws have been published.

The Creek clans follow, those marked with an asterisk being extinct; the final *algi* means 'people': Ahalakalgi (Bog potato), Aktayatsalgi, Atchialgi (Maize), \*Chukotalgi, Fusualgi (Bird), Halpadalgi (Alligator), Hlahloalgi (Fish), Hutalgalgi (Wind), \*Isfanalgi, Itamalgi, Itchhasualgi (Beaver), Itchualgi (Deer), Katsalgi (Panther), Koakotsalgi (Wild-cat), Kunipalgi (Skunk), \*Muklasalgi, Nokosalgi (Bear), \*Odshisalgi (Hickory-nut), \*Okilisa, \*Oktchunualgi (Salt), Osanalgi (Otter), Pahosalgi, Sopaktalgi (Toad), Takusalgi (Mole), Tsulalgi (Fox), \*Wahlakalgi, Wotkalgi (Raccoon), Yahalgi (Wolf).

Below is a list of the Creek towns and villages. The smaller contained 20 to 30 cabins and the larger as many as 200. Tukabatchi, the largest, is said to have had 386 families in 1832. The towns were composed of irregular clusters of 4 to 8 houses, each cluster being occupied by the representative of a clan.

*Upper Creek towns.*—Abihka, Abikudshi, Alkehatchee, Anatichapko, Assilanapi, Atasi, Atchinaalgi, Atchinabatchi, Aucheucaula, Canjauda, Cayomulgi, Chakihlako, Chananagi, Chatoksofki, Chatukchufaula, Chiaha, Cholocco Litabixee, Conaliga, Coosahatchi, Cow Towns, Eufaula, Fusihatchi, Ghuaclahatche, Guaxule, Hatcheuxhau, Hatchichapa, Hillabi, Hlanudshiapala, Hlaphlako, Hlahlokalka, Huhliwahli, Ikanachaka, Ikanhatki, Imukfa, Ipisoga, Istapoga, Istudshilaika, Kailaidshi, Keroff, Kitchopataki, Kohamutkikatska, Kulumi, Kusa, Littefutchi, Lutchapoga, Massi (?), Muklassa, New Eufaula, Ninnipaskulgee, Niuyaka, Oakfuskee, Oakfuskudshi, Okchayi, Okchayudshi, Opilhlako, Osonee (?), Otituchina, Pakan, Tallahassee, Pinhoti, Potchushatchi, Sakapatatayi, Sambella, Satapo, Saugahatchi, Sukaispoka, Taladega, Talasse, Talassehatchi, Talapoosa, Taliposehogy, Taluamutchasi, Tukabatchi, Tukabatchi

Tallahassee, Tukpafka, Tukhtukagi, Tuskegee, Uktahasasi, Ullibahali, Wakokayi, Weogufka, Wetumpka, Wewoka, Woksoyudshi.  (See also *Alibamu*.)

*Lower Creek and Hitchiti towns.*—Amakalli, Apalachicola, Apatai, Chattahoochee, Chiaha, Chiahudshi, Chihlakonini, Chiskatalofa, Chukahlako, Cotohautustennuggee, Donally's Town, Ematlochee, Finhalui, Hatchichapa, Hihagee, Hlekatska, Hotalihuyana, Huhlitaiga, Itahasiwaki, Kasihta, Kawaiki, Kawita, Nipky, Ocheese, Ocmulgee, Ocon, Oconee, Okitiyakni, Osotchi, Sawokli, Sawokliudshi, Secharlecha, Suolanocha, Tamali, and Telmocresses.

Ani'-Gu'să.—Mooney in 19th Rep. A. B. E., 509, 1900 (Cherokee name, from Kusa, their principal ancient town). Anikoēssa.—ten Kate, Reizen in N. A., 422, 1885 (Cherokee name). Ani'-Ku'să.—Mooney, op. cit. (alternative form of Cherokee name). Copas.—Carver, Trav., map, 1778 (possibly the same; see *Kópa*, the Yuchi name, below). Creek Indians.—Craven (1712) in N. C. Col. Rec., I, 898, 1886. Greek nation.—H. R. Rep. 854, 27th Cong., 2d sess., 12, 1842 (misprint). Humásko.—Gatschet, Creek Migr. Leg., I, 60, 1884 (Shawnee name, singular). Humaskógi.—Ibid. (pl. form). Kópa.—Gatschet, Yuchi MS., B. A. E., 1885 (Yuchi name, from *ko* 'man,' *pa* 'to burn,' referring to their custom of burning prisoners at the stake). Kreeks.—Mandrillon, Spectateur Américain, map, 1785. Krichos.—Hervas, Idea dell' Universo, XVII, 90, 1784. Krihk.—Gatschet, inf'n (German form of several writers). Kúsa.—Gatschet, inf'n (Cherokee name, pl. *Anikúsa;* so called after Kusa, their earliest center). Ku-û'-sha—Gatschet, Creek Migr. Leg., I, 59, 1884 (Wyandot name, after Cherokee name). Machecous.—Smith, Bouquet's Exped., 69, 1766 (probably misspelled for *Mashcouqui;* misspelling handed down by Hutchins, Jefferson, and Schoolcraft). Mackóꭓe.—Dorsey, Kansas MS. vocab., B. A. E., 1882 (Kansa name). Macku'ꭓe.—Dorsey, Osage MS. vocab., B. A. E., 1883 (Osage name). Maskógi.—Gatschet, Creek Migr. Leg., I, 59, 1884. Maskókálgi.—Ibid. (own name, plural). Maskóki.—Ibid. Maskokúlki.—ten Kate, Reizen in N. A., 411, 1885 (*úlki* trans. 'people'). Masquachki.—Heckewelder in Barton, New Views, app., 9, 1798 (Delaware name: 'swampy land', 'Swampylanders'). Mobilian.—Shea, Cath. Miss., 22, 1855. Mo-cko'-ꭓi.—Dorsey, Kwapa MS. vocab., B. A. E., 1891 (Quapaw name). Moskoky.—Morse, Rep. to Sec. War, 311, 1822. Mucogulgee.—Schoolcraft, Ind. Tribes, III, 511, 1853. Musaogulge.—Ker, Travels, 337, 1816 (misprint). Muscagee.—N. Y. Doc. Col. Hist., VI, 709, 1855. Muscogee.—Ind. Aff. Rep., 71, 1849. Muscogeh.—Brinton, Floridian Penin., 144, 1859. Muscogulges.—Bartram, Travels, 149, 1791. Muscolgees.—Rafinesque, introd. to Marshall's Ky., I, 30, 1824. Muscows.—Brinton, Floridian Penin., 144, 1859. Musgogees.—Schoolcraft, Ind. Tribes, I, 134, 1851. Muskogee.—Pike, Travels, 159, 1811. Muskogolgees.—Nuttall, Jour., 277, 1821. Muskohge.—Adair, Am. Ind., 257, 1775. Muskohgee.—Worsley, View of Am. Inds., 95, 1828. Muskokes.—Smith, Cabeça de Vaca, 164, note, 1871. Mus-koo-gee.—Bollaert in Jour. Ethnol. Soc. Lond., II, 265, 1850. Musqua.—Woodward, Reminiscences, 13, 1859. Sko'-ki haⁿ-ya'.—Dorsey, Biloxi MS. Dict., B. A. E., 1892 (Biloxi name). Umashgohak.—Gatschet, inf'n (Fox name). Western Indians.—Brinton, Floridian Penin., 144, 1859.

**Cremation.** See *Mortuary customs.*

**Crescents.** See *Banner stones.*

**Cristone.** A ruined pueblo on Gallinas cr., s. of Tierra Amarilla, N. w. N. Mex.—Cope in Wheeler Survey Rep., VII, 355, 1879.

**Croatan.** A village in 1585 on an island then called by the same name, which appears to have been that on which C. Lookout is situated, on the coast of Carteret co., N. C. The inhabitants seem to have been independent of the chiefs of Secotan. It is thought that the lost colony of Lane, on Roanoke id., joined them and that traces of the mixture were discernible in the later Hatteras Indians. (J. M.)

Croatan.—Lane (1586) in Smith (1629), Virginia, I, 92, repr. 1819. Croatoan.—Strachey (*ca.* 1612), Virginia, 43, 145, 1849. Crooton.—Lane, op. cit., 86.

**Croatan Indians.** The legal designation in North Carolina for a people evidently of mixed Indian and white blood, found in various E. sections of the state, but chiefly in Robeson co., and numbering approximately 5,000. For many years they were classed with the free negroes, but steadily refused to accept such classification or to attend the negro schools or churches, claiming to be the descendants of the early native tribes and of white settlers who had intermarried with them. About 20 years ago their claim was officially recognized and they were given a separate legal existence under the title of "Croatan Indians," on the theory of descent from Raleigh's lost colony of Croatan (q. v.). Under this name they now have separate school provision and are admitted to some privileges not accorded to the negroes. The theory of descent from the lost colony may be regarded as baseless, but the name itself serves as a convenient label for a people who combine in themselves the blood of the wasted native tribes, the early colonists or forest rovers, the runaway slaves or other negroes, and probably also of stray seamen of the Latin races from coasting vessels in the West Indian or Brazilian trade.

Across the line in South Carolina are found a people, evidently of similar origin, designated "Redbones." In portions of w. N. C. and E. Tenn. are found the so-called "Melungeons" (probably from French *melangé*, 'mixed') or "Portuguese," apparently an offshoot from the Croatan proper, and in Delaware are found the "Moors." All of these are local designations for peoples of mixed race with an Indian nucleus differing in no way from the present mixed-blood remnants known as Pamunkey, Chickahominy, and Nansemond Indians in Virginia, excepting in the more complete loss of their identity. In general, the physical features and complexion of the persons of this mixed stock incline more to the Indian than to the white or negro. See *Métis, Mixed bloods.* (J. M.)

**Cross.** This symbol or device, which in some of its familiar forms is known as the swastika, was in common use all over America in pre-Columbian times. N. of the Rio Grande it assumed many forms, had varied significance and use, and doubtless originated in many different ways. Some of these ways may be briefly suggested: (1) Primitive man adjusts himself to his environment, real and imaginary, by keeping in mind the cardinal points as he understands them. When the Indian considers the world about

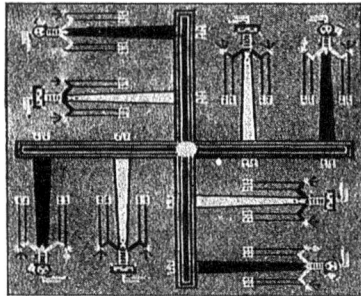

NAVAHO ALTAR-FLOOR SYMBOL OF THE FOUR WORLD-QUARTERS. (J. STEVENSON)

him he thinks of it as divided into the four quarters, and when he communicates with the mysterious beings and powers with which his imagination peoples it—the rulers of the winds and rains—he turns his face to the four directions in stipulated order and addresses them to make his appeals and his offerings. Thus his worship, his ceremonies, his games, and even his more ordinary occupations in many cases are arranged to conform to the cardinal points, and the various symbolic representations associated with them assume the form of the cross (see *Color symbolism, Orientation*). This was and is true of many peoples and is well illustrated in the wonderful altar paintings of the tribes of the arid region (see *Dry-painting*). Such

SHELL GORGET WITH FIGURE OF SPIDER AND CONVENTIONAL- IZED CROSS MARKING. (2-5)

crosses, although an essential part of symbolism and religious ceremony, exist only for the purposes of the occasion and are brushed away when the ceremony is ended, but nevertheless they pass into permanent form as decorations of ceremonial objects — as pottery,

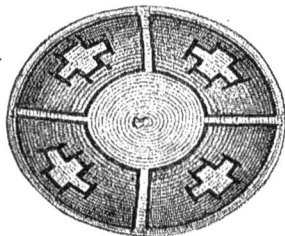

NAVAHO BASKET TRAY WITH CROSSES REPRESENTING THE FOUR WORLD-QUARTERS AND STARS OR CLOUDS. (1-15)

basketry, and costumes—retaining their significance indefinitely. (2) Distinct from the crosses thus derived in form and significance are those having a pictorial origin; such are the conventional delineations of animal and vegetal forms or their markings, or those representing the cos-

mic bodies, as the sun and the stars, particularly the morning and evening stars as among the tribes of the S. W. These figures, generally very simple in form, may

CROSS FORMED BY THE ORNA- MENTAL AR- RANGEMENT OF FOUR TIPI FIG- URES ON AN ARAPAHO MEDI- CINE-CASE LID. (KROEBER)

be symbols of mythic powers and personages; and when used in non-symbolic art they may in time lose the symbolic character and remain in art as mere formal decorative patterns. (3) Distinct from these again are a large class of crosses and cross-like forms which have an adventitious origin, being the result of the combined mechanical and esthetic requirements of embellishment. In nearly all branches of art in which surface ornament is an important factor the spaces available for decorative designs are squares, rectangles, circles, and ovals, or are borders or zones which are divided into squares or parallelograms for ready treatment. When simple figures, symbolic or non-symbolic, are filled into these spaces, they are introduced, not singly, since the result would be unsatisfactory from the point of view of the decorator; not in pairs, as that would be little better, but in fours, thus filling the spaces evenly and symmetrically. This quadruple arrangement in a multitude of cases produces the cross which, although a

PIMA BASKET WITH PSEUDO CROSS (SWASTIKA) FORMED ADVENTI- TIOUSLY OF THE INTERSPACES OF FOUR SCROLL-FRET UNITS. (1-12)

pseudo cross, is not always to be distinguished from the cross symbol. The separate elements in such crosses may be figures of men, insects, mountains, clouds, frets, and scrolls, or what not, and of themselves symbolic, but the cross thus produced is an accident and as a cross is without significance. (4) In very many cases designs are invented by the primitive decorator who fills the available spaces to beautify articles manufactured, and the arrangement in fours is often the most natural and effective that can be devised. These designs, primarily nonsignificant, may have meanings read into them by the woman as she works the stitches of her basketry or beadwork, or by others subsequently, and these ideas may be wholly

SILVER CROSS (ROMAN CATHOLIC) FROM A MOUND IN WISCONSIN; 1-3. (THOMAS)

distinct from those associated with the cross through any other means.

It is thus seen that the cross naturally and freely finds its way into the art of primitive peoples, and that it may have great variety of form and diversity of meaning. There seems no reason whatever for supposing that the cross of the American aborigines, in any of its phases, is derived from the cross of the Old World, or that the ideas associated with it are at all analogous with those that cluster about the Christian cross. It is well known, however, that the Christian cross was introduced everywhere among the American tribes by the conquerors and colonists as a symbol of the religion which they sought to introduce, and being adopted by the tribes it is embodied to some extent in the post-Columbian native art. Crosses of silver, such as were commonly worn as pendants on rosaries, are frequently recovered from mounds and burial places of the aborigines.

Consult Barrett in Am. Anthrop., VII, no 4, 1905; Beauchamp in Bull. 73, N. Y. State Mus., 1903; Blake, The Cross, Ancient and Modern, 1888; Brinton in Proc. Am. Philos. Soc., XXVI, 1889; J. O. Dorsey (1) in 11th Rep. B. A. E., 1894, (2) in The Archæologist, 1894; Fletcher in Rep. Peabody Mus., III, 1884; Holmes (1) in 20th Rep. B. A. E., 1903, (2) in Am. Anthrop., II, 1889; Jones in Smithson. Rep. 1881, 1883; Kroeber in Bull. Am. Mus. Nat. Hist., XVIII, 1902; McAdams, Records of Ancient Races, 58, 1887; Stevenson in 8th Rep. B. A. E., 1891; Tooker in Am. Antiq., XX, no. 6, 1898; Wilson in Rep. Nat. Mus. 1894, 1896. (W. H. H.)

**Crossweeksung** ('the house of separation' (?).—Boudinot). A former Delaware village in Burlington co., N. J., probably about the present Crosswicks. A mission was established there by Brainerd in 1745. (J. M.)
Crossweeckes.—Doc. of 1674 in N. Y. Doc. Col. Hist., II, 682, 1858. Crossweeksung.—Boudinot, Star in the West, 278, 1816. Crosweek.—Ibid., 117.

**Croton-bug.** The water cockroach (*Blatta germanica*), from Croton, the name of a river in Westchester co., N. Y., which has been applied also to the metropolitan reservoir system. Tooker considers the word a personal name and derives it from *kloltin*, in the Delaware dialect of Algonquian, signifying 'he contends.' (A. F. C.)

**Crow Dog** (*Kangisunka*). An Oglala Sioux chief. He took no prominent part in the Sioux war of 1876, but in 1881 he shot Spotted Tail in a brawl, and for this was tried before a jury and sentenced to be hanged, but the United States Supreme Court ordered his release on habeas corpus, ruling that the Federal courts had no jurisdiction over crimes committed on reservations secured to Indian tribes by treaty. Other deeds attested his fearless nature, and when the Ghost-dance craze emboldened the Oglala to go upon the warpath, angered by a new treaty cutting down their reservation and rations, Crow Dog was one of the leaders of the desperate band that fled from Rosebud agency to the Bad-lands and defied Gen. J. A. Brooke's brigade. He was inclined to yield when friendlies came to persuade them, and when the irreconcilables caught up their rifles to shoot the waverers he drew his blanket over his head, not wishing, as he said, to know who would be guilty of slaying a brother Dakota. When the troops still refrained from attacking, and the most violent of his companions saw the hopelessness of their plight, he led his followers back to the agency toward the close of Dec., 1890. (F. H.)

**Crowmocker** (transl. of *Kâg'-ahyelis'kĕ*, a chief's name). A former Cherokee settlement on Battle cr., which falls into Tennessee r. below Chattanooga, Tenn. (J. M.)
Crow Mockers Old Place.—Royce in 5th Rep. B. A. E., map, 1887.

**Crow People.** A division of the Crows, distinguished from the Minesetperi.—Culbertson in Smithson. Rep. 1850, 144, 1851.

**Crows** (trans., through French *gens des corbeaux*, of their own name, *Absároke*, crow, sparrowhawk, or bird people). A Siouan tribe forming part of the Hidatsa group, their separation from the Hidatsa having taken place, as Matthews (1894) believed, within the last 200 years. Hayden, following their tradition, placed it about 1776. According to this story it was the result of a factional dispute between two chiefs who were desperate men and nearly equal in the number of their followers. They were then residing on Missouri r., and one of the two bands which afterward became the Crows withdrew and migrated to the vicinity of the Rocky mts., through which region they continued to rove until gathered on reservations. Since their separation from the Hidatsa their history has been similar to that of most tribes of the plains, one of perpetual war with the surrounding tribes, their chief enemies being the Siksika and the Dakota. At the time of the Lewis and Clark expedition (1804) they dwelt chiefly on Bighorn r.; Brown (1817) located them on the Yellowstone and the E. side of the Rocky mts.; Drake (1834) on the s. branch of the Yellowstone, in lat. 46°, long. 105°. Hayden (1862) wrote: "The country usually inhabited by the Crows is in and near the Rocky mts., along the sources of

Powder, Wind, and Bighorn rs., on the s. side of the Yellowstone, as far as Laramie fork on the Platte r. They are also often found on the w. and N. side of that

CROW MAN

river, as far as the source of the Mussel-shell and as low down as the mouth of the Yellowstone.''

According to Maximilian (1843) the tipis of the Crows were exactly like those of the Sioux, set up without any regular order, and on the poles, instead of scalps were small pieces of colored cloth, chiefly red, floating like streamers in the wind. The camp he visited swarmed with wolf-like dogs. They were a wandering tribe of hunters, making no plantations except a few small patches of tobacco. They lived at that time in some 400 tents and are said to have possessed between 9,000 and 10,000 horses. Maximilian considered them the proudest of Indians, despising the whites; "they do not, however, kill them, but often plunder them." In stature and dress they corresponded with the Hidatsa, and were proud of their long hair. The women have been described as skilful in various kinds of work, and their shirts and dresses of big-horn leather, as well as ther buffalo robes, embroidered and ornamented with dyed porcupine quills, as particularly handsome. The men made their weapons very well and with much taste, especially their large bows, covered with horn of

the elk or bighorn and often with rattle-snake skin. The Crows have been described as extremely superstitious, very dissolute, and much given to unnatural practices; they are skilful horsemen, throwing themselves on one side in their attacks, as is done by many Asiatic tribes. Their dead were usually placed on stages elevated on poles in the prairie.

The population was estimated by Lewis and Clark (1804) at 350 lodges and 3,500 individuals; in 1829 and 1834, at 4,500; Maximilian (1843) counted 400 tipis; Hayden (1862) said there were formerly about 800 lodges or families, in 1862 reduced to 460 lodges. Their number in 1890 was 2,287; in 1904, 1,826. Lewis (Stat. View, 1807) said they were divided into four bands, called by themselves Ahaharopirnopa, Ehartsar, Noota, and Pareescar. Culbertson (Smithson. Rep. 1850, 144, 1851) divides the tribe into (1) Crow People, and (2) Minesetperi, or Sapsuckers. These two divisions he subdivides into 12 bands, giving as the names only the English equivalents. Morgan (Anc. Soc., 159, 1877) gives the following bands: Achepabecha, Ahachik, Ashinadea, Ashbochiah, Ashkanena, Booadasha, Esachkabuk, Esekepkabuk, Hokarutcha, Ohotdusha, Oosabotsee, Petchaleruhpaka, and Shiptetza.

The Crows have been officially classified as Mountain Crows and River Crows, the former so called because of their custom

CROW WOMAN

of hunting and roaming near the mountains away from Missouri r., the latter from the fact that they left the mountain section about 1859 and occupied the country along the river. There was no ethnic, linguistic, or other difference between them. The Mountain Crows numbered 2,700 in 1871 and the River Crows 1,400 (Pease in Ind. Aff. Rep., 420, 1871). Present aggregate population, 1,826. See Hayden, Ethnog. and Philol. Mo. Valley, 1862; Maximilian, Trav., 1843; Dorsey in 11th and 15th Reps. B. A. E., 1894, 1897; McGee in 15th Rep. B. A. E., 1897; Simms, Traditions of the Crows, 1903.

**Absaraka.**—Brackett, Absaraka MS. vocab., B. A. E.. 1879. **Absarakos.**—Warren, Nebr. and Ariz., 50, 1875. **Absaroka.**—Schoolcraft, Ind. Tribes, I, 259, 1851. **Ab-sar'-o-kas.**—Morgan in N. Am. Rev., 47, 1870. **Absarokes.**—Schoolcraft, Ind. Tribes, I, 523, 1851. **Absároki.**—Am. Natur., 523, 1882. **Absoroka.**—Drake, Bk. Inds., x, 1848. **A-i-nun'.**—Hayden, Ethnog. and Philol. Mo. Valley, 326, 1862 ('Crow people': Arapaho name). **Ap-sah-ro-kee.**—Bonner, Life of Beckwourth, 298, 1856 (trans. :'sparrowhawk people'). **Ápsárräkă.**—Everette in Pilling, Proof Sheets, 942, 1885. **Apsa-ruka.**—Maximilian, Trav., 174, 1843. **Ap-shâ-roo-kee.**—Orig. Jour. Lewis and Clark, VI, 267, 1905. **Atsharoke.**—Smet, Letters, 51, 1843 (trans. 'crow', attributed to their robberies). **Aub-sa'-ro-ke.**—Hayden, Ethnog. and Philol. Mo. Valley, 402, 1862 (own name: 'anything that flies'). **Corbeaus.**—Orig. Jour. Lewis and Clark, VI, 103, 1905. **Corbeaux.**—Perrin du Lac, Voy. dans les Louisianes, 337, 1805. **Crow Indians.**—Orig. Jour. Lewis and Clark, I, 189, 1904. **De Corbeau.**—Clark (1804) in Orig. Jour. Lewis and Clark, I, 130, 1904. **de Curbo.**—Ibid. **Gens des Corbeau.**—Lewis and Clark, Discov., 41, 1806 (French name). **Hahderuka.**—Maximilian, Trav., 174, 1843 (Mandan name). **Haideroka.**—Ibid. (Hidatsa name). **Hapsa-ro-kay.**—Gebow, Sho-sho-nay Vocab., 8, 1868 (Shoshoni name). **Hapsaroke.**—Burton, City of Saints, 151, 1861. **Hounena.**—A. L. Kroeber, inf'n, 1905 (Arapaho name: 'crow men'). **I-sa-po'-a.**—Hayden, Ethnog. and Philol. Mo. Valley, 264, 1862 (Siksika name). **Issáppo'.**—Tims, Blackfoot Gram. and Dict., 125, 1889 (Siksika name; sing. Issáppo'-ekuŭn). **Kaṅgitoka.**—Iapi Oaye, XIII, no. 9, 33, 1884 (Yankton name: 'raven foes'). **Kaṅ-ġi'-wi-ca-śa.**—Cook, MS. Yankton vocab., B. A. E., 184, 1882. **Ka'-xi.**—Dorsey, Winnebago MS., B. A. E., 1886 (Winnebago name). **Kee'-hât-sâ.**—Orig. Jour. Lewis and Clark, VI, 103, 1905. **Keeheet-sas.**—M'Vickar, Hist. Exped. Lewis and Clark, I, map, 1842. **Kee'-kât'-sâ.**—Lewis and Clark, Discov., 41, 1806. **Kiĥnatsa.**—Matthews, Hidatsa Inds., 39, 1877 (Hidatsa name: 'they who refused the paunch'). **Kikastas.**—Keane in Stanford, Compend., 518, 1878. **Kiqatsa.**—Am. Naturalist, 829, Oct., 1882. **Kite.**—Orig. Jour. Lewis and Clark, I, 130, 1904 (De Corbeau or). **Kokokiwak.**—Gatschet, Fox MS., B. A. E., 1882 (Fox name). **Long Haired Indians.**—Sanford, U. S., clxvii, 1819. **O-e'-tun'-i-o.**—Hayden, Ethnog. and Philol. Mo. Valley, 290, 1862 (Cheyenne name). **O-tun-nee.**—Bonner, Life of Beckwourth, 452, 1856 (Cheyenne name: 'crow'). **Pâr-is-câ-ŏh-pân-gâ.**—Long, Exped. Rocky Mts., II, lxxxiv, 1823 (Hidatsa name: 'crow people'). **Ravin Indians.**—Orig. Jour. Lewis and Clark, I, 220, 1904. **Stéǎmtshi.**—Hoffman in Proc. Am. Philos. Soc., 371, 1886 (Salish name). **Stěmchi.**—Giorda, Kalispelm Dict., pt. 2, 81, 1879 (Kalispel name). **Stémtchi.**—Gatschet, Salish MS., B. A. E., 1884 (Salish name). **Stimk.**—Gatschet, Okinagin MS., B. A. E., 1884 (Okinagan name). **Upsàraukas.**—Browne in Beach, Ind. Miscel., 83, 1877. **Upsaro-cas.**—Keane in Stanford, Compend., 470, 1878. **Ŭp-sâ-rŏ-kâ.**—Long, Exped. Rocky Mts., II, lxxix, 1823 (own name). **Up-shar-look-kar.**—Orig. Jour. Lewis and Clark (1806), V, 21, 1905 (Chopunnish name). **Upsook.**—Schoolcraft, Ind. Tribes, IV, 181, 1854. **Ŭp-sor-ah-kay.**—Anon. Crow MS. vocab., B. A. E. **Yaχ-ka'-a.**—Gatschet, Wandot MS., B. A. E., 1881 (Wyandot name: 'crow').

**Crow Town** (trans. of *Kâgûnyĭ*, 'crow place,' from *kâ'gû* 'crow,' *yĭ* locative).

A former Cherokee town on the left bank of Tennessee r., near the mouth of Raccoon cr., Cherokee co., N. E. Ala. It was one of the so-called "five lower towns" built by those Cherokee, called Chickamauga, who were hostile to the American cause during the Revolutionary period, and whose settlements farther up the river had been destroyed by Sevier and Campbell in 1782. The population of Crow Town and the other lower settlements was augmented by Creeks, Shawnee, and white Tories until it reached a thousand warriors. The towns were destroyed in 1794. See Mooney in 19th Rep. B. A. E., 54, 1900.

**Crow-wing.** Mentioned by Neill (Hist. Minn., 386, 1858) as one of the Chippewa bands that took part in the treaty of 1826. There was a village of the same name at the mouth of Crow Wing r., in N. central Minnesota, which was the home of Hole-in-the-Day in 1838.

**Cuaburidurch.** A former Maricopa rancheria on the Rio Gila, Ariz.; visited by Father Sedelmair in 1744.—Bancroft, Ariz. and N. Mex., 366, 1889.

**Cuactataugh.** A village, probably belonging to the Patuxent, on the E. bank of Patuxent r., in Anne Arundel co., Md., in 1608.—Smith (1629), Virginia, I, map, repr. 1819.

**Cuampis.** Mentioned as a division of the Faraon Apache.
**Cuampes.**—Orozco y Berra, Geog., 59, 1864. **Cuampis.**—Villa Señor y Sanchez, Theatro Am., II, 413, 1748.

**Cuanrabi.** Given as the name of a Hopi village in 1598 in connection with Naybí (Oraibe), Xumupamí (Shumopovi), and Esperiez (Oñate, 1598, in Doc. Inéd., XVI, 137, 1871). Not identified.

**Cubac.** A former rancheria, probably of the Papago, visited by Father Garcés in 1771; situated in the neighborhood of San Francisco Atí, w. from the present Tucson, s. Ariz. Distinct from Tubac.
**Cubac.**—Arricivita (1791) quoted by Bancroft, Ariz. and N. Mex., 387, 1889. **Cubic.**—Orozco y Berra, Geog., 348, 1864.

**Cubero** (from Pedro Rodriguez Cubero, governor of New Mexico, 1697–1703). Formerly a pueblo, established in 1697 by rebel Queres from Santo Domingo, Cieneguilla, and Cochiti, 14 m. N. of Acoma, at the site of the present town of that name in New Mexico. It was probably abandoned in the early part of the 18th century (Bancroft, Ariz. and N. Mex., 221, 1889). According to Laguna tradition Cubero was formerly a pueblo of the Laguna and Acoma people, who were driven out by the Mexican colonists a century ago. (F. W. H.)
**Covera.**—Bancroft, Ariz. and N. Mex., 281, 1889 (or Cubero). **Covero.**—Emory, Recon., 133, 1848. **Cubero.**—Bancroft, op. cit. **Cuvarro.**—Hughes, Doniphan's Exped., 149, 1848. **Govero.**—Eastman, map in Schoolcraft, Ind. Tribes, IV, 24–25, 1854. **Punyeestye.**—Powell in 7th Rep. B. A. E., 83, 1891.

**Punyitsiama.**—Hodge, field notes, B. A. E., 1895 (Laguna name).

**Cubo Guasibavia.** A former rancheria, apparently Papago, visited by Kino and Mange in 1701; situated in a volcanic desert in N. W. Sonora, Mexico, between the Rio Salado and the Gulf of California, 2 m. from the shore.
**Cubo Guasibavia.**—Kino (1701) quoted by Bancroft, No. Mex. States, I, 495, 1884. **Duburcopota.**—Ibid.

**Cucamonga.** A former Gabrieleño rancheria in Los Angeles co., Cal.—Taylor in Cal. Farmer, June 8, 1860.
**Coco Mongo.**—Pac. R. R. Rep., III, pt. 3, 34, 1856. **Cucamungabit.**—Caballeria, Hist. San Bernardino Val., 1905. **Cucomogna.**—Ried (1852) quoted by Taylor in Cal. Farmer, June 8, 1860.

**Cuchendado.** A Texas tribe, the last that Cabeza de Vaca met before he left the Gulf coast to continue inland.—Cabeza de Vaca, Nar. (1542), Smith trans., 137, 1871.

**Cuchillones** (Span: 'knifers,' 'knife people'). A former Costanoan division or village E. of San Francisco bay, Cal. In 1795, according to Engelhardt (Franciscans in Cal., 1897), they became involved in a quarrel with the neophytes of San Francisco mission, whereupon their rancheria was attacked by the Spaniards.
**Cuchian.**—Taylor in Cal. Farmer, Oct. 18, 1861.

**Cuchiyaga** ('place where there has been suffering'). A former Calusa village on one of the keys on the S. W. coast of Florida, about 1570.
**Cuchiaga.**—Fontaneda (ca. 1575) in French, Hist. Coll. La., 2d s., II, 256, 1875. **Cuchiyaga.**—Fontaneda, Mem., Smith trans., 19, 1854.

**Cucho.** An Indian province or settlement of New Mexico, noted, with Cibola (Zuñi), Cicuich (Pecos), and others, in Ramusio, Nav. et Viaggi, III, 455, map, 1565. Probably only another form of Cicuich or Cicuyé, duplication being common in early maps of the region.

**Cuchuta.** A former Opata pueblo and the seat of a Spanish mission founded in 1653; situated in N. E. Sonora, Mexico, near Fronteras; pop. 227 in 1678, 58 in 1730. It was abandoned on account of depredations by the Suma and Jano, warlike Mexican tribes.
**Chu-ui-chu-pa.**—Bandelier in Arch. Inst. Papers, IV, 59, 1890 (same?). **Cuchuta.**—Doc. of 1730 cited by Bancroft, No. Mex. States, I, 514, 1884. **San Francisco Javier Cuchuta.**—Zapata (1678) in Doc. Hist. Mex., 4th s., III, 369, 1857.

**Cuchuveratzi** ('valley or torrent of the fish called matalote [the Gila trout].'—Bandelier). A former Opata settlement a few miles N. E. of Fronteras, on the headwaters of the Rio Bavispe, in the N. E. corner of Sonora, Mexico.—Bandelier in Arch. Inst. Papers, IV, 520, 1892.

**Cuclon.** Given as a Cherokee town in a document of 1799 (Royce in 5th Rep. B. A. E., 144, 1887). Not identified.

**Cucoomphers.** Mentioned as a tribe living in the mountains near Mohave r., S. E. Cal., not speaking the same language as the Mohave or the Paiute (Antisell in Pac. R. R. Rep., VII, 104, 1854). They were perhaps Serranos.
**Cucompners.**—Taylor in Cal. Farmer, Jan. 31, 1862 (misprint).

**Cuculato.** A Yuman tribe living w. of lower Rio Colorado in 1701, when they were visited by Father Kino. Consag (1746) classes them with the gulf or southern divisions of the Cocopa.
**Cuculato.**—Venegas, Hist. Cal., I, 58, 1759. **Cuculutes.**—Taylor in Browne, Res. Pac. Slope, app., 54, 1869.

**Cucurpe.** A Eudeve pueblo, containing also some Tegui Opata, and the seat of a Spanish mission subordinate to Arivechi, founded in 1647; situated on the headwaters of the Rio San Miguel de Horcasitas, the w. branch of the Rio Sonora, Mexico, about 25 m. s. E. of Magdalena. Pop. 329 in 1678, 179 in 1730. It is still inhabited by Opata. (F. W. H.)
**Cucurpe.**—Doc. of 1730 cited by Bancroft, No. Mex. States, I, 513, 1884. **Cucurpo.**—Kino, map (1702) in Stöcklein, Neue Welt-Bott, 74, 1726. **Reyes de Cucurpe.**—Zapata (1678) in Doc. Hist. Mex., 4th s., III, 344, 1857. **Santos Reyes Cucurpe.**—Bancroft, No. Mex. States, I, 245, 1884.

**Cudurimuitac.** A former Maricopa rancheria on the Rio Gila, s. Ariz., visited by Father Sedelmair in 1744.—Bancroft, Ariz. and N. Mex., 366, 1889.

**Cuercomache.** Apparently a division or rancheria of the Yavapai on one of the heads of Diamond cr., near the Grand Canyon of the Colorado, Ariz., in the 18th century. They lived N. E. of the Mohave, of whom they were enemies, and are said to have spoken the same language as the Havasupai. (F. W. H.)
**Yabipais Cuercomaches.**—Garcés (1776), Diary, 231, 410, 1900. **Yavipai cuercomache.**—Orozco y Berra, Geog., 41, 1864 (after Garcés).

**Cuerno Verde** (Span.: 'green horn'). A celebrated Comanche warrior who led various raids against the Spanish settlements along the Rio Grande in New Mexico in the latter part of the 18th century. A force of 645 men, including 85 soldiers and 259 Indians, was led against him by Juan de Anza, governor of New Mexico, in 1778, and in a fight that took place 95 leagues N. E. of Santa Fe, Cuerno Verde was killed, together with 4 of his subchiefs, his "high priest," his eldest son, and 32 of his warriors. His name is commemorated in Greenhorn r. and mt., Colo. (F. W. H.)

**Cueva Pintada** (Span.: 'painted cave,' on account of numerous pictographs on its walls). A natural cave in the s. wall of the Potrero de las Vacas, about 25 m. w. of Santa Fe, N. Mex., anciently used for ceremonial purposes and still one of the points to which ceremonial pilgrimages are made by the Queres. A few cliff-dwellings of the excavated type occur near by in the face of the cliff overlooking the Cañada de la Cuesta Colorada. The small excavated rooms within and about the rim of the cave were probably not used for places of abode, but rather as shrines where idols and other ceremonial objects were deposited. (E. L. H.)

Tsé-ki-a-tán-yi.—Lummis in Scribner's Mag., 96, 1893. **Tsíkyätitans'.**—Hodge, field notes, B. A. E., 1895. **Tzek-iat-a-tanyi.**—Bandelier, in Arch. Inst. Papers, IV, 156, 1892 (Queres name).

**Cuiapaipa.** A rancheria and reservation of 36 Mission Indians in s. California. Their land, consisting of 880 acres, is an unproductive waterless tract 125 m. from Mission Tule River agency.

Cuiapaipa.—Lummis in Out West, XXI, 578, 1904. **Cuyapipa.**—Ind. Aff. Rep., 175, 1902. **Cuyapipe.**—Lummis, op. cit. (given as common but incorrect form). **Guaypipa.**—Ind. Aff. Rep., 146, 1903.

**Cuirimpo.** A Mayo settlement on the Rio Mayo, between Navajoa and Echojoa, s. w. Sonora, Mexico.

Concepcion Cuirimpo.—Orozco y Berra, Geog., 356, 1864. **Corimpo.**—Kino, map (1702) in Stöcklein, Neue Welt-Bott, 1726. **Couirimpo.**—Orozco y Berra, op. cit., map. **Curinghóa.**—Hardy, Travels, 438, 1829.

**Cuitciabaqui.** A former rancheria of the Papago, visited by Father Kino in 1697; situated on the w. bank of the Rio Santa Cruz, in the vicinity of the present Tucson, s. Ariz. According to Father Och a mission was established at the Papago settlement of "Santa Catharina" in 1756 by Father Mittendorf, but he was forced to abandon it, evidently shortly afterward, on account of cruel treatment by the natives. This is doubtless the same. (F. W. H.)

S. Catharina,—Och (1756), Nachrichten, I, 71, 1809. **Sta. Catalina.**—Kino, map (1701) in Bancroft, Ariz. and N.Mex.,360,1889. **Sta Catalina Cuitciabaqui.**—Bernal (1697) quoted by Bancroft, ibid., 356. **Sta. Catarina.**—Mange, ibid., 358. **Sta Catarina Caituagaba.**—Ibid.

**Cuitoas.** A tribe mentioned in connection with the Escanjaques (Kansa). Their habitat and identity are unknown.—Duro, Don Diego de Peñalosa, 57, 1882.

**Cuitoat.** A former settlement, evidently of the Papago, between San Xavier del Bac and Gila r., s. Ariz; visited by Father Garcés in 1775. The name has been confused with Aquitun.

Cuitoa.—Font (1775) quoted by Coues, Garcés Diary, I, 84, 1900. **Cuitoat.**—Arricivita, Crónica Seraf., II, 416, 1792. **Cuytoa.**—Font, op cit. **Quitoac.**—Coues, op cit. **Quitoa.**—Garcés (1775), Diary, 65, 1900. **Quitoac.**—Ibid., 64.

**Cujant.** Apparently a former Papago rancheria in N. w. Sonora, Mexico, between the mouth of the Gila and the settlement of Sonoita in 1771.—Coues, Garcés Diary, 37, 1900.

**Cultus-cod.** A name of the blue, or buffalo, cod (*Ophiodon elongatus*), an important food fish of the Pacific coast from Santa Barbara to Alaska; so called from *cultus*, signifying 'worthless,' in the Chinook jargon, a word ultimately derived from the Chinook dialect of the Chinookan stock and in frequent use on the Pacific coast. (A. F. C.)

**Cumaro.** A Papago village in s. Arizona, near the Sonora border, having 200 families in 1871.

Camaro.—Ind. Aff. Rep., 135, 1865. **Cumaro.**—Taylor in Cal. Farmer, June 19, 1863. **Cumera.**—Browne, Apache Country, 291, 1869 (misquoting Poston). **Cumero.**—Poston in Ind. Aff. Rep. 1863, 385, 1864. **Del Cumero.**—Bailey, ibid., 208, 1858.

**Cummaquid.** A village subject to the Wampanoag, formerly at Cummaquid harbor, Barnstable co., Mass. Qyannough, from whom Hyannis takes its name, was chief in 1621–23. Hyanaes village still existed in 1755. (J. M.)

Cummaquid.—Mourt (1622) in Mass. Hist. Soc. Coll., 2d s., IX, 53, 1822. **Hyanaes.**—Douglass, Summary, I, 188, 1755. **Wayanaes,**—Ibid.

**Cumpa.** Located as a Navaho settlement by Pike (Exped., 3d map, 1810). It is more likely either the name of a locality or a confounding of the Kwiumpus division of the Paiute of s. w. Utah.

**Cumpus.** A Teguima Opata pueblo and the seat of a Spanish mission founded in 1644; situated on the Rio Soyopa (or Moctezuma), N. of Oposura, lat. 30° 20′, N. E. Sonora, Mexico. Pop. 887 in 1678, 146 in 1730.

Asuncion Amipas.—Doc. of 1730 quoted by Bancroft, No. Mex. States, 246, 1884 (or Comupas). **Comupas.**—Ibid. **Cúmpas.**—Hardy, Travels, 437, 1829. **Cumupas.**—Ribas (1645) quoted by Bandelier in Arch. Inst. Papers, III, 58, 1890.

**Cumshewa** (corrupted from *Gô′mshewa*, or *Gô′msewa*, the name of its chief). A former Haida town at the N. entrance of Cumshewa inlet, Queen Charlotte ids., Brit. Col. By the natives it was known as Hlkenul. It was almost entirely occupied by the Stawas-haidagai, q. v. According to John Work's estimate, 1836–41, there were then 20 houses in the place and 286 people. This agrees closely with that still given by Cumshewa people as the former number. Cumshewa was one of the last towns abandoned when all the Indians of this region went to Skidegate.—Swanton, Cont. Haida, 279, 1905.

Casswer.—Downie in Jour. Roy. Geog. Soc., XXXI, 251, 1861. **Comshewars.**—Dunn, Hist. Oreg., 281, 1844. **Crosswer.**—Downie, op. cit. **Cumshawas.**—Scouler in Jour. Roy. Geog. Soc., XI, 219, 1841. **Cumshewa.**—Dawson, Q. Charlotte Ids., 168B, 1880. **Cumshewes.**—Scouler in Jour. Ethnol. Soc. Lond., I, 233, 1848. **Cumshuwaw.**—Can. Ind. Aff., 128, 1879. **Gumshewa.**—Deans, Tales from Hidery, 82, 1899. **Kit-ta-wäs.**—Dawson, Q. Charlotte Ids., 168, 1880 (Tsimshian name). **Koumchaouas.**—Duflot de Mofras, Oreg., I, 337, 1844. **Kumshahas.**—Latham in Trans. Philol. Soc. Lond., 73, 1856. **Kumshewa.**—Dawson, op. cit., 168. **Kumshiwa.**—Tolmie and Dawson, Vocabs. Brit. Col., 26, 1884. **Łkê′nAl.**—Swanton, Cont. Haida, 279, 1905 (Haida name). **Tlkinool.**—Dawson, op. cit., 168 (Haida name).

**Cumumbah.** A division of the Ute, formerly living in Salt Lake, Weber, and Ogden valleys, Utah. They are said to have been a mixture of Ute and Shoshoni, the Ute element largely predominating in their language; pop. 800 in 1885. They are not now separately enumerated.

Cawaupugos.—Collins in Ind. Aff. Rep., 125, 1861.

**Cum-i-um-has.**—Hurt, ibid., 1856, 230, 1857. **Cum-min-tahs.**—Head, ibid., 149, 1868. **Cumpes.**—Pino, Noticias Hist. N. Mex., 83, 1849. **Cumumbah.**—West (1858) in H. R. Ex. Doc. 29, 37th Cong., 2d sess., 113, 1862. **Cum-um-pahs.**—Simpson (1859), Exped. Across Utah, 34, 460, 1876. **Cun-i-um-hahs.**—Hurt in Ind. Aff. Rep. 1856, 228, 1857. **Kumumbar.**—Doty in Ind. Aff. Rep. 1864, 175, 1865. **Treaber Utes.**—Hurt in Ind. Aff. Rep. 1855, 197, 1856 (misprint for *Weber*). **Weber River Yutas.**—Burton, City of Saints, 578, 1861. **Weber-Utes.**—Cooley in Ind. Aff. Rep., 17, 1865.

**Cumuripa.** A Nevome pueblo and the seat of a Spanish mission founded in 1619; situated on the w. tributary of the Rio Yaqui, about 12 m. N. N. E. of Buena Vista, and about 20 m. N. of Cocori, in Sonora, Mexico; pop. 450 in 1678 and 165 in 1730, but the village contained only 4 families in 1849. It is now practically a white Mexican town. The inhabitants, also called Cumuripa, probably spoke a dialect slightly different from the Nevome proper.                (F. W. H.)
**Comoripa.**—Kino, map (1702) in Stöcklein, Neue Welt-Bott, 74, 1726. **Comuripa.**—Rivera (1730) quoted by Bancroft, No. Mex. States, I, 513, 1884. **Cumuripa.**—Escudero, Noticias Son. y Sin., 99, 1849. **S. Pablo Comuripa.**—Zapata (1678) quoted by Bancroft, op. cit., 246. **S. Pedro.**—Sonora Catalogo quoted by Bancroft, ibid.

**Cuñeil.** A tribe, evidently Yuman, described by Garcés in 1775–76 (Diary, 444, 450, 1900) as inhabiting the territory between San Diego, s. Cal., and the mouth of the Rio Colorado. They were friendly with the Cocopa. From their habitat and the similarity in their names they would seem to be identical with the Comeya, but Garcés mentions the latter, under the name Quemayá, as if distinct. On the map of Father Pedro Font (1777), who was a companion of Father Garcés, the Cuñeil are located in N. Lower California, between lat. 31° and 32°. According to Gatschet the name *Kunyil*, or *Kuneyil*, in the Comeya dialect, signifies 'all men,' 'people.'                (F. W. H.)
**Cuñai.**—Orozco y Berra, Geog., 353, 1864. **Cunyeel.**—Font (1777), map in Coues, Garcés Diary, 1900.

**Cunitcacahel** ('water of the great rocks'). A rancheria, probably Cochimi, connected with Purísima mission, which was near the w. coast of Lower California, about lat. 26° 20′.—Doc. Hist. Mex., 4th s., v, 188, 1857.

**Cunquilipinoy.** Mentioned as a pueblo of the province of Atripuy, in the region of the lower Rio Grande, N. Mex., in 1598.—Oñate (1598) in Doc. Inéd., XVI, 115, 1871.

**Cupheag** ('a place shut in,' from *kuppi*, 'closed'). The Algonquian name of Stratford, Fairfield co., Conn. There was probably a village of the same name there before the English settlement in 1639.—Benj. Trumbull, Hist. Conn., I, 109, 1818; J. H. Trumbull, Ind. Names Conn., 13, 1881.

**Cuppunaugunnit.** Mentioned as if a Pequot village in 1637, probably in New London co., Conn.

**Cuppunaugunnit.**—Williams (1637) in Mass. Hist. Soc. Coll., 4th s., VI, 201, 1852. **Cuppunnaugunnit.**—Ibid.

**Cups.**   See *Receptacles*.

**Cupstones.** Blocks of stone unworked except for small cavities made in them. These cups vary from a rough pecking, probably the initial stage, to smooth, hemispherical depressions 2 in. in diameter; at the bottom of many of the latter is a secondary pit as though made with a flint drill or gouge. They range in number from 1 to 20, though rarely one stone may contain 50 or 100. In a majority of cases they are of sandstone. On irregular blocks the pits are on one side only, extending over less than half the surface; on flat slabs they are always on both sides. Many theories have been advanced to account for these cupstones; but while any suggestion may apply to a few specimens, it will not fit the majority. There is a prevalent idea that they were used for cracking nuts in, for which reason the blocks are sometimes called nutstones; but only casual inspection is necessary to prove this belief incorrect. The holes are not often on the same level, and in any case it would be necessary to pick the stone up and turn it over each time it was used. They are also supposed to be for grinding paint, or to steady drills, spindles, or firesticks; but it is evident that only one pit could

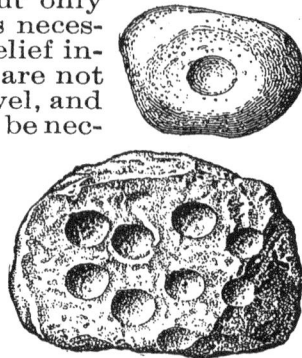

CUPSTONES; OHIO. (1-10)

be used at a time for any of these purposes. Undoubtedly the real explanation awaits determination. Cupstones are the most abundant and widespread of the larger relics. They not only occur on many village sites but are scattered at random over the country, often in places where diligent search fails to disclose aboriginal relics of any other form. See *Problematical objects*. Consult Fowke in 13th Rep. B. A. E., 1896; Rau in Cont. N. A. Ethnol., v, 1881.                (G. F.)

**Cuquiarachi.** A former pueblo of the Teguima Opata and the seat of a Spanish mission founded in 1653; situated about 6 m. southward from Fronteras, N. E. Sonora, Mexico. Pop. 380 in 1678; 76 in 1730. When visited by Bartlett in 1850 it was deserted, apparently on account of the Apache.                (F. W. H.)
**Cocuiárachi.**—Bartlett, Personal Narrative, I, 273, 1854. **Cuquiarachi.**—Bandelier in Arch. Hist. Papers, IV, 529, 1892 (wrongly identified with Fronteras). **Cuquiaratzi.**—Orozco y Berra, Geog., 343, 1864. **Cuquiarichi.**—Mange (ca. 1700) quoted by Bancroft, No. Mex. States, I, 233, 1884. **Cuquiurachi.**—Hamilton, Mexican Handbook, 47, 1883. **San Ignacio Cuquiarachi.**—Zapata (1678) quoted by Bancroft, op. cit., 246.

**Curepo.**—A Chinipa rancheria in Chihuahua, Mexico, in 1601.—Bancroft, No. Mex. States, I, 211, 1886.

**Curly Head** (*Babisigandibe*). A chief of the Mississippi (or Sandy lake) Chippewa, born about the middle of the 18th century, on the s. shore of L. Superior. He removed to the upper Mississippi about 1800 with a number of the Crane (Businausee) gens, of which he was a member, and settled near the site of the present Crow Wing, Minn. Here his band was augmented by the bravest warriors and hardiest hunters of the eastern Chippewa until it became a bulwark against the Sioux raiders who hitherto had harried the Chippewa as far as the shores of L. Michigan. The white traders lavished gifts upon him, which he freely shared with his followers. His lodge was always well supplied with meat, and the hungry were welcomed. The peace and friendship that generally prevailed between the white pioneers and the Chippewa were due chiefly to Curly Head's restraining influence. He was visited in 1805 by Lieut. Z. M. Pike, who passed the winter in his neighborhood. He died while returning from the conference, known as the treaty of Prairie du Chien, held Aug. 19, 1825, in which his name appears as "Babaseekeendase, Curling Hair." According to Warren (Hist. Ojibway, 47, 1885) he was both civil and war chief of his people.

**Cusabo.** A collective term used to designate the Combahee, Coosa, Edisto, Etiwaw, Kiawaw, St Helena, Stono, and Wapoo Indians, formerly living between Charleston, S. C., and Savannah r. Their territory was the Chicora of Ayllon and other early Spanish adventurers, and it is probable that some, if not most of the tribes mentioned, belonged to the Muskhogean stock. They early became reduced through the raids of Spanish slavers and the connivance of the colonists. In Jan., 1715, they were reported to number 295 inhabitants in 4 villages, but during the Yamasi war in that year they and other tribes were expelled or exterminated. See Mooney, Siouan Tribes of the East, Bull. B. A. E., 86, 1894.

Corsaboys.—Doc. of 1719 in Rivers, Hist. S. C., 93, 1874. Cusabees.—Rivers, Hist. S. C., 38, 1856. Cussobos.—Simms, Hist. S. C., 56, 1860.

**Cusarare** (corruption of *Usárare*, from *usáka*, 'eagle'). A small Tarahumare rancheria situated a short distance s. of Bocoyna, on the E. slope of the Sierra Madre, in lat. 28°, w. Chihuahua, Mex.—Lumholtz (1) in Scribner's Mag., XVI, 40, 1894; (2) Unknown Mex., I, 136, 1902.

**Cusawatee** (*Kúsăwetíyĭ*, 'old Creek place'). A former important Cherokee settlement on lower Coosawatee r., in Gordon co., Ga.

**Coosawatee.**—Mooney, in 19th Rep. B. A. E., 526, 1900. **Coosawaytee.**—Doc. of 1799 quoted by Royce in 5th Rep. B. A. E., 144, 1887. **Kúsăwetíyĭ.**—Mooney, op. cit. (proper Cherokee name). **Tensawattee.**—Doc. quoted by Mooney, ibid.

**Cuscarawaoc** ('place of making white beads.'—Tooker). A division of the Nanticoke; mentioned by Capt. John Smith as a tribe or people living at the head of Nanticoke r., in Maryland and Delaware, and numbering perhaps 800 in 1608. Their language was different from that of the Powhatan, Conestoga, and Atquanachuke. Heckewelder believed them to be a division of the Nanticoke, the correctness of which Bozman (Maryland, I, 112–121, 1837) has clearly demonstrated. For a discussion of the name see Tooker, Algonquian Series, IX, 65, 1901.　　　　　　　　　　(J. M.)

Cuscarawaoke.—Simons in Smith (1629), Virginia, I, 178, repr. 1819. Cuskarawaocks.—Bozman, Maryland, I, 110, 1837. Huokarawaocks.—Schoolcraft, Ind. Tribes, VI, 131, 1857. Kuscarawaoks.—Smith (1629), op. cit., 74. Kuscarawocks.—Brinton, Lenape Leg., 23, 1885. Kuskaranaooke.—Prier in Purchas, Pilgrimes, IV, 1713, 1626. Kuskarawack.—Smith's map (1615) in Purchas, ibid., p. 1692. Nuskarawaoks.—Strachey (ca. 1612), Virginia, 41, 1849.

**Cuscatomiu.** See *Kiskitomas.*

**Cuscowilla.** The principal Seminole town on Cuscowilla lake, Alachua co., Fla. It was established by Creeks from Oconee, Ga., who first settled at Alachua Old Town but abandoned it on account of its unhealthfulness.—Bartram (Travels, 1791) found 30 houses there in 1775.

**Cushaw.** See *Cashaw.*

**Cushna.** A division of the Maidu on the upper waters of the s. fork of Yuba r., Sierra co., Cal.; pop. about 600 in 1850.—Ind. Aff. Rep., 124, 1850; Taylor in Cal. Farmer, May 31, 1861.

**Cushook.** A band residing in 1806 on the E. bank of Willamette r., Oreg., just below the falls, their number estimated at 650. Probably a branch of the Chinookan tribe of Clowwewalla.

Cashhooks.—Orig. Jour. Lewis and Clark, IV, 233, 1905. Cashook.—Lewis and Clark, Exped., II, 216, 1814. Clishhooks.—Cass (1834) quoted by Schoolcraft, Ind. Tribes, III, 609, 1853. Cushhooks.—Lewis and Clark, Exped., II, 474, 1814. Cushhouks.—Nouv. Ann. Voy., XII, map, 1821.

**Cushtusha** (*Kashtih-asha*, 'fleas are there'). A former Choctaw town on the s. side of Cushtusha cr., about 3 m. s. w. of the old town of Yazoo, Neshoba co., Miss.—Halbert in Miss. Hist. Soc. Publ., VI, 431, 1902.

Castachas.—Charlevoix, Hist. Nouv. France, Shea ed., VI, 104, 1872. Cuctachas.—Romans, Florida, map, 1775. Custachas.—West Fla. map, ca. 1775. Custusha.—Halbert in Ala. Hist. Soc. Trans., 73, 1899.

**Cusihuiriachic** ('where the upright pole is'). A former Tarahumare settlement, now a white Mexican town, on the headwaters of the Rio San Pedro, lat. 28° 12′, long. 106° 50′, w. central Chihuahua, Mexico.

Cusihuirachic.—Orozco y Berra, Geog., map, 1864. Cusihuiriachic.—Lumholtz in Scribner's Mag., XVI, 32; July, 1894.

**Cussewago.** A village of the Seneca and of remnants of other wandering tribes, situated in 1750 where Ft Le Bœuf was afterward built, on the site of the present Waterford, Erie co., Pa.

Casewago.—N. Y. Doc. Col. Hist., X, 259, 1858. Cussewago.—Gist (1753) in Mass. Hist. Soc. Coll., 3d s., v, 104, 1836.

**Custaloga's Town.** The Delawares had two villages, each known as Custaloga's Town, from the name of its chief, probably one and the same person. The first village was near French cr., opposite Franklin, Venango co., Pa., in 1760; the other was on Walhonding r., near Killbucks cr., in Coshocton co., Ohio, in 1766. The chief of this second village was chief of the Unalachtigo Delawares, and had probably removed from the first village about 1763. The name is also written Costeloga, Custalaga, Custologa, Custologo, Kustaloga. (J. M.)

**Cutalchich.** A tribe or subtribe that visited the Avavare, in whose country Cabeza de Vaca (Smith trans., 72–74, 84, 1851) stayed during the latter part of his sojourn in Texas in 1528–34. They spoke a language different from that of the Avavare, and lived inland near the Maliacon and the Susola. Learning of Cabeza de Vaca's success in treating the sick, the Cutalchich applied to him for help, and in return for his services gave "flints a palm and a half in length, with which they cut," and which "were of high value among them." They showed their gratitude also by leaving with him, as they departed, their supply of prickly pears, one of their staple foods. Although the Cutalchich dwelt in the region occupied in part by agricultural Caddoan tribes, they seem not to have cultivated the soil, but to have subsisted on roots and fruits, as did the tribes nearer the coast. Their ethnic relations are not determined. (A. C. F.)

Cutalchulches.—Cabeza de Vaca (1529), Smith trans., 137, 1871. Cutalches.—Ibid., note, 127. Cutalchiches.—Ibid., note, 139. Cuthalchuches.—Ibid., 121.

**Cutans.** A name used by Rafinesque (introd. to Marshall, Ky., I, 23, 1824) for the people of an imaginary prehistoric empire of North America.

**Cutchogue.** The present Cutchogue in Suffolk co., Long id., N. Y., occupies the site of a former Indian village, probably of the same name, which was in the Corchaug territory.—Thompson, Long Island, I, 392, 1843.

Catsjajock.—Stuyvesant (1647) in N. Y. Doc. Col. Hist., XIV, 79, 1883. Catsjeyick.—Doc. of 1645, ibid., 60.

**Cuteco.** A former division of the Varohio in w. Chihuahua, Mexico, probably in Chinipas valley.—Orozco y Berra, Geog., 58, 1864.

**Cutespa.** A Calusa village on the s. w.

coast of Florida, about 1570.—Fontaneda Memoir (ca. 1575), Smith trans., 19, 1854.

**Cutha Aimethaw.** A former Choctaw village placed by Romans (Florida, map, 1775) in the present Kemper co., Miss., on the headwaters of an affluent of Sukinatcha cr.

**Cuthi Uckehaca** (possibly a corruption of *Kati Oka-hikia*, 'thorn-bush standing in water'). A former Choctaw town which seems to have been near the mouth of Parker cr., which flows into Petickfa cr., Kemper co., Miss.—Halbert in Miss. Hist. Soc. Publ., VI, 426, 1902.

Cuthi Uskehaca.—Romans, Florida, map, 1775.

**Cuts.** An unidentified band of the Sihasapa.—Culbertson in Smithson. Rep. 1850, 141, 1851.

Des Coupes.—Culbertson, ibid.

**Cuttatawomen.** According to Capt. John Smith, the name of 2 tribes of the Powhatan confederacy in Virginia in 1608, each having a principal village of the same name. One village was on the Rappahannock, at Corotoman r., in Lancaster co., and the tribe numbered about 120. The other was about Lamb cr., on the Rappahannock, in King George co., and the tribe numbered about 80. (J. M.)

Cuttatawoman.—Smith (1629), Virginia, I, map, repr. 1819. Cuttatawomen.—Smith, ibid., 117. Cuttawomans.—Jefferson, Notes, 139, 1801.

**Cuyamaca.** A former Diegueño village about 50 m. E. N. E. from San Diego mission, s. Cal.—Hayes (1850) quoted by Bancroft, Nat. Races, I, 458, 1882.

**Cuyamunque.** A former Tewa pueblo on Tesuque cr., between Tesuque and Pojoaque, about 15 m. N. W. of Santa Fé, N. Mex. With Nambe and Jacona the population was about 600 in 1680, when the Pueblo rebellion, which continued with interruptions until 1696, resulted in the abandonment of the village in the latter year and the settlement of its surviving inhabitants in the neighboring Tewa pueblos. In 1699 the site of Cuyamunque was granted to Alonzo Rael de Aguilar, and regranted in 1731 to Bernardino de Sena, who had married the widow of Jean l'Archévèque, the murderer of La Salle. It is now a "Mexican" hamlet. See Bandelier in Arch. Inst. Papers, IV, 85, 1892; Meline, Two Thousand Miles, 231, 1867. (F. W. H.)

Coyamanque.—Cope in Ann. Rep. Wheeler Surv., app. LL, 76, 1875. Ouya Mangue.—Vetancurt, Teatro Mex., III, 317, 1871. Cuyamanque.—Domenech, Deserts, I, 443, 1860. Cuyammique.—Vargas (1692) quoted by Bancroft, Ariz. and N. Mex., 199, 1889. Cuyamonge.—Pullen in Harper's Weekly, 771, Oct. 4, 1890. Cuya-mun-ge.—Bandelier in Ritch, New Mexico, 201, 1885. Cuyamunguè.—Buschmann, Neu-Mexico, 230, 1858. Cuyamunque.—Bandelier in Arch. Inst. Papers, I, 23, 1881. Cuyo, Monque.—Davis, El Gringo, 88, 1857. Ku Ya-mung-ge.—Bandelier in Arch. Inst. Papers, IV, 85, 1892.

**Cuyamus.** A Chumashan village formerly on the mesa near Santa Barbara, Cal.—Taylor in Cal. Farmer, Apr. 24, 1863.

**Cuyuhasomi** ('fish people,' from *cuyu* 'fish,' *hasomi* 'people'). A phratry of the ancient Timucua of Florida.—Pareja (1617) quoted by Gatschet in Proc. Am. Philos. Soc., XVII, 492, 1878.

**Cuyuhasomiaroqui.** A clan of the Cuyuhasomi phratry of the Timucua of Florida.—Pareja (1617) quoted by Gatschet in Proc. Am. Philos. Soc., XVII, 492, 1878.

**Cuyuhasomiele.** A clan of the Cuyuhasomi phratry of the Timucua of Florida.—Pareja (1617) quoted by Gatschet in Proc. Am. Philos. Soc., XVII, 492, 1878.

**Daahl.** The Earth or Sand clan of Jemez pueblo, N. Mex. A corresponding clan existed also at the former related pueblo of Pecos.
Daáhl.—Hodge in Am. Anthrop., IX, 350, 1896 (Pecos form). Dâ′ât‘hl.—Ibid. (Jemez form). Pâh-käh-täh.—Hewett in Am. Anthrop., n. s., VI, 431, 1904 (Pecos form).

**Dachizhozhin** ('renegades'). A division of the Jicarillas whose original home was around the present Jicarilla res., N. N. Mex.
Dáchizh-ó-zhĭ′n.—Mooney, field notes, B. A. E., 1897. Náchizh-ó-zhĭ′n.—Ibid.

**Dadens** (*Da′dens*). A Haida town on the s. coast of North id., fronting Parry passage, Queen Charlotte ids., British Columbia. It was the chief town of the Yaku-lanas previous to their migration to Prince of Wales id.; afterward the site was used as a camp, but, it is said, was not reoccupied as a town. It figures prominently in accounts of early voyagers, from which it would appear either that it was still occupied in their time or that it had only recently been abandoned.　　　(J. R. S.)
Da′dens lnagā′-i.—Swanton, Cont. Haida, 281, 1905 (lnagā′-i = 'town'). Tartanee.—Douglas quoted by Dawson, Queen Charlotte Ids., 162, 1880.

**Dadjingits** (*Dadjĭ′ñgits*, 'common-hat village'). A Haida town on the N. shore of Bearskin bay, Skidegate inlet, Queen Charlotte ids., Brit. Col. It was occupied for a brief time by part of the Gitins of Skidegate, afterward known as Nasagas-haidagai, during a temporary difference with the other branch of the group.—Swanton, Cont. Haida, 279, 1905.

**Dagangasels** (*Dāgañasėls*, 'common food-steamers'). A subdivision of the Kona-kegawai of the Haida. They were of low social rank, and the name was used probably in contempt.—Swanton, Cont. Haida, 273, 1905.

**Daggers.** Sharp-pointed, edged implements, intended to thrust and stab. Daggers of stone do not take a prominent place among the weapons of the northern tribes, and they are not readily distinguished from knives, poniards, lance-heads, and projectile points, save in rare cases where the

DAGGER OF STEEL; TLINGIT (NIBLACK)

handle was worked in a single piece with the blade. Bone was well suited for the making of stabbing implements and the long 2-pointed copper poniard of the region of the great lakes was a formidable weapon. The exact use of this group of objects as employed in prehistoric times must remain largely a matter of conjecture. The introduction of iron soon led to the making of keen-pointed knives, as the dirk, and among the N. W. coast tribes the manufacture of broad-bladed daggers of copper and iron or steel, modeled after European and Asiatic patterns, became an important industry.

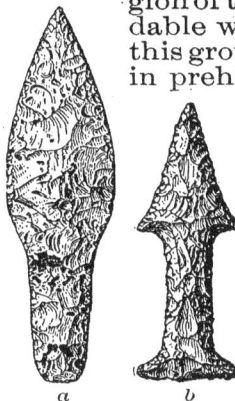

STONE DAGGERS. *a*, OF CHALCEDONY; ILLINOIS; LENGTH 10 IN. *b*, OF FLINT; ALABAMA; LENGTH 7 1-4 IN.

For daggers of stone consult Moorehead, Prehist. Impls., 1900; Rau in Smithson. Cont., XXII, 1876; Thruston, Antiq. of Tenn., 1897; for metal daggers, see Niblack in Rep. Nat. Mus. 1888, 1890.
　　　(W. H. H.)

**Dahet** (*Daxē′t*, 'fallen stunned'). A former Tlingit village in the Sitka country, Alaska.　　　(J. R. S.)

**Dahnohabe** ('stone mountain'). A Pomo village said to have been on the w. side of Clear lake, Lake co., Cal., with 70 inhabitants in 1851.
Dah-no-habe.—Gibbs (1851) in Schoolcraft, Ind. Tribes, III, 109, 1853. Do-no-ha-be.—McKee (1851) in Sen. Ex. Doc. 4, 32d Cong., spec. sess., 136, 1853.

**Dahoon.** An American holly, *Ilex dahoon*. The term was first applied by Catesby (1722–26), probably from one of the Indian languages of the s. Atlantic states, though nothing definite seems to be known about the word.　　　(A. F. C.)

**Dahua** (*Da′xua*). A Haida town N. of Lawn hill, at the mouth of Skidegate inlet, Queen Charlotte id., Brit. Col. It belonged to the Djahui-skwahladagai, and was noted in legend as the place where arose the troubles which resulted in separating the later w. coast Indians from those of Skidegate inlet. It was also the scene of a great battle between the inlet people and those of the w. coast, in which the latter were defeated.—Swanton, Cont. Haida, 279, 1905.

**Daiyu** (*Daiyū′*, 'giving-food-to-others town'). A Haida town on Shingle bay, E. of Welcome point, Moresby id., w. Brit. Col. It was owned by a small band, the Daiyuahl-lanas or Kasta-kegawai, which received one of its names from that of the town.—Swanton, Cont. Haida, 279, 1905.

**Daiyuahl-lanas** (*Daiyū ał lā′nas*, 'people of the town where they always give away food'). A division of the Raven

clan of the Haida, named from one of its towns. A second name for the band was Kasta-kegawai (Q!ā′sta qē′gawa-i), 'those born at Skidegate cr.' It formerly occupied the coast between Alliford bay and Cumshewa point, but is now nearly extinct.—Swanton, Cont. Haida, 269, 1905.
**K·āstak·ē′rauāi.**—Boas, Fifth Rep. N. W. Tribes Canada, 26, 1889. **Q!ā′sta qē′gawa-i.**—Swanton, op. cit. **Tai′ōtl lā′nas.**—Boas, Twelfth Rep. N. W. Tribes Canada, 24, 1898.

**Dakanmanyin** ('walks shining'). A subgens of the Han gens of the Kansa.
**Dakaⁿ manyiⁿ.**—Dorsey in 15th Rep. B. A. E., 231, 1897.

**Dakota** ('allies'). The largest division of the Siouan family, known commonly as Sioux, according to Hewitt a French-Canadian abbreviation of the Chippewa *Nadowe-is-iw*, a diminutive of *nadowe*, 'an adder,' hence 'an enemy.' *Nadoweisiw-eg* is the diminutive plural. The diminutive singular and plural were applied by the Chippewa to the Dakota, and to the Huron to distinguish them from the Iroquois proper, the true 'adders' or 'enemies.' According to Chippewa tradition the name was first applied to a body of Indians living on an island somewhere E. of Detroit (W. Jones).

Dakota, Nakota, Lakota are the names used by themselves, in the Santee, Yankton, and Teton dialects respectively. J. O. Dorsey, in his classification of the Siouan languages, divides the Dakota group into 4 dialects: Santee, Yankton, Assiniboin, and Teton. The Assiniboin, however, constitute a separate tribe. The close linguistic relation of the divisions—the differences being largely dialectic—indicates that they are branches of an original group, the development probably being augmented by incorporations. At the time of Long's expedition (1825), when the bands were still near their respective localities, the country inhabited by the group was, according to him, bounded by a curved line extending E. of N. from Prairie du Chien on the Mississippi, so as to include all the E. tributaries of the Mississippi, to the first branch of Chippewa r.; thence by a line running w. of N. to Spirit lake; thence westwardly to Crow Wing r., Minn., and up that stream to its head; thence westwardly to Red r., and down that stream to Pembina; thence southwestwardly to the E. bank of the Missouri near the Mandan villages; thence down the Missouri to a point probably not far from Soldiers r.; thence E. of N. to Prairie du Chien, Wis. This tract includes the territory between lat. 42° to 49°, and long. 90° 30′ to 99° 30′, but omits entirely the vast region occupied by the various bands of the Teton Sioux w. of the Missouri from the Yellowstone southward to the Platte.

The first positive historical mention of this people is found in the Jesuit Relation for 1640, where it is said that in the vicinity of the "Nation des Puans" (Winnebago) are the "Nadvesiv" (Nadowessioux), "Assinipour" (Assiniboin), etc. In the Jesuit Relation for 1642 it is stated that the Nadouessis are situated some 18 days' journey N. w. or w. of Sault Ste Marie, "18 days farther away." According to their tradition, the Chippewa first encountered the Dakota at Sault Ste Marie. Dr Thomas S. Williamson, who spent several years among the Dakota of the Mississippi, says (Schoolcraft, Ind. Tribes, I, 247, 1851) that they claimed to have resided near the confluence of the Mississippi and Minnesota rs. for several generations; that before they came to the Mississippi they lived at Mille lac, which they call Isanta-mde, 'knife lake,' from which is probably derived the name Isanyati, 'dwelling at the knife,' by which the Dakota of the Missouri call those who lived on Mississippi and Minnesota rs. Rev. A. L. Riggs asserts that Isanyati, from which Santee is derived, was properly applied only to the Mdewakanton, which would seem to identify this tribe with Hennepin's Issati. He also remarks that most of these Indians with whom he conversed could trace their history no further back than to Mille lac, but that some could tell of wars they had with the Chippewa before they went thither and trace their history back to Lake of the Woods. He adds that all their traditions show that they came from the N. E. and have been moving toward the s. w., which would imply that they came from some point N. of the lakes. Du Luth (1678) and Hennepin (1680) found some of the Dakota at and in the region of Mille lac, named by the latter in his text L. Issati, and in his autograph map L. Buade. These included the Mdewakanton, part of the Sisseton, part if not all of the Wahpeton, and probably the Wahpekute. Hennepin's map places the Issati (Mdewakanton) close to L. Buade, the Oüa de Battons (Wahpeton) a little to the N. E. of the lake, the Hanctons (Yankton or Yanktonai) some distance to the N., and the Tinthonha or Gens des Prairies (Teton) to the w., on the upper Mississippi. If this may be considered even approximately correct, it indicates that parts at least of some of the western tribes still lingered in the region of the upper Mississippi, and indeed it is well known that very few of the Sioux crossed the Missouri before 1750. Mallery's winter count (10th Rep. B. A. E., 266, 1894) places their entrance into the Black-hills, from which they dispossessed the Cheyenne and the Kiowa, at about 1765. Referring to their location in the latter part of the 17th century, Hennepin (Descr. La., Shea trans., 201, 1880) says: "Eight leagues above St. Anthony of Padua's falls on the right, you find the river of the Issati or Nadoussion [Rum r.], with a very narrow mouth, which you can ascend to the N. for about 70 leagues to L. Buade [Mille lac] or of the Issati where it rises. . . . In the neighborhood of L. Buade are many other lakes, whence issue several rivers, on the banks of which live the Issati, Nadouessans, Tinthonha (which means 'prairiemen'), Ouadebathon River People, Chongaskethon Dog, or Wolf tribe (for *chonga* among these nations means dog or wolf), and other tribes, all which we comprise under the name Nadonessiou." Here the Issati are distinguished from the Tinthonha (Teton), Ouadebathon (Wahpeton), Chongaskethon (Sisseton), and Nadouessans (perhaps the Wahpekute). From the time of Le Sueur's visit (1700) the Dakota became an important factor in the history of the N. W. Their gradual movement westward was due chiefly to the persistent attacks of the Chippewa, who received firearms from the French, while they themselves were forced to rely almost wholly on bows and arrows.

Lieut. Gorrell, an English officer, mentions their condition in this respect as late as 1763 (Wis. Hist. Soc. Coll., I, 36, 1855): "This day, 12 warriors of the Sous came here [Green Bay, Wis.]. It is certainly the greatest nation of Indians ever yet found. Not above 2,000 of them were ever armed with fire-arms, the rest depending entirely on bows and arrows and darts, which they use with more skill than any other Indian nation in North America. They can shoot the wildest and largest beasts in the woods at 70 or 100 yds. distance. They are remarkable for their dancing; the other nations take the fashion from them." He mentions that they were always at war with the Chippewa. On the fall of the French dominion the Dakota at once entered into friendly relations with the English. It is probable that the erection of trading posts on L. Pepin enticed them from their old residence on Rum r. and Mille lac, for it was in this section that Carver (1766) found those of the eastern group. He says (Travels, 37, 1796): "Near the river St. Croix reside three bands of the Naudowessie Indians, called the River bands. This nation is composed, at present, of 11 bands. They were originally 12, but the Assinipoils [Assiniboin] some years ago, revolting, and separating themselves from the others, there remain only at this time 11. Those I met here are termed the River bands, because they chiefly dwell near the banks of this river: the other 8 are generally distinguished by the title,

Naudowessies of the Plains, and inhabit a country that lies more to the westward. The names of the former are Nehogatawonahs, the Mawtawbauntowahs, and Shahsweentowahs." During an investigation by Congress in 1824 of the claim by Carver's heirs to a supposed grant of land, including the site of St Paul, made to Carver by the Sioux, Gen. Leavenworth stated that the Dakota informed him that the Sioux of the Plains never owned any land E. of the Mississippi.

During the Revolution and the War of 1812 the Dakota adhered to the English. There was, however, one chief who sided with the United States in 1812; this was Tohami, known to the English as Rising Moose, a chief of the Mdewakanton who joined the Americans at St Louis, where he was commissioned by Gen. Clark. By the treaty of July, 1815, peace between the Dakota and the United States was established, and by that of Aug., 1825, the boundary lines between them and the United States and between them and the various tribes in the N. W. were defined. The boundaries of the Sioux and other northwestern tribes were again defined by the treaty of Sept. 17, 1851. Their most serious outbreak against the whites occurred in Minnesota under Little Crow in 1862, when about 700 white settlers and 100 soldiers lost their lives and some of the most horrible cruelties known to history were committed by the Indians; but the entire Dakota group never participated unitedly in any of the modern wars or outbreaks. The bands engaged in the uprising mentioned were the Mdewakanton, Wahpekute, Wahpeton, and Sisseton. Although this revolt was quelled and the Sioux were compelled for a time to submit to the terms offered them, a spirit of unrest continued to prevail. By the treaty of 1867 they agreed to relinquish to the United States all their territory s. of Niobrara r., w. of long. 104°, and N. of lat. 46°, and promised to retire to a large reservation in s. w. Dakota before Jan. 1, 1876. On the discovery of gold in the Black-hills the rush of miners thither became the occasion of another outbreak. This war was participated in by such well-known chiefs as Sitting Bull, Crazy Horse, Spotted Tail, Rain-in-the-face, Red Cloud, American Horse, Gall, and Crow King, and was rendered famous by the cutting off of Maj. Gen. George A. Custer and five companies of cavalry on the Little Bighorn, June 25, 1876. A final rising during the Ghost-dance excitement of 1890–91 was subdued by Gen N. A. Miles.

The Dakota are universally conceded to be of the highest type, physically, mentally, and probably morally, of any of the western tribes. Their bravery has never been questioned by white or Indian, and they conquered or drove out every rival except the Chippewa. They are educated in their own language, and through the agency of missionaries of the type of Riggs, Williamson, Cleveland, and Cook, many books in the Dakota language have been printed, and papers in Dakota are issued regularly. (See Pilling, Bibliog. Siouan Lang., Bull. B. A. E., 1887.)

Socially, the Dakota originally consisted of a large number of local groups or bands, and, although there was a certain tendency to encourage marriage outside the band, these divisions were not true gentes, remembered blood relationship, according to Clark, being the only bar to marriage. Personal fitness and popularity determined chieftainship more than heredity, but where descent played any part it was usually from father to son. The tipi might belong to either parent and was obtained by that parent through some ancestor who had had its character revealed in a dream or who had captured it in war. The authority of the chief was limited by the band council, without whose approbation little or nothing could be accomplished. War parties were recruited by individuals who had acquired reputation as successful leaders, while the shamans formulated ceremonial dances and farewells for them. Polygamy was common, the wives occupying different sides of the tipi. Remains of the dead were usually, though not invariably, placed on scaffolds.

Early explorers usually distinguished these people into an Eastern or Forest and a Western or Prairie division. A more complete and accurate classification, one which is also recognized by the people themselves, is the following:

1. Mdewakanton; 2. Wahpeton; 3. Wahpekute; 4. Sisseton; 5. Yankton; 6. Yanktonai; 7. Teton, each of which is again subdivided into bands and subbands. These seven main divisions are often known as "the seven council fires." The first four named together constitute the Isanyati, Santee, or eastern division, of which the Mdewakanton appear to be the original nucleus, and speak one dialect. Their home was in Minnesota prior to the outbreak of 1862. The Yankton and Yanktonai—the latter subdivided into (a) Upper and (b) Hunkpatina or Lower—held the middle territory between L. Traverse and Missouri r. in E. Dakota, and together spoke one dialect, from which the Assiniboin was an offshoot. The great Teton division, with its subdivisions, Upper and Lower Brulé, Oglala, Sans Arcs, Sihasapa or Blackfoot, Miniconjou, Oohenonpa or Two Kettle, Hunkpapa, etc., and comprising together more than half the nation, held the whole

tribal territory w. of the Missouri and spoke one dialect.

The following are names of divisions, groups, or bands that are spoken of as pertaining to the Dakota. Some of these have not been identified; others are mere temporary geographical or local bands: Black Tiger, Broken Arrows, Cascarba, Cazazhita, Chanshushka, Chasmuna, Cheokhba, Cheyenne Sioux, Congewichacha, Farmer's band, Fire Lodge, Flandreau Indians, Gens du Large, Grand Saux, Grey Eagle, Late Comedu, Lean Bear, Long Sioux, Menostamenton, Micacoupsiba, Minisha, Neecoweegee, Nehogatawonahs, Newastarton, Northern Sioux, Ocatameneton, Ohankanska, Oughetgeodatons, Oujatespouitons, Peshlaptechela, Pineshow, Psinchaton, Psinoumanitons, Psinoutanhinhintons, Rattling Moccasin, Red Leg's band, Redwood, Sioux of the Broad Leaf, Sioux of the Des Moyan, Sioux of the East, Sioux of the Meadows, Sioux of the West, Sioux of the Woods, Sioux of the Lakes, Sioux of the River St Peter's, Souon, Star band, Talonapi, Tashunkeeota, Tateibombu's band, Tatkannai, Ticicitan, Touchouasintons, Traverse de Sioux, Upper Sioux, Waktonila, White Cap Indians, White Eagle band, Wiattachechah.

In 1904 the Dakota were distributed among the following agencies and school superintendencies: Cheyenne River (Miniconjou, Sans Arcs, and Two Kettle), 2,477; Crow Creek (Lower Yanktonai), 1,025; Ft Totten school (Sisseton, Wahpeton, and Pabaksa), 1,013; Riggs Institute (Santee), 279; Ft Peck (Yankton), 1,116; Lower Brulé (Lower Brulé), 470; Pine Ridge (Oglala), 6,690; Rosebud (Brulé, Wagluhe, Lower Brulé, Northern, Two Kettle, and Wazhazha), 4,977; Santee (Santee), 1,075; Sisseton (Sisseton and Wahpeton), 1,908; Standing Rock (Sihasapa, Hunkpapa, and Yanktonai), 3,514; Yankton (Yankton), 1,702; under no agency (Mdewakanton in Minnesota), 929; total, 26,175. Including the Assiniboin the total for those speaking the Dakota language is 28,780. A comparison of these figures with those taken in previous years indicates a gradual decline in numbers, but not so rapid a decrease as among most North American tribes.

**Ab-boin-ee Sioux.**—Ramsey in Ind. Aff. Rep., 83, 1850. **Ab-boin-ug.**—Warren in Minn. Hist. Coll., v, 36, 1885 (Chippewa name: 'roasters,' from their custom of torturing foes). **Abbwoi-nug.**—Tanner, Narr., 57, 1830. **Ab-oin.**—Warren in Minn. Hist. Coll., v, 162, 1885. **Aboinug.**—Schoolcraft, Ind. Tribes, II, 141, 1852. **Abwoinug.**—Schoolcraft, Ind. Tribes, v, 39, 1855. **Ba-akush'.**—Gatschet, Caddo and Yatassi MS. vocab., B. A. E., 82 (Caddo name). **Ba-ra-shŭp'-gi-o.**—Hayden, Ethnog. and Philol. Mo. Val., 402, 1862 (Crow name). **Bevan-acs.**—Ramsey in Ind. Aff. Rep., 70, 1849 (usual Chippewa name; ev misprint for w). **Bewanacs.**—Lapham, Blossom and Dousman, Inds. of Wis., 15, 1870. **Boin-acs.**—Ramsey in Ind. Aff.

Rep., 70, 1849 (French notation of Bwanacs). **Boines.**—Long, Exped. St Peter's R., I, 389, 1824. **Bwaⁿ.**—Trumbull, MS. letter to Dorsey, Aug. 25, 1876. **Bwan-acs.**—Ramsey in Ind. Aff. Rep., 74, 1849. **Bwoinug.**—Tanner, Narr., 316, 1830. **Bwoirnug.**—Ibid.,144. **Caaⁿ'.**—Dorsey in Cont. N. A. Ethnol., VI, pt. 1, 339, 1890 (Omaha and Ponca, and Pawnee name). **Caaⁿ'qti.**—Dorsey, Dhegiha MS. Dict., B. A. E., 1878 (Omaha name: 'real Dakota'). **Ca'haⁿ.**—Dorsey, Tciwere MS. vocab., B. A. E., 1879 (so called by Iowa, Oto, Missouri, Kansa, and Osage). **Caⁿ-haⁿ.**—David St Cyr in Dorsey, Winn. MS., B. A. E., 1886 (Winnebago name). **Chah'-ra-rat.**—Grinnell, Pawnee Hero Tales, 92, 1889 (Pawnee name). **Chi8.**—Charlevoix, New France, ed. Shea, III, 31, 1868. **Ciou.**—Doc. of 1695 in N. Y. Doc. Col. Hist., IX, 611, 1855. **Cioux.**—Doc. of 1693, ibid., 570. **Coupegorge.**—Blackmore in Jour. Ethnol. Soc. Lond., I, 301, 1869 ('cutthroats': so called by the French from their gesture). **Coupes-gorges.**—Burton, City of Saints, 95, 1862. **Cruel.**—Shea, Cath. Miss., 348, 1855. **Cuouex.**—Lewis and Clark, Exped., I, 70, note, 1893. **Cutthroats.**—Marcy, Army Life on Border, 33, 1866 (given erroneously as the translation of Dakota). **Dacorta.**—Lewis and Clark, Exped., I, 61, 1814. **Dacota.**—Long, Exped. St Peter's R., II, 245, 1824. **Dacotah.**—Howe, Hist. Coll., 357, 1851 (translated 'allied tribes'). **Dahcotah.**—Tanner, Narr., 18, 1830. **Dahcotas.**—Gallatin in Trans. Am. Antiq. Soc., II, 121, 1836. **Dahkota.**—Parker, Minn. Handbk., 13, 1857. **Dahko-tah.**—Tanner, Narr., 146, 1830. **Dakoias.**—Shea, Early Voy., 120, note, 1861 (misprint for Dakotas). **Dakotah.**—Neill, Hist. Minn., xliv, note, 1858. **Dakotas.**—Ramsey in Ind. Aff. Rep., 69, 1849. **Dakotha.**—Smet, Mission de l' Oregon, 264, 1848. **Darcota.**—Lewis and Clark, Exped., I, 183, 1817. **Darcotar.**—Lewis and Clark, Discov., 30, 1806. **Dareotas.**—Rafinesque in Marshall, Hist. Ky., I, 28, 1824. **Dawta.**—Domenech, Deserts of N. Am., II, 28, 1860. **Docota.**—Drake, Bk. Inds., vii, 1848. **Guerriers.**—Jes. Rel. 1658, 21, 1858. **Hadovesaves.**—Alcedo, Dict. Geog., III, 213, 1788 (misprint). **Hadovessians.**—Harris, Coll. Voy. and Trav., II, 919, 1705 (misprinted from Lahontan). **Hand Cutters.**—Burton, City of Saints, 124, 1862 (Ute name). **I ta há tski.**—Matthews, Ethnog. Hidatsa, 159, 1877 (Hidatsa name: 'long arrows'). **Ít-áns-ké.**—Long, Exped. Rocky Mts., II, lxxxiv, 1823. **Kaispa.**—Wilson in Rep. N. W. Tribes Can., 11, 1888 (Sarsi name). **Kious.**—La Metairie (1682) in French, Hist. Coll. La., II, 25, 1875. **K'odalpä-K'iñago.**—Mooney in 14th Rep. B. A. E., 1057, 1896 ('necklace people': Kiowa name). **Lacota.**—Morgan in Beach, Ind. Misc., 220, 1877. **La-cotahs.**—Ruxton, Life in Far West, 112, 1849. **La-ko'-ta.**—Riggs, Dakota Gram. and Dict., 135, 1851. **La Sues.**—Croghan (1765), Jour., 38, 1831. **Madowesians.**—Lewis and Clark, Exped., I, 61, 1814. **Ma-ko'-ta.**—Hayden, Ethnog. and Philol. Mo. Val., 402, 1862 (Crow name). **már-án-shó-bísh-kó.**—Long, Exped. Rocky Mts., II, lxxix, 1823 (Crow name: 'cutthroats'). **Mattaugwessawacks.**—Sproat, Scenes Sav. Life, 188, 1868. **Maudowessies.**—McIntosh, Orig. N. Am. Inds., 103, 1853. **Minishúpsko.**—Col. H. L. Scott, inf'n, 1906 (Crow name, of opprobrious meaning). **Nacotah.**—Featherstonhaugh, Canoe Voy., I, 168, 1847. **Nadawessi.**—Ramsey in Ind. Aff. Rep., 71, 1849. **Na-da-wessy.**—Ibid., 70. **Naddouwessioux.**—Brackenridge, Views of La., 77, 1815. **Nadesis.**—Güssefeld, Charte von Nord Am., 1797. **Nadiousioux.**—Long, Exped. St Peter's R., II, 323, 1824. **Nadissioux.**—N. Y. Doc. Col. Hist., index, 304, 1861. **Nadoeses.**—Barcia, Ensayo, 291, 1723. **Nadoessi.**—Coues and Kingsley, Stand. Nat. Hist., pt. 6, 167, 1883. **Nadoessians.**—Salverte, Hist. Men, Nat., and Places, I, 66, 1864. **Nadoessious.**—La Chesnaye (1697) in Margry, Déc., VI, 6, 1886. **Nadonaisi.**—Burton, City of Saints, 96, 1862 (Chippewa name: 'enemies'). **Nadonaisioug.**—Domenech, Deserts N. Am., II, 26, 1860. **Nadonechiouk.**—Ibid. **Nadonessioux.**—Blackmore in Jour. Ethnol. Soc. Lond., I, 301, 1869 (misprint). **Nadonessis.**—Lahontan, New Voy., I, 115, 1703. **Nadooessis.**—Jefferys, Am. Atlas, map 8, 1776. **Nadouags.**—Bacqueville de la Potherie, Hist. Am., II,

49, 1753. **Nadouagssioux.**—Ibid., 147. **Nadouaissious.**—Ibid., 179. **Nadouaissioux.**—Ibid., 62. **Nadouayssioux.**—Ibid., 56. **Nad8echi8ec.**—Charlevoix, New France, III, 31, 1868. **Nadouechiouec.**—Rel. of 1660 in Margry, Déc., I, 54, 1876. **Nadouechiouek.**—Jes. Rel. 1658, 21, 1858. **Nadoüechio8ec.**—Ibid., 1660, 27. **Nadoüecious.**—Ibid., 1670, 98. **Nadoüecis.**—Ibid., 1670, 97. **Nad8e8is.**—Shea, Discov. Miss. Val., xxi, 1852. **Nadouesans.**—Hennepin, New Discov., map, 1698. **Nadouesciouz.**—Domenech, Deserts N. Am., II, 26, 1860. **Nadouesiouack.**—Neill, Hist. Minn., 102, 1858. **Nadouesiouek.**—Jes. Rel. 1656, 39, 1858. **Nadouesioux.**—Perrot (1689) in Margry, Déc., V, 33, 1883. **Nadouesioux.**—Williamson in Minn. Hist. Coll., I, 297, 1872. **Nadouessans.**—La Salle's Exped. (1679–81), in Margry, Déc., I, 481, 1876. **Nadouesse.**—French map (1710) in Minn. Hist. Coll., II, 256, 1872. **Nadouessians.**—Niles (1760) in Mass. Hist. Col., 4th s., V, 541, 1861. **Nadouessies.**—Hayden, Ethnog. and Philol. Mo. Val., 380, 1862. **Nadouessions.**—La Metairie (1682) in French, Hist. Coll. La., II, 25, 1875. **Nadouessiou.**—Hennepin (1683) quoted by Shea, Discov., 131, 1852. **Nadoüessioüak.**—Jes. Rel. 1665, 7, 1858. **Nadouessiouek.**—Ibid. 1667, 23. **Nadoüessious.**—Ibid. 1670, 99. **Nadouessioux.**—Doc. of 1681 in N. Y. Doc. Col. Hist., IX, 161, 1855. **Nadoüessous.**—Jes. Rel. 1642, 97, 1858. **Nadouessons.**—Coxe, Carolana, 42, 1741. **Nadouessoueronons.**—Sanson, map of Can. (1657) in Am. Antiq., I, 233, 1879. **Nadoussians.**—Hennepin, New Discov., I, 178, 1698 (made equivalent to Issati). **Nadoussieux.**—Du Chesneau (1681) in N.Y. Doc. Col. Hist., IX, 153, 1855. **Nadoussioux.**—Doc. (1679), ibid., 795. **Nadouwesis.**—Hayden, Ethnog. and Philol. Mo. Val., 380, 1862. **Nadovesaves.**—Barcia, Ensayo, 238, 1723. **Nadovessians.**—Hennepin (1680) in French, Hist. Coll. La., I, 211, 1846. **Nä-do-wa-see-wug.**—Morgan in N. Am. Rev., 53, 1870. **Nadowasis.**—Mackenzie, Voy., lx, 1802. **Nadowassis.**—Maximilian, Trav., 148, 1843. **Nadowaysioux.**—Schoolcraft, Ind. Tribes, III, 51, 1853. **Nadowesee.**—Schiller quoted by Neill, Hist. Minn., 89, 1858. **Nadowesi.**—Mooney in 14th Rep. B. A. E., 1057, 1896 ('little snakes,' or 'little enemies': common Algonquian name). **Nadowesioux.**—Kingsley, Stand. Nat. Hist., VI, 167, 1885. **Nadowesioux.**—Rafinesque in Marshall, Hist. Ky., I, 28, 1824. **Nadowessien.**—Adelung, Mithridates, III, 244, 1816. **Nadowessies.**—Henry, Trav., 46, 1809. **Nado-wessiouex.**—Shea, Cath. Miss., 348, 1855. **Nadowessioux.**—Henry, Trav., 197, 1809. **Nadowesteaus.**—McKenney and Hall, Ind. Tribes, III, 80, 1854. **Nadsnessiouck.**—Domenech, Deserts N. Am., II, 26, 1860. **Nadussians.**—Jefferys, Am. Atlas, map 5, 1776. **Naduwessi.**—Ramsey in Ind. Aff. Rep., 70, 1849. **Nadvesiv.**—Le Jeune in Jes. Rel. 1640, 35, 1858. **Nahcotah.**—Featherstonhaugh, Canoe Voy., I, 223, 1847. **Nahdawessy.**—Ramsey in Minn. Hist. Coll., I, 45, 1872. **Nahdowaseh.**—Jones, Ojibway Inds., 129, 1861. **Nahtooessies.**—Snelling, Tales of Northwest, 137, 1830. **Nakota.**—Burton, City of Saints, 95, 1862. **Nandawissees.**—Umfreville (1790) in Me. Hist. Coll., 6th s., 270, 1859. **Nandoesi.**—Maximilian, Trav., 148, 1843. **Nandoessies.**—Lahontan quoted by Ramsey in Ind. Aff. Rep., 72, 1849. **Nandowese.**—Drake, Ind. Chron., 186, 1836. **Nandowessies.**—Prichard, Phys. Hist. Mankind, V, 410, 1847. **Nandswesseis.**—Harmon, Jour., 165, 1820 (misprint). **Naoudoouessis.**—B. de Lozières, Voy. à la Louisiane, 348, 1802. **Narcotah.**—Schoolcraft, Trav., 291, 1821. **Natenéhima.**—Mallery in Proc. A. A. A. S., XXVI, 352, note, 1877. **Nate-ne'-hin-a.**—Hayden, Ethnog. and Philol. Mo. Val., 326, 1862 (Arapaho name: 'cutthroats'). **Natni.**—Mooney in 14th Rep. B. A. E., 1057, 1896 (Arapaho name). **Natnihina.**—Ibid. **Na'-towo-na.**—Hayden, Ethnog. and Philol. Mo. Val., 290, 1862 (Cheyenne name, applied to Mdewakanton, Sisseton, Wahpekute, and Wahpeton). **Nátuesse.**—Gatschet, MS., B. A. E., 1878 (Potawatomi name: 'small snake,' because farther w., therefore less to be dreaded). **Nátuessuag.**—Gatschet in Am. Antiq., II, 78, 1879 (Potawatomi name). **Naudawissees.**—Umfreville quoted by Hayden, Ethnog. and Philol. Mo. Val., 380, 1862. **Naudewessioux.**—Trumbull in Johnson Cyclop., II, 1156, 1877. **Naudoessi.**—Ramsey in Ind. Aff. Rep., 72, 1849. **Naudouescioux.**—Morgan in N.

Am. Rev., 53, 1870. **Naudoüessi.**—Ramsey in Ind. Aff. Rep., 69, 1849. **Naudouisioux.**—Raymbault (1642) quoted by Brackett in Smithson. Rep. 1876, 466, 1877. **Naudouisses.**—Ibid. **Naudouwessies.**—Brown, West. Gaz., 360, 1817. **Naud-o-wa-se.**—Warren in Minn. Hist. Coll., v, 280, 1885. **Naud-o-wa-se-wug.**—Ibid., 72. (Chippewa name: 'like unto adders'). **Naudowasses.**—Schuyler et al. (1702) in N. Y. Doc. Col. Hist., IV, 979, 1854. **Naudowesies.**—Carver, Trav., IX, 1778. **Naudowesse.** — Lewis, Trav., 233, 1809. **Naudowesseeg.**—Tanner, Narr., 316, 1830 (Ottawa name: 'roasters'). **Naudowessies.**—Carver, Trav., 56, 1778. **Naudowissies.**—Morgan in N. Am. Rev., 53, 1870. **Naudussi.**—Jefferys, Am. Atlas, map, 2, 1776. **Nauduwassies.**—Schermerhorn (1812) in Mass. Hist. Coll., 2d s., II, 12, 1814. **Nawdowessie.**—Carver, Trav., 59, 1778. **Nawdowissnees.**—Schoolcraft, Ind. Tribes, VI, 34, 1857 (Algonquian nickname: 'our enemies'). **Ndakotahs.**—Nicollet, Rep. on Upper Mississippi, 10, 1843. **Nedouessaus.**—Hennepin quoted by Neill in Minn. Hist. Coll., I, 256, 1872. **Noddouwessces.**—Brackenridge, Views of La., 77, 1815. **Nod-o-way-se-wug.**—Schoolcraft, Ind. Tribes, II, 139, 1852. **Nodoweisa.**—Linn (1839) in Sen. Ex. Doc. 204, 26th Cong., 1st sess., I, 1840. **Nodowessies.**—Bradbury, Trav., 41, 1817. **Nord oüests.**—Bradford quoted by Ramsey in Ind. Aff. Rep., 70, 1849 (evident corruption of *Nadouessiou*). **Nottawessie.**—Adelung, Mithridates, III, 264, 1816. **Nottoweasses.**—Croghan (1759), Hist. West. Penn., 146, note, 1851. **Nuktú-sĕm.**—Gatschet. MS., 1884 (Salish name: 'cut-throats'). **Nŭqtu'.**—Hoffman in Proc. Am. Philos. Soc., 371, 1886 (Salish name). **Nχtúsum.**—Gatschet MS., B. A. E., 1884 (Okinagan name). **O-bwah-nug.**—Schoolcraft, Ind. Tribes, v, 193, 1855 (Chippewa name). **Óceti śakowiɲ.**—Riggs, Dakota Gram. and Dict., XV, 1851 (own name: 'seven council fires'). **Ochente Shakoan.**—Long, Exped. St Peters R., I, 377, 1824. **Ochente Shakons.**—Coues and Kingsley, Stand. Nat. Hist., pt. 6, 169, 1883. **Ocheti Shaowni.**—Warren, Dacota Country, 15, 1855. **Ohó-hómo.**—ten Kate, Synonymie, 8, 1884 ('those on the outside'). **Ohò-omò-yo.**—Mallery in Proc. A. A. A. S., XXVI, 352, note, 1877. **O-o'-ho-mo-i'-o.**—Hayden, Ethnog. and Philol. Mo. Val., 290, 1862 (Cheyenne name). **Óshahak.**—Gatschet, MS., 1883 (Fox name). **Osheti Shakowin.**—Burton, City of Saints, 95, 1862. **Otchenti-Chakoang.**—Balbi, Atlas Ethnog., 55, 1826. **Pain-pe-tse-menay.** — Gebow, Sho-sho-nay Vocab., 18, 1868 (Shoshoni name). **Pakota.**—U. S. Stat., X, 173, 1853 (misprint). **Pambizimina.**—Mooney in 14th Rep. B. A. E., 1057, 1896 ('beheaders': Shoshoni name). **Pámpe Chyimina.**—Burton, City of Saints, 124, 1862 (Ute name: 'hand-cutters'). **Pani.**—Schuyler et al (1702) in N. Y. Doc. Col. Hist., IV, 979, 1854 (given as French name; confused with Pawnee). **Papitsinima.**—Mooney in 14th Rep. B. A. E., 1057, 1896 ('beheaders': Comanche name). **Píshakulk.**—Mooney, inf'n, 1892 (Yakima name: 'beheaders'). **Ponarak.**—Jes. Rel. 1656, 39, 1858 (misprint). **Poualac.**—Mallery in Proc. A. A. A. S., XXVI, 352, note, 1877. **Poualak.**—Jes. Rel. 1658, 21, 1858 (Chippewa name; incorrectly transl. 'warriors'). **Poualakes.**—McKenney and Hall, Ind. Tribes, III, 81, 1854. **Poualaks.**—Boucher (1660) in Margry, Déc., I, 55, 1875. **Pouanak.**—Tailhan, Perrot Mém., 232, note, 1864. **Roasters.**—Ramsey in Ind. Aff. Rep., 83, 1850 (Ab-boin-ee Sioux, or). **Sáhagi.**—Gatschet, MS., B. A. E., 1879 (Shawnee name). **Saoux.**—Schermerhorn (1812) in Mass. Hist. Coll., 2d s., II, 12, 1814. **Saux.**—Hurlbert in Jones, Ojebway Inds., 178, 1861. **Sceouex.**—Lewis and Clark, Exped., I, 70, note, 1893. **Sceoux.**—Clark, MS., Codex B, quoted in Lewis and Clark Exped., I, 101, note, 1893. **Scieux.** — Henry (1801) quoted by Neill in Minn. Hist. Coll., v, 453, 1885. **Sciou.**—Neill, Hist. Minn., 149, 1858. **Scioux.**—Doc. (1693) in N. Y. Doc. Col. Hist., IX, 570, 1855. **Scouex.**—Lewis and Clark, Exped., I, 70, note, 1893. **Seauex.**—Clark, Codex B, quoted in Lewis and Clark Exped., I, 128, note, 1893. **Seaux.**—Lewis and Clark, Exped., I, 70, note, 1893. **Shahañ.**—Dorsey quoted by Mooney in 14th Rep. B. A. E., 1057, 1896 (Osage, Kansa, and Oto name). **Shánana.**—Gat-

schet, MS., B. A. E., 1884 (Kiowa Apache name). **Sicouex.**—Lewis and Clark, Exped., I, 70, note, 1893. **Sieouex.**—Ibid. **Sieux.**—Coxe, Carolana, 20, 1741. **Siooz.**—Jefferys, Am. Atlas, map 8, 1776. **Sios.**—Alegre, Hist. Comp. Jesus, I, 336, 1841. **Siou.**—Lamothe Cadillac (1703) in Margry, Déc., v, 329, 1883. **Siouse.**—Perrot, Mém., 232, 1864. **Sioust.**—Doc. (1767) in N. Y. Doc. Col. Hist., VII, 989, 1856. **Sioux.**—Morel (1687) in Margry, Déc., v, 32, 1883. **Siouxes.**—Bacqueville de la Potherie, Hist. Am., IV, 33, 1753. **Siouxs.**—Lewis and Clark, Discov., 7, 1806. **Sioxes.**—Poole, Among the Sioux, 153, 1881. **Siroux.**—Perrot, Mém., 55, 1864. **Sivux.**—Boudinot, Star in the West, 128, 1816 (misprint). **Siwer.**—Balbi, Atlas Ethnog., 55, 1826. **Soo.**—Lewis and Clark, Discov., 30, 1806. **Soues.**—Lewis and Clark, Exped., I, 70, note, 1893. **Souex.**—Ibid. **Souix.**—Gorrell (1761) in Wis. Hist. Soc. Coll., I, 26, 1855. **Soux.**—Lewis and Clark, Exped., I, 70, note, 1893. **Su.**—Gatschet, Kaw vocab., B. A. E., 27, 1878 (Kansa form). **Sue.**—Croghan (1765), Jour., 38, 1831. **Suil.**—Ibid., 37. **Sun-nun'-at.**—Hayden, Ethnog. and Philol. Mo. Val., 357, 1862 (Arikara name). **Suouex.**—Lewis and Clark, Exped., I, 70, note, 1893. **Tsaba'kosh.**—Mooney in 14th Rep. B. A. E., 1057, 1896 ('cut-throats': Caddo name). **Túyĕtchískĕ.**—ten Kate, Synonymie, 9, 1884 (Comanche name: 'cut-throats'). **Wadoüissians.**—Hennepin quoted by Ramsey in Ind. Aff. Rep., 72, 1849. **Wanak.**—Belcourt (1850–56) in Minn. Hist. Coll., I, 235, 1872 (Chippewa name). **Wä-sä-sa-o-no.**—Morgan in N. Am. Rev., 52, note, 1870 (Iroquois name). **Wäsä'-seh-o-no.**—Morgan, League of Iroquois, 268, 1851 (Seneca name). **Yuɲssáha.**—Gatschet, Wyandot MS., B. A. E., 1879 (Wyandot name: 'birds'). **Zue.**—Croghan (1759), Hist. West. Penn., 146, note, 1851 (given as French form).

**Dakota turnip.** See *Tipsinah*.

**Daktlawedi.** A Tlingit clan belonging to the Wolf phratry. It is found at Tongas, Killisnoo, and among the Chilkat, while the Tsaguedi of Kake is a branch. **Dăklá-wĕti.** — Krause, Tlinkit Ind., 118, 1885. **DAq! ḷawe'dî.**—Swanton, field notes, B. A. E., 1904. **Takla-uĕdi.**—Krause, op. cit., 116. **Taktla-uĕdi.**—Ibid., 120.

**Dakubetede.** A group of Athapascan villages formerly on Applegate cr., Oreg. The inhabitants spoke a dialect practically identical with that employed by the Taltushtuntede who lived on Gallice cr. not far from them. They were intermarried with the Shasta, who, with the Takilman, were their neighbors. With other insurgent bands they were removed to the Siletz res. in 1856.

**Applegate Creek.**—Palmer in Ind. Aff. Rep., 464, 1854. **Da'-ku-be tĕ'-de.**—Dorsey in Jour. Am. Folk-lore, III, 235, 1890 (own name). **Do-dah-ho.**—Gibbs, letter to Hazen, B. A. E., 1856. **Etch-kah-taw-wah.**—Palmer in Ind. Aff. Rep., 464, 1854. **Ní'ckito hitclûm.**—Dorsey, Alsea MS. vocab., B. A. E., 1884 (Alsea name: 'people far up the stream'). **Spena.**—Gibbs, letter to Hazen, 1856, B. A. E. **Ts'û-qûs-li'-qwŭt-me' ɉûnnĕ.**—Dorsey in Jour. Am. Folk-lore, III, 235, 1890 (Naltûnnetûnnĕ name).

**Dalles Indians.** The Chinookan tribes formerly living at The Dalles, Oreg., and on the opposite side of Columbia r. While tribes of other stocks, notably Shahaptian, frequently visited The Dalles during the summer, they were not permanent residents. Of the Chinookan tribes the Wasco were important, and the term is sometimes limited to that tribe.　(L. F.)

Dalles.—U. S. Ind. Treat. (1855), 622, 1873. **Dalles Indians.**—White in Ind. Aff. Rep., 204, 1844. **Dalls Indians.** — Lee and Frost, Oregon, 96, 1844. **La Dalle Indians.**—M'Vickar, Hist. Exped. Lewis and Clark, II, 386, note, 1842. **La Dalles Indians.**—Parker, Jour., 140, 1846.

**Dance.** Nature is prodigal of life and energy. The dance is universal and instinctive. Primarily the dance expresses the joy of biotic exaltation, the exuberance of life and energy; it is the ready physical means of manifesting the emotions of joy and of expressing the exultation of conscious strength and the ecstasy of successful achievement—the fruitage of well-directed energy. Like modern music, through long development and divergent growth the dance has been adapted to the environment of many and diverse planes of culture and thought; hence it is found among both savage and enlightened peoples in many complex and differing forms and kinds. But the dance of the older time was fraught with symbolism and mystic meaning which it has lost in civilization and enlightenment. It is confined to no one country of the world, to no period of ancient or modern time, and to no plane of human culture.

Strictly interpreted, therefore, the dance seems to constitute an important adjunct rather than the basis of the social, military, religious, and other activities designed to avoid evil and to secure welfare. A contrary view renders a general definition and interpretation of the dance complex and difficult, apparently requiring a detailed description of the various activities of which it became a part. For if the dance is to be regarded as the basis of these activities, then these ceremonies and observances must be defined strictly as normal developments of the dance, a procedure which is plainly erroneous. The truth appears to be that the dance is only an element, not the basis, of the several festivals, rites, and ceremonies performed in accordance with well-defined rules and usages, of which it has become a part. The dance was a powerful impulse to their performance, not the motive of their observance.

Among the Indians N. of Mexico the dance usually consists of rhythmic and not always graceful gestures, attitudes, and movements of the body and limbs, accompanied by steps usually made to accord with the time of some form of music, produced either by the dancer or dancers or by one or more attendant singers. Drums, rattles, and sometimes bone or reed flutes are used to aid the singers. Every kind and class of dance has its own peculiar steps, attitudes, rhythm, figures, song or songs with words and accompanying music, and costumes.

The word or logos of the song or chant in savage and barbaric planes of thought and culture expressed the action of the *orenda*, or esoteric magic power, regarded as immanent in the rite or ceremony of which the dance was a dominant adjunct and impulse. In the lower planes of thought the dance was inseparable from the song or chant, which not only started and accompanied but also embodied it.

Some dances are peculiar to men and others to women. Some dances are performed by a single dancer, others belong respectively to individuals, like those of the *Onthonrontha* ('one chants') among the Iroquois; other dances are for all who may wish to take part, the number then being limited only by the space available; still others are for specified classes of persons, members of certain orders, societies, or fraternities. There are, therefore, personal, fraternal, clan or gentile, tribal, and inter-tribal dances; there are also social, erotic, comic, mimic, patriotic, military or warlike, invocative, offertory, and mourning dances, as well as those expressive of gratitude and thanksgiving. Morgan (League of the Iroquois, I, 278, 1904) gives a list of 32 leading dances of the Seneca Iroquois, of which 6 are costume dances, 14 are for both men and women, 11 for men only, and 7 for women only. Three of the costume dances occur in those exclusively for men, and the other 3 in those for both men and women.

In general among the American Indians the heel and the ball of the foot are lifted and then brought down with great force and swiftness in such wise as to produce a resounding concussion. Usually the changes of position of the dancer are slow, but the changes of attitude are sometimes rapid and violent. The women employ several steps, sometimes employed also by the men, among which are the shuffle, the glide, and the hop or leap. Holding both feet together and usually facing the song altar, the women generally take a leap or hop sidewise in advance and then a shorter one in recoil, so that after every two hops the position is slightly advanced. They do not employ the violent steps and forceful attitudes in vogue among the men. They keep the body quite erect, alternately advancing either shoulder slightly, which gives them a peculiar swaying or rocking motion, resembling the waving of a wind-rocked stalk of corn. Indeed, among the Onondaga, Cayuga, and other Iroquois tribes, one of the names for "woman" (*wathonwisas*, 'she sways or rocks') is a term taken from this rocking or swaying motion.

Among some tribes, when the warriors were absent on a hunting or war expedition, the women performed appropriate dances to insure their safety and success. Among the same people in the dances in which women may take part, these, under the conduct of a leader with one or more aids, form a circle around the song altar (the mat or bench provided for the singer or singers), maintaining an interval of from 2 to 5 feet. Then, outside of this circle the men, under like leadership, form another circle at a suitable distance from that of the women. Then the two circles, which are usually not closed between the leaders and the ends of the circles, move around the song altar from the right to the left in such manner that at all times the heads of the circles of dancers move along a course meeting the advancing sun (their elder brother), whose apparent motion is conversely from the left to the right of the observer. In the Santee Dakota dance a similar movement around the center of the circle from right to left is also observed. Among the Muskhogean tribes, however, the two circles move in opposite directions, the men with the course of the sun and the women contrary to it (Bartram). Among the Santee the women may dance only at the meeting of the "medicine" society of which they are members; they alone dance the scalp dance while the warriors sing. Rev. John Eastman says that in dancing the Santee form 3 circles, the innermost composed of men, the middle of children, and the outermost of women. According to Le Page Du Pratz, these circles, among the Natchez, moved in opposite directions, the women turning from left to right, and the men from right to left. This movement of the circles from right to left seems designed to prevent the dancer in the entire course around the song altar from turning his back to the sun.

The Mandan and other Siouan tribes dance in an elaborate ceremony, called the Buffalo dance, to bring game when food is scarce, in accordance with a well-defined ritual. In like manner the Indians of the arid region of the S. W. perform long and intricate ceremonies with the accompaniment of the dance ceremonies which, in the main, are invocations or prayers for rain and bountiful harvests and the creation of life. Among the Iroquois, in the so-called green-corn dance, the shamans urge the people to participate in order to show gratitude for bountiful harvests, the preservation of their lives, and appreciation of the blessings of the expiring year. The ghost dance, the snake dance, the sun dance, the scalp dance, and the calumet dance (q. v.), each performed for one or more purposes, are not developments from the dance, but rather the dance has become only a part of the ritual of each of these

important observances, which by metonymy have been called by the name of only a small but conspicuous part or element of the entire ceremony.

Consult Bartram, Travels, 1792; Jesuit Relations, Thwaites ed., I–LXXIII, 1896–1901; Margry, Déc., I–VI, 1875–86; Morgan, League of the Iroquois, 1857, 1904; Lafitau, Mœurs des Sauvages, 1724; Le Page Du Pratz, Hist. de la Louisiane, 1758.

(J. N. B. H.)

**Danokha** (*Danoχa*). A former Pomo village on the N. shore of Clear lake, Cal.

(S. A. B.)

**Dapishul** (*Dá-pi-shūl*, 'high sun'). A former Pomo village in Redwood valley, Mendocino co., Cal.—Powers in Cont. N. A. Ethnol., III, 155, 1877.

**Daquinatinno** (Caddo: *atino* 'red'). A tribe of N. E. Texas in 1687, said to be allies of the Caddo, and probably related to them.—Joutel (1687) in Margry, Déc., III, 410, 1878. Cf. *Daquio, Daycao.*

**Daquio.** One of the bands, mostly Caddoan, who were allies of the Caddo in Texas in 1687 (Margry, Déc., III, 410, 1878). Possibly the same as the Daycao of the narratives of De Soto's expedition of 1542 (Gentl. of Elvas (1557) in Bourne, Narr. De Soto, I, 182, 1904).

**Darby's Village.** A former Huron village on upper Darby cr., about midway between the present Columbus and Marysville, Ohio.—Royce in 18th Rep. B. A. E., pl. clvi, 1899.

**Dart sling.** See *Throwing-stick.*

**Dasamonquepeuc.** An Algonquian village on the coast of Dare co., N. C., opposite Roanoke id., in 1587.

Dasamanquepeio.—Strachey (ca. 1612), Virginia, 147, 1849. **Dasamanquepeuk.**—Ibid., 152. **Dasamonpeack.**—Lane (1586) in Smith (1629), Virginia, I, 91, repr. 1819. **Dasamonquepeio.**—Hakluyt (1600), Voy., III, 344–345, repr. 1810. **Dasamonquepeuk.**—Strachey, op. cit., 151. **Dasamoquepeuk.**—Ibid., 150. **Dasamotiquepero.** — Dutch map (1621) in N. Y. Doc. Col. Hist., I, 1856 (misprint). **Dassamonpeack.**—Lane, op. cit., 92. **Dassamopoque.**—Smith (1629), Virginia, I, map, repr. 1819. **Dessamonpeake.**—Morse, N. Am., 159, 1776. **Dessamopeak.**—Schoolcraft, Ind. Tribes, VI, 93, 1857.

**Dasoak** ('flying'). A clan of the Huron.

**Datcho.** An unidentified Texan tribe or division hostile to the Caddo in 1687.—Joutel (1687) in Margry, Déc., III, 409, 1878. Cf. *Kadohadacho.*

**Daupom Wintun** ('sloping-ground Wintun'). A Wintun tribe formerly living in Cottonwood valley, Shasta co., Cal.

Cottonwoods.—Powers in Cont. N. A. Ethnol., III, 230, 1877. **Daú-pum Wintūn.**—Ibid. **Valley Indians.**—Ibid. **Waikemi.**—Kroeber, inf'n, 1903 (Yuki name of Cottonwood Creek Wintun; probably the same).

**Davis, John.** A full-blood Creek, born in the "Old Nation." In the War of 1812, when a boy, he was taken prisoner, and was reared by a white man. He emigrated from Alabama in 1829, and was educated at the Union Mission after reaching Indian Territory. He had good talents, and in early manhood became a valuable helper to the missionaries as interpreter and speaker in public meetings. He was an active worker in 1830, and died about 10 years later. Two daughters survive him, who were educated in the Presbyterian boarding school, one of whom, Susan, wife of John McIntosh, rendered important service to Mrs A. E. W. Robertson in her Creek translations. Davis was joint author with J. Lykens in translating the Gospel of John into Creek, published at the Shawanoe Baptist Mission, Ind. Ter., in 1835, and was also a collaborator with R. M. Loughridge, D. Winslett, and W. S. Robertson in the translation into Creek of two volumes of hymns.—Pilling, Bibliog. Muskhogean Lang., Bull. B. A. E., 1889.

**Dawes Commission.** See *Commission to the Five Civilized Tribes.*

**Daycao.** A territory that lay 10 days' journey beyond the extreme westerly point reached by Moscoso, of De Soto's expedition, in 1542. The name was strictly that of a stream, possibly Trinity r., Texas, and is spoken of also as if designating an Indian "province." See Gentl. of Elvas in Hakluyt Soc. Publ., IX, 138–140, 1851.

**Dayoitgao** ('there where it issues'). A former Seneca village situated at Squakie hill, on Genesee r., near Mt Morris, N. Y. It received the name Squawkiehah from the fact that 700 Fox (Muskwaki) captives were settled there by the Iroquois in 1681–83. The site was sold by the Seneca in 1825 and relinquished by them in 1827. See *Squawkihow.* (J. N. B. H.)
Da-yo-it-gä-o.—Morgan, League Iroq., 435, 1851. Squakie Hill village.—Ibid., 468. Squawkie Hill.—Conover, Kanadesaga and Geneva MS., B. A. E. (= Squawkiehah Ganadahah, 'Squawkiehah village lying high'). Squawkihows.—Cusick, Sketches Six Nations, 20, 1828. Squawky Hill.—Morris treaty (1797) in U. S. Ind. Treat., 820, 1873.

**De.** The Coyote clans of the Tewa pueblos of San Juan, Tesuque, and San Ildefonso, N. Mex. Those of Tesuque and San Ildefonso are extinct.
Dé-tdóa.—Hodge in Am. Anthrop., IX, 350, 1896 (*tdóa*='people').

**Deadoses.** A small Texan tribe which in the 18th century lived with other tribes on San Xavier r., probably the San Miguel, which joins Little r. and flows into the Brazos about 150 m. from the gulf. In 1767–68 they were said to reside between Navasota and Trinity rs., and in 1771 were mentioned with the Tonkawa, Comanche, Towash (Wichita), and others as northern Texas tribes in contradistinction to the Cocos (Coaque), Karankawa, and others of the coast region. If the Mayeyes were really related to the Tonkawa, as has been asserted, the fact that this tribe is mentioned with them may indicate that the language of the Deadoses resembled that of the Tonkawa. They may have been swept away by the epidemic that raged among the Indians of Texas in 1777–78.
(H. E. B.   J. R. S.)

**Decoration.** See *Adornment, Art, Clothing, Ornament.*

**Deep Creek Spokan.** A former Spokan colony that lived 17 m. s. w. of Spokane falls, now Spokane, Wash. The colony was established for farming purposes; pop. about 30 in 1880.—Warner in Ind. Aff. Rep., 67, 1880.

**Deer Skins.** Apparently a division of the northern Athapascans, as they are mentioned as belonging to a group including the Beaver Hunters, Flatside Dogs (Thlingchadinne), and Slaves.—Smet, Oregon Missions, 164, 1847.

**Defense.** See *Fortification.*

**Deformation.** See *Artificial head deformation.*

**Degataga.** See *Stand Watie.*

**Dekanawida** ('two river-currents flowing together.'—Hewitt). An Iroquois prophet, statesman, and lawgiver, who lived probably during the second and third quarters of the 15th century, and who, conjointly with Hiawatha, planned and founded the historical confederation of the five Iroquois tribes. According to a circumstantial tradition, he was born in the vicinity of Kingston, Ontario, Canada, in what then was probably Huron territory. He was reputed to have been one of 7 brothers. Definite tradition gives him rank with the demigods, owing to the masterful *orenda* or magic power with which he worked tirelessly to overcome the obstacles and difficulties of his task, the astuteness he displayed in negotiation, and the wisdom he exhibited in framing the laws and in establishing the fundamental principles on which they were based and on which rested the entire structure of the Iroquois confederation. Omens foreshadowed his birth, and portents accompanying this event revealed the fact to his virgin mother that Dekanawida would be the source of evil to her people, referring to the destruction of the Huron confederation by that of the Iroquois. Hence at his birth his mother and grandmother, with true womanly patriotism, sought to spare their country woes by attempting to drown the new-born infant by thrusting it through a hole made in the ice covering a neighboring river. Three attempts were made, but in the morning after each attempt the young Dekanawida was found unharmed in the arms of the astonished mother. Thereupon the two women decided that it was decreed that he should live, and so resolved to rear him. Rapidly he grew to man's estate, and then, saying that he must take up his foreordained work, departed southward, first assuring his mother that in the event of his death by violence or sorcery, the otter skin flayed entire which, with the head downward, he had hung in a corner of the lodge, would vomit blood. Dekanawida was probably a Huron by blood, but perhaps an Iroquois by adoption. In the long and tedious negotiations preceding the final establishment of the historical confederation of the five Iroquois tribes, he endeavored to persuade the Erie and the Neuter tribes also to join the confederation; these tribes, so far as known, were always friendly with the Huron people, and their representatives probably knew of Dekanawida's Huron extraction. Many of the constitutional principles, laws, and regulations of the confederation are attributed to him. His chiefship did not belong to the hereditary class, but to the merit class, commonly styled the 'pine-tree chiefs.' Hence, he could forbid the appointment of a successor to his office, and could exclaim, "To others let there be successors, for like them they can advise you. I have established your commonwealth, and none has done what I have." But it is probable that prohibition was attributed to him in later times when the true nature of the merit chiefs had become obscured. Hence it is the peculiar honor of the merit chiefs of to-day not to be condoled officially after death, nor to have successors to their chieftaincies. For these reasons the title Dekanawida does not belong to the roll of 50 federal league chiefships. (J. N. B. H.)

**Dekanisora.** An Onondaga chief who came into prominence in the latter part of the 17th century, chiefly through his oratorical powers and his efforts to maintain peace with both the French and the English. He was first mentioned by Charlevoix in 1682 as a member of an embassy from the Iroquois to the French at Montreal. He was also one of the embassy to the French in 1688, which was captured by Adario (Le Rat), and then released by the wily captor under the plea that there had been a mistake, blaming the French for the purpose of widening the breach between them and the Iroquois. Colden (Hist. Five Nat., I, 165, 1755) says Dekanisora was tall and well made, and that he "had for many years the greatest reputation among the Five Nations for speaking, and was generally employed as their speaker in their negotiations with both French and English." His death is supposed to have occurred about 1730, as he was a very old man

when he was a member of an embassy at Albany in 1726. (C. T.)

**Dekanoagah** ('between the rapids.'—Hewitt). A village, inhabited by Seneca, Nanticoke, Conoy, and remnants of other tribes, placed by Gov. Evans (Day, Penn., 391, 1843) in 1707 on Susquehanna r., about 9 m. from Pequehan, the Shawnee village on the E. side of the Susquehanna, just below Conestoga cr., in Lancaster co., Pa.

**Dekaury, Choukeka.** A chief of the Winnebago tribe, born about 1730. He was the son of Sabrevoir De Carrie, an officer of the French army in 1699, and Hopoekaw, daughter of a principal Winnebago chief, whom he married in 1729, spoken of by Carver (Travels, 20, 1796) as the queen of the Winnebago. Their son, Choukeka ('Spoon'), was known to the whites as Spoon Dekaury. After having been made chief he became the leader of attacks on the Chippewa during a war with the Winnebago, but he maintained friendly relations with the whites. It was principally through his influence that the treaty of June 3, 1816, at St Louis, Mo., was brought about. His wife was a daughter of Nawkaw. He died at Portage, Wis., in 1816, leaving 6 sons and 5 daughters.

**Dekaury, Konoka.** The eldest son and successor of Choukeka Dekaury, born in 1747. He was named Konoka ('Eldest') Dekaury, and is often mentioned as "Old Dekaury," but is equally well known as Schachipkaka. Before his father's death, in 1816, Konoka had joined a band of Winnebago who took part, in 1813, in the attack led by Proctor on Ft Stephenson, on lower Sandusky r., Ohio, which was gallantly defended by Maj. George Croghan. He fought also in the battle of the Thames, in Canada. He was held for a time, in 1827, as a hostage at Prairie du Chien for the delivery of Red Bird. His band usually encamped at the portage of Wisconsin r., the site of the present Portage, Wis. Mrs Kinzie (Wau-Bun, 89, 1856) describes him as "the most noble, dignified, and venerable of his own or indeed of any other tribe," having a fine Roman countenance, his head bald except for a solitary tuft of long, silvery hair neatly tied and falling back on his shoulders, and exhibiting a demeanor always courteous, while his dress was always neat and unostentatious. He signed the treaty of Prairie du Chien Aug. 19, 1825, on behalf of the Winnebago, and died on Wisconsin r. Apr. 20, 1836.

Other members of the family, whose name has been variously written DeKaury, DeKauray, DayKauray, Day Korah, Dacorah, and DeCorrah, were noted. From Choukeka's daughters, who married white men, are descended several well-known families of Wisconsin and Minnesota.

(C. T.)

**Delaware.** A confederacy, formerly the most important of the Algonquian stock, occupying the entire basin of Delaware r. in E. Pennsylvania and S. E. New York, together with most of New Jersey and Delaware. They called themselves Lenápe or Leni-lenápe, equivalent to 'real men,' or 'native, genuine men'; the English knew them as Delawares, from the name of their principal river; the French called them Loups, 'wolves,' a term probably applied originally to the Mahican on Hudson r., afterward extended to the Munsee division and to the whole group. _ To the more remote Algonquian

JACK HARRY (WAIAWAKWAKUMAU, TRAMPING EVERYWHERE)— DELAWARE

tribes they, together with all their cognate tribes along the coast far up into New England, were known as Wapanachki, 'easterners,' or 'eastern land people,' a term which appears also as a specific tribal designation in the form of Abnaki. By virtue of admitted priority of political rank and of occupying the central home territory, from which most of the cognate tribes had diverged, they were accorded by all the Algonquian tribes the respectful title of "grandfather," a recognition accorded by courtesy also by the Huron. The Nanticoke, Conoy, Shawnee, and Mahican claimed close connection with the Delawares and preserved the tradition of a common origin.

The Lenápe, or Delawares proper, were composed of 3 principal tribes, treated by

Morgan as phratries, viz: Munsee, Unami, and Unalachtigo (q. v.), besides which some of the New Jersey bands may have constituted a fourth. Each of these had its own territory and dialect, with more or less separate identity, the Munsee particularly being so far differentiated as frequently to be considered an independent people.

The early traditional history of the Lenápe is contained in their national legend, the Walam Olum (q. v.). When they made their first treaty with Penn, in 1682, the Delawares had their council fire at Shackamaxon, about the present Germantown, suburb of Philadelphia, and under various local names occupied the whole country along the river. To this early period belongs their great chief, Tamenend, from whom the Tammany Society takes its name. The different bands frequently acted separately but regarded themselves as part of one great body. About the year 1720 the Iroquois assumed dominion over them, forbidding them to make war or sales of lands, a condition which lasted until about the opening of the French and Indian war. As the whites, under the sanction of the Iroquois, crowded them out of their ancient homes, the Delawares removed to the Susquehanna, settling at Wyoming and other points about 1742. They soon crossed the mountains to the headwaters of the Allegheny, the first of them having settled upon that stream in 1724. In 1751, by invitation of the Huron, they began to form settlements in E. Ohio, and in a few years the greater part of the Delawares were fixed upon the Muskingum and other streams in E. Ohio, together with the Munsee and Mahican, who had accompanied them from the E., being driven out by the same pressure and afterward consolidating with them. The Delawares, being now within reach of the French and backed by the western tribes, asserted their independence of the Iroquois, and in the subsequent wars up to the treaty of Greenville in 1795 showed themselves the most determined opponents of the advancing whites. The work of the devoted Moravian missionaries in the 17th and 18th centuries forms an important part of the history of these tribes (see *Gnadenhuetten, Missions*). About the year 1770 the Delawares received permission from the Miami and Piankishaw to occupy the country between the Ohio and White rs., in Indiana, where at one time they had 6 villages. In 1789, by permission of the Spanish government, a part of them removed to Missouri, and afterward to Arkansas, together with a band of Shawnee. By 1820 the two bands had found their way to Texas, where the Delawares numbered at that time probably at least 700. By the year 1835 most of the tribe had been gathered on a reservation in Kansas, from which they removed, in 1867, to Indian Ter. and incorporated with the Cherokee Nation. Another band is affiliated with the Caddo and Wichita in w. Oklahoma, besides which there are a few scattered remnants in the United States, with several hundred in Canada, under the various names of Delawares, Munsee, and Moravians.

It is impossible to get a definite idea of the numbers of the Delawares at any given period, owing to the fact that they have always been closely connected with other tribes, and have hardly formed one compact body since leaving the Atlantic coast. All the estimates of the last century give them and their connected tribes from about 2,400 to 3,000, while the estimates within the present century are much lower. Their present population, including the Munsee, is about 1,900, distributed as follows: Incorporated with Cherokee Nation, Ind. T., 870; Wichita res., Oklahoma, 95; Munsee, with Stockbridges, in Wisconsin, perhaps 260; Munsee, with Chippewa, in Kansas, perhaps 45; "Moravians of the Thames," Ontario, 347; "Munsees of the Thames," Ontario, 122, with Six Nations on Grand r., Ontario, 150.

According to Morgan (Anc. Soc., 171, 1877) the Delawares have 3 clans (called by him gentes), or phratries, divided into 34 subclans, not including 2 subclans now extinct. These clans, which are the same among the Munsee and Mahican, are: (1) Took-seat ('round paw,' 'wolf'). (2) Pokekooungo ('crawling,' 'turtle'). (3) Pullaook ('non-chewing,' 'turkey'). These clans—Wolf, Turtle, and Turkey—are commonly given as synonymous with Munsee, Unami, and Unalachtigo, the 3 divisions of the Delawares, exclusive of the New Jersey branch. According to Brinton they are not clans, but mere totemic emblems of the 3 geographic divisions above named. Of these the Unami held the hereditary chieftainship. The New Jersey branch probably formed a fourth division, but those bands broke up at an early period and became incorporated with the others. Many of them had originally removed from the w. bank of Delaware r. to escape the inroads of the Conestoga. The 3 clans as given by Morgan are treated under the better known geographic names.

The Took-seat, or Wolf clan, has the following 12 subdivisions: (1) Maangreet (big feet); (2) Weesowhetko (yellow tree); (3) Pasakunamon (pulling corn); (4) Weyarnihkato (care enterer, i. e. cave enterer?); (5) Tooshwarkama (across the river); (6) Olumane (vermilion); (7)

Punaryou (dog standing by fireside); (8) Kwineekcha (long body); (9) Moonhartarne (digging); (10) Nonharmin (pulling up stream); (11) Longushharkarto (brush log); (12) Mawsootoh (bringing along).

The Pokekooungo, or Turtle clan, has the following 10 subdivisions, 2 others being extinct: (1) Okahoki (ruler); (2) Takoongoto (high bank shore); (3) Seeharongoto (drawing down hill); (4) Oleharkarmekarto (elector); (5) Maharolukti (brave); (6) Tooshkipakwisi (green leaves); (7) Tungulungsi (smallest turtle); (8) Welunungsi (little turtle); (9) Leekwinai (snapping turtle); (10) Kwisaesekeesto (deer).

The Pullaook, or Turkey clan, has the following 12 subdivisions: (1) Moharala (big bird); (2) Lelewayou (bird's cry); (3) Mookwungwahoki (eye pain); (4) Mooharmowikarnu (scratch the path); (5) Opinghaki (opossum ground); (6) Muhhowekaken (old shin); (7) Tongonaoto (drift log); (8) Noolamarlarmo (living in water); (9) Muhkrentharne (root digger); (10) Muhkarmhukse (red face); (11) Koowahoke (pine region); (12) Oochukham (ground scratcher).

The divisions of the Munsee, according to Ruttenber, were the Minisink, Waoranec, Waranawonkong, Mamekoting, Wawarsink, and Catskill. He names among the Unami divisions the Navasink, Raritan, Hackensack, Aquackanonk, Tappan, and Haverstraw, all in N. New Jersey, but there were others in Pennsylvania. Among the Unalachtigo divisions in Pennsylvania and Delaware were probably the Neshamini, Shackamaxon, Passayonk, Okahoki, Hickory Indians (?), and Nantuxets. The Gachwechnagechga, or Lehigh Indians, were probably of the Unami division. Among the New Jersey bands not classified are the Yacomanshaghking, Kahansuk, Konekotay, Meletecunk, Matanakons, Eriwonec, Asomoche, Pompton (probably a Munsee division), Rancocas, Tirans, Siconesses (Chiconessex), Sewapoo (perhaps in Delaware), Kechemeche, Mosilian, Axion, Calcefar, Assunpink, Naraticon, and Manta (perhaps a Munsee division). The Nyack band, or village, in Rockland co., N. Y., may have belonged to the Unami. The Papagonk band and the Wysox probably belonged to the Munsee. See also *Munsee, Unami, Unalachtigo.*

The following were Delaware villages: Achsinnink, Ahasimus (Unami?), Alamingo, Allaquippa, Alleghany, Aquackanonk, Au Glaize, Bald Eagle's Nest, Beaversville, Bethlehem (Moravian), Black Hawk, Black Leg's Village, Buckstown, Bullets Town (?), Cashiehtunk (Munsee?), Catawaweshink (?), Chikohoki (Unalachtigo),

Chilohocki (?), Chinklacamoose (?), Clistowacka, Conedogwinit, Communipaw (Hackensack), Conemaugh, Coshocton, Crossweeksung, Custaloga's Town, Edgpiiliik, Eriwonec, Frankstown (?), Friedenshuetten (Moravian), Friedensstadt (Moravian), Gekelemukpechuenk, Gnadenhuetten (Moravian), Goshgoshunk, Grapevine Town (?), Greentown (?), Gweghkongh (Unami ?), Hespatingh (Unami ?), Hickorytown, Hockhocken, Hogstown (?), Hopocan, Jacob's Cabins (?), Jeromestown (?), Kalbauvane (?), Kanestio, Kanhanghton, Katamoonchink (?), Kickenapawling (?), Killbuck's Town, Kiskiminetas, Kiskominitoes, Kittaning, Kohhokking, Kuskuski, Lackawaxen (?), Languntennenk (Moravian), Lawunkhannek (Moravian), Lichtenau (Moravian), Macharienkonck (Minisink), Macock, Mahoning, Mamalty, Matawoma, Mechgachkamic (Unami ?), Meggeckessou (?), Meniolagomeka, Meochkonck (Minisink), Minisink (Minisink), Mohickon John's Town (Mahican ?), Munceytown (Munsee), Muskingum, Nain (Moravian), Nescopeck, Newcomerstown, New Town, Nyack (Unami), Ostonwackin, Outaunink (Munsee), Owl's Town, Pakadasank (Munsee ?), Pakataghkon, Papagonk (?), Passayonk, Passycotcung (Munsee ?), Peckwes (?), Peixtan (mixed), Pematuning (?), Pequottink (Moravian), Playwickey, Pohkopophunk, Queenashawakee, Rancocas, Remahenonc (Unami ?), Roymount, Salem, (Moravian), Salt Lick, Sawcunk (with Shawnee and Mingo), Sawkin (?), Schepinaikonck (Munsee), Schipston (?), Schoenbrunn (Moravian), Seven Houses, Shackamaxon, Shamokin (with Seneca and Tutelo), Shannopin's town, Shenango (with others), Sheshequin, Skehandowa (with Mahicans and Shawnee), Snakestown (?), Soupnapka (?), Three Legs Town, Tioga (with Munsee and others), Tom's Town, Tullihas, Tuscarawas, Venango (?), Wakatomica (with Mingo), Wechquetank (Moravian), Wekeeponall, Welagamika, White Eyes, White Woman, Will's Town (?), Wapeminskink, Wapicomekoke, Wyalusing, Wyoming, Wysox (?).     (J. M.)

**Abnaki.**—For various forms applied to the Delawares, see under *Abnaki*. **Ă-ko-tcă-kă' nĕⁿ'.**—Hewitt, Mohawk MS. vocab., B. A. E., 1882 ('one who stammers in his speech': Mohawk name used in derision of the strange tongue. See other forms under *Mahican*). **Ă-ko-tcă-kă-nhă'.**—Hewitt, Oneida MS. vocab., B. A. E. (Oneida name). **A-kots-ha-ka-nen.**—Hewitt, Mohawk MS. vocab., B. A. E. (Mohawk form). **Ă-ku-tcă-ka''-nhă'.**—Hewitt, inf'n, 1886 (Tuscarora form). **Anakwan'kĭ.**—Mooney in 19th Rep. B. A. E., 508, 1900 (Cherokee name; an attempt at the Algonquian *Wapanaqti*, 'easterners'). **Auquitsaukon.**—Stiles (1756) in Mass. Hist. Soc. Coll., 1st s., VII, 74, 1801. **Delawar.**—Lords of Trade (1756) in N. Y. Doc. Col. Hist., VII, 120, 1856. **Delawaras.**—Mt Johnson Conference (1755), ibid., VI, 977, 1855.

**Delawares.**—Lords of Trade (1721), ibid., v, 623, 1855. **De Lawarrs.**—Watts (1764) in Mass. Hist. Soc. Coll., 4th s., x, 524, 1871. **Delaways.**—Cowley (1775) in Arch. of Md., Jour. of Md. Convention, 94, 1892. **Deleawares.**—Glen (1750) in N. Y. Doc. Col. Hist., VI, 588, 1855. **Delewars.**—Campbell (1761) in Mass. Hist. Soc. Coll., 4th s., IX, 423, 1871. **Deleways.**—Croghan (1760), ibid., 248. **Deluas.**—Soc. Geog. Mex., 268, 1870. **Dillewars.**—Lewis and Clark, Trav., 12, 1806. **Lenais.**—Boudinot, Star in the West, 127, 1816. **Lenalenape.**—Am. Pion., I, 408, 1842. **Lenalinepies.**—Jefferson (1785?), quoted by Schoolcraft, Ind. Tribes, v, 669, 1855. **Lenap.**—Rafinesque, introd. to Marshall, Ky., I, 31, 1824. **Lenape.**—Heckewelder in Mass. Hist. Soc. Coll., 2d s., x, 98, 1823. **Lenapegi.**—Gatschet, Shawnee MS. vocab., B. A. E., 1879 (Shawnee name). **Lenappe.**—Boyd, Ind. Local Names, 44, 1885. **Lenappys.**—Gordon (1728) quoted by Brinton, Lenape Leg., 33, 1885. **Lenawpes.**—Schoolcraft, Ind. Tribes, I, 65, 1851. **Lenelenape.**—Am. Pion., II, 189, 1843. **Lenelenoppes.**—Proud, Penn., II, 295, 1798. **Lenepee.**—Gale, Upper Miss., map, 1867. **Leni-Lenape.**—Nuttall, Jour., 250, 1821. **Lenna-lenape.**—Drake, Bk. Inds., vii, 1848. **Lennape.**—Ibid., bk. 5, 179. **Lennapewi.** — Squier quoted in Beach, Ind. Miscel., 28, 1877. **Lenni-Iappe.**—Maximilian, Trav., 39, note, 1843. **Lenni-Lenápe.**—Loskiel (1794) quoted by Barton, New Views, app. 1, 1798. **Lenni-Lennápe.**—Barton, ibid., x. **Lenno Lenapees.**—Schoolcraft in N. Y. Hist. Soc. Proc., 80, 1844. **Lenno Lenapi.**—Schoolcraft, Ind. Tribes, VI, 573, 1857. **Lenno-Lennape.**—Gallatin in Trans. Am. Antiq. Soc., II, 44, 1836. **Lenopi.**—Easton treaty (1757) in N. Y. Doc. Col. Hist., VII, 294, 1856. **Lenoppea.**—Vater, Mith., pt. 3, sec. 3, 366, 1816. **Leonopi.**—Thompson in Jefferson, Notes, 283, 1825. **Leonopy.**—Conference of 1759 quoted by Brinton, Lenape Leg., 34, 1885. **Linapis.**—Rafinesque, Am. Nations, I, 121, 1836. **Linapiwi.**—Squier quoted in Beach, Ind. Miscel., 28, 1877. **Linnelinopies.**—Croghan (1759) quoted by Jefferson, Notes, 142, 1825. **Linni linapi.**—Rafinesque (1833) quoted by Brinton, Lenape Leg., 162, 1885. **Linnilinopes.**—Boudinot, Star in the West, 127, 1816. **Linnope.**—McCoy, Ann. Reg. Ind. Aff., 27, 1836. **Llenilenapés.**—Nuttall, Jour., 283, 1821. **Loup.**—'Wolf,' the name applied by the French to the Delawares, Munsee, and Mahican; for forms see under *Mahican*. **Mochomes.**—Yates and Moulton in Ruttenber, Tribes Hudson R., 47, 1872 ('Grandfather': title given to the Delawares by those Algonquian tribes claiming descent from them). **Nar-wah-ro.**—Marcy, Red River, 273, 1854 (Wichita name). **Renapi.**—Gallatin in Trans. Am. Antiq. Soc., II, 44, 1836 (given as Swedish form, but properly the form used by the New Jersey branch of the tribe). **Renni Renape.**—Duponceau in Mass. Hist. Soc. Coll., 2d s., VII, note, 1822 (form used in New Jersey and Delaware). **Sag-a-na'-gä.**—Morgan, League Iroq., 338, 1851 (Iroquois name). **Tcă-kă'-nĕⁿ.**—Smith and Hewitt, Mohawk and Onondaga MS. vocabs., B. A. E., 1881 (Mohawk and Onondaga name). **Tcă-kă'-nhă'.**—Smith and Hewitt, Tuscarora, Cayuga, Seneca, Oneida, and Onondaga MS. vocabs., B. A. E., 1884 (Cayuga, Oneida, and Onondaga name). **Tsă-kă-nhă'-o-näⁿ.**—Ibid. (Seneca name). **Wapanachki.**—For various forms applied to the Delawares see under *Abnaki*.

**Deluge myths.** See *Mythology*.

**Descent.** See *Clan and Gens, Family. Kinship, Social organization*.

**Des Chutes.** A loosely defined Shahaptian group living formerly on and about Deschutes r., Oreg. The term probably included remnants of several tribes. The name has passed out of use, and the Indians, if any survive, are probably on the Warm Springs res., Oreg., under other names.     (L. F.)

**De Chentes.**—Meek in H. R. Ex. Doc. 76, 30th Cong., 1st sess., 10, 1848 (misprint). **De Chute river.**—Farnham, Trav., 112, 1843. **De Chutes.**—

Lane in Ind. Aff. Rep., 160, 1850. **Des Chutes.—** Wilkes in Pac. R. R. Rep., I, 417, 1855. **Des Chute's River.—**Gibbs in Pac. R. R. Rep., I, 417, 1855. **Deshoot.—**Palmer in Ind. Aff. Rep., 194, 1855. **Deshoots.—**Palmer in H. R. Ex. Doc. 93, 34th Cong., 1st sess..23, 1856. **Fall Indians.—**Parker, Jour., 137, 1842. **Falls Indians.—**M'Vickar, Hist. Exped. Lewis and Clark, II, 386, note, 1842.

**Deshu.** A former Chilkat town at the head of Lynn canal, Alaska.
**Dashu.—**Emmons in Mem. Am. Mus. Nat. Hist., III, pl. v, 1903. **Decu'.—**Swanton, field notes, B. A. E., 1904.

**Deshuhittan** ('people of the house at the end of the road'). A Tlingit clan at Killisnoo, Alaska, belonging to the Raven phratry. Formerly they lived at Angun.
**Dashiton.—**Emmons in Mem. Am. Mus. Nat. Hist., III, pl. xiii, 1903. **De'citan.—**Swanton, field notes, B. A. E., 1904 (contracted form of name). **Decū'hît tān.—**Ibid. **Dēschĭtān.—**Krause, Tlinkit Ind., 118, 1885.

**Desnedekenade** ('people of the great river'). A tribe of the Chipewyan group of the Athapascan family living along the banks of Great Slave r., Athabasca, Canada. There were 122 enumerated at Ft Resolution and 256 at Smith Landing in 1904.
**Des-nèdhè-kkè-nadè.—**Petitot, Autour du lac des Esclaves, 363, 1891.

**Desnedeyarelottine** ('people of the great river below'). An Etchareottine division living on the banks of upper Mackenzie r., British America.
**Des-nèdhè-yaρè-l'Ottinè.—**Petitot, Autour du lac des Esclaves, 363, 1891. **Gens du Fort Norman.—**Petitot, Dict. Dènè-Dindjié, xx, 1876. **Tess-cho tinneh.—**Ross quoted by Gibbs, MS., B. A. E., 1866. **Tρi-kka-Gottinè.—**Petitot, Autour, op. cit. ('people on the water').

**Dest.** A former village, probably Timuquanan, in Florida, lat. 28° 30', near a small lake.—Bartram, Voy., I, map, 1799.

**Destcaraguetaga.** Named by La Salle (Margry, Déc., II, 149, 1877) with the Mahican, Manhattan, Minisink, and others as a New England tribe in 1681. Unidentified.

**Destchetinaye** ('tree in a spring of water'). A Coyotero band or clan at San Carlos agency, Ariz., in 1881; considered by Bourke (Jour. Am. Folk-lore, III, 112, 1890) to be an offshoot of a former clan of which the Titsessenaye also formed part.

**Destchin** ('red paint'). An Apache band or clan at San Carlos agency and Ft Apache, Ariz., in 1881 (Bourke in Jour. Am. Folk-lore, III, 111, 1890); coordinate with the Chie of the Chiricahua and the Theshchini of the Navaho.
**Deshtchin.—**Gatschet, Apache MS., B. A. E., 1883. **Dis-cheiné.—**White, Apache Names of Ind. Tribes, MS., B. A. E.

**Detsanayuka** (*Detsănáyuka*, 'bad campers'). A division of the Comanche, formerly called Nokoni ('wanderers'), but on the death of a chief bearing the latter name their designation was changed. In 1847 they were said to number 1,750, in 250 lodges, evidently a gross exaggeration;

in 1869 their number was 312, and in 1872 they were reported at 250. Their present population is unknown, as no official account is now taken of the various Comanche divisions.      (J. M.)
**Detsănáyuka.—**Mooney in 14th Rep. B. A. E., 1044, 1896. **Go-about band.—**Sen. Ex. Doc. O, 39th Cong., 1st sess., 4, 1866. **Nacanes.—**Pénicaut (1712) in Margry, Déc., v, 504, 1883. **Nacanne.—**Jefferys (1763), Am. Atlas, map 5, 1776. **Naconômes.—**Rivera, Diario, leg. 2, 602, 1736. **Nacunes.—**Boudinot, Star in the West, 127, 1816. **Na-ko-nies.—**Neighbors in Ind. Aff. Rep., 577, 1848. **No-co-me.—**Leavenworth (1868) in H. R. Misc. Doc. 139, 41st Cong., 2d sess., 6, 1870. **Noconee.—**Neighbors in Ind. Aff. Rep. 1856, 175, 1857. **Noconi.—** Pimentel, Cuadro Desc., II, 347, 1865 (or Yiuhta, confused with Ute). **Noconi Comanches.—**Leavenworth in Sen. Ex. Doc. 60, 40th Cong., 2d sess., 3, 1869. **No-coo-nees.—**Butler in H. R. Doc. 76, 29th Cong., 2d sess., 6, 1847. **No'koni.—**Hoffman in Proc. Am. Philos. Soc., XXIII, 300, 1886 (trans. 'movers'). **No-ko-nies.—**Neighbors in Schoolcraft, Ind. Tribes, II, 127, 1852. **People in a Circle.—**Butler in H. R. Doc. 76, 29th Cong., 2d sess., 6, 1847. **Tist'shinoie'ka.—**Hoffman in Proc. Am. Philos. Soc., XXIII, 299, 1886 (trans. 'bad movers'). **Tistshnoie'ka.—**Ibid., 300. **Tüχtchĕnóyika.—**Gatschet, Comanche MS., B. A. E., 1893 (trans. 'people removing from place to place'). **Wanderers.—**Alvord in H. R. Ex. Doc. 240, 41st Cong., 2d sess., 151, 1870.

**Devil.** See *Religion*.

**Devil's Medicine-man Band.** A Sihasapa band; not identified.—Culbertson in Smithson. Rep. 1850, 141, 1851.

**Deyodeshot** ('there is a spring,' from the neighboring Avon Springs.—Hewitt). A modern Seneca settlement that formerly stood about 2 m. s. E. of the present site of East Avon, on the site of the ancient Seneca settlement of Keinthe.     (J. M.)
**De-o'-de-sotª.—**Morgan, League Iroq., 468, 1851. **Dĕyodĕ's'hot.—**Hewitt, inf'n, 1886 (correct Seneca form). **Dyudoosot.—**Shea, note in Charlevoix, New France, III, 289, 1868. **Gandachioragon.—**Jes. Rel. 1672, 24, 1858. **Gandachiragou.—**Jes. Rel. 1670, 69, 1858. **Gannondata.—**Denonville (1687) quoted by Morgan, League Iroq., 316, 1851. **Gannounata.—**Denonville (1687) in N. Y. Doc. Col. Hist., IX, 367, 1855. **Ganochiaragon.—**La Salle (1682) in Margry, Déc., II, 217, 1877. **Keint-he.—**Greenhalgh (1677) in N. Y. Doc. Col. Hist., III, 251, 1853. **Onnenatu.—**Belmont (1687) quoted by Conover, Kanadesaga and Geneva MS., B. A. E. **Ounnenatu.—**Ibid. **Saint Jean.—**Mission name about 1670. **Saint John.—**The same. **Tanochioragon.—**Writer of 1686 in Margry, Déc., II, 99, 1877.

**Deyohnegano** ('at the cold spring'). (1) A former Seneca village near Caledonia, N. Y.; (2) A former Seneca village on Allegany res., Cattaraugus co., N. Y., near Allegheny r.
**Allegany Village.—**Morgan, League Iroq., 466, 1851. **Cananouagan.—**La Tour, map, 1779. **Cold Spring Village.—**Brown, West. Gaz., 355, 1817. **Deónagäno.—**Morgan, League Iroq., 466, 1851. **Dĕyo-hne-gă'-no.—**Hewitt, inf'n, 1886. **Dunewangua.—**Procter (1791) in Am. State Papers, Ind. Aff., I, 152, 1832.

**Deyonongdadagana** ('two little hills close together.'—Hewitt). An important Seneca village formerly on the w. bank of Genesee r. near Cuylerville, N. Y. The tract was sold by the Indians in 1803.
**De-o-nun'-dä-gä-a.—**Morgan, League Iroq., 426, 1851. **De-yo-noñ-dä-dä-gäⁿ'-ă.—**Hewitt, inf'n, 1886. **Little Beard's Town.—**Morris deed (1797) in Am. State Papers, Ind. Aff., I, 627, 1832.

**Dhatada.** One of the four gentes of the Hangashenu subdivision of the Omaha.

The meaning is lost, although Dorsey translates it 'bird.'

Ɵatada.—Dorsey in 3 1 Rep. B. A. E., 219, 1885; 15th Rep. B. A. E., 226, 1897. **Lä'-tä-dä.**—Morgan, Anc. Soc., 155, 1877.

**Dhegiha** ('on this side.'—Fletcher). A term employed by J. O. Dorsey to distinguish a group of the Siouan family comprising the Omaha, Ponca, Osage, Kansa, and Quapaw tribes. Dorsey arranged the group in two subdivisions: the Quapaw or Lower Dhegiha, consisting of the Quapaw only; and the Omaha, or Upper Dhegiha, including with the Omaha, the Osage, Kansa, and Ponca. See *Chiwere.*

Ɵegiha.—Dorsey in 3d Rep. B. A. E., 211, 1885 (Ponca and Omaha name for themselves). Ɵeχaha.—Dorsey, Osage MS., B. A. E., 1883 (name of Osage for themselves). **Dʝe-tú'.**—Dorsey, Kwapa MS. vocab., B. A. E., 1891 (used by the Quapaw in speaking of themselves). **Dhegiha.**—Dorsey in Am. Antiq., 168, 1879. **Yegaha.**—Dorsey, Kansas MS., B. A. E., 1883 (name of Kansa for themselves on their own land).

**Dhighida.** A Ponca gens, divided into the subgentes Sindeagdhe and Wamiitazhi, according to Dorsey. The meaning of the name is lost.

Ɵixida.—Dorsey in 15th Rep. B. A. E., 228, 1897 (trans. 'bird'). **De-a-ghe'-ta.**—Morgan, Anc. Soc., 155, 1877 (trans. 'many people').

**Dhiu.** Mentioned by Oñate (Doc. Inéd., XVI, 114, 1871) as a pueblo of New Mexico in 1598. Doubtless situated in the Salinas, in the vicinity of Abo, E. of the Rio Grande, and in all probability a village of the Piros or the Tigua.

**Dictionaries.** Dictionaries have been made of at least 63 different North American Indian languages belonging to 19 linguistic families, besides many vocabularies of other languages. Of 122 dictionaries mentioned below more than half are still in manuscript.

Beginning with the Eskimauan family, vocabularies of Greenland Eskimo have been supplied by the labors of Egede (1750), Fabricius (1804), Kleinschmidt (1871), Rink (1877), and Kjer and Rasmussen (1893); of Labrador Eskimo, by Erdmann (1864); of Chiglit (Kopagmiut), by Petitot (1876); and there are collections by Pinart of the Aleutian Fox (Unalaskan Aleut) dialect (1871, MS.), and of that of the Kaniagmiut (1871–72, MS.).

In the Athapascan languages there are the dictionaries of Végréville for the Chipewyan (1853–90, MS.), the threefold dictionary of Petitot for the Montagnais (Chipewyan), Peau de Lièvre (Kawchodinne), and Loucheux (Kutchin) (1876); of Radloff for the Kenai (Knaiakhotana) (1874); of Garrioch (1885) for the Beaver (Tsattine); of Morice for the Tsilkotin (1884, MS.); of Matthews (1890, MS.) and Weber (1905, MS.) for the Navaho; and of Goddard for the Hupa (1904, MS.).

Of the languages of the Algonquian family, the Cree has dictionaries by Watkins (1865), Lacombe (1874), and Végréville (*ca.* 1800, MS.); the Montagnais, by Silvy (*ca.* 1678, MS.), Favre (1696, MS.), Laure (1726, MS.), and Lemoine (1901); the Algonkin, 3 by anonymous Jesuit fathers (1661, 1662, 1667, all MS.) and 1 each by André (*ca.* 1688, MS.), Thavenet (*ca.* 1815, MS.), and Cuoq (1886); the Micmac, by Rand (Micmac-English, 1854, MS., and English-Micmac, 1888); the Malecite-Passamaquoddy, by Demillier (*ca.* 1840, MS.); the Abnaki, by Rasles (1691, first printed in 1833), Aubéry (1712–15, MS.), Lesueur (*ca.* 1750, MS.), Nudénans (1760, MS.), Mathevet (*ca.* 1780, MS.), and Vetromile (1855–75, MS.); the Natick Massachuset, by Trumbull (1903); the Delaware, by Ettwein (*ca.* 1788, MS.), Dencke (*ca.* 1820, MS.), Henry (1860, MS.), Zeisberger (1887), and Brinton and Anthony (1888); the Ojibwa (Chippewa), by Belcourt (*ca.* 1840, MS.), Baraga (1853, new ed. 1878–80), Wilson (1874), and Férard (1890, MS.); the Potawatomi, by Bourassa (*ca.* 1840, MS.) and Gailland (*ca.* 1870, MS.); the Ottawa, by Jaunay (*ca.* 1740, MS.); the Shawnee, by Gatschet (1894, MS.); the Peoria Illinois, by Gravier (*ca.* 1710, MS.) and Gatschet (1893, MS.); the Miami Illinois, by Le Boulanger (*ca.* 1720, MS.); the Menominee, by Krake (1882–89, MS.) and Hoffman (1892); the Blackfoot (Siksika), by Lacombe (1882–83, MS.), Tims (1889), and McLean (1890, MS.).

In the Iroquoian languages there are dictionaries of the Huron (Wyandot), by Le Caron (1616–25, MS.), Sagard (1632, repr. 1865), Brebœuf (*ca.* 1640, MS.), Chaumonot (*ca.* 1680, MS.), and Carheil (1744, MS.); of the Iroquois Mohawk, by Bruyas (1862), Marcoux (1844, MS.), and Cuoq (1882); of the Iroquois Seneca, by Jesuit fathers (MS.); the Iroquois Onondaga, by Jesuit fathers (printed in 1860); of the Iroquois Tuscarora, by Mrs E. A. Smith (1880–82, MS.) and Hewitt (1886, MS.); besides extended glossaries of the Cherokee, by Gatschet (1881, MS.) and Mooney (1885, MS.; and 1900, 19th Rep. B. A. E.).

In the Muskhogean languages there are the dictionaries of the Choctaw by Byington (*ca.* 1865, MS.), Wright (1880), and Rouquette (*ca.* 1880, MS.); of the Maskoki (Creek), by Robertson (1860–89, MS.) and Loughridge (1882, MS.).

The Siouan family is provided with dictionaries of the Santee Dakota by Riggs (1852, 1890) and Williamson (1871, 1886); of the Yankton Dakota, by Williamson (1871); of the Quapaw, the Biloxi, the Winnebago, and the Dhegiha

(Omaha), by Dorsey (1891–95, MS.); of the Hidatsa, by Matthews (1873–74); and of the Kansa, by Bourassa (*ca.* 1850, MS.).

Other linguistic families are represented by dictionaries or extended glossaries as follows: Natchesan, Natchez lexicon, by Gatschet (1893, MS.); Chitimachan, Shetimasha (Chitimacha), by Gatschet (*ca.* 1880, MS.); Caddoan, Pawnee, by Dunbar (1880, MS.); Tonkawan, Tonkawa, by Gatschet (*ca.* 1877, MS.); Kiowan, Kiowa, by Mooney (1900, MS.); Shoshonean, Snake (Shoshoni), by Gebow (1864, 1868), and Comanche, by Rejon (1866); Koluschan, Chilkat, by Everette (*ca.* 1880, MS.); Chimmesyan, Tsimshian, by Boas (1898, MS.); Salishan, Kalispel by Giorda (1877–79), Twana by Eells (*ca.* 1880, MS.), and Nisqualli by Gibbs (1877); Chinookan, Chinook by Gibbs (1863) and Boas (1900, MS.), and Chinook jargon by Blanchet (1856), Gibbs (1863), Demers (1871), Gill (1882), Prosch (1888), Tate (1889), Coones (1891), Bulmer (1891, MS.), St Onge (1892, MS.), and Eells (1893, MS.); Kitunahan, Kutenai, by Chamberlain (1891–1905, MS.); Shahaptian, Nez Percé by McBeth (1893, MS.) and Gatschet (1896, MS.); Lutuamian, Klamath by Gatschet (1890); Shastan, Shasta, by Gatschet (1877, MS.); Piman, Cora by Ortega (1732, repr. 1888), Opata by Pimentel (1863), and Tarahumare by Steffel (1791) and Lumholtz (1894, MS.).        (w. e.)

**Diegueños.** A collective name, probably in part synonymous with Comeya, applied by the Spaniards to Indians of the Yuman stock who formerly lived in and around San Diego, Cal., whence the term; it included representatives of many tribes and has no proper ethnic significance; nevertheless it is a firmly established name and is here accepted to include the tribes formerly living about San Diego and extending s. to about lat. 31° 30′. A few Diegueños still live in the neighborhood of San Diego. There are about 400 Indians included under this name as attached to the Mission agency of California, but they are now officially recognized as part of the "Mission Indians." The rancherias formerly occupied by the Diegueños, so far as known, are: Abascal, Awhut, Cajon, Camajal, Campo, Capitan Grande, Cenyowpreskel(?), Cojuat, Coquilt, Corral, Cosoy, Cuyamaca, Ekquall, Focomae, Gueymura, Hasoomale, Hassasei, Hataam, Hawai, Honwee Vallecito, Icayme, Inomassi, Inyaha, Kwalwhut, Laguna, La Punta, Lorenzo, Mactati, Maramoydos, Mataguay, Matamo, Matironn, Mattawottis, Melejo, Mesa Chiquita, Mesa Grande, Meti, Nellmole, Nipaguay, Otai, Otat, Pocol, Prickaway, San Dieguito, San Felipe, San José, San Luis, San Pascual, Santa Isabel, Sequan,

Suahpi, Tacahlay, Tahwie, Tapanque, Toowed, Valle de las Viejas, Wahti, Xamacha, Xana, and Yacum. The Conejos and the Coyotes are mentioned as former bands of the Diegueños.        (h. w. h.)
Daigano.—Palmer in Am. Nat., XI, 736, 1877. **Diagano.**—Ibid., 743. **Diegana.**—Ind. Aff. Rep., 361, 1859. **Diegeenos.**—Whipple, Exp'n from San Diego to the Colorado, 2, 1851. **Diegenes.**—Sleigh (1873) in H. R. Ex. Doc. 91, 43d Cong., 1st sess., 6, 1874. **Diegino.**—Burton (1856) in H. R. Ex. Doc. 76, 34th Cong., 3d sess., 115, 1857. **Diegmons.**—Jackson and Kinney, Rep. Miss. Ind., 20, 1883. **Dieguinos.**—Wozencraft (1852) in Sen. Ex. Doc. 4, 32d ong., spec. sess., 288, 1853. **Diegunos.**—Whipple (1849) in Schoolcraft, Ind. Tribes, II, 100, 1852. **Digenes.**—Ind. Aff. Rep., 13, 1879. **Diogenes.**—Ind. Aff. Rep. 1902, 595, 1903. **Disguino.**—Burton (1856) in H. R. Ex. Doc. 76, 34th Cong., 3d sess., 127, 1857. **Kamia.**—A. L. Kroeber, inf'n, 1905 (Mohave name; cf. *Comeya*). **Llégeenos.**—Whipple, Exp'n from San Diego to the Colorado, 2, 1851 (misprint). **Lligunos.**—Whipple (1849) in Schoolcraft, Ind. Tribes, II, 100, 1852 (misprint).

**Digger.** Said by Powell to be the English translation of Nuanuints, the name of a small tribe near St George, s. w. Utah. It was the only Paiute tribe practising agriculture, hence the original signification of the name, "digger." In time the name was applied to every tribe known to use roots extensively for food and hence to be "diggers." It thus included very many of the tribes of California, Oregon, Idaho, Utah, Nevada, and Arizona, tribes speaking widely different languages and embracing perhaps a dozen distinct linguistic stocks. As the root-eaters were supposed to represent a low type of Indian, the term speedily became one of opprobium.        (h. w. h.)

**Digging sticks.** See *Agriculture, Perforated stones.*

**Dighton Rock.** A mass of silicious conglomerate lying in the margin of Taunton r., Bristol co., Mass., on which is an ancient, probably prehistoric, inscription. The length of the face measured at the base is 11½ ft. and the height a little more than 5 ft. The whole face, to within a few inches of the ground, is covered with the inscription, which consists of irregular

DIGHTON ROCK, MASS.    (LENGTH ABOUT 12 FT)

lines and outline figures, a few having a slight resemblance to runes; others triangular and circular, among which can be distinguished 3 outline faces. The earliest copy was that of Danforth in 1680. Cotton Mather copied a part as early as 1690 and sent a rude woodcut of the entire inscription to the Royal Society of Great Britain in 1712. Copies were also made by Isaac Greenwood in 1730; by Stephen Sewell, of Cambridge, in 1768; by Prof. Winthrop in 1788; by Joseph Gooding in 1790; by Edward A. Kendall in 1807; by Job Gardner in 1812, and one for the Rhode Island Historical Society in 1830. Soon after this the suggestion was made that it was a runic inscription of the Norsemen, and the interest excited by this caused it to be frequently copied and published. The subject, with accompanying figures, was thoroughly discussed by Danish antiquaries, especially by Rafn, in Antiquitates Americanæ (1837). The earlier drawings mentioned above are reproduced by Mallery (10th Rep. B. A. E., pl. xi, 1893). The annexed illustration from a photograph is perhaps the most nearly correct of any published. The opinions advanced in regard to the origin and signification of the inscription vary widely. The members of the French Academy, to whom a copy was sent, judged it to be Punic; Lort, in a paper in Archæologia (London, 1786), expressed the opinion that it was the work of a people from Siberia; Gen. Washington, who saw Winthrop's drawings at Cambridge in 1789, pronounced the inscription similar to those made by the Indians; Davis and Kendall also ascribed it to the Indians, the former thinking it represented an Indian deer hunt. The Danish antiquaries decided that it was the work of the Northmen; Prof. Finn Magnusen interpreted the central portion, assuming it to consist of runes, as meaning that Thorfinn with 151 men took possession of the country; and even Dr De Costa was persuaded that the central part is runic. Buckingham Smith, according to Haven (Proc. Am. Antiq. Soc., Apr. 29, 1863), was inclined to believe it to consist of ciphers used by the Roman Catholic Church. Schoolcraft, although charged with wavering in his opinion, decided without reservation in 1853 that it was entirely Indian. The latter author submitted several drawings of the inscription to an Algonquian chief, who, rejecting a few of the figures near the center, interpreted the remainder as the memorial of a battle between two native tribes. Although this Indian's explanation is considered doubtful, the general conclusion of students in later years, especially after Mallery's discussion, is that the inscription is the work of Indians and belongs to a type found in Pennsylvania and at points in the W.

Following are the more important writings on the subject of Dighton Rock: Antiquitates Americanæ, 1837; Archæologia, viii, 1786; T. Ewbank, N. Am. Rockwriting, 1866; Gravier in Compte-rendu Cong. Internat. des Américanistes, i, 1875; Haven in Proc. Am. Antiq. Soc., Apr. 29, 1863, Oct. 21, 1864, Oct., 1867; Kendall, Trav., ii, 1809; Mallery in 10th Rep. B. A. E., 1893; Mem. Am. Acad. Arts and Sci., ii, pt. 2, 1804, iii, pt. 1, 1809; Philos. Trans. Roy. Soc. Lond., xxviii, 1714; Rau (1) in Am. Antiq., i, 1878; (2) in Mag. Am. Hist., Feb., 1878, Apr., 1879; Schoolcraft, Ind. Tribes, i, 1851, iv, 1854; Trans. Soc. Antiquaries, Lond., 1732; Winsor, Hist. Am., i, 1884. (C. T.)

**Dippers and Ladles.** See *Receptacles*.

**Discoidal stones.** Prehistoric objects of unknown use (see *Problematical objects*) whose most typical form is that of a double-convex or double-concave lens. The perimeter is a circle and the sides range from considerably convex through plane to deeply concave. The diameter varies from 1 in. to 8 in., the thickness from one-fourth of an inch to 6 in., very rarely passing these limits; the two dimensions have no definite relation to each other. Some specimens are convex on one face and plane on the other; but when one face is concave the other is also. Of the latter form many have a secondary depression at the center; others have a perforation which is sometimes enlarged until the disk becomes a ring. They are made principally of very hard rock, as quartz, flint, jasper, novaculite, quartzite, porphyry, syenite, and the like, though stone as soft as marble, sandstone, barite, and even steatite was sometimes chosen. No type of relics is more difficult to classify than these disks.

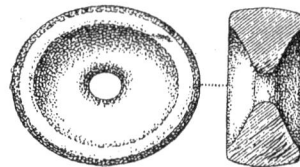

DISK OF GRANITE; VIRGINIA. (1-6)

The name first given them, and by which they are still commonly known, is "chunkey stones," from the native name of the game played with analogous disks by southern Indians. But the description of the game, considered in connection with the great variation in size and material of the specimens, shows that only a small percentage of them could have been thus utilized. Culin believes that a limited number may be definitely regarded as chunkey stones. He recognizes three types: (1) perforated (least common); (2) symmetrical, unperforated; (3) asymmetrical, unperforated. A similar diversity is observed in the stones used in the analogous Hawaiian game of *maika* (24th Rep. B. A. E., 1906). From the smooth, symmetrical, highly polished chunkey stone they merge by insensible gradations into mullers, pestles, mortars, pitted stones, polishing and grinding stones, hammers, sinkers, club heads, and ornaments, for all of which purposes except the last they may have been used in some of their stages, so that no dividing line is possible. They present various styles and degrees of finish. Many retain their natural surface on both sides with the edge worked off by grinding or pecking, the latter marks possibly resulting from use as hammers. The sides may be ground down while the edge remains untouched; or, when made from a thick pebble, the sides may be pecked and the edge ground. Some specimens which are entirely unworked require very close examination to distinguish them from others whose whole surface has been artificially produced. It is possible, however, to arrange a large number of specimens from one locality in a regular series from a roughly chipped disk to a finished product of the highest polish and symmetry. The finest specimens, in greatest numbers, come from the states s. of the Ohio r., and from Arkansas eastward to the Atlantic. The territory within a radius of 100 m. around Chattanooga, Tenn., and for about the same distance around Memphis, is especially rich in them. From s. E. Ohio to central Missouri a considerable number has been found, though few of them are as well wrought as those from the S. Rather rough ones occur along the Delaware r. Beyond the limits indicated the type practically disappears. Discoidal stones corresponding closely with eastern types, save that the faces are rarely concave, are found in the Pueblo country and in the Pacific states. See *Chunkey*.

Objects of the class here described are referred to by numerous authors, including Fowke (1) Archæol. Hist. Ohio, 1902, (2) in 13th Rep. B. A. E., 1896; Jones, Antiq. So. Inds., 1873; Moorehead, Prehist. Impls., 1900; Squier and Davis, Ancient Monuments, 1848; Rau, Archæol. Coll. Nat. Mus., 1876; Thruston, Antiq. Tenn., 1897.                          (G. F.)

**Disease.** See *Health.*

**Dishes.** Vessels for the preparation and serving of food and other purposes were manufactured by all Indian tribes. While their use as receptacles prescribes a concavity of circular, oval, or oblong outline, there is a great variety of shape, decoration, etc., according to individual taste or tribal custom, and a wide range of material, as stone, shell, bone, ivory, horn, rawhide, bark, wood, gourd, pottery, and basketry.

The vessels for serving food were not used to hold individual portions, for the Indians ate in common; but the little dishes held salt and other condiments, small quantities of delicate foods, etc. The larger dishes contained preparations of corn or other soft vegetables, and the trays and platters were for game, bread, etc., or for mixing or preparing food. In many cases the cooking pot held the common meal, and portions were taken out by means of small dishes and ladles, in which they were cooled and eaten. Some dishes had special uses, as platters, mats, and trays for drying fruits, roasting seeds, etc., and as ceremonial bowls, baskets, etc.

From archeological sites have been collected many examples of dishes. Some made of soapstone were found in several Eastern and Southern states, and in Wyoming and California. Vessels formed of seashells, cut principally from *Busycon*, and also from *Cassis, Strombus*, and *Fasciolaria*, were found in Ohio, Indiana, Illinois, Iowa, Arkansas, Georgia, and Florida. Dishes of pottery come from many parts of the United States and some made of wood from Florida.

The Indians in general used dishes of wood, and even where pottery, basketry, and bark were common, wooden vessels were made. Each region supplied suitable woods. A predilection for burl wood and knots was general. The majority of existing wooden vessels were fashioned with iron tools, but before metal was introduced they were excavated by means of fire and stone tools. Eskimo wooden dishes were sometimes cut from a single piece, but they usually had a rim of bent wood fastened to the excavated bottom and were oval in shape. Those of the N. W. coast tribes were boxes of rectangular shape, with scarfed and bent sides attached to the bottom; but the Indians also had excavated dishes carved to represent animal forms in great variety, and small bowls of horn occur. The Salishan tribes made dishes of wood and horn which were elaborately carved. The northern Athapascans as a rule used dishes, platters, and trays of birch bark folded and sewed, but among some tribes the dishes were like those of the Eskimo.

The Chippewa had well-finished wooden dishes of rectangular, oval, or circular shape. The Iroquois made excellent dishes, cups, bowls, etc., of burl wood, and sometimes furnished them with handles. The Plains Indians also used in preference burl or knot wood, and while as a rule their dishes were simple in outline and homely, some specimens were well carved and finished. The Virginia and other Southern Indians cut dishes, often of large size, from soft wood; of these the Cherokee and Choctaw bowls and platters made of tupelo are noteworthy. The Ute made rude oval bowls with projections at the ends, and oblong platters and knot bowls with handles. The Paiute used for dishes the carapace of the box turtle. The Pueblos, while relying mainly on pottery and basketry, had dishes wrought from knots and mountain-sheep horn. The Pima and Papago made oblong trays and shallow platters from mesquite wood. The Hupa of N. California cut large, flat trays from redwood. The tribes of the Santa Barbara region, California, inlaid wooden vessels with mother-of-pearl.

Bark dishes were extensively used by tribes within the birch area and to some extent by all the forest Indians. Those of the S. made great use of gourds.

The Pueblo Indians employed pottery and to some extent basketry for dishes, and the same is true in a lesser degree of some of the Plains and Eastern tribes. Southwestern and Californian Indians made use of basketry almost exclusively. See *Bark, Basketry, Bowls, Implements, Pottery, Receptacles, Woodwork.*

Consult Goddard in Univ. Cal. Publ., Am. Archæol. and Ethnol., I, no. 1, 1903; Holmes in 20th Rep. B. A. E., 1903; Moore in Jour. Acad. Nat. Sci. Phila., X–XII, 1894–1903; Murdoch in 9th Rep. B. A. E., 1892; Nelson in 18th Rep. B. A. E., 1899; Niblack in Rep. Nat. Mus. 1888, 1890; Swanton in Mem. Am. Mus. Nat. Hist., V, 1905; Turner in 11th Rep. B. A. E., 1894. (W. H.)

**Distancia.** One of the villages of the Opata.—Hrdlicka in Am. Anthrop., VI, 72, 1904.

**Ditsakana** (*Ditsä′kăna*, 'sewers'). A Comanche division, the name of which was formerly Widyu ('awl'), but on the death of a chief bearing the same name it was changed to Ditsakana. They were also popularly known as Yamparika, from their habit of eating yampa root. They were estimated to number 356 in 1869, and 200 in 1872, but their present population is unknown, as the Comanche divisions are not officially recognized. (J. M.)
Ditsä′kăna.—Mooney in 14th Rep. B. A. E., 1044, 1896. Etsitü′biwat.—Ibid. ('northerners'). Gūi-yūs.—Butcher and Lyendecher, MS. Comanche vocab., B. A. E., 1867. It-chit-a-bud-ah.—Neighbors in Schoolcraft, Ind. Tr., II, 128, 1852. Jupes.—Bol. Soc. Mex., V, 318, 1857. Lamparacks.—Bollaert in Jour. Ethnol. Soc. Lond., II, 265, 1850. Lemparack.—Latham in Trans. Philol. Soc. Lond., 1856. Llamparicas.—Escudero, Noticias Nuevo Mex., 83, 1849. Root Diggers.—Butler in H. R. Doc. 76, 29th Cong., 2d sess., 6, 1847. Root-Eaters.—Schoolcraft, Ind. Tribes, I, 522, 1851. Samparicka.—Maximilian, Trav., 510, 1843. Tapparies Comanches.—Alvord in Sen. Ex. Doc. 18, 40th Cong., 3d sess., 23, 1869 (misprint). Teachatzkennas.—Ibid., 36. Teckat Kenna.—McKusker in Sen. Ex. Doc. 40, 40th Cong., 3d sess., 14, 1869. Ted-Chath-Kennas.—Ibid. Tedchat-kenna.—Ibid. Titsakanai.—Hoffman in Proc. Am. Philos. Soc., XXIII, 300, 1886 ('the sewing people'). Tupes.—Domenech, Deserts, II, 21, 1860. Wi′dyu.—Mooney in 14th Rep. B. A. E., 1044, 1896 ('awl'). Wiuini′em.—Hoffman in Proc. Am. Philos. Soc., XXIII, 300, 1886. Yachakeenees.—Penney in Ind. Aff. Rep. 1869, 101, 1870 (probably the same; Yamparakas also given). Yamhareek.—Ruxton, Life in Far West, 201, 1849. Yamparack.—Burnet in Schoolcraft, Ind. Tribes, I, 230, 1851. Yamparakas.—Penney in Ind. Aff. Rep. 1869, 101, 1870. Yamparecks.—Keane in Stanford, Compend., 544, 1878. Yampareekas.—Hazen in Ind. Aff. Rep. 1869, 388, 1870. Yamparicas.—Mayer, Mexico, II, 123, 1853. Yam′pari′ka.—Hoffman in Proc. Am. Philos. Soc., XXIII, 299, 1886 ('yampa eaters'). Yam-pa-se-cas.—Neighbors in Ind. Aff. Rep., 574,

1848. Yampatéka.—ten Kate, Reizen in N. Am., 384, 1885. Yampaxicas.—Domenech, Deserts, II, 21, 1860. Yamperack.—Drake, Bk. Inds., xii, 1848. Yamperethka.—Battey, Advent., 90, 1875. Yamper-rikeu.—Leavenworth in H. R. Misc. Doc. 139, 41st Cong., 2d sess., 6, 1870. Yam-pe-uc-coes.—Butler in H. R. Doc. 76, 29th Cong., 2d sess., 6, 1847. Yampirica.—Sen. Ex. Doc. O, 39th Cong., 1st sess., 4, 1866. Yam-pi-rio-coes.—Butler in H. R. Doc. 76, 29th Cong., 2d sess., 8, 1847. Yäpä.—Mooney in 14th Rep. B. A. E., 1044, 1896. Yapainé.—Pimentel, Cuadro Descr., II, 347, 1865. Yaparehca.—Ibid. Yā-pă-rēs-kă.—Butcher and Lyendecher, Comanche MS. vocab., B. A. E., 1867. Ya′pa-re′χka.—Gatschet, MS. vocab., B. A. E., 1884. Yapparickoes.—McKusker in Sen. Ex. Doc. 40, 40th Cong., 3d sess., 13, 1869. Yappariko.—Alvord in Sen. Ex. Doc. 18, 40th Cong., 3d sess., 6, 1868.

**Diwa′lĭ.** See *Bowl.*

**Djahui-gitinai** (*Djaxui′ gitĭnā′i*, 'seaward Eagles'). A division of the Eagle clan of the Haida. They considered themselves a part of the Gitins of Skidegate, being simply those who lived farthest outward down Skidegate inlet, Queen Charlotte ids., Brit. Col. They formed the main part of the Eagle population at Naikun and C. Ball.—Swanton, Cont. Haida, 274, 1905.
Dj′āaquīg′it ′ena′i.—Boas, 5th Rep. N. W. Tribes Can., 26, 1889; ibid., 12th Rep., 25, 1898. Tsāagwī′ gyit′inai′.—Ibid.

**Djahui-hlgahet-kegawai** (*Djaxui′lgā′xet qē′gawa-i*, 'those born on the seaward side of Pebble town'). A subdivision of the Hlgahet-gitinai, of the Haida of Queen Charlotte ids., Brit. Col.—Swanton, Cont. Haida, 274, 1905.

**Djahui-skwahladagai** (*Djaxui′ sqoā′ładaga-i*, 'down-the-inlet Skwahladas'). A division of the Raven clan of the Haida. They were probably once a part of the Skwahladas who lived on the w. coast of Queen Charlotte ids., Brit. Col., being distinguished from them by the fact that they lived seaward (*djahui*) down Skidegate inlet.—Swanton, Cont. Haida, 269, 1905.
Djāaqui′sk·uatl′adagā′i.—Boas, 5th Rep. N. W. Tribes Can., 26, 1889. Tsāagwīsguatl′adegai′.—Ibid., 12th Rep., 25, 1898.

**Djestyedje** ('long lake'). A former village of the Kansa on Kansas r., near Lawrence, Kans.—Dorsey, Kansa MS. vocab., B. A. E., 1882.

**Djigogiga** (*Djigogi′ga*). A legendary Haida town of the Kasta-kegawai on Copper bay, Moresby id., Queen Charlotte ids., Brit. Col.—Swanton, Cont. Haida, 279, 1905.

**Djigua** (*Djĭ′gua*). A legendary Haida town on the N. shore of Cumshewa inlet, Queen Charlotte ids., Brit. Col., whence the ancestress of the Djiguaahl-lanas, Kaiahl-lanas, Kona-kegawai, and Stawas-haidagai is said to have come.—Swanton, Cont. Haida, 94, 1905.

**Djiguaahl-lanas** (*Djĭ′gua ał lā′nas*, 'Djĭ′gua town people'). A prominent division of the Eagle clan of the Haida, so named from a legendary town on the N. side of Cumshewa inlet, whence their ancestress, who was also the ancestress of the Kai-ahl-lanas, Kona-kegawai, and Stawas-hai-dagai, is said to have come. They lived in the town of Kloo.—Swanton, Cont. Haida, 273, 1905.

Tsēgoatl lā′nas.—Boas, 12th Rep. N. W. Tribes Can., 25, 1898.

**Djihuagits** (*Djixuágĭts*, Masset dialect *Chawagis*, 'always low water'). A Haida town on a creek just s. of Naikun, E. coast of Graham id., N. w. Brit. Col. Anciently it belonged to the Naikun-kegawai, but afterward to the Chawagis-stustae.—Swanton, Cont. Haida, 280, 1905.

**Djishtangading.** A Hupa village at a bend in Trinity r. at the extreme s. end of Hupa valley, Cal., below the mouth of Tishtangatang cr. (P. E. G.)

Djictañadĭñ.—Goddard, Life and Culture of the Hupa, 12, 1903. Pa-tes-oh.—McKee (1851) in Sen. Ex. Doc. 4, 32d Cong., spec. sess., 194, 1853. Pat-isch-oh.—Meyer, Nach dem Sacramento, 282, 1855. Peht-sau-an.—Gibbs, MS., B. A. E., 1852. Pepht-soh.—Gibbs in Schoolcraft, Ind. Tribes, III, 139, 1853. Pétsawan.—Goddard, inf'n, 1903 (Yurok name). Tish-tan′-a-tan.—Powers in Cont. N. A. Ethnol., III, 73, 1877.

**Djus-hade** (*Djus xade′*, 'people of Djus island'). A division of the Eagle clan of the Haida, living on an island of the same name at the entrance of Tsooskahli, Queen Charlotte ids., and closely related to the Widja-gitunai, Tohlka-gitunai, and Chets-gitunai. They afterward moved to the mouth of Masset inlet. A branch of the Kuna-lanas received the same name.—Swanton, Cont. Haida, 275, 1905.

Dzōs hāedrai′.—Boas, 12th Rep. N. W. Tribes Can., 23, 1898.

**Dockmackie.** A name of the maple-leaved arrowwood (*Viburnum acerifolium*). The Indians used this plant for external application in tumors, etc. The terminal -*ie* suggests that the word came from them first to the Dutch, and from these to English-speakers. According to Miss L. S. Chamberlain (Am. Nat., XXXV, 3, 1901), the Delawares smoked *dogekumak*. W. R. Gerard (Gard. and For., IX, 262, 1896) says it is from a Mahican word meaning 'it is cooling,' which would be related to the Chippewa *takaiamagad*, 'it is cool.' A Delaware origin is however more probable. (A. F. C.)

**Doestoe** ('live where there are large falls of water'). A subdivision of Apache under chiefs Chiquito and Disalin in 1875.

Does-to′-e.—White, Apache Names of Ind. Tribes, MS., B. A. E.

**Dog.** A former division of the Foxes.

**Dog.** See *Many Horses.*

**Dog Creek.** A Shuswap village or band on upper Fraser r. below the mouth of Chilcotin r., Brit. Col. Pop. 14 in 1904.—Can. Ind. Aff. 1904, pt. 2, 72, 1904.

**Dogachamus.** A name for *Cornus circinata*, cited by Gerard (Gard. and For., IX, 263, 1896), who states that it is a corruption of *damaganatikwamosi*, 'pipe-

stem bush,' in the Penobscot dialect of Algonquian. The word is also spelled *dogackerme*. (A. F. C.)

**Dogekumak.** See *Dockmackie.*

**Dogi.** Mentioned by Lederer (Discov., 2, 1672) as a people who inhabited the piedmont region of Virginia before the appearance of the historic tribes in that section. They were extinct at the time of his journey in 1670. Apparently distinct from the Doeg (Nanticoke).

Tacci.—Lederer, op. cit.

**Do-gitunai** (*Dō-gĭtAnā′-i*, 'Gitans of the west coast'). A division of the Eagle clan of the Haida. They are said to have branched off from the Mamun-gitunai, and, as the name implies, their towns and camping places were on the w. coast of Queen Charlotte id., Brit. Col.—Swanton, Cont. Haida, 275, 1905.

Tōgyit′inai′.—Boas, 12th Rep. N. W. Tribes Can., 22, 1898.

**Dogs.** A band or a secret order of the Hidatsa.—Culbertson in Smithson. Rep. 1850, 143, 1851.

**Dogs.** See *Domestication.*

**Dog Soldiers.** See *Military societies.*

**Doguenes.** A tribe or division of a tribe met by Cabeza de Vaca about 1527, when they were living on the mainland near the coast, probably in the vicinity of San Antonio bay, Tex. The region was probably occupied by Karankawan people, but the data are too meager to determine the ethnic relations of the Doguenes. See Gatschet, Karankawa Inds., 46, 1891.

Aguenes.—Cabeza de Vaca (1555), Bandelier trans., 120, 1905. Deaguanes.—Ibid., 79. Deguenes.—Ibid., 123. Doguenes.—Cabeza de Vaca, Smith trans., 137, 1871. Draguanes.—Ibid., 56, ed. 1851.

**Dohasan** (*Dohásän*, 'little bluff'; also *Dohá, Doháte*, 'bluff'). The hereditary name of a line of chiefs of the Kiowa for nearly a century. It has been borne by at least four members of the family, viz: (1) The first of whom there is remembrance was originally called Pá-do‘gá′-i or Padó′gâ, 'White-faced-buffalo-bull,' and this name was afterward changed to Dohá or Doháte. He was a prominent chief. (2) His son was originally called Ä′añoñ′te (a word of doubtful etymology), and afterward took his father's name of Doháte, which was changed to Dohásän, 'Little Dohate,' or 'Little-bluff,' for distinction. He became a great chief, ruling over the whole tribe from 1833 until his death on Cimarron r. in 1866, since which time no one has had unquestioned allegiance in the tribe. His portrait was painted in 1834 by Catlin, who calls him Teh-toot-sah, and his name appears in the treaty of 1837 as "To-ho-sa, the Top of the Mountain." (3) His son, whose widow is An-kímä, inherited his father's name, Dohásän. He was also a distinguished warrior, and died about 1894. His scalp shirt and war-bonnet case are in the National Museum. (4) The nephew of the great Dohásän II and cousin of the last mentioned (3) was also called Dohásän, and always wore a silver cross with the name "Tohasan" engraved upon it. He was the author of the Scott calendar and died in 1892. Shortly before his death he changed his name to Dánpä′, 'shoulder-blade,' from *dán*, 'shoulder' (?), leaving only Ankímä's husband (3) to bear the hereditary name, which is now extinct. Dohasan II, the greatest chief in the history of the Kiowa tribe, in 1833 succeeded A′dáte, who had been deposed for having allowed his people to be surprised and massacred by the Osage in that year. It was chiefly through his influence that peace was made between the Kiowa and Osage after the massacre referred to, which has never been broken. In 1862, when the Cheyenne, Arapaho, Comanche, Kiowa, and Kiowa Apache were assembled on Arkansas r. to receive annuities, the agent threatened them with punishment if they did not cease their raids. Dohasan listened in perfect silence to the end, when he sprang to his feet, and calling the attention of the agent to the hundreds of tipis in the valley below, replied in a characteristic speech: "The white chief is a fool. He is a coward. His heart is small—not larger than a pebble stone. His men are not strong—too few to contend against my warriors. They are women. There are three chiefs—the white chief, the Spanish chief, and myself. The Spanish chief and myself are men. We do bad toward each other sometimes—stealing horses and taking scalps—but we do not get mad and act the fool. The white chief is a child, and, like a child, gets mad quick. When my young men, to keep their women and children from starving, take from the white man passing through our country, killing and driving away our buffalo, a cup of sugar or coffee, the white chief is angry and threatens to send his soldiers. I have looked for them a long time, but they have not come. He is a coward. His heart is a woman's. I have spoken. Tell the great chief what I have said." In addition to the treaty of 1837 Dohasan was also a signer of the treaty of Ft Atkinson, Ind. T., July 27, 1853, and that of Oct. 18, 1865, on Little Arkansas r., Kansas. See Mooney in 17th Rep. B. A. E., pt. 1, 1898.

**Dokis Band.** A Chippewa band, so named from their chief, residing on a reservation of 30,300 acres at the head of French r., where it leaves L. Nipissing, Ontario. They have a large admixture of French blood, are Roman Catholics, and obtain a livelihood by hunting and fishing and by working in adjacent lumber camps. The band numbered 62 in 1884 and 78 in 1904. (J. M.)

**Dolls.** Dolls were common among all the American tribes. They were fashioned from stone, wood, clay, skin, dough, corncobs, plants, and rags. Those used merely as playthings were frequently elaborately dressed by the mother in accordance with tribal costumes. Human hair was sometimes fastened to the head and arranged in the tribal style, the face was painted, the eyebrows were marked, and tattoo lines were indicated. Labrets of bone or shell were put in place among the tribes which used these objects, and the doll was further adorned with earrings, bracelets, and necklaces. The Eskimo father carved the small bone or ivory dolls more or less elaborately, and made them stand upright, to the great delight of the

EASTERN ESKIMO DOLL　　　WESTERN ESKIMO DOLL

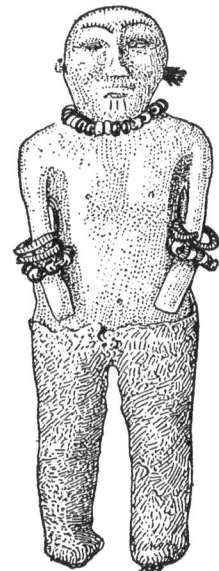

children. Among these people there was a festival in which small figures or dolls were used to represent the dead, at which time the people prepared and partook of food in their presence in memory of the time when those represented were living. The corncob and rag dolls were usually of the child's own manufacture. Those made of dough were used in a social ceremony among the Iroquois. Dolls were provided with cradles, clothing, tents, and vessels and utensils of clay.

In the S. W. and the extreme N. little figures were made for ceremonies in which mythic ancestors or dead relatives were remembered. Travelers have sometimes mistaken these figures for idols. Among the Hopi these little figures are of soft cottonwood, so cut and painted as to indicate in miniature the elaborate headdress, decorated face, body, and clothing of those who represent kachinas, or impersonations of ancestral "breath bodies" or spirits of men. These dolls are not worshipped, but are made by the priests in their kivas during the great spring ceremonies as presents for the little girls, to whom they are presented on the morning of the last day of the festival by men personating kachinas (Fewkes). In this way the young become familiar with the com-

HOPI KACHINA DOLL OF WOOD (1-4)

HOPI DOLL OF CLAY (1-2)

plicated and symbolic masks, ornaments, and garments worn during tribal and religious ceremonies. See *Amusements, Child life, Games.*

Consult Dorsey and Voth in Field Columb. Mus. Publ., 55 and 66; Fewkes in 17th, 19th, and 21st Reps. B. A. E., and Internat. Archiv. Ethnog., VII, 1894; Mooney in 17th Rep. B. A. E., 1898; Nelson in 18th Rep. B. A. E., 1899; Turner in 11th Rep. B. A. E., 1894. (A. C. F.)

**Dolores** (contracted from Span. *Nuestra Señora de los Dolores*, 'Our Lady of Sorrows'). A mission established among the Pima by Father Kino in 1687, just above Cucurpe on the headwaters of the w. branch of the Rio Sonora, in N. w. Sonora, Mexico. According to Venegas it had 2 visitas (probably Remedios and Cocospera) in 1721. Pop. 29 in 1730.
Dolores.—Mange (1699) in Bancroft, Ariz. and N. Mex., 352, 1889. **Los Dolores.**—Orozco y Berra, Geog., 347, 1864. **Nuestra Señora de los Dolores.**—Kino (1694) in Doc. Hist. Mex., 4th s., I, 248, 1856.

**Dolores.** A Spanish Franciscan mission established in California within the site of the city of San Francisco on Oct. 9, 1776. When Gov. Portola, in searching for Monterey, came to the bay of San Francisco, that had remained hidden to all previous explorers, Father Junipero Serra regarded it as a miraculous discovery, for the visitador-general in naming the missions to be established at the havens of the coast had said to the mission president, who was disappointed be-

cause the name of the founder of the order was omitted, that if St Francis desired a mission he must show his port. The missionaries impatiently brooked the obstacles that delayed planting a mission at the port that their patron saint had revealed. The site was beside the lagoon of Nuestra Señora de los Dolores, hence the mission of San Francisco de Assisi came to be known as Dolores mission. There were no natives present when the mission was opened. The inhabitants, the Romonan, had been driven from the peninsula by a hostile tribe who burned their rancherias and killed all who did not escape on rafts. When the fugitives returned to find their home occupied by the Spaniards they were disposed to contend for its possession. In the first fight the soldiers fired in the air, in the next they shot a native, upon which the savages begged for peace, but fled when the Spaniards released after a whipping those that they had captured, and were not seen again until spring. The missionaries gradually won their confidence after they returned and in October baptized 17 adults. At the end of 5 years there were 215 converts, and in 1796 they numbered 720. The neophytes when harshly treated could escape easily by water, and after 280 had run away and the soldiers were unable to stay the exodus the head missionary sent out a party of 15 Christian Indians, of whom 7 were slain by the Cuchillones. A priest, Father Fernandez, brought charges against the missionary fathers, and Gov. Borica demanded that they reform their treatment—long tasks, scant rations, and cruel punishments, evidenced by 200 escapes and as many deaths within a year. Although Father Lasuen, the mission president, promised and endeavored to remedy the alleged evils, the Indians continued to run away, and the missionaries, in 1797, sent out another party of neophytes to gather in the lost flock, but the former barely escaped the fate of the preceding party. The Saclan harbored the fugitives and threatened to kill the mission Indians if they continued to work and the soldiers if they interfered. The governor sent a detachment of troops to punish them, and in the fight 2 soldiers were wounded and 7 natives killed. The Cuchian were also attacked and the soldiers returned with 83 of the fugitive Christians. During the decade 1,213 natives were baptized and 1,031 buried, and at the end of the 18th century the neophyte population was 644. The cattle had increased to 8,200 head, and the crop in 1800 was 4,100 bushels, half of it wheat. The land about the mission was sterile, and fields 12 m. distant were planted. The neophytes first dwelt in rude huts of willow poles and tule, but between 1793 and 1798 adobe houses were built for every family and the thatched roofs of the church and mission buildings were replaced with tiles. On looms made by the Indians woolen cloth was produced in quantities sufficient to clothe the converts and blankets were woven for the presidio. In 1796 the manufacture of coarse pottery was begun. In 1820 the neophyte population was 622, but the mortality continued to be greater than in any other mission. In 1830 the population was 219. The sheep fell off to one-fifth of the former number and only a third as much grain was produced as in 1810. The decline was due to the division of the mission when San Rafael was founded in a healthier location in 1817 and San Francisco Solano in 1823. While the baptisms were exceeded only at San José, there were 2,100 deaths at San Francisco Dolores and San Rafael, whither half the neophytes were removed, in the 10 years ending with 1820. Solano, founded with the intention of transferring the entire mission, received half the neophytes of the parent mission, but returned a part when it was constituted an independent establishment. The buildings fell into ruin, except the church, which is still standing as part of the Dolores mission church of San Francisco. The number of neophytes fell to 204 in 1832, and in 1840 there were 89 at San Mateo and about 50 scattered about the district. The civilian administrator found little property in 1834 and soon none was left. The neophytes received nothing; they were never organized in a pueblo, but were apportioned among the settlers and held in servitude against their will. In 1843 the last remnant, 8 aged starvelings, appealed to the Government for help.

The tribes that came first under the influence of the Dolores mission were the Ahwaste, Altahmo, Olhon, Romonan, and Tulomo, all speaking the same language, the Costanoan, as did some other tribes, not so numerous, that lived on or near the thickly peopled shores of San Francisco bay. They subsisted by hunting and fishing. Both sexes often wore their hair short, having the custom of cutting it when afflicted by sorrow or misfortune. Those of the s. allowed their hair to grow and wore the long carefully dressed braids adorned with beads and trinkets wound about the head like a turban. The medicine-men, through their incantations, pretended to be able to bring fish as well as to cure the sick. Of the blubber of stranded whales and of seals they were extremely fond, and they ate nuts, berries, and camas bulbs, and made bread of seeds and acorns. The people who came to the mission from the opposite shore of the bay and the estuary were of lighter hue and more corpulent than the coast Indians. The men went naked, coating themselves with mud on cold mornings; the women wore an apron of sedge or rushes reaching before and behind to the knees and a cloak of the same material over their shoulders. People are said to have married and parted without ceremony, mothers taking their children with them, and men often took whole families of sisters for their wives. These Indians burned their dead.

The following list of rancherias and tribes from which the mission drew its neophytes is adapted from those recorded in the parish books (Taylor in Cal. Farmer, Oct. 18, 1861):

Abmoctac, Acnagis, Acyum, Aleta, Altahmo, Aluenchi, Amutaja, Anamas, Anamon, Anchin, Aramay, Assunta, Atarpe, Cachanegtac, Caprup, Carascan, Cazopo, Chagunte, Chanigtac, Chapugtac, Chayen, Chipisclin, Chipletac, Chiputca, Chuchictac, Chupcan, Churmutce, Chutchin, Chynau, Conop, Elarroyde, Flunmuda, Gamchines, Genau, Guanlen, Guloismistac, Halchis, Horocroc, Huimen, Hunctu, Itaes, Joquizara, Josquigard, Juniamuc, Juris, Lamsim, Libantone, Livangebra, Livangelva, Luianeglua, Luidneg, Macsinum, Malvaitac, Mitline, Muingpe, Naig, Naique, Napa, Olestura, Ompivromo, Otoacte, Ousint, Patnetac, Petaluma, Proqueu, Pructaca, Pruristac, Puichon, Purutea, Puycone, Quet, Sadaues, Sagunte, Saraise, Sarontac, Satumuo, Saturaumo, Sicca, Sipanum, Siplichiquin, Siscastac, Sitintajea, Sitlintaj, Sittintac, Ssalayme, Ssichitca, Ssipudca, Ssiti, Ssogereate, Ssupichum, Subchiam, Suchui, Sunchaque, Talcan, Tamalo, Tatquinte, Timigtac, Timsin, Titivu, Torose, Totola, Tubisuste, Tuca, Tupuic, Tupuinte, Tuzsint, Uchium, Urebure, Ussete, Vagerpe, Vectaca, Yacmui, Yacomui, Zomiomi, Zucigin. The names of the tribes which furnished the early converts were Ahwaste, Bolbone, Chiguau, Cuchillones, Chuscan, Cotejen, Junatca, Karkin, Khulpuni, Olemos, Olhon, Olmolococ, Olpen, Quemelentus, Quirogles, Saclan, Suisun, Sanchines, Saucou, Sichican, Uchium, Uquitinac.

See Hittell, Hist. Cal., 1885–97; Bancroft, Hist. Cal., 1886–90; Palou, Life of Serra, 102, 1884.

**Domestication.** The Indian learned a great deal from and was helped in his efforts by the actions of animals in their wild state. The period of domestication began when he held them in captivity for the gratification of his desires or they became attached to him for mutual benefit. In this process there are gradations:

1. Commensalism begins when food is left for serviceable animals to devour,

so that these may give notice of danger or advantage. The coyote is said to reveal the presence of the mountain lion. Small animals are tolerated for their skins and flesh. Plants would be sown to attract such creatures as bees, and tame animals would be regularly fed at later stages.

2. Confinement is represented by such activities as keeping fish and other aquatic animals in ponds; caging birds and carrying off their young, gallinaceous fowl last; tying up dogs or muzzling them; corralling ruminants, and hobbling or tethering wild horses so as to have them near, keep them away from their enemies, or fatten them for eating. The aborigines had no difficulty in breeding some animals in confinement, but few wild birds will thus propagate, and the Indians could obtain those to tame only by robbing nests. Lawson says of the Congaree of North Carolina that "they take storks and cranes before they can fly and breed them as tame and familiar as dung-hill fowls."

3. Keeping animals for their service or produce, as dogs for retrieving game or catching fish, hawks for killing birds; various creatures for their fleece, hides, feathers, flesh, milk, etc., and taming them for amusement and for ceremonial or other purposes, were a later development. Roger Williams says the Narraganset Indians of Rhode Island kept tame hawks about their cabins to frighten small birds from the fields.

4. Actually breaking them to work, training dogs, horses, and cattle for packing, sledding, hauling travois, and, later, for riding, constitutes complete domestication.

In pre-Columbian times the dog was the most perfectly subdued animal of the North Americans, as much so as the llama in w. South America. But other species of mammals, as well as birds, were in different degrees rendered tractable. After the coming of the whites the methods of domesticating animals were perfected, and their uses multiplied. Moreover, horses, sheep, cattle, donkeys, hogs, and poultry were added to the list, and these profoundly modified the manners and customs of many Indian tribes.

Domestication of animals increased the food supply, furnished pets for old and young, aided in raising the Indian above the plane of low savagery, helped him to go about, multiplied his wants, furnished a standard of property and a medium of exchange, took the load from the back of women, and provided more abundant material for economic, artistic, and ceremonial purposes.

Domestication had a different development in each culture area. In the Arctic region the dog was preeminent; it was reared with unremitting care, the women often suckling the puppies; all its life it was trained to the sled. As the dogs were never perfectly tamed, it was no easy task to drive a team of them; yet by the aid of dogs and sleds, in combination with umiaks, the whole polar area of America was exploited by the Eskimo, who found these an excellent means of rapid transit from Asia to the Atlantic. In recent years the successful introduction of the reindeer among the Alaskan tribes has proved a blessing. The Mackenzie-Yukon district is a canoe country, and domestication of the dog was not vigorously prosecuted until the Hudson's Bay Company gave the stimulus. But southward, among the Algonquian and Siouan tribes of the great lakes and the plains, this animal attained its best as a hunter and a beast of burden and traction. It was also reared for food and for ceremonial purposes. Not more than 50 pounds could be borne by one dog, but twice that amount could be moved on a travois. The coming of the horse (q. v. ) to the great plains was a boon to the Indian tribes, all of which at once adopted the new instrument of travel and transportation. The horse was apotheosized; it became a standard of value, and fostered a greater diversity of occupations. But the more primitive methods of domestication were still practised throughout the middle region. In the N. Pacific area dogs were trained to hunt; but here and elsewhere this use of the dog was doubtless learned from the whites. Morice writes of the Athapascan tribes of the interior of British Columbia: "Owing to the semi-sedentary state of those Indians and the character of their country, only the dog was ever domesticated among them in the common sense of the word. This had a sort of wolfish aspect, and was small, with pointed, erect ears, and uniformly gray, circumstances which would seem to imply that the domesticating process had remained incomplete. The flesh of those wolf dogs was relished by the employees of the Northwestern and Hudson's Bay companies, who did not generally eat that of those of European descent. In a broader sense, those aborigines also occasionally domesticated and have continued to domesticate other animals, such as black bears, marmots, foxes, etc., which they took when young and kept as pets, tied up to the tent post or free. Such animals, as long as they remained in a state of subjection, were considered as members of the family and regarded as dogs, though often called by the endearing names of 'sons,' 'daughters,' 'grandsons,' etc. Birds were never caged, but might be seen at times hobbling about with the tips of their wings cut."

In the California-Oregon area birds of gay plumage were caged, plucked, and then set free. On Santa Catalina id. birds called large crows by the Spaniards were kept and worshipped, recalling Boscana's story of the Shoshonean condor cult on the adjacent California coast. In the S. W., the desert area, the whole development of domestication is seen. The coyote was allowed to feed about the camps. The Querecho (Vaquero Apache) of Coronado in 1541 had a great number of large dogs which they obliged to carry their baggage when they moved from place to place (see *Travois*). Some of the Pueblo tribes practised also the caging of eagles, the rearing of turkeys, and, since the coming of the Spaniards, the herding of sheep, goats, burros, and horses.　(O. T. M.)

**Donacona.** A Huron chief found by Jacques Cartier, in 1535, residing with his people at the junction of St Croix and St Lawrence rs., Canada. Although Cartier was well received and kindly treated by this chief, he managed, partly by stratagem and partly by force, to convey the latter aboard his vessel and carry him to France where he soon died.　(C. T.)

**Donally's Town.** A (Creek?) settlement mentioned in 1793 as situated on Flint r., Ga.—Melton in Am. State Papers, Ind. Aff., II, 372, 1832.

**Dooesedoowe** ('plover.'—Hewitt). A clan of the Iroquois.
Asco.—French writer (1666) in N. Y. Doc. Col. Hist., IX, 47, 1855. **Doo-ese-doo-wé.**—Morgan, League Iroq., 46, 1851 (Seneca form). **Nicohès.**—French writer (1666), op. cit. **Tä-wis-tä-wis.**—Hewitt, inf'n, 1886 (Tuscarora name).

**Dostlan-lnagai** (*Dō-sL!an-lnagā'-i*, 'west-coast rear-town people'). A local subdivision of the Stlenga-lanas, one of the larger Haida divisions on the Raven side, who lived on the N. w. coast of Queen Charlotte ids., Brit. Col. A small section of them was called Kaiihllanas.—Swanton, Cont. Haida, 271, 1905.
Dü Hāadē.—Harrison in Proc. and Trans. Roy. Soc. Can., 2d s., II, sec. 2, 124, 1895. **TōstlEngilnagai'.**—Boas, 12th Rep. N. W. Tribes Can., 22, 1898.

**Dotame.** A tribe of which Lewis and Clark learned from Indian informants. They were said to speak the Comanche language and to number 30 warriors, or 120 souls, in 10 lodges. No traders had been among them; they trafficked usually with the Arikara, were hostile toward the Sioux, but friendly with the Mandan, the Arikara, and with their neighbors. From the use of the name in connection with Cataka (Kiowa Apache) and Nemousin (Comanche), the Dotame are seemingly identifiable with the Kiowa.
Detame.—Fisher, New Trav., 26, 1812. **Do-ta ma.**—Orig. Jour. Lewis and Clark, VI, 102, 1905. **Do-ta-me.**—Ibid.

**Dotchetonne.** An unidentified Texan tribe allied to the Caddo in 1687 (Joutel in Margry, Déc., III, 409, 1878). The ending suggests *dinne, tinne,* the Athapascan term for 'people,' and hence a possible Apache connection.

**Dotle.** A Koyukukhotana village on Koyukuk r., Alaska; pop. 12 in 1885.
Dotlèkákat.—Allen, Rep. on Alaska, 140, 1887.

**Dotuskustl** (*Dō't!Ask!AsL*, 'those who left the west coast'). A subdivision of the Sagua-lanas, a division of the Eagle clan of the Haida. The name seems to imply that they formerly lived on the w. coast of Queen Charlotte ids., Brit. Col., but in historical times they were in the town of Kung, in Naden harbor, with the other Sagua-lanas.—Swanton, Cont. Haida, 275, 1905.

**Doughnut stones.** See *Perforated stones.*

**Douglas.** The local name for a body of Lower Lillooet between Lillooet and Harrison lakes, Brit. Col.; pop. 76 in 1904.—Can. Ind. Aff. 1904, pt. II, 74, 1905.

**Doustioni.** A tribe, formerly living on Red r. of Louisiana, that from its proximity to the Natchitoches and the Yatasi was probably kindred thereto and belonged to the Caddo confederacy. The people are mentioned by Joutel, in 1687, as allies of the Kadohadacho. Pénicaut, in 1712, met them with a party of Natchitoches, and remarks that for the 5 years previous they had been constantly wandering, and living by the chase (Margry, Déc., V, 488). Their warriors at that time numbered about 200. The cause of the abandonment of their village is unknown, but when in 1714 they accepted the invitation of St Denys to settle near the Natchitoches, and seed was given them, they seem to have returned to their agricultural and village life. In 1719 La Harpe speaks of them as numbering 150 and dwelling on an island in Red r. not far distant from the French post among the Natchitoches. If any survive they are merged with the kindred Caddo in Oklahoma.　(A. C. F.)
Douesdonqua.—Joutel (1687) in Margry, Déc., III, 409, 1878. **Doustiany.**—Pénicaut (1712), ibid., V, 498, 1883. **Doustionis.**—Pénicaut (1713) in French, Hist. Coll. La., n. s., I, 117, 1869.

**Dragging-canoe** (translation of his Indian name, Tsíyu-gûnsíni̤; known also as Cheucunsene and Kunnesee). A prominent leader of those Cherokee who were hostile to the Americans during the Revolutionary war. He moved with his party to the site of Chickamauga, where he continued to harass the Tennessee settlements until 1782, when the Chickamauga towns were broken up. His people then moved farther down the river and established the "five lower towns," but these also were destroyed in 1794. In accounts of the Creek war Dragging-canoe is mentioned as one of the prominent Cherokee chiefs in alliance with Jackson, and a participant in the last great encounter at Horseshoe Bend.—Mooney in 19th Rep. B. A. E., 54, 63, 97, 1900.

**Dramatic representation.** Among many tribes ceremonies were dramatic in character. Every religious rite had its dramatic phases or episodes expressive of beliefs, emotions, or desires, but in certain instances the dramatic element dominated and became differentiated from the ceremony. In such cases there were masked and costumed actors with stage setting, effigies, and other properties, and events, historical or mythic, in the cultural history or life of the tribe were represented. The most elaborate of these exhibitions were those of the Pueblo peoples and the tribes of the N. W. coast. Among the Hopi a dramatic representation occurs yearly in March either in the open plaza or in a kiva. The space between the fire and one end of the room is set apart as the stage; at the rear a decorated screen is placed, behind which are men who sound shell trumpets and manipulate the effigies of a plumed serpent, which, at times, are projected through the screen and contend with the actors in front. Marionettes of the Corn-maids are occasionally employed and are skilfully managed; birds walk about and whistle; imitation fields of corn are swept over by serpent effigies, and men representing primal gods struggle with the effigies in an effort to overcome them. The stage setting and personnel are changed for every act, and during the change blankets are held around the fire to darken the kiva.

In the large wooden dwellings of the N. W. myths and legends were dramatized. The performance took place at one end of the house, where concealed openings in the painted wall admitted the actors who personated gods and heroes, and there were devices to give realistic effect to strange and magical scenes. Songs and dances accompanied the dramatic presentation.

Some of the great tribal ceremonies of the inland peoples, while religious in initiative, were social in general character. They portrayed episodes in the past history of the tribe for the instruction of the younger generation. There were societies a part of whose function was to preserve the history of its membership. This was done by means of song and the dramatic representation of the acts the song commemorated.

The Pawnee were remarkable for their skill in sleight-of-hand performances. Seeds were sown, plants grew, blossomed, and yielded fruit; spears were thrust through the body and many other surprising feats performed in the open lodge with no apparent means of concealment. During many dramatic representations,

particularly those which took place in the open air, episodes were introduced in which a humorous turn was given to some current event in the tribe. Sometimes clowns appeared and by their antics relieved the tensity of the dramatic presentation. Among the Pueblo Indians these "delight-makers," as Bandelier translates the name of the *Koshare* of the Queres villagers, constitute a society which performs comedies in the intervals of the public dances. See *Ceremony, Dance.*

Consult Bandelier, Delight Makers, 1900; Boas in Rep. Nat. Mus., 1895; Dorsey and Voth in Field Columb. Mus. Publ., Anthrop. ser.; Fewkes (1) in 15th and 19th Reps. B. A. E., 1897, 1900; (2) Proc. Wash. Acad. Sci., II, 1900; (3) various articles in Am. Anthrop. and Jour. Am. Folklore; Fletcher in Proc. A. A. A. S., XLV, 1896; Matthews in Mem. Am. Mus. Nat. Hist., VI, 1902; Powell in 19th Rep. B. A. E., 1900; Stevenson in 23d Rep. B. A. E., 1905.   (A. C. F.)

**Dreams and Visions.** Most revelations of what was regarded by the Indians as coming from the supernatural powers were believed to be received in dreams or visions. Through them were bestowed on man magical abilities and the capacity to foresee future events, to control disease, and to become able to fill the office of priest or of leader. It was the common belief of the Indians that these dreams or visions must be sought through the observance of some rite involving more or less personal privation; an exception is found in the Mohave who believe that the dream seeks the individual, coming to him before birth, or during infancy, as well as in mature life. In general the initiation of a man's personal relations to the unseen through dreams and visions took place during the fast which occurred at puberty, and the thing seen at that time became the medium of supernatural help and knowledge, and in some tribes determined his affiliations. It was his sacred object. It had no reference to his kindred, but was strictly personal in its efficacy, and he painted it on his person or his belongings as a prayer for assistance—a call for help in directing his actions. Any dream of ordinary sleep in which this object appeared had meaning for him and its suggestions were heeded. Men with a natural turn of mind toward the mysterious frequently became shamans and leaders in rites which dealt with the occult. Such persons, from the time of their first fast, cultivated their ability to dream and to have visions; the dreams came during natural sleep, the visions during an ecstasy when the man was either wholly or partially unconscious of his surroundings. It was generally believed that such men had power to bring or to avert disaster through direct communication with the unseen.

Many of the elaborate ceremonies observed among the tribes were said to have been received through visions, the actual performance following faithfully in detail the prefiguration of the vision. So, too, many of the shrines and their contents were believed to have been supernaturally bestowed in a vision upon some one person whose descendants were to be the hereditary keepers of the sacred articles. The time for the performance of rites connected with a shrine, and also other ceremonies, frequently depended on an intimation received in a dream.

The dreams of a man filling an important position, as the leader of a war party, were often regarded as significant, especially if he had carried with him some one of the sacred tribal objects as a medium of supernatural communication. This object was supposed to speak to him in dreams and give him directions which would insure safety and success. Forecasting the future was deemed possible by means of artificially induced visions. The skin of a freshly killed animal, or one that had been well soaked for the purpose, was wound around the neck of a man until the gentle pressure on the veins caused insensibility, then in a vision he saw the place toward which his party was going and all that was to take place was prefigured. In some tribes a skin kept for this special purpose was held sacred and used for divining by means of an induced vision. Some Indians employed plants, as the peyote, or mescal button, for like purposes. That the spirit left the body and traveled independently, and was able to discern objects distant both in time and space, was believed by certain tribes; others thought that the vision came to the man as a picture or in the form of a complete dramatic ceremony.

The general belief concerning dreams and visions seems to have been that the mental images seen with closed eyes were not fancies but actual glimpses of the unseen world where dwelt the generic types of all things and where all events that were to take place in the visible world were determined and prefigured.

Consult Fletcher in 22d Rep. B. A. E., 1903; Kroeber in Am. Anthrop., IV, no. 2, 1902; Mooney in 14th Rep. B. A. E., 1896. (A. C. F.)

**Dress.** See *Adornment, Clothing.*

**Drills and Drilling.** The first drill was a development of the primitive awl, a sharp-pointed instrument of bone, stone, or copper which was held in one hand, pressed against the object, and turned back and forth until a hole was bored.

The point was set in a socket of bone or wood. By setting it in a transverse handle increased pressure and leverage were obtained, with increased penetrating power. Artificially perforated objects of bone, fish bones, ivory, pottery, stone, and wood, common to all periods of the world's history, are found in mounds, caves, shellheaps, and burial places of the Indians. The holes vary from an eighth to a half inch in diameter, and from a fourth of an inch to 6 in. or more in depth. Shell, bone, and stone were drilled to make beads. Stone pipes with bowl and stem openings of different sizes were common, and whistles were made of stone and bone. Tubes in stone, several inches long, with walls scarcely an eighth of

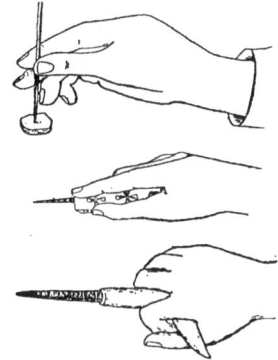

SINGLE HAND DRILLS

an inch thick, were accurately drilled. The columella of the Busycon shell was bored through for beads. The graceful butterfly-shaped objects found throughout E. United States were perforated with surprising accuracy. It has been said that in prehistoric times the natives bored holes through pearls by means of heated copper spindles. The points of drills were made of copper rolled into a hollow cylinder or of pieces of reed, or of solid metal, stone, shell, or wood. Boring by means of hollow drills was usual among all early races of Europe, Asia, and Africa; it was common also in Mexico, and instances are not rare in the mounds of Ohio and elsewhere in the United States, but in North

TUBULAR DRILL OF SHEET-COPPER AND SECTION OF BORING

America solid drill points were generally employed. Grass and bristles were also used as drills, being worked by twirling between the thumb and the index finger. Points of hard stone or metal usually cut by direct contact, but where the points were of wood, dry or wet sand proved more effectual. At times the points were separate from the shafts and were firmly attached to the latter by strings of hide or vegetal fiber. The rapidity with which a drill cuts depends on the velocity of the revolution, the weight and size of its different parts, the hardness of the abrading material and of the object drilled, the diameter of the hole, and its depth. The point used is indicated by the form of the perforation. The frequency with which objects are found bored from both sides is proof that the Indian appreciated the advantage of reducing friction. Progress in the elaboration of drills consisted mainly in heightening speed of revolution.

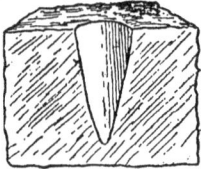

If the drill-point be of wood much depends on its hardness, for when too hard the wood grinds the sand to powder, while if it be too soft the grains catch at the base of the cavity and cut away the shaft. Only wood of proper texture holds the sand as in a matrix and enables it to cut to the best advantage. The insides of drill holes show by the character of their striæ whether the cutting was accomplished by direct pressure or with the aid of sand.

DRILL-POINT OF STONE AND SECTION OF BORING

The simplest form of drill was a straight shaft, varying from a fourth to three-fourths of an inch in diameter and from 10 in. to 2 ft in length. This shaft was revolved in alternating directions between the hands, or, when the shaft was held horizontally, it was rolled up and down the thigh with the right hand, the point of the drill being pressed against the object held in the left hand; or at times the object was held between the naked feet while the drill was revolved

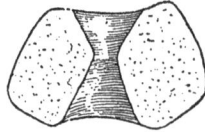

SECTION OF BEAD WITH BICONICAL PERFORATION

between the hands. This drill was in use at the time of Columbus and is the only one represented in the Mexican codices (Kingsborough, Antiq. of Mex., I, pl. 39). With the exception of the strap drill, which was apparently used only in the far N., this is the only form of drill referred to by early American writers.

THE REVOLVING SHAFT DRILL USED BY A HUPA

The strap drill, used both as a fire drill and as a perforator, is an improvement on the shaft drill, both in the number of its revolutions and in the pressure which may be imparted to the shaft. The shaft is kept in position by means of the head-piece of wood, which is held in the teeth. A thong that is wound once round the shaft, one end being held in each hand, is pulled alternately to the right and to the left. The thong was sometimes furnished with hand pieces of bone or bear's teeth to give a firmer grip to the strap. This drill, apparently known to the cave people of France, as it certainly was to the early peoples of Greece, Egypt, and India, has been used by the Greenlanders from early times and is employed also by the Aleut. To a person using the strap drill the jar to the teeth and head is at first quite severe, but much of the disagreeable sensation disappears with use.

STRAP DRILL USED BY ESKIMO OF ALASKA

Closely related to the strap drill, but a great improvement over the latter, is the bow drill, which can be revolved with much greater speed. The head piece of the bow drill is held in position with the left hand, while the strap is attached to the two ends of a bow, and after wrapping around the shaft, as with the strap drill, is alternately revolved by a backward and forward motion of the bow.

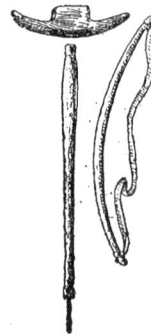

ESKIMO BOW DRILL SHOWING PARTS

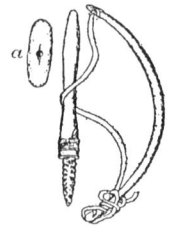

BOW DRILL WITH STONE POINT. a, HAND-PIECE

The pump drill, still employed in the arts, is said to have been known to the Iroquois and is used by the Pueblo Indians. This drill consists of a shaft which passes through a disk of stone, pottery, or wood, and a crosspiece through which the shaft also runs; to each end of the crosspiece is attached a string or buckskin thong having sufficient play to allow it to cross the top of the shaft and to permit the crosspiece to reach close to the disk. This

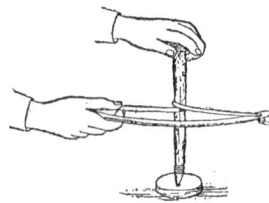

USE OF BOW DRILL

disk is turned to wind the string about the shaft; this raises the crosspiece. By pressing down the crosspiece after a few turns have been taken, the shaft is made to revolve and the disk receives sufficient impetus to rewind the string, which by successive pressure and re-

USE OF PUMP DRILL BY A ZUÑI                PUMP DRILL

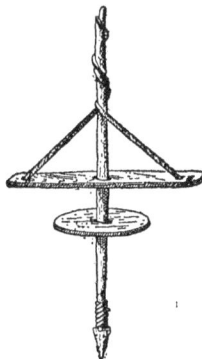

lease, continues the reciprocal movement necessary to cutting. The speed attained by the pump drill is much greater than with the bow drill or the strap drill, and the right hand is left free to hold the object that is being drilled. The pump drill, although long in common use among the Pueblo Indians, is probably of foreign origin.

A remarkable and unique drill was recently used by the Indians of Round valley, Cal., for drilling small holes through hard white shells. Its shaft is of hard wood, the disk taking the place of the crosspiece and the weight of the shaft giving sufficient impetus. The thong of this drill passes over the shaft and through opposite sides of the disk, and is attached to the shaft near the bottom. The disk moves freely up and down the shaft, and the thong is so wrapped that as the string unwinds from the top of the shaft it winds below, and vice versa. This drill revolves little if any

DISK DRILL; CALIFORNIA

faster than the shaft drill, and appears to cut chiefly, but not entirely, with the downward pressure. The use of this drill is apparently confined to a very restricted area. See *Shellwork, Stonework.*

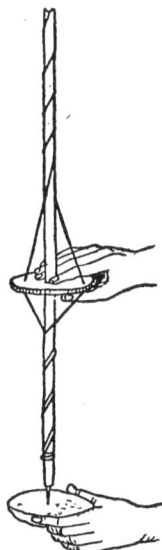

Consult Hough, Firemaking Apparatus, Rep. Nat. Mus. for 1888; McGuire, A Study of the Primitive Methods of Drilling, Rep. Nat. Mus. for 1894. (J. D. M.)

**Dry-painting.** An art existing among the Indians, especially those of the S. W., the products of which have been named sand altars, sand pictures or paintings, and sand mosaics by various authors. It is doubtless of aboriginal origin and of great antiquity, but it has come to the knowledge of white people only within the last 25 years. The art has been found among various Pueblo tribes of New Mexico and Arizona, among the wilder Navaho and Apache of the same region, and, in crude form, among the Cheyenne, Arapaho, and Siksika. According to Navaho information, dry-painting was practised also by the Ute and the cliff-dwellers, but the latter may refer to one or more of the Hopi clans that occupied Canyon de Chelly, Arizona, within comparatively recent time (see *Asa*). There is evidence of a wide extent of the art among the Indians, but it is probable that it has been yet more widely practised in the past, or may even be more widely practised at the present among tribes who have concealed it from civilized men.

So far as can be learned dry-painting has reached its greatest perfection among the Navaho, whose designs are larger, more numerous, and more elaborate than those of any other tribe. These Indians make their pictures almost exclusively in connection with religious ceremonies and draw them of various sizes. Some of their larger pictures, in their great 9 days' ceremonies, are 10 or 12 ft in diameter, and represent, in conventional forms, various gods of their mythology, divine ceremonies, lightning, sunbeams, rainbows, mountains, animals, and plants, having a mythic or traditional significance. Among this people, in order to prepare a groundwork for a sacred picture in the lodge, several young men collect, with ceremonial observances, a quantity of dry sand, which is carried in blankets, thrown on the floor of the lodge, spread over a surface of sufficient size and to the depth of 2 or 3 in., and made smooth and level by means of the broad oaken battens used in weaving. The pigments represent the 5 sacred colors of Navaho mythology—white, blue, yellow, black, and red. For the greater part of the work the white, yellow, and red are made of finely powered sandstone of these colors; the black of powdered charcoal mixed with a little sandstone to give it stability; and the " blue " (really gray) of black and white mixed. These powders are prepared before the picture is begun and are kept on improvised trays of juniper bark. Sometimes, for certain ornamental parts of the work, more precious pigments than these are used. To apply the pigments the artist picks up a small quantity between his first and second fingers and his opposed thumb and allows it to flow slowly as he moves his hand. When he takes up his pinch of powder, he blows on his fingers to remove aberrant particles and to keep them from falling on the picture out of place. When he makes a mistake he does not brush away the colored powder, but obliterates it by pouring sand on it, then draws the correct design on the new surface. The drawings are begun as near the center as the design will permit, due regard being paid to the points of the compass, which have an established order of precedence in Navaho ceremony. The figures in the periphery of the picture are made last, in order that the operators may not have to step over and thus possibly spoil the finished work. The pictures are drawn according to an exact system, except in certain well-defined cases where the artist is allowed to indulge his fancy. On the other hand, some parts are measured by palms, and not the slightest deviation can be made from the established design. Straight and parallel lines are drawn with the aid of a tightened cord. The naked bodies of the gods are first drawn and then the clothing is put on. The shaman who enacts the part of master of ceremonies does little more than direct and criticize the work. A number of men who have been initiated into the mystery of the ceremony perform the labor, each working on a different part, and often spending many hours on one picture. When it is finished, ceremonies are performed over it, and then with song and ceremony it is obliterated. When no semblance of it remains, the sand of which it was made is gathered in blankets and thrown away at a distance from the lodge. In the ceremonies of the Pueblo Indians a picture is allowed to remain several days, while the Navaho make and destroy a picture in a day. No permanent copies of the dry-paintings are preserved by the Navaho; indeed, until recently they had no means of making such copies. The paintings are not made in the summer, hence their designs must be carried from winter to winter in the fallible memories of men; yet the shamans declare that the pictures have been transmitted unaltered for many generations. Although this declaration may reasonably be doubted, there is some evidence in its favor.

During the Sun-dance ceremony of the Cheyenne a dry-painting is made in a lodge to represent the morning star. The field of the painting is of plain sand, and the design is made in a strictly prescribed manner by the use of black, red, yellow, and white dry paint, in order. Dotted lines representing stars form part of the painting, in this case those in white being drawn first because the white stars appear first in the morning. The unbroken lines are roads; the white represents the lodge-maker and his wife, the red line the road of the Cheyenne, the black the trail of the buffalo, and yellow the path of the sun. The dry-painting made by the Arapaho in their Sun-dance ceremony, while of symbolic significance, is of a much simpler character.

The sand pictures of the Hopi differ considerably from those of the Navaho. Some of the best are made in midsummer during the ceremonies of the Antelope society. In making dry-paintings the Hopi chief of the ceremony commonly begins at the periphery and follows the ceremonial circuit of the cardinal points in the use of pigments—first drawing yellow (north), then green or blue (west), then red (south), and finally white (east). The field of the picture, which is always made secretly in kivas among the Hopi, is valley sand sifted on the floor from a basket. These Indians never use cords or other measuring instruments. When the dry-painting is effaced pinches of the sand used in making it are deposited in prescribed places; e. g., a portion of the sand of an Antelope dry-painting is placed in a shrine of each cardinal point by the Snake chief (Fewkes).

See Dorsey in Field Columb. Mus. Publ., Anthrop. ser., IV, 1903, and IX, no. 2, 1905; Voth, ibid., III, nos. 2, 4, 1901, 1903; Dorsey and Voth, ibid., III, nos. 1, 3, 1901, 1902; Fewkes in Jour. Am. Ethnol. and Archæol., IV, 1894, and in various reports of the B. A. E.; Matthews (1) in 5th Rep. B. A. E., 1887, (2) in Mem. Am. Mus. Nat. Hist., VI, 1902, (3) Navaho Legends, 1897; Stevenson in 8th Rep. B. A. E., 1891.                                   (W. M.)

**Dsihlnaothihlni** ('encircled mountain'). A Navaho clan, so named from Dsilnaothil mt., its original home.
Dsilanoọí'lni.—Matthews in Jour. Am. Folk-lore, III, 103, 1890 (misprint). Dsilnaoọílọine.—Ibid., 91. Dsilnaoọílni. — Ibid.    Dsǐ'lnaotǐ'lni. — Matthews, Navaho Leg., 30, 1897.

**Dsihlthani** ('brow of the mountain'). A Navaho clan.
Biọàni.—Matthews in Jour. Am. Folk-lore, III, 104, 1890 (distinct from Bǐtá'ni, 'folded arms'; see *Bithani*).    Bǐtáni.—Matthews, Navaho Leg., 30, 1897.    Dsilọàni.—Matthews in Jour. Am. Folk-lore, III, 104, 1890.    Dsǐltáni.—Matthews, Navaho Leg., 30, 1897.

**Dsihltlani** ('base of the mountain'). A Navaho clan.
Dsǐltlá'ni.—Matthews, Navaho Leg., 30, 1897. Dsiltlá'ni.—Matthews in Jour. Am. Folk-lore, III, 103, 1890.

**Dtakhtikianpandhatazhi** ('does not eat deer and elk'). Given as a subgens of the Ponca gens Nikapashna, but seemingly an error.
ʇaqti kǐ Aⁿpaⁿ ɵatajǐ —Dorsey in 15th Rep. B. A. E., 228, 1897.

**Dtedhezedhatazhi** ('does not eat buffalo tongues'). A subgens of the Ponca gens

Washabe. J. O. Dorsey also gives it as a Nikapashna gens, but this is seemingly an error.

Ŧe ǥeze ǥatajĭ.—Dorsey in 15th Rep. B. A. E., 228, 229, 1897.

**Dtepaitazhi** ('touch no buffalo head'). A subgens of the Dhatada gens of the Omaha.

Ŧe-ḍa it‘ajĭ.—Dorsey in 15th Rep. B. A. E., 226, 1897.

**Dtepaitazhi** ('does not touch a buffalo head or skull'). A subgens of the Washabe gens of the Ponca.

Ŧe-ḍa it‘ajĭ.—Dorsey in 15th Rep. B. A. E., 229, 1897.

**Dtesanhadtadhishan** (pertaining to the sacred skin of an albino buffalo cow). Given as a subgens of the Hanga gens of the Omaha, but it is seemingly an error.

Hañga-qti.—Dorsey in 15th Rep. B. A. E., 227, 1897 ('real Hanga'). Ŧe-ǥeze-ǥatajĭ.—Ibid. ('do not eat buffalo tongues'). Ŧesaⁿhaᶾa-ǥicaⁿ.—Ibid. Wacabe.—Ibid. ('dark buffalo').

**Dtesinde** ('buffalo tail'). Given as a subgens of the Washabe gens of the Ponca.

Ŧe-ǥeze ǥatajĭ.—Dorsey in 15th Rep. B. A. E., 229, 1897 ('does not eat buffalo tongues'). Ŧe-jiñga ǥatajĭ.—Ibid. ('does not eat a very young buffalo calf'). Ŧe-sĭnde.—Ibid., 228.

**Dtesindeitazhi** ('does not touch a buffalo tail'). Given as a subgens of the Ponca gens Nikapashna.

Ŧe-sĭnde-it‘ajĭ.—Dorsey in 15th Rep. B. A. E., 228, 1897.

**Duahe.** Mentioned by Oviedo (Hist. Gen. Indies, iii, 628, 1853) as one of the provinces or villages visited by Ayllon in 1520; probably on the South Carolina coast.

**Duasno.** A former Kawia village on or near the Cahuilla res., s. Cal. (Jackson and Kinney, Rep. Miss. Ind., 18, 1883). Possibly intended for Durazno (Span. 'peach').

**Dubois.** Mentioned only by McKenney and Hall (Ind. Tribes, iii, 79, 1854) in a list of tribes. Possibly intended for Gens des Bois (Hankutchin, Tschantoga, etc.); otherwise unidentified.

**Duck Lake.** A local name for a band of Okinagan in s. w. British Columbia; pop. 24 in 1901.—Can. Ind. Aff. for 1901, pt. ii, 166.

**Duck tablets.** Prehistoric objects of undetermined use, made of wood, bone, and metal, and representing in a conventional manner the figure of a duck. The most typical examples are certain paddle-like objects of wood found by Cushing in excavations at Key Marco, Fla., and connected by him with other similar forms in stone and silver found also in Florida, as well as

DUCK TABLET OF WOOD; FLORIDA; ABOUT 1-30. (CUSHING)

with various other classes of objects thought to embody the duck motive, such as the birdstone (q.v.), the banner stone (q.v.), and the calumet (q.v.). Although these tablets were undoubtedly symbolic, the exact significance and manner of use can not

be determined, and they are therefore classed with problematical objects (q. v.). See Cushing in Proc. Am. Philos. Soc., xxxv, 1897.　　　　(w. h. h.)

**Ducoigne, Jean Baptiste.** A Kaskaskia chief at the beginning of the 19th century, noted mainly for his firm adherence to the United States and friendship for the whites. Reynolds (Pion. Hist., iii, 22, 1887) describes him as a cunning half-blood of considerable talent. In his Memoirs, Gen. W. H. Harrison, who had dealings with Ducoigne, speaks of him as ''a gentlemanly man, by no means addicted to drink, and possessing a very strong inclination to live like a white man; indeed has done so as far as his means would allow.'' Writing to the Secretary of War, he says: ''Ducoigne's long and well-proved friendship for the United States has gained him the hatred of all the other chiefs and ought to be an inducement with us to provide as well for his happiness, as for his safety.'' According to Reynolds, Ducoigne asserted that neither he nor his people had shed the blood of white men. He was a signer of the treaties of Vincennes, Aug. 7 and 13, 1803; by the latter the United States agreed to build a house and inclose 100 acres of land for him. He had two sons, Louis and Jefferson, and a daughter, Ellen, who married a white man and in 1850 was living in Indian Ter. The name of Louis appears on behalf of the Kaskaskia in the treaty of Edwardsville, Ill., Sept. 25, 1818. Ducoigne's death probably occurred shortly before Oct., 1832, as it is stated in the treaty at Castor Hill, of that date, that there should be reserved ''to Ellen Ducoigne, the daughter of their late chief,'' a certain tract of land. The name is perpetuated in that of the town of Duquoin, Perry co., Ill.　　　　(c. t.)

**Duel.** See *Nith songs*.

**Dueztumac.** A former Maricopa rancheria about 45 leagues (120 m.) above the mouth of the Rio Gila in s. w. Arizona; visited by Father Sedelmair in 1744.—Bancroft, Ariz. and N. Mex., 366, 1889.

Santa María del Agua Caliente.—Ibid., 367 (probably the same).

**Dugh-sokum.** Given as the name of a tribe (Mallet in Ind. Aff. Rep., 198, 1877), but really that of the place where Port Madison, Wash., now stands. (Boulet in letter, Mar. 22, 1886).

**Duharhe.** A country on the coast of Florida, seen by Lucas Vazquez de Ayllon in 1520, whose people were light in color and had abundant hair. The chief who ruled over this and other provinces was said to have been nourished on a certain food that caused him to grow to a gigantic size.—Barcia, Ensayo, 4, 1723.

**Dukes, Joseph.** An interpreter, the son of half-blood Choctaw parents, born in the old Choctaw country, in the present Mississippi, in 1811. He attended one of the early mission schools at Mayhew, where he made such progress that he often acted as interpreter for Rev. Cyrus Kingsbury, the pioneer missionary, who never learned the Choctaw language. After the Choctaw had ceded to the United States their lands in the E., he remained in Mississippi for some years, helping Rev. Cyrus Byington prepare a Choctaw grammar and dictionary. In 1851 or 1852 he preached under the direction of Rev. Allen Wright at Wheelock, Ind. Ter., and assisted Mr Wright in translating the Old Testament. When Mr Wright was succeeded by Rev. John Edwards, in 1853, Dukes taught the latter Choctaw and aided him in translation in addition to his preaching. The first draft of the whole of the Old Testament from Genesis to II Kings, as well as of the Psalms, is attributed to him, and he probably translated also some portions of the New Testament. He died in 1861. He was the author of The History of Joseph and His Brethren (Utica, 1831, repr. 1836).—Pilling, Bibliog. Muskh. Lang., Bull. B. A. E., 1889.

**Dulastunyi** (*Dulastûñ'yĭ,* 'potsherd place'). A former Cherokee settlement on Nottely r., Cherokee co., N. C., near the Georgia line. A half-breed Cherokee ball captain who formerly lived there, John Butler, or Tsanugásita (Sour John), having been defeated in a ball game, said, in contempt of his men, that they were of no more use than broken pots.—Mooney in 19th Rep. B. A. E., 406, 1900.

**Dulchioni.** A tribe, probably Caddoan, formerly living in villages on Red r. of Louisiana, 3 leagues below those of the Natchitoches. They were visited by Bienville and St Denys in 1700, when on their journey up Red r. to open trade between the Spanish and French provinces, and by La Harpe in 1719. Further than these brief references little is known of this tribe or of its subsequent fate. (A. C. F.)
Dulchanois.—La Harpe (1719) in French, Hist. Coll. La., III, 19, 1851. **Dulchinois.**—Ibid., 72. **Oulchionis.**—La Harpe in Margry, Déc., VI, 277, 1886.

**Duldulthawaiame** ('village where there are plenty of humming insects'). A former village of the Mishikhwutmetunne on Coquille r., Oreg.
Dul-dul' ça-wai'-ă-mĕ.—Dorsey in Jour. Am. Folklore, III, 232, 1890.

**Dull Knife.** A chief of a band of Northern Cheyenne who first came into public notice in 1868 when, as one of the representatives of his tribe, he signed the treaty of Ft Laramie, May 10, made by the Northern Cheyenne and Northern Arapaho with the United States, his name appearing as "Tah-me-la-pash-me, or Dull Knife." In 1875, or early in 1876, Dull Knife's band, numbering about 400 warriors, suddenly attacked Washakie's band of Shoshoni, at that time on Bighorn r. near the mouth of Gray Bull r. In 1876 the Northern Cheyenne, including Dull Knife's band, joined the Sioux under Sitting Bull in their general uprising during this and the following year. They were present at and were participants in the Custer massacre on the Little Bighorn in June, 1876, and according to Chief Gall's statement, at the beginning of the battle the Cheyenne fought Custer's command while the Sioux attacked Reno's force, and after the latter had been driven back, the entire body of warriors turned on Custer's command. On Nov. 25, 1876, the cavalry under Col. Mackenzie attacked Dull Knife's camp at daybreak, destroying 173 lodges and capturing 500 ponies. Although the Indians escaped, with heavy loss, they later surrendered and were moved to Oklahoma and placed with the Southern Cheyenne. Greatly dissatisfied with their new home, an attempt was made by a large party under Dull Knife to escape to the N. in Sept., 1878. They were pursued and a part of them captured and confined at Ft Robinson, Nebr., whence they made a desperate attempt to escape on the night of Jan. 9, 1879, during which most of them, including Dull Knife, were killed. Consult Dunn, Massacres, 1886; Ellis, Ind. Wars, 1892; Ind. Aff. Rep. 1877–79; Mooney in 14th Rep. B. A. E., 1896. See the article *Cheyenne.* (c. t.)

**Durango.** A former Tepehuane settlement, now the capital of the Mexican state of the same name.—Orozco y Berra, Geog., 318, 1864.

**Dustayalunyi** (*Dústăyalûñ'yĭ,* 'where it made a noise, as of thunder or shooting,' apparently referring to a lightning stroke). A former Cherokee settlement about the mouth of Shooting cr., an affluent of Hiwassee r., near Hayesville, Clay co., N. C.—Mooney in 19th Rep. B. A. E., 517, 1900.

**Dutch influence.** The influence of the Dutch on the Indians N. of Mexico was confined to the period (1609–64) from Hudson's visit to the surrender of New Amsterdam and its dependencies to the English. The region in which this influence was exerted lies between the Susquehanna and Connecticut rs., and between the Atlantic and L. Ontario. Ft Orange, now the city of Albany, was a noted trading post of the Dutch, and there they came in contact with the Iroquoian tribes of the N., in addition to the Algonquian tribes of the S. The harsh conduct of Hudson toward the Indians met by him on Hudson r. was in part responsible for many subsequent conflicts between the Dutch and the natives. The Dutch were agents in furnishing brandy to the Indians of their territory and to the surrounding tribes, thereby undoing much of the good sought to be accomplished by the French authorities. The United Company of the New Netherlands, which exercised the first controlling influence in the region of Hudson r., was succeeded in 1621 by the powerful West India Company, and in 1632 was founded the fort on Connecticut r. where is now the city of Hartford. The trade in furs with the Pequot and other tribes was extensive. Disputes soon occurred that proved detrimental to trade, and De Forest (Hist. Inds. of Conn., 73, 1852) considers that it was the loss of the Dutch trade which induced the Pequot to invite the English of Massachusetts bay to settle in Connecticut, an act that led ultimately to their own destruction. Quarrels between the Dutch of New Amsterdam and the Indians, and the savage conduct of Gov. Kieft in 1642, led to much slaughter of natives during the next 2 years, and stirred up many of the Connecticut tribes against both the English and the Dutch. Some of them had engaged in intriguing, now against one, now against the other party of the whites. Friederici (Indianer und Anglo-Americaner, 16, 1900) takes a more favorable view of the attitude of the Dutch toward the Indians in general than that entertained by many authorities. The Dutch helped the Iroquois confederacy against the northern Algonquian hordes, and the wars thus initiated were in progress when the English conquest took place. They also aided the Mahican against the Mohawk (Ruttenber, Ind. Tribes of Hudson R., 56, 1872) and the Seneca against the Munsee, to whom the Swedes had supplied arms. Many troubles arose from the cupidity of the traders and settlers who sold firearms and liquors to the Indians, regardless of the general policy of the government (Nelson, Inds. of New Jersey, 1894). An interesting relic of Dutch influence is the title "Kora" given by the modern Iroquois of Canada to the governor-general, or to the King of England, a corruption of Corlaer, the name of one of the Dutch governors of New Amsterdam. (A. F. C.)

**Dwamish.** A small body of Salish near Seattle, Wash., which city was named from a chief of this and the Suquamish tribes. Their proper seat, according to Gibbs, was at the outlet of L. Washington. In 1856 they were removed to the E. shore of Bainbridge id., but owing to the absence of a fishing ground were shortly afterward taken to Holderness point, on the w. side of Elliot bay, which

was already a favorite place for fishing. The name, being well known, has been improperly applied collectively to a number of distinct bands in this neighborhood. Their population about 1856 is variously given from 64 to 312. The remnant is incorporated with the Snohomish and others under the Tulalip school, N. W. Wash., altogether numbering 465 in 1904. (J. R. S.)

Dawamish.—Simmons (1856) in H. R. Ex. Doc. 37, 34th Cong., 3d sess., 73, 1857. Dewamish.—Shaw (1856), ibid., 113. Du-a+bo′.—McCaw, Puyallup, MS. vocab., B. A. E., 1885 (Puyallup name). Dughdwabsh.—Mallet in Ind. Aff. Rep., 198, 1877. Dwahmish.—Maynard (1856) in H. R. Ex. Doc. 37, 34th Cong., 3d sess., 86, 1857. Dwa-mish.—Stevens in Ind. Aff. Rep., 453, 1854. D'Wamish.—Gibbs in Pac. R. R. Rep., I, 436, 1855. Lake Indians.—Page (1856) in H. R. Ex. Doc. 37, 34th Cong., 3d sess., 82, 1857. Neamitch.—Farnham, Travels, 111, 1843. Nee-wam-ish.—Starling in Ind. Aff. Rep., 170, 1852. Nowamish.—Gibbs in Pac. R. R. Rep., I, 432, 1855. Nuna-mish.—Starling in Ind. Aff. Rep., 171, 1852. N'Wamish.—Gibbs in Pac. R. R. Rep., I, 432, 1855. Port Orchard.—Wilkes, ibid., 435. Tsa-bah-bish.—Maynard (1856) in H. R. Ex. Doc. 37, 34th Cong., 3d sess., 86, 1857. Tsa-bah-bobs.—Ibid., 82. Tsahbahbish.—Ibid., 86. T'sakbahbish.—Stevens (1856), ibid., 46.

**Dwarfs.** See *Anatomy, Physiology, Popular fallacies.*

**Dyami** (*D'ya'-mi*). The Eagle clans of the Keresan pueblos of Laguna, Acoma, Santa Ana, Sia, San Felipe, and Cochiti, N. Mex. The Eagle clan of Laguna claims to have come originally from Acoma; that of Acoma forms a phratry with the Soshka (Chaparral-cock) clan, while that of Cochiti is extinct. (F. W. H.)

D'yámi-háno.—Hodge in Am. Anthrop., IX, 350, 1896 (Sia, San Felipe, and Santa Ana forms; *háno*='people'). Dyámi-hánuch.—Ibid. (Cochiti form). Ti-ä′-mi.—Stevenson in 11th Rep. B. A. E., 19, 1894 (Sia form). Tya-me.—Bandelier in Arch. Inst. Papers, III, 293, 1890 (applied to the clan fetish). Tyame hanutsh.—Bandelier, Delight Makers, 181, 1890. Tyámi-hánoch.—Hodge, op. cit. (Laguna form). T'yámi-hánoqoh.—Ibid. (Acoma form).

**Dyani** (*Dya'-ni*). The Deer clans of Sia and San Felipe pueblos, N. Mex.; the latter clan is extinct.

Dyáni-hano.—Hodge in Am. Anthrop., IX, 350, 1896 (*háno*='people'). Tä/ñe.—Stevenson in 11th Rep. B. A. E., 19, 1894.

**Dyapige.** A prehistoric Tano pueblo S. E. of Lamy, "some distance in the mountains," N. central New Mexico.

Dyap-i-ge.—Bandelier in Arch. Inst. Papers, IV, 100, 1892 (Tewa name).

**Dye** (*D'ye*). The Gopher clans of the Tewa pueblos of San Juan, Santa Clara, San Ildefonso, and Tesuque, N. Mex.

Dyé-tdóa.—Hodge in Am. Anthrop., IX, 351, 1896 (*tdóa*='people').

**Dyea.** A former Chilkat village which became noted subsequently in the time of the Yukon gold excitement, but is now practically dead owing to the building of the Yukon and White Pass railway to Skagway.

Daiye′.—Swanton, field notes, B. A. E., 1904.

**Dyes and Pigments.** Most of the Indian tribes of North America made permanent dyes from organic materials. The demand for these dyes arose when basketry, quillwork, and other textile industries had reached a considerable degree of advancement, and there was need of diversity of color in ornamentation, as well as permanency of color, which pigments alone could not supply.

*Dyes.*—The California tribes and many others who made baskets were usually satisfied with natural colors. These are the red and black of bark, the white of grass stems, the pale yellow of peeled rods or rushes, and the brown of root bark. A few dyes were known, however, notably a black or dark gray on splints which had been buried in mud. The Hupa obtained bright yellow from lichens, another color from the roots of the Oregon grape, and a brownish red from alder bark. Most of the tribes of the S. W. use only black for designs on baskets, and, rarely, red dyes. The Hopi, however, have a larger number of native dyes for basketry splints than any other tribe, and the Apache, Walapai, and Havasupai have a number of vegetal dyes that are not used in basketry. The Abnaki and other tribes made fugitive stains from pokeberries and fruits of the blueberry and elder. Lichens, golden-seal, bloodroot, and the bark of the butternut and other trees were also used by the northern and eastern tribes, and in southern regions the prickly pear. The Virginia Indians, according to Hariot, used sumach, a kind of seed, a small root, and the bark of a tree to dye their hair, as well as to color their faces red and to dye mantles of deerskin and the rushes for baskets and mats. The tribes of the N. W. coast employed a number of harmonious vegetal colors in their baskets. Most of the native dyes of the Indians were superseded by others introduced, especially in late years by aniline colors.

Quillwork, formerly widespread, was generally superseded by beadwork, and the native dyes employed in the art have fallen almost into disuse. Some of the N. W. coast tribes, the Eskimo, and the northern Athapascans alone practise quillworking in its purity, but its former range was extensive.

Native vegetal blanket dyes are found in use only among the Chilkat of Alaska, who still retain them in weaving their ceremonial shawls. The Nez Percés and the Navaho formerly used permanent vegetal dyes of pleasing colors for wool. With the latter these dyes have given way so recently to aniline colors that the details of their manufacture have not become lost. The use of dyes required a knowledge of mordants; for this purpose urine was commonly employed by the Navaho, Hopi, and Zuñi, besides an impure native alum, and an iron salt mixed with organic acids to produce black. It has been assumed that, since the weaver's art seems to be accultural with the Navaho, the mordant dyes may have been derived from the Pueblos, who, in turn, may have received them from the Spaniards. Matthews, however, controverts the opinion that the Navaho learned the art of weaving from the Pueblos; and indeed there is no reason why the Indians should not have become acquainted with various mordants through the practise of the culinary art or other domestic arts in which fire is employed.

*Pigments.*—The inorganic colors used by the Indians were mostly derived from iron-bearing minerals, such as ochers and other ores, and stained earths. These furnished various tints, as brown, red, green, blue, yellow, orange, and purple. The search for good colors was assiduously pursued; quarries were opened and a commerce in their products was carried on. White was derived from kaolin, limestone, and gypsum; black from graphite, powdered coal, charcoal, or soot; green and blue from copper ores, phosphate of iron, etc. Pigments were used for facial decoration, red being most prized, for which reason the vermilion of the trader was eagerly adopted, but the intent of face painting was generally totemic or religious and not merely ornamental. Pigments were rubbed into soft tanned skins, giving the effect of dye, and were mixed with various media for painting the wood and leather of boxes, arrows, spears, shields, tipis, robes, parfleche cases, etc. Among the Southwestern tribes in particular pigments were mixed with sand for dry-paintings (q. v.), while pigments of iron earths or kaolin were employed for decorating pottery. In connection with the preparation and use of pigments are grinding slabs and mullers, mortars and pestles, brushes and paint sticks, and a great variety of pouches and pots for carrying or for preserving them. The media for applying the pigments varied with the objects to be decorated and with tribal or personal usage. In general, face paint was mixed with grease or saliva, while the medium for wood or skin was grease or glue. The N. W. coast Indians put grease on their faces before applying the paint. Among some of the Pueblos, at least, an emulsion of fat seeds was made with the pigment, and this was applied by spurting from the mouth. See *Adornment, Art, Dry-painting, Mines and Quarries, Ornament, Painting.*

Consult Dorsey in Field Columb. Mus. Publ., Anthrop. ser.; Fewkes in 17th Rep. B. A. E., 1898; Goddard, Life and Culture of the Hupa, 1903; Holmes in Am. Anthrop., v, no. 3, 1903; Hough

(1) in Am. Anthrop., XI, May, 1898; (2) in Rep. Nat. Mus., 1900 and 1901; Kroeber in Bull. Am. Mus. Nat. Hist., XVIII, pt. 1, 1902; Mason, Aboriginal American Basketry, 1902; Matthews in 3d Rep. B. A. E., 1884; Pepper, Native Navajo Dyes, in Papoose, Feb., 1902; Stephen in Internat. Folk-lore Cong., I, 1898; Wissler in Bull. Am. Mus. Nat. Hist., XVIII, pt. 3, 1904. (W. H.)

**Dyosyowan** ('it is oil-covered.'—Hewitt). An important former Seneca village on Buffalo cr., Erie co., N. Y.
Buffalo.—Kirkland (1788) in Am. State Pap., Ind. Aff., I, 211, 1832. **Dyo'-syo-wän.**—Hewitt, inf'n, 1887 (Seneca name). **Tehoseroron.**—Treaty of Oct. 22, 1784, in U. S. Ind. Treat., 922, 1873. **Teyoheghscolea.**—Kirkland, op. cit.

**Dyrnaeskirk.** A former Eskimo missionary station on Eriksfjord, s. Greenland.—Crantz, Hist. Greenland, I, map, 1767.

**Eagle.** Among the many birds held in superstitious and appreciative regard by the aborigines of North America, the eagle, by reason of its majestic, solitary, and mysterious nature, became an especial object of worship. This is expressed in the employment of the eagle by the Indian for religious and esthetic purposes only. The wing-bones were fashioned into whistles to be carried by warriors or used in ceremonies, and the talons formed powerful amulets or fetishes, having secondary value as ornaments; the feathers were, however, of greatest importance. The capture of eagles for their feathers was a hazardous branch of hunting, requiring great skill. Among some tribes eagle-killing was delegated to certain men. Owing to the difficulty of getting within bowshot of the bird, it was often trapped or the eyrie was visited to secure the young. Eagles are still kept in captivity by the Pueblo Indians as in the time of Coronado (14th Rep. B. A. E., 516, 1896). The striking war-bonnet of the Plains tribes was made of eagle feathers and was highly valued, for it is said that one pony was the price of a perfect tail of 12 feathers of the "war eagle," i. e., the white plumes with black tips. Other varieties, with bars across the feathers, are regarded as inferior (Mooney). Warriors of the Plains tribes usually wore the feathers of the golden eagle only, and it is probable that the customs of many tribes prescribed like discriminations as to feathers of different species. Many tribes wore one or more eagle feathers in the hair, and these feathers were often cut, colored, or otherwise decorated with some cognizance of the wearer (see *Heraldry*). It was the custom of the Pillager Chippewa to allow a warrior who scalped an enemy to wear on his head two eagle feathers, and the act of capturing a wounded prisoner on the battlefield earned the distinction of wearing five. Fans made of the primary feathers of the eagle formed an accessory to the costume of the Sioux and other tribes. Eagle feathers were also attached as ornaments to the buckskin shirts worn by men, and war costumes and paraphernalia, including shields, were ornamented with them. As one of the prominent totemic animals, the eagle gave its name to many clans and religious fraternities. It is probable that nearly every tribe in the United States recognizing clan or gentile organization had an eagle clan or gens at some period in its history.

The eagle held an important place in symbolic art. It was depicted by all the methods of art expression known to the Indian, appearing on pottery, basketry, textiles, beadwork, quillwork, shields, crests, totem poles, house and grave posts, pipes, rattles, and objects pertaining to cult and ceremony. It was also represented in the primitive drama connected with ceremonies. Many tribes possessed eagle deities, as the Kwahu, the eagle kachina of the Hopi of Arizona, and the Eagle god of the Miwok of California.

Among the Haida, passes made with eagle fans were thought to be effectual in conjuring, and this use reappears in many tribes. The wing-bones were often employed as sucking tubes, with which medicine-men pretended to remove disease. The Tlingit and other North Pacific tribes used eagle down for ceremonial sprinkling on the hair, masks, and dance costume; it was also scattered in the air, being blown through a tube or sprinkled by hand. The Pawnee and other Plains tribes as well as the Pueblos also used the down in ceremonies, and it was probably a general custom. Among the Hopi the eagle is generally associated with the Sky god, and its feathers are used with disks to represent the Sun god (Fewkes).

The use of eagle feathers in religion is nowhere better shown than among the Pueblos, when downy plumes are attached to masks, rattles, prayer-sticks (q. v.), and other cult objects entering into ceremonies. For this purpose a great quantity of feathers is yearly required. The Hopi clans claimed the eagle nests in the localities where they formerly resided, and caught in traps or took from the nests eaglets, whose down was used in ceremonies. The eaglets, when required for feathers, have their heads washed; they are killed by pressure on the thorax, and buried with appropriate rites in special cemeteries, in which offerings of small wooden images and bows and arrows are yearly deposited. The interior Salish also are said by Teit to have property in eagles. Near the present Hopi villages there are shrines in which offerings of eagle eggs carved from wood are placed during the winter solstice for the increase of eagles. Among the Zuñi, feathers shed by their captive eagles have special significance, though the feathers are also regularly plucked and form a staple article of trade.

The mythology of almost every tribe is replete with eagle beings, and the widespread thunderbird myth relates in some cases to the eagle. In Hopi myth the Man-eagle is a sky-being who lays aside his plumage after flights in which he spreads devastation, and the hero who slays him is carried to the house in the sky by eagles of several species, each one in its turn bearing him higher. The Man-eagle myth is widely diffused, most tribes regarding this being as a manifestation of either helpful or maleficent power.

See Fewkes, Property Rights in Eagles among the Hopi, Am. Anthrop., II, 690–707, 1900; Hoffman in 14th Rep. B. A. E., 1896; Mooney (1) ibid., (2) in 19th Rep. B. A. E., 1900.
(w. h.)

**Eagle Hills Assiniboin.** A band of Assiniboin of 35 lodges living in 1808 between Bear hills and South Saskatchewan r., Assiniboia, Canada.—Henry-Thompson Jour., Coues ed., II, 523, 1897.

**Earth lodge.** A dwelling partly underground, circular in form, from 30 to 60 ft in diameter, with walls about 6 ft high, on which rested a dome-shaped roof with an opening in the center to afford light within and to permit the egress of smoke. The entrance was a projecting passageway from 6 to 14 ft long. The method of construction was first to draw a circle on the ground and excavate the earth within it from 2 to 4 ft deep. About 1½ ft within the circle were set crotched posts some 8 or 10 ft apart, on which were laid beams. Outside these posts were set others, one end of them braced against the bottom of the bank of earth at the periphery of the circle, and the other end leaning against the beams, forming a close stockade, an opening being left at the E. side for the entrance. Midway between the center of the excavation and the stockade were planted 4, 6, or 8 tall crotched posts, forming an inner circle. In the crotches were laid heavy beams to support the roof. The bark was stripped from all the posts and beams. The roof was formed of long, slender, tapering tree trunks, stripped of bark. The large ends were tied with strings of the inner bark of the elm to the beams at the top of the stockade, and the middle to those resting in the crotches of the inner circle of posts. The slender ends were cut so as to form the circular opening in the center of the roof, 2 or 3 ft in diameter. Outside this framework branches of willow were placed close together across the posts of the wall and the beams of the roof, and bound tightly to each pole, beginning at the ground and continuing upward to the central opening. Over the willow branches a heavy thatch of coarse dried grass was laid, tied in bundles and arranged so that it would shed water. Over the thatch was placed a thick coating of sods, cut so that they could be lapped, and laid like shingles. The wall and roof were afterward carefully tamped with earth and made impervious to rain. The long entranceway was built in the same manner as the lodge, and thatched and sodded at the

PAWNEE EARTH LODGE

same time. The grass of the sod continued to grow, and wild flowers brightened the walls and roof of the dwelling. The blackened circle around the central opening in the roof, produced by the heat and smoke, was the only suggestion that the verdant mound was a human abode. Within, the floor was made hard by a series of tampings, in which both water and fire were used. The fireplace was circular in shape and slightly excavated. A curtain of skin hung at the opening from the passageway into the lodge. The outer door was covered with a skin that was stiffened by sticks at the top and bottom, which was turned to one side to give entrance to the passageway. The couches of the occupants were placed around the wall, and frequently were inclosed by reed mats which could be raised or lowered. More than one family sometimes occupied a lodge, and in such case the families took different sides. The back part, opposite the entrance, was reserved for the keeping of sacred objects and the reception of guests. In the winter curtains of skin were hung from the beams of the inner circle of posts, making a smaller room about the fireplace. The shields and weapons of the men were suspended from these inner posts, giving color to the interior of the dwelling, which was always picturesque, whether seen at night, when the fire leaped up and glinted on the polished blackened roof and when at times the lodge was filled with men and women in their gala dress at some social meeting or religious ceremony, or during the day when the shaft of sunlight fell through the central opening over the fireplace, bringing into relief some bit of aboriginal life and leaving the rest of the lodge in deep shadow. Few, if any, large and well-built earth lodges exist at the present day. Even with care a lodge could be made to last only a generation or two.

Ceremonies attended the erection of an earth lodge from the marking of the circle to the putting on of the sods. Both men and women took part in these rites and shared in the labor of building. To cut, haul, and set the heavy posts and beams was the men's task; the binding, thatching, and sodding that of the women.

The earth lodge was used by the Pawnee, Arikara, Omaha, Ponca, Osage, and other tribes. A similar abode was found in the Aleutian ids., on Kodiak id., and in s. w. Alaska. There were habitations among some of the California tribes that had features in common with the earth lodge, and there are evidences of relationship between it, the Navaho hogan, and one form of Pima dwelling.

Among the Pawnee are preserved the most elaborate ceremonies and traditions pertaining to the earth lodge. These tribes are said to have abandoned the grass house of their kindred at some distant period and, under the teaching of aquatic animals, to have learned to construct the earth lodge. According to their ceremonies and legends, not only the animals were concerned with its construction—the badger digging the holes, the beaver sawing the logs, the bears carrying them, and all obeying the directions of the whale—but the stars also exercised authority. The earlier star cult of the people is recognized in the significance attached to the four central posts. Each stood for a star—the Morning and Evening stars, symbols of the male and female cosmic forces, and the North and South stars, the direction of chiefs and the abode of perpetual life. The posts were painted in the symbolic colors of these stars—red, white, black, yellow. During certain ceremonies corn of one of these colors was offered at the foot of the post of that color. In the rituals of the Pawnee the earth lodge is made typical of man's abode on the earth; the floor is the plain, the wall the distant horizon, the dome the arching sky, the central opening the zenith, dwelling place of Tirawa, the invisible power which gives life to all created beings.

The history of the distribution of this kind of dwelling among peoples widely scattered is a problem not yet fully solved. See *Grass lodge, Habitations.*    (A. C. F.)

**East Abeika.** (*Aiabeka*, 'unhealthful place'). A former Choctaw town at the mouth of Straight cr., an affluent of the Sukenatcha, in Kemper co., Miss. Called East Abeika to distinguish it from another town of the same name.—Halbert in Miss. Hist. Soc. Publ., VI, 425, 1902. See *Abihka.* **Abeeka.**—Romans, Florida, 313, 1775. **Aiabeka.**—Halbert, op. cit. **East Abeoka.**—Ibid., 309. **East Abeika.**—West Florida map, *ca.* 1775.

**Eastern Indians.** A collective term applied by the early New England writers to all the tribes N. E. of Merrimac r. It is used by Hubbard as early as 1680. These tribes, including the Pennacook, Abnaki, Malecite, and Micmac, were generally in the French interest and hostile to the English.    (J. M.)

**Eastern Indians.**—Form used by most early English writers. **Eastward Indians.**—Winthrop (1700) in N. Y. Doc. Col. Hist., IV, 612, 1854. **Estward Indians.**—Owaneco (1700), ibid., 614 ("the Nowonthewog or the Estward Indians").

**Eastern Shawnee.** A division of the Shawnee now living in Indian Ter. They formerly lived with the Seneca (Mingo) near Lewistown, Ohio, but sold their lands in 1831 and removed with the latter tribe to Kansas. In 1867 they separated from the Seneca and removed to Indian Ter. under the name of Eastern Shawnee. They are now under the Seneca school and numbered 95 in 1904.    (J. M.)

**East Greenlanders.** The Eskimo inhabiting the E. coast of Greenland. They are divided into two groups: The Angmagsalingmiut, inhabiting the fjords about C. Dan; and the southern group, formerly scattered along the coast southward. They have long lived in complete isolation, three-fourths of them in the Angmagsalik district, others farther s. about Iluilek, C. Bille, and Tingmiarmiut. (Nansen, First Crossing of Greenland, I, 321–371, 1890). They have developed some of the peculiar arts of the Eskimo to their highest perfection, especially the use of harpoons with shafts that become detached and float in the water, while the seal swims off with the line and bladder, and of flexible-jointed lances also for killing the struggling animal. The more easily handled double bladder is their invention. They employ the double-bladed paddle altogether, wear skin-tight garments that fit in the waist of the kaiak so closely that no water can enter, and when overturned in the sea they are able to right themselves single handed with the paddle. The ornamental arts of the East Greenlanders are neglected, except among one isolated band in the remote N. E. Their winter houses, made of stones and sod, are long and narrow, with family benches on one side, and can be stretched out to accommodate more people than the square houses of Alaska. The large public buildings of the western tribes they know only by tradition. The East Greenlanders numbered 548, comprising 245 males and 303 females, in 1884, not counting a few scattered families of unknown numbers living N. of 68° (Rink, Eskimo Tribes, 1887). The entire southern group of the East Greenlanders, all the pagan Eskimo of Tingmiarmiut and the other places s. of Angmagsalik, 114 individuals altogether, emigrated between 1887 and 1900 to Kernertok, near C. Farewell.

The villages and settlements of the East Greenlanders, past and present, are as follows: Akernivak, Akorninarmiut, Aluik, Aluk, Amivik, Anarnisok, Angmagsalik, Anoritok, Aputitek, Atangime, Auarkat, Estale, Igdluarsuk, Ikatek, Ikerasak, Iluilek, Imarsivik, Ingmikertok, Inigsalik, Inugsiut, Ivimiut, Kangarsik, Kangigdlek, Kemisak, Kernertok, Kialinek, Kikertarsoak, Kinarbik, Koremiut, Kumarmiut, Kutek, Manitsuk, Nanusek, Narsuk, Norajik, Norsit, Nualik, Nunakitit, Okiosorbik, Orkua, Patuterajuit, Pikiutdlek, Sangmisok, Sarkarmiut, Sermiligak, Sermilik, Sivinganek, Sivingarnarsik, Tarsia, Tasiusarsik, Taterat, Tingmiarmiut, Umanak, Umivik, Utorkarmiut.          (H. W. H.)

**Eastman, Charles Alexander** (*Ohiyesa*, 'the Winner'). A Santee Dakota physician and author, born in 1858 near Redwood Falls, Minn. His father was a full-blood Sioux named Many Lightnings, and his mother the half-blood daughter of a well-known army officer. His mother dying soon after his birth, he was reared by his paternal grandmother and an uncle, who after the Minnesota massacre in 1862 fled with the boy into Canada. Here he lived the life of a wild Indian until he was 15 years of age, when his father, who in the meantime had accepted Christianity and civilization, sought him out and brought him home to Flandreau, S. Dak., where a few Sioux families had established themselves as farmers and homesteaders. Ohiyesa was placed in the mission school at Santee, Nebr., where he made such progress in 2 years that he was selected for a more advanced course and sent to Beloit College, Beloit, Wis. After 2 years spent there in the preparatory department he went to Knox College, Galesburg, Ill., thence to Kimball Academy and Dartmouth College, New Hampshire. He was graduated from Dartmouth in 1887, and immediately entered the Boston University school of medicine, receiving the degree of M. D. in 1890. Dr Eastman was then appointed Government physician to the Pine Ridge agency, S. Dak., and served there nearly 3 years, through the ghost-dance disturbance and afterward. In 1893 he went to St Paul, Minn., and entered there on the practice of medicine, also serving for 3 years as traveling secretary of the Young Men's Christian Association among the Indians. Afterward he was attorney for the Sioux at Washington, and later again Government physician at Crow Creek, S. Dak. In 1903 he was appointed by the Office of Indian Affairs to the special

CHARLES ALEXANDER EASTMAN.    (HARPER & BROS.)

work of revising the allotment rolls and selecting permanent family names for the Sioux. His first book, "Indian Boyhood," appeared in 1902, and "Red Hunters and the Animal People" in 1904. He is an occasional contributor to the magazines and lectures frequently on Indian life and history. In 1891 Dr Eastman married Miss Elaine Goodale, of Massachusetts, and they have 6 children.          (E. G. E.)

**Eastman, John** (*Mahpiyawakankidan*, 'Sacred Cloud Worshipper'). A Santee Dakota of three-fourths blood, brother of Charles Alexander Eastman, noted as a Presbyterian clergyman; born in Mar., 1849, at Shakopee, Minn. His father was Many Lightnings, a full-blood Sioux, who, on becoming a Christian in 1864, took the name of Jacob Eastman. His mother, Mary Nancy Eastman, was the daughter of Capt. Seth

Eastman, an American army officer, and maternal granddaughter of Cloudman, a Sioux chief. He was taught during two winters by Rev. A. L. Riggs at Sisseton mission, walking there about 100 m. from his home at Flandreau, S. Dak., and back again in spring. Afterward he was sent to live for 9 mos. in the family of Robert Riggs at Beloit, Wis., who taught him. In 1876 he was ordained as a Presbyterian minister at Flandreau and installed as pastor of the Indian church of Flandreau township, which had been organized in 1871 and provided by the Presbyterian Mission Board with a building in 1874. Mr Eastman took charge of a Government school and began teaching the youth of the Santee res. in 1878, but resigned this charge in 1885 in order to accept the position of overseer of the band then living in Flandreau township. He retired from this position in 1896 and now devotes much of his attention to the work of his ministry and the cultivation of a small farm purchased some years ago. His church now numbers 96 communicants. In 1874 Mr Eastman married Miss Mary J. Faribault, a half-blood Santee. They are parents of 6 children. Mr Eastman is still active in tribal affairs, and since about 1880 has annually served in the capacity of delegate of his people at Washington.

**Ebahamo.** An extinct tribe formerly dwelling on Matagorda bay, Tex. La Salle constructed his Ft St Louis within the territory of this tribe and of the Quelanhubeches, or Karankawa, who probably were a cognate people. Joutel (1687) states in his narrative (French, Hist. Coll. La., I, 134, 1846) that La Salle recorded a vocabulary of their language, which is very different from that of the Cenis (Caddo) and more difficult; that they were neighbors and allies of the latter people and understood some of their words. "At our fort at St Louis bay," he says, "we made some stay to cultivate the friendship of our Bracamos (as the Indian nation that dwells near our fort is called), in order to leave protectors to the people whom we would have to leave in the fort." (A. S. G.)

Apayxam.—Massanet MS. (1690) cited by H. E. Bolton, inf'n, 1906 (same?). **Bahamos.**—Early writer quoted by Gatschet, Karankawa Inds., 24, 1891. **Bracamos.**—Cavelier (1685) quoted by Shea, Early Voy., 21, 1861. **Ebahamo.**—Joutel (1687) in Margry, Déc., III, 276, 1878. **Ebahumo.**—Ibid., 300. **Hebahamo.**—Joutel (1687) in French, Hist. Coll. La., I, 134, 1846. **Hebohamos.**—Joutel quoted by Gatschet, op. cit.

**Ebiamana.** An unidentified village in N. Florida about 1565.—De Bry, Brev. Nar., II, map, 1591.

**Ebita Poocola Chitto** (*Ibetap okla chitto*, 'fountain-head big people'). A former Choctaw town, noted by Romans, believed to have been situated on the head of Straight cr., in Kemper co., Miss., hence the name.—Halbert in Miss. Hist. Soc. Publ., VI, 425, 1902.

Ebita-poocolo-chitto.—West Florida map, ca. 1772. Ebitap-oocoolo-cho.—Romans, Florida, 310, 1775. Ibetap okla chitto.—Halbert, op. cit.

**Ebita Poocola Skatane** (*Ibetap okla iskitini*, 'fountain-head little people'). A former Choctaw town on the w. or main prong of Yazoo cr., a N. affluent of Petickfa cr., in Kemper co., Miss.—Halbert in Miss. Hist. Soc. Publ., VI, 423, 1902.

Ebeetap Oocoola.—Romans, Florida, 310, 1775. Ibetap okla iskitini.—Halbert, op. cit.

**Ecatacari.** A rancheria of either the Eudeve or the Nevome of Sonora, Mexico, in the early part of the 18th century. It was probably situated near Matape.—Writer of 1702(?) in Doc. Hist. Mex., 4th s., V, 126, 1857.

**Echantac.** A village, presumably Costanoan, formerly connected with San Juan Bautista mission, Cal.—Engelhardt, Franciscans in Cal., 398, 1897.

**Echilat.** A former village of the Rumsen division of the Costanoan family situated 12 m. S. E. of San Carlos mission, Cal.

Echilat.—Taylor in Cal. Farmer, Apr. 20, 1860. San Francisquita.—Ibid.

**Echojoa.** A Mayo settlement on the Rio Mayo, above Santa Cruz, S. W. Sonora, Mexico; pop. 444 in 1900.

Echehóa.—Hardy, Trav. in Mex., 438, 1829. Echojoa.—Orozco y Berra, Geog., 356, 1864. Echonova.—Ibid. (Echojoa, or). Hetschojoa.—Kino, map (1702) in Stöcklein, Neue Welt-Bott, 1726.

**Echota** (corruption of *Itsă'tĭ*, meaning unknown). The name of several Cherokee towns. (1) the most important—often distinguished as Great Echota—was on the s. side of Little Tennessee r., a short distance below Citico cr., in Monroe co., Tenn. It was the ancient capital and sacred "peace town" of the nation. At that place there is a large mound. (2) Little Echota was on Sautee (Itsâ'tĭ) cr., a head-stream of the Chattahoochee, w. of Clarkesville, Ga. (3) New Echota, the capital of the nation for some years before the removal, was established at a spot, originally known as Gănsági, at the junction of Oostanaula and Conasauga rs., in Gordon co., Ga. It was sometimes called Newtown. (4) The old Macedonian mission on Soco cr., of the North Carolina res., is also known to the Cherokee as Itsâ'tĭ, as was also (5) the great Nacoochee mound. See Mooney in 19th Rep. B. A. E., 523, 1900.

Choquata.—Mooney, op. cit. (cited as former misprint). Chota.—Doc. of 1799 quoted by Royce in 5th Rep. B. A. E., 144, 1887. Chote.—Timberlake, Mem., map, 1765 (on Little Tennessee r.). Chote great.—Bartram, Trav., 371, 1792 (on Tenn. r.).

**Echulit.** A Tolowa village at a lagoon on the coast about 5 m. N. of Crescent, Cal. (P. E. G.)

E'-tcu-lĕt ʒûn-nĕ.—Dorsey, MS. Chetco vocab., B. A. E., 1884. E-tcu'-lĭt.—Dorsey in Jour. Am. Folklore, III, 236, 1890 (Tututunne named). E-tc'u'-lĭt.—

Ibid. (Naltunnetunne name). **Tc'ĕs-qan'-me.**—Ibid. (another Naltunnetunne name).

**Eclauou.** A village of the Utina (Timucua) confederacy in central Florida in the 16th century.—Laudonnière (1564) in French, Hist. Coll. La., n. s., 243, 1869.

**Ecochee.** A former Cherokee settlement on a head stream of Savannah r., in N. W. South Carolina or N. E. Georgia. It was destroyed during the Revolutionary war. (J. M.)

**Ecorce.** A band of Nipissing living at Oka, Canada, in 1736. Their totem was the birch. Chauvignerie calls them L' Ecoree, evidently intended for L' Ecorce.
**Bark tribe.**—Chauvignerie (1736) transl. in N. Y. Doc. Col. Hist., IX, 1053, 1855. **L'Ecoree.**—Chauvignerie quoted by Schoolcraft, Ind. Tribes, III, 554, 1853.

**Ecureuil** (French: 'squirrel'). Spoken of as a tribe formerly living between Tadoussac and Hudson bay, Quebec province, Canada; destroyed by the Iroquois in 1661. Probably a Montagnais band living about the headwaters of Three rs., possibly about the lake named Ouapichiouanon in the Jesuit Relations.
**Escurieux.**—Jes. Rel., 20, 1661. **L'Ecureuil.**—McKenney and Hall, Ind. Tribes, III, 79, 1854.

**Ecushaw.** See *Cashaw.*

**Edelano.** An unidentified village on an island in St Johns r., Fla., in the 16th century.—Laudonnière (1564) in French, Hist. Coll. La., n. s., 287, 1869.

**Edenshaw** (or Edensaw, from a Tlingit word referring to the glacier). The Haida chief best known to the whites. He succeeded early in the 19th century to the chieftainship of the strong Stustas kinship group which centered in the town of Kioosta on the coast of Graham id. opposite North id., Brit. Col. Shortly after 1860, his people having fallen off in numbers, he moved with them to Kung, at the mouth of Naden harbor, where he erected a large house, which is still standing. Through the exercise of his exceptional abilities in trade and in various other ways he became one of the wealthiest of the Haida chiefs. His relations with the whites were always cordial, and it was through his influence that a missionary was sent to Masset. Among other good offices to the whites, he protected the crew of an American vessel when threatened by other natives. He died about 1885. A monument mentioning his kind treatment of the whites stands in Masset. (J. R. S.)

**Edgpiiliik.** A Delaware village in w. New Jersey in 1792.
**Edgpiiliik.**—Brinton, Lenape Leg., 46, 1885. **Edgpüluk.**—Keane in Stanford, Comp., Cent. and S. Am., 512, 1878.

**Edisto.** A small tribe, now extinct, which appears to have occupied lower Edisto r., S. C., which derived its name from that of the tribe. The Huguenots of Ribault's colony were kindly welcomed by them in 1562, and the Span-

iards for a time had a mission among them. They were included in the Cusabo group, and are mentioned in connection with the Stono, Westo, and Savannah as still living in the region named in 1670, when English colonization began. With the Westo and Stono they were possibly driven out by the Shawnee in 1680. Gatschet thinks it probable that they spoke the Uchean language. See Mooney, Siouan Tribes of the East, Bull. B. A. E., 1894.
**Adusta.**—De Bry, Brev. Nar., II, map, 1591. **Audusta.**—Laudonnière (1587) in Hakluyt, Voy., 379, 1600. **Edistoes.**—Gallatin in Trans. Am. Antiq. Soc., II, 83, 1836. **Edisto.**—Adair, Hist. Inds., 325, 1775. **Edistow.**—Harris, Voy. and Trav., I, map, 1705. **Orista.**—Fontaneda (*ca.* 1570) in Ternaux-Compans, Voy., XX, 16, 1841. **Oristanum.**—Brigstock (1623) quoted by French, Hist. Coll. La., II, 186, 1875.

**Edjao** (ᵍ*I'djao*). A Haida town situated around a hill of the same name, at the E. end of Masset village, Queen Charlotte ids., Brit. Col. It was occupied by the Aoyaku-lnagai, a branch of the Yaku-lanas, and, according to the old men, consisted in later times of about 6 houses, which would have contained nearly a hundred persons. Later it came to be included within the limits of Masset.—Swanton, Cont. Haida, 99, 1905.
**Hai'ts'au.**—Boas, Twelfth Rep. N. W. Tribes Can., 23, 1898. **Hā-jū hādē.**—Krause, Tlinkit-Indianer, 304, 1885 ('people of Edjao'; probably the same).

**Edjieretrukenade** ('buffalo people'). An Athapascan tribe of the Chipewyan group living along the banks of Buffalo r., Athabasca, Canada.
**Edjiére-tρou-kkè-nadé.**—Petitot, Autour du lac des Esclaves, 363, 1891 ('buffalo people').

**Education.** The aborigines of North America had their own systems of education, through which the young were instructed in their coming labors and obligations, embracing not only the whole round of economic pursuits—hunting, fishing, handicraft, agriculture, and household work—but speech, fine art, customs, etiquette, social obligations, and tribal lore. By unconscious absorption and by constant inculcation the boy and girl became the accomplished man and woman. Motives of pride or shame, the stimulus of flattery or disparagement, wrought constantly upon the child, male or female, who was the charge, not of the parents and grandparents alone but of the whole tribe (Heckewelder). Loskiel (p. 139) says the Iroquois are particularly attentive to the education of the young people for the future government of the state, and for this purpose admit a boy, generally the nephew of the principal chief, to the council and solemn feast following it.

The Eskimo were most careful in teaching their girls and boys, setting them difficult problems in canoeing, sledding, and hunting, showing them how to solve them, and asking boys how they would meet a given emergency (see *Child life*). Everywhere there was the closest association, for education, of parents with children, who learned the names and uses of things in nature. At a tender age they played at serious business, girls attending to household duties, boys following men's pursuits. Children were furnished with appropriate toys; they became little basket makers, weavers, potters, water carriers, cooks, archers, stone workers, watchers of crops and flocks, the range of instruction being limited only by tribal custom. Personal responsibilities were laid on them, and they were stimulated by the tribal law of personal property, which was inviolable. Among the Pueblos cult images and paraphernalia were their playthings, and they early joined the fraternities, looking forward to social duties and initiation. The Apache boy had for pedagogues his father and grandfather, who began early to teach him counting, to run on level ground, then up and down hill, to break branches from trees, to jump into cold water, and to race, the whole training tending to make him skilful, strong, and fearless. The girl was trained in part by her mother, but chiefly by the grandmother, the discipline beginning as soon as the child could control her movements, but never becoming regular or severe. It consisted in rising early, carrying water, helping about the home, cooking, and minding children. At 6 the little girl took her first lessons in basketry with yucca leaves. Later on decorated baskets, saddle-bags, beadwork, and dress were her care.

On the coming of the whites a new era of secular education, designed and undesigned, began. All the natives, young and old, were pupils, and all the whites who came in contact with them were instructors, whether purposely or through the influence of their example and patronage. The undesigned instruction can not be measured, but its effect was profound. The Indian passed at once into the iron age; the stone period, except in ceremony, was moribund. So radical was the change in the eastern tribes that it is difficult now to illustrate their true life in museum collections.

An account of the designed instruction would embrace all attempts to change manners, customs, and motives, to teach reading and writing in the foreign tongue, to acquaint the Indians with new arts and industries, and to impress or force upon them the social organization of their conquerors. The history of this systematic instruction divides itself into the period of (1) discovery and exploration, (2) colonization and settlement, (3) Colonial and Revolutionary times, (4) the growth

of the national policy, and (5) the present system.

Parts of the area here considered were discovered and explored by several European nations at dates wide apart. All of them aroused the same wonder at first view, traded their manufactures for Indian products, smoked the pipe of peace, and opened friendly relations. The Norwegians began their acculturation of Greenland in the year 1000. The Spanish pioneers were Ponce de León, Narvaez, Cabeza de Vaca, Marcos de Niza, De Soto, Coronado, Cabrillo, and many others. The French appeared in Canada and in the Mississippi valley, and were followed by the English in Virginia and in New England, the Dutch in New York, the Swedes in New Jersey, the Quakers in Pennsylvania, and the Russians in Alaska. Instruction, designed and undesigned, immediately ensued, teaching the Indians many foreign industrial processes, the bettering of their own, and the adoption of firearms, and metal tools and utensils. Domestic animals (horses, donkeys, cattle, sheep, goats, poultry) and many vegetables found congenial environment. It was through these and other practical lessons that the missionaries and teachers of the early days, who came to Christianize young Indians and bestow on them an education, were more successful instructors than they knew. By the subtle process of suggestion, the inevitable action of mind upon mind, the Indians received incalculable training in all arts and the fashion of living. Failures to accomplish the most cherished object of the missionaries grew out of the great distance which separated the two races, and of the contrary influences of many of the whites who were first on the spot, not from lack of zeal or ability. The Roman Catholic clergy were at first the most efficient agents of direct instruction; besides carrying on their proper missionary work they exerted themselves to mitigate the harsh treatment visited on the Indian. In the 16th century the expedition of Narvaez to Florida was accompanied by Franciscans under Padre Juan Juarez, and the appearance of Cabeza de Vaca in Mexico prompted Fray Marcos de Niza's journey to the N. as far as Zuñi, and of the expedition of Coronado, who left Fray Juan de Padilla and a lay brother in Quivira, on the Kansas plains, as well as a friar and a lay brother at Tiguex and Pecos, respectively, all destined to be killed by the natives. The subsequent history of the S. W. records a series of disasters to the immediate undertakings, but permanent success in practical education.

In 1567 the agricultural education of Indians was tried in Florida by the Jesuit

Fray Rogel, who selected lands, procured agricultural implements, and built commodious houses (Shea).

Early in the 17th century Franciscan missions were established among the Apalachee and neighboring tribes, afterward to be abandoned, but forming the first link in the chain of causes which has brought these Indians through their minority under guardianship to mature self-dependence. Concentration for practical instruction was established in California by the Franciscans (see *California, Indians of*). The results achieved by the missions in the S. W. were chiefly practical and social. Domestic animals, with the art of domestication and industries depending on their products, were permanently acquired. Foreign plants, including wheat, peaches, and grapes, were introduced, gunpowder was adopted in place of the bow, and new practices and customs, good and bad, came into vogue. The early French missions in North America were among (1) the Abnaki in Maine, (2) the Huron in Ontario, Michigan, and Ohio, (3) the Iroquois in New York, (4) the Ottawa in Wisconsin and Michigan, (5) the Illinois in the middle W., and (6) the tribes of Louisiana. Bishop Laval founded a school at Quebec for French and Indian youth, Father de Smet planted the first Catholic mission among the Salish tribes, and Canadian priests visited the natives on Puget sd. and along the coast of Washington.

One of the objects in colonizing Virginia, mentioned in the charter of 1606 and repeated in that of 1621, was to bring the infidels and savages to human civility and a settled and quiet government (Neill). Henrico College was founded in 1618. The council of Jamestown in 1619 voted to educate Indian children in religion, a civil course of life, and in some useful trade. George Thorpe, superintendent of education at Henrico, gave a cheering account of his labors in 1621. Many youths were taken to England to be educated. William and Mary College was founded in 1691, and special provisions were made in the charter of Virginia for the instruction of Indians (Hist. College of William and Mary, 1874). Brasserton manor was purchased through the charity of Robert Boyle, the yearly rents and profits being devoted to a boarding-school foundation in William and Mary College. In Maryland no schools were founded, but the settlers and Indians exchanged knowledge of a practical kind. The interesting chapter of Indian education in New England includes, during the 17th century, the offering of their children for instruction, the translation of the Bible (1646–90) into their language by Eliot (see *Eliot Bible*), the founding of Natick, the

appointment of a superintendent of Indians (Daniel Gookin, 1656–86), and the provision for Indian youth in Harvard. The spirit and methods of instruction in the 18th century are revealed in the adoption of Indian children by the colonists (Samson Occum, for example), the founding of Moor's charity school, Bishop Berkeley's gift to Yale, the labors of Eleazer Wheelock (1729), and the founding of Dartmouth College in 1754 (see Fletcher, Ind. Education and Civilization, 1888). In New York and other northern states large sums of money were appropriated for the instruction of Indians, and in Princeton College special provisions were made for their education.

The Moravians, models of thrift and good will, had in their hearts wherever they went the welfare of the aborigines as a private and public burden.

Between 1741 and 1761 began, under Vitus Bering and his successors, the series of lessons given for the acculturation of the Aleut, Eskimo, and Indians of Alaska. Schools were formally opened in Kodiak in 1794, and a little later in Sitka. This chapter in education includes the Russian Company's schools, as well as military, Government, and church schools. Pupils were taught the Russian and English languages, geography, history, arithmetic, geometry, trigonometry, and navigation. Industrial training was compulsory in many cases. Dall (Alaska, 1870) speaks of the great aptness of the Aleuts in receiving instruction. In all areas the voyageur, the trapper, the trader, the missionary, the settler, the school-teacher, and Government authorities were partners in education. The contact, whenever it took place, had its effect in a generation or two. The making of treaties with the Indians afforded an object lesson in practical affairs. Old things passed away whose nature and very existence and structure can be proved now only by impressions on ancient pottery or remains in caverns and graves. The two-fold education embraced new dietaries, utensils, and modes of preparing and eating food; new materials and fashions in dress and implements for making clothing; new or modified habitations and their appurtenances and furniture; new productive industries and new methods of quarrying and mining, woodcraft, hunting, trapping, and fishing; the introduction of gunpowder, domestic animals, and foreign handicrafts; the adoption of calendars and clocks, and the habit of steady employment for wages; new social institutions, manners, customs, and fashions, not always for the better; foreign words and jargons for new ideas and activities; new esthetic ideas; changes in the clan and tribal life, and accessions to native beliefs and forms of worship borrowed from the conquerors.

In the Canadian colonies little was done for secular and industrial education by the provincial governments prior to confederation. The Roman Catholic missions inherited from the French, Anglican missions sent from the mother country, the New England Company's missions among the Six Nations and Mohawk, and Methodist schools founded by Lord Elgin and others, as well as those managed by Presbyterians, Baptists, and Congregationalists, all combined common school instruction and training in the practical arts with their special work (see *Missions*). After the confederation (1867) the subject was taken up systematically and contract schools were established and put into the hands of the Christian denominations. In the older provinces agriculture and other industries had largely taken the place of primitive arts. After the admission of British Columbia, Manitoba, and the Northwest Territory into the Dominion, steps were taken to establish systematic training in those provinces. In 1904 there were 24 industrial, 46 boarding, and 228 day schools in operation. Day schools among the tribes aim to secure the cooperation of parents; the boarding schools especially cultivate industrial training for various bread-winning trades; normal schools and girls' homes have been established to teach self-support under new conditions. Improvement in dwellings has developed a stronger attachment to home, as well as bettered health and raised the moral tone, for when houses are furnished with stoves, beds, tables, chairs, musical instruments, and sewing machines, the tastes of the occupants are elevated and other thoughts stimulated. Indians become individual owners of farms and of flocks and herds and sell the produce; they partake of the benefits of commerce and transportation and acquire thrift. Competition in fairs and exhibitions stimulates proficiency in both the old and the new activities. The purpose of the Canadian government has been to encourage the Indians to emerge from a condition of tutelage and continue voluntarily what they have learned under close supervision. The schools discourage premature marriages and educate the young prospective mothers. Education has made the aborigines law-respecting, prosperous, and contented. Far from being a menace to or a burden upon the commonwealth, they contribute in many ways to its welfare. The able-bodied in the mixed farming districts have become practically self-supporting (Pedley in Can. Ind. Aff. for 1904).

57008°—Bull. 30—12——27

After the establishment of the United States government the following Christian bodies either instituted secular day and boarding schools among the Indians or continued those already in existence, and these schools have borne a large part in Indian education: Roman Catholic and Moravians from colonial times; Friends (Orthodox), 1795; Baptist, 1807; American Board of Commissioners for Foreign Missions, 1810; Episcopal, 1815; Methodist Episcopal, 1816; Presbyterian (North), 1833; Old School Presbyterians, 1837; Methodist Episcopal (South), 1844; Congregational American Missionary Association, 1846; Reformed Dutch, 1857; Presbyterian (South), 1857; Friends (Hicksite), 1869; United Presbyterian, 1869; Unitarian, 1886. Miss Alice C. Fletcher affirms that the missionary labors among the Indians have been as largely educational as religious. Until 1870 all Government aid for this object passed through the hands of the missionaries.

On July 12, 1775, a committee on Indian affairs was appointed in the Continental Congress, with Gen. Schuyler as chairman, and in the following year a standing committee was created. Money was voted to support Indian students at Dartmouth and Princeton colleges. After the War Department was created, in 1789, Indian affairs were left in the hands of its Secretary until 1849, when the Department of the Interior was established and the Indian Bureau was transferred thereto. Gen. Knox, Washington's Secretary of War, urged industrial education, and the President was of the same mind. In his message of 1801 President Adams noted the success of continued efforts to introduce among the Indians the implements and practices of husbandry and the household arts.

The first petition of an Indian for schools among his tribe was made by David Folsom, a Choctaw, in 1816. The Ottawa, in their treaty (1817) and in their address to President Monroe (1822), stipulated for industrial and literary education. In 1819 a first appropriation of $10,000 was made by Congress for Indian education, the superintendents and agents to be nominated by the President. In 1823 there were 21 schools receiving Government aid, and the number was increased to 38 in 1825. The first contract school was established on the Tulalip res., Wash., in 1869, but it was not until 1873 that Government schools proper were provided. In the beginning there were only day schools, later boarding schools on the reservations, and finally boarding schools remote from them. The training in all these schools was designed to bring the Indians nearer to civilized life, with a view to ultimate citizenship by enabling them to assimilate the speech, industrial life, family organization, social manners and customs, civil government, knowledge, modes of thinking, and ethical standards of the whites. The change to agriculture and sedentary industries had a profound effect in developing a sense of continuous responsibility. A school was established at Carlisle, Pa., in 1879, by Capt. R. H. Pratt, U. S. A., for the purpose of educating Indian boys and girls by separating them from their tribal life so as to prepare them to live and labor in contact with white people (see *Carlisle School*). To this end they are taught in the school as far as the high-school grade, and instruction is given in mechanical trades and domestic work. In order to facilitate association with the white population the "outing system" was adopted, by which pupils are permitted to go out during vacations to earn money. Boys and girls are also placed in families where they may work for their board, and perhaps more, and attend school. Thus the young Indians are trained in home life and associate with white children. Contract schools were abandoned June 30, 1900; the religious societies have since taken care of their own schools, and the appropriation for Indian education is applied under the law entirely to Government schools. About 100 students receive higher instruction in Hampton Institute. One of the latest experiments is that of Rev. Sheldon Jackson in connection with the introduction of domesticated reindeer into Alaska. These are allotted to mission and other schools, and instruction in the care and use of them is a part of the training.

The present scheme of education adopted by the Indian Office is to teach the pupils English, arithmetic, geography, and United States history, and also to train them in farming and the care of stock and in trades, as well as gymnastics. This requires the maintenance of day, boarding, and training schools, 253 now in all, with 2,300 employees, involving an annual expenditure of nearly $5,000,000. Some of these Indian schools are models (see *Chilocco Indian Industrial School*). Allotment of land has been the means of sending Indian children to district schools with white children. Indian teachers are being employed and parents are coming to be interested.

While on some reservations there are still Indian children who never saw a school, the great mass have ceased to be indifferent. The results of a century's efforts are immeasurable. Indians now take their places beside whites in many of the industrial pursuits and in the higher walks as well. The best evidence that the Indian is capable of civilization is the list of those who have succeeded. The Government has been stimulated, advised, and aided all along by associations of benevolent men and women who have freely given their time and means for the education and uplifting of the Indians, with various motives, some seeking the preservation of tribal life, arts, and customs, some their extinction. See *Carlisle School*, *Chilocco Indian Industrial School*, *Dutch influence*, *English influence*, *French influence*, *Spanish influence*, etc., *Governmental policy*, *Missions*.

In addition to the works cited, see Reps. Ind. Aff., especially for 1898 and subsequent years; Bureau of Education Reports for 1870, 339–354; 1871, 402–411; 1872, 405–418; 1873, 469–480; 1874, 506–516; 1875, 519–528; 1878, 281–286; 1879, 278–280; 1880, 372–376; 1886, app. 8 and 657–660; 1888, 999–1004; 1897, 1520–1522; also circulars 3, 1883, 58–73; 4, 34–43; Bulletin 1 of the New Orleans Exposition, 541–544 and 746–754, 1889; Archæologia Americana, 1820–60; Bacon, Laws of Md., 1765; Camden Soc. Publications, I–CIX, 1838–72; Canadian Ind. Aff. Reps.; Catesby, Nat. Hist. Carolina, II, XII, 1743; Eastman, Indian Boyhood, 1902; Doc. Hist. N. Y., I–IV, 1849–51; Fletcher, Indian Education and Civilization, 1888; Hailmann, Education of the Indian, 1904; Hall, Adolescence, 1904; Heckewelder, Narr. of the Mission of the United Brethren, 1820; Jenks, Childhood of Ji-shib', 1900; Hist. College of William and Mary, 1660–1874; La Flesche, The Middle Five, 1900; Loskiel, Hist. of the Mission of the United Brethren, 1794; Mass. Hist. Soc. Coll., I–X, 1792–1809; Neill, Hist. Va. Co., 1869; Parkman, Old Régime in Canada; Pratt, Reps. on Carlisle School in An. Rep. Commr. Ind. Aff., especially 20th and 24th; Rawson et al., Rep. of Commissioners on Indian Education in 1844 (Jour. Leg. Assemb. Prov. of Can., VI, 1847); Shea, Catholic Missions, 1855; Smet (1) Oregon Miss., 1845, (2) New Indian Sketches, 1865, (3) Western Missions and Missionaries, 1863; Spencer, Education of the Pueblo Child, 1899; Spotswood, Off. Letters (1710–22), Va. Hist. Soc., I–II, 1882–85; Stevenson, Religious Life of the Zuñi Child, 1887; Stith, Hist. Va., repr. 1865.　(o. t. m.)

**Eeh.** A band or division of the Iruwaitsu of Scott valley, Siskiyou co., Cal.; noted by Gibbs as living with the Watsahewa in 1851.

E-eh.—Gibbs (1851) in Schoolcraft, Ind. Tribes, III, 171, 1853. E-oh.—McKee (1851) in Sen. Ex. Doc. 4, 32d Cong., spec. sess., 171, 1853.

**Eeksen** (*Ē'exsen*). A Salish tribe about Oyster bay, E. coast of Vancouver id., speaking the Comox dialect.—Boas, MS., B. A. E., 1887.

**Eel River Indians.** A part of the Miami, formerly living in Indiana. Their village was at Thorntown, Boone co., where they had a reservation, which was sold in 1828, the band removing to the Miami res. between the Wabash and Eel rs., in Miami co. They afterward shared the general fortunes of the tribe.
(J. M.)
Eel River Indians.—Knox (1792) in Am. St. Papers, I, 235, 1832. Eelrivers.—Brown, West. Gaz., 72, 1817. Elk river tribe.—Ibid., 349 (misprint). Isle-River Indians.—Imlay, West. Ter., 371, 1793 (Eel r., through a corruption of l'Anguille into 'Long-isle'). l'Anguille.—French name of the band and settlement ('The eel'). Long-isle.—Imlay, op. cit. (misrendering of French l'Anguille). Thornton party.—Gale, Upper Miss., 178, 1867. Thorntown party.—Wyandot Vil. treaty (proclaimed 1828) in U. S. Ind. Treat., 520, 1873.

**Eesteytoch.** Given as a tribe on Cascade inlet, Brit. Col.; probably a village group of the Bellacoola.
Ees-tey-toch.—Kane, Wand. in N. Am., app., 1859.

**Efaca.** A Timucua clan belonging to the Acheha phratry.—Pareja (1612–14) quoted by Gatschet in Proc. Am. Philos. Soc., XVII, 492, 1878.

**Egan.** An Algonquian settlement in Maniwaki township, Ottawa co., Quebec, containing 225 Indians in 1884.

**Egedesminde.** A missionary station on Davis str., w. Greenland.—Crantz, Hist. Greenland, I, 14, 1767.

**Eguianna-cahel** ('water-hole of the mountain'). A rancheria, probably Cochimi, connected with Purísima (Cadegomo) mission, Lower California, in the 18th century.—Doc. Hist. Mex., 4th s., V, 189, 1857.
Egusanna cahel.—Ibid.

**Ehartsar.** A band of the Crows, one of the four into which Lewis divided the tribe.
E-hârt'-sâr.—Lewis, Trav., 175, 1809. Ĕh-hä-tzä.—Long, Exped. Rocky Mts., II, lxxxiv, 1823 (Hidatsa name: 'leaf people').

**Ehatisaht.** A Nootka tribe on Esperanza inlet, w. coast of Vancouver id., Brit. Col.; pop. 101 in 1902, 95 in 1904. Their principal village is Oke. From their waters came the larger part of the supply of dentalium shells extensively used on the Pacific coast as media of exchange.
Ai-tiz-zarts.—Jewitt, Nar., 36, 1849. Aitzarts.—Armstrong, Oregon, 136, 1857. Ayhuttisaht.—Sproat, Sav. Life, 308, 1868. Eh-aht-tis-aht.—Can. Ind. Aff., 52, 1875. Ehateset.—Mayne, Brit. Col., 251, 1862. Ehatisaht.—Can. Ind. Aff. 1901, pt. 2, 158. Ĕ'hatisath.—Boas, 6th Rep. N. W. Tribes Can., 31, 1890. Ehatt-is-aht.—Can. Ind. Aff. 1897, 357.

**Ehouae** ('one battered it.'—Hewitt). A village of the Tionontati existing in 1640.
Eh8ae.—Jes. Rel. 1641, 69, 1858.—Ehwae.—Shea, note in Charlevoix, New France, II, 153, 1866. Sainct Pierre et sainct Paul.—Jes. Rel. 1640, 95, 1858.

**Ehressaronon.** The Huron name of a tribe mentioned by Ragueneau in 1640 as living s. of St Lawrence r. (Jes. Rel. 1640, 35, 1858). It can not now be identified with any tribe s. of the St Lawrence. Perhaps Iroquoian, as are some of the tribes mentioned in the same list.

**Ehutewa.** A Luiseño village formerly in the neighborhood of San Luis Rey mission, s. Cal. (Taylor in Cal. Farmer, May 11, 1860). Possibly the same as Hatawa.

**Eidenu** (perhaps an Eskimo rendering of 'I don't know'). A Kinugumiut coast settlement at C. Prince of Wales.
Ei-dan-noo.—Beechy (1826) quoted by Baker, Geog. Dict. Alaska, 1901. Iden-noo.—Ibid. Wales.—Post-route map, 1903.

**Eider** (trans. of *Igognak*, 'eider duck'). An Aleut village on Captain bay, Unalaska, Alaska, at a point of the same name. Pop. 39 in 1830, according to Veniaminoff.
Igognak.—Kotzebue (1816) quoted by Baker, Geog. Dict. Alaska, 1901 ('eider duck'). Igonok.—Coxe, Russ. Discov., 166, 1787. Paystravskoi.—Elliott, Cond. Aff. Alaska, 225, 1875. Pestriakof.—Baker, Geog. Dict. Alaska, 1901 (Russian: 'eider duck'). Pestriakovskoje.—Holmberg, Ethnol. Skizz., map, 1855. Pestryakovskoe.—Veniaminoff, Zapiski, II, 202, 1840.

**Einake** (*Ĕ-in'-a-ke*, 'catchers,' or 'soldiers'). A society of the Ikunuhkatsi, or All Comrades, in the Piegan tribe; it has been obsolete since about 1860, and perhaps earlier.—Grinnell, Blackfoot Lodge Tales, 221, 1892.

**Eiwhuelit.** A division of the Yuit Eskimo on St Lawrence id., Bering sea. Bogoras says "they are plainly a colony from the nearest [Siberian] shore, probably from Indian point." The villages are Chibukak, Chitnak, Kialegak, Kukuliak, Puguviliak, and Punuk.
Eiwhue'lit.—Bogoras, Chukchee, 20, 1904 (Chukchi name). Kikhtŏg'āmūt.—Dall in Cont. N. A. Ethnol., I, 15, 1877 ('islanders'). Oomoojeks.—Kelly, Arctic Eskimo in Alaska, 11, 1890. Shiwo-kŭg-mūt.—Dall in Proc. A. A. A. S., XXXIV, 377, 1885. Umudjek.—Woolfe in 11th Census, Alaska, 130, 1893.

**Ekaentoton.** The Huron name of Manitoulin id. and of the Indians (Amikwa) living on it in 1649. It was the ancient home of the Ottawa.
Ekaentoton.—Jes. Rel. 1649, II, 6, 1858. l'Isle de Sainote Marie.—Ibid.

**Ekaloaping.** A Padlimiut Eskimo settlement in Padli fjord, Baffin land.
Eχaloaping.—Boas in 6th Rep. B. A. E., 441, 1888.

**Ekaluakdjuin.** A summer settlement of the Saumingmiut subtribe of the Okomiut Eskimo, N. of Cumberland sd.
Eχaluaqdjuin.—Boas in 6th Rep. B. A. E., 439, 1888.

**Ekalualuin.** A summer settlement of the Akudnirmiut Eskimo on Home bay, Baffin land.
Eχalualuin.—Boas in 6th Rep. B. A. E., 441, 1888.

**Ekaluin.** A summer settlement of the Nugumiut Eskimo of Baffin land at the head of Frobisher bay.
Eχaluin.—Boas in 6th Rep. B. A. E., map, 1888.

**Ekaluin.** A summer settlement of Talirpingmiut Eskimo on the s. shore of Cumberland sd.
Eχoluin.—Boas in 6th Rep. B. A. E., map, 1888.

**Ekalukdjuak.** A summer settlement of the Kingua Okomiut Eskimo at the head of Cumberland sd.
Eχaluqdjuaq.—Boas in 6th Rep. B. A. E., map, 1888.

**Ekaluktaluk.** An Eskimo village in the Kuskokwim district, Alaska; pop. 24 in 1893.
Ekaluktalugumiut.—11th Census, Alaska, 164, 1893.

**Ekarenniondi** ('there a tree lies extended.'—Hewitt). A Tionontati village of the Deer clan where the Jesuits had their mission of St Mathias in 1648.
Ekarenniondi.—Garnier (1648) in Charlevoix, New Fr., II, 228, note, 1866. **Sainct Matthieu.**—Jes. Rel. 1640, 95, 1858. **Saint Mathias.**—Jes. Rel. 1648, 61, 1858.

**Ekatopistaks** ('half-dead meat'—Morgan'; 'the band that have finished packing'—Hayden). A division of the Piegan tribe of the Siksika (q. v.), probably extinct.
e-ka-to'-pi-staks.—Hayden, Ethnog. and Philol. Mo. Val., 264, 1862. **E-ko'-to-pis-taxe.**—Morgan, Anc. Soc., 171, 1878.

**Ekgiagan.** A village of the Chalone division of the Costanoan family, formerly near Soledad mission, Cal.—Taylor in Cal. Farmer, Apr. 20, 1860.

**Ekilik.** A Togiagamiut village on Togiak r., near its mouth, in Alaska. Pop. 192 in 1880; 60 in 1890.
Ekilígamut.—Spurr and Post quoted by Baker, Geog. Dict. Alaska, 1901. **Ikalinkamiut.**—11th Census, Alaska, 5, 1893. **Ikaliukha.**—Petroff, 10th Census, Alaska, 17, 1884.

**Ekiondatsaan.** A Huron village in Ontario about 1640.
Ekhiondaltsaan.—Jes. Rel. 1637, 162, 1858. **Ekiondatsaan.**—Jes. Rel., III, index, 1858. **Khiondaësahan.**—Jes. Rel. 1637, 70, 1858.

**Ekoolthaht** ('bushes-on-hill people'). A Nootka tribe formerly inhabiting the shores of Barclay sd., w. coast of Vancouver id.; pop. 48 in 1879. They have now joined the Seshart.
E-koolth-aht.—Can. Ind. Aff., 308, 1879. **Ekū'-lath.**—Boas, 6th Rep. N. W. Tribes Can., 31, 1890. **Equalett.**—Kelley, Oregon, 68, 1830.

**Ekquall.** A former rancheria, possibly of the Diegueño, under San Miguel de la Frontera mission, in the mountains of w. Lower California, about 30 m. s. of San Diego, Cal.—Taylor in Cal. Farmer, May 18, 1860.

**Ekuhkahshatin.** A Shuswap village on a small branch of Deadman cr., a N. affluent of Thompson r., Brit. Col. Pop., with Skichistan (q. v.), 118 in 1904.
E-kuh-kah'-sha-tin.—Dawson in Trans. Roy. Soc. Can. for 1891, sec. II, 44.

**Ekuk.** A Nushagagmiut village near the mouth of Nushagak r., Alaska. Pop. 112 in 1880; 65 in 1890.
Ekouk.—Lutke (1828) quoted by Baker, Geog. Dict. Alaska, 1901. **Ekuk.**—Petroff, Rep. on Alaska, 17, 1884. **Yekuk.**—11th Census, Alaska, 164, 1893.

**Ekuks.** A Squawmish village community on the right bank of Squawmisht r., w. Brit. Col.
E'kuiks.—Boas, MS., B. A. E., 1887. **Ēk·ūks.**—Hill-Tout in Rep. Brit. A. A. S., 474, 1900.

**Ekupabeka.** A Hidatsa band.

**Bonnet.**—Morgan, Anc. Soc., 159, 1877. **E-ku'-pä-be-ka.**—Ibid.

**Elahsa** ('village of the great willows'). A former Hidatsa village on the N. bank of Knife r., N. Dak., about 3 m. from Missouri r.
Biddahatsi-Awatiss.—Maximilian, Voy. dans l'int. de l'Am., III, 3, 1843. **Eláh-Sá.**—Maximilian, Trav., 178, 1843. **Hidatsa.**—Matthews, Ethnog. Hidatsa, 38, 1877 (see Hidatsati).

**Elakulsi** (E'lăkŭl'sĭ, referring to ela, 'earth'; or Alagulsa). A Cherokee settlement in N. Georgia about 1800–35. (J. M.)
Ailigulsha.—Doc. of 1799 quoted by Royce in 5th Rep. B. A. E., 144, 1887.

**Elarroyde.** A former village, presumably Costanoan, connected with Dolores mission, San Francisco, Cal.—Taylor in Cal. Farmer, Oct. 18, 1861.

**Eleidlinottine** ('people of the fork'). An Etchareottine tribe at the confluence of Liard and Mackenzie rs., whose territory extends to La Martre, Grandin, and Taché Lakes.
Él'é-idlin-Gottine.—Petitot, Autour du lac des Esclaves, 363, 1891. **Élè-idlin-ottinè.**—Petitot in Bull. Soc. de Geog. Paris, chart, 1875. **Gens de la fourche du Mackenzie.**—Petitot. Dict. Dènè Dindjié, xx, 1876.

**Elephant Mound.** A noted effigy mound, 4 m. s. of Wyalusing, Grant co., Wis., first brought to public notice in 1872 through a pencil sketch and brief description by Jared Warner (Smithson. Rep. 1872, 1873). From its massive form and an apparent prolongation of the nose, supposed to be a part of the original mound, giving the tumulus a slight resemblance to an elephant, the name Elephant Mound was applied to it. Although frequently mentioned and illustrated, the figures are copies of Warner's sketch, no reexamination having been made until Nov., 1884, when the Bureau of American Ethnology surveyed and platted the mound; the result of this work appears in its Twelfth Report (91–93, fig. 44, 1894). The immediate situation is a long rectangular depression forming a *cul de sac*, the level of which is only a few feet above the Mississippi at high water. Although the tract had been cultivated for many years, the mound at the time of the survey distinctly showed the rounded surface, the highest point being at the hip of the effigy, where the height was 4 ft. The measurements were: length, 140 ft; width across the body and to the lower end of the hind leg, 72 ft. At the time of the survey no indication of an elephant-like proboscis was found. After an examination of similar effigies it was determined that this mound was designed to represent a bear, and that the supposed nasal prolongation seen by Warner was accidental, due probably to washed or drifted earth. In addition to the references cited, see Am. Antiq., VI, 178, 1884; Strong (1) in Rep. Wis. Geol. Surv. for

1873–4, (2) in Smithson. Rep. 1876, 431, 1877; Thomas, Catalogue Prehist. Works, Bull. B. A. E., 232, 1891.　　(c. t.)

**Eleunaxciay.** A Chumashan village formerly near Santa Barbara, Cal.—Bancroft, Nat. Races, I, 459, 1874.

**Elhlateese.** The principal village of the Uchucklesit (q. v.) at the head of Uchucklesit harbor, Alberni canal, Vancouver id.; pop. 45 in 1902.—Can. Ind. Aff., 263, 1902.

**Eliot Bible.** The translation of the Scriptures into the Algonquian language of the Massachuset, made by John Eliot (1604–90), the Apostle to the Indians, was the first Bible printed in America by English-speaking people. The first edition of the whole Bible was published at Cambridge, Mass., in 1663, the New Testament having appeared two years before. The books of Genesis and Matthew seem to have been printed in 1655 and a portion of the Psalms in 1658, by which time the translation of the whole Bible was completed. Eliot was the author of other works in the language of the Massachuset, and of books about the language and the natives (Pilling, Bibliog. Algonq. Lang., Bull. B. A. E., 1891). Trumbull's Dictionary of the Eliot Bible, which is not exhaustive, has been published as the Natick Dictionary (Bull. 25, B. A. E., 1903). The Eliot Bible is one of the monuments of missionary endeavor and prescientific study of the Indian tongues. In his linguistic labors Eliot was assisted by his two sons and by several Indians. See *Bible translations, Cockenoe.*　　(a. f. c.)

**Eljman.** A former Chumashan village described as situated near the windmill of La Patera, near Santa Barbara, Cal.
Aljiman.—Bancroft, Nat. Races, I, 459, 1874. Eljiman.—Taylor in Cal. Farmer, Apr. 24, 1863. Eljman.—Ibid. Elmian.—Bancroft, op. cit. San Marcos.—Taylor, op. cit.

**Elks.** A mythical people, said by Pidgeon (Traditions of De-coo-dah, 162, 1858), on information said to have been obtained from the Dakota, "to have come from the N., and once held dominion over all this country, from the Mississippi r., E. and N., to the great waters."

**Ellijay** (from *Elătsé*, abbr. of *Elătséyĭ*, possibly 'green [verdant] earth'). The name of several former Cherokee settlements. One was on the headwaters of Keowee r., S. C.; another was on Ellijay cr. of Little Tennessee r., near the present Franklin, Macon co., N. C.; another about the present Ellijay in Gilmer co., Ga., and a fourth on Ellejoy cr. of Little r., near the present Maryville, in Blount co., Tenn.—Mooney in 19th Rep. B. A. E., 517, 1900.
Allagae.—Bartram, Travels, 372, 1792. Elijoy.—Doc. of 1775 quoted by Royce in 5th Report B. A. E., 143, 1887. Ellijay.—Doc of 1799, ibid.

**El Morro** (Span.: 'the castle'). A prehistoric ruined pueblo, consisting of the remains of two blocks of dwellings, situated on the summit of a rock mesa called El Morro, or Inscription Rock, about 35 m. E. of Zuñi, Valencia co., N. Mex. The pueblo is reputed to be of Zuñi origin, but there is only legendary testimony of this. The peñol is called El Morro on account of its fancied resemblance to a castle from a distance, and Inscription Rock from the occurrence thereon of numerous inscriptions carved by early Spanish explorers. The earliest in date is that of Juan de Oñate in 1605. For description see Bandelier in Arch. Inst. Papers, IV, 328, 1892; Coues, Garcés Diary (1775–76), 1900; Fewkes in Jour. Am. Ethnol. and Archæol., I, 1890; Hoopes and Broomall in Proc. Del. Co. (Pa.) Inst. of Sci., I, pt. 1, 1905; Lummis, Strange Corners, 164–182, 1892; Simpson, Jour., 121, 1850.　　(f. w. h.)
El Morro.—Vargas (1692) quoted by Bancroft, Ariz. and N. Mex., 200, 1889 (applied to the peñol). Héshotayá'hlto.—Hodge, inf'n, 1895 ('ruins on top or above': Zuñi name). Hesho-ta Yashtok.—Bandelier in Arch. Inst. Papers, IV, 328, 1892 (given as Zuñi name).

**Elochuteka.** A former village, probably Seminole, between Hillsboro and Big Withlacoochee rs., Fla.—H. R. Doc. 78, 25th Cong., 2d sess., map, 768–769, 1838.

**Elogio.** A Papago settlement, probably in Pima co., s. Ariz., with 66 inhabitants in 1858.—Bailey in Ind. Aff. Rep., 208, 1858.

**Eloquale.** An unidentified village in N. Florida in 1564.—De Bry, Brev. Nar., II, map, 1591.

**Eloquence.** See *Oratory.*

**Elothet.** Given by Kelley (Oregon, 68, 1830) as a Nootka town on Vancouver id. under chief Wickaninish; possibly intended for Ucluelet.

**El Paso.** A mission established among the Mansos at the present Juarez, Chihuahua, opposite El Paso, Tex., by Fray Garcia de Zuñiga (or de San Francisco) in 1659. The settlement contained also some Piros from Tabira in 1684, and it became prominent as the seat of the New Mexican government during the Pueblo rebellion of 1680–92.　　(f. w. h.)
Guadalupe del Paso.—Bancroft, Ariz. and N. Mex., 168, 1889. Nuestra Señora de Guadalupe de los Mansos del Paso del Norte.—Garcia (1659) quoted by Bandelier in Arch. Inst. Papers, III, 86, 1890. Nuestra Señora de Guadalupe del Paso del Rio del Norte.—MS. of 17th century quoted by Bandelier, ibid., IV, 248, 1892. Nuestra Señora de Guadalupe del Passo.—Villa-Señor, Theatro Am., pt. 2, 422, 1748. Paso.—Shea, Cath. Miss., 83, 1855. Paso del Rio del Norte.—Arch. Santa Fé, MS. quoted by Bancroft, op. cit. Passo del Norte.—Villa-Señor, op. cit., 424.

**El Peñon** (Span.: 'the large rocky hill or height'). A former small settlement, probably Seminole, on an island 13 leagues N. of Mosquito r., at the entrance of Matanzas r., Fla.
El Penon.—Smyth, Tour in U. S., II, 21, 1784.

**Elquis.** A Chumashan village w. of Pueblo de las Canoas (San Buenaventura), Ventura co., Cal., in 1542.—Cabrillo, Nar. (1542) in Smith, Colec. Doc. Fla., 181, 1857.

**Elskwatawa.** See *Tenskwatawa*.

**El Turco.** See *Turk*.

**Eluaxcu.** A former Chumashan village near Santa Barbara, Cal.—Bancroft, Nat. Races, I, 459, 1874.

**Elwha.** A Clallam village at the mouth of the river of the same name in Washington.

Él'-hwa.—Eells, letter, B. A. E., Feb., 1886 (own name). **Elkwah.**—Gibbs in Pac. R. R. Rep., I, 429, 1855. **Elwahs.**—Colyer in Ind. Aff. Rep., 191, 1871. **Elwha.**—Swan in Smithson. Cont., XVI, 50, 1869. **Iraqua Indians.**—Lee and Frost, Oregon, 274, 1844.

**Emamoueta.** An unidentified tribe placed by Marquette on his map of 1673 w. of the Mississippi, apparently on the lower Arkansas.

Emam8eta.—Marquette, map (1673) in Shea, Discov. Miss. Val., 268, 1852.

**Emanuelito.** See *Manuelito*.

**Ematlochee** (*imatla*, 'leader'). A former Creek town on Apalachicola r.; exact location unknown.

Emarhe.—Ex. Doc. 425, 24th Cong., 1st sess., 299, 1836. **Ematlochees town.**—U. S. Ind. Treat. (1833), 578, 1837.

**Emet.** A small tribe met by De León and Manzanet near lower Guadalupe r., Texas, in 1689. They occupied a village with the Cava Indians near the crossing place, apparently about 15 leagues from the French Fort St Louis on Matagorda bay. To the northward they encountered several other Emet "ranchitos." Within a year these Indians appear to have moved farther E., for in 1690 De León encountered them on that side of the Rio Colorado, living with the Cava, Too, and Toaa Indians, their former neighbors. They were perhaps related to the Karankawa. Possibly the Meghty of Joutel are identical.            (H. E. B.)

Emat.—De León MS. (1690) in Texas Archives. **Emet.**—Manzanet (1689) quoted in Tex. Hist. Quar., VIII, 214, 1905.

**Emistesigo.** Known also as Guristersigo. An Upper Creek chief and noted warrior who came prominently into notice in the latter part of the 18th century. The British being in possession of Savannah, Ga., in June, 1782, Gen. Wayne was dispatched to watch their movements. On May 21, Col. Brown, of the British force, marched out of Savannah to meet, according to appointment, a band of Indians under Emistesigo, but was intercepted and cut to pieces by Wayne. Meanwhile Emistesigo succeeded in traversing the entire state of Georgia without discovery, except by two boys, who were captured and killed. Wayne, who was not anticipating an attack, was completely surprised by the Indians, who captured 2 of his cannon, but succeeded in extricating his troops from their danger, and, after severe fighting, in putting the Creeks to flight. Emistesigo was pierced by bayonets, and 17 of his warriors fell by his side. He was at this time only 30 years of age, and is described as being 6 ft 3 in. in height and weighing 220 pounds.

(C. T.)

**Emitahpahksaiyiks** ('dogs naked'). A division of the Siksika.

Dogs Naked.—Grinnell, Blackfoot Lodge Tales, 208, 1892. **E'-mi-tah-pahk-sai-yiks.**—Ibid.

**Emitaks** (*E'-mi-taks*, 'dogs'). A society of the Ikunuhkahtsi, or All Comrades, in the Piegan tribe; it is composed of old men who dress like, and dance with and like, the Issui, though forming a different society.—Grinnell, Blackfoot Lodge Tales, 221, 1892.

**Empress of the Creek Nation.** See *Bosomworth, Mary*.

**Emussa** (*imúsa*, 'affluent,' 'tributary'). Mentioned as a Lower Creek town formerly on lower Chattahooche r., Henry co., Ala., 2 m. above Wikaiva, near the junction of Omussee cr., with 20 inhabitants in 1820. It seems to be equally probable that the settlement, which is not mentioned by early writers, was composed of Yamasi, from whom it derived its name.

Emusas.—Drake, Bk. Inds., vii, 1848. **Emussas.**—Morse, Rep. to Sec. War, 364, 1822.

**Encaquiagualcaca.** Mentioned by Oñate (Doc. Inéd., XVI, 115, 1871) as a pueblo of the province of Atripuy, in the region of the lower Rio Grande, N. Mex., in 1598.

**Encinal** (Span.: 'oak grove'). Formerly a summer village of the Lagunas, now a permanently occupied pueblo, situated 6 m. N. W. of Laguna, N. Mex. In 1749 an attempt was made by Father Menchero to establish a mission there for the Navaho, but it was abandoned in the following year.            (F. W. H.)

Hapuntíka.—Hodge, field notes, B. A. E., 1895 (Laguna name: 'place of the oaks'). **Lespaía.**—Ibid. (Acoma name). **Pun-ye-kia.**—Pradt quoted by Hodge in Am. Anthrop., IV, 346, 1891 (another Laguna name: 'house to the west').

**Enecappe.** A village on middle St Johns r., Fla., belonging to the Utina (Timucua) confederacy in the 16th century.

Enacapen.—Barcia, Ensayo, 48, 1723 (cacique's name). **Enecappe.**—Laudonnière (1567) in French, Hist. Coll. La., n. s., 243, 1869. **Enecaq.**—De Bry, Brev. Nar., II, map, 1591. **Enecaque.**—Laudonnière, op. cit., 305. **Eneguape.**—Laudonnière, op. cit., 287. **Enequaque.**—Barcia, op. cit., 72. **Helmacape.**—Laudonnière, op. cit., 349.

**Eneeshur.** Shahaptian bands, aggregating 1,200 population in 41 mat lodges, found by Lewis and Clark in 1805 on both sides of Columbia r. near the mouth of the Deschutes, in Washington. The term probably refers more specifically to the Tapanash.            (L. F.)

Eioestures.—Robertson in H. R. Ex. Doc. 76, 30th Cong., 1st sess., 9, 1848. **Eivesteurs.**—Robertson, Oregon, 129, 1846. **E-ne-churs.**—Clark (1806) in Orig. Jour. Lewis and Clark, III, 342, 1905. **E-neesher.**—Lewis and Clark, Exped., II, map, 1814.

**Enesher.**—Lewis (1806) in Orig. Jour. Lewis and Clark, III, 164 1905. **E-nee-shur.**—Clark (1805), ibid., 164. **E-neé-Shur.**—Ibid., 183. **E-ne-show.**—Gibbs in Pac. R. R. Rep., I, 417, 1855. **E-ne-shur.**—Lewis and Clark, op. cit., I, map. **Eneshure.**—Ibid., II, 472. **Enesteurs.**—Wilkes, Hist. Oregon, 44. 1845.

**Enekelkawa.** A former Luiseño village near the site of San Luis Rey mission, s. Cal.—Taylor in Cal. Farmer, May 11, 1860.

**Enempa.** A Calusa village on the s. w. coast of Florida, about 1570.—Fontaneda Memoir (*ca.* 1575), Smith trans., 19, 1854.

**Enfrenado** (Span.: 'bridled'). An Indian village about 40 leagues from C. Santa Helena, in s. South Carolina, visited by Juan Pardo in 1565.—Vandera (1567) in Smith, Colec. Doc. Fla., I, 16, 1857.

**English influence.** The first English visitors to the coast of Virginia-Carolina were well received by the Indians, whom the early chroniclers, as Hariot, for example, describe as peaceful and amiable people. So, too, were in the beginning the natives of the New England coast, but in 1605 Capt. Weymouth forcibly carried off five Indians, and he soon had many imitators. The good character ascribed by Pastor Cushman in 1620 to the Indians of Plymouth colony was forgotten when theological zeal saw in the aborigines of the New World "the accursed seed of Canaan," which it was the duty of good Christians to exterminate (see *Lost Ten Tribes*). When the political ambitions of the English colonists were aroused conflicts with the Indians soon occurred, and the former came to regard the latter as the natural enemies of the whites in the onward march of civilization. Unlike the French, they paid little attention to the pride of the Indians, despising the heathen ways and institutions more and more as their power grew and their land hunger increased. With a few noble exceptions, like Roger Williams and John Eliot, the clergy of the English colonies were not nearly so sympathetic toward the natives as were the French missionaries in Acadia and New France. Scotchmen, however, in the S., in the W., in the old provinces of Canada, and in the territories handed over to the Hudson's Bay Company have played a conspicuous part as associates and leaders of the Indians. Even men like Canonicus were always suspicious of their English friends, and never really opened their hearts to them. The introduction of rum and brandy among the Indians worked infinite damage. Some of the New England tribes, such as the Pequot, for example, foreseeing perhaps the result of their advent, were inimical to the English from the first, and the extermination of these Indians ensued when the whites were strong enough to accomplish it. It appears, however, that the English colonists paid for most of the land that they took from the Indians (Thomas in 18th Rep. B. A. E., 549, 1899). English influence on tribal government and land tenure was perceptible as early as 1641. The success of deliberately planned educational institutions for the benefit of the Indian during the early periods of American history does not seem to have been proportionate to the hopes and ideals of their founders. Harvard, Dartmouth, and the College of William and Mary all began, in whole or in part, as colleges for Indian youth, but their graduates of aboriginal blood have been few indeed, while they are now all high-class institutions for white men (see *Education*). The royal charter of Dartmouth College (1769) specifically states that it is to be "for the education and instruction of youths of the Indian tribes in this land," and "for civilizing and Christianizing the children of pagans." That of Harvard looked to "the education of the English and Indian youth in knowledge and godliness." Harvard had during the colonial period one Indian graduate, Caleb Cheeshateaumuck, of whom hardly more than his name is known (see James, English Institutions and the American Indian, 1894). The aim of the English has ever been to transform the aborigines and lift them at once to their own plane. When commissioners visited the Cherokee they induced these to elect an "emperor," with whom treaties could be made. The Friends, from the time of William Penn (1682) down to the present (see Mooney in 17th Rep. B. A. E., 193, 1898), seem to have furnished many individuals capable, like the Baptist Roger Williams (1636), of exercising great personal influence over the Indians. The Quakers still continue their work, e. g., among the eastern Cherokee (Mooney in 19th Rep. B. A. E., 176, 1900) and the Tlingit of Alaska. The New England Company established for the propagation of the gospel in America (1649), whose operations were transferred to Canada in 1822, carries on at the present time work on the Brantford Iroquois reserve and in other parts of Ontario, at Kuper id., Brit. Col., and elsewhere. Its Mohawk institute, near Brantford, has had a powerful influence among the Iroquois of Ontario. The pagan members of these Indians have recently been investigated by Boyle (Jour. Anthrop. Inst. G. B., n. s., III, 263–273, 1900), who tells us that "all for which Iroquois paganism is indebted to European culture" is the possession of some ideas about God or the Great Spirit and "a few suggestions respecting conduct, based on the Christian code of morals." The constant mingling of the young men with their white neighbors and the going of the young women out to service are nevertheless weakening more and more the old ideas which are doomed "to disappear as a system long before the people die out." That they have survived so long is remarkable.

English influence made itself felt in colonial days in the introduction of improved weapons, tools, etc., which facilitated hunting and fishing and made possible the manufacture with less labor and in greater abundance of ornaments, trinkets, and other articles of trade. The supplying of the Indians with domestic animals also took place at an early period. Spinning wheels and looms were introduced among the Cherokee shortly before the Revolution, and in 1801 the agent reported that at the Cherokee agency the wheel, the loom, and the plow were in pretty general use. The intermarriage of Englishmen and Indians has been greater all over the country than is commonly believed, and importance must consequently be attached to the effects of such intermingling in modifying Indian customs and institutions. Clothing and certain ornaments, and, after these, English beds and other furniture were adopted by many Indians in colonial days, as is now being done by the tribes of the N. Pacific coast.

English influence on the languages of some of the aborigines has been considerable. The word *Kinjames*, 'King James,' in use among the Canadian Abnaki, testifies to the power of English ideas in the 17th century. The vocabularies of the eastern Algonquian tribes who have come in contact with the English contain other loan-words. Rand's English-Micmac Dictionary (1888) contains, among others, the following: *Jak-ass; cheesawa,* 'cheese'; *koppee,* 'coffee'; *mulugech,* 'milk'; *gubulnol,* 'governor.' Brinton and Anthony's Lenape-English Dictionary (1889), representing the language of about 1825, has *amel,* 'hammer'; *apel,* 'apple'; *mbil,* 'beer'; *mellik,* 'milk'; *skulin,* 'to keep school,' which may be partly from English and partly from German. A Shawnee vocabulary of 1819 has for 'sugar' *melassa,* which seems to be English 'molasses'; and a Micmac vocabulary of 1800 has *blaakeet,* 'blanket.' The English 'cheese' has passed into the Nipissing dialect of Algonquian as *tchis.* The Chinook jargon (q. v.) contained 41 words of English origin in 1804, and 57 in 1863, while in 1894, out of 1,082 words (the total number is 1,402) whose origin is known, Eells cites 570 as English. Of recent years "many words of Indian origin have been dropped, English words having taken their places." In colonial days English doubtless had some influence on the grammatical form and sentence-construction of Indian languages,

and this influence still continues: the recent studies by Prince and Speck of the Pequot-Mohegan (Am. Anthrop., n. s., VI, 18–45, 469–476, 1904) contain evidence of this. English influence has made itself felt also in the languages of the N. W. Hill-Tout (Rep. Ethnol. Surv. Can., 18, 1902) observes, concerning certain Salishan tribes, that "the spread and use of English among the Indians is very seriously affecting the purity of the native speech." Even the Athapascan Nahane of N. British Columbia have, according to Morice (Trans. Canad. Inst., 529, 1903), added a few English words to their vocabulary. See also Friederici, Indianer und Anglo-Amerikaner, 1900; MacMahon, The Anglo-Saxon and the North American Indian, 1876; Manypenny, Our Indian Wards, 1880. (A. F. C.)

**Englishman.** See *Sagaunash.*

**Engraved tablets.** See *Notched plates.*

**Engraving.** Although extensively employed in pictographic work and in decoration, the engraver's art did not rise to a high degree of artistic excellence among the tribes N. of Mexico. As no definite line can be drawn between the lower forms of relief sculpture and engraving, all ordinary petroglyphs may be classed as engravings, since the work is executed in shallow lines upon smooth rock surfaces (see *Pictography*). Point work is common on wood, bone, horn, shell, bark, metal, clay, and other surfaces. Each material has its own particular technique, and the designs run the entire gamut of style from graphic to purely conventional representations, and the full range of significance from purely symbolic through esthetic to simply trivial motives.

Perhaps the most artistic and technically perfect examples of engraving are those of the N. W. coast tribes of the present day, executed on slate utensils and on ornaments of metal (Niblack), yet the graphic

ANIMAL FIGURES ENGRAVED ON SILVER BRACELETS; HAIDA

productions of the Eskimo on ivory, bone, and antler have sometimes a considerable degree of merit (Boas, Hoffman, Murdoch, Nelson, Turner). With both of these peoples the processes employed and the style of representation have probably undergone much change in recent times through contact with white people. The steel point is superior to the point of stone, and this alone would have a marked effect on the execution. The picture writings on bark of many of the northern tribes, executed with bone or other hard points, are good examples of the native engraver's art, although these are not designed either for simply pictorial or for decorative effect. The ancient mound builders were clever engravers, the technical excellence of their work being well illustrated by examples from the mounds and dwelling sites of Ross co., Ohio (Putnam and Willoughby), and by others from the Turner mounds in Hamilton co., Ohio. Shell also was a favorite material for the graver's point, as is illustrated by numerous ornaments recovered from mounds in the middle Mississippi valley.

ENGRAVINGS ON OBJECTS OF IVORY; ESKIMO

In decorating their earthenware the native tribes often used the stylus with excellent effect. The yielding clay afforded a tempting surface, and in some cases considerable skill was shown, especially by the ancient potters of the lower Gulf states, who executed elaborate scroll designs with great precision (Moore, Holmes). The point was used for incising, trailing, and indenting, and among ancient Pueblo potters was sometimes used upon dark-painted surfaces to develop delicate figures in the light color of the underlying paste. Examples of engraving are given by Boas in 6th Rep. B. A. E., 1888; Fewkes in 17th Rep. B. A. E., 1898; Hoffman in Nat. Mus. Rep. 1895, 1897; Holmes (1) in 2d Rep. B. A. E., 1883, (2) in 20th Rep. B. A. E., 1903; Hough in Nat. Mus. Rep., 1901; Moore, various memoirs in Jour. Acad. Nat. Sci. Phila., x–xii, 1894–1903; Murdoch in 9th Rep. B. A. E., 1892; Nelson in 18th Rep. B. A. E., 1899; Niblack in Rep. Nat. Mus. 1888, 1890; Putnam and Willoughby in Proc. A. A. A. S., xliv, 1896; Turner in 11th Rep. B. A. E., 1894. See *Art, Ornament*. (w. h. h.)

ENGRAVING ON A SHELL GORGET FROM A MISSOURI MOUND. (1-4)

**Enias.** A local name for a body of Upper Lillooet on Seton lake, in 1902 reduced to a single individual.—Can. Ind. Aff., pt. ii, 72, 1902.

**Enipeu.** A Yurok village on Klamath r., Cal., 15 m. above the mouth.

**Enitunne** ('people at the base of a plateau'). A village of the Tututni near the mouth of a southern affluent of Rogue r., Oreg.
Ĕni′ tûnnĕ′.—Dorsey in Jour. Am. Folk-lore, iii, 236, 1890.

**Enitunne.** A part of the Mishikwut-metunne in a village on upper Coquille r., Oreg.
Ĕ-ni′ tûnnĕ′.—Dorsey in Jour. Am. Folk-lore, iii, 232, 1890.

**Enmegahbowh** ('The one who stands before his people'). An Indian preacher. He was an Ottawa by birth, but was adopted while young by the Chippewa and was converted to the Methodist faith in Canada, educated at the Methodist mission school at Jacksonville, Ill., and ordained as a preacher with the name of the Rev. John Johnson. In 1839 he accompanied Elder T. B. Kavanaugh to the upper Mississippi, where he was a missionary among the Chippewa for 5 years, when the Methodist church withdrew from that field. In 1852, at Johnson's solicitation, the Episcopal church sent a minister into this section, and a mission and school were established at Gull lake, Minn., in which he served as assistant and interpreter. In 1858 Johnson was admitted by Bishop Kemper to the first order of the Episcopal ministry at Faribault, and in 1859 was left in charge of the mission at Gull lake, where he continued until the Sioux outbreak of 1862, when he alone of the Episcopal missionaries remained in the field. In 1869 the Gull lake mission was removed to the reservation at White Earth, whither Johnson followed and was given charge, bringing into the church a number of his tribesmen and erecting a chapel and parsonage. Here the Rev. Joseph A. Gilfillan, who was assigned to White Earth as an Episcopal missionary in 1873, with Johnson's aid established a school for the training of Indian clergy, and in a few years 9 Chippewa were ordained to the ministry. Johnson was living in 1898, at which time he was spoken of as the "aged Indian pastor and co-worker of Bishop Whipple."

**Enmitahin** ('cliff's end'). A Yuit Eskimo village of the Nabukak or Nookalit division, n. of East cape, n. e. Siberia; pop. 42 in 8 houses about 1895.
Enmita′hin.—Bogoras, Chukchee, 30, 1904 (Chukchi name).

**Eno.** A tribe associated with the Adshusheer and Shakori in North Carolina in the 17th century. Mooney thinks it doubtful that the Eno and the Shakori were of Siouan stock, as they seem to have differed in physique and habits from their neighbors, although their alliances were all with Siouan tribes. Little is known of them, as they disappeared from history as tribal bodies about 1720, having been incorporated with the Catawba on the s. or with the Saponi and their confederates on the N., although they still retained their distinct dialect in 1743. The Eno and Shakori are first mentioned by Yardley in 1654, to whom a Tuscarora described, among other tribes of the interior, living next to the Shakori, "a great nation" called Haynoke, by whom the northern advance of the Spaniards was valiantly resisted (Hawks, N. C., II, 19, 1858). The next mention of these two tribes is by Lederer, who heard of them in 1672 as living s. of the Occaneechi about the headwaters of Tar and Neuse rs. The general locality is still indicated in the names of Eno r. and Shocco cr., upper branches of these streams. In 1701 Lawson found the Eno and Shakori confederated and the Adshusheer united with them in the same locality. Their village, which he calls Adshusheer, was on Eno r., about 14 m. E. of the Occaneechi village, which was near the site of the present Hillsboro. This would place the former not far N. E. of Durham, N. C. Eno Will, a Shakori by birth, was at that time, according to Lawson, chief of the three combined tribes, and at this period the Shakori seem to have been the principal tribe. They had some trade with the Tuscarora. Later, about 1714, with the Tutelo, Saponi, Occaneechi, and Keyauwee, together numbering only about 750 souls, they moved toward the settlements. Lawson includes Eno in his list of Tuscarora villages at that date, and as the Eno lived on the Neuse adjoining the Tuscarora, it was natural that they were sometimes classed with them. In 1716 Gov. Spotswood, of Virginia, proposed to settle the Eno, Sara, and Keyauwee at Eno town, on "the very frontiers" of North Carolina; but the project was defeated by North Carolina on the ground that all three tribes were then at war with South Carolina. From the records it can not be determined clearly whether this was the Eno town of Lawson or a more recent village nearer the Albemarle settlements. Owing to the objection made to their settlement in the N., the Eno moved southward into South Carolina. They probably assisted the other tribes of that region in the Yamasi war of 1715. At least a few of the mixed tribe found their way into Virginia with the Saponi, as Byrd speaks of an old Indian, called Shacco Will, living near Nottoway r. in 1733, who offered to guide him to a mine on Eno r. near the old country of the Tuscarora. The name of Shockoe cr., at Richmond, Va., may possibly have been derived from that of

the Shakori tribe, while the name of Enoree r. in South Carolina may have a connection with that of the Eno tribe.

Lederer speaks of the Eno village as surrounded by large cultivated fields and as built around a central plaza where the men played a game described as "slinging of stones," in which "they exercise with so much labor and violence and in so great numbers that I have seen the ground wet with the sweat that dropped from their bodies." This was probably the chunkey game played with round stones among the Creeks. Lederer agrees with Yardley as to the small size of the Eno, but not as to their bravery, though they were evidently industrious. They raised plentiful crops and "out of their granary supplied all the adjacent parts." "The character thus outlined," says Mooney, "accords more with that of the peaceful Pueblos than with that of any of our eastern tribes and goes far to indicate a different origin." It should be remembered, however, that Lederer is not a leading authority, as it is doubtful if he was ever in North Carolina. The houses of the Eno are said to have been different in some respects from those of their neighbors. Instead of building of bark, as did most Virginia and Carolina tribes, they used interwoven branches or canes and plastered them with mud or clay, like the Quapaw Indians of E. Arkansas. The form was usually round. Near every house was a small oven-shaped structure in which they stored corn and nuts. This was similar to the storehouse of the Cherokee and some other southern tribes. Their government was democratic and patriarchal, the decision of the old men being received with unquestioned obedience. See Mooney, Siouan Tribes of the East, Bull. B. A. E., 1896.

Anoeg.—Strachey (1612), Hist. Va., 48, 1849 (probably identical). Eano.—McKenney and Hall, Ind. Tr., III, 81, 1854. Eenó.—Adair (1743), Hist. Am. Inds., 224, 1775. Enoe.—Lawson (1709), N. C., 97, 1860. Haynokes.—Yardley (1654) quoted by Hawks, N. C., II, 19, 1858. Œnock.—Lederer, Discov., 15, 1672. Oenock.—Ibid.

Enoqua. An unidentified village or tribe mentioned to Joutel, in 1687 (Margry, Déc., III, 410, 1878), while he was staying with the Kadohadacho on Red r. of Louisiana, by the chief of that tribe, as one of his allies.

Enpishemo (from apishĭmun.—W. J.). According to Bartlett (Dict. Americanisms, 201, 1877), "a word used w. at the Rocky mts. to denote the housings of a saddle, the blanket beneath it, etc." Another form seems to be 'apishamore'. In the Medicine Lodge treaty made with the Comanche, Kiowa, and others in 1867, Fish-e-more appears as the name of one of the signers. (A. F. C.)

Ensenore. A chief of Wingandacoa (Secotan), N. C., previous to 1585, noted as the earliest chief of the E. coast between Hudson r. and St Helena sd. of whom there is any notice. He was the father of Wingina and Granganameo (q. v.), and a firm friend of the English colony on Roanoke id. in 1585–86. While he lived he restrained Wingina from wreaking vengence on Lane's company for killing some of the natives. His death occurred in 1585 or 1586. (c. t.)

**Entubur.** A former rancheria, probably of the Papago, visited by Kino and Mange in 1694; situated between Tubutama and Busanic, lat. 31°, N. w. Sonora, Mexico.— Mange (*ca.* 1701) quoted by Bancroft, No. Mex. States, I, 258, 1884.

**Environment.** The natural phenomena that surrounded the aborigines of North America, stimulating and conditioning their life and activities, contrasted greatly with those of the European-Asiatic continent. The differences in the two environments do not lie alone in physical geography and in plant and animal life, but are largely meteorologic, the sun operating on air, land, and water, producing variations in temperature and water supply, and as a result entirely new vegetal and animal forms. The planets and stars also affected cultural development, since lore and mythology were based on them. Within the American continent N. of Mexico there were ethnic environments which set bounds for the tribes and modified their industrial, esthetic, social, intellectual, and religious lives. Omitting the Eskimo, practically all the peoples dwelt in the temperate zone. Few impassable barriers separated the culture areas, as in Asia. In some respects, indeed, the entire region formed one environment, having easy communications N. and s. and few barriers E. and w. The climate zones which Merriam has worked out for the U. S. Department of Agriculture in regard to their animal and vegetal life correspond in a measure with the areas of linguistic families as delimited on Powell's map (see *Linguistic families*). The environmental factors that determine cultural development of various kinds and degrees are (1) physical geography; (2) climate, to which primitive peoples are especially amenable; (3) predominant plants, animals, and minerals that supply the materials of drink, food, medicines, clothing, ornaments, houses, fuel, furniture and utensils, and the objects of hunting, war, the industrial arts, and activities connected with travel, transportation, and commerce. Twelve ethnic environments may be distinguished. There are cosmopolitan characters common to several, but in each area there is an ensemble of qualities that impressed themselves on their inhabitants and differentiated them.

(1) *Arctic.*—The characteristics of this environment are an intensely cold climate; about six months day and six months night; predominance of ice and snow; immense archipelagos, and no accessible elevations; good stone for lamps and tools; driftwood, but no timber and little fruit; polar bear, blue fox, aquatic mammals in profusion, migratory birds, and fish, supplying food, clothing, fire, light, and other wants in the exacting climate.

(2) *Yukon-Mackenzie.*—This is Merriam's transcontinental coniferous belt, separated from the arctic environment by the timber line, but draining into arctic seas. It has poor material resources, and barren grounds here and there. Its saving riches are an abundance of birch, yielding bark utensils, canoes, binding materials, and houses, and of spruce, furnishing textile roots and other necessaries; caribou, muskox, bear, red fox, wolf, white rabbit, and other fur-bearing mammals, and porcupines, migrating birds, and fish. Snow necessitates snowshoes of fine mesh, and immense inland waters make portages easy for bark canoes. Into this area came the Athapascan tribes who developed through its resources their special culture.

(3) *St Lawrence and Lake region.*—This is a transition belt having no distinct lines of separation from the areas on the N. and s. It occupies the entire drainage of the great lakes and includes Manitoba, E. Canada, and N. New England. It was the home of the Iroquois, Abnaki, Chippewa, and their nearest kindred. The climate is boreal. There are a vast expanse of lowlands and numerous extensive inland waters. The natural products are abundant—evergreens, birch, sugar maple, elm, berries, and wild rice in the w.; maize, squash, and beans in the s.; moose, deer, bear, beaver, porcupines, land and water birds in immense flocks, whitefish, and, on the seacoast, marine products in greatest variety and abundance. Canoe travel; pottery scarce.

(4) *Atlantic slope.*—This area, occupied principally by tribes allied to the Delawares, but also by detached Iroquoian tribes and perhaps some Siouan and Uchean bands, included the region of the fertile piedmont, poor foothills, rich lowlands, bays and rivers abounding in aquatic life, and vast salt meadows. The low mountains were not ethnic barriers, but the differences in physical conditions on the two sides were marked enough to produce separate cultures. Minerals for tools and weapons were present in great variety, and ochers, clays, and some copper were found. Plant life was varied and abundant. Forests of hard wood, birch, elm, maple,

and evergreens furnished materials for supplying a great diversity of wants. From the soft wood were made dugout canoes. The dense forest growth rendered foot traveling irksome. Nuts, berries, roots, and maize furnished food; flax and tough pliant woods and bark gave textile materials. The life conditions for economic animals were as varied as possible. Beginning with the shallow marshes and numerous salt-water inlets, furnishing clams, oysters, crabs, cod, mackerel, herring, halibut, shad, sturgeon, eels, and terrapin, as shell-heaps attest, it terminated in the trout streams of the mountains. There were birds of the air, like the eagle and wild pigeon, ground birds, like the quail and the turkey, and water birds innumerable. Mammals of the water were the muskrat, otter, and beaver; of the land, moose, elk, deer, bear, rabbit, squirrel, raccoon, opossum, and woodchuck. The wide range of latitude necessitated different dwellings for different climates, as the bark tipi, the mat house, and the arbor house. For clothing, garments of hide, rabbit skin, and feathers were used. Stone was abundant for making tools, for flaking or grinding, but neither materials nor motives for artistic work of a high order were present.

(5) *Gulf coast.*—The Southern states, from Georgia to Texas, were inhabited by Muskhogean tribes and several small linguistic families. The characteristics of this area are a climate ranging from temperate to subtropical, with abundant rain, low mountains, and rich river valleys and littoral with varied and profuse mineral, vegetal, and animal resources. The environment yielded a diet of meat, fish, maize, pulse, melons, and fruits. It was favorable to meager dress and furnished materials and incentives for featherwork and beadwork, stonework, earthwork, and pottery. Traveling on foot and in dugout canoes was easy.

(6) *Mississippi valley.*—This area includes the states of the Middle West beyond the Great Lake divide, extending to the loosely defined boundary of the great plains. Its characteristics in relation to Indian life were varied climate, abundant rainfall, numerous waterways, fertile lands, alternate timber and prairie, and minerals in great variety and abundance, including clay for pottery. The economic plants were soft and hard woods, and plants yielding nuts, berries, fruits, and fiber. The fertile land was favorable to the cultivation of maize and squashes. Animals of the chase were buffalo, deer, small rodents, and wild pigeons and other land birds; but there was a poor fish supply, and the only shellfish were river mussels. This environment developed hunting and agricultural tribes,

chiefly of Algonquian lineage, including sedentary tribes that built remarkable mounds.

(7) *Plains.*—This environment lies between the Rocky mts. and the fertile lands w. of the Mississippi. To the n. it stretches into Athabasca, and it terminates at the s. about the Rio Grande. The tribes were Siouan, Algonquian, Kiowan, Caddoan, and Shoshonean. The Missouri and Arkansas and many tributaries drain the area. The plants were bois d'arc and other hard woods for bows, cedar for lodge poles, willows for beds, the pomme blanche for roots, etc., but there were no fine textile fibers. Dependence on the buffalo and the herbivorous animals associated with it compelled a meat diet, skin clothing and dwellings, a roving life, and industrial arts depending on the flesh, bones, hair, sinew, hide, and horns of those animals. Artistic and symbolic designs were painted on the rawhide, and the myths and tales related largely to the buffalo. Travel was on foot, with or without snowshoes, and transportation was effected by the aid of the dog and travois. The horse afterward wrought profound changes. The social order and habit of semi-nomadic wandering about fixed centers were the direct result of the surroundings and discouraged agriculture or much pottery. No canoes or other craft than the Mandan and Hidatsa skin boats.

(8) *North Pacific coast.*—From Mt St Elias to the Columbia mouth, lying along the archipelago and cut off from the interior by mountains covered with snow, was the area inhabited by the Tlingit, Haida, Tsimshian, Nootka, and coast Salish. It has a moist, temperate climate, a mountainous coast, with extensive island groups and landlocked waters favorable to canoe travel. The shores are bathed by the warm current of the n. Pacific. The days in different seasons vary greatly in length. The material resources are black slate for carving and good stone for pecking, grinding, and sawing; immense forests of cedar, spruce, and other evergreen trees for houses, canoes, totem-posts, and basketry; mountain goat and bighorn, bear, beaver, birds, and sea food in great variety and in quantities inexhaustible by savages. This environment induced a diet of fish, mixed with berries, clothing of bark and hair, large communal dwellings, exquisite twined and checkered basketry to the discouragement of pottery, carving in wood and stone, and unfettered travel in dugout canoes, which provided opportunity for the full development of the dispersive clan system.

(9) *Columbia-Fraser region.*—This includes the adjoining basins of these streams and contiguous patches, inhab-

ited principally by Salishan, Shahaptian, and Chinookan tribes. In the s. is a coast destitute of islands. At the head-waters of its rivers it communicates with the areas lying to the E. across the mountains. Rich lands, a mild climate, good minerals for industries, textile plants, excellent forests, and an abundance of edible roots and fruits, fish, mollusks, and water-fowl ready at hand characterize this environment, with skin and wool for clothing. The manifold resources and varied physical features fostered a great variety of activities.

(10) *Interior basin.*—This is embraced between the Rocky mts. and the Sierras of the United States, terminating in a regular line in the s., and is the home of the great Shoshonean family. It partly coincides with the arid Sonoran area of Merriam, consisting of partial deserts, with rich wooded patches among the mountains. Good stone for various crafts is present. Timber is scarce, but wild seeds are abundant for food, and excellent woods and roots for basketry. Animals available were buffalo, rabbit, deer, antelope, wolf, mountain sheep, and birds, but fish were scarce. The environment made necessary the brush shelter and the cave dwelling. Little pottery was made, but the sinew-backed bow was developed. Traveling was necessarily done on foot, and carrying effected by dogs and women, as there was no transportation by water.

(11) *California-Oregon.*—This includes s. Oregon and the greater part of California—that embraced in the drainage basins of the Sacramento, San Joaquin, and smaller rivers flowing into the Pacific. The temperature is mild, neither cold in winter nor hot in summer, and the year is divided into wet and dry seasons. The Sierras form a mountain boundary, and mountain groups of some height are obstructions within the area, but the Coast range is low and broken and not a barrier. Obsidian, steatite, and other good stones for the arts were plentiful. There was clay, but no pottery. The region was well but not heavily timbered, consisting of open plains, with hillsides and ranges covered more or less with brush and scattered oaks, many species furnishing acorns for food. The open spaces alternating with the wooded lands yielded grasses and medicinal herbs. Other useful plants were the buckeye, manzanita, nut pine, redwood, and tule in the s. for balsas, baskets, matting, and houses, and edible and textile roots were also found. The animals entering into Indian economy were the deer, rabbit, bear, coyote, squirrel, jaguar, condor, salmon, sturgeon, eel, trout, smelt, mussel, clam, haliotis, and other shellfish whose shells furnished media of exchange. This environment

was the Caucasus of North America, where 25 linguistic families were assembled. On Merriam's bio-geographic maps, published by the Department of Agriculture, a great variety of life is shown, due to vertical zones of temperature, only the lower of which were inhabited by Indians. The more elevated of these were just as effectual as boundaries as though they were impassable. Owing to the peculiar nature of materials, the arts of this environment were well defined.

(12) *Pueblo country.* This area includes s. Utah, s. w. Colorado, all of New Mexico and Arizona together with the Mohave desert, and extends southward into Mexico. It embraces the drainage basin of the San Juan in the N., the Rio Grande and the Pecos in the E., and the Colorado in the w. In physiographic character it ranges from semiarid to desert. There are deep canyons, elevated mesas, narrow fertile valleys, broad stretches of plains, and isolated mountain masses. The climate demands little clothing in the lowlands, but on the plateaus the nights are cold and the summer temperature that of Maine. Rain is irregular and periodic, being plentiful for weeks, followed by months of drought; most of the streams are therefore intermittent. Useful minerals are gypsum, obsidian, varieties of quartz, potter's clay, adobe, ochers, lignite, salt, and turquoise. Plant life, except after rains, is comparatively meager, the species giving rise to native industries being chiefly cactus, yucca, cottonwood, greasewood, willow, scrub oak, conifers, and rushes. Maize, beans, and cotton were cultivated from a very early period. Wild animals hunted or trapped were the rabbit, deer, bear, turkey, prairie dog, mountain lion, wild-cat, wood-rat, mountain sheep, coyote, and wolf. Dogs were trained, and burros, sheep, goats, and cattle found a congenial home in this area after their introduction by the Spaniards. Travel was formerly done on foot only, and goods had to be carried chiefly on the heads and backs of men and women, there being few navigable waters. This peculiar environment impelled tribes coming into the region to lead the life of the Pueblo. The outskirts of the region were even less favored with resources, hence the Pueblos were brought into conflict with predatory tribes like the Ute, and later the Navaho, the Apache, and the Comanche, who robbed them and constantly threatened to consume what they raised. These conflicts developed the cliff-dwelling as means of protection. Southwest of the region proper are Piman and Yuman tribes and the Mission Indians, dwelling in oases of the desert that extends into Mexico. Here grow mesquite, ironwood, agave,

palo verde, cacti in the greatest variety, and, along the water courses, cottonwood and rushes. The people live a life partly sedentary, housed in shelters of brush and grass. The effects of this environment, where the finding of springs was the chief desideratum in the struggle for existence, were to influence social structure and functions, manners and customs, esthetic products and motives, lore and symbolism, and, most of all, creed and cult, which were conditioned by the unending, ever-recurring longing for water.

Consult Morice (1) W. Dénés, 1894, (2) N. Inter. Brit. Col., 1904; Merriam (1) Life Zones, Bull. 20, Biol. Surv. Dept. Agr., (2) N. A. Fauna, ibid., Bull. 3 and 16, (3) Bio.-Geo. maps, 1892 and 1893; Powell, Linguistic Families, 7th Rep. B. A. E., 1891; Sargent (1) Distrib. Forest Trees, 10th Census, (2) Trees of N. Am., 1905, (3) Silva N. Am.; Chesnut (1) Poisonous Plants, Bull. 20, Div. Bot. Dept. Agr., (2) Plants used by Inds. Mendocino Co., Cal., Cont. U. S. Nat. Herb., VII, 3, 1902; Elliott, Mammals of N. Am., Fewkes in Internat. Geog. Cong., 1903; Field Columb. Mus. Publ., Zool., II, 1901; McGee, Beginning Agr., Am. Anthrop., VIII, no. 4, 1895; Mason, Influence of Environment, Smithson. Rep. 1895, 1896; Barrows, Ethno-botany of Coahuilla Inds., 1900; Miller, N. Am. Land Mammals, Boston Soc. Nat. Hist., XXX, no. 1, 1901; Farrand, Basis of Am. Hist., 1904; Dellenbaugh, North Americans of Yesterday, 1901. (O. T. M.)

**Eototo** (name of a supernatural being). One of the clans of the Kokop (Wood) phratry of the Hopi.

Eototo wiñwû.—Fewkes in 19th Rep. B. A. E., 584, 1900 (*wiñwú*='clan'). E-o'-to-to wüñ-wû.—Fewkes in Am. Anthrop., VII, 404, 1894.

**Epanow.** One of the first Indians to be taken across the Atlantic by the English from New England—a member of the party forcibly taken from Marthas Vineyard, Mass., by Capt. Harlow in 1611. He was shown in England as a wonder, and managed to escape from the English on the return voyage by pretending to pilot them to a gold mine. In 1619 he was at the island of Capoge, near C. Cod, and in that year a body of Indians under his guidance attacked Capt. Dormer's men while attempting to land on Marthas Vineyard. Epanow is spoken of as artful and daring. He may be the same as Apannow, a signer of the Plymouth treaty of 1621. See Drake, Inds. N. Am., 72, 1880.

**Epiminguia.** A tribe formerly living on Mississippi r., 20 leagues above Arkansas r. (Coxe, Carolana, 11, 1741); probably a division of the Quapaw.

**Epinette.** A Chippewa band which formerly lived on the N. shore of L. Superior, E. of Michipicoton r., Ontario.—Dobbs, Hudson Bay, 32, 1744.

**Episok.** An Eskimo settlement in N. w. Greenland.—Kane, Arct. Explor., II, 278, 1856.

**Epley's Ruin.** A large prehistoric pueblo ruin on the outskirts of Solomonsville, on the Gila, S. E. Ariz. So called from the owner of the ranch on which it is situated.—Fewkes in 22d Rep. B. A. E., 171, 1904.

**Erie** (Huron: *yĕñresh*, 'it is long-tailed', referring to the eastern puma or panther; Tuscarora, *kĕn'räks*, 'lion', a modern use, Gallicised into *Eri* and *Ri*, whence the locatives *Eri'e*, *Rigué*, and *Riqué*, 'at the place of the panther', are derived. Compare the forms Erieehronon, Eriechronon, and Riquéronon of the Jesuit Relations, signifying 'people of the panther'. It is probable that in Iroquois the puma and the wild-cat originally had generically the same name and that the defining term has remained as the name of the puma or panther). A populous sedentary Iroquoian tribe, inhabiting in the 17th century the territory extending s. from L. Erie probably to Ohio r., E. to the lands of the Conestoga along the E. watershed of Allegheny r. and to those of the Seneca along the line of the w. watershed of Genesee r., and N. to those of the Neutral Nation, probably on a line running eastward from the head of Niagara r. (for the Jesuit Relation for 1640–41 says that the territory of the Erie and their allies joined that of the Neutral Nation at the end of L. Erie), and w. to the w. watershed of L. Erie and Miami r. to Ohio r. Their lands probably adjoined those of the Neutral Nation w. of L. Erie. The Jesuit Relation for 1653, speaking of L. Erie, says that it "was at one time inhabited toward the s. by certain peoples whom we call the Cat Nation; but they were forced to proceed farther inland in order to escape their enemies whom they have toward the w." In this eastward movement of the Erie is probably found an explanation of the emigration of the Awenrehronon (Wenrohronon) to the Huron country in 1639 from the E. border of the lands of the Neutral Nation, although the reason there given is that they had for some unknown reason ruptured their relations with the Neutral Nation, with whom, it is stated, they had been allied, and that, consequently, losing the powerful support of the populous Neutral Nation, the Wenrohronon, were left a prey to their enemies, the Iroquois. But the earlier Jesuit Relation (for 1640–41), referring undoubtedly to this people, says that a certain strange nation, the Awenrehronon, dwelt beyond the Cat Nation, thus placing them at this time E. of the Erie and apparently separate from the Neutral Nation; so that at that time the Wenrohronon may have been either entirely independent or else confederated with the Erie.

Historically little is definitely known of the Erie and their political and social organization, but it may be inferred to have been similar to that of the Hurons. The Jesuit Relations give only a few glimpses of them while describing their last wars with the Iroquois confederation; tradition, however, records the probable fact that the Erie had had many previous wars with these hostile tribes. From the Relations mentioned it is learned that the Erie had many sedentary towns and villages, that they were constituted of several divisions, and that they cultivated the soil and spoke a language resembling that of the Hurons, although it is not stated which of the four or five Huron dialects, usually called "Wendat" (Wyandot) by themselves, was meant. From the same source it is possible to make a rough estimate of the population of the Erie at the period of this final war. At the taking of the Erie town of Riqué in 1654 it is claimed that the defenders numbered between 3,000 and 4,000 combatants, exclusive of women and children; but as it is not likely that all the warriors of the tribe were present, 14,500 would probably be a conservative estimate of the population of the Erie at this period.

The Jesuit Relation for 1655–56 (chap. xi) gives the occasion of the final struggle. Thirty ambassadors of the Cat Nation had been delegated, as was customary, to Sonontouan, the Seneca capital, to renew the existing peace. But through the misfortune of an accident one of the men of the Cat Nation killed a Seneca. This act so incensed the Seneca that they massacred all except 5 of the ambassadors in their hands. These acts kindled the final war between the Erie and the confederated tribes of the Iroquois, especially the Seneca, Cayuga, Oneida, and Onondaga, called by the French the 'upper four tribes', or 'les Iroquis supérieurs'. It is further learned from the Jesuit Relation for 1654 that on the political destruction of their country some Hurons sought asylum among the Erie, and that it was they who were actively fomenting the war that was then striking terror among the Iroquois tribes. The Erie were reputed brave and warlike, employing only bows and poisoned arrows, although the Jesuit Relation for 1656 declares that they were unable to defend one of their palisades against the Iroquois on account of the failure of their munitions, especially powder, which would indicate that they used firearms. It is also said that they "fight like Frenchmen, bravely sustaining the first

charge of the Iroquois, who are armed with our muskets, and then falling upon them with a hailstorm of poisoned arrows," discharging 8 or 10 before a musket could be reloaded. Following the rupture of amicable relations between the Erie and the Iroquois tribes in 1653, the former assaulted and burned a Seneca town, pursued an Iroquois war party returning from the region of the great lakes, and cut to pieces its rear guard of 80 picked men, while the Erie scouts had come to the very gates of one of the Iroquois palisaded towns and seized and carried into captivity Annenraes (Annencraos), "one of the greatest captains." All this roused the Iroquois tribes, which raised 1,800 men to chastise the Erie for these losses. A young chief, one of the two leaders of this levy, was converted by Father Simon Le Moine, who chanced to be in the country at the time, and was baptized. These two chiefs dressed as Frenchmen, in order to frighten the Erie by the novelty of their garments. When this army of invaders had surrounded one of the Erie strongholds, the converted chief gently asked the besieged to surrender, lest they be destroyed should they permit an assault, telling them: "The Master of Life fights for us; you will be ruined if you resist him." "Who is this Master of our lives?" the Erie defiantly replied. "We acknowledge none but our arms and hatchets." No quarter was asked or given on either side in this war. After a stubborn resistance the Erie palisade was carried, and the Onondaga "entered the fort and there wrought such carnage among the women and children that blood was knee-deep in certain places." This was at the town of Riqué, which was defended by between 3,000 and 4,000 combatants, exclusive of women and children, and was assailed by about 1,800 Iroquois. This devastating war lasted until about the close of 1656, when the Erie power was broken and the people were destroyed or dispersed or led into captivity. Six hundred surrendered at one time and were led to the Iroquois country to be adopted as one of the constituent people of the Iroquois tribes. The victory at Riqué was won at a great loss to the Iroquois, who were compelled to remain in the enemy's country two months to care for the wounded and to bury the dead.

Only two of the Erie villages are known by name—Riqué and Gentaienton. A portion of the so-called Seneca now living in Indian Ter. are probably descendants of Erie refugees.          (J. N. B. H.)

Cat Indians.—Smith quoted by Proud, Penn., II, 300, 1798. Cat Nation.—Cusic (ca. 1824) quoted by Schoolcraft, Ind. Tribes, VI, 148, 1857. Ehriehronnons.—Jes. Rel. for 1654, 9, 1858. Erians.—Macauley, N. Y., II, 180, 1829. Erieckronois.—Hennepin, New Discov., map, 1698. **Erieehronons.**—Jes. Rel. for 1641, 71, 1858. **Eriehronon.**—Jes. Rel. for 1640, 35, 1858. **Erielhonons.**—Schoolcraft, Ind. Tribes, IV, 207, 1854. **Erieronons.**—Rafinesque, introd. Marshall, Ky., I, 36, 1824. **Eries.**—Jefferys, Fr. Doms., I, 103, 1760. **Eriez.**—Esnauts and Rapilly, map, 1777. **Erigas.**—Evans (1646?) quoted by Barton, New Views, lxv, 1798. **Errieronons.**—Lahontan, New Voy., I, 217, 1703. **Eves.**—McKenney and Hall, Ind. Tribes, III, 79, 1854 (misprint). **Gahkwas.**—Ruttenber, Tribes Hudson R., 52, 1872. **Gä-quä'-ga-o-no.**—Morgan, League Iroq., 41, 1851. **Heries.**—Browne in Beach, Ind. Misc., 110, 1877. **Irrironnons.**—Day, Penn., 309, 1843. **Irrironons.**—Harvey quoted by Day, ibid., 311. **Kah-Kwah.**—Gale, Upper Miss., 37, 1867. **Kahquas.**—Schoolcraft, Ind. Tribes, III, 290, 1853 (Seneca name). **Kakwas.**—Schoolcraft, Ind. Tribes, II, 344, 1852. **Nation des Chats.**—Jes. Rel. for 1660, 7, 1858. **Nation du Chat.**—Jes. Rel. for 1641, 71, 1858. **Pungelika.**—Rafinesque, Am. Nat., I, 138, 1836 ('lynx-like': Delaware name). **Rhiierrhonons.**—Jes. Rel. for 1635, 33, 1858 (probably their Huron name). **Rigneronnons.**—Jes. Rel. for 1661, 29, 1858 (misprint). **Rigueronnons.**—Jes. Rel. for 1666, 3, 1858. **Riquehronnons.**—Jes. Rel. for 1660, 7, 1858.

**Erigoanna.** A tribe living near St Louis (Matagorda) bay, Tex., in 1687, and referred to as at war with the Ebahamo, q. v. (Douay quoted by Shea, Discov. and Expl. Miss., 209, 1852). Not identified, unless the same as the Kohani (q. v.). Probably a Karankawa band.

**Erilite.** A mineral, according to Dana (Text-book of Mineral., 426, 1888), "acicular, wool-like crystals of unknown nature occurring in a cavity in the quartz from Herkimer co., N. Y.": from *Erie*, the name of a lake, and *-lite* from the Greek λιθος, a stone. The lake was named from one of the peoples of Iroquoian stock. (A. F. C.)

**Erio** (*E-ri′-o*). A name given by the Spaniards to the Pomo living at the mouth of Russian r., Sonoma co., Cal.—Powers in Cont. N. A. Ethnol., III, 194, 1877.

**Eriwonec.** A former Delaware village on the E. bank of Delaware r., about Old Man's cr., in Salem or Gloucester co., N. J. The village was next above the Asomoche and 5 m. below the Rancocas. In 1648 the population numbered about 200, but had just been at war with the Conestoga.
**Armeomeks.**—De Laet (*ca.* 1633) in N. Y. Hist. Soc. Coll., 2d s., I, 303, 1841. **Armewamen.**—Shea, note in Alsop, Md., 118, 1880. **Armewamus.**—Hudde (1663) in N. Y. Doc. Col. Hist., XII, 430, 1877. **Aroenemeck.**—Beekman (1660), ibid., 300 (settlement). **Eriwoneck.**—Evelin (*ca.* 1648) in Proud, Pa., I, 113, 1797. **Ermomex.**—Van der Donck, map (1656) cited by Brinton, Lenape Leg., 42, 1885. **Esewonecks.**—Sanford, U. S., cxlvi, 1819.

**Erner.** A Yurok village on Klamath r., at the mouth of Blue cr., in Del Norte co., N. W. Cal. (A. L. K.)

**Ernivwin** (*Er′nivwiñ*). An Utkiavinmiut Eskimo summer camp inland from Pt Barrow, Alaska.—Murdoch in 9th Rep. B. A. E., 83, 1892.

**Ertlerger.** A Yurok village on lower Klamath r., at the mouth of the Trinity, opposite Pekwuteu and Weitspus, in Humboldt co., Cal. (A. L. K.)

**Erusi** (*E-rus′-si*). A name said by Powers (Cont. N. A. Ethnol., III, 194, 1877) to have been applied to the Pomo formerly living near Ft Ross, Sonoma co., Cal., by the Pomo living N. of them. The people referred to now live near Stewart's Point and on the Haupt ranch a few miles E. of that place. Powers suggests that the name is a relic of the Russian occupancy, which is probably correct, as it is not an Indian name. (S. A. B.)

**Ervipiames.** A tribe of central Texas in the 18th century. Domingo Ramón was met by some of them a few leagues W. of Trinity r., not far from the country of the Bidai. They are mentioned in unpublished documents as among the tribes which in company with other northern tribes petitioned for a mission on San Javier r., and they are included among the northern Indians as distinguished from the coast tribes. If they belonged to any of the large recognized divisions in this neighborhood it was probably Tonkawan. (H. E. B.)
**Enepiahe.**—Joutel, Jour. Voy., 90, 1719. **Enepiahœ.**—Shea, note in Charlevoix, New France, IV, 78, 1870. **Enepiahoes.**—Barcia, Ensayo, 271, 1723. **Ervipiames.**—Rivera, Diario, leg. 2602, 1736. **Exepiahohé.**—Joutel in Margry, Déc., III, 288, 1878. **Hierbipiames.**—Barrios, MS., 1771. **Yerbipiame.**—Ramón, MS., Texas Memorias, XVII, 151. **Yorbipianos.**—Informe de Misiones, ibid., XXVIII, 179, 1762. **Yrbipias.**—Bosque (1675) in Nat. Geog. Mag., XIV, 343, 1903. **Yrbipimas.**—Ibid., 340.

**Esachkabuk** ('bad leggings'). A Crow band.
**Bad Leggins.**—Culbertson in Smithson. Rep. 1850, 144, 1851. **E-sach′-ka-buk.**—Morgan, Anc. Soc., 159, 1877.

**Esahateaketarpar** ('toward the Santee', from *Isanyate* 'Santee', *ektapa* 'toward'). A division of the Brulé Dakota which had Tartonggarsarpar (Tatónka-tsapa, Black Buffalo Bull) for its principal chief in 1804.
**E-sah-a-te-ake-tar-par.**—Lewis and Clark, Discov., 34, 1806.

**Esbataottine** (? 'bighorn people'). A Nahane tribe living in the mountains between Liard and Peace rs., Brit. Col. They are said to be of a very low grade of culture and to practise cannibalism, probably under stress of hunger.
**Dounie′ Espa-tρa-Ottinè.**—Petitot, Autour du grand lac des Esclaves, 301, 1891 (='goat people'). **Esba-t'a-ottinè.**—Petitot, Ethnog. chart in Bull. Soc. de Géogr. Paris, July, 1875 (='dwellers among the argali'). **Es-pā-to-ti-na.**—Dawson in Rep. Geol. Surv. Can. for 1887, 202B, 1889. **Espa-tρa-Ottinè.**—Petitot, Autour du lac des Esclaves, 362, 1891 (trans. 'bighorn people'). **Gens des Bois.**—Dall in Cont. N. A. Ethnol., I, 32, 1877 (so called by Hudson bay people). **Gens des chèvres.**—Petitot, Autour du lac des Esclaves, 301, 1891. **Knife Indians.**—Campbell quoted by Dawson, op. cit.

**Escaba.** A former tribe, probably Coahuiltecan, on the lower Rio Grande.
**Escabaca-Cascastes.**—Fernando del Bosque (1675) in Nat. Geog. Mag., XIV, 340, 1903 (combined with the name of another tribe, the Cascastes, and corrupted). **Escabas.**—Revillagigedo (1793) quoted by Bancroft, Nat. Races, I, 611, 1886.

**Escambuit.** See *Assacumbuit*.

**Escooba** (*Oski holba*, 'cane-like', referring to reed-brakes). A former Choctaw town, noted by Romans; evidently situated a few miles E. or N. E. of Ayanabi, perhaps on or near Petickfa cr., Kemper co., Miss.—Halbert in Miss. Hist. Soc. Publ., VI, 424, 1902.

**Escoumains** (probably from *ashkĭmĭn*, or *askĭmĭn*, 'early berry'.—W. J.). A Montagnais band living on a reserve of 97 acres on the s. w. side of Escoumains r., on the N. shore of the St Lawrence, in Saguenay co., Quebec. They numbered 53 in 1884, 43 in 1904.
Escoumains.—Can. Ind. Aff. Rep. for 1884, pt. I, 185, 1885.

**Escumawash.** A former Chumashan village at San José, about 6 m. from Santa Barbara mission, Cal.—Timeno (1856) quoted by Taylor in Cal. Farmer, May 4, 1860.

**Esekepkabuk.** A band of the Crow tribe adopted from the Sihasapa.
Bad Coup.—Culbertson in Smithson. Rep. 1850, 144, 1851. Bad Honors.—Morgan, Anc. Soc., 159, 1877. Ese-kep-kä'-buk.—Ibid.

**Eshhulup.** The name of "the rancheria of the mission of San Buenaventura," Cal. (Taylor in Cal. Farmer, May 4, 1860). The native name usually given to San Buenaventura was Mishkanakan, or Mitskanakan (see *Miscanaka*).

**Eshkebugecoshe** ('Flat-mouth', 'Wide-mouth'). A chief of the Pillager Chippewa; born in 1774, died about 1860. He belonged to the Awausee gens. In his youth Eshkebugecoshe engaged in distant expeditions, lived among the Cree and Assiniboin, and visited in war or peace the tribes of the upper Missouri, spending some time among the Hidatsa. His father, Yellow-hair (Wasonaunequa), was not a chief by descent, but gained ascendency over the Pillagers through his knowledge of medicine, and it is said that whoever incurred his hatred died mysteriously. The son was different, enjoying the respect of whites as well as Indians throughout his long life. He was much impressed by the prophecies of Tenskwatawa, and through his influence poisoning ceased among the Pillagers, as among other Chippewa. In the later contests with the Sioux for the headwaters of the Mississippi he bore a valiant part. Although his band at Leech lake, Minn., was decimated in the exterminating war, it continued to grow through accessions of the bravest spirits of the eastern villages. When a political agent sought to enlist the Pillagers in the British interest at the beginning of the war of 1812, Flat-mouth returned the proffered wampum belts, saying that he would as soon invite white men to aid him in his wars as take part in a quarrel between the whites. (F. H.)

**Eshpeu.** A Yurok village on the coast between the mouths of Klamath r. and Redwood cr., at Gold bluff, Cal. The dialect differed slightly from that of the Klamath River Yurok. (A. L. K.)

**Eskegawaage.** One of the 7 districts of the territory of the Micmac as recognized by themselves. It includes E. Nova Scotia from Canso to Halifax.—Rand, First Micmac Reading Book, 81, 1875.

**Eskimauan Family.** A linguistic stock of North American aborigines, comprising two well-marked divisions, the Eskimo and the Aleut (q. v.). See Powell in 7th Rep. B. A. E., 71, 1891. (The following synonymy of the family is chronologic.)
>Eskimaux.—Gallatin in Trans. and Coll. Am. Antiq. Soc., II, 9, 305, 1836; Gallatin in Trans. Am. Ethnol. Soc., II, pt. 1, xcix, 77, 1848; Gallatin in Schoolcraft, Ind. Tribes, III, 401, 1853. =Eskimo.—Berghaus (1845), Physik. Atlas, map 17, 1848; ibid., 1852; Latham, Nat. Hist. Man, 288, 1850 (general remarks on origin and habitat); Buschmann, Spuren der aztek. Sprache, 689, 1859; Latham, Elem. Comp. Philol., 385, 1862; Bancroft, Nat. Races, III, 562, 574, 1882. >Esquimaux.—Prichard, Phys. Hist. Mankind, v, 367–371, 1847 (follows Gallatin); Latham in Jour. Ethnol. Soc. Lond., I, 182–191, 1848; Latham, Opuscula, 266–274, 1860. >Eskimo.—Dall in Proc. A. A. A. S., 266, 1869 (treats of Alaskan Eskimo and Tuski only); Berghaus, Physik. Atlas, map 72, 1887 (excludes the Aleutian). >Eskimos.—Keane, app. to Stanford's Compend., Cent. and So. Am., 460, 1878 (excludes Aleutian). >Ounángan.—Veniaminoff, Zapiski, II, 1, 1840 (Aleutians only). >Ŭnŭgŭn.—Dall in Cont. N. A. Ethnol., I, 22, 1877 (Aleuts a division of his Orarian group). >Unangan.—Berghaus, Physik. Atlas, map 72, 1887. ×Northern.—Scouler in Jour. Roy. Geog. Soc., XI, 218, 1841 (includes Ugalentzes of present family). ×Haidah.—Scouler, ibid., 224, 1841 (same as his Northern family). >Ugaljachmutzi.—Gallatin in Schoolcraft, Ind. Tribes, III, 402, 1853 (lat. 60°, between Prince Williams sd. and Mt St Elias, perhaps Athapascan). >Aleuten.—Holmberg, Ethnog. Skizzen, 1855. >Aleutians.—Dall in Proc. A. A. A. S., 266, 1869; Dall, Alaska, 374, 1870 (in both places a division of his Orarian family). >Aleuts.—Keane, app. to Stanford's Compend., Cent. and So. Am., 460, 1878 (consist of Unalaskans of mainland and of Fox and Shumagin ids., with Akkhas of rest of Aleutian arch.). >Aleut.—Bancroft, Nat. Races, III, 562, 1882 (two dialects, Unalaska and Atkha). >Konjagen.—Holmberg, Ethnog. Skizzen, 1855 (Island of Koniag or Kadiak). =Orarians.—Dall in Proc. A. A. A. S., 265, 1869 (group name; includes Innuit, Aleutians, Tuski); Dall, Alaska, 374, 1870; Dall in Cont. N. A. Ethnol., I, 8, 9, 1877. ×Tinneh.—Dall in Proc. A. A. A. S., 269, 1869 (includes "Ugalense"). >Innuit.—Dall in Cont. N. A. Ethnol., I, 9, 1877 ("Major group" of Orarians: treats of Alaska Innuit only); Berghaus, Physik. Atlas, map 72, 1887 (excludes the Aleutians).

**Eskimo.** A group of American aborigines, forming part of the Eskimauan linguistic stock, which formerly occupied nearly all the coasts and islands of Arctic America from E. Greenland and the N. end of Newfoundland to the westernmost Aleutian ids., even extending to the E. coast of Siberia, a distance of more than 5,000 m. From remains found in Smith sd. it is evident that bands formerly wintered as far N. as lat. 79° and had summer camps up to 82°. At the present time they have receded from this extreme range and in the S. have abandoned the N. shore of the Gulf of St Lawrence, the N. end of Newfoundland, James bay, and the s. shores of Hudson bay, while in Alaska one Eskimo tribe, the Ugalakmiut, has practically become Tlingit through intermarriage. The name Eskimo (in the form

SUKUUK, A KINUGUMIUT ESKIMO OF ALASKA. (NELSON)

Excomminquois) seems to have been first given by Biard in 1611. It is said to come from the Abnaki *Esquimantsic*, or from *Ashkimeq*, the Chippewa equivalent, signifying 'eaters of raw flesh.' They call themselves Inuit, meaning 'people.' The Eskimo constitute physically a distinct type. They are of medium stature, but possess uncommon strength and endurance; their skin is light brownish yellow with a ruddy tint on the exposed parts; their hands and feet are small and well formed; their eyes, like those of other American tribes, have a Mongoloid character, which circumstance has induced many ethnographers to class them with the Asiatic peoples. They are characterized by very broad faces and narrow, high noses; their heads are also exceptionally high. This type is most marked among the tribes E. of Mackenzie r. In disposition the Eskimo may be described as peaceable, cheerful, truthful, and honest, but exceptionally loose in sexual morality.

The Eskimo have permanent settlements, conveniently situated for marking certain hunting and fishing grounds. In summer they hunt caribou, musk-oxen, and various birds; in winter they live principally on sea mammals, particularly the seal. Although their houses differ with the region, they conform in the main to three types: In summer, when they

travel, they occupy tents of deer or seal skins stretched on poles. Their winter dwellings are made either in shallow excavations covered with turf and earth laid upon a framework of wood or whale ribs, or they are built of snow. Their clothing is of skins, and their personal adornments are few. Among most tribes, however, the women tattoo their faces, and some Alaskan tribes wear studs in openings through their cheeks. Considering their degree of culture, the Eskimo are excellent draftsmen and carvers, their designs usually consisting either of simple linear incisions or of animal forms executed with much life and freedom. The people about Bering strait make some use of paints.

There has always been extensive intertribal communication. The Eskimo have an exceptional knowledge of the geography of their country. Poetry and music play an important part in their life, especially in connection with their religious observances.

The Eskimauan social organization is exceedingly loose. In general the village is the largest unit, although persons inhabiting a certain geographical area have sometimes taken the name of that area as a more general designation, and it is often convenient for the ethnographer to make

KERLUNGNER, A KINUGUMIUT ESKIMO WOMAN OF ALASKA. (NELSON)

a more extended use of this native custom. In matters of government each settlement is entirely independent, and the same might almost be said for each family, although there are customs and precedents, especially with regard to hunting and fishing, which define the relations existing between them. Although hardly deserving the name of chief, there is usually some advisory head in each settlement whose dictum in certain matters, particularly as to the change of village sites, has much weight, but he has no power to enforce his opinions.

The men engage in hunting and fishing, while all the household duties fall to the lot of the women—they must cook, make and mend clothes, and repair the kaiaks and boat covers, pitch the tents, and dry the fish and meat and stow them away for the winter. In some tribes skin-dressing is done by the men, in others by the women. Monogamy, polygamy, and polyandry are all practised, their occurrence being governed somewhat by the relative proportion of the sexes; but a second marriage is unusual where a man's first wife has borne him children. The execution of law is largely left to the individual, and blood-revenge is universally exacted.

The Eskimo believe in spirits inhabiting animals and inanimate objects. Their chief deity, however, is an old woman who resides in the ocean and may cause storms or withhold seals and other marine animals if any of her tabus are infringed. Her power over these animals arises from the fact that they are sections of her fingers cut off by her father at the time when she first took up her abode in the sea. The chief duty of angakoks, or shamans, is to find who has infringed the tabus and thus brought down the wrath of the supernatural beings and to compel the offender to make atonement by public confession or confession to the angakok. The central Eskimo suppose two spirits to reside in a man's body, one of which stays with it when it dies and may temporarily enter the body of some child, who is then named after the departed, while the other goes to one of several lands of the souls. Some of the lands of souls lie above the earth's surface, some beneath, and the latter are generally more desirable.

Although the theory of Asiatic origin of the Eskimo was long popular, many of their ethnic peculiarities are opposed to such a notion, and recent researches seem to indicate that their movements have rather been from E. to W. They are peculiar as being the only race of American aborigines who certainly had contact with white people before the days of Columbus, for Greenland was occupied during the 10th and 11th centuries by Norwegians, whose expeditions extended even as far as the American mainland.

Later Frobisher and other European navigators encountered Eskimo along the E. coasts, while the Russians discovered and annexed the w. part of their domain. This occupancy in its earlier period proved disastrous to the Aleut (q. v.) in particular, who were harshly dealt with and whose number was greatly reduced during the Russian domination (see *Russian influence*). The larger portion of the Greenland and Labrador Eskimo have been Christianized by Moravian and Danish missionaries, while the Alaskan representatives of the family have had Russian missionaries among them for more than a century. Those of the central groups, however, owing to the remoteness of their situation, have always been much less affected by outside influences. The Eskimo have proved almost indispensable assistants to Arctic explorers.

The Eskimauan stock embraces two well-marked divisions, the Eskimo proper and the inhabitants of the Aleutian ids., the Aleut. Other divisions are rather geographical than political or dialectic, there being great similarity in language and customs from one end of the Eskimo domain to the other. They can be separated, however, into the following fairly well marked ethnological groups (based on information furnished by Dr Franz Boas):

I. The Greenland Eskimo, subdivided into the East Greenlanders, West Greenlanders, and Ita Eskimo, the last transitional between the Greenland Eskimo proper and the next group.

II. The Eskimo of s. Baffin land and Labrador, embracing the following divisions: Akudnirmiut, Akuliarmiut, Itivimiut, Kaumauangmiut, Kigiktagmiut, Nugumiut, Okomiut, Padlimiut, Sikosuilarmiut, Suhinimiut, Tahagmiut.

III. The Eskimo of Melville penin., North Devon, N. Baffin land, and the N. W. shore of Hudson bay, embracing the Agomiut, Aivilirmiut, Amitormiut, Iglulirmiut, Inuissuitmiut, Kinipetu, Koungmiut, Pilingmiut, Sauniktumiut.

IV. The Sagdlirmiut of Southampton id., now extinct.

V. The Eskimo of Boothia Felix, King William land, and the neighboring mainland. These include the Netchilirmiut, Sinimiut, Ugjulirmiut, Ukusiksalirmiut.

VI. The Eskimo of Victoria land and Coronation gulf, including the Kangormiut and Kidnelik, which may, perhaps, be one tribe.

VII. The Eskimo between C. Bathurst and Herschel id., including the mouth of Mackenzie r. Provisionally they may be divided into the Kitegareut at C. Bathurst and on Anderson r., the Nageuktormiut at the mouth of Coppermine r., and the Kopagmiut of Mackenzie r. This group approximates the next very closely.

VIII. The Alaskan Eskimo, embracing all those within the American territory. This group includes the Aglemiut, Chingigmiut, Chnagmiut, Chugachigmiut, Ikogmiut, Imaklimiut, Inguklimiut, Kaialigmiut, Kangmaligmiut, Kaniagmiut, Kaviagmiut, Kevalingamiut, Kiatagmiut, Kinugumiut, Kowagmiut, Kukpaurungmiut, Kunmiut, Kuskwogmiut, Magemiut, Malemiut, Nunatogmiut, Nunivagmiut, Nuwukmiut, Nushagagmiut, Selawigmiut, Sidarumiut, Tikeramiut, Togiagmiut, Ugalakmiut, Unaligmiut, Utukamiut, and Utkiavinmiut.

IX. The Yuit of Siberia.

Holm (1884–85) placed the number of East Greenland Eskimo at 550. The w. coast Greenlanders were given as 10,122 by the Royal Greenland Co. in 1888, and the Ita Eskimo numbered 234 in 1897, giving a total for this group of 10,906. The Eskimo of Labrador were estimated at 1,300 in a recent report by the Government of Newfoundland, and Boas in 1888 gave the number of Eskimo in the central groups as 1,100. According to the census of 1890, there were on the Arctic coast of Alaska from the British border to Norton sd., 2,729 Eskimo; on the s. shore of Norton sd. and in the Yukon valley, 1,439; in Kuskokwim valley, 5,254; in the valley of Nushagak r., 1,952; on the s. coast, 1,670. The Ugalakmiut of Prince William sd., numbering 154, are reckoned with the Tlingit, but they were originally Eskimo, and for our present purposes are best placed in that category. Adding these, therefore, the total for this group,

WESTERN ESKIMO COSTUME. (MURDOCH)

exclusive of the 968 Aleut, is 13,298. The Yuit of Siberia are estimated by Bogoras at 1,200. The Eskimo proper therefore number about 27,700, and the stock about 28,670. (H. W. H. J. R. S.)

Aguskemaig.—Tanner, Narr., 316, 1830. A'lvayê'lĭlĭt.—Bogoras, Chukchee, 11, 1904 (Chukchi: 'those of alien language'). Anda-kρœn.—Petitot, Dict. Dènè Dindjié, 169, 1876 (Loucheux name: trans. 'ennemis-pieds'). Ara-k'è.—Ibid. (Bastard Loucheux name, same meaning). Enna-k'è.—Ibid. (Peaux de Lièvre name, same meaning). En-na-k'iè.—Ibid. (Slave name: trans. 'steppesennemis'). Escoumins.—Jes. Rel., III, index, 1858. Eshkibod.—Baraga, Otchipwe-Eng. Dict., 114, 1880 (Ojibwa: 'those who eat their food raw'). Eskeemoes.—Gordon, Hist. Mem. of N. Am., 117, 1820. Eskima.—Dobbs, Hudson Bay, 203, 1744. Eskimantsik.—Hervas, Idea dell' Universo, XVII, 87, 1784. Eskīma'ntzik.—Dall in Cont. N. A. Ethnol., I, 9, 1877 (Abnaki name). Eskimauk.—Morse, N. Am., map, 1776. Eskimaux.—Lahontan, New Voy., I, 208, 1703. Eskimeaux.—Jeffreys, French Dom. Am., pt. 1, map, 1760. Eskimesi.—Hervas, Idea dell' Universo, XVII, 86, 1784. Eskimo.—Buschmann, Spuren d. Aztek. Spr., 669, 1859. Eskimos.—Hutchins (1770) quoted by Richardson, Arct. Exped., II, 38, 1851. Esquimantsic.—Prichard, Phys. Hist., V, 367, 1847. Esquimau.—Petitot, Dict. Dènè Dindjié, 169, 1876. Esquimaux.—Morse, Hist. Am., 126, 1798. Esquimeaux Indians.—McKeevor, Voy. Hudson's Bay, 27, 1819. Esquimones.—Hennepin, Cont. of New Discov., 95, 1698. Eusquemays.—Potts (1754) quoted by Boyle, Archæol. Rep. Ont., 1905. Excomminqui.—Jes. Rel. 1612–14, Thwaites ed., II, 67, 1896 (= 'excommunicated'). Excomminquois.—Biard in Jes. Rel. 1611, 7, 1858. Huskemaw.—Packard in Am. Natural., XIX, 555, 1885 (name given by a missionary in Labrador). Hŭs'ky.—Dall in Cont. N. A. Ethnol., I, 9, 1877 (Hudson bay jargon). Innoït.—Petitot in Bib. Ling. et Ethnol. Am., III, pt. 2, 29, 1876 (sing. Innok). In-nu.—Lyon, Repulse Bay, 40, 1825. Innuees.—Parry, Sec. Voy., 414, 1824. In'nüit.—Dall in Cont. N. A. Ethnol., I, 9, 1877 (own name). Inuin.—Murdoch in 9th Rep. B. A. E., 42, 1892. Inuit.—Bessels in Archiv f. Anthrop., VIII, 107, 1875. Kaladlit.—Nansen, Eskimo Life, 13, 1893 (name which the Greenland Eskimo give themselves, said to be a corruption of Danish Skraeling). Kālālik.—Richardson, Polar Regions, 300, 1861. Kalalit.—Keane in Stanford's Compend., 517, 1878. Karaler.—Crantz, Greenland, II, 291, 1820. Karalit.—Mass. Hist. Soc. Coll., 2d s., IX, 233, 1822. Keralite.—Heriot, Travels, 34, 1813. Kĭ'ĭmĭlĭt.—Bogoras, Chukchee, 21, 1904 (from kĭ'xmi, an inhabitant of C. Prince of Wales: Yuit name). Nochways.—Dobbs, Hudson Bay, 12, 1744 (Algonkin: 'snakes', 'enemies,' applied to people of alien race regarded as natural enemies). Nodways.—Dobbs, Hudson Bay, 12, 1744 ('snakes': Siksika name). Œnné.—Petitot, Dict. Dènè Dindjié, 169, 1876 (Loucheux name: 'enemies'). Orarians.—Dall in Proc. A. A. A. S., XVIII, 265, 1870. Ot'el'nna.—Petitot, Dict. Dènè Dindjié, 169, 1876 (Montagnais name: trans. 'steppes-ennemis'). Pa-erks.—Hooper, Tents of Tuski, 137, 1853 (Chukchi name for Eskimo of American coast). Payairkets.—Ibid., 103. Ro'č'hĭlĭt.—Bogoras, Chukchee, 21, 1904 ('opposite shore people': Yuit name). Seymòs.—Richardson, Arct. Exped., I, 340, 1851 (used by sailors of Hudson's Bay Co.'s ships: derived from the Eskimo cry of greeting: Seymo or Teymo). Skraelingas.—Schultz in Trans. Roy. Soc. Can., XIII, pt. 2, 114, 1895. Skrællingar.—Richardson, Polar Regions, 298, 1861 (Scandinavian name: 'small people'). S Krællings.—Crantz, Greenland, I, 123, 1820 (applied by the Norwegians). Skrellings.—Amer. Hist. Soc., 2d ser., I, Portland, 1869. Skroelingues.—Morse, Hist. Am., 126, 1778. Sŭckĕmòs.—Richardson, Arct. Exped., I, 340, 1851 (same derivation as Seymòs). Ta-kutchi.—Ibid. (Kutchin name: 'ocean people'). Tchiechrone.—Pyrlæus (ca. 1748) quoted in Am. Antiq., IV, 75, 1881 (German form of Seneca name: 'seal people'). Tciě'k-rúnĕn.—Hewitt, inf'n (Seneca name). Ultsehaga.—Richardson,

Arct. Exped., I, 408, 1851 (Kenai name: 'slaves'). **Ultsehna.**—Ibid. **Uskee-mès.**—Ibid., 55. **Uskee'-mi.**—Dall in Cont. N. A. Ethnol., I, 9, 1877 (Athapascan name). **Uskees.**—O'Reilly, Greenland, 59, 1818. **Uskimay.**—Middleton in Dobbs, Hudson Bay, 189, 1744. **Ŭsquemows.**—Coats, Geog. of Hudson Bay, 15, 1852. **Weashkimek.**—Belcourt (before 1853) in Minn. Hist. Coll., I, 226, 1872 (Saulteur name: 'eaters of raw flesh'). **Yĭkĭrga'-ulĭt.**—Bogoras, Chukchee, 21, 1904 (Yuit name).

**Eskini.** A Maidu village formerly situated on the site of Durham, Butte co., Cal., the people of which are extinct except for a few survivors at Chico. The Maidu creation myth centers about this spot. (R. B. D.)
**Erskins.**—Ind. Aff. Rep., 124, 1850. **Es'-kin.**—Powers in Cont. N. A. Ethnol., III, 282, 1877. **Éskini.**—Curtin, MS. vocab., B. A. E., 1885.

**Esksinaitupiks** ('worm people'). A division of the Piegan.
**Esk'-sin-ai-tŭp-ĭks.**—Grinnell, Blackfoot Lodge Tales, 209, 1892. **is-ksi'-na-tup-i.**—Hayden, Ethnog. and Philol. Mo. Val., 264, 1862. **Worm People.**—Grinnell, Blackfoot Lodge Tales, 225, 1892.

**Eskusone.** A Micmac village formerly in Cape Breton.—Rand, First Micmac Reading Book, 87, 1875.

**Eslanagan.** A village, supposed to be of the Chalone division of the Costanoan family, but possibly Esselenian, formerly connected with Soledad mission, Monterey co., Cal.—Taylor in Cal. Farmer, Apr. 20, 1860.

**Esmischue.** A former Chumashan village near Purísima mission, Santa Barbara co., Cal.—Taylor in Cal. Farmer, Oct. 18, 1861.

**Esnispele.** A former Chumashan village near Purísima mission, Santa Barbara co., Cal.—Taylor in Cal. Farmer, Oct. 18, 1861.

**Esopus** (*sip* 'river,' *-us* 'small'). A division of the Munsee that lived along the w. bank of Hudson r. in Greene and Ulster cos., N. Y., above the Minisink, who formed the main division. Esopus is the old name of Kingston, which was their principal rendezvous. Under this name were included the Catskill, Mamekoting, Waoranec, Warranawonkong, and Wawarsink, sometimes called the five tribes of the Esopus country. They continued to reside about Kingston until some joined the Moravian Munsee and Mahican in Pennsylvania, and others placed themselves under the protection of the Iroquois. About the year 1775 the remnant were at Oquanga, with fragments of other tribes. (J. M.)
**Æsopus.**—Smitt (1660) in N. Y. Doc. Col. Hist., XIII, 157, 1881. **Aesopus.**—Doc. of 1658, ibid., 81. **Asopus.**—Writer ca. 1742 in Drake, Bk. Inds., bk. 5, 18, 1848. **Esopes.**—Doc. of 1665 in N. Y. Doc. Col. Hist., XIII, 401, 1881. **Esopus.**—De Laet (1633) quoted by Ruttenber, Tribes Hudson R., 72, 1872. **Esopuz.**—Map ca. 1614 in N. Y. Doc. Col. Hist., I, 1856. **Sapes.**—Doc. of 1665, ibid., XIII, 399, 1881. **Sepus.**—Schuyler (1693), ibid., IV, 66, 1854 (settlement). **Soopis.**—Stoll (1658), ibid., XIII, 77, 1881 (locality). **Soopus.**—Ibid., 96. **Sopes.**—Nicolls (1665), ibid., 399. **Sopez.**—Smith (1659), ibid., 114 (place). **Sopus.**—Doc. of 1668, ibid., 418. **Zopus.**—Ingoldsby (1691), ibid., III, 793, 1853 (settlement).

**Espachomy.** A village on lower Hudson r., N. Y., near Poughkeepsie, under English protection in 1664.—Albany treaty (1664) in N. Y. Doc. Col. Hist., III, 68, 1853.

**Espamichkon.** A small Montagnais tribe N. of the St Lawrence in 1643 (Jes. Rel. 1643, 38, 1858), probably about the headwaters of Saguenay or St Maurice r.

**Espejos** (named from their chief Espejo (Span.: 'mirror'). A branch of the Mescaleros inhabiting the plains of Chihuahua, Mexico, about 1859.—Froebel, Seven Years' Trav., 352, 1859.

**Espeminkia.** A band, apparently part of the Illinois, mentioned with the Tamaroa and Tapouaro (Peoria?).—La Salle (1681) in Margry, Déc., II, 134, 1877.

**Esperiez.** Given by mistake as the name of one of the Hopi pueblos in 1598.—Oñate (1598) in Doc. Inéd., XVI, 137, 1871.

**Espiiluima.** A former Chumashan village near Purísima mission, Santa Barbara co., Cal.—Taylor in Cal. Farmer, Oct. 18, 1861.

**Espiritu Santo de Zuñiga.** A mission established by the Marquis de San Miguel Aguayo, in March or April, 1722, near and under the protection of the newly established fort of Santa María de Loreto de la Bahía del Espíritu Santo, commonly called La Bahía, which was built on the site of La Salle's ill-fated Ft St Louis, on Lavaca r., Matagorda bay, Tex., in the territory of the Karankawa. The Spanish mission, of which Fray Agustin Patron was the first missionary, was abandoned before 1726, its priest establishing a new one among the Tamique and Juranames (Aranama), who lived 10 leagues inland, on lower San Antonio r., and in 1749 it was moved upstream opposite the site of the modern Goliad. The presidio of La Bahía was shifted with the mission. In 1768 its population was 300, and to that date there had been 623 baptisms; there were also 1,500 cattle and 100 horses, and it is said once to have had 15,000 cattle. The population, which consisted of Aranama, Tamique, Piguican, Manos de Perro, Kohani, and Karankawa Indians, had dwindled to 116 in 1785 (in which year there were also 3,000 cattle), and to only 33 Indians in 1793. See Bancroft, No. Mex. States, I, 1886; Garrison, Texas, 1903.

**Espopolames.** A former tribe, probably Coahuiltecan, in the neighborhood of the lower Rio Grande.
**Espopolames.**—Fernando del Bosque (1675) in Nat. Geog. Mag., XIV, 341, 1903. **Isipopolames.**—Revillagigedo (1793) quoted by Bancroft, Nat. Races, I, 611, 1886.

**Esqugbaag.** Formerly a rancheria, probably of the Sobaipuri, and a visita of the mission of Suamca about 1760–67; situated on or near the Rio San Pedro, near the Arizona-Sonora boundary.
**Badz.**—Bancroft, No. Mex. States, I, 563, 1884. **S. Andrès Esqugbaag.**—Ibid.

**Esquimalt.** The local name for a body of Songish at the s. e. end of Vancouver id., under the Cowichan agency; pop. 15 in 1901, 20 in 1904.—Can. Ind. Aff., pt. 2, 66, 1902; pt. 2, 69, 1904.

**Esquimaux Point.** A Montagnais mission settlement on the n. bank of the St Lawrence, about 20 m. e. of Mingan, Quebec.
Esquimaux Point.—Stearns, Labrador, 271, 1884. Pointe des Esquimaux.—Hind, Lab. Penin., ii, 180, 1863.

**Esquipomgole.** Defined by Bartlett (Dict. of Americanisms, 202, 1877) as "another name for kinnickinnick, or a mixture of tobacco and cornel bark"; said to be an Indian word, possibly Algonquian.    (A. F. C.)

**Essanape** (Algonq.: *asīnapă* 'stone person'.—W. J.). A tribe located by Lahontan (New Voy., i, 114, 1703) on his "Long r.," identified with Minnesota r. His voyage up this stream is probably fictitious, and so may be the tribe, which was certainly not the Assiniboin, as has been suggested, since these under the name Assimpoual were correctly placed by Lahontan in the region of L. Winnipeg. The tribe, if not imaginary, may have been, as Ramsey supposed, the Santee, known as Isanyati, for the Mdewakanton band dwelt at that time on Minnesota r.
Esanapes.—Harris, Coll. Voy. and Trav., ii, map, 1705. Esanopes.—Barcia, Ensayo, 291, 1723. Essan-a-pis.—Ramsey in Ind. Aff. Rep. 1849, 78, 1850. Essannapes.—Neill in Minn. Hist. Coll., i, 31, 1872. Essenapes.—Vaugondy, map, 1778.

**Esselen.** A tribe of Californian Indians, constituting the Esselenian family, most of the members of which on the founding of Carmelo mission, near Monterey, in 1770, were brought under civilizing influences, resulting, as was the case with the Indians at all the Californian missions, in their rapid decrease (see *California Indians, Mission Indians, Missions*). A portion of the tribe seems to have been taken to the mission at Soledad, for Arroyo de la Cuesta (MS., B. A. E.) in 1821 says of an Esselen vocabulary obtained by himself, "Huelel language of Soledad; it is from the Esselenes, who are already few." The original territory of the Esselen lay along the coast s. of Monterey, though its exact limits are diversely given. Henshaw (Esselen MS., B. A. E.) states that they lived on the coast s. of Monterey, in the mountains. The Rumsen Indians of the present day at Carmel and Monterey state (Kroeber, MS., Univ. Cal.) that the Esselen originally lived at Agua Caliente (Tassajara springs), which is near the head of Carmel r., in a line between Sur and Soledad. Powell's map (7th Rep. B. A. E.) makes the Esselen territory comprise Sur r., the head of Carmel r., and the country about as far s. as Santa Lucia peak, which is probably approximately correct. In any case the Es-

selen territory was confined to a limited area and was bordered only by Salinan and Costanoan tribes. La Perouse's statement that it extended more than 20 leagues e. of Monterey is incorrect. Almost nothing is known of the mode of life and practices of the Esselen, but they were certainly similar to those of the neighboring tribes. What little is known in regard to the Esselen language shows it to have been simple and regular and of a type similar to most of the languages of central California, but, notwithstanding a few words in common with Costanoan, of entirely unrelated vocabulary and therefore a distinct stock.

Taylor gives a list of Esselen villages connected with San Carlos mission, namely: Chachat, Coyyo, Fyules, Gilimis, Jappayon, Nennequi, Noptac, Santa Clara, Sapponet, Soccorondo, Tebityilat, Triwta, Tushguesta, Xumis, Yampas, and Yanostas. He mentions also Xaseum, 10 leagues from Carmelo, in the sierra, and Pachhepes near Xaseum, among the Esselen. He gives still other names, such as Excellemaks and Eslanagan; but none of the settlements named by him have been proved to be Esselen and not Costanoan.
Carmelo Eslenes.—Taylor in Cal. Farmer, Apr. 20, 1860. Ecclemachs.—Lamanon in La Perouse, Voy., ii, 291, 1797. Eclemaches.—Chamisso quoted by Kotzebue, Voy., iii, 49, 1821. Ecselenas.—Taylor in Cal. Farmer, Apr. 20, 1860. Ecselenes.—Ibid. Ekklemaches.—Ludewig, Abor. Lang. Am., 68, 1858. Ensenes.—Taylor in Cal. Farmer, Apr. 20, 1860. Escelen.—Humboldt, Essai Pol., 321, 1811. Escelenes.—Mayer, Mexico, ii, 39, 1853. Escellens.—Taylor in Cal. Farmer, Apr. 20, 1860. Eselenes.—Ibid. Eskelen.—Ludewig, Abor. Lang. Am., 68, 1858. Eslen.—Galiano, Viaje Sutil y Mexicana, 167, 1802. Eslenes.—Ibid., 172. Esselen.—Henshaw in Am. Anthrop., iii, 45, 1890. Excellemaks.—Taylor in Cal. Farmer, Apr. 20, 1860.

**Esselenian Family.** A small linguistic stock in w. California, first positively established by Henshaw (Am. Anthrop., iii, 45, 1890). At the time of the Spanish settlement, this family, which has become extinct, consisted of a single group, the Esselen, q. v.
=Esselen.—Dixon and Kroeber in Am. Anthrop., n. s., v, no. 1, map, 1903. =Esselenian.—Powell in 7th Rep. B. A. E., 75, 1891. <Salinas.—Latham in Trans. Philol. Soc. Lond., 85, 1856 (includes Gioloco?, Ruslen, Soledad, Eslen, Carmel, San Antonio, and San Miguel, cited as including Eslen); Latham, Opuscula, 350, 1860.

**Estait.** A former Chumashan village near Purísima mission, Santa Barbara co., Cal.—Taylor in Cal. Farmer, Oct. 18, 1861.

**Estale.** A former settlement of the southern group of E. Greenland Eskimo.—Meddelelser om Grönland, xxv, 26, 1902.

**Estame.** A Calusa village on the s. w. coast of Florida, about 1570.—Fontaneda Memoir (*ca.* 1575), Smith trans., 19, 1854.

**Estancia** (a Spanish term with many meanings, but here probably signifying 'sojourning or staying place'). A Pima rancheria visited by Anza in 1774; situ-

ated 4 leagues s. of the mission of Saric, which was just s. of the Arizona boundary.
La Estancia.—Anza quoted by Bancroft, Ariz. and N. Mex., 389, 1889.

**Estatoee.** Two former Cherokee settlements, one on Tugaloo r. below the junction of Chattooga and Tallulah rs., in Oconee co., S. C., the other in the N. w. part of Pickens co. The former was generally known as Old Estatoee.
Estalaoe.—Royce in 18th Rep. B. A. E., pl. clxi, 1900. Estatoe.—Royce in 5th Rep. B. A. E., map, 1887. Estatoie.—Doc. of 1755 quoted by Royce, ibid., 143. Estotowe.—Bartram, Travels, 372, 1792 (on Tugaloo r.). Estotowe great.—Ibid. (town on another river).

**Estero.** An unidentified tribe mentioned by Langsdorff (Voy., II, 163, 1814) as inhabiting the coast of California.

**Estocoloco.** A Chumashan village on one of the northern Santa Barbara ids., Cal., in 1542.—Cabrillo, Narr. (1542) in Smith, Colec. Doc. Fla., 186, 1857.
Coloco.—Cabrillo, op. cit., 186. Estilococo.—Taylor in Cal. Farmer, Apr. 17, 1863.

**Estuc.** A former Chumashan village near San Marcos, in the vicinity of Santa Barbara, Cal.—Taylor in Cal. Farmer, Apr. 24, 1863.

**Estufa.** See *Kiva*.

**Etaa.** The Turtle clan of the Zuñi of New Mexico. It appears to be extinct.
Étáa-kwe.—Cushing in 13th Rep. B. A. E., 386, 1896 (*kwe*='people').

**Etaatthatunne** ('people at the cove'). A village of the Tututni of Oregon.
E'-ta-a'-tça ʠûn'nĕ.—Dorsey in Jour. Am. Folklore, III, 233, 1890 (Tututni name). E'-ta-a-t'ộut' ʠûnne'.—Ibid. (Naltunnetunne name).

**Etagottine** ('people in the air'). A Nahane band or division in the valleys of the Rocky mts. between the Esbataottine and the Tukkuthkutchin, lat. 66°, British America. Their totem is the lynx.
Dābo'-tenā.—Ross quoted by Dawson in Rep. Geol. Surv. Can. 1887–88, 200B, 1889. Daha-dinneh.—Dunn, Hist. Oregon, 79, 1844. Dahadinnès.—Richardson, Arct. Exped., I, 180, 1851. Dahâ-dtinné.—Richardson quoted by Petitot, Dict. Dènè-Dindjié, XX, 1876. Da-ha-dumies.—Hind, Expl. Exped., I, 159, 1860. Dahodinni.—Latham in Trans. Philol. Soc. Lond., 66, 1856. Daho-tena.—Bancroft, Native Races, I, 149, 1882. Dāho'-tenā'.—Dall in Cont. N. A. Ethnol., I, 33, 1877. Dawhoot-dinneh.—Franklin, Narr., II, 84, 1824. Ehta-Gottinè.—Petitot, Autour du lac des Esclaves, 362, 1891. Eta-gottiné.—Petitot, Dict. Dènè-Dindjié, XX, 1876 (trans. 'mountain people'). Éta-Gottinè.—Petitot, Autour du Grand lac des Esclaves, 301, 1891. Éta-Ottinè.—Petitot, Grand lac des Ours, 66, 1893 (trans. 'Rocky mountain people'). Gens de la montagne.—Petitot, Dict. Dènè-Dindjié, XX, 1876. Gens d' En-haut.—Petitot, Autour du Grand lac des Esclaves, 363, 1891. Gens des Montagnes-Rocheuses.—Petitot, Grand lac des Ours, 66, 1893. Gens en l'air.—Petitot, Autour, op. cit., 262. Hunters.—Prichard, Phys. Hist., V, 377, 1847. Mountain Indian.—Richardson, Arct. Exped., I 400, 1851. Naha-'tdinné.—Ibid. Noh'ha-i-è.—Ibid., II, 7, 1851 (so called by Kutchin). Sicanees.—Dall in Cont. N. A. Ethnol., I, 33, 1877 (sometimes so called by traders). Yéta-ottiné.—Petitot, Autour du Grand lac des Esclaves, 363. 1891 (trans. 'dwellers in the air').

**Etah.** An Ita Eskimo village at C. Ohlsen, on Smith sd., w. Greenland, lat. 78° 20'. See *Ita*.
Ahipa.—Markham in Trans. Ethnol. Soc. Lond., 9, 1866. Appah.—Kane, Arct. Explor., II, 212,

1856. Etah.—Bessels, Am. Nordpol. Exped., map, 1878. Igita.—Kroeber in Bull. Am. Mus. Nat. Hist., XII, 269, 1900.

**Etakmehu.** A division of Salish now on Port Madison res., Wash.
Etak-bush.—Mallett in Ind. Aff. Rep., 198, 1877. Etakmehu.—Boulet, letter, B. A. E., Mar. 22, 1886. Etakmurs.—Ind. Aff. Rep., 176, 1875.

**Etanie.** A former Seminole town in Putnam co., Fla., of which Checota Hajo was chief in 1823. There is now a town of Etoniah in the w. part of the county, and also a creek of the same name. See H. R. Ex. Doc. 74 (1823), 19th Cong., 1st sess., 27, 1826.

**Etarita.** A village of the Wolf clan of the Tionontati, where the Jesuits established the mission of St Jean; destroyed by the Iroquois in 1649.
Etarita.—Parkman, Jes., 403, 1883. Etharita.—Garreau (1648) quoted in Hist. Mag., 1st s., V, 263, 1861. Sainct Iean.—Jes. Rel. for 1640, 95, 1858. Saint Iean.—Jes. Rel. for 1648, 61, 1858. St. John's.—Shea, Cath. Miss., 192, 1855.

**Etatchogottine** ('hair people'). A division of the Kawchodinne dwelling N. and E. of Great Bear lake and on Great cape, Mackenzie Ter., Can. Their totem is a white wolf.
Ehta-tchô-Gottinè.—Petitot, Grand lac des Ours, 66, 1893.

**Etchaottine.** An Etchareottine division living w. and N. w. of Great Slave lake between Liard r. and the divide, along Black, Beaver, and Willow rs., British America. The Bistchonigottine and Krayiragottine are two of the divisions.
Dènè Étcha-Ottinè.—Petitot, Autour du lac des Esclaves, 301, 1891. Esclaves.—Ibid. Étcha-Ottinè.—Ibid. Gens du lac la Truite.—Petitot, Dict. Dènè-Dindjié, XX, 1876. Slaves proper.—Kennicott, MS. vocab., B. A. E.

**Etchareottine** ('people dwelling in the shelter'). An Athapascan tribe occupying the country w. of Great Slave lake and upper Mackenzie r. to the Rocky mts., including the lower Liard valley, British America. Their range extends from Hay r. to Ft Good Hope, and they once lived on the shores of L. Athabasca and in the forests stretching northward to Great Slave lake. They were a timid, pacific people, called 'the people sheltered by willows' by the Chipewyan, indicating a riparian fisher folk. Their Cree neighbors, who harried and plundered them and carried them off into bondage, called them Awokanak, 'slaves,' an epithet which in its French and English forms came to be the name under which they are best known. Early in the 18th century they were dispossessed of their home, rich in fish and game, and driven northward to Great Slave lake whither they were still followed by the Cree, known only as Enna, 'the enemy,' a name still mentioned with horror as far as Great Bear lake. On the islands where they took refuge a fresh carnage took place. The Thlingchadinneh and Kawchodinneh, who speak the same dialect with

them and bear a like reputation for timid-
ity, probably comprehended under the
name Awokanak by the Cree, began their
northerly migration at the same time,
probably under the same impulsion (Petitot, La Mer Glaciale, 292, 1887). Petitot
found among them a variety of physiognomy that he ascribed to a mixture of
races. Many of the males are circumcised
in infancy; those who are not are called
dogs, not opprobriously, but rather affec-
tionately. The bands or divisions are
Eleidlinottine, Etchaottine, Etcheridiegottine, Etechesottine, Klodesseottine,
and Desnedeyarelottine (Petitot, Autour
du lac des Esclaves, 363, 1891). In his
monograph on the Dènè-Dindjié, Petitot
restricted the term to the Etcheridigot-
tine, whom he distinguished from the
Slaves proper, making the latter a separate
tribe with divisions at Hay r., Great Slave
lake, Horn mts., the fork of the Mackenzie, and Ft Norman.

**A-cha′-o-tin-ne.**— Morgan, Consang. and Affin.,
289, 1871 (trans. 'people of the lowlands'). **Acheo-
tenne.**— Morgan in N. Am. Rev., 58, 1870. **A-che-
to-e-ten-ni.**— Ross, MS. notes on Tinne, B. A. E.
**Acheto-e-Tinne.**— Kennicott, MS. vocab., B. A. E.
**Acheto-tenà.**— Dall, Alaska, 429, 1870. **Achoto-e-
tenni.**— Pope, MS. Sicanny vocab., B. A. E., 1865.
**A-tsho-to-tï-na.**— Dawson in Rep. Geol. Surv. Can.,
1887–88, 200 B, 1889. **Awokànak.**— Petitot, La Mer
Glaciale, 293, 1887 ('slaves': Cree name). **Brushwood Indians.**— Franklin, Journ. to Polar Sea, II, 87,
1824. **Cheta-ut-tdinnè.**— Richardson, Arct. Exped.,
II, 7, 1851, **Danè Esclaves.**— Petitot, Autour du lac
des Esclaves, 289, 1891. **Danites Esclaves.**— Ibid.,
305. **Edchautawoot.**— Schoolcraft, Ind. Tribes,
II, 27, 1852. **Edchawtawhoot dinneh.**— Franklin,
Journ. to Polar Sea, 262, 1824. **Edchawtawhoot tinneh.**— Tanner, Narr., 293, 1830. **Edchawtawoot.**—
Gallatin in Trans. Am. Antiq. Soc., II, 19, 1836.
**Edshawtawoots.**— Schoolcraft, Ind. Tribes, III, 542,
1853. **Esclaves.**— Petitot, Autour du lac des Esclaves, 363, 1891. **Etchapè-ottiné.**— Petitot, Dict.
Dènè-Dindjié, xx, 1876. **Etsh-tawút-dinni.**— Latham in Trans. Philol. Soc. Lond., 69, 1856 (trans.
'thickwood-men'). **Slave Indians.**— Hooper,
Tents of Tuski, 303, 1853. **Slaves.**— Petitot, Autour
du lac des Esclaves, 363, 1891 (English form).
**Slavey.**— Ross, MS. notes on Tinne, B. A. E. (so
called by fur-traders).

**Etcheridiegottine** ('people of the rapids'). An Etchareottine division which
hunt along Liard r. and neighboring
regions to the border of the Etchaottine
country near old Ft Halkett, British
America. They have intermarried with
the Etchaottine and with the Tsattine in
the s., and have absorbed their manners
and customs and adopted their dialectal
forms to such a degree that they have
been frequently confounded with the one
tribe or the other.

**Bastard Beaver Indians.**— Ross in Smithson. Rep.
1866, 308, 1872. **Beaver.**— Franklin, Journ. to Polar
Sea, 262, 1824. **Erèttchi-ottinè.**— Dawson in
Rep. Geol. Surv. Can., 1887–88, 200B, 1889 ('people of the rapids': Kawchodinneh name). **Et-
tchéri-dié-Gottinè.**— Petitot, Autour du lac des
Esclaves, 363, 1891. **Liards Indians.**— Ross quoted
by Gibbs, MS., B. A. E. **Liard Slaves.**— Pope, MS.
Sicanny vocab., B. A. E, 1865. **Ndu-tchô-ottinnè.**—
Dawson, op. cit. **Sceth-tessesay-tinneh.**— Ross
quoted by Gibbs, MS., B. A. E. ('people of the
mountain river'). **Slave Indians of Ft. Liard.**— Ross,
MS. notes on Tinne, B. A. E. **Strong bow.**— Mac-

kenzie in Mass. Hist. Coll., 2d s., II, 43, 1814. **Tsilla-
ta-ut' tiné.**— Richardson quoted by Petitot, Dict.
Dènè-Dindjié, xx, 1876. **Tsilla-ta-ut'-tinné.**— Richardson, Arct. Exped., II, 6, 1851. **Tsillawadoot.**—
Schoolcraft, Ind. Tribes, II, 28, 1852. **Tsillaw-
awdoot.**— Gallatin in Trans. Am. Antiq. Soc., II,
19, 1836. **Tsillaw-awdút-dinni.**— Latham in Trans.
Philol. Soc. Lond., 69, 1856 (trans.: 'bush-wood-
men'). **Tsillawdawhoot-dinneh.**— Franklin, Journ.
to Polar Sea, II, 87, 1824. **Tsillawdawhoot Tinneh.**—
Bancroft, Nat. Races, I, 145, 1882.

**Etechesottine** ('horn mountain people'). A division of the Etchareottine
occupying the country between Great
Slave and La Martre lakes, Mackenzie
Ter., Can. Franklin erroneously considered them Thlingchadinneh.

**Deerhorn mountaineers.**— Franklin, Narr., II, 181,
1824. **Étè-ches-ottinè.**— Petitot in Bull. Soc. de
Geog. Paris, chart, 1875. **Gens de la montagne la
Corne.**— Petitot, Dict. Dènè-Dindjié, xx, 1876.
**Horn Mountain Indians.**— Franklin, Narr., 260, 1024.

**Etheneldeli** ('caribou-eaters'). An
Athapascan tribe living e. of L. Caribou
and L. Athabasca, in the barren grounds
which extend to Hudson bay (Petitot,
Dict. Dènè-Dindjié, xx, 1876). Franklin
(Journ. Polar Seas, II, 241, 1824) placed
them between Athabasca and Great
Slave lakes and Churchill r., whence
they resorted to Ft Chipewyan. Ross
(MS., B. A. E.) makes them a part of the
eastern Tinne, their habitat being to the
N. and E. of the head of L. Athabasca,
extending to the end of Great Slave lake.
Rocky r. separates them from the Tatsanottine. In the E. are the barren
grounds to which they resort every year
to hunt the caribou, which supplies
practically all their needs. They were
a part of the migrating Chipewyan who
descended from the Rocky mts. and
advanced eastward from Peace r. to dispute the Hudson bay region with the
Maskegon and Cree. One of their women
who was held in captivity by the Maskegon was astonished at the weapons, utensils, and clothing of European manufacture that she saw among her captors, who
told her that they made these articles
themselves. Finding at last that they
got them in barter for furs at Ft Prince
of Wales, she made her escape to the
English and told them of her own people
on Peace r. who held the choicest furs
cheap. The British traders, eager to extend their trade, sent her with a safe
conduct to her people, whom she persuaded to migrate to the barren grounds
near Hudson bay, where caribou were
abundant. They settled around Reindeer, Big, and North Indian lakes, and
were called the Northern Indians by the
English and the Mangeurs de Cariboux
by the Canadian French, while the neighboring tribes called them by the same
name that they had given to the English,
Men of the Stone House. Hearne saw
them in 1769 and Petitot found them
there still a century later, numbering
900. About 300 traded at Ft Fond du

Lac at the head of L. Athabasca. There were 248 enumerated at Fond du Lac in 1902, and 368 in 1904.

**Cariboo eaters.**—Ross in Smithson. Rep. 1866, 306, 1872. **Eastern Folks.**—Richardson, Arct. Exped., II, 5, 1851. **Ethen-eldèli.**—Petitot, Dict. Dènè-Dindjié, xx, 1876. **Éthen-eltèli.**—Petitot, Autour du lac des Esclaves, 363, 1891. **Ettine-tinney.**—Ross quoted by Gibbs, MS. notes, B. A. E. ('caribou people'). **Gens du Fort-de-pierre.**—Petitot, Autour du Grand lac des Esclaves, 363, 1891. **Mangeurs de cariboux.**—Petitot, Dict. Dène-Din-djié xx, 1876. **Michinipicpoets.**—Dobbs, Hudson Bay, 25, 1744 ('people of stone of the great lake': Cree name). **Northern Indians.**—Ibid, 17. **Rising Sun Folks.**—Richardson, Arct. Exped., II, 5, 1851. **Rising Sun men.**—Prichard, Phys. Hist., v, 376, 1847. **Sa-essau-dinneh.**—Schoolcraft, Ind. Tribes, II, 27, 1852 (trans. 'eastmen'). **Sah-se-sah tinney.**—Ross quoted by Gibbs, MS. notes, B. A. E. (trans. 'eastern people'). **Sa-i-sa-'dtinnè.**—Richardson, Arct. Exped., II, 5, 1851 ('people of the rising sun'). **Sawassaw-tinney.**—Keane in Stanford, Compend., 534, 1878. **Saw-cesaw-dinneh.**—Franklin quoted by Schoolcraft, Ind. Tribes, III, 542, 1853. **Saw-cessaw-dinnah.**—Schoolcraft, ibid., v, 172, 1855. **Saw-eessaw-dinneh.**—Franklin, Journ. Polar Sea, II, 241, 1824 (trans. 'Indians from the rising sun,' or 'eastern Indians).' **Sawessaw tinney.**—Keane in Stanford, Compend., 464, 1878. **See-issaw-dinni.**—Latham in Trans. Philol. Soc. Lond., 69, 1856 (trans. 'rising-sun-men'). **Thé-Ottiné.**—Petitot, MS. vocab., B. A. E., 1865 ('stone people'). **Thé-yé Ottiné.**—Petitot in Jour. Roy. Geog. Soc., 651, 1883. **Thè-yé-Ottiné.**—Petitot, Autour du lac des Es-claves, 363, 1891 ('people of the stone fort').

**Ethics and Morals.** It is difficult for a person knowing only one code of morals or manners to appreciate the customs of another who has been reared in the knowledge of a different code; hence it has been common for such a one to conclude that the other has no manners or no morals. Every community has rules adapted to its mode of life and surroundings, and such rules may be found more rigorously observed and demanding greater self-denial among savages than among civilized men. Notwithstanding the differences which necessarily exist between savage and civilized ethics, the two systems must evidently have much in common, for from the days of Columbus to the present travelers have given testimony of customs and manners of Indians, who were still in the barbarous or the savage stage, which displayed a regard for the happiness and well-being of others.

It is often difficult to tell how much of Indian manners and morals may have been derived from white people; but there are still some tribes which have held aloof from the intrusive race and have been little contaminated by it, and we have the testimony of early writers to guide us. The latter may be narrow in their judgment of Indian conduct while they are accurate in describing it.

To discuss the rise of ethics among primitive peoples would lead too far afield; but it is clear from all that is known of the natives of this continent that there existed among them standards of right conduct and character. Both from folklore and other sources we learn of conscience among the Indians and of their dread of its pangs. The Navaho designate conscience by a term which signifies "that standing within me which speaks to me." Abundant evidence might be adduced to show that Indians are often actuated by motives of pure benevolence and do good merely from a generous delight in the act.

Social ethics obtained among all the tribes, and public opinion was the power that compelled the most refractory to obedience. A system of ethics having once taken shape, the desire for the approval of one's associates and the wish to live at peace furnished sufficient incentive for compliance with the less onerous rules. But these motives were not sufficient in matters of graver import. Some tribes had executive bands, which had limited power to punish offenders in certain cases, such as violation of the orders of the tribal council; but among other tribes there was no established power to punish, nor were there even the rudiments of a court of justice. The pagan Indian is destitute of the faith in heaven and hell, which affords a strong incentive to moral life among many of our own people; but he has faith in good and bad luck, and frequently attaches different imaginary punishments to different offenses. Some regard various inanimate objects as the agents of these punishments. "May the cold freeze you!" "May the fire burn you!" "May the waters drown you!" are their imprecations.

When during the tribal hunt runners were sent out to seek a herd of buffalo, they had to give, on their return to camp, their report in the presence of sacred emblems in attestation of the truth of their statement. Scouts must report accurately or meet disgrace. The successful warrior must not claim more than his due; otherwise he would not be permitted to receive the badge of honors rightfully won. The common punishment for lying in many of the tribes was the burning of the liar's tent and property by tribal sanction. Not to keep a promise deliberately given was equivalent to lying. There are many instances of Indians keeping their word even at the risk of death.

Honesty was inculcated in the young and exacted in the tribe. In some communities the rule was limited in its operation to those within the tribe itself, but it was not uncommon to find its obligations extended to allies and to all friendly tribes. As war removed all ethical barriers, pillage was legitimate. The stealing of horses was a common object of war parties, but only from a hostile tribe. When a theft was committed the tribal authorities demanded restitution; the loss of the property taken, flogging, and a degree of social ostracism constituted the punishment of the thief. Instances could be multiplied to show the security of personal effects in a tribe. The Zuñi, for example, on leaving home, close and seal the door with clay, and it remains inviolate. The Nez Percés and many other tribes lean a pole across the door to indicate the absence of the family, and no one molests the dwelling.

Murder within the tribe was always punished, either by exile, by inexorable ostracism and the making of gifts to the kindred of the slain, or by suffering the murderer to become the lawful victim of their vengeance.

Truth, honesty, and the safeguarding of human life were everywhere recognized as essential to the peace and prosperity of a tribe, and social customs enforced their observance; the community could not otherwise keep together, much less hold its own against enemies, for except where tribes were allies, or bound by some friendly tie, they were mutual enemies. An unaccredited stranger was always presumably an enemy.

Adultery was punished. The manner of punishment varied among the tribes, the choice being frequently left to the aggrieved party. Among the Apache it was the common custom to disfigure an erring woman by cutting off her nose.

The care of one's family was regarded as a social duty and was generally observed. This duty sometimes extended to one's relations.

While the young were everywhere taught to show respect to their elders, and while years and experience were supposed to bring wisdom, yet there were tribes among which it was the custom to abandon or to put to death the very old. Where this custom prevailed the conditions of life were generally hard, and the young and active found it difficult to secure food for themselves and their children. As the aged could not take care of themselves, and were an encumbrance to travel, they acquiesced in their fate as a measure of prudence and economy, dying in order that the young might live and the tribe maintain its existence.

The cruel punishment of witchcraft everywhere among the tribes had its ethical side. The witch or wizard was believed to bring sickness or death to members of the community; hence for their security the sorcerer must be put to death. The custom was due to a lack of knowledge of the causes of disease and to mistaken ethics.    (A. C. F.   W. M.)

**Etipsikya** (the name of a shrub). A traditional village of the Squash people of the Hopi; situated on the s. side of Rio Colorado Chiquito, on the brink of a canyon, not far from the point where the river is crossed by the Santa Fé Pac. R. R., Arizona.—Stephen and Mindeleff in 8th Rep. B. A. E., 26, 1891.

**Etiquette.** The interior of most native dwellings was without complete partitions, yet each member of the family had a distinct space, which was as inviolable as a separate apartment inclosed by walls. In this space the personal articles of the occupant were stored in packs and baskets, and here his bed was spread at night. Children played together in their own spaces and ran in and out of that belonging to the mother, but they were forbidden to intrude elsewhere and were never allowed to meddle with anyone's possessions. When more than one family occupied a dwelling, as the earth lodge, the long bark house, or the large wooden structure of the N. W., every family had its well-known limits, within which each member had a place. A space was generally set apart for guests, to which, on entering, a visitor made his way. Among the Plains tribes this place was at the back part of the dwelling, facing the entrance, and the visitor when entering a lodge and going to this place must not pass between his host and the fire. Among many tribes the place of honor was at the w., facing the entrance. If he was a familiar friend, greetings were at once exchanged, but if he had come on a formal mission, he entered in silence, which was unbroken for some little time after he was seated. On such occasions conversation was opened by reference to trivial matters, the serious purpose of the visit not being mentioned until considerable time had elapsed. When a delegation was received, only the older men of the party or of the tribe spoke; the younger members kept silent unless called on to say something. Among all the tribes haste was a mark of ill breeding, particularly during official or ceremonial proceedings. No visitor could leave the dwelling of his host without some parting words to show that his visit was at an end.

Among many tribes etiquette required that when speaking to a person a term of relationship rather than the personal name should be used. An elderly man or woman was usually addressed as grandfather or grandmother, and a similar title was also applied to a man of distinction. Uncle or aunt might be used for persons of about the same age as the speaker, but to a younger man or woman the term of address would signify younger brother or sister. A friendly visitor from outside the tribe was addressed by a term meaning "friend." A member of the tribe, although of a different clan or gens, was spoken to by a term of relationship; among the Iroquois, for example, one of the opposite phratry was greeted as "my father's clansman," or "my cousin."

When the bearer of an invitation entered a lodge, the person invited did not respond if a relative or friend was present, who would accept for him, saying, "Your uncle (or aunt) has heard." Among the Hopi, in entering a kiva, according to Dr Fewkes, one must ask, "Am I welcome?" before his left foot leaves the lowest rung of the ladder. He must always approach the altar on the right and leave it on the left. Among the Zuñi a person, whether friend or stranger, on appearing at a doorway is invited to enter and sit; if at meal time, and often at other times, he is offered food.

Among a number of tribes etiquette required that there should be no direct speech between a woman and her son-in-law, and in some instances a similar restriction was placed on a woman addressing her father-in-law. In many tribes also the names of the dead were not likely to be mentioned, and with some Indians, for a space of time, a word was substituted for the name of a deceased person, especially if the latter were prominent. In some tribes men and women used different forms of speech, and the distinction was carefully observed. A conventional tone was observed by men and women on formal occasions which differed from that employed in everyday life.

Etiquette between the sexes demanded that the man should precede the woman while walking or in entering a lodge "to make the way safe for her." Familiar conversation could take place only between relatives; reserve characterized the general behavior of men and women toward each other.

Respect must be shown to elders in both speech and behavior. No one could be interrupted when speaking or forced to speak when inclined to be silent, nor could personal questions be asked or private matters mentioned. During certain ceremonies no one may speak above a whisper. If it was necessary to pass between a person and the fire permission must be asked, and if one brushed against another, or trod upon his foot, an apology must be made. At meal time, if one could not eat all that had been put upon his dish, he must excuse himself to show that it was through no dislike of the food, and when he had finished he must not push away his dish but return it to the woman, speaking a term of relationship, as mother, aunt, wife, which was equivalent to thanks. Among some tribes, if a cooking vessel had been borrowed, it must be returned with a portion of what had been cooked in it to show the owner the use that had been made of the utensil, and also, in courtesy, to share the food.

There was an etiquette in standing and sitting that was carefully observed by the women. They stood with the feet straight and close together, and if the hands were free, the arms hung down, a little toward the front, the fingers extended and the palms lightly pressed against the dress. Women sat with both feet under them, turned to one side. Men usually sat cross-legged.

The training of children in tribal etiquette and grammatical speech began at an early age, and the strict observance of etiquette and the correct use of language indicated the rank and standing of a man's family. Class distinctions were everywhere more or less observed. On the N. Pacific coast the difference between high caste and low caste was strongly marked. Certain lines of conduct, such as being a too frequent guest, were denounced as of low caste. So, too, among the Haida, it was of low caste to lean backward; one must sit on the forward part of the seat in an alert attitude to observe good form. Lolling in company was considered a mark of bad manners among the tribes; and among the Hopi one would not sit with legs extended during a ceremony. Smoking, whether social or ceremonial, had its etiquette; much form was used in exchanging smoking materials and in passing the pipe in smoking and in returning it. In certain societies, when a feast was served, particular parts of the animal belonged by etiquette to the noted warriors present, and these were presented by the server with ceremonial speech and movements. Among some tribes when a feast was given a pinch of each kind of food was sacrificed in the fire before eating. Ceremonial visitors usually made their approach known according to the local custom. Among some of the Plains tribes the visitors dispatched a runner bearing a little bunch of tobacco to apprise their host of their intended visit; should their coming prove to be ill timed, the tobacco could be returned with an accompanying gift, and the visit would be postponed without any hard feeling. There was much and varied detail in the etiquette of family life, social gatherings, and the ceremonies of the various tribes living N. of Mexico. See *Child life, Ethics and Morals, Hospitality, Salutation.*                    (A. C. F.)

**Etishoka** (*E-tish-sho'-ka*, 'hill people'). An Hidatsa band.—Morgan, Anc. Soc., 159, 1877.

**Etiwaw** (Catawba: 'pine tree'). A small tribe, now extinct, forming part of the Cusabo group and living about Ashley and Cooper rs., Berkeley co., S. C., extending E. to the present Monk's Corner, where their hunting grounds bordered the Sewee country. The Santee and Congaree were above them. They were never prominent historically, and in Jan., 1715, had a single village with 240 inhabitants (Rivers, Early Hist. S. C., 94, 1874). Nothing is heard of them after the Yamasi war in 1715, until 1751, when they are mentioned as one of the small tribes for which the South Carolina government made peace with the Iroquois. From this time they seem to have become lost to history. Their name is preserved in Eutaw Springs, and in Pine Tree, another name for Camden, S. C.—Mooney, Siouan Tribes of the East, Bull. B. A. E., 1894.

**Ashley River Indians.**—Williamson, N. C., I, 201, 1812. **Etewaus.**—Glen (1751) in N. Y. Doc. Col. Hist., VI, 721, 1855. **Etiwans.**—Rivers, Hist. S. C., 37, 1856. **Ittawans.**—Ibid.

**Etleuk.** A Squawmish village community on the right bank of Squawmisht r., w. British Columbia.

**Ela-a-who.**—Brit. Adm. Chart, No. 1917. **Etlē′uq.**—Hill-Tout in Rep. Brit. A. A. S., 474, 1900.

**Etnataek** (perhaps *ă'tanataheg i*, 'where the fight, battle, or clubbing took place.'—W. J.). Given as the name of an old fortification said to have stood formerly near the Kickapoo village on Sangamon r., Ill. It is supposed to have been built by the Kickapoo and Foxes, who were defeated there by the combined forces of the Ottawa, Potawatomi, and Chippewa.—Long, Exped., I, 173, 1823.

**Etoluk.** An Alaskan Eskimo village in the Kuskokwim district; pop. 25 in 1890.

**Etohlugamiut.**—11th Census, Alaska, 164, 1893.

**Etotulga.** A former Seminole town, 10 m. E. of the old Mickasuky town, in Florida.—H. R. Ex. Doc. 74 (1823), 19th Cong., 1st sess., 26, 1826.

**Etowah** (properly *I'tăwă'*, of unknown meaning). A Cherokee settlement that existed, until the removal of 1838, on Etowah r., about the present Hightower (a corruption of *I'tăwă'*), in Forsyth co., Ga. Another settlement of the same name may have been on Hightower cr. of Hiwassee r., in Towns co., Ga.—Mooney in 19th Rep. B. A. E., 522, 1900.

**Hightower.**—Doc. of 1799 quoted by Royce in 5th Rep. B. A. E., 144, 1887. **I'tăwă'.**—Mooney, op. cit. (Cherokee name.)

**Etowah mound.** A large artificial mound on the N. bank of Etowah r., 3 m. s. E. of Cartersville, Bartow co., Ga. With 4 or 5 smaller mounds it is on a level bottom in a bend of the stream, the immediate area, covering about 56 acres, flanked on one side by an artificial ditch which extends in a semicircle from a point on the river above to the river below. The large mound, which is a quadrilateral truncated pyramid, 61 ft. high, has a broad roadway ascending the s. side to within 18 or 20 ft. of the top, and was formerly provided with steps made with crossbeams imbedded in the earth, remains of which were visible as late as 1885. The diameters of the base are respectively 380 and 330 ft, and of the top 170 and 176 ft. The area of the base is a little less than 3 acres, and of the top about seven-tenths of an acre. The solid contents of the mound, including the roadway, are about 4,300,000 cu. ft. On the E. side there is a narrow extension from the summit to the base, which appears to have been a sort of refuse slide. The village situated here was possibly the Guaxule of De Soto's chroniclers (1540), and the large mound the one mentioned by Garcilasso de la Vega (Florida, lib. III, cap. xx, 139, 1723), although Mooney (19th Rep. B. A. E., 520, 1900) is of the opinion that Guaxule was probably about at Nacoochee mound in White co.

The earliest description of the Etowah mound in modern times is by Cornelius (Silliman's Am. Jour. Sci. and Art., 1st s., I, 322, 1818). C. C. Jones (Antiq. So. Ind., 136, 1873)

ETOWAH MOUND, GEORGIA.   (HEIGHT, 61 FT; GREATEST LENGTH OF BASE, 380 FT)

and Whittlesey (Smithson. Rep., 624, 1881) also describe and illustrate it. A careful survey of the large mound and group, and a partial exploration of the smaller mounds, were made by the Bureau of American Ethnology and an account thereof was published (5th Rep., 95–105, 1887; 12th Rep., 292, 1894). Cornelius states that "the Cherokees in their late war with the Creeks secured its [the large mound's] summit by pickets and occupied it as a place of protection for hundreds of their women and children." The smallest of the 3 larger mounds, the surrounding space, and 1 or 2 small tumuli have been explored. Parts of 3 or 4 stone images, copper plates with stamped figures bearing some resemblance to Mexican designs, and other copper plates with pieces attached by rivets have been found. Other articles, such as pipes, earthenware, copper celts, stone plates, etc., have also been unearthed. For further information see the works above cited; also Squier and Davis, Ancient Monuments, 1852; Thomas (1) Burial Mounds of the Northern Section,

5th Rep. B. A. E., 1887, (2) Catalogue of Prehistoric Works, Bull. B. A. E., 45, 1891; Holmes in Science, III, 437, 1884.    (C. T.)

**Etsekin.** A winter village of the Kwakiutl proper on Havannah channel, w. coast of British Columbia.

Et-se-kin.—Boas in Bull. Am. Geog. Soc., 229, 1887. Etsi-kin.—Dawson in Trans. Roy. Soc. Can., sec. II, 65, 1887.

**Etskainah** (*Ĕts-kai'-nah*, 'horns'). A society of the Ikunuhkahtsi, or All Comrades, among the Siksika; it is obsolete among the southern Piegan, but still exists with the northern Piegan and the Kainah. It is regarded as having originated with the latter and extended to the other divisions. The Sinopah (Kit-fox) society among the southern Piegan is practically identical with it. The present Etskainah society is said to have taken on some of the functions of the Stumiks (Bulls), now extinct. The members carry a crooked staff and are supposed to have magical powers (Wissler, inf'n, 1906). See Grinnell, Blackfoot Lodge Tales, 221, 1892.

**Etsowish - simmegee - itshin** ('grizzly-bear standing'). A Kalispel chief in the first half of the 19th century, baptized by Father De Smet about 1842 or 1843 under the name Loyola, by which name he was known to the whites. His early history is not known, but he was distinguished in his later years for his firm adherence to the Roman Catholic religion and his zealous efforts to lead his people to observe the teachings of the missionaries and the services and ordinances of the church. Although strict in repressing disorder, Loyola was highly regarded by his people, who regarded him as a father. He died Apr. 6, 1854, and was succeeded by Victor Alamiken, distinct from Victor of the Flathead (Salish) tribe of about the same period.    (C. T.)

**Ettchaottine** ('people who act contrarily'). A Nahane tribe of which one division lives on Francis lake, British Columbia, another in the neighborhood of old Ft Halkett (Hardisty in Smithson. Rep. 1866, 311, 1872). Their name came from their warlike habits. Ross (MS., B. A. E.) gave their pop. in 1858 as 435.

Bad-people.—Morice, Notes on W. Dénés, 16, 1893. 'Dtcha-ta-'uttinnnè.—Richardson, Arct. Exped., II, 6, 1851. Ettcha-ottiné.—Petitot, Dict. Dènè-Dindjié, xx, 1876 ('people who act contrarily'). Mauvais Monde.—Latham in Trans. Philol. Soc. Lond., 66, 1856. Netsilley.—Richardson, Arct. Exped., I, 401, 1851. Slávè Indians.—Dall, Alaska, 429, 1870. Wild Nation.—Richardson, op. cit.

**Etuck Chukke** ('blue wood'). A former Choctaw town near East Abeika, Kemper co., Miss.—Romans, Fla., 309, 1775.

**Eudeve.** A division of the Opata of Sonora, Mexico, inhabiting the divide of the Rio Sonora and Rio San Miguel, and extending southward from about lat. 30°

30′ to the villages of Matape and Nacori on the Rio Matape in lat. 29°, exclusive of Ures, which for the greater part was a Nevome pueblo, although containing some Opata. The language of the Eudeve—also called Heve, Dohme, etc.—is a dialect of the Opata. Like the other Opata, they have almost lost their former customs, religion, and habits, and have become Mexicanized. Population of the division unknown. The villages and settlements that have been mentioned are: Alamos, Bacanora, Batuco, Cucurpe, Matape, Nacori, Opodepe, Robesco, Saracachi, Sahuaripa,* Soyopa,* Tepuspe, Toape,* and Tonichi.* Those marked with an asterisk were settled in part by Nevome.    (F. W. H.)

Batucos.—Orozco y Berra, Geog., 344, 1864 (used here as a synonym of the language). Cudeves.—Cancio (1768) in Doc. Hist. Mex., 4th s., II, 270, 1856 (misprint). Dohema.—Pimentel, Lenguas de Mex., II, 153, 1865 (corruption of *dohme*, 'man,' 'pueblo,' 'nation'). Dohme.—Orozco y Berra, op. cit. Egues.—Rivera, Diario, leg. 1352, 1736 (doubtless identical, although mentioned as distinct from Eudeve at leg. 1514). Equi.—Orozco y Berra, op. cit. Eudebe.—Ibid., 63. Eudeva.—Ibid. Eudeve.—Rivera, op. cit., leg. 1514. Hegue.—Orozco y Berra, op. cit. Hequi.—Ibid., 63. Heve.—Ibid., 64.

**Eufaula.** A former Upper Creek town on Eufaula cr., 5 or 6 m. s. of the present town of Talladega, Ala.

Eufala's.—Campbell (1836) in H. R. Doc. 274, 25th Cong., 2d sess., 20, 1838. Eufalee.—Flint, Ind. Wars, 202, 1833. Eufaulahatche.—Pickett, Hist. Ala., II, 341, 1851. Eufaula Old Town.—Royce in 18th Rep. B. A. E., pl. cviii, 1899. Eu-fau-lau-hat-che.—Hawkins (1799), Sketch, 42, 1848. Eufaulies.—Finnelson (1792) in Am. State Pap., Ind. Aff., I, 289, 1832. Euphalau.—Alcedo, Dic. Geog., II, 113, 1787. Euphalees.—U. S. Ind. Treat. (1797), 70, 1837. Huphale.—Adair, Am. Inds., 278, 1775. Little Eufauly.—Finnelson (1792) in Am. State Pap., Ind. Aff., I, 289, 1832. Little Ufala.—Swan in Schoolcraft, Ind. Tribes, V, 262, 1855. Ufaula.—H. R. Doc. 274, 25th Cong., 2d sess., 142, 1838. Ufauley.—Schoolcraft, Ind. Tribes, VI, 371, 1857. Uphaulie towns.—Robertson (1793) in Am. State Pap., Ind. Aff., I, 467, 1832. Upper Eufalla.—U. S. Ind. Treat. (1827), 420, 1837. Upper Euphaules.—Ibid. (1797), 68. Upper Ufale.—Bartram, Travels, 462, 1791. Usauleys.—Cherokee council (1792) in Am. State Pap., Ind. Aff., I, 273, 1832. Usawla.—H. R. Ex. Doc. 276, 24th Cong., 140, 1836. Usawles.—Harris, Voy. and Trav., II, 385, 1705. Yofale.—Jefferys, French Dom. Am., I, 134, map, 1761. Yofate.—Jefferys, Am. Atlas, 7, 1776.

**Eufaula.** A former Upper Creek town on the w. bank of Tallapoosa r., near the site of the present Dadeville, Tallapoosa co., Ala.

Big Ufala.—Swan in Schoolcraft, Ind. Tribes, V, 262, 1855. Eufaula.—Royce in 18th Rep. B. A. E., pl. cviii, 1899. Eu-fau-lau. — Hawkins (1799), Sketch, 48, 66, 1848.

**Eufaula.** A former Lower Creek town on the E. bank of Chattahoochee r., 15 m. below Sawokli, Quitman co., Ga. In 1799 a portion of its inhabitants settled at several points downstream as far as the mouth of Flint r.; the settlements here made also became known as Eufaula.

Eufantees.—Gatschet, Creek Migr. Leg., II, 26, 1888. Eufath.—Seagrove (1792) in Am. State Pap., Ind. Aff., I, 311, 1832. Eufaule.—Drake, Bk. Inds., bk. 4, 29, 1848. Eufollahs.—Schoolcraft, Ind. Tribes,

VI, 469, 1857. **Eufowlas.**—Woodward, Reminis., 38, 1859. **Lower Enfalla.**—Robin, Voy., II, map, 1807. **Lower Enfula.**—Jesup (1836) in H. R. Doc. 78, 25th Cong., 2d sess., 48, 1838 (misprint). **Lower Ufale.**—Bartram, Trav., 461, 1791. **Nafoli.**—Bartram, Voy., Benoist trans., I, map, 1799. **Ufalees.**—Holmes (1799) in Am. State Pap., Ind. Aff., I, 386, 1832. **Ufallahs.**—Morse, Rep. to Sec. War, 364, 1822. **Ufallays.**—Drake, Bk. Inds., bk. 4, 94, 1848. **Ufawlas.**—McCall, Hist. Georgia, I, 363, 1811. **Ufewles.**—Barnard (1793) in Am. State Pap., Ind. Aff., I, 395, 1832. **Youfalloo.**—H. R. Ex. Doc. 276, 24th Cong., 300, 1836. **Yufala.**—Romans, Florida, I, 280, 1775. **Yufalis.**—Gatschet, Creek Migr. Leg., II, 26, 1888.

**Eufaula.** A former Lower Creek town on the w. bank of Chattahoochee r., in Henry co., Ala.
**Eufala Town.**—Royce in 18th Rep. B. A. E., pl. cviii, 1899.

**Eufaula.** A town of the Creek Nation on the s. side of Deep fork of Canadian r., near Ocmulgee, Ind. T.
**Yufala hupáyi.**—Gatschet, Creek Migr. Leg, I, 122, 1884.

**Eufaula.** Formerly a town, now a city, of the Creek Nation, near the mouth of North fork of Canadian r., on the Mo., Kans. and Tex. R. R., Ind. T.
**Yufála.**—Gatschet, Creek Migr. Leg., II, 185, 1888.

**Eulachon.** One of the names of the candle-fish (*Thaleichthys pacificus*), of the family *Salmonidæ*, closely related to the smelt: from the name of this fish in one of the Chinookan dialects. It is found in the waters of the N. Pacific coast of America and is much used by the Indians of that region for food and the production of grease and oil. Other forms (Christian Union, Mar. 22, 1871) are *hoolikan* and *oolichan*, and Irving (Astoria, II) cites the form *uthlecan*. (A. F. C.)

**Eushtat** (*E'-ushtat*). The principal settlement of the Klamath on lower Williamson r., near lower Klamath lake, Klamath co., Oreg.—Gatschet in Cont. N. A. Ethnol., II, pt. 2, 32, 1890.

**Evea.** A Comanche chief, prominent between 1772 and 1778. In June, 1772, he went to San Antonio Béxar and ratified a treaty with the governor of Texas. Gov. Ripperdá, referring to this event in a letter of July 4, 1772, called him Evea, "capitan" of the Comanche nation, and in a letter written the next day he referred to him as "Pubea ó Evea, principal capitan" of that tribe. He was apparently still chief in 1778, for Mezières tells of meeting in Texas a party of Comanche under the son of Evea, a chief held in high estimation among his people. (H. E. B.)

**Evil Peace.** A village seen by De Soto's army in 1539, between Utinama and Cholupaha, Fla.—Gentl. of Elvas (1557) in French, Hist. Coll. La., II, 130, 1850.

**Ewawoos.** A Cowichan tribe whose town was Skeltem, 2 m. above Hope, Fraser r., Brit. Col.; pop. 27 in 1904.
**Ewahoos.**—Can. Ind. Aff., 309, 1879. **Ewa-woos.**—Ibid., 1901, pt. 2, 158. **Ēwā'wus.**—Boas, MS., B. A. E., 1891.

**Exchange, media of.** Before the arrival of Europeans intertribal trade had resulted almost everywhere in America in the adoption of certain standards of value of which the most important were shell beads and skins. The shell currency of the Atlantic coast consisted of small white and black or purplish beads cut from the valves of quahog and other shells and familiarly known as wampum, q. v. These were very convenient, as they could be strung together in quantities and carried any distance for purposes of trade, in this respect having a decided advantage over skins. In exchange two white beads were equivalent to one black one. During the early colonial period wampum was almost the only currency among white people as well; but inferior, poorly finished kinds, made not only out of shell, but of stone, bone, glass, horn, and even wood, were soon introduced, and in spite of all attempted regulation the value of wampum dropped continually until in 1661 it was declared to be legal tender no longer in Massachusetts, and a year or two later the same fate overtook it in the other New England colonies. In New York it appears to have held on longer, its latest recorded use as currency being in 1693. Holm says, speaking of the Delawares of New Jersey: "In trade they measure those strings [of wampum] by their length," each fathom of them being worth 5 Dutch guilders, reckoning 4 beads for every stiver. "The brown beads are more valued than the others and fetch a higher price; a white bead is of the value of a piece of copper money, but a brown one is worth a piece of silver." Holm quotes another authority, however, to the effect that a white bead was worth one stiver and a black bead two. The latter says also that "their manner of measuring the strings is by the length of their thumbs; from the end of the nail to the first joint makes 6 beads."

On the Pacific coast between S. E. Alaska and N. California shell currency of another kind was employed. This was made from the *Dentalium pretiosum* (money tooth-shell), a slender univalve found on the w. coasts of Vancouver and Queen Charlotte ids. In the Chinook jargon it was called *hiaqua*. The principal place where it was obtained is said to have been the territory of a Nootka tribe, the Ehatisaht, in Esperanza inlet, w. coast of Vancouver id., but it was collected as far N. as Quatsino inlet. The method of procuring it is described in one of the earliest accounts of this region, the Narrative of John Jewitt. According to Boas, a block of cedar was split up at one end so that it formed a kind of brush which opened when pushed down into the water and closed when pulled up, thus entangling the shells. These shells were valued in proportion to their individual lengths. In w. Washington the standard of value was 40 to the fathom, and the value fell off rapidly above that number, while very long single shells were worth more than a dollar. A fathom of 40 was formerly equivalent to a slave, according to Gibbs, and in his time would bring $5. In California and on the plateaus farther N. the shells had incised designs. Among the Hupa of California they are decorated by being wrapped spirally with fish skin or snake skin, and in addition usually bear a tuft of red feathers, probably from the woodpecker's crest. The following further description of these is given by Goddard:

"The individual shells are measured and their value determined by the creases on the left hand. The longest known shells were about 2½ in. long. One of them would reach from the crease of the last joint of the little finger to the crease on the palm opposite the knuckle joint of the same finger. The value of such a piece in early days was about $5. Shells of this length were called diñket. The next smaller shells were called kiketúkútxoi, and measured about 2⅜ in. They were worth about $1.50 each. A shell about 1⅛ in. long was called tcwōlahit. Their value was from 25 to 50 cents. Shells smaller than these were not rated as money and had no decoration. The length of the shells smaller than the first mentioned was determined by applying them to the creases of the middle and other fingers of the left hand.

"This money was strung on strings which reached from the thumb nail to the point of the shoulder. Eleven of the largest size filled such a string and was therefore called mōanala. Twelve shells of the next smaller size composed a string and were called mōananax. Thirteen shells are called mōanatak, and 14 of the smallest shells, called mōanadiñk, was the largest number placed on a string. These strings are approximately 25 in. long. This, as it appears, was the least common multiple of the individual standard lengths.

"Since all hands and arms are not of the same length, it was necessary for the man, when he reached his maturity, to establish the values of the creases on his hand by comparison with money of known length as measured by someone else. He also had a set of lines tattooed on the inside of the left forearm. These lines indicated the length of 5 shells of the several standards. The measures were subdivided, there being lines of mōanala long and mōanala short, and so on. This was the principal method of

estimating the money. The first 5 on the string were measured by holding the tip of the first shell at the thumb nail and drawing the string along the arm and noting the tattooed mark reached by the butt of the fifth shell. In like manner the last and intermediate sets of 5 were measured." This shell money was carried in special elk-horn boxes.

Among the coast tribes N. of Vancouver id., dentalia were not so much in vogue, but were used for ornamental purposes and in trade with the interior Indians. The standard of value among the Kutchakutchin and neighboring tribes consisted of lines of beads 7 ft long joined together at the distance of a foot, and called naki eik ('bead clothing'). The whole naki eik, according to Jones, "is equal to 24 made beaver, and one of the lines is one or more beaver skins, according to the value of the beads."

In central and s. California circular, disk-shaped shell beads were used. Among the Maidu they were counted instead of being measured in strings, although for each 10 beads a stick was laid down as a counter (Dixon). According to Powers the Miwok rated shell beads at $5 a yard, while the Yokuts valued a string reaching from the point of the middle finger to the elbow at 25 cents. These latter sometimes strung with them a section of bone very white and polished, about 2½ in. long, which they rated at 12½ cents. The Miwok strung together other shells which Powers believed to be olivella, valuing them at $1 a yard, as well as fancy marine shells, rated from $3 to $10 or $15 a yard, according to their beauty.

So far inland were these shells carried that dentalia were found among the Dakota, and it is probable that shells from both the Atlantic and the Pacific reached the same tribes.

A more usual standard of value among interior people, however, was the pelt, especially the skin of the beaver. Even on the Atlantic coast it was used from the very earliest times side by side with wampum, and in 1613 the statement is made that it was the basis of all trade between the French of Canada and the Indians. In 1670 (Margry, Déc., I, 164, 1878) it is learned that a beaver skin was worth a fathom of tobacco, a fourth of a pound of powder, 6 knives, or a portion of little blue beads. According to Hunter it was also the standard of value among the Osage, Kansa, Oto, Omaha, and their neighbors. He adds that 2 good otter skins, from 10 to 12 raccoon, or 4 or 5 wildcat skins were valued at one beaver skin. Here this standard passed out very rapidly with the coming of white men; but in the great fur regions of Canada it remained the basis of value first between French and Indians, and afterward between English and Indians. Up to the present time everything is valued in "skins," meaning beaver skins, but the term has come to have a fixed value of 50 cents in Canadian money.

In former days, before the arrival of the Russians, the unit of value among the Eskimo of the lower Yukon was a full grown land-otter skin, to which was equivalent the skin of the large hair seal. This has now given place to the beaver; and all other skins, furs, and articles of trade are sold as "a skin" and multiples and fractions of "a skin." "In addition to this," says Nelson, "certain small, untanned skins, used for making fur coats or blouses, are tied in lots sufficient to make a coat, and are sold in this way. It requires 4 skins of reindeer fawns, or 40 skins of Parry's marmot or of the muskrat for a coat, and these sets are known by terms designating these bunches." The pelt of a wolf or wolverene is worth several "skins" in trade, while a number of pelts of muskrats or Parry's marmot are required to make the value of "a skin."

Among the northern tribes in the N. Pacific coast area, where dentalia were not so much valued, elk and moose skins seem formerly to have constituted one of the standards of value, although the skins of other animals were no doubt used to some extent as well. In later times all these were replaced by blankets introduced by the Hudson's Bay Company, which were distinguished by points or marks on the edge, woven into their texture, the best being 4-point, the smallest and poorest 1-point. The acknowledged unit of value, at least among the Haida, was a single 2½-point blanket, worth in 1880 a little more than $1.50, but on the coast farther s. it is now rated at about 50 cents. Everything was referred to this unit, according to Dawson, even a large 4-point blanket being said to be worth so many "blankets."

Another standard universal in this region was slaves, and perhaps the remarkable copper plates should also be mentioned, though strictly speaking they were legal tender of varying value which had to be fixed by means of some other standard, such as blankets or slaves. Pieces of cedar bark prepared for roofing sometimes appear as units of value also.

By the interior Salish of British Columbia Indian hemp bark was put up in bundles about 2 ft long and 2 in. in diameter, and tied at both ends, and 6 of these bundles constituted a "package," while dried salmon was generally sold by the "stick," each stick numbering 100 fish (Teit).

In addition to their dentalia the Hupa and the peoples of Klamath r., in N. California, use scalps of woodpeckers. They employ those of both the pileated and smaller woodpecker for this purpose, the present exchange values of which are now $1 and 10 cents, respectively (Goddard). According to Bourke, eagle feathers were an article of commerce with a determinate value among the Pueblo Indians. The Mandan standards were skin corn measures of different dimensions which were kept in the council lodge; and the Arikara measure was a stone mortar. In later years an important unit of value on the great plains was the horse.

The standards among the Hopi and probably other Pueblo tribes were a kind of basket tray, a fixed variety of blue blanket, and turquoise and shell beads.

On the Pacific coast canoes were valued according to the length in fathoms, but among the Hupa, where the length is constant, by their height and breadth, the natives providing themselves with marks on their legs for this particular purpose. Many other long articles seem to have been appraised in the same manner.

Although including the more prominent standards, the foregoing list by no means exhausts their number, for where articles of various kinds were continually bartered, numerous standards of a more or less evanescent nature arose. For a list of comparative valuations in one tribe see Teit, cited below, p. 260. See *Beadwork, Commerce, Fur-trade, Horses, Measurements, Shellwork, Wampum.*

Consult Bourke, Snake Dance of the Moquis, 1885; Chittenden, Am. Fur Trade, 1902; Dawson, Report on Queen Charlotte Ids., Geol. Surv. of Can., 1880; Dixon in Bull. Am. Mus. Nat. Hist., XVII, pt. 3, 1905; Gibbs in Cont. N. A. Ethnol., I, 1877; Goddard in Univ. Cal. Publ., Am. Archæol. and Ethnol., 1903; Hardesty in Smithson. Rep. 1866, 1872; Holm, Descr. New Sweden, 1834; Holmes in 2d Rep. B. A. E., 1883; Hunter, Captivity, 1823; Jewitt, Narrative, 1815; Jones in Smithson. Rep. 1866, 1872; Loskiel, Missions, 1794; Nelson in 18th Rep. B. A. E., 1899; Powers in Cont. N. A. Ethnol., III, 1877; Teit, Thompson Indians, Mem. Am. Mus. Nat. Hist., II, 1900.                                   (J. R. S.)

**Eyak.** An Ugalakmiut Eskimo village at the entrance of Prince William sd., Alaska; pop. 94 in 1890, 222 in 1900. Near by is a cannery called Odiak, where 273 people live.

Eyak.—Baker, Geog. Dict. Alaska, 1901. Hyacks.—Halleck in Rep. Sec. of War. I, pt. 1, 1869 (probably identical). Ikhiak.—Petroff, 10th Census, Alaska, 29, 1884. Odiak.—Moser (1899), quoted by Baker, op. cit.

**Eyeish.** A tribe of the Caddo confederacy which spoke a dialect, now practically extinct, very different from the dialects of the other tribes; hence it is probable they were a part of an older confederacy which was incorporated in the Caddo when the latter became dominant. The early home of the tribe was on Eyeish cr. between the Sabine and Neches rs. of Texas. Moscoso led his troops through their country in 1542, encountering herds of buffalo. From the statements of Joutel and Douay, the Eyeish were not on good terms with the tribes w. of them on the Trinity, nor with those on Red r. in the N. at the time the French entered their country late in the 17th century; but, judging from the confusion of names by early writers, it is likely that only some of the subdivisions or villages were represented in the war parties. The mission of Nuestra Señora de los Dolores (q. v.) was established among them by the Franciscans who accompanied Don Domingo Ramon on his tour in 1716–17. They were, however, very little amenable to Spanish influence, for after 50 years of missionary effort, the mission register showed, according to Solis (MS., cited by H. E. Bolton, inf'n, 1906), only 11 baptisms, 7 interments, and 3 marriages performed at the mission, although the tribe had not been backward in receiving material aid from the missionaries. Solis reported in 1768 that this tribe was the worst in Texas—drunken, thievish, licentious, impervious to religious influence, and dangerous to the missionaries. Their villages were not far from the road between the French post at Natchitoches and the Spanish post at Nacogdoches, and the tribe was thus exposed to the contentions of the period and to the ravages of smallpox, measles, and other new diseases introduced by the white race. In the latter part of the 18th century the Eyeish were placed under the jurisdiction of the officials residing at Nacogdoches; in 1779 Mezières stated that there were 20 families of the "Ays" and that they were hated by both Indians and Spaniards (Bolton, op. cit.). In 1785 there were reported to have been 300 "Ahijitos" on Atoyac r., opposite the Nacogdoches (Bancroft, No. Mex. States, I, 666, 1886). In 1805 Sibley stated that only 20 members of the tribe were then living; but in 1828 (Soc. Geog. Mex., 1870) they were said to number 160 families between Brazos and Colorado rs. These differences in the estimates would seem to indicate that the Eyeish were considerably scattered during this period. Those who survived the vicissitudes which befell the Caddo in the 19th century are with their kindred on the Wichita res. in Oklahoma. Nothing definite is known of their customs and beliefs, which, however, were

probably similar to those entertained and practised by other tribes of the confederacy, and no definite knowledge of their divisions and totems has survived. While in New Mexico in 1540–41 Coronado learned from a Plains Indian known as The Turk, probably a Pawnee, of a province or settlement called Ayas, 6 or 7 days' journey distant, at which the Spanish army could obtain provisions on its way to Copala and Quivira. This place may have been imaginary, or the Eyeish people may have been meant. It was The Turk's intention to lead the Spaniards astray, hence locality plays but little part in the identification. (A. C. F.)

Aas.—Villa-Señor, Theatro Am., pt. II, 412, 1748. Aays.—Gentl. of Elvas (1557) in Hakluyt Soc. Pub., IX, 136, 1851. Aes.—Rivera, Diario y Derrotero, leg. 2165, 1736. Ahiahichi.—Thevenot quoted by Shea, Discov., 268, 1852. Ahijados.—Freytas, Peñalosa (1662), 35, 66, 1882. Ahijitos.—Morfi, MS. Hist. Tejas, bk. 2, ca. 1781–82. Ahijaos.—Freytas, op. cit., 34. Ahyches.—Doc. ca. 1735 in Margry, Déc., VI, 233, 1886. Aiaichi.—Marquette, map (1673) in Shea, Discov., 1852. A'-ic.—Dorsey, Caddo MS., B. A. E., 1882. Aiches.—La Harpe (1716) in Margry, Déc., VI, 193, 1886. Aijados.—Bancroft, Ariz. and N. Mex., 150, 1889. Aijaos.—Ibid., 163. Aijas.—Vetancurt (ca. 1693), Teatro Mex., III, 303, 1871. Ais.—Uhde, Länder, 182, 1861. Aise.—Morse, Rep. to Sec. War, 373, 1822. A'-ish.—Gatschet, Creek Migr. Leg., I, 44, 1884. Aix.—Bull. Soc. Geog. Mex., 268, 1870. Aixai.—Sanson, L'Amérique, map 27, 1657. Aixaj.—Linschoten, Descr. l'Amérique, map 1, 1638. Aixaos.—Benavides, Memorial, 85, 1630. Aizes.—Tex. St. Arch., Nacogdoches, 1832. Aleche.—Schermerhorn (1812) in Mass. Hist. Soc. Coll., 2d s., II, 24, 1814. Alich.—Latham in Trans. Philol. Soc. Lond., 101, 1856. Aliche.—Sibley (1805), Hist. Sketches, 70, 1806. Alickas.—McKenney and Hall, Ind. Tribes, III, 80, 1854. Alish.—Latham, Essays, 401, 1860. Alishes.—Brackenridge, Views of La., 87, 1814. Apiches.—Shea, Discov., xxxii, 1852 (misprint). Auches.—Garcilasso de la Vega, Fla., 213, 1723 (seemingly the same). Axtaos.—Oñate (1606) cited by Prince, N. Mex., 166, 1883 (possibly identical). Ayache.—Flint, Ind. Wars, 30, 1833. Ayas.—Mota-Padilla, Hist. de la Conq., 164, 1742. Ayays.—Gentl. of Elvas (1557) in Hakluyt Soc. Pub., IX, 115, 1851. Ayche.—La Harpe (1716) in Margry, Déc., VI, 194, 1886. Ayches.—Jefferys (1763), Am. Atlas, map 5, 1776. Aychis.—Baudry des Lozières, Voy. à la Louisiane, 241, 1802. Ayeche.—Gravelin (ca. 1717) quoted by Winsor, Hist. Am., V, 30, note, 1887. Ayes.—Villa-Señor (1748) quoted by Buschmann, Spuren. d. azt. Spr., 418, 1854. Ayiches.—La Harpe (1717) in French, Hist. Coll. La., III, 48, 1851. Ayish.—Kennedy, Tex., I, 25, 1841 (the bayou). Ayjados.—Bandelier in Arch. Inst. Pap., III, 169, 1890. Ayjaos.—Zarate-Salmeron (ca. 1629), Rel., in Land of Sunshine, 46, Dec., 1899. Ays.—Barcia, Ensayo, 322, 1723. Ayses.—Tex. St. Arch., census of 1790. Ayzes.—Ibid. Egeish.—Schermerhorn (1812) in Mass. Hist. Soc. Coll., 2d s., II, 24, 1814 (misprint). Eyeish.—Sibley, Hist. Sketches, 70, 1806. Eyish.—Brackenridge, Views of La., 81, 1815. Haïish.—ten Kate, Reizen in N. Am., 374, 1885. Hais.—Biedma (1544) in Hakluyt Soc. Pub., IX, 197, 1851. Ha'-ish.—Gatschet, Caddo and Yatassi MS., B. A. E., 42. Haychis.—Joutel (1687) in Margry, Déc., III, 410, 1878. Heiche.—Brown, West, Gaz., 214, 1817. Yais.—Soc. Geog. Mex., 504, 1869. Yayecha.—D'Anville, Carte des Isles de l'Amér., 1731.

**Fabrics.** See *Clothing, Cotton, Featherwork, Quillwork, Weaving.*

**Face.** See *Anatomy.*

**Face painting.** See *Adornment, Ornament, Painting, Tattooing.*

**Fallacies.** See *Popular fallacies.*

**Faluktabunnee.** A Choctaw town, mentioned in the treaty of 1805, on the right bank of Tombigbee r., in Choctaw co., Ala.—Am. State Papers, Ind. Aff., I, 749, 1832; Royce in 18th Rep. B. A. E., pl. cviii, 1899.

Fuketcheepoonta.—Am. State Papers, op. cit.

**Family.** There are important material differences in the organization and in the functions of the family as found respectively in savagery, barbarism, and civilization, and even within each of these planes of culture several marked types of the family, differing radically one from another in many characteristic features, exist.

To determine definitely even the main organic features of the family systems in a majority, not to say all, of the Indian tribes N. of Mexico, is not yet possible, owing to lack of material. In communities like those of the Muskhogean and the Iroquoian tribes, in which the clan system has been so highly developed, two radically different organic groups of persons exist to which the term family may properly be applied; and within each of these groups a more or less complex system of relationships definitely fixes the status of every person, a status that, acquired by birth or adoption, determines the civil or other rights, immunities, and obligations of the person. Among the Iroquois the *ohwachira* (the common Iroquoian name for the maternal blood family) was becoming merged into the clan (q. v.), so that in specific cases the two are virtually identical, although in other cases several ohwachira are comprised under one clan. The term ohwachira is common to all the known dialects of the Iroquoian stock. On the other hand there are found in these dialects several different names designating the group called a clan, seemingly indicating the probability that the family as an institution existed long before the development of the clan organization, when the several tribes still had a common history and tradition. But it is not strictly accurate to call an ohwachira a family, or a clan a family. The first and larger group includes the entire body of kindred of some one person, who is usually denominated the *propositus.*

In view of the rights and obligations of the father's clan to a person, in addition to those inherited from the clan of the mother, it appears that the family group among the Iroquois and Muskhogean tribes is composed of the maternal and paternal clans. The clan owes the child of its son certain civil and religious rights, and is bound to the child by obligations which vitally concern the latter's life and welfare, present and future. The youth's

equipment for life would not be regarded as complete were the performance of these clan duties neglected. The tutelar of every person is named and made by the members of the paternal clan. The duties just mentioned do not end with the death of the person; if occasioned by war or by murder the loss must be made good by the paternal clan supplying a prisoner or the scalp of an enemy.

Some of the duties and obligations of the clan or clans whose sons have taken wives from a clan stricken by death are to condole with it, prepare the death feasts, provide suitable singers to chant the dirges at the wake lasting one or more nights, guard and care for the body lying in state and prepare it for burial, make the bark burial case or wooden coffin, construct the scaffold or dig the grave, and to perform all the other needful duties due from clans bound together by marriage. It was regarded as unseemly for the stricken clan to do anything but mourn until the body of the dead had been placed in its final resting place and until after the feast of "reassociating with the public," held ten days subsequent to the death of the deceased, at which his property was divided among his heirs and friends. In case of the death of a chief or other noted person the clan mourned for an entire year, scrupulously refraining from taking part in public affairs until the expiration of this period and until after the installation of a successor to the dead officer. During the interim the bereaved clan was represented by the clan or clans bound to it by the ties of marriage and offspring.

These two clans are exogamic groups, entirely distinct before the child's birth, and form two subdivisions of a larger group of kindred—the family—of which any given person, the propositus, is the focal point or point of juncture. Strictly speaking, both clans form incest groups in relation to him. Every member of the community is therefore the point of contact and convergence of two exogamic groups of persons, for in these communities the clan is exogamic; that is to say, each is an incest group in so far as its own members are concerned. Within these clans or exogamic groups the members are governed by rules of a more or less complex system of relationships, which fix absolutely the position and status of everyone in the group, and the clan is thus organized and limited. Those, then, who have common blood with one another, or with a third person, belong to the same family and are kindred. Both of these clans owe the offspring the rights and obligations of kindred, but in differing degrees. Thus a person may be said to have two clans, in some measure—that of his mother and that of his father. Both clans exercise rights and are bound by obligations to the household of which he is a member; both have, moreover, in different measure, the rights and obligations of kinship to him.

The second and smaller group, the fireside or household, includes only the husband, his wife or wives, and their children. Where there are several wives from several different families, this group in its family relations becomes very intricate, but is nevertheless under the rigid control of family law and usage.

It is thus apparent that these two groups of persons are in fact radically distinct, for the lesser group is not merely a portion of the larger. The relative status of the husband and his wife or wives and their children makes this evident.

Custom, tradition, and the common law do not regard the wife or wives of the household as belonging to the clan of the husband. By marriage the wife acquires no right of membership in her husband's clan, but remains a member of her own clan, and, equally important, she transmits to her children the right of membership in her clan; and she acquires no rights of inheritance of property either from her husband or from his clan. On the other hand, the husband acquires no rights from his wife or from her clan, and he, likewise, does not become a member of his wife's clan.

But the fireside, or household, is the product of the union by marriage of two persons of different clans, which does not establish between the husband and wife the mutual rights and obligations arising from blood feud and from inheritance. It is precisely these mutual rights and obligations that are peculiarly characteristic of the relations between clansmen, for they subsist only between persons of common blood, whether acquired by birth or by adoption. Therefore, husband and wife do not belong to the same clan or family.

As there is a law of the clan or exogamic kinship group governing acts and relations as between members of the same clan group, so there are rules and usages governing the household or fireside and defining the rights and obligations belonging to its jurisdiction. The relations of the various members of the fireside are affected by the fact that every member of it is directly subject to the general rule of the clan or higher kinship group—the husband to that of his clan, the wife or wives to those of their respective clans, and the children to those of both parents, but in different kind and degree.

The dominating importance of the family in the social organization of a primitive people is apparent; it is one of the most vital institutions founded by private law and usage. In such a community every member is directly obligated to the family, first of all, for the protection that safeguards his welfare. The members of the family to which he belongs are his advocates and his sureties. In the grim blood feud the family defends him and his cause, even with their lives, if need be, and this care ends not with his death, for if he be murdered the family avenges his murder or exacts payment therefor. In the savage and barbaric ages, even to the beginning of civilization, the community placed reliance largely on the family for the maintenance of order, the redress of wrongs, and the punishment of crime.

Concerned wholly with the intimate relations of private life, family custom and law are administered within the family and by its organs; such customs and laws constitute daily rules of action, which, with their underlying motives, embody the common sense of the community. In a measure they are not within the jurisdiction of public enactment, although in specific cases the violation of family rights and obligations incurs the legal penalties of tribal or public law, and so sometimes family government comes into conflict with public law and welfare. But by the increasing power of tribal or public law through centralization of power and political organization the independence of the family in private feuds, regarded as dangerous to the good order of the community, is gradually limited. And when the family becomes a unit or is absorbed in a higher organization the individual acquires certain rights at the expense of the family—the right of appeal to the higher tribunal is one of these.

The wealth and power of a clan or family depend primarily on the dearth or abundance of its numbers. Hence the loss of a single person is a great loss, and there is need that it be made good by replacing the departed with another or by many others, according to the relative standing and importance of the person to be restored. For example, Aharihon, an Onondaga chieftain of the 17th century, sacrificed 40 men to the shade of his brother to show the great esteem in which he held him. But among the Iroquois the duty of restoring the loss does not devolve directly on the stricken clan or exogamic kinship group, but upon all allied to it by the ties of what is termed *hontoññishoñ'*—i. e., upon those whose fathers are clansmen of the person to be replaced. So the birth or the adoption of many men in a clan or exogamic kinship group is a great advantage to it; for although these men become separated through the obligation of marrying into clans or such groups other than their own, the children of such unions are bound in a measure to the clan or exogamic kinship group of their fathers. This is a principle so well established that the chief matron of the paternal clan or exogamic kinship might oblige these offspring of diverse households (as many as might suffice) to go to war in fulfilment of their obligation, as seemed good to her; or she might stop them if they wished to undertake a war which was not, from its expediency, pleasing to her and her advisers. Therefore this chief matron, having decided that the time was at hand ''to raise again the fallen tree'' or ''to put back on the vacant mat'' one of the clan whom death removed, would inform one of the children whose fathers were her clansmen, their *hoñthoñni'*, that it was her desire that he form and lead a war party against their enemies for the purpose of securing a prisoner or a scalp for the purpose named. The person whom she selected was one judged most capable of executing her commission. This was soon accomplished. She enforced and confirmed this commission with a belt of wampum. So powerful was this chief matron of a clan that when the council chiefs did not favor the designs of certain ambitious war chiefs in raising levies for military purposes, fearing that they might injure the best interests of the tribe, one of the surest methods they might employ to frustrate these enterprises was to win the chief matrons of the clans whose clansmen were the fathers of the recruits from the other clans, for these chief matrons had only to interpose their influence and authority to bring to naught the best concerted designs and enterprises of these ambitious war chiefs. This is ample evidence that these women had an influence in some degree exceeding that of the council of the ancients and tribal chiefs.

In the blood feud the paternal kin did not interfere except by counsel; but to avenge the death of a clansman of their father was an obligation. Outlaws were denied family and tribal rights. The renunciation of clan kinship entailed the loss of every right and immunity inhering in kinship. The fundamental concept in the organic structure of the family with its rights, immunities, and obligations is that of protection. To exercise the right of feud was lawful only to avenge the guilty murder of a clansman.

The clan or family was made useful by the tribe as a police organization, through which control was exercised over lawless men who otherwise were beyond restraint. Every clan had jurisdiction over the lives and property of its members, even to the taking of life for cause.

The mutual obligations of kindred subsist between persons who can act for themselves; but there are duties of protection by these toward those who can not act for themselves for any reason whatever, for it is a principle of humanity that they who are legally independent should protect those who are legally dependent. The modern law of guardianship of minors and imbeciles is evidently but a survival and extension of this obligation of protection in the primitive family and clan.

Speaking generally of the tribes of the N. W. coast, Swanton (Am. Anthrop., n. s., VII, no. 4, 1905) says that in addition to the ''husband, wife, and children, a household was often increased by a number of relations who lived with the house owner on almost equal terms, several poor relations or protégés who acted as servants, and on the N. Pacific coast as many slaves as the house owner could afford or was able to capture.''

In tribes where a clan or gentile organization similar to that of the Iroquoian and the Muskhogean tribes does not exist, it is known that the incest groups on the maternal and the paternal sides are largely determined by the system of relationships, which fixes the position and status of every person within an indefinite group, and the incest group is reckoned from each propositus. That is to say, marriage and cohabitation may not subsist between persons related to each other within prescribed limits on both the maternal and paternal sides, although kinship may be recognized as extending beyond the prescribed limit. Among the Klamath these relationships are defined by reciprocal terms defining the relation rather than the persons, just as the term ''cousin'' is employed between cousins.

In speaking of the fierce, turbulent, and cruel Athapascan tribes of the valley of the Yukon, Kirkby (Smithson. Rep. 1864, 1865), says: ''There is, however, another division among them, of a more interesting and important character than that of the tribes just mentioned. Irrespective of tribe they are divided into three classes, termed, respectively, Chit-sa, Nate-sa, and Tanges-at-sa, faintly representing the aristocracy, the middle classes, and the poorer orders of civilized nations, the former being the most wealthy and the latter the poorest. In one respect, however, they greatly differ, it being the *rule* for a man *not* to marry in his own, but to take a wife from either of the other classes. A Chit-sa gentleman will marry a Tanges-at-sa peasant without the least feeling *infra dig.* The offspring in every case belong to the class of the mother. This arrangement has had a most beneficial effect in allaying the deadly feuds formerly so frequent among them.'' As no further data are given, it is impossible to say what, if any, was the internal structure and organization of these three exogamic classes, with female descent, mentioned above. Apparently a similar social organization existed among the Natchez, but no detailed information on the subject is available.

See *Adoption, Captives, Clan and Gens, Government, Labor, Kinship, Marriage, Slavery, Social organization, Women.*
(J. N. B. H.)

**Faraon** ('Pharaoh'). A tribe of Apache. From references in early Spanish writings to the "Apache hordes of Pharaoh," it is assumed that the name of the Faraon Apache was thus derived. This tribe, no longer known by name, seems to have formed the s. division of the Querecho of Coronado (1541), the Vaqueros of Benavides (1630) and other 17th century writers, and part at least of the Llaneros of more recent times. Their principal range was that part of New Mexico lying between the Rio Grande and the Pecos, although their raids extended beyond this area. Nothing is known of their ethnic relations, but judging from their habitat, they were probably more closely related to the Mescaleros than to any other of the Apache tribes, if indeed they were not a part of them. They made numerous depredations against the Spanish and Pueblo settlements of the Rio Grande in New Mexico, as well as in Chihuahua, and for a time at least their principal rendezvous was the Sandia mts. in the former territory. Several expeditions were led against them by the Spanish authorities, and treaties of peace were made, but these did not prove to be binding. According to Orozco y Berra (Geog., 59, 1864) their divisions were Ancavistis, Jacomis, Orejones, Carlanes, and Cuampes, but of these the Carlanes at least belonged to the Jicarillas.
(F. W. H.)

Apache hoards of Pharaoh.—Doc. of 1714 quoted by Bancroft, Ariz. and N. Mex., 232, 1889. **Apaches Faraones.**—Autos de guerra (1704) quoted by Bandelier in Arch. Inst. Papers, V, 183, 1890. **Apaches Farones.**—Bollaert in Jour. Ethnol. Soc. Lond., II, 265, 1850. **Apaches Pharaones.**—Rivera, Diario, leg. 784, 1736. **Apaches Taraones.**—Bandelier, Gilded Man, 253, 1893 (misprint). **Faraona.**—Doc. of 1714 quoted by Bandelier in Arch. Inst. Papers, III, 180, 1890. **Faraon Apaches.**—Bancroft, Ariz. and N. Mex., 223, 1889. **Faraones.**—Villa-Señor, Theatro Am., pt. 2, 416, 1748. **Fardones.**—Humboldt, Kingd. of N. Sp., II, 238, 1822 (misprint). **Farreon Apaches.**—Vargas (1694) quoted by Davis, Span. Conq. N. Mex., 396, 1869. **Intujen-né.**—Escudero, Noticias Estad. de Chihuahua, 212, 1834 (misprint). **Pharaona.**—Valverde (1720) quoted by Bandelier in Arch. Inst. Papers, V, 184, 1890. **Pharaones.**—Rivera, Diario, leg. 950, 1736. **Southern Apaches.**—Bandelier in Arch. Inst. Papers, V, 183, 1890. **Taracone.**—Villa-Señor, Theatro Am., pt. 2, 416, 1748. **Taraones.**—Mota-Padilla, Hist. de la Conquista, 516, 1742. **Tarracones.**—Domenech, Deserts of N. Am., II, 7, 1860. **Yuta-jenne.**—Orozco y Berra, Geog., 59, 1864.

**Far Indians.** A general term used by English writers about the beginning of the 18th century to designate the Indians of any tribe remote from the English settlements of the N. Atlantic coast. It was applied more especially to the tribes of the upper great lakes and to the Shawnee before their removal from the S. The word occurs also as "Farr." (J. M.)

**Farmers Band.** A Dakota division, probably of the Mdewakanton, whose habitat was below L. Traverse, Minn.

Civilized Farmers.—Ind. Aff. Rep. 1859, 100, 1860. **Iasica.**—Hinman, MS. notes, B. A. E., 1881. **Farmers' band.**—Ind. Aff. Rep., 68, 1860. **New civilized band.**—Ind. Aff. Rep. 1859, 102, 1860. **Saopi.**—Gale, Upper Miss., 252, 1867 (probably misprint for Taopi). **Taopi's band.**—McKusick in Ind. Aff. Rep., 315, 1863.

**Farmer's Brother.** A Seneca chief, known among his people as Honanyawus, of vulgar meaning, born in 1716, or 1718, or 1732, according to varying authorities; died in 1814 (Drake, Biog. and Hist. Inds., bk. V, 108, 1837; Haines, Am. Indian, 579, 1888). He is often mentioned in connection with Red Jacket, but does not appear to have come into prominence until about 1792. One of his most celebrated speeches was delivered before a council at Genesee r., N. Y., in 1798. He signed the treaties of Genesee, Sept. 15, 1797, and Buffalo cr., June 30, 1802. He espoused the cause of the United States in the war of 1812, and although 80 years of age engaged actively in the strife and was present in the action near Ft George, N. Y., Aug. 17, 1813. He died soon after the battle of Lundy's Lane and was buried with military honors by the fifth regiment of U. S. infantry. Farmer's Brother was always an advocate of peace and more than once prevented his tribe from going on the warpath. (C. T.)

**Fasting.** A rite widely observed among the Indians and practised both in private and in connection with public ceremonies. The first fast took place at puberty, when the youth was sometimes sent to a sequestered place and remained alone, fasting and praying from 1 to 4 days, or even longer (see *Child life*). At this time or during similar fasts which followed, he was supposed to see in a dream the object which was to be his special medium of communication with the supernatural. Simple garments or none were worn when fasting. Among some tribes clay was put upon the head, and tears were shed as the appeals were made to the unseen powers. At the conclusion of a long fast the quantity of food taken was regulated for several days. It was not uncommon for an adult to fast, as a prayer for success, when about to enter upon an important enterprise, as war or hunting. Fasting was also a means by which occult power was believed to be acquired; a shaman had to fast frequently in order to be able to fulfill the duties of his office.

Initiation into religious societies was accompanied by fasting, and in some of the great ceremonies all the principal actors were obliged to fast prior to taking part. The length of these fasts varied with the ceremony and the tribe, and ranged from midnight to sunset, or continued 4 days and nights. Fasting generally included abstinence from water as well as food. The reason for fasting has been explained by a Cherokee priest as "a means to spiritualize the human nature and quicken the spiritual vision by abstinence from earthly food." Other tribes have regarded it as a method by which to remove "the smell" of the common world. Occasionally chiefs or leaders have appointed a tribal fast in order to avert threatening disaster. See *Feasts*.

Consult Dorsey and Voth in Field Columbian Mus. Publ., Anthrop. ser., III, 1900–03; Fewkes (1) in Jour. Am. Ethnol. and Archæol., IV, 1894, (2) in 19th Rep. B. A. E., 1900; Matthews in Mem. Am. Mus. Nat. Hist., VI, 1902; Mooney in 19th Rep. B. A. E., 1900.     (A. C. F.)

**Fax.** A former Chumashan village near Purísima mission, Santa Barbara co., Cal.—Taylor in Cal. Farmer, Oct. 18, 1861.

**Feasts.** Among all tribes there were feasts, ranging in importance from that of the little child to its playmate up to those which were a part of the great sacred ceremonies. These so-called feasts were never elaborate and were simply served, each portion being ladled from the kettle by the hostess, or by one appointed for the task.

Feasts were held at stated times. On the N. Pacific coast the coming of the salmon was celebrated in a feast of thanksgiving by all the tribes able to secure the fish from inlets or rivers. Farther s. the ripening of acorns and other fruits was similarly observed. The maturing of the maize was the occasion for tribal festivities; at that time the Creeks held their 8-days' ceremony known as the *Busk* (q. v.), when the new corn was eaten, the new fire kindled, new garments worn, and all past enmities forgiven. In November, when the Eskimo had gathered their winter store, they held a feast, at which time gifts were exchanged; by this a temporary relationship was formed between the giver and taker, which tended to good feeling and fellowship. During the full moon of December the Eskimo held a feast to which the bladders of animals killed during the year were brought. These were "supposed to contain the *inuas*, or shades of the animals." On the sixth and last day the bladders were taken out to a hole made in the ice, and thrust into the water under the ice. They "were supposed to swim far out to sea and then enter the bodies of unborn animals of their kind, thus becoming reincarnated and rendering game more plentiful" (Nelson). Among the Iroquois a feast was held to keep the medicine alive. Religious ceremonies to insure fruitfulness took place at the planting of the maize, at which time a feast was held.

Feasts were given on the completion of a house, at a marriage, and when a child was named. Feasts in honor of the dead were widely observed. The time which must elapse after a death before the feast could be given varied among the tribes. Among some of the Plains Indians it occurred after 4 days, with the Iroquois after 10 days, and with other tribes after nearly a year. The Eskimo held their memorial feast late in November. The near relatives were the hosts, and the dead were supposed to be present beneath the floor of the dwelling where they enjoyed the festivities in their honor, partaking of the food and water cast there for them, and receiving the clothing put as a gift upon their namesakes. At the feast for the dead held by the tribes on the N. Pacific coast, the spirits of the departed were also supposed to be present, but the portions of food intended for them were passed through the fire and reached them in this manner. The Huron held their ceremonial feast in the fall, when all who had died during the year were disinterred by their kindred, the flesh stripped from the bones, and these wrapped in new robes and laid in the clan burial pit. The feast was one of tribal importance and was accompanied with religious rites.

It was incumbent on an aspirant to tribal honor to give feasts to the chiefs, and one who desired initiation into a society must provide feasts for the society. Respect to chiefs and leading men was expressed by a feast. On such an occasion the host and his family did not eat with their guests; they provided the food and the dishes, but the head chief appointed one of the guests to act as server. At all feasts the host was careful not to include in the food or the dishes used anything that would be tabu to any of his guests; a failure to observe this important point would be considered an insult.

The meetings of secular societies among the Plains tribes, whether the membership was of one or both sexes, were always accompanied with a feast. There was no public invitation, but the herald of the society went to each lodge and gave notice of the meeting. The food was provided by the family at whose lodge the society met, or by certain other duly appointed persons. The preparation for the feast varied in different societies within the same tribe. In some instances the food was brought ready cooked to the lodge, in others it was prepared in the presence of the assembly. The people brought their own eating vessels, for at these feasts one had to eat all that was served to him or take what was left to his home.

In most tribal ceremonies sacred feasts occurred, for which certain prescribed food was prepared and partaken of with special ceremony. Feasts of this kind often took place at the close of a ceremony, rarely at the beginning, although sometimes they marked a particular stage in the proceedings. Among the Iroquois, and perhaps other tribes, the owner feasted his fetish (q. v.), and the ceremony of the calumet (q. v.), according to early writers, was always concluded with a feast, and was usually accompanied by an exchange of presents.

Among the Omaha and cognates there was a gathering called "the fire-place feast." A company of young men or of young women, never of both sexes, met together by invitation of one of their number. When the company took their places around the fire, a space at the w. was left, where a bowl and spoon were placed to represent the presence of Wakanda, the giver of food.

At every feast of any kind, on any occasion where food was to be eaten, a bit or small portion was first lifted to the zenith, sometimes presented to the four cardinal points, and then dropped upon the earth at the edge of the fire or into the fire. During this act, which was an offering of thanks for the gift of food, every one present remained silent and motionless. See *Etiquette, Fasting, Food, Potlatch.*

Consult Dorsey and Voth in Field Columbian Mus. Publ., Anthrop. ser., III, 1900–03; Fewkes in 15th, 16th, and 19th Rep. B. A. E., 1897–1900; Fletcher in Publ. Peabody Museum; Gatschet, Creek Migr. Leg., I, 177, 1884; Hoffman in 7th and 14th Reps. B. A. E., 1891, 1896; Jenks in 19th Rep. B. A. E., 1900; Jesuit Relations, Thwaites ed., I–LXXIII, 1896–1901; Matthews in Mem. Am. Mus. Nat. Hist., VI, 1902; Mindeleff in 17th Rep. B. A. E., 1898; Nelson in 18th Rep. B. A. E., 357, 1899.                          (A. C. F.)

**Featherwork.** The feathers of birds entered largely into the industries, decorations, war, and worship of the Indians. All common species lent their plumage on occasion, but there were some that were especially sought: in the Arctic regions, water birds during their annual migrations; the eagle everywhere; wild turkeys in their habitat; ravens and flickers on the N. Pacific coast; woodpeckers, meadow larks, crested quail, mallard ducks, jays, blackbirds, and orioles in California; and in the Pueblo region, eagles, hawks, turkeys, and parrots especially. The prominent species in every area were used.

Not willing to depend on the fortunes of the hunt, the Pueblo and Virginia Indians held eagles and turkeys in captivity until such time as their feathers were wanted. Property right in eagles of certain localities were recognized by the Pueblos. In the Arctic regions parkas were made of bird skins sewed together, the feathers forming an excellent barrier against the cold. To the southward the skins of young waterfowl, while covered with down, were sewed together for robes. The historic tribes of the E. cut bird skins into strips and wove them into blankets in the same way that the western tribes used rabbit skins. In the turkey robes described by Capt. John Smith and other early explorers the pretty feathers of these birds were tied in knots to form a network, out of which beautiful patterned cloaks were wrought. Fans and other accessories of dress were made of wings or feathers by the Iroquois and other tribes. The uses of feathers in decoration were numberless. The Western Eskimo sewed little sprays of down into the seams of garments and bags made of intestinal membranes, and the California Indians decorated their exquisite basketry in the same manner. The quills of small birds, split and dyed, were used for beautiful embroidery and basketry in the same way as porcupine quills. For giving directness to the flight of arrows, feathers were usually split so that the halves could be tied or glued to the shaftment in twos or threes. Among the Eskimo and some of the southwestern Indians the feathers were laid on flat. Among California tribes bird scalps were used as money, being both a standard of value and a medium of exchange. The most striking uses of feathers were in connection with social customs and in symbolism. The masks and the bodies of performers in ceremonies of the N. Pacific coast were copiously adorned with down. Feathers worn by the Plains tribes in the hair indicated rank by their kind and number, or by the manner of mounting or notching. The decoration of the stem of the calumet (q. v.) was of feathers, the colors of which depended on the purpose for which the calumet was offered. Whole feathers of eagles were made into warbonnets, plumes, and long trails for dances and solemnities. In the Pueblo region feathers played an important rôle in symbolism and worship—prayersticks, wands, altar decorations, and aspergills were made of them. The downy feather was to the mind of the Indian a kind of bridge between the spirit world and ours. Creation and other myths spring out of feathers.

Feather technic in its highest development belongs to South America, Central America, and Polynesia, but there is continuity in the processes from the N. part of America southward. See *Adornment, Art, Clothing, Color symbolism, Eagle, Exchange, Horse, Ornament, Quillwork, Weaving.*

Consult Bancroft, Native Races, I–V, 1874–75; Boas in 6th Rep. B. A. E., 1888; Dixon in Bull. Am. Mus. Nat. Hist., XVII, pt. 3, 1905; Goddard in Publ. Univ. Cal., Am. Archæol. and Ethnol., I, 1903; Holmes (1) in 6th Rep. B. A. E., 1888, (2) in 13th Rep. B. A. E., 1896; Mallery in 10th Rep. B. A. E., 1893; Mason (1) in Rep. Nat. Mus. 1902, 1904, (2) in Smithson. Rep. 1886, 1889; Murdoch in 9th Rep. B. A. E., 1892; Nelson in 18th Rep. B. A. E., 1899; Turner in 11th Rep. B. A. E., 1894; Winship in 14th Rep. B. A. E., 1896. (o. t. m.)

**Features.** See *Anatomy.*

**Fejiu.** A prehistoric pueblo of the Tewa at the site of the present town of Abiquiu, on the Rio Chama, Rio Arriba co., N. Mex.

Fe-jiu.—Bandelier in Arch. Inst. Papers, IV, 54, 1892. Fe-jyu.—Ibid., 55.

**Fermentation.** Instances are few among the North American tribes of the employment of fermentation for a definite purpose. The phenomena of the "turning" or souring of cooked vegetal food or of ripe fruit must frequently have been observed, but the isolation of a pure culture, the starting and control of its action to furnish a desired product or result, was practically unknown. The rare examples of primitive American brewing and yeast making, however, are instructive as bearing on the development of the knowledge of the process of fermentation. Some Californian tribes prepare manzanita cider by mashing the berries of the *Arctostophylos manzanita*, collecting the juice and allowing it to ferment from natural causes—by means of minute organisms, such as yeast and bacteria, which are constantly present in human surroundings and for which the juice of ripened fruit presents a proper medium. This, however, was perhaps not knowingly used as a fermented drink or intoxicant in aboriginal times. A step in advance of this is observed in the preparation of tiswin by the Apache of Arizona; corn is soaked, sprouted, dried, and ground, and this is mixed in water and kept in a warm place to ferment, producing a kind of beer. The fermenting agent is natural, as in the case of the manzanita cider, but the production of malt as a culture for the yeast germs seems to indicate that tiswin is not an Apache invention. The Apache also ferment pine bark by a process more primitive

than that employed in the manufacture of tiswin. In the crude fermentations described, the Indians have learned to put their brew in a jar long used for the purpose, and thus retaining in its pores the organisms causing fermentation. What appears to be an approach to the discovery of beer is found in the sour corn gruel made by the Cherokee and other southern tribes, and by the Huron and other tribes of the N. This is a thin gruel of corn meal and water allowed to sour. It was a popular food, and there is no evidence that it had an intoxicating effect. Among the Pueblos is found the highest advance in the process of fermentation—the preparation and preservation of yeast for bread making. This is made by retaining corn meal in the mouth for several hours, when the magma is ejected into the food mass designed to be fermented. By this method the starch of the corn meal is acted on by the ptyalin of the saliva, rendering it a culture medium for the yeast which, once "set," continues its action indefinitely. The Zuñi have discovered that by means of salt and lime this saliva yeast may be preserved for future use. Saliva yeast was known to most beer-drinking agricultural tribes of the Old World; in America it is known to various tribes of s. Mexico and of Central and South America, but so far as known the Pueblos and neighboring tribes are the only ones in northern America acquainted with its use. See *Food.*

Consult Cushing, Zuñi Breadstuff, The Millstone, IX, X, Indianapolis, 1884–85; Goddard in Univ. of Cal. Publ., Am. Archæol. and Ethnol., I, 1903; Hrdlicka, Tesvino among the White River Apaches, Am. Anthrop., VI, 190, 1904. (w. H.)

**Fesere.** A prehistoric pueblo of the Tewa on a mesa w. or s. of the Rio Chama, near Abiquiu, Rio Arriba co., N. Mex.

Fe-se-re.—Bandelier in Arch. Inst. Papers, IV, 58, 1892.

**Fetish** (Portuguese: *feitiço*, 'a charm', 'sorcery', 'enchantment' (whence the English *fetish*); adjective, 'made by art', 'artificial', 'skilfully contrived'; Latin *factitious*, 'made by art', 'artful by magic'). Among the American Indians an object, large or small, natural or artificial, regarded as possessing consciousness, volition and immortal life, and especially *orenda* (q. v.), or magic power, the essential characteristic, which enables the object to accomplish, in addition to those that are usual, abnormal results in a mysterious manner. Apparently in any specific case the distinctive function and sphere of action of the fetish depends largely on the nature of the object which is supposed to contain it. It is the imagined possession of this potent mysterious power that causes an object to be regarded as indispensable to the welfare of its possessor.

In the belief of the Indians, all things are animate and incarnate—men, beasts, lands, waters, rocks, plants, trees, stars, winds, clouds, and night—and all possess volition and immortal life; yet many of these are held in perpetual bondage by weird spells of some mighty enchantment. So, although lakes and seas may writhe in billows, they can not traverse the earth, while brooks and rivers may run and bound over the land, yet even they may be held by the potent magic power of the god of winter. Mountains and hills may throb and quake with pain and grief, but they can not travel over the earth because they are held in thraldom by the powerful spell of some potent enchanter. Thus it is that rocks, trees, roots, 'stocks and stones', bones, the limbs and parts of the body, and the various bodies of nature are verily the living tombs of diverse beings and spirits. Of such is the kingdom of the fetish, for even the least of these may be chosen. Moreover, a fetish is an object which may also represent a vision, a dream, a thought, or an action.

The following extract from Cushing's Zuñi Fetiches (2d Rep. B. A. E., 1883) will show the reputed connection between the object and its quickener, between the object and the thing it represents. In speaking of the Two Sun Children, Cushing says: "Now that the surface of the earth was hardened, even the animals of prey, powerful and like the fathers (gods) themselves, would have devoured the children of men; and the Two thought it was not well that they should all be permitted to live, 'for,' said they, 'alike will the children of men and the children of the animals of prey multiply themselves. The animals of prey are provided with talons and teeth; men are but poor, the finished beings of earth, therefore the weaker.'

"Whenever they came across the pathway of one of these animals, were he a great mountain lion or but a mere mole, they struck him with the fire of lightning which they carried in their magic shield. *Thlu!* and instantly he was shriveled and burned into stone.

"Then said they to the animals that they had changed into stone: 'That ye may not be evil unto men, but that ye may be a great good unto them, have we changed you into rock everlasting. By the magic breath of prey, by the heart that shall endure forever within you, shall ye be made to serve instead of to devour mankind.'"

"Thus was the surface of the earth hardened and scorched and many of all kinds of beings changed to stone. Thus, too, it happened that we find, here and there throughout the world, their forms, sometimes large like the beings themselves, sometimes shriveled and distorted. And we often see among the rocks the forms of many beings that live no longer, which shows us that all was different in the 'days of the new.'

"Of these petrifactions, which are of course mere concretions or strangely eroded rock forms, the Zuñi say, 'Whomsoever of us may be met with the light of such great good fortune may *see* (discover, find) them and should treasure them for

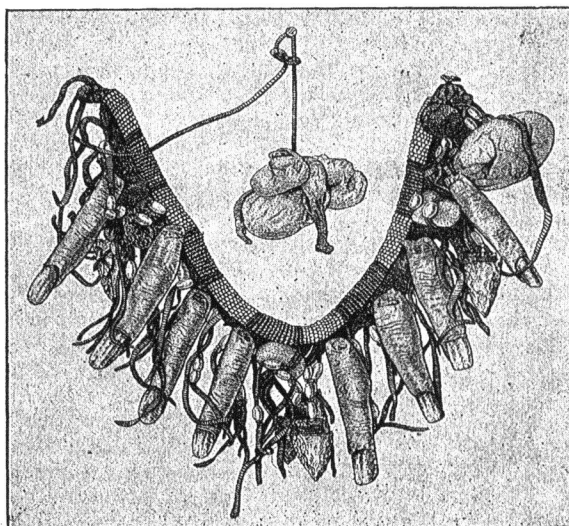

FETISH NECKLACE OF HUMAN FINGERS; CHEYENNE. (BOURKE)

the sake of the sacred (magic) power which was given them in the days of the new.'" Such is the Zuñi philosophy of the fetish.

A fetish is acquired by a person, a family, or a people for the purpose of promoting welfare. In return, the fetish requires from its owner worship in the form of prayer, sacrifice, feasts, and protection, and from its votaries it receives ill or good treatment in accordance with the character of its behavior toward them. Some fetishes are regarded as more efficacious than others. The fetish which loses its repute as a promoter of welfare gradually becomes useless and may degenerate into a sacred object—a charm, an amulet, or a talisman—and finally into a mere ornament. Then other fetishes are acquired, to be subjected to the same severe test of efficiency in promoting the well-being of their possessors.

The fetish is clearly segregated from the group of beings called tutelars, or guardian spirits, since it may be bought or sold, loaned or inherited, while, so far as known, the tutelar is never sold, loaned, or, with the Iroquois, inherited.

Among the Santee and the Muskhogean and Iroquoian tribes the personal tutelar, having a different origin, is scrupulously discriminated from all those objects and beings which may be called fetishes. The tutelar has a particular name as a class of beings. Rev. John Eastman says that this is true of the Santee, and it is probably true of many other tribes. Some fetishes are inherited from kindred, while others are bought from neighboring tribes at a great price, thus constituting a valuable article of intertribal commerce. It is also acquired by choice for multifarious reasons.

A person may have one or many fetishes. The name fetish is also applied to most of the articles found in the medicine sack of the shaman, the *pindikosan* of the Chippewa. These are commonly otter, snake, owl, bird, and other skins; roots, bark, and berries of many kinds; potent powders, and a heterogeneous collection of other things employed by the shaman.

A fetish is not a product of a definite phase of religious activity, much less is it the particular prerogative of any plane of human culture; for along with the adoration of the fetish goes the worship of the

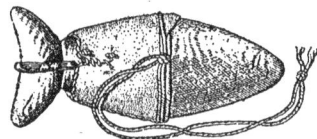

WHALE FETISH OF WOOD; WESTERN ESKIMO. (MURDOCH)

sun, moon, earth, life, trees, rivers, water, mountains, and storms as the embodiment of as many personalities. It is therefore erroneous to assign the fetish to the artificial stage of religion sometimes called hecastotheism. The fetish must be carefully distinguished from the tutelar of every person. Among the Iroquois these are known by distinct names, indicative of their functions: *ochina'kĕn'da'* for fetish, and *oiäron'* for the tutelar.

Mooney says, in describing the fetish, that it may be "a bone, a feather, a carved or painted stick, a stone arrowhead, a curious fossil or concretion, a tuft of hair, a necklace of red berries, the stuffed skin of a lizard, the dried hand of an enemy, a small bag of pounded charcoal mixed with human blood—anything, in fact, which the owner's medicine

WILDCAT FETISH OF THE CHASE; ZUÑI. (CUSHING)

dream or imagination might suggest, no matter how uncouth or unaccountable, provided it be easily portable and attachable. The fetish might be the inspiration of a dream or the gift of a medicine-man, or even a trophy taken from a slain enemy, or a bird, animal, or reptile; but, however insignificant in itself, it had always, in the owner's mind at least, some symbolic connection with occult power. It might be fastened to the scalp-lock as a pendant, attached to some part of the dress, hung from the bridle bit, concealed between the covers of a shield, or guarded in a special repository in the dwelling. Mothers sometimes tied the fetish to the child's cradle.

"A fetish noted among the Sioux is described as the image of a little man, which was inclosed in a cylindrical wooden case and enveloped in sacred swan's down (Riggs). A hunting and divining fetish among the Cherokee consisted of a transparent crystal, which its owner kept wrapped up in buckskin in a sacred cave and occasionally fed by rubbing over it the blood

FETISH OF DRIED BEES IN BOX; WESTERN ESKIMO. (MURDOCH)

of a deer. The Pueblo tribes have numerous war and hunting fetishes of stone, small figurines cut to resemble various predatory animals, with eyes of inlaid turquoise and one or more arrowheads bound at the back or side, and smeared with frequent oblations of blood from the slain game. The protective amulet sometimes took the form of a small figurine of a bird or other animal swift in flight, as the hawk; silent in movement, as the owl; or expert in dodging, as the dragonfly. In all tribes the nature and mysterious origin of the personal fetish or 'medicine' were the secret of the individual owner or of the maker, who, as a rule, revealed it only to one formally chosen as heir to the mystic possession and pledged in turn to the same secrecy."

Consult Bourke in 9th Rep. B. A. E., 1892; Clark, Indian Sign Language, 1885; Cushing, Zuñi Fetishes, 2d Rep. B. A. E., 1883; Jesuit Relations, Thwaites ed., 1896–1901; Lafitau, Mœurs des Sauvages Ameriquains, 1724; Maximilian, Travels, 1843; Müller, Orig. and Growth of Religion, 1879; Murdoch in 9th Rep. B. A. E., 1892; Nelson in 18th Rep. B. A. E., 1899; Riggs, Gospel Among the Dakotas, 1869.
(J. N. B. H.)

**Fetkina.** A Chnagmiut village on the N. arm of the Yukon delta, Alaska; pop. 30 in 1880.—Petroff in 10th Census, Alaska, 111, 1884.

**Fetutlin.** A Hankutchin village of 106 people on upper Yukon r., Alaska, near the mouth of Forty-mile cr.—Petroff, 10th Census, Alaska, map, 1884.
David's people.—Petroff, Rep. on Alaska, 62, 1880.
Fetoutlin.—Petroff, 10th Census, Alaska, 12, 1884.

**Few that Lived (The).** A former Yanktonai band under chief Two Bears.—Culbertson in Smithson. Rep. 1850, 141, 1851.

**Fife.** An Upper Creek chief, called James or Jim Fife, who flourished in the early years of the 19th century, and whose importance arose chiefly from the aid he rendered Gen. Jackson in the latter's fight with the Creeks, Jan. 22, 1814, on Tallapoosa r. near the mouth of Emuckfau cr., Ala. In this battle, Fife, who had joined Jackson with 200 warriors at Talladega, not only saved Coffee's division from defeat when hard pressed by fearful odds, but turned the tide of battle in favor of Jackson's army. "But for the promptness of Fife and his warriors," says Drake (Ind. Chiefs, 104, 1832), "doubtless the Americans must have retreated." He signed the treaty of Indian Springs, Ga., Feb. 12, 1825, only as representing Talladega, and is not included among "the chiefs and headmen of the Creek nation" who signed the supplementary treaty. (C. T.)

**Fife's Village.** A former Upper Creek village situated a few miles E. of Talladega, Ala.—Royce in 18th Rep. B. A. E., pl. cviii, 1899.

**Fightingtown** (mistranslation of *Walâs'-unûlsti'yǐ*, 'place of the plant walâs'-unûl'stǐ', i. e., 'frog fights with it'). A former Cherokee settlement on Fightingtown cr., near Morganton, Fannin co., Ga.—Mooney in 19th Rep. B. A. E., 545, 1900.

**Finhalui** (*Fin-'hálui*, 'high log'). A former Lower Creek town, probably in Georgia, with 187 heads of families in 1832. A swamp bearing the name Finholoway is in Wayne co., Ga., between lower Altamaha and Satilla rs. (A. S. G.) Fin-'hálui.—Gatschet, Creek, Migr. Leg., I, 130, 1884. High Log.—Schoolcraft, Ind. Tribes, IV, 578, 1854.

**Finhioven** (*Fin-hi-öven*). A chief of the Kadohadacho in 1771. He guided the Wichita from upper Red r. to Natchitoches, La., and witnessed the treaty made between the latter tribe and the Spanish governors of Louisiana and Texas, Oct. 27, 1771. He is referred to in the manuscript record of this event as "gran casique" of the Kadohadacho. (H. E. B.)

**Fire Lodge.** One of the former Dakota bands below L. Traverse, Minn.—Ind. Aff. Rep. 1859, 102, 1860.

**Fire-making.** Two methods of making fire were in use among the American aborigines at the time of the discovery. The first method, by flint-and-pyrites (the progenitor of flint-and-steel), was practised by the Eskimo and by the northern Athapascan and Algonquian tribes ranging across the continent from Stikine r. in Alaska to Newfoundland and around the entire Arctic coast, and also throughout New England; as well as by the tribes of the N. Pacific coast. The inference is that this method of fire-making at one time was general in this area, but the observations on which its distribution is based are from widely separated localities in which it is invariably used in connection with fire-making by wood friction. It appears probable that flint-and-pyrites, in view of its distribution in northern Europe, was introduced into America through Scandinavian contact, or is accultural either from Europe or Asia. The flint-and-steel is clearly an introduction of recent times.

The second method, by reciprocating motion of wood on wood and igniting the ground-off particles through heat generated by friction, was widespread in America, where it was the most valued

MAKING FIRE WITH SIMPLE ROD DRILL REVOLVED BETWEEN THE HANDS; HUPA

as well as the most effectual process known to the aborigines. The apparatus, in its simplest form, consists of a slender rod or drill and a lower piece or hearth, near the border of which the drill is worked by twisting between the palms, cutting a socket. From the socket a narrow canal is cut in the edge of the hearth, the function of which is to collect the powdered wood ground off by the friction of the drill, as within this wood meal the heat rises to the ignition point. This is the simplest and most widely diffused type of fire-generating apparatus known to uncivilized man. Among the Eskimo and some other tribes the simple two-piece fire drill became a machine by the use of a hand or mouth rest containing a stone, bone, or wood socket for the upper end of the drill, and a cord with two handles or string on a bow for revolving the drill. By these inventions uniform and rapid motion and great pressure were effected, rendering it possible to make fire with inferior wood. The four-part drill consisted of two kinds: (*a*) The cord drill, which requires the cooperation of two persons in its working, and (*b*) the bow drill, which enables one person to make fire or to drill bone and ivory. The distribution of these varieties, which are confined to the Eskimo and their neighbors, follows no regular order; they may be used together in the same tribe, or one or the other may be used alone, although the presumption is that the cord drill is the older. The hearth alone embodies two interesting modifications which reflect the environment. In one the canal leads down to a step or projection from the side of the hearth, and in the other the drilling is done on a longitudinal slot in the middle of the hearth, the object in both cases being to prevent the fire from falling into the snow. These features also seem to have an indiscriminate distribution in the area mentioned.

The pump drill has been employed for fire-making only among the Onondaga of Canada, who used it in making sacred fire for the White-dog feast; but the pump drill is of little practical use in fire-making. From the Onondaga also there is an example of the fire plow like that of the Polynesians, in which a stick is held at an angle between the hands and rubbed back and forth along a plane surface, cutting a groove in which the wood meal produced by friction igitnes. The appearance of these diverse methods in one tribe, in an area where the simple drill was common, leads to the assumption that they are of recent introduction. There is no other evidence that the fire plow ever existed in the western hemisphere.

The wood selected for the fire drill varied in different localities, the proper kinds and qualities being a matter of acquired knowledge. Thus the weathered roots of the cottonwood were used by the Pueblos; the stems of the yucca by the Apache; the root of the willow by the Hupa and Klamath; cedar by the N. W. coast tribes; elm, maple, and buttonwood by the eastern Indians. In some instances sand was placed in the fire cavity to increase friction; often two men twirled the drill alternately for the purpose of saving labor or when the wood was intractable.

A similar discrimination is observed in the selection of tinder. The Eskimo prized willow catkins; the Indians of the N. W. coast used frayed cedar bark; other tribes used fungi, softened bark, grass, or other ignitible material. Touchwood or punk for preserving fire was obtained from decayed trees, or some form of slow match was prepared from bark. From the striking of a spark to the well-started campfire considerable skill and forethought were required. The glowing coal from the fire drill was usually made to fall into a small heap of easily ignitible material, where it was encouraged by faning or blowing until actual flame was produced; or the spark with the small kindling was gathered in a bunch of grass or a strip of bark and swung in the air.

Fire-making formed an important feature of a number of ceremonies. New fire was made in the Green-corn ceremony of the Creeks (see *Busk*), the White-dog feast of the Iroquois, the New-fire and Yaya ceremonies of the Hopi, and among many other tribes in widely separated localities. There are also many legends and myths grouped about the primitive method of obtaining fire at will. The Cherokee and other southern tribes believed that a perpetual fire burned beneath some of the mounds in their country, and the Natchez built their mounds with a view, it is said, of maintaining a perpetual fire. On the introduction of flint-and-steel and matches the art of fire-making by the old methods speedily fell into disuse among most tribes and was perpetuated only for procuring the new fire demanded by religious rites. See *Drills and Drilling, Illumination.*

Consult Dixon in Bull. Am. Mus. Nat. Hist., xvii, pt. 3, 1905; Hough in Rep. Nat. Mus., 1888 and 1890.          (w. h.)

**First Christian Party.** A division of the Oneida at the period of the removal to Green bay, Wis., and afterward.—Washington treaty (1828) in U. S. Ind. Treat., 621, 1873.

**Fish-eating Creek.** A Seminole settlement with 32 inhabitants in 1880, situated 5 m. from the mouth of a creek that empties into L. Okeechobee, Manatee co., Fla.—MacCauley in 5th Rep. B. A. E., 478, 1887.

**Fish-e-more.** See *Enpishemo.*

**Fishhooks.** Starting from the simple device of attaching the bait to the end of a line, the progressive order of fishhooks used by the Indians seems to be as follows: (*a*) The gorge hook, a spike of bone or wood, sharpened at both ends and fastened at its middle to a line, a device used also for catching birds; (*b*) a spike set obliquely in the end of a pliant shaft; (*c*) the plain hook; (*d*) the barbed hook; (*e*) the barbed hook combined with sinker and lure. This series does not exactly represent stages in invention; the evolution may have been effected by the habits of the different species of fish and their increasing wariness. The material used for hooks by the Indians was wood, bone, shell, stone, and copper. The Mohave employed the recurved spines of certain species of cactus, which are natural hooks.

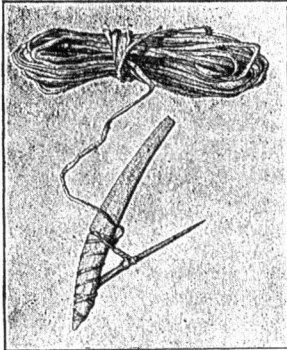

FISHHOOK AND LINE; HUDSON BAY ESKIMO. (TURNER)

Data on the archeology of the fishhook have been gathered from the Ohio mounds and the shell-heaps of Santa Barbara, Cal., unbarred hooks of bone having been found on a number of Ohio sites and gorge hooks at Santa Barbara. The fishhook of recent times may be best studied among the N. Pacific tribes and the Eskimo of Alaska. The Makah of Washington have a modified form of the gorge hook, consisting of a sharpened spine of bone attached with a pine-root lash to a whalebone. British Columbian and s. Alaskan tribes used either a simple hook of bent wood having a barb lashed to a point, or a compound hook consisting of a shank of wood, a splint of pine-root lashed at an angle of 45° to its lower end, and a simple or barbed spike of bone, wood, iron, or copper lashed or set on the outer end of the splint. Eskimo hooks consisted frequently of a shank of bone with a curved, sharpened spike of metal set in the lower end, or several spikes were set in, forming a gig. Usually, however, the Eskimo hook had the upper half of its shank made of stone and the lower half of ivory, in which the unbarbed curved spike of metal was set, the parts being fastened together by lashings of split quill. A leader of quill was attached to the hook and a bait of crab carapace was hung above the spike. This is the most complex hook known in aboriginal America.

FISHHOOKS OF WESTERN ESKIMO. (MURDOCH)

BONE FISHHOOK; ARKANSAS; ACTUAL SIZE. (RAU)

COPPER FISHHOOK; WISCONSIN; ACTUAL SIZE. (RAU)

Lines and poles varied like the hook with the customs of the fishermen, the habits of the fish, and the environment. The Eskimo used lines of knotted lengths of whalebone quill, hair, or sinew; the N.

Pacific tribes, lines of twisted bark, pine root, and kelp; and other tribes lines of twisted fiber. Short poles or none were used by the Eskimo and N. Pacific tribes. In other regions it is probable that long poles of cane or saplings were used. In some regions, as on the N. W. coast, a trawl, consisting of a series of hooks attached by leaders to a line, was used for taking certain species of fish. The Haida, according to Swanton, made a snap hook, consisting of a hoop of wood, the ends of which were held apart by a wooden peg. This peg was displaced by the fish on taking the bait, and the ends of the hoop snapped together, holding the fish by the jaw. (See *Fishing*.)

Consult Boas in 6th Rep. B. A. E., 1888; Goddard in Univ. Cal. Publ., Am. Archæol. and Ethnol., i, 1903; Hoffman in 14th Rep. B. A. E. pt 2, 1896; Holmes in 2d Rep. B. A. E., 1883; Mills (1) in Ohio Archæol. and Hist. Quar., ix, no. 4, 1901, (2) ibid., xv, no. 1, 1906; Moore (1) in Jour. Acad. Nat. Sci. Phila., xi, 1899, (2) ibid., xii, 1903, (3) ibid., xiii, 1905; Murdoch in 9th Rep. B. A. E., 1892; Nelson in 18th Rep. B. A. E., pt 1, 1899; Niblack in Rep. Nat. Mus. 1888, 1890; Palmer in Am. Nat., xii, no. 6, 1878; Putnam in Wheeler Surv. Rep., vii, 1879; Rau in Smithson. Cont., xxv, 1884; Teit in Mem. Am. Mus. Nat. Hist., ii, Anthrop. i, 1900; Turner in 11th Rep. B. A. E., 1894.　　　　　　　　　　　　(w. h.)

**Fishing.** At the first coming of the Europeans the waters of this continent were found teeming with food fish, the great abundance of which quickly attracted fleets of fishermen from all civilized parts of the Old World. The list of species living in American waters utilized by the Indians would fill a volume. The abundance or scarcity of this food on the Atlantic coast varied with the season. In spring the fish made their appearance in vast shoals in the spawning beds of the coast and in the bays and rivers. Capt. John Smith relates, in his History of Virginia, early in the 17th century, that on one occasion fish were encountered in such numbers in the Potomac as to impede landing from his boat. The annual spring run of herring above Washington is still almost great enough to warrant the assertion. Fish life varied with locality and season. On the northern and eastern coasts the fish disappeared to a great extent when the waters became cold at the approach of winter, and many northern fishes went to more southerly waters. Among the better known food products furnished by the waters of the country may be mentioned the whale, sea lion, seal, otter, swordfish, sturgeon, porpoise, cod, haddock, halibut, pollock, salmon, trout, herring, shad, perch, bass, mackerel, flounder, eel, plaice, turbot, whitefish, catfish, smelt, pike, dogfish, and all varieties of shellfish. By some tribes, as the Apache, Navaho, and Zuñi, fish were tabu as food; but where fish was used at

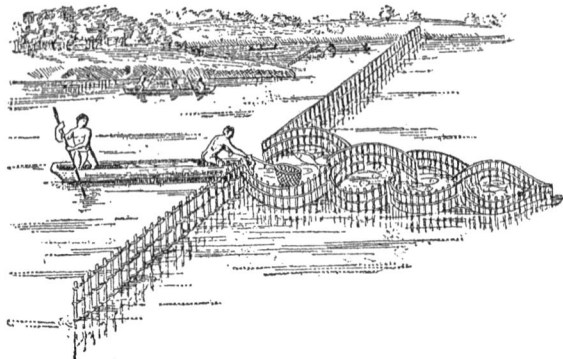

WATTLE-WORK FISH TRAP OF THE VIRGINIA INDIANS. (HARIOT, 1585)

all by the Indians, practically everything edible that came from the water was consumed. The salmon of the Pacific coast are still found in enormous schools, and in the canning industry hundreds of persons are employed. Lobsters and crabs furnished no inconsiderable food supply, while the vast deposits of shells along all tidewater regions, as well as many of the interior rivers, testify to the use made of shellfish by the aborigines; they not only supplied a large part of the daily food of the people but were dried for time of need. Shellfish were dug or

CARRYING FISH IN A BASKET; VIRGINIA INDIANS. (HARIOT)

taken by hand in wading and by diving. Salmon and herring eggs formed one of the staple articles of diet of the tribes of the N. Pacific coast. To collect herring eggs these tribes laid down under water at low tide a row of hemlock branches, which were held in position with weights; then branches were fastened together, and a float was fixed at one end, bearing the owner's mark. When these boughs were found to be covered with eggs they were taken into a canoe, carried ashore, and elevated on branches of a tree stripped of its smaller limbs, where they were left to dry. When first placed in position the eggs adhered firmly to the boughs, but on taking them down great care had to

ALASKAN ESKIMO HARPOON; FORESHAFT AND HEAD. (MURDOCH)

be exercised, because they were very brittle and were easily knocked off. Those not immediately consumed were put up in the intestines of animals and laid aside for winter use. It is recorded in the Jesuit Relations that many eels came to the mouth of St Lawrence r. and were trapped by the Indians, who made long journeys to get the season's supply.

On the middle and s. Atlantic coast fish are found during the greater portion of, if not throughout, the year, while farther N. fishing is confined more to the spawning seasons and to the months when the waters are free of ice. Experience taught the natives when to expect the coming of the fish and the time when they would depart. In methods of capturing sea food the native had little to learn from the white man, even in killing the whale (which was treated as royal game on the

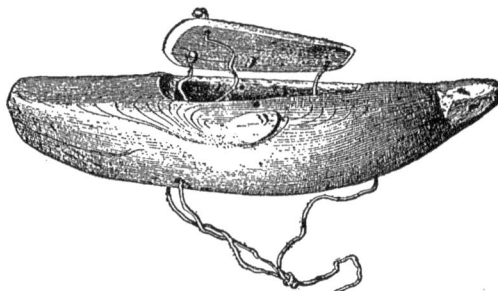

ALASKAN ESKIMO BOX FOR CONTAINING HARPOON HEADS. (MURDOCH)

coast of Vancouver id.), the sea lion, or the seal, or in taking shellfish in the waters of the ocean and in the smallest streams.

Large fish and marine mammals were captured by means of the harpoon, while the smaller ones were taken by the aid of bow and arrow, gigs, net, dull, trap, or weir. Fires or torches were used along the shore or on boats, the gleam of which attracted the game or fish to the surface, when they were easily taken by hand or with a net. Among the Cherokee, Iroquois, and other tribes, fish were drugged with poisonous bark or other parts of plants; in parts of California extensive use was made of soap root and other plants for this purpose. Carved fishhooks (q. v.) of shell and bone have been found in shellheaps and graves in the interior. In shape these

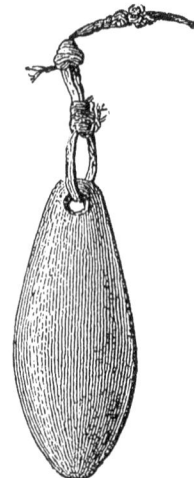

ALASKAN ESKIMO STONE SINKER; 1-2. (RAU)

resemble the hooks of metal from Europe, though the natives of the Pacific coast used fishhooks of wood and bone combined, made in so primitive a manner as to indicate aboriginal origin. Another ingenious device employed along the N. Pacific coast for catching fish consisted of a straight pin, sharp at both ends and fastened to a line by the middle; this pin was run through a dead minnow, and, being gorged by another fish, a jerk of the string caused the points to pierce the mouth of the fish, which was then easily taken from the water. Artificial bait, made of stone and bone combined, was used as a lure, and was quite as attractive to fish as is the artificial bait of the civilized fisherman.

Still another ingenious way of catching fish was by "pinching," by means of a split stick, which, like the gig, held the fish fast.

In shallow rivers low walls were built from one side of the stream to the other, having a central opening through which

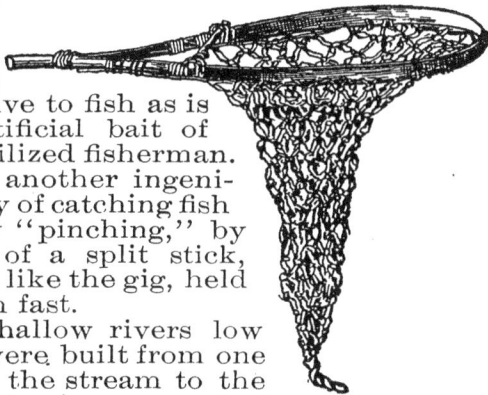

DIPNET OF THE HAIDA. (NIBLACK)

fish were forced into a trap. Brushwood mats were also made, which were moved along like seines, so as to drive the fish into shallow or narrow places, where they were readily taken by the hand or with dipnets. Along the shores of rapid streams men stationed themselves on rocks or staging and speared fish as they passed up or down stream. During winter, when the northern waters were frozen, holes were cut in the ice, and through these fish were shot, speared, or netted.

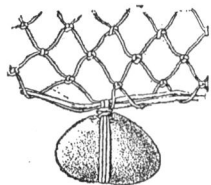

ALASKAN ESKIMO NET SINKER. (NELSON)

Probably the most primitive of all methods of fishing, however, by which many salmon were and doubtless are still captured, was that of knocking them on the head with a club. After a great run of fish had subsided, single ones were caught in shallow water by any of the above methods. There are still indications that from an early period a trade existed between the fishing Indians and those of the interior who gained their livelihood by other means. Great supplies of fish were cured by drying in the sun or over fires, and sometimes the product was finely ground and packed in skins or baskets for future use. See *Food*.

Consult Adair, Hist. Am. Inds., 1775; Boas (1) in 6th Rep. B. A. E., 1888, (2) in Bull. Am. Mus. Nat. Hist., xv, pt. 1, 1901; Dawson, Queen Charlotte Ids., 1880; Dixon in Bull. Am. Mus. Nat. Hist., xvii,

pt. 3, 1905; Gatschet in Am. Anthrop., v, 361, 1892; Goddard in Univ. Cal. Publ., Am. Archæol. and Ethnol., i, 1903; Jesuit Relations, Thwaites ed., i–lxxiii, 1896–1901; Lawson, Hist. Carolina, 340, 1714, repr. 1860; Lewis and Clark, Orig. Jour., i–viii, 1904–05; Margry, Découvertes, v, 81, 1883; Morice in Trans. Can. Inst., 1893; Murdoch in 9th Rep. B. A. E., 1892; Nelson in 18th Rep. B. A. E., pt. 1, 1889; Rau, Prehistoric Fishing, 1884; Smith, Hist. Va., repr. 1819. Turner in 11th Rep. B. A. E., 1894.                        (J. D. M.)

**Fiskernaes.** An Eskimo settlement and Danish trading post, 90 miles s. of Godthaab, w. Greenland.—Kane, Arct. Explor., i, 21, 1856.

**Five Civilized Tribes.** A term used both officially and unofficially in modern times to designate collectively the Cherokee, Chickasaw, Choctaw, Creek, and Seminole tribes in Indian Ter., applied on account of the advance made by these tribes toward civilized life and customs. The term appears in the reports of the Indian Office as early as 1876, when the agent reported (p. 61) that each tribe "had a constitutional government, with legislative, judicial, and executive departments, conducted upon the same plan as our State governments, the entire expenses of which are paid out of their own funds." There was, however, at that date no court with jurisdiction to try cases where an Indian was one party and a citizen of the United States or a corporation was the other, but this lack has since been supplied. Some of the tribes, notably the Cherokee, have had their laws and the acts of their councils printed.

ALASKAN ESKIMO FISH SPEAR; 1–8. (MURDOCH)

These five tribes differed from most others in the fact that their lands were held not on the same basis as reservations but by patents or deeds in fee simple, with certain restrictions as to alienation and reversion—those conveyed to the Cherokee Nation, Dec. 31, 1838, forever upon condition that they "shall revert to the United States if the said Cherokee Nation becomes extinct or abandons the same"; those to the Choctaw Nation, Mar. 23, 1842, in fee simple to them and their descendants, "to inure to them while they shall exist as a nation, and live on it, liable to no transfer or alienation, except to the United States or with their consent"; those to the Creek tribe, Aug. 11, 1852, "so long as they shall exist as a nation and continue to occupy the country hereby conveyed to them." Although the lands were held in fee simple, the right to alienate them except to the United States or with its consent does not appear to have passed to the grantees. The title is defined as a "base, qualified, or determinable fee, with only a possibility of reversion to the United States (U. S. *v.* Reese, 5 Dill., 405). The right of these tribes to cut, sell, and dispose of their timber, and to permit mining and grazing within the limits of their respective tracts was for a time limited to their own citizens, but this right has been somewhat extended, though the exercise of it is still subject to approval by the proper United States authorities. The title of the Chickasaw Nation to their lands in Indian Ter. was obtained from the Choctaw in accordance with treaties with the United States, while that of the Seminole was obtained from the Creeks, these two tribes being granted their lands on the same basis and with the same title and privileges as the United States granted the lands to the Choctaw and the Creeks. The territory thus assigned to these five tribes within the limits of Indian Ter. amounted to 19,475,614 acres, or about 30,431 sq. m., an area equal to that of South Carolina, and equivalent to 230 acres for each man, woman, and child of the entire population (84,507) of the five tribes.

The treaties of 1866 with the several tribes all provided for the holding of a general council to be composed of delegates from each tribe in Indian Ter., and the Choctaw and Chickasaw treaty also provides that this general council shall elect a delegate to Congress whenever Congress shall authorize the admission into its body of an official who shall represent Indian Ter. Although some of the tribes have made an effort to bring about the results contemplated in these treaty stipulations, nothing effectual in this direction has been accomplished. By act of Congress Feb. 8, 1887, every Indian born in the United States who receives land in allotment and takes up "his residence separate and apart from any tribes of Indians therein and has adopted the habits of civilized life," is declared a citizen of the United States; but the Five Civilized Tribes were excepted from the provisions of this act. By act of Mar. 3, 1901, however, this section was amended by inserting after the words "civilized life" the words "and every Indian in Indian Territory," thus declaring every Indian of that territory to be a citizen of the United States. By act of May 2, 1890, the laws of Arkansas, so far as applicable, were extended over Indian Ter. until Congress should otherwise provide. United States courts and courts of special jurisdiction have also been established in the Territory. By sec. 16 of the act of Mar. 3.

1893, the President was authorized to appoint three commissioners (subsequently changed to five), to negotiate with the five tribes for the allotment in severalty of their lands, thus extinguishing the tribal title thereto. (See *Commission to the Five Civilized Tribes.*)

On the abolition of slavery the problem of determining the status and relations of the freedmen in the Five Civilized Tribes became a difficult one, though by treaties of 1866 it was agreed that they should be subject to the same laws as the Indians and be entitled to a portion of the land (the rights in this respect differing in the different tribes); but questions respecting other matters, as school privileges, have proved troublesome factors. In some of the tribes negroes have separate schools, and by the act of Congress of June 28, 1898, the freedmen were excluded from participating in the royalties on coal and asphalt, or in the school funds arising therefrom. By the same act and the acts of Mar. 1, 1901, and July 1, 1902, the tribal governments of these tribes were to cease Mar. 4, 1906, but by resolution of Feb. 27, 1906, the time was extended one year. Freedmen are, however, citizens in all the tribes. Consult the articles on the tribes composing the Five Civilized Tribes. (c. t.)

**Flakes.** The term flake is often used by archeologists synonymously with chip and spall, but it is most commonly applied to the long, thin slivers of flint or other brittle stone designed for use as cutting implements or produced without particular design in the ordinary course of implement making. When systematically made in numbers for use as knives or scrapers or for other purposes, a roughly cylindrical or somewhat conical piece of fine-grained material was selected or made, and the

FLINT FLAKES FOR USE AS KNIVES.

flakes were removed by strokes with a hammer delivered on one of the ends near the margin, the fracture extending the entire length or most of the length of the core and producing a flake, flat or slightly convex on the inside, sharp on the edges, and having an outer surface or back with one or more angles or facets according to the previous contour of the particular part of the original surface of the core removed. The manufacture of flakes for knives, extensively carried on by the ancient Mexicans, is described as being accomplished by abrupt pressure with a wooden implement, one end placed against the shoulder of the operator and the other set upon the core at the proper point. The exact manner of utilizing the flake blades by the northern tribes is not known, but they were probably set in suitable handles as knives, or employed in making small arrowheads, scrapers, and the like. Flakes and chips are produced by identical implements, the latter term being generally applied to the shorter, more abrupt flakes or bits produced in the ordinary work of shaping implements by both percussion and pressure processes. The expression "chipped implements" is however very generally applied to all forms shaped by fracture processes. See *Cores, Flaking implements, Hammers, Stonework.* (w. h. h.)

**Flaking implements.** The shaping of stone by fracture processes is one of the earliest as well as one of the most important arts of primitive men. Two distinct classes of processes as well as two widely differing classes of implements are employed. Fracture by percussion is accomplished by means of hammers of stone or other hard material (see *Hammers, Stonework*), and fracture by pressure

FLAKER; ALASKAN ESKIMO. THE FLAKING POINT OF HARD BONE IS AT THE LEFT. (MURDOCH)

employs a number of devices, perhaps the most usual among the northern tribes being bits of hard bone, antler, or ivory, somewhat resembling an awl in shape and often set in handles of wood or other suitable material. These are employed where the edges of the stone under treatment are sharp and rather thin. In using them the edge is firmly placed crosswise on the sharp edge of the brittle stone, or the point is set near the edge, and by a quick movement accompanied with strong pressure the flake is driven off. This operation is rapidly repeated, passing along the outline of the implement, alternating the sides, until the desired form is produced. The pieces under treatment may be held in various ways; for deep notching, which requires strong force, they are often laid flat on a pad of buckskin or other yielding material supported on a stable surface, and the bone point is made to remove the chips by a quick downward movement. Implements of metal are effectual in this particular form of the chipping work. Other devices mentioned by some writers are notched bones and pincers of bone, by means of which the sharp edge of the flint was chipped. For heavier work various contrivances enabling the operator

to apply greater force were employed, but these are not well understood. It appears that a punch-like tool of bone or antler was sometimes used, the point being set, at the proper point, on the stone to be fractured, while the other end was struck with a hammer or mallet to remove the flake. For writings on the subject, see *Stonework.* (w. h. h.)

**Flandreau Indians.** A part of the Santee who separated from the Mdewakanton and Wahpekute of the Santee agency, Nebr., in 1870, and settled in 1876 at Flandreau, S. Dak.—Ind. Aff. Rep. 27, 1876.

Flandreau Sioux.—Barber in Am. Nat., XVII, 750, 1885.

**Flathead.** A name applied to several different tribes usually owing to the fact that they were accustomed to flatten the heads of their children artificially. In s. e. United States the Catawba and Choctaw were sometimes designated by the term Flatheads, and the custom extended to nearly all Muskhogean tribes as well as to the Natchez and the Tonika. In the N. W. the Chinook of Columbia r., many of the Vancouver id. Indians, and most of the Salish of Puget sd. and British Columbia were addicted to the practice, and the term has been applied to all as a body and to some of the separate divisions. Curiously enough, the people now known in official reports as Flatheads—the Salish proper (q. v.)—never flattened the head. Dawson implies (Trans. Roy. Soc. Can. for 1891, sec. II, 6) that they were so named (Têtes-Plates) by the first Canadian voyageurs because slaves from the coast with deformed heads were among them. For the names of the tribes to which the term has been applied, see *Flatheads* in the index; consult also *Artificial head deformation.* (J. R. S.)

**Flat-mouth.** See *Eshkebugecoshe.*

**Flechazos** (Span: 'arrow or dart blows'). A name applied by the Spaniards in the latter part of the 18th century to the upper village of the Tawakoni settlement on the w. side of Brazos r., near Waco, Tex. The one below it was called Quiscat. One or the other of these villages was the Waco village. (H. E. B.)

**Flint.** Until recently the use of the term flint was restricted to nodular concretions found in chalk beds of Cretaceous age mainly in England, France, and other European countries, but recently obtained from Cretaceous strata in Arkansas and Texas. Although flint is classed as a variety of chalcedony, the name has been extended in popular usage to include various forms of chalcedonic minerals, as chert, hornstone, basanite, jasper, agate, and the like. The principal constituent of all these minerals is silica, and notwithstanding their great dissimilarity the distinctions are due almost entirely to manner of formation and included foreign substances. Such impurities, though they make up a very small percentage of the stone, produce upon exposure to atmospheric influences an infinite variety of coloring and great diversity of texture. The flints as thus defined were extensively employed by the aborigines in the manufacture of chipped implements, and the implements themselves are sometimes referred to as "flints." See *Chalcedony, Chert, Quartz, Mines and Quarries.* (G. F. W. H. H.)

**Flint disks.** Flattish objects of circular, elliptical, or almond-like outline produced by chipping away the outer portions of nodules having these approximate forms. The question has been earnestly debated whether these and kindred forms were for any practical or economic use, or whether they had some occult significance as votive offerings. They are very seldom found in graves and infrequently on village sites or about shops where implements were made. Many of them are of the blue nodular hornstone found in s. Illinois, in the vicinity of Wyandotte cave in s. Indiana, and in w. Kentucky and

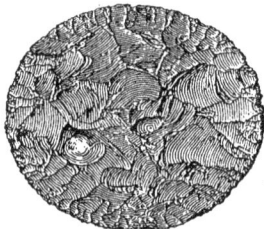

FLINT DISK; TENNESSEE.
(DIAM., 9 IN.)

Tennessee, but no record has yet been made of the discovery in large numbers of such disks in any of these localities except the first. The range in size is generally from 3 to 8 in. in length or diameter, though a few exceed the latter dimension. The finest specimen known is from Tennessee; it is almost exactly circular, made of the Stewart co. flint, about 1 in. thick and 9 in. across. Flint disks as well as the more leaf-like blades are usually found in deposits or caches containing numerous nearly identical specimens. See *Cache disks and blades, Storage and Caches.* (W. H. H.)

**Florida Indians.** A term almost as vague as the ancient geographic conception of Florida itself, used (Doc. Col. Hist. N. Y., VI, 243, 1855) to designate Indians who robbed a vessel stranded on the Florida keys in 1741–42. Schoolcraft (Ind. Tribes, VI, 47, 1857) refers to it as a term vaguely applied to the "Apalachian group of tribes." (A. S. G.)

**Flowpahhoultin.** A small body of Salish of Fraser superintendency, Brit. Col., in 1878.—Can. Ind. Aff., 79, 1878.

**Flunmuda.** A former village, presumably Costanoan, connected with Dolores mission, San Francisco, Cal.—Taylor in Cal. Farmer, Oct. 18, 1861.

**Focomae.** A Diegueño rancheria represented in the treaty of 1852 at Santa Isabel, s. Cal.—H. R. Ex. Doc. 76, 34th Cong., 3d sess., 132, 1857.

**Folk-lore.** See *Mythology.*

**Fond du Lac.** A Chippewa band residing on St Louis r., near Fond du Lac, E. Minnesota. They are now under the White Earth agency, numbering 107 in 1905.                    (J. M.)

**Food.** The areas occupied by the Indians may be classed as supplying, predominantly, animal food, vegetal food, and mixed diet. No strict lines separate these classes, so that in regions where it is commonly said that the tribes are meat eaters exclusively, vegetal food is also of importance, and vice versa. Vegetal food stuffs are (1) preagricultural, or the gathering of self-sown fruits, nuts, seeds, and

MONO WOMEN HARVESTING SEEDS.    (SANTA FÉ RAILWAY)

roots; and (2) agricultural, or (*a*) the raising of root crops, originating in the harvesting of roots of wild plants, and (*b*) of cereal products, consisting chiefly of maize (q. v.) grown by the majority of the tribes, and wild rice (q. v.) in the area of the upper lakes, where a sort of semiagriculture was practised to some extent. (See *Agriculture.*)

Animal food was obtained from the game of the environment, and the settlement and movements of some tribes depended largely on the location or range of animals, such as the buffalo, capable of furnishing an adequate food supply; while on the other hand, the limit of habitat of water animals, as the salmon, tended to restrict the range of other tribes to the places where the supply could be gathered. No pure hunter stage can be found, if it ever existed, for while the capture of animals devolved on the man and the preparation of food on the woman, the latter added to the diet substances derived from the vegetal kingdom. Similarly no purely agricultural stage with exclusively vegetal diet existed, and no aboriginal domestication (q. v.) of animals N. of Mexico is found except in the case of the turkey and the dog.

In general, in the N. portion of the continent the diet was three-fourths animal food; in the S. part it was three-fourths vegetal; while with the tribes of the coast, mountains, lakes, and plains, it varied according to the food supply. The absence of milk food, other than the maternal lactation, to a considerable extent limited the natural increase of population. The food supply also changed with the seasons, causing the diet at different periods of the year to vary in its ratio of animal to vegetal constituents, and another feature depended on religious customs and habits which modified or regulated the food used. For example, the Apache and Navaho will not eat fish or the flesh of the bear or beaver, and other tribes had tabu or totemic animals which, though useful for food, were not eaten (see *Tabu*). In inhospitable regions, such as that inland from the Texas coast in the 16th century, the natives subsisted on whatsoever they could find. Cabeza de Vaca wrote of the Yguazas: "Their support is principally roots, which require roasting two days; many are very bitter. Occasionally they take deer, and at times take fish; but the quantity is so small and the famine so great, that they eat spiders and the eggs of ants, worms, lizards, salamanders, snakes, and vipers that kill whom they strike; and they eat earth and wood, and all that there is, the dung of deer, and other things that I omit to mention; and I honestly believe that were there stones in that land they would eat them. They save the bones of the fishes they consume, of snakes, and other animals, that they may afterward beat them together and eat the powder." Almost as much may be said of the Maidu of California who, in addition to consuming every edible vegetal product, ate badgers, skunks, wildcats, and mountain lions; practically all birds except the buzzard; yellowjacket larvæ, grasshoppers, locusts, and crickets, and even salmon bones and deer vertebræ (Dixon).

Vegetal food comprised a vast array of the products of plant life, of which roots and seeds were the most valuable. The most important food plant possessed by the Indians was maize (q. v.) which formed and still forms their principal subsistence. Following maize in order of importance came beans, peas, potatoes, squashes, pumpkins, melons, and chile, which were grown in variety. Uncultivated plants also entered into the dietary, as seeds, roots, and flowers of grasses and other plants, or parts of plants used as greens, for flavoring, etc. In number-

less cases wild plants have preserved tribes from starvation when cultivated crops failed. In the S. W., cactus and yucca fruits, mesquite beans, and the agave were most important elements of the food supply. As in Mexico, the roasted fleshy leaves and leaf matrix of the agave were prized as sweet, nourishing food (see *Mescal*). Tuckaho and other fungi were used for food by the eastern Indians; "tuckaho bread" was well known in the S. The N. Pacific tribes made much use of the sweet inner bark of the hemlock and spruce. Savors, flavors, and condiments, as well as sweets, were valued by the Indian, who was also fond of chewing gum. While salt was tabued by the Onondaga and lye substituted by some of the southern Indians, the former was in general use. In some cases salt was made by the evaporation of the water of salt springs; in other localities it was obtained in crystal form from salt lakes and springs, and commerce in this product was widespread. Chile, which is of Mexican origin, became known throughout the S. W., and saffron, an introduced plant, is still in use there to flavor and color food, as are also the yellow flowers of the squash vine. Throughout New England and S. E. Canada sugar was produced by the evaporation of maple sap (see *Maple sugar*); in the S. W. it was derived from the willow and the agave. In some localities clay was eaten, either alone or mixed with food or taken in connection with wild potatoes to mitigate the griping effect of this acrid tuber. In general, buffalo, the deer family, and fish were the animals most useful for food. Some woodland tribes depended on deer, while the coast and river tribes usually made special use of fish and other products of the waters. Amphibious mammals sustained the Eskimo, while the porcupine is said to have been the chief food animal of the Montagnais. The range of game animals influenced the range of man in America quite as much as the distribution of food plants predetermined his natural diffusion.

Contrary to popular belief the Indians, as a rule, preferred cooked food. The Eskimo, whose name signifies 'eaters of raw flesh', ate uncooked meat only when absence of fuel prohibited cooking, or as a side dish. Vegetal food especially requires the agency of fire to render it fit for human digestion, whereas animal food may be consumed in a raw state, certain parts, as the liver, often being eaten in this way. All the edible portions of the animal were put to use, and in many cases both animal and vegetal substances advanced toward putrefaction were preferred, as salmon eggs which were stored in sand, by the Alaskans, and immature corn in the ear which the Hurons are said to have soaked in water until it became putrid, when soup was made of it.

Among the Pueblo Indians cooking is carried to a remarkable degree of proficiency, approaching in variety and methods the art among civilized peoples. Most

STONE-BOILING—LIFTING THE HOT STONES INTO THE FOOD BASKET; CALIFORNIA INDIANS. (HOLMES)

tribes knew how to prepare savory and nourishing dishes, some of which have been adopted by civilized peoples (see *Hominy, Maize, Samp, Succotash*, etc.). The methods of cooking among the meat-eating tribes were, in order of importance,

STONE-BOILING—REMOVING THE STONES FROM THE BOILING BASKET; CALIFORNIA INDIANS. (HOLMES)

broiling, roasting, and boiling, the last-named process often being that known as "stone boiling." The tribes whose diet was approximately vegetarian practised all the methods. (See *Ovens.*)

The preparation of maize as food involved almost numberless processes, varying with the tribes. In general, when maize reached the edible stage the ears were roasted in pit ovens, and after the feasting the surplus of roasted ears was dried for future use. The mature grain was milled raw or parched, the meal entering into various mushes, cakes, pones, wafers, and other bread. The grain was soaked in lye obtained from wood ashes to remove the horny envelope and was then boiled, forming hominy; this in turn was often dried, parched and ground, reparched and reground, making a concentrated food of great nourishing power in small bulk, which was consumed dry or in water as gruel. Pinole, consisting of

ground parched corn, forms the favorite food of S. W. desert tribes. The fermentation of corn to make beer was not generally practised, and it is doubtful if the process was known in America before the discovery. A yeast formed by chewing corn has long been known to the Zuñi and Hopi at least, and the former know how to preserve it through the agency of salt. (See *Fermentation.*)

The Iroquois and other eastern tribes cooked maize with beans, meat, or vegetables. The Pueblos add wood-ash lye to their "paper bread," and prepare their bread and mushes with meat, greens, or oily seeds and nuts, besides using condiments, especially chile.

Vegetal food stuffs were preserved by drying, and among the less sedentary tribes were strung or tied in bundles for facility of transportation or storage. The preservation of maize, mesquite beans, acorns, etc., gave rise to granaries and other storage devices. Animal food, from its perishable character, was often dried or frozen, but at times was preserved by smoking. Dried meat was sometimes pulverized and mixed with berries, grease, etc., forming pemmican (q. v.), valued for use on journeys on account of its keeping properties. Fruits were pulped and dried for preservation. Nuts were often ground before being stored, as were also maize, grass seeds, and the legumes. Tubers were frequently stored in the ground or near the fireplace; the Virginian tribes preserved tubers for winter use in this way. (See *Agriculture, Storage.*)

Infusions of leaves, roots, etc., of various herbs were drunk by the Indians as medicine (see *Black drink*), but no stimulating beverage of the character of tea or coffee has been observed. Drinks made from fruit, as cider from manzanita berries, used by the tribes of California, and a beverage made from cactus fruit by the Pima and neighboring tribes of Arizona, are the fermented beverages best known.

In addition to the reports of the Bureau of American Ethnology, consult Barber, Moqui Food Preparation, Am. Nat., XII, 456, 1878; Barrows, Ethnobotany of Coahuilla Inds., 1900; Carr, Food of Certain American Indians and their Method of Preparing It, Proc. Am. Antiq. Soc., X, 155–190, 1895; Cabeza de Vaca, Narr., Smith trans., 1871; Coville, Wokas, A Primitive Food of the Klamath Inds., 1902; Cushing, Zuñi Breadstuffs, The Millstone, IX and X, Indianapolis, 1884–85; Dixon in Bull. Am. Mus. Nat. Hist., XVII, pt. 3, 1905; Fewkes in Am. Anthrop., IX, 1896; Goddard in Univ. Cal. Publ., Am. Archæol. and Ethnol., I, 1903; Holm, Descr. New Sweden, 1834; Hough (1) in Am. Anthrop., X, 1897, (2) ibid., XI, 1898; Jenkins, The Moki Bread, Pop. Sci.

Month., Jan., 1900; Jenks in 19th Rep. B. A. E., 1900; Mason (1) Migration and the Food Quest, Smithsonian Rep., 1894, (2) Aboriginal American Zootechny, Am. Anthrop., I, Jan., 1899; Palmer (1) in Am. Nat., XII, 402, 1878, (2) in Rep. Com'r of Agr. 1870, 1871; Payne, Hist. America, I, 376-400, 1892; Powers in Cont. N. A. Ethnol., III, 1877; Sagard-Theodat, Grand Voy., 1632, repr. 1865; Schoolcraft, Ind. Tribes, I–VI, 1851–57; Sturtevant, Indian Corn and the Indian, Am. Nat., XIX, 225, 1885. See also the bibliographies under the articles above cited. (w. H.)

**Foolish Dogs.** An Hidatsa band according to Culbertson (Smithson. Rep., 1850, 143, 1851), but properly a warrior society.

**Footprint sculptures.** Among relics of undetermined use and significance left by the vanished tribes are numerous representations of human footprints, often regarded as actual footprints made while the rock material was still plastic. They are sculptured in slabs or masses, generally of sandstone, and show varying degrees of skill in execution. Representations of tracks of men and beasts also occur frequently in pictographs painted and sculptured on rock surfaces (see *Track rock*). In this connection they probably served to designate particular creatures or beings, the direction of their movements, the number of individuals, etc., but the larger well-sculptured footprints represented in museum collections probably had special significance as the reputed tracks of ancestors, of giants, or monsters, and may have been designed by cunning persons to deceive the uninitiated. The carvings represent sometimes a single footprint and again two or more in association, and are usually shallow, being rarely more than an inch in depth (see *Pictography, Problematical objects*). Consult Rau in Smithson. Cont., XXII, 22, 1876. (w. H. H.)

**Foreman, Stephen.** A Cherokee who became an active coworker with the Presbyterian missionaries among his people. He received an elementary education at the mission school at Candy's Creek, w. of Cleveland, Tenn., and after pursuing some preparatory studies under Rev. S. A. Worcester at New Echota, Ga., spent a year at Union Theological Seminary in Virginia and another at Princeton, N. J., in the study of theology. He was licensed to preach by the Union Presbytery of Tennessee about Oct. 1, 1833. Foreman is said to have preached with animation and fluency in the Cherokee language. With Mr Worcester he translated the Psalms and a large part of Isaiah into the Cherokee language.—Pilling, Bibliog. Iroq. Lang., Bull. B. A. E., 1888.

**Forked Horn.** One of the Dakota bands below L. Traverse, Minn.; probably Wahpeton or Sisseton.—Ind. Aff. Rep., 102, 1859.

**Forks of the River Men.** A band of the Arapaho, q. v.

**Fort Ancient.** A prehistoric Indian fortification in Warren co., Ohio. It is situated on a headland, from 260 to 280 ft high, which projects from a plateau and overlooks the E. bank of Miami r. The slopes are mostly steep and in several places precipitous. The place is naturally a strong one, the elevated area being flanked by two ravines that approach each other some distance back from the point of the bluff, forming a peninsula of this front part with a narrow isthmus behind it. This divides the fort into two unequal portions, the smaller one embracing the peninsula known as the "Old Fort," the other, known as the "New Fort," extending back and eastwardly on the plateau to a second but wider neck of land. The total area is estimated at about 100 acres.

FORT ANCIENT EMBANKMENT

The wall, which is chiefly of earth, follows closely the zigzag course of the bluff, except where it crosses the level neck of land in the rear of the fort. The work has been often described and figured, the first notice and plan being that given in the "Portfolio" (1809), from which Atwater's plan and description (Trans. Am. Antiq. Soc., I, 1820) appear to have been in large part copied. About 20 years later a survey was made by Locke, whose description and plat appear in Trans. Assn. Am. Geologists, I, 1843. Locke's plat was copied by Squier and Davis, and is the one from which most subsequent figures have been taken; it is accurate in the main, but the elements have somewhat changed the configuration in subsequent years, additional ravines having been formed by water breaking through the wall at certain points. Evidences of wearing are observable at some of the ravines crossed by the wall, and a few of the smaller gullies appear to have been worn since the wall was built, although in most cases the adaptation of the wall to the slopes shows that these existed when it was erected. That gaps were left in the wall at the bottom of the few deep ravines that it crosses is evident from the form of the wall at these points, but nothing remains to indicate how these gaps were closed in case of attack. Although the wall is built chiefly of earth (mostly of clay) cast up from an inside ditch, it is partially underlaid at numerous points with stone. The total length of the wall, following all the bends, is 18,712 ft, or a little more than 3½ m.; the height varies from 6 to 10 ft, except across the neck at the back of the fort where it reaches 18 or 19 ft. The solid contents probably do not exceed 3,000,000 cu. ft.

That Ft Ancient, so called, is a work of defense is evident from its character and situation, exhibited especially by the different methods adopted for defending its more vulnerable points. The only level approach was at the rear, which was protected by a high wall. On the N. the points more easily approached are usually narrow, sloping ridges, generally crossed at the upper terminus by a wall of ordinary height, the ridge immediately outside being cut down several feet in order to present a steep slope corresponding to the outer slope of the wall. On the other hand, where similar ridges form approaches from the S., and at some other points, the defenses are formed by raising the wall considerably above the normal height. The most vulnerable point appears to be at the isthmus separating the two forts, where the opposite walls have their nearest approach. Here a short space was undefended, though the ascent is by no means difficult. A short distance E. of the posterior wall of the new fort are two small mounds, a short distance apart, from each of which extends a low wall, or road as Atwater terms it, elevated about 3 ft, running nearly parallel about ¼ m., and forming an irregular semicircle about another small mound. A part of the area between these walls was paved with flat stones, remains of which now lie at a depth of 2 ft in the soil. Several small mounds and a number of stone graves which contained human remains were within the fort; these were explored by Moorehead, but nothing of special interest was found except the human remains. The greater portion of the area included in this inclosure is now the property of the State of Ohio and has been made a reservation under the care of the Ohio Archæological and Historical Society. The first purchase was made in accordance with an act of the legislature, Apr. 28, 1890, and the second purchase in pursuance of the act of Apr. 16, 1896.

For further information see, in addition to the works cited, Allen, Prehistoric World, 1885; Drake, Pictures of Cincinnati, 1815; Howe, Historical Collections of Ohio, 1898; MacLean, Mound Builders, 1879; Moorehead, Fort Ancient, 1890; Peet in Am. Antiq., Apr., 1878; Shepherd, Antiquities of Ohio, 1887; Thomas in Science, VIII, Dec. 10, 1886. (C. T.)

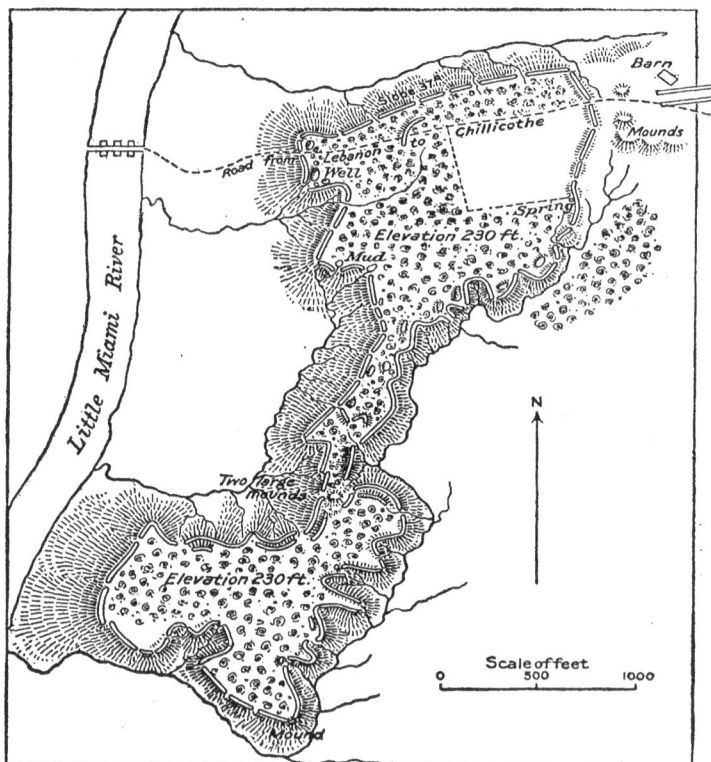

MAP OF FORT ANCIENT, OHIO.    (SQUIER AND DAVIS)

**Fortification and Defense.** The simplest defenses were furnished to the Indians by nature. In the forest regions battles were fought in the shelter of trees, and in stony sections from sheltering rocks. That war was waged and defensive measures were necessary in prehistoric times is shown by the remains of fortifications in the mound area of the United States. These are of different types, the most common being the so-called hill forts, where defensive walls of earth or stone surround a peak or hilltop or skirt a bluff headland, as at Ft Ancient (q. v.), Ohio. There are also circular, square, octagonal, and other inclosures on the lowlands which are generally supposed to have been built for defensive purposes, but they could hardly have been effectual unless stockaded. There are, or were until recently, earthen embankments and inclosures in New York which, as Squier has shown, mark the sites of palisaded forts similar to those of the Iroquois observed by Champlain and Cartier. These were often polygonal, of double or triple stockades, as that at Hochelaga which Cartier says was of "three courses of rampires, one within another." Some were strengthened by braces and had beams running round them near the top, where stones and other missiles were placed ready to be hurled upon besiegers. The walls of some of these fortifications were 20 ft high. One of the polygonal forts in w. New York, however, was overlooked by a hill from which arrows could easily be shot into the inclosure. Most of the early figures of these forts represent them as having a single entrance between overlapping ends of the stockade; there is one, however (Underhill, News from America, 1638), which shows two overlappings. When first seen by the whites most of the villages from Florida to the Potomac were protected with surrounding stockades, which are represented in De Bry as single with one opening where the ends overlap. The construction of these surrounding palisades was practically the same, whether they inclosed a single house or 50 houses. In some sections a ditch was usually dug, both within and outside of the palisade. A few of the forts in s. New England were square, but the circular form generally prevailed (Willoughby in Am. Anthrop., VIII, no. 1, 1906). The fortress built by King Philip in the swamp at South Kensington, R. I., consisted of a double row of palisades, flanked by a great abatis, outside of which was a deep ditch. At one corner a gap of the length of one log was left as an entrance, the breastwork here being only 4 or 5 ft high; and this passage was defended by a well-constructed blockhouse, whilst the ditch was crossed by a single log which served as a bridge. Stockaded villages were also common as far w. as Wisconsin. Stone walls, which C. C. Jones considered defensive, have been observed on Stone mtn., Mt Yona, and other peaks of N. Georgia. De Soto found strongly fortified villages in his passage through the Gulf states and Arkansas.

Vancouver (Voy., III, 289, 1798) mentions villages on Kupreanof id., situated on the summits of steep, almost inaccessible rocks and fortified with strong platforms of wood laid upon the most elevated part of the rock, which projected at the sides so as to overhang the declivity. At the edge of the platform there was usually a sort of parapet of logs placed one upon another. This type, according to Swanton, was quite common on the N. W. coast. The Skagit tribe, ac-

cording to Wilkes, combined dwellings and forts, and a similar custom was followed by some of the Haida clans. Wilkes mentions also inclosures 400 ft long, which were constructed of pickets about 30 ft long thrust deep into the ground, the interior being divided into roofed lodges. The Clallam also had a fort of pickets, 150 ft square, roofed over, and divided into compartments for families. No stockades seem to have been used by the Ntlakyapamuk, but fortresses or fortified houses were at one time in use in a few places. These defenses, according to Boas, consisted of logs placed lengthwise on the ground one above another and covered with brush and earth, loopholes being left at places between the logs. According to the same authority, some of the stockades of British Columbia were provided with underground passages as a means of escape. It has been a general custom of the Indians of the plains, when in danger of being attacked by a superior force, to dig a pit or pits in the loose, generally sandy soil, throwing the earth around the margin to increase the height of the defense, the bank of a creek or a gully being selected when within reach, as defense of one side only was necessary. Native drawings of some of these defenses are given by Mooney (17th Rep. B. A. E., 271–274, 1898). In the S. W. the cliff-dwellings (q. v.) were places of security, easy of defense. The large compound structures known as pueblos (q. v.), in which the lower stories formerly had few or no wall openings, were fortifications as well as habitations, while in some cases the mesas on which they are built are in themselves well-nigh impregnable. In the drainage area of the Gila and Salado of s. Arizona there were defensive structures, as shown by their massive walls, in which the former inhabitants could take refuge in time of danger. Many of the isolated peaks of s. Arizona, N. Sonora, and Chihuahua contain the remains of stone breastworks and fortifications. See *Architecture, Casa Grande, Cliff-dwellings, Habitations, Mounds, Pueblos, War and War discipline.*

In addition to the authorities cited, consult Bancroft, Native Races, I, 1886; Bry, Collectiones Peregrinationem, 1590–1634; Jesuit Relations, Thwaites ed., I–LXXIII, 1896–1901; V. Mindeleff in 8th Rep. B. A. E., 1891; C. Mindeleff in 13th and 16th Reps. B. A. E., 1896, 1897; Squier, Antiq. of N. Y., 1851; Squier and Davis, Ancient Monuments, 1848; Thomas in 12th Rep. B. A. E., 1894.                         (c. t.)

**Fort Yukon.** A Kutchakutchin village and trading post of 107 inhabitants at the junction of Yukon and Porcupine rs., Alaska.—Petroff in 10th Census, Alaska, 62, 1884.

**Foskey.** See *Black drink, Busk.*

**Fotshou's Village.** A summer camp of one of the Taku chiefs of the Tlingit named Gochaí; 24 people were there in 1880.—Petroff in 10th Census, Alaska, 32, 1884.

**Fountain.** A band of Upper Lillooet, inhabiting, with the Shuswap, the village of Huhilp, on the E. bank of Fraser r., above Lillooet, Brit. Col.; pop. 205 in 1904.—Can. Ind. Aff. 1904, pt. II, 73, 1905.

**Four Creek Tribes.** A collective name for the Yokuts tribes or bands that resided on the four streams tributary to L. Tulare, Cal.—McKee (1851) in Sen. Ex. Doc. 4, 32d Cong., spec. sess., 80, 1853; Henley in Ind. Aff. Rep., 511, 1854.

**Four Mile Ruin.** A prehistoric ruin on a branch of the Little Colorado, 4 m. from Snowflake, Navajo co., Ariz. The ruin was excavated in 1897 by the Bureau of American Ethnology, the mortuary deposits unearthed indicating relations with both Zuñi and Hopi clans. See Fewkes in 22d Rep. B. A. E., 136–164, 1904.

**Four Nations.** Mentioned with the Kawita and Kasihta as having a conference with the English near the mouth of Apalachicola r., Fla., in 1814 (Hawkins in Am. State Papers, Ind. Aff., I, 859, 1832). Probably the Oakfuskee, with their 3 villages on the Chattahoochee, were meant. (A. S. G.)

**Fowl Town.** A former Seminole town in N. W. Florida, about 12 m. E. of Ft Scott, on Apalachicola r. at the Georgia boundary, containing about 300 inhabitants in 1820. The name has been given also in the plural as though including more than one town. It is distinct from Tutalosi, also called Fowl Town.
Foul Town.—Drake, Bk. Inds., bk. 4, 64, 1848. **Fowl Towns.**—Morse, Rep. to Sec. War, 364, 1822.

**Foxes** (trans. in plural of *wagosh*, 'red fox,' the name of a clan). An Algonquian tribe, so named, according to Fox tradition recorded by Dr William Jones, because once while some Wagohŭgᴵ, members of the Fox clan, were hunting, they met the French, who asked who they were; the Indians gave the name of their clan, and ever since the whole tribe has been known by the name of the Fox clan. Their own name for themselves, according to the same authority, is Mĕshkwaʻkihŭgᴵ, 'red-earth people,' because of the kind of earth from which they are supposed to have been created. They were known to the Chippewa and other Algonquian tribes as Utŭgamig, 'people of the other shore'.

When they first became known to the whites, the Foxes lived in the vicinity of L. Winnebago or along Fox r., Wis. Verwyst (Missionary Labors, 178, 1886) says they were on Wolf r. when Allouez visited them in 1670. As the tribe was inti-

mately related to the Sauk, and the two were probably branches of one original stem, it is probable that the early migrations of the former corresponded somewhat closely with those of the latter. The Sauk came to Wisconsin through the lower Michigan peninsula, their traditional home having been N. of the lakes, and were comparatively newcomers in Wisconsin when they first became known to the French. One of their important villages was for some time on Fox r. The conclusion of Warren (Hist. Ojibways, 95, 1885) that the Foxes

FOX CHIEF

early occupied the country along the S. shore of L. Superior and that the incoming Chippewa drove them out, has the general support of Fox tradition. Nevertheless there is no satisfactory historical evidence that the Foxes ever resided farther N. than Fox r. in Wisconsin, and in none of their treaties with the United States have they claimed land N. of Sauk co. This restless and warlike people was the only Algonquian tribe against whom the French waged war. In addition to their disposition to be constantly at strife with their neighbors, they had conceived a hatred of the French because of the aid which the latter gave the Chippewa and others by furnishing firearms, and because they gathered the various tribes for the purpose of destroying the Foxes. The proposal to exterminate them was seriously considered in the French councils, and their destruction would earlier have been attempted but for the pleas interposed by Nicolas Perrot. Their character is briefly described by Charlevoix (Shea trans., v, 305, 1881) when he says they "infested with their robberies and filled with murders not only the neighborhood of the Bay [Green bay], their natural territory, but almost all the routes communicating with the remote colonial posts, as well as those leading from Canada to Louisiana. Except the Sioux, who often joined them, and the Iroquois, with whom they had formed an alliance, . . . all the nations in alliance with us suffered greatly from these hostilities." It was this tribe that in 1712 planned the attack on the fort at Detroit, and but for the timely arrival of friendly Indians and the bravery of the French commandant, Buisson, would undoubtedly have destroyed it. They were almost constantly at war with the Illinois tribes s. of them, and finally succeeded, in conjunction with the Sauk, in driving them from a large part of their country, of which they took possession. From their earliest known history they were almost constantly at war with the Chippewa dwelling N. of them, but usually without decided success, though often aided by the Sioux. It was by the Chippewa, together with the Potawatomi, Menominee, and the French, that their power was finally broken. About 1746, and perhaps for some few years previous, the Foxes lived at the Little Butte des Morts on the w. bank of Fox r., about 37 m. above Green bay. They made it a point, whenever a trader's boat approached, to place a torch upon the bank as a signal for the traders to come ashore and pay the customary tribute, which they exacted from all. To refuse was to incur their displeasure, and robbery would be the mildest penalty inflicted. Incensed at this exaction, Morand, a leading trader, raised a volunteer force of French and Indians, and after inflicting severe punishment on the Foxes in two engagements drove them down Wisconsin r. They settled on the N. bank about 20 m. from the mouth. About 1780, in alliance with the Sioux, they attacked the Chippewa at St Croix falls, where the Foxes were almost annihilated. The remnant incorporated with the Sauk, and although long officially regarded as one, the two tribes have preserved their identity.

According to Dr William Jones (inf'n, 1906) the culture of the Foxes is that of the tribes of the eastern woodlands with some intrusive streaks from the plains. They were acquainted with wild rice, and raised corn, beans, squashes, and tobacco. They lived in villages in summer, the bark house being the type of the warm-weather dwelling; in winter they scattered and dwelt in oval flag-reed lodges. The social organization is rigid and is based on gentes with marriage outside of the gens. The gens and, with some exceptions, the name, followed the father. The Fox gentes are the Bear, Fox, Wolf, Elk, Big Lynx, Buffalo, Swan, Pheasant, Eagle, Sea, Sturgeon, Bass, Thunder, and Bear Potato. The mythology of the Foxes is rich. Beast fable prevails. The deities are many and some have clear definite character. The principal deity is Wisa'kä$^n$, the culture hero. His brother is Kiyapa'tä$^n$, or Chĭpayabosw$^n$, who presides over the spirit world at the setting of the sun. The belief in a cosmic substance called mănĭtowĭw$^i$, or mănĭtowĭwĭn$^i$, is an essential element in their philosophy. Objects, animate or inanimate, imbued with this substance become the recipients of marked adoration. The Foxes practise many ceremonies, the principal one being the feast festival of the gentes. There is probably no other Algonquian community within the limits of the United States, unless it be that of the Mexican band of Kickapoo in Oklahoma, where a more primitive state of society exists.

Besides being warlike, the Foxes were described by neighboring tribes as stingy, avaricious, thieving, passionate, and quarrelsome; their bravery, however, was proverbial. Like most of the tribes of the region of the great lakes they were polygamists. They were familiar with both dug-out and birch-bark canoes. Spears and clubs were among their weapons of war. Schoolcraft states that a band of warriors seen by him wore headdresses consisting of red-dyed horse-hair tied in such manner to the scalplock as to present the shape of the decoration of a Roman helmet. The rest of the head was completely shaved and painted. They wore breech-cloths, moccasins, and leggings, and the upper part of their bodies was painted; often the print of a hand in white clay was marked on the back or shoulder. They bore flags of feathers. Their "coat of arms" is described by Lahontan in heraldic terms: "A meadow sinople, crossed by a winding pale, with two foxes' gules at the two extremities of the river, in chief and point"—in other words, as his figure shows, an oblique mark representing a stream, with a fox at each end on opposite sides. He explains this "coat of arms" as the mark or symbol which, after a victory or successful raid, they paint on trees. (See Owen, Folk-lore of the Musquakie Inds., 1904.)

Guignes estimated them in 1728 at 200 warriors, but most of the estimates before the last half century give them from 1,500 to 2,000 souls. Lewis and Clark estimated them at 300 warriors, or 1,200 souls, in 1805. Since about 1850 the two tribes have been enumerated together. The 345 "Sauk and Fox of Mississippi" still (1905) in Iowa are said to be all Foxes. There are also 82 "Sauk and Fox of Missouri" under the Kickapoo school in Kansas. See *Sauk*. (J. M. C. T.)

Be-àde'-ke.—Riggs, Dakota Dict., 34, 1852 (Dakota name). **Outagamies.**—Lapham, Inds. of Wis., 16, 1870 (misprint). **Dutagamis.**—Lahontan, New Voy., I, 172, 1703 (misprint). **Foxers.**—Dalton (1783) in Mass. Hist. Soc. Coll., 1st s., x, 123, 1809. **Foxes.**—Albany conf. (1737) in N. Y. Doc. Col. Hist., VI, 104, 1855. **Mechecaukis.**—French trader (1766) quoted by Schoolcraft, Ind. Tribes, III, 554, 1853. **Mechecouakis.**—French trader quoted by Smith, Bouquet's Exped., 69, 1766. **Mechuouakis.**—Heckewelder quoted by Buchanan, Sketches of N. Am. Inds., 156, 1824. **Meskwä'kï'àgⁱ.**—Jones in Am. Anthrop., VI, 370, 1904 ('red-earth people': own name). **Messenacks.**—Hennepin, New Discov., 230, 1698 (Sioux name). **Messenecqz.**—Hennepin (1683) quoted by Shea, Discov. Miss. Val., 134, 1852. **Miscouaquis.**—Coxe, Carolana, map, 1741. **Miskwukeeyuk.**—Jones, Ojebway Inds., 178, 1861 (trans. 'red-earth men'; said to be so called from wearing red blankets). **Moshkos.**—Loskiel (1794) quoted by Ruttenber, Tribes Hudson R., 336, 1872 (may be Mascouten). **Mus-kwä-ka-uk.**—Morgan, Consang. and Affin., 288, 1871. **Muskwake.**—Tanner, Narr., 325, 1830. **Muskwaki.**—McGee in Am. Anthrop., XI, 88, 1898. **Musquacki.**—Maximilian, Trav., 106, 1843. **Mus-quack-ki-uck.**—Ibid. **Musquakees.**—Croghan (1759) quoted by Rupp, West Penn., 146, 1846. **Musquakes.**—Ibid., app., 132. **Musquakies.**—N. Y. Doc. Col. Hist., IX, 161, note, 1855. **Musquakkink.**—Meigs in Smithson. Rep. 1867, 414, 1872. **Musquattamies.**—Croghan (1765) in N. Y. Doc. Col. Hist., VII, 780, 1856. **Musquawkée.**—Featherstonhaugh, Canoe Voy., II, 26, 1847. **Musquiakis.**—Army officer (1812) quoted by Schoolcraft, Ind. Tribes, III, 555, 1853. **Odagami.**—Kelton, Ft Mackinac, 154, 1884. **Odagumaig.**—Schoolcraft, Ind. Tribes, V, 39, 1855. **O-dug-am-eeg.**—Warren (1852) in Minn. Hist. Soc. Coll., V, 33, 1885 (Chippewa name: 'those who live on the opposite side'; from *agaming*, 'on the other side of the water,' and *od*, a personal and tribal prefix). **Odugamies.**—Ibid., 242. **O-dug-aumeeg.**—Ramsey in Ind. Aff. Rep., 83, 1850. **Onlogamies.**—Brackenridge, La., 16, note, 1815 (misprint). **Ontagamies.**—Schoolcraft, Ind. Tribes, V, 184, 1855. **Ootagamis.**—Maximilian, Trav., 102, 1843. **Osheraca.**—Morse, Rep. to Sec. War, 21, 1822 (Winnebago name). **Otagamies.**—Kendall, Trav., II, 295, 1809. **Otogamies.**—Hutchins (1778) quoted by Jefferson, Notes, 144, 1825. **Ottagamies.**—Boudinot, Star in the West, 128, 1816. **Ottagaumies.**—Carver, Trav., 105, 1778. **Ottar-car-me.**—Orig. Jour. Lewis and Clark, VII, 93, 1905. **Ot-târ-gâr-me.**—Lewis and Clark, Trav., 30, 1806. **Ottigamie.**—Schoolcraft, Ind. Tribes, II, 335, 1852. **Ottigaumies.**—Carver, Trav., 39, 1778. **Ottiquamies.**—Pike, Trav., 30, 1811. **Ottogamis.**—Vater, Mith., pt. 3, sec. 3, 266, 1816. **Ouagoussac.**—Jes. Rel. for 1673, quoted by Lapham, Inds. Wis., 4, 1870 (plural of *wagosh*, 'fox'). **Outagami.**—Jes. Rel. for 1667, 21, 1858. **Outagamie-ock.**—Owen, Folk-lore of Musquakie Inds., 18, 1904 ('other side of river people'). **Outagamiouek.**—Ibid. **Outagamy.**—Ibid. **Outagomies.**—Minn. Hist. Soc. Coll., V, 32, note, 1885. **Outaouagamis.**—Hennepin (1683), La., 119, 1698. **Outigamis.**—Nuttall, Jour., 184, 1821. **Outoagamis.**—Hennepin, New Discov., 257, 1698. **Outogamis.**—Coxe, Carolana, 48, 1741. **Outouagamis.**—Hennepin, New Discov., 244, 1698. **Outougamis.**—Coxe, Carolana, map, 1741. **Outtagamies.**—Croghan (1765) quoted in Monthly Am. Jour. Geol., 272, 1831. **Outtagaumie.**—Keane in Stanford, Compend., 513, 1878. **Outtagomies.**—Hutchins (1778) in Schoolcraft, Ind. Tribes, VI, 714, 1857. **Outtongamis.**—Prise de Possession (1671) in N. Y. Doc. Col. Hist., IX, 803, 1855. **Outtouagamis.**—Hennepin, New Discov., 98, 1698. **Outtougamis.**—Prise de Possession (1671) in Margry, Déc., I, 97, 1875. **Penard.**—Esnauts and Rapilly, map U. S., 1777 (misprint). **Quacksis.**—Albany conf. (1726) in N. Y. Doc. Col. Hist., V, 791, 1855. **Red Fox.**—McGee in Am. Anthrop., XI, 88, 1898. **Reiners.**—Dalton (1783) in Mass. Hist. Soc. Coll., 1st s., X, 123, 1809. **Renais.**—McKenney and Hall, Ind. Tribes, III, 79, 1854. **Renards.**—Du Chesneau (1681) in Margry, Déc., II, 267, 1877. **Renars.**—Lewis and Clark, Trav., 15, 1806. **Renarz.**—Orig. Jour. Lewis and Clark, VI, 93, 1905. **Reynards.**—Pike (1806) quoted in Minn. Hist. Soc. Coll., V, 457, 1855. **Skäxshurunu.**—Gatschet, Wyandot MS. vocab., B. A. E., 1881 ('fox people,' from *skäxshu*, 'the red fox': Huron name). **Skenchíohronon.**—Jes. Rel. for 1640, 35, 1858 (Huron name). **Skuakísagi.**—Gatschet, Shawnee MS. vocab., B. A. E., 1882 (sing. Skuakísa; Shawnee name, from *M'skuakisagi*). **Squaghkies.**—Stone, Life of Brant, II, 4, 1864. **Squatchegas.**—Jour. Maj. Gen. Jno. Sullivan, 300, 1887. **Squawkiehah.**—Conover, Kanadesaga and Geneva MS., B. A. E. (Seneca name). **Squawkihows.**—Macauley, N. Y., II, 180, 1829 (improperly said to be the Erie). **To-chewah-coo.**—Clark (1804) in Orig. Jour. Lewis and Clark, I, 190, 1904 (Arikara name?). **Utagāmĭg.**—Jones in Am. Anthrop., VI, 370, 1904 (Chippewa name: 'people of the other shore'). **Wa'gushag.**—Gatschet, Ojibwa MS. vocab., B. A. E., 1878 ('foxes,' from *wa'gush*, 'fox'; a modern Chippewa name). **Wākushég.**—Gatschet, Potawatomi MS. vocab., B. A. E., 1878 ('foxes,' from *wākushe'*, 'fox': Potawatomi name, probably recent).

**Foxes.** An Arikara band.—Culbertson in Smithson. Rep. 1850, 143, 1851.

**Foxes.** A gens or secret order of the Hidatsa, according to Culbertson (Smithson. Rep. 1850, 143, 1851), but properly one of the war and dance societies.

**Francisco.** A Yuma chief. The Tonto Apache who murdered Royse Oatman and most of his family at the Gila bend, Ariz., Mar. 18, 1850, carried off Olive and Mary, the youngest children, 12 and 7 years of age, into slavery, and in 1852 sold them to the Mohave. These Indians treated them better than had the Tonto until a famine came, during which Mary died from starvation and cruelty. Young Lorenzo Oatman, who had escaped after being left for dead, endeavored to interest people in California in the fate of his sisters, but a searching party sent out from Ft Yuma returned without finding trace of them. Finally Francisco, who happened to be at the fort in Jan., 1856, betrayed knowledge of the lost girls, and, impressed with fear of the troops, said he would bring the surviving captive if he had four blankets and some beads to pay for her. When Francisco came to the village the Mohave denied having Olive, having stained her skin with berries, but she spoke out and told who she was. Francisco then addressed them with such eloquent conviction that they consented to release the girl, and on the day set he brought her to the fort, where she was soon joined by her brother. Owing to his service in saving his tribe from chastisement by the militia, or to the rewards and praise he received from the whites, Francisco was chosen chief. He grew overbearing, but remained friendly to the whites. To this friendship his people attributed the ill luck that befell them in a raid that the river tribes undertook in 1857 against the Maricopa. The latter, reenforced by the Papago, won the battle at Maricopa wells, Ariz. Of 75 Yuma warriors all were slain save 3, and when the day turned against them they are believed to have killed the chief who led them to disaster. (F. H.)

**Francis the Prophet.** See *Hillis Hadjo.*

**Frankstown.** A village, probably of the Delawares, which seems to have been near the site of the present Frankstown, Blair co., Pa., in 1756. (J. M.)
Franckstown.—Pouchot map (1758) in N. Y. Doc. Col. Hist., x, 694, 1858. **Franks Town.**—Weiser (1748) in Rupp, West. Pa., app. 13, 1846. **Frankstown.**—Ibid., 20.

**Frauds.** See *Pseudo Indian.*

**Frederiksdal.** A Moravian missionary station in s. Greenland, close to C. Farewell.
Fredericstahl.—Kane, Arct. Explor., I, 453, 1856.

**Frederikshaab.** A missionary station in s. w. Greenland.—Crantz, Hist. Greenland, I, map, 1767.

**French Indians.** A term used by early English writers to designate the tribes in the French interest, especially the Abnaki and their congeners on the New England frontier.

**French influence.** The influence of the French colonists on the Indians began very early. The use of glass beads in barter gave an impetus to the fur trade, and the speedy introduction of other commodities of trade led to long-continued associations with the Iroquoian tribes in particular. The influence of the French missionaries on many of the Indian tribes was marked; for example, the Montagnais and the Huron in the early days. The supply of peltries was increased by furnishing the Indians with firearms, which enabled them to travel with impunity and gave them a superiority over the neighboring tribes which they were not slow to take advantage of; hence almost from the beginning the French settlers and the government of New France came into more or less sympathetic contact with several tribes of the country. This state of affairs arose both from the peaceful efforts of the missionaries and from the desire of the authorities to use the aborigines as a bulwark against the power of the English in North America. To her alliances with the Algonquian tribes of the great lakes and the region s. and e. of them, including New France

and Acadia, France owed in great part her strength on this continent, while on the other hand the confederacy of the Iroquois, the natural enemies of the Algonquian peoples, contributed largely to her overthrow. The French character impelled the colonists to see in the Indian a fellow human being, and it is no wonder that the greatest intermixture between the Indian and the European, N. of the Mexican boundary, is represented by the mixed-bloods of Canada and the N. W. and their descendants, who form no small element in the population of these regions of civilized America (see *Mixed-bloods*). The French recognized the Indian's pride and prejudices, and won his confidence by respecting his institutions and often sharing in his ceremonies. They ruled while seeming to yield. Least of all did they despise the languages of the aborigines, as the rich records of the missionaries abundantly prove. The existence of a large number of mixed-bloods able to speak both their own tongue and French was a distinct advantage to the colonists. The relations between the French and the Acadian Indians, as pictured by Lescarbot, were, to use the word of Friederici, "idyllic," though there is doubtless some exaggeration in these old accounts.

Several words of French origin crept very early into the eastern Algonquian tongues, such as Montagnais, Nascapi, and Micmac, and later a corresponding French element is to be found in the Algonquian languages of the region beyond Montreal (Chamberlain in Canad. Indian, Feb., 1891). The Chippewa vocabulary (Carver, Trav., 421, 1778) contains the word *kapotewian,* 'coat,' which is the French *capote,* with the Chippewa radical suffix *-waian,* 'skin.' In a Missisauga vocabulary of 1801 appears *napané,* 'flour.' The French *bon jour!* in the form *boju!* is now the salutation in several Algonquian dialects. From *(les) anglais* is supposed to be derived the word for 'English' in a number of these languages: Micmac *aglaseãoo,* Montagnais *agaleshu,* Nipissing *aganesha,* formerly *angalesha,* Chippewa *shaganash,* Cree *akayâsiw,* etc. Another example of French influence is the contribution of Canadian French to the Chinook jargon (q. v.). There is also a French element in the modern tales and legends of the Indians of the Canadian Northwest and British Columbia, partly due to missionary teaching, partly to the campfires of the trappers, voyageurs, coureurs de bois, etc. In tales of the N. Pacific coast appears 'Shishé Tlé' (i. e., Jésus Christ), and in some of those of Indians on the E. side of the Rocky mts., 'Mani' (i. e., the Virgin Mary). The French are also the subject of many Indian stories from the Atlantic to the Pacific. Among the Abnaki intermixture began very early. With them the term for mixed-blood is *malouidit*, 'of (St) Malo,' indicative of the source of the fathers in most of these marriages. The wheat introduced from France was termed *maloumenal*, 'grains of (St) Malo.' In the 17th century the Abnaki called peas *wenutsiminar*, 'French seeds.' The Micmac term for apple is *wenjoosoon*, 'French cranberry.' In the Iroquoian languages an example of French influence is seen in *Onontiio* ('Big Mountain'), the term applied by the Mohawk to the kings of France, which seems to translate Montmagny, the name of Champlain's successor as governor of Canada. Another example, noted by Hewitt, is that the Mohawk of Caughnawaga and other settlements on St Lawrence r. speak far more rapidly than do their brethren on Grand River res., Ontario, and they also have a more copious lexicon of modern terms.

Under the leadership of Mgr. de Laval the clergy of New France made strenuous opposition to the sale of liquor to the Indians, and succeeded in getting Colbert to prohibit the traffic; but the necessities of the political schemes of Frontenac and the fact that the Indians turned to the English and Dutch, from whom they could easily procure rum and brandy, caused the reversal of this policy, against the protests of missionaries and the church. To salve their feelings the matter was referred to the Sorbonne and the University of Toulouse, the former pronouncing against the sale of liquor to the Indians, the latter declaring it permissible. Finally a sort of theoretical prohibition but actual toleration of liquor selling resulted.

Consult Parkman (1) Jesuits in North America, (2) Conspiracy of Pontiac, (3) Pioneers of France in the New World, and other works; Jesuit Relations, Thwaites ed., I–LXXIII, 1896–1901.

(A. F. C.)

**Fresnal** (Span.: 'ash grove'). A Papago village, probably in Pima co., s. Ariz.; pop. about 250 in 1863.—Poston in Ind. Aff. Rep. 1863, 385, 1864.

**Friedenshuetten** (German: 'huts of peace'). A village formerly on Susquehanna r. a few miles below Wyalusing, and probably in Wyoming co., Pa. It was established in 1765 by Mahican and Delaware converts under direction of the Moravian missionaries, and seems to have been on the site of an older town. In 1770 the Indians removed to Friedenstadt, in Beaver co. According to Loskiel (Miss. United Breth., pt. 3, 1794) the name Friedenshuetten was also applied to a temporary village adjoining Bethlehem in Northampton co., settled in 1746 by Moravian converts from Shecomico, who

soon afterward removed to Gnadenhuetten in Carbon co. (J. M.)

Freidenshutten.—Ruttenber, Tribes Hudson R., 198, 1872. Frieden Huetten.—Rupp, Northampton, etc., Cos., 86, 1845. Friedenshuetten.—Loskiel (1794) in Rupp, West. Pa., app., 355, 1846. Friedenshutten.—Loskiel in Day, Penn., 103, 1843.

**Friedensstadt** (Germ.: 'town of peace'). A village in Beaver co., Pa., probably near the present Darlington, settled in May, 1770, by the Moravian Delawares from Friedenshuetten. In 1773 they removed to Gnadenhuetten and Schoenbrunn on the Muskingum. See *Languntennenk*. (J. M.)

Friedensstadt.—Loskiel, Missions, map, 1794. Friedenstadt.—Ibid., pt. 3, 57. Town of Peace.—Ibid.

**Friendly Village.** The name given by Mackenzie (Voy., 351, 1802) to an Athapascan village, probably of the Takulli, on upper Salmon r., Brit. Col., on account of his kind treatment there.

**Frogtown** (trans. of *Walâsi'yĭ*, 'frog place'). A former Cherokee settlement on a creek of the same name, N. of Dahlonega, Lumpkin co., Ga.—Mooney in 19th Rep. B. A. E., 545, 1900.

**Fugitive.** A former Kaniagmiut Eskimo village at Hobson harbor, Sitkalidak id., near Kodiak, Alaska.—Lisiansky, Voy., 178, 1814.

**Furniture.** There was little regular furniture among the Indians, as home life was simple and wants were few. The furniture of the tipi differed from that used in the communal dwelling, for the character of the habitation controlled its furnishing. In all classes of habitations seats were generally arranged along the walls. Mats of plaited bark or of woven rushes and skins dressed only on one side were spread as seats, and pillows, formerly having skin cases, were stuffed with feathers, the hair of the deer or elk, in some cases scrapings from the hide, or, as in the S., the long gray Spanish moss, and used as cushions to sit on. Among some tribes a bearskin was the seat of honor. In the pueblos seats were of stone, or were rectangular stools made from a single block of wood, in addition to a masonry bench extending round or partly round the room. In N. California stools were circular in form. In the houses of the N. W. coast long settees were placed facing the fire, against the partitions that marked a family's space in the communal dwelling.

In the earth lodge and similar habitations stationary couches, which served as seats by day and as beds by night, were arranged against the walls. These were made by planting in the floor four tall posts on which were supported two shelves, or bunks, of wattled twigs, on which the bedding was placed. Sometimes both shelves were used as beds, but generally the upper one was used for storing the property of the person to whom the compartment belonged. In the lodges of some tribes, hung on a rod fastened across the two front poles was a reed curtain, which could be rolled up or dropped to give seclusion to the occupant of the berth. Another form of bed consisted of a mat of willows stretched upon a low platform, its tapering ends raised and fastened to tripods which formed head and foot boards. The skin of an animal, as the buffalo bull, killed in winter, was trimmed to fit the bed and served as the mattress, on which robes or blankets were spread as bedding. Pillows such as are described above were used, but in N. California were of wood and were

BED FRAME OF THE CHIPPEWA. (HOFFMAN)

used only in the men's sleeping lodge. Little children occupied cradles (q. v.), which varied in form and ornamentation, but were all constructed on the general plan of a portable box and adapted to the age of the child. Among some tribes a hammock, made by folding a skin about two ropes, was hung between posts and used to swing children to sleep. A crotched stick was thrust slanting into the edge of the fireplace, and from the crotch hung one or more smaller crotched sticks directly over the fire, serving as hooks for kettles in cooking. The household meal

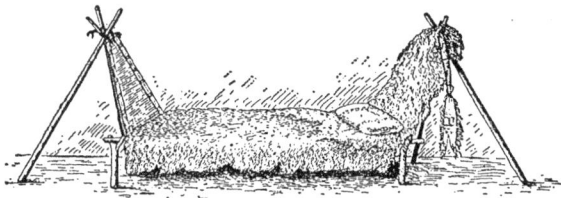

COUCH OF THE PLAINS TRIBES. (MOONEY)

was often served on a mat. In the dwellings of the corn-growing Plains Indians the wooden mortar used for pounding maize was set at the right of the entrance and held firmly in place by sinking its pointed base well into the earthen floor. In every habitation a suspended pole or rack was placed near the fire for the drying of moccasins or other clothing. In the Pueblo house the mealing trough occupied a corner of the room, and was set at a sufficient distance from the wall to permit the women to kneel comfortably at their work and face the apartment. The trough was of stone and generally contained three metates, varying in coarse-

ness, for hulling, cracking, and mealing the grain. Niches in the walls served as shelves or closets. Utensils varied with the methods of cooking in the different parts of the country; they were baskets, wooden and pottery vessels, and later metal kettles. Household utensils, for cooking, eating, and drinking, were usually kept in or near the space belonging to the housewife, and consisted of baskets, boxes, platters, and bowls of wood or pottery, spoons of horn, wood, gourd, or pottery, and ladles. Some of the household utensils were ornamented with carving or painting, and not infrequently were treasured as heirlooms. Brooms of coarse grass or twigs were used to sweep the floor, and the wing of a bird served as a brush to keep the central fireplace tidy. The Pueblos tied a bunch of coarse grass near the middle, using the butt end for brushing the hair and the other for sweeping the floor. Some of the Plains and Rocky mtn. tribes used a wooden spade-like implement to remove the snow from the ground about the entrance of the lodge, and the Pueblos employed a similar implement for passing bread in and out of the ovens. The Plains tribes stored their food and other articles in packs made of parfleche and ornamented with painted designs; for preserving feathers until needed the Pueblos used wooden receptacles cut from a single stick, usually of cottonwood, and provided with a countersunk lid; on the N. W. coast elaborately carved boxes and trays were made for this purpose.

Mural decoration was confined to the Pueblos and the houses on the N. Pacific coast. Frequently in the latter the posts, beams, and doors were carved and painted, as were also the screens, which served several purposes, domestic and ceremonial.

In the lodges of the Plains tribes the ornamented shields, weapons, saddles, bridles, and various accouterments were always hung on the posts within the lodge, and gave color and decorative effect to the otherwise plain interior of the native dwelling. In winter painted or embroidered skins were suspended between the inner circle of posts of the earth lodge and, like an arras, inclosed the space about the fire, adding much to the attractiveness of this picturesque habitation. Among the Eskimo the stone lamp was the essential article of the household. It furnished light and heat and served as a stove for cooking. Such lamps, cut from steatite or basalt, cost much labor, and were handed down from one generation to another. See *Boxes and Chests, Dishes, Habitations, Implements.*

Consult Boas (1) in Rep. Nat. Mus., 1895, (2) in 6th Rep. B. A. E., 1888; Dixon in Bull. Am. Mus. Nat. Hist., XVII, pt 3, 1905; Dorsey and Voth in Field Columb. Mus. Publ., Anthrop. ser.; J. O. Dorsey in 13th Rep. B. A. E., 1896; Goddard in Univ. Cal. Publ., Am. Archæol. and Ethnol., I, 1903; Hoffman in 14th Rep. B. A. E., 1896; Holm, Descr. New Sweden, 1834; Hough in Rep. Nat. Mus., 1896; Kroeber in Bull. Am. Mus. Nat. Hist., XVIII, pt 1, 1902; Mindeleff in 8th Rep. B. A. E., 1891; Nelson in 18th Rep. B. A. E., 1899.                    (A. C. F.)

**Fur trade.** The fur trade was an important factor in the conquest and settlement of North America by the French and the English. Canada and the great W. and N. W. were long little more to the world than the "Fur Country." Lahontan (New Voy., I, 53, 1703) said: "Canada subsists only upon the trade of skins or furs, three-fourths of which come from the people that live around the great lakes." Long before his time the profit to be gained in the fur traffic with distant tribes encouraged adventurers to make their way to the Mississippi and beyond, while the expenses of not a few ambitious attempts to reach Cathay or Cipangu through a N. W. passage to the South sea were met, not out of royal treasuries, but from presents and articles of barter received from the Indians. The various fur and trading companies established for traffic in the regions w. of the great lakes and in the Hudson bay country exercised a great influence upon the aborigines by bringing into their habitat a class of men, French, English, and Scotch, who would intermarry with them, thus introducing a mixed-blood element into the population. Manitoba, Minnesota, and Wisconsin in particular owe much of their early development to the trader and the mixed-blood. The proximity of hunting grounds to the settlements beyond the Alleghanies favored the free hunter and the single trapper, while the remote regions of the N. W. could best be exploited by the fur companies. The activity of the free trapper and solitary hunter meant the extermination of the Indian where possible. The method of the great fur companies, which had no dreams of empire over a solid white population, rather favored amalgamation with the Indians as the best means of exploiting the country in a material way. The French fur companies of early days, the Hudson's Bay Company (for two centuries ruler of a large part of what is now Canada), the Northwest Company, the American Fur Company (in the initiation of which patriotism played a part), the Missouri Fur Company, the Russian-American Company, the Alaska Commercial Company, and others have influenced the development of civilization in North America. The forts and fur-trading stations of these companies long represented to the Indian tribes the white man and his civilization. That the Hudson's Bay Company abandoned its line of forts on the seacoast and went to the Indian hunting grounds, ultimately taking possession of the vast interior of Canada, was due largely to the competition of rival fur traders, such as the Northwest Company. Intimate contact with Indian tribes was thus forced on rather than initiated by the Hudson's Bay Company. The pioneers of the fur trade were the solitary trappers and buyers, whose successors are the free traders on the upper Mackenzie today. They blazed the way for canoe trips, fur brigades, trading posts, and, finally, settlements. It was often at a portage, where there were falls or rapids in a river, that the early white trader established himself. At such places afterward sprang up towns whose manufactures were developed by means of the water power. The Indian village also often became a trading post and is now transformed into a modern city. Portages and paths that were first used by the Indian and afterward by the fur trader are now changed to canals and highways, but other routes used by fur traders are still, in regions of the far N., only primitive paths. Some, like the *grande route* from Montreal to the country beyond Hudson bay, are followed by white men for summer travel and pleasure. In the N. W. the fur trade followed the course of all large streams, and in some parts the leading clans derived much of their power from the control of the waterways.

The appearance and disappearance of fur-bearing animals, their retreat from one part of the country to another, influenced the movements of Indian tribes. This is particularly true of the movements of the buffalo (q. v.), though the decrease of other large game was often the compelling motive of tribal migration. The hunt of the buffalo led to certain alliances and unions for the season of the chase among tribes of different stocks, a few of which may have become permanent. Thus the Kutenai, Sarsi, Siksika, and Atsina have all hunted together on the plains of the Saskatchewan and the upper Missouri. The occasional and finally complete disappearance of the buffalo from these regions has weighed heavily upon the Indian tribes, the buffalo having been to some of them what the bamboo is to the Malay and the palm to the West African, their chief source of food, fuel, clothing, and shelter. The extermination of the wild buffalo caused the discontinuance of the Kiowa sun dance (Mooney in 17th Rep. B. A. E., 346, 349, 1898) and affected likewise the ceremonies of other tribes. In several tribes the buffalo dance was an important ceremony and buffalo chiefs seem to have been elected for duty during the hunting season. The importance of the northern hare, whose skin was used to make coats and tipis by certain Indians of the Canadian Northwest, is shown in the designation "Hareskins" for one of the Athapascan tribes (Kawchogottine). The Tsattine, another Athapascan tribe, received their name for a like reason. The Iroquois war against the Neutral nation was partly due to the growing scarcity of beavers in the Iroquois country. The recent inroads of the whites upon the muskox of arctic Canada are having their effect upon the Indian tribes of that region. Bell (Jour. Am. Folk-lore, XVI, 74, 1903) has noted the advance of the free trader on Athabasca r. and lake, giving rise to a barbarous border civilization, like that of the whaler on the shores of Hudson bay and the rancher and miner on the Peace and other mountain streams, which is having its due effect on the natives: "The influx of fur traders into the Mackenzie r. region, and even to Great Bear lake, within the last two years, has, I believe, very much altered the character of the northern Indians." The effect upon the Indians of the s. Atlantic region of the coming of the white trader was early noted by Adair and others. Here, too, the trader not infrequently married into the tribe and became an agent in modifying aboriginal culture by the introduction of European ideas and institutions.

Before the advent of the Europeans the fur trade had assumed considerable proportions in various parts of the continent (Mason, Rep. Nat. Mus., 586–589, 1894). In the 16th century the Pecos obtained buffalo skins from the Apache and bartered them again with the Zuñi. The people of Acoma obtained deerskins from the Navaho. The trade between Ottawa r. and Hudson bay was well known to the Jesuit missionaries in the beginning of the 17th century. In the time of Lewis and Clark the Arikara obtained furs from other tribes and bartered them with the whites for various articles, and the Skilloot used to get buffalo skins from tribes on the upper Missouri to barter off with other Indian tribes. The Chilkat proper and the Chilkoot even now act as middlemen in the fur trade between the whites and other Indian tribes. The tribes about the mouth of the Columbia were also middlemen, and their commerce influenced the conditions of their social institutions, making possible, perhaps, slavery, the existence of a class of nobles, certain changes in the status of women, etc. The trade in furs between the Eskimo of Alaska and the peoples of extreme N. E. Asia existed long before the advent of Europeans. At Kotzebue sd. there is

still held a summer fair (Nelson in 18th Rep. B. A. E., 229, 1899). Fur-trading voyages are common in this region.

The development of intertribal commerce among the Plains Indians was much stimulated by the hunt of the buffalo and its material rewards. By inducing the natives to trap and hunt the wild animals of the northern part of the continent on a large scale for the sake of their valuable skins the fur companies stimulated the aboriginal talent in the production and use of snares and other devices, even if they did not improve the morals of the Indians. The introduction of the horse (q. v.) and the gun led to the extermination of the buffalo by Plains Indians and whites. In certain parts of the continent skins were a basis of value—primitive money. A Kutenai, when he draws a beaver, produces a picture, not of the animal, but of its cured skin. With the Eskimo of the Yukon, even before the advent of the Russians, the unit of value was "one skin"; that is, the skin of the full-grown land otter, and of late years this has been replaced by the skin of the beaver (Nelson, op. cit., 232). Skins of sea otters, beavers, and other animals were the basis of the wealth, also, of many tribes of the N. Pacific coast, until the practical extermination of some of these species made necessary a new currency, provided in the blankets of the Hudson's Bay Company, which were preferred to most other substitutes that were offered by white men. Toward the interior the beaver skin was the ruling unit, and to-day in some parts such unit is the skin of the muskrat. Among the Kutenai of s. E. British Columbia the word for a quarter of a dollar is *khanko* ('muskrat'). English traders reckoned prices in skins and French traders in "plus" (*pelus, peaux*). Indians counted their wealth in skins, and in the potlatch of some tribes the skin preceded the blanket as a unit of value in the distribution. During the colonial period furs were legal tender in some parts of the country; also at various times and places during the pioneer occupancy of the W. and N. Altogether the fur trade may be considered one of the most important and interesting phases of the intercourse between the Europeans and the North American Indians. See *Buffalo, Commerce, Exchange, Trading posts, Trails and Trade routes, Travel and Transportation.*

Consult Bryce, Remarkable History of the Hudson's Bay Company, 1900; Chittenden, American Fur Trade of the Far West, 1902; Laut, Story of the Trapper, 1902; Morice, History of Northern British Columbia, 1904; Willson, The Great Company, 1900.　　　　　　(A. F. C.)

**Fu Sang.** A land E. of China which, according to Chinese annals, was visited in a voyage made by Buddhist monks in the 5th century A. D. Some have sought to identify it with America; there is good reason to believe that Fu Sang was Corea, Japan, Sakhalin, or the Liu-kiu ids., or all of them. Japan has played a part in the myths of the Chinese similar to the garden of the Hesperides in Greek story. De Guignes was an early propagator of the Fu Sang theory; more recent advocates were C. G. Leland (Fu-Sang, 1875) and Vining (An Inglorious Columbus, 1885). Arguments on the other side have been advanced by W. H. Dall in Science, Nov. 5, 1886; H. Mueller in Verh. d. Berl. Ges. F. Anthr., 1883, and A. F. Chamberlain in Am. Notes and Queries, II, 84, 1888, but the whole matter has been effectually disposed of by the authoritative investigations of Gustav Schlegel, an eminent Chinese scholar, in his *Fou-Sang* (1892). Schlegel attributes what is not mythical in the Chinese legends to the island of Sakhalin, etc. (A. F. C.)

**Fusihatchi** (Creek: *fu'swa* 'bird,' *ha'-tchi* 'creek,' 'river'). A former Upper Creek town in Macon co., Ala., on the N. bank of lower Talapoosa r., 2 m. below Huhliwahli. Remains of a walled town were visible from the opposite bank of the river at the close of the 18th century. (A. S. G.)

Foosce-hat-che.—Hawkins (1799), Sketch, 33, 1848. Fooschatchee.—Hawkins (1813) in Am. State Papers, Ind. Aff., I, 854, 1832. Foose Hatchee.—Ibid., 848. Fooskahatche.—Schoolcraft, Ind. Tribes, IV, 380, 1854. Fusahatche.—Bartram, Trav., 461, 1791. Tusehatche.—Barnard (1793) in Am. State Papers, Ind. Aff., I, 386, 1832 (misprint,).

**Fusualgi.** The Bird clan of the Creeks.

Bird.—Morgan, Anc. Soc., 161, 1878. Fúsualgi.—Gatschet, Creek Migr. Leg., I, 155, 1884. Tus'-wă.—Morgan, op. cit. (misprint).

**Fwaha.** The Fire clan of the former pueblo of Pecos, N. Mex.

Fwah.—Hewett in Am. Anthrop., n. s., VI, 451, 1904. Fwa-ha'.—Hodge, ibid., IX, 350, 1896.

**Fyules.** A former village in California, said to have been Esselen.—Taylor in Cal. Farmer, Apr. 20, 1860.

**Gaandowanang** (*Gă'-än-do-wă-nän̄*, 'it is a great tree.'—Hewitt). A former Seneca village on Genesee r., near Cuylerville, N. Y.

Big Tree.—Morris deed (1797) in Am. State Papers, Ind. Aff., I, 627, 1832. Chenondoanah.—Johnson (1754) in N. Y. Doc. Col. Hist., VI, 899, 1855. Gă'-än-do-wă-nän̄. — Hewitt, inf'n, 1886 (Seneca name). Gä-un-do'-wä-na.—Morgan, League Iroq., 468, 1851. Kanvagen.—Pouchot, map (1758) in N. Y. Doc. Col. Hist., X, 694, 1858.

**Gabacamanini.** A rancheria, probably Cochimi, connected with Purisima (Cadegomo) mission, Lower California, in the 18th century.—Doc. Hist. Mex., 4th s., V, 190, 1857.

**Gabrieleño.** A Shoshonean division and dialectic group which formerly occupied all of Los Angeles co., Cal., s. of the San Bernardino mts., with the probable exception of a strip of coast from Santa

Monica westward, and Orange co. to Alisos cr.; the territory did not extend very far E. of the Los Angeles co. line. Santa Catalina id. also was occupied by them, and possibly San Nicolas id. The name has been loosely applied by the Spanish inhabitants from the name of the mission of San Gabriel, near Los Angeles, where many were at one time collected. This, in the absence of an appropriate native term, may be accepted as the most convenient designation. Their rancherias were: Acuragna, Ahapchingas, Alyeupkigna, Awigna, Azucsagna, Cahuenga, Chokishgna, Chowigna, Cucamonga, Hahamogna, Harasgna, Houtgna, Hutucgna, Isanthcogna, Kowanga, Mapipinga, Maugna, Nacaugna, Okowvinjha, Pascegna, Pasinogna, Pubugna, Pimocagna, Saway-yanga, Sibagna, Sisitcanogna, Sonagna, Suangna, Taybipet, Techahet, Tibahagna, and Yangna.

Gabrileños.—Loew in Ann. Rep. Chief of Eng., pt. III, 542, 1876. Kij.—Hale, Ethnog. and Philol., 222, 1846. Kizh.—Ibid., 569; Gatschet in Rep. Chief of Eng., III, 556, 1876 (trans. 'houses'). Playsanos.—Hoffman in Bull. Essex Inst., XVII, 26, 1885 (seems to be applied to the California Shoshoni living in the lowlands, and especially near the coast in the region of Los Angeles). San Gabriel.—Hale, op. cit., 222. Tobikhars.—Gatschet, op. cit., 556 (said to mean 'settlers,' but probably taken from Tobohar, the mythical first man). Tumangamalum.—A. L. Kroeber, inf'n, 1905 (Luiseño name: 'northerners').

**Gachigundae** (*Gatcligu'nda-i*, 'village always moving to and fro'). A Haida town on the N. E. shore of Alliford bay, Moresby id., Queen Charlotte ids., Brit. Col., occupied by a socially low branch of the Djahui-skwahladagai.—Swanton, Cont. Haida, 279, 1905.

**Gachwechnagechga** ('islanders.'—Hewitt). The name applied to the Lehigh Indians formerly on Lehigh r., Pa.; so called, according to Pyrlæus, after the island they occupied.

Gachwechnágechga.—Gatschet in Am. Antiq., IV, 75, 1881–82. Lecha.—Ibid. Lehigh.—Ibid.

**Gadaho** (*Gă-'dä'-ho'*, 'sand bank.'—Hewitt). A former Seneca village that occupied the site of Castile, Genesee co., N. Y.

Gă'd'ä'ho'.—Hewitt, inf'n, 1886 (Seneca form). Gä-dă'-o'.—Morgan, League Iroq., 435, 1851. Gardeau.—Morris deed (1797) in Am. State Papers, Ind. Aff., I, 627, 1832. Gardow.—Morgan, op. cit., 467. Guardou.—Conover, Kanadega and Geneva MS., B. A. E.

**Gadinchin** ('rush,' 'reed grass'). Given as a clan of the Pinal Coyotero living in 1881 at San Carlos agency, Ariz.—Bourke in Jour. Am. Folk-lore, III, 112, 1890.

**Gado** (*Gadō'*). A Haida town said to have stood on the s. side of De la Beche inlet, Moresby id., Queen Charlotte ids., Brit. Col. Another town of the same name is said to have stood on the E. side of Lyell id., near the town of Hlkia.—Swanton, Cont. Haida, 278, 1905.

**Gaedi** (*Gă'-idî*, the name of a fish). A Haida town on the N. E. shore of a small inlet just N. E. of Huston inlet, Queen Charlotte ids., Brit. Col. It belonged to the Tadji-lanas, a band of Ninstints.—Swanton, Cont. Haida, 277, 1905.

**Gaesigusket** (*Ga-isiga's-q!eit*, 'strait town where no waves come ashore'). A Haida town on Murchison id., at a point opposite Hot Springs id., Queen Charlotte ids., Brit. Col. So named because it fronted on smooth water. It belonged to the Hagilanas of the Ninstints.—Swanton, Cont. Haida, 277, 1905.

**Gagihetnas-hadai** ( *G·ɛgihē't-nas-:had'ă'i*, 'land-otter house people'). Given by Boas (5th Rep. N. W. Tribes Can., 27, 1889) as the name of a subdivision of the Yaku-lanas, a division of the Raven clan of the Haida in Alaska. It is in reality only a house name belonging to that band. The Gagihet (Gagixi't) is a human being who, in native mythology, has been made insane by land otters. (J. R. S.)

**Gahato** ('floating branch.'—Hewitt). A village, probably of the Seneca, in Chemung co., N. Y., which was burned by Sullivan in 1779. (J. M.)
Chamong.—Pemberton (*ca.* 1792) in Mass. Hist. Soc. Coll., 1st s., II, 175, 1810. Chemeney.—Ibid., 176. Chemung.—Brown (1803), ibid., IX, 120, 1804 (probably the Delaware name). Gähă'to.—Morgan, League Iroq., 469, 1851.

**Gahayanduk** ( *Gă-'hä\*ⁿyă-yăⁿñ'-dă'k*, 'there was a forest, or orchard.'—Hewitt). A Seneca village destroyed by Denonville's expedition in 1687.—Shea, note in Charlevoix, New France, III, 289, 1868.

**Gahko** ('crane'). A Mahican clan.

**Gahlinskun** (*Gălĭ'nskun*, 'high up on a point'). A Haida town N. of C. Ball, on the E. coast of Graham id., Brit. Col., occupied by the Naikun-kegawai. Work assigned to it 120 people in 9 houses in 1836–41. A-se-guang, the name given by him, is said to have been applied to some high land back of the town.—Swanton, Cont. Haida, 280, 1905.
A se guang.—Schoolcraft, Ind. Tribes, V, 489, 1855 (after Work, 1836–41). A-se-quang.—Kane, Wand. in N. A., app., 1859 (misprint from Work). Gălĭ'nskun.—Swanton, Cont. Haida, 280, 1905.

**Gaiagunkun** (*GaiɛgA'n kun*). A Haida town said to have stood near Hot Spring id., Brit. Col.—Swanton, Cont. Haida, 278, 1905.

**Gaibanipitea.** Apparently a former settlement of the Pima or of an allied tribe, possibly the Sobaipuri, described as situated on a hill on the w. bank of the Rio San Pedro. Visited by Father Kino in 1697. Probably identical with the ruins known as Santa Cruz, a few miles w. of Tombstone, s. Ariz.
Jaibanipitea.—Bancroft, No. Mex. States, I, 274, 1884. Santa Cruz de Gaibanipitea.—Bernal (1697) in Doc. Hist. Mex., 4th s., I, 277, 1856. Santa Cruz del Cuervo.—Bancroft, No. Mex. States, I, 274, 1884. Sta. Cruz de Gaibauipetea.—Ibid., 264. Sta. Cruz de Jaibanipitea de Pimas.—Kino (1698), ibid., 290.

**Gakhulin** ('village on a stream'). One of the 4 Kansa villages in 1820.
Gaqúliⁿ.—Dorsey, Kansa MS. vocab., B. A. E., 1882.

**Gakhulinulinbe.** A former Kansa village near the head of a s. tributary of Kansas r., on which a trading post was established.
Gaqúliⁿ uliⁿ'be.—Dorsey, Kansa MS. vocab., B. A. E., 1882.

**Gakpomute** ('little turtle'). A Mahican clan.

**Galena.** The ore of lead occurs in beds, pockets, and in true veins in connection with various geological formations in the United States and in British America, being especially abundant in Illinois and Missouri. The Indians of the Mississippi valley, especially the mound builders, seem to have prized this ore very highly in the form in which it usually occurs—masses of blue-gray, glistening cubical crystals. It was probably valued for its beauty, as was also the yellow crystals of iron pyrites, and possibly had special significance with the mound-building tribes, as it is found among the articles placed upon the sacrificial altars. In some cases the heat of the altar fires has been sufficient to melt part of the ore, but it does not appear that the Indians had learned to make any practical use of the lead. Squier and Davis found 30 pounds of the ore, in pieces varying from 2 ounces to 3 pounds, on an altar in one of the Mound City mounds in Ohio; and it is at times found also on pueblo sites. Galena was sometimes shaped into the simpler forms of ceremonial objects, such as spheres, hemispheres, cones, plummets, and boatstones (q. v.). Consult Moorehead in The Antiquarian, I, 1897; Rau in Smithson. Rep. 1872, 1873; Squier and Davis in Smithson. Cont., I, 1848. (W. H. H.)

**Galiano Island.** A band of the Penelakut (q. v.) who speak a Cowichan dialect, residing in s. E. Vancouver id.; pop. 32 in 1904.—Can. Ind. Aff. 1904, pt. II, 69, 1905.

**Galilali** (*Galīlali*, 'the houses'; i. e., ancient cave houses). A Tarahumare rancheria in the Sierra Madre, w. Chihuahua, Mexico.—Lumholtz, inf'n, 1894.

**Galisteo.** A former Tano pueblo 1½ m. N. E. of the present hamlet of the same name, and about 22 miles s. of Santa Fé, N. Mex. Identified by Bandelier (Arch. Inst. Papers, IV, 122, 1892) with the Ximena of Coronado, who visited the village in 1541, when it consisted of 30 houses. Galisteo was the seat of a Franciscan mission perhaps as early as 1617—certainly in 1629—and in 1680 contained 800 neophytes and a fine church; San Cristóbal was a visita at this date. In the revolt of the Pueblos in August of the latter year the Indians of Galisteo killed the resident priest, besides the father custodian of New Mexico, the missionaries of San Marcos and Pecos, who were on their way to give warning, and several colonists. After the remaining Spanish colonists had been driven out of the country the Tano of Galisteo removed to Santa Fé and erected a village on the ruins of the old Palace, but were expelled by Vargas in 1692. In 1706 the town was reestablished with 90 Indians by the governor of the province under the name Nuestra Señora de los Remedios de Galisteo, but it was also called Santa María. It remained an inconsiderable village until between 1782 and 1794, when the inhabitants, decimated by smallpox and by the persistent hostilities of the Comanche, removed to Santo Domingo pueblo, where their descendants still live, preserving the language of their ancestors and in part their tribal autonomy. At one time, according to Bandelier, Galisteo probably had a population of 1,000. In 1712 it numbered 110 souls; in 1748, 50 families, and but 52 souls in 1782 just before its abandonment. (F. W. H.)

Galisteo.—Vaugondy, map Amérique, 1778. Calixteo.—Kitchin, map N. A., 1787. Calixto.—Güssefeld, Charte America, 1797. Galasteo.—Mendoza (1742) quoted by Meline, Two Thousand Miles, 213, 1867. Galiste.—Alcedo, Dic. Geog., II, 131, 1787. Galisteo.—Zarate Salmeron (ca. 1629) cited by Bancroft, Nat. Races, I, 600, 1882. Gallisteo.—Eaton in Schoolcraft, Ind. Tribes, IV, 220, 1854. Glistéo.—Oñate (1598) in Doc. Inéd., XVI, 258, 1871. Jimena.—Mota-Padilla, Hist. de la Conq., 164, 1742. Kimena.—Peet in Am. Antiq., XVI, 354, 1895 (misprint). Nuestra de Señora de los Remedios de Galisteo.—MS. of 1720 quoted by Bandelier in Arch. Inst. Papers, V, 194, 1890. San Lucas.—Sosa (1590) in Doc. Inéd., XV, 251, 1871 (identified with Galisteo by Bandelier, Arch. Inst. Papers, IV, 101, 1892). Santa Ana.—Oñate (1598), ibid., XVI, 258, 1871 (Glistéo or). Santa Cruz de Galisteo.—Vetancurt, Teatro Mex., III, 322, 1871 (mission name prior to 1706). Santa María de Galisteo.—Cuervo (1706) quoted by Bancroft, Ariz. and N. Mex., 228, 1889 (mission name from 1706). S$^{ta}$ Cruz de Galisteo.—D'Anville, map Amér. Sept., 1746. S$^{ta}$ Maria.—Ibid. S$^{ta}$ Mario.—Jefferys, Amer. Atlas, map 5, 1776. S$^{t}$ Maria.—D'Anville, map N. A., Bolton ed., 1752. T'a-ge Uing-ge.—Bandelier in Arch. Inst. Papers, IV, 100, 1892 (native name). Ta-ge-uing-ge.—Ibid., III, 125, 1890 (native name). Tage-unge.—Bandelier, Gilded Man, 221, 1893. Tanoque.—Schoolcraft, Ind. Tribes, III, 298, 1853 (trans. 'the lower settlement': native name; but it seemingly means 'Tano village'). Ximena.—Castañeda (ca. 1565) in 14th Rep. B. A. E., 523, 1896. Ximera.—Castañeda in Ternaux-Compans, Voy., IX, 177, 1838.

**Gall** (*Pizi*). A chief of the Hunkpapa Teton Sioux, born on Moreau r., S. Dak., in 1840; died at Oak cr., S. Dak., Dec. 5, 1894. He was of humble parentage, but was well brought up, receiving the usual consideration of his people for an orphan, his mother being a poor widow. As a young man he was a warrior of note, and that he was possessed of military genius of high order was shown by the disposition he made of his forces at the battle of the Little Bighorn, June 25, 1876, where he led the Sioux. He was the lieutenant of Sitting Bull, but had the quality of leadership in the field that was

lacking in his chief. He fled to Canada with Sitting Bull after the Custer affair, but in 1880 he and Crow Chief withdrew from the Sitting Bull following, leaving the latter with but few people. With his followers he surrendered to Maj. Ilges at Poplar r. camp, Mont., Jan. 1, 1881, and settled as a farmer on Standing Rock res., N. and S. Dak. He denounced Sitting Bull as a coward and a fraud and became a friend to the whites, wielding a potent influence in procuring the submission of the Indians to the plan of the Government for the education of the children. He was a man of noble presence and much esteemed for his candor

CHIEF GALL

and sagacity by the whites with whom he came in contact. He was influential in bringing about the ratification of the act of Mar. 2, 1889, the last agreement with the Sioux by which their great reservation was divided into separate reservations and certain portions were ceded to the United States. From 1889 he was a judge of the court of Indian offenses at Standing Rock agency. (J. M'L.)

**Galley.** A Cherokee settlement of about 12 families in 1819 (Nuttall, Arkansa, 122, 1821), on the Galley hills, in Yell co., Ark., about midway between Danville and Dardenelle. (J. M.)

**Gallinomero.** A name more usually rendered *Kainomero* by the Indians to whom it is applied. It was given by the Spaniards of San Rafael mission to the Pomo from the vicinity of Healdsburg and Santa Rosa, Sonoma co., Cal., on the occasion of their being brought into the mission in the early part of the 19th century. The name is now used to designate in particular the few remaining Indians whose former homes were in the Russian r. valley from the vicinity of Healdsburg s. to the southern limit of the territory occupied by the Pomo, or a point about halfway between Santa Rosa and Petaluma. In a still broader sense it is made to include the remainder of the people speaking the same dialect and formerly living about Cloverdale and the upper part of Dry cr. The name is not of Indian origin and its significance is not known.

(S. A. B)

Cainameros.—Bancroft, Hist. Cal., IV, 71, 1886. Calajomanes.—Bancroft, Nat. Races, I, 363, 1877. Canaumanos.—Taylor in Cal. Farmer, Mar. 30, 1860. Canimairo.—Ibid., June 8, 1860. Canimares.—Ibid., Feb. 22, 1860. Gal-li-no-me'-ro.—Powers in Cont. N. A. Ethnol., III, 174, 1877. Kai-nama.—Wrangell, Ethnog. Nachr., 80, 1839. Kai-na-méah.—Gibbs (1851) in Schoolcraft, Ind. Tribes, III, 102, 1853. Kai-na-mé-ro.—Ibid. Kai-no-méahs.—Ibid., 112. Kanamara.—Taylor in Cal. Farmer, Mar. 30, 1860. Kanimares.—Ibid. Kanimarres.—Ibid. Kianamaras.—Ind. Aff. Rep. 1864, 119, 1865. Kyanamara.—Ibid., 1856, 257, 1857.

**Galpa.** A former Tepehuane pueblo and the seat of a mission; situated in central Durango, Mexico, on the headwaters of Rio San Pedro.

S Lúcas de Galpa.—Orozco y Berra, Geog., 319, 1864.

**Gamacaamanc** ('ravine of palms'). A rancheria, probably Cochimi, connected with Purísima (Cadegomo) mission, Lower California, in the 18th century.—Doc. Hist. Mex., 4th s., V, 189, 1857.

**Gamacaamancxa** ('mouth of the ravine of palms'). A rancheria, probably Cochimi, connected with Purísima (Cadegomo) mission, Lower California, in the 18th century.—Doc. Hist. Mex., 4th s. V, 190, 1857.

**Gambling.** See *Games*.

**Gamchines.** A former village, presumably Costanoan, connected with Dolores mission, San Francisco, Cal.—Taylor in Cal. Farmer, Oct. 18, 1861.

**Games.** Indian games may be divided into two general classes: games of chance and games of dexterity. Games of pure skill and calculation, such as chess, are entirely absent. The games of chance fall into one of two categories: (1) games in which implements corresponding with dice are thrown at random to determine a number or numbers, the counts being kept by means of sticks, pebbles, etc., or upon an abacus or counting board or circuit; (2) games in which one or more of the players guess in which of two or more places an odd or particularly marked counter is concealed, success or failure resulting in the gain or loss of counters. The games of dexterity may be designated as (1st) archery in its various modifications; (2d) a game of sliding javelins or darts upon the hard ground or ice; (3d) a game of shooting at a moving target consisting of a netted hoop or a ring; (4th) the game of ball in several highly specialized forms; and (5th) the racing games, more or less interrelated and complicated with the ball games (q. v.). In addition, there is a sub-class, related to the game of shooting at the moving target, of which it is a miniature form, corresponding with the European game of cup-and-ball. Games of all the classes designated are found among all the Indian tribes of North America, and constitute the games, *par excellence*, of the Indians. The children have a variety of other amusements such as top spinning, mimic fights, and similar imitative sports (see *Amusements*); but the games first described are played only by men and women, youths and maidens, not by children, and usually at fixed seasons as the accompaniment of certain festivals or religious rites. A well-marked affinity exists between the manifestation of the same game even among the most widely separated tribes; the variations are more in the materials employed, due to environment, than the object or method of plays. Precisely the same games are played by tribes belonging to unrelated linguistic stocks, and in general the variations do not follow the differences in language. At the same time there appears to be a progressive change from what seems to be the older forms of existing games from a center in S. W. United States along lines radiating from the same center southward into Mexico. There is no evidence that any of the games above described were ever imported into America; on the contrary, they appear to be the direct and natural outgrowth of aboriginal American institutions. They show no modification due to white influence other than the decay which characterizes all Indian institutions under existing conditions. It is probable, however, that the wide dissemination of certain games, as, for example, the hand game, is a matter of comparatively recent date, due to wider and less restricted intercourse through the abolition of tribal wars. Playing cards and probably the simple board game, known by the English as merrels, are practically the only games borrowed by the Indians from the whites. On the other hand we have taken *lacrosse* in the N. and *racket* in the S., and the Mexicans of the Rio Grande play all the old Indian games under Spanish names. In the dice games, it appears, the original number of dice was four, and that they were made of canes, being the shaftments of arrows painted or burned with marks corresponding with those used to designate the arrows of the four world-quarters. In one of the earliest forms of the guessing game the number of the places of concealment was four, and the implements used in hiding were derived from the four marked arrow shaftments. In general, in all Indian games, the arrow or the bow, or some derivative of them, is found to be the predominant implement, and the conceptions of the four world-quarters the fundamental idea. From this it became apparent that the relation of the games to each other in the same area, and of each to its counterpart among all the tribes, was largely dependent on their common origin in ceremonies from which games produced as amusements were uniformly derived. Back of each game is found a ceremony in which the game was a significant part. The ceremony has commonly disappeared; the game survives as an amusement, but often with traditions and observances which serve to connect it with its original purpose. The ceremonies appear to have been to cure sickness, to cause fertilization and reproduction of plants and animals, and, in the arid region, to produce rain. Gaming implements are among the most significant objects that are placed upon many Hopi altars, and constantly reappear as parts of the masks, headdresses, and other ceremonial adornments of the Indians generally. These observations hold true both of the athletic games as well as of the game of chance. The ball was a sacred object not to be touched with the hand, and has been identified as symbolizing the earth, the sun, or the moon. In the ring-and-pole game, the original form of the ring was a netted hoop derived from the spider web, the emblem of the Earth mother. The performance of the game was bound up with ceremonies of reproduction and fertility. In the kicked-stick and ball-race games of the S. W., the primary object seems to have been to protect the crops against sand storms within the circuit traversed.

Following are brief descriptions of the principal games played by the Indians N. of Mexico:

*Arrow games.*—A variety of games was played with actual arrows. In one of the commonest, an arrow was tossed with the hand by one of the players and the others then threw at it and endeavored to cause their arrows to fall across it.

*Ball games.*—The two common ball games which are widely distributed are racket ball, a man's game played with one or two netted bats or rackets, and shinny, commonly played by women.

In addition, women had a game with a double or tied ball which was tossed with long slender rods. In all of these it was not permitted to touch the ball with the hands. Among the Plains tribes the women played with a small buckskin-covered ball of buffalo hair. (See *Ball play.*)

BALL RACKETS

SHINNY BALL AND STICK

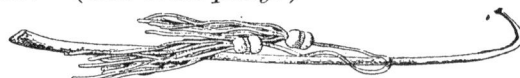

DOUBLE BALL AND STICK

*Bowl game.*—A kind of dice game widely played by women among the Algonquian, Iroquois, Sioux, and other northern tribes. The dice consist of bone disks, or of peach or plum stones, which are tossed in a wooden bowl or a basket. Some California tribes use a large flat basket.

BOWL GAME

*Cat's cradle.*—The trick of weaving patterns with string upon the fingers, which we call cat's cradle, is very generally known, but the designs are different and much more intricate.

BASKET DICE GAME

The Zuñi and Navaho attribute the origin of this amusement to the spider and associate the figures with the spider-web net shield of the war gods.

*Children's games.*—Indian children play a variety of games, which are practically identical with those played by the children of civilization. They are all mimetic in their character, and have no relation to the ceremonial and divinatory games of their elders, except so far as they may be imitations of them. (See *Amusements, Child life.*)

*Chunkey.*—The ring-and-pole game of the Creeks and neighboring tribes, in which a stone ring or disk was employed. From specimens of the stones found in the mounds it is shown that this form of the game had a wide distribution. Stone rings were used until recently in a similar game by some of the tribes on the N. W. coast.

*Cup-and-pin game.*—An amusement analogous to the cup-and-ball, or bilboquet, of Europe. The game is universal among the Indians, and exists in a great

ESKIMO CUP-AND-PIN GAME

variety of forms, all of which may be referred to the spider-web shield. Among the Dakota the game is called the 'deer-toe game' and played with a string of phalan-

CUP-AND-PIN GAME

geal bones which are caught on a needle. The Eskimo use solid bone or ivory objects which are caught in the same way.

*Football.*—The game commonly spoken of as football is a ball race, chiefly confined to the S. W., in which a small wooden or stone ball is kicked around a long course, the original object having been the magical protection of the fields against sand storms. The Tarahumare derive their name from this game. Football proper exists among the Eskimo.

*Four-stick game.*—A game in which 4 marked sticks or billets of two different

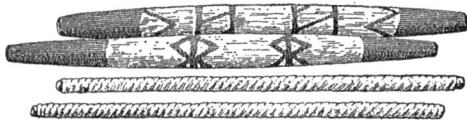

FOUR-STICK GAME

sizes are hidden under a flat basket, the object being to guess their relative positions.

*Hand game.*—The commonest and most widely distributed of Indian guessing games. Two (or four) bone or wooden

HAND GAME

cylinders, one plain and one marked, are held in the hands by one player, the other side guessing in which hand the unmarked cylinder is concealed. The game is commonly counted with sticks and is played to the accompaniment of songs or incantations.

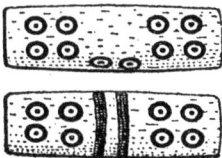

*Hidden-ball game.*—The common guessing game of the Southwestern tribes, played with four wooden tubes or cups, under one of which a ball or stick is hidden. The opposing side endeavors to guess where the object is concealed. The four cups or tubes refer to the four world-quarters, and the game is sacred to the war gods.

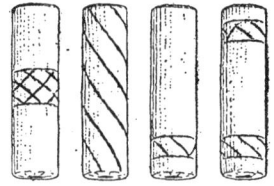

HIDDEN-BALL GAME

*Hoop-and-pole.*—A widely distributed athletic game in which a hoop or ring, frequently covered with network, is rolled along the ground and shot at with arrows or javelins, the counts being determined by the way in which the latter fall with reference to the ring. The game exists in a great variety of forms, all more or less related to and associated

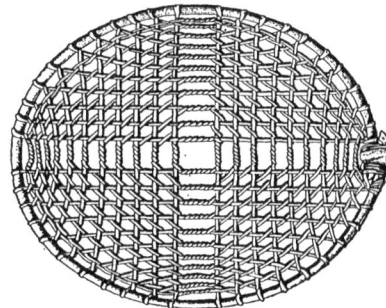

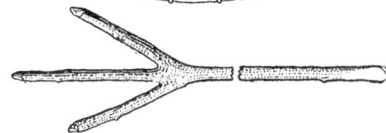

HOOP-AND-POLE GAME

with ideas of fertility and generation.

*Juggling.*—Juggling with balls, sometimes made of clay especially for the purpose, is practised by the women of some tribes. They keep two or more in the air at one time, and endeavor to see which can thus maintain them longest.

*Kicked stick.*—A game of the Southwestern Indians, notably the Zuñi, in which two small painted sticks are kicked in a race around a ceremonial circuit inclosing the fields beyond the village.

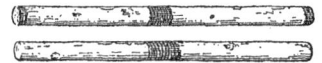

KICKED STICK GAME

*Moccasin game.*—A common guessing game of the northern tribes. Four moccasins are commonly employed and a small object, such as a bullet, or a ball of buffalo hair, is hidden in one of them. The opposing side endeavors to guess where it is concealed. The game is counted with sticks, and is clearly a derivative of the hidden-ball game played with wooden tubes.

*Patol.*—The Spanish or Mexican name of the stick-dice game among the Hopi Indians and some of the Pueblos of the Rio Grande. Derived from the Aztec word *patolli*, which the old Mexicans are described as having played on a painted mat, using beans as dice.

*Snow snake.*—A gaming implement, sometimes carved to represent a snake,

SNOW SNAKES

which is hurled along the ice or frozen ground, the object being to see whose 'snake' will go farthest.

*Stick game.* — A common guessing game of the tribes of California and the N. Pacific

STICK GAME

coast, one that extends entirely across the continent to Canada and the Atlantic. The sticks, probably originally arrow shaftments, are shuffled and divided, the object being to guess in which bundle either the odd or a particularly marked stick is concealed. (See *Straw game*, below.)

*Stick dice game.*—A widely distributed game in which several 2-faced lots are

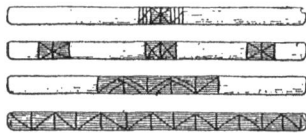

STICK DICE GAME

tossed in the air like dice, the counts being kept on a diagram or with sticks. The number of the dice ranges from 3 upward, 4 being the most common.

*Stilts.*—Stilt-walking is a children's sport among the Hopi and Shoshoni, and from its existence in Mexico is probably indigenous among the Indians.

*Straw, game of.*—The name given by early writers to a guessing game played by Huron and other tribes of the Atlantic slope. The implements consisted of fine splints or reeds, and the object of the game was to guess the number, odd or even, when the bundle was divided at random.

*Tops.*—The top is almost universal as a child's plaything among the Indian tribes of the United States and appears to be indigenous. The common form is a whip top made of horn, bone, stone, or wood, spun on the ice or on frozen ground.

Consult Culin, American Indian Games, 24th Rep. B. A. E., 1906.          (s. c.)

**Gamgamtelatl.** A gens of the Tenaktok, a Kwakiutl tribe.

Ḏa'mǝ'amtᴇlaʟ.—Boas in Rep. Nat. Mus., 331, 1895.

**Gamiskwakoka-wininiwak** (*Kamĭskwa-waʻkuʻka-winĭnĭwag*, 'men or people of the place of much red cedar.'—Jones). A Chippewa band about Cass lake, near the head of the Mississippi, in Minnesota.

Cass Lake band.—Common name. **Gamiskwakoka-wininiwak.**—Gatschet, Ojibwa MS., B. A. E., 1882. **Kāmĭskwāwā'kuʻkā-winiwiwag.**—Wm. Jones, inf'n, 1905 (correct Chippewa form).

**Ganadoga** ('it is a divided village.'—Hewitt). A former Oneida village in Oneida co., N. Y., near Oneida Castle.

**Ganadoga.** A former Iroquois village on the Canadian shore of L. Ontario, near the site of Toronto.

Ganadoke.—Homann Heirs' map, 1756. **Gä-nä'-doque.**—Morgan, League Iroq., 473, 1851. **Kanada-gerea.**—Doc. of 1676 in Doc. Col. Hist. N. Y., XIII, 502, 1881.

**Ganagweh** ('one took it out.'—Hewitt). A former Seneca village about the site of Palmyra, N. Y.

Gä'-nă-gweh.—Morgan, League Iroq., 469, 1851.

**Ganahadi** ('people of Ganak,' an island somewhere near the s. end of Alaska). A Tlingit division which is said to have moved from below the present town of Port Simpson, Brit. Col., and to have separated into several branches, of which one settled at Tongas, another at Taku, a third at Chilkat, a fourth at Yakutat, and, according to one informant, a fifth at Klawak.          (J. R. S.)

Gānaxạ'dî.—Swanton, inf'n, 1904. Gānaxte'dî.—Ibid. Kar̄ách-ắdi.—Krause, Tlinkit Ind., 120, 1885. Kanach-tēdi.—Ibid., 116.

**Ganasarage** ('at the place of mandrakes.'—Hewitt). A former Tuscarora village on Canaseraga cr., at the present site of Sullivan, N. Y.

Canaseraga.—N. Y. Doc. Col. Hist., VII, 512, note, 1856. Canesraca.—Esnauts and Rapilly, map, 1782. Ganaghsaragey.—Johnson (1762) in N. Y. Doc. Col. Hist., VII, 512, 1856. Ganaghsaragues.—German Flats conf. (1770), ibid., VIII, 229, 1857. Gä-nă-sä-rä'-ge.—Hewitt, inf'n, 1886 (Seneca form). Kanadasero.—Johnson (1763) in N. Y. Doc. Col. Hist., VII, 582, 1856. Kanassarago.—Canajoharie conf. (1759), ibid., 382.

**Ganawagus** ('it has a swampy smell.'—Hewitt). A former Seneca village on Genesee r., near Avon, N. Y.

Canawagus.—Deed of 1797 in Am. State Papers, Ind. Aff., I, 627, 1832. Conewaugus.—Cornplanter (1822) quoted by Drake, Bk. Inds., bk. v, 115, 1848. Gä'-nă-wä'-gus.—Hewitt, inf'n, 1886 (Seneca form). Gänowaúges.—Morgan, League Iroq., 468, 1851.

**Gandaseteiagon.** A Cayuga village existing about 1670 near Port Hope, Ontario, on the shore of L. Ontario.

Ganadatsiagon.—Vaugondy, map (1753), cited in N. Y. Doc. Col. Hist., IX, 112, 1855. Ganatcheskia-gon.—Frontenac (1673) in Margry, Déc., I, 233, 1875. Ganatoheskiagon.—Frontenac (1673) in N. Y. Doc. Col. Hist., IX, 112, 1855 (misprint). Gandas-chekiagon.—Frontenac (1674), ibid., 117. Gan-daseteiagon.—Shea, note in Charlevoix, New France, III, 110, 1868. Gandatsiagon.—Bellin, map, 1755. Gandatskiagon.—Homann Heirs' map, 1756.

**Ganedontwan** (*Găʻ-ne-doⁿ-twäⁿ*, 'one put hemlock in the fire.'—Hewitt). A former Seneca village on the site of Moscow, N. Y.

Gä-năh'-dä-on-tweh.—Morgan, League Iroq., 468, 1851.

**Ganeraske.** An Iroquois village that stood about 1670 at the mouth of Trent r., Ontario, near the N. E. end of L. Ontario.

Ganaraské.—Bellin, map, 1756. Ganeraské.—Frontenac (1673) in Margry, Déc., I, 233, 1875. Ganeroske.—Alcedo, Dic. Geog., II, 183, 1787. Gannaraské.—Denonville (1687) in N. Y. Doc. Col. Hist., IX, 369, 1855. Gonaraske.—Homann Heirs' map, 1756. Quandarosque.—Crepy, map, *ca.* 1755.

**Gangasco** (from *shingascui*, 'level, wet, and grassy ground.'—Heckewelder). A village of the Powhatan confederacy formerly near the present Eastville, Northampton co., Va. It was the most important village on the lowest part of the E. shore in 1722. The inhabitants, who were of the Accomac or the Accohanoc tribe, were known as Gingaskins and remained there until they were driven off in 1833, being then much mixed with negroes.
(J. M.)
Gangascoe.—Beverly, Va., 199, 1722. Gingaskins.—Wise in Schoolcraft, Ind. Tribes, V, 36, 1855 (name used for the band).

**Ganneious.** A former Iroquois village on the N. shore of L. Ontario, on the present site of Napanee, Ontario.
Ganciou.—Lotter, map, *ca.* 1770. Gancydoes.—Esnauts and Rapilly, map, 1777. Ganeidos.—Alcedo, Dic. Geog., II, 183, 1787. Ganeious.—Frontenac (1673) in Margry, Déc., I, 233, 1875. Ganejou.—Homann Heirs' map, 1756. Ganeousse.—Lahontan (1773), New Voy., I, 32, 1735. Ganeyont.—Parkman, Frontenac, 140, 1883. Ganneious.—Denonville (1687) in N. Y. Doc. Col. Hist., IX, 362, 1855. Gannejouts.—Bellin, map, 1755. Ganneous.—Hennepin, New Discov., 101, 1698. Ganneouse.—Lahontan (1703) quoted by Macauley, N. Y., II, 191, 1829. Gonejou.—Crepy, map, *ca.* 1755.

**Gannentaha** ('beside the mountain.'—Hewitt). The Huron form of the name of Onondaga lake, N. Y. In 1656 the French established on its shore, about 5 leagues from Onondaga, a mission, composed of Onondaga, Hurons, and Neutrals, which was called Notre Dame de Ganentaa, from the name of the lake. It was abandoned in 1658 on account of the hostility of the pagan Iroquois.　(J. M.)
Canainda.—Hansen (1700) in N. Y. Doc. Col. Hist., IV, 803, 1854. Caneenda.—Bleeker (1701), ibid., 891. Cannenda.—Schuyler (1711), ibid., V, 246, 1855. Ganentaa.—Shea, Cath. Miss., 224, 1855. Ganentaha.—Esnauts and Rapilly, map, 1777. Gannentaha.—Macauley, N. Y., I, 113, 1829. Gä-non-dä'-ä'.—Hewitt, inf'n, 1886. Gä-nun-ta'-ah.—Morgan, League Iroq., 471, 1851. Kaneenda.—Bleeker (1701) in N. Y. Doc. Col. Hist., IV, 891, 1854. Notre Dame de Ganentaa.—Shea, Cath. Miss., 228, 1855 (French name of mission). St. Mary's.—Ibid.

**Ganogeh** (*Gă-än-no''-ge*, 'place of floating oil.'—Hewitt). The principal Cayuga village formerly on the site of Canoga, N. Y.
Canoga.—Macauley, N. Y., II, 177, 1829. Gă-än-no''-ge.—Hewitt, inf'n, 1886. Gä-no'-geh.—Morgan, League Iroq., 423, 1851.

**Ganondasa** ('it is a new town.'—Hewitt). A former Seneca village on the site of Moscow, N. Y.
Cánádáràggo.—Amherst (1763) in N. Y. Doc. Col. Hist., VII, 568, 1856. Canadasaggo.—Johnson (1763), ibid., 550. Canaderagey.—Johnson Hall conf. (1763), ibid., 556. Gă-non-dä'-sä'.—Hewitt, inf'n, 1886. Gä-nun'-dä-sa.—Morgan, League Iroq., 435, 1851. Kanadaraygo.—Johnson (1763) in N. Y. Doc. Col. Hist., VII, 576, 1856. Kanaderagey.—Ibid., 582.

**Ganosgagong** ('among the milkweeds.'—Hewitt). A small Seneca village formerly on the site of Dansville, N. Y.

Gä-nose'-gä-go.—Morgan, League Iroq., 437, 1851. Gä-nos'-gä-goñ.—Hewitt, inf'n, 1886. Gä-nus'-gä-go.—Morgan, op. cit., 468. Ganuskago.—Johnson (1756) in N. Y. Doc. Col. Hist., VII, 92, 1856. Kanuskago.—Ft Johnson conf. (1756), ibid., 57.

**Ganowarohare** ('skull is fastened to the top of it.'—Hewitt). One of the former principal Oneida towns, situate on Oneida cr., at the site of Vernon, N. Y. At this place the Jesuit mission of St François Xavier was established in 1667. In 1777 it was destroyed by the Indians who had espoused the British cause.　(J. N. B. H.)
Cahnowellahella.—Macauley, N. Y., II, 298, 1829. Canawagore.—Guy Park conf. (1775) in N. Y. Doc. Col. Hist., VIII, 550, 1857. Canawaroghere.—Johnson Hall conf. (1774), ibid., 476. Canowaloa.—Ibid., VII, 101, note, 1856 (Oneida form). Canowarighare.—Guy Park conf., ibid., VIII, 535, 1857. Canowaroghere.—Johnson (1762), ibid., VII, 512, 1856. Conawaroghere.—Johnstown conf. (1774), ibid., VIII, 504, 1857. Gä-no-ä-o'-ä.—Morgan, League Iroq., chart, 394, 1851 (Cayuga name). Gä-no'ä-o-hä.—Ibid. (Seneca name). Gänoⁿwăro'häre'.—Hewitt, inf'n, 1886 (a Seneca form). Gä-no-wä'-lo-hale.—Morgan, League Iroq., chart, 394, 1851 (Oneida name). Gä'-no-wä-lo-har'-la.—Ibid. (Mohawk name). Gä-no-wi'hä.—Ibid. (Onondaga name). Kahnonwolo-hale.—Belknap and Morse in Mass. Hist. Soc. Coll., 1st s., V, 13, 1806. Kahnowolohale.—Macauley, N. Y., II, 298, 1829. Kä-no-wa-no'-häte.—Morgan, op. cit. (Tuscarora name). Kononwarohare.—Oneida address (1775) in Williams, Vermont, II, 437, 1809. Old Oneida.—Sergeant (1796) in Mass. Hist. Soc. Coll., 1st s., V, 18, 1806. Onawaraghhare.—Johnson (1756) in N. Y. Doc. Col. Hist., VII, 101, 1856. Oneida Castle.—Sauthier, map, 1777. Onnosarage Castle.—Ibid. Orisca.—Johnson Hall conf. (1765) in N. Y. Doc. Col. Hist., VII, 729, 1856. Oriska.—Sergeant (1796) in Mass. Hist. Soc. Coll., 1st s., V, 18, 1806. Oriske.—Oneida letter (1776) in N. Y. Doc. Col. Hist., VIII, 690, 1857. Tgănⁿeo''hă'.—Hewitt, inf'n, 1886 (a Seneca form).

**Gantlet.** See *Captives, Ordeals.*

**Gaodjaos** (*Gaodja'os*, 'drum village'). A Haida town on the S. shore of Lina id., Bearskin bay, Queen Charlotte ids., Brit. Col., occupied by the Hlgaiu-lanas family. It is often referred to in the native stories.—Swanton, Cont. Haida, 279, 1905.

**Gao-haidagai** ('inlet people'). The name by which the Haida of Masset inlet and of the N. coast of Queen Charlotte ids. generally were known to those farther s.　(J. R. S.)

**Gaousge** (*Gä-onᵉsage-on*, 'place of basswood.'—Hewitt). Probably a former Seneca village, located by Morgan on Niagara r., N. Y.
Gä-o-ŭs'-ge'.—Hewitt, inf'n, 1886. Gä-o-us-geh.—Morgan, League Iroq., map, 1851.

**Gapkaliptoua.** A Malemiut Eskimo village on Norton bay, Alaska.—Zagoskin in Nouv. Ann. Voy., 5th s., XXI, map, 1850.

**Garabato** (a Spanish term with various meanings, but here referring to the pictographs). A cave in a gorge on the W. slope of Arroyo Garabato, which drains into the Rio Chico, in the Sierra Nacori, W. of the Rio Casas Grandes, in N. W. Chihuahua, that contains the well-preserved remains of an ancient aboriginal habitation on the walls of which are numerous paintings that give the cave its name. The remains are possibly those of the Tarahumare.—Lumholtz, Unknown Mex., I, 103, 1902.

**Garakonthie** (*Ga-ra'-kón-ti-e'*, 'Moving Sun'), **Daniel**. An Onondaga chief during the middle of the 17th century; died at Onondaga, N. Y., in 1676. When the French missionaries fled from Onondaga in 1658, Garakonthie aided them, perhaps secretly, to make their escape, but soon openly became the protector of the Christians and an advocate of peace. In 1661 he induced the Onondaga to send an embassy to Quebec and to return 9 French captives with a view of establishing peace. He accompanied the prisoners to Montreal, where he was well received, and obtained the release of a number of his people. In 1662 he succeeded in temporarily checking the chiefs who wished to make war on the French, and frustrated a plot to kill the missionary Le Moyne. During the war that followed he exercised his authority in protecting the French in his country. He declared himself a convert and was baptized in 1669 in the cathedral at Quebec, receiving the name Daniel. Garakonthie was not only an able, humane leader, but an orator of considerable ability; his strong attachment to the whites lessened his influence with the more warlike element of his tribe, yet when an embassy was to be sent either to the French or to the English, his services were in demand.                              (c. t.)

**Garangula.** See *Grangula*.

**Garganwahgah.** See *Cornplanter*.

**Garomisopona.** A Chumashan village between Goleta and Pt Conception, Cal., in 1542.—Cabrillo, Narr. (1542) in Smith, Colec. Doc. Fla., 183, 1857.

**Gash.** The winter town of the Sanyakoan (q. v.), a Tlingit clan near C. Fox, s. Alaska. Most of the people have now moved to Ketchikan.                    (j. r. s.)

**Gasins** (*Gasí'ns*, perhaps 'gambling sticks'). A Haida town on the N. W. shore of Lina id., Bearskin bay, Queen Charlotte ids., Brit. Col.; occupied by the family Hlgaiu-lanas.—Swanton, Cont. Haida, 279, 1905.

**Gaskosada** ('it is a waterfall.'—Hewitt). A former Seneca village on Cayuga cr., w. of Lancaster, N. Y.
Falls Village. Morgan, League Iroq., 466, 1851 (common English name). Gǎ'-skō'-sǎ-dǎ'.—Hewitt, inf'n, 1886.

**Gaspesien** (*Gaspé* is from *gachepe*, or *kéchpi*, 'the end.'—Vetromile). A name given by early French writers to a part of the Micmac living about Gaspé bay on the Gulf of St Lawrence, Quebec province. Their dialect differs somewhat from that of the other Micmac. They frequently crossed the gulf and made war on the Eskimo and Papinachois. In 1884 the "Micmacs of Gaspé" numbered 71 persons.                              (j. m.)
Gaspesians.—Lahontan, New Voy., i, 230, 1703 (common English form). Gaspesies.—Hennepin, New Discov., map, 1698.

**Gatagetegauning** (probably for *Kǎ-'tǎgǐ'tǐganǐng*, 'at the ancient field.'—W. J.) A former Chippewa village on Lac (Vieux) Desert or Gatagetegauning, on the Michigan-Wisconsin state line. The present Vieux Desert Chippewa in Michigan numbered, with the L'Anse band, 668 in 1903.
Ga-ta-ge-te-gaun-ing.—Warren (1852) in Minn. Hist. Soc. Coll., v, 38, 1885. Gete'kitigan.—Baraga Eng.-Otch. Dict., 185, 1878. Kǎ'tǎgi'tigāning.—Wm. Jones, inf'n, 1905 (correct Chippewa form). Old Field.—Ibid. Vieux Desert.—Ibid. Vieux De Sert band.—La Pointe treaty (1854) in U. S. Ind. Treat., 223, 1873.

**Gatga-inans** (*Gǎ'tgaǐna'ns*). A Haida town on Hippa id., Queen Charlotte ids., Brit. Col. It is in possession of the family Do-gitinai.—Swanton, Cont. Haida, 280, 1905.

**Gatûñ'wa'li.** See *Big-mush*.

**Gaudekan** ('bell town'). The principal Huna town, now generally called Huna, in Port Frederick, on the N. shore of Chichagof id., Alaska. Pop. 800 in 1880; 447 (including whites) in 1900.
Gāot!ā'k-ān.—Swanton, field notes, B. A. E., 1904. Gaud-ah-kan.—Emmons in Mem. Am. Mus. Nat. Hist., iii, pl. xii, 1903. Gaudēkān.—Krause, Tlinkit Ind., 104, 118, 1885. Koudekan.—Petroff in Tenth Census, Alaska, 31, 1884.

**Gawababiganikak** (*Kawapabikŭnǐ'kag*, 'place of much white earth.'—W. J.). A Chippewa band about White Earth lake, N. W. Minn., officially reported to number 1,735 in 1905.
Gawababiganikak.—Gatschet, Ojibwa MS., B. A. E., 1882. Kāwāpābikani'kǎg.—Wm. Jones, inf'n, 1905. White Earth band.—Common name.

**Gawunena.** A band of the Arapaho, q. v.

**Gayagaanhe** (*Gǎ-yǎ'-gǎ'-ǎⁿ'-he'*, 'its body is inclined.'—Hewitt). The former principal village of the Cayuga, situate near the E. shore of Cayuga lake, 3½ miles s. of Union Springs, N. Y. St Joseph's mission was established there in 1668, and the settlement was destroyed by Gen. Sullivan in 1779.                    (j. m.)
Cayuga Castle.—Machin, map (1779), cited by Conover, Kanadesaga and Geneva MS., B. A. E. Gǎ-yǎ'-gǎ-an'-ha.—Morgan, League Iroq., 423, 1851. Gǎ-yǎ'-gǎ-ǎⁿ'he'.—Hewitt, inf'n, 1886. Goiogouin.—See *Cayuga*. Gwa-u-gweh.—Morgan, League, Iroq., map, 1851. Saint Joseph.—Jes. Rel. for 1670, 63, 1858.

**Gayanthwahgeh, Gayehtwageh, Gayenthwahgih.** See *Cornplanter*.

**Gay Head.** A village, probably of the Wampanoag, formerly on the w. end of Marthas Vineyard, off the s. E. coast of Massachusetts. It contained 260 souls in 1698, and in 1809 there were still 240 Indian and negro mixed-bloods, who probably represented the entire Indian population of the island.                    (j. m.)

**Gearksutite.** A fluorine mineral resembling kaolin, found in Greenland. The word is compounded of *arksutite* (q. v.) and the Greek *γῆ*, 'earth.'        (a. f. c.)

**Geguep.** A former Chumashan village near Santa Inez mission, Santa Barbara co., Cal.—Taylor in Cal. Farmer, Oct. 18, 1861.

**Geies** (or *Geier*). One of the non-Caddoan tribes reported by Father Damian Massanet, comisario for the missions of Texas, on the road from Coahuila (probably the presidio rather than the province) to the Tejas (Texas) country in the 18th century.—Dictamen Fiscal, Mexico, Nov. 30, 1716, cited by H. E. Bolton, inf'n, 1906.

**Gekelemukpechuenk.** A Delaware village in Ohio in 1770–73 and the residence of Netawatwees, the principal chief of the tribe. Perhaps identical with White Eyes' town. It was abandoned in 1773 or 1774, the inhabitants removing to Coshocton, on the E. side of the Muskingum, which Netawatwees henceforth made his chief residence.—Loskiel, Missions, 1794.

**Gelelemend** ('leader'). A Delaware chief, born about 1722; known also as Killbuck, the name borne by his father, one of the best educated Indians of his time. He was chosen on the death of White Eyes, about 1778, to succeed him as acting chief of the nation during the minority of the hereditary sachem of the Turtle or Unami division, having in the council won a reputation for sagacity and discretion. Like his predecessor he strove to maintain friendship with the whites, and was encouraged in this by the Indian agents and military commandants at Pittsburg, who promised the aid of the American Government in the uplifting and civilization of the Indians if lasting peace could be effected. The war party, led by Hopocan, prevailed, however, in the council. Gelelemend was therefore invited by the officer commanding the garrison to remove with others of the peace party to an island in Allegheny r., where they could be under the protection of the soldiery, but they were not protected from a party of murderous white men that fell upon them when returning from the massacre of nearly 100 Christian Delawares at Gnadenhuetten in 1782, when the young chief and all the others except a few were slain. Gelelemend made his escape by swimming, but the documents that William Penn had given to the Indians were destroyed. His services were of value in bringing about a general peace, but the Munsee held him responsible for the misfortunes that had befallen the Delawares, and to escape their vengeance he remained with his family at Pittsburg long after peace was proclaimed. He joined the Moravian Indians in the end and lived under the protection of the settlement, still sedulously avoiding his vindictive foes. He was baptized by the name of William Henry and lived till Jan., 1811.

**Geliac.** A former Chumashan village on Patera ranch, near Santa Barbara, Cal.
Geliac.—Taylor in Cal. Farmer, Apr. 24, 1862. Geliec.—Bancroft, Nat. Races, I, 459, 1874. Gelo.—Ibid.

**Génau.** A former village, presumably Costanoan, connected with Dolores mission, San Francisco, Cal.—Taylor in Cal. Farmer, Oct. 18, 1861.

**Genega's Band** (named from its chief, Genega, 'Dancer'). A Paviotso band formerly living at the mouth of Truckee r., w. Nevada, said to number 290 in 1859. They are no longer recognized under this name.
Dancer band.—Burton, City of Saints, 472, 1862. Ge-nega's band.—Dodge in Ind. Aff. Rep. 1859, 374, 1860. Gonega.—Burton, op. cit.

**Geneseo** (*Tyo'nesi'yo'*, 'there it has fine banks.'—Hewitt). An important Seneca settlement formerly situated about the site of Geneseo, N. Y. In 1750 it contained 40 or more large houses. It was destroyed by Sullivan in 1779.
Cenosio.—Ft Johnson conf. (1757) in N. Y. Doc. Col. Hist., VII, 254, 1856. Chenceses.—Bouquet (1764) quoted by Rupp, West Penn., app., 147, 1846. Chenesee Castle.—Machin (1779) quoted by Conover, MS., B. A. E. Chenessies.—Croghan (1765) quoted by Rupp, West Penn., app., 172, 1846 (band). Chenessios.—Colden (1764) in N. Y. Doc. Col. Hist., VII, 609, 1856. Chenissios.—Ibid., 610. Chennesse Castle.—Machin (1779) quoted by Conover, op. cit. Chennussios.—N. Y. Doc. Col. Hist., index, 291, 1861. Chenosio.—Johnson (1759), ibid., VII, 376, 1856. Chenusies.—Watts (1764) in Mass. Hist. Soc. Coll., 4th s., x, 522, 1871. Chenusios.—Johnson (1763) in N. Y. Doc. Col. Hist., VII, 522, 1856. Chenussio.—Johnson (1759), ibid., 379. Chinesee.—Sullivan (1779) quoted by Conover, MS., B. A. E. Chinesse.—Jones (1780) in N. Y. Doc. Col. Hist., VIII, 786, 1857. Chinnesee.—Pemberton (ca. 1792) in Mass. Hist. Soc. Coll., 1st s., II, 177, 1810. Chinosiā.—Ft Johnson conf. (1757) in N. Y. Doc. Col. Hist., VII, 264, 1856. Genesee.—Livermore (1779) in N. H. Hist. Soc. Coll., VI, 328, 1850. Geneseo.—Knox (1791) in Am. State Papers, Ind. Aff., I, 226, 1832. Genessees.—Mallery in Proc. A. A. A. S., XXVI, 352, 1877. Genneces.—Goldthwait (1766) in Mass. Hist. Soc. Coll., 1st s., x, 121, 1809. Gennesse.—Machin, map (1779), quoted by Conover, MS., B. A. E. Ginnacee.—McKendry (1779) quoted by Conover, ibid. Ischua.—Day, Penn., 644, 1843. Jennessee.—Drake, Bk. Inds., bk. 5, 111, 1848. Kanonskegon.—Pouchot, map (1758) in N. Y. Doc. Col. Hist., x, 694, 1858. Tsinusios.—Claus (1777), ibid., VIII, 702, 1857. Tyo'nesi'yo'.—Hewitt, inf'n, 1890 (correct Seneca form). Upper Senecas.—Claus (1777) in N. Y. Doc. Col. Hist., VIII, 702, 1857. Zeneschio.—Loskiel (1794) misquoted by Day, Penn., 644, 1843. Zoneschio.—Loskiel, Missions, pt. 3, 32, 1794. Zoneshio.—Ibid., pt. 2, 122. Zonesschio.—Zeisberger (1750) quoted by Conover, MS., B. A. E. Zonneschio.—Conover, ibid.

**Genizaros** (Span. transl. of Turkish *yeñicheri* (Eng. *janizary*), lit. 'new troops,' referring to a former body of Turkish infantry largely recruited from compulsory conscripts and converts taken from Christian subjects). A term applied to certain Indians who were purchased or captured from predatory tribes and settled by the Spaniards in villages along the Rio Grande, N. Mex. One of these "pueblos de Genizaros" was established at Abiquiu before 1748; another at Tome, farther down on the Rio Grande, at a subsequent date, and a third apparently at Belen. See Villa-Señor, Theatro Am., 416, 1748; Bandelier in Arch. Inst. Pap., III, 197, 1890; IV, 54, 1892. (F. W. H.)

**Genobey.** A large Jumano settlement E. of the Rio Grande, in N. Mex., in

1598.—Oñate (1598) in Doc. Inéd., XVI, 114, 1871.

**Xenopué.**—Ibid., 123.

**Gens.** See *Clan and Gens.*

**Gens de la Sapinière** (French: 'people of the fir tree'). A numerous tribe formerly living N. N. W. of L. Superior and trading with the English on Hudson bay. Du Lhut, in 1684, endeavored to draw their trade to the French. They were distinct from the Cree, Chippewa, and Assiniboin, and may have been a part of the Maskegon.—La Chesnaye (1697) in Margry, Déc., VI, 7, 1886.

**Gens de Paise** (corruption of French *Gens du Pais*, 'people of the land'; or of *Gens du Panse*, 'band of the paunch'). Given as a band of Sioux at the Mandan subagency, N. Dak., in 1832 (Ex. Doc. 90, 22d Cong., 1st sess., 63, 1832), but probably intended for the Hidatsa, q. v.

**Gens de Pied** (French: 'foot people'). A former band of Assiniboin in 33 lodges w. of Eagle hills, Assiniboia, Canada.—Henry (1808) in Coues, New Light, II, 491, 1897.

**Foot Assiniboines.**—Ibid., 523.

**Gens des Lacs** (French: 'people of the lakes'). One of the 5 tribes into which Badin (Ann. de la Prop. de la Foi, IV, 536, 1843) in 1830 divided the Sioux nation. What people he includes has not been ascertained, possibly only the Mdewakanton. Prichard (Phys. Hist. Mankind, V, 140, 1847) uses the term Gens du Lac as equivalent to People of the Leaves, and includes the 4 most easterly Dakota tribes, not only the Mdewakanton (the true Gens des Lacs), but the Wahpeton (Leaf villages), Wahpekute (Leaf-shooters), and Sisseton.

**Gens du Large** (French: 'wandering people'). One of the two divisions of the Dakota, as given by Long (Exped. St Peters r., I, 380, 1824), comprising the following tribes: Kahra (a Sisseton band), Miakechakesa (Sisseton), Tetoans (Teton), Wahkpakota (Wahpekute), Wahkpatoan (Wahpeton), Yanktoanan (Yanktonai), Yanktoan (Yankton). It embraces all the group except the Mdewakanton, his Gens du Lac.

**Dacota errans.**—Balbi, Atlas Ethnog., 55, 1826. **Roving Dakotas.**—Long, op. cit., I, 380.

**Gentaienton** ('meadows lying together.'—Hewitt). One of the chief villages of the Erie, q. v. Its location is not known, but the name indicates that it was on a plain.

**Gentagega.**—Jes. Rel., Thwaites ed., LVIII, 75, 1899. **Gentaguetehronnons.**—Ibid., XLII, 197, 1899. **Gentaienton.**—Ibid., LXI, 195, 1900. **Kentaienton.**—Shea, note in Charlevoix, New France, II, 266, 1866.

**Gergecensens.** A subdivision of the so-called Thamien group of the Costanoan Indians of California.

**Gergecensens.**—Taylor in Cal. Farmer, June 22, 1860. **Gerguensens.**—Ibid. **Gerzuensens.**—Bancroft, Nat. Races, I, 452, 1874.

**German influence.** German influence on the aborigines N. of Mexico has made itself felt in three particular regions—among the Eskimo of Labrador and Greenland; among the Delawares, Mahican, and some of the Iroquois in Pennsylvania, New York, and Ontario; and among the Cherokee of South Carolina. In those regions Moravian missionaries have endeavored to convert the natives with considerable success. The Moravian missions in Greenland began in 1721 under Egede. The station of Ny Herrnhut dates from 1734. From the account given by Thompson (Moravian Missions, 211, 1890) the native Christians in Greenland number some 1,500, and their customs and habits have been much changed for the better, especially where the influence of whalers and traders has not been too strong. The Moravian efforts in Labrador began at Hopedale in 1752 under Ehrhardt, but the first successful establishment was made in 1771. The general result has been to modify considerably the dress, implements, habits, and beliefs of the natives, and particularly their sexual morality (Delabarre in Bull. Geog. Soc. Phila., 145–151, 1902). The disappearance of the Eskimo pirates, who once infested the straits of Belleisle, and the general improvement of Arctic navigation have been brought about through the change in Eskimo life and character. Turner observed that some of the Eskimo children of the Labrador missions use the German words for numbers up to 10 in their counting-out games, having caught them from the missionaries. Much of what the Moravians have accomplished in Greenland has been done in spite of the Danish authorities rather than with their cooperation. Moravian missionaries in the 18th century and the early years of the 19th, labored among the Mahican of E. New York (Rauch having begun the work in 1740), among the Delawares and other tribes of Pennsylvania, Zeisberger being "the apostle of the Delawares," and among the Iroquois in parts of Pennsylvania, New York, and Canada (Thompson, op. cit., 267–341). They exercised restraint on the Indians during the French-English and Revolutionary wars, when their converts generally were illtreated by all sorts of white men. According to Thompson (p. 276) the Moravian mission of 1735 to Georgia was the first company from any quarter that reached the shores of America with the express and leading object of evangelizing natives. Their labors began among the Creeks. Moravian missions were established also among the Cherokee (Mooney in 19th Rep. B. A. E., 83, 1900). According to some the father of Sequoya, the inventor of the Cherokee alphabet, was a German of the Georgia colony.　　　　　　　　　(A. F. C.)

**Geronimo** (Spanish for *Jerome*, applied by the Mexicans as a nickname; native name Goyathlay, 'one who yawns'). A medicine-man and prophet of the Chiricahua Apache who, in the latter part of the 19th century, acquired notoriety through his opposition to the authorities and by systematic and sensational advertising; born about 1834 at the headwaters of Gila r., N. Mex., near old Ft Tulerosa. His father was Taklishim, 'The Gray One,' who was not a chief, although his father (Geronimo's grandfather) assumed to be a chief without heredity or election. Geronimo's mother was known as Juana. When it was decided, in 1876, in consequence of depredations committed in Sonora, of

GERONIMO

which the Mexican government complained, to remove the Chiricahua from their reservation on the s. frontier to San Carlos, Ariz., Geronimo and others of the younger chiefs fled into Mexico. He was arrested later when he returned with his band to Ojo Caliente, N. Mex., and tilled the ground in peace on San Carlos res. until the Chiricahua became discontented because the Government would not help them irrigate their lands. In 1882 Geronimo led one of the bands that raided in Sonora and surrendered when surrounded by Gen. George H. Crook's force in the Sierra Madre. He had one of the best farms at San Carlos, when trouble arose in 1884 in consequence of the attempt of the authorities to stop the making of tiswin, the native intoxi-

cant. During 1884–85 he gathered a band of hostiles, who terrorized the inhabitants of s. Arizona and New Mexico, as well as of Sonora and Chihuahua, in Mexico. Gen. Crook proceeded against them with instructions to capture or destroy the chief and his followers. In Mar., 1886, a truce was made, followed by a conference, at which the terms of surrender were agreed on; but Geronimo and his followers having again fled to the Sierra Madre across the Mexican frontier, and Gen. Miles having been placed in command, active operations were renewed and their surrender was ultimately effected in the following August. The entire band, numbering about 340, including Geronimo and Nachi, the hereditary chief, were deported as prisoners of war, first to Florida and later to Alabama, being finally settled at Ft Sill, Okla., where they now reside under military supervision and in prosperous condition, being industrious workers and careful spenders. Geronimo died there Feb. 17, 1909.　　　　　　　(J. M. C. T.)

**Gewauga** (*Odji'wăgĕnʻ*, 'it is bitter, salty.'—Hewitt). A Cayuga village on the site of the present Union Springs, town of Springport, on the E. side of Cayuga lake, N. Y. It was destroyed by Sullivan's troops, Sept. 22, 1779.　　(J. N. B. H.)
Ge-wä'-ga.—Morgan, League Iroq., 470, 1851. Ge-wau'-ga.—Ibid., 423. Ge-waw-ga.—Adams in Cayuga Co. Hist. Soc. Coll., no. 7, 176, 1889.

**Ghost dance.** A ceremonial religious dance connected with the messiah doctrine, which originated among the Paviotso in Nevada about 1888, and spread rapidly among other tribes until it numbered among its adherents nearly all the Indians of the interior basin, from Missouri r. to or beyond the Rockies. The prophet of the religion was a young Paiute Indian, at that time not yet 35 years of age, known among his own people as Wovoka ('Cutter'), and commonly called by the whites Jack Wilson, from having worked in the family of a ranchman named Wilson. Wovoka seems already to have established his reputation as a medicine-man when, about the close of 1888, he was attacked by a dangerous fever. While he was ill an eclipse spread excitement among the Indians, with the result that Wovoka became delirious and imagined that he had been taken into the spirit world, and there received a direct revelation from the God of the Indians. Briefly stated, the revelation was to the effect that a new dispensation was close at hand by which the Indians would be restored to their inheritance and reunited with their departed friends, and that they must prepare for the event by practising the songs and dance ceremonies which the prophet gave them. Within a very short time the dance spread to the tribes E. of the mountains, where it became known commonly as the Spirit or Ghost dance. The dancers, men and women together, held hands, and moved slowly around in a circle, facing toward the center, keeping time to songs that were sung without any instrumental accompaniment. Hypnotic trances were a common feature of the dance. Among the Sioux in Dakota the excitement, aggravated by local grievances, led to an outbreak in the winter of 1890–91. The principal events in this connection were the killing of Sitting Bull, Dec. 15, 1890, and the massacre at Wounded Knee, Dec. 29. The doctrine has now faded out, and the dance exists only as an occasional social function. In the Crow dance of the Cheyenne and Arapaho, a later development from the Ghost dance proper, the drum is used, and many of the ordinary tribal dances have incorporated Ghost-dance features, including even the hypnotic trances.

The belief in the coming of a messiah, or deliverer, who shall restore his people to a condition of primitive simplicity and happiness, is probably as universal as the human race, and takes on special emphasis among peoples that have been long subjected to alien domination. In some cases the idea seems to have originated from a myth, but in general it may safely be assumed that it springs from a natural human longing. Both the Quichua of Peru and the Aztec of Mexico, as well as more cultured races, had elaborate messiah traditions, of which the first Spanish invaders were quick to take advantage, representing themselves as the long-expected restorers of ancient happiness. Within the United States nearly every great tribal movement originated in the teaching of some messianic prophet. This is notably true of the Pontiac conspiracy in 1763–64, and of the combination organized by Tecumseh (q. v.) and his brother, the prophet Tenskwatawa (q. v.), shortly before the War of 1812. Of similar nature in more recent times is the doctrine formulated on Columbia r. by Smohalla. See Mooney, Ghost Dance Religion, 14th Rep. B. A. E., pt. II, 1896. See *Dance, Mythology, Religion.*          (J. M.)

**Ghuaclahatche.** A former Upper Creek town on lower Tallapoosa r., Ala., between Kulumi and the Atasi towns.—Bartram, Travels, 461, 1791.

**Giants.** See *Popular fallacies.*

**Gidanemuk** (or *Gikidanum*). A band of Serranos (q. v.) living on Tejon and neighboring creeks in the Tehachapi mts., s. Cal. The term is that which they apply to themselves.          (A. L. K.)

**Giguay.** A former village, presumably Costanoan, connected with San Juan Bautista mission, Cal.—Engelhardt, Franciscans in Cal., 398, 1897.

**Gila Apache.** The name Gila, or Xila, was apparently originally that of an Apache settlement w. of Socorro, in s. w. New Mexico, and as early as 1630 was applied to those Apache residing for part of the time on the extreme headwaters of the Rio Gila in that territory, evidently embracing those later known as Mimbreños, Mogollones, and Warm Springs (Chiricahua) Apache, and later extended to include the Apache living along the Gila in Arizona. The latter were seemingly the Arivaipa and Chiricahua, or a part of them. There were about 4,000 Indians under this name in 1853, when some of their bands were gathered at Ft Webster, N. Mex., and induced by promise of supplies for a number of years to settle down and begin farming. They kept the peace and made some progress in industry, but were driven back to a life of pillage when the supplies were stopped, the treaty not having been confirmed. They are no longer recognized under this name. The term Gileños has also been employed to designate the Pima residing on the Gila in Arizona.          (F. W. H.)

Apaches de Xila.—Benavides, Memorial, 53, 1630. Apaches gileños.—Garcés (1769) in Doc. Hist. Mex., 4th s., II, 371, 1856.     Apaches jileños.—Escudero, Notic. de Sonora y Sinaloa, 69, 1849.     Cileños.—Orozco y Berra, Geog., map, 1864. Gelinos.—Hamy in Bull. Soc. d'Anthrop. de Paris, 788, 1883. Gila Apaches.—Ind. Aff. Rep., 436, 1853.   Gilans.—Hughes, Doniphan's Exped., 216, 1848.   Gilas.—Rivera, Diario y Derrotero, leg. 950, 1736.   Gileñas.—Ind. Aff. Rep., 122, 1861.   Gileno.—Adelung and Vater, Mithridates, III, 178, 1816.   Gileños.—Arricivita (1791) quoted by Bancroft, Ariz. and N. Mex., 388, 1889.   Gileños Apaches.—Garcés (1769) in Doc. Hist. Mex., 4th s., II, 375, 1856.   Southern Apache.—Ind. Aff. Rep. 1871, 191, 1872.   Tjuiccujen-ne.—Orozco y Berra, Geog., 59, 1864.   Tjusceujen-né.—Escudero, Notic. Estad. de Chihuahua, 212, 1834 (native name).   Xilenos.—Rudo Ensayo (*ca.* 1763), Smith ed., 20, 1863.   Xileños.—Alegre, Hist. Comp. Jesus, I, 336, 1841.   Yabipais Gileños.—Garcés (1776), Diary, 452, 1900.

**Gilak.** A Magemiut settlement near C. Romanzoff, Alaska; pop. 22 in 1890. Gilakhamiut.—11th Census, Alaska, 111, 1893.

**Gilimis.** A former village, said to have been Esselen, connected with San Carlos mission, Cal.—Taylor in Cal. Farmer, Apr. 20, 1860.

**Gimiels.** A band of almost pure Yuma in N. Lower California (Taylor in Browne, Res. Pac. Slope, app., 53–54, 1869). Perhaps the *Comeya.*

**Gipuy.** A village occupied by the ancestors of the present Queres of Santo Domingo pueblo, 1½ m. E. of Thornton, on the brink of Arroyo de Galisteo, N. central N. Mex. In consequence of a flood which destroyed a portion of the pueblo, Gipuy was abandoned prior to 1591, and another village bearing the same name was built 4 m. w., nearly on the site of the present Santo Domingo. It was the latter Gipuy that was visited and named Santo Domingo (q. v.) by Castaño de Sosa in 1591; but after 1605 this pueblo was also destroyed by a freshet, the inhabitants moving farther w., where they built another village on the banks of the Rio Grande, naming it Huashpa Tzena. See Bandelier in Arch. Inst. Papers, IV, 185–187, 1892.　　　(F. W. H.)

Gi-pu-i.—Bandelier in Ausland, 814, 1882. Gi-pu-y.—Bandelier in Arch. Inst. Papers, IV, 22, 185, 1892. Guiperi.—Oñate cited by Bandelier in Arch. Inst. Bull., I, 18, 1883 (misprint). Guipui.—Oñate (1598) in Doc. Inéd., XVI, 102, 1871 (or Santo Domingo). Gui-pu-y.—Bandelier in Arch. Inst. Papers, III, 34, 1890.

**Girty's Town.** A Shawnee village in 1795 on St Marys r., E. of Celina reservoir, Auglaize co., Ohio. It took its name from Simon Girty, an Indian trader living with the Shawnee.　　　(J. M.)

**Gist, George.** See *Sequoya*.

**Gitin-gidjats** (*Gitin-gī'djats*, 'servants of the Gitins'). A family of the Eagle clan of the Haida. This family, who are of low social rank and are distributed among the houses of the Gitins of Skidegate, once had a town in connection with the Lana-chaadus, on Shingle bay, Queen Charlotte ids., Brit. Col., but people of Kloo enslaved so many of them that they gave up their town and independent family organization, entering the different houses of the Gitins as servants.—Swanton, Cont. Haida, 273, 1905.

Gyitingīts'ats.—Boas, Twelfth Rep. N. W. Tribes Can., 24, 25, 1898. Gyit'îngyits'ats.—Boas, Fifth Rep., ibid., 26, 1889.

**Gitinka-lana** (*Gī'tinq!a-lā'na*). A town of the Yagunstlan-lnagai of the Haida, on the N. shore of Masset inlet, Brit. Col., where it expands into the inner bay.—Swanton, Cont. Haida, 281, 1905.

**Gitins** (*Gitī'ns*). An important subdivision of the Eagle clan of the Haida. Gitins is a synonym for Eagle clan, and the name of the subdivision would naturally have been Hlgaiu-gitinai, but the family was so prominent that, as in a similar case at Masset, it came to be called simply Gitins. This was the subdivision or family that owned the town of Skidegate, Queen Charlotte ids., Brit. Col. It was divided into two principal branches— Nayuuns-haidagai and Nasagas-haidagai. Subordinate branches were the Lagalaiguahl-lanas and the Gitin-gidjats.— Swanton, Cont. Haida, 273, 1905.

Gyit'i'ns.—Boas, Twelfth Rep. N. W. Tribes Can., 24, 1898.

**Gitlapshoi** ('grassland people'). A division of the Chinook tribe living at Sealand, Pacific co., Wash.

GiLā'pcō-i.—Boas, Chinook Texts, 260, 1894.

**Gituns** (*GitAns*, dialectic variant of *Gitins*). An important family group of the Haida, living at Masset, Queen Charlotte ids., Brit. Col. Its prominence at Masset, like that of the Gitins at Skidegate, was such that no further designation was used. Two principal subdivisions recognized were the Mamun-gitunai and the Undlskadjins-gitunai; inferior divisions were the Tees-gitunai and the Sadjugahl-lanas.　　　(J. R. S.)

Gyit'i'ns.—Boas, 12th Rep. N. W. Tribes Can., 23, 1898. Kitāns.—Harrison in Proc. and Trans. Roy. Soc. Can., sec. II, 125, 1895.

**Glacial man.** See *Antiquity, Archeology*.

**Glaglahecha** ('slovenly ones'). A band of the Sihasapa Teton Sioux, possibly identical with Tizaptan, q. v.

Bad looking ones.—Culbertson in Smithson. Rep. 1850, 141, 1851. Glagla-heċa.—Dorsey in 15th Rep. B. A. E., 219, 1897. Glagla-hetca.—Ibid.

**Glaglahecha.** A band of the Miniconjou Teton Sioux.

Glagla-heċa.—Dorsey in 15th Rep. B. A. E., 220, 1897. Glagla-hetca.—Ibid.

**Glen-Vowell Band.** A band of Kitksan living on the right bank of upper Skeena r., 4 m. above Hazelton, Brit. Col.; pop. 73 in 1904.—Can. Ind. Aff., 209, 1902; 212, 1904.

**Gleuaxcuqu.** A former Chumashan village near Santa Barbara, Cal.—Taylor in Cal. Farmer, Apr. 24, 1863.

**Glikhikan.** A Delaware warrior and orator. He was one of the chief captains of the Delawares, who, in an argument with the French priests in Canada had, in the opinion of the Indians, refuted the Christian doctrine. Thinking to achieve a similar victory and win back to paganism the Christian Delawares, he challenged the Moravian missionaries to a debate in 1769. To the dismay of his admirers he was himself converted to Christianity, and in the following year went to live with the United Brethren. In the Revolutionary war his diplomacy saved the Christian settlements from destruction at the hands of the Hurons under Half-King in 1777, and when the latter, on Sept. 4, 1781, captured him and the German missionaries, their chief interfered to save Glikhikan from the wrath of his Munsee tribesmen who were with the Hurons. Glikhikan was murdered and scalped at Gnadenhuetten on Mar. 8, 1782, by the white savages under Col. David Williamson.

**Glooscap.** See *Nanabozo*.

**Glue.** See *Cement*.

**Gluskap.** See *Nanabozo*.

**Gnacsitare.** A tribe, supposed to be imaginary, mentioned by Lahontan as living, about 1690, on a long river emptying into the Mississippi in Minnesota, in about the same latitude as Minnesota r.

Gnacsitares.—Lahontan, Voyages, I, 119, 1703. Gnacsitaries.—Janson, Stranger in Am., 277, 1807. Gnasitaries.—Coxe, Carolana, 19, 1741. Knacsitares.—Dobbs, Hudson Bay, map, 1744.

**Gnadenhuetten** (German: 'huts of grace'). The name of several mission villages (5, according to Brinton) established at different periods among the Mahican, Munsee, and Delawares by the Moravian missionaries. The first was settled in 1746 by Moravian Mahican from Shecomeco and Scaticook on the N. side of Mahoning cr., near its junction with the Lehigh, about the present Lehighton, Carbon co., Pa. In 1754 it was abandoned for a new village, called New Gnadenhuetten, on the site of Weissport, Carbon co., Pa. Delawares and Mahican occupied the village together. Soon after removing here the old village was burned by hostile Indians in 1755, and the new place was for a time deserted. In 1763 the Indians abandoned the settlement for a short time on account of the troubles arising from Pontiac's war. The last and best known village of the name was established on the Muskingum, about the site of the present Gnadenhuetten, Tuscarawas co., Ohio, in 1772. Toward the close of the Revolution the inhabitants were removed to Sandusky by the hostile Indians, and on returning to gather their corn were massacred by the Americans in 1782. Consult Heckewelder, Narr., 1820; Howells, Three Villages, 1884; Loskiel, Hist. Miss. United Brethren, 1794.            (J. M.)

Gnaden Auetten.—Rupp, Northampton, etc., Cos., 220, 1845 (misprint). Gnadenhuetten.—Loskiel, Hist. Miss. United Brethren, pt. 3, 82, 1794. Guaden Huetten.—Rupp, op. cit., 86 (misprint).

**Goasila** ('north people'). A Wakashan tribe of Smith inlet, Brit. Col., speaking the Kwakiutl subdialect. The gentes are Gyigyilkam, Sisintlae, and Komkyutis. One of their towns is Waitlas. Pop. 48 in 1901; 36 in 1904.

Gua-shil-la.—Kane, Wand. in N. Am., app., 1859. Guasi'la.—Boas, 6th Rep. N. W. Tribes Can., 53, 1890. Kwashilla.—Tolmie and Dawson, Vocabs. Brit. Col., 117B, 1884. Kwasila.—Boas in Bull. Am. Geog. Soc., 226, 1887. Kwawshela.—Can. Ind. Aff. 1904, pt. 2, 70, 1905. Kwaw-she-lah.—Can. Ind. Aff., 145, 1879. Qoasi'la.—Boas in Petermanns Mitt., pt. 5, 131, 1887. Quatsinas.—Scott in Ind. Aff. Rep., 316, 1868. Quaw-she-lah.—Boas in Bull. Am. Geog. Soc., 226, 1887. Quoisillas.—Brit. Col. map, 1872. Quisillas.—Can. Ind. Aff., 113, 1879.

**Goch** ('wolf'). The name given by the southern Tlingit to one of the two sides or phratries into which the Tlingit are divided. The northern Tlingit call this phratry *Chak*, q. v.

Gōtc.—Swanton, field notes, 1904, B. A. E. Khanúkh.—Dall, Alaska, 414, 1870 (the word for petrel is here used erroneously).

**Godbout.** A trading station of the Montagnais and Nascapee at the mouth of Godbout r., on the St Lawrence, Quebec. In 1904 the Indians there numbered 40, the population having been stationary for 20 years.

**Godthaab.** The chief Danish residence and Eskimo missionary station on the w. coast of Greenland, about lat. 64°.—Crantz, Hist. Greenland, I, map, 1767.

**Goggles.** Inventions related to the visor and eyeshade, to reduce the amount of sunlight penetrating the eye. After the long Arctic winter comes the trying season of the low sun which, glancing over the snow and Arctic waters, nearly blinds the hunter and fisher. All northern peoples wear vizors of some kind, but it is not enough that the Eskimo should have his eyes shaded; he must have a device through which the eyes look out of narrow slits or small elliptical holes. In-

deed, in many localities the shade and goggles are united. From E. to the farthest W. the Eskimo have succeeded in perfecting such apparatus. The Eskimo and Aleut spend much pains and skill in the manufacture of their goggles. They differ in materials, form, workmanship, method of attachment, and amount of foreign acculturation according to locality and exposure. Goggles or eyeshades were rarely worn by the Indians. In the

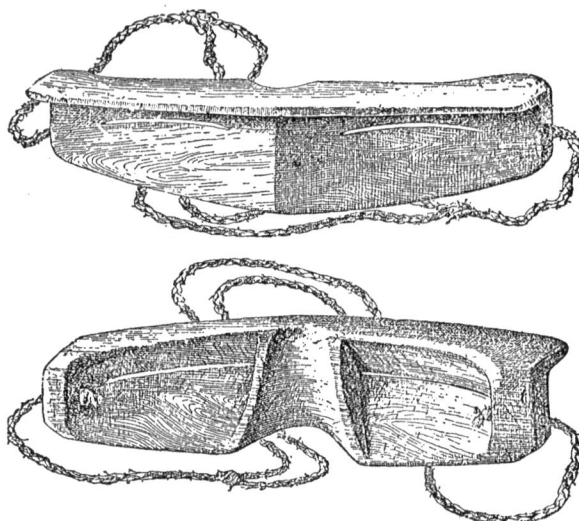

WOODEN GOGGLES; HUDSON BAY ESKIMO.    (TURNER)

Report of the National Museum for 1894 (pp. 281–306, figs. 15–35) this device is well illustrated. Consult also Boas, Murdoch, Nelson, and Turner in the Reports of the Bureau of American Ethnology. In the writings of Arctic explorers also goggles are mentioned.            (O. T. M.)

**Gohate.** A former Maricopa rancheria on the Rio Gila in s. Arizona; visited by Sedelmair in 1744 (Bancroft, Ariz. and N. Mex., 366, 1889). Apparently distinct from Cohate.

**Gohlkahin** (*Goʻlkáhĭn*, 'prairie people'). A division of the Jicarillas. See *Guhlkainde*.            (J. M.)

**Going Snake** (*Iʻnădû-naʼĭ*, signifying that a person is 'going along in company with a snake'). A Cherokee chief, prominent about 1825.—Mooney in 19th Rep. B. A. E., 522, 1900.

**Goiogouen** (*Gwĕñioʼ gwĕnʻ*, 'place where locusts were taken out of a liquid.'—Hewitt). One of the chief towns of the Cayuga in 1670, and from which the tribe took its name, situated at this time on the E. side of Cayuga lake, on Great Gully brook, about 4 m. s. of the present Union Springs, and 4 leagues from the town of Tiohero (Kiohero), lying at the N. end of Cayuga lake, and 6 leagues from Onnontare, these three being the principal towns of the Cayuga when first known. The inhabitants of Goiogouen were composed in part of Cayuga and in part of adopted captives from the Hurons, the Conestoga, and the Neutral Nation. This town or 'Bourg d'Oiogouen,' in 1668, according to the Jesuit Relation for 1669, contained more than 2,000 souls and could muster more than 300 warriors. While the Cayuga were proud-spirited, the missionaries found them more tractable and less fierce than were the Onondaga and the Oneida. At this town Father de Carheil dedicated the mission of St Joseph on Nov. 9, 1668, and 7 days later witnessed the horrible spectacle of the burning and the eating of a captive Conestoga woman. Archeologic evidence indicates, what is usual in regard to the permanency of Indian village sites, that this town has been removed from site to site within a radius of 10 miles or more.

In 1779 Gen. Sullivan's army found three places named Cayuga; namely, (1) Cayuga Castle, containing about 15 very large houses of squared logs, superior to anything seen before among these Indians; the troops destroyed here 110 acres of corn; (2) Upper Cayuga, containing 14 houses, situated about 1 m. s. of the Castle; (3) East Cayuga, 'Old Town,' containing about 13 houses, situated about 1 m. N. E. from the Castle. In these towns the troops found apples, peaches, potatoes, turnips, onions, pumpkins, squashes, cucumbers, watermelons, and vegetables of various kinds in great abundance. These with other hamlets of the Cayuga were burned and the fruit and vegetables destroyed by the troops, Sept. 23–24, 1779.                                        (J. N. B. H. )

Caiougo.—N. Y. Doc. Col. Hist., index, 1861. Cajouge.—Doc. of 1687, ibid., III, 446, 1853. Cayauge.—Ibid., 480. Cayuga.—Proc. at Johnson Hall (1765), ibid., VII, 737, 1856. Gajuka.—Beauchamp, Hist. N. Y. Iroquois, 162, 1905. Gä′-u-gwa.—Morgan, League Iroq., 159, 1851. Goiogoüen.—Jes. Rel. 1668–69, Thwaites ed., LII, 184, 1899. Goiogouin.—Ibid., 1673–74, LVIII, 225, 1899. Goiogwen.—Ibid., 1696, LXV, 25, 1900. Goiog8en.—Ibid., 24. Goyogouh.—Cusick, Sketches, 19, 1828. Goyogouin.—Jes. Rel., index, 1858. Gué-u-gweh.—Morgan, League Iroq., 51, 65, 1851. Gweugweh.—Ibid., 170. Mission de St Joseph.—Jes. Rel., 1670, 63, 1858. Oigoien.—Jes. Rel., Thwaites ed., index, LXXIII, 1901. Oiogoen.—Ibid., 1656–57, XLIII, 185, 1899. Oiogoien.—Ibid., 1655–56, XLII, 99, 1899. Oiogouan.—Ibid., 1656–57, XLIII, 167, 1899. Oiogouen.—Ibid., 1660–61, XLVII, 81, 1899. Oiogouin.—Ibid., 1673–77, LIX, 77, 1900. Oioguen.—Ibid., 1659–61, XLVI, 181, 1899. Oiogwen.—Ibid., 1666–67, L, 197, 1899. Oiog8en.—Ibid., 106. Ojogoüen.—Ibid., 1668–69, LII, 172, 1899. Oneyoté.—Jes. Rel., index, 1858. Onioen.—Ibid. Onneioté.—Ibid., 1653, 18 (given as the chief 'bourg' or capital of the Onionenhronnons, but probably a mistake for Onnontare, q. v.). Ouïoen.—Ibid., index. Ouoguens.—Jes. Rel., 1676–77, Thwaites ed., LX, 173, 1900.

**Gold.** Although gold in the form of nuggets occurs in more than one section of the continent N. of Mexico, the tribes in general were practically without knowledge of its use. In a few cases objects of gold have been obtained from mounds in the Ohio valley, notably in the Turner group, Hamilton co., Ohio, where a small copper pendant was found retaining traces of a thin plating of gold, and bits of the filmy sheet were also found in the débris (Putnam). This plating with thin sheet gold is suggestive of well-known Mexican work, and along with other evidence obtained from mounds in Ross co., Ohio, tends to strengthen the belief that the mound-builders of this region had more or less indirect intercourse with the people of central Mexico. Some rudely shaped and perforated gold beads were found in one of the Etowah mounds in Georgia (Jones), and finds of slight importance are reported from other localities.

GOLD PENDANT FROM A MOUND; ORANGE CO., FLORIDA. (KUNZ)

The most interesting objects of gold found in connection with native remains come from Florida, and several of these have been published by Kunz. One of the specimens described was obtained from a mound in Orange co.—a flat rectangular pendant notched at the upper end for the attachment of a cord. It was associated with a human skeleton, and had been worn as a pendant in connection with a necklace of glass beads. Its weight is 75½ dwts. A second specimen is a pendant ornament 2¾ in. in length and nearly 1 in. wide, and weighing 61½ dwts. It is convex on one face and flat on the other, and is grooved at the upper end for the attachment of a cord. A third specimen is a disk of thin sheet gold, 3½ in. in diameter and weighing 19 dwts., with repoussé embellishment about the edge and a circular boss at the center. It was found in a mound in Orange co., and in appearance closely resembles gold ornaments found in large numbers in the Isthmian region. A fourth specimen, also from an Orange co. mound, is a plain disk of thin metal nearly 2½ in. in diameter and having a central perforation. A very interesting object of gold, or rather of gold-silver alloy, was obtained from a mound in Manatee co., s. Fla., and is described by Rau. It is cut from a piece of thin gold plate, and graphically represents the head of a crested bird, probably the ivory-bill woodpecker, the neck being prolonged in a

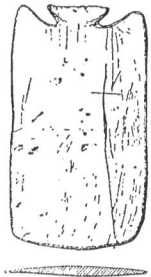

GOLD ORNAMENT FROM A MOUND; SUMTER CO., FLORIDA. (KUNZ)

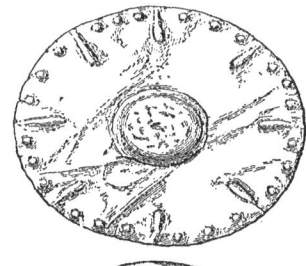

GOLD ORNAMENT FROM A MOUND; ORANGE CO., FLORIDA. (KUNZ)

thin knife-like blade. The conventional treatment of the bird is characteristically Floridian, and the object is almost certainly of native make. The alloy consists of 893 parts of gold to 107 of silver, and may be of Spanish origin, although it is more likely to have been derived from Central America or Mexico.

Although the early Spanish explorers of Florida found some gold in possession of the natives and were led to believe that

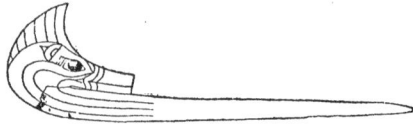

GOLD ORNAMENT FROM A MOUND; MANATEE CO., FLORIDA. LENGTH 9 IN. (RAU)

it had been mined in the mountains to the N., the evidence on this point is unsatisfactory, and it seems highly probable, as stated Sir John Hawkins, that most of the gold observed in Florida had been derived from Spanish vessels wrecked on the coast on their homeward voyage from the gold-producing districts of middle America.

Consult Cabeza de Vaca, Relation, Smith trans., 1871; Douglas in Proc. A. A. A. S., XXXVIII, 1890; Jones, Antiq. Southern Inds., 1873; Hawkins in Hakluyt, Voyages, III, 615, 1800; Kunz in Am. Antiq., IX, no. 4, 1887; Le Baron in Smithson. Rep. 1882, 1884; Moore, various memoirs in Jour. Acad. Nat. Sci. Phila., 1894–1905; Putnam in Peabody Mus. Rep., XVI, 1884; Rau in Smithson. Rep. 1877, 1878; Thomas in 12th Rep. B. A. E., 1894.    (W. H. H.)

**Golden Lake.** A band of Algonkin occupying a reservation on Golden lake, Renfrew co., Ontario, near Ottawa r.; pop. 86 in 1900, 97 in 1904.

**Golok.** An Eskimo village in the Nushagak district, Alaska; pop. 29 in 1890.
Gologamiut.—Eleventh Census, Alaska, 164, 1893.

**Gonaho.** A former Tlingit town at the mouth of Alsek r., Alaska. Cf. *Gunachonken.*
Gonā'xo.—Swanton, field notes, B. A. E., 1904. Gun-nah-ho.—Emmons in Mem. Am. Mus. Nat. Hist., III, 232, 1903.

**Gontiel** ('broad river'). Given as an Apache clan at San Carlos agency and Ft Apache, Ariz., in 1881 (Bourke in Jour. Am. Folk-lore, III, 112, 1890). The name indicates a former habitat on Gila r.

**Goolkizzen** ('spotted country'). A band of Apache, probably Coyoteros, formerly under chief Nakaidoklini, q. v.—White, Apache Names of Indian Tribes, MS., B. A. E., 1875.

**Gorgets.** A term applied to objects worn in some proximate relation with the gorge or throat. They may be suspended from a string or chain encircling the neck, or may be attached to the dress. They may be simple ornaments not differing materially in form or significance

from those used to embellish the ears, hair, wrists, or waist, or they may have special significance as symbols, insignia, charms, etc. They may be plain, or embellished with designs, significant, ornamental, or trivial. They may be natural objects selected because of their beauty, or they may be made of any material presenting an attractive appearance. On account of its beauty of color and its probable sacred significance as being a product of the water, shell was a favorite material and the numerous engraved disks obtained from burial mounds in the middle Eastern states are typical pendant gorgets (see *Shellwork*). Sheet copper was extensively employed by many of the tribes (see *Copper*), and stone was in universal use. Gorgets may have

SHELL GORGET FROM A MOUND; TENNESSEE. (DIAMETER 4 1-4 IN.)

one or two marginal perforations for suspension, or they may be pierced centrally or otherwise for attachment, against a supporting surface, as illustrated by the pierced tablets much used by the former Eastern tribes. The name gorget is also applied to composite ornaments of various kinds suspended on or fixed against the chest, the showy breast ornament composed of two rows of bone beads or tubes employed by the Plains tribes being a good example (see *Adornment*). Gorgets are described in various publications on ethnology and archeology, and a somewhat extended discussion of these and allied ornaments and other objects, by Peabody and Moorehead, appears in Bull. II, Dept. of Archæol., Phillips Acad., 1906. See *Pendants, Pierced tablets, Problematical objects.*    (W. H. H.)

**Goshgoshunk** ('hog place.'—Hewitt). A large settlement of the Munsee and Delawares, with perhaps some Seneca, consisting of 3 villages, on Allegheny r. in 1767, about the upper part of Venango co., Pa. It was visited by the missionary Zeisberger in the year named, and in 1768 it became the seat of a Moravian mission.
Goschegoschuenk.—Loskiel (1794) quoted by Rupp, West Pa., app., 356, 1846. Goschgoschuenk.—Loskiel (1765), Hist. United Brethren, pt. 3, 16, 1794. Goshgoshink.— Ibid., map. Goshgoshunk.—Day, Pa., 102, 1843.

**Gosiute** (*kŭtsĭp,* or *gŭtsĭp,* 'ashes,' 'parched or dry earth,'+*Ute.*—R. V. Chamberlin). A Shoshonean tribe formerly inhabiting Utah W. of Salt and Utah lakes, and E. Nevada. Jacob Forney, superintendent of Indian affairs for Utah, reported in 1858 that he had visited a small tribe called the Go-sha-utes, who lived about 40 m. W. of Salt Lake City. "They are," he says, "without exception, the most miserable looking set of human beings I ever beheld. They have heretofore subsisted principally on snakes, lizards, roots, etc." Writing in 1861, Burton (City of Saints, 475, 1862) says: "Gosh Yuta, or Gosha Ute, is a small band, once protégés of the Shoshonee, who have the same language and limits. Their principal chief died about 5 years ago, when the tribe was broken up. A body of 60, under a peaceful leader, were settled permanently on the Indian farm at Deep cr., and the remainder wandered 40 to 200 m. w. of Great Salt Lake City. During the late tumults they have lost 50 warriors, and are now reduced to about 200 men. Like the Ghuzw of Arabia, they strengthen themselves by admitting the outcasts of other tribes, and will presently become a mere banditti." The agent in 1866 said they "are peaceable and loyal, striving to obtain their own living by tilling the soil and laboring for the whites whenever an opportunity presents, and producing almost entirely their own living." In 1868 the superintendent at Utah agency wrote of them: "These Indians range between the Great Salt lake and the land of the western Shoshones. Many of them are quite industrious, maintaining themselves in good part by herding stock and other labor for the settlers." It appears that later they cultivated land to some extent, being scattered over the country in spots where springs and streams afforded arable land. It is asserted by some authors that they are a mixture of Shoshoni and Ute. Their language indicates a closer relationship with the Shoshoni proper than with the Ute and Paiute, though they affiliate chiefly with the latter and have largely intermarried with them. According to Powell they numbered 460 in 1873; in 1885 they were said to number 256.

The following are divisions or subtribes: Pagayuats, Pierruiats, Torountogoats, Tuwurints, and Unkagarits.

Go-sha-utes.—Forney in Ind. Aff. Rep., 212, 1858. Goshee Utes.—Hatch in Ind. Aff. Rep. 1863, 116, 1864. Goshen Utes.—Head, ibid., 1867, 174, 1868. Goship.—Ibid., 349, 1866. Goship Shoshones.—Sen. Misc. Doc. 136, 41st Cong., 2d sess., 21, 1870. Go-ship-Utes.—Simpson (1859), Rep. of Explor. across Utah, 36, 1876 (so named from Goship, their chief). Goshiss.—U.S. Statutes, XIII, 177, 1866. Goshoots.—Taylor in Cal. Farmer, June 26, 1863. Go-shutes.—Simpson, op. cit., 36. Gosh Yuta.—Burton, City of Saints, 475, 1862. Go-si Utes.—Powell in H. R. Misc. Doc. 86, 43d Cong., 1st sess., 6, 1874. Gos-ta Utes.—Huntington (1857) in H. R. Ex. Doc. 29, 37th Cong., 2d sess., 85, 1862. Kusi-Utahs.—Remy and Brenchley, Journ. to Great Salt Lake, II, 412, 1861.

**Got** (*Gŏt*, 'eagle'). One of the two great exogamic phratries or clans of the Haida. A synonym for the term was Gitins, the meaning of which is uncertain. The Masset dialect made these ᵍōt and *Gituns*, respectively.         (J. R. S.)

Gŏt.—Swanton, Cont. Haida, passim, 1905. Koot.—Dawson, Queen Charlotte Ids., 134B., 1880.

**Gouges.** Stone implements resembling celts or adzes, with one face hollowed out, giving a curved edge. Early writers speak of their use as spiles, in some sections, for tapping sugar-maple trees, the sap running through the groove into the vessel placed beneath. Examples grooved for hafting are rare. Held in the hand and struck with a mallet, or hafted after the manner of a hoe or an adz, they would be serviceable for hollowing out wooden canoes, troughs, mortars, and other vessels, especially in connection with charring. The distribution of these implements does not favor the theory of their use in making canoes, as they are most numerous in the N. where these vessels were mostly of birch-bark, and are rare in the S. where the dugout was the prevailing craft. The gouge is of somewhat rare occurrence w. of the Alleghanies. See *Adzes, Celts.*

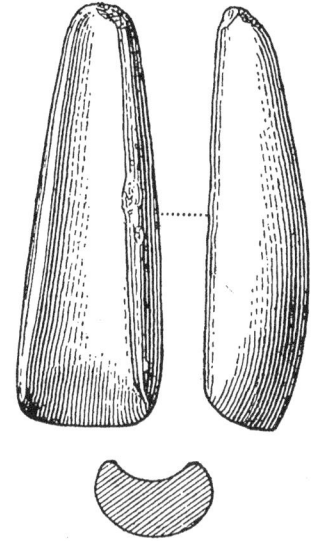

STONE GOUGE; NEW YORK. (1-3)

Consult Abbott, Prim. Indus., 1881; Fowke in 13th Rep. B. A. E., 1896; Moorehead, Prehist. Impl., 1900; Rau, Archæol. Coll. Nat. Mus., 1876.    (G. F.)

**Gourds.** The shells of gourds were employed by the Indians for storage and carrying, as water jugs, dippers, spoons, and dishes, and for mixing bowls, pottery smoothers, rattles, sounders for the rasping stick, roof-drains, masks, parts of ornaments, and other purposes, and the flowers were used as food, coloring material, and in ceremonies. A number of species and varieties were commonly raised, producing fruit of different shapes and sizes—globose, lenticular, pyriform, and tubular, with necks of varying length and curve, or without necks, but all of value for the general or special purpose for which they were selectively grown. Gourds were sometimes shaped by pressure or bandaging while growing. Wild species were eaten green, or were used as medicine, but these were rarely made into utensils, while the larger and varied gourds, which were early distributed, like corn, from regions to the S. or derived during the historic period from the Old World, adapted themselves more fully to Indian needs. Aside from their use as domestic utensils they were extensively made into rattles, those E. of the Rocky mts. being almost universally of pyriform gourds, while the shape of the Pueblo gourd rattles is globular, lenticular, and pyriform. The Pueblos also made of gourd-shell heads for certain effigies, noses for masks, the bell ends of flageolets, ornaments for paraphernalia, and resonators for the notched rattle; and the Hopi imitate with a gourd trumpet behind a ceremonial altar the supposed sound made by the mythical plumed serpent. Gourd rattles for ceremonial use by various tribes were sometimes painted, burnt, or etched in symbolic designs. A Navaho specimen bears the outlines of several constellations scratched on the surface. Among the Iroquois gourd rattles were the special sacred objects of the medicine societies. The Cherokee, according to Mooney, fastened hollow gourds to tops of long poles set up near their houses so that the black house-martin might build their nests in them and frighten away the crows. Some of the Pueblos have Gourd or Calabash clans. See *Dishes, Rattles, Receptacles.*

(w. H.)

**Government.** Government is the basis of the welfare and prosperity of human society. A government is an organic institution formed to secure the establishment of justice by safeguarding rights and enforcing the performance of duties in accordance with the experience and the established customs and rules of conduct of the governed. The superlative measure of justice obtainable by government is found in the care and protection of the young and the aged, the ready assistance rendered to comrades and the unfortunate, the maintenance of peace, the preservation of the equivalency of rights, the recognition of the equality of persons, the liberty of judgment and personal activity, and the substitution of mercy for vengeance in the punishment of crime. Among primitive folk rules of conduct, formulated by common consent or by customs derived from high ancestral usage, are observed, and these are enforced ultimately by corrective punitive measures. But justice is not secured thereby, and so some other method whereby causes in contention may be more promptly adjudicated is devised, and governments are organized.

Among the Indians of North America there are found many planes of culture, every one of which is characterized by widely differing forms of government— from the simplest family group and village community to the most complex confederation of highly organized tribes. In this area there are scores of distinct political governments, all differing widely in degrees of structural complexity. These differences in organization are determined largely by the extent to which the functions of government are discriminated and by the correlative specialization of organs thus made necessary. For most of the tribes of North America a close study and analysis of the social and political organization are wanting, hence the generalizations possible may as yet be applied safely only to those peoples that have been most carefully studied. However, it may be said in general that kinship, real or fictitious, is the basis of government among the Indians of North America, for the fundamental units of the social structure are groups of consanguine kindred, tracing descent of blood through the male or the female line.

The known units of the social and political organization of the North American Indians are the family, the clan or gens, the phratry, the tribe, and the confederation (q. v.). Of these the tribe and the confederation are the only units completely organized. The structures of only two or three confederations are known, and that of the Iroquois is the type example. The confederation of tribes was not usual, because the union of several tribes brought together many conflicting interests which could not be adjusted without sacrifices that appeared to overbalance the benefits of permanent confederation, and because statesmanship of the needed breadth and astuteness was usually wanting. Hence tribal government remains as the prevailing type of social organization in this area. In most tribes the military were carefully discriminated from the civil functions. The civil government was lodged in a chosen body of men usually called chiefs, of whom there were commonly several grades. Usually the chiefs were organized in a council exercising legislative, judicial, and executive functions in matters pertaining to the welfare of the tribe. The civil chief was not by virtue of his office a military leader. Among the Iroquois the civil chief in order to go to war had to resign his civil function during his absence on the warpath.

In tribal society every structural unit has, so far as known, the right to hold a council. The *ohwachira* (q. v.) can hold a council, the family can hold a council, and the united ohwachira councils with their officers form the council of the clan or gens. The clan or gens has the right to hold a council. The chiefs of the clans and gentes are the tribal chiefs, who form the tribal council; but on occasions of great emergencies a grand council is held, composed of the chiefs and subchiefs, the matrons and head warriors of the ohwachira, and the leading men of the tribe. Besides, there is the council of the confederation. So there are family councils, clan councils, gentile councils, tribal councils, and confederation councils, respectively exercising sway in separate and independent jurisdictions.

In some regions nature is so niggard of her bounties to man that savagery and barbarism had not devised means to enable their sons to dwell there in organized political communities; hence here may be found some of the lowest forms of social organization, if such it may be named. Kroeber says: "In general rudeness of culture the California Indians are scarcely above the Eskimo; and whereas the lack of development of the Eskimo on many sides of their nature is reasonably attributable in part to their difficult and limiting environment, the Indians of California inhabit a country naturally as favorable, it would seem, as might be. If the degree of civilization attained by people depends in any large measure on their habitat, as does not seem likely, it might be concluded from the case of the California Indians that natural advantages were an impediment rather than an incentive to progress" (Univ. Cal. Publ., Am. Archæol. and Ethnol., II, no. 3, 81, 1904). This question of the effect of environment on the activities and development of peoples is one still requiring much scientific study.

Dixon (Bull. Am. Mus. Nat. Hist., XVII, pt. 3, 1905), in treating of the northern Maidu of California, describes a state of society largely similar to that of the Hupa as noted in general terms by Goddard. Among the Maidu he finds no trace of gentile or totemic grouping. Aside from the village communities there was no definite organization. Every village or group of small villages had a headman or chief (the office being in no case hereditary), who was chosen largely through the aid of the shaman, who was thought to reveal to the electors the choice of the spirits. Mature years and wealth, ability, and generosity were strong recommendations in making a selection. Tenure of office lasted only during good behavior. The functions of the chief were largely advisory, although force of character and ability might in some cases secure a larger measure of respect and obedience. There also appears to have been "a rather indeterminate council, composed of the older members of the Secret Society."

Goddard (Univ. Cal. Publ., Am. Archæol. and Ethnol., I, no. 1, 1903) says there were no organization and no formalities in the government of the village or tribe among the Hupa. "Formal councils were unknown, although the chief might, and often did, take the advice of his men in a collected body." Each village had a headman, whose wealth gave

him the power of a chief and maintained him in that power, and he was obeyed because from him food was obtained in times of scarcity. If trouble arose, he settled the dispute with money. While the people obeyed him, whatever he had was at their service. "His power descended to his son at his death, if his property also so descended. On the other hand, anyone who, by industry or extraordinary abilities, had acquired more property might obtain the dignity and power." The family and the village communities were the units of the social organization.

According to Powers (Overland Mo., VIII, 530, 1872), among the Karok of California the chief exercises no authority beyond his own village, wherein his functions are chiefly advisory. He can state the law or the custom and the facts, and he may give his opinion, but he can hardly pronounce and execute judgment.

Kroeber (op. cit., 83), in speaking of the Indians of California generally, says that the social structure was simple and loose, there being no trace of a gentile organization and that it is hardly correct to speak of tribes. Above the family the only units of organization were the village and the dialect; the common bond was similarity of language or frequency and cordiality of intercourse; in most cases the larger groups were nameless, while the village communities were usually named from localities; the lack of organization generally made the systematic classification of the divisions of any large body of Indians difficult; in population and social life the village approximated a localized clan, but, being the largest political unit, it corresponded in a measure to a tribe. In so simple a condition of society difference of rank naturally found but little scope. The influence of chiefs was small, and no distinct classes of nobles or slaves were known.

Mooney says that the Kiowa government was formerly lodged in a council of chiefs, composed of the presiding chief, the chiefs of the several bands, and the war chiefs. Women had no voice in the government. The Cheyenne have no head chief, but instead have a council composed of 40 chiefs and 4 ex-chiefs.

Some of the tribes, like the Five Civilized Tribes, the eastern Cherokee, and the Seneca of New York, have written constitutions patterned largely after European ideas. That of the Seneca is confirmed by the legislature of New York.

See *Chiefs, Clan and Gens, Confederation, Family, Kinship, Social organization, Tribe.* (J. N. B. H.)

**Governmental policy.** The policy of the several governments toward the Indians and their methods of pursuing it were often at variance, and therefore should not be confused. The policy itself may have been just, equitable, and humane, while the method of carrying it into effect by those to whom this duty was intrusted was sometimes unjust, oppressive, and dishonest. The governments, other than those of the United States and the colonies, which have had control of parts of the territory N. of Mexico are Great Britain, France, Spain, Russia, Denmark, Sweden, and the Netherlands. Although the policy adopted by them in their dealings with the Indians differed in some important respects, all agreed in assuming the right of dominion, based on discovery, without regard to the natives. In all the contests between the European nations regarding their claims to territory in the New World the rights of the Indians nowhere were allowed to intervene. The earliest charters, as those to Raleigh and Gilbert, make no allusion to the natives, while most of those of the 17th century call briefly for their Christianization, and efforts to this end were made to some extent in most of the colonies. The questions of most importance in the relations of the whites with the Indians were those relating to the title to the soil. Although each government insisted on the right of dominion in its acquired territory and that of granting the soil, the rights of the original inhabitants were in but few instances entirely disregarded, though they were necessarily to a considerable extent curtailed (Johnson and Graham's lessee *v.* McIntosh, 8 Wheaton, 583 et seq.). The Indians were admitted to be the rightful occupants of the lands, with right of possession over so much as was necessary for their use; yet the policy of the various governments differed in the extent to which the exercise of this right was conceded. While Spain limited it to the lands actually occupied or in use (Recop. de Leyes de los Reynos de las Indias, I, lib. ii, 1774), the United States usually allowed it to the land claimed, whenever the boundaries between the different tribes were duly recognized.

It was the usual policy of the United States and other governments, as well as of the colonies, in dealing with the Indians to treat them as tribes. The Articles of Confederation gave to Congress the "sole and exclusive right and power of regulating the trade and managing all affairs with the Indians" not under State jurisdiction. By the Constitution, the power of Congress in this respect is briefly expressed as follows: "To regulate commerce with foreign nations and among the several States, and with the Indian tribes." The authority to act in this respect must therefore be found in this clause, in that relating to the making of treaties, and in the general powers granted to Congress and the Executive. The term "tribes" in the clause quoted would indicate that the framers of the Constitution contemplated dealing with the Indians as autonomous groups, through treaties; this was the method followed by the United States until it was changed by the act of Mar. 3, 1871, and was that of the colonies and the mother country. The effect of the act cited was to bring under the immediate control of Congress, as specified in art. I, section 8, clause 3, of the Constitution, all transactions with the Indians, and to reduce to simple agreements what before had been accomplished by solemn treaties. Laws were enacted in the various colonies, and also by the United States, forbidding and rendering void the sale of lands by Indians to individuals. By the act of Congress of Feb. 8, 1887, the later policy of the Government, that the Indian tribes should cease to exist as independent communities and be made part of the body politic, found legislative expression. This act permits tribal lands, including reservations, to be divided so as to give to each man, woman, and child of the tribe an individual holding and, after a limited probation, confers citizenship upon the allottees, and makes them subject to the laws of the states or territories within which they live. Previous, however, to this final step intervened the reservation policy. The plan of forming Indian reservations was adopted from the necessity of bringing tribes under the more complete control of the Government and of confining them to definite limits for the better preservation of order, and aimed especially to restrict them to less territory in order that the whites might obtain the use of the residue. This was a most important step in the process of leading the natives to abandon the hunter stage and to depend for their subsistence on agriculture and home industries (see *Reservations*). The same policy was followed in Canada under both French and English rule, and to some extent by the colonies, and it was inaugurated by the United States in 1786. An incident indicative of one phase of the policy of the colonies in their dealings with and management of the Indians is that Indian captives were held as slaves in some of the colonies, while, under various pretexts, during a period in the history of South Carolina Indians were forced to submit to the same fate. In 1702 the Virginia assembly decreed that no Indian could hold office, be a capable witness, or hunt over patented land; an Indian child was classed as a mulatto, and Indians, like slaves, were liable to be taken on execution for the payment of debt (Hening, Stat. Va.,

III, 224, 250–252, 298, 333, 447). In 1644 the county courts of Massachusetts were invested with jurisdiction over the Indians in their respective districts (Rec. Mass., II, 134). Through the efforts of John Eliot and Thomas Mayhew many Indians in Massachusetts were brought under religious influence and gathered into towns on lands set apart for them by the General Court in accordance with the act of 1633 (Thomas and Homans, Laws of Colonial and State Govts., 9, 1812). In 1655 the Indians were placed nominally under law and required to pay taxes.

Though the brief rule of the Dutch in New York was marked chiefly by an irregular and vacillating policy in their dealings with their Algonquian neighbors, they established a trading post at Albany in 1615 and entered into treaties with the Iroquois that were never broken. In 1664 New Netherlands passed under English control, and the ill-advised English policy relative to the Indians of the northern districts prevailed until 1765, when, through the efforts of Sir William Johnson, a more satisfactory and practical method of dealing with the Indians, especially as to their territorial rights, was adopted.

Preeminent among the difficulties in the way of carrying out a just, humane, and consistent policy has been and is still the antagonism, born of the ignorance of both races of each other's mode of thought, social ideals and structure, and customs, together with persistent contention about land, one race defending its birthright, the other race ignoring native claims and regarding the territory as vacant. As a result a dual condition has existed—on the one side, a theoretic Government plan, ideal and worthy; on the other, modifications of this plan in compliance with local ignorance and greed. The laws and regulations of the U. S. Government applying to the Indian tribes, with few exceptions, have been framed to conserve their rights. The wars, which have cost much blood and treasure, the enforced removals, the dishonest practices and degrading influences that stain the page of history have all come about in violation of these laws and of solemn compacts of the Government with native tribes. In spite of adverse circumstances the theoretic purpose of the Government policy has slowly made headway. On July 13, 1787, an ordinance was passed by the Continental Congress for the government of the territory of the United States N. W. of the Ohio r., in which article 3 provides: "The utmost good faith shall always be observed toward the Indians; their land and property shall never be taken from them without their consent; and in their prop-

erty, rights, and liberty they shall never be invaded or disturbed, unless in just and lawful wars authorized by Congress; but laws founded in justice and humanity shall from time to time be made, for preventing wrongs being done to them, and for preserving peace and friendship with them " (U. S. Stat., I, 52, 1854). This ordinance was confirmed by the act of Aug. 7, 1789 (ibid., 50). Acts organizing the following states and territories contain an article reaffirming the above ordinance: Alabama, Colorado, Dakota, Idaho, Illinois, Iowa, Kansas, Michigan, Minnesota, Mississippi, Montana, Nebraska, Nevada, Oregon, Wisconsin, and Wyoming.

The Republic of Texas in its need made solemn treaties which were afterward repudiated; consequently no tribe within its limits could claim tribal lands. When Texas was admitted into the Union it retained its laws and the control of its public lands. The Indian tribes appealed to the U. S. Government for protection, and for their relief they were removed to reservations set apart for them in what was then a part of the Indian Ter., and there the remnant of them are now, holding their lands in severalty, subject to the laws and regulations of Oklahoma.

In 1792 the Russians established a school at Kodiak, and in 1805 one at Sitka, the Government and the church cooperating in behalf of education for the mixed-bloods and natives. When the transfer of Alaska to the United States took place in 1867 the teachers were recalled to Russia and the schools were closed. Within a month the American residents voted to establish schools, but little was accomplished. After 10 years of persistent effort Dr John Eaton, Commissioner of Education, assisted by Dr Sheldon Jackson, secured the first Presidential appeal to Congress for civil government and schools for the "self-supporting natives of the territory." Four years later Congress passed the needed law in which the natives' "right of occupancy" was recognized, the sale of liquor prohibited, and education ordered to be provided for the children of school age "without reference to race." In the following year public schools were opened and some of the mission schools were turned over to the Government. The sufferings of the Eskimo consequent upon the decline of the whaling industry and the killing of the fur animals prompted the introduction of reindeer from Siberia in 1892. In the following year the Government made its first appropriation for the purchase of reindeer. Herds have been placed in charge of some of the schools, and Laplanders were imported to instruct the natives in the care and breeding of reindeer, which have very largely multiplied. Not only has a new vocation thus been opened to the natives, but a valuable means of support has been given to the rapidly increasing population of the territory (see Jackson, Rep. on Introd. of Reindeer, 1904).

On May 22, 1792, the following declaration was made in instructions given to Brig. Gen. Rufus Putnam, who was sent to negotiate with the lately hostile Indians near L. Erie: "That the United States are highly desirous of imparting to all the Indian tribes the blessings of civilization, as the only means of perpetuating them on the earth; that we are willing to be at the expense of teaching them to read and write, to plow and to sow in order to raise their own bread and meat with certainty, as the white people do" (Am. State Papers, I, 235). The first treaty providing for any form of education was made on Dec. 2, 1794, with the Oneida, Tuscarora, and Stockbridge Indians, who had faithfully adhered to the colonies during the Revolution. Two persons were to be employed to instruct them in the "arts of the miller and sawyer" (U. S. Stat., II, 48). The Committee on Indian Affairs reported to the House of Representatives on Jan. 22, 1818, in favor of increasing the number of trading posts and establishing schools on or near the frontier for the education of Indian children as measures that " would be attended with beneficial effects both to the United States and to the Indian tribes" (Am. State Papers, II, 151). In 1819 the first general appropriation ($10,000 a year) for Indian education was made. The maintenance of shops, supported, however, by tribal funds, was one of the means used for industrial training, and many tribes through treaty stipulations supported and still support the schools on their reservations. The money appropriated by the Government for Indian education from 1819 to 1873 was mainly expended with the cooperation of various missionary societies that had established missions. From 1873 to the present time the Government has maintained public schools for the Indians.

About 1875 the Indians began to modify the tribal form of government by depriving chiefs of power and transferring their authority to a representative council, limited in number. The movement met with opposition in some tribes, but was accepted in others as a means of countervailing undue conservatism and giving to the progressive element a voice in the management of tribal affairs. About the same time Congress passed a law prohibiting agents from distributing supplies and ammunition to able-bodied Indians, between 18 and 45 years of age, except after the performance of some service "for the benefit of themselves or the tribe, at a reasonable rate to be fixed by the agent in charge and to an amount equal in value to the supplies to be delivered." The Secretary of the Interior might "by written order except any particular tribe or portion of tribe from the operation of this provision when he deems it proper or expedient" (U. S. Stat., XVIII, 176, 449, 1875).

A court of Indian offenses was instituted in 1882 in order to familiarize the Indian with some of the methods which his white neighbors use in trying and punishing offenders. Though the practice of this court has been crude, it has yet assisted in preparing the Indian to conform to the general customs of the country. The judges are appointed by the Indian bureau to serve one year. No compensation is given. The agents all report faithful service on the part of the Indian judges.

The method of establishing reservations has not been uniform, some having been created by treaty, some by Executive order, and others by act of Congress; but those established by Executive order without an act of Congress were not held to be permanent before the general allotment act of 1887 was passed. The various Indian titles recognized by the Government are (1) the original right of occupancy, alienable to the Government only; (2) the title to reservations, which differs from the original title chiefly in the fact that it is derived from the United States. The tenure since the act of 1887 is the same as before, and the power to alienate or transfer is subject to the same limitation, the absolute title being in the Government. Another class of titles is (3) where reservations have been patented to Indian tribes, as those to the Cherokee, Choctaw, and Creek nations, or where grants made by Spain have been confirmed by treaty, as in the case of the Pueblo Indians of New Mexico. The right of the Indians on reservations to sell timber or to grant mining privileges has been restricted, though it is now being gradually extended.

The policy of the United States in dealing with the Indians has, as a rule, been humane and just. The chief exceptions are: First, that arid or semi-arid lands have been selected for some of the reservations, defeating the effort to change some tribes from the hunter to the agricultural stage and entailing misery and death; second, that the pressure brought to bear by white settlers to eject the Indians from their favorite sections, where they were promised permanent homes, has too often been successful. See *Agency system, Dutch influence, Education, English influence, French influence, German influence, Land tenure, Missions, Office of Indian Affairs, Reservations, Russian influence, Spanish influence, Treaties.* (A. C. F.)

**Goyathlay.** See *Geronimo.*

**Grail.** The name of a chief and of a band of Sisseton and Yankton Sioux occupying a village of 627 people on Big Stone lake, 280 m. from the agency in Minnesota in 1836, the other chief being Mazahpatah. Grail was probably a Sisseton Sioux. See Schoolcraft, Ind. Tribes, III, 612, 1853.

**Granaries.** See *Receptacles, Storage.*

**Grand Bois.** A former village, probably of the Potawatomi, about 6 m. s. E. of Geneva, Kane co., Ill.; also known as Shaytee's village.—Royce in 18th Rep. B. A. E., pl. cxxv, 1899.

**Grande Gueule.** See *Grangula.*

**Grand Portage.** A Chippewa band formerly at this place, on the N. shore of L. Superior in N. E. Minnesota; mentioned in La Pointe treaty (1854) in U. S. Ind. Treat., 224, 1873.

**Grand River Indians.** The Iroquois living on Grand r., Ontario. They numbered 3,230 in 1884, 4,050 in 1902, 4,195 in 1904.

Sweke-áka.—Gatschet, Tuscarora MS., B. A. E., 1885 (Tuscarora name).

**Grand River Ute.** A band of the Yampa. Under Chief Piah they formerly ranged as far E. as Denver, Colo. They numbered 350 in 1873.

Denver Ute.—Ind. Aff. Rep., 246, 1877. Grand River Utahs.—Nicolay in Ind. Aff. Rep. 1863, 151, 1864. Pe-ah's band of Utes.—Ind. Aff. Rep. 1873, 340, 1874. Piah band.—Barber in Bull. U. S. Geol. Surv. Terr., III, no. 3, 533, 1877.

**Grand Saux.** Given apparently as equivalent to the Dakota of the plains, as distinguished from "Saux [Sioux] of the wood."—Trumbull, Ind. Wars, 185, 1851.

**Grand Soleil** (French: 'Great Sun'). The title of a noted Natchez chief, whose individual name is unknown, in the first half of the 18th century. He was a friend of the whites until the French commandant demanded the site of his village, White Apple, situated a few miles s. w. of the present Natchez, Miss., which the Natchez had occupied, as their chief replied, for more years than there were hairs in the governor's peruke. The haughty commandant, Chopart, would not allow them to have even their growing crops until it was agreed to compensate him for the concession. The chief then sent out bundles of sticks to the Natchez villages to indicate, ostensibly, their quota of the promised tribute, but really the number of days that were to elapse before making a concerted attack on the French. The docile and submissive Natchez were not suspected, even though a Natchez woman warned the

French officers. On Nov. 30, 1729, the Indians massacred every white person in the settlement, 700 in number, and with his allies the Grand Soleil went on laying waste French plantations in Louisiana until the governor of the French colony assembled a force of French and Choctaw with which he recaptured the fort at Natchez. Then the chief ostensibly agreed to terms of peace that were offered, but in the night he and his people disappeared in different directions. One division he led 180 miles up Red r., where he built a fort and an expedition found him a year later. His warriors sallied out to attack the French, who drove them back into the fort and bombarded them there until the great chief and some others surrendered themselves. The chief was taken to New Orleans and probably executed with most of his warriors, while the women and children who did not die of an epidemic that befell them were transported to Haiti to labor as slaves on the French plantations. The title "Great Sun" was always borne by the head chief of the Natchez to distinguish him from other members of the class of nobles, all of whom were called "Suns."

**Grand Traverse.** A former settlement of the Chippewa near the site of Flint, Genesee co., Mich.; so named by French traders because at this point was the great ford of Flint r. on the Indian trail from the Saginaw to Detroit. The place became a popular hunting place and camping ground, game and fish being abundant in the neighborhood.

**Granganameo.** A son of Ensenore and brother of Wingina, chiefs of Wingandacoa (Secotan), N. C., and leading man of the tribe in 1585. He is noted chiefly for the friendly aid shown by him to Amidas and Barlow and to Grenville and the accompanying English sent out by Sir Walter Raleigh in the year named. His residence was on Roanoke id., Albemarle sd. As Wingina was confined to his house by a wound when Amidas and Barlow arrived, Granganameo, as acting sachem, received the adventurers kindly and, according to the account given by them, sent them "commonly every day" deer, rabbits, fish, and sometimes various fruits and vegetables. Unfortunately for the English colonists he died before a year expired. (C. T.)

**Grangula** (from French *grande gueule*, 'big mouth'). An Onondaga chief, whose right name was Haaskouan ('His mouth is large'), but who also known as Otreouati. The governor of Canada equipped an army in 1684 to crush the Five Nations because they interfered with French trade. Sickness among the troops having prevented the expedition, Governor de la Barre crossed L. Ontario to offer peace, which he sought to make conditional on the restoration to French merchants of the trade that the Iroquois had diverted to the English. Grangula, representing the Five Nations, replied defiantly that the Iroquois would trade with English or French as they chose, and would continue to treat as enemies French traders who supplied the Miami, Illinois, Shawnee, and other tribes with arms and ammunition to fight them.

**Granite.** A term applied to igneous rocks consisting essentially of quartz and orthoclase feldspar, with mica, hornblende, and other accessories. The name, however, is often made to include a variety of siliceous rocks with similar structure, as the coarser gabbros and diabases, gneiss, syenite, etc. These rocks are generally massive in structure, and were much used by the Indian tribes for their heavier implements, such as sledges for quarry work, hammers for breaking up stone and roughing out implements, and for axes, celts, mortars, pestles, mullers, discoidal stones, and the larger varieties of so-called ceremonial objects. On account of the toughness of these rocks they were difficult to fracture or to flake, and were therefore shaped almost exclusively by the pecking and grinding processes. Very generally the natives selected water-worn fragments approximating the form of the implement to be made, so that the minimum of shaping work was necessary. (w. h. h.)

**Grape Island.** A former Missisauga settlement, probably in N. Minnesota.—Jones, Hist. Ojeb. Inds., 138, 1861.

**Grapevine Town.** A former village, perhaps belonging to the Delawares, situated 8 m. up Captina cr., Belmont co., Ohio.—Washington (1770) in Rupp, West Pa., app., 397, 1846.

**Graphic art.** With the tribes N. of Mexico the arts that may be comprehended under the term graphic are practically identical with the pictorial arts; that is to say, such as represent persons and things in a manner so realistic that the semblance of the original is not entirely lost. Graphic delineations may be (1) simply pictorial; that is, made to gratify the pictorial or esthetic impulse or fancy; (2) trivial, intended to excite mirth, as in caricature and the grotesque; (3) simply decorative, serving to embellish the person or object to which they are applied; (4) simply ideographic, standing for ideas to be expressed, recorded, or conveyed; (5) denotive, including personal names and marks of ownership, distinction, direction, enumeration, etc.; and (6) symbolic, representing some religious, totemic, heraldic, or other occult concept. It is manifest, however, that in very many cases there must be uncertainty as to the motives prompting these graphic representations; and the significance attached to them, even where the tribes using them come directly under observation, is often difficult to determine.

The methods of expression in graphic art are extremely varied, but may be classified as follows: (1) Application of color by means of brushes and hard or soft points or edges, and by developing the form in pulverized pigments (see *Dry painting, Painting*); (2) engraving, which is accomplished by scratching and pecking with hard points (see *Engraving*); (3) indenting and stamping where the surfaces are plastic (see *Pottery*); (4) tattooing, the introduction of coloring matter into designs pricked or cut in the skin (see *Tattooing*); (5) textile methods, as in weaving, basketry, beadwork, featherwork, and embroidery (see *Textile arts*); and (6) inlaying, as in mosaic, where small bits of colored material are so set as to form the figures (see *Mosaic*). The figures are drawn in outline simply, or are filled in with color or other distinctive surfacing. The elaboration or embellishment of sculptured or modeled figures or images of men and beasts by adding details of anatomy, markings, etc., in color or by engraving, thus increasing the realism of the representation, comes also within the realm of the graphic as here defined. In recent times, as the result of contact with the whites, much progress has been made by some of the native tribes in the pictorial art; but the purely aboriginal work, although displaying much rude vigor, shows little advance toward the higher phases of the art. Aboriginally, there was little attempt at effective grouping of the subject save as required in decoration, and light and shade and perspective were entirely unknown. Portraiture and landscape belong apparently to much more advanced stages of culture than have been reached by any of the northern tribes. When the delineations are devoted to the presentation of non-symbolic ideas merely, as in pictography and denotive devices, there is a tendency in frequently recurring use to progressive simplification; the picture as such has no reason to be perpetuated, and this simplification in time reaches a stage where a part takes the place of the whole, or where semblance to the original is entirely lost, the figure becoming the formal sign of an idea. The graphic art of the northern tribes, however, shows no very significant progress in this kind of specialization, unless modern alphabets, like those of the Micmac, or certain inscriptions of somewhat problematical origin, as the Grave Creek Mound tablet (see *Grave Creek Mound*) and the Davenport tablet (Farquharson), are considered.

Graphic delineations are most extensively employed by the tribes in pictography (q. v.), examples of which, engraved or painted on rock surfaces, are found in nearly every section of the country. Similar work was executed by many of the tribes on dressed skins, on birch-bark, and on objects of wood, ivory, bone, horn, and shell. The delineation of life forms in decorative and symbolic art is hardly less universal than in simple pictography, and is especially exemplified in the work of the more advanced peoples, as the pottery of the mound builders and Pueblos, the utensils and the carvings of the tribes of the N. Pacific coast, and ceremonial costumes, and walls and floors of sacred chambers among various tribes. The graphic work of the Eskimo has a peculiar interest, since it seems to have been somewhat recently superposed upon an earlier system in which simple geometric figures predominated, and is much more prevalent where these people have been for a long time in contact with the whites, and more especially with the Athapascan and other Indian tribes skilled in graphic work (Hoffman). A special feature of the art of the Eskimo is the engraving of hunting scenes and exploits of various kinds on objects of ivory and bone—works paralleled among the Indian tribes in the S. by such examples as the Thruston tablet (Thruston, Holmes), the Davenport tablet (Farquharson), and the battle and hunting scenes of the Plains tribes (Mallery, Mooney).

Skill in graphic work was highly regarded among many of the tribes, and the artist took particular pride in his work, and when especially successful became in a sense professional. Usually decorative designs were executed without pattern or copy, and with much directness. The most intricate patterns, applied to earthenware vessels and other objects, were not sketched out but were drawn at once, and often with remarkable skill. Among the N. W. coast tribes, however, patterns were often cut out of cedar bark and the conventional life forms worked in their handsome blankets and capes were drawn out full size on a pattern board. The native artist did not draw directly from nature, but kept in view rather the presentation of the idea, delineating it in the conventional form common to his tribe. He might have been able to produce a portrait, for example, but the desirability of portraiture does not seem to have occurred to him. He might have delineated a species of animal with accuracy, but was apparently content to suggest the particular subject of his thought in a striking and forcible though conventional manner. See *Art, Basketry, Ornament, Painting, Pottery.*

Among the numerous authorities to be consulted on this topic are Boas, Cushing, Fewkes, Holmes, Mallery, Mooney, Murdoch, Nelson, J. and M. C. Stevenson, and Turner in Reps. B. A. E.; Boas, Hoffman, Mason, and Niblack in Reps. Nat. Mus.; Dixon, Kroeber, Matthews, Swanton, Wissler, and others in Memoirs and Bulletins Am. Mus. Nat. Hist.; Farquharson in Proc. Davenport Acad. Sci., II, 1877–1880; Grosse, Beginnings of Art, 1897; Haddon, Evolution in Art, 1895; Kroeber in Am. Anthrop., n. s., III, 1901; Moore, various memoirs in Jour. Acad. Nat. Sci. Phila., 1894–1905; Schoolcraft, Ind. Tribes, I–VI, 1851–57; Thruston, Antiq. of Tenn., 1897; various authors in the ethnological and archeological journals.

(W. H. H.)

**Grass house.** A dwelling having the shape of an old-fashioned beehive, often

WICHITA GRASS HOUSE IN PROCESS OF CONSTRUCTION. (MOONEY)

described by Spanish and French travelers of the 16th and 17th centuries, which was the typical habitation of the Caddoan tribes, except the Pawnee and Arikara. Its construction was begun by drawing a circle on the ground, and on the outline setting a number of crotched posts, in which beams were laid. Against these, poles were set very closely in a row so as to lean inward; these in turn were laced with willow rods and their tops brought together and securely fastened so as to form a peak. Over this frame a heavy thatch of grass was laid and bound down by slender rods, and at each point where the rods joined an ornamental tuft of grass was tied. Two poles, laid at right angles, jutting out in four projecting points, were fastened to the apex of the roof, and over the center, where they crossed, rose a spire, 2 ft high or more, made of bunches of grass. Four doors, opening to each point of the compass, were formerly made, but now, except when the house is to be used for ceremonial purposes, only two are provided, one on the E. to serve for the morning, and one on the W. to go in and out of when the sun is in that quarter. The fireplace was a circular excavation in the center of the floor, and the smoke found egress through a hole left high up in the roof toward the E. The four projecting beams at the peak pointed toward and were symbolic of the four points of the compass, where were the paths down which the powers descend to help man. The spire typified the abode in the zenith of the mysterious permeating force that animates all nature. The fireplace was accounted sacred; it was never treated lightly even in the daily life of the family. The couches of the occupants were placed against the wall. They consisted of a framework on which was fitted a woven covering of reeds. Upon this robes or rush mats were spread. The grass house is a comely structure. Skill is required to build it, and it has an attractive appearance both without and within. It is adapted to a warm climate only, and is still in use among the Wichita. Temporary dwellings of poles covered with grass were common among the Plains tribes, and similar houses for storage purposes were used by tribes on the coast of Oregon (Boas). See *Earth lodge, Habitations*.

Consult Catlin, No. Am. Inds., I–II, 1841; Winship, Coronado Exped., 14th Rep. B. A. E., 1896; G. A. Dorsey, Mythology of the Wichita, 1904; Manzanet Diary in Tex. Hist. Ass'n Quar., II, 303, 1899. (A. C. F.)

**Grasswork.** The Indian found the widely diffused grasses of the United States of great value, almost a necessity, and adapted them in numerous ways to his needs. The obvious needs supplied by loose grass were for house building (see *Grass house*), bedding, for lining caches, etc.; it was also worked into baskets (southern Indians, Hopi, Pima, Tlingit, Aleut, Eskimo), mats, leggings (Ntlakyapamuk), socks, towels (Eskimo), and other articles. The polished yellow or white stems were used by various tribes to ornament basketry, and by the Hupa of California as fringes of garments. Stiff stems were gathered into bundles and used as hair and floor brushes by the Pueblos and cliff-dwellers. Slender, flat grass stems, sometimes dyed, were applied to dressed skins by some tribes with sinew thread for ornamental purposes, just as were porcupine quills (Grinnell).

Grass was generally found useful as tinder; some species furnished excellent fiber for cord, and some were employed as perfumery. The Cheyenne burned grass and mixed the ashes with blood and tallow to produce paint. So far as is known the Indian invented no implements for cutting grass; basketry fans, gathering baskets, etc., were used in harvesting seeds for food. In ceremony grass had an important place. It was a component of various prayer-sticks and wands of the Hopi, and the sacred buffalo skull of some of the Plains tribes was thought to be made to live by stuffing balls of grass into the eye sockets and nose. Sweet grass was also burned to produce consecrating smoke and for lighting the pipe in sacred rites of the Plains Indians. The sod used in the *Hako* altar of the Pawnee, described by Miss Fletcher (22d Rep. B. A. E., 1903) was in Indian thought a symbol of life and growth. (W. H.)

**Grave Creek mound.** A noted prehistoric Indian mound, situated near Moundsville, Marshall co., W. Va., at the point where Grave cr. unites with Ohio r. It was visited as early as 1734, as appears from this date cut on a tree growing from its summit, but was first described by

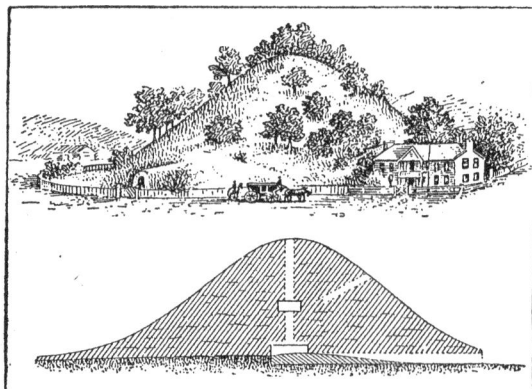

GRAVE CREEK MOUND AND SECTION. (SQUIER AND DAVIS)

Hart in 1797 (Imlay, Topog. Desc. W. Ter. N. Am., 296–304), since which time it has been repeatedly described and figured, attention of scholars having been called to it chiefly by an inscription on a small stone which was reputed to have been found in the mound during its excavation. The mound is conical in form, being probably the largest example of this type in the United States, having a diameter at the base of about 320 ft, a height of 70 ft, and 1,870,000 cu. ft of solid contents. It is symmetrical in form and has a dish-shaped depression in the top. It was excavated in 1838 by the proprietor, who first carried a horizontal drift at the base to the center and a shaft from the top to connect with the drift. Two burial vaults were discovered, one at the base and another 30 ft above, each constructed of logs and covered with stones, which had sunk as the wood decayed, leaving the depression in the summit. Squier and Davis (Anc. Mon., 169, 1848) assert that under the center of the mound there was a slight natural elevation into which the lower vault had been sunk. This vault contained two human skeletons, the upper vault but one. Accompanying the skeletons were 3,000 to 4,000 shell beads, ornaments of mica, several copper bracelets, and various articles of stone, including the inscribed stone mentioned, the inscription on which has received various interpretations. An illustration of this inscription was first published in the Cincinnati Chronicle, Feb. 2, 1839; another in the American Pioneer, II, no. 5, 1843. Rafn, whose tendency was to give a foreign interpretation to Indian inscriptions, inclined to the opinion that the inscribed characters were Anglo-Saxon runes, while Schoolcraft concluded that they belonged to some 8 or 9 different alphabets, as old Greek, Etruscan, etc. A committee of the Ohio Archæological and Historical Society in 1877 reached the following conclusions: "1. The inscription is not necessarily to be regarded as alphabetical. 2. If it is assumed to be alphabetical, it can not be referred to any known language. 3. It is precisely of such a character as would be the result of an ordinary attempt to manufacture an inscription. 4. Its manufacture is within the capacity of any laborer of ordinary intelligence who may have been employed in the work of exploring the mound. 5. At the time of its discovery there was no proper scrutiny of the inscription to determine whether it was of recent manufacture or not. 6. The evidence that it came from the mound is by no means conclusive. 7. Its history is such that the subsequent discovery of unquestioned ancient inscriptions with similar characters would warrant us in concluding that this also is ancient. 8. Until its authenticity is thus fully established, it ought not to be regarded as any evidence of the character, ethnical relationship, or intellectual culture of the builders of the mounds." Whittlesey, in 1872, expressed the belief that the inscription was a forgery. Consult Clemens in Morton, Crania Americana, 221, 1839; Schoolcraft in Trans. Am. Ethnol. Soc., I, 369–420, 1846; Squier and Davis, Anc. Monuments, 168–170, 1848; Thomas (1) in 5th Rep. B. A. E., 51, 1887; (2) Cat. Prehistoric Works, 222, 1891, with bibliographic references; Whittlesey in Tracts West. Res. Hist. Soc., I, nos. 9 and 33, 1877, and II, no. 44, 1888.                                      (C. T.)

**Gray Village.** A former Natchez village.
Grays.—Dumont in French, Hist. Coll. La., V, 49, 1853. Gray Village.—Ibid., 48.

**Greasy Faces.** A band of the Arapaho, q. v.

**Great Island Village.** A former settlement, probably of the Delawares, on the Susquehanna opposite the present Lock Haven, Clinton co., Pa.—Royce in 18th Rep. B. A. E., Pa. map, 1899.

**Great Mortar** (Yayatustenuggee). A Creek chief; an ally of the French in the Seven Years' war. When the English superintendent of Indian affairs called a council of the Creeks with the object of winning them over, he refused the pipe of peace to Great Mortar because the chief had favored the French, and the latter withdrew with his followers, confirmed in his hostility to the British. He received a commission from the French, and after killing or driving out the English traders and settlers took up a position on the border, where he could raid the Georgia settlements, obtaining his arms and supplies from the French fort on Alabama r. Many Creeks and Cherokee joined him there until the Chickasaw surprised the camp and put his warriors to flight. He settled at another place whence he could resume his depredations and continued to ravage the scattered settlements, including Augusta, Ga. In 1761 Col. James Grant, at the head of 2,600 Americans and friendly Indians, brought all the hostiles to terms, and a peace was made which fixed the watershed of the Allegheny mts. as the boundary between the British colonies and the lands of the natives.—Drake, Aborig. Races, 384, 1880.

**Great Spirit.** See *Popular fallacies, Religion.*

**Great Sun.** See *Grand Soleil.*

**Green-corn dance.** See *Busk.*

**Greentown.** A former Delaware village on the Black fork of Mohican r., near the boundary of Richland and Ashland cos., Ohio. See Treaty of Maumee Rapids (1819) in U. S. Ind. Treat., 204, 1873; Royce in 18th Rep. B. A. E., Ohio map, 1899.

**Greeting.** See *Salutation.*

**Grenadier Squaw's Town.** A Shawnee village situated in 1774 on Scippo cr., Pickaway co., Ohio. The name was derived from Grenadier Squaw, a sister of Cornstalk, the Shawnee chief, who made this her home.                           (J. M.)
Grenadier Squaws T.—Howe, Hist. Coll. Ohio, II, 402, 1896. Squaw Town.—Royce in 18th Rep. B. A. E., Ohio map, 1899.

**Grey Eagle Band.** One of the Dakota bands below L. Traverse, Minn. (Ind. Aff. Rep. 1859, 102, 1860), evidently taking its name from the chief; not identified.

**Grigras.** A French nickname and the only known name of a small tribe already incorporated with the Natchez confederacy in 1720; it was applied because of the frequent occurrence of *grigra* in their language. There is uncertainty in regard to the language and ethnic relations, but unless affiliated with the Tonica, the tribe was evidently distinct from every other, since, as indicated by the sound *grigra*, their language possessed an *r*.

Grigas.—Richebourg (1713) in French, Hist. Coll. La., III, 248, 1851. Grigras.—Le Page du Pratz, Hist. La., II, 222, 1758.

**Grinaiches.** Mentioned by Baudry de Lozières (Voy. Louisiane, 242, 1802) in a list of tribes with no indication of habitat. Probably a misprint of some well-known tribal name.

**Grinding stones.** See *Abrading implements*.

**Grizzly Bear Erect.** See *Etsowish-simmegee-itshin*.

**Gros** (Les). A Wea village on the Wabash in 1718 (Memoir of 1718 in N. Y. Doc. Col. Hist., IX, 891, 1855); perhaps in Tippecanoe co., Ind.

**Grosse Tête** (Fr.: 'big head'). A former Chitimacha village in Louisiana. Grosse Tête namu.—Gatschet in Trans. Anthrop. Soc. Wash., II, 152, 1883 (*namu* = 'village').

**Gros Ventres** (French, 'big bellies') A term applied by the French, and after them by others, to two entirely distinct tribes: (1) the Atsina (q. v.), or Hitunena, a detached band of the Arapaho, and (2) the Hidatsa (q. v.), or Minitari. In the Lewis and Clark narrative of 1806 the former are distinguished as Minitarees of Fort de Prairie and the latter as Minitarees of the Missouri, although there is no proper warrant for applying the name Minitari to the Atsina. The two tribes have also been distinguished as Grosventres of the Missouri (Hidatsa) and Grosventres of the Prairie (Atsina). The name as applied to the Atsina originates from the Indian sign by which they are designated in the sign language—a sweeping pass with both hands in front of the abdomen, intended to convey the idea of 'always hungry,' i. e., 'beggars.' A clew to its application to the Hidatsa is given in the statement of Matthews (Hidatsa, 43, 1877) that the Hidatsa formerly tattooed parallel stripes across the chest, and were thus sometimes distinguished in picture writings. The gesture sign to indicate this style of tattooing would be sufficiently similar to that used to designate the Atsina to lead the careless observer to interpret both as "Gros Ventres." The ordinary sign now used by the southern Plains tribes to indicate the Hidatsa is interpreted to mean 'spreading tipis' or 'row of lodges.' (J. M.)
Big-bellys.—Gass, Journal, 76, 1807. Big bellied.—Mackenzie, Voy., lxiv, 1801. Bigbellies.—Lewis and Clark, Exped., I, 132, 1814. Big Pauch.—Lewis and Clark, Travels, 15, 1807 (misprint). Big Paunch.—Lewis and Clark, Discov., 18, 1806. Gos ventres.—De Smet, Letters, 62, 1843. Great Belly Indians.—Writer of 1786 in Mass. Hist. Soc. Coll., 1st s., III, 24, 1794. Grosse Ventres.—Brown, West. Gaz., 212, 1817. Gross Vantres.—Orig. Jour. Lewis and Clark (1804), I, 210, 1904. Grossventers.—Gass, Jour., 76, 1807. Gross Ventres.—Orig. Jour. Lewis and Clark, I, 243, 1904. Gross Ventres proper.—Schoolcraft, Ind. Tribes, I, 259, 1851 (intended for the Hidatsa). Grosvantres.—Orig. Jour. Lewis and Clark, I, 209, 1904. Gros-Ventres.—Saint Pierre (1753) in Margry, Déc., VI, 640, 1886. Gros Ventres of the Missouri.—Hale, Ethnog. and Philol., 220, 1846 (intended for the Hidatsa). Gros-Vents.—Kane, Wanderings of an Artist, 366, 1859. Grovan.—Bonner, Life of Beckwourth, 162, 1856.

**Groton.** A former Mohegan village about the present Groton, New London, Conn. In 1825 the population was reduced to 50 souls. (J. M.)

**Gua.** A Chumashan village w. of Pueblo de las Canoas (San Buenaventura), Ventura co., Cal., in 1542. In the Muñoz manuscript of Cabrillo's narration (Smith, Colec. Doc. Fla., 181, 1857) this name is united, probably correctly, with the prefix Quanmu, forming Quanmugua.

**Guacata.** An inland Calusa village on L. "Mayaimi," or Okechobee, s. Fla., about 1570. Elsewhere in his memoir Fontaneda refers to it as a distinct but subordinate tribe. Guacata.—Fontaneda Memoir (*ca.* 1575), Smith trans., 19, 1854. Guasaca.—Fontaneda in French, Hist. Coll. La., 2d s., II, 245, 1875.

**Guacaya.** Mentioned by Oviedo (Hist. Gen. Indies, III, 628, 1853) as one of the provinces or villages on or in the general vicinity of the South Carolina coast, visited by Ayllon in 1520.

**Guachochic** ('place of the blue herons'). A rancheria of "civilized" Tarahumare on the headwaters of Rio Fuerte, about lat. 26° 50′, long. 106° 55′, in s. Chihuahua, Mexico; entire population 1,147 in 1900. The inhabitants gain a livelihood mainly as servants of the Mexicans.—Lumholtz (1) in Scribner's Mag., XVI, 32, 39, 1894; (2) Unknown Mexico, I, 194, 205, 1902.

**Guachoya.** A palisaded village, probably of the Quapaw, containing 300 houses in the 16th century, on the w. bank of the Mississippi, apparently a short distance below the mouth of the Arkansas. It was here De Soto died, May 21, 1542. Guachoia.—Shipp, De Soto and Florida, 432, 1881. Guachoya.—Gentl. of Elvas (1557) in French, Hist. Coll. La., II, 186, 1850. Guachoyanque.—Biedma (1544) in French, Hist. Coll. La., II, 107, 1850.

**Guadalupe.** Mentioned as a Navaho settlement in 1799 (Cortez in Pac. R. R. Rep., III, pt. 3, 119, 1856), but more likely the Spanish name of a locality, as the Navaho are not villagers. Guadelupe.—Domenech, Deserts of N. A., II, 7, 1860.

**Guadalupe.** A Papago village about 10 leagues s. of Areitorae, in Sonora, Mexico. Guadalupe.—Box, Adventurers, 264, 1869. Guadalupe-Pa-Pagoe.—Ibid. (i. e., "Papago").

**Guadalupe y Ocotan.**—A Huichol pueblo near Rio Chapalagana, Jalisco, Mexico. See Lumholtz (1) Huichol Indians, 5, 1898; (2) Unknown Mexico, II, 16, map, 1902.

**Guaes.** A people of whom Coronado learned in 1542. They evidently lived E. of Quivira, the Wichita country of E. central Kansas, of whose people they were enemies. The name bears a resemblance to Kaws, but as this is the French traders' contraction of Kansa, first applied not earlier than the first quarter of

the 19th century, the two peoples were probably not the same, Guas or Guaes being apparently a Wichita or Pawnee name, or a corruption thereof.   (F. W. H.)
Guaes.—Castañeda (ca. 1560) in 14th Rep. B. A. E., 503, 1896. Guas.—Ibid., 529. Guyas.—Castañeda in Ternaux-Compans, Voy., IX, 194, 1838 (misprint).

Guagejohe.—Given as one of the Comanche divisions, living about 1857 on the plains N. of Texas. Possibly a misprint Spanish form of Kwahari, q. v.
Gúä-gĕ-jö-hĕ.—Butcher and Lyendecher, MS. Comanche vocab., B. A. E., 1867.

Guaguatu. An unidentified people described early in the 17th century, by the Acoma and Jemez Indians of New Mexico, as resembling the Mexicans in language and dress, and as living in straw-covered houses in a mild country somewhere to the westward of the Navaho, toward the Pacific. The name suggests the pueblo of Awatobi, q. v.
Guaguatu.—Zarate-Salmeron (ca. 1629), Rel., in Land of Sunshine, 183, Feb., 1900. Guaputu.—Ibid.

Guahate. A fertile province, probably in the present s. w. Arkansas, heard of by De Soto in 1541 at Quipana as being 8 days s. of that place.—Gentl. of Elvas (1557) in French, Hist. Coll. La., II, 182, 1850.

Guailopo. A subdivision of the Varohio in w. Chihuahua, Mexico. They lived with the Chinipa in the pueblo of San Andres Chinipas.—Orozco y Berra, Geog., 58, 325, 1864.

Guainonost. A former Chumashan village near Santa Barbara mission, Cal.—Taylor in Cal. Farmer, Apr. 24, 1863.

Guaislac. A former Chumashan village near Santa Inés mission, Santa Barbara co., Cal.— Taylor in Cal. Farmer, Oct. 18, 1861.

Guajochic ('place of the guajo,' a small variety of mosquito). A small rancheria of the Tarahumare, not far from Norogachic, Chihuahua, Mexico.—Lumholtz, Unknown Mexico, I, 218, 1902.

Gualala. A name applied by Powers to the Pomo living along Gualala r., in Sonoma co., Cal. The people living along this stream belong to two dialectic groups, one occupying the territory chiefly along the lower course of Russian r., the other that along the immediate coastline w. of Gualala r.; but as Powers' statements are not explicit, it is not possible to say whether the people speaking one or the other of these dialects is meant. The name itself comes undoubtedly from waláli, a name applied to the point at which the waters of any two streams flow together, or at which any stream flows into the ocean.   (S. A. B.)
Gua-la-la.—Powers in Cont. N. A. Ethnol., III, 186, 1877. Walhalla.—Bancroft, Nat. Races, I, 362, 1874.

Guale. The Indian name by which the Spaniards knew the present Amelia id.,

N. coast of Florida, and a part of the adjacent Florida and Georgia coast, in the 16th century. There is strong probability that the tribe in occupancy was that known later as Yamasi. In 1597 the son of the chief of Guale led a revolt against the missions that had been established by the Spanish Franciscans a few years before. There were then on the island at least 3 mission villages—Asao, Asopo, and Ospo. The missions were reestablished in 1605 and may have continued until their destruction by the English and their Indian allies in 1704–06.   (J. M.)
Gualdape.—Fontaneda Memoir (ca. 1575), Smith trans., 16, 1854. Guale.—Ibid. Quale.—Fontaneda in Ternaux-Compans, Voy., XX, 16, 1841. Quate.—Fontaneda misquoted by Shipp, De Soto and Fla., 585, 1881.

Gualta. Given by the Yavapai to Fray Francisco Garcés in 1776 as the name of a tribe, possibly in the vicinity of the Rio Colorado.—Garcés, Diary (1775–76), 405, 1900.

Guamua. The Yavapai name of a tribe evidently on or in the vicinity of the Rio Colorado in Arizona or California, in the 18th century.—Garcés (1775–76), Diary, 404, 1900. Cf. Gueymura.
Guamoa.—Cortez (1799) in Pac. R. R. Rep., III, pt. 3, 126, 1856.

Guanabepe. The Yavapai name of a tribe, evidently Yuman, on the lower Colorado in Arizona or California, in the 18th century.
Guanabepe.—Garcés (1776), Diary, 404, 1900. Guanavepe.—Orozco y Berra, Geog., 349, 1864 (after Garcés).

Guanacos (Span.: Los Guanacos.) A group of ruined pueblos 8 m. s. of Tempe, in the Salt River valley, Ariz. So named from a number of figurines, resembling the guanaco, found there.—Cushing in Compte-rendu Internat. Cong. Am., VII, 178, 1890.

Guancane. Mentioned by Garcilasso de la Vega (Florida, 201, 1723) as a province visited by De Soto's army in 1542. Situated probably in s. w. Arkansas, near Naguatex, q. v.
Guacane.—Shipp, De Soto and Florida, 430, 1881.

Guanipas. A former Coahuila tribe, belonging perhaps to the Coahuiltecan stock.—Revillagigedo (1793) quoted by Orozco y Berra, Geog., 306, 1864.

Guanlen. A former village, presumably Costanoan, connected with Dolores mission, San Francisco, Cal.—Taylor in Cal. Farmer, Oct. 18, 1861.

Guarungunve ('town of weeping'). A Calusa village on one of the keys of the s. w. coast of Florida, about 1570. Brinton (Floridian Penin., 114, 1859) thinks the word is another name for Old Matacumbe (Metacumbe) key, described by Romans (1775) as one of the last refuges of the Calusa Indians.   (J. M.)
Guaragunve.—Fontaneda quoted by Ternaux-Compans, Voy., XX, 10, 1841. Guardgumve.—Fontaneda quoted by French, Hist. Coll. La., 2d s., II,

262, 1875 (misprint). **Guarugumbe.**—Fontaneda quoted by Ternaux-Compans, op. cit., 32. **Guarugunve.**—Fontaneda Mem. (*ca.* 1575), Smith trans., 13, 1854. **Guarungunve.**—Ibid., 19. **Guarunguve.**—Fontaneda quoted by Ternaux-Compans., op. cit., 22. **Metacumbe.**—Present map form for the key. **Old Matacombe.**—Romans, Fla., app., xxxiv, 1775 (the key; same?).

**Guasamota.** A Cora pueblo on the upper Rio Jesus María, on the E. slope of the Sierra de Nayarit, in the N. part of the territory of Tepic, Mexico (Lumholtz, Unknown Mexico, I, 487; II, 16, map, 1902). Orozco y Berra records it as a Tepehuane settlement.
**Guasamota.**—Lumholtz, op. cit. **Guazamota.**—Orozco y Berra, Geog., 281, 1864. **Santa María Guazamota.**—Ibid., 318–319.

**Guasas.** A tribe mentioned in Spanish narratives and reports on Texas in the latter part of the 18th century as enemies of the "northern Indians," particularly of the Comanche. According to one narrative they were the only people able to defeat the latter. They are described as having lived in permanent villages defended by adobe towers; they called their warriors together by means of drums in time of danger. They were reputed to be of great stature and of remarkable skill in horsemanship. Although many of the things told about them are entirely fabulous, a real tribe appears to be referred to, probably one of those which erected earth lodges. This may have been the Osage (*Wasash*) or, since an annotator of a letter written by Ripperdá in 1772 enumerates "Guasers" and Osage separately, possibly they were the Kansa or the Pawnee. (J. R. S.)
**Guasas.**—Prieto, Hist. de Tamaulipas, 137, 1873. **Guasers.**—Annotator of a letter of Ripperdá, 1772, MS. cited by H. E. Bolton, inf'n, 1906. **Guazas.**—Report of council at San Antonio in 1778, MS. cited by H. E. Bolton, inf'n, 1906.

**Guasco.** A province, possibly Caddoan, visited in 1542 by Moscoso, of De Soto's army, who there found much maize; situated probably in s. w. Arkansas or N. W. Louisiana. See Gentl. of Elvas (1557) in French, Hist. Coll. La., II, 199, 1850.

**Guasigochic** ('a flat'). A small rancheria of the Tarahumare, N. E. of Norogachic, Chihuahua, Mexico.—Lumholtz, inf'n, 1894.

**Guaslaique.** A former Chumashan village near Purísima mission, Santa Barbara co., Cal.—Taylor in Cal. Farmer, Oct. 18, 1861.

**Guatitruti.** Mentioned by Oñate in 1598 (Doc. Inéd., xvi, 114, 1871) as a pueblo of the Jemez in New Mexico. It has not been identified with the present native name of any ruins in the vicinity of Jemez. In Oñate's second list of Jemez villages (ibid., 102) Fiapuzi and Triyti are given. Comparison shows the first name to be a misprint of the name of the preceding pueblo mentioned ('Trea'), improperly compounded with a misprint ('puzi') of 'Guati,' the first part of the

name Guatitruti; the other pueblo mentioned in the second list ('Triyti') being a corruption of the latter portion ('truti') of the name Guatitruti. (F. W. H.)
**Friyti.**—Bancroft, Ariz. and N. Mex.,136, 1889(misprint). **Guatitritti.** — Columbus Memorial Vol., 155, 1893 (misprint). **Trivti.**—Bandelier in Arch. Inst. Papers, IV, 207, 1892 (misquoting Oñate). **Triyti.**—Oñate (1598) in Doc. Inéd., XVI, 102,1892.

**Guauaenok.** A Kwakiutl tribe living on Drury inlet, Brit. Col. The gentes are Gyigyilkam, Kwakowenok, and Kwikoaenok. Summer villages are Hohopa and Kunstamish. Pop. 46 in 1885.
**Guau'aēnoq.**—Boas in 6th Rep. N. W. Tribes Can., 55, 1890. **Guau'aēnox.**—Boas in Rep. Nat. Mus., 331, 1895. **Kwauaenoq.**—Boas in Bull. Am. Geog. Soc., 228, 1887. **Kwā-wa-ai-nuk.**—Dawson in Trans. Roy. Soc. Can., sec. II, 73, 1887. **Kwā-wa-a-nuk.**—Ibid. **Quai-iunough.**—Brit. Col. map, 1872. **Quai-nu.**—Kane, Wand. in N. Am., app., 1859. **Quáūaē-noq.**—Boas in Petermanns Mitt., pt. 5, 130, 1887.

**Guaxule.** A village, apparently of the Creeks, visited by De Soto in 1540. Coxe seems to locate it near the head of Mobile r.; Shipp places it on the Chattahoochee, and Thomas (12th Rep. B. A. E., 649, 1894) near Cartersville, in Bartow co., Ga. The Spaniards were entertained so well at this place that to the army its name became a synonym for good fortune. See *Etowah mound*.
**Guachoula.**—Shipp, De Soto and Florida, 368, 1881. **Guachoule.**—Mooney in 19th Rep. B. A. E., 520, 1900 (given as an early form). **Guachule.**—Mooney, Siouan Tribes of the East, 57, 1894. **Guasili.**—Mooney in 19th Rep., op. cit. **Guasula.**—Ibid. **Guasuli.**—Biedma (1544) in Hakluyt Soc. Pub., IX, 182, 1851. **Guaxula.**—Coxe, Carolana, 23, 1741. **Guaxule.**—Gentleman of Elvas (1557) in French, Hist. Coll. La., II, 147, 1850.

**Guaya.** A former village of the Calusa confederacy near the s. end of Florida (Fontaneda, *ca.* 1575, in Ternaux-Compans, Voy., xx, 22, 23, 1841). The village is not given in B. Smith's translation of Fontaneda's narrative.

**Guayabas.** A Huichol rancheria and religious place, containing a temple; situated about 2½ m. s. w. of San Andres Coamiata, q. v.—Lumholtz, Unknown Mex., II, 52, 1902.
**Temolikíta.**—Lumholtz, ibid. ('where trees and flowers are budding': native name).

**Guaycones.** An unidentified tribe visited by Cabeza de Vaca (Smith trans., 84, 1851) during his sojourn in Texas in 1528–34.
**Gualciones.**—Barcia, Historiadores, I, 1749.

**Guaynamota.** A former Cora pueblo and the seat of a mission, situated on the E. bank of Rio San Pedro, lat. 22° 30′, Jalisco, Mexico.
**S. Ignacio Guaynamota.**—Orozco y Berra, Geog., 280, 1864.

**Guayoguia.** Mentioned by Oñate in 1598 (Doc Inéd., XVI, 114, 1871) as a pueblo of the Jemez in New Mexico. It has not been identified with the present native name of any ruins in the vicinity of Jemez. In Oñate's second list (ibid., 207) Yxcaguayo and Quiamera are mentioned. The names are obviously misprinted, the latter part of the first name and a misprint of the first part of the other forming "Guayoquia."

**Guayotri.** Apparently a Tigua pueblo in New Mexico in 1598. Mentioned by Oñate (Doc. Inéd., xvi, 115, 1871) in connection with Puaray. See *Tiguex*.

**Guayusta.** A village of the Rumsen division of the Costanoan family, formerly at Pt Pinos, near Monterey, Cal., the inhabitants of which were connected with San Carlos mission.
Guayusta.—Taylor in Cal. Farmer, Apr. 20, 1860. Point Pinos.—Ibid.

**Guazapar.** A division of the Tarahumare occupying the village of Guazapares, w. Chihuahua, Mexico. It includes also the Temoris who inhabit the pueblos of Santa María Magdalena, Nuestra Señora del Valle Humbroso, and Cerocahui. The Guazapar dialect is said to resemble more closely the Tarahumare proper than the Varohio. (F. W. H.)
Guazapar.—Orozco y Berra, Geog., map, 1864. Guazápare.—Ibid., 58.

**Guazapares.** A village of the Guazapar division of the Tarahumare in the district of Arteaga, w. Chihuahua, Mexico; pop. 542 in 1900.
Guazayepo.—Orozco y Berra, Geog., 324, 1864. Santa Teresa de Guazápares.—Ibid.

**Guazarachic.** A Tarahumare settlement in the Hidalgo district, Chihuahua, Mexico.
Guasarochic.—Orozco y Berra, Geog., 322, 1864. Guazarachis.—Ibid., 59 (given as Apache, but doubtless Piman).

**Guazavas** (probably from Opata *guasaca*, 'where the (pitahaya) fruit ripens first.'—Rudo Ensayo). A former Coguinachi Opata pueblo, containing also some Apache, and the seat of a Spanish mission founded in 1645, on Rio Bavispe, about lat. 29° 40', Sonora, Mexico. Its inhabitants numbered 632 in 1678, and 191 in 1730. A new church was built in 1764. The place is now civilized, but 50 Yaqui were settled in and about the town in 1900. (F. W. H.)
Buasdabas.—Ribas (1645) quoted by Bandelier in Arch. Inst. Papers, iii, 58, 1890. Goasavas.—de Croix (1769) in Doc. Hist. Mex., 4th s., ii, 25, 1856. Guasavas.—Orozco y Berra, Geog., 343, 1864. Guayavas.—Hamilton, Mex. Handbook, 47, 1883. Guazaca.—Doc. of 1730 quoted by Bandelier in Arch. Inst. Papers, iv, 505, 1892. Guazava.—Mange (ca. 1700) quoted by Bancroft, No. Mex. States, i, 233, 1884. Huassabas.—Bandelier in Arch. Inst. Papers, iii, 58, 1890. Huassavas.—Ibid., 56. San Francisco Guazava.—Rivera (1730) quoted by Bancroft, op. cit., 514. San Francisco Javier de Guazava.—Zapata (1678), ibid., 246.

**Guazave.** A subdivision of the Vacoregue, formerly occupying the pueblos of San Pedro Guazave and Tamazula, on Rio Sinaloa, about lat. 25° 45', N. w. Sinaloa, Mexico. The Vacoregue were also sometimes known as Guazave. A Jesuit mission was established among them in 1600, but the natives burned the church and fled. They were brought back, however, and the offenders hanged. Between 1646

and 1649 they again threatened trouble, but they later became Christianized and noted for their faith in the new religion. Orozco y Berra (Geog., 332, 1864) says: "In Guazave were united several factions, and although they were known as Guazaves they speak the Mexican tongue between themselves; this is the civilized language in all parts." (F. W. H.)

**Gubo.** A former rancheria, probably of the Papago, visited by Father Kino in 1694; situated 13 leagues E. of Sonoita, which was on the Rio Salado of Sonora, just below the Arizona boundary.
Gubo.—Kino (1694) in Doc. Hist. Mex., 4th s., i, 252, 1856. Guvoverde.—Kino (1699) quoted by Bancroft, No. Mex. States, i, 267, 1884.

**Gueguachic.** A former Tarahumare settlement in Chihuahua, Mexico.—Orozco y Berra, Geog., 322, 1864.

**Gueiquesales.** A former tribe of s. Texas, probably Coahuiltecan, living near the Manos Prietas, Bocores, Haeser, Pinanaca, Escaba, Cacastes, Cocobipta, Codame, Contotores, Colorados, Babiamares, and Taimamares. Perhaps identical with the Guisoles, and probably the Susolas of Cabeza de Vaca. (J. R. S.)
Gueiquesales.—Fernando del Bosque (1675) in Nat. Geog. Mag., xiv, 340, 1903. Gueiquizales.—Revillagigedo MS. (1793) quoted by Bancroft, Nat. Races, i, 611, 1886.

**Guepacomatzi.** A former Opata rancheria N. of Oputo, E. Sonora, Mexico. It was abandoned in the 18th century owing to the hostility of the Apache, Suma, and Jocome. Not to be confounded with Huepac.
Guepa Comatzi.—Doc. of 18th cent. quoted by Bandelier in Arch. Inst. Papers, iv, 525, 1892.

**Guerachic.** Mentioned as a Tepehuane pueblo on the Upper Rio Fuerte, in the Sierra Madre, Chihuahua, Mexico.
Guerachic.—Orozco y Berra, Geog., 324, 1864. Guerechic.—Ibid., 322 (apparently the same). Huerachic.—Lumholtz, Unknown Mexico, i, 299, note, 1902.

**Guess, George.** See *Sequoya*.

**Guetela** ('northern people'). A sept of the true Kwakiutl which formerly formed one tribe with the Komoyue, but separated on account of some quarrel. The clans are Maamtagyıla, Kukwakum, Gyeksem, Laalaksentaio, and Sisintlae. They now live at Ft Rupert, Brit. Col.
Guē'tEla.—Boas in Nat. Mus. Rep., 330, 1895. Kuē'xāmut.—Ibid. (='fellows of the Kueha').

**Guetela.** A clan of the Wikeno, a Kwakiutl tribe.—Boas in Nat. Mus. Rep., 330, 1895.

**Guevavi.** A former Sobaipuri settlement and the seat of a Spanish mission established about 1720–32; situated on the w. bank of Rio Santa Cruz, below Tubac, at or near the present Nogales, Arizona-Sonora boundary. In 1750 it was plundered by the Indians and abandoned, but was reoccupied two years later as a mission under the protection of Tubac. In 1760–64 Guevavi contained 111 natives;

in 1772, 86, and with its visitas (Calabazas, Jamac, Sonoita, and Tumacacori), 337. It was abandoned before 1784, Tumacacori becoming head of the mission establishment.　　　　　　　　　　　　(F. W. H.)

Genevavi.—Kino, map (1701) in Bancroft. Ariz. and N. Mex., 360, 1889 (misprint). **Guazavez.**—Writer (ca. 1713) in Doc. Hist. Mex., 4th s., v, 175, 1857. **Guebavi.**—Kino, map (1701) in Stöcklein, Neue Welt-Bott, 74, 1726. **Guevavi.**—Mange (1699) quoted by Bancroft, op. cit., 358. **Guevaví-Gussudao.**—Orozco y Berra, Geog., 347, 1864. **Gusudac.**—Rudo Ensayo (1763), 149, 1863 (Pima name: 'great water'). **Gusutaqui.**—Mange quoted by Bancroft, op. cit., 358. **San Felipe de Jesus Guevavi.**—Villa-Señor quoted by Bancroft, No. Mex. States, I, 531, 1884. **San Miguel.**—Bancroft, Ariz. and N. Mex., 384, 1889 (Jesuit name). **San Miguel de Guevavi.**—Ibid., 362 (probably not so named until 1732). **San Rafael.**—Ibid., 384 (Jesuit name). **Santos Angeles.**—Ibid. (Franciscan name). **S. Luis Guebavi.**—Venegas, Hist. Cal., I, map, 1759.

**Guevu.** A Calusa village on the s. w. coast of Florida, about 1570.

Gueva.—Fontaneda quoted in Doc. Inéd., v, 539, 1866. **Guevu.**—Fontaneda Mem. (ca. 1575), Smith trans., 19, 1854.

**Gueymura.** A tribe speaking the Diegueño dialect, formerly living about Santa Catalina mission, N. Lower California. (Duflot de Mofras, Voy., I, 217, 228, 1844). Cf. *Comeya, Guamua, Quilmur.*

**Gueyniotiteshesgue** ('four tribes'). A phratry of the Caughnawaga Iroquois.

**Gueza.** An Indian settlement in w. South Carolina, probably in the present Edgefield co., visited by Juan Pardo in 1565.—Vandera in Smith, Colec. Doc. Fla., I, 17, 1857.

**Guhlaniyi** (*Gŭʻlani'yĭ*). A Cherokee and Natchez settlement formerly at the junction of Brasstown cr. with Hiwassee r., a short distance above Murphy, Cherokee co., N. C.—Mooney in 19th Rep. B. A. E., 520, 1900.

**Guhlga** (*Gū'tga*). A legendary Haida town on the N. shore of Skidegate inlet, just above the present town of Skidegate, Queen Charlotte ids., Brit. Col., where there are now works for refining dog-fish oil. No native pretends to say what family occupied this town.　　(J. R. S.)

Gū'tga.—Swanton, Cont. Haida, 279, 1905. **Quilhcah.**—Deans, Tales from Hidery, 67, 1899.

**Guhlkainde** (*Gŭ'lʻka-ï'nde*, 'plains people'). A division of the Mescalero Apache who claim as their original habitat the Staked plains region E. of Pecos r., in New Mexico and Texas. See *Gohlkahin.*
　　　　　　　　　　　　　　　　(J. M.)

Cuelcajen-né.—Escudero, Not. de Chihuahua, 212, 1834 (probably identical). **Gŭ'lʻka-ï'nde.**—Mooney, field notes, B. A. E., 1897. **Llaneros.**—Orozco y Berra, Geog., 59, 1864 (Cuelcajen-ne or).

**Guia.** An unidentified ruined pueblo on the Rio Grande in the vicinity of Albuquerque, N. Mex.—Loew in Wheeler Survey Rep., VII, 338, 1879.

**Guias.** A Maricopa rancheria on the Rio Gila, s. Ariz., in 1744.—Sedelmair quoted by Bancroft, Ariz. and N. Mex., 366, 1889.

**Guika.** A former Tanos pueblo on the Rio Grande, in the vicinity of Albuquer-

que, N. Mex.—Loew in Wheeler Survey Rep., VII, 338, 1879.

**Gui-k'ati.** See *Sleeping Wolf.*

**Guilitoy.** A tribe of the Patwin division of the Copehan family, formerly living in Napa co., Cal.; one of the seven which made peace with Gov. Vallejo in 1836.

Guilitoy.—Bancroft, Hist. Cal., IV, 71, 1886. **Guillicas.**—Taylor in Cal. Farmer, Mar. 30, 1860. **Guilucos.**—Bancroft, op. cit., 72. **Ulucas.**—Taylor in Cal. Farmer, June 7, 1861.

**Guima.** A former Chumashan village near Santa Barbara, Cal.—Taylor in Cal. Farmer, Apr. 24, 1863.

**Guimen.** A division of the Olamentke branch of the Moquelumnan family of California, according to Choris and Kotzebue, who state that the people spoke the same language as the Tamal and Sonomi.

Guimen.—Choris, Voy. Pitt., 6, 1822. **Guymen.**—Chamisso in Kotzebue, Voy., III, 51, 1821.

**Guiomaer.** A village said to be 40 leagues from St Helena, probably in or near the present Barnwell co., S. C.; visited by Juan Pardo in 1566.—La Vandera (1569) in Smith, Colec. Doc. Fla., I, 16, 1857.

**Guipago.** See *Lone Wolf.*

**Guismanes.** An imaginary province, located in the great plains, in the region of Quivira.—Zarate-Salmeron (ca. 1629), Relacion, in Land of Sunshine, 187, 1900.

**Guisoles.** A tribe of Coahuila or Texas, probably Coahuiltecan, noted in a manuscript quoted by Orozco y Berra, Geog., 306, 1864. It may be identical with the Gueiquesales, or with the Quitoles of Cabeza de Vaca.

**Gulhlgildjing** (*GAltgĭ'ldjiñ*, probably 'mussel-chewing town'). A Haida town on the s. shore of Alliford bay, Moresby id., Queen Charlotte ids., Brit. Col. Another name for this place (or for one near it) was Skama. It was occupied by a low social division of the Djahuiskwahladagai.—Swanton, Cont. Haida, 279, 1905.

Sqā'ma.—Ibid. (probably identical with above: 'woman's needle case').

**Gull Lake Band.** A Chippewa band formerly on Gull lake, on the upper Mississippi, in Cass co., Minn. They sold their lands in 1863.　　　　　　　　(J. M.)

Gulf Lake reservation.—Washington treaty (1867) in U. S. Ind. Treat., 273, 1873 (misprint). **Gull Lake band.**—Washington treaty (1863), ibid., 215.

**Guloismistac.** A former village, presumably Costanoan, connected with Dolores mission, San Francisco, Cal.—Taylor in Cal. Farmer, Oct. 18, 1861.

**Gumisachic** ('arroyo'). A Tarahumare rancheria about 20 m. N. E. of Norogachic, Chihuahua, Mexico.—Lumholtz, inf'n, 1894.

**Gunachonken.** Given by Krause as one of the Tlingit social groups living at Yakutat, Alaska, but it is actually only a name for the people of Gonaho (*Gŏ'naxo*), q. v., a small town in that neighborhood.

**Gŏ'naxo qoan.**—Swanton, field notes, B. A. E., 1904.
**Gūnăchokon.**—Krause, Tlinkit Ind., 116, 1885.

**Gunakhe.** The principal village of the Lakweip, situated on a branch of upper Stikine r., Brit. Col.
**Gunaqä'**—Boas, 10th Rep. N. W. Tribes Can., 34, 1895.

**Gunasquamekook** ('long gravel bar joining the island'). A former Passamaquoddy village on the site of St Andrews, New Brunswick, on Passamaquoddy bay. The Indians were dispossessed by the whites and were finally settled at Pleasant Point, Me.—Vetromile, Abnakis, 55, 1866.

**Gunghet-haidagai** ('Ninstints people'). A part of the Haida living about the s. end of Queen Charlotte ids., Brit. Col. In the Masset dialect their name is Anghethade. The whites formerly called them Ninstints people, from the name by which their chief town was generally known. Their language differs somewhat from that spoken by the Haida farther N. The remnant lives principally at Skidegate.                (J. R. S.)
**Āngīt Hāadē.**—Harrison in Proc. Royal Soc. Can., sec. II, 125, 1895. **Cape St. James tribe.**—Poole, Queen Charlotte Ids., 195, 1872. **GA'ñxet Xā'-idAga·i.**—Swanton, Cont. Haida, 272, 1905. **Kunqit.**—Swanton, field notes, 1900–1901. **Kunχit.**—Dawson, Queen Charlotte Ids., 169, 1880 (proper name of the village, Ninstance being the name of the chief).

**Gunghet-kegawai** ( GA'ñxet-qē'qawa-i, 'those born in the Ninstints country'). A subdivision of the Stasaos-kegawai, a division of the Raven clan of the Haida, probably descended from women who had married in the Ninstints country. It is to be distinguished from another and more important division of the same name at Ninstints which belonged to the Eagle clan.—Swanton, Cont. Haida, 270, 1905.

**Gunghet-kegawai.** A subdivision of the Eagle clan of the Haida, belonging, as the name implies, to one of the Ninstints or Gunghet group. They were sometimes called also Gunghet-gitinai.—Swanton, Cont. Haida, 270, 1905.

**Gupa.** A former Agua Caliente village on the headwaters of San Luis Rey r., s. Cal., better known as Agua Caliente (q. v.). Its inhabitants were removed to Pala res. in 1902.
**Agua Caliente.**—Ind. Aff. Rep. 1902, 175, 1903. **Aqua Caliente.**—Jackson and Kinney, Rep. Miss. Ind., 20, 1883. **Gupa.**—A. L. Kroeber, inf'n, 1905 (own name). **Gupa-nga-git-om.**—Ibid. (own name: 'Gupa-at-people'). **Ha-koo-pin.**—Taylor in Cal. Farmer, May 11, 1860. **Hakupin.**—A. L. Kroeber, inf'n, 1905 (Diegueño name). **Ko-pa.**—Barrows, Ethno-Bot. Coahuilla Ind., 34, 1900 (Kawia name).

**Gusti** ( Gustĭ'). A traditional Cherokee settlement on Tennessee r., near Kingston, Roane co., Tenn.—Mooney in 19th Rep. B. A. E., 521, 1900.

**Gutgunest-nas-hadai** ( Gutgunē'st nas:-had'ā'i 'owl-house people'). Given by Boas (Fifth Rep. N. W. Tribes Can., 26, 1889) as the name of a subdivision of the

Yaku-lanas, a division of the Raven clan of the Haida. It is really only a house name belonging to that family. (J. R. S.)

**Gutheni** ( GAt-hĭ'nĭ, 'salmon creek'). A former Tlingit town situated N. of Dry bay, Alaska. (J. R. S.)

**Gutubur.** A Pima rancheria visited by Father Kino in 1694; definite locality unknown.—Kino in Doc. Hist. Mex., 4th s., I, 251, 1856.

**Guwisguwi.** See *Cooweescoowee; Ross* ( *John*).

**Guyasuta.** See *Kiasutha*.

**Gwaeskun** ( Gwā-iskún, 'end of island'). Formerly the northernmost Haida town on Queen Charlotte ids., Brit. Col. It was named from the cape near by and is said to have been owned by the Stustas, but it has long been abandoned.—Swanton, Cont. Haida, 281, 1905.

**Gwaidalgaegins** ( Gwai-dalga'-igins, 'island that floats along'). A former Haida fort belonging to the Kadusgo-kegawai of Kloo. It was near the mountain called Kinggi, famous in native legend, on Queen Charlotte ids., Brit. Col. (J. R. S.)

**Gwalgahi** ( Gwal'gá'hĭ, 'frog place'). A place on Hiwassee r., in the Cherokee country, just above the junction of Peachtree cr., near Murphy, Cherokee co., N. C.; about 1755 the site of a village of refugee Natchez, and later of a Baptist mission.—Mooney in 19th Rep. B. A. E., 521, 1900.

**Gwaugweh** ('one took out a locust.'—Hewitt). Probably a former Seneca village near Niagara r., N. Y.
**Carrying Place Village.**—Morgan, League Iroq., 466, 1851. **Gwa-u-gueh.**—Ibid., map. **Gwä'-u-gweh.**—Ibid., 466.

**Gweghkongh.** A village in 1657, probably belonging to the Unami Delawares and apparently situated in N. New Jersey, near Staten id., or in the adjacent part of New York.
**Gweghkongh.**—Deed of 1657 in N. Y. Doc. Col. Hist., XIV, 393, 1883. **Hweghkongh.**—Ibid.

**Gweundus** ( Gwēā'ndAs). A subdivision of low social rank of the Hlgahet-gitinai, a family of the Eagle clan of the Haida.—Swanton, Cont. Haida, 274, 1905.

**Gwinwah.** A former Niska village on Nass r., Brit. Col.
**Gu'nwa.**—Swanton, field notes, 1900-01 (name obtained from the Haida). **Gwinwah.**—Dorsey in Am. Antiq., XIX, 281, 1897.

**Gyagyilakya** ( G·āg·g·ilak·a, 'always wanting to kill people'). A gens of the Tsawatenok, a Kwakiutl tribe.—Boas in Rep. Nat. Mus., 331, 1895.

**Gyaushk** ('gull'). A gens of the Chippewa (q. v.).
**Gi-oshk.**—Tanner, Narr., 315, 1830. **Gyaushk.**—Warren in Minn. Hist. Soc. Coll., v, 44, 1885.

**Gyazru.** The Parrot clan of the Hopi.
**Gyarzobi.**—Mindeleff in 8th Rep. B. A. E., 120, 1891. **Gya'-zro**—Stephen, ibid., 39. **Gyazru wiñwû.**—Fewkes in 19th Rep. B. A. E., 584, 1900 ( wiñwú= 'clan'). **Káro.**—Voth, Hopi Proper Names, 81, 1905. **Karro.**—Dorsey and Voth, Mishongnovi Ceremonies, 175, 1902.

**Gyegyote** (*G·'ēg·'ō'tē*, 'descendants of Gyote'). A subdivision of the Lalauitlela, a gens of the Tlatlasikoala.—Boas in Rep. Nat. Mus., 332, 1895.

**Gyekolekoa** (*G·ēg'ō'lqEoa*). A gens of the Koskimo, a Kwakiutl tribe.—Boas in Rep. Nat. Mus., 329, 1895.

**Gyeksem** ('chiefs'). The principal gens in the following Kwakiutl tribes and septs: Koskimo, Nakomgilisala, Tlatlasikoala, Nakoaktok, Guetela, Walaskwakiutl, Matilpe, Tenaktak, Hahuamis, and Wiwekae.
G·ē'xsEm.—Boas in Rep. Nat. Mus., 329–331, 1895.
Gyē'qsEm.—Boas in 6th Rep. N. W. Tribes Can., 53–55, 1890.

**Gyeksemsanatl** (*G·ē'xsEms'anaL*, 'highest chiefs'). A gens of the Koskimo, a Kwakiutl tribe.—Boas in Rep. Nat. Mus., 329, 1895.

**Gyigyekemae** (*G·ī'g·EqEmaē*, 'chiefs'). A gens of the Tsawatenok, a Kwakiutl tribe.—Boas in Rep. Nat. Mus., 331, 1895.

**Gyigyilkam** ('those who receive first'). A gens, or gentes, having the same name, in the following Kwakiutl tribes and septs: Wikeno, Tlatlasikoala, Goasila, Komoyue sept of the true Kwakiutl, Koeksotenok, Tlauitsis, Nimkish, Awaitlala, Guauaenok, Hahuamis, Wiwekae sept of the Lekwiltok.
G·ī'g·îlqam.—Boas in Rep. Nat. Mus., 328–331, 1895. Gyī'gyElk·am.—Boas in 6th Rep. N. W. Tribes Can., 55, 1890. Gyī'gyilk·am.—Ibid. Hamalak-yauœ.—Boas in Petermanns Mitt., pt. 5, 130, 1887 (name of ancestor).

**Gyilaktsaoks** (*Gyilaχtsǎ'oks*, 'people of the canoe planks'). A Tsimshian family living at Kitzilas, on the N. side of Skeena r., Brit. Col.—Boas in Ztschr. f. Ethnol., 232, 1888.

**Gyisgahast** (*Gyîsg·'ahā'st*, 'grass people'). A Niska division of the Gyispawaduweda clan, living in the town of Kitwinshilk, on Nass r., and a Kitksan division living in the town of Kitzegukla, on Skeena r., Brit. Col.—Boas in 10th Rep. N. W. Tribes Can., 49–50, 1895.

**Gyiskabenak** (*Gyisk·ab'Enā'q*). A Niska division of the Lakskiyek clan, living in the town of Lakkulzap, on Nass r., Brit. Col.—Boas in 10th Rep. N. W. Tribes Can., 49, 1895.

**Gyispawaduweda** (*Gyispawaduw E'da*, 'bear'). One of the four Tsimshian clans.—Boas in 10th Rep. N. W. Tribes Can., 49, 50, 1895.
GyīspōtuwE'da.—Boas in 5th Rep., ibid., 9, 1889.

**Gyitgyigyenik** (*Gyîtgyîgyē'niH*). A Niska division of the Lakyebo clan, now in the town of Andeguale, on Nass r., Brit. Col.—Boas in 10th Rep. N. W. Tribes Can., 49, 1895.

**Gyitkadok** (*GyîtHk·'adô'k·*). A Niska division of the Kanhada clan, now living in the town of Lakkulzap, at the mouth of Nass r., Brit. Col.—Boas in 10th Rep. N. W. Tribes Can., 49, 1895.

**Gyitktsaktl** (*Gyitχtsǎ'χtl*, 'people of the lake shore'). A subdivision of the Kitzilas living in a village on the s. side of Skeena r., Brit. Col.—Boas in Ztschr. f. Ethnol., 232, 1888.

**Gyitsaek** (*Gyits'ǎ'eʀ*). A Niska division of the Lakskiyek clan living in the town of Kitwinshilk, on Nass r., Brit. Col.—Boas in 10th Rep. N. W. Tribes Can., 49, 1895.

**Gyitwulnakyel** (*Gyîtwulnaky'ē'l*). A Niska division of the Lakyebo clan living in the town of Kitlakdamix, on Nass r., Brit. Col.—Boas in 10th Rep. N. W. Tribes Can., 49, 1895.

**Gypsum.** A mineral (hydrous sulphide of calcium) embracing three principal varieties—gypsum, satin-spar, and selenite—and occuring in both crystallized and massive forms in connection with stratified rocks. The light-colored compact forms are known as alabaster, a name sometimes erroneously applied to certain forms of travertine and stalagmite. Having no considerable degree of hardness, gypsum was not used for implements by the aborigines, but the pleasing colors and translucent effects made the massive forms valuable for ornaments and carvings generally. Selenite, which has the foliate structure, is readily separated into thin sheets and until recent years was used for window lights instead of glass by some of the Pueblo tribes. The same people crush the gypsum and use it as whitewash on the walls of their houses, generally using a piece of sheep skin as a brush. The Plains Indians, according to Mooney, roast the blocks of gypsum and use the resulting powder to clean and whiten dressed skins and to whiten the gummed tips of feathers in decorative work. (w. h. h.)

**Gyusiwa.** Formerly one of the western group of Jemez pueblos, ½ m. N. of Jemez hot springs, on a slope descending to the river from the E., in Sandoval co., New Mexico. Judging from the extent of the ruins of the village, it at one time contained probably 800 inhabitants. It was the seat of the Spanish mission of San Diego de Jemez, and had a chapel, erected probably previous to 1617, at which date it was the principal Jemez village. The pueblo was abandoned in 1622 on account of the persistent aggressiveness of the Navaho, who had succeeded in scattering the Jemez tribe; but in 1627 Fray Martin de Arvide gathered the scattered members and resettled them in Gyusiwa and Amushungkwa (Patoqua?) pueblos. The latter was deserted prior to 1680, but Gyusiwa was occupied when the pueblos revolted in that year. It was, however, finally abandoned shortly afterward. The walls of the ruined church, in some places 8 feet thick, are still standing. See Bandelier, cited below; Holmes in Am. Anthrop., VII, no. 2, 1905.
(f. w. h.)

Cuunsiora.—Orozco y Berra in Anales Minis. Fom. Mex., 196, 1882 (evidently the same). **Gin-se-ua.**—Bandelier in Arch. Inst. Papers, IV, 204, 1892. **Guimzique.**—Ibid., 205 (misprint of Zarate-Salmeron's Quiunzique). **Guin-se-ua.**—Bandelier in Compte-rendu Internat. Cong. Am., VII, 452, 1890. **Qicinzigua.**—Zarate-Salmeron (*ca.* 1629) quoted by Bancroft, Nat. Races, I, 600, 1882. **Quicinzigua.**—Vargas quoted by Orozco y Berra in Anales Minis. Fom. Mex., 196, 1882. **Quinsta.**—Bancroft, Ariz. and N. Mex., 136, 1889 (misquoting Oñate). **Quiumzi-qua.**—Zarate-Salmeron (*ca.* 1629) Rel., in Land of Sunshine, 183, Feb., 1900. **Quiumzique.**—Zarate-Salmeron quoted by Bandelier in Arch. Inst. Papers, III, 127, 1890. **Quiunzique.**—Ibid., IV, 205, 1892. **Quiusta.**—Oñate (1598) in Doc. Inéd., XVI, 102, 1871 (probably the same). **San Diego.**—Bandelier in Arch. Inst. Papers, I, 23, 27, 1881. **San Diego de James.**—Ind. Aff. Rep. 1867, 213, 1868. **San Diego de Jemes.**—Alencaster (1805) quoted by Meline, Two Thousand Miles, 212, 1867. **San Diego de Jemez.**—Alencaster (1805) quoted by Prince, New Mex., 37, 1883. **San Diego de los Emex.**—MS. of 1643 quoted by Bandelier in Arch. Inst. Papers, IV, 206, 1892. **San Diego de los Hemes.**—Vetancurt, Menolog. Fran., 275, 1871. **San Diego de los Temes.**—Orozco y Berra in Anales Minis. Fom. Mex., 255, 1882. **S. Diego.**—D'Anville, map Am. Sept., 1746.

**Gyuungsh.** The Oak clan of the former pueblo of Pecos, N. Mex.

**Gyuúⁿsh.**—Hodge in Am. Anthrop., IX, 351, 1896 (usually with the suffix -*ash*, 'people').

www.ingramcontent.com/pod-product-compliance
Lightning Source LLC
Chambersburg PA
CBHW080408270326
41929CB00018B/2947